HEADS OF STATE AND GOVERNMENT

2ND EDITION
JOHN V DA GRAÇA

HEADS OF STATE AND GOVERNMENT

2ND EDITION
JOHN V DA GRAÇA

© John V da Graça, 2000.

All rights reserved.
No part of this publication may be reproduced, stored in or introduced into a retrieval system, or transmitted, in any form or by any means (electronic, mechanical, photocopying, recording or otherwise) without prior written permission of the publisher unless in accordance with the provisions of the Copyright Designs and Patents Act 1988, or under the terms of any licence permitting limited copying issued by the Copyright Licensing Agency, 90 Tottenham Court Road, London W1P 9HE, UK.
Further, any person, company or firm found to be reproducing or assisting others in producing mailing lists, or machine-readable versions derived from this publication will be prosecuted for copyright infringement.

Published in the United States and Canada by
ST. MARTIN'S PRESS, 2000
175 Fifth Avenue, New York, NY 10010

St. Martin's Press ISBN: 1-56159-269-2

A catalog record for this book is available from the Library of Congress

Published in the United Kingdom by
MACMILLAN PRESS LTD, 2000
Brunel Road, Houndmills, Basingstoke, Hants RG21 6XS
London and Oxford
Companies and representatives throughout the world

British Library Cataloguing in Publication Data:
da Graça, John V.
    Heads of state and government. – 2nd ed.
    1. Heads of state – Biography
    I. Title
    320.9'22

Macmillan ISBN: 0-333-78615-7

Distributed by Macmillan Distribution Ltd
Brunel Road, Houndmills, Basingstoke, Hants RG21 6XS

Typeset by York House Typographic, London

Printed and bound in Great Britain by Antony Rowe Ltd, Chippenham, Wiltshire

CONTENTS

Preface vi

Statistical Records vii

Abbreviations viii

Section A – Major International Organizations 1

Section B – Countries and Regions 51

Index 1103

PREFACE TO SECOND EDITION

The title of the first edition "Heads of State and Government" has been retained for the second, even though it does not clearly describe all the lists of leaders. Whilst reigning monarchs, presidents and their equivalents are all heads of state, i.e. the person who represents the country in terms of international law, the position of head of government is less clear. In some countries, such as the USA, the President is both head of state and head of government, whilst in others such as the UK, the monarch is head of state and the prime minister is head of government. In some other countries such as France, the head of state is also the head of government, but there is also a prime minister whose duties are often described as being in charge of day-to-day government business. I have not attempted to distinguish between the different types of prime minister, since in terms of diplomatic protocol, they are equivalent. The roles of heads of state also vary from executive leaders (USA), through figureheads with some constitutional role in government (UK), to a complete separation from government business (Sweden). The Swiss presidency is an unusual position – the incumbent has no powers attached to the position; simply functioning as a chairman of the cabinet and a contact for foreign heads of state for protocol purposes.

In addition to Monarchs, Presidents and Prime Ministers, there are other positions included because of the authority vested in them, such as heads of ruling communist parties, military junta heads who did not assume the presidency, and some personalities who held no formal post yet wielded supreme authority.

The purpose of the first edition was to present an easy-to-use reference guide to the leaders of mostly present-day nations. This second edition has the same function and updates the first, quite a task considering the major political changes which many countries have undergone in recent years, including the disintegration of the USSR, Yugoslavia and Czechoslovakia and the consequent emergence of several new states. The scope of the book has also been broadened to include more international organizations, more regional government leaders, more governments-in-exile and colonial governors of the twentieth century, this last limitation because of the excellent coverage of the topic by Henige.

The information comes from many sources, including various encyclopedias, yearbooks (especially Europa, The Statesman's Yearbook and Whitaker's Almanac), Keesing's Record of World Events, specific history books, and correspondence with many libraries, archives and government offices. I am most grateful for all the assistance I received. Ths book is not the only chronological list of leaders, but an examination of the following will show that there are differences. I nevertheless acknowledge them all as having been extremely useful for my compilation:

Carpenter, C. (1978). *The Guinness Book of Kings, Rulers and Statesmen*. Guinness Superlatives Ltd, Enfield.

Henige, D. P. (1970). *Colonial Governors from the Fifteenth Century to the Present*. University of Wisconsin Press, Madison.

Ross, M. (1978). *Rulers and Governments of the World Vol.I*. Bowker, London & New York.

Spuler, B. (1978). *Rulers and Governments of the World Vols.II & III*. Bowker, London & New York.

Truhart, P. (1984-88). *Regents of Nations, Part I* (1984), *Part II* (1985), *Part III (1)* (1986), *Part III (2)* (1988). K.G.Saur, Munchen.

http://www.geocities.com/Athens/1058/rulers.html

I am also indebted to friends and contacts in various countries who took the time and trouble to find information for me.

STATISTICAL RECORDS

Longest reign by a hereditary ruler:
Prince Heinrich XI (Reuss-Greiz). March 1723–June 1800. 77 years 3 months.
(Longest serving current hereditary ruler: Raja Tuanku Syed Putra (Perlis, Malaysia) since December 1945.)

Longest reign by a king:
King Louis XIV (France). 72 years 4 months.
King Minhti (Arakan, now in Myanmar) reputed to have reigned 1279–1374. 95 years.
Pharaoh Pepi II (Phiops) (Egypt) believed to have reigned c2281BC–c2107BC. 94 years.
(Longest current reigning king: Bhumibol Adulyadej (Thailand) since June 1946.)

Longest rule by a head of state (other than a monarch):
Francisco Franco Bahamonde (Spain). April 1939–November 1975. 36 years 7 months.

Longest presidency:
Alfredo Stroessner (Paraguay). August 1954–February 1989. 34 years 6 months.
(Longest serving current President: Gnassingbé Eyadéma (Togo) since April 1967.)

Longest premiership:
Ibrahim Didi (Maldives). 1883–1925. 42 years.
(Longest serving current PM: Fidel Castro (Cuba) since February 1959.)

Longest governor-generalship (Commonwealth):
Florizel Glasspole (Jamaica). June 1973–March 1991. 17 years 9 months.
(Longest serving current Governor-General: Howard Cooke (Jamaica) since August 1991.)

Longest leadership of a ruling communist party:
Kim Il Sung (North Korea). September 1948–July 1984. 36 years 10 months.
(Longest serving current party leader: Fidel Castro (Cuba) since October 1965.)

Shortest reign by a monarch:
King Louis XIX (France). A few hours on 2 August 1830.
Luis II (Portugal) was technically king for 20 minutes on 1 February 1908.

Shortest presidency:
Pedro Lascurain (Mexico). Approximately 1 hour on 18 February 1913.

Shortest premiership:
Siaka Stevens (Sierra Leone). A few minutes on 21 March 1967.

Shortest governor-generalship (Commonwealth):
John Paul (Bahamas). July–August 1973. 21 days.

Shortest leadership of a ruling communist party:
Georgy Malenkov (USSR). 6–14 March 1953. 8 days.

First female president:
a. independent state – Maria Estela de Perón (Argentina). 1974–76.
b. regional state – A. F. Nuorteva (Karelia, Russia). 1924–28.

First female prime minister:
a. traditional – Kaakumana (Hawaii). 1819–32.
b. modern – Sirimavo Bandaranaike (Sri Lanka). 1960–65.

First female governor-general (Commonwealth):
Elmira Gordon (Belize). 1981–93.

First female state governor:
Nellie Ross (Wyoming, USA). 1925–27.

Note: Of the more than 20,000 names listed in this book, just over 200 are female, and more than 160 of them have held office in the last 50 years.

Highest number of separate reigns by one monarch:
Emperor Takla Giyorghis I (Ethiopia). 6 reigns between 1779 and 1800.

Highest number of separate presidencies:
Antonio de Santa Anna (Mexico). 6 times between 1833 and 1855.

Highest number of separate premierships:
Alexandros Koumoundouros (Greece). 11 times between 1865 and 1882.

Most presidents:
Switzerland: 83

Most prime ministers:
France: 117

ABBREVIATIONS

b = born
f = formerly
† = died in office
Political party abbreviations are shown under the respective country/region

SECTION A

MAJOR INTERNATIONAL ORGANIZATIONS

ARAB MAGHREB UNION (AMU)

Formation date: 17 February 1989

Headquarters: Rabat

The Arab Maghreb Union was formed to encourage joint ventures and to create a single market, especially in view of the single market being created by the European Union.

Member states:

Algeria	Libya
Mauritania	Morocco
Tunisia	

Secretary-General:

Oct 1991- Mohammed Amanou (Tunisia)

ASIA-PACIFIC ECONOMIC CO-OPERATION (APEC)

Date formed: November 1989
Headquarters: Singapore

APEC was founded to devise programmes of co-operation between the countries of the Pacific rim, ie those that line the two sides of the Pacific Ocean. A summit meeting is held annually to discuss mainly economic matters.

Member states:

Australia	Brunei
Canada	China
Hong Kong	Indonesia
Japan	Korea (South)
Malaysia	Mexico
New Zealand	Papua New Guinea
Peru	Philippines
Russia	Singapore
Taiwan (Chinese Taipeh)	Thailand
USA	Vietnam

Executive-Secretaries:

Feb 1993-Dec 1996	Rusli Noor (Indonesia)
Jan-Dec 1997	Jack Whittleton (Canada)
Jan-Dec 1998	Noor Adlan (Malaysia)
Jan-Dec 1999	Timothy Hannah (New Zealand)
Jan-Dec 2000	Serbini Ali (Brunei)

ASSOCIATION OF SOUTH EAST ASIAN NATIONS (ASEAN)

Formation date: 7 August 1967

Headquarters: Jakarta (Indonesia)

In 1967 five south east Asian nations formed ASEAN to promote co-operation and assistance in economic, social, cultural, technical, scientific and administrative fields. Brunei became the sixth member in 1984, and ten years later the first communist ruled country, Vietnam, was admitted.

Member states:

Brunei (1984)	Cambodia (1999)
Indonesia	Laos (1997)
Malaysia	Myanmar (1997)
Philippines	Singapore
Thailand	Vietnam (1994)

Secretaries-General:

Feb 1976-Feb 1978	Hartono Dharsono (Indonesia)
Feb-July 1978	Umarjadi Njotowijona (Indonesia)
July 1978-July 1980	Datuk Ali bin Abdullah (Malaysia)
July 1980-July 1982	Narciso Reyes (Philippines)
July 1982-July 1984	Chan Kai Yau (Singapore)
July 1984-July 1986	Phan Wannamethee (Thailand)
July 1986-July 1989	Roderick Yong Yin Fatt (Brunei)
July 1989-July 1993	Rusli Noor (Indonesia)
July 1993-Jan 1998	Arjit Singh (Malaysia)
Jan 1998-	Rodolfo Severino (Philippines)

CARIBBEAN COMMUNITY (CARICOM)

Formation date: 1 August 1973

Headquarters: Georgetown (Guyana)

In 1973 a group of Caribbean nations signed a treaty establishing the Caribbean community for co-operation in economic affairs and co-ordination in health, education, culture, sport, science and technology.

Member state: (admission dates)

Antigua & Barbuda (1974)	Bahamas (1983)
Barbados (1973)	Belize (1974)
Dominica (1974)	Grenada (1974)
Guyana (1973)	Haiti (1999)
Montserrat (1974)	Jamaica (1973)
St Lucia (1974)	St Christopher & Nevis (1974)
Surinam (1995)	St Vincent (1974)
Trinidad & Tobago (1973)	

Secretaries-General:

1973-74	William Demas (Trinidad & Tobago)
1974-Aug 1977	Alistair McIntyre (Grenada)
Aug 1977-Aug 1978	Joseph Tyndall (Guyana)(acting)
Nov 1978-Sept 1983	Kurleigh King (Barbados)
Sept 1983-Aug 1992	Roderick Rainford (Jamaica)
Aug 1992-	Edwin Carrington (Trinidad & Tobago)

CENTRAL TREATY ORGANIZATION (CENTO)

Previous name: Baghdad Pact 1955-1959
Formation date: 24 February 1955
Dissolution date: September 1979
Headquarters: Baghdad (1955-1959), Ankara (1959-1979)

A mutual defence pact was signed by Turkey and Iraq in 1955, which was then joined by the other members. Iraq formally withdrew in 1959, while the others maintained CENTO for the next 20 years.

Member states:

Iran	Iraq (1955-1959)
Pakistan	Turkey
UK	USA

Secretaries-General:

1955-Oct 1958	Awni Khalidi (Iraq)
1959-61	Mirza Baig (Pakistan)
1962-Jan 1968	Abbas Khalatbary (Iran)
Jan 1968-1972	Turgut Menemencioğlu (Turkey)
1972-75	Nassi Assar (Iran)
1975-Aug 1977	Umit Bayulken (Turkey)
Aug 1977-March 1978	Sidar Hasan Mahmud (Pakistan)(acting)
March 1978-Sept 1979	Kamuren Gürün (Turkey)

COMMONWEALTH OF INDEPENDENT STATES (CIS)

Formation date: 8 December 1991

Headquarters: Minsk

After the collapse of the Soviet Union at the end of 1991, all the former constituent republics, except the three Baltic states of Estonia, Latvia and Lithuania, formed an association for both military and economic cooperation.

Member states:

Armenia	Azerbaijan (1993)
Belarus	Georgia (1993)
Kazakhstan	Kyrgyzstan
Moldova	Russia
Tajikistan	Turkmenistan
Ukraine	Uzbekistan

Executive Secretaries:

Oct 1992-April 1998	Ivan Korotchenya	(Belarus)
April 1998-April 1999	Boris Berezovsky	(Russia)
April 1999-	Yury Yazrov	(Russia)

COMMONWEALTH OF NATIONS

Formation date: 31 December 1931 (Statute of Westminster)
Headquarters: London

The Imperial Conference of 1926 defined Great Britain and the Dominions as being equal in status and freely associated as members of the British Commonwealth of Nations. This became law with the Statute of Westminster in 1931. The nature of the Commonwealth changed in 1950 to allow membership of republics. Most former British territories have, on achieving independence, joined the Commonwealth. A secretariat was established in 1965. Mozambique was the first country without any British-linked colonial past to be admitted.

Member states: (admission dates)

Antigua & Barbuda   (1981)
Australia   (1901/31)
Bahamas   (1973)
Bangladesh   (1972)
Barbados   (1966)
Belize   (1981)
Botswana   (1966)
Brunei   (1984)
Cameroon   (1995)
Canada   (1867/1931)
Cyprus   (1961)
Dominica   (1978)
Fiji   (1970-87, 1997)
Gambia   (1965)
Ghana   (1957)
Grenada   (1974)
Guyana   (1966)
India   (1947)
Jamaica   (1962)
Kenya   (1963)
Kiribati   (1979)
Lesotho   (1966)
Malawi   (1963)
Malaysia   (1957)
Maldives   (1982)
Malta   (1964)
Mauritius   (1968)
Mozambique   (1995)
Namibia   (1990)
Nauru   (1968, full member 1999)
New Zealand   (1907/31)
Nigeria   (1960) (suspended 1995-99)
Pakistan   (1947-72, 1989)
Papua New Guinea   (1975)
St Christopher & Nevis   (1983)
St Lucia   (1979)
St Vincent   (1979)
Samoa   (1970)
Seychelles   (1976)
Sierra Leone   (1961)
Singapore   (1965)
Solomon Islands   (1978)
South Africa   (1910/31-61, 1994)
Sri Lanka   (1948)
Swaziland   (1968)
Tanzania   (1961)
Tonga   (1970)
Trinidad & Tobago   (1962)
Tuvalu*   (1978)
Uganda   (1962)
United Kingdom
Vanuatu   (1980)
Zambia   (1964)
Zimbabwe   (1980)

* Special membership
Former member: Ireland   (1922/31-49)

Secretaries-General:

July 1965-July 1975	Arnold Smith (Canada)
July 1975-July 1990	Shridath (Sonny) Ramphal (Guyana)
July 1990-April 2000	Chukwumeka (Emeka) Anyaoku (Nigeria)
April 2000-	Donald McKinnon (New Zealand)

COMMUNITY OF PORTUGUESE SPEAKING COUNTRIES

Formation date: July 1996

Headquarters: Lisbon

Portugal, five of its former colonies in Africa and Brazil formed an organization of Portuguese-speaking states in 1996 to develop co-operation between them in various fields and to promote the use of their language in international affairs.

Member states:

Angola
Cape Verde
Mozambique
São Tomé & Principe

Brazil
Guinea-Bissau
Portugal

Executive Secretary:

July 1996- Marcolino Moco (Angola)

COUNCIL OF EUROPE

Formation date: 5 May 1949
Headquarters: Strasbourg

In 1948 a Congress of Europe called for the creation of a united Europe; this meeting was the basis for the Council of Europe formed a year later. Its aim is to bring European nations closer together.

Member states: (admission dates)

Albania (1995)	Andorra (1994)
Austria (1956)	Belgium (1949)
Bulgaria (1992)	Croatia (1996)
Cyprus (1961)	Czech Republic (1993)
Denmark (1949)	Estonia (1993)
Finland (1989)	France (1949)
Georgia (1999)	Germany (West until 1990) (1951)
Greece (1949)	Hungary (1990)
Iceland (1950)	Ireland (1949)
Italy (1949)	Latvia (1995)
Liechtenstein (1978)	Lithuania (1993)
Luxembourg (1949)	Macedonia (1995)
Malta (1965)	Moldova (1995)
Netherlands (1949)	Norway (1949)
Poland (1991)	Portugal (1976)
Romania (1993)	Russia (1996)
San Marino (1988)	Slovakia (1993)
Slovenia (1993)	Spain (1977)
Sweden (1949)	Switzerland (1963)
Turkey (1949)	Ukraine (1995)
United Kingdom (1949)	

Secretaries-General:

Aug 1949-July 1953	Jacques Camille-Paris (France)
July 1953-May 1957	Léon Marchal (France)
May 1957-Jan 1964	Ludovico Benvenuti (Italy)
Jan 1964-May 1969	Peter Smithers (UK)
May 1969-May 1974	Lujo Tončić-Sorinj (Austria)
May 1974-May 1979	Georg Kahn-Ackermann (West Germany)
May 1979-May 1984	Franz Karasek (Austria)
May 1984-May 1989	Marcelino Orega Aguirre (Spain)
May 1989-May 1994	Catherine Lalumière (France)
May 1994-Sept 1999	Daniel Tarschys (Sweden)
Sept 1999-	Walter Schwimmer (Austria)

COUNCIL FOR MUTUAL ECONOMIC ASSISTANCE (CMEA)

Formation date: 25 January 1949
Dissolution date: 28 June 1991
Headquarters: Moscow

The CMEA, known as Comecon in the West, was formed in 1949 to strengthen the economic collaboration of the socialist (communist) countries. Following the collapse of communism in eastern Europe it was dissolved in 1991.

Member states:

Albania   (1949-62)
Cuba   (1972-91)
Hungary   (1949-91)
Poland   (1950-91)
USSR   (1949-91)
Bulgaria   (1949-91)
German Democratic Republic   (1950-90)
Mongolia   (1962-91)
Romania   (1949-91)
Vietnam   (1978-91)

Secretaries:

June 1962-Oct 1983   Nikolai Faddeyev   (USSR)
Oct 1983-June 1991   Vyacheslav Sychev   (USSR)

EAST AFRICAN CO-OPERATION

Previous names: East African Common Services Organization 1961-67, East African Community 1967-77

Formation date: 9 December 1961, Relaunched March 1996

Dissolution date: 1 July 1977

Headquarters: Arusha (Tanzania)

Prior to independence the British-ruled states of East Africa shared many facilities under the direction of the East African High Commission. When Tanganyika gained independence the EACSO was formed, and in 1967 was transformed into the East African Community. Tensions between the member states led to its dissolution in 1977. In the 1990s relations between the three states improved and in 1996 it was effectively re-established under a new name, East African Co-operation.

Member states:

Kenya   Tanzania
Uganda

Secretaries-General:

1964-68	Dunstan Omari (Kenya)
1968-71	Zerubaberi Bigirwenkya (Uganda)
1971-74	Charles Maina (Kenya)
1974-77	Edwin Mtei (Tanzania)
(1977-96	organization abolished

Executive Secretary:

March 1996-   Francis Muthura   (Kenya)

ECONOMIC COMMUNITY OF WEST AFRICAN STATES (ECOWAS)

Formation date: May 1975

Headquarters: Lagos

The Lagos Treaty setting up ECOWAS was signed by 15 states in 1975. Its aim is to promote trade, co-operation and self-reliance of West Africa. Military forces of ECOWAS have provided peace-keeping roles during civil strife in Liberia and Sierra Leone.

Member states:

Benin	Burkina Faso
Cape Verde (1977)	Côte d'Ivoire
Gambia	Ghana
Guinea	Guinea-Bissau
Liberia	Mali
Mauritania	Niger
Nigeria	Senegal
Sierra Leone	Togo

Executive Secretaries:

Nov 1976-Nov 1984	Aboubacar Diabey-Ouattara (Côte d'Ivoire)
Nov 1984-Nov 1988	Momodu Munu (Sierra Leone)
(Nov 1988-Feb 1989	post vacant)
Feb 1989-Sept 1993	Abbas Bundu (Sierra Leone)
Sept 1993-Sept 1997	Edouard Benjamin (Guinea)
Sept 1997-	Lansana Kouyalé (Guinea)

EUROPEAN FREE TRADE ASSOCIATION (EFTA)

Formation date: 3 May 1960
Headquarters: Geneva

EFTA was set up in 1960 by Western European nations not in the European Communities (now Union) to achieve free trade in industrial products. Denmark, Portugal, UK, Austria, Sweden and Finland have since left to join the European Union. In 1992 (effective 1994), EFTA and EU established a European Economic Area for free movement of goods, services, capital and labour.

Member states: (admission dates)

Iceland (1970)	Liechtenstein (1991)
Norway (1960)	Switzerland (1960)

Former members:

Austria (1960-95)	Denmark (1960-73)
Finland (1985-95)	Portugal (1960-86)
Sweden (1960-95)	United Kingdom (1960-73)

Secretaries-General:

May 1960-Nov 1965	Frank Figgures (UK)
Nov 1965-Feb 1972	John Coulson (UK)
Feb 1972-Nov 1975	Bengt Rabaeus (Sweden)
Nov 1975-Sept 1981	Charles Müller (Switzerland)
Oct-Nov 1981	Magnus Vahlqvist (Sweden) (acting)
Dec 1981-April 1988	Per Kleppe (Norway)
April 1988-Sept 1994	Georg Reisch (Austria)
Sept 1994-	Kjartan Jóhannsson (Iceland)

EUROPEAN UNION

Previous name: European Communities 1958-93

Formation date: 1 January 1958

Headquarters of the European Commission: Brussels

Six Western European countries established three communities, namely the European Coal and Steel Community, the European Atomic Energy Community and the European Economic Community. With the formation of the latter two in 1958 a commission to oversee the affairs of all three was formed. The eventual aim of the communities is to achieve political unity in Europe. In 1993 the Maastricht Treaty on closer monetary union came into effect, and the name European Union was adopted.

Member states: (admission dates)

Austria (1995)	Belgium (1958)
Denmark (1973)	Finland (1995)
France (1958)	Germany (1958) (West Germany until 1990),
Greece (1981)	Ireland (1973)
Italy (1958)	Luxembourg (1958)
Netherlands (1958)	Portugal (1986)
Spain (1986)	Sweden (1995)
United Kingdom (1973)	

Commission Presidents:

Jan 1958-June 1966	Walter Hallstein (West Germany)
June 1966-May 1970	Jean Rey (Belgium)
May 1970-March 1972	Franco Malfatti (Italy)
May 1972-Jan 1973	Sicco Mansholt (Netherlands)
Jan 1973-Jan 1977	François-Xavier Ortoli (France)
Jan 1977-Jan 1981	Roy Jenkins (UK)
Jan 1981-Jan 1985	Gaston Thorn (Luxembourg)
Jan 1985-Jan 1995	Jacques Delors (France)
Jan 1995-Sept 1999	Jacques Santer (Luxembourg)
Sept 1999-	Romani Prodi (Italy)

Associated organization

AFRICAN, CARIBBEAN & PACIFIC GROUP (ACP)

Formation date: 1 April 1976
Headquarters: Brussels

The agreement between the EU and 70 developing countries, known as the Lomé Conventions, provides for co-operation in the fields of trade, agriculture, industry, finance and technology.

Secretaries-General:

1976-79	Tissoulé Konaté	(Mali)
1979-84	T.Okelo-Odongo	(Kenya)
1984-89	Edwin Carrington	(Trinidad & Tobago)
1989-94	Ghebray Berhane	(Ethiopia)
1994-96	Carl Greenidge (acting)	(Guyana)
July 1996-	Ng'andu Magande	(Zambia)

LA FRANCOPHONIE

Date formed: 1970

Headquarters: Paris

La Francophonie organizes a conference of the heads of state of member countries every two years to promote co-operation throughout the French-speaking world. In recent years some countries without French speaking communities have been admitted because of their interest in promoting the language. A secretariat was formed in 1997.

Member states: (admission dates)

Belgium (1970)	Benin (1970)
Bulgaria (1991)	Burkina Faso (1970)
Burundi (1970)	Cambodia (1991)
Cameroon (1991)	Canada (1970)
Cape Verde (1996)	Central African Republic (1973)
Chad (1970)	Comoros (1977)
Congo-B (1981)	Congo-K (1977)
Côte d'Ivoire (1970)	Djibouti (1977)
Dominica (1979)	Egypt (1983)
Equatorial Guinea (1989)	France (1970)
Gabon (1970)	Guinea (1980)
Guinea-Bissau (1979)	Haiti (1970)
Laos (1991)	Lebanon (1973)
Luxembourg (1970)	Madagascar (1970)
Mali (1970)	Mauritius (1970)
Mauritania (1980)	Morocco (1981)
Monaco (1970)	Niger (1970)
Romania (1993)	Rwanda (1970)
St Lucia (1970)	Senegal (1970)
Seychelles (1976)	Switzerland (1996)
Togo (1970)	Tunisia (1970)
Vanuatu (1979)	Vietnam (1970)

Secretary-General:

Nov 1997-   Butros Butros-Ghali   (Egypt)

GULF CO-OPERATION COUNCIL (GCC)

Official name: Co-operation Council of the Arab States of the Gulf
Formation date: 25 May 1981
Headquarters: Riyadh

The GCC was set up in 1981 for co-operation in economic, social and cultural affairs. Defence co-operation was added later.

Member states:

Bahrain   Kuwait,
Oman   Qatar
Saudi Arabia   United Arab Emirates   (UAE)

Secretaries-General:

May 1981-April 1993   Abdullah Bishara   (Kuwait)
April 1993-April 1996 Shaikh Fahim bin Sultan al-Qasimi   (UAE)
April 1996-   Jameel al-Hujilan   (Saudi Arabia)

INTERNATIONAL OLYMPIC COMMITTEE (IOC)

Formation date: June 1894

Headquarters: Lausanne

The formation of the IOC was due largely to the efforts of Count Pierre de Coubertin, who was convinced of the need to recreate the Olympic spirit of ancient Greece. The first modern Olympic games were held in Greece in 1896. The organization of the games and the co-ordination of the Olympic movement is the responsibility of the IOC.

Members:

National Olympic Committees of 197 countries

Presidents:

1894-96	Dimitrios Vikelas (Greece)
1896-25	Pierre de Coubertin (France)
1925-42	Henri de Baillet-Latour (Belgium)
(1942-46	post vacant)
1946-July 1952	J.Sigfrid Edstrom (Sweden)
July 1952-Sept 1972	Avery Brundage (USA)
Sept 1972-Aug 1980	Lord Killanin (Michael Morris) (Ireland)
Aug 1980-	Juan Antonio Samaranch (Spain)

LEAGUE OF ARAB STATES (ARAB LEAGUE)

Formation date: 22 March 1945

Headquarters: Cairo, (Tunis 1979-90)

The leaders of the Arab movement in the nineteenth century and of the Arab revolt against their Turkish rulers during the first World War to establish a united independent Arab state. But the 1919 peace settlement divided the region largely into foreign spheres of influence, and the formation of separate states. As more of these states became independent, an Arab conference was organised in 1944 which laid down the outlines of a league of Arab states. There were seven founding members, but this has since increased to 22. Egypt was suspended from 1979 until 1989 for signing a peace treaty with Israel; during this time the headquarters were located in Tunis.

Member states: (admission dates)

Algeria (1962)	Bahrain (1971)
Comoros (1993)	Djibouti (1977)
Egypt (1945)	Iraq (1945)
Jordan (1945)	Kuwait (1961)
Lebanon (1945)	Libya (1953)
Mauritania (1973)	Morocco (1958)
Oman (1971)	Palestine* (1976)
Qatar (1971)	Saudi Arabia (1945)
Somalia (1974)	Sudan (1956)
Syria (1945)	Tunisia (1958)
United Arab Emirates (1971)	Yemen (1945-North, 1967-South)

*mostly under Israeli occupation; represented by the PLO

Secretaries-General:

March 1945-Sept 1952	Abdul Azzem	(Egypt)
Sept 1952-June 1972	Abdul Hassouna	(Egypt)
June 1972-March 1979	Mahmoud Riad	(Egypt)
June 1979-Sept 1990	Chedli Klibi	(Tunisia)
Sept 1990-May 1991	Assad al-Assad	(Lebanon) (acting)
May 1991-	Esmat Meguib	(Egypt)

LEAGUE OF NATIONS

Formation date: 29 April 1919
Dissolution date: 19 April 1946
Headquarters: Geneva

The League of Nations was formed after World War I with the objective of promoting international peace. The USA never joined, Germany withdrew in 1933, and the USSR ceased participating in 1934. Its failure in preventing Italian occupation of Ethiopia in 1936 and the outbreak of World War II in 1939 lead to its formal dissolution in 1946.

Member states: (admission/membership dates)

Afghanistan (1934)	Albania (1920-39
Argentina (1919)	Australia (1919)
Austria (1920-38)	Belgium (1919)
Bolivia (1919)	Brazil (1919-26)
Bulgaria (1920)	Canada (1919)
Chile (1919-38)	China (1919)
Colombia (1919)	Costa Rica (1920-25)
Cuba (1919)	Czechoslovakia (1919)
Denmark (1919)	Dominican Republic (1924)
Ecuador (1934)	Egypt (1937)
El Salvador (1919-37)	Estonia (1921)
Ethiopia (1923)	Finland (1920)
France (1919)	Germany (1926-33)
Guatemala (1919-36)	Haiti (1919-42)
Honduras (1919-36)	Hungary (1922- 39)
India (1919)	Iraq (1932)
Ireland (1923)	Italy (1919-37)
Japan (1919-33)	Latvia (1921)
Liberia (1919)	Lithuania (1921)
Luxembourg (1920)	Mexico (1931)
Netherlands (1919)	New Zealand (1919)
Nicaragua (1919-36)	Norway (1919)
Panama (1919)	Paraguay (1919-35)
Persia (Iran) (1919)	Peru (1919-39)
Poland (1919)	Portugal (1919)
Romania (1919-40)	Siam (Thailand) (1919)
South Africa (1919)	Spain (1919-39)
Sweden (1919)	Switzerland (1919)
Turkey (1932)	UK (1919)

USSR   (1934-39)
Venezuela   (1919-38)
Uruguay   (1919)
Yugoslavia   (1919)

Secretaries-General:

April 1919-June 1933   J. Eric Drummond   (UK)
June 1933-Aug 1940   Joseph Avenol   (France)
Aug 1940-April 1946   Seán Lester   (Ireland)

NORTH ATLANTIC TREATY ORGANIZATION (NATO)

Formation date: 24 August 1949
Headquarters: Brussels

In 1948 Canada suggested that a 'security league' of free nations on both sides of the Atlantic be formed. A year later foreign ministers of 12 nations signed the treaty forming NATO, four other countries joining later. In 1999 the first former members of the Warsaw Pact joined NATO.

Member states: (admission dates)

Belgium (1949)	Canada (1949)
Czech Republic (1999)	Denmark (1949)
France (1949)	Germany (1955) (West Germany until 1990),
Greece (1952)	Hungary (1999)
Iceland (1949)	Italy (1949)
Luxembourg (1949)	Netherlands (1949)
Norway (1949)	Poland (1999)
Portugal (1949)	Spain (1982)
Turkey (1952)	UK (1949)
USA (1949)	

Secretaries-General:

March 1952-May 1957	Hastings Ismay (UK)
May 1957-Feb 1961	Paul-Henri Spaak (Belgium)
Feb-April 1961	Alberico Casardi (Italy) (acting)
April 1961-May 1964	Dirk Stikker (Netherlands)
May 1964-Oct 1971	Manlio Brosio (Italy)
Oct 1971-June 1984	Joseph Luns (Netherlands)
June 1984-July 1988	Lord Carrington (Peter Carrington) (UK)
July 1988-Aug 1994	Manfred Wörner (Germany) (†)
Aug-Oct 1994	Sergio Balanzino (Italy) (acting) (1st)
Oct 1994-Oct 1995	Willy Claes (Belgium)
Oct-Dec 1995	Sergio Balanzino (Italy) (acting) (2nd)
Dec 1995-Oct 1999	Javier Solana (Spain)
Oct 1999	Lord Robertson (George Robertson) (UK)

ORGANIZATION OF AFRICAN UNITY (OAU)

Formation date: 25 May 1963
Headquarters: Addis Ababa

In 1963 the heads of state of 30 African countries signed a charter establishing the OAU with the object of furthering African unity and solidarity, the co-ordination of policies in various fields, the elimination of colonialism in Africa, and the common defence of members.

Member states: (admission dates)

Algeria   (1963)
Benin   (1963)
Burkina Faso   (1963)
Cameroon   (1963)
Central African Republic   (1963)
Comoros   (1975)
Congo-K   (1963)
Djibouti   (1977)
Equatorial Guinea   (1968)
Ethiopia   (1963)
Gambia   (1965)
Guinea   (1963)
Kenya   (1963)
Liberia   (1963)
Madagascar   (1963)
Mali   (1963)
Mauritius   (1968)
Namibia   (1990)
Nigeria   (1963)
Saharwi Republic   (1982)
Senegal   (1963)
Sierra Leone   (1961)
South Africa   (1994)
Swaziland   (1968)
Togo   (1963)
Uganda   (1963)
Zimbabwe   (1980)

Angola   (1975)
Botswana   (1966)
Burundi   (1963)
Cape Verde   (1975)
Chad   (1963)
Congo-B   (1963)
Côte d'Ivoire   (1963)
Egypt   (1963)
Eritrea   (1993)
Gabon   (1963)
Ghana   (1963)
Guinea-Bissau   (1974)
Lesotho   (1966)
Libya   (1963)
Malawi   (1964)
Mauritania   (1963)
Mozambique   (1975)
Niger   (1963)
Rwanda   (1963)
São Tomé & Principe   (1975)
Seychelles   (1976)
Somalia   (1963)
Sudan   (1963)
Tanzania   (1963)
Tunisia   (1963)
Zambia   (1964)

Former member: Morocco (1963-82)

Secretaries-General:

July 1964-July 1972	Diallo Telli (Guinea)
July 1972-July 1974	Nzo Ekangaki (Cameroon)
July 1974-July 1978	William Eteki Mbomua (Cameroon)
July 1978-July 1983	Edem Kodjo (Togo)
July 1983-July 1985	Peter Onu (Nigeria) (acting)
July 1985-July 1989	Ide Oumarou (Niger)
July 1989-	Salim Ahmed Salim (Tanzania)

ORGANIZATION OF AMERICAN STATES (OAS)

Formation date: 30 April 1948
Headquarters: Washington DC

The OAS traces its origins back to 1890 when the First International Conference of American States was held. Successive conferences led to the adoption in 1948 of the charter of the OAS.

Member states: (admission dates)

Antigua & Barbuda (1981)
Bahamas (1982)
Belize (1991)
Brazil (1948)
Chile (1948)
Costa Rica (1948)
Dominica (1979)
Ecuador (1948)
Grenada (1975)
Guyana (1991)
Honduras (1948)
Mexico (1948)
Panama (1948)
Peru (1948)
St Lucia (1979)
Surinam (1977)
USA (1948)
Venezuela (1948)
Argentina (1948)
Barbados (1967)
Bolivia (1948)
Canada (1990)
Colombia (1948)
Cuba (1948, suspended 1962)
Dominican Republic (1948)
El Salvador (1948)
Guatemala (1948)
Haiti (1948)
Jamaica (1969)
Nicaragua (1948)
Paraguay (1948)
St Christopher & Nevis (1984)
St Vincent (1981)
Trinidad & Tobago (1967)
Uruguay (1948)

Secretaries-General:

May 1948-Aug 1954	Alberto Lleras (Colombia)
Aug 1954-Oct 1956	Carlos Dávila (Chile)
Oct 1956-Feb 1968	José Mora Otero (Uruguay)
Feb 1968-May 1975	Galo Plaza Lasso (Ecuador)
May 1975-March 1984	Alejandro Orfila (Argentina)
March-June 1984	Valerie McComie (Barbados) (acting)
June 1984-June 1994	João Baena Soares (Brazil)
June-Sept 1994	Christopher Thomas (Trinidad & Tobago) (acting)
Sept 1994-	César Gaviria Trujillo (Colombia)

ORGANISATION COMMUNE AFRICAINE ET MAURICIENNE (OCAM)

Previous name: Organisation Commune Africaine et Malgache de Cooperation Economique (until 1974)

Formation date: February 1965

Dissolution date: 23 March 1985

Headquarters: Bangui (CAR)

OCAM was formed by French-speaking African states to accelerate economic, social, technical and cultural development between them. After several members withdrew, the organization was dissolved in 1985.

Member states: (membership dates)

Benin (1965-85)	Burkina Faso (1965-85)
Cameroon (1965-74)	Central African Republic (1965- 85)
Chad (1965-74)	Congo-B (1965-73)
Congo-K/Zaire (1965-73)	Côte d'Ivoire (1965-85)
Gabon (1965-78)	Madagascar (1965-74)
Mauritania (1965)	Mauritius (1969-85)
Niger (1965-85)	Rwanda (1965-85)
Senegal (1965-85)	Seychelles (1977-78)
Togo (1965-85)	

Secretaries-General:

1965-68	Diakha Dieng	(Senegal)
1968-74	Falilou Kane	(Senegal)
1974	Regis Franchet	(Mauritius)
1974-79	Sydney Moutia	(Mauritius)
1979-85	Ismail Amri Sued	(Rwanda)

ORGANIZATION FOR ECONOMIC CO-OPERATION AND DEVELOPMENT (OECD)

Previous name: Organization for European Economic Co-operation (OEEC)
Formation dates: 1948 (OEEC) ; 30 September 1961 (OECD)
Headquarters: Paris

The OEEC was formed to promote economic co-operation amongst members. When in 1961 it broadened its membership to include developed nations outside Europe, it also extended its purpose into the field of development, especially to stimulate and harmonize its members' efforts in favour of developing countries.

Member states:

Australia	Austria
Belgium	Canada
Czech Republic (1995)	Denmark
Finland	France
Germany (West Germany until 1990)	Greece
Hungary (1996)	Iceland
Italy	Japan
Korea (South) (1996)	Luxembourg
Mexico (1994)	Netherlands
New Zealand	Norway
Poland (1996)	Portugal
Spain	Sweden
Switzerland	Turkey
UK	USA

Secretaries-General:

April 1948-April 1955	Robert Marjolin (France)
April 1955-July 1960	René Sergent (France)
July 1960-Sept 1969	Thorkil Kristensen (Denmark)
Sept 1969-Sept 1984	Emile van Lennep (Netherlands)
Sept 1984-Sept 1994	Jean-Claude Paye (France) (1st)
Sept-Nov 1994	Staffan Sohlman (Sweden) (acting)
Nov 1994-May 1996	Jean-Claude Paye (France) (2nd)
June 1996-	Donald Johnson (Canada)

ORGANIZATION OF THE ISLAMIC CONFERENCE (OIC)

Formation date: May 1971

Headquarters: Jeddah (Saudi Arabia)

The OIC was founded to promote Islamic solidarity, and to establish economic, technical, commercial, cultural, humanitarian and political co-operation.

Member states:

Afghanistan	Algeria
Azerbaijan (1991)	Bahrain
Bangladesh	Benin
Burkina Faso	Cameroon
Chad	Comoros
Djibouti	Egypt
Gabon	Gambia
Guinea	Guinea-Bissau
Indonesia	Iran
Iraq	Jordan
Kuwait	Lebanon
Libya	Malaysia
Maldives	Mali
Mauritania	Morocco
Niger	Oman
Pakistan	Palestine*
Qatar	Saudi Arabia
Senegal	Somalia
Sudan	Syria
Tunisia	Turkey
Uganda	United Arab Emirates
Yemen	Zanzibar (Feb-Aug 1993)

*mostly under Israeli occupation; represented by the PLO

Secretaries-General:

1971-1973	Tunku Abdul Rahman Putra (Malaysia)
1973-1976	Hassan al-Tuhamy (Egypt)
1976-Jan 1979	Amadou Karim Gaye (Senegal)
Jan 1979-Jan 1985	Habib Chatti (Tunisia)
Jan 1985-Jan 1989	Sharifuddin Pirzada (Pakistan)
Jan 1989-Jan 1997	Hamid Algabid (Niger)
Jan 1997-	Azzedine Laraki (Morocco)

ORGANIZATION OF PETROLEUM EXPORTING COUNTRIES (OPEC)

Formation date: September 1960
Headquarters: Vienna

OPEC was established by several oil producing states to safeguard interests of its members, and to determine ways of co-operation within the petroleum industry. It gained major importance during the energy crisis of the 1970s.

Member states:

Algeria	Ecuador
Gabon	Iran
Iraq	Indonesia
Kuwait	Libya
Nigeria	Qatar
Saudi Arabia	United Arab Emirates

Secretaries-General:

Jan 1961-April 1964	Fuad Rouhani (Iran)
May 1964-April 1965	Abdul Rahman Bazzaz (Iraq)
May 1965-Dec 1966	Ashraf Lutfi (Kuwait)
Jan-Dec 1967	Mohammed Jukhdar (Saudi Arabia)
Jan-Dec 1968	Francisco Parra (Venezuela)
Jan-Dec 1969	Elrich Sanger (Indonesia)
Jan-Dec 1970	Omar el-Badri (Libya)
Jan 1971-Dec 1972	Nadim Pachachi (Iraq)
Jan 1973-Dec 1974	Abderrahman Khene (Algeria)
Jan 1975-Dec 1976	Mesach Feyide (Nigeria)
Jan 1977-Dec 1978	Ali Mohammed Jaidah (Qatar)
Jan 1979-July 1981	René Ortiz (Ecuador)
July 1981-July 1983	Marc Nan Nguema (Gabon)
July 1983-June 1988	Fadhil al-Chalabi (Iraq) (acting)
June 1988-June 1994	Subroto (Indonesia)
June-Dec 1994	Abdallah al-Badri (Libya) (acting)
Jan 1995-	Rilwanu Lukman (Nigeria)

ORGANIZATION FOR SECURITY AND CO-OPERATION IN EUROPE (OCSE)

Previous name: Conference on Security and Co-operation in Europe (until 1995)
Formation date: 1975
Headquarters: Prague and Vienna

The organization was launched in 1975 in Helsinki. Agreements between all but one European nation (Albania) and Canada and the USA established agreements on security in Europe, as well as scientific, technological and environmental co-operation. Humanitarian co-operation was also covered. After the end of the Cold War the organization was re-vitalized, and it now committed its members to support multi-party democracy, free market economies and human rights. Albania joined in 1991.

Member states:

- Albania (1991)
- Austria
- Belarus (1992)
- Bosnia & Herzegovina (1992)
- Canada
- Cyprus
- Denmark
- Finland
- Georgia (1992)
- Greece
- Iceland
- Italy
- Kyrgyzstan (1992)
- Liechtenstein
- Luxembourg
- Monaco
- Norway
- Portugal
- Russia
- Slovakia
- Spain
- Switzerland
- Turkey
- Ukraine (1992)
- USA
- Vatican City
- Armenia (1992)
- Azerbaijan (1992)
- Belgium
- Bulgaria
- Croatia (1992)
- Czech Republic
- Estonia (1991)
- France
- Germany
- Hungary
- Ireland
- Kazakhstan (1992)
- Latvia (1991)
- Lithuania (1991)
- Moldova (1992)
- Netherlands
- Poland
- Romania
- San Marino
- Slovenia (1992)
- Sweden
- Tajikistan (1992)
- Turkmenistan (1992)
- UK
- Uzbekistan (1992)
- Yugoslavia (suspended 1992)

Secretaries-General:

June 1993-June 1996   Wilhelm Höynck   (Germany)
June 1996-June 1999   Giancarlo Aragona   (Italy)
June 1999-   Ján Kubiš   (Slovakia)

PACIFIC COMMUNITY

Previous name: South Pacific Commission 1948-98
Formation date: 29 July 1948
Headquarters: Nouméa (New Caledonia)

The Community's main function is to advise and consult on the development activities in each territory of the region.

Member states:

American Samoa	Australia
Cook Islands	Fiji
France	French Polynesia
Guam	Kiribati
Marshall Islands	Micronesia
Nauru	New Caledonia
New Zealand	Niue
Norfolk Island	Northern Marianas
Palau	Papua New Guinea
Pitcairn Island	Samoa
Solomon Islands	Tokelau
Tonga	Tuvalu
UK	USA
Vanuatu	Wallis & Futuna

Former member: Netherlands (1949-62)

Secretaries-General:

1949-Nov 1951	William Forsythe (Australia) (1st)
Nov 1951-March 1955	Brian Freeston (UK)
March 1955-Oct 1957	Ralph Bedell (USA)
Oct 1957-March 1963	Thomas Bell (New Zealand)
March 1963-66	William Forsythe (Australia) (2nd)
1966-69	Gawain Bell (UK)
1969-71	Afioga Afoafouvale Misimoa (Western Samoa)
1971-Oct 1975	Gustav Betham (Western Samoa)
Oct 1975-Oct 1979	Esika Salato (Fiji)
Oct 1979-Oct 1981	M.Young Vivian (Niue)
Oct 1981-Oct 1986	Francis Bugotu (Solomon Islands)
Oct 1986-Oct 1989	Palauni Tuiasosopo (American Samoa)
Oct 1989-93	Atanraoi Baiteke (Kiribati)
1993-96	George Sokomanu (Vanuatu)
1996-2000	Robert Dun (Australia)
Jan 2000	Lourdes Pangelinan (Guam)

SOUTH ASIAN ASSOCIATION FOR REGIONAL CO-OPERATION (SAARC)

Formation date: 8 December 1985

Headquarters: Katmandu

The SAARC was formed to promote co-operation between its members especially in economic development.

Member states:

Bangladesh Bhutan
India Maldives
Nepal Pakistan
Sri Lanka

Secretaries-General:

Jan 1987-Oct 1989	Abdul Alisan (Bangladesh)
Oct 1989-Jan 1992	Kant Bhargava (India)
Jan 1992-Jan 1994	Hussain Zaki (Maldives)
Jan 1994-Jan 1997	Yadav Kant Silval (Nepal)
Jan 1997-Jan 1999	Naeemuddin Hasan (Pakistan)
Jan 1999-	Nihal Rodrigo (Sri Lanka)

SOUTHERN AFRICAN DEVELOPMENT COMMUNITY (SADC)

Previous name: Southern African Development Co-ordination Conference (SADCC) 1979-92

Formation date: July 1979

Headquarters: Gaberone

SADCC was founded in 1979 by nine countries in southern Africa to reduce the region's economic dependence on South Africa. In 1992 it was converted to an economic community. After the installation of a democratically elected government in South Africa in 1994, the organization altered its role to include co-operation with South Africa which was then admitted as a member.

Member states:

Angola	Botswana
Lesotho	Malawi
Mauritius (1995)	Mozambique
Namibia (1990)	South Africa (1994)
Swaziland	Tanzania
Zambia	Zimbabwe

Executive Secretaries:

1980-82	Lebang Mpotokwane (Botswana) (acting)
July 1982-84	Arthur Blumeris (Zimbabwe)
1984-93	Simbarashe Makoni (Zimbabwe)
Dec 1993-	Kaire Mbuende (Namibia)

SOUTH EAST ASIA TREATY ORGANIZATION (SEATO)

Formation date: 8 September 1954
Dissolution date: 30 June 1977
Headquarters: Bangkok

In 1954 eight nations signed a collective defence pact covering the general areas of South-East Asia and the South-West Pacific. In addition the pact allowed for economic and technical co-operation. By 1977 it was felt that the pact had outlived its usefulness and was therefore terminated.

Member states:

Australia	France
New Zealand	Pakistan
Philippines	Thailand
UK	USA

Secretaries-General:

July-Sept 1957	Pote Sarasin (Thailand) (1st)
Sept 1957-Jan 1958	William North (Australia) (acting)
Jan 1958-Dec 1963	Pote Sarasin (Thailand) (2nd)
Feb 1964-July 1965	Konthi Suphamongkhon (Thailand)
July 1965-72	Jesus Vargas (Philippines)
1972-June 1977	Sunthorn Hongladarom (Thailand)

SOUTH PACIFIC FORUM (SPF)

Formation date: 5 August 1971
Headquarters: Suva (Fiji)

The forum is a gathering of the government leaders of the independent and self-governing states of the Pacific for discussions of common interests. The Secretariat of the South Pacific Bureau for Economic Co-operation (founded 17 April 1973) acted as the Secretariat of the Forum until 1988 when it formally became the Forum Secretariat.

Member states:

Australia	Cook Islands
Fiji	Kiribati
Marshall Islands	Micronesia
Nauru	New Zealand
Niue	Papua New Guinea
Samoa	Solomon Islands
Tonga	Tuvalu
Vanuatu	

Directors:

1975-83	Gabriel Gris (Papua New Guinea)
1983-86	Mahe Tupouniua (Tonga)
1986-91	Henry Faati Naisali (Fiji)
1991-98	Ieremia Tabai (Kiribati)
Jan 1998-	Noel Levi (Papua New Guinea)

UNITED NATIONS (UN)

Formation date: 24 October 1945
Headquarters: New York

In 1944 discussions were held between USA, USSR, UK and China to agree on proposals to draw up a charter to maintain international peace and security. These proposals were presented to delegates of 50 countries at a conference in San Francisco in June 1945, and the United Nations formally came into existence in October of that year. There are now 189 member states.

Member states: (admission dates)

Afghanistan (1946)
Algeria (1962)
Antigua & Barbuda (1981)
Armenia (1992)
Austria (1955)
Bahamas (1973)
Bangladesh (1974)
Belgium (1945)
Belarus (1945)
Bhutan (1971)
Bosnia & Herzegovina (1992)
Brazil (1945)
Bulgaria (1955)
Burundi (1962)
Cameroon (1960)
Cape Verde (1975)
Chad (1960)
China (1945)
Comoros (1975)
Congo (Kinshasa) (1960)
Côte d'Ivoire (1960)
Cuba (1945)
Czech Republic (1993)
Djibouti (1977)
Dominican Republic (1945)
Egypt (1945)
Equatorial Guinea (1968)
Estonia (1991)
Fiji (1970)
France (1945)
Gambia (1965)

Albania (1955)
Andorra (1993)
Argentina (1945)
Australia (1945)
Azerbaijan (1992)
Bahrain (1971)
Barbados (1966)
Belize (1981)
Benin (1960)
Bolivia (1945)
Botswana (1966)
Brunei (1984)
Burkina Faso (1960)
Cambodia (1955)
Canada (1945)
Central African Republic (1960)
Chile (1945)
Colombia (1945)
Congo (Brazzaville) (1960)
Costa Rica (1945)
Croatia (1992)
Cyprus (1960)
Denmark (1945)
Dominica (1978)
Ecuador (1945)
El Salvador (1945)
Eritrea (1993)
Ethiopia (1945)
Finland (1955)
Gabon (1960)
Germany (1973, East & West separate until 1990)

Georgia (1992)
Greece (1945)
Guatemala (1945)
Guinea-Bissau (1974)
Haiti (1945)
Hungary (1955)
India (1945)
Iran (1945)
Ireland (1955)
Italy (1955)
Japan (1956)
Kazakhstan (1992)
Kiribati (1999)
Korea (South) (1991)
Kyrgyzstan (1992)
Latvia (1991)
Lesotho (1966)
Libya (1955)
Lithuania (1991)
Macedonia (1993)
Malawi (1964)
Maldives (1965)
Malta (1964)
Mauritania (1961)
Mexico (1945)
Moldova (1992)
Mongolia (1961)
Mozambique (1975)
Namibia (1990)
Nepal (1955)
New Zealand (1945)
Niger (1960)
Norway (1945)
Pakistan (1947)
Panama (1945)
Paraguay (1945)
Philippines (1945)
Portugal (1955)
Romania (1955)
Rwanda (1962)
St Lucia (1979)
Samoa (1976)
São Tome & Principe (1975)
Senegal (1960)
Sierra Leone (1961)

Ghana (1957)
Grenada (1974)
Guinea (1958)
Guyana (1966)
Honduras (1945)
Iceland (1946)
Indonesia (1950)
Iraq (1945)
Israel (1949)
Jamaica (1962)
Jordan (1955)
Kenya (1963)
Korea (North) (1991)
Kuwait (1963)
Laos (1955)
Lebanon (1945)
Liberia (1945)
Liechtenstein (1990)
Luxembourg (1945)
Madagascar (1960)
Malaysia (1957)
Mali (1960)
Marshall Islands (1991)
Mauritius (1968)
Micronesia (1991)
Monaco (1993)
Morocco (1956)
Myanmar (1948)
Nauru (1999)
Netherlands (1945)
Nicaragua (1945)
Nigeria (1960)
Oman (1971)
Palau (1994)
Papua New Guinea (1975)
Peru (1945)
Poland (1945)
Qatar (1971)
Russia (1945)
St Christopher & Nevis (1983)
St Vincent (1980)
San Marino (1992)
Saudi Arabia (1945)
Seychelles (1976)
Singapore (1965)

Slovakia   (1993)
Solomon Islands   (1978)
South Africa   (1945)
Sri Lanka   (1955)
Surinam   (1975)
Sweden   (1946)
Tajikistan   (1992)
Thailand   (1946)
Tonga   (1999)
Tunisia   (1956)
Turkmenistan   (1992)
Uganda   (1962)
United Arab Emirates   (1971)
USA   (1945)
Uzbekistan   (1992)
Venezuela   (1945)
Yemen (North-1947; South-1967)
Zambia   (1964)
Slovenia   (1992)
Somalia   (1960)
Spain   (1955)
Sudan   (1956)
Swaziland   (1968)
Syria   (1945)
Tanzania   (1961)
Togo   (1960)
Trinidad & Tobago   (1962)
Turkey   (1945)
Tuvalu   (2000)
Ukraine   (1945)
UK   (1945)
Uruguay   (1945)
Vanuatu   (1981)
Vietnam   (1977)
Yugoslavia   (1945)
Zimbabwe   (1980)

Former members:

Czechoslovakia (1945-92 - Country divided into Czech Republic & Slovakia) Taiwan (replaced in 1971 as the representative of China), USSR (seat taken by Russia in 1991), Zanzibar (1964, united with Tanganyika to form Tanzania), Indonesia withdrew 1965-66. Syria gave up its separate seat during its union with Egypt (1958-61). The two Yemens and the two Germanies united in 1990.

Observer states:

Switzerland, Vatican City

Secretaries-General:

Feb 1946-April 1953	Trygve Lie (Norway)
April 1953-Sept 1961	Dag Hammerskjöld (Sweden) († air accident)
Nov 1961-Dec 1971	U Thant (Burma) (acting Nov 1961-Nov 1962)
Jan 1972-Dec 1981	Kurt Waldheim (Austria)
Jan 1982-Dec 1991	Javier Pérez de Cuellar (Peru)
Jan 1992-Dec 1996	Butros Butros-Ghali (Egypt)
Jan 1997-	Kofi Annan (Ghana)

United Nations Agencies

FOOD AND AGRICULTURAL ORGANIZATION (FAO)

Formation date: 16 October 1945
Headquarters: Rome

Directors-General:

May 1946-April 1948	John Boyd Orr (UK)
April 1946-Dec 1953	Norris Dodd (USA)
Dec 1953-Sept 1956	Philip Cardon (USA)
Sept 1956-June 1968	Binay Sen (India)
June 1968-June 1976	Addeke Boerma (Netherlands)
June 1976-Jan 1994	Edouard Saouma (Lebanon)
Jan 1994-	Jacques Diouf (Senegal)

INTERNATIONAL ATOMIC ENERGY AGENCY (IAEA)

Formation date: 29 July 1957
Headquarters: Vienna

Directors-General:

Oct 1957-Oct 1961	W.Sterling Cole (USA)
Oct 1961-Oct 1981	R.Sigvard Eklund (Sweden)
Oct 1981-97	Hans Blix (Sweden)
1997-	Mohammed el-Baradei (Egypt)

INTERNATIONAL BANK FOR RECONSTRUCTION AND DEVELOPMENT (WORLD BANK)

Formation date: June 1946
Headquarters: Washington DC

Presidents:

June-Dec 1946	Eugene Meyer (USA)
Dec 1946-July 1949	John McCloy (USA)
July 1949-Jan 1963	Eugene Black (USA)
Jan 1963-April 1968	George Woods (USA)
April 1968-July 1981	Robert McNamara (USA)
July 1981-July 1986	Alden (Tom) Clausen (USA)
July 1986-July 1991	Barber Conable (USA)
July 1991-May 1995	Lewis Preston (USA) (†)
May-June 1995	Ernest Stern (USA) (acting)
June 1995-	James Wolfensohn (USA)

INTERNATIONAL CIVIL AVIATION ORGANIZATION (ICAO)

Formation date: 4 April 1947
Headquarters: Montréal

Secretaries-General:

May 1947-Nov 1951	Albert Roper (France)
Nov 1951-July 1959	Ernst Ljungberg (Sweden)

July 1959-Aug 1964	Ronald Macdonnell (Canada)
Aug 1964-Aug 1970	Bernardus Twigt (Netherlands)
Aug 1970-Aug 1976	Assad Kotaite (Lebanon)
Aug 1976-89	Yves Lambert (France)
1989-91	Shivinder Singh Sidhu (India)
Aug 1991-Aug 1997	Philippe Rochat (Switzerland)
Aug 1997-	Renato Costa Pereira (Brazil)

INTERNATIONAL FUND FOR AGRICULTURAL DEVELOPMENT (IFAD)

Formation date: June 1976
Headquarters: Rome

Presidents:

Dec 1977-Nov 1984	Abdelmuhsin al-Sudeary (Saudi Arabia)
Nov 1984-Jan 1993	Idriss Jazairy (Algeria)
Jan 1993-	Fawzi al-Sultan (Kuwait)

INTERNATIONAL LABOUR ORGANIZATION (ILO)

Formation date: 1919
Headquarters: Geneva

Directors-General:

1919-May 1932	Albert Thomas (France) (†)
July 1932-June 1938	Harold Butler (UK)
July 1938-Feb 1941	John Winant (USA)
Feb 1941-June 1948	Edward Phelan (Ireland)
June 1948-May 1970	David Morse (USA)
May 1970-Oct 1973	Wilfred Jenks (UK) (†)
Oct 1973-Feb 1989	Francis Blanchard (France) (acting Oct 1973-Feb 1974)
Feb 1989-March 1999	Michel Hansenne (Belgium)
March 1999-	Juan Somavía (Chile)

INTERNATIONAL MARITIME ORGANIZATION (IMO)

Previous name: Inter-Governmental Maritime Consultative Organization 1959-1982
Formation date: January 1959
Headquarters: London

Secretaries-General:

Jan 1959-Nov 1961	Ove Nielsen (Denmark) (†)
Nov 1961-Jan 1963	William Graham (UK) (acting)
Jan 1963-Jan 1968	Jean Rouiller (France)

Jan 1968-Jan 1974	Colin Goad (UK)
Jan 1974-Jan 1990	Chadrika Srivastava (India)
Jan 1990-	William O'Neil (Canada)

INTERNATIONAL MONETARY FUND (IMF)

Formation date: 27 December 1945
Headquarters: Washington DC

Managing Directors:

May 1946-May 1951	Camille Gutt (Belgium)
May 1951-Dec 1956	Ivar Rooth (Sweden)
Dec 1956-May 1963	Per Jacobsson (Sweden) (†)
Sept 1963-Sept 1973	Pierre-Paul Schweitzer (France)
Sept 1973-Sept 1978	Hendrickus Witteveen (Netherlands)
Sept 1978-Jan 1987	Jacques de Larosière de Champfeu (France)
Jan 1987-Feb 2000	Michel Camdessus (France)
Feb-May 2000	Peter Fischer (USA) (acting)
May 2000-	Horst Köhler (Germany)

INTERNATIONAL TELECOMMUNICATIONS UNION (ITU)

Formation date: 17 May 1865
Headquarters: Geneva

Secretaries-General:

Director 1869-1949

Jan 1869-May 1872	Louis Curchad (Switzerland) (1st)
May 1872-Jan 1873	Charles Lendi (Switzerland)
Feb 1873-Oct 1889	Louis Curchad (Switzerland) (2nd)
Feb-June 1890	August Frey (Switzerland)
Nov 1890-Feb 1897	Timothie Rothen (Switzerland)
March 1897-Aug 1921	Emile Frey (Switzerland)
Aug 1921-Dec 1927	Henri Etienne (Switzerland)
Feb 1928-Oct 1934	Joseph Raber (Switzerland)
Jan 1935-Dec 1949	Frans von Ernst (Switzerland)
Jan 1950-Dec 1953	Léon Mulatier (France)
Jan 1954-June 1958	Marco Andrada (Argentina) (†)
June 1958-Dec 1965	Gerald Gross (USA) (acting June 1958-Jan 1959)
Jan 1966-Feb 1967	Manohar Sarwate (India) (†)
Feb 1967-Dec 1982	Mohammed Mili (Tunisia)
Jan 1983-Oct 1989	Richard Butler (Australia)
Nov 1989-Jan 1999	Pekka Tarjanne (Finland)
Feb 1999-	Yashio Utsumi (Japan)

UNITED NATIONS EDUCATION, SCIENTIFIC AND CULTURAL ORGANIZATION (UNESCO)

Formation date: 4 November 1946
Headquarters: Paris

Directors-General:

May 1947-Nov 1948	Julian Huxley (UK)
Nov 1948-Nov 1952	Jaime Torres Bodet (Mexico)
Nov 1952-June 1953	John Taylor (USA) (acting)
June 1953-Nov 1958	Luther Evans (USA)
Nov 1958-Nov 1961	Vittorino Veronese (Italy)
Nov 1961-Nov 1974	Pierre Maheu (France)
Nov 1974-Nov 1987	Amadou M'Bow (Senegal)
Nov 1987-Nov 1989	Federico Mayor Zaragoza (Spain)
Nov 1989-	Koichiro Matsuura (Japan)

UNITED NATIONS INDUSTRIAL DEVELOPMENT ORGANIZATION (UNIDO)

Formation date: 1 January 1986
Headquarters: Vienna

Directors-General:

Jan 1986-Jan 1993	Domingo Siazon (Philippines)
Jan-March 1993	Louis Alexandrenne (Senegal) (acting)
March 1993-Dec 1997	Mauricio de María y Campos (Mexico)
Dec 1997-	Carlos Magariños (Argentina)

UNIVERSAL POSTAL UNION (UPU)

Formation date: 1 July 1875
Headquarters: Berne

Directors:

1945-Jan 1950	Alois Muri (Switzerland)
Jan 1950-Jan 1961	Fritz Hess (Switzerland)
Jan 1961-Dec 1966	Edward Weber (Switzerland)
Jan 1967-Jan 1975	Michel Rahi (Egypt)
Jan 1975-Jan 1985	Mohammed Sobhi (Egypt)
Jan 1985-Jan 1995	Advaldo Cardoso Botto de Barros (Brazil)
Jan 1995-	Thomas Leavey (USA)

WORLD HEALTH ORGANIZATION (WHO)

Formation date: 7 April 1948
Headquarters: Geneva

Directors-General:

July 1948-May 1953	Brock Chisholm (Canada)
June 1953-June 1973	Marcolino Gomes Candau (Brazil)
June 1973-July 1988	Halfdan Mahler (Denmark)
July 1988-July 1998	Hiroshi Nakajima (Japan)
July 1998-	Gro Harlem Brundtland (Norway)

WORLD INTELLECTUAL PROPERTY ORGANIZATION (WIPO)

Formation date: April 1970
Headquarters: Geneva

Directors-General:

April 1970-Dec 1973	G.Bodenhausen (Netherlands)
Dec 1973-Oct 1997	Arpad Bogsch (USA)
Nov 1997-	Kamil Idris (Sudan)

WORLD METEOROLOGICAL ORGANIZATION (WMO)

Formation date: 23 March 1950
Headquarters: Geneva

Directors-General:

April 1951-55	Gustav Swoboda (Switzerland)
1955-Jan 1980	David Davies (UK)
Jan 1980-Jan 1984	Akel Wiin-Nielsen (Denmark)
Jan 1984-	Godwin Obasi (Nigeria)

WORLD TRADE ORGANIZATION (WTO)

Previous name: General Agreement on Tariffs and Trade (GATT) 1948-95
Formation date: 1 January 1948
Headquarters: Geneva

Directors-General:

Executive Secretary 1948-1966

Jan 1948-May 1968	E.Wyndham White (UK)
May 1968-April 1980	Olivier Long (Switzerland)
April 1980-June 1993	Arthur Dunkel (Switzerland)
June 1993-May 1995	Peter Sutherland (Ireland)
May 1995-April 1999	Renato Ruggiero (Italy)
May 1999-Sept 1999	David Hartridge (UK) (acting)
Sept 1999-	Michael Moore (New Zealand)

WARSAW PACT

Official name: Warsaw Treaty of Friendship, Co-operation and Mutual Assistance
Formation date: 14 May 1955
Dissolution date: 31 March 1991
Headquarters: Moscow

In 1955 the USSR and seven Eastern European nations signed a mutual defence treaty. Albania ceased to participate after 1962, and formally withdrew in 1968. After the collapse of communism the Pact was dissolved in 1991.

Member states:

Albania   (1955-68)
Bulgaria   (1955-91)
Czechoslovakia   (1955-91)
German Democratic Republic   (1955-90)
Hungary   (1955-91)
Poland   (1955-91)
Romania   (1955-91)
USSR   (1955-91)

Secretary-General:

1969-91   Nikolai Firyubin   (USSR)

WESTERN EUROPEAN UNION (WEU)

Formation date: 6 May 1955

Headquarters: London

The WEU is based on The Brussels Treaty of 1948 and its members seek to co-ordinate defence policy and equipment, and to co-operate in other fields.

Member states: (admission dates)

Belgium (1955)	France (1955)
Germany (1955)	Greece (1995)
Italy (1955)	Luxembourg (1955)
Netherlands (1955)	Portugal (1988)
Spain (1988)	UK (1955)

Secretaries-General:

May 1955-Jan 1962	Louis Goffin (France)
Jan 1962-Jan 1971	Iweins d'Eeckhoutte (Belgium)
Jan 1971-Sept 1973	Georges Heisbourg (Luxembourg)
Sept 1973-March 1977	Karl von Plehwe (West Germany) (acting)
March 1977-April 1985	Edouard Longerstaey (Belgium)
April 1985-89	Alfred Cahen (Belgium)
1989-Nov 1994	Willem van Eekelen (Netherlands)
Nov 1994-Nov 1999	José Cutileiro (Portugal)
Nov 1999-	Javier Solana (Spain) (see NATO)

WORLD COUNCIL OF CHURCHES (WCC)

Formation date: 23 August 1948
Headquarters: Geneva

The WCC was formally constituted in 1948 in Amsterdam by an assembly representing 147 churches from 44 countries. It is a fellowship of Christian churches, with Protestant, Anglican, Orthodox and Old Catholic Confessions as members.

Members:

306 Christian churches in over 100 countries

General Secretaries:

Aug 1948-Dec 1966	Willem Visser't Hoft	(Netherlands)
Dec 1966-Aug 1972	Eugene Carson Blake	(USA)
Aug 1972-Jan 1985	Philip Potter	(Dominica)
Jan 1985-Dec 1993	Emilio Castro	(Uruguay)
Dec 1993-	Konrad Raiser	(Germany)

SECTION B

COUNTRIES AND REGIONS

AFGHANISTAN

Official name: Islamic Emirate of Afghanistan

Previous names: Kingdom of Afghanistan until 1973; Republic of Afghanistan 1973-1978 & 1987-92; Democratic Republic of Afghanistan 1978-1987; Islamic State of Afghanistan 1992-97

State founded: July 1747

Capital: Kandahar (1747-74), Kabul (since 1774)

Afghanistan was ruled for many centuries by various powers. Persian rule was overthrown in 1747 and a monarchy was established. This lasted until 1973 when the king was deposed and a republic proclaimed. Another coup in 1978 established a pro-Soviet government, and in 1979 Soviet troops entered the country. Continued armed resistance to the Soviet presence by Islamic guerilla groups led to an agreement in 1988 for their withdrawal. In 1992 the communist government collapsed and the Islamic groups took power, but civil war continued between these groups. One group, Taliban, gained control of southern areas during 1995, and in 1996 seized Kabul, forcing the government to relocate to the north of the country.

Emirs:

July 1747-Oct 1772	Ahmad Shah Durrani	(*f* Ahmad Khan Abdali)
Oct 1772-May 1793	Timur	(*son*)
May 1793-1800	Zaman Mirza	(*son*)
1800-03	Mahmud	(*brother*) (1st)
July 1803-June 1809	Shuja-ul-Mulk	(*brother*) (1st)
June 1809-18	Mahmud	(2nd)
(1818-26	anarchy)	
1826-3	Dost Mohammed	(1st) (abdicated)
April 1839-April 1842	Shuja-ul-Mulk	(2nd)
April 1842-June 1863	Dost Mohammed	(2nd)
June 1863-May 1866	Sher Ali Khan	(*son*) (1st)
May 1866-Oct 1867	Afzal Khan	(*brother*)
Oct 1867-March 1868	Azam Khan	(*brother*)
March 1868-Feb 1879	Sher Ali Khan	(2nd)
Feb-Dec 1879	Yakub Khan	(*son*) (abdicated)
Dec 1879-March 1880	Musa Khan	(*son*)
March 1880-Oct 1881	Ayub Khan	(*uncle*)
Oct 1881-Oct 1901	Abdur Rahman	(*son of Afzal Khan*)
Oct 1901-Feb 1919	Habibullah Khan	(*son*) (assassinated)
20-22 Feb 1919	Nasrullah Khan	(*brother*)
Feb 1919-Jan 1929	Amanullah Khan	(*nephew*) (abdicated)
14-17 Jan 1929	Inayatullah Khan	(*brother*)
Jan-Oct 1929	Habibullah Ghazi	(*f* Baccao Saqqao) (usurper) (deposed, executed)

Kings:

Oct 1929-Nov 1933   Mohammed Nadir Shah   (grand-nephew of Dost Mohammed) (assassinated)
Nov 1933-July 1973   Mohammed Zahir Shah   (son) (deposed)

Presidents:
President of the Revolutionary Council 1978-87

July 1973-April 1978   Mohammed Daoud   (*cousin*) (deposed, assassinated)
April 1978-Sept 1979   Nur Taraki   (deposed, executed)
Sept-Dec 1979   Hafizullah Amin   (deposed, assassinated)
Dec 1979-Nov 1986   Babrak Karmal
Nov 1986-Sept 1987   Mohammed Chamkani   (acting)
Sept 1987-April 1992   Najibullah   (executed 1996)
21-28 April 1992   Abdul Rahim Hatef   (acting) (deposed)
April-June 1992   Sibghatullah Mujadidi
June 1992-Sept 1996   Burhanuddin Rabbani   (deposed)

Leader:
Emir since Oct 1997

Sept 1996-   Mohammed Omar

Prime Ministers:
Chairman of the Executive Committee of the Council of Ministers 1989-90
Chairman of the Interim Council since Sept 1996

May 1927-Jan 1929   Sidar Shir Ahmed Sura-i-Milli
Jan-Oct 1929   Shir Ghiyam
Nov 1929-March 1946   Sidar Hashim Khan
March 1946-Sept 1953   Shah Mahmud Khan
Sept 1953-March 1963   Mohammed Daoud   (1st)
March 1963-Nov 1965   Mohammed Yusuf
Nov 1965-Oct 1967   Mohammed Maiwandwal
Oct-Nov 1967   Abdallah Yakta   (acting)
Nov 1967-June 1971   Nur Etemadi
June 1971-Dec 1972   Abdul Zahir
Dec 1972-July 1973   Mohammed Shafeq
July 1973-April 1978   Mohammed Daoud   (2nd)
April 1978-March 1979   Nur Taraki
March-Dec 1979   Hafizullah Amin
Dec 1979-June 1981   Babrak Karmal
June 1981-May 1988   Soltan Ali Keshtmand   (1st)
May 1988-Feb 1989   Mohammed Sharq
Feb 1989-May 1990   Soltan Ali Keshtmand   (2nd)
May 1990-April 1992   Fazil-ul-Haq Khalikyar
(April-July 1992   post vacant)

July-Aug 1992	Abdul Sabur Fareed
(Aug 1992-June 1993	post vacant)
June 1993-June 1994	Gulbuddin Hekmatyar (1st)
(June-Nov 1994	post vacant)
Nov 1994-95	Arsala Rahmani (acting)
1995-June 1996	Ahmadshah Ahmadzai (acting)
June-Sept 1996	Gulbuddin Hekmatyar (2nd)
Sept 1996-	Mohammed Rabbani

Communist Party* Leaders:

* People's Democratic Party until 1990, Homeland Party
General Secretary

April 1978-Sept 1979	Nur Taraki
Sept-Dec 1979	Hafizullah Amin
Dec 1979-May 1986	Babrak Karmal
May 1986-April 1992	Najibullah

GOVERNMENT-IN-EXILE 1989-92

Operated against communist government in Kabul
Headquarters: Peshawar (Pakistan)

President:

Feb 1989-April 1992	Sibghatullah Mujadidi

Prime Ministers:

June 1988-Feb 1989	Ahmed Shah
Feb 1989-April 1992	Abdulrab Rasul Sayyaf

RIVAL GOVERNMENT

Operates from northern Afghanistan after the capture of Kabul by the fundamentalist Taliban movement in 1996.
Headquarters: Mazar-i-Sharif (until Aug 1998)

President:

Sept 1996-	Burhanuddin Rabbani

Prime Ministers:

Sept 1996-Aug 1997	Gulbuddin Hekmatyar
Aug 1997	Abdul Rahman Ghafurzai († air accident)
Aug 1997-	Mohammed Ali Jawid (acting)

ALBANIA

Official name: Republic of Albania, Republika Shqipërisë

Previous names: Kingdom of Albania 1928-1946; People's Republic of Albania 1946-1976; Socialist People's Republic of Albania 1976-91

Independence date: 28 November 1912

Capital: Tirana

Albania was ruled by Turkey from 1468 until 1912 when independence was proclaimed. During and just after World War I it was occupied by several nations, its independence being restored in 1920. From 1925 to 1928 it was a republic, and then a monarchy. During World War II Albania was occupied first by Italy and then by Germany. After liberation in 1944 a communist government took over and proclaimed a republic in 1946. Because of its adherence to Stalinist policies Albania broke off relations with the USSR in 1961, and became increasingly isolated until 1991 when, in line with other east European countries, a multi-party democracy was introduced.

Heads of State:

March-Sept 1914	Prince William of Wied
Sept 1914	Burhan Eddin
(Sept 1914-April 1920	Austrian, French & Italian occupation)

Regents:

April 1920-Dec 1921	Aqif Pasha Elbasini/Luigi Bumçi/Mihal Turtulli/Abdi Toptani
Dec 1921-Feb 1922	Omer Vrioni/Antoine Pistulli
Dec 1921-Jan 1925	Sotir Peçi/Refik Toptani
Feb 1922-Jan 1925	Xhafar Ypi/Gjon Çoba

President:

Jan 1925-Aug 1928	Ahmed Zogu

King:

Aug 1928-April 1939	Zog I (*b* Ahmed Zogu) (exiled)

Governors:

7-23 April 1939	Alfredo Guzzoni
April 1939-March 1943	Francesco Jacomini di San Lavino
March-June 1943	Alberto Pariani
(Sept 1943-Oct 1944	German occupation)
(Nov 1944-Jan 1946	Provisional government)

Presidents:

Chairman of the Presidium of the People's Assembly Jan 1946-March 1991

Jan 1946-July 1953	Omer Nishani
July 1953-Nov 1982	Haxhi Lleshi
Nov 1982-April 1992	Ramiz Alia
April 1992-July 1997	Sali Berisha (DP)
July 1997-	Rexhep Mejdani (SPA)

Prime Ministers:

Chairman of the Council of Ministers 1946-92

Nov 1912-March 1914	Ismail Kemal Vlora
March-Oct 1914	Turkhan Pasha Permeti (1st)
Oct 1914-Feb 1916	Essad Toptani Pasha (not recognised by occupying powers)
(Feb 1916-Dec 1918	post vacant)
Dec 1918-March 1920	Turkhan Pasha Permeti (2nd)
March-Nov 1920	Suleyman Delvina
Dec 1920-Oct 1921	Elias Vrioni (1st)
Oct-Dec 1921	Pandeli Evangheli (1st)
7-12 Dec 1921	Hassan Pristina
12-25 Dec 1921	Xhafar Ypi (1st)
Dec 1921-Dec 1922	Omer Vrioni
Dec 1922-1923	Ahmed Zogu (1st)
1923-May 1924	Shefqet Verlaçi (1st)
May-June 1924	Elias Vrioni (2nd)
June-Dec 1924	Theophanes (Fan) Noli
Jan 1925-Sept 1928	Ahmed Zogu (2nd)
Sept 1928-March 1930	Kostaq Kolta (1st)
March 1930-Oct 1935	Pandeli Evangheli (2nd)
Oct 1935-Nov 1936	Mehdi Frashëri (1st)
Nov 1936-April 1939	Kostaq Kolta (2nd)
9-12 April 1939	Xhafar Ypi (2nd)
April 1939-Dec 1941	Shefqet Verlaçi (2nd)
Dec 1941-Jan 1943	Mustafa Merlika-Kruja
Jan-Feb 1943	Ekrem Lubohova (1st)
Feb-May 1943	Maliq Bushati
May-Sept 1943	Ekrem Lubohova (2nd)
Sept-Oct 1943	Ibrahim Bicakçiu
Oct-Nov 1943	Mehdi Frashëri (2nd)
Nov 1943-July 1944	Rexhep Mitrovica
July-Oct 1944	Fiori Dine
Nov 1944-July 1954	Enver Hoxha
July 1954-Dec 1981	Mehmet Shehu († suicide)
Jan 1982-Feb 1991	Adil Çarçani
Feb-June 1991	Fatos Nano (1st) (APL, SPA)
June-Dec 1991	Ylli Bufi (SPA)

Dec 1991-April 1992   Vilson Ahmeti
April 1992-March 1997   Alexander Meksi   (DP)
March-July 1997   Bashkim Fino   (SPA)
July 1997-Oct 1998   Fatos Nano   (2nd) (SPA)
Oct 1998-Oct 1999   Pandeli Majko   (SPA)
Oct 1999   Ilir Meta   (SPA)

APL = Albanian Party of Labour (sole legal party until 1991)
DP = Democratic Party
SPA = Socialist Party of Albania (*f* APL)

Communist Party* Leaders:

* Albanian Party of Labour
Secretary-General 1944-July 1954
First Secretary of the Central Committee July 1954-91

Nov 1944-April 1985   Enver Hoxha (†)
April 1985-June 1991   Ramiz Alia
(1991   multi-party system introduced)

ALGERIA

Official name: Democratic People's Republic of Algeria, Jamhuriya al-Jazairiya al-Democratia as-Shabiya
Previous name: Algerian Republic 1962-1963
Independence date: 3 July 1962
Capital: Algiers (Al-Jazair)

After three centuries of Turkish rule Algeria came under French control between 1830 and 1860. In 1946 the colony was transformed into a group of French departments. An armed struggle for independence led by the National Liberation Front began in 1954. In 1962 referenda in both France and Algeria approved the granting of self-determination, and the independence of Algeria was proclaimed on 3 July. After 30 years of one-party rule, multi-party elections were held, but were annulled when it appeared that an Islamist party was winning. Armed Islamic groups were then formed and began an insurrection resulting in many civilian deaths.

Governors-General:

1900-01	Célestin Jonnart	(1st)
1901-03	Amedée Revoil	
1903	Maurice Varnier	
1903-11	Célestin Jonnart	(2nd)
1911-18	Charles Lutaud	
1918-19	Célestin Jonnart	(3rd)
1919-21	Jean-Baptiste Abel	
1921-25	Jules Steeg	
1925	Henri Dubief	
1925-27	Maurice Viollette	
1927-30	Pierre-Louis Bordes	
1930-35	Jules-Gaston Carde	
1935-40	Georges Le Beau	
1940-41	Jean-Charles Abrial	
1941-43	Yves-Charles Châtel	
1943	Bernard-Marcel Peyrouton	
1943-44	Georges Catroux	
1944-48	Yves Chataigneau	
1948-51	Marcel-Edmond Naegelen	
1951-55	Roger Leonard	
1956	Jacques-Émile Soustelle	

Ministers-Resident:

1956	Georges Catroux

Feb 1956-May 1958   Robert Lacoste
12-25 May 1958   André Mutter

Delegates-General:

June-Dec 1958   Robert Salan
Dec 1958-Nov 1960   Paul Delouvrier
Nov 1960-March 1962   Jean Morin

High Commissioner:

March-July 1962   Christian Fouchet

Presidents:

Chairman of the Revolutionary Committee July 1965-Dec 1976
Chairman of the High Council of State Jan 1992-Jan 1994

Sept 1962-Sept 1963   Ferhat Abbas
Sept 1963-July 1965   Ahmed Ben Bella   (deposed)
July 1965-Dec 1978   Houari Boumédienne   (*b* Mohammed Boukarouba) (†)
Dec 1978-Feb 1979   Rabah Bitat   (acting)
Feb 1979-Jan 1992   Chadli Benjedid
11-12 Jan 1992   Abdelmalek Benhabyles   (acting)
Jan-June 1992   Mohammed Boudiaf   († assassinated)
July 1992-Jan 1994   Ali Kafi
Jan 1994-April 1999   Liamine Zeroual
April 1999-   Abdelaziz Bouteflika

Prime Ministers:

April-July 1962   Abderrahman Farès
July-Sept 1962   Youssef Ben Khedda
Sept 1962-July 1965   Ahmed Ben Bella
July 1965-Dec 1978   Houari Boumédienne   (†)
(Dec 1978-Feb 1979   post vacant)
Feb 1979-Jan 1984   Mohammed Abdelghani
Jan 1984-Nov 1988   Abdelhamid Brahimi
Nov 1988-Sept 1989   Kasdi Merbah   (assassinated 1993)
Sept 1989-June 1991   Mouloud Hamrouche
June 1991-July 1992   Sid Ahmed Ghozali
July 1992-Aug 1993   Belaid Abdessalam
Aug 1993-April 1994   Redha Malek
April 1994-Dec 1995   Mokdad Sifi
Dec 1995-Dec 1998   Ahmed Ouyahia
Dec 1998-Dec 1999   Smail Hamdani
Dec 1999   Ahmed Benbitour

GOVERNMENT-IN-EXILE 1958-62

Headquarters: Cairo
Operated during the independence war against France

Prime Ministers:

Sept 1958-Aug 1961	Ferhat Abbas
Aug 1961-July 1962	Youssef Ben Khedda

ANDORRA

Official name: Principality of Andorra, Principat d'Andorra (Catalan)
Previous name: Valleys of Andorra until 1982
State founded: 1278
Capital: Andorra la Vella

The origins of Andorra can be traced back to the 9th century when the emperor Charlemagne established a buffer state in the Pyrrenes against the Moors in Spain. Andorra's status was settled in 1278 when it was placed under the joint suzerainty of the Bishop of Urgel in Spain and the Compte de Foix as co-princes, the latter's rights now being exercised by the President of France. A change in the system of government was introduced in 1982 when the first ministerial cabinet was formed. In 1993 the co-princes accepted the results of a referendum conferring full sovereignty on Andorra.

Co-Princes:
1. Heads of State of France
2. Bishops of Urgel (Spain) -

1879-1900	Salvador Casañas y Pages
1901-02	Raimundo Riu y Calañas
1903-07	Juan Laguarda y Fenollera
1907-18	Juan Bennloch y Viva
1918-40	Justino Guitart y Vilardebo
1942-69	Ramón Iglesias Navarra
June 1969-Nov 1970	Ramón Malla Call (acting)
Nov 1970-	Joan Marti Alanis

First Syndics (since 1903):

1903-6	Bonaventura Maestre (1st)
1906-11	Pere Moles
1911-15	Bonaventura Maestre (2nd)
1915-17	Pere Font (1st)
1917-20	Josep Vilanova
1920-23	Bonaventura Villarubia
1923-27	Pere Font (2nd)
1927-33	Roc Pallares
1933-36	Pere Torres
1936-Dec 1960	Francesc Cairat
Dec 1960-Dec 1966	Julià Reig Ribó (1st)
Dec 1966-Dec 1972	Francesc Escude Ferrero
Dec 1972-Dec 1978	Julià Reig Ribó (2nd)

Dec 1978-Jan 1982   Estanislau Sangrà Font

(after Jan 1982 the First Syndics ceased to exercise any executive function)

Prime Ministers:
President of the Government

Jan 1982-April 1984	Oscar Ribas Reig	(*nephew of J.Reig Ribó*) (1st)
April 1984-Jan 1990	Josep Pintat Solens	
Jan 1990-Dec 1994	Oscar Ribas Reig	(2nd)
Dec 1994-	Marc Forné Molné	(LU)

LU = Liberal Union

ANGOLA

Official name:	Republic of Angola, República de Angola
Previous name:	People's Republic of Angola 1975-92
Independence date:	11 November 1975
Capital:	Luanda

Portuguese settlements were established in Angola in 1491 and until 1951 it was a Portuguese colony. Its status was then changed to Overseas Territory, and from 1955 it was a province of metropolitan Portugal. In 1961 a guerilla war aimed at winning independence began, and the 1974 coup in Portugal began moves towards independence. A transitional government bringing together the three independence movements (MPLA, UNITA and FNLA) was formed but collapsed after 7 months. In November 1975 Portugal withdrew from Angola, and the MPLA proclaimed a government in Luanda, which received widespread recognition. The other two parties proclaimed a rival government which did not function for long. Cuban troops assisted the Luanda government to extend control over most of the country, but UNITA maintained armed opposition to it until the 1991 peace agreement which led to multi-party elections in 1992. UNITA rejected the results and resumed the war. Another peace agreement was signed in 1995, but fighting resumed in late 1998.

Governors:

1900-03	Francesco Moncada	
1903-04	Eduardo da Costa	(1st)
1904	Custodio de Borja	
1904-06	António Curto	
1906-07	Eduardo da Costa	(2nd)
1907-09	Henrique Couceira	
1909	Alvaro Ferreira	
1909-10	José Rocadas	
1910-11	Caetano Gonçalves	
1911-12	Manuel Coelho	
1912-15	José de Matos	(1st)
1915-16	António de Eca	
1916-17	Pedro do Amorim	
1917-18	Jaime Morais	
1918-19	Filomeno Cabral	(1st)
1919-20	Francesco Reis	

Governors-General:

1921-24	José de Matos	(2nd)
1924	João Soares	
1924-25	Antero de Carvalho	

1925-26	Francesco Chaves
1926-28	António Ferreira
1928-29	António Mora
1929-30	Filomeno Cabral (2nd)
1930-31	José Faro
1931-34	Eduardo Viana
1934-35	Julio Lencastre
1935-39	António Mateus
1939-41	Manuel Mano
1941-42	Abel Souto-Maior
1942-43	Alvaro Morna
1943	Manuel Figueira
1943-47	Vasco Alves
1947	Fernando Mena
1947-55	José Carvalho
1955-59	Horacio Rebelo
1960-61	Alvaro Tavares
1961-62	Venancio Deslandes
1962-66	Jaime Marques
1966-72	Camilo Rebocho Vaz
1972-74	Fernando Castro
June-July 1974	Silvino Marques (see Cape Verde)
July 1974-Jan 1975	António Rosa Coutinho

High Commissioner:

Jan-Nov 1975	António Cardoso

Presidents:

Nov 1975-Sept 1979	Agostinho Neto (MPLA) (†)
Sept 1979-	José Eduardo dos Santos (MPLA)

Prime Ministers:

Jan-Aug 1975	Lopo do Nascimento (MPLA) (1st)/Johnny Eduardo (UNITA)/ José N'Dele (FNLA)
(Aug-Nov 1975	post abolished)
Nov 1975-Dec 1978	Lopo do Nascimento (2nd)
(Dec 1978-July 1991	post abolished)
July 1991-Dec 1992	Fernando Van-Dúnem (1st)
Dec 1992-June 1996	Marcolino Moco
June 1996-Jan 1999	Fernando Van-Dúnem (2nd)
(Jan 1999	post abolished)

FNLA = Frente Nacional de Libertação de Angola
MPLA = Movimento Popular de Libertação de Angola (sole legal party 1975-91)
UNITA = União Nacional para a Independência Total de Angola

GOVERNMENT-IN-EXILE 1962-72

Headquarters: Leopoldville, later renamed Kinshasa
Operated during part of the independence war against Portugal.

Prime Minister:

April 1962-Dec 1972   Holden Roberto   (FNLA)

RIVAL GOVERNMENT

Democratic Republic of Angola
Headquarters: Huambo

President:

Dec 1975-Jan 1976   Jonas Savimbi   (UNITA)

Prime Ministers:

Dec 1975-Jan 1976   Johnny Eduardo   (UNITA)/José N'Dele (FNLA)

Secessionist State

CABINDA

Secessionist governments were proclaimed twice in the enclave of Cabinda, but neither functioned for long.

Presidents:

Aug 1975   Luis Ranque Franque
May 1977   Henrique N'Zita Tiago

Prime Minister:

Aug 1975   François-Xavier Lubota

ANTIGUA AND BARBUDA

Official name: State of Antigua and Barbuda
Independence date: 1 November 1981
Capital: St John's

Antigua was visited by Christopher Columbus in 1493, and colonized by British settlers from 1632. It was part of the Leeward Islands Federation from 1871 until 1956, when it became a separate Crown Colony. A measure of self-government was granted in 1960, and from 1958 until 1962 Antigua was part of the West Indies Federation. In 1967 it became a UK Associated State and full independence followed in 1981.

Administrators:

1936	Hubert Bode
1936-41	James Harford
1941-44	Herbert Boon
1944-46	F.S.Harcourt
1946-47	Leslie Greening
1947-54	Richard Wayne
1954-58	Alec Lovelace
1958-64	Ian Turbott
1964-66	David Rose
1966-67	Wilfred Jacobs

Governor:

Feb 1967-Nov 1981	Wilfred Jacobs

Governors-General:

Represent monarch who is concurrently British monarch

Nov 1981-June 1993	Wilfred Jacobs
June 1993-	John Carlisle

Chief Minister:

Jan 1960-Feb 1967	Vere Bird (ALP)

Prime Ministers:

Premier 1967-81

Feb 1967-Feb 1971	Vere Bird (1st) (ALP)
Feb 1971-Feb 1976	George Walter (PLM)

Feb 1976-March 1994	Vere Bird	(2nd) (ALP)
March 1994-	Lester Bird	(son) (ALP)

ALP = Antigua Labour Party
PLM = Progressive Labour Movement

Dependency

BARBUDA

Capital: Codrington

Council Chairmen:

1981-85	T. Hilbourne Frank	
1985-?	Arthur Nibbs	(1st)
?-?	John Thomas	
1997	Arthur Nibbs	(2nd)

ARGENTINA

Official name: Argentine Republic, República Argentina
Previous name: Argentine Confederation 1852-62
Independence date: 9 July 1816
Capital: Buenos Aires (Confederal capital 1852-62: Paraná)

Argentina was first colonized by Spain in 1534 and at first formed part of the Vice-Royalty of Peru but was later separated under the name La Plata. In 1816 Argentina proclaimed its independence. Civil wars plagued the early years; from 1827 to 1852 there was no central government. In that year a confederation was formed by the regional governments, excluding Buenos Aires. It rejoined the rest of Argentina in 1862 to form the Argentine Republic. The most important developments of the twentieth century were the two periods of populist Peronist rule (1946-55 & 1973-76), and the military regime of 1976-83 during which many opponents were killed, and the Falkland Islands War with Britain in 1982 was lost. Democracy was restored in 1983.

Heads of State:

July 1816-June 1819	Juan Puerreydon
June 1819-Feb 1820	José Rondeau
(Feb 1820-Feb 1826	period of disintegration)

Presidents:

Feb 1826-July 1827	Bernardino Rivadavia
July-Aug 1827	Vicente López y Planes
(1827-52	no central government)
May 1852-Feb 1860	Justo de Urquiza († assassinated)
Feb 1860-Sept 1861	Santiago Derqui (acting)
Sept 1861-Oct 1862	Juan Esteban Pedernera (acting)
Oct 1862-Oct 1868	Bartolomé Mitre
Oct 1868-Oct 1874	Domingo Sarmiento
Oct 1874-Oct 1880	Nicolás Avellaneda
Oct 1880-Oct 1886	Julio Roca (1st)
Oct 1886-Aug 1890	Miguel Juárez Celmán (*son-in-law*)
Aug 1890-Oct 1892	Carlos Pellegrini
Oct 1892-Jan 1895	Luis Sáenz Peña
Jan 1895-Oct 1898	José E. Uriburu
Oct 1898-Oct 1904	Julio Roca (2nd)
Oct 1904-March 1906	Manuel Quintana (†)
March 1906-Oct 1910	José Alcorta
Oct 1910-Aug 1914	Roque Sáenz Peña (*son of L.Sáenz Peña*) (†)
Aug 1914-Oct 1916	Victorino de la Plaza (acting)

COUNTRIES AND REGIONS

Oct 1916-Oct 1922	Hipólito Irigoyen (1st) (UCR)
Oct 1922-Oct 1928	Marcello Torcuato de Alvear (UCR)
Oct 1928-Sept 1930	Hipólito Irigoyen (2nd) (deposed) (UCR)
Sept 1930-Feb 1932	José F.Uriburu (*son of J.E.Uriburu*)
Feb 1932-Feb 1938	Agustín Justo
Feb 1938-June 1942	Roberto Ortiz
June 1942-June 1943	Ramón Castillo (deposed)
5-7 June 1943	Arturo Rawson
June 1943-March 1944	Pedro Ramírez
March 1944-June 1946	Edelmiro Farrell
June 1946-Sept 1955	Juan Perón (1st) (deposed) (FJL)
Sept-Nov 1955	Eduardo Lonardi (deposed)
Nov 1955-April 1958	Pedro Aramburu (assassinated 1970)
April 1958-March 1962	Arturo Frondizi (UCR-Intransigent)
March 1962-Oct 1963	José Guido
Oct 1963-June 1966	Arturo Illia (deposed) (UCR del Puebla)
June 1966-June 1970	Juan Onganía
June 1970-March 1971	Roberto Levingston
March 1971-May 1973	Alejandro Lanusse
May-July 1973	Héctor Campora (FJL)
July-Oct 1973	Raúl Lastiri (acting)
Oct 1973-July 1974	Juan Perón (2nd) (†) (FJL)
July 1974-March 1976	María Estela de Perón (*b* M.E.Martínez) (*widow*) (deposed) (FJL)
March 1976-March 1981	Jorge Videla (see Tucumán)
March-Dec 1981	Roberto Viola
Dec 1981-June 1982	Leopoldo Galtieri
June-July 1982	Alfredo Saint-Jean (acting)
July 1982-Dec 1983	Reynaldo Bignone
Dec 1983-July 1989	Raul Alfonsín Foulkes (UCR)
July 1989-Dec 1999	Carlos Menem (PJ) (see La Rioja)
Dec 1999	Fernando de la Rúa (UCR)

FJL = Frente Justicialista Liberacion
PJ = Partido Justicialista (*f* FJL)
UCR = Union Civica Radical

Chiefs of Cabinet:

May 1995-March 1996	Eduardo Bauzá
March 1996-Dec 1999	Jorge Rodríguez
Dec 1999-	Rodolfo Terragno

Provinces

Governors since the return to civilian rule in 1958 are listed, and include the military appointed ones of 1962-63, 1966-73 and 1976-83

BUENOS AIRES

Capital: La Plata

Governors:

May 1958-March 1962	Oscar Alende
March-April 1962	Jorge Bermudez Emparanza (see Córdoba)
April-June 1962	Roberto Etchepareborda
June-Oct 1962	Félix Viera
Oct 1962-April 1963	Francisco Imaz (1st)
April 1963-June 1966	Anselmo Marini
June-July 1966	Jorge Von Stecher (acting)
July 1966-June 1969	Francisco Imaz (2nd)
June 1969-June 1970	Saturnino Llorente
June 1970-Sept 1971	Horacio Rivara
Sept 1971-May 1973	Miguel Moraques
May 1973-Jan 1974	Oscar Bidegain
Jan 1974-March 1976	Victorio Calabro
24-30 March 1976	Adolfo Sigwald
March 1976-March 1981	Ibérico Saint Jean
March 1981-Jan 1982	Oscar Gallino
Jan 1982-Dec 1983	Jorge Aguado
Dec 1983-Dec 1987	Alejandro Armendariz
Dec 1987-Dec 1991	Antonio Cafiero
Dec 1991-Dec 1999	Eduardo Duhalde (PJ)
Dec 1999-	Carlos Ruckauf (PJ)

CATAMARCA

Capital: Catamarca

Governors:

May 1958-April 1962	Juan Manuel Salas
April 1962-June 1966	Armando Navarro
June 1966-June 1971	Guillermo Brizuela
June 1971-May 1973	Agustín Perneartti
May 1973-March 1976	Hugo Mott
March-May 1976	Alberto Lucena

May 1976-Dec 1978	Jorge Carlucci
Dec 1978-April 1981	Oscar Barcena
April 1981-Dec 1983	Arnoldo Castillo (1st)
Dec 1983-Dec 1987	Vicente Saadi
Dec 1987-April 1991	Ramón Saadi
(April-Dec 1991	Federal government trusteeship)
Dec 1991-Dec 1999	Arnoldo Castillo (2nd) (UCR)
Dec 1999-	Oscar Castillo (*son*) (UCR)

CHACO

Capital: Resistencia

Governors:

May 1958-April 1962	Anselmo Zoilo Duca
1962	Víctor Fleytas
1962	Manrique Mom
1962-63	Marcelino Castelan
1963	Osvaldo Núñez
1963-66	Deolindo Bittel (1st)
1966	Ricardo Miro
1966-67	Rafael Torrado
1967-71	Miguel Basail
1971-73	Oscar Mazza
May 1973-March 1976	Deolindo Bittel (2nd)
1976	Oscar Zucconi
1976-81	Antonio Serrano
1981-83	José Ruiz Palacios
Dec 1983-Dec 1987	Florencio Tenev (PJ)
Dec 1987-Dec 1991	Danilo Baroni (UCR)
Dec 1991-Dec 1995	Rolando Tauguinas (AC)
Dec 1995-	Angel Rozas (UCR)

AC = Accion Chaqueña

CHUBUT

Capital: Rawson

Governors:

May 1958-April 1962	Jorge Galina
May-June 1962	Fernando Elizondo
June-Oct 1962	Julio Petrochi
Oct-Nov 1962	José Quintans
Nov 1962-April 1963	Pedro Priani

May-Oct 1963   Carlos Miranda Naon
Oct 1963-Oct 1965   Roque González
15-25 Oct 1965   Armando Knischnik   (acting)
Oct 1965 June 1966   Manuel Pio Raso
28-29 June 1966   Carlos Vellegal
June-July 1966   Gerardo Ojanguren
Aug 1966-Jan 1967   Rodolfo Varela
Jan 1967-March 1968   Osvaldo Guaita
March 1968-July 1970   Guillermo Pérez Piton
Aug 1970-May 1973   Jorge Costa
May 1973-March 1976   Benito Fernández
March-April 1976   Rafael de Piano
April 1976-Nov 1978   Julio Etchegoyen
Nov-Dec 1978   Alberto Rueda
Dec 1978-April 1981   Angel Martín
April 1981-Dec 1983   Niceto Ayerra
Dec 1983-Dec 1987   Atilio Viglione
Dec 1987-Sept 1990   Nestor Perl
Oct 1990-Dec 1991   Fernando Cosentino
Dec 1991-Dec 1999   Carlos Maestro
Dec 1999-   José Lizarume

CORDOBA

Capital: Córdoba

Governors:

May 1958-June 1960   Arturo Zanichelli
June 1960-March 1961   Juan de Larrechea
March 1961-March 1962   Jorge Bermudez Emparanza
March-April 1962   Mario Atencio
April-June 1962   Aniceto Pérez
June 1962-Oct 1963   Rogelio Nores Martínez
Oct 1963-June 1966   Justo Páez Molina
June-July 1966   Gustavo Martínez Zuviria
July-Sept 1967   Miguel Ferrer Deheza
Sept 1967-June 1969   Carlos Caballero
June-July 1969   Jorge Carcagno
July 1969-April 1970   Roberto Huerta
April-June 1970   Juan Carlos Reyes
June 1970-Feb 1971   Bernardo Dag
Feb-March 1971   Carlos Gigena Parker
2-16 March 1971   José Uriburu
March 1971-May 1973   Helvio Gouzden   (see La Pampa)
May 1973-Feb 1974   Ricardo Obregon Cano

Feb-March 1974	Mario Agodino (acting)
March-Sept 1974	Duilio Rafael Brunello
Sept 1974-Sept 1975	Raúl Lacabanne
Sept 1975	Luciano Menéndez
Sept 1976-March 1976	Raúl Bercovich Rodríguez
March-April 1976	José Vaquero
April 1976-Jan 1979	Carlos Chasseling
Jan-March 1979	Miguel Marini
March 1979-Jan 1982	Adolfo Sigwald (see Buenos Aires)
Jan 1982-Dec 1983	Rubén Pellanda
Dec 1983-July 1995	Eduardo Angeloz (UCR)
July 1995-Dec 1998	Ramón Mestre (UCR)
Dec 1998-	José Manuel de la Sota (PJ)

CORRIENTES

Capital: Corrientes

Governors:

May 1958-March 1962	Fernando Piargine Niveira
1962	Raúl Fait
1962-63	Walter Alsina
April 1963-June 1966	Nicolás Díaz Colodrero
1966	Mario Laprida
1966-67	Gustavo Revidatti
1967-69	Hugo Garay Sánchez
1969-72	Adolfo Navajas Artaza
1972-73	Roberto Tiscornia
May 1973-March 1976	Julio Romero
1976-81	Luis Gómez Centurion
1981-83	Juan Pita
Dec 1983-Dec 1987	José Romero Feris
Dec 1987-Dec 1991	Ricardo Leconte
Dec 1991-July 1999	Raúl Romero Feris
July-Dec 1999	Pedro Braillard Poccard
Dec 1999-	Ramón Mestre (see Córdoba)

ENTRE RIOS

Capital: Paraná

Governors:

1958-62	Raúl Uranga
1963-66	Carlos Contín

1966-73	Ricardo Favre
1973-March 1976	Enrique Cresto
April 1976-Aug 1978	Ruben Di Bello
Aug 1978-April 1981	Carlos Aguirre
April 1981-Feb 1983	Jorge Washington Ferreira
Feb-Dec 1983	Mario Bertozzi
Dec 1983-Dec 1987	Sergio Montiel (UCR)
Dec 1987-Dec 1991	Jorge Busti (1st)
Dec 1991-Dec 1995	Mario Moine
Dec 1995-Dec 1999	Jorge Busti (2nd)
Dec 1999-	Alberto Montiel (UCR)

FORMOSA

Capital: Formosa

Governors:

April-Dec 1958	Luis Gutnisky (†)
Dec 1958-April 1962	Emilio Tomás
April-Dec 1962	Guillermo Sosa Laprida (1st)
Dec 1962-Oct 1963	Italo Occhilupo
Oct 1963-June 1966	Alberto Montoya
July 1966	Héctor Oliveira
July 1966-May 1973	Guillermo Sosa Laprida (2nd)
May-Nov 1973	Antenor Gauna
Nov 1973	A.Rodríguez Foz
Dec 1973-Nov 1975	Juan Carlos Taparelli
Nov 1975-March 1976	Horacio Gorlori
March-April 1976	Agustín Alturria
April 1976-Nov 1981	Juan Carlos Colombo
Dec 1981-April 1983	Rodolfo Rhinera
April-Dec 1983	Essio Massa
Dec 1983-Dec 1987	Floro Bogado
Dec 1987-Dec 1995	Vicente Joga
Dec 1995-	Gildo Insfrán (PJ)

JUJUY

Capital: San Salvador de Jujuy

Governors:

May 1958-April 1962	Horacio G.Guzmán (1st)
April-May 1962	Oigimer Silva Ballbe
May-Oct 1962	Fortunato Daud

Oct 1962-Oct 1963	Roberto Pomarez
Oct 1963-Aug 1964	Horacio G.Guzmán (2nd)
Aug 1964-June 1965	Antonio de la Rúa
June 1965-Jan 1966	Carlos Fernández Jensen
Jan-Feb 1966	Roberto Hansen
Feb-June 1966	José Martiarena
June-Aug 1966	Fernando Guillen
Aug 1966-Jan 1967	Héctor Puente Pistarini
Jan 1967-June 1970	Dario Arias
June-Aug 1970	Eduardo Episcopo
Aug 1970-June 1971	Julio Aranguren
June-Nov 1971	Carlos González López
Nov 1971-May 1973	Manuel Pérez
May 1973-March 1976	Carlos Snopek (1st)
March-April 1976	Carlos Bulacios
April 1976-April 1981	Fernando Vicente
April 1981-Jan 1982	Rafael Zenon Jauregui
Jan-Oct 1982	Horacio Guzmán
Oct 1982-Dec 1983	Nestor Ulloa
Dec 1983-Dec 1987	Carlos Snopek (2nd)
Dec 1987-Dec 1991	Ricardo de Aparici
Dec 1991-April 1993	Roberto Dominguez
2-14 April 1993	José Ficoseco (acting)
April 1993-96	Oscar Perassi (†)
1996-Dec 1999	Carlos Ferraro
Dec 1999-	Gerardo Morales

LA PAMPA

Capital: Santa Rosa

Governors:

May 1958-Dec 1959	Ismael Amit (1st)
10-23 Dec 1959	Héctor Fazzini
Dec 1959-May 1960	Angel Lagomarsino
May 1960-April 1962	Ismael Amit (2nd)
April 1962-Oct 1963	Mario Pensotti
Oct 1963-June 1966	Ismael Amit (3rd)
June-Aug 1966	Jorge Granada
Aug 1966-Jan 1967	Carlos González
23-27 Jan 1967	Abelardo de Campos
Jan 1967-March 1971	Helvio Gouzden
March-May 1971	Floreal Conte
May 1971-May 1973	Angel Trapaglia
May 1973-March 1976	Aquiles Regazzoli
March-April 1976	Flavio Iriart

April 1976-Nov 1978	Carlos Aguirre
Nov 1978-April 1981	Julio Etchegoyen
April 1981-Feb 1983	Ricardo Telleriarte
Feb-Dec 1983	Eduardo Fraire
Dec 1983-Dec 1987	Rubén Marin (1st)
Dec 1987-Dec 1991	Nestor Rufino Ahuad
Dec 1991-	Rubén Marin (2nd)

LA RIOJA

Capital: La Rioja

Governors:

May 1958-April 1962	Herminio Torres Brizuela
April 1962-Oct 1963	Manuel Fernández Valdez
Oct 1963-June 1966	Juan de Caminos
June 1966-Jan 1967	Julio Krause
Jan 1967-71	Guillermo Iribarren
1971-72	Juan Bilmezis
1972-May 1973	Julio Luchessi
May 1973-March 1976	Carlos Menem (1st) (FJL)
March 1976-March 1981	Francisco Llerena
March-Dec 1983	Guillermo Piastrellini
Dec 1983-July 1989	Carlos Menem (2nd) (FJL)
July 1989-Dec 1991	Armando Cavero
Dec 1991-Dec 1995	Bernabé Arnaudo
Dec 1995-	Angel Maza (PJ)

MENDOZA

Capital: Mendoza

Governors:

May 1958-May 1961	Ernesto Weltschi
May 1961-April 1962	Francisco Gabrielli (1st)
April-June 1962	Segundo Armanini
June 1962-Feb 1963	Joaquín Guevara Civit
Feb-April 1963	Augusto Lavalle Cobo
April-Oct 1963	Sergio Moretti
Oct 1963-June 1966	Francisco Gabrielli (2nd)
June-Aug 1966	Tomás Caballero
Aug 1966-July 1970	José Blanco
July 1970-April 1972	Francisco Gabrielli
5-14 April 1972	Luis Gómez Centurion

April 1972-March 1973	Félix Gibbs
March-May 1973	Ramón Díaz Bessone
May 1973-June 1974	Alberto Martínez Baca
June-Aug 1974	Carlos Mendoza
Aug 1974-June 1975	Antonio Cafiero
June-Nov 1975	Luis Rodríguez
Nov 1975-March 1976	Pedro Lucero
March-April 1976	Tamer Yapur
April 1976-Feb 1980	Jorge Fernández
Feb 1980-Jan 1982	Rolando Ghisani
Jan 1982-Feb 1983	Bonifacio Cejuela
Feb-Dec 1983	Eliseo Vidart Villanueva
Dec 1983-Dec 1987	Felipe Yaber
Dec 1987-Dec 1991	José Bordon (FJL)
Dec 1991-Dec 1995	Rodolfo Gabrielli
Dec 1995-Dec 1999	Arturo Lafalla
Dec 1999-	Roberto Iglesias

MISIONES

Capital: Posadas

Governors:

May 1958	Pedro Rebollo
May 1958-March 1959	Rodolfo Prower de Kroning
March 1959-Jan 1960	César Ayrauld (1st)
Jan-May 1960	Francisco Marios
May 1960-April 1962	César Ayrauld (2nd)
April-June 1962	Wilde Santa Cruz
June-Oct 1962	Emilio Gueret
Oct 1962-Oct 1963	Pablo Luzuriaga
Oct 1963-Aug 1966	Mario Losada
Aug 1966-July 1967	Manuel Galeano
July 1967-Nov 1969	Hugo Montiel
Nov 1969-May 1973	Angel Rossi
May-Nov 1973	Juan Irrazabal (†)
Nov 1973-Jan 1975	Luis Ripoll
Jan-May 1975	Juan Taparelli
May 1975-March 1976	Miguel Alterach
March-April 1976	Juan Beltrametti
April 1976-March 1977	René Buteler
March 1977-Dec 1978	Rodolfo Poletti
Dec 1978-March 1981	Norberto Pacagnini
March 1981-Dec 1983	Juan Bayon
Dec 1983-Sept 1987	Ricardo Barrios Arrechea

Sept 1987-Dec 1991	Julio Humada
Dec 1991-Dec 1995	Federico Fuerta
Dec 1995-	Ramón Puerta (PJ)

NEUQUEN

Capital: Neuquén

Governors:

May 1958-April 1959	Angel Edelman
April 1959-April 1962	Alfredo Asmar
May-June 1962	Guillermo Villegas
June 1962-Oct 1963	Francisco Olano
Oct 1963-June 1966	Felipe Sapag (1st)
June-Aug 1966	Jorge Elizagaray
Aug 1966-Feb 1970	Rodolfo Rosauer
Feb 1970-Aug 1972	Felipe Sapag (2nd)
Aug 1972-May 1973	Pedro Salvatori (1st)
May 1973-March 1976	Felipe Sapag (3rd)
March-April 1976	Eduardo Contreras Santillan
April 1976-Dec 1978	José Martínez Waidner
Dec 1978-Dec 1983	Manuel Trimarco
Dec 1983-Dec 1987	Felipe Sapag (4th)
Dec 1987-Dec 1991	Pedro Salvatori (2nd)
Dec 1991-Dec 1995	Jorge Sobisch (PNM) (1st)
Dec 1995-Dec 1999	Felipe Sapag (5th)
Dec 1999-	Jorge Sobisch (PNM) (2nd)

PNM = Popular Neuquén Movement

RIO NEGRO

Capital: Viedma

Governors:

May 1958-March 1962	Edgardo Castello
March-May 1962	Francisco Muñoz
June 1962-Oct 1963	Carlos Mejía
Oct 1963-June 1966	Carlos Nielsen
28-30 June 1966	José Fasseri (acting)
June-Aug 1966	Navio Uhalde
Aug 1966-Aug 1969	Luis Lanari
Aug-Sept 1969	Juan Figueroa Bunge
Sept 1969-Aug 1972	Roberto Requeijo

Aug 1972-May 1973	Oscar Lava
May 1973-March 1976	Mario Franco
March-April 1976	Nestor Castelli
April 1976-Nov 1978	Aldo Bachmann
Nov 1978-Aug 1982	Julio Acuña
Aug 1982-Dec 1983	Carlos San Juan
Dec 1983-Dec 1987	Osvaldo Alvarez Guerrero
Dec 1987-Dec 1995	Horacio Massaccesi (UCR)
Dec 1995-	Pablo Verani

SALTA

Capital: Salta

Governors:

May 1958-Nov 1961	Bernardino Biella
Nov 1961-April 1962	Enrique Escobar Cuello
April-June 1962	Federico Toranzo Montero
June-Oct 1962	Julio Castellanos
Oct 1962-Oct 1963	Pedro Remy Sola
Oct 1963-June 1966	Ricardo Durand
June-Aug 1966	Carlos Moyano
Aug 1966-April 1968	Héctor d'Andrea
April 1968-Aug 1969	Hugo Rovaletti
21-29 Aug 1969	Julio Díaz Villalba
Aug 1969-June 1970	Carlos Ponce Martínez
June-Aug 1970	Hernán Risso Patrón
Aug 1970-April 1971	Raúl Aguirre Molina
April 1971-May 1973	Ricardo Spangenberg
May 1973-Nov 1974	Miguel Ragone
Nov 1974-Oct 1975	José Mosquera
Oct-Nov 1975	Jorge Aranda
Nov 1975-Feb 1976	Ferdinando Pedrini
Feb-March 1976	Dante Lovaglio
1-23 March 1976	René Orsi
March-April 1976	Carlos Mulhall
April 1976-April 1977	Héctor Gadea
April 1977-Feb 1983	Roberto Ulloa (1st)
Feb-Dec 1983	José Plaza
Dec 1983-Dec 1987	Roberto Romero
Dec 1987-Dec 1991	Hernán Cornejo
Dec 1991-Dec 1995	Roberto Ulloa (2nd)
Dec 1995-	Juan Carlos Romero

SAN JUAN

Capital: San Juan

Governors:

Nov 1958-April 1962	Américo García
April-June 1962	Fernando Pérez Méndez
June 1962-April 1963	Miguel Pedrozo
April-May 1963	Jorge Gattoni
May-Oct 1963	Pedro Avalia
Oct 1963-June 1966	Leopoldo Bravo (1st)
28-29 June 1966	Horacio de la Colina
June-July 1966	Arturo Cordón Aguirre
July 1966-Aug 1969	Edgardo Gómez
Aug 1969-March 1971	José López
March-April 1971	Ruperto Godoy
April-May 1971	Julio Arroyo Iglesia
May 1971-May 1973	Carlos Gómez Centurion (1st)
May 1973-March 1976	Eloy Camus
March-April 1976	Carlos Tragant
April 1976-Nov 1978	Alberto Lombardi
Nov 1978-April 1981	Angel Zamboni
April 1981-Jan 1982	Rodríguez Castro
Jan-Dec 1982	Leopoldo Bravo (2nd)
Dec 1982-Dec 1983	Eduardo Posleman
Dec 1983-Nov 1985	Leopoldo Bravo (3rd)
Nov 1985-Dec 1987	Jorge Ruiz Aguilar
Dec 1987-Dec 1991	Carlos Gómez Centurion (2nd) (SJBP)
Dec 1991-Dec 1999	Jorge Escobar
Dec 1999-	Alfredo Avelin

SJBP = San Juan Bloquista Party

SAN LUIS

Capital: San Luis

Governors:

May 1958-April 1962	Alberto Domeniconi
April-July 1962	Jorge Naveiro
July-Nov 1962	Alberto Vázquez
Nov 1962-Oct 1963	Luis Garzo (1st)
Oct 1963-June 1966	Santiago Besso
June-July 1966	Eduardo Federik
July 1966-Jan 1967	Luis Garzo (2nd)
Jan 1967-July 1970	Matías Laborda Ibarra

July-Aug 1970	Enrique Viola
Aug 1970-May 1972	Angel Vivas
May 1972-May 1973	Rafael Blanco Moreno
May 1973-March 1976	Elías Adre
March-April 1976	Aldo Barbuy
April-June 1976	Cándido Capitan
June 1976-April 1981	Hugo Marcilese
April 1981-Dec 1983	Hugo Di Risio
Dec 1983-	Adolfo Rodríguez Saa (PJ)

SANTA FE

Capital: Santa Fé

Governors:

May 1958-April 1962	Carlos Begnis (1st)
April-June 1962	Ernesto Cordés
June 1962-Oct 1963	Jorge Nocetti Campos
Oct 1963-June 1966	Aldo Tessio
June-Aug 1966	Eleodoro Sánchez Lahoz
Aug 1966-July 1970	Eladio Vázquez
14-27 July 1970	Roberto Fonseca
July 1970-May 1973	Guillermo Sánchez Almeyra
May 1973-March 1976	Carlos Begnis (2nd)
March-April 1976	José González
April 1976-March 1981	Jorge Desimoni
March 1981-Jan 1982	Rodolfo Luchette
Jan 1982-Feb 1983	Roberto Casis
Feb-Dec 1983	Héctor Salvi
Dec 1983-Dec 1987	José Vernet
Dec 1987-Dec 1991	Víctor Reviglio
Dec 1991-Dec 1995	Carlos Reutemann (1st)
Dec 1995-Dec 1999	Jorge Obeid
Dec 1999-	Carlos Reutemann (2nd)

SANTA CRUZ

Capital: Rio Gallegas

Governors:

1958-60	Mario Castulo Paradelo
1960-62	Luis Carrizo
1962	Carlos López
1962	Pedro Priani

1962-63	Horacio Agulla
1963	Carlos Pardos
1963	Hugo Pernice
1963-66	Rodolfo Matinović
1966	Ricardo Borselli
1966-71	Carlos Ravnelli
1971	Julio Tartara
1971-73	Fernando García
1973-74	Jorge Cepernić
1974-75	Augusto Saffores
1975-76	Orlando Parolin
March-April 1976	Alberto Amoresano
April 1976-Aug 1977	Ulderico Carnighi
Aug-Sept 1977	Heraldo Amoresano
Sept 1977-April 1981	Juan Carlos Favergiotti
April 1981-Dec 1983	Antonio López
Dec 1983-Dec 1987	Arturo Puricelli
Dec 1987-May 1990	Ricardo del Val
May 1990-May 1991	José Granero
May-Dec 1991	Héctor García
Dec 1991-	Nestor Kirchner

SANTIAGO DEL ESTERO

Capital: Santiago del Estero

Governors:

1958-62	Eduardo Miguel
1962	Agustín de la Vega
1962	Adolfo Scillingo
1962	Pedro Molinari
1962-63	Gabriel Maleville
1963	Germán Quintana
1963-66	Benjamin Zavalia
1966-67	Jorge Nallar
1967-70	Carlos Uriondo
1970-73	Carlos Jensen (1st)
1973	Pedro Garro
1973	Ernesto Fattigati
1973	Juan Jiménez Dominguez
1973-76	Carlos Juárez (1st)
1976-82	César Ochoa
1982-83	Carlos Jensen (2nd)
Dec 1983-Dec 1987	Carlos Juárez (2nd)
Dec 1987-Dec 1991	César Iturre

Dec 1991-93	Carlos Mujica
1993-95	Fernando Martín Lobo
Dec 1995-	Carlos Juárez (3rd)

TIERRA DEL FUEGO

Capital: Ushuaia
Provincial status: 1990

Governors:

| Dec 1995-Dec 1999 | José Estabillo |
| Dec 1999- | Carlos Manfredotti (PJ) |

TUCUMAN

Capital: San Miguel de Tucumán

Governors:

April 1958-March 1962	Celestino Celsi
March-April 1962	Julio Sueldo
April-May 1962	Carlos Imabud (1st)
May-Nov 1962	Ricardo Arandia
Nov 1962-Oct 1963	Alberto Gordillo Gómez
Oct 1963-June 1966	Lazaro Barbieri
June-Aug 1966	Delfor Otero
Aug 1966-March 1968	Fernando Aliaga García
March 1968-July 1969	Jorge Nanclares
July 1969-Aug 1970	Roberto Avellaneda
Aug-Sept 1970	Jorge Videla
Sept 1970-Feb 1971	Carlos Imabud (2nd)
Feb 1971-May 1973	Oscar Sarrulle
May 1973-March 1976	Amado Juri
March 1976-Dec 1977	Antonio Bussi (1st)
Dec 1977-April 1981	Lino Montiel Forzano
April 1981-July 1983	Antonio Merlo
July-Dec 1983	Mario Fattor
Dec 1983-Dec 1987	Fernando Riera
Dec 1987-Dec 1991	José Domato
Dec 1991-Dec 1995	Ramón Ortega
Dec 1995-June 1998	Antonio Bussi (2nd)
June-July 1998	Raúl Topa (acting)
July 1998-Dec 1999	Antonio Bussi (3rd)
Dec 1999-	Julio Mirando

ARMENIA

Official name: Republic of Armenia, Haikakan Hanrapetoutioun
Previous name: Armenian Soviet Socialist Republic 1920-90
Independence dates: 26 May 1918; 23 September 1991
Admission to USSR: 30 December 1922 (member of Transcaucasian Federation 1922-36)
Capital: Yerevan

An independent Armenian state existed in the first century BC, but was then a vassal state of Rome and the Parthians. Independence was revived in the 9th century, lasting until the 11th. The Mamluks ruled until the 14th century when Turkey took over the country. This lasted until 1918 when Armenian independence was declared. In 1920 a soviet republic was established, and Armenia became a member of the Soviet Union, first as part of the Transcaucasian Federation, and after 1936 as a full member. In 1990 a non-communist government was elected, and in 1991 independence was again declared as the Soviet Union collapsed. Armenia and Azerbaijan are in dispute over Nagorno-Karabakh, an Armenian-populated autonomous region of Azerbaijan whose local authorities regard the area as part of Armenia.

Presidents:
Chairman of the National Council 1918-20
Chairman of the Central Executive Committee 1922-38
President of the Presidium of the Supreme Soviet 1938-90
Chairman of the Supreme Soviet Aug 1990-Oct 1991

May 1918-Dec 1920	Avetis Aharonyan
(Dec 1920-April 1922	post vacant)
April 1922-April 1925	Sargis Ambartsumyan
April 1925-July 1928	Artashes Karinyan
July 1928-Dec 1930	Sargis Kasyan (S.Ter-Gasparyan)
Dec 1930-Jan 1935	Armenek Ananyan
Jan 1935-Nov 1936	Sergei Martikyan
Dec 1936-Nov 1937	Gevorg Anecoglyan
Nov 1937-May 1954	Matsak Papyan
May 1954-April 1963	Shmavon Arushanyan
April 1963-July 1975	Nagush Arutiunyan
July 1975-Jan 1986	Babken Sarkisov
Jan 1986-Aug 1990	Grant Voskanyan
Aug 1990-Feb 1998	Levon Ter-Petrosyan (ANM)
Feb 1998-	Robert Kocharyan (acting Feb-April 1998)

Prime Ministers:
Chairman of the Council of People's Commissars 1922-46
Chairman of the Council of Ministers 1946-95

July 1918-Aug 1919	Ruben Kachaznuni
Aug 1919-May 1920	Aleksander Khatissyan

May-Nov 1920	Hamazasp Ohandianyan
Nov-Dec 1920	Simon Vratsyan
Dec 1920-Feb 1921	Sargis Kasyan
April 1921-March 1922	Aleksandr Myasnikyan (A.Myasnikov) (see Belarus)
March 1922-June 1925	Sargis Lukashin (S.Sraponyan)
June 1925-March 1928	Sargis Ambartsumyan (1st)
March 1928-Feb 1935	Saak Ter-Gabrielyan
Feb 1935-37	Abram Goulyan
1937	Sargis Ambartsumyan (2nd)
Nov 1937-45	Aram Piruzyan
1945-March 1947	Agasi Sarkisyan
March 1947-Nov 1952	Saak Karapetyan
Nov 1952-Feb 1966	Anton Kochinyan
Feb 1966-Nov 1972	Badal Muradyan
Nov 1972-Nov 1976	Grigory Arzumanyan
Nov 1976-Jan 1989	Fadei Sarkisyan
Jan 1989-Aug 1990	Vladimir Markaryants
Aug 1990-Sept 1991	Vazguen Manukyan
Nov 1991-Aug 1992	Gagik Arutiunyan
Aug 1992-Feb 1993	Khostrov Arutiunyan
Feb 1993-Nov 1996	Grant Bagratyan
Nov 1996-March 1997	Armen Sarkisyan
March 1997-April 1998	Robert Kocharyan (see Nagorno-Karabakh)
April 1998-June 1999	Armen Darbinyan
June-Oct 1999	Vazguen Sarkisyan (RP) († assassinated)
Nov 1999-	Aram Sarkisyan (*brother*)

ANM = Armenian National Movement
RP = Republican Party

Communist Party Leaders:
First Secretary

1919-20	Sargis Kasyan
1921-22	Sargis Lukashin
1922-27	Ashot Ionnisyan
July 1927-April 1928	Haik Hovsepyan
April 1928-May 1930	Haik Kostanyan
May 1930-July 1936	Aghasi Khandjyan (†)
July 1936-Sept 1937	A. S. Amatouni
Sept 1937-Nov 1953	Grigor Arutiuman (G.Arutinov)
Nov 1953-Dec 1960	Suren Tovmasyan
Dec 1960-Feb 1966	Yakov Zarobyan
Feb 1966-Nov 1974	Anton Kochinyan
Nov 1974-May 1988	Karen Demichyan
May 1988-April 1990	Suren Arutiunyan
April-Aug 1990	Vladimir Movisyan
(Aug 1990	non-communist party government elected)

AUSTRALIA

Official name: Commonwealth of Australia
State founded: 1 January 1901
Capital: Melbourne (1901-27), Canberra (since 1927)

The first authenticated visit to Australia by Europeans was by the Dutch in the 17th century. The east coast was visited by James Cook in 1770, and he took possession for Britain what is now New South Wales. British penal settlements were established there from 1788. During the 19th century the settlement expanded considerably and separate colonies were set up. Self-government was granted to these colonies during the latter half of the 19th century. In 1901 the six colonies formed the Commonwealth of Australia, their status being changed to that of states.

Governors-General:
Represent monarch who is concurrently British monarch

Jan 1901-July 1902	Earl of Hopetoun (John Hope)
July 1902-Jan 1904	Lord Tennyson (Hallam Tennyson)
Jan 1904-Sept 1908	Lord Northcote (Henry Northcote)
Sept 1908-July 1911	Earl of Dudley (William Ward)
July 1911-May 1914	Lord Denman (Thomas Denman)
May 1914-Oct 1920	Viscount Novar (Ronald Munro-Ferguson)
Oct 1920-Oct 1925	Lord Forster (Henry Forster)
Oct 1925-Oct 1930	Lord Stonehaven (John Baird)
Oct 1930-Jan 1931	Baron Somers (Arthur Somers Cocks) (acting)
Jan 1931-Jan 1936	Isaac Isaacs
Jan 1936-July 1944	Lord Gowrie (Alexander Hore-Ruthven)
July 1944-Jan 1945	Winston Dugan (acting) (1st)
Jan 1945-Jan 1947	Prince Henry (Duke of Gloucester)
Jan-March 1947	Winston Dugan (acting) (2nd)
March 1947-May 1953	William McKell (see New South Wales)
May 1953-Feb 1960	Viscount Slim (William Slim)
Feb 1960-Feb 1961	Lord Dunrossil (William Morrison) (†)
Feb-Aug 1961	R.Dallas Brooks (acting)
Aug 1961-May 1965	Lord De L'Isle (William Sidney)
May-Sept 1965	Kenry Smith (acting)
Sept 1965-April 1969	Lord Casey (Richard Casey)
April 1969-June 1974	Paul Hasluck
June 1974-Dec 1977	John Kerr
Dec 1977-July 1982	Zelman Cowen
July 1982-Feb 1989	Ninian Stephen
Feb 1989-Feb 1996	William Hayden
Feb 1996-	William Deane

Prime Ministers:

Jan 1901-Sept 1903	Edmund Barton
Sept 1903-April 1904	Alfred Deakin (1st) (LPA)
April-Aug 1904	John Watson (ALP)
Aug 1904-July 1905	George Reid
July 1905-Nov 1908	Alfred Deakin (2nd) (LPA)
Nov 1908-June 1909	Andrew Fisher (1st) (ALP)
June 1909-April 1910	Alfred Deakin (3rd) (LPA)
April 1910-June 1913	Andrew Fisher (2nd) (ALP)
June 1913-Sept 1914	Joseph Cook
Sept 1914-Oct 1915	Andrew Fisher (3rd) (ALP)
Oct 1915-Feb 1923	William Hughes (ALP,NP)
Feb 1923-Oct 1929	Stanley Bruce (NP)
Oct 1929-Jan 1932	James Scullin (ALP)
Jan 1932-April 1939	Joseph Lyons (see Tasmania) (UAP)
7-20 April 1939	Earl Page (acting) (CP)
April 1939-Aug 1941	Robert Menzies (1st) (UAP)
Aug-Oct 1941	Arthur Fadden (CP)
Oct 1941-July 1945	John Curtin (†) (ALP)
6-13 July 1945	Francis Forde (acting)
July 1945-Dec 1949	Joseph Chifley (ALP)
Dec 1949-Jan 1966	Robert Menzies (2nd) (LPA)
Jan 1966-Dec 1967	Harold Holt (†) (LPA)
Dec 1967-Jan 1968	John McEwan (acting) (CP)
Jan 1968-March 1971	John Gorton (LPA)
March 1971-Dec 1972	William McMahon (LPA)
Dec 1972-Nov 1975	E.Gough Whitlam (ALP)
Nov 1975-March 1983	Malcolm Fraser (LPA)
March 1983-Dec 1991	Robert Hawke (ALP)
Dec 1991-March 1996	Paul Keating (ALP)
March 1996-	John Howard (LPA)

ALP = Australian Labour Party
CP = Country Party
LPA = Liberal Party of Australia
NP = National Party
UAP = United Australia Party

States

Governors since the formation of the Commonwealth are listed

NEW SOUTH WALES

Capital: Sydney

Governors:

Jan-April 1901	Earl Beauchamp (William Lygon)
April 1901-May 1902	Frederick Darley (acting)
May 1902-March 1909	Harry Rawson
March-May 1909	George Simpson (acting)
May 1909-March 1913	Baron Chelmsford (Frederic Thesiger)
March 1913	William Cullen (acting) (1st)
March 1913-Oct 1917	Gerald Strickland
Oct 1917-Feb 1918	William Cullen (acting) (2nd)
Feb 1918-Sept 1923	Walter Davidson
Sept 1923-Feb 1924	William Cullen (acting) (3rd)
Feb 1924-April 1930	Dudley De Chair
April-May 1930	William Cullen (acting) (4th)
May 1930-Jan 1935	Philip Game
Jan-Feb 1935	Philip Street (acting) (1st)
Feb 1935-Jan 1936	Alexander Hore-Ruthven (see Australia)
Jan-Aug 1936	Philip Street (acting) (2nd)
Aug-Oct 1936	David Anderson
Oct 1936-April 1937	Philip Street (acting) (3rd)
April 1937-June 1945	Baron Wakehurst (John de Vere Loder)
June 1945-Aug 1946	Frederick Jordan (acting)
Aug 1946-July 1957	John Northcott
Aug 1957-Aug 1965	Eric Woodward
Aug 1965-Jan 1966	Kenneth Street (acting)
Jan 1966-Jan 1981	Roden Cutler
Jan 1981-Jan 1989	James Rowland
Jan 1989-Aug 1990	David Martin
Aug 1990-Jan 1996	Peter Sinclair
Jan 1996-	Gordon Samuels

Premiers:

June-Aug 1856	Stuart Donaldson
Aug-Oct 1856	Charles Cowper (1st)
Oct 1856-Sept 1857	Henry Parkes (1st)
Sept 1857-Oct 1859	Charles Cowper (2nd)
Oct 1859-March 1860	William Forster
March 1860-Jan 1861	John Robertson (1st)

Jan 1861-Oct 1863	Charles Cowper (3rd)
Oct 1863-Feb 1865	James Martin (1st)
Feb 1865-Jan 1866	Charles Cowper (4th)
Jan 1866-Oct 1868	James Martin (2nd)
Oct 1868-Jan 1870	John Robertson (2nd)
Jan-Dec 1870	Charles Cowper (5th)
Dec 1870-May 1872	James Martin (3rd)
May 1872-Feb 1875	Henry Parkes (2nd)
Feb 1875-March 1877	John Robertson (3rd)
March-Aug 1877	Henry Parkes (3rd)
Aug-Dec 1877	John Robertson (4th)
Dec 1877-Dec 1878	James Farnell
Dec 1878-Jan 1883	Henry Parkes (4th)
Jan 1883-Oct 1885	Alexander Stuart
Oct-Dec 1885	George Dibbs (1st)
Dec 1885-Feb 1886	John Robertson (5th)
Feb 1886-Jan 1887	Patrick Jennings
Jan 1887-Jan 1889	Henry Parkes (5th)
Jan-March 1889	George Dibbs (2nd)
March 1889-Oct 1891	Henry Parkes (6th)
Oct 1891-Aug 1894	George Dibbs (3rd)
Aug 1894-Sept 1899	George Reid
Sept 1899-March 1901	William Lyne
March 1901-June 1904	John See
June-Aug 1904	Thomas Waddell
Aug 1904-Oct 1907	Joseph Carruthers
Oct 1907-Oct 1910	Charles Wade (LPA)
Oct 1910-June 1913	James McGowen (ALP)
June 1913-April 1920	William Holman (ALP,NP)
April 1920-Oct 1921	John Storey (ALP)
Oct-Dec 1921	James Dooley (1st) (NP)
20 Dec 1921	George Fuller (1st) (ALP)
Dec 1921-April 1922	James Dooley (2nd) (NP)
April 1922-June 1925	George Fuller (2nd) (ALP)
June 1925-Oct 1927	John Lang (1st) (ALP)
Oct 1927-Nov 1930	Thomas Bavin (ALP)
Nov 1930-May 1932	John Lang (2nd) (ALP)
May 1932-Aug 1939	Bertram Stevens (NP)
Aug 1939-May 1941	Alexander Mair (NP)
May 1941-Feb 1947	William McKell (ALP) (see Australia)
Feb 1947-April 1952	James McGirr (ALP)
April 1952-Oct 1959	John Cahill (†) (ALP)
Oct 1959-April 1964	Robert Heffron (ALP)
April 1964-May 1965	John Renshaw (ALP)
May 1965-Dec 1974	Robin Askin (LPA)
Dec 1974-May 1976	Eric Willis (LPA)

May 1976-May 1983	Neville Wran (1st) (ALP)
May-July 1983	Jack Ferguson (acting) (ALP)
July 1983-July 1986	Neville Wran (2nd) (ALP)
July 1986-March 1988	Barrie Unsworth (ALP)
March 1988-June 1992	Nick Greiner (LPA)
June 1992-April 1995	John Fahey (LPA)
April 1995-	Robert Carr (ALP)

QUEENSLAND

Capital: Brisbane

Governors:

Jan-Dec 1901	Baron Lamington (Charles Baillie)
Dec 1901-March 1902	Samuel Griffith (acting)
Mar 1902-Oct 1904	Herbert Chermside
Oct 1904-Nov 1905	Hugh Nelson (acting)
Nov 1905-May 1909	Baron Chelmsford (Frederic Thesiger) (see NSW)
May-Dec 1909	Arthur Morgan (acting) (1st)
Dec 1909-July 1914	William Macgregor
July 1914-March 1915	Arthur Morgan (acting) (2nd)
March 1915-Feb 1920	Hamilton Good-Adams
Feb-Dec 1920	William Lennon (acting) (1st)
Dec 1920-Oct 1925	Matthew Nathan
Oct 1925-June 1927	William Lennon (acting) (2nd)
June 1927-April 1932	Thomas Goodwin
April-June 1932	James Blair (acting) (1st)
June 1932-May 1937	Leslie Wilson (1st)
May-Nov 1937	James Blair (acting) (2nd)
Nov 1937-April 1946	Leslie Wilson (2nd)
April-Sept 1946	Frank Cooper (acting)
Sept 1946-Dec 1957	John Lavarack
Dec 1957-March 1958	Alan Mansfield (acting)
March 1958-March 1966	Henry Abel-Smith
March 1966-March 1972	Alan Mansfield
9-21 March 1972	Mostyn Hanger (acting) (1st)
March 1972-March 1977	Colin Hannah
March-April 1977	Mostyn Hanger (acting) (2nd)
April 1977-July 1985	James Ramsay
July 1985-July 1992	Walter Campbell
July 1992-July 1997	Mary Leneen Forde
July 1997-	Peter Arnison

Premiers:

Dec 1859-Feb 1866	Robert Herbert (1st)
Feb-July 1866	Arthur Macalister (1st)

July-Aug 1866	Robert Herbert (2nd)
Aug 1866-Aug 1867	Arthur Macalister (2nd)
Aug 1867-Nov 1868	Robert Mackenzie
Nov 1868-May 1870	Charles Lilley
May 1870-Jan 1874	Arthur Palmer
Jan 1874-June 1876	Arthur Macalister (3rd)
June 1876-March 1877	George Thorn
March 1877-Jan 1879	John Douglas
Jan 1879-Nov 1883	Thomas McIlwraith (1st) (NP)
Nov 1883-June 1888	Samuel Griffith (1st) (LPA)
June-Nov 1888	Thomas McIlwraith (2nd) (NP)
Nov 1888-Aug 1890	Boyd Morehead
Aug 1890-March 1893	Samuel Griffith (2nd) (LPA)
March-Oct 1893	Thomas McIlwraith (3rd) (NP)
Oct 1893-April 1898	Hugh Nelson
April-Oct 1898	Thomas Byrnes
Oct 1898-Dec 1899	James Dickson
1-7 Dec 1899	Andrew Dawson (ALP)
Dec 1899-Sept 1903	Robert Philp (1st) (LPA)
Sept 1903-Jan 1906	Arthur Morgan (LPA)
Jan 1906-Nov 1907	William Kidston (1st) (LPA)
Nov 1907-Feb 1908	Robert Philp (2nd) (LPA)
Feb 1908-Feb 1911	William Kidston (2nd) (LPA)
Feb 1911-June 1915	Digby Denham (LPA)
June 1915-Oct 1919	Thomas Ryan (ALP)
Oct 1919-Feb 1925	Edward Theodore (ALP)
Feb-Oct 1915	William Gillies (ALP)
Oct 1925-May 1929	William McCormack (ALP)
May 1929-June 1932	Arthur Moore (LPA)
June 1932-Sept 1942	W.Forgan Smith (ALP)
Sept 1942-March 1946	Frank Cooper (ALP)
March 1946-Jan 1952	Edward Hanlon (ALP)
Jan 1952-Aug 1957	Vincent Gair (ALP)
Aug 1957-Jan 1968	Francis Nicklin (CP)
Jan-July 1968	Jack Pizzey (†) (CP)
1-8 Aug 1968	Gordon Chalk (acting) (CP)
Aug 1968-Dec 1987	Johannes Bjelke-Petersen (CP,NP)
Dec 1987-Sept 1989	Michael Ahern (NP)
Sept-Dec 1989	Russell Cooper (NP)
Dec 1989-March 1996	Wayne Goss (ALP)
March 1996-June 1998	Robert Borbidge (NP)
June 1998-	Peter Beattie (ALP)

SOUTH AUSTRALIA

Capital: Adelaide

Governors:

Jan 1901-July 1902	Lord Tennyson (Hallam Tennyson)
July 1902-July 1903	Samuel Way (acting) (1st)
July 1903-Feb 1909	George Ruthven Le Hunte
Feb-Mar 1909	Samuel Way (acting) (2nd)
March 1909-March 1914	Day Bosanquet
March-April 1914	Samuel Way (acting) (3rd)
April 1914-April 1920	Henry Galway
April-June 1920	George Murray (acting) (1st)
June 1920-May 1922	William Weigall
May-Dec 1922	George Murray (acting) (2nd)
Dec 1922-Dec 1927	George Bridges
Dec 1927-May 1928	George Murray (acting) (3rd)
May 1928-April 1934	Alexander Hore-Ruthven
April-July 1934	George Murray (acting) (4th)
July 1934-Feb 1939	Winston Dugan (see Victoria)
Feb-Aug 1939	George Murray (acting) (5th)
Aug 1939-April 1944	Charles Barclay-Harvey
April-Dec 1944	J.Mellis Napier (acting) (1st)
Dec 1944-June 1952	Charles Norrie (later Gov-Gen)
June 1952-Feb 1953	J.Mellis Napier (acting) (2nd)
Feb 1953-March 1960	Robert George
March 1960-April 1961	J.Mellis Napier (acting) (3rd)
April 1961-June 1968	Edric Bastyan (see Tasmania)
June-Dec 1968	J.Mellis Napier (acting) (4th)
Dec 1968-Sept 1971	James Harrison
Sept-Dec 1971	J.Mellis Napier (acting) (5th)
Dec 1971-Nov 1976	Mark Oliphant
Dec 1976-April 1977	Douglas Nichols
April-Sept 1977	Walter Crocker (acting) (1st)
Sept 1977-March 1982	Keith Seaman
March-April 1982	Walter Crocker (acting) (2nd)
April 1982-Feb 1991	Donald Dunstan
Feb 1991-July 1996	Roma Mitchell
July 1996-	Eric Neal

Premiers:

April-Aug 1857	Boyle Finniss
Aug-Sept 1857	John Baker
1-29 Sept 1857	Robert Torrens
Sept 1857-May 1860	Richard Hanson

May 1860-Oct 1861	Thomas Reynolds
Oct 1861-July 1863	George Waterhouse
4-14 July 1863	Francis Dutton (1st)
July 1863-Aug 1864	Henry Ayers (1st)
Aug 1864-March 1865	Arthur Blyth (1st)
March-Sept 1865	Francis Dutton (2nd)
Sept-Oct 1865	Henry Ayers (2nd)
Oct 1865-March 1866	John Hart (1st)
March 1866-May 1867	James Boucaut (1st)
May 1867-Sept 1868	Henry Ayers (3rd)
Sept-Oct 1868	John Hart (2nd)
Oct-Nov 1868	Henry Ayers (4th)
Nov 1868-May 1870	Henry Strangeways
May 1870-Nov 1871	John Hart (3rd)
Nov 1871-Jan 1872	Arthur Blyth (2nd)
Jan 1872-July 1873	Henry Ayers (5th)
June 1873-June 1875	Arthur Blyth (3rd)
June 1875-June 1876	James Boucaut (2nd)
June 1876-Oct 1877	John Colton (1st)
Oct 1877-Sept 1878	James Boucaut (3rd)
Sept 1878-June 1881	William Morgan
June 1881-June 1884	John Bray
June 1884-June 1885	John Colton (2nd)
June 1885-June 1887	John Downer (1st)
June 1887-June 1889	Thomas Playford (1st)
June 1889-Aug 1890	John Cockburn
Aug 1890-Jan 1892	Thomas Playford (2nd)
Jan-Oct 1892	Frederick Holder (1st)
Oct 1892-June 1893	John Downer (2nd)
June 1893-Dec 1899	Charles Kingston
1-8 Dec 1899	Vaiben Solomon
Dec 1889-May 1901	Frederick Holder (2nd)
May 1901-March 1905	John Jenkins
March-July 1905	Richard Butler (1st)
July 1905-June 1909	Thomas Price (ALP)
June 1909-June 1910	Archibald Peake (1st) (ALP)
June 1910-Feb 1912	John Verran
Feb 1912-April 1915	Archibald Peake (2nd) (ALP)
April 1915-July 1917	Crawford Vaughan
July 1917-April 1920	Archibald Peake (3rd) (ALP)
April 1920-April 1924	Henry Barwell
April 1924-Aug 1926	John Gunn
Aug 1926-April 1927	Lionel Hill (1st) (ALP)
April 1927-April 1930	Richard Butler (2nd) (LPA)
April 1930-Feb 1933	Lionel Hill (2nd) (ALP)
Feb-April 1933	Robert Richards (ALP)

April 1933-Nov 1938	Richard Butler (3rd) (LPA)
Nov 1938-March 1965	Thomas Playford (*grandson of T.Playford*) (LPA)
March 1965-May 1967	Frank Walsh (LPA)
June 1967-April 1968	Donald Dunstan (1st) (ALP)
April 1968-June 1970	Raymond Hall (LPA)
June 1970-Feb 1979	Donald Dunstan (2nd) (ALP)
Feb-Sept 1979	Desmond Corcoran (ALP)
Sept 1979-Nov 1982	David Tonkin (LPA)
Nov 1982-Sept 1992	John Bannon (ALP)
Sept 1992-Nov 1993	Lynn Arnold (ALP)
Nov 1993-Oct 1996	Dean Brown (LPA)
Oct 1996-	John Olsen (LPA)

TASMANIA

Capital: Hobart

Governors:

Jan-Nov 1901	John Dodds (acting) (1st)
Nov 1901-April 1904	Arthur Havelock
April-Oct 1904	John Dodds (acting) (1st)
Oct 1904-May 1909	Gerald Strickland (see NSW, W.Australia, & Malta)
May-Sept 1909	John Dodds (acting) (3rd)
Sept 1909-March 1913	Harry Barron
March-June 1913	John Dodds (acting) (4th)
June 1913-Mar 1917	William Macartney
March-July 1917	Herbert Nicholls (acting) (1st)
July 1917-Feb 1920	Francis Newdegate (see W.Australia)
Feb-April 1920	Herbert Nicholls (acting) (2nd)
April 1920-Jan 1922	William Allardyce
Jan 1922-Dec 1924	Herbert Nicholls (acting) (3rd)
Dec 1924-Dec 1930	James O'Grady
Dec 1930-Aug 1933	Herbert Nicholls (acting) (4th)
Aug 1933-Aug 1945	Ernest Clark
Aug-Dec 1945	John Morris (acting)
Dec 1945-May 1951	Hugh Binney
May-Aug 1951	Stanley Burbury (acting) (1st)
Aug 1951-June 1958	Ronald Cross
June 1958-Oct 1959	Stanley Burbury (acting) (2nd)
Oct 1959-March 1963	Lord Rowallan (Thomas Corbett)
March-Sept 1963	Stanley Burbury (acting) (3rd)
Sept 1963-July 1968	Charles Gairdner
July-Dec 1968	Stanley Burbury (acting) (4th)
Dec 1968-Nov 1973	Edric Bastyan (see S.Australia)
Nov-Dec 1973	Guy Green (acting) (1st)

Dec 1973-Sept 1982   Stanley Burbury
Sept-Oct 1982   Guy Green   (acting) (2nd)
Oct 1982-May 1987   James Plimsoll   (†)
May-Oct 1987   Guy Green   (acting) (3rd)
Oct 1987-Oct 1995   Phillip Bennett
Oct 1995-   Guy Green

Premiers:

Nov 1856-Feb 1857   William Champ
Feb-April 1857   Thomas Gregson
April-May 1857   William Weston   (1st)
May 1857-Nov 1860   Francis Smith
Nov 1860-Aug 1861   William Weston   (2nd)
Aug 1861-Jan 1863   Thomas Chapman
Jan 1863-Nov 1866   James Whyte
Nov 1866-Aug 1869   Richard Dry
Aug 1869-Nov 1872   James Wilson
Nov 1872-Aug 1873   Frederick Innes
Aug 1873-June 1876   Alfred Kennerley
June 1876-Aug 1877   Thomas Reibey
Aug 1877-March 1878   Philip Fysh   (1st)
March-Dec 1878   William Giblin   (1st)
Dec 1878-Oct 1879   William Crowther
Oct 1879-Aug 1884   William Giblin   (2nd)
Aug 1884-March 1886   Adye Douglas
March 1886-March 1887   James Agnew
March 1887-Aug 1892   Philip Fysh   (2nd)
Aug 1892-April 1894   Henry Dobson
April 1894-Oct 1899   Edward Braddon
Oct 1899-April 1903   Neil Lewis   (1st)
April 1903-July 1904   William Propsting
July 1904-June 1909   John Evans
June-Oct 1909   Neil Lewis   (2nd) (LPA)
20-27 Oct 1909   John Earle   (1st) (ALP)
Oct 1909-June 1912   Neil Lewis   (3rd) (LPA)
June 1912-April 1914   Albert Solomon   (LPA)
April 1914-April 1916   John Earle   (2nd) (ALP)
April 1916-Aug 1922   William Lee   (1st) (LPA)
Aug 1922-Aug 1923   John Hayes   (LPA)
Aug-Oct 1923   William Lee   (2nd) (LPA)
Oct 1923-June 1928   Joseph Lyons   (see Australia) (ALP)
June 1928-June 1934   John McPhee   (NP)
June 1934-June 1939   Albert Ogilvie   (ALP) (†)
June-Dec 1939   Edmund Dwyer-Gray   (ALP)
Dec 1939-Dec 1947   Robert Cosgrove   (1st) (ALP)

Dec 1947-Feb 1948   Edward Brooker   (ALP)
Feb 1948-Aug 1958   Robert Cosgrove   (2nd) (ALP)
Aug 1958-May 1969   Eric Reece   (1st) (ALP)
May 1969-May 1972   W.Angus Bethune   (LPA)
May 1972-March 1975   Eric Reece   (2nd) (ALP)
March 1975-Nov 1977   William Neilson   (ALP)
Nov 1977-Nov 1981   Douglas Lowe   (ALP)
Nov 1981-May 1982   Harry Holgate   (ALP)
May 1982-June 1989   Robert Gray   (LPA)
June 1989-Jan 1992   Michael Field   (ALP)
Jan 1992-March 1996   Raymond Groom   (LPA)
March 1996-Sept 1998   Anthony Rundle   (LPA)
Sept 1998-   James Bacon   (ALP)

VICTORIA

Capital: Melbourne

Governors:

Jan-Dec 1901   John Madden   (acting) (1st)
Dec 1901-Nov 1903   George Clarke
Nov 1903-April 1904   John Madden   (acting) (2nd)
April 1904-July 1908   Reginald Talbot
July 1908   John Madden   (acting) (3rd)
July 1908-May 1911   Thomas Carmichael
May 1911   John Madden   (acting) (4th)
May 1911-Jan 1914   John Fuller
Jan-Feb 1914   John Madden   (acting) (5th)
Feb 1914-Jan 1920   Arthur Stanley
Jan 1920-Feb 1921   William Irvine   (acting) (1st)
Feb 1921-April 1926   Earl of Stradbroke   (George Rous)
April-June 1926   William Irvine   (acting) (2nd)
June 1926-June 1931   Baron Somers   (Arthur Somers Cocks) (see Australia)
June 1931-May 1934   William Irvine   (acting) (3rd)
May 1934-April 1939   Baron Huntingfield   (William Vanneck)
April-July 1939   Frederick Mann   (acting)
July 1939-Feb 1949   Winston Dugan
Feb-Oct 1949   Edmund Herring   (acting)
Oct 1949-May 1963   R.Dallas Brooks
May 1963-May 1974   Rohan Delacombe
June 1974-March 1982   Henry Winneke
March-May 1982   John Young   (acting) (1st)
May 1982-Oct 1985   Brian Murray
Oct 1985-Feb 1986   John Young   (acting) (2nd)
Feb 1986-April 1992   Davis McCaughey

April 1992-April 1997   Richard McGarvie
April 1997-   James Gobbo

Premiers:

Nov 1855-March 1857   William Haines   (1st)
March-April 1857   John O'Shanassy   (1st)
April 1957-March 1858   William Haines   (2nd)
March 1858-Oct 1859   John O'Shanassy   (2nd)
Oct 1859-Nov 1860   William Nicholson
Nov 1860-Nov 1861   Richard Heales
Nov 1861-June 1863   John O'Shanassy   (3rd)
June 1863-May 1868   James McCulloch   (1st)
May-July 1868   Charles Sladen
July 1868-Sept 1869   James McCulloch   (2nd)
Sept 1869-April 1870   John MacPherson
April 1870-June 1871   James McCulloch   (3rd)
June 1871-June 1872   Charles Duffy
June 1872-July 1874   James Francis
July 1874-Aug 1875   George Kerferd
Aug-Oct 1875   Graham Berry   (1st)
Oct 1875-May 1877   James McCulloch   (4th)
May 1877-March 1880   Graham Berry   (2nd)
March-Aug 1880   James Service   (1st)
Aug 1880-July 1881   Graham Berry   (3rd)
July 1881-March 1883   Bryan O'Loghlen
March 1883-Feb 1886   James Service   (2nd)
Feb 1886-Nov 1890   Duncan Gillies
Nov 1890-Feb 1892   James Munro
Feb 1892-Jan 1893   William Shiels
Jan 1893-Sept 1894   James Patterson
Sept 1894-Dec 1899   George Turner   (1st)
Dec 1899-Nov 1900   Allan McLean
Nov 1900-Feb 1901   George Turner   (2nd)
Feb 1901-June 1902   Alexander Peacock (1st)
June 1902-Feb 1904   William Irvine   (LPA)
Feb 1904-Jan 1909   Thomas Bent
Jan 1909-May 1912   John Murray
May 1912-Dec 1913   William Watt   (1st) (LPA)
9-22 Dec 1913   G.A.Elmslie   (ALP)
Dec 1913-June 1914   William Watt   (2nd) (LPA)
June 1914-Nov 1917   Alexander Peacock (2nd)
Nov 1917-March 1918   John Bowser
March 1918-April 1924   Harry Lawson   (ALP)
April-July 1924   Alexander Peacock (3rd)

July-Nov 1924	George Prendergast (ALP)
Nov 1924-May 1927	John Allan (CP)
May 1927-Nov 1928	Edmond Hogan (1st) (ALP)
Nov 1928-Dec 1929	W.H.McPherson (NP)
Dec 1929-May 1932	Edmond Hogan (2nd) (ALP)
May 1932-April 1935	Stanley Argyle (NP)
April 1935-Sept 1943	Albert Dunstan (1st) (CP)
14-18 Sept 1943	Jonathan Cain (1st) (ALP)
Sept 1943-Oct 1945	Albert Dunstan (2nd) (CP)
Oct-Nov 1945	Ian MacFarlan (LPA)
Nov 1945-Nov 1947	Jonathan Cain (2nd) (ALP)
Nov 1947-June 1950	Thomas Hollway (1st) (ALP)
June 1950-Oct 1952	James McDonald (1st) (CP)
27-31 Oct 1952	Thomas Hollway (2nd) (ALP)
Oct-Dec 1952	James McDonald (2nd) (CP)
Dec 1952-June 1955	Jonathan Cain (3rd) (ALP)
June 1955-Aug 1972	Henry Bolte (LPA)
Aug 1972-June 1981	Rupert Hamer (LPA)
June 1981-April 1982	Lindsay Thompson (LPA)
April 1982-Aug 1990	John Cain (*son of Jonathan Cain*) (ALP)
Aug 1990-Oct 1992	Joan Kirner (ALP)
Oct 1992-Oct 1999	Jeffery Kennett (LPA)
Oct 1999-	Steve Bracks (ALP)

WESTERN AUSTRALIA

Capital: Perth

Governors:

Jan-March 1901	Alexander Onslow (acting)
March-April 1901	Edward Stone (acting) (1st)
May 1901-Aug 1902	Arthur Lawley
Aug 1902-March 1903	Edward Stone (acting) (2nd)
March 1903-April 1909	Frederick Bedford
April-May 1909	Edward Stone (acting) (3rd)
May 1909-March 1913	Gerald Strickland (see NSW & Malta)
4-16 March 1913	Edward Stone (acting) (4th)
March 1913-Feb 1917	Harry Barron
Feb-April 1917	Edward Stone (acting) (5th)
April 1917-April 1920	William Macartney
April 1920-June 1924	Francis Newdegate
June-Oct 1924	Robert McMillan (acting)
Oct 1924-June 1931	William Campion
June 1931-July 1933	John Northmore (acting)
July 1933-June 1951	John Mitchell (acting July 1933-Oct 1948)

July-Aug 1951	John Dwyer (acting) (1st)
7-27 Aug 1951	Albert Wolff (acting) (1st)
Aug-Nov 1951	John Dwyer (acting) (2nd)
Nov 1951-Aug 1963	Charles Gairdner
Aug-Oct 1963	John Dwyer (acting) (3rd)
Oct 1963-Oct 1973	Douglas Kendrew
Oct 1973-Jan 1974	Albert Wolff (acting) (2nd)
Jan 1974-April 1975	Hughie Edwards
April-Nov 1975	James Ramsay (acting)
Nov 1975-May 1980	Wallace Kyle
16-24 May 1980	Francis Burt (acting) (1st)
25-27 May 1980	John Lavan (acting) (1st)
May-Aug 1980	Francis Burt (acting) (2nd)
Aug-Nov 1980	John Lavan (acting) (2nd)
10-24 Nov 1980	Francis Burt (acting) (3rd)
Nov 1980-Nov 1983	Richard Trowbridge
Nov 1983-July 1984	Francis Burt (acting) (4th)
July 1984-Sept 1989	Gordon Reid
Sept 1989-Sept 1993	Francis Burt (acting 1989-90) (5th)
Sept-Nov 1993	D.K.Malcolm (acting)
Nov 1993-	Michael Jeffery

Premiers:

Dec 1890-Feb 1901	John Forrest
Feb-May 1901	George Throssell
May-Nov 1901	George Leake (1st)
Nov-Dec 1901	Alfred Morgans
Dec 1901-June 1902	George Leake (2nd)
June-July 1902	Frederick Illingworth
July 1902-Aug 1904	Walter James
Aug 1904-Aug 1905	Henry Daglish
Aug 1905-May 1906	Cornthwaite Rason
May 1906-Sept 1910	Newton Moore
Sept 1910-Oct 1911	Frank Wilson (1st)
Oct 1911-July 1916	John Scadden
July 1916-June 1917	Frank Wilson (2nd)
June 1917-April 1919	Henry Lefroy
April-May 1919	Hal Colebatch
May 1919-April 1924	James Mitchell (1st)
April 1924-April 1930	Philip Collier (1st) (ALP)
April 1930-April 1933	James Mitchell (2nd)
April 1933-Aug 1936	Philip Collier (2nd) (ALP)
Aug 1936-Aug 1945	John Willcock (ALP)
Aug 1945-April 1947	Frank Wise (ALP)

April 1947-Feb 1953	Duncan McLarty (LPA)
Feb 1953-April 1959	Albert Hawke (ALP)
April 1959-March 1971	David Brand (LPA)
March 1971-April 1974	John Tonkin (ALP)
April 1974-Jan 1982	Charles Court (LPA)
Jan 1982-Feb 1983	Raymond O'Connor (LPA)
Feb 1983-Jan 1988	Brian Burke (ALP)
Jan 1988-Feb 1990	Peter Dowding (ALP)
Feb 1990-Feb 1993	Carmen Lawrence (ALP)
Feb 1993-	Richard Court (LPA)

Territories

AUSTRALIAN CAPITAL TERRITORY

Capital: Canberra

Chief Ministers:

May-Dec 1989	Rosemary Follett (1st) (ALP)
Dec 1989-June 1991	Trevor Kaine (ALP)
June 1991-Feb 1995	Rosemary Follett (2nd) (ALP)
Feb 1995-	Katherine Carnell (LPA)

NORTHERN TERRITORY

Capital: Darwin

Administrators:

1911-12	Samuel Mitchell (acting)
1912-19	John Gilruth
1919-21	Miles Smith (acting)
1921	E.T.Leane (acting)
1921-26	Frederick Urquhart
1926-27	E.C.Playford (acting)
1927-37	R.H.Weddel
1937-46	Charles Abbott
1946	Leslie Giles (acting)
1946-51	Arthur Driver
1951-56	Frank Wise
1956-61	James Archer
1961-64	Roger Nott
1964-70	Roger Dean
1970-75	Frederick Chaney

1975-76	Eric Dwyer (acting)
1976-81	John England
1981-88	Eric Johnston
1988-93	James Muirhead
1993-97	Austin Asche
1997-	Neil Conn

Chief Ministers:

July 1978-Oct 1984	Paul Everingham (CP,CLP)
Oct 1984-May 1986	Ian Tuxworth (CLP)
May 1986-July 1988	Steve Hatton (CLP)
July 1988-May 1995	Marshall Perron (CLP)
May 1995-Feb 1999	Shane Stone (CLP)
Feb 1999-	Denis Burke (CLP)

CLP = Country-Liberal Party

External Territories

CHRISTMAS ISLAND

Capital: The Settlement

Administrators:

1970-73	J.G.White
1973-76	C.H.Webb
1976-79	W.Worth
1979-80	F.C.Boyle
1980-82	R.M.Holten
1982-84	W.Yates
1984-86	T.F.Paterson
1986-90	A.D.Taylor
1990-91	W.McKenzie
1991-93	Michael Grimes
1993-96	Danny Gillespie
1996-97	Merrilyn Chilvers
Oct 1997-Nov 1998	Ron Harvey (also Cocos Islands)
Nov 1998-Feb 1999	Graham Nicholls (also Cocos Islands)
Feb 1999-	Bill Taylor (also Cocos Islands)

Shire Council President:

1992-95	Lillian Oh

COCOS (KEELING) ISLANDS

Headquarters: West Island

Administrators:

1975-78	R.J.Linford
1978-82	Charles Buffett
1982-84	Eric Hanfield
1984-86	K.Chan
1986-89	Carolyn Stuart
1989-91	A.Dawn Laurie
1991-92	W.Young
1992-93	Barry Cunningham
1993-95	John Read
1995-96	Martin Mowbray
1996-97	Jarl Andersson
1997	Maureen Ellis (acting)
Oct 1997-Nov 1998	Ron Harvey
Nov 1998-Feb 1999	Graham Nicholls (acting)
Feb 1999-	Bill Taylor

Island Council Chairman:

1979-July 1992	Parson bin Yaput

Shire Council Presidents:

July 1992-98	Ronald Grant
1998-	Yakin Capstan

NORFOLK ISLAND

Capital: Kingston

Administrators:

1896-98	Warner Spalding
1898-1903	Charles King
1903-07	Walton Drake
1907-13	Charles Elliot
1913-20	Michael Murphy (1st)
1920-24	John Parnell
1924-26	Edwin Leane
1926	Henry Edgar (1st)
1926-27	Michael Murphy (2nd)
1927-28	Victor Sellheim
1928	Henry Edgar (2nd)

1928-29	Charles Herbert
1929-32	Alfred Bennett
1932-37	Charles Pinney
1937-46	Charles Rosenthal
1946-53	Alexander Wilson
1953-58	Colin Norman
1958-62	Reginald Leydin (see Nauru)
1962-64	Robert Wordsworth
1964-66	Roger Nott (see Northern Territory)
1966-68	Reginald Marsh
1968-74	Robert Dalkin
1974-78	E.T.Pickard
1978-80	D.V.O'Leary
1980-82	W.P.Coleman
1982-85	E.Trebilco
1985-89	John Matthew
1989-92	H.B.MacDonald
April 1992-Aug 1997	Alan Kerr
Aug 1997-	Anthony Messner

Chief Ministers:

Aug 1979-Feb 1982	David Buffett (1st)
(Feb 1982-May 1983	post not designated)
May 1983-May 1986	David Buffett (2nd)
(May 1986-April 1997	post not designated)
April 1997-	George Smith

AUSTRIA

Official name: Republic of Austria, Republik Österreich
Previous names: Empire of Austria until 1918, Austrian State 1934-38
State founded: 9th century
Capital: Vienna (Wien)

'Österreich', the eastern province of the Holy Roman Empire, was founded in the 9th century. It came under Habsburg rule in 1276, and in 1453 the Duke was proclaimed Archduke. The Archdukes held the title of Holy Roman Emperor from the reign of Maximilian I until Napoleon I suppressed the title in 1806. However, the Habsburgs had adopted the style 'Emperor of Austria' in 1804 and ruled over central Europe, northern Italy and parts of the Balkans. In 1867, after Austria's defeat by Prussia, self-government was granted to Hungary and the empire became the Dual Monarchy of Austria-Hungary. After World War I Austria became a republic, losing all non-German regions. In 1938 Austria was annexed by Germany and became part of the German Reich. The republic was reconstituted in 1945 under Allied occupation, regaining full sovereignty in 1955.

Archdukes/Archduchess:

1453-Aug 1493	Friedrich III
Aug 1493-Jan 1519	Maximilian I
May 1519-April 1521	Karl I (*grandson*) (Carlos I of Spain) (abdicated)
April 1521-July 1564	Ferdinand I (*brother*)
July 1564-Oct 1576	Maximilian II (*son*)
Oct 1576-Jan 1612	Rudolf V (*son*)
Jan 1612-March 1619	Matthias (*brother*)
March 1619-Feb 1637	Ferdinand II (*cousin*)
Feb 1637-April 1657	Ferdinand III (*son*)
April 1657-May 1705	Leopold I (*son*)
May 1705-April 1711	Josef I (*son*)
April 1711-Oct 1740	Karl II (*brother*)
Oct 1740-Nov 1780	Maria Theresa (*daughter*) (co-ruler Aug 1765-Nov 1780)
Aug 1765-Feb 1790	Josef II (*son*) (co-ruler Aug 1765-Nov 1780)
Feb 1790-March 1792	Leopold II (*brother*) (Leopold I of Tuscany)
March 1792-Aug 1804	Franz (*son*)

Emperors:

Aug 1804-March 1835	Franz
March 1835-Dec 1848	Ferdinand (*son*) (abdicated)
Dec 1848-Nov 1916	Franz Josef (*nephew*)
Nov 1916-Nov 1918	Karl (*grand nephew*)

Presidents:

Feb 1919-Dec 1920	Karl Seitz (acting) (see Vienna)
Dec 1920-Dec 1928	Michael Hainisch
Dec 1928-March 1938	Wilhelm Miklas
(March 1938-April 1939	German occupation)
(April 1939-April 1945	Union with Germany)
(April-Dec 1945	Provisional government)
Dec 1945-Dec 1950	Karl Renner (†)
Dec 1950-May 1951	Leopold Figl (acting)
May 1951-Jan 1957	Theodor Körner (see Vienna) (†)
Jan-May 1957	Julius Raab (acting)
May 1957-Feb 1965	Adolf Schärf (†)
Feb-June 1965	Josef Klaus (acting)
June 1965-April 1974	Franz Jonas (see Vienna) (†)
April-July 1974	Bruno Kreisky (acting)
July 1974-July 1986	Rudolf Kirchschläger
July 1986-July 1992	Kurt Waldheim (see United Nations)
July 1992-	Thomas Klestil

Chancellors:

May 1821-March 1848	Clemens von Metternich
13-20 March 1848	Alfred von Windisch-Grätz

Prime Ministers:

March-April 1848	Franz Kolowrat
April-May 1848	Karl Ficquelmont
May-July 1848	Franz von Pillersdorf
July 1848	Anton von Doblhoff-Dier
July-Nov 1848	Johann Wessenberg-Ampringen
Nov 1848-April 1852	Felix Scharzenberg (†)
April 1852-Aug 1859	Karl Buol-Schauenstein
Aug 1859-Feb 1861	Johann Rechberg und Rothenlöwen
Feb 1861-June 1865	Archduke Rainier
June-July 1865	Alexander Mensdorff-Pouilly
July 1865-Feb 1867	Richard Belcredi
Feb-Dec 1867	Ferdinand von Beust
Dec 1867-Sept 1868	Karl von Auersperg (1st)
Sept 1868-Dec 1869	Eduard von Taaffe (1st)
Dec 1869-April 1870	Leopold Hasner
April 1870-Feb 1871	Alfred Potocki
Feb-Oct 1871	Karl von Hohenwart
Oct-Nov 1871	Ludwig Holzgethan
Nov 1871-Feb 1879	Karl von Auersperg (2nd)
Feb-Aug 1879	Karl von Stremayr

Aug 1879-Nov 1893   Eduard von Taaffe   (2nd)
Nov 1893-June 1895   Alfred Windisch-Grätz
June-Sept 1985   Erich Kielmansegg
Sept 1895-Nov 1897   Kasimir Badeni
Nov 1897-March 1898   Paul Gautsch von Frankenthurn   (1st)
March 1898-Oct 1899   Franz Thun und Hohenstein
Oct-Dec 1899   Manfred von Clary-Aldnugen
Dec 1899-Jan 1900   Heinrich von Wittek
Jan 1900-Dec 1904   Ernst von Körber   (1st)
Dec 1904-April 1906   Paul Gautsch von Frankenthurn   (2nd)
2-28 May 1906   Conrad von Hohenlohe-Schillingfurst
June 1906-Nov 1908   Max Beck
Nov 1908-June 1911   Richard Bienerth
June-Oct 1911   Paul Gautsch von Frankenthurn   (3rd)
Oct 1911-Oct 1916   Otto Sturgkh   (†)
Oct-Dec 1916   Ernst von Körber   (2nd)
Dec 1916-June 1917   Richard Clam-Martinitz
June 1917-July 1918   Ernst Seidler von Feudhtenegg
July-Oct 1918   Max Hussarek von Heinlein
Oct-Nov 1918   Heinrich Lammasch

Chancellors:

Nov 1918-June 1920   Karl Renner   (1st) (SDP)
June 1920-June 1921   Michael Mayr   (CSP)
June 1921-May 1922   Johann Schober   (1st) (GNP)
May 1922-Nov 1924   Ignaz Siepel   (1st) (CSP)
Nov 1924-Oct 1926   Rudolph Ramek   (CSP)
Oct 1926-April 1929   Ignaz Siepel   (2nd) (CSP)
April-Sept 1929   Ernst Streeruwitz
Sept 1929-Sept 1930   Johann Schober   (2nd) (GNP)
Sept-Nov 1930   Karl Vaugoin   (CSP)
Dec 1930-June 1931   Otto Ender   (CSP) (see Vorarlberg)
June 1931-May 1932   Karl Buresch   (CSP) (see Lower Austria)
May 1932-July 1934   Engelbert Dollfuss   († assassinated) (CSP)
26-29 July 1934   Ernst Starhemberg   (acting) (HG)
July 1934-March 1938   Kurt von Schuschnigg
March 1938-April 1939   Arthur Seyss-Inquart   (executed 1946)
(April 1939-April 1945   Union with Germany)
April-Nov 1945   Karl Renner   (2nd) (SPA)
Nov 1945-April 1953   Leopold Figl   (APP) (see Lower Austria)
April 1953-April 1961   Julius Raab   (APP)
April 1961-April 1964   Alfons Gorbach   (APP)
April 1964-April 1970   Josef Klaus   (APP) (see Salzburg)
April 1970-May 1983   Bruno Kreisky   (SPA)
May 1983-June 1986   Alfred Sinowatz   (SPA)

June 1986-Jan 1997	Franz Vranitzky (SPA,SDPA)
Jan 1997-Feb 2000	Viktor Klima (SDPA)
Feb 2000	Wolfgang Schüssel (APP)

APP = Austrian People's Party
CSP = Christian Social Party
GNP = German National Party
HG = Home Guard
SDP = Social Democratic Party
SDPA = Social Democratic Party of Austria (*f* SPA)
SPA = Socialist Party of Austria

Provinces

BURGENLAND

Capital: Eisenstadt

Governors:

July 1922-July 1923	Alfred Rausnitz
July 1923-Jan 1924	Alfred Walheim (1st) (PP)
Jan 1924-Jan 1928	Josef Rauhofer (CSP)
Jan 1928-July 1929	Anton Schreiner (1st) ((CSP)
July 1929-Dec 1930	Johann Thullner (CSP)
Dec 1930-Nov 1931	Anton Schreiner (2nd) (CSP) (assassinated 1932)
Nov 1931-Feb 1934	Alfred Walheim (2nd) (PP)
Feb 1934-March 1938	Hans Sylvester (CSP)
(March 1938-Oct 1945	post abolished)
Oct 1945-Jan 1946	Ludwig Leser (SPA)
Jan 1946-June 1956	Lorenz Karall (APP)
June 1956-Aug 1961	Johann Wagner (APP)
Aug 1961-June 1964	Josef Lentsch (APP)
June 1964-June 1966	Hans Boegl (SPA)
June 1966-Oct 1987	Theodor Kery (SPA)
Oct 1987-July 1991	Hans Sipoetz (SPA,SDPA)
July 1991-	Karl Stix (SDPA)

PP = Peasants Party

CARINTHIA

Karnten

Capital: Klagenfurt

Governors:

Nov 1918-July 1921	Arthur Lemisch (1st) (PP)
July 1921-Nov 1923	Florian Gröger (SDP)
Nov 1923-May 1927	Vinzenz Schumy (APP)

May 1927-Dec 1930	Arthur Lemisch (2nd) (APP)
Dec 1930-March 1934	Ferdinand Kernmaier (APP)
March 1934-Feb 1936	Ludwig Hülgerth
Feb 1936-March 1938	Arnold Sucher (CSP)
(March 1938-May 1945	post abolished)
May 1945-April 1947	Hans Piesch (SPA)
April 1947-April 1965	Ferdinand Wedenig (SPA)
April 1965-April 1974	Hans Sima (SPA)
April 1974-Sept 1988	Leopold Wagner (SPA)
Sept 1988-May 1989	Peter Ambrosy (SPA)
May 1989-June 1991	Jörg Haider (1st) (FP)
June 1991-April 1999	Christof Zernatto (APP)
April 1999-	Jörg Haider (2nd) (FP)

FP = Freedom Party

LOWER AUSTRIA
Niederösterreich

Capital: Vienna (1918-86), St.Pölten (since 1986)

Governors:

Nov 1918-May 1919	Leopold Steiner (CSP)
May 1919-Nov 1920	Albert Sever (SDP)
Nov 1920-June 1922	Johann Mayer (CSP)
June 1922-July 1931	Karl Buresch (1st) (CSP) (later Chancellor)
July 1931-May 1932	Josef Reither (1st) (CSP)
May 1932-May 1933	Karl Buresch (2nd) (CSP)
May 1933-Oct 1934	Josef Reither (2nd) (CSP)
Nov 1934-Oct 1935	Eduard Baar von Baarenfels (CSP)
Nov 1935-Feb 1938	Josef Reither (3rd) (CSP)
(Feb 1938-May 1945	post abolished)
May-Oct 1945	Leopold Figl (1st) (APP) (later Chancellor)
Oct 1945-May 1949	Josef Reither (4th) (APP)
May 1949-Jan 1962	Johann Steinbock (APP)
Jan 1962-May 1965	Leopold Figl (2nd) (APP)
June 1965-Oct 1966	Eduard Hartmann (APP)
Nov 1966-Jan 1981	Andreas Maurer (APP)
Jan 1981-Oct 1992	Siegfried Ludwig (APP)
Oct 1992-	Erwin Pröll (APP)

SALZBURG

Capital: Salzburg

Governors:

Jan 1909-April 1919	Alois Winkler (CSP)
April 1929-May 1922	Oskar Meyer (CSP)

May 1922-March 1938	Franz Rehrl
(March 1938-May 1945	post abolished)
May-Dec 1945	Adolf Schemel (APP)
Dec 1945-Dec 1947	Albert Hochleitner (APP)
Dec 1947-Dec 1949	Josef Rehrl (APP)
Dec 1949-April 1961	Josef Klaus (APP) (later Chancellor)
April 1961-April 1977	Hans Lechner (APP)
April 1977-May 1989	Wilfried Haslauer (APP)
May 1989-April 1997	Hans Katschthaler (APP)
April 1997-	Franz Schausberger (APP)

STYRIA
Steiermark

Capital: Graz

Governors:

Nov 1918-May 1919	Wilhelm Edler von Kaan (GFP)
May 1919-June 1926	Anton Rintelen (1st) (CSP)
June-Oct 1926	Franz Prisching (CSP)
Oct 1926-May 1927	Alfred Gurtler (CSP)
May 1927-April 1928	Hans Paul (CSP)
April 1928-Nov 1934	Anton Rintelen (2nd) (CSP)
Nov 1934-1938	Karl Stepan
March 1938	Rolph Trummer
(March 1938-May 1945	post abolished)
May-Dec 1945	Reinhard Machold (SPA)
Dec 1945-July 1948	Anton Pirchegger (APP)
July 1948-Nov 1971	Josef Krainer (APP)
Nov 1971-July 1980	Friedrich Niederl (APP)
July 1980-Jan 1996	Josef Krainer Jr (APP) (*son of J.Krainer*)
Jan 1996-	Waltraud Klasnic (APP)

GFP = German Freedom Party

TIROL

Capital: Innsbruck

Governors:

1917-1921	Joseph Schaffl (TPP)
June 1921-Feb 1935	Franz Stumpf (TPP)
March 1935-May 1938	Joseph Schumacher
(1938-1945	post abolished)

May-Oct 1945	Karl Gruber (APP)
Oct 1945-Feb 1951	Alfons Weissgatterer (APP)
Feb 1951-Nov 1957	Alois Grauss (APP)
Nov 1957-March 1963	Hans Tschiggfrey (APP)
March 1963-March 1987	Eduard Wallnofer (APP)
March 1987-Sept 1993	Alois Partl (APP)
Sept 1993-	Wendelin Weingartner (APP)

TPP = Tirol People's Party

UPPER AUSTRIA
Oberösterreich

Capital: Linz

Governors:

May 1908-Feb 1927	Johann Hauser (CSP)
Feb 1927-Feb 1934	Josef Schlegel (CSP)
Feb 1934-March 1938	Heinrich Gleissner (1st) (CSP)
(March 1938-May 1945	post abolished)
May-Aug 1945	Adolf Eigl
Oct 1945-May 1971	Heinrich Gleissner (2nd) (APP)
May 1971-Oct 1977	Erwin Wenzl (APP)
Oct 1977-March 1995	Josef Ratzenbock (APP)
March 1995-	Josef Pühringer (APP)

VIENNA
Wien

Capital: Vienna

Governors:

May 1919-Nov 1923	Jakob Reumann (SDLP)
Nov 1923-Feb 1934	Karl Seitz (SDLP)
Feb 1934-March 1938	Richard Schmitz (CSP)
(March 1938-April 1945	post abolished)
April 1945-June 1951	Theodor Körner (SPA) (later President)
June 1951-June 1965	Franz Jonas (SPA) (later President)
June 1965-Dec 1970	Bruno Marek (SPA)
Dec 1970-July 1973	Felix Slavik (SPA)
July 1973-Sept 1984	Leopold Gratz (SPA)
Sept 1984-Nov 1994	Helmut Zilk (SPA,SDPA)
Nov 1994-	Michael Haüpl (SDPA)

SDLP = Social Democratic Labour Party

VORARLBERG

Capital: Bregenz

Governors:

1918-Dec 1930	Otto Ender (1st) (CSP)
Dec 1930-July 1931	Ferdinand Redler (CSP)
July 1931-July 1934	Otto Ender (2nd) (CSP)
July 1934-March 1938	Ernst Winsauer (CSP)
(March 1938-Nov 1945	post abolished)
Nov 1945-Sept 1964	Ulrich Ilg (APP)
Sept 1964-July 1987	Herbert Kessler (APP)
July 1987-April 1997	Martin Purtscher (APP)
April 1997-	Herbert Sausgruber (APP)

AZERBAIJAN

Official name: Republic of Azerbaijan, Azarbaijchan Respublikasy
Previous names: Azerbaijan Republic 1918-20
Azerbaijan Soviet Socialist Republic 1920-90
Independence dates: 28 May 1918; 30 August 1991
Admission to USSR: 30 December 1922 (member of Transcaucasian Federation 1922-36)
Capital: Baku

Azerbaijan was under Persian rule continually from the 11th century until 1813, except for 8 years in the 18th century. In 1813 Russia acquired some of the khanates of the area, the remainder staying under Persian control. In 1918 Azerbaijan proclaimed its independence from Russia, but lost it with the invasion by the Russian Red Army and the proclamation of a soviet republic in 1920. It was incorporated into the Soviet Union in 1922 as a member of the Transcaucasian Federation. In 1936 it became a full member of the union. As the Soviet Union collapsed in 1991 Azerbaijan again declared independence. Azerbaijan and Armenia have had armed clashes over Nagorno-Karabakh, an autonomous region of Azerbaijan but whose Armenian population regard as part of Armenia.

Presidents:
Chairman of the Central Executive Committee 1920-38
President of the Presidium of the Supreme Soviet 1938-May 1990

May 1918-April 1920	Mehmet Resulzade	
April 1920-Dec 1922	Nariman Narimanov	
Dec 1922-29	Samed Agamaly	
1929-32	Gazanfar Musabekov	(see Transcaucasia) (executed 1938)
Jan 1932-37	Sultan Efendiev	
1937-April 1949	Mir Kasumov	
May 1949-March 1954	Nazar Geydarov	
March 1954-Jan 1958	Mirza Ibrahimov	
Jan 1958-Nov 1959	Ilyas Abdullayev	
Nov 1959-Nov 1961	Saftar Djafarov	
Nov 1961-Dec 1969	Mamed Iskanderov	
Dec 1969-Dec 1985	Kurban Halilov	
Dec 1985-June 1989	Suleiman Tatliyev	
June 1989-May 1990	Elmira Kafarova	
May 1990-March 1992	Ayaz Mutalibov (1st)	
March-May 1992	Yagub Mamedov (acting)	
14-15 May 1992	Ayaz Mutalibov (2nd) (deposed)	
May-June 1992	Isa Kamberov (acting)	
June 1992-June 1993	Abulfaz Elchibey (PFA) (deposed)	
June 1993-	Geidar Aliev (NAP) (acting June-Oct 1993)	

Prime Ministers:

Chairman of the Council of People's Commissars 1920-46
Chairman of the Council of Ministers 1946-95

May 1918-April 1919	Fath Ali Khan Choi
April 1919-April 1920	Nasib Yusofbeli
April 1920-Dec 1922	Nariman Narimanov
Dec 1922-28	Gazanfar Musabekov
1928-32	Dadash Buniatzade
1932-33	Mir Bakirov (1st)
1933-37	Gusein Rakhmanov
Nov 1937-April 1953	Timur Kuliev (1st)
April-July 1953	Mir Bakirov (2nd) (executed 1956)
July 1953-March 1954	Timur Kuliev (2nd)
March 1954-July 1958	Sadik Rakhimov
July 1958-July 1959	Veli Akhundov
July 1959-Dec 1961	Mamed Iskanderov
Dec 1961-April 1970	Enver Alikhanov
April 1970-Jan 1981	Ali Ibrahimov
Jan 1981-Jan 1989	Gasan Seidov
Jan 1989-Jan 1990	Ayaz Mutalibov
Jan 1990-April 1992	Gasan Gasanov
April-June 1992	Feirus Mustafayev
June 1992-Jan 1993	Rakhim Guseinov
Jan-April 1993	Ali Masimov (acting)
April-June 1993	Panakh Guseinov
June 1993-Oct 1994	Surat Guseinov
Oct 1994-July 1996	Fuad Kutiyev (acting Oct 1994-May 1995)
July 1996-	Artur Rasizade (acting July-Nov 1996)

NAP = New Azerbaijan Party
PFA = Popular Front of Azerbaijan

Communist Party Leaders:

First Secretary

April-Dec 1920	Anastas Mikoyan
July 1921-25	Sergei Kirov (S.Kostrikov)
1925-26	Mirza Guseinov
1926-29	Levon Mirzoyan
1929-30	Nikolai Gikalo
Aug 1930-33	Vladimir Polonski
1933-July 1953	Mir Bakirov
July 1953-55	Mir Yakabov
1955-July 1959	Imam Mustafayev
July 1959-July 1969	Veli Akhundov
July 1969-Nov 1982	Geidar Aliev

Dec 1982-May 1988	Kyamran Bagirov
May 1988-Jan 1990	Abdul Vezirov
Jan 1990-Aug 1991	Ayaz Mutalibov
(Aug 1991	party suspended)

Autonomous Republic

NAKHICHEVAN
Naxcivan

Official name: Nakhichevan Republic
Previous name: Nakhichevan Autonomous Soviet Socialist Republic 1924-91
Republic formed: 9 February 1924
Capital: Nakhichevan

Presidents:
Chairman of the Central Executive Committee 1924-38
President of the Presidium of the Supreme Soviet 1938-90
Chairman of the Supreme Soviet (Majlis) since 1990

? -37	G.Babayev
1937	Mamed Ragimov
Nov 1937-40	Saftar Dzharfarov
1940-52	?
Sept 1952-Sept 1964	Gusein Mamedov
Sept 1964-Sept 1990	Sakina Alieva
Sept 1990-Sept 1991	Afiyaddin Dzhalilov
Sept 1991-Oct 1993	Geidar Aliev (see Azerbaijan)
(Oct 1993-April 1994	post vacant)
April 1994-96	Natig Gasanov
1996-	Vasif Talibov

Prime Ministers:
Chairman of the Council of People's Commissars 1925-46
Chairman of the Council of Ministers since 1946

1925-29	Gamid Sultanov
Sept 1925-32	Teimur Aliev
1932-38	?
July 1938-42	Yuz Ahmed Balametov
1942-53	I.Gyulmamedov
1953-55	Neimat Novruzov
1955-Oct 1965	M.G.Askerov
Oct 1965-Aug 1967	R.Ismailov
Aug 1967-Jan 1979	Yusif Nabiyev
Jan 1979-May 1983	Imran Mekhtiyev
May 1983-March 1988	Salekh Gadzhiyev

March-Nov 1988	Geidar Isayev
Nov 1988-89	Sakina Alieva
1989-90	Afiyaddin Dzhalilor
Sept 1990-91	Mir Ismail Aliev
1991-93	Bedzhan Farziliyev
1993-	Shamsaddin Khanbabayev

Communist Party Leaders:
First Secretary

1926-37	Ali Jarov
1943	G. Nadzhafov
1952-61	P. Aliev
Oct 1961-April 1970	Gadzhi Ibragimov
April 1970-Dec 1975	Aslan Guseinov
Dec 1975-Dec 1983	Kamran Ragimov
Dec 1983-Nov 1988	Nurradin Mustafayev
Nov 1988-Jan 1990	Geidar Isayev
Jan 1990-April 1991	Afetin Jalilov
April-Aug 1991	Akper Aliev

Autonomous Region

NAGORNO-KARABAKH

Republic of Nagornyi-Karabakh
Region established: 7 July 1923
Self-declared republic: 8 September 1991
Capital: Stepanakert

Armed conflict occurred between Armenian and Azerbaijan over the region, which is inhabited by Armenians. The Armenians declared the part of the region considered as Armenia's a republic in 1992.

Presidents:
Chairman of the Supreme Soviet 1992-95

Jan-April 1992	Artur Mkrtchyan	(† assassinated)
April-Aug 1992	Georgy Petrosyan	(acting)
Aug 1992-June 1995	Karen Baguryan	(acting 1992-93)
June 1995-March 1997	Robert Kocharyan	
March-Sept 1997	Artur Tovmassyan	(acting)
Sept 1997-	Arkady Gukasyan	

Prime Ministers:
Chairman of the Executive Committee until Jan 1992

Jan 1949-March 1963	R.T. Shakhramanyan

March 1963-Aug 1967	M.G.Ogandzhanyan
Aug 1967-Feb 1974	Yusif Nabiyev
Feb 1974-Aug 1988	Armais Aslanov
Aug 1988-Jan 1989	S.A.Babayan
(Jan 1989	post suspended)
Jan-Aug 1992	Oleg Yesayan
Aug 1992-June 1995	Levon Shakhnazaryan (acting)
June 1995-June 1998	Leonard Petrosyan (assassinated 1999)
July 1998-June 1999	Zhirayr Pogosyan
June 1999-	Arkady Gukasyn

Chairman of the Defence Committee:

Aug 1992-June 1995	Robert Kocharyan
(June 1995	post abolished)

Communist Party Leaders:

First Secretary

April 1960-Sept 1963	N.S.Shakhnazarov
Sept 1963-April 1970	G.A.Melkumyan
April 1970-Oct 1983	Aslan Guseinov
Oct 1983-Feb 1988	Boris Kevorkov
Feb 1988-Jan 1989	Genrikh Pogosyan

BAHAMAS

Official name: Commonwealth of the Bahamas
Independence date: 10 July 1973
Capital: Nassau

The Bahamas were discovered by Columbus in 1492. British settlers arrived in the 17th century and the islands became a British colony in 1717. Nassau was captured by the American navy in 1776; in 1782 it was surrendered to Spain but returned to Britain in 1783. Full internal self-government was introduced in 1964 and independence was granted in 1973.

Governors:

1898-1904	Gilbert Carter
1904-12	William Grey-Wilson (see Falkland Is)
1912-14	George Haddon-Smith
1914-20	William Allardyce
1920-26	Harry Cordeaux
1926-32	Charles Orr
1932-36	Bede Clifford
1936-40	Charles Dundas
1940-45	Edward, Duke of Windsor (*f* King Edward VIII)
1945-50	William Murphy
1950-51	George Sandford
1951-53	Robert Neville
1953-56	Earl of Ranfurly (Thomas Knox)
1956-60	Oswald Arthur
1960-64	Robert de Stapleton
1964-68	Ralph Grey (see British Guiana)
1968-72	Francis Cumming-Bruce
1972-73	John Paul (see British Honduras)

Governors-General:

Represents monarch who is concurrently British monarch

July-Aug 1973	John Paul
Aug 1973-Jan 1979	Milo Butler (incapacitated Sept 1976) (†)
Sept 1976-June 1988	Gerald Cash (acting Sept 1976-Sept 1979)
June 1988-Jan 1992	Henry Taylor
Jan 1992-Jan 1995	Clifford Darling
Jan 1995-	Orville Turnquest

Prime Ministers:

Jan 1964-Jan 1967	Roland Symonette (UBP)
Jan 1967-Aug 1992	Lynden Pindling (PLP)
Aug 1992-	Hubert Ingraham (FNM)

FNM = Free National Movement
PLP = Progressive Liberal Party
UBP = United Bahamas Party

BAHRAIN

Official name: State of Bahrain, Dowlat al Bahrain
State founded: 1783
Independence date: 15 August 1971
Capital: Manama

Bahrain was occupied by Portugal in 1507, but in 1602 it was seized by Arab subjects of the Shah of Persia. In 1783 it was occupied by Arabs from the mainland led by the Khalifa family, which has ruled since then. Treaties with Britain in 1882 and 1892, under which Britain was responsible for Bahrain's defence and foreign relations, were replaced by a treaty of friendship in 1971 when Bahrain declared its independence.

Heads of State:
Emir since 1971

1783-96	Shaikh Ahmed bin Khalifa al-Khalifa
1796-1800	Shaikh Sulaiman bin Ahmed al-Khalifa (*son*)
(1800-10	Foreign occupation)
1810-25	Shaikh Abdullah bin Ahmed al-Khalifa (*brother*)
1825-34	Shaikh Khalifa bin Sulaiman al-Khalifa (*nephew*)
1834-67	Shaikh Mohammed bin Khalifa al-Khalifa (*son*)
1867-9	Shaikh Ali bin Khalifa al-Khalifa (*brother*)
1869-1923	Shaikh Isa bin Ali al-Khalifa (*son*)
1923-Feb 1942	Shaikh Hamed bin Isa al-Khalifa (I) (*son*)
Feb 1942-Nov 1961	Shaikh Sulman bin Hamed al-Khalifa (*son*)
Nov 1961-March 1999	Shaikh Isa bin Sulman al-Khalifa (*son*)
March 1999-	Shaikh Hamed bin Isa al-Khalifa (II) (*son*)

Prime Minister:

Nov 1971-	Shaikh Khalifa bin Sulman al-Khalifa (*brother of Shaikh Isa*)

BANGLADESH

Official name: People's Republic of Bangladesh, Ganaprojatantri Bangladesh (Bengali)
Previous names: East Bengal 1947-55, East Pakistan 1955-71
Independence date: 16 December 1971
Capital: Dhaka (Dacca)

The state of Bangladesh was formerly the eastern province of Pakistan, which came into being on the partition of British India in 1947. In elections called in 1969 the Awami League, which called for independence, won an overall majority in East Pakistan. Attempts to suppress the League led to rebellion and civil war and in 1971 India invaded East Pakistan to support the independence movement. Indian victory led to the establishment of an independent Bangladesh. The country has experienced two periods of military rule (1975-79 and 1982-86).

Presidents:

Dec 1971-Jan 1972	Sayed Nazrul Islam (acting) (executed 1975)
10-12 Jan 1972	Mujibur Rahman (1st) (AL)
Jan 1972-Dec 1973	Abu Sayed Chowdhury
Dec 1973-Jan 1975	Mohammedullah
Jan-Aug 1975	Mujibur Rahman (2nd) (AL) (deposed, assassinated)
Aug-Nov 1975	Khondakar Mushtaq Ahmed (deposed)
Nov 1975-April 1977	Abusadat Sayem
April 1977-May 1981	Ziaur Rahman (BNP) († assassinated)
May 1981-March 1982	Abdus Sattar (acting May-Nov 1981) (BNP) (deposed)
March 1982-Dec 1983	Ahsanuddin Chowdhury
Dec 1983-Dec 1990	Hussain Ershad (JP)
Dec 1990-Oct 1991	Shahabuddin Ahmed (acting)
Oct 1991-Oct 1996	Abdur Rahman Biswas
Oct 1996-	Shahabuddin Ahmed

Prime Ministers:

Chief Adviser March-June 1996

Dec 1971-Jan 1972	Tajuddin Ahmed (executed 1975)
Jan 1972-Jan 1975	Mujibur Rahman (AL)
Jan-Aug 1975	Mansoor Ali (deposed, executed)
(Aug 1975-March 1979	post abolished)
March 1979-March 1982	Azizur Rahman
(March 1982-March 1984	post abolished)
March 1984-Jan 1985	Ataur Rahman Khan
(Jan 1985-July 1986	post abolished)
July 1986-March 1988	Mizanur Rahman Chowdhury

March 1988-Aug 1989	Moudud Ahmed
Aug 1989-Dec 1990	Kazi Zafar Ahmed
(Dec 1990-March 1991	post vacant)
March 1991-March 1996	Khaleda Zia (*widow of Ziaur Rahman*) (BNP)
March-June 1996	Mohammed Habibur Rahman
June 1996-	Hasina Wajed (*daughter of Mujibur Rahman*) (AL)

Martial Law Administrators:

Nov 1975	Ziaur Rahman (1st)
Nov 1975-Nov 1976	Abusadat Sayem
Nov 1976-April 1979	Ziaur Rahman (2nd)
(April 1979-March 1982	martial law lifted)
March 1982-Nov 1986	Hussain Ershad
(Nov 1986	martial law lifted)

AL = Awami League
BNP = Bangladesh National Party
JP = Jatiya Party

At partition in 1947 the Indian province of Bengal was divided into the Indian state of West Bengal and the Pakistani province of East Pakistan.

BENGAL

Prime Ministers:

1937-July 1943	A.K.Fazlul Huq
July 1943-Aug 1945	Khawaja Nazimuddin
(Aug 1945-June 1946	Governor's rule)
June 1946-Aug 1947	Hussein Suhrawardy (see Pakistan)

EAST PAKISTAN

Previous name: East Bengal until 1955

Governors:

Aug 1947-1950	Frederick Bourne
1950-March 1953	Firoz Khan Noon (see Pakistan)
March 1953-Nov 1954	Chaudhuri Khaliquzzan
Nov 1954-June 1955	Mohammed Shahabuddin (†)
June 1955-March 1956	Aminuddin Ahmed (acting)
March 1956-April 1958	A.K.Fazlul Huq
1-26 April 1958	Hamid Ali (acting)
April-Oct 1958	Sultanuddin Ahmed
Oct 1958-April 1960	Zakir Hussein

April 1960-May 1962	Azam Khan
May-Oct 1962	Ghulam Faruk
Oct 1962-March 1969	Abdul Monem Khan
March-Sept 1969	M.N.Huda
Sept 1969-March 1971	S.M.Ahsan
March-Aug 1971	Tikka Khan
Aug-Dec 1971	Abdul Malik

Chief Ministers:

Aug 1947-Sept 1948	Khawaja Nazimuddin (see Pakistan) (ML)
Sept 1948-April 1954	Nurul Amin (see Pakistan) (ML)
April-May 1954	A.K.Fazlul Huq (UF)
(May 1954-June 1955	post vacant)
June 1955-Aug 1956	Abu Sarkar (1st) (KSP)
Aug 1956-March 1958	Ataur Rahman Khan (1st) (AL)
31 March 1958	Abu Sarkar (2nd) (KSP)
April-June 1958	Ataur Rahman Khan (2nd) (AL)
20-25 June 1958	Abu Sarkar (3rd) (KSP)
(June-Aug 1958	post vacant)
Aug-Oct 1958	Ataur Rahman Khan (3rd) (AL)
(Oct 1958	post abolished)

KSP = Krishak Sramik Party
ML = Moslem League
UF = United Front

BARBADOS

Official name: Barbados
Independence date: 30 November 1966
Capital: Bridgetown

Spanish explorers are known to have landed on Barbados before 1518 and by 1536 all Arawak inhabitants had either been killed or deported. British settlements were established in 1627 and British rule was instituted in 1652. Partial self-government was granted in 1954, followed by full self-government in 1961. From 1958 to 1962 Barbados was part of the West Indies Federation. Barbados became independent in 1966.

Governors:

1900-04	Frederick Hodgson
1904-11	Gilbert Carter (see Bahamas)
1911-18	Leslie Probyn
1918-25	Charles O'Brien
1925-33	William Robertson
1933	Harry Newlands
1933-38	Mark Young
1938-41	E. John Waddington
1941-47	Harry Newlands
1947-49	Hilary Blood (see the Gambia)
1949-53	Alfred Savage
1953-59	Robert Arundell
1959-66	John Stow

Governors-General:

Represents monarch who is currently British monarch

Nov 1966-May 1967	John Stow
May 1967-Aug 1976	Winston Scott (†)
Aug-Nov 1976	William Douglas (acting) (1st)
Nov 1976-Jan 1984	Deighton Ward (†)
Jan-Feb 1984	William Douglas (acting) (2nd)
Feb 1984-June 1990	Hugh Springer
June 1990-Dec 1995	Nita Barrow (sister of E.Barrow) (†)
Dec 1995-June 1996	Denys Williams (acting)
June 1996-	Clifford Husbands

Prime Ministers:

Feb 1954-April 1958	Grantley Adams (see West Indies Federation) (BLP)
April 1958-Dec 1961	Hugh Cummins (BLP)

Dec 1961-Sept 1976   Errol Barrow   (1st) (DLP)
Sept 1976-March 1985   John   (Tom) Adams (*son of G.Adams*) (BLP) (†)
March 1985-May 1986   Bernard St.John   (BLP)
May 1986-June 1987   Errol Barrow   (2nd) (DLP) (†)
June 1987-Sept 1994   Erskine Sandiford   (DLP)
Sept 1994-   Owen Arthur   (BLP)

BLP = Barbados Labour Party
DLP = Democratic Labour Party

BELARUS

Official name:	Republic of Belarus, Respublika Belarus
Previous names:	Belorussian People's Republic 1918-19, Belorussian Soviet Socialist Republic 1919-91
Independence dates:	March 1918; 25 August 1991
Admission to USSR:	30 December 1922
Capital:	Minsk

Belarus was part of Kievan Rus until its breakup in the 13th century, when most of it passed to Lithuania. Polish influence and control occurred with the union of Lithuania and Poland in 1569. Belarus became Russian between 1771 and 1795 as a result of the three partitions of Poland. In 1918 it proclaimed independence, but in 1919 a soviet republic was established which was one of the founding members of the Soviet Union. During World War II Belarus was occupied by Germany. In 1991 it again declared independence with the breakup of the Union.

Presidents:

Rada President 1918
Chairman of the Central Executive Committee 1919-38
President of the Presidium of the Supreme Soviet 1938-90
Chairman of the Supreme Soviet March 1990-July 1994

March-May 1918	Ivan Serada
May 1918	Pavel Aliaksuk
May-Dec 1918	Iosif Lesik
Jan-April 1919	Aleksei Chervyakov (1st)
(April-Dec 1919	Polish occupation)
Dec 1919-June 1937	Aleksei Chervyakov (2nd) († suicide)
June-Nov 1937	Mikhail Stakun (acting)
Nov 1937-June 1941	Nikifor Natalevich (1st)
(June 1941-July 1944	German occupation)
July 1944-Jan 1948	Nikifor Natalevich (2nd)
Jan 1948-Dec 1967	Vasili Kozlov
Jan 1968-July 1971	Sergei Pritytsky
July 1971-Dec 1976	Fyodor Surganov
(Dec 1976-Feb 1977	post vacant)
Feb 1977-Nov 1985	Ivan Polyakov
Nov 1985-July 1989	Georgi Tarazevich
July 1989-Aug 1991	Nikolai Dementei
Sept 1991-Jan 1994	Stanislav Shushkevich
Jan-July 1994	Mecheslav Grib
July 1994-	Aleksandr Lukashenko

Prime Ministers:

Chairman of the Council of People's Commissars 1919-46
Chairman of the Council of Ministers since 1946

March-April 1918	I.Varonka
April-May 1918	Roman Skirmunt
May 1918	Ivan Serada
May-Dec 1918	Anton Luckevich
Jan-Feb 1919	Dmitri Zhilunovich
March-April 1919	Vikenti Mitskevich-Kapsukas (also PM of Lithuania)
(April-Dec 1919	Polish occupation)
Dec 1919-July 1920	Vatslav Lastowski
July 1920-March 1924	Aleksei Chervyakov
March 1924-May 1927	Iosif Adamovich
May 1927-June 1937	Nikolai Goloded
June-Sept 1937	Daniil Volkavich
Sept 1937-July 1938	Afanasi Kovalev
July 1938-June 1940	Kuzma Kisialev
June 1940-June 1941	Ivan Bylinski (in exile June 1941-Feb 1944)
(June 1941-July 1944	German occupation)
July 1944-March 1947	Panteleimon Ponomarenko
March 1947-July 1953	Aleksei Kleschev
July 1953-July 1956	Kirill Mazurov
July 1956-April 1959	Nikolai Avkhimovich
April 1959-Dec 1978	Tikhon Kiselyov
July 1978-July 1983	Aleksandr Aksyonov
July 1983-Dec 1985	Vladimir Brovikov
Dec 1985-April 1990	Mikhail Kovalev
April 1990-July 1994	Vyacheslav Kebich
July 1994-Nov 1996	Mikhail Chigir
Nov 1996-Feb 2000	Syargey Ling (acting Nov 1996-Feb 1997)
Feb 2000-	Vladimir Yermoshin

Communist Party Leaders:

First Secretary

1920	Aleksandr Myasnikov (A.Myasnikyan) (see Armenia)
Nov 1920-23	Wilgelm Knorinsh (1st)
1923-24	Aleksandr Osatkin-Vladimirsky
1924-27	Aleksandr Krinitsky
May 1927-Nov 1928	Wilgelm Knorinsh (2nd)
Nov 1928-Oct 1929	Yan Gamarnik
Jan 1930-Jan 1932	Konstantin Gei
Jan 1932-March 1937	Nikolai Gikalo
March-Aug 1937	Vasili Sharangovich
Aug 1937-June 1938	Aleksei Volkov
June 1938-March 1947	Panteleimon Ponomarenko (in exile 1941-44) (see Kazakhstan)

March 1947-July 1950	Nikolai Gusarov
July 1950-July 1956	Nikolai Patolichev
July 1956-March 1965	Kirill Mazurov
March 1965-Oct 1980	Pyotr Masherov († motor accident)
Oct 1980-Jan 1983	Tikhon Kiselyov (†)
Jan 1983-Feb 1987	Nikolai Slyunkov
Feb 1987-Dec 1990	Yefrem Sokolov
Dec 1990-Aug 1991	Anatoly Malofeyev
(Aug 1991	party suspended)

BELGIUM

Official name: Kingdom of Belgium, Royaume de Belgique, Koninkrijk België
Independence date: 4 October 1830
Capital: Brussels (Bruxelles)

The Belgian provinces of Burgundy became part of the Habsburg lands in 1477 with the marriage of Mary of Burgundy to the Emperor Maximilian I. The provinces were therefore ruled by the Habsburg kings of Spain until 1580 and Austria until 1795, when they were annexed by France. At the Treaty of Vienna in 1815, Belgium and the Netherlands were united under the king of the Netherlands, but in 1830 Belgium declared independence and Prince Leopold of Saxe-Coburg was chosen as king. Belgium's neutrality was guaranteed by Britain and France, and Germany's invasion in 1914 marked the beginning of World War I. Belgium was again occupied by Germany during World War II. To satisfy demands for autonomy by the different language groups, a federal form of government was gradually introduced in the 1980s and 1990s.

Regent:

Feb-July 1831	Erasme Surlet de Chokier

Kings:

July 1831-Dec 1865	Leopold I
Dec 1865-Dec 1909	Leopold II (*son*)
Dec 1909-Aug 1914	Albert I (*nephew*) (1st)

Governors-General:

Oct 1914	Colmar von der Goltz
Nov 1914-April 1917	Moritz von Bissing
April 1917-Nov 1918	Ludwig von Falkenhausen

Kings:

Nov 1918-Feb 1934	Albert I (2nd)
Feb 1934-May 1940	Leopold III (*son*) (1st)

Commissioner:

May 1940-Sept 1944	Alexander von Falkenhausen

Regent:

Sept 1944-July 1950	Prince Charles (*brother of Leopold III*)

Kings:

July 1950-July 1951	Leopold III (2nd) (abdicated)
July 1951-July 1993	Baudouin (*son*) (Prince Royal Aug 1950-July 1951) (abdicated 4-5 April 1990)
Aug 1993-	Albert II (*brother*)

Prime Ministers:

Sept 1830-Feb 1831	Charles Rogier (1st)
Feb-July 1831	Erasme Surlet de Chokier
July 1831-Oct 1832	Charles de Brouckère
Oct 1832-Aug 1834	Charles Rogier (2nd)
Aug 1834-Aug 1840	Barthélémy Theux de Meylandt (1st)
Aug 1840-April 1841	Joseph Lebeau (CP)
April 1841-June 1845	Jean-Baptiste Nothomb
June 1845-March 1846	Sylvain van de Weyer (LP)
March 1846-Aug 1847	Barthélémy Theux de Meylandt (2nd) (CP)
Aug 1847-Sept 1852	Charles Rogier (3rd) (LP)
Sept 1852-March 1855	Henri de Brouckère (LP)
March 1855-Oct 1857	Pierre de Decker (MCP)
Oct 1857-Jan 1868	Charles Rogier (4th) (LP)
Jan 1868-July 1870	Hubert Frère-Orban (1st) (LP)
July 1870-Dec 1871	Jules d'Anethan (CP)
Dec 1871-Aug 1874	Barthélémy Theux de Meylandt (3rd) (CP) (†)
Aug 1874-June 1878	Jules Malou (1st) (CP)
June 1878-June 1884	Hubert Frère-Orban (2nd) (LP)
June-Oct 1884	Jules Malou (2nd) (CP)
Oct 1884-March 1894	Auguste Beernaert (MCP)
March 1894-Feb 1896	Jules de Burlet
Feb 1896-Jan 1899	Paul de Smet de Nayer (1st) (CP)
Jan-Aug 1899	Julius van den Peereboom (CP)
Aug 1899-May 1907	Paul de Smet de Nayer (2nd) (CP)
May 1907-Jan 1908	Jules de Trooz (CP)
Jan 1908-June 1911	François Schollaert (CP)
June 1911-Aug 1914	Charles de Broqueville (1st) (CP)
(Aug 1914-Nov 1918	German occupation)
Nov 1918-Nov 1920	Léon Delacroix
Nov 1920-Dec 1921	Henri Carton de Wiart (CaP)
Dec 1921-May 1925	Georges Theunis (1st) (CaP)
May-June 1925	Alois van der Vyvere (CaP)
June 1925-May 1926	Prosper Poullet (CaP)
May 1926-June 1931	Henri Jaspar (CaP)
June 1931-Oct 1932	Jules Renkin (CaP)
Oct 1932-Nov 1934	Charles de Broqueville (2nd) (CaP)
Nov 1934-March 1935	Georges Theunis (2nd) (CaP)
March 1935-Nov 1937	Paul van Zeeland (CaP)

Nov 1937-May 1938	Paul Janson (LP)
May 1938-Feb 1939	Paul-Henri Spaak (1st) (SP)
Feb 1939-May 1940	Hubert Pierlot (1st) (CaP)
(May 1940-Sept 1944	German occupation)
Sept 1944-Feb 1945	Hubert Pierlot (2nd) (CaP)
Feb 1945-March 1946	Achille van Acker (1st) (SP)
21-27 March 1946	Paul-Henri Spaak (2nd) (SP)
March-Aug 1946	Achille van Acker (2nd) (SP)
Aug 1946-March 1947	Camille Huysmans (SP)
March 1947-Aug 1949	Paul-Henri Spaak (3rd) (SP) (see NATO)
Aug 1949-June 1950	Gaston Eyskens (1st) (CSP)
June-Aug 1950	Jean Duvieusart (CSP)
Aug 1950-Jan 1952	Joseph Pholien (CSP)
Jan 1952-April 1954	Jean van Houtte (CSP)
April 1954- June 1958	Achille van Acker (3rd) (SP)
June 1958-April 1961	Gaston Eyskens (2nd) (CSP)
April 1961-July 1965	Théodore Lefèvre (CSP)
July 1965-March 1966	Pierre Harmel (CSP)
March 1966-June 1968	Paul van den Boeynants (1st) (CSP)
June 1968-Jan 1973	Gaston Eyskens (3rd) (CSP)
Jan 1973-April 1974	Edmond Leburton (SP)
April 1974-Dec 1978	Leo Tindemans (CSP)
Dec 1978-April 1979	Paul van den Boeynants (2nd) (CSP)
April 1979-April 1981	Wilfried Martens (1st) (CSP)
April-Dec 1981	Mark Eyskens (*son of G.Eyskens*) (CSP)
Dec 1981-March 1992	Wilfried Martens (2nd) (CSP)
March 1992-July 1999	Jean-Luc Dehaene (CSP)
July 1999-	Guy Verhoefstadt (FLP)

CaP = Catholic Party
CP = Clerical Party
CSP = Christian Social Party   (f CaP)
FLP = Flemish Liberal Party
LP = Liberal Party
MCP = Moderate Clerical Party
SP = Socialist Party

GOVERNMENTS-IN-EXILE 1914-18 & 1940-44

Operated during German occupations
Headquarters: Le Havre (1914-18), London (1940-44)

King:

Aug 1914-Nov 1918	Albert I

Prime Ministers:

Aug 1914-June 1918	Charles de Broqueville

June-Nov 1918   Gerhard Cooreman
June 1940-Sept 1944   Hubert Pierlot

Autonomous Regions

BRUSSELS

Capital: Brussels

Ministers-Presidents:

July 1989-July 1999   Charles Picque
July 1999-   Jacques Simonet

FLANDERS

Vlanderen

Capital: Ghent

Ministers-Presidents:

Dec 1981-Jan 1992   Gaston Geens   (CSP)
Jan 1992-July 1999   Luc van den Brande   (CSP)
July 1999-   Patrick Dewael

WALLONIA

Capital: Namur

Ministers-Presidents:

Dec 1981-Jan 1982   Jean-Marie Dehousse   (1st) (SP)
Jan 1982-Oct 1985   André Damseaux   (LRP)
Oct-Dec 1985   Jean-Marie Dehousse   (2nd) (SP)
Dec 1985-Feb 1988   Melchior Wathelet   (CSP)
Feb-May 1988   Guy Coëme   (SP)
May 1988-Jan 1992   Bernard Anselme   (SP)
Jan 1992-Jan 1994   Guy Spitaels   (SP)
Jan 1994-July 1999   Robert Collignon   (SP)
July 1999-   Elio Di Rupo

LRP = Liberal Reform Party

Communities

FLEMISH

Functions carried out by Flanders Council

FRENCH

Headquarters: Brussels

Council Chairmen:

Dec 1981-May 1988	Philippe Moreaux
May 1988-Jan 1992	Valmy Féaux
Jan 1992-May 1993	Bernard Anselme (see Wallonia)
May 1993-July 1994	Laurette Onkelinx
July 1999-	Hervé Hasquin

GERMAN

Headquarters: Eupen

Council Chairmen:

Jan 1984-Nov 1986	Bruno Fagnoul
Nov 1986-July 1999	Joseph Maraite
July 1999-	Karl-Heinz Lambertz

BELIZE

Official name: Belize
Previous name: British Honduras until 1973
Independence date: 21 September 1981
Capital: Belize City (until 1970), Belmopan

In about 1638 British woodcutters established settlements in the region of present-day Belize. In 1780 Britain appointed a superintendent, and in 1862 British Honduras was declared a British colony subordinate to Jamaica. It became a separate colony in 1884. In 1961 a measure of self-government was granted, followed by full self-government in 1964. Full independence was delayed until 1981 because of territorial claims by Guatemala.

Governors:

1884-91	Roger Goldsworthy
1891-97	Cornelius Moloney
1897-1904	David Wilson
1904-06	Ernest Sweet-Escott (see Seychelles)
1906-13	Eric Swayne
1913-18	Wilfred Collet
1918-19	William Bennett
1919-25	Eyre Hutson
1925-32	John Burdon
1932-34	Harold Kittermaster (see British Somaliland)
1934-40	Alan Burns
1940-47	John Hunter
1947-48	Edward Hawkesworth
1948-52	Ronald Garvey
1952-55	Patrick Renison
1955-61	Colin Thornley
1961-66	Peter Stallard
1966-72	John Paul (see the Gambia)
1972-76	Richard Posnett
1976-80	Peter McEntee
1980-81	James Hennessy

Governors-General:

Represent monarch who is concurrently British monarch

Sept 1981-Nov 1993	Elmira Gordon
Nov 1993-	Colville Young

First Minister:

April 1961-Jan 1964　　　　George Price　(PUP)

Prime Ministers:

Premier 1964-81

Jan 1964-Dec 1984	George Price　(1st) (PUP)
Dec 1984-Sept 1989	Manuel Esquivel　(1st) (UDP)
Sept 1989-July 1993	George Price　(2nd) (PUP)
July 1993-Aug 1998	Manuel Esquivel　(2nd) (UDP)
Aug 1998-	Said Musa　(PUP)

PUP = People's United Party
UDP = United Democratic Party

BENIN

Official name: Republic of Benin, République du Benin
Previous names: Republic of Dahomey until 1975, People's Republic of Benin 1975-90
Independence date: 1 August 1960
Capital: Porto Novo

The four kingdoms that made up the southern part of present-day Benin became French protectorates in the 1890s. French control was extended to the north and in 1904 the territory was consolidated as the colony of Dahomey and became part of French West Africa. Dahomey became an Overseas Territory in 1946. Self-government was granted in 1958, and independence followed in 1960. The country experienced several coups during the first decade. In 1972 a Marxist state was proclaimed, and in 1975 the name was changed to Benin. Marxism was abandoned in 1989 and a multi-party system introduced in 1991.

Lieutenant-Governors:

1891-1900	Victor Ballot
1900-06	Victor-Théophile Liotard
1906-08	Charles Marchal (see French Guiana)
1908-09	Jean Peuvergne
1909-11	Henri Malan
1911-12	Émile Merwart (see French Guiana)
1912-17	Charles Noufflard
1917-28	Gaston Fourn
1929-31	Dieudonné Reste
1931-32	Théophile Tellier
1932	Louis-Placide Blacher
1932-34	Jules-Marcel de Coppet (see Chad)
1934-35	Marcel Marchessou
1935-37	Maurice-Léon Bourgine

Governors:

1937-38	Louis Bonvin
1938-40	Armand-Léon Annet
1940-43	Léon-Hippolyte Truitard
1943-45	Charles Assier de Popignan (see Gabon)
1945-46	Marc de Villedeul
1946-48	Robert Legendre
1948	Jean-Georges Chambon
1948-49	Jacques-Alphonse Boissier
1949-51	Claude Valluy

1951-55	Charles-Henri Bonfils
1955-58	Casimir-Marc Biros

High Commissioner:

1959-60	René Tirant

Presidents:

Aug 1960-Oct 1963	Hubert Maga (1st) (DDR) (deposed)
Oct 1963-Jan 1964	Christophe Soglo (1st)
Jan 1964-Nov 1965	Sourou-Migan Apithy (RPD) (deposed)
Nov-Dec 1965	Tairou Congacou
Dec 1965-Dec 1967	Christophe Soglo (2nd) (deposed)
20-21 Dec 1967	Maurice Kouandété
Dec 1967-July 1968	Alphonse Alley
July 1968-Dec 1969	Émile Zinsou (deposed)
Dec 1969-May 1970	Paul-Émile de Souza
May 1970-May 1972	Hubert Maga (2nd)
May-Oct 1972	Justin Ahomadegbe (deposed)
Oct 1972-April 1991	Mathieu Kerekou (1st) (PPRB)
April 1991-April 1996	Nicéphore Soglo (BRP)
April 1996-	Mathieu Kerekou (2nd)

Prime Ministers:

July 1958-May 1959	Sourou-Migan Apithy (PPD)
May 1959-Aug 1960	Hubert Maga (DDR)
(Aug 1960-Jan 1964	post abolished)
Jan 1964-Nov 1965	Justin Ahomadegbe
Nov-Dec 1965	Tairou Congacou
Dec 1965-Dec 1967	Christophe Soglo
Dec 1967-July 1968	Maurice Kouandété
July 1968-Dec 1969	Émile Zinsou
(Dec 1969-March 1990	post abolished)
March 1990-April 1991	Nicéphore Soglo
(April 1991-April 1996	post abolished)
April 1996-May 1998	Adrien Houngbédjie (DRP)
(May 1998	post abolished)

BRP = Benin Renaissance Party
DDR = Democratic Dahomey Rally
DRP = Democratic Renewal Party
PPD = Popular Party of Dahomey
PPRB = Party of the Popular Revolution of Benin (sole party 1975-90)
RPD = Republican Party of Dahomey (*f* PPD)

BHUTAN

Official name: Kingdom of Bhutan, Druk-yul (Dzongkha)
State founded: 16th century
Capital: Thimphu (Previous capitals until 1992: Punakha (winter); Paro & Tashichodzong (Thimphu) (summer))

The state of Bhutan in the eastern Himalayas was consolidated in the mid-16th century, and until 1907 was ruled by a diarchy of temporal and spiritual rajas. In 1907 the governor of eastern Bhutan was elected as the first hereditary king. The British government acted as advisor on external relations until 1947, when India took over this role. Since 1971 Bhutan has asserted its independence.

Dharna Rajas (from 1791):
Spiritual heads

1791-1830	Ngawang Jigme Dakpa II
1830-61	Ngawang Jigme Norbu
1862-1904	Ngawang Jigme Chogyal

Deb Rajas (from 1864):
Temporal heads

1864-66	Tsewing Situp
1866-70	Tsondu Pekar
1870-73	Jigme Namgyal (1st)
1873-77	Kyitselpa Dorji Namgyal (1st)
1877-78	Jigme Namgyal (2nd)
1878-79	Kyitselpa Dorji Namgyal (2nd)
1879-80	Chogyal Zangpo
1880-81	Jigme Namgyal (3rd)
1881-83	Lama Tsewang
1883-85	Kawa Zangpo
1885-1901	Yanglob Singye Dorji
1901-05	Chokyul Yeshe Ngodrup

Kings:

Dec 1907-Aug 1926	Ugyen Wangchuk
Aug 1926-Oct 1952	Jigme Wangchuk (*son*)
Oct 1952-July 1972	Jigme Dorji Wangchuk (*son*)
July 1972-	Jigme Singye Wangchuk (*son*)

Prime Ministers:
Chairman of the Council of Ministers

1907- ?	Kazi Ugyen Dorji
? -1952	Debzunpon S.T.Dorji
1952-April 1964	Jigme Dorji (*son*) († assassinated)
(April-July 1964	post vacant)
July-Nov 1964	Lendup Dorji (*brother*)
Nov 1964-July 1972	King Jigme Dorji Wangchuk (†)
July 1972-July 1998	King Jigme Singye Wangchuk
July 1998-	Jigme Thinley

BOLIVIA

Official name: Republic of Bolivia, República de Bolivia
Independence date: 6 August 1825
Capital: La Paz

Following the Spanish conquest in the 16th century, a territory known as Upper Peru was constituted as a dependency of the Viceroyalty of Peru. In 1825 it declared itself independent, choosing the name Bolivia in honour of Simón Bolívar, leader of the independence movement. In the war with Chile and Peru (1879-83) Bolivia lost its coastal region to Chile. Further territory was lost to Paraguay in 1930. Bolivia has suffered from considerable political instability throughout its history, with many of its leaders being overthrown. Bolivia has had democratically elected governments since 1982.

Presidents:

Aug 1825-Oct 1826	Simón Bolívar (also President of Colombia, Peru & Venezuela)
Oct 1826-April 1828	Antonio de Sucre (1st)
April-Aug 1828	Pedro Blanco (acting) († assassinated)
Aug 1828-Jan 1829	José de Velasco (1st) (deposed)
Jan-March 1829	Antonio de Sucre (2nd) (deposed)
March 1829-Jan 1839	Andrés Santa Cruz (also President of Colombia)
Feb-June 1839	José Serrano (acting)
June 1839-Sept 1841	José de Velasco (2nd)
Sept 1841	Mariano Calvo
Sept 1841-Dec 1847	José Ballivián (deposed)
Dec 1847-Jan 1848	Eusebio Guilarte (deposed)
Jan-Dec 1848	José de Velasco (3rd)
Dec 1848-Aug 1855	Manuel Belzú (acting Dec 1848-Aug 1850)
Aug 1855-Nov 1857	Jorge Cordova (deposed)
Nov 1857-Jan 1861	José Linares (acting) (deposed)
(Jan-May 1861	post vacant)
May 1861-Dec 1864	José de Acha (acting May-Aug 1861) (deposed)
Dec 1864-June 1871	Mariano Melgarejo (acting Dec 1864-Feb 1865) (deposed, assassinated)
June 1871-Oct 1872	Agustín Morales (deposed, assassinated)
Oct-Nov 1872	Tomás Frias (1st)
Nov 1872-Feb 1874	Adolfo Ballivián († assassinated)
Feb 1874-May 1876	Tomás Frias (2nd) (deposed)
May 1876-Dec 1879	Hilarion Daza (deposed) (assassinated 1894)
Dec 1879-Aug 1884	Narciso Campero (acting Dec 1879-June 1880)
Aug 1884-Aug 1888	Gregorio Pacheco
Aug 1888-Aug 1892	Aniceto Arce
Aug 1892-Aug 1896	Mariano Baptista
Aug 1896-April 1899	Sergio Fernández Alonso (deposed)

(April-Oct 1899	post vacant-rule by military junta)
Oct 1899-Aug 1904	José Pando (assassinated 1917)
Aug 1904-Aug 1909	Ismael Montes (1st)
Aug 1909-Aug 1913	Eliodoro Villazon
Aug 1913-Aug 1917	Ismael Montes (2nd)
Aug 1917-July 1920	José Gutiérrez Guerra (deposed)
July 1920-Sept 1925	Juan Bautista Saavedra (deposed)
Sept 1925-Jan 1926	Felipe Guzmán (acting)
Jan 1926-May 1930	Hernando Siles (deposed)
May-June 1930	David Toro (1st) (deposed)
June 1930-Feb 1931	Carlos Blanco Galindo
Feb 1931-Nov 1934	Daniel Salamanca (acting Feb-March 1931)
Nov 1934-May 1936	Luis Tejeda Sorzano (deposed)
May 1936-July 1937	David Toro (2nd) (deposed)
July 1937-Aug 1939	Germán Busch († suicide)
Aug 1939-March 1940	Carlos Quintanilla (acting)
March 1940-Dec 1943	Enrique Peñaranda (deposed)
Dec 1943-July 1946	Gualberto Villaroel (deposed, assassinated)
July-Aug 1946	Nestor Guillen (acting)
Aug 1946-March 1947	Tomás Monje Gutiérrez
March 1947-Oct 1949	Enrique Hertzog
Oct 1949-May 1951	Mamerto Urriolagoitia (deposed)
May 1951-April 1952	Hugo Ballivián Rojas (deposed)
9-16 April 1952	Hernán Siles Zuazo (acting)
April 1952-Aug 1956	Víctor Paz Estenssoro (1st) (NRM)
Aug 1956-Aug 1960	Hernán Siles Zuazo (1st) (NRM)
Aug 1960-Nov 1964	Víctor Paz Estenssoro (2nd) (NRM) (deposed)
Nov 1964-Jan 1966	René Barrientos Ortuño (1st) (Co-President May 1965-Jan 1966)
May 1965-Aug 1966	Alfredo Ovando Candía (1st) (Co-President May 1965-Jan 1966)
Aug 1966-April 1969	René Barrientos Ortuño (2nd) († air accident) (BRF)
April-Sept 1969	Luis Siles Salinas (BRF) (deposed)
Sept 1969-Oct 1970	Alfredo Ovando Candía (2nd) (deposed)
Oct 1970-Aug 1971	Juan Torres González (deposed) (assassinated 1976)
Aug 1971-July 1978	Hugo Banzer Suárez (1st) (deposed)
July-Nov 1978	Juan Pereda Asbún (deposed)
Nov 1978-Aug 1979	David Padilla Arancibia
Aug-Nov 1979	Walter Guevara Arce (deposed)
1-16 Nov 1979	Alberto Natusch Busch (*nephew of G.Busch*)
Nov 1979-July 1980	Lidia Gueiler Tejada (deposed)
July 1980-Aug 1981	Luis García Meza
Aug-Sept 1981	Waldo Bernal Pereira
Sept 1981-July 1982	Celso Torrelio Villa
July-Oct 1982	Guido Vildoso Calderón
Oct 1982-Aug 1985	Hernán Siles Zuazo (2nd) (NRM-Leftist)
Aug 1985-Aug 1989	Víctor Paz Estenssoro (3rd) (NRM)
Aug 1989-Aug 1993	Jaime Paz Zamora (*nephew*) (LRM)

Aug 1993-Aug 1997   Gonzalo Sánchez de Lozada   (NRM)
Aug 1997-   Hugo Banzer Suárez   (2nd) (DNA)

BRF = Bolivian Revolutionary Front
DNA = Democratic Nationalist Action
LRM = Leftist Revolutionary Movement
NRM = National Revolutionary Movement

BOSNIA AND HERZEGOVINA

Official name: Republic of Bosnia and Herzegovina
Previous name: Socialist Republic of Bosnia-Herzegovina 1945-91
Independence date: 5 April 1992
Capital: Sarajevo

The area was conquered by the Turks in 1463. In 1878 the Congress of Berlin assigned it to Austrian rule under nominal Turkish suzerainty. Its annexation by Austria in 1908 caused internal tensions which contributed to the outbreak of World War I. In 1918 it became part of the new state of Yugoslavia, attaining republic status in 1945. As communism collapsed in eastern Europe, it declared independence in 1992. Ethnic divisions soon caused civil war and the declaration of Serb and Croat states. In 1994 the Croats and the Muslims formed a federal state, and in 1995 a cease fire with the Serbs was declared. The peace treaty of 1996 provided for the division of the country into two states (a Serb republic and a Muslim-Croat federation) with a small central government.

Presidents:
President of the People's Assembly 1945-74
President of the State Presidency April 1974-Sept 1996
President of the Collective Presidency since Sept 1996

1945-1946	Vojslav-Djedo Kećmanović
1946-1948	Djuro Pućar-Sjari (1st)
1948-1953	Vlado Segrt
1953-1963	Djuro Pućar-Sjari (2nd)
1963-1967	Rato Dugonjić (1st)
1967-1971	Dzemal Bijedic
1971-April 1974	Hamidija Pozderac
April 1974-April 1978	Rato Dugonjić (2nd)
April 1978-April 1982	Raif Dizdarević
April 1982-April 1983	Branko Mikulić
April 1983-April 1985	Milanko Renovica
April 1985-April 1987	Munir Mesihović
April 1987-April 1988	Mato Andrić
April 1988-April 1989	Nikola Filipović
April 1989-Dec 1990	Obrad Piljak
Dec 1990-Oct 1998	Alija Izetbegović (1st) (PDA)
Oct 1998-June 1999	Zivko Radisić (SPSRS)
June 1999-Feb 2000	Ante Jelavić (CDU)
Feb 2000-	Alija Izetbegović (2nd) (PDA)

Prime Ministers:

President of the Executive Council 1945-91
Chairmen of the Council of Ministers since Jan 1997

1945-48	Rodoljub Colaković
1948-53	Djuro Pućar-Sjari
1953-55	Avdo Humo
1955-63	Osman Karabegović
1963-65	Hasan Brkić
1965-67	Rudi Kolak
1967-69	Branko Mikulić
1969-April 1974	Dragutin Kosavac
April 1974-April 1982	Milanko Renovica
April 1982-April 1984	Seid Maglajlija
April 1984-April 1986	Gojko Ubiparip
April 1986-April 1988	Josip Lovrenović
April 1988-Dec 1990	Marko Ceranić
Dec 1990-Nov 1992	Jure Pelivan (CDU)
Nov 1992-Aug 1993	Mile Akmadžić
(Aug-Oct 1993	post vacant)
Oct 1993-Jan 1996	Haris Silajdžić (1st)
Jan 1996-Jan 1997	Hasan Muratović
Jan 1997-	Haris Silajdžić (2nd) (co-PM)
Jan 1997-Feb 1999	Boro Bošić (co-PM)
Feb 1999-	Svetozar Mihajlović (co-PM)

CDU = Croatian Democratic Union
PDA = Party of Democratic Action
SPRS = Socialist Party of Serbia for Republika Srpska

Communist Party Leaders:

1945-64	Djuro Pućar-Sjar
1964-69	Cvijetin Mijatović
1969-April 1978	Branko Mikulić
April 1978-May 1982	Nikola Stojanović
May 1982-May 1984	Hamidija Pozderac
May 1984-May 1986	Mato Andrić
May 1986-May 1988	Milan Uzelac
May 1988-June 1989	Abdulah Mutapćić
June 1989-Dec 1990	Nijaz Duraković
(Dec 1990	non-communist government elected)

Republics

The Serbian and Croatian communities proclaimed their own republics, but were not recognised by the central government. In 1994 the Croats and the Muslims formed a federation for those parts of the country under their control. The Croat state was dissolved after the peace settlement was implemented.

CROAT REPUBLIC OF HERCEG-BOSNA

Croat Community proclaimed: 4 July 1992
Republic proclaimed: 28 August 1993
Dissolved: 17 December 1996
Capital: Mostar (*Headquarters*: Grude)

Presidents:
Chairman of the Presidential Council 1994-96

July 1992-Feb 1994	Mate Boban (CDU)
Feb 1994-Dec 1996	Kresimir Zubak (CDU)
(June 1994-Dec 1996	Ivan Bender (acting))

Prime Ministers:

Aug 1993-June 1996	Jadranko Prlić
June-Dec 1996	Pero Marković

SERBIAN REPUBLIC OF BOSNIA
Republika Srpska

Republic declared: 27 March 1992
Capital: Banja Luka (*Seat of government*: Pale 1992-98)

Presidents:

March 1992-July 1996	Radovan Karadžić (SDP)
July 1996-Nov 1998	Biljana Plavsić (acting July-Sept 1996) (SDP, AC)
Nov 1998-March 1999	Nikola Poplasen (SDP)
(March 1999-Jan 2000	post vacant)
Jan 2000-	Mirko Sarović

Prime Ministers:

March 1992-1993	Branko Djerić
1993-Aug 1994	Vladimir Lukić
Aug 1994-Dec 1995	Dusan Kozić
Dec 1995-May 1996	Rajko Kasagić
May 1996-Jan 1998	Gojko Klićković
Jan 1998-	

AC = Accord Coalition
SDP = Serb Democratic Party

BOSNIAN FEDERATION OF MUSLIMS AND CROATS

Formation date: 31 March 1994
Capital: Sarajevo

Presidents:

June 1994-March 1997	Kresimir Zubak (CDU)
March-Dec 1997	Vladimir Soljić
Dec 1997-Jan 1999	Ejup Ganić (1st)
Jan 1999-Jan 2000	Ivo Andrić-Luzanski
Jan 2000-	Ejup Ganić (2nd)

Prime Ministers:

June 1994-Jan 1996	Haris Silajdžić
Jan-Dec 1996	Izudin Kapetanović
Dec 1996-	Edhem Bicakćić

Self-declared Autonomous Province

WESTERN BOSNIA

Capital: Bihać

President:

Sept 1993-Aug 1994   Fikret Abdić   (DPC)

Prime Minister:

Sept 1993-Aug 1994   Zlatko Jusić

(Captured by Bosnian government forces Aug 1994)

DPC = Democratic Peoples Community

BOTSWANA

Official name: Republic of Botswana
Previous name: Bechuanaland until 1966
Independence date: 30 September 1966
Capital: Gaberone

In 1884 Bechuanaland became a British protectorate. The area south of the Molopo River was transferred to the Cape Colony in 1895 and the rest of the territory remained a protectorate. Self-government was granted in 1965 and full independence the following year.

Commissioners:

1885-95	Sidney Shippard
1895-97	Francis Newton
1897-1901	Hamilton Goold-Adams
1901-06	Ralph Williams
1907-16	Francis Panzera
1916-17	Edward Garraway
1917-23	James MacGregor
1923-27	Jules Ellenberger
1928-30	Rowland Daniel
1930-37	Charles Rey
1937-42	Charles Arden-Clarke
1942-46	Aubrey Thompson
1946-50	Anthony Sillery
1950-53	Edward Beetham
1953-55	William MacKenzie
1955-59	Martin Wray
1959-65	Robert Fawcus
1965-66	Hugh Norman-Walker

Presidents:

Sept 1966-July 1980	Seretse Khama (DP) (†)
July 1980-March 1998	Q. Ketumile Masire (DP)
April 1998-	Festus Mogae (DP)

Prime Minister:

March 1965-Sept 1966	Seretse Khama (DP)
(Sept 1966	post abolished)

DP = Democratic Party

BRAZIL

Official name: Federative Republic of Brazil, República Federativa do Brasil
Previous names: Empire of Brazil 1822-1889, United States of Brazil 1889-1937, Brazil 1937-1967
Independence date: 7 September 1822
Capital: Rio de Janeiro (until 1960), Brasília (since 1960)

Portuguese settlement in Brazil dates from 1500. In 1815 the colony was declared a kingdom, and in 1822 Dom Pedro, son of the king of Portugal was named Perpetual Defender. Later that year he declared Brazil's independence and took the title Emperor. A revolution in 1889 abolished the monarchy and established a federal republic. After two decades of military rule Brazil returned to democracy in 1985.

Emperors:

Oct 1822-April 1831	Pedro I (Pedro IV of Portugal) (abdicated)
April 1831-Nov 1889	Pedro II (*son*) (deposed)
	Regents:
	1831-5 Regency Council
	1835-7 Diogo Feijo
	1837-40 Pedro Lima

Presidents:

Nov 1889-Nov 1891	Deodoro da Fonseca
Nov 1891-Nov 1894	Floriano Peixoto (acting)
Nov 1894-Nov 1898	Prudente Barros
Nov 1898-Nov 1902	Manuel Salles
Nov 1902-Nov 1906	Francisco Alves
Nov 1906-June 1909	Affonso Penna (†)
June 1909-Nov 1910	Nilo Peçanha (acting)
Nov 1910-Nov 1914	Hermes da Fonseca (*nephew of D.da Fonseca*) (see Bahia)
Nov 1914-Nov 1918	Wenceslão Braz Gomes (see Minas Gerais)
(1918	Francisco Alves, President-elect, did not assume office due to illness)
Nov 1918-July 1919	Delphim Moreira (acting)
July 1919-Nov 1922	Epitácio Pessôa
Nov 1922-Nov 1926	Arthur Bernardes
Nov 1926-Oct 1930	Washington de Souza (deposed)
Oct 1930-Oct 1945	Getúlio Vargas (see Rio Grande do Sul) (1st)
Oct 1945-Jan 1946	José Linhares
Jan 1946-Jan 1951	Eurico Dutra (SDP)
Jan 1951-Aug 1954	Getúlio Vargas (2nd) (BLP) († suicide)
Aug 1954-Nov 1955	João Café (SPP)

8-11 Nov 1955	Carlos da Luz (acting) (deposed)
Nov 1955-Jan 1956	Nereu Ramos (acting)
Jan 1956-Jan 1961	Juscelino Kubitschek (see Minas Gerais)
Jan-Aug 1961	Jânio Quadros (see São Paulo)
Aug 1961-March 1964	João Goulart (BLP) (deposed)
March-April 1964	Ranieri Mazzilli (acting)
April 1964-March 1967	Humberto Castello Branco
March 1967-Oct 1969	Arthur Costa e Silva
Oct 1969-March 1974	Emilio Médici
March 1974-March 1979	Ernesto Geisel
March 1979-March 1985	João Figuereido (ARENA)
(1985	Tancredo Neves (see Minas Gerais) (BDM (President-elect, did not assume office due to illness)
March 1985-March 1990	José Sarney (b J.Costa) (BDM) (acting March-April 1985) (see Maranhão)
March 1990-Dec 1992	Fernando Collor de Mello (NRP) (see Alagoas) (suspended Oct 1992)
Dec 1992-Jan 1995	Itamar Franco (acting Oct-Dec 1992)
Jan 1995-	Fernando Henrique Cardoso (SDP)

Prime Ministers:

July 1847-March 1848	Manuel Branco
March-Aug 1848	Visconde de Macaé (José Torres)
Aug-Sept 1848	Bernardo Campos
Sept 1848-Oct 1849	Visconde de Olinda (Pedro Lima) (1st)
Oct 1849-May 1852	Visconde de Monte Alegre (José Carvalho)
May 1852-Sept 1853	Visconde de Itaborai (Joaquim Torres) (1st)
Sept 1853-Sept 1856	Visconde de Paraná (Horacio Leão)
Sept 1856-May 1857	Marquês de Caxias (Luiz de Lima e Silva) (1st)
May 1857-Dec 1858	Visconde de Olinda (Pedro Lima) (2nd)
Dec 1858-Aug 1859	Visconde de Abaeté (António de Abreu)
Aug 1859-March 1861	Angelo Ferraz
March 1861-May 1862	Marquês de Caxias (Luiz de Lima e Silva) (2nd)
May-Oct 1862	Visconde de Olinda (Pedro Lima)
Oct-Nov 1862	Marquês de Abrantes (Miguel du Pin e Almeida)
Nov 1862-Jan 1864	Visconde de Olinda (Pedro Lima) (4th)
Jan-Aug 1864	Zacarias de Góis e Vasconcelos (1st)
Aug 1864-May 1865	Francisco Furtado
May 1865-Aug 1866	Visconde de Olinda (Pedro Lima) (5th)
Aug 1866-July 1868	Zacarias de Góis e Vasconcelos (2nd)
July 1868-Sept 1870	Visconde de Itaborai (Joaquim Torres) (2nd)
Sept 1870-March 1871	Visconde de São Vicente (José Bueno)
March 1871-June 1875	Visconde de Rio Branco (José Paranhos)
June 1875-Jan 1878	Marquês de Caxias (Luiz de Lima e Silva) (3rd)
Jan 1878-March 1880	João de Sinimbu
March 1880-Jan 1882	José Saraiva (1st)

Jan-July 1882	Martinho Campos
July 1882-May 1883	Visconde de Paranaguá (João Paranaguá)
May 1883-June 1884	Lafaiete Pereira
June 1884-May 1885	Manuel Dantas
May-Aug 1885	José Saraiva (2nd)
Aug 1885-March 1888	Barão de Cotegipe (João Wanderley)
March 1888-June 1889	João de Oliveira
June-Nov 1889	Visconde de Ouro Preto (Afonso Figuereido)
(Nov 1889-Sept 1961	post abolished)
Sept 1961-June 1962	Tancredo Neves
3-4 July 1962	Auro Andrade
July-Sept 1962	Francisco da Rocha
Sept 1962-Jan 1963	Hermes Lima
(Jan 1963	post abolished)

ARENA = Aliiança Renovadora Nacional
BDM = Brazil Democratic Movement
BLP = Brazilian Labour Party
NRP = National Reconstruction Party
SDP = Social Democratic Party
SPP = Social Progress Party

Parties in state lists:
BSP = Brazilian Socialist Party
DLP = Democratic Labour Party
LFP = Liberal Front Party
PRP = Progressive Reform Party
SCP = Social Christian Party
UDN = Union of Democratic Nationalists
WP = Workers' Party

States

ACRE

Statehood: 15 June 1962
Capital: Rio Branco

Governors:

June 1962-March 1963	Aníbal da Silva
1-25 March 1963	José de Araújo
March-Sept 1963	Edgard de Cerqueira
Sept 1966-March 1971	Jorge Kalume
March 1971-March 1975	Francisco Dantas
March 1975-March 1979	Geraldo de Mesquita (ARENA)
March 1979-March 1983	Joaquim Falcão Macedo (ARENA)
March 1983-May 1986	Nabor Teles da Rocha (BDM)

May 1986-March 1987   Iolanda Fleming   (BDM)
March 1987-March 1991   Flaviano Baptista de Melo   (BDM)
March 1991-May 1992   Edmundo Pinto   (SDP) († assassinated)
May 1992-Jan 1995   Romildo Magalhães
Jan 1995-Jan 1999   Orleir Camelli   (PRP)
Jan 1999-   Jorge Viana   (WP)

ALAGOAS

Capital: Maceió

Governors:

Nov-Dec 1889	Tibúrcio de Araújo
Dec 1889-Dec 1890	Pedro de Fonseca (1st)
Dec 1890-June 1891	Manoel de Araújo Góes (1st)
12-14 June 1891	Pedro da Fonseca (2nd)
June-Nov 1891	Manoel de Araújo Góes (2nd)
Nov 1891-April 1892	Manoel Ribeiro (1st)
April 1892-June 1894	Gabino Besouro
July-Oct 1894	Tibúrcio da Rocha Lins
Oct 1894-Jan 1896	Manoel Ribeiro (2nd)
Jan 1896-June 1897	José Peixoto
June 1897-June 1899	Manoel Duarte
June 1899-June 1900	Francisco Pacheco
June 1900-June 1903	Euclides Malta (1st)
June 1906-March 1909	Joaquim Malta
March-June 1909	José de Vasconcelos
June 1909-March 1912	Euclides Malta (2nd)
March-June 1912	Macário Lessa
June 1912-June 1915	Clodoaldo da Fonseca
June 1915-June 1918	João Acioly
June 1918-May 1921	José de Barros Lima (1st)
May-June 1921	Manoel Carvalho
June 1921-June 1924	José de Barros Lima (2nd)
June 1924-June 1928	Pedro Rêgo
12 June 1928	José Cansanção
June 1928-Oct 1930	Alvaro Paes

Administrators:

Oct 1930-Aug 1931	Hermilio Melro
Aug-Oct 1931	Luiz Albuquerque (1st)
Oct 1931-Oct 1932	Tasso Tinoco
Oct 1932-Jan 1933	Luiz Albuquerque (2nd)
Jan 1933-March 1934	Francisco de Carvalho
March-May 1934	Temístocles de Azevedo

May 1934-March 1935	Osman de Farias (1st)
March-May 1935	Edgar Monteiro (1st)
10-27 May 1935	Benedito da Silva
May 1935-Oct 1940	Osman de Farias (2nd)
Oct 1940-Feb 1941	José das Neves
Feb 1941-Nov 1945	Ismar Monteiro
Nov-Dec 1945	Edgar Monteiro (2nd)
Dec 1945-March 1947	António de Miranda

Governors:

March 1947-Jan 1951	Silvestre Monteiro
Jan 1951-Jan 1956	Arnon Mello
Jan 1956-Jan 1961	Sebastião Falção
Jan 1961-Jan 1966	Luiz Cavalcante (UDN)
Jan-Aug 1966	João Tubino
Aug 1966-March 1971	António de Lamenha
March 1971-March 1975	Afrânio Lages
March 1975-Aug 1978	Divaldo Suruagy (1st) (ARENA)
Aug-Sept 1978	Ernandes Dorvillé
Sept 1978-March 1979	Geraldo de Melo
March 1979-March 1982	Guilherme Palmeira (ARENA)
March 1982-March 1983	Theobaldo Barbosa
March 1983-May 1986	Divaldo Suruagy (SDP) (2nd)
May 1986-March 1987	José Tavares
March 1987-89	Fernando Collor de Mello (BDM)
1989-March 1991	Moacir de Andrade
March 1991-Jan 1995	Geraldo Bulhões (SCP)
Jan 1995-Jan 1999	Divaldo Suruagy (3rd) (BDM)
Jan 1999-	Ronaldo Lessa (BSP)

AMAPÁ

Statehood: 5 October 1988
Capital: Macapá

Governors:

Oct 1988-March 1991	Jorge Nova da Costa
March 1991-Jan 1995	Annibal Barcellos (LFP)
Jan 1995-	João Capiberibe (SP)

AMAZONAS

Capital: Manaus

Governors:

Jan-Nov 1890	Augusto de Vileroy
Nov 1890-May 1891	Eduardo Ribeiro (1st)
5-25 May 1891	Guilherme Moreira (1st)
May-June 1891	António Pimentel
June-Sept 1891	Guilherme Moreira (2nd)
Sept 1891-Feb 1892	Gregório Azevedo
Feb-March 1892	José Machado
March 1892-July 1896	Eduardo Ribeiro (2nd)
July 1896-April 1898	Fileto Ferreira
April 1898-July 1900	José Ramalho
July 1900-July 1904	Silvério Néry
July 1904-July 1908	António Néry
July 1908-Jan 1913	António Bittencourt
Jan 1913-Jan 1917	Jônathas Pedrosa
Jan 1917-Jan 1921	Pedro Bacellar
Jan 1921-Aug 1924	César Monteiro
Aug-Dec 1924	Raymundo Barbosa
Dec 1924-Jan 1926	Alfredo Sá
Jan 1926-Jan 1930	Ephigênio de Salles
Jan-Oct 1930	Dorval Pôrto

Administrators:

1-20 November 1930	Floriano Machado
Nov 1930-Oct 1933	Álvaro Maia (1st)
Oct 1933-Feb 1935	Nélson de Mello
Feb 1935-Nov 1945	Álvaro Maia (2nd)
Nov 1945-Feb 1946	Emiliano Afonso
Feb-May 1946	Júlio Néry
May-Aug 1946	Raimundo da Silva
Aug-Sept 1946	João da Mata
Sept 1946-March 1947	Siseno Sarmento

Governors:

March-May 1947	João da Mata
May 1947-Jan 1951	Leopoldo Neves
Jan 1951-March 1955	Álvaro Maia
March 1955-March 1959	Plínio Coelho (1st)
March 1959-March 1963	Gilberto Mestrinho (1st) (BLP)
March 1963-June 1964	Plínio Coelho (2nd)
June 1964-Sept 1966	Arthur Reis
Sept 1966-March 1971	Danilo Areosa
March 1971-March 1975	João de Andrade
March 1975-March 1979	Henoch Reis (ARENA)

March 1979-May 1982 José Lindoso   (ARENA)
May 1982-March 1983 Paulo Néry
March 1983-March 1987 Gilberto Mestrinho   (2nd) (BDM)
March 1987-March 1991 Amazonino Mendes   (1st) (BDM)
March 1991-Jan 1995 Gilberto Mestrinho   (3rd) (BDM)
Jan 1995- Amazonino Mendes   (2nd) (PRP)

BAHIA

Capital: Salvador

Governors:

18-23 Nov 1889 Virgílio Damásio   (1st)
Nov 1889-April 1890 Manoel Pereira
April-Sept 1890 Hermes da Fonseca   (later President)
Sept-Nov 1890 Virgílio Damásio   (2nd)
Nov 1890-Nov 1891 José da Silva
Nov-Dec 1891 Tude Neiva
Dec 1891-May 1892 Leal Ferreira
May 1892-May 1895 Joaquim Lima
May 1896-May 1900 Luiz Viana
May 1900-May 1904 Severino Vieira
May 1904-May 1908 José de Souza
May 1908-Dec 1911 João Pinho
Dec 1911-Jan 1912 Aurélio Viana
Jan-March 1912 Bráulio Pereira
March 1912-March 1916 José Seabra   (1st)
March 1916-March 1920 António de Aragão
March 1920-March 1924 José Seabra   (2nd)
March 1924-March 1928 Francisco Calmon
March 1928-July 1930 Vital Soares
July-Oct 1930 Frederico da Costa

Administrators:

Oct-Nov 1930 Jacintho Osório
Nov 1930-Feb 1931 Leopoldo do Amaral
Feb-July 1931 Artur Neiva
July-Sept 1931 Raymundo Barbosa
Sept 1931-Nov 1937 Juracy Magalhães
Nov 1937-March 1938 António Dantas
March 1938-Nov 1942 Landulfo de Almeida
Nov 1942-Oct 1945 Renato Aleixo
Oct 1945-Feb 1946 João Viana
Feb-July 1946 Guilherme Marback

July 1946-April 1947   Cândido Caldas

Governors:

April 1947-Jan 1951	Octávio Mangabeira
Jan 1951-April 1955	Luís Pereira
April 1955-April 1959	António de Carvalho
April 1959-April 1963	Juracy Magalhães
April 1963-April 1967	António Lomanto
April 1967-March 1971	Luiz Viana Filho
March 1971-March 1975	António Magalhães (1st)
March 1975-March 1979	Roberto Santos (ARENA)
March 1979-March 1983	António Magalhães (2nd) (ARENA)
March 1983-March 1987	João Carneiro (SDP)
March 1987-89	Francisco Pires de Souza (BDM)
1989-March 1991	Nilo Coelho (BDM)
March 1991-Jan 1995	António Magalhães (3rd) (LFP)
Jan 1995-Jan 1999	Paulo Souto (LFP)
Jan 1999-	César Borges (LFP)

CEARÁ

Capital: Forteleza

Governors:

Nov 1889-Feb 1891	Luís Ferraz
Feb 1891-April 1891	Benjamin Barroso (1st)
April 1891-Feb 1892	José de Queiroz
Feb-July 1892	Benjamin Barroso (2nd)
July-Aug 1892	António Acióli (1st)
Aug 1892-July 1897	José Fontenelle
July 1897-July 1900	António Acióli (2nd)
July 1900-July 1904	Pedro Borges
July 1904-Jan 1912	António Acióli (3rd)
Jan-July 1912	António Mota
July 1912-March 1914	Marcos Rabelo
March-June 1914	Fernando de Carvalho
June 1914-July 1916	Benjamin Barroso (3rd)
July 1916-July 1920	João de Sabóia e Silva
July 1920-Aug 1923	Justiniano de Serpa
Aug 1923-July 1924	Ildefonso Albano
July 1924-May 1928	José da Rocha
May-July 1928	Eduardo Girão
July 1928-Aug 1930	José Peixoto
Aug 1930-Sept 1931	Manoel Távora

Administrators:

Sept 1931-Sept 1934	Roberto de Mendonça
Sept 1934-May 1935	Felipe Lima
May 1935-Oct 1945	Francisco Pimentel
Oct 1935-Jan 1946	Benedito dos Santos
Jan-Feb 1946	Acrísio da Rocha
Feb-Oct 1946	Pedro Firmeza
Oct 1946-Feb 1947	José Lopes
Feb-March 1947	José de Ataíde

Governors:

March 1947-Jan 1951	Faustino de Albuquerque e Sousa
Jan 1951-June 1954	Raul Barbosa
June 1954-March 1955	Stênio da Silva
March 1955-July 1958	Paulo Lopes
July 1958-March 1959	Flávio Marcilio
March 1959-March 1963	José Barroso
March 1963-Sept 1966	Virgílio Távora (1st)
Sept 1966-March 1971	Placido Castelo
March 1971-March 1975	César de Oliveira
March 1975-March 1978	José Bezerra (ARENA)
March 1978-March 1979	José de Alcantara e Silva
March 1979-May 1982	Virgílio Távora (2nd) (ARENA)
May 1982-March 1983	Manoel de Castro
March 1983-March 1987	Luiz Motta (SDP)
March 1987-March 1991	Tasso Jereissati (1st) (BDM)
March 1991-Sept 1994	Ciro Gomes (SDP)
Sept-Dec 1994	Francisco Aguiar
Jan 1995-	Tasso Jereissati (2nd) (SDP)

ESPÍRITO SANTO

Capital: Vitória

Governors:

Nov 1889-Jan 1890	Afonso Rosa
Jan-Sept 1890	José Costa
Sept-Nov 1890	Constante Sodré
Nov 1890-March 1891	Henrique Coutinho (1st)
March-June 1891	António Aguirre
June-Dec 1891	Alfeu de Andrade e Almeida
(Dec 1891-May 1892	junta)
May 1892-May 1896	José Freire

May 1896-Sept 1897	Graciano Neves
Sept 1897-Jan 1898	Constante Sodre
Jan 1898-May 1900	José de Vasconcelos
May 1900-May 1904	José Freire
May-June 1904	Argeu Monjardim
June 1904-May 1908	Henrique Coutinho (2nd)
May 1908-May 1912	Jerônimo Monteiro
May 1912-May 1916	Marcondes de Sousa
May 1916-May 1920	Bernardino Monteiro
May 1920-May 1924	Nestor Gomes
May 1924-June 1928	Florentino Ávidos
June 1928-Oct 1930	Aristeu de Aguiar

Administrators:

Oct-Nov 1930	José de Paula
Nov 1930-Jan 1943	João Bley
Jan 1943-Oct 1945	Jones Neves
Oct-Nov 1945	José Sette
Nov 1945-Feb 1946	Otávio Lengruber
Feb-June 1946	Aristides Campos
June-Oct 1946	Ubaldo Maia
Oct 1946-March 1947	Moacyr da Silva

Governors:

March 1947-Jan 1951	Carlos Lindenberg (1st)
Jan 1951-Oct 1952	Jones Neves
Oct 1952-Jan 1955	Francisco Ataíde
Jan 1955-Jan 1959	Francisco de Aguiar (1st)
Jan-Oct 1959	Carlos Lindenberg (2nd)
Oct 1959-July 1962	Raul Giuberti
July-Aug 1962	Hélsio Cordeiro
Aug 1962-Jan 1963	Asdrúbal Soares
Jan 1963-April 1966	Francisco de Aguiar (2nd)
April 1966-Jan 1967	Rubens Rangel
Jan 1967-March 1971	Cristiano Lopes
March 1971-March 1975	Artur Santos
March 1975-March 1979	Élcio Alvares (ARENA)
March 1979-March 1983	Eurico Resende (ARENA)
March 1983-May 1986	Gérson Camata (BDM)
May 1986-March 1987	José Moraes
March 1987-March 1991	Max Mauro (BDM)
March 1991-Jan 1995	Albuíno Azeredo (DLP)
Jan 1995-Jan 1999	Vitor Buaiz (WP)
Jan 1999-	José Ignacio (SDP)

GOIÁS

Statehood: 24 October 1933
Capital: Goiânia

Administrator:

Sept 1933-April 1935   Pedro Teixeira   (1st)

Governor:

April 1935-Nov 1937   Pedro Teixeira   (1st)

Administrators:

Nov 1937-Nov 1945   Pedro Teixeira   (2nd)
Nov 1945-Feb 1946   Eládio de Amorim
Feb-Sept 1946   Felipe de Barros
Sept-Oct 1946   Belarmino Cruvinel
Oct 1946-March 1947   Joachim de Araújo

Governors:

March 1947-June 1950   Jerônymo Bueno
June 1950-Jan 1951   Hosannah Guimarães
Jan 1951-July 1954   Pedro Teixeira   (2nd)
July 1954-Jan 1955   Jonas Duarte
Jan-March 1955   Bernardo Araújo
March 1955-Jan 1959   José de Almeida
Jan 1959-Jan 1961   José Ferreira
Jan 1961-Nov 1964   Mauro Teixeira
Nov 1964-Jan 1965   Carlos Mattos
Jan 1965-Jan 1966   Emilio Ribas
Jan 1966-March 1971   Otavio de Siqueira
March 1971-March 1975   Leonino Caiado
March 1975-March 1979   Irapuan Costa   (ARENA)
March 1979-March 1983   Ary Valadão   (ARENA)
March 1983-Feb 1986   Iris Rezende Machado   (1st) (BDM)
Feb 1986-March 1987   Onofre Quinan   (BDM)
March 1987-March 1991   Henrique Santillo   (BDM)
March 1991-Jan 1995   Iris Rezende Machado   (2nd) (BDM)
Jan 1995-Jan 1999   Maguito Vilela   (BDM)
Jan 1999-   Marconi Perillo   (SDP)

GUANABARA

Statehood: 21 April 1960
Dissolution: 15 March 1975 (merged with Rio de Janeiro)
Capital: Rio de Janeiro

Governors:

April-Dec 1960	José Camara
Dec 1960-Oct 1965	Carlos de Lacerda
Oct-Dec 1965	Rafael Magalhães
4-5 Dec 1965	Martinho Neto
Dec 1965-March 1970	Francisco de Lima
March 1970-March 1975	António Freitas

MARANHÃO

Capital: São Luis

Governors:

Dec 1889-Jan 1890	Pedro Tavares
Jan-July 1890	Eleutério Varela
4-5 July 1890	José de Porciúncula
5-25 July 1890	Augusto de Castro
July-Oct 1890	Manoel Vieira (1st)
Oct 1890-March 1891	José Vaz
4-14 March 1891	Tarquínio Lopes
March-Dec 1891	Lourenço de Sá e Albuquerque
(Dec 1891-Jan 1892	junta)
Jan-Nov 1892	Manoel Vieira (2nd)
Nov 1892-Oct 1893	Alfredo Martins (1st)
Oct 1893-Feb 1895	Casemiro Vieira (1st)
Feb-Aug 1895	Manoel Vieira (3rd)
Aug 1895-March 1897	Casemiro Vieira (2nd)
March 1897-March 1898	Alfredo Martins (2nd)
March-Aug 1898	José Braga
Aug 1898-March 1902	João da Costa
March 1902-March 1906	Manuel da Cunha
March 1906-May 1908	Benedito Leite
May 1908-Feb 1909	Artur Moreira
Feb-June 1909	Mariano Neto
June 1909-Feb 1910	Américo dos Reis
Feb-March 1910	Frederico Filgueiras
March 1910-March 1914	Luís da Silva
March-April 1914	Afonso de Mattos
April 1914-March 1917	Herculano Praga
March 1917-March 1918	António de Araújo
March-Oct 1918	José Marques
9-21 Oct 1918	Raul Machado (1st)
Oct 1918-Feb 1922	Urbano Araújo
Feb 1922-Jan 1923	Raul Machado (2nd)

Jan 1923-March 1926 Godofredo Viana
March 1926-March 1930 José de Almeida
March-Oct 1930 José Sexto

Administrators:

15-27 Nov 1930 José Torres
Nov 1930-Jan 1931 José Perdigão
Jan-Aug 1931 Astoldo Serra
Aug-Sept 1931 Joaquim Correia
Sept 1931-Feb 1933 Lourival da Mota
Feb-April 1933 Américo Wanick
April-June 1933 Álvaro Saldanha
June 1933-July 1935 António de Almeida
July 1935-June 1936 Aquiles Lisboa
June-Aug 1936 Roberto de Mendoça
Aug 1936-April 1945 Paulo Ramos
April-Nov 1945 Clodomir Cardoso
Nov 1945-Feb 1946 Eleazar Campos
Feb 1946-April 1947 Saturnino Belo

Governors:

10-14 April 1947 João Ferreira
April 1947-Jan 1951 Sebastião da Silva
Jan-Feb 1951 Traiaú Moreira
Feb-March 1951 Eugênio Barros (1st)
March-Sept 1951 César Aboud
Sept 1951-Jan 1956 Eugênio Barros (2nd)
Jan-March 1956 Alderico Machado
March 1956-July 1957 Eurico Ribeiro
July 1957-Jan 1961 José Carvalho
Jan 1961-Jan 1966 Newton Belo
Jan 1966-March 1971 José Sarney (later President)
March 1971-March 1975 Pedro de Santana
15-31 March 1975 José Murad
March 1975-March 1979 Oswaldo Freire (ARENA)
March 1979-May 1982 João Gonçalves (ARENA)
May 1982-March 1983 Ivar Saldanha
March 1983-March 1987 Luiz da Rocha (SDP)
March 1987-March 1991 Epitácio Pereira (BDM)
March 1991-Jan 1995 Edison Lobão (LFP)
Jan 1995- Roseana Sarney (LFP)

MATO GROSSO

Capital: Cuiabá

Governors:

Dec 1889-Feb 1891	António Coelho
Feb-March 1891	José Rondon
June-Aug 1891	Frederico de Medeiros-Mallet
Aug 1891-Aug 1895	Manoel Murtinho
Aug 1895-July 1899	Pedro da Costa (1st)
July-Aug 1899	António de Figuereido
Aug 1899-Aug 1903	António Alves de Barros
Aug 1903-July 1906	António Paes de Barros
July 1906-Aug 1907	Pedro Osorio
Aug 1907-Oct 1908	Generosa Ponce
Oct 1908-Sept 1911	Pedro da Costa (2nd)
Sept 1911-Aug 1915	Joaquim Marques
Aug 1915-Feb 1917	Caetano Albuquerque
Feb-Aug 1917	Camile de Moura
Aug 1917-Jan 1918	Cipriano Ferreira
Jan 1918-Jan 1922	Francisco Correa
Jan 1922-Oct 1924	Pedro da Costa (3rd)
Oct 1924-Jan 1926	Esterão Correa
Jan 1926-Jan 1930	Mario da Costa
Jan-Oct 1930	Anibal de Toledo

Administrators:

Oct-Nov 1930	Sebastião Leite
Nov 1930-April 1931	Antonino Gonçalves
April 1931-June 1932	Arthur Maciel
June 1932-Oct 1934	Leonidas de Mattos
Oct 1934-March 1935	Cesar Serva
March-Aug 1935	Fenelon Müller
Aug-Sept 1935	Newton Cavalcanti
Sept 1935-Sept 1937	Manoel Pires

Governor:

Sept-Nov 1937	Julio Müller

Administrators:

Nov 1937-Oct 1945	Julio Müller
Oct 1945-Aug 1946	Olegário de Barros
8-18 Aug 1946	Wladislau Gomes
Aug 1946-April 1947	José Moreira

Governors:

April 1947-June 1950	Arnaldo de Figueireido
June 1950-Jan 1951	Jary Gomes
Jan 1951-Jan 1956	Fernando da Costa (1st)
Jan 1956-Oct 1961	João de Arruda
Oct 1961-Jan 1966	Fernando da Costa (2nd)
Jan 1966-Jan 1971	Pedro Pedrossian (see Mato Grosso do Sul)
Jan 1971-March 1975	José Fragelli
March 1975-Aug 1978	José Neto (ARENA)
Aug 1978-March 1979	Cassio de Barros
March 1979-March 1983	Frederico Campos (ARENA)
March 1983-May 1986	Julio de Campos (SDP)
May 1986-March 1987	Wilmar de Farias
March 1987-March 1991	Carlos Bezerra (BDM)
March 1991-Jan 1995	Jaime Campos (LFP)
Jan 1995-	Dante de Oliveira (DLP)

MATO GROSSO DO SUL

Statehood: 1 January 1979
Capital: Campo Grande

Governors:

Jan-June 1979	Harry Amorin
June-July 1979	Londres Machado (1st)
July 1979-Nov 1980	Marcelo Soares (1st)
4-7 Nov 1980	Londres Machado (2nd)
Nov 1980-March 1983	Pedro Pedrossian (1st) (ARENA)
March 1983-May 1986	Wílson Martins (1st)
May 1986-March 1987	Ramez Tebet
March 1987-March 1991	Marcelo Soares (2nd) (BDM)
March 1991-Jan 1995	Pedro Pedrossian (2nd) (BLP)
Jan 1995-Jan 1999	Wílson Martins (2nd) (BDM)
Jan 1999-	José (Zeca) Miranda dos Santos (WP)

MINAS GERAIS

Capital: Belo Horizonte

Governors:

16-24 Nov 1889	António Pires
Nov 1889-Feb 1890	José Alvim
Feb-April 1890	João da Silva (1st)
April-July 1890	Domingos da Rocha
July 1890-Feb 1891	Chrispim Bias Fortes (1st)

Feb-March 1891	Frederico da Silva
March-June 1891	António de Lima
June 1891-Sept 1894	Eduardo Cerqueira
Sept 1894-Sept 1898	Chrispim Bias Fortes (2nd)
Sept 1898-Sept 1902	Francisco Brandão
Sept 1902-Sept 1906	Francisco de Salles
Sept 1906-Oct 1908	João da Silva (2nd)
Oct 1908-April 1909	Júlio Brandão (1st)
April 1909-Sept 1910	Wenceslau Braz Gomes (later President)
Sept 1910-Sept 1914	Júlio Brandão (2nd)
Sept 1914-Sept 1918	Delfim Ribeiro
Sept 1918-Sept 1922	Arthur Bernardes
Sept 1922-Aug 1924	Raul de Moura
Aug-Dec 1924	Olegário Maciel (1st)
Dec 1924-Sept 1926	Fernando Viana
Sept 1926-Sept 1930	António de Andrada
Sept-Nov 1930	Olegário Maciel (2nd)

Administrators:

Nov 1930-Sept 1933	Olegário Maciel
Sept-Dec 1933	Gustavo Capanema
Dec 1933-Nov 1945	Benedito Ribeiro
Nov 1945-Feb 1946	Nísio de Oliveira
Feb-Aug 1946	João Beraldo
Aug-Nov 1946	Júlio de Carvalho
Nov-Dec 1946	Noraldino Lima
Dec 1946-March 1947	Alcides Lins

Governors:

March 1947-Jan 1951	Milton Campos
Jan 1951-March 1955	Juscelino Kubitschek (later President)
March 1955-Jan 1956	Clovis da Gama
Jan 1956-Jan 1961	José Bias Fortes
Jan 1961-Jan 1966	José Pinto
Jan 1966-March 1971	Israel Pinheiro
March 1971-March 1975	Rondon Pacheco
March 1975-July 1978	António Chaves de Mendoça (ARENA)
July 1978-March 1979	Levindo Coelho
March 1979-March 1983	Francelino dos Santos (ARENA)
March 1983-Aug 1984	Tancredo Neves (BDM) (later President-elect)
Aug 1984-March 1987	Hélio Garcia (1st)
March 1987-March 1991	Newton Cardoso (BDM)
March 1991-Jan 1995	Hélio Garcia (2nd) (SRF)
Jan 1995-Jan 1999	Eduardo Azeredo (SDP)
Jan 1999-	Itamar Franco (BDM) (f President)

PARÁ

Capital: Belém

Governors:

Dec 1889-May 1890	Justo Chermont (1st)
May-July 1890	José de Carvalho (1st)
July 1890-Feb 1891	Justo Chermont (2nd)
Feb-March 1891	Augusto Bittencourt (1st)
March-June 1891	Duarte Guedes
June-Dec 1891	Lauro Sodré e Silva (1st)
Dec 1891-July 1892	Augusto Bittencourt (2nd)
July 1892-Sept 1894	Lauro Sodré e Silva (2nd)
Sept 1894-Feb 1895	Augusto Bittencourt (3rd)
Feb 1895-Jan 1897	Lauro Sodré e Silva (3rd)
Jan 1897-Jan 1901	José de Carvalho (2nd)
Jan 1901-Oct 1904	Augusto Montenegro (1st)
Oct 1904-Oct 1905	João Coelho (1st)
Oct 1905-Jan 1909	Augusto Montenegro (2nd)
Jan 1909-Feb 1913	João Coelho (2nd)
Feb 1913-Jan 1917	Eneas Martins
Jan 1917-Jan 1921	Lauro Sodré e Silva (4th)
Jan 1921-Dec 1922	António Castro (1st)
Dec 1922-Feb 1923	Cipriano dos Santos
Feb 1923-Jan 1925	António Castro (2nd)
Jan 1925-Jan 1929	Dionisio Bentes
Jan 1929-Oct 1930	Eurico Valle

Administrators:

Nov 1930-April 1935	Joaquim Barata (1st)
April-May 1935	Roberto de Mendonça

Governor:

May 1935-Nov 1937	José Malcher

Administrators:

Nov 1937-Jan 1943	José Malcher
Jan-Feb 1943	Miguel Pernambuco
Feb 1943-Oct 1945	Joaquim Barata (2nd)
29-30 Oct 1945	João Bittencourt
Oct-Nov 1945	Alexandre de Assunção
Nov 1945-Feb 1946	Manuel Neto
Feb-Dec 1946	Otávio Meira
Dec 1946-March 1947	José dos Santos e Silva

Governors:

March 1947-June 1950	Luís Carvalho (1st)
June-July 1950	Waldir Bouhid (acting) (1st)
July 1950-Jan 1951	Alberto Engelhard
24-27 Jan 1951	Waldir Bouhid (acting) (2nd)
Jan-Feb 1951	Arnaldo Lobo (acting)
9-20 Feb 1951	Abel de Figuereido
Feb 1951-Jan 1956	Alexandre de Assunção
Jan-June 1956	Edward Pinheiro
June 1956-May 1959	Joaquim Barata
May 1959-Jan 1961	Luís Carvalho (2nd)
Jan 1961-June 1964	Aurelio do Carmo
12-15 June 1964	Dionisio de Carvalho
June 1964-Jan 1966	Jarbas Passarinho
Jan 1966-March 1971	Alacid Nunes (1st)
March 1971-March 1975	Fernando Guilhon
March 1975-Aug 1978	Aloysio Chaves (ARENA)
Aug 1978-March 1979	Clovis Rego
March 1979-March 1983	Alacid Nunes (2nd) (ARENA)
March 1983-March 1987	Jader Barbalho (1st) (BDM)
March 1987-March 1991	Hélio Gueiros (BDM)
March 1991-Jan 1995	Jader Barbalho (2nd) (BDM)
Jan 1995-	Almir Gabriel (SDP)

PARAÍBA

Capital: João Pessoa

Governors:

Dec 1889-Nov 1891	Venâncio Neiva
(Nov 1891-Feb 1892	junta)
Feb 1892-Oct 1896	Álvaro Machado (1st)
Oct 1896-Oct 1900	António da Gama e Melo
Oct 1900-Oct 1904	José de Araújo
Oct 1904-Oct 1905	Álvaro Machado (2nd)
Oct 1905-Oct 1908	Walfredo Leal
Oct 1908-Oct 1912	João Machado
Oct 1912-July 1915	João Pinto
July 1915-July 1916	António Pessoa
July-Oct 1916	Solon de Lucena (1st)
Oct 1916-Oct 1920	Francesco de Holanda
Oct 1920-Oct 1924	Solon de Lucena (2nd)
Oct 1924-Oct 1928	João Suassuna
Oct 1928-July 1930	João de Albuquerque
July-Oct 1930	Álvaro de Carvalho

Administrators:

Oct-Nov 1930	José de Almeida
Nov 1930-April 1932	Antenor Navarro
April 1932-Dec 1934	Gratuliano Brito
Dec 1934-Jan 1935	José Mariz
Jan 1935-Jan 1940	Argemiro de Figueireido
Jan-Aug 1940	António Guedes
Aug 1940-July 1945	Rui Carneiro
July-Nov 1945	Samuel Duarte
Nov 1945-Feb 1946	Severino Montenegro
Feb-Sept 1946	Odon Cavalcânti
Sept 1946-March 1947	José Gomes da Silva

Governors:

March 1947-Jan 1951	Oswaldo Melo
Jan 1951-Jan 1956	José de Almeida
Jan 1956-Jan 1958	Flávio Coutinho
Jan 1958-March 1960	Pedro Gondim (1st)
March 1960-Jan 1961	José de Lima
Jan 1961-Jan 1966	Pedro Gondim (2nd)
Jan 1966-March 1971	João Agripino
March 1971-March 1975	Ernâni Satyro e Souza
March 1975-Aug 1978	Ivan Sobreira (ARENA)
Aug 1978-March 1979	Dorgival Neto
March 1979-May 1982	Tarcísio Burity (1st) (ARENA)
May 1982-March 1983	Clovis Cavalcânti
March 1983-May 1986	Wílson Braga (SDP)
May-June 1986	Rivando Cavalcânti
June 1986-March 1987	Milton Cabral
March 1987-March 1991	Tarcísio Burity (2nd) (BDM)
March 1991-Jan 1995	Ronaldo Cunha Linha (BDM)
Jan-Sept 1995	António Mariz (BDM) (†)
Sept 1995-	José Maranhão (BDM)

PARANÁ

Capital: Curitiba

Governors:

Nov-Dec 1889	Francisco Cardoso (1st)
Dec 1889-Feb 1890	José Guimarães
Feb-March 1890	Uladislau de Freitas (acting)
March-July 1890	Americo Pereira
July-Aug 1890	Joaquim de Carvalho e Silva (acting) (1st)

Aug-Nov 1890　　　　　　　Innocêncio Correia
Nov-Dec 1890　　　　　　　Joaquim de Carvalho e Silva　(acting) (2nd)
Dec 1890-June 1891　　　　José Lima
June-Nov 1891　　　　　　Generosa dos Santos
(Nov 1891-Feb 1892　　　　junta)
Feb 1892-April 1893　　　　Francisco da Silva　(1st)
April 1893-Jan 1894　　　　Vicente Lima　(1st)
Jan 1894　　　　　　　　　Théofilo Gomes
Jan-March 1894　　　　　　João Dória
March-April 1894　　　　　Francisco Cardoso　(2nd)
April-May 1894　　　　　　Tertuliano de Freitas
May 1894　　　　　　　　　António Braga
May 1894-Feb 1896　　　　Francisco da Silva　(2nd)
Feb 1896-Feb 1900　　　　　José Andrade
Feb 1900-Feb 1904　　　　　Francisco da Silva　(3rd)
Feb 1904-April 1906　　　　Vicente Lima　(2nd)
April 1906-July 1907　　　　João Ferreira
July 1907-Feb 1908　　　　　Joaquim de Carvalho e Silva　(acting) (3rd)
Feb-April 1908　　　　　　Manoel Guimarães
April 1908-Feb 1912　　　　Francisco da Silva　(4th)
Feb 1912-Feb 1916　　　　　Carlos de Albuquerque
Feb 1916-Feb 1920　　　　　Afonso de Camargo　(1st)
Feb 1920-Feb 1928　　　　　Caetano da Rocha
Feb 1928-Oct 1930　　　　　Afonso de Camargo　(2nd)

Administrator:

Oct 1930-Dec 1931　　　　　Mario Tourinho

Governor:

Dec 1931-Jan 1932　　　　　João Perneta

Administrator:

Jan 1932-Jan 1935　　　　　Manoel Ribas　(1st)

Governor:

Jan 1935-Nov 1937　　　　　Manoel Ribas

Administrators:

Nov 1937-Nov 1945　　　　Manoel Ribas　(2nd)
Nov 1945-Feb 1946　　　　　Clotário Portugal
Feb-Oct 1946　　　　　　　Brasil Machado
Oct 1946-Feb 1947　　　　　Mario da Silva
Feb-March 1947　　　　　　António Chaves

Governors:

March 1947-Jan 1951	Moysés Lupion (1st)
Jan 1951-April 1955	Bento da Rocha Netto
April-May 1955	António Anibelli (acting)
May 1955-Jan 1956	Adolpho Franco
Jan 1956-Jan 1961	Moysés Lupion (2nd)
Jan 1961-Nov 1965	Ney Braga (1st)
17-20 Nov 1965	António Ruppel (acting)
Nov 1965-Jan 1966	Algacir Guimarães
Jan 1966-March 1971	Paulo Pimental
March-Nov 1971	Haroldo Peres
Nov 1971-July 1973	Pedro de Souza
July-Aug 1973	João Mansur
Aug 1973-March 1975	Emilio Gomes
March 1975-March 1979	Jayme Canet (ARENA)
March 1979-May 1982	Ney Braga (2nd) (ARENA)
May 1982-March 1983	José de Novaes
15 March 1983	José Richa
March 1983-March 1987	João de Campos (BDM)
March 1987-March 1991	Álvaro Dias (BDM)
March 1991-Jan 1995	Roberto Requião (BDM)
Jan 1995-	Jaime Lerner (DLP)

PERNAMBUCO

Capital: Recife

Governors:

1889	José Lima
1889-90	José de Oliveir
1890	Albino de Vasconcellos
1890	Ambrosio Cavalcanti
189	Barão de Lucena (Henrique de Lucena)
1890-91	José da Silva
1891	José Mello
1891	Barão de Contendas (Epaminondas Correia)
1892-96	Alexandre Lima
1896-99	Joaquim de Araújo
1899-1900	Sigismundo Gonçalves (1st)
1900-4	António Ferreira
1904-8	Sigismundo Gonçalves (2nd)
1908-11	Herculano de Mello
1911	Estacio Coimbra (1st)
1911	João de Carvalho
1911-15	Emygdio Barreto

1915-19 Manoel Borba
1919 José da Cunha
1919-21 José Cavalcânti
1921-22 Severino Pinheiro
Oct 1922-Oct 1926 Sergio Loreto
Oct-Dec 1926 Julio de Melo (1st)
Dec 1926-Oct 1930 Estacio Coimbra (2nd)

Administrators:

Oct 1930-July 1931 Carlos Cavalcânti (1st)
July-Aug 1931 Jurandir Mamedo (1st)
Aug 1931-July 1932 Carlos Cavalcânti (2nd)
July 1931-Sept 1934 Luís de Almeida
Sept 1934-April 1935 Jurandir Mamedo (2nd)

Governor:

April 1935-Nov 1937 Carlos Cavalcânti

Administrators:

Nov-Dec 1937 Amaro Vilanova
Dec 1937-Feb 1945 Agamenon Magalhães
Feb-Nov 1945 Etelvino de Albuquerque
Nov 1945-Feb 1946 José Neves
Feb-Aug 1946 José da Silva
Aug 1946-March 1947 Demerval Peixoto

Governors:

March-July 1947 Amaro Pedrosa
July 1947-Feb 1948 Otávio de Araújo
Feb 1948-Jan 1951 Alexandre Sobrinho
Jan 1951-Dec 1952 Agamenon Magalhães
Dec 1952-Nov 1953 António Galvão
Nov-Dec 1953 José de Melo Cavalcânti (acting)
Dec 1953-Jan 1955 Etelvino de Albuquerque
Jan 1955-Jan 1959 Osvaldo de Farias
Jan 1959 Constantino Maranhão
Jan 1959-Jan 1963 Cid Feijo Sampião
Jan 1963-April 1964 Miguel de Alencar
April 1964 Valfredo de Sequeira (acting)
April 1964-Jan 1967 Paulo Guerra
Jan 1967-March 1971 Nilo de Souza Coelho
March 1971-March 1975 Eraldo Leite
March 1975-March 1979 José de Moura Cavalcânti
March 1979-March 1983 Marco Maciel (ARENA)

March 1983-1986	Roberto Magalhães (SDP)
1986-March 1987	Gustavo Sobrinho
March 1987-March 1991	Miguel Arraes de Aleucar (1st) (BDM)
March 1991-Jan 1995	Joaquim Cavalcânti (LFP)
Jan 1995-Jan 1999	Miguel Arraes de Aleucar (2nd) (SP)
Jan 1999-	Jarbas Vasconcelos (BDM)

PIAUÎ

Capital: Teresina

Governors:

Dec 1889-June 1890	Gregório Azevedo
June-Aug 1890	Joaquim Paranaguá
Aug-Oct 1890	Gabino Besouro
Oct-Dec 1890	Barão de Uruçui (João da Cruz e Santos)
Dec 1890-May 1891	Alvaro Lima
May-Dec 1891	Gabriel Ferreira
Dec 1891-Feb 1892	João Ramos
Feb 1892-July 1896	Coriolano de Carvalho e Silva
July 1896-July 1900	Raimundo de Vasconcelos
July 1900-July 1904	Arlindo Nogueira
July 1904-Dec 1907	Álvaro Mendes
Dec 1907-March 1908	Areolino de Abreu
March-July 1908	José de Morais e Silva
July 1908-Dec 1909	Anísio de Abreu
Dec 1909-March 1910	Manuel da Paz
March 1910-July 1912	Antóninio da Silva
July 1912-July 1916	Miguel Rosa
July 1916-July 1920	Euripides de Aguiar
July 1920-July 1924	João Ferreira
July 1924-July 1928	Matias de Melo
July 1928-Oct 1930	João Leal

Administrators:

Oct 1930-Jan 1931	Humberto Leão
Jan-May 1931	Joaquim Cunha
May 1931-May 1935	Landry Gonçalves
May 1935-Nov 1945	Leônidas Melo
Nov-Dec 1945	António Ferraz
Dec 1945-March 1946	Benedito do Rego
March-Sept 1946	José Correia
Sept-Oct 1946	Manoel da Silveira
Oct 1946-March 1947	Teodoro Sobral

Governors:

March-April 1947	Waldir Gonçalves
April 1947-Jan 1951	José Furtado
Jan 1951-March 1955	Pedro Freitas
March 1955-March 1959	Jacob Gayoso e Almendra
March 1959-July 1962	Francisco Rodrigues
July 1962-March 1963	Tibério Nunes
March 1963-Aug 1966	Petrônio Nunes
Aug-Sept 1966	José Alencar
Sept 1966-May 1970	Helvídio de Barros
14-15 May 1970	João de Santana
May 1970-March 1971	João d'Almeida
March 1971-March 1975	Alberto Silva (1st)
March 1975-Aug 1978	Dirceu Arcoverde (ARENA)
Aug 1978-March 1979	Djalma Veloso
March 1979-March 1983	Lucídio Nunes (ARENA)
March 1983-May 1986	Hugo Neto
May 1986-March 1987	José Medeiros
March 1987-March 1991	Alberto Silva (2nd)
March 1991-Jan 1995	Feitas Neto (LFP)
Jan 1995-	Francisco Souza (Mão Santo) (BDM)

RIO DE JANEIRO

Capital: Niterói (to 1894, 1903-1975), Petropolis (1894-1903), Rio de Janeiro (since 1975)

Governors:

15-16 Nov 1889	Francisco da Fonseca e Silva
Nov 1889-Dec 1891	Fransisco Portela
10-11 Dec 1891	José Guimarães
Dec 1891-May 1892	Carlos da Silveira
May 1892-Dec 1894	José de Porciúncula
Dec 1894-Dec 1897	Joaquim de Abreu
Dec 1897-Dec 1900	Alberto Torres
Dec 1900-Dec 1903	Quintino Bocaiúva (*b* Q.de Sousa)
Dec 1903-Nov 1906	Nilo Peçanha (1st)
Nov-Dec 1906	Francisco Botelho (1st)
Dec 1906-Dec 1910	Alfredo Backer
Dec 1910-Dec 1914	Francisco Botelho (2nd)
Dec 1914-Sept 1917	Nilo Peçanha (2nd)
7-19 Sept 1917	Francisco Guimarães (acting)
Sept 1917-Dec 1918	Angelo Collet
Dec 1918-Dec 1922	Raul Veiga
Dec 1922-Jan 1923	Raul Fernandes

Jan-Dec 1923 Aurelino Leal
Dec 1923-Dec 1927 Feliciano Sodré
Dec 1927-Oct 1930 Manuel Silva

Administrators:

24-27 Oct 1930 Demócrito Barbosa
Oct 1930-May 1931 Plínio Casado
May-Nov 1931 João Barreto
Nov-Dec 1931 Pantaleão Pessôa
Dec 1931-Nov 1935 Ari Parreiras
7-12 Nov 1935 Newton Cavalcânti

Governor:

Nov 1935-Nov 1937 Protógenes Guimarães

Administrators:

Nov 1937-Oct 1945 Ernâni Peixoto
Nov 1945-Feb 1946 Abel Magalhães
Feb-Sept 1946 Lúcio Meira
Sept 1946-Feb 1947 Hugo Silva
6-8 Feb 1947 Francisco Santos
8-24 Feb 1947 Álvaro da Silva

Governors:

Feb 1947-Jan 1951 Edmundo Soares e Silva
Jan 1951-Jan 1955 Ernâni Peixoto
Jan 1955-July 1958 Miguel Couto
July 1958-Jan 1959 Togo de Barros
30-31 Jan 1959 Osmar de Carvalho
Jan 1959-Feb 1961 Roberto Silveiro
Feb 1961-July 1962 Celso Peçanha (acting)
July 1962-Jan 1963 José Janotti
18-31 Jan 1963 Luís Pinaud (acting)
Jan 1963-May 1964 Badger da Silveiro
1-4 May 1964 Cordolino Ambrósio
May 1964-Aug 1966 Paulo Torres
Aug 1966-Jan 1967 Teutônio de Araújo
Jan 1967-March 1971 Jeremias Fontes
March 1971-March 1975 Raimundo Padilha
March 1975-March 1979 Floriano Lima (ARENA)
March 1979-March 1983 António Freitas (BDM)
March 1983-March 1987 Leonel Brizola (1st) (DLP)
March 1987-March 1991 Wellington Franco (BDM)
March 1991-94 Leonel Brizola (2nd) (DLP)

1994-Jan 1995	Nilo Batista
Jan 1995-Jan 1999	Marcello Alencar (SDP)
Jan 1999-	Anthony Garotinho

RIO GRANDE DO NORTE

Capital: Natal

Governors:

Nov-Dec 1889	Pedro Maranhão (1st)
Dec 1889-Feb 1890	Adolfo Gordo
Feb-March 1890	Jerônimo da Câmara (1st)
March-Sept 1890	Joaquim da Silveira
Sept-Nov 1890	Pedro Maranhão (2nd)
Nov-Dec 1890	João Ribeiro
Dec 1890-March 1891	Manuel Castro e Silva
March-June 1891	Francisco Barros
June-Aug 1891	José Barros
Aug-Sept 1891	Francisco de Oliveira
Sept-Nov 1891	Miguel Castro
(Nov 1891-Feb 1892	junta)
22-28 Feb 1892	Jerônimo da Câmara (2nd)
Feb 1892-March 1896	Pedro Maranhão (3rd)
March 1896-March 1900	Joaquim Chaves (1st)
March 1900-March 1904	Alberto Maranhão (1st)
March 1904-Nov 1906	Augusto de Lyra
Nov 1906-Feb 1907	Manuel Dias
Feb 1907-March 1908	António de Melo e Sousa (1st)
March 1908-Jan 1914	Alberto Maranhão (2nd)
Jan 1914-Jan 1920	Joaquim Chaves (2nd)
Jan 1920-Jan 1924	António de Melo e Sousa (2nd)
Jan 1924-Jan 1928	José Medeiros
Jan 1928-Oct 1930	Juvenal de Faria

Administrators:

Oct 1930-Jan 1931	Irineu Jofili
Jan-July 1931	Aluízio Moura
July 1931-June 1932	Hercolino Cascardo
June 1932-Aug 1938	Bertino da Silva
Aug 1933-Oct 1935	Mário da Câmara
27-29 Oct 1935	Liberato Barroso
Oct 1935-July 1943	Rafael Gurjão
July 1943-Aug 1945	António Dantas
Aug-Nov 1945	Georgino Avelino
Nov 1945-Feb 1946	Miguel Fagundes

Feb 1946-Jan 1947   Ubaldo de Melo
Jan-July 1947   Orestes Lima

Governors:

March 1947-Jan 1951   José Varela
Jan-July 1951   Jerônimo Maia
July 1951-Jan 1956   Sílvio Pedrosa
Jan 1956-Jan 1961   Dinarte Mariz
Jan 1961-Jan 1966   Aluízio Alves
Jan 1966-March 1971   Walfredo Gurgel
March 1971-March 1975   José de Araújo
March 1975-March 1979   Tarcísio Maia   (ARENA)
March 1979-March 1983   Lavoisier Sobrinho   (ARENA)
March 1983-May 1986   José Maia   (SDP)
May 1986-March 1987   Radir de Araújo
March 1987-March 1991   Geraldo de Melo   (BDM)
March 1991-Jan 1995   Agripino Maia   (LFP)
Jan 1995-   Garibaldi Alvis Filho   (BDM)

RIO GRANDE DO SUL

Capital: Pôrto Alegre

Governors:

Nov 1889-Feb 1890   José Câmara   (1st)
Feb-May 1890   Júlio da Frota
6-13 May 1890   Francisco Tavares   (acting)
13-24 May 1890   Carlos de Bittencourt
May 1890-March 1981   Cândido da Costa
March-July 1891   Fernando Abbott   (acting)
July-Nov 1891   Júlio de Castilhos   (1st)
(Nov 1891-June 1892   junta)
8-17 June 1892   José Câmara   (2nd)
June-Sept 1892   Vitoriano Monteiro
Sept 1892-Jan 1893   Fernando Abbott
Jan 1893-Jan 1898   Júlio de Castilhos   (2nd)
Jan 1898-Jan 1908   António de Medeiros   (1st)
Jan 1908-Jan 1913   Carlos Gonçalves
Jan 1913-Jan 1928   António de Medeiros   (2nd)
Jan 1928-Oct 1930   Getúlio Vargas   (later President)

Administrators:

Oct-Nov 1930   Oswaldo Aranha
27-28 Nov 1930   Sinval Saldanha

Nov 1930-Oct 1937	José da Cunha
Oct 1937-Jan 1938	Manuel Daltro
Jan-March 1938	Joaquim Cardoso
March 1938-Sept 1943	Oswaldo de Farias
Sept 1943-Nov 1945	Ernesto Dornelles
Nov 1945-Feb 1946	Samuel da Silva
Feb 1946-March 1947	Pompílio Rosa

Governors:

March 1947-Jan 1951	Válter Jobim
Jan 1951-March 1955	Ernesto Dornelles
March 1955-March 1959	Ildo Meneghetti (1st)
March 1959-March 1963	Leonel Brizola (see Rio de Janeiro)
March 1963-Sept 1966	Ildo Meneghetti (2nd)
Sept 1966-March 1971	Wálter Barcelos
March 1971-March 1975	Euclides Triches
March 1975-March 1979	Sinval Guazzelli
March 1979-March 1983	José de Souza (ARENA)
March 1983-March 1987	Jair Soares (SDP)
March 1987-March 1991	Pedro Simon (BDM)
March 1991-Jan 1995	Alceu Colarres (DLP)
Jan 1995-Jan 1999	António Britto (BDM)
Jan 1999-	Olívio Dutra (WP)

RONDÔNIA

Statehood: 16 December 1981
Capital: Pôrto Velho

Governors:

1981-82	João Neto
1982-86	Jorge de Oliveira (SDP)
1986-87	Angelo Angelin
March 1987-March 1991	Jerônimo Santana (BDM)
March 1991-Jan 1995	Osvaldo Pianna (WP)
Jan 1995-Jan 1999	Vladir Raupp (BDM)
Jan 1999-	José Bianco (LFP)

RORAIMA

Statehood: 5 October 1988
Capital: Boa Vista

Governors:

Oct 1988-March 1991	Romero Jucá Filho

March 1991-Jan 1995   Otomar Pinto   (BLP)
Jan 1995-   Neudo Campo   (BDM)

SANTA CATARINA

Capital: Florianópolis

Governors:

Dec 1889-Dec 1891   Lauro Müller   (1st)
(Dec 1891-March 1892   junta)
March 1892-April 1894   Manoel Machado
April-Sept 1894   António César
Sept 1894-Sept 1898   Hercílio da Luz   (1st)
Sept 1898-Sept 1902   Felipe Schmidt   (1st)
Sept-Nov 1902   Lauro Müller   (2nd)
Nov 1902-March 1905   António da Silva e Oliveira   (1st)
March-Oct 1905   Vidal Ramos   (1st)
Oct 1905-Sept 1906   António da Silva e Oliveira   (2nd)
Sept-Nov 1906   Abdon Batista
Nov 1906-Sept 1910   Gustavo Richard
Sept 1910-Sept 1914   Vidal Ramos   (2nd)
Sept 1914-Sept 1918   Felipe Schmidt   (2nd)
Sept 1918-Oct 1924   Hercílio da Luz   (2nd)
Oct 1924-Sept 1926   António da Silva e Oliveira   (3rd)
Sept 1926-Sept 1930   Adolpho Kônder
Sept-Oct 1930   Fúlvio Aducci

Administrators:

Oct 1930-Oct 1932   Ptolomeu Brasil
Oct 1932-March 1933   Rui Zobaran
March-April 1933   Manoel da Silveira
April 1933-May 1935   Aristiliano Ramos
May 1935-Nov 1945   Nereu Ramos
Nov 1945-Feb 1946   Luiz Gallotti
Feb 1946-March 1947   Udo Deeke

Governors:

March 1947-Jan 1951   Aderbal da Silva
Jan 1951-Jan 1956   Irineu Bornhausen
Jan 1956-June 1958   Jorge Lacerda
June 1958-Jan 1961   Heriberto Hulse
Jan 1961-Jan 1966   Celso Ramos
Jan 1966-March 1971   Ivo Silveira
March 1971-March 1975   Colombo Salles

March 1975-March 1979	António Reis (ARENA)
March 1979-May 1982	Jorge Bornhausen (ARENA)
May 1982-March 1983	Henrique de Córdova
March 1983-March 1987	Esperidão Helou (SDP)
March 1987-March 1991	Pedro Campos (BDM)
March 1991-Jan 1995	Vilson Kleinubing (LFP)
Jan 1995-Jan 1999	Paulo Vieira (BDM)
Jan 1999-	Esperidão Amin

SÃO PAULO

Capital: São Paulo

Governors:

Dec 1889-Oct 1890	Prudente Barros
Oct 1890-March 1891	Jorge Tibiriça (1st)
March-Dec 1891	Américo Mello
15-16 Dec 1891	Sergio Castelo Branco
Dec 1891-Aug 1892	José Cesar
Aug 1892-April 1896	Bernardino de Campos (1st)
15-30 April 1896	Francisco Gomide (acting) (1st)
May 1896-Oct 1897	Manoel Sales
Oct 1897-Nov 1898	Francisco Gomide (acting) (2nd)
Nov 1898-April 1900	Fernando de Albuquerque
May 1900-Feb 1902	Francisco Alves (1st)
Feb-July 1902	Domingos de Moraes (acting)
July 1902-April 1904	Bernardino de Campos (2nd)
May 1904-April 1908	Jorge Tibiriça (2nd)
May 1908-April 1912	Manoel Lins
May 1912-April 1916	Francisco Alves (2nd)
May 1916-April 1920	Altino Marques
May 1920-April 1924	Washington Pereira
May 1924-April 1927	Carlos de Campos
April-July 1927	António Bueno (acting)
July 1927-May 1930	Júlio de Albuquerque
May-Oct 1930	Heitor Penteado (acting)
24-29 October 1930	Hastínfilo de Moura
Oct-Nov 1930	José Whitacker
6-24 Nov 1930	Plínio Barreto

Administrators:

Nov 1930-July 1931	João de Barros
July-Nov 1931	Laudo de Camargo
Nov 1931-March 1932	Mandel Rabelo
March-Oct 1932	Pedro de Toledo

2-5 Oct 1932	Herculano de Carvalho e Silva
Oct 1932-July 1933	Valdomiro de Lima
July-Aug 1933	Manoel Daltro
Aug 1933-April 1935	Armando Oliveira

Governors:

April-Dec 1936	Armando Oliveira
Dec 1936-Jan 1937	Henrique Bayma
Jan-Nov 1937	José Neto

Administrators:

Nov 1937-April 1938	José Neto
25-26 April 1938	Francsico da Silva
April 1938-June 1941	Ademar de Barros
June 1941-Oct 1945	Fernando Costa
Oct-Nov 1945	Sebastião de Lima
Nov 1945-March 1947	José Soares

Governors:

March 1947-Jan 1951	Ademar de Barros (1st)
Jan 1951-Jan 1955	Lucas Garcez
Jan 1955-Jan 1959	Jânio Quadros (later President)
Jan 1959-Jan 1963	Carlos Pinto
Jan 1963-June 1966	Ademar de Barros (2nd)
June 1966-Jan 1967	Laudo Natel (1st)
Jan 1967-March 1971	Roberto Sodre
March 1971-March 1975	Laudo Natel (2nd)
March 1975-March 1979	Paulo Martens (ARENA)
March 1979-May 1982	Paulo Maluf (ARENA)
May 1982-March 1983	José Marin
March 1983-March 1987	André Montoro (BDM)
March 1987-March 1991	Orestes Quércia (BDM)
March 1991-Jan 1995	Luís Fleury (BDM)
Jan 1995-	Mário Covas (SDP)

SERGIPE

Capital: Aracajú

Governors:

Dec 1889-Aug 1890	Felisbello Freire
Aug-Nov 1890	Augusto da Silva
Nov 1890-Jan 1891	Lourenço Dantas
Jan-May 1891	Luís de Morais

May-Nov 1891	Vicente Ribeiro
(Nov 1891-May 1892	junta)
May 1892-Sept 1894	José de Calasans (1st)
Sept-Oct 1894	João Leite (acting)
Oct 1894-July 1896	Manuel Valladão (1st)
July-Oct 1896	António Dantas (acting)
Oct 1896-Aug 1899	Martinho Garcez
Aug-Oct 1899	Apulchro Motta
Oct 1899-Oct 1902	Olympio Campos
Oct 1902-Oct 1905	Josino Menezes
Oct 1905-Oct 1908	Guilherme Campos
Oct 1908-Oct 1911	José Doria
Oct 1911-July 1914	José Menezes
July-Oct 1914	Pedro de Carvalho
Oct 1914-Oct 1918	Manuel Valladão (2nd)
Oct 1918-Oct 1922	José Lobo
Oct 1922-Oct 1926	Mauricio Cardoso
Oct 1926-Jan 1927	Ciro de Azevedo
March 1927-Oct 1930	Manoel Dantas
Oct-Nov 1930	José de Calasans (2nd)
4-10 Nov 1930	Marcelino Jorge
10-16 Nov 1930	José de Calasans (3rd)

Administrators:

Nov 1930-March 1935	Augusto Gomes (1st)
March-April 1935	Aristides de Carvalho
April 1935-July 1941	Eronides de Carvalho
July 1941-March 1942	Milton de Azevedo
March 1942-Oct 1945	Augusto Gomes (2nd)
Oct-Nov 1945	Francisco Neto
Nov 1945-March 1946	Hunald Cardoso
March 1946-Jan 1947	António Brandão
Jan-March 1946	Joaquim Ribeiro

Governors:

March 1947-Jan 1951	José Leite (1st)
Jan-Feb 1951	João dos Reis (acting)
Feb-March 1951	Edelzio de Melo (acting)
March 1951-Jan 1955	Arnaldo Garcez
Jan 1955-Oct 1958	Leandro Maciel
Jan 1959-July 1962	Luís Garcia
July 1962-Jan 1963	Dionízio Machado
30-31 Jan 1963	Horácio de Góes (acting)
Jan 1963-March 1964	João Doria
March 1964-Jan 1967	Sebastião de Carvalho

Jan 1967-May 1970	Lourival Baptista
May-June 1970	Wolney de Melo (acting)
June 1970-March 1971	João Garcez
March 1971-March 1975	Paulo de Meneses
March 1975-March 1979	José Leite (2nd) (ARENA)
March 1979-May 1982	Augusto Franco (ARENA)
May 1982-March 1983	Djenal de Queiroz
March 1983-March 1987	João Alves (1st) (SDP)
March 1987-March 1991	António Valadares (LFP)
March 1991-Jan 1995	João Alves (2nd) (LFP)
Jan 1995-	Albano Franco (SDP)

TOCANTINS

Statehood: 5 October 1988 (*f* part of Goiás)
Capital: Palmas

Governors:

Oct 1988-March 1991	José Siqueira Campos (1st)
March 1991-Jan 1995	Moises Alvelino (BDM)
Jan 1995-	José Siqueira Campos (PRP) (2nd)

BRUNEI

Official name: State of Brunei, Negeri Brunei Darussalam (Malay)
State founded: 1405
Independence date: 1 January 1984
Capital: Bandar Seri Begawan (*f* Brunei Town)

In the 15th century Brunei was a powerful state controlling most of Borneo. However, its power declined from the end of the century and concessions were made to Britain reducing the Sultanate to its present boundaries. In 1888 Brunei became a British protectorate until 1984 when it regained independence.

Sultans:

1405-15	Mohammed	
1415-25	Ahmad	(*brother*)
1425-33	Sharif Ali	(*son*)
1433-73	Sulaiman	(*uncle*)
1473-1521	Bolkiah	(*son*)
1521-75	Abdul Kahar	(*son*)
1575-1600	Saiful Rijal	(*son*)
1600-5	Shah Berunai	(*son*)
1605-19	Hassan	(*brother*)
1619-49	Abdul Jalilul Akhbar	(*son*)
1649-52	Abdul Jalilul Jabbar	(*son*)
1652-60	Mohammed Ali	(*son of Hassan*)
1660-73	Abdul Mubin	(*grandson of Saiful Rijal*)
1673-90	Muhyiddin	(*son of Abdul Jalilul Akhbar*)
1690-1705	Nassaruddin	(*grandson*)
1705-30	Kamaluddin	(*son of Mohammed Ali*) (1st)
1730-45	Mohammed Alauddin	(*grandson of Muhyiddin*)
1745-62	Kamaluddin	(2nd)
1762-95	Omar Ali Saifuddin I	(*son of Mohammed Alauddin*)
1796-1807	Mohammed Tajuddin	(*son*)
1807	Mohammed Jamalul Alam I	(*son*)
1807-29	Mohammed Kanzul Alam	(*son of Omar Ali Saifuddin I*)
1825-28	Mohammed Alam (Co-Sultan)	(*grandson of Omar Ali Saifuddin I*)
1829-52	Omar Ali Saifuddin II	(*son of Mohammed Jamalul Alam I*)
1852-85	Abdul Momin	(*grandson of Omar Ali Saifuddin I*)
1885-May 1906	Hashim Jalilul Alam Akamuddin	(*son of Omar Ali Saifuddin II*)
May 1906-Sept 1924	Mohammed Jamalul Alam II	(*son*)
Sept 1924-June 1950	Ahmed Tajuddin	(*son*)

June 1950-Oct 1967	Omar Ali Saifuddin III *(son)* (abdicated)
Oct 1967-	Hassanal Bolkiah *(son)*

Chief Ministers:

Sept 1959-1962	Ibrahim bin Mohammed
1962-67	Marsal bin Maun
1967-72	Mohammed Yusuf bin Abdul Rahim
1972-81	Abdul Momin bin Ismail (acting 1972-73)
1981-Dec 1983	Abdul Aziz (acting 1981-82)

Prime Minister:

Jan 1984-	Sultan Hassanal Bolkiah

BULGARIA

Official name: Republic of Bulgaria, Republika Bulgaria
Previous names: Principality of Bulgaria 1879-1908, Kingdom of Bulgaria 1908-1946, People's Republic of Bulgaria 1946-90
Independence date: 22 September 1908
Capital: Sofia

After 500 years of Ottoman rule, the Principality of Bulgaria was constituted under Turkish suzerainty by the Treaty of Berlin in 1878. In 1908 Bulgaria declared its independence from Turkey. During World War II Bulgaria sided with Germany and in 1944 Soviet troops entered the country. A communist government was established and in 1946 a people's republic was proclaimed. In 1990, along with other communist states of eastern Europe, a multi-party system was introduced.

Princes:

July 1879-Sept 1886	Aleksander *(nephew of Emperor Aleksandr II of Russia)*
Sept 1886-July 1887	Co-regents: Stefan Stambolov/Petko Karavelov/Sava Mutkurov
July 1887-Oct 1908	Ferdinand

Kings:

Oct 1908-Oct 1918	Ferdinand (abdicated)
Oct 1918-Aug 1943	Boris III *(son)*
Aug 1943-Sept 1946	Simeon II *(son)*
	Co-regents:
	Aug 1943-Sept 1944 Prince Kyril/Bogdan Filov/Nikolai Michov
	Sept 1944-Sept 1946 Venelin Ganev/Zvetko Boboshevsky/Todor Pavlov

Presidents:

Chairman of the Presidium of the National Assembly 1946-71
Chairman of the Council of State 1971-90

Sept 1946-Dec 1947	Vasil Kolarov
Dec 1947-May 1950	Mintso Neychev
May 1950-Nov 1958	Georgi Damianov (†)
Nov 1958-April 1964	Dimitar Ganev (†)
April 1964-April 1971	Georgi Traikov
April 1971-Nov 1989	Todor Zhivkov
Nov 1989-July 1990	Petŭr Mladenov
Aug 1990-Jan 1997	Zheliu Zhelev (UDF)
Jan 1997-	Petŭr Stoyanov (UDF)

Prime Ministers:

Chairman of the Council of Ministers 1946-91

July-Nov 1879	Todor Burmov
Nov 1879-March 1880	Archbishop Kliment (*b* Vasil Drumev) (1st)
March-Nov 1880	Dragan Tsankov (1st) (LP)
Nov 1880-April 1881	Petko Karavelov (1st) (LP)
April 1881-July 1882	Iohan Erenroth
July 1882-Sept 1883	Leonid Sobolev
Sept 1883-June 1884	Dragan Tsankov (2nd) (LP)
June 1884-Aug 1886	Petko Karavelov (2nd) (LP)
9-12 Aug 1886	Archbishop Kliment (2nd)
12-16 Aug 1886	Petko Karavelov (3rd) (LP)
Aug 1886-June 1887	Vasil Radoslavov (1st)
June-Aug 1887	Constantin Stoilov (1st)
Aug 1887-May 1894	Stefan Stambolov (LP)
May 1894-Oct 1908	Constantin Stoilov (2nd)
Oct 1908-March 1911	Aleksander Malinov (1st) (DP)
March 1911-July 1913	Ivan Gheshov (NP)
14-18 July 1913	Stoyan Danev
July 1913-June 1918	Vasil Radoslavov (2nd)
June-Nov 1918	Aleksander Malinov (2nd) (DP)
Nov 1918-Oct 1919	Todor Todorov
Oct 1919-June 1923	Aleksander Stamboliski (deposed, executed) (AP)
June 1923-Jan 1926	Aleksander Tsankov
Jan 1926-June 1931	Andrei Liapchev (DP)
June-Oct 1931	Aleksander Malinov (3rd) (DP)
Oct 1931-May 1934	Nikola Mushanov (deposed) (DP)
May 1934-Jan 1935	Kimon Gheorghiev (1st)
Jan-April 1935	Pencho Zlatev
April-Nov 1935	Andrei Toshov
Nov 1935-Feb 1940	Georgi Kiosseivanov
Feb 1940-Aug 1943	Bogdan Filov (executed 1945)
Aug 1943-May 1944	Dobri Bozhilov (executed 1945)
May-Sept 1944	Ivan Bagrianov
2-9 Sept 1944	Kosta Muraviev (deposed) (AP)
Sept 1944-Oct 1946	Kimon Gheorghiev (2nd) (RP)
Oct 1946-July 1949	Georgi Dimitrov (†) (BCP)
July 1949-Jan 1950	Vasil Kolarev (†) (BCP)
Jan 1950-April 1956	Vulko Chervenkov (*brother-in-law of G.Dimitrov*) (BCP)
April 1956-Nov 1962	Anton Yugov (BCP)
Nov 1962-April 1971	Todor Zhivkov (BCP)
April 1971-June 1981	Stanko Todorov (BCP)
June 1981-March 1986	Grisha Filipov (BCP)
March 1986-Feb 1990	Georgi Atanasov (BCP)
Feb-Dec 1990	Andrei Lukanov (BSP)

Dec 1990-Nov 1991   Dimitar Popov
Nov 1991-Dec 1992   Filip Dimitrov   (UDF)
Dec 1992-Oct 1994   Lyuben Berov   (MRF)
Oct 1994-Jan 1995   Reneta Indjova
Jan 1995-Feb 1997   Zhan Videnov   (BSP)
Feb-May 1997   Stefan Sofianski (UDF)
May 1997-   Ivan Kostov   (UDF)

AP = Agrarian Party
BCP = Bulgarian Communist Party (dominant role constitutionally defined 1948-90)
BSP = Bulgarian Socialist Party (*f* BCP)
DP = Democratic Party
LP = Liberal Party
MRF = Movement for Rights and Freedom
NP = National Party
RP = Republican Party
UDF = Union of Democratic Forces

Communist Party Leaders:

General Secretary 1946-54 and 1981-90
First Secretary of the Central Committee 1954-81

Oct 1946-March 1954   Vulko Chervenkov
March 1954-Nov 1989   Todor Zhivkov
Nov 1989-Feb 1990   Petŭr Mladenov
(1990   multi-party system introduced)

BURKINA FASO

Official name: People's Republic of Burkina Faso, République Populaire du Burkina Faso
Previous name: Republic of Upper Volta until 1984
Independence date: 5 August 1960
Capital: Ouagadougou

The French colony of Upper Volta was created in 1919 by detaching districts from Upper Senegal (now Mali) and Niger. In 1932 the colony was abolished and the area became part of Ivory Coast. In 1948 it was reconstituted, and self-government was granted in 1958. In 1960 Upper Volta became an independent republic, changing its name to Burkina Faso in 1984.

Governors:

1919-28	Frédéric Hesling
1928-31	Alberic-Auguste Fournier
1931-32	Gabriel-Omer Descemet
1932	Henri Chessé
(1932-47	post abolished)
1947-48	Gaston Mourgues
1948-52	Albert-Jean Mouragues
1952-53	Roland Pré (see French Guinea)
1953-56	Salvador-Jean Etcheber
1956-58	Yvon Bourges

High Commissioner:

1959-60	Paul Masson

Presidents:

Aug 1960-Jan 1966	Maurice Yameogo (deposed)
Jan 1966-Nov 1980	Sangoulé Lamizana (deposed)
Nov 1980-Nov 1982	Saye Zerbo (deposed)
Nov 1982-Aug 1983	Jean-Baptiste Ouédraogo (deposed)
Aug 1983-Oct 1987	Thomas Sankara (deposed, assassinated)
Oct 1987-	Blaise Campaoré (OPD-LM)

Prime Ministers:

July-Oct 1958	Ouézzin Coulibaly (†) (VDU)
Oct 1958-Dec 1960	Maurice Yameogo (VDU)
(Dec 1960-Jan 1966	post abolished)
Jan 1966-Feb 1971	Sangoulé Lamizana (1st)

Feb 1971-Feb 1974	Gerard Ouédraogo (VDU)
Feb 1974-July 1978	Sangoulé Lamizana (2nd)
July 1978-Nov 1980	Joseph Conombo (VDU)
Nov 1980-Nov 1982	Saye Zerbo
(Nov 1982-Jan 1983	post abolished)
Jan-May 1983	Thomas Sankara
(May 1983-June 1992	post abolished)
June 1992-March 1994	Youssouf Ouédraogo
March 1994-Feb 1996	Roch Kaboré
Feb 1996-	Kadré Ouédraogo

OPD-LM = Organization for Popular Democracy-Labour Movement
VDU = Volta Democratic Union

BURUNDI

Official name: Republic of Burundi, République du Burundi, Republika Y'Uburundi (Kirundi)
Previous names: Urundi until 1962, Kingdom of Burundi 1962-66
Independence date: 1 July 1962
Capital: Bujumbura (*f* Usumbura)

The kingdom of Urundi was established in the 16th century. In 1895 it was incorporated into German East Africa. After World War I it passed into Belgian control and then became a League of Nations (later United Nations) trust territory. Urundi was administrated together with its neighbour Rwanda. Self-government was granted in 1961 and independence in 1962. In 1966 the monarchy was overthrown and a republic established. Ethnic rivalry between Hutus and Tutsis over the years has resulted in the loss of many lives.

Kings:

1765-95	Mwambutsa III
1795-1852	Ntare IV
1852-Aug 1908	Mwezi II (*son*)
Aug 1908-Dec 1915	Mutaga II (*son*)
Dec 1915-July 1966	Mwambutsa IV (*son*) (regency council 1915-30?) (deposed)
July-Nov 1966	Ntare V (*b* Charles Ndideye) (*son*) (deposed) (assassinated 1972)

Presidents:
Chairman of the National Committee of Public Safety (Oct 1993)

Nov 1966-Nov 1976	Michel Micombero (UNP) (deposed)
Nov 1976-Sept 1987	Jean-Baptiste Bagaza (UNP) (deposed)
Sept 1987-July 1993	Pierre Buyoya (1st) (UNP)
July-Oct 1993	Melchior Ndadaye (FDB) (deposed, executed)
21-25 Oct 1993	François Ngeze (nominal)
(Oct 1993-Feb 1994	post vacant)
Feb-April 1994	Cyprien Ntaryamira (FDB) († air crash)
April 1994-July 1996	Sylvestre Ntibantuganya (acting April-Sept 1994) (deposed)
July 1996-	Pierre Buyoya (2nd)

Prime Ministers:

Jan-Sept 1961	Joseph Cimpaye
Sept-Oct 1961	Prince Louis Rwagasore (UNP) († assassinated)
Oct 1961-June 1963	André Muhirwa
June 1963-April 1964	Pierre Ngendandumwe (1st)
April 1964-Jan 1965	Albin Nyamoya (1st)

COUNTRIES AND REGIONS

11-15 Jan 1965	Pierre Ngendandumwe (2nd) († assassinated)
Jan-Sept 1965	Joseph Bamina (removed, executed)
Sept 1965-July 1966	Leopold Biha
July 1966-July 1972	Michel Micombero (1st)
July 1972-June 1973	Albin Nyamoya (2nd)
June 1973-Nov 1976	Michel Micombero (2nd)
Nov 1976-Oct 1978	Edouard Nzambimana
(Oct 1978-Nov 1988	post abolished)
Nov 1988-July 1993	Adrien Sibomana
July 1993-Feb 1994	Sylvie Kinigi
Feb 1994-Feb 1995	Anatole Kanyenkiko
Feb 1995-July 1996	Antoine Nduwayo
July 1996-June 1998	Pascal-Firmin Ndimira
(June 1998	post abolished)

FDP = Front for Democracy in Burundi (FRODEBU)
UNP = Union for National Progress (UPRONA) (sole legal party until 1993)

Former Trust Territory

RUANDA-URUNDI

Capital: Usumbura

Governors:

1916-19	Justin Malfeyt
1920-30	Alfred Marzorali
1930-32	Charles Voisin
1932-46	Eugène Jungers
1946-52	Léon Petillon
1952-55	Alfred Claeys-Bouaert
1955-62	Jean-Paul Harroy

CAMBODIA

Official name: Cambodia, Kampuchea

Previous names: Kingdom of Cambodia until 1970, Khmer Republic 1970-75, Democratic Kampuchea 1975-79, People's Republic of Kampuchea 1979-89, State of Cambodia 1989-93

State founded: 1st century AD

Independence date: 9 November 1953

Capital: Phnom Penh

The kingdom of Funan was founded in the 1st century and covered present day Cambodia as well as most of south east Asia. In the 6th century the area was taken over by the Khmers. In the colonial era, a French protectorate was established in Cambodia 1863. In 1945 the Japanese ousted the French and an independent Cambodia was proclaimed, but within months the British entered Phnom Penh and re-established French control. In 1949 Cambodia became a French Associated State, with full independence following in 1953. A right-wing coup in 1970 replaced the monarchy with a republic. Communist guerilla forces (the Khmer Rouge), took Phnom Penh in 1975 and established a pro-Chinese government. Vietnam invaded Cambodia in 1978/79 and installed a rival communist regime. The ousted leaders continued to oppose the new rulers and in 1982 formed an opposition coalition with other anti-Vietnamese groups. A peace agreement in 1991 set up a joint council to run the country under UN supervision until elections in 1993. The monarchy was then restored.

Kings/Queen:

1796-1835	Chan II
1835-48	Mey (*daughter*)
1848-Oct 1860	Ang Duong (*brother*)
Oct 1860-April 1904	Norodom I (*son*)
April 1904-Aug 1927	Sisowath (*brother*)
Aug 1927-April 1941	Sisowath Monivong (*son*)
April 1941-March 1955	Norodom Sihanouk (*grandson*) (1st) (abdicated)
March 1955-April 1960	Norodom Suramarit (*father*)
April-June 1960	Regency Council President: Prince Monireth

Heads of State:

June 1960-March 1970	Norodom Sihanouk (1st) (deposed)
March 1970-March 1972	Cheng Heng

Presidents:

Chairman of the Supreme Committee 12-16 April 1975

March 1972-April 1975	Lon Nol

1-12 April 1975   Saukham Khoy   (acting)
12-16 April 1975   Sak Sutsakhan

Head of State:

April 1975-April 1976   Norodom Sihanouk   (2nd)

Presidents:

President of the State Presidium 1976-79
President of the Revolutionary Council 1979-81
Chairman of the Council of State 1981-91

April 1976-Jan 1979   Khieu Samphan   (deposed)
Jan 1979-Nov 1991   Heng Samrin

Head of State:

Nov 1991-Sept 1993   Norodom Sihanouk   (3rd)

King:

Sept 1993-   Norodom Sihanouk   (2nd)

Prime Ministers:

Chairman of the Council of Ministers 1981-93

March-Oct 1945   Son Ngoc Thanh   (1st)
Nov 1945-Sept 1946   Prince Monireth
Sept 1946-Aug 1947   Prince Youthevong
Aug 1947-Feb 1948   Sam Sary
Feb-Nov 1948   Chean Van
Nov 1948-Sept 1949   Penn Nouth   (1st)
Sept 1949-May 1950   Yem Sambaur
June 1950-March 1951   Prince Moniphong
March-Oct 1951   Oum Cheang Sun   (1st)
Oct 1951-June 1952   Huy Kanthoul
June 1952-Jan 1953   King Norodom Sihanouk   (1st)
Jan-Nov 1953   Penn Nouth   (2nd)
Nov 1953-March 1954   Chann Ak
March-April 1954   King Norodom Sihanouk   (2nd)
April 1954-Jan 1955   Penn Nouth   (3rd)
Jan-Sept 1955   Leng Ngeth
Sept 1955-Jan 1956   Prince Norodom Sihanouk   (f King) (3rd)
Jan-March 1956   Oum Cheang Sun   (2nd)
1-30 March 1956   Prince Norodom Sihanouk   (4th)
April-Aug 1956   Khim Tit
Sept-Oct 1956   Prince Norodom Sihanouk   (5th)
Oct 1956-April 1957   San Yun

April-June 1957	Prince Norodom Sihanouk (6th)
June 1957-Jan 1958	Sim Var (1st)
8-17 Jan 1958	Ek Yi Oun
Jan-April 1958	Penn Nouth (4th)
April-July 1958	Sim Var (2nd)
July 1958-April 1960	Prince Norodom Sihanouk (7th)
April 1960-Jan 1961	Pho Proeung
Jan 1961-Oct 1962	Penn Nouth (5th)
Oct 1962-Oct 1966	Prince Norodom Kantol
Oct 1966-May 1967	Lon Nol (1st)
May-Dec 1967	Son Sann
Jan 1968-Aug 1969	Penn Nouth (6th)
Aug 1969-March 1972	Lon Nol (2nd)
11-13 March 1972	Sirik Matak (executed 1975)
March-Oct 1972	Son Ngoc Thanh (2nd)
Oct 1972-April 1973	Hang Thun Hak
May-Dec 1973	In Tam
Dec 1973-April 1975	Long Boret (deposed, executed)
April 1975-April 1976	Penn Nouth (7th)
April 1976-Jan 1979	Pol Pot (*b* Saloth Sar) (deposed)
(Sept-Dec 1976	Nuon Chea (acting))
(Jan 1979-June 1981	post abolished)
June-Dec 1981	Pen Sovan
Dec 1981-Dec 1984	Chan Si (acting Dec 1981-Feb 1982) (†)
Dec 1984-	Hun Sen (acting Dec 1984-Jan 1985) (2nd co-PM June 1993-Nov 1998) (CPP)
June 1993-July 1997	Prince Norodom Ranariddh (*son of Norodom Sihanouk*) (1st co-PM) (FUNCINPEC)
Aug 1997-Nov 1998	Ung Huot (1st co-PM) (FUNCINPEC)

CPP = Cambodian People's Party (*f* Communist Party)
FUNCINPEC = United Front for an Independent, Neutral, Peaceful & Co-operative Cambodia

Communist Party* Leaders:

*Kampuchean People's Revolutionary Party 1979-91
Secretary of the Central Committee until June 1981
General Secretary 1981-91

April 1975-Jan 1979	Pol Pot (deposed)
April 1979-Dec 1981	Pen Sovan
Dec 1981-Oct 1991	Heng Samrin

GOVERNMENT-IN-EXILE 1970-75

Headquarters: Beijing
Operated in opposition to the government in Phnom Penh

Head of State:

May 1970-April 1975	Norodom Sihanouk

Prime Minister:

May 1970-April 1975   Penn Nouth

RIVAL GOVERNMENTS

1. Democratic Kampuchea (1979-90)
   National Government of Cambodia (1990-93)
   No established headquarters - members moved to Phnom Penh in 1991
   Operated in opposition to the Vietnamese supported government in Phnom Penh and retained the United Nations seat.

Presidents:

Jan 1979-June 1982	Khieu Samphan
June 1982-July 1988	Norodom Sihanouk (1st)
(July 1988-Feb 1989	post vacant)
Feb 1989-July 1991	Norodom Sihanouk (2nd)
July 1991-1993	Son Sann (acting)

Prime Ministers:

Jan-Dec 1979	Pol Pot
Dec 1979-June 1982	Khieu Samphan
June 1982-1993	Son Sann

2. Provisional government
   Headquarters: Pailin
   Set up by Khmer Rouge after failure to reach settlement with central government. Defections, loss of most areas to government forces in 1997-98 led to its effective demise.

Prime Minister:

July 1994-98   Khieu Samphan

CAMEROON

Official name: Republic of Cameroon, République du Cameroun
Previous names: State of Cameroon 1960-61, Federal Republic of Cameroon 1961-72, United Republic of Cameroon 1972-82
Independence date: 1 January 1960
Capital: Yaoundé

Germany established a protectorate in the Cameroons in 1884. The territory was occupied by French and British troops in 1915-16, and in 1919 the greater part was placed under French administration and the rest under British control as League of Nations (later United Nations) trusteeship territories. In 1956 partial self-government was granted in the French area, with full self-government in 1959 and independence in 1960. The British region, Southern Cameroons, became self-governing in 1958, and in 1961 joined Cameroon to form a federation; a unitary republic was established in 1972.

Governors:

1885-91	Julius von Soden
1891-95	Eugen von Zimmerer
1895-1907	Jesko von Puttkamer
1907-10	Theodor Seitz
1910-12	Otto Gleim
1912-16	Karl Ebermaier
1916	Joseph Aymerich
1916-20	Lucien Fourneau (see of French Congo)
1920-21	Jules Carde

High Commissioners:

1921-23	Jules Carde
1923-32	Théodore-Paul Marchand
1932-35	Auguste-François Bonnecarrère (see Togo)
1935-36	Jules-Vincent Repiquet (see Reunion)
1936-39	Pierre-François Boisson
1939-40	Richard Brunot (see Chad)
1940	Philippe Leclerc de Hautecloque
1940-43	Pierre Cournarie
1943-44	Hubert Carras
1944-46	Henri-Pierre Nicolas
1946-47	Robert-Louis Delavignette
1947-49	René Hoffherr
1949-54	Jean Soucadeux
1954-56	Roland Pré (see French Somaliland)

1956-57   Pierre Messmer   (see Ivory Coast)
1958   Jean-Paul Ramadier   (see Niger)
1958-59   Xavier-Antoine Torré

Presidents:

Jan 1960-Nov 1982   Ahmadou Ahidjo   (CNU, DRCP)
Nov 1982-   Paul Biya   (DRCP)

Prime Ministers:

May 1956-Jan 1959   André-Marie Mbida   (CD)
Jan 1959-Jan 1960   Ahmadou Ahidjo   (CNU)
(Jan 1960-July 1975   post abolished)
July 1975-Nov 1982   Paul Biya
Nov 1982-Aug 1983   Bello Maigari
Aug 1983-Jan 1984   Luc Ayang
(Jan 1984-April 1991   post abolished)
April 1991-April 1992   Sadou Hayatou
April 1992-Sept 1996   Simon Achidi Achu
Sept 1996-   Peter Mafany Musonge

CD = Cameroon Democrats
CNU = Cameroon National Union
DRCP = Democratic Rally of the Cameroon People (*f* CNU) (sole legal party 1966-91)

Former provinces

EAST CAMEROON

Capital: Yaoundé

Prime Ministers:

Oct 1961-Feb 1965   Charles Assalé   (CNU)
Feb-Nov 1965   Vincent Ahanda   (CNU)
Nov 1965-July 1972   Simon-Pierre Tchoungi   (CNU)
(July 1972   post abolished)

WEST CAMEROON

Previous name: Southern Cameroons until 1961
Capital: Buea

Commissioner:

1960-61   John Field

Prime Ministers:

May 1958-Feb 1959   Emmanuel Enderley   (KNC)

Feb 1959-May 1965   John Foncha   (KNDP)
May 1965-Jan 1968   Augustine Jua   (KNDP, CDU)
Jan 1968-July 1972   Salomon Muna   (CDU)
(July 1972   post abolished)

KNC = Kamerun National Convention
KNDP = Kamerun National Democratic Party (merged with CDU in 1966)

CANADA

Official name: Dominion of Canada, Dominion du Canada
State formed: 1 July 1867
Capital: Ottawa

The first European visitors to the Atlantic coast of North America were probably Norse explorers, but colonial exploration dates from the voyages of the Englishman John Cabot in 1497 and the Frenchman Jacques Cartier in 1534. British and French colonies were established and rivalry between the colonial powers culminated in the British capture of Quebec in 1759; at the Treaty of Utrecht in 1763 Canada was formally ceded to Britain. Responsible government was granted to Nova Scotia in 1848, to Upper and Lower Canada (now Ontario and Quebec) jointly in 1851, and to New Brunswick, Prince Edward Island and Newfoundland by 1855. In 1867 Upper and Lower Canada, New Brunswick and Nova Scotia were united to form the Dominion of Canada. The other six provinces that make up modern Canada joined the Dominion between 1870 and 1949. Recent referenda in the mainly French speaking province of Quebec have shown growing support for independence from the rest of Canada.

Governors-General:

Represent monarch who is concurrently British monarch
Acting Governors-General are officially called Administrators

July 1867-Nov 1868	Viscount Monck (Charles Monck)
Nov 1868	Charles Windham (acting)
Nov 1868-June 1872	Lord Lisgar (John Young)
June 1872	Charles Doyle (acting)
June 1872-Nov 1878	Earl of Dufferin (Frederick Blackwood)
Nov 1878	Patrick MacDougall (acting)
Nov 1878-Oct 1883	Marquess of Lorne (John Campbell)
Oct 1883-May 1888	Marquess of Lansdowne (Henry Petty-Fitzmaurice)
May-June 1888	John Ross (acting)
June 1888-Sept 1893	Lord Stanley of Preston (Frederick Stanley)
Sept 1893	A.G.Montgomery Moore (acting)
Sept 1893-Nov 1898	Marquess of Aberdeen (John Gordon)
Nov 1898-Nov 1904	Earl of Minto (Gilbert Elliot-Murray-Kynynmound)
Nov-Dec 1904	H.Elzear Taschereau (acting)
Dec 1904-Oct 1911	Earl Grey (Albert Grey)
Oct 1911-Oct 1916	Prince Arthur,Duke of Connaught (see South Africa)
Oct-Nov 1916	Charles Fitzpatrick (acting)
Nov 1916-July 1921	Duke of Devonshire (Victor Cavendish)
July-Aug 1921	Louis Davies (acting) (see Prince Edward Island)
Aug 1921-Sept 1926	Viscount Byng of Vimy (Julian Byng)
Sept-Oct 1926	Francis Anglin (acting)
Oct 1926-April 1931	Viscount Willington (Freeman Freeman-Thomas)

April 1931-Sept 1935	Earl of Beesborough (Vere Ponsonby)
Sept-Nov 1935	Lyman Duff (acting) (1st)
Nov 1935-Feb 1940	Lord Tweedsmuir (John Buchan) (†)
Feb-June 1940	Lyman Duff (acting) (2nd)
June 1940-April 1946	Earl of Athlone (Prince Alexander of Teck) (see South Africa)
April 1946-Feb 1952	Viscount Alexander (Harold Alexander)
Feb 1952-Sept 1959	Vincent Massey
Sept 1959-March 1967	Georges Vanier (†)
March-April 1967	Robert Taschereau (acting) (*son of Louis Taschereau*)
April 1967-Jan 1974	Roland Michener
Jan 1974-Jan 1979	Jules Léger
Jan 1979-May 1984	Edward Schreyer (see Manitoba)
May 1984-Jan 1990	Jeanne Sauvé (*b* J.Benoît)
Jan 1990-Feb 1995	Ramon Hnatyshyn
Feb 1995-Oct 1999	Roméo Leblanc
Oct 1999-	Adrienne Clarkson

Prime Ministers:

Upper and Lower Canada

Oct 1851-Sept 1854	Francis Hincks/Augustin Morin
Sept 1854-Jan 1855	Alan McNab/Augustin Morin
Jan 1855-May 1856	Alan McNab/Étienne Tache (1st)
May 1856-Nov 1857	John Alexander MacDonald (1st)/Étienne Tache
Nov 1857-Aug 1858	John Alexander MacDonald/George Cartier (1st)
2-5 Aug 1858	George Brown/Antoine Dorion (1st)
Aug 1858-May 1862	John Alexander MacDonald (2nd)/George Cartier (2nd)
May 1862-May 1863	John Sandfield MacDonald/Louis Sicotte
May 1863-March 1864	John Sandfield MacDonald/Antoine Dorion (2nd)
March 1864-July 1865	John Alexander MacDonald (3rd)/Étienne Tache (2nd) (†)
Aug 1865-July 1867	John Alexander MacDonald/Narcisse Belleau

Dominion of Canada

July 1867-Nov 1873	John Alexander MacDonald (CP)
Nov 1873-Oct 1878	Alexander MacKenzie (LP)
Oct 1878-June 1891	John Alexander MacDonald (CP) (4th) (†)
June 1891-Nov 1892	John Abbott (CP)
Dec 1892-Dec 1894	John Thompson (see Nova Scotia) (CP)
Dec 1894-April 1896	MacKenzie Bowell (CP)
May-July 1896	Charles Tupper (see Nova Scotia) (CP)
July 1896-Oct 1911	Wilfred Laurier (LP)
Oct 1911-July 1920	Robert Borden (CP, UP)
July 1920-Dec 1921	Arthur Meighen (1st) (UP)
Dec 1921-June 1926	W.Mackenzie King (1st) (LP)
June-Sept 1926	Arthur Meighen (2nd) (CP)

Sept 1926-Aug 1930	W.MacKenzie King (2nd) (LP)
Aug 1930-Oct 1935	Richard Bennett (CP)
Oct 1935-Nov 1948	W.MacKenzie King (3rd) (LP)
Nov 1948-June 1957	Louis St.Laurent (LP)
June 1957-April 1963	John Diefenbaker (PCP)
April 1963-April 1968	Lester Pearson (LP)
April 1968-June 1979	Pierre Trudeau (1st) (LP)
June 1979-Feb 1980	Joseph Clark (PCP)
Feb 1980-June 1984	Pierre Trudeau (2nd) (LP)
June-Sept 1984	John Turner (LP)
Sept 1984-June 1993	Brian Mulroney (PCP)
June-Nov 1993	Kim Campbell (PCP)
Nov 1993-	Jean Chrétien (LP)

CP = Conservative Party
LP = Liberal Party
PCP = Progressive Conservative Party (*f* CP)
UP = Unionist Party

Parties in Provinces and Territories:
CCP = Co-operative Commonwealth Party
NDP = New Democratic Party   (*f* CCP)
PP = Peoples' Party
PQ = Parti Québecois
SCP = Social Credit Party
UN = Union Nationale
UFP = United Farmers' Party
YP = Yukon Party

Provinces

ALBERTA

Admitted to Dominion: 1 September 1905
Capital: Edmonton

Lieutenant-Governors:

Sept 1905-Oct 1915	George Bulyea
Oct 1915-Oct 1925	Robert Brett
Oct 1925-April 1931	William Egbert
April 1931-Sept 1936	William Walsh
Sept 1936-March 1937	Philip Primrose (†)
March 1937-Feb 1950	John Bowen
Feb 1950-Feb 1959	John Bowlen
Feb 1959-Jan 1966	J.Percy Page
Jan 1966-July 1974	J.W.Grant MacEwan
July 1974-Oct 1979	Ralph Steinhauer
Oct 1979-Jan 1985	Frank Lynch-Staunton

Jan 1985-March 1991   Helen Hunley
March 1991-April 1996 Gordon Towers
April 1996-Feb 2000   Horace (Bud) Olson
Feb 2000-   Lois Hole

Premiers:

Sept 1905-May 1910   Alexander Rutherford   (LP)
May 1910-Oct 1917   Arthur Sifton   (LP)
Oct 1917-Aug 1921   Charles Stewart   (LP)
Aug 1921-Nov 1925   Herbert Greenfield   (UFP)
Nov 1925-July 1934   John Brownlee   (UFP)
July 1934-Sept 1935   Richard Reid   (UFP)
Sept 1935-May 1943   William Aberhart   (SCP)
May 1943-Dec 1968   Ernest Manning   (SCP)
Dec 1968-Sept 1971   Harry Strom   (SCP)
Sept 1971-Oct 1985   Peter Lougheed   (PCP)
Oct 1985-Dec 1992   Donald Getty   (PCP)
Dec 1992-   Ralph Klein   (PCP)

BRITISH COLUMBIA

Admitted to Dominion: 20 July 1871
Capital: Victoria

Lieutenant-Governors:

July 1871-June 1876   Joseph Trutch
June 1876-June 1881   Albert Richards
June 1881-Feb 1887   Clement Cornwall
Feb 1887-Nov 1892   Hugh Nelson
Nov 1892-Nov 1897   Edgar Dewdney
Nov 1897-June 1900   Thomas McInnes
June 1900-May 1906   Henri Joly de Lotbinière   (see Quebec)
May 1906-Dec 1909   James Dunsmuir
Dec 1909-Dec 1914   Thomas Paterson
Dec 1914-Dec 1919   Frank Barnard
Dec 1919-Dec 1920   Edward Prior   (†)
Dec 1920-Jan 1926   Walter Nichol
Jan 1926-July 1931   R.Randolph Bruce
July 1931-April 1936   J.W.Fordham Johnson
April 1936-Aug 1941   Eric Hamber
Aug 1941-Oct 1946   William Woodward
Oct 1946-Oct 1950   Charles Banks
Oct 1950-Oct 1955   Charles Wallace
Oct 1955-Oct 1960   Frank Ross

Oct 1960-July 1968   George Pearkes
July 1968-March 1973   John Nicholson
March 1973-May 1978   Walter Owen
May 1978-July 1983   Henry Bell-Irving
July 1983-Sept 1988   Robert Rogers
Sept 1988-April 1995   David See-chai Lam
April 1995-   Garde Gardom

Premiers:

Nov 1871-Dec 1872   John McCreight
Dec 1872-Feb 1874   Amor De Cosmos   (*b* William Smith)
Feb 1874-Feb 1876   George Walkem   (1st)
Feb 1876-June 1878   Andrew Elliot
June 1878-June 1882   George Walkem   (2nd)
June 1882-Jan 1883   Robert Beaver
Jan 1883-May 1887   William Smythe
May 1887-Aug 1889   Alexander Davie
Aug 1889-July 1892   John Robson
July 1892-March 1895   Theodore Davie   (*brother of A.Davie*)
March 1895-Aug 1898   John Turner
Aug 1898-Feb 1900   Charles Semlin
Feb-June 1900   Joseph Martin
June 1900-Nov 1902   John Dunsmuir
Nov 1902-June 1903   Edward Prior
June 1903-Dec 1915   Richard McBride   (CP)
Dec 1915-Nov 1916   William Bowser   (CP)
Nov 1916-March 1918   Harlan Brewster   (LP)
March 1918-Aug 1927   John Oliver   (CP)
Aug 1927-Aug 1928   John MacLean   (LP)
Aug 1928-Nov 1933   Simon Tolmie   (CP)
Nov 1933-Dec 1941   Thomas Pattullo   (LP)
Dec 1941-Jan 1947   John Hart   (LP)
Jan 1947-Aug 1952   Byron Johnson   (LP)
Aug 1952-Sept 1972   William A.Bennett   (SCP)
Sept 1972-Dec 1975   David Barrett   (NDP)
Dec 1975-Aug 1986   William R.Bennett   (*son of W.A.Bennett*) (SCP)
Aug 1986-April 1991   William Vander Zalm   (SCP)
April-Oct 1991   Rita Johnston   (*b* R. Leichert) (SCP)
Oct 1991-Feb 1996   Michael Harcourt   (NDP)
Feb 1996-Aug 1999   Glen Clark   (NDP)
Aug 1999-Feb 2000   Dan Miller   (NDP)
Feb 2000-   Ujjal Dosanjh   (NDP)

MANITOBA

Admitted to Dominion: 15 July 1870
Capital: Winnipeg

Lieutenant-Governors:

May 1870-April 1872	Adams Archibald
April-Dec 1872	Francis Johnson
Dec 1872-Oct 1877	Alexander Morris
Oct 1877-Sept 1882	Joseph Cauchon
Sept 1882-July 1888	James C.Aikens
July 1888-Sept 1895	John Schultz
Sept 1895-Oct 1900	James Patterson
Oct 1900-Aug 1911	Daniel McMillan
Aug 1911-Aug 1916	Douglas Cameron
Aug 1916-Oct 1926	James A.Aikens (*son of J.C.Aikens*)
Oct 1926-Jan 1929	Thomas Burrows (†)
Jan 1929-Dec 1934	James McGregor
Dec 1934-Nov 1940	William Tupper (*son of C.Tupper*)
Nov 1940-Aug 1953	Roland McWilliams
Aug 1953-Jan 1960	John McDiarmid
Jan 1960-Sept 1965	Errick Willis
Sept 1965-Sept 1970	Richard Bowles
Sept 1970-March 1976	William McKeag
March 1976-Oct 1981	Francis Jobin
Oct 1981-Dec 1986	Pearl McGonigal
Dec 1986-March 1993	George Johnson
March 1993-	W.Yvon Dumont

Premiers:

Sept 1870-Dec 1871	Alfred Boyd (CP)
Dec 1871-March 1872	Marc Girard (1st) (CP)
March 1872-July 1874	J.H.Clarke (CP)
July-Dec 1874	Marc Girard (2nd) (CP)
Dec 1874-Oct 1878	Robert Davis (CP)
Oct 1878-Dec 1887	John Norquay (CP)
Dec 1887-Jan 1888	David Harrison (CP)
Jan 1888-Jan 1900	Thomas Greenway (LP)
Jan-Oct 1900	Hugh MacDonald (CP)
Oct 1900-May 1915	Rodmond Roblin (CP)
May 1915-Aug 1922	Tobias Norris (CP)
Aug 1922-Jan 1943	John Bracken (CP)
Jan 1943-Nov 1948	Stuart Garson (PCP)
Nov 1948-June 1958	Douglas Campbell (LP)
June 1958-Nov 1967	Dufferin Roblin (*grandson of R.Roblin*) (PCP)

Nov 1967-July 1969	Walter Weir (PCP)
July 1969-Oct 1977	Edward Schreyer (later Gov-Gen) (PCP)
Oct 1977-Nov 1981	Sterling Lyon (PCP)
Nov 1981-May 1988	Howard Pawley (NDP)
May 1988-Oct 1999	Gary Filmon (PCP)
Oct 1999-	Gary Doer (NDP)

NEW BRUNSWICK

One of the original provinces
Capital: Fredericton

Lieutenant-Governors:

July-Oct 1867	Charles Hastings Doyle
Oct 1867-July 1868	Francis Harding
July 1868-Nov 1873	Lemuel Wilmot
Nov 1873-July 1878	Samuel Tilley (1st)
July 1878-Feb 1880	E.Barron Chandler (†)
Feb 1880-Oct 1885	Robert Wilmot
Oct 1885-Sept 1893	Samuel Tilley (2nd)
Sept-Dec 1893	John Boyd (†)
Dec 1893-Nov 1896	John Fraser (†)
Dec 1896-Jan 1902	Abner McClenan
Jan 1902-Feb 1907	Jabez Snowball (†)
March 1907-March 1912	Lemuel Tweedie
March 1912-June 1916	Josiah Wood
June 1916-Oct 1917	Gilbert Ganong (†)
Nov 1917-Feb 1923	William Pugsley
Feb 1923-Dec 1928	William Todd
Dec 1928-Feb 1935	Hugh McLean
Feb 1935-March 1940	Murray MacLaren
March 1940-Nov 1945	William G.Clark
Nov 1945-June 1958	David MacLaren
June 1958-June 1965	J.Leonard O'Brien
June 1965-Feb 1968	John McNair
Feb 1968-Oct 1971	Wallace Bird
Oct 1971-Jan 1982	Hedard Robichaud
Jan 1982-Aug 1987	George Stanley
Aug 1987-June 1994	Gilbert Finn
June 1994-April 1997	Margaret McCain
April 1997-	Marilyn Trenholm Counsell

Premiers:

Nov 1854-May 1856	Charles Fisher (1st) (LP)

May 1856-May 1857	Edward Chandler (CP)
May 1857-March 1861	Charles Fisher (2nd) (LP)
March 1861-March 1865	Samuel Tilley (LP)
March 1865-April 1866	Albert Smith
April 1866-July 1867	Peter Mitchell
July 1867-Feb 1871	Andrew Wetmore (CP)
Feb 1871-July 1872	George Hathaway
July 1872-78	George King (LP)
1878-82	John Fraser (CP)
1882-83	Daniel Hanington (CP)
1883-July 1896	Andrew Blair (LP)
July 1896-Oct 1897	James Mitchell (CP)
Oct 1897-Aug 1900	Henry Emmerson (LP)
Aug 1900-March 1907	Lemuel Tweedie (CP)
March-May 1907	William Pugsley (LP)
May 1907-March 1908	Clifford Robinson (LP)
March 1908-Oct 1911	John Hazen (CP)
Oct 1911-Dec 1914	James Flemming (CP)
Dec 1914-Feb 1917	George Clarke (CP)
Feb-April 1917	James Murray (CP)
April 1917-Feb 1923	Walter Foster (LP)
Feb 1923-Sept 1925	Peter Veniot (LP)
Sept 1925-May 1931	John Baxter (CP)
May 1931-June 1933	Charles Richards (CP)
June 1933-July 1935	Leonard Tilley (CP)
July 1935-March 1940	A.Allison Dysart (LP)
March 1940-Oct 1952	John McNair (LP)
Oct 1952-July 1960	Hugh Flemming (*son of J.Flemming*) (PCP)
July 1960-Nov 1970	Louis Robichaud (LP)
Nov 1970-Oct 1987	Richard Hatfield (PCP)
Oct 1987-Oct 1997	Frank McKenna (LP)
Oct 1997-May 1998	J.Raymond Frenette (LP)
May 1998-June 1999	Camille Thériault (LP)
June 1999-	Bernad Lord (PCP)

NEWFOUNDLAND AND LABRADOR

Admitted to Dominion: 31 March 1949
Capital: St.John's

Governors:

1898-1901	Henry McCallum
1901-04	Cavendish Boyle
1904-09	William Macgregor
1909-13	Ralph Williams

1913-17	Walter Davidson
1917-22	Charles Hams
1922-28	William Allardyce
1928-32	John Middleton
1932-35	David Anderson
1935-46	Humphrey Walwyn
1946-49	Gordon Macdonald

Lieutenant-Governors:

April-Sept 1949	Albert Walsh
Sept 1949-Dec 1957	Leonard Outerbridge
Dec 1957-March 1963	Campbell Macpherson
March 1963-April 1969	Fabian O'Dea
April 1969-July 1974	E.John Harnum
July 1974-July 1981	Gordon Winter
July 1981-Sept 1986	W.Anthony Paddon
Sept 1986-Nov 1991	James McGrath
Nov 1991-Feb 1997	Frederick Russell
Feb 1997-	A.Maxwell House

Prime Ministers:

May 1855-1858	Philip Little (LP)
1858-May 1861	John Kent (LP)
May 1861-Nov 1865	Hugh Hoyles (CP)
Nov 1865-Nov 1869	Frederick Carter (1st) (LP)
Nov 1869-Nov 1874	Charles Bennett (CP)
Nov 1874-Nov 1878	Frederick Carter (2nd) (LP)
Nov 1878-Nov 1885	William Whiteway (1st) (LP)
Nov 1885-Nov 1889	Robert Thorburn (CP)
Nov 1889-April 1894	William Whiteway (2nd) (LP)
April-Dec 1894	Augustus Goodridge (CP)
Dec 1894-Feb 1895	Daniel Green (LP)
Feb 1895-Oct 1897	William Whiteway (3rd) (LP)
Oct 1897-Nov 1900	James Winter (CP)
Nov 1900-May 1909	Robert Bond (LP)
May 1909-Jan 1918	Edward Morris (PP)
Jan-Oct 1918	John Crosbie (acting)
Oct 1918-May 1919	William Lloyd (LP)
May-Nov 1919	Michael Cashin (CP)
Nov 1919-July 1923	Richard Squires (1st) (LP)
July 1923-April 1924	William Warren (CP)
May-June 1924	Albert Hickman (LP)
June 1924-Oct 1928	Walter Monroe (CP)
Oct-Nov 1928	Frederick Alderdice (1st) (CP)
Nov 1928-June 1932	Richard Squires (2nd) (LP)

June 1932-Feb 1934	Frederick Alderdice (2nd) (CP)
(Feb 1934-April 1949	post abolished)

Premiers:

April 1949-Jan 1972	Robert Smallwood (LP)
Jan 1972-March 1979	Frank Moores (PCP)
March 1979-Jan 1989	Brian Peckford (PCP)
Jan-March 1989	John Collins (acting)
March-April 1989	Thomas Rideout (PCP)
April 1989-Jan 1996	Clyde Wells (LP)
Jan 1996-	Brian Tobin (LP)

NOVA SCOTIA

One of the original provinces
Capital: Halifax

Lieutenant-Governors:

July-Oct 1867	William Williams
Oct 1867-July 1873	Charles Hastings Doyle (see New Brunswick)
May-July 1873	Joseph Howe
July 1873-July 1883	Adams Archibald (see Manitoba)
July 1883-July 1888	Matthew Richey
July 1888-June 1890	Archibald McLelan (†)
July 1890-July 1900	Malachy Bowes Daly
July 1900-March 1906	Alfred Jones (†)
March 1906-Oct 1910	Duncan Fraser (†)
Oct 1910-Oct 1915	James McGregor
Oct 1915-Nov 1916	David MacKeen (†)
Nov 1916-Jan 1925	MacCallum Grant
Jan-Sept 1925	J.Robson Douglas
Sept 1925-Nov 1930	James Tory
Nov 1930-Sept 1931	Frank Stanfield (†)
Oct 1931-April 1937	Walter Covert
April 1937-May 1940	Robert Irwin
May 1940-Nov 1942	Frederick Mathers
Nov 1942-Aug 1947	H.Ernest Kendall
Aug 1947-Sept 1952	John McCurdy
Sept 1952-Jan 1958	Alistair Fraser
Jan 1958-March 1963	Edward Plow
March 1963-July 1968	Henry MacKeen (*son of D.MacKeen*)
July 1968-Oct 1973	Victor Oland
Oct 1973-Dec 1978	Clarence Gosse
Dec 1978-Feb 1984	John Shaffner
Feb 1984-Feb 1989	Alan Abraham

Feb 1989-June 1994	Lloyd Crouse
June 1994-	J.James Kinley

Premiers:

Feb 1848-April 1854	James Uniacke (LP)
April 1854-Feb 1857	William Young (1st) (LP)
Feb 1857-Feb 1860	James Johnston (1st) (CP)
Feb-Aug 1860	William Young (2nd) (LP)
Aug 1860-June 1863	Joseph Howe (LP)
June 1863-May 1864	James Johnston (2nd) (CP)
May 1864-July 1867	Charles Tupper (later PM of Canada) (CP)
July-Nov 1867	Hiram Blanchard (CP)
Nov 1867-May 1875	William Annand (LP)
May 1875-Oct 1878	Philip Hill (LP)
Oct 1878-May 1882	Simon Holmes (CP)
May-Aug 1882	John Thompson (later PM of Canada) (CP)
Aug 1882-July 1884	William Pipes (LP)
July 1884-July 1896	William Fielding (LP)
July 1896-Jan 1923	George Murray (LP)
Jan 1923-July 1925	Ernest Armstrong (LP)
July 1925-Aug 1930	Edgar Rhodes (CP)
Aug 1930-Sept 1933	Gordon Harrington (CP)
Sept 1933-July 1940	Angus Macdonald (1st) (LP)
July 1940-Sept 1945	Alexander MacMillan (LP)
Sept 1945-April 1954	Angus Macdonald (2nd) (LP)
April-Sept 1954	Harold Connolly (LP)
Sept 1954-Nov 1956	Henry Hicks (LP)
Nov 1956-Sept 1967	Robert Stanfield (PCP)
Sept 1967-Oct 1970	George Smith (PCP)
Oct 1970-Oct 1978	George Regan (LP)
Oct 1978-Sept 1990	John Buchanan (PCP)
Sept 1990-Feb 1991	Roger Bacon (acting)
Feb 1991-May 1993	Donald Cameron (PCP)
May 1993-July 1997	John Savage (LP)
July 1997-Aug 1999	Russell MacLellan (LP)
Aug 1999-	John Hamm (PCP)

ONTARIO

One of the original provinces
Capital: Toronto

Lieutenant-Governors:

July 1867-July 1878	Henry Stisted
July 1878-Nov 1873	William Howland

Nov 1873-May 1875	John Crawford (†)
May 1875-June 1880	Donald MacDonald
June 1880-Feb 1887	John Robinson
Feb 1887-May 1892	Alexander Campbell (†)
May 1892-Nov 1897	George Kirkpatrick
Nov 1897-April 1903	Oliver Mowat (†)
April 1903-Sept 1908	William M. Clark
Sept 1908-Sept 1914	John Gibson
Sept 1914-Nov 1919	John Hendrie
Nov 1919-Sept 1921	Lionel Clarke
Sept 1921-Dec 1926	Henry Cockshut
Dec 1926-Oct 1932	William Ross
Oct 1932-Nov 1937	Herbert Bruce
Nov 1937-Dec 1946	Albert Matthews
Dec 1946-Jan 1952	Ray Lawson
Jan 1952-Dec 1957	Louis Breithaupt
Dec 1957-May 1963	John Mackay
May 1963-July 1968	W. Earl Rowe
July 1968-Jan 1974	W. Ross MacDonald
Jan 1974-Sept 1980	Pauline McGibbon
Sept 1980-Sept 1985	John Black Aird
Sept 1985-Dec 1991	Lincoln Alexander
Dec 1991-Jan 1997	Henry (Hal) Jackman
Jan 1997-	Hilary Weston

Premiers:

July 1867-Dec 1871	John Sandfield Macdonald (see Upper & Lower Canada) (CP)
Dec 1871-Oct 1872	Edward Blake (LP)
Oct 1872-July 1896	Oliver Mowat (LP)
July 1896-Oct 1899	Arthur Hardy (LP)
Oct 1899-Feb 1905	George Ross (LP)
Feb 1905-Oct 1914	James Whitney (CP)
Oct 1914-Nov 1919	William Hearst (CP)
Nov 1919-July 1923	Ernest Drury (UFP)
July 1923-Dec 1930	George Ferguson (CP)
Dec 1930-July 1934	George Henry (CP)
July 1934-Oct 1942	Mitchell Hepburn (LP)
Oct 1942-May 1943	Gordon Conant (LP)
May-Aug 1943	Harry Nixon (LP)
Aug 1943-Oct 1948	George Drew (PCP)
Oct 1948-May 1949	Thomas Kennedy (PCP)
May 1949-Nov 1961	Leslie Frost (PCP)
Nov 1961-March 1971	John Robarts (PCP)
March 1971-Jan 1985	William Davis (PCP)
Jan-June 1985	Frank Miller (PCP)

June 1985-Sept 1990	David Peterson (LP)
Sept 1990-June 1995	Robert Rae (NDP)
June 1995-	Michael Harris (PCP)

PRINCE EDWARD ISLAND

Admitted to Dominion: 1 July 1873
Capital: Charlottetown

Lieutenant-Governors:

June 1873-June 1874	William Robinson
June 1874-July 1879	Robert Hodgson
July 1879-Sept 1884	Thomas Haviland
Sept 1884-Sept 1889	Andrew Macdonald
Sept 1889-Feb 1894	Jedediah Carvell (†)
Feb 1894-May 1899	George Howlan
May 1899-Oct 1904	Peter McIntyre
Oct 1904-June 1910	Donald MacKinnon
June 1910-June 1915	Benjamin Rogers
June 1915-Aug 1919	Augustine Macdonald (†) (*brother of Andrew Macdonald*)
Sept 1919-Sept 1924	Murdoch McKinnon
Sept 1924-Nov 1930	Frank Heartz
Nov 1930-Dec 1933	Charles Dalton (†)
Dec 1933-Sept 1939	George DeBlois
Sept 1939-May 1945	Bradford LePage
May 1945-Oct 1950	Joseph Bernard
Oct 1950-March 1958	Thomas Prowse
March 1958-Aug 1963	F. Walter Hyndman
Aug 1963-Oct 1969	William MacDonald
Oct 1969-Oct 1974	J. George MacKay
Oct 1974-Jan 1980	Gordon Bennett
Jan 1980-Aug 1985	Joseph Doiron
Aug 1985-Aug 1990	Lloyd MacPhail
Aug 1990-Aug 1995	Marion Reid (*b* M. Doyle)
Aug 1995-	Gilbert Clements

Premiers:

April 1851-54	George Coles (1st) (LP)
1854-55	John Holl (CP)
1855-59	George Coles (2nd) (LP)
1859-63	Edward Palmer (CP)
1863-65	John Gray (CP)
1865-67	James Pope (1st) (CP)
1867-69	George Coles (3rd) (LP)

1869	Joseph Hensley (LP)
1869-70	Robert Haythorne (1st) (LP)
1870-72	James Pope (2nd) (CP)
1872-April 1873	Robert Haythorne (2nd) (LP)
April-Sept 1873	James Pope (3rd) (CP)
Sept 1873-Aug 1876	Lemuel Owen (CP)
Aug 1876-April 1879	Louis Davies (LP) (later acting Gov-Gen)
April 1879-Nov 1889	William Sullivan (CP)
Nov 1889-April 1891	Neil McCleod (CP)
April 1891-Oct 1897	Frederick Peters (LP)
Oct 1897-Aug 1898	Alexander Warburton (LP)
Aug 1898-Dec 1901	Donald Farquharson (LP)
Dec 1901-Feb 1908	Arthur Peters (*brother of F.Peters*) (LP)
Feb 1908-May 1911	Francis Haszard (LP)
May-Dec 1911	Herbert Palmer (LP)
Dec 1911-June 1917	John Mathieson (CP)
June 1917-Sept 1919	Aubin Arsenault (CP)
Sept 1919-Sept 1923	John Bell (LP)
Sept 1923-Aug 1927	James Stewart (1st) (CP)
Aug 1927-May 1930	Albert Saunders (LP)
May 1930-Aug 1931	Walter Lea (1st) (LP)
Aug 1931-Oct 1933	James Stewart (2nd) (CP)
Oct 1933-Aug 1935	William MacMillan (CP)
Aug 1935-Jan 1936	Walter Lea (2nd) (LP)
Jan 1936-May 1943	Thane Campbell (LP)
May 1943-May 1953	J.Walter Jones (LP)
May 1953-Sept 1959	Alexander Matheson (LP)
Sept 1959-July 1966	Walter Shaw (PCP)
July 1966-Sept 1978	Alexander Campbell (*son of T.Campbell*) (LP)
Sept 1978-May 1979	Bennett Campbell (LP)
May 1979-Nov 1981	Angus MacLean (PCP)
Nov 1981-April 1986	James Lee (PCP)
April 1986-Jan 1993	Joseph Ghiz (LP)
Jan 1993-Sept 1996	Catherine Callbeck (LP)
Oct-Nov 1996	Keith Milligan (LP)
Nov 1996-	Patrick Binns (PCP)

QUÉBEC

One of the original provinces
Capital: Québec

Lieutenant-Governors:

July 1867-Feb 1873	Narcisse Belleau
Feb 1873-Dec 1876	René-Edouard Caron (†)

Dec 1876-July 1879   Luc Letellier de Saint-Just
July 1879-Oct 1884   Théodore Robitaille
Oct 1884-Oct 1887   Louis Masson
Oct 1887-Dec 1892   Auguste-Réal Angers
Dec 1892-Jan 1898   Joseph-Adolphe Chapleau
Jan 1898-Sept 1908   Louis-Amable Jette
Sept 1908-April 1911   Charles Pelletier   (†)
May 1911-Feb 1915   François Langelier   (†)
Feb 1915-Oct 1918   Pierre-Evariste LeBlanc   (†)
Oct 1918-Oct 1923   Charles Fitzpatrick
Oct 1923-Jan 1924   Louis-Philippe Brodeur   (†)
Jan 1924-Dec 1928   Narcisse Pérodeau
Dec 1928-March 1929   Lomer Gouin   (†)
April 1929-April 1934   Henry Carroll
April 1934-Dec 1939   Esioff Patenaude
Dec 1939-Oct 1950   Eugène Fiset
Oct 1950-Feb 1958   Gaspard Fauteux
Feb 1958-Oct 1961   Onésime Gagnon
Oct 1961-Feb 1966   Paul Comptois
Feb 1966-April 1978   Hughues Lapointe
April 1978-March 1984   Jean-Pierre Coté
March 1984-Aug 1990   Gilles Lamontagne
Aug 1990-Sept 1996   Martial Asselin
Sept-Nov 1996   Jean-Louis Roux
Jan 1997-   Lise Thibault

Premiers:

July 1867-Feb 1873   Pierre Chauveau   (CP)
Feb 1873-Sept 1874   Gédéon Ouimet   (LP)
Sept 1874-March 1878   Charles Boucherville   (1st) (CP)
March 1878-Oct 1879   Henri Joly de Lotbinière   (LP)
Oct 1879-Aug 1882   Joseph-Adolphe Chapleau   (CP)
Aug 1882-Jan 1884   Joseph-Alfred Mousseau   (CP)
Jan 1884-Jan 1887   John Ross   (CP)
Jan 1887   Louis-Olivier Taillon   (1st) (CP)
Jan 1887-Dec 1891   Honoré Mercier   (LP)
Dec 1891-Dec 1892   Charles Boucherville   (2nd) (CP)
Dec 1892-May 1896   Louis-Olivier Taillon   (2nd) (CP)
May 1896-May 1897   Edmund Flynn   (LP)
May 1897-Oct 1900   Félix-Gabriel Marchand   (LP)
Oct 1900-March 1905   Simon-Napoléon Parent   (LP)
March 1905-July 1920   Jean Gouin   (LP)
July 1920-June 1936   Louis-Alexandre Taschereau   (LP)
June-Aug 1936   J.Adelard Godbout   (1st) (LP)
Aug 1936-Nov 1939   Maurice Duplessis   (1st) (UN)

Nov 1939-Aug 1944	J.Adelard Godbout (2nd) (LP)
Aug 1944-Sept 1959	Maurice Duplessis (2nd) (UN)
Sept 1959-Jan 1960	Jean-Paul Sauvé (UN)
Jan-July 1960	Antonio Barrette (UN)
July 1960-June 1966	Jean Lesage (LP)
June 1966-Sept 1968	Daniel Johnson (†) (UN)
Oct 1968-May 1970	Jean-Jacques Bertrand (UN)
May 1970-Nov 1976	Robert Bourassa (1st) (LP)
Nov 1976-Sept 1985	René Lévesque (PQ)
Sept-Dec 1985	Pierre-Marc Johnson (PQ) (*son of D.Johnson*)
Dec 1985-Jan 1994	Robert Bourassa (2nd) (LP)
Jan-Sept 1994	Daniel Johnson (LP) (*son of D.Johnson*)
Sept 1994-Jan 1996	Jacques Parizeau (PQ)
Jan 1996-	Lucien Bouchard (PQ)

SASKATCHEWAN

Admitted to Dominion: 1 September 1905 (*f* part of Northwest Territories)
Capital: Regina

Lieutenant-Governors:

Sept 1905-Oct 1910	Amedee Forget (see Northwest Territories)
Oct 1910-Oct 1915	George Brown
Oct 1915-Feb 1921	Richard Lake
Feb 1921-March 1931	Henry Newlands
March 1931-Sept 1936	Hugh Munroe
Sept 1936-Feb 1945	Archibald McNab
Feb-June 1945	Thomas Miller (†)
June 1945-March 1948	Reginald Parker (†)
March 1948-July 1951	John Uhrich
July 1951-Sept 1958	William Patterson
Sept 1958-March 1963	Frank Bastedo
March 1963-Feb 1970	Robert Hanbidge
Feb 1970-Feb 1976	Stephen Worobetz
Feb 1976-Feb 1978	George Porteous
Feb 1978-July 1983	Cameron McIntosh
July 1983-Sept 1988	Frederick Johnson
Sept 1988-May 1994	Sylvia Fedoruk
May 1994-Feb 2000	John (Jack) Wiebe
Feb 2000-	Lynda Haverstock

Premiers:

Sept 1905-Oct 1916	Walter Scott (LP)
Oct 1916-April 1922	William Martin (LP)
April 1922-Feb 1926	Charles Dunning (LP)

Feb 1926-Sept 1929	James Gardiner (1st) (LP)
Sept 1929-July 1934	James Anderson (CP)
July 1934-Nov 1935	James Gardiner (2nd) (LP)
Nov 1935-July 1944	William Patterson (LP)
July 1944-Nov 1961	Thomas Douglas (CCP)
Nov 1961-May 1964	Woodrow Lloyd (CCP,NDP)
May 1964-June 1971	Ross Thatcher (LP)
June 1971-May 1982	Allan Blakeney (NDP)
May 1982-Oct 1991	Grant Devine (PCP)
Oct 1991-	John Romanow (NDP)

Territories

NORTHWEST TERRITORIES

Included Saskatchewan until 1905

Capital: Regina until 1905, Ottawa 1905-67, Yellowknife since 1967

Lieutenant-Governors:

1872-76	Alexander Morris
1876-81	David Laird
1881-88	Edgar Dewdney
1888-93	Joseph Royal
1893-98	Charles Mackintosh
1898-1905	Amedee Forget

Commissioners:

Aug 1905-19	Frederick White
June 1919-Feb 1931	William Cory
March 1931-April 1934	Hugh Rowatt
(April 1934-Dec 1936	post vacant)
Dec 1936-Dec 1946	Charles Camsel
Jan 1947-Sept 1950	Hugh Keenleyside
Nov 1950-Nov 1953	Hugh Young
Nov 1953-July 1963	R.Gordon Robertson
Nov 1963-Jan 1967	Bent Sivertz
March 1967-April 1979	Stuart Hodgson
April 1979-July 1989	John Parker
Oct 1989-Sept 1994	Daniel Norris
Jan 1995-March 1999	Helen Maksagak
March 1999-	Daniel Marion

Premier:

1897-Sept 1905	Frederick Haultain
(Sept 1905	post abolished)

Government Leaders:

June 1980-Jan 1984	George Braden
Jan 1984-Nov 1985	Richard Nerysoo
Nov 1985-Nov 1987	Nick Sibbeston
Nov 1987-Nov 1991	Dennis Patterson
Nov 1991-Feb 1994	Nellie Cournoyea

Premiers:

Feb 1994-Nov 1995	Nellie Cournoyea
Nov 1995-Dec 1998	Don Morin
Dec 1998-Jan 2000	James (Jim) Antoine
Jan 2000-	Stephen Kakfwi

NUNAVUT

Part of Northwest Territories until 1999

Capital: Iqaluit

Commissioners:

April 1999-April 2000	Helen Maksagak (see Northwest Territories)
April 2000-	Peter Irniq

Premier:

April 1999-	Paul Okalik

YUKON

Capital: Dawson (until 1952), Whitehorse (since 1952)

Commissioners:

1898-1901	William Ogilvie
1901-02	James Ross
1903-04	Frederick Congdou
1904-07	William Innes
1907-12	Alexander Henderson
1912-16	George Black
1916-27	George Mackenzie
1927-31	G.I.MacLean
1932-47	George Jeckell
1947-50	J.E.Gibben
1950-51	A.H.Gibson
1951-53	F.Fraser
1953-56	W.G.Brown

1956-62   F.H.Collins
1962-66   Gordon Cameron
Nov 1966-July 1976 James Smith
July 1976-Jan 1979 Arthur Pearson
Jan 1979-March 1986 Douglas Bell
March 1986-June 1995 Ken McKinnon
June 1995-   Judy Gingell

Premiers:

Oct 1979-March 1985   Christopher Pearson   (PCP)
March-May 1985   Willard Thelps   (PCP)
May 1985-Nov 1992   Tony Penikett   (NDP)
Nov 1992-Sept 1996   John Ostashek   (YP)
Sept 1996-April 2000 Piers McDonald   (NDP)
April 2000-   Pat Duncan   (LP)

CAPE VERDE

Official name: Republic of Cape Verde, República de Cabo Verde
Independence date: 5 July 1975
Capital: Praia

The Cape Verde islands were discovered by the Portuguese in 1460, and the first settlers arrived in 1462. In 1587 a Portuguese governor was appointed. The colony became an Overseas Province in 1951. Independence was granted in 1975. A multi-party system was introduced in 1991.

Governors:

1900-02	Arnaldo de Rebelo
1902-03	Francisco de Paulo Cid
1903-04	António de Freitas
1904-07	Amancio Cabral (see São Tomé & Principe)
1907-09	Bernardo de Mecedo
1909-10	Martinho Montenegro
1910-11	António Ortigão
1911	Artur de Campos
1911-15	Joaquim Biker (see Portuguese Guinea)
1915-18	Abel da Costa
1918-19	Teofilo Duarte
1919-21	Manuel Magalhães
1921-22	Filipe de Carvalho
1924-26	Júlio de Abreu
1927-31	António Guedes Vaz
1931-41	Amadeu de Figueiredo
1941-43	José Martins
1943-49	João de Figueiredo
1949-53	Carlos Roçadas
1953-57	Manuel Amoral
1957-58	António Correia
1958-63	Silvino Marques
1963-73	Leão Monteiro
1973-74	António dos Santos
1974-75	Henrique Horta

Presidents:

July 1975-March 1991	Aristides Pereira (APICV)
March 1991-	António Mascarenhas Moreira (MD)

Prime Ministers:

July 1975-Jan 1991	Pedro Pires	(APICV)
Jan 1991-	Carlos Veiga	(MD)

APICV = African Party for the Independence of Cape Verde (PAICV) (sole legal party 1975-90)
MD = Movement for Democracy

CENTRAL AFRICAN REPUBLIC

Official name: Central African Republic, République Centrafricaine
Former names: Ubangui-Chari until 1958, Central African Republic 1958-76, Central African Empire 1976-79
Independence date: 13 August 1960
Capital: Bangui

Ubangui-Chari was separated from the French Congo in 1891 and in 1908 joined other French territories to form French Equatorial Africa. In 1958 the country became self-governing and full independence was granted in 1960. In 1976 President Bokassa proclaimed himself Emperor, but after his overthrow in 1979 the country reverted to a republic.

Lieutenant-Governors:

1920-22	Henri Dirat
1922-26	Auguste Lamblin (1st)
1926-28	Georges-David Prouteaux
1928-29	Auguste Lamblin (2nd)
1930-35	Adolphe Deitte (see of Chad)
1935-36	Richard Brunot
1936	Émile Buhot-Launay
1936-39	Charles de Saint-Félix (see French Guiana)
1939-42	Pierre de Saint-Mart
1942-46	Henri-Camille Sautot

Governors:

1946-48	Jean Calvet
1949-50	Pierre Delteil
1950-51	Ignace Colombani
1951-54	Aimé Grimald
1954-58	Louis Sanmarco
1958	Pierre-Camille Bordier

High Commissioner:

1959-60	Pierre-Camille Bordier

Presidents:

Aug 1960-Jan 1966	David Dacko (1st) (MESAN) (deposed)
Jan 1966-Dec 1976	Jean-Bédel Bokassa (*cousin*) (MESAN)

Emperor:

Dec 1976-Sept 1979   Bokassa I   (J.-B.Bokassa) (deposed)

Presidents:

Sept 1979-Sept 1981   David Dacko   (2nd) (DUC) (deposed)
Sept 1981-Oct 1993   André Kolingba   (DCR)
Oct 1993-   Ange-Félix Patassé   (MLCAP)

Prime Ministers:

July 1958-March 1959   Barthélémy Boganda   (MESAN) († air accident)
March 1959-Jan 1966   David Dacko   (*cousin*) (MESAN)
Jan 1966-Jan 1975   Jean-Bédel Bokassa   (*cousin*) (1st)
Jan 1975-April 1976   Elizabeth Domitien
April-Dec 1976   Jean-Bédel Bokassa   (2nd)
Dec 1976-July 1978   Ange-Félix Patassé
July 1978-Sept 1979   Henri Maidou
Sept 1979-Aug 1980   Bernard Ayandho
(Aug-Nov 1980   post vacant)
Nov 1980-April 1981   Jean-Pierre Lebouder
April-Sept 1981   Simon Bozanga
Sept 1981-March 1991   André Kolingba
March 1991-Dec 1992   Edouard Franck
Dec 1992-Feb 1993   Timothée Malendoma
Feb-Oct 1993   Enoch Lakoué
Oct 1993-April 1995   Jean-Luc Mandaba
April 1995-June 1996   Gabriel Koyambounou
June 1996-Jan 1997   Jean-Paul Ngoupande
Jan 1997-Feb 1999   Michel Gbezera-Bria
Feb 1999-   Anicet Dologuélé

DCR = Democratic Central African Rally (sole legal party 1987-92)
DUC = Democratic Central African Union
MESAN = Mouvement d'evolution sociale de l'Afrique noire (sole legal party 1960-79)
MLCAP = Movement for the Liberation of the Central African People

CHAD

Official name: Republic of Chad, République du Tchad
Independence date: 11 August 1960
Capital: N'djamena (*f* Fort Lamy)

French sovereignty over Chad was recognized by the Franco-German agreement of 1894. In 1900 a French protectorate was proclaimed and in 1906 the territory was incorporated into French Equatorial Africa. It became a colony in 1920. Self-government was granted in 1958 and full independence in 1960. Much of the post-independence period has been plagued by civil war.

Lieutenant-Governors:

1920-25	Fernand Lavil
1925	Antoine Touzet
1925-28	Dieudonné Reste
1928-29	Adolphe Deitte
1929-32	Jules-Marcel de Coppet
1932-34	Richard Brunot
1934-38	Charles Dagain
1939-41	Adolphe Éboué
1941-42	Pierre-Olivier Lapie
1943-44	André Latrille
1944-46	Jacques Rogué

Governors:

1946-49	Jacques Rogué
1949	Pierre Le Layec
1950-51	Henri de Mauduit (see Mauritania)
1951	Carles-Émile Manin
1951-56	Ignace Colombani (see Ubangui-Shari)
1956-58	Jean-René Troadec

High Commissioner:

1959-60	Daniel-Marius Doustin

Presidents:
Chairman of the Council of State March-April 1979

Aug 1960-April 1975	Ngarta Tombolbaye (*f* François Tombolbaye) (PCP, NMCSR) (deposed, assassinated)
April 1975-March 1979	Félix Malloum

March-April 1979	Goukouni Ouedei (1st)
April-Sept 1979	Lol Mohammed Shawa
Sept 1979-June 1982	Goukouni Ouedei (2nd) (deposed)
June 1982-Dec 1990	Hissène Habré (deposed)
Dec 1990-	Idriss Deby

Prime Ministers:

July 1958-Feb 1959	Gabriel Lisette (PCP)
Feb-March 1959	Gontchome Sahoulba (GIRT)
13-24 March 1959	Ahmed Koulamallah (ASM)
March 1959-April 1975	François Tombolbaye (PCP)
April 1975-Aug 1978	Félix Malloum
Aug 1978-March 1979	Hissène Habré
(March 1979-May 1982	post abolished)
May-June 1982	Djidingar Domo Ngardou (*b* Michel Djidingar)
(June 1982-March 1991	post abolished)
March 1991-May 1992	Jean Bawoyeu Alingué
May 1992-April 1993	Joseph Yodoyman
April-Oct 1993	Fidèle Moungar
Nov 1993-April 1995	Delwa Koumakoye
April 1995-May 1997	Koibla Djimasta
May 1997-Dec 1999	Nassour Ouaidou
Dec 1999-	Nagoum Yamassoum

ASM = African Socialist Movement
GIRT = Groupement des Independents et Ruraux du Tchad
PCP = Progressive Chadian Party (sole party after 1962-75)
NMCSR = National Movement for Cultural and Social Revolution (*f* PCP)

RIVAL GOVERNMENT

After President Goukouni Ouedei was ousted in 1982 he fled to Libya and reformed his government which was initially based in Bardai in northern Chad. After the N'djamena government gained control over the northern areas it moved into exile, first in Libya and later in Algeria. This opposition government suffered from internal divisions and by 1989 had ceased to exist.

Presidents:

Oct 1982-Oct 1986	Goukouni Ouedei (1st)
Oct 1986-March 1988	Acheikh bin Oumar
March 1988-1989?	Goukouni Ouedei (2nd)

CHILE

Official name: Republic of Chile, República de Chile
Independence date: 12 February 1818
Capital: Santiago

Chile was ruled by Spain from the 16th century. In 1810 a national government was formed, and complete independence was proclaimed in 1818. In recent times Chile experienced four decades of democratic government which was ended by the military takeover of 1973. Democracy was restored in 1990.

Presidents:

Sept 1818-Jan 1823	Bernardo O'Higgins
Jan 1823-May 1827	Ramón Freire
May 1827	Manuel Blanco Encalada
May 1827-Sept 1831	Francisco Pinto
Sept 1831-Sept 1841	Joaquín Pietro
Sept 1841-Sept 1851	Manuel Bulnes
Sept 1851-Sept 1861	Manuel Montt
Sept 1861-Sept 1871	José Pérez
Sept 1871-Sept 1876	Federico Errázurez Zañartu
Sept 1876-Sept 1881	Aníbal Pinto
Sept 1881-Sept 1886	Domingo Santa Maria
Sept 1886-Sept 1891	José Balmaceda († suicide)
Sept 1891-Sept 1896	Jorge Montt
Sept 1896-July 1901	Federico Errázurez Echaurrea (*son of F.Errázurez Zañartu*) (†)
Aug 1901-Jan 1905	Germán Riesco (acting Aug-Sept 1901)
Jan 1905-Sept 1906	Rafael Reyes (acting)
Sept 1906-Aug 1910	Pedro Montt (*son of M.Montt*) (†)
Aug-Sept 1910	Elias Fernández Albano (acting) (†)
Sept 1910-Sept 1911	Emiliano Figueroa Larrain (acting)
Sept 1911-Dec 1915	Ramón Barros Luca
Dec 1915-June 1920	Juan Sanfuentes Adonaegui
June 1920-Sept 1924	Arturo Alessandri Palma (1st) (deposed)
Sept 1924-Jan 1925	Luis Altamirano
Jan-March 1925	Emilio Bello Codecido
March-Oct 1925	Arturo Alessandri Palma (2nd)
Oct-Dec 1925	Luis Barros Borgoño (acting)
Dec 1925-April 1927	Emiliano Figueroa Larrain (deposed)
April 1927-July 1931	Carlos Ibáñez del Campo (1st) (deposed)
26-28 July 1931	Pedro Opazo (acting)
July-Aug 1931	Juan Esteban Montero (acting) (1st)

Aug-Nov 1931	Manuel Trucco (acting)
Nov 1931-June 1932	Juan Esteban Montero (acting) (2nd)
July-Sept 1932	Carlos Dávila Espinoza (acting) (deposed)
Sept-Oct 1932	Bartolome Blanche (acting)
Oct-Dec 1932	Abraham Oyanedel (acting)
Dec 1932-Dec 1938	Arturo Alessandri Palma (3rd)
Dec 1938-Nov 1941	Pedro Aguirre Cerda (†)
Nov 1941-April 1942	Gerónimo Méndez
April 1942-June 1946	Juan Rios (†)
June-Aug 1946	Alfredo Duhalde (acting)
Aug-Nov 1946	Vicente Merino Bielich (acting)
Nov 1946-Nov 1952	Gabriel González Videla (RP)
Nov 1952-Nov 1958	Carlos Ibáñez del Campo (2nd)
Nov 1958-Nov 1964	Jorge Alessandri Rodríguez (*nephew of A.Alessandri Palma*) (CLP)
Nov 1964-Nov 1970	Eduardo Frei Montalva (CDP)
Nov 1970-Sept 1973	Salvador Allende Gossens (SP) (deposed, assassinated)
Sept 1973-March 1990	Augusto Pinochet Ugarte
March 1990-March 1994	Patricio Aylwin Azócar (CDP)
March 1994-March 2000	Eduardo Frei Ruiz-Tagle (CDP) (*son of E.Frei Montalva*)
March 2000-	Ricardo Lagos (PD)

CDP = Christian Democratic Party
CLP = Conservative-Liberal Party
PD = Party for Democracy
RP = Radical Party
SP = Socialist Party

CHINA

Official name: People's Republic of China, Zhonghua Renmin Gongheguo
Previous names: Empire of China until 1911, Republic of China 1911-49 (see China (Taiwan))
State founded: 2nd century BC
Capital: Beijing (Peking) until 1928, and since 1949; Nanning (Nanking) 1928-38 and 1946-49; Chongqing (Chungking) 1938-46

The Chinese Empire appears to have arisen in the 2nd century BC with the Shang dynasty. The Mongols invaded China in 1210 but were driven out by 1372, and the Ming dynasty then ruled until 1616 when the Manchu (Ching) dynasty was founded. The revolution of 1911 ended imperial rule and a republic was formed. During the 1920's and 1930's there was considerable political instability and several rival governments were formed. From 1937 to 1945 parts of China were occupied by Japan. After World War II communist forces gained control of the country proclaiming a people's republic in 1949. The nationalist forces retreated to Taiwan. In an attempt to revive a revolutionary spirit, a cultural revolution was launched in the late 1960s, causing considerable damage. In recent times, more liberal policies has resulted in large-scale economic growth.

(Note: The Wade-Giles transliteration is used for names up to 1949, after which the Pinyin system is used. For some of the first leaders of the people's republic the Wade-Giles spellings are given in parenthesis)

Emperors:
Temple name (reign/era name) (personal name)

1368-June 1398	T'ai Tsu (Hung-wu) (*b* Chu Yuan-chang)
June 1398-1402	Hui Ti (Chien-wen) (*b* Chu Yun-wen) (*grandson*)
1402-Aug 1424	Ch'eng Tsu (Yung-lo) (*b* Chu Ti) (*uncle*)
Aug 1424-1425	Jen Tsung (Hung-hsi) (*b* Chu Kao-chih) (*son*)
1425-35	Hsuan Tsung (Hsuan-te) (*b* Chu Chan-chi) (*brother*)
1435-49	Ying Tsung (Ch'eng-t'ung) (*b* Chu Ch'i-chen) (*son*) (deposed) (1st)
1449-57	Ching Ti (Ching t'ai) (*b* Chu Ch'i-yu) (*brother*)
1457-64	Ying Tsung (T'ien-shun) (2nd)
1464-87	Hsien Tsung (Ch'eng-hua) (*b* Chu Chien-shen) (*son*)
1487-1505	Hsiao Tsung (Hung-chih) (*b* Chu Yu-t'ang) (*son*)
1505-21	Wu Tsung (Chang-te) (*b* Chu Hou-chao) (*son*)
1521-66	Shih Tsung (Chia-ching) (*b* Chu Hou-tsung) (*grandson of Hsien Tsung*)
1566-72	Mu Tsung (Lung-ch'ing) (*b* Chu Tsai-kou) (*son*)
1572-Aug 1620	Shen Tsung (Wan-li) (*b* Chu I-chun) (*son*)
1620	Kuang Tsung (T'ai-ch'ang) (*b* Chu Ch'ang-lo) (*son*)
1620-27	Hsi Tung (T'ien-ch'i) (*b* Chu Yu-chao) (*son*)
1627-April 1644	Chuang Lieh-ti (Chung-chen) (*b* Chu Yu-tsung) (*brother*) (deposed, suicide)

April-June 1644	Li Tzu-ch'eng (usurper)
June 1644-Feb 1661	Shih-tsu (Shun-Chih) (*b* Fu-lin)
	Regents: 1644-50 Dorgan
	1650-57 Jirgalang
Feb 1661-Dec 1722	Sheng-tsu (K'ang Hsi) (*b* Hsuan-yeh) (*son*) (Regency council)
Dec 1722-Oct 1735	Shih Tsung (Yung-cheng) (*b* Yin-chen) (*son*) (murdered?)
Oct 1735-1796	Kao Tsung (Ch'ien-lung) (*b* Hung-li) (*son*) (abdicated)
1796-Sept 1820	Jen Tsung (Chia-ch'ing) (*b* Yung-yen) (*son*)
Sept 1820-Feb 1850	Hsuan Tsung (Tao-kuang) (*b* Min-ning) (*son*)
Feb 1850-Aug 1861	Wen Tsung (Hsien-feng) (*b* Yi-chu) (*son*)
Aug 1861-Jan 1875	Mu Tsung (T'ung-chih) (*b* Tsai-ch'un) (*son*)
	Regents: 1861-72 Tz'u-An/Tz'u-Hsi
Jan 1875-Nov 1908	Te Tsung (Kuang-hsu) (*b* Tsai-t'ien) (*cousin*) (assassinated)
Nov 1908-Jan 1912	Hsuan T'ung (*b* P'u-yi) (*nephew*) (see Manchukuo) (abdicated)
	Regent: Prince Chun (*father*)

Presidents:

Chairman of the Republic Oct 1949-Jan 1975
From Jan 1975 to June 1983 the post of President was abolished, the ceremonial functions of head of state being conducted by the Chairman of the Standing Committee of the National People's Congress

In Beijing:
Jan-Feb 1912	Sun Yat-sen
Feb 1912-June 1916	Yuan Shih-kai (†)
June 1916-Aug 1917	Li Yuan-hung (1st)
Aug-Sept 1917	Feng Kuo-chang
Sept 1917-June 1922	Hsu Chih-ch'ang
June 1922-June 1923	Li Yuan-hung (2nd)
Oct 1923-Nov 1924	Ts'ao K'un (1st)
Nov 1924-April 1926	Tuan Ch'i-jui
April-May 1926	Ts'ao K'un (2nd)
(May 1926-June 1927	post vacant)
June 1927-June 1928	Chang Tso-lin (†)

In Nanjing (1928-38, 1946-49) & Chongqing (1938-46):
Oct 1928-Dec 1931	Chiang Kai-shek (Chiang Chung-cheng) (1st)
Dec 1931-Jan 1932	Ch'eng Ming-hsu
Jan 1932-May 1943	Lin Sen (†)
May 1943-Jan 1949	Chiang Kai-shek (2nd)
Jan-Sept 1949	Li Tsung-jen (acting)

In Beijing:
Oct 1949-April 1959	Mao Zedong (Mao Tse-tung)
April 1959-Oct 1968	Liu Shaoqi (Liu Shao-chi)
Oct 1968-Jan 1975	Dong Biwu (Tung Pi-wu) (acting)
Jan 1975-July 1976	Ju De (Chu Teh) (†)
July 1976-March 1978	Song Qingling (Soong Ching-ling) (*widow of Sun Yat-sen*) (*de facto* acting)

March 1978-June 1983	Ye Jianying (Yeh Chien-ying)
June 1983-April 1988	Li Xiannian (Li Hsien-nien)
April 1988-March 1993	Yang Shangkun
March 1993-	Jiang Zemin (see Shanghai)

Prime Ministers:

President of the Executive Yuan 1928-49
Premier of the State Council since 1949

In Beijing:

Oct-Dec 1911	Yuan Shih-k'ai
Dec 1911-March 1912	Huang Hsin
March-June 1912	T'ang Shao-yi (1st)
June-Sept 1912	Lu Cheng-hsiang
Oct 1912-July 1913	Ch'ao Ping-chun
July 1913-Feb 1914	Hsiung Hsi-ling
Feb-May 1914	Sun Pao-chi
May 1914-Dec 1915	Hsu Shih-chang (1st)
Dec 1915-March 1916	Lu Cheng-hsiang (acting)
March-May 1916	Hsu Shih-chang (2nd)
May 1916-May 1917	Tuan Ch'i-yui (1st)
23-28 May 1917	Wu T'ing-fang (acting)
May-June 1917	Li Ching-hsi (1st)
13-14 June 1917	Chiang Chao-tsung
June-July 1917	Li Ching-hsi (2nd)
July-Nov 1917	Tuan Ch'i-jui (2nd)
Nov 1917-Oct 1918	Wang Shih-chen (1st)
Oct 1918-June 1919	Ch'ien Neng-hsun
June-Sept 1919	Kung Hsin-chan (acting)
Sept 1919-May 1920	Chin Yun-p'eng (1st)
May-Aug 1920	Sa Chen-ping (acting)
Aug 1920-Dec 1921	Chin Yun-p'eng (2nd)
18-24 Dec 1921	Yen Hui-ch'ing (acting)
Dec 1921-Jan 1922	Liang Shih-yi
Jan-April 1922	Yen Hui-ch'ing (1st)
April-May 1922	Chou Tzu-ch'i
May-June 1922	Wang Shih-chen (2nd)
June-July 1922	Yen Hui-ch'ing (2nd)
July-Sept 1922	T'ang Shao-yi (2nd)
Sept-Nov 1922	Wang Ch'ung-hui
Nov-Dec 1922	Wang Ta-hsieh
Dec 1922-Jan 1923	Wang Cheng-t'ung (acting)
Jan 1923-Jan 1924	Chang Shao-tseng
Jan-July 1924	Sun Pao-Ch'i (2nd)
July-Sept 1924	Ku Wei-chun (Wellington Koo) (1st)
Sept-Oct 1924	Yen Hui-ching (3rd)
3-24 Nov 1924	Huang Fu (acting)

Nov 1924-Dec 1925	Tuan Ch'i-jui (3rd)
Dec 1925-Feb 1926	Hsu Shih-ying (George Hsu)
Feb-April 1926	Chia Teh-yao
April-May 1926	Hu Wei-teh (acting)
May-June 1926	Yen Hui-ching (4th)
June-Oct 1926	Tu Hsi-kua
Oct 1926-June 1927	Ku Wei-chun (2nd)
June 1927-Oct 1928	P'an Fu

In Nanjing (1927-38,1946-49) & Chongqing (1938-46):

April-Aug 1927	Chiang Kai-shek (1st)
Aug-Sept 1927	T'an Yen-kai (1st)
(Sept 1927-Feb 1928	post vacant)
Feb 1928-Sept 1930	T'an Yen-kai (2nd) (†)
Sept-Dec 1930	Sung Tsu-wen (T.V.Soong) (acting) (*brother-in-law of Sun Yat-sen*)
Dec 1930-Dec 1931	Chiang Kai-shek (2nd)
Dec 1931-Jan 1932	Sun Fo (1st) (*son of Sun Yat-sen*)
Jan-Aug 1932	Wang Ching-wei (Wang Chao-ming) (1st)
Aug 1932-March 1933	Sung Tsu-wen (2nd)
March 1933-July 1935	Wang Ching-wei (2nd)
July-Aug 1935	Kung Hsian-hsi (acting)
Aug-Dec 1935	Wang Ching-wei (3rd)
Dec 1935-April 1937	Chiang Kai-shek (3rd)
April 1937-Jan 1938	Wang Chung-hui
Jan 1938-Nov 1939	Kung Hsian-hsi
Nov 1939-Dec 1944	Chiang Kai-shek (4th)
Dec 1944-March 1947	Sung Tsu-wen (3rd)
March-April 1947	Chiang Kai-shek (acting)
April 1947-May 1948	Chung Ch'un
May-Nov 1948	Wong Wen-hao
Nov 1948-March 1949	Sun Fo (2nd)
March-June 1949	Ho Ying-ch'in
June-Sept 1949	Yen Hsi-shan

In Beijing:

Oct 1949-Jan 1976	Zhou Enlai (Chou En-lai) (†)
(Jan-Feb 1976	Deng Xiaoping, *de facto* acting)
Feb 1976-Sept 1980	Hua Guofeng (Hua Kuo-feng) (acting Feb-April 1976)
Sept 1980-Nov 1987	Zhao Ziyang (Chao Tzu-yang) (see Guangdong and Sichuan)
Nov 1987-March 1998	Li Peng (acting Nov 1987-April 1988) (*adopted son of Zhou Enlai*)
March 1998-	Zhu Rongji (see Shanghai)

Communist Party Leaders:

Chairman of the Central Committee 1949-82
General-Secretary since Sept 1982

Oct 1949-Sept 1976	Mao Zedong (†)
Oct 1976-June 1981	Hua Guofeng

June 1981-Jan 1987	Hu Yaobang
Jan 1987-June 1989	Zhao Ziyang (acting Jan-Nov 1987)
June 1989-	Jiang Zemin

Paramount Leader:

Not a formal post. Dates refer to Chairmanship of Military Affairs Commission. Remained influential after officially retiring in 1989 until his death in Feb 1997.

June 1981-Nov 1989	Deng Xiaoping (Teng Hsiao-ping) (*b* Deng Xiansheng)

RIVAL GOVERNMENTS

1. In Canton (Guangzhou)

Presidents:

Sept 1917-June 1922	Sun Yat-sen (1st) (deposed)
June 1922-March 1923	Chen Chu-hsuan
March 1923-March 1925	Sun Yat-sen (2nd) (†)
March 1925-27	Hu Han-min

Prime Ministers:

July 1925-March 1926	Wang Ching-wei (1st)
April 1926-27	T'an Yen-k'ai
(1927	government dissolved)
June 1931-Jan 1932	Wang Ching-wei (2nd)

2. In Tianjin (Tientsin)

Prime Ministers:

June 1917	Hsu Shih-chang
(1917-23	government dissolved)
June-Sept 1923	Li Ken-yuan
Sept 1923-24	Kao Lin-wei

3. In Wuhan

Prime Ministers:

Dec 1926-March 1927	Hsu Shih-ying (George Hsu)
March-Aug 1927	Wang Ching-wei

4. In Beijing

Prime Ministers:

July-Oct 1930	Wang Ching-wei
Oct-Nov 1930	Yen Hsi-shan

5. Soviet governments in Jui-chen (1931-4) and Yenan (1936-49)

Prime Minister:

Dec 1931-Oct 1934	Mao Tse-tung (1st)
(1934-36	no government)
1936-49	Mao Tse-tung (2nd)

6. In Fuzhou

President:

Sept 1933-Jan 1934   Li Chi-sen

7. Governments in Japanese-occupied China

a) In Beijing

Prime Minister:

Dec 1937-April 1940   Wang Keh-min

b) In Nanjing

Prime Minister:

May 1938-April 1940   Liang Hung-chi

The two governments were united in 1940 in Nanjing

Presidents:

April 1940-Nov 1944	Wang Ching-wei (†)
Nov 1944-Aug 1945	Chen Kung-po

Secessionist States

EAST TURKISTAN

Xinjiang attempted to secede under the name East Turkistan
Capital: Aqsu

President:

Nov 1933-Feb 1934   Hwaga Niyaz Heggi

Prime Ministers:
Government Chairman 1934-36 & 1944-46

Nov 1933-Feb 1934	Abdul-Bakr Tabit Damla
1934-36	Ma Hushan (in Khotan)
(1936-44	no government)
Nov 1944-June 1946	Ali Khan Ture

MANCHUKUO
Government established during Japanese occupation

Capital: Mukden

Head of State:

March 1932-March 1934   P'u-Yi   (*f* Emperor of China)

Emperor:

March 1934-May 1945   Kang Teh   (*b* P'u-Yi)

Prime Ministers:

Nov 1931-Jan 1932	Yuan Chin-kai
Jan 1932-May 1935	Chang Hsiao-hsin
May 1935-May 1945	Chang Ching-hui (*son*)

MENGKIANG
Federal Autonomous Government of Mongolia
Government established in Inner Mongolia during Japanese occupation

State proclaimed: 1 September 1939
Capital: Huhehot

President:

Sept 1939-Aug 1945   Prince Teh Wang   (Demchukdondup)

Former Independent State

TIBET

Capital: Lhasa

Kings:

1642-55	Gusri
1655-68	Daya Khan
1668-97	Tenzin Dalai Khan
	Regent: 1668-79 Sange Gyatso Lhabzang Khan
1697-1720	Lhabzang Khan
(1720-28	Chinese occupation)
1728-47	Phola Sonam Tobgye
1747-50	Gyurme

Rulers:
(The first date is the date of birth. Enthronement dates are given in brackets)

1708(1750)-57   Kelzang Gyatso   (7th Dalai Lama)

1758-1804	Jampal Gyatso	(8th Dalai Lama)
1806-15	Lungtok Gyatso	(9th Dalai Lama)
1816-37	Tsultrim Gyatso	(10th Dalai Lama)
1838(March 1855)-56	Khendrup Gyatso	(11th Dalai Lama)
1856(1873)-75	Trinley Gyatso	(12th Dalai Lama)
1876(Oct 1895)-Dec 1933	Thubten Gyatso	(13th Dalai Lama)
1935(Nov 1950)-March 1959	Tenzin Gyatso	(*b* Lhamo Tontrup) (14th Dalai Lama) (exiled)
March 1959-Sept 1965	Chokyi Gyaltsen	(6th Panchen Lama)

Regents:

1757-77	Demo Trulku Jampel Delek (†)
1777-April 1791	Tsemoling Ngawang Tsultrim (†)
1791-1810	Tenpai Gonpo Kindeling (†)
1811-19	Demo Thubten Jigme (†)
1819-Sept 1844	Jampel Tsultrim Tsemoling
1844-May 1845	Administrator: Tenpai Nyima (4th Panchen Lama)
May 1845-62	Yeshe Gyatso Rating
1864-73	Khenrab Wangchuk Dedrug
1875-86	Choskyi Gyaltsen Kundeling (†)
1886-95	Demo Trinley Rabgyas
1895-1913	Ganden Tripa Tsemoling
(1913-33	Rule by Dalai Lama)
Jan 1934-Feb 1941	Rating Rimpoche (*b* Jampal Yeshe)
Feb 1941-Nov 1950	Taktra Rimpoche Ngawang Sungrab

Prime Ministers:

(Usually Co-Prime Ministers)

1862-Sept 1864	Wangchuk Gyalpo Shatra
(1864-1907	post abolished)
1907-20	Changkhyim (†)
1907-23	Paljor Dorje Shatra (†)
1907-26	Sholkhang (†)
1926-40	Silong Yakkyi Langdun (*nephew of 13th Dalai Lama*)
(1940-50	post abolished)
1950-April 1952	Lozang Tashi/Lukhangwa Tsewongroutsen

GOVERNMENT-IN-EXILE

Headquarters: Dharamsala (India)

Head of State:

March 1959-	Tenzin Gyatso (14th Dalai Lama)

Senior-Most Kalons:

1959-60	Jangsa Tsang
1960-75	Woeser G.Kundeling
1975-March 1980	Wangdu Dorjee
March 1980-90	Juchen Thupten Namgyal
1990-92	Kalsang Yeshi (1st)
1992-93	Galo Thondup
1993-96	Tenzin Namgyal Tethong
1996-97	Kalsang Yeshi (2nd)
1997-	Sonam Togyal

Autonomous Regions

GUANGXI-ZHUANG

Capital: Nanning

Governors:

1949-55	Zhang Yunyi (Chang Yun-yi)
Feb 1955-58	Wei Guoqing (Wei Kuo-ch'ing)

Government Chairmen:

1958-Dec 1975	Wei Guoqing
Dec 1975-Feb 1977	An Pingsheng (An P'ing-sheng)
Feb 1977-Dec 1979	Qiao Xiaoguang (Chiao Hsiao-kuang)
Dec 1979-April 1983	Qin Yingji (Chin Ying-chi)
April 1983-Jan 1990	Wei Chunshu
Jan 1990-April 1998	Cheng Kejie
April 1998-	Li Zhaozhuo

NEI MONGGOL

Inner Mongolia

Capital: Hohhot (Huhehot)

Government Chairmen:

1947-Nov 1967	Ulanfu
Nov 1967-70	Deng Haijiong (Teng Hai-ching)
1970-79	Yu Taizhong (Yu Tai-chung)
Dec 1979-April 1983	Kong Fei (Kung Fei)
April 1983-93	Bu He (Pu Heh)
1993-98	Wu Liji
1998-	Yun Longbo

NINGXIA-HUI

Capital: Yinchuan

Governors:

Sept 1949-Nov 1951	Pan Cili
Nov 1951-Sept 1954	Xing Zhaotang
(1954-58	part of Gansu Province)

Government Chairmen:

Oct 1958-Sept 1960	Liu Geping (Liu Keh-ping)
Sept 1960-67	Yang Jingren (Yang Ching-jen)
April 1968-Jan 1977	Kang Jianmen (K'ang Chien-min)
Jan 1977-78	Huo Shihlian (Huo Shih-wen)
June 1979-April 1983	Ma Xin (Ma Hsin)
April 1983-March 1987	Hei Bole (Hei Po-leh)
March 1987-May 1997	Bai Lichen
May 1997-	Ma Qizhi (acting 1997-98)

XINJIANG

Capital: Urumqi (Urumchi)

Governors:

Oct-Dec 1949	Bao Erhan (Burhan Sahidi)
Dec 1949-1951	Peng Dehuai

Government Chairmen:

Sept 1955-Sept 1968	Saifuddin (1st)
Sept 1968-July 1973	Long Shujin (Lung Shu-chin)
July 1973-78	Saifuddin (2nd)
1978-Sept 1979	Wang Feng
Sept 1979-Dec 1985	Ismayil Aymat
Dec 1985-93	Tamur Dawamat
1993-	Abdulahat Abdurixit

XIZANG
Tibet

Capital: Lhasa

Government Chairmen:

Sept 1965-Sept 1968	Ngapo Ngawang Jigme (1st)
Sept 1968-June 1971	Zeng Yongyu (Tseng Yung-ya)
June 1971-Aug 1979	Ren Rong (Jen Jung)

Aug 1979-April 1981   Tian Bao   (Tian Pao)
April 1981-March 1983   Ngapo Ngawang Jigme   (2nd)
March 1983-Dec 1985   Doje Cedain
Dec 1985-May 1990   Doje Cering
May 1990-98   Gyainvain Norbu
1998-   Legqog

Provinces

ANHUI

Capital: Hefei

Governors:

Chairman of the Revolutionary Committee 1968-80

Aug 1952-March 1955   Zeng Xisheng   (Tseng Hsi-sheng)
March 1955-1965   Huang Yan
April 1968-74   Li Desheng   (Li Te-sheng)
June 1975-June 1977   Song Peizhang   (Sung Pei-chang)
June 1977-Dec 1979   Wan Li
Dec 1979-March 1981   Zhang Jingfu
March 1981-April 1983   Zhou Zijian
April 1983-86   Wang Yuzhao
1986-88   Wang Guangyu
1988-89   Lu Rongjing   (acting)
1989-94   Fu Xishou
1994-99   Hui Liangyu
Sept 1999-Jan 2000   Wang Taihua
Jan 2000-   Xu Zhongling

FUJIAN

Capital: Fuzhou

Governors:

Chairman of the Revolutionary Committee 1968-80

1949-April 1955   Zhang Dingcheng   (Chang Ting-cheng)
April 1955-59   Ye Fei   (Yeh Fei)
1959-Dec 1962   Jiang Yizhen   (Chiang Yi-chen)
Dec 1962-68   Wei Jinghui   (Wei Ching-hui)
Aug 1968-Jan 1975   Han Xianchu   (Han Hsien-ch'u)
Jan 1975-Dec 1979   Liao Zhigao   (Liao Chih-kao)
Dec 1979-April 1983   Ma Xingyan
April 1983-87   Hu Ping
1987-90   Wang Zhaoguo
1990-93   Jia Qinglin   (acting 1990-91)

1993-April 1997	Chen Mingyi
April 1997-Feb 2000	He Guoqiang
Feb 2000-	Xie Jinping

GANSU

Capital: Lanzhou

Governors:
Chairman of the Revolutionary Committee 1968-80

1949-66	Deng Baoshan	(Teng Pao-shan)
Jan 1968-June 1977	Xian Henghan	(Hsien Heng-han)
June 1977-Dec 1979	Sung Ping	
Dec 1979-Jan 1981	Feng Jixin	
Jan 1981-May 1983	Li Dengying	
May 1983-May 1986	Chen Guangyi	
May 1986-1992	Jia Zhijie	
1992-Sept 1993	Yan Haiwang	
Sept 1993-96	Zhang Wule	(acting 1993-94)
1996-98	Wu Yixia	
1998-	Song Zhaosu	

GUANGDONG

Capital: Guangzhou (Canton)

Governors:
Chairman of the Revolutionary Committee 1968-80

Oct 1949-Feb 1955	Ye Jianying	(Yeh Chien-ying) (later President)
Feb 1955-Aug 1957	Tao Zhu	(Tao Chu)
Aug 1957-68	Chen Yu	
Feb 1968-April 1972	Liu Xingyuan	(Liu Hsiang-yuan)
April 1972-73	Ding Sheng	(Ting Sheng)
April 1974-Oct 1975	Zhao Ziyang	(Chao Tzu-yang)
Oct 1975-Dec 1978	Wei Guoqing	(Wei Kuo-ching)
Dec 1978-March 1981	Xi Zhongxun	(Hsi Chung-hsun)
March 1981-April 1983	Liu Tianfu	
April 1983-Aug 1985	Liang Lingguang	
Aug 1985-May 1991	Ye Xuanping	
May 1991-May 1996	Zhu Senlin	
May 1996-	Lu Ruihua	

GUIZHOU

Capital: Guiyang

Governors:

Chairman of the Revolutionary Committee 1967-80

Dec 1949-55	Yang Yong
1955-July 1965	Zhou Lin (Chou Lin)
July 1965-Feb 1967	Li Li
Feb 1967-Aug 1974	Li Zaihan (Li Tsai-han)
Aug 1974-March 1977	Lu Ruilin (Lu Jui-lin)
March 1977-Jan 1980	Ma Li
Jan 1980-April 1983	Su Gang
April 1983-1992	Wang Chaowen
1992-98	Chen Shineng
Dec 1998-	Qian Yunluo

HAINAN

Part of Guangdong until 1988

Capital: Qiongshan

Governors:

Chairman of the Revolutionary Committee 1968-80

1952-58	Lin Tie
1958-67	Liu Zihou (Liu Tzu-hou) (1st)
Feb 1968-April 1973	Liu Xuefeng (Liu Hsueh-feng)
April 1973-Feb 1980	Liu Zihou (2nd)
Feb 1980-April 1983	Li Erzhong
April 1983-May 1986	Zhang Shuguang
May 1986-88	Xie Feng
1988-89	Yue Qifeng
1989-91	Cheng Weigao (see Henan)
1991-92	Liu Jianfeng
1992-98	Ye Liansong
Feb 1998-	Wang Xiaofeng

HEBEI

Capital: Shijiazhuang

Governors:

Chairman of the Revolutionary Committee 1967–80

1949-52	Yang Xiufeng
1952-58	Lin Tie
1958-67	Liu Zihou (1st)
Feb 1968-April 1973	Li Xuefeng
April 1973-Feb 1980	Liu Zihou (2nd)

Feb 1980-Aug 1982   Li Erzhong
Aug 1982-April 1983   Liu Bingyan   (acting)
April 1983-89   Zhang Shugang
1989-93   Cheng Weigao   (see Henan)
1993-98   Ye Liansong
May 1998-   Liu Maosheng

HEILONGJIANG

Capital: Harbin

Governors:
Chairman of the Revolutionary Committee 1967-80

Sept 1958-66   Li Fanwu
Jan 1967-72   Ban Fushang   (Pan Fu-shang)
1972-76   Wang Jiadao   (Wang Chia-tao)
1976-77   Liu Guangdao   (Liu Kuang-tao) (acting)
1977-79   Yang Yi-chen   (Yang Yichen)
Dec 1979-Feb 1985   Chen Lei
Feb 1985-89   Hou Jie
1989-93   Shao Qihui
1993-2000   Tian Fengshan
Jan 2000-   Song Fatang

HENAN

Capital: Zhengzhou (Chengchow)

Governors:
Chairman of the Revolutionary Committee 1968-80

1949-July 1962   Wu Zhipu   (Wu Chi-pu)
July 1962-67   Wen Minsheng
Jan 1968-Aug 1978   Liu Jianxun   (Liu Chien-hsun) (see Hubei)
Aug 1978-Sept 1979   Duan Junyi   (Tuan Chun-yi)
Sept 1979-May 1981   Liu Jie
May 1981-April 1983   Dai Suli   (acting May-Dec 1981)
April 1983-July 1987   He Zhukang
July 1987-89   Cheng Weigao
1989-92   Li Changchun   (acting 1989-90)
1992-99   Ma Zhongchen
Feb 1999-   Li Keqiang

HUBEI

Capital: Wuhan

Governors:

Chairman of the Revolutionary Committee 1968-80

Oct 1951-Oct 1954	Liu Jianxun (Liu Chien-hsun)
Oct 1954-Jan 1956	Liu Zihou (Liu Tsi-hou)
Jan 1956-67	Zhang Tixue (Chang Ti-hsui)
Feb 1968-74	Zeng Siyu (Tseng Ssu-yu)
1975-78	Zhao Xinchu (Chao Hsin-chu)
Aug 1978-Jan 1980	Chen Pixian (Chen Pi-hsien)
Jan 1980-Aug 1982	Han Ningfu
Aug 1982-May 1986	Huang Zhizhen (acting Aug 1982-April 1983)
May 1986-March 1990	Guo Zhengqian
March 1990-93	Guo Shuyan
1993-95	Jia Zhijie
1995-	Jiang Zhuping

HUNAN

Capital: Changsha

Governors:

Chairman of the Revolutionary Committee 1968-80

1949-50	Chen Mingren (Chen Ming-jen)
Feb 1950-Dec 1952	Wang Shoudai
Dec 1952-April 1968	Cheng Jian
April 1968-May 1970	Li Yuan (1st)
May 1970-73	Hua Guofeng (Hua Kuo-feng) (later PM)
1973-76	Li Yuan (2nd)
1976-77	Zhang Binghua (Chang Ping-hua)
June 1977-Dec 1979	Mao Ziyong (Mao Chih-yung)
Dec 1979-May 1983	Sun Gouzhu
May 1983-85	Liu Zheng
1985-89	Xiong Qingquan
1989-96	Chen Bangzhu
Jan 1996-May 1999	Yang Zhengwu
May 1999-	Chun Bo

JIANGSU

Capital: Nanjing (Nanking)

Governors:

Chairman of the Revolutionary Committee 1968-80

1952-Feb 1955	Dan Zhenlin (Tan Chen-lin)
Feb 1955-67	Hui Yuyu (1st)

March 1968-73	Xu Shiyou (Hsu Shih-yu)
Nov 1974-Dec 1977	Peng Chong (Peng Chung)
Dec 1977-Dec 1979	Xu Jiatun (Hsu Chia-tun)
Dec 1979-April 1983	Hui Yuyu (2nd)
April 1983-April 1989	Gu Xiulian
April 1989-93	Chen Huanyou
1993-99	Zheng Silin (acting 1993-94)
1999-	Ji Yunshi

JIANGXI

Capital: Nanchang

Governors:
Chairman of the Revolutionary Committee 1968-80

June 1949-March 1965	Shao Shiping
March 1965-67	Fang Zhichun
Jan 1968-Jan 1975	Cheng Shiqing (Cheng Shih-ching)
Jan 1975-Dec 1979	Jiang Weiqing (Chiang Wei-ching)
Dec 1979-April 1983	Bao Dongcai
April 1983-July 1985	Zhao Zengyi
July 1985-86	Ni Xiance
1986-95	Wu Guanzhong
1995-	Shu Shenyou

JILIN

Capital: Changchun

Governors:
Chairman of the Revolutionary Committee 1968-80

Feb 1955-66	Li Yuwen
March 1968-77	Wang Huaixiang (Wang Huai-hsiang)
1977-81	Wang Enmao
1981-83	Yu Ke
May 1983-June 1985	Zhao Xiu
June 1985-June 1987	Gao Dezhan
June 1987-89	He Zhukang (see Henan)
1989-91	Wang Zhongyu
1991-95	Gao Yan
1995-99	Wang Yunkun
1999-	Hong Hu

LIAONING

Capital: Shenyang

Governors:

Chairman of the Revolutionary Committee 1968-80

1954-58	Du Zheheng (Tu Cheh-heng)
1958-67	Huang Oudong (Huang Ou-tung)
May 1968-74	Chen Xilian (Chen Hsi-lien)
1975-78	Zeng Shaoshen (Tseng Shao-shan)
1978-80	Ren Zhongyi
1980	Guo Feng
Jan 1980-May 1983	Chen Puru
May 1983-March 1987	Quan Shuren
March 1987-89	Li Changchun
1989-93	Yue Qifeng (acting 1989-91)
1993-97	Wen Shizhen (acting 1993-94)
1997-	Zhang Guogang

QINGHAI

Capital: Xining

Governors:

Chairman of the Revolutionary Committee 1967-80

1949-Nov 1952	Zhao Shoushan
Nov 1952-Dec 1954	Zhang Zhongliang
Dec 1954-58	Sun Zuobin
Feb 1959-Dec 1962	Yuan Renyuan
Dec 1962-67	Wang Zhao (Wang Chao)
Aug 1967-76	Liu Xianquan (Liu Hsien-chuan)
1976-77	Jiang Jianglin (Chiang Chiang-lin) (acting)
March 1977-Dec 1979	Tan Qilong (Tan Ch'i-lung) (see Zheijiang)
Dec 1979-Dec 1982	Zhang Guosheng
Dec 1982-June 1985	Huang Jingbo (acting Dec 1982-April 1983)
June 1985-Nov 1989	Song Ruixiang
Nov 1989-92	Jin Jipeng
1992-97	Tian Chengping
1997-99	Bai Enpei
Sept 1999-	Zhao Leji

SHAANXI

Capital: Xian

Governors:

Chairman of the Revolutionary Committee 1968-80

1949-52	Ma Mingfang

1952-59	Zhao Shoushan (see Quinghai)
Oct 1959-63	Zhao Boping (Chao Po-p'ing)
1963-67	Lin Qiming (Lin Ch'i-ming)
May 1968-78	Liu Ruishan (Liu Jui-shan)
1978-79	Huo Shilian
Jan-Dec 1979	Ma Wenrui
Dec 1979-Feb 1983	Yu Mingtao
Feb 1983-Dec 1986	Li Qingwei
Dec 1986-Jan 1988	Zhang Boxing (acting)
Jan 1988-April 1990	Hou Zongbin
April 1990-Jan 1995	Bai Qingcai
Jan 1995-96	Cheng Andong (1st)
1996-99	Wang Shousen
1999-	Cheng Andong (2nd)

SHANDONG

Capital: Jinan

Governors:
Chairman of the Revolutionary Committee 1967-80

March 1949-Dec 1954	Kang Sheng
Dec 1954-March 1955	Tan Qilong (Tan Ch'i-lung) (acting) (see Zheijiang)
March 1955-Nov 1958	Zhao Jianmin (Chao Rian-min)
Nov 1958-Dec 1963	Tan Qilong
Dec 1963-Feb 1967	Bai Rubing (Pai Ju-ping) (1st)
Feb 1967-July 1975	Wang Xiayu
July 1975-Dec 1979	Bai Rubing (2nd)
Dec 1979-Dec 1982	Su Yirian
Dec 1982-June 1985	Liang Buting
June 1985-July 1987	Li Changyan
July 1987-March 1989	Jiang Chunyun (acting July 1987-Feb 1988)
March 1989-95	Zhao Zhihao
1995-97	Li Chuting
May 1997-	Wu Guangzheng

SHANXI

Capital: Taiyuan

Governors:
Chairman of the Revolutionary Committee 1967-80

Aug 1949-50	Cheng Zihua (Cheng Tzu-hua)
Feb-Dec 1951	Lai Ruoyu (Lai Jo-yu)
Dec 1951-April 1956	Pei Lisheng (P'ei Li-sheng)

April 1956-Oct 1957	Wang Shiying
Oct 1957-Feb 1967	Wei Heng
Feb 1967-69	Liu Geping (Liu Ke-ping)
(1969-72	post vacant)
Nov 1972-Sept 1975	Xie Zhenhua (Hsieh Ch'en-hua)
Sept 1975-Dec 1979	Wang Qian (Wang Chien)
Dec 1979-April 1983	Luo Guibo
April 1983-Aug 1992	Wang Senhao
Aug 1992-Sept 1993	Hu Fuguo
Sept 1993-Sept 1999	Sun Wensheng (acting 1993-94)
Sept 1999-	Liu Zhenghua

SICHUAN

Capital: Chengdu

Governors:
Chairman of the Revolutionary Committee 1968-80

Aug 1952-Jan 1955	Li Jingquan (Li Ching-ch'uan)
Jan 1955-May 1968	Li Dazhang (Li Ta-chang)
May 1968-72	Zhang Guohua (Chang Kuo-hua)
Feb 1973-78	Liu Xingyuan (Liu Hsing-yuan)
1978-Dec 1979	Zhao Ziyang (later PM)
Dec 1979-April 1983	Lu Dadong
April 1983-May 1985	Yang Xizong
May 1985-88	Jiang Minjuan
1988-92	Zhang Haoruo
1992-96	Xiao Yang
Feb 1996-Jan 2000	Song Baorui
Jan 2000-	Zhang Zhongwei

TAIWAN

See China (Taiwan)

YUNNAN

Capital: Kunming

Governors:
Chairman of the Revolutionary Committee 1968-80

1950-55	Chen Geng (Chen Keng)
1955-58	Guo Yingqin (Kuo Ying-ch'in)
March 1958-Sept 1964	Yu Yichuan (Yu Yi-ch'uan)

Sept 1964-Feb 1965	Liu Mingchin (acting)
Feb 1965-68	Zhou Xing (Chou Hsing) (1st)
Aug 1968-70	Tan Furen (Tan Fu-jen)
(1970-72	post vacant)
Nov 1972-74	Zhou Xing (2nd)
1975-Feb 1977	Jia Qiyun (Chia Chi-yan)
Feb 1977-Jan 1980	An Pingsheng (see Guangxi-Zhuang)
Jan 1980-April 1983	Liu Minghui
April 1983-Aug 1985	Pu Chauzhu
Aug 1985-97	He Zhiqiang
1997-	Li Jiating

ZHEIJIANG

Capital: Hangzhou

Governors:
Chairman of the Revolutionary Committee 1968-80

Aug 1949-Nov 1952	Dan Zhenlin (Tan Chen-lin)
Nov 1952-55	Tan Qilong (Tan Ch'i-lung) (1st)
1955-57	Sha Wenhan
Jan 1958-May 1968	Zhou Jianren (Chou Chien-jan)
May 1968-Sept 1972	Nan Ping (Nan P'ing)
Sept 1972-March 1977	Tan Qilong (2nd)
March 1977-Dec 1979	Tieh Ying
Dec 1979-April 1983	Li Fengping
April 1983-Feb 1988	Xue Ju
Feb 1988-90	Shen Zulun
1990-92	Ge Hongsheng (acting 1990-91)
1993-97	Wan Xueyuan
1997-	Chai Songyue

Special Muncipalities

BEIJING

Mayors:
Chairman of the Revolutionary Committee 1967-80

Jan-Sept 1949	Ye Jianying (Yeh Chien-ying) (later President)
Sept 1949-51	Nie Rongzhen (Nieh Jung-chen)
1951-66	Peng Zhen (Peng Ch'en)
1966-67	Wu De (Wu Teh) (acting)
1967-68	Xie Fuzhu (Hsieh Fu-chu)

1968-Oct 1980	Wu De
Oct 1980-Jan 1981	Lin Hujia (see Tianjin)
Jan 1981-March 1983	Jiao Ruoyu
March 1983-Feb 1993	Chen Xitong
Feb 1993-Oct 1996	Li Qiyan
Oct 1996-Feb 1999	Jia Qinglin (acting 1996-97)
Feb 1999-	Liu Qi

CHONGQING

Mayors:

1997-2000	Pu Haiqing
Jan 2000-	Bao Xuding

SHANGHAI

Mayors:

Chairman of the Revolutionary Committee 1967-80

1949-58	Chen Yi
1958-Dec 1965	Ke Qingshi (K'e Ch'ing-shih)
Dec 1965-Feb 1967	Cao Diqiu (Ts'ao Ti-ch'iu)
Oct 1967-Oct 1976	Zhang Chunqiao (Chang Ch'un-ch'iao)
Nov 1976-79	Su Zhenhua (Su Chen-hua)
1979-81	Chen Guodong
April 1981-July 1985	Wang Daohan
July 1985-April 1988	Jiang Zemin
April 1988-April 1991	Zhu Rongji
April 1991-1998	Huang Ju
March 1998-	Xu Kuangdi

TIANJIN

Mayors:

Chairman of the Revolutionary Committee 1967-80

Dec 1967-May 1978	Xie Xuegung (Hsieh Hsueh-kung)
May-Oct 1978	Lin Hujia
Oct 1978-June 1980	Chen Weida
June 1980-May 1982	Hu Qili
May 1982-90	Li Ruihan
1990-93	Nie Bichin
1993-98	Zhang Lichang
May 1998-	Li Shenglung

Special Autonomous Regions

HONG KONG

Xianggang

Hong Kong island and part of Kowloon were ceded to Britain by China in 1842, and the rest of the territory was leased in 1898. On 1 July 1997 the whole territory was returned to China.

Capital: Government located in Central District, Hong Kong island; the designation 'Victoria' is no longer used.

Governors:

1898-1903	Henry Blake
1904-07	Matthew Nathan
1907-12	Frederick Lugard
1912-19	Francis May
1919-25	Reginald Stubbs
1925-30	Cecil Clementi
1930-35	William Peel
1935-37	Andrew Caldecott
1937-40	Geoffrey Northcote
1940-41	Edward Norton
1941	Mark Young (1st)
1941-45	Rensuka Isogai (during Japanese occupation)
1945-47	Mark Young (2nd)
1948-58	Alexander Grantham
1958-64	Robert (Robin) Black (see Singapore)
1964-71	David Trench
1971-82	C.Murray MacLehose
1982-Dec 1986	Edward Youde (†)
Dec 1986-May 1987	David Akers-Jones (acting)
May 1987-July 1992	Lord Wilson (David Wilson)
July 1992-June 1997	Christopher Patten

Chief Executive:

July 1997-	Tung Chee-hwa

MACAU

Macau became a Portuguese colony in 1557. This was confirmed with China by the 1887 treaty. On 21 December 1999 Macau was returned to Chinese sovereignty.

Governors:

1900-02	José Horta e Costa	(2nd)
1902-03	Arnoldo Rebelo	
1904-07	Martinho Montenegro	
1907-08	Pedro Coutinho	
1908-09	José Rocadas	
1909-10	Eduardo Marques	
1910-12	Alvaro Machado	
1912-14	Anibal Sanches e Miranda	
1914-16	José de Maia	
1917-18	Fernando da Malos	
1918-19	Artur Barbosa	(1st)
1919-22	Henrique da Silva	
1922-23	Luís Correia	
1923-24	Rodrigo Rodrigues	
1924-25	Joachim dos Santos	
1925-26	Manuel Magalhães	
1926-29	Artur Barbosa	(2nd)
1929-31	João Magalhães	(1st)
1931	Joaquim da Mala e Oliveira	
1931-32	João Magalhães	(2nd)
1932-35	António de Miranda	
1935-36	João Barbosa	
1936-37	António da Silva Junior	
1937-40	Artur Barbosa	(3rd)
1940-46	Gabriel Teixeira	
1947-51	Albano de Oliveira	
1951-57	Joaquim Esparteiro	
1957-58	Pedro Barros	
1958-59	Manuel Nunes	
1959-62	Jaime Marques	
1962-66	António dos Santos	
1966-74	José Nobre de Carvalho	
1974-78	José Leandro	
1978-79	Vitor Santos	(acting)
1979-81	Nuno de Melo Egidio	
June 1981-May 1986	Vasco Almeida e Costa	
May 1986-July 1987	Joaquim Machado	
July 1987-Sept 1990	Carlos Melancia	
Sept 1990-March 1991	Francisco Nabo	
March 1991-Dec 1999	Vasco Vieira	

Chief Executive:

Dec 1999-	Edmund Ho Hau-wah

CHINA (TAIWAN)

Official name: Republic of China, Chung-hua Min Kuo
Previous name: Republic of Taiwan May-Nov 1895
Capital: Taipeh

After the Sino-Japanese war in 1895 Taiwan was ceded to Japan by China. In an attempt to prevent the Japanese takeover, an independent Republic of Taiwan was declared but was soon defeated. After World War II the island surrendered to Chinese forces. When the People's Republic was proclaimed in Peking in 1949, the nationalist forces retreated to Taiwan where in December 1949 they re-established the government of the Republic of China.

Presidents:

a. Republic of Taiwan:

May-June 1895	T'ang Ching-sung
June-Nov 1895	Liu Yung-fu
(1895-1945	Japanese rule)

b. Republic of China:

March 1950-April 1975	Chiang Kai-shek (†) (KMT)
April 1975-May 1978	Yen Chia-kan (KMT)
May 1978-Jan 1988	Chiang Ching-kuo (*son of Chiang Kai-shek*) (†) (KMT)
Jan 1988-May 2000	Lee Teng-hui (KMT)
May 2000-	Chen Shui-bian (DDP)

Prime Ministers:
President of the Executive Yuan

Dec 1949-March 1950	Yen Hsi-chan
March 1950-June 1954	Chen Cheng (*b* Ching Tien) (1st)
June 1954-June 1958	Yui Hung-chun (O.K.Yui)
June 1958-Dec 1963	Chen Cheng (2nd)
Dec 1963-June 1972	Yen Chia-kan
June 1972-May 1978	Chiang Ching-kuo
May 1978-May 1984	Sun Yun-suan
May 1984-May 1989	Yu Kuo-hwa
May 1989-June 1990	Lee Huan
June 1990-Feb 1993	Hau Pei-tsun
Feb 1993-Sept 1997	Lien Chan
Sept 1997-May 2000	Vincent Siew (Hsiao Wan-chang)
May 2000-	Tang Fei

DPP = Democratic People's Party
KMT = Kuomintang

Province

TAIWAN

Governors:

Oct 1945-March 1947	Chen Yi
March 1947-Dec 1948	Wei Tao-ming
Dec 1948-Dec 1949	Chen Cheng
Dec 1949-April 1953	Wu Kuo-chen
April 1953-June 1954	Yui Hung-chun (O.K. Yui)
June 1954-Aug 1957	Yen Chia-kan
Aug 1957-Dec 1962	Chou Chih-jou
Dec 1962-69	Huang Chieh
1969-May 1972	Shen Ta-ching
May 1972-May 1978	Hsieh Tung-ming
May 1978-Dec 1981	Lin Yang-kuang
Dec 1981-May 1984	Lee Teng-hui
May 1984-89	Chiu Chuang-huan
1989-Feb 1993	Lien Chan
March 1993-Dec 1998	James Soong Chu-yu
Dec 1998-	Chao Shou-po

COLOMBIA

Official name: Republic of Colombia, República de Colombia

Previous names: Republic of Greater Colombia 1819-30 (included Ecuador & Venezuela), Republic of New Granada 1830-5, Granadine Confederation 1858-61, United States of Colombia 1861-86

Independence date: 17 December 1819

Capital: Bogotá

Colombia was ruled by Spain from the 16th century as the Vice-Royalty of New Granada. In 1819 it declared its independence together with Ecuador and Venezuela, forming Greater Colombia. The union broke up in 1830. Colombia has had several periods of democratic rule, the present dating from 1958. In recent years governments have struggled against left-wing guerilla movements and drugs cartels.

Presidents:

Dec 1819-Jan 1830	Simón Bolívar (also President of Bolivia & Peru)
Jan-June 1830	Andrés Santa Cruz (also President of Bolivia)
June-Aug 1830	Joaquín Mosquera y Arboleda
Aug 1830-Sept 1831	Rafael Urdaneta (acting)
Sept-Nov 1831	Domingo Caicedo (acting)
Nov 1831-March 1832	José Obando (acting)
March-Oct 1832	José de Marquez (acting)
Oct 1832-March 1837	Francisco de Paula Santander
March 1837-May 1841	José de Marquez
May 1841-March 1844	Pedro Alcantara Herran
March 1844-March 1849	Tomás de Mosquera (acting March 1844-April 1845) (1st)
March 1849-April 1853	José López
April 1853-April 1854	José Obando (deposed)
April-Dec 1854	José Melo
April 1855-April 1857	Manuel Mallarino
April 1857-March 1861	Mariano Ospina Rodríguez
March-Nov 1861	Julio Arboleda (†)
Nov 1861-July 1862	Bartolomé Calvo
Nov 1862-Feb 1863	Tomás de Mosquera (2nd)
Feb-June 1863	Froilan Largarcha (acting)
June 1863-April 1864	Tomás de Mosquera (3rd)
April 1864	Juan Uricoechea (acting)
April 1864-March 1866	Manuel Murillo Toro (1st)
April-May 1866	José Rojas Garrido (acting)
May 1866-May 1867	Tomás de Mosquera (4th) (deposed)
May 1867-April 1868	Santos Acosta

April 1868-April 1870	Santos Gutiérrez
April 1870-April 1872	Eustorjio Salgar
April 1872-April 1874	Manuel Murillo Toro
April 1874-April 1876	Santiago Pérez
April 1876-April 1878	Aquillo Parra
April 1878-April 1880	Julian Trujillo
April 1880-April 1882	Rafael Núñez (1st)
April-Dec 1882	Francisco Zaldúa (†)
Dec 1882-April 1883	Climacho Calderón (acting)
April 1883-April 1884	José Otalora
April-Aug 1884	Ezequiel Hurtado
Aug 1884-April 1886	Rafael Núñez (2nd) (deposed)
April 1886-Dec 1887	José Campo Serrano (acting)
Dec 1887-Feb 1888	Eliseo Payan
Feb-Aug 1888	Rafael Núñez (3rd)
Aug 1888-Aug 1892	Carlos Holguín
Aug 1892-Sept 1894	Rafael Núñez (4th) (†)
Sept 1894-March 1896	Miguel Caro (1st)
March 1896	Guillermo Quintero Calderón (acting)
March 1896-Aug 1898	Miguel Caro (2nd)
Aug 1898	José Marroquín (acting)
Aug 1898-July 1900	Manuel Sanclemente
July 1900-Aug 1904	José Marroquín
Aug 1904-July 1908	Rafael Reyes (1st)
July-Aug 1908	Euclides de Angelo
Aug 1908-Aug 1909	Rafael Reyes (2nd)
Aug 1909	Jorge Holguín (acting) (1st)
Aug 1909-Aug 1910	Ramón González Valencia
Aug 1910-Aug 1914	Carlos Restrepo
Aug 1914-Aug 1918	José Concha
Aug 1918-Nov 1921	Marco Suárez
Nov 1921-Aug 1922	Jorge Holguín (acting) (2nd)
Aug 1922-Aug 1926	Pedro Nel Ospina
Aug 1926-Aug 1930	Miguel Abadía Méndez (CP)
Aug 1930-Aug 1934	Enrique Olaya Herrera (LP)
Aug 1934-Aug 1938	Alfonso López Pumarejo (1st) (LP)
Aug 1938-Aug 1942	Eduardo Santos (LP)
Aug 1942-July 1945	Alfonso López Pumarejo (2nd) (LP)
July 1945-Aug 1946	Alberto Lleras Camargo (acting July-Aug 1945) (1st) (LP)
Aug 1946-Aug 1950	Mariano Ospina Pérez (CP)
Aug 1950-June 1953	Laureano Gómez Castro (CP) (deposed)
June 1953-May 1957	Gustavo Rojas Pinilla (deposed)
May 1957-Aug 1958	Gabriel París (junta leader)
Aug 1958-Aug 1962	Alberto Lleras Camargo (2nd) (LP)
Aug 1962-Aug 1966	Guillermo Valencia (CP)

Aug 1966-Aug 1970	Carlos Lleras Restrepo	(*cousin of A.Lleras Camargo*) (LP)
Aug 1970-Aug 1974	Misael Pastrana Borrero	(CP)
Aug 1974-Aug 1978	Alfonso López Michelson	(*son of A.Lopez Pumarejo*) (LP)
Aug 1978-Aug 1982	Julio Turbay Ayala	(LP)
Aug 1982-Aug 1986	Belisario Betancur Cuartas	(CP)
Aug 1986-Aug 1990	Virgilio Barco Vargas	(LP)
Aug 1990-Aug 1994	César Gaviria Trujillo	(LP)
Aug 1994-Aug 1998	Ernesto Samper Pizano	(LP)
Aug 1998-	Andrés Pastrana Arango	(*son of M.Pastrana*) (SCP)

CP = Conservative Party
LP = Liberal Party
SCP = Social Conservative Party (*f* CP)

COMOROS

Official name: Federal and Islamic Republic of the Comoros, République Federale et Islamique des Comores, Jumhuriyat al-Qumur al-Itthadiyah al-Islamiyah
Independence date: 6 July 1975
Capital: Moroni

In 1841 the island of Mayotte was ceded to France by the local ruler. The other three islands in the Comoros were ceded to France between 1886 and 1902. In 1912 the Comoros were proclaimed a French colony and in 1914 placed under the control of the Governor-General of Madagascar. In 1946 they were removed from this control, and in 1961 internal autonomy was granted. In 1975 the Comoros declared independence, but the island of Mayotte decided to remain French. The country has experienced political instability since independence, and in 1997 two of the islands, Anjouan and Moheli attempted to secede.

Governors:

1946-48	Eugène Alaniou
Dec 1948-Dec 1950	Marie-Emmanuel Remy
Dec 1950-April 1956	Pierre Coudert
April 1956-April 1959	Georges Arnaud
April 1959-Dec 1960	Gabriel Savignac (acting)
Dec 1960-Dec 1961	Louis Saget

High Commissioners:

Dec 1961-May 1962	Louis Saget
May 1962-Feb 1963	Yves de Daruvar
Feb 1963-April 1966	Henri Bernard
April 1966-Nov 1969	Antoine Colombani
Nov 1969-73	Jacques Mouradien (see New Hebrides)

Delegate-General:

1973-75	Henri Beaux (see St Pierre & Miquelon)

Presidents:

July-Aug 1975	Ahmed Abdallah Abderemane (1st) (deposed)
Aug 1975-Jan 1976	Said Mohammed Jaffar
Jan 1976-May 1978	Ali Soilih (deposed, assassinated)
May-Oct 1978	Abdallah Mohammed Ahmed (Co-President)
May 1978-Nov 1989	Ahmed Abdallah Abderemane (2nd) (CUP) (Co-President May-Oct 1978) († assassinated)

Nov 1989-Sept 1995	Said Mohammed Djohar (acting Nov 1989-March 1990) (1st) (CUP) (deposed)
Sept-Oct 1995	Ayouba Combo (junta head)
2-4 Oct 1995	Mohammed Taki Abdoulkarim (1st) /Said Ali Kamal
Oct 1995-March 1996	Said Mohammed Djohar (2nd) (exiled Oct 1995-Jan 1996)
(Oct 1995-Jan 1996	Caabi el-Yachroutou Mohammed (acting))
March 1996-Nov 1998	Mohammed Taki Abdoulkarim (2nd) (†) (NUCD)
Nov 1998-April 1999	Tadjidine Ben Said Massonde (acting) (deposed)
April 1999-	Azzaly Assoumani

Prime Ministers:

Co-ordinator of Government Jan-May 1992

Dec 1961-March 1970	Said Mohammed Cheikh (†) (UNR, CDU)
April 1970-June 1972	Prince Said Ibrahim (CDU)
June-Oct 1972	Said Mohammed Jaffar (CPDR)
Oct 1972-Aug 1975	Ahmed Abdallah Abderemane (CDU)
(Aug 1975-Jan 1976	post abolished)
Jan 1976-April 1977	Abdelahi Mohammed (1st)
(April 1977-May 1978	post abolished)
May-Dec 1978	Abdelahi Mohammed (2nd)
Dec 1978-Feb 1982	Salim Ben Ali
Feb 1982-Jan 1985	Ali Mroudjae
(Jan 1985-Jan 1992	post abolished)
Jan-July 1992	Mohammed Taki Abdoulkarim (NUCD)
(July 1992-Jan 1993	post vacant)
Jan-May 1993	Halidi Abderamane Ibrahim
May-June 1993	Said Ali Mohammed
June 1993-Jan 1994	Ahmed Ben Cheikh Attoumane
Jan-Oct 1994	Mohammed Abdou Madi
Oct 1994-April 1995	Halifa Houmadi
April-Sept 1995	Caabi el-Yachroutou Mohamed (1st)
(Sept-Oct 1995	post vacant during coup)
Oct 1995-March 1996	Caabi el-Yachroutou Mohamed (2nd)
March-Dec 1996	Tadjidine Ben Said Massonde
Dec 1996-Sept 1997	Ahmed Abdou
(Sept-Dec 1997	post vacant)
Dec 1997-May 1998	Nourdine Bourhane
(May-Nov 1998	post vacant)
Nov 1998-April 1999	Abbas Djoussouf
(April-June 1999	post vacant)
Aug-Dec 1999	Azzaly Assoumani
Dec 1999-	Bianrifi Tarmidi

CDU = Comoros Democratic Union(*f* UNR)
CPDR = Comoro People's Democratic Rally

CUP = Comoran Union for Progress (sole legal party 1982-89)
NUCD = National Union for Comoron Democracy
UNR = Union for a New Republic

Secessionist states

ANJOUAN

Independence declared: 3 August 1997
Capital: Mutsamudu

Presidents:

Aug 1997-Aug 1999	Abdullah Ibrahim
Aug 1999-	Said Abeid

Prime Ministers:

Aug 1997-March 1998	Abdou Mohammed Mindhi
March-July 1998	Chamassi Said Omar
July 1998-Jan 1999	Abdou Mohammed Hussain
June 1999-	Said Abeid

MOHELI

Independence declared: 11 August 1997
Capital: Fomboni

President:

Aug 1997-	Said Mohammed Soefou

Prime Minister:

Aug 1997-	Soidri Ahmed

CONGO (BRAZZAVILLE)

Official name: Republic of the Congo, République du Congo
Former names: Middle Congo until 1958, People's Republic of the Congo 1969-91
Independence date: 15 August 1960
Capital: Brazzaville

The Middle (French) Congo, which then included Gabon and Ubangui-Chari, was occupied by France in 1882, and became one of the federated territories of French Equatorial Africa in 1908. In 1958 the Congo was granted self-government and it became independent in 1960. In 1969 a people's republic was proclaimed. A multi-party system was introduced in 1992, but rivalry between factions led to civil strife in 1997 and the overthrow of the elected government.

Lieutenant-Governors:

1889-94	Fortune de Chavannes
1894-99	Albert Dolisie
1899-1902	Jean Lemaire
1902-06	Émile Gentil
1906-11	Adolphe-Louis Cureau
1911-12	Charles Vergnes
1912-16	Lucien Fourneau
1916-17	Jules Carde
1917-19	René-Victor Fournier
1919-23	Mathieu-Maurice Alfassa
1923-25	Jean-Henri Marchand
(1925-29	post abolished)
1929-30	Adolphe Deitte (see Chad)
1930-31	Pierre Bonnefort (acting)
1931-32	Charles de Saint-Félix
(1932-41	post abolished)
1941-45	Gabriel-Émile Fortune
1945-46	Ange Bayardelle
1946	Christian Laigret (acting)

Governors:

Nov 1946-Dec 1947	Numa Sadoul (see Gabon)
Dec 1947-March 1950	Jacques-Georges Fourneau (see French Guinea)
March 1950-April 1952	Paul Le Layac (see Chad)
April 1952-Aug 1953	Jean-Jacques Chambon
Aug 1953-Nov 1956	Ernest-Eugène Rouys

Nov 1956-Dec 1958	Jean-Michel Soupault
Jan 1959	Paul-Charles Deriaud (acting)

High Commissioner:

Jan 1959-Aug 1960	Guy-Noël Georgy

Presidents:

Aug 1960-Aug 1963	Fulbert Youlou (deposed)
(Aug-Dec 1963	post vacant)
Dec 1963-Sept 1968	Alphonse Massamba-Débat (deposed, executed 1977)
Sept 1968-Jan 1969	Alfred Raoul
Jan 1969-March 1977	Marien Ngouabi (CLP) († assassinated)
April 1977-Feb 1979	Joachim Yhombi-Opango (CLP)
Feb 1979-Aug 1992	Denis Sassou-Nguesso (1st) (CLP)
Aug 1992-Oct 1997	Pascal Lissouba (PAUSD) (deposed)
Oct 1997-	Denis Sassou-Nguesso (2nd)

Prime Ministers:

July-Nov 1958	Jacques Opangault (PCP)
Nov 1958-Aug 1960	Fulbert Youlou (DUDAI)
(Aug 1960-Aug 1963	post abolished)
Aug-Dec 1963	Alphonse Massamba-Débat (1st)
Dec 1963-April 1966	Pascal Lissouba
April 1966-Jan 1968	Ambroise Noumazalay
Jan-Aug 1968	Alphonse Massamba-Débat (2nd)
Aug 1968-Jan 1970	Alfred Raoul
(Jan 1970-Aug 1973	post abolished)
Aug 1973-Dec 1975	Henri Lopes
Dec 1975-Aug 1984	Louis-Sylvain Goma (1st)
Aug 1984-Aug 1989	Ange Poungui
Aug 1989-Dec 1990	Alphonse Poati-Souchlaty
Dec 1990-Jan 1991	Pierre Moussa (acting)
Jan-June 1991	Louis-Sylvain Goma (2nd)
June 1991-Sept 1992	André Milongo
Sept-Dec 1992	Stephane Bongho-Nouarra
Dec 1992-June 1993	Claude-Antoine Dacosta
June 1993-Aug 1996	Joachim Yhombi-Opango
Aug 1996-Sept 1997	Charles Ganao
Sept-Oct 1997	Bernard Kolelas
(Oct 1997	post abolished)

CLP = Congolese Labour Party (sole legal party 1969-91)
DUDAI = Democratic Union for the Defence of African Interests
PAUSD = Pan-African Union for Social Democracy
PCP = Popular Congolese Party

Former Federation

FRENCH EQUATORIAL AFRICA

Capital: Brazzaville
Member states: Chad, Gabon, Middle Congo, Ubangui-Chari

Governors-General:

1910-17	Martial-Henri Merlin (see Guadeloupe)
1918-19	Gabriel-Louis Angoulvant
1920-24	Jean-Victor Augagneur
1924-34	Raphaël Antonetti (see Ivory Coast)
1934-35	Georges Renard
1935-39	Dieudonné Reste (see Ivory Coast)
1939-40	Pierre-François Boisson
1940	Louis Husson
1940	René de Larminet
1940-44	Félix Eboué (†)
1944-47	Ange Bayardelle (see French Somaliland)
1947	Charles-Jean Luizet

High Commissioners:

1947-51	Bernard Cornut-Gentille
1951-58	Paul Chauvet
1958	Pierre Messmer (see Ivory Coast)
1958	Yves Bourges (see Upper Volta)

High Commissioner-General:

1958-60	Yves Bourges

CONGO (KINSHASA)

Official name: Democratic Republic of Congo, République Democratique du Congo

Previous names: Congo Free State 1885-1908, Belgian Congo 1908-60, Republic of the Congo 1960-64, Democratic Republic of Congo 1964-71, Republic of Zaire 1971-97

Independence date: 30 June 1960

Capital: Boma (1886-1926), Kinshasa (f Leopoldville) (since 1926)

In 1885 the Congo became the personal property of King Leopold II of Belgium as the 'Congo Free State'; in 1908 it became a Belgian colony. In 1960 the Belgian Congo was granted independence but this was soon followed by an army mutiny, the secession of the province of Katanga and other internal troubles. The intervention of United Nations forces led to the collapse of the Katangan secession in 1963. In 1971 Congo changed its name to Zaire. After the overthrow of President Mobutu in 1997 it reverted to its previous name.

Governors-General:

1887-90	Camille Janssen
1890-91	Herman Ledeganck
1891	Henri-Ernest Gondry
1891-92	Camille-Aimé Coquilhat
1892-96	Théophile Wahis (1st)
1896-1900	François Dhanis
1900-12	Théophile Wahis (2nd)
1912-16	Félix-Alexandre Fuchs
1916-21	Eugène Henry
1921-23	Maurice Lippens
1923-27	Martin Rutten
1927-34	Auguste-Constant Tilkens
1934-46	Pierre Ryckmans
1946-52	Eugène Jungers
1952-58	Léon Petillon
1958-60	Henri Cornelis

Presidents:

June 1960-Nov 1965	Joseph Kasabuvu (AB) (deposed)
Nov 1965-May 1997	Mobutu Sese Seko (b Joseph Mobutu) (PRM) (deposed)
May 1997-	Laurent Kabila

Prime Ministers:

President of the College of Commissioners Sept 1960-Feb 1961
First State Commissioner 1977-94

June-Sept 1960	Patrice Lumumba (CNM) (assassinated 1961)
10-14 Sept 1960	Joseph Iléo (1st) (deposed)
Sept 1960-Feb 1961	Justin Bomboko
Feb-Aug 1961	Joseph Iléo (2nd)
Aug 1961-July 1964	Cyrille Adoula
July 1964-Oct 1965	Moïse Tshombe (see Katanga)
Oct-Nov 1965	Evariste Kimba (deposed, executed 1966)
Nov 1965-Oct 1966	Leonard Mulamba
Oct 1966-June 1967	Joseph Mobutu (1st)
(June 1967-July 1977	post abolished)
July 1977-March 1979	Mpinga Kasenda
March 1979-Aug 1980	Bo-Boliko Lokonga (*b* André Bo-Boliko)
Aug 1980-April 1981	Nguza Karl-I-Bond (*b* Jean Nguza) (1st)
April 1981-Nov 1982	N'Singa Udjuu (*b* Joseph N'Singa)
Nov 1982-Oct 1986	Kengo Wa Dondo (*b* Léon Kengo) (1st)
Oct 1986-Jan 1987	Mobutu Sese Seko (*b* Joseph Mobutu) (2nd)
Jan 1987-March 1988	Mabi Mulumba
March-Nov 1988	Sambwa Pida Nbagui
Nov 1988-April 1990	Kengo Wa Dondo (2nd)
April 1990-March 1991	Lunda Bululu
March-Sept 1991	Mulumba Lukoji
Sept-Oct 1991	Étienne Tshisekedi (1st)
Oct-Nov 1991	Bernardin Mungul-Diaka
Nov 1991-Aug 1992	Nguza Karl-I-Bond (2nd)
Aug 1992-June 1994	Étienne Tshisekedi (2nd) (ignored presidential dismissal Dec 1992)
March 1993-June 1994	Faustin Birindwa (rival PM)
June 1994-April 1997	Kengo Wa Dondo (3rd)
3-9 April 1997	Étienne Tshisekedi (3rd)
April-May 1997	Likulia Bolongo
(May 1997	post abolished)

AB = Alliance of Ba-Kongo (ABAKO)
CNM = Congolese National Movement
PRM = Popular Revolutionary Movement (sole legal party 1967-91)

RIVAL GOVERNMENTS 1960-64

Republic of the Congo 1960-63, People's Republic of the Congo 1964
Headquarters: Stanleyville (now called Kisangani)

Set up by supporters of Patrice Lumumba in November 1960 in opposition to the Leopoldville government. It collapsed in January 1963, but was briefly resurrected in 1964.

Prime Ministers:

Nov 1960-Jan 1963	Antoine Gizenga
Sept-Nov 1964	Christophe Gbenye

Secessionist states

KATANGA

State of Katanga
Independence date: 11 July 1960
Secession ended: 15 January 1963
Capital: Elisabethville (now called Lubumbashi)

President:

Aug 1960-Jan 1963   Moïse Tshombe

Prime Minister:

June 1960-Jan 1963   Moïse Tshombe

SOUTH KASAI

Autonomous State of South Kasai
State formed: 9 August 1960
Secession ended: October 1962
Capital: Luluabourg (now called Kananga)

Regarded as a secessionist state, but proclaimed itself as autonomous within the Congo.

Presidents:

June 1960-Jan 1962	Albert Kalonji (1st) (imprisoned in the Congo Jan-Sept 1962)
Jan-Sept 1962	Ferdinand Kazadi (acting)
Sept-Oct 1962	Albert Kalonji (2nd)
Oct 1962	Joseph Ngalula

Prime Minister:

Aug 1960-Oct 1962   Joseph Ngalula

Provinces

From 1960 to 1962 there were six autonomous provinces. This number was then changed to 21, reduced to 12 in 1966, and then to 8 in 1967. In 1972 they became regions with reduced autonomy.

EQUATEUR

Capital: Mbandaka (*f* Coquilhatville until 1966)

President:

June 1960-Aug 1962   Laurent Eketebi
(1962-1966   divided into Cuvette-Central, Moyen Congo and Ubangi)

Prime Minister:

1960-61 — — Boukango

Governors:

1966-67 Léon Engulu
1967-68 Jonas Mukamba
1968-72 Denis Paluku   (see Congo-Centrale)

Provinces 1962-66

Cuvette-Central

Capital: Coquilhatville

President:

Sept 1962-Aug 1965 Léon Engulu

Governor:

Aug 1965-April 1966 Léon Engulu

Moyen Congo

Capital: Lisala

Presidents:

1962-June 1964 Laurent Eketebi   (see Equateur)
June 1964-Aug 1965 Augustin Engwanda

Governor:

Aug 1965-April 1966 Denis Sakombi

Ubangi

Capital: Gemena

President:

Sept 1962-July 1965 Alfred Nzondomyo

Governor:

July 1965-April 1966 Michel Denge

KASAI

Following the secession of South Kasai in August 1960 Kasai was effectively divided into two:

NORTH KASAI

Capital: Lodja

Presidents:

June 1960-Dec 1961	Barthélémy Mukenge	(1st)
Dec 1961-May 1962	André Lubaya	
June 1962-Aug 1962	Barthélémy Mukenge	(2nd)

For South Kasai, see Secessionist States above.

Divided into Lomami, Luluabourg, Sankuru, Sud-Kasai and Unité Kasienne 1962-66, and then reorganized into Kasai-Orientale and Kasai-Occidentale in 1966.

Provinces 1962-66

Lomami

Capital: Kabinda

President:

Sept 1962-Aug 1965   Dominique Manono

Governors:

Aug 1965-April 1966   Dominique Manono
18-25 April 1966   Jean-Marie Kikalango

Luluabourg

Capital: Luluabourg

Presidents:

Sept 1962-Sept 1963	François Luakabwanga	(1st)
Sept 1963-Sept 1964	André Lubaya	
Sept 1964-Sept 1965	François Luakabwanga	(2nd)

Governors:

Aug-Dec 1965	François Luakabwanga	(1st)
Jan-April 1966	Constantin Tshilumba	
18-25 April 1966	François Luakabwanga	(2nd)

Sankuru

Capital: Lodja

Presidents:

Sept 1962-Dec 1963	André Diumasumbu
Dec 1963-June 1965	Paul-Marcel Sumbu

Governors:

June 1965-Jan 1966	Benoît Wetshindjadi
18-25 April 1966	Étienne Kihuyu

Sud-Kasai

Capital: Bakwanga

President:

Oct 1962-July 1965	Joseph Ngalula

Governor:

Aug 1965-April 1966	Jonas Mukamba

Unité Kasienne

Capital: Tshikapa

Presidents:

Sept 1962-Dec 1963	Gregoire Kamamga
Jan 1964-Aug 1965	François Mbengele

Governors:

Aug-Dec 1965	François Mbengele
Jan-April 1966	Robert Mbombo

Provinces 1966-72

Kasai-Occidental

Capital: Kananga (*f* Luluabourg)

Governors:

1966-68	Paul Muhona
1968-72	André Ntikala

Kasai-Oriental

Capital: Mbuyi-Mayi (*f* Bakwanga)

Governors:

1967-68	Henri-Desiré Takizala (see Bandundu)
1968-72	Bernard Ndebo (see Congo-Central)

KATANGA

Seceeded from the Congo (1960-63) (see above), then divided into Nord-Katanga and Sud-Katanga, the latter being further divided into Katanga-Oriental and Lualuba (1963-66), and then reconstituted. Katanga was reconstituted in 1967.

Governors:

1967	Foster Manzikala
1967-68	Denis Paluku (see Congo-Central)
1968-72	Léon Engulu (see Kivu)

Provinces 1963-66

Lualuba

Capital: Jadotville (later Likasi)

President:

June 1963-April 1966	Dominique Diur

Katanga-Oriental

Capital: Elisabethville

Presidents:

June 1963-June 1965	Edouard Bulundwe
June 1965-66	Godefroid Munongo

Nord-Katanga

Capital: Albertville (later Kalemi)

Presidents:

Oct 1960-March 1961	Prosper Mwamba-Ilunga (1st)
(March 1961-Sept 1962	post vacant)
Sept 1962-Sept 1963	Prosper Mwamba-Ilunga (2nd)
Sept 1963-March 1964	Jason Sendwe (1st)

March-April 1964	Kabangui-Fortunat Nimba (1st)
April-June 1964	Jason Sendwe (2nd)
June-July 1964	Ildephonse Massengho
July 1964	Gaston Soumialot (rebel leader)
July 1964-Nov 1966	Henri Ndala Kambola

Sud-Katanga

Capital: Elisabethville (later Lubumbashi)

Governors:

April-Nov 1966	Godefroid Munungo
1966-67	Foster Manzikala

KIVU

Capital: Bukavu

Presidents:

1960-61	— — Muwandu
Jan-Dec 1960	Jean Miruho (1st)
Jan-Feb 1961	Anicet Kashamura
Feb-Aug 1961	Taris Omari
Sept 1961-May 1962	Jean Miruho (2nd)
(1962-66	Divided into Kivu-Central, Maniema and Nord-Kivu)

Governors:

1966-68	Léon Engulu (see Cuvette-Central)
1968-72	Henri-Desiré Takizala (see Kasai-Oriental)

Provinces 1962-66

Kiva-Central

Capital: Bukavu

Presidents:

July 1963-July 1964	Simon Malago
Aug 1964-Aug 1965	Dieudonné Boji

Governor:

Aug 1965-April 1966	Dieudonné Boji

Maniema

Capital: Kindu

Presidents:

Sept-March 1962	Ignace Kanga
March 1962-Sept 1963	Hilaire Kisanga
June-July 1964	Joseph Tshomba-Fariah (1st)
July-Oct 1964	Charles Malembe
Oct 1964-Aug 1965	Joseph Tshomba-Fariah (2nd)

Governors:

Aug 1965-Jan 1966	Joseph Tshomba-Fariah
Jan-April 1966	Pascal Luanghy

Nord-Kivu

Capital: Kiroba

President:

Sept 1962-July 1965   Benezeth Moley

Governor:

July 1965-Dec 1966   Denis Paluku

LEOPOLDVILLE

Capital: Leopoldville

Presidents:

June 1960-Feb 1962	Cleophas Kamitatu
Feb-Aug 1962	Gaston Diomi
(1962-66	Divided into Congo-Central, Kwango, Kwilu and Maindombe)

Provinces 1962-66

Congo-Central

Capital: Kasangula

President:

Sept 1962-Jan 1967   Faustin-Vital Moanda

Governors:

1966-68	Denis Paluku
1968-69	François Luakabwanga (see Bandundu)
1969-72	Bruno Ndala

Kwango

Capital: Kenge

Presidents:

Sept-Nov 1962	Albert Delvaux
Nov 1962	Emmanuel Mayamba
Nov 1962-April 1963	Alphonse Pashi
Aug 1963-April 1964	Pierre Masikita
April-Sept 1964	Belunda Kavunzu
Sept 1964-Aug 1965	Joseph Kulumba

Governor:

Aug 1965-April 1966	Pierre Masikita

Kwilu

Capital: Kikwit

Presidents:

Sept 1962-Jan 1964	Norbert Leta
Jan 1964-Jan 1966	Pierre Mulele

Governor:

Jan-April 1966	Henri-Desiré Takizala

Maindombe

Capital: Inongo

Presidents:

Sept 1962-Dec 1963	Victor Koumoriko
Jan-Dec 1964	Gabriël Zangabie

Governor:

July 1965-April 1966	Daniel Mongiya

Kwango, Kwilu and Maindombe were combined to form Bandundu

Bandundu

Capital: Bandundu (*f* Banneville)

Governors:

1966-67	Henri-Desiré Takizala
1967	François Kupa
1967-68	François Luakabwanga (see Luluabourg)
1969-72	Paul Muhona (see Kasai-Occidental)

ORIENTALE

Capital: Stanleyville

Presidents:

June-Oct 1960	Jean-Pierre Finant
Oct-Dec 1960	Charles Badjoko
Dec 1960-Oct 1961	Jean Foster Manzikala
Oct 1961-July 1962	Simon Losala
(1962-66	Divided into Kibali-Ituri, Haut-Congo and Uele)

Prime Minister:

1960	— — Bonekwe

Governors:

1966-67	Faustin-Vital Moanda (see Congo-Central)
1967-68	Michel Denge
1968-72	Jonas Mukamba (see Equateur)

Provinces 1962-66

Kibali-Ituri

Capital: Bunia

President:

Sept 1962-Dec 1966	Jean Manzikala

Haut-Congo

Capital: Stanleyville

Presidents:

Jan-June 1963	Georges Grenfell
June 1963-June 1964	Paul Isombuma
June-Aug 1964	François Arudjaba
(Sept-Nov 1964	rebel Congolese government in Stanleyville)
1964-66	?

Uele

Capital: Paulis (later renamed Isiro)

President:

Sept 1962-May 1965	Paul Mambaya

Governor:

July 1965-Dec 1966	François Kupa

COSTA RICA

Official name: Republic of Costa Rica, República de Costa Rica
Independence date: 15 September 1821
Capital: San José

Central America was conquered by Spain in the 16th century. In 1821 Costa Rica declared independence, along with El Salvador, Guatemala, Honduras and Nicaragua. From 1823 until 1838 these countries formed the Central American Confederation. Costa Rica has had democratically elected governments since 1948.

Presidents:

Jan 1823-Sept 1824	José Santos Lombardo
Sept 1824	Agustín Lizano Zabal (1st)
Sept 1824-March 1833	Juan Mora Fernández
March 1833-June 1834	José de Gallegos Alvaredo (1st)
June 1834	Juan Lara
June 1834-May 1835	Agustín Lizano Zabal (2nd)
May 1835-April 1837	Braulio Carillo (1st)
April 1837-May 1838	Manuel Aguilar
June 1838-June 1842	Braulio Carillo (acting April-June 1842) (2nd)
July-Sept 1842	Francisco Morazan (deposed)
Sept 1842-Nov 1844	José Alfaro (1st)
Nov-Dec 1844	Francisco Oreamuno
Dec 1844-May 1845	Rafael Moya (†)
May 1845-June 1846	José de Gallegos Alvaredo (2nd)
June 1846-May 1847	José Alfaro (2nd)
May 1847-Jan 1849	José Castro (1st)
Jan 1849-Aug 1859	Juan Rafael Mora (deposed)
Aug 1859-April 1863	José Montealegra (acting Aug 1859-Feb 1860)
April 1863-May 1866	Jesús Jiménez (1st)
May 1866-Sept 1868	José Castro (2nd)
Sept 1868-April 1870	Jesús Jiménez (acting Sept-Nov 1868) (2nd)
April-Aug 1870	Bruno Carranza
Aug 1870-Nov 1873	Tomás Guardia (1st)
Nov-Dec 1873	Salvador González
Dec 1873-Feb 1874	Rafael Barroeta
Feb 1874-May 1876	Tomás Guardia (2nd)
May-July 1876	Aniceto Esquivel
July-Sept 1876	Vicente Herrera
Sept 1876-May 1877	Tomás Guardia (3rd)

May 1877	Sergio Camargo
May 1877-July 1882	Tomás Guardia (4th) (†)
July 1882-March 1885	Prospero Fernández
May 1885-Nov 1889	Bernardo Soto y Alfaro
Nov 1889-May 1890	Carlos Durán Cartin
May 1890-May 1894	José Rodríguez
May 1894-May 1902	Rafael Iglesias y Castro
May 1902-May 1906	Ascensión Esquivel
May 1906-May 1910	Cleto González Viquez (1st)
May 1910-May 1912	Ricardo Jiménez Oreamuno (1st)
May 1912-May 1914	Cleto González Viquez (2nd)
May 1914-Jan 1917	Alfredo González Flores (deposed)
Jan 1917-May 1919	Federico Tinoco Granados
May-Aug 1919	Julio Acosta García (1st)
Aug 1919	Francisco Aguilar Barquero (acting)
Aug 1919-May 1920	Juan Bautista Quiros
May 1920-May 1924	Julio Acosta García (2nd)
May 1924-May 1928	Ricardo Jiménez Oreamuno (2nd)
May 1928-May 1932	Cleto González Viquez (3rd)
May 1932-May 1936	Ricardo Jiménez Oreamuno (3rd)
May 1936-May 1940	León Cortes Castro
May 1940-May 1944	Rafael Calderón Guardia
May 1944-April 1948	Teodoro Picado Michalski (deposed)
April-May 1948	Santos León Herrera (acting)
May 1948-Jan 1949	José Figueres Ferrer (1st) (NLP)
Jan 1949-Sept 1952	Otilio Ulate Blanco (NUP)
Sept 1952-June 1953	Alberto Oreamuno Flores
June 1953-May 1958	José Figueres Ferrer (2nd) (NLP)
May 1958-May 1962	Mario Echandi Jiménez (*son of R.Jiménez Oreamuno*) (NUP)
May 1962-May 1966	Francisco Orlich Bolmarich (NLP)
May 1966-May 1970	José Trejos Fernández (NUP)
May 1970-May 1974	José Figueres Ferrer (3rd) (NLP)
May 1974-May 1978	Daniel Oduber Quiros (NLP)
May 1978-May 1982	Rodrigo Carazo Odio (UOP)
May 1982-May 1986	Luis Monge Alvarez (NLP)
May 1986-May 1990	Oscar Arias Sánchez (NLP)
May 1990-May 1994	Rafael Calderón Fournier (*son of R.Calderón Guardia*) (USCP)
May 1994-May 1998	José-María Figueres Olsen (*son of J.Figueres Ferrer*) (NLP)
May 1998-	Miguel Rodríguez Echeverría (USCP)

NLP = National Liberation Party
NUP = National Unification Party
UOP = United Oppostion Party
USCP = United Social Christian Party

CÔTE D'IVOIRE (IVORY COAST)

Official name: Republic of Côte d'Ivoire, République de Côte d'Ivoire
Independence date: 7 August 1960
Capital: Abidjan (until 1983), Yamoussoukro (since 1983)

In 1842 France concluded treaties with villages along the Ivory Coast, and in 1889 the first French resident was appointed, followed in 1893 by the first French governor. In 1904 the Ivory Coast became part of French West Africa. Its status was changed from that of a colony to an overseas territory in 1946. Self-government was granted in 1959 and independence in 1960. A multi-party system was introduced in 1990.

Lieutenant-Governors:

1893-95	Louis-Gustave Binger
1895-96	Pierre Pascal
1896	Eugène Berlin
1896-98	Louis Mottet
1898-99	Adrien Bonhoure
1899-1902	Henri Roberdeau
1902-08	Marie-François Clozel
1908-16	Gabriel-Louis Angoulvant
1916-18	Maurice-Pierre Lapalud (1st)
1918-24	Raphaël Antonetti (see French Soudan)
1924-25	Richard Brunot
1925-30	Maurice-Pierre Lapalud (2nd)
1930	Jules Brévié
1931-35	Dieudonné Reste (see Chad)
1935-36	Adolphe Deitte (see Ubangui-Chari)
1936-37	Gaston Mondou

Governors:

1937-39	Gaston Mondou
1939-41	Horace Crocicchia
1941-42	Hubert-Jules Deschamps (see French Somaliland)
1942-43	Georges-Pierre Rey (see Senegal)
1943-47	André Latrille
1947-48	Oswald Durand
1948	Georges Orselli (see Martinique)
1948-51	Laurent-Élisée Pechoux
1951-52	Pierre-François Pelieu

1952-54 Camille-Victor Bailly
1954-56 Pierre Messmer (see Mauritania & France)
1956-57 Pierre Lami
1957-58 Ernest de Nattes

High Commissioners:

1959 Ernest de Nattes
1959-60 Yves Guena

Presidents:

Aug 1960-Dec 1993 Félix Houphouët-Boigny (DPCI) (†)
Dec 1993-Dec 1999 Henri Konan-Bédié (DPCI) (deposed)
Dec 1999 Robert Guéi

Prime Ministers:

July 1958-May 1959 Auguste Denise
May 1959-Aug 1960 Félix Houphouët-Boigny
(Aug 1960-Nov 1990 post abolished)
Nov 1990-Dec 1993 Alassane Ouattara
Dec 1993-Dec 1999 Daniel Kablan-Duncan
Dec 1999- post abolished)

DPCI = Democratic Party of Côte d'Ivoire (sole legal party until 1990)

CROATIA

Official name: Republic of Croatia, Republika Hrvatska
Previous names: Independent Croat State 1941-45, Socialist Republic of Croatia 1945-90 (as part of Yugoslavia)
Independence date: 25 June 1991
Capital: Zagreb

Croatia was united with Hungary in 1091 and remained under Hungarian domination until 1918 when it became part of the new state of Yugoslavia. In 1941 when Yugoslavia was occupied by Germany Croatia became nominally independent under German control. In 1945, a communist republic was proclaimed in Yugoslavia and Croatia became one of the constituent republics. When multi-party elections were held in 1990 a non-communist government was elected. Independence was declared in 1991. This was followed by civil strife as Serbs in the republic, supported by Yugoslav federal forces, fought against the Croat government and proclaimed their own state. In 1995 most of this territory was forcibly re-incorporated.

Head of State:

April 1941-May 1945	Ante Pavelić
(May 1941	Tomislav, nominated as king but never enthroned)

Presidents:

President of the People's Assembly 1945-74
President of the State Presidency 1974-90

1945-49	Vladimir Nazor
1949-52	Karlo-Gaspar Mrazović
1952-53	Vicko Krutulović
1953	Zlatan Sremec
1953-63	Vladimir Bakarić
1963-74	Ivan Krajaćić
May 1974-May 1982	Jakov Blažević
May 1982-May 1983	Marijan Cvetković
May 1983-May 1984	Milutin Baltić
May 1984-May 1985	Jaksa Petrić
May-Nov 1985	Pero Car (†)
Nov 1985-May 1986	Ema Derosi-Bjelajac
May 1986-May 1988	Ante Marković (see Yugoslavia)
May 1988-May 1990	Ivo Latin
May 1990-Dec 1990	Franjo Tudjman (CDU) (incapacitated Nov 1999) (†)
Dec 1990-Feb 2000	Vlatko Pavetić (acting)

2-18 Feb 2000	Zlatho Tomćić (acting)
Feb 2000-	Stjepan (Stipe) Mesić (CCP)

Prime Ministers:

President of the Executive Council 1945-90

April 1941-Sept 1943	Ante Pavelić
Sept 1943-April 1945	Nikola Mandić
April 1945-Dec 1953	Vladimir Bakarić
Dec 1953-July 1962	Jakov Blažević
July 1962-June 1963	Zvonko Brkić
June 1963-May 1967	Mika Špiljak
May 1967-May 1969	Savka Dabčević-Kućar
May 1969-Dec 1971	Dragutin Haramija
Dec 1971-May 1974	Ivo Perisin
May 1974-April 1978	Jakov Sirotković
April 1978-May 1982	Petar Fleković
May 1982-May 1986	Ante Marković
May 1986-May 1990	Ante Milović
May-Aug 1990	Stjepan (Stipe) Mesić (CDU) (see Yugoslavia)
Aug 1990-Aug 1991	Josip Manolić (CDU)
Aug 1991-Aug 1992	Franjo Gregurović
Aug 1992-March 1993	Hrovje Sarinić
March 1993-Nov 1995	Nikica Valentić (CDU)
Nov 1995-Jan 2000	Zlatko Mateša (CDU)
Jan 2000-	Ivaca Račan (SDP)

CDU = Croatian Democratic Union
CDP = Croat People's Party
SDP = Social Democratic Party

Communist Party Leaders:

1945-47	Djuro Špoljarić
1948-68	Vladimir Bakarić
1969-Dec 1971	Savka Dabčević-Kućar
Dec 1971-May 1982	Milka Planinc (see Yugoslavia)
May 1982-May 1983	Jure Bilić
May 1983-May 1984	Josip Vrhovec
May 1984-May 1986	Mika Špiljak (see Yugoslavia)
May 1986-May 1990	Stanko Stojćević
(May 1990	non-communist government elected)

Republic

The Serb community in Croatia declared their own republic after Croatia became independent. In 1995 Croatian troops overran most of the area.

KRAJINA

Republic of Serbian Krajina
Autonomy declared: 28 February 1991
Republic declared: 19 December 1991
Capital: Knin

Presidents:

Dec 1991-Feb 1992	Milan Babić
Feb 1992-Jan 1994	Goran Hadzić
Jan 1994-Aug 1995	Milan Martić

Prime Ministers:

June-Dec 1991	Milan Babić (1st)
Dec 1991-March 1993	Zdravko Zečević
March 1993-April 1994	Djordje Bjegović
April 1994-May 1995	Borislav Mikelić
June-Aug 1995	Milan Babić (2nd)

CUBA

Official name: Republic of Cuba, República de Cuba
Independence date: 10 December 1898
Capital: Havana (Habana)

Cuba was a Spanish colony from 1511 until 1898 when Spanish rule was overthrown. A republic was proclaimed in 1901, but the country was soon under American occupation until independence was restored in 1909. The revolutionary movement against the Batista dictatorship achieved power on 1 January 1959, and established a Marxist regime.

Governors:

Jan-Dec 1899	John Brooke
Dec 1899-May 1902	Leonard Wood

President:

May 1902-Sept 1906	Tomás Estrada Palma

Governors:

Sept-Oct 1906	William Taft
Oct 1906-Jan 1909	Charles Magoon

Presidents:
President of the State Council since 1976

Jan 1909-May 1913	José Gómez
May 1913-May 1921	Mario García Menocal
May 1921-May 1925	Alfredo Zayas y Alfonso
May 1925-Aug 1933	Gerardo Machado y Morales (deposed)
12 Aug 1933	Alberto Herrera y Franch
Aug-Sept 1933	Carlos de Céspedes y Quesada (deposed)
Sept 1933-Jan 1934	Ramón Grau San Martin (1st)
15-17 Jan 1934	Carlos Hevia (acting)
Jan 1934-Dec 1935	Carlos Mendieta
Dec 1935-May 1936	José Barnet y Vinageras
May-Dec 1936	Miguel Gómez y Arias (*son of J.Gómez*)
Dec 1936-Oct 1940	Federico Laredo Bru
Oct 1940-Oct 1944	Fulgencio Batista y Zaldívar (1st)
Oct 1944-Oct 1948	Ramón Grau San Martin (2nd)
Oct 1948-March 1952	Carlos Prio Socarras (deposed)

March 1952-Jan 1959	Fulgencio Batista y Zaldívar (2nd) (deposed)
(1958/59	Andrés Rivero Agüero President-elect; did not assume office)
1-2 Jan 1959	Carlos Piedra (acting)
Jan-July 1959	Manuel Urrutia Lleo
July 1959-Dec 1976	Osvaldo Dorticós Torrado
Dec 1976-	Fidel Castro Ruz

Prime Ministers:
Chairman of the Council of Ministers since 1976

Nov 1940-June 1942	Carlos Saladrigas y Zayas
June 1942-March 1944	Ramón Zaydin y Marquez Sterling
March-Oct 1944	Anselmo Alliegro y Milá
Oct 1944-Oct 1945	Felix Lancís Sánchez (1st)
Oct 1945-April 1947	Carlos Prio Socarras
April 1947-Oct 1948	Raúl López del Castillo
Oct 1948-Oct 1950	Manuel de Varona y Loredo
Oct 1950-March 1951	Felix Lancís Sánchez (2nd)
March 1951-March 1952	Oscar Gans y Martínez
(March 1952-Feb 1955	post abolished)
Feb 1955-March 1957	Jorge García Montes
March 1957-March 1958	Andrés Rivero Agüero
6-12 March 1958	Emilio Núñez Portuondo
March 1958-Jan 1959	Gonzalo Güell y Morales
Jan-Feb 1959	José Miro Cardono
Feb 1959-	Fidel Castro Ruz

Communist Party Leader:
First Secretary of the Central Committee

Oct 1965-	Fidel Castro Ruz

CYPRUS

Official name: Republic of Cyprus, Kypriaki Dimokratia, Kibris Cumhuriyeti
Independence date: 16 August 1960
Capital: Nicosia (Lefkosia)

Cyprus was captured from the Venetians by the Turks in 1571 and remained under Turkish rule until 1878 when administration was ceded to Britain. In 1914 Cyprus was annexed by Britain and it became a crown colony in 1925. Independence was granted in 1960. Communal disturbances between the Greek and Turkish populations began in 1963 and a United Nations peace-keeping force was sent in. In 1974 President Makarios was deposed in a coup backed by Greece. Turkey then invaded and occupied the northern area. Later that year Makarios returned to power, and in 1975 the Turks proclaimed an autonomous state in the north. In 1983 this state declared itself independent, but is recognised only by Turkey.

Governors:

1925-26	Malcolm Stevenson
1926-32	Ronald Storrs
1932-33	Reginald Stubbs
1933-39	Herbert Palmer
1939-41	William Battershill
1941-46	Charles Wooley
1946-49	Baron Winster (Reginald Fletcher)
1949-53	Andrew Wright (see Gambia)
1953-55	Robert Armitage
1955-58	John Harding
1958-60	Hugh Foot (see Jamaica)

Presidents:

Aug 1960-July 1974	Archbishop Makarios III (*b* Michael Mouskos) (1st) (deposed)
15-23 July 1974	Nikos Sampson
July-Dec 1974	Glafkos Clerides (acting)
Dec 1974-Aug 1977	Archbishop Makarios III (2nd) (†)
Aug 1977-Feb 1988	Spyros Kyprianou (DP)
Feb 1988-Feb 1993	Georgios Vassiliou
Feb 1993-	Glafkos Clerides (DR)

DP = Democratic Party
DR = Democratic Rally

Secessionist state

NORTHERN CYPRUS

Official name: Turkish Republic of Northern Cyprus, Kuzey Kibris Türk Cumhuriyeti
Previous name: Turkish Cypriot Federated State 1975-83
Independence date: 15 November 1983 (recognised only by Turkey)
Capital: Nicosia (Lefkosa)

President:

Feb 1975-	Rauf Denktaş

Prime Ministers:

July 1976-April 1978	Nejat Konuk (1st)
April-Dec 1978	Osman Örek
Dec 1978-Dec 1983	Mustapha Cağatay (NUP)
Dec 1983-July 1985	Nejat Konuk (2nd)
July 1985-Jan 1994	Derviş Eroğlu (1st) (NUP)
Jan 1994-Aug 1996	Hakki Atun (DP)
Aug 1996-	Derviş Eroğlu (2nd) (NUP)

DP = Democratic Party
NUP = National Unity Party

CZECH REPUBLIC

Official name: Czech Republic, Česká Republika
Previous name: Czech Socialist Republic 1969-90 (as part of Czechoslovakia)
Independence date: 1 January 1993
Capital: Prague (Praha)

Bohemia was an independent state from the 9th century, becoming a kingdom in the 12th. From the 16th century it was ruled by the Habsburgs and gradually became part of the Austro-Hungarian Empire until 1918, when an independent Czechoslovak republic was established. In 1939 Czechoslovakia was invaded by Germany and divided into two parts, the protectorate of Bohemia-Moravia and a nominally independent Slovakia. After liberation in 1945 Czechoslovakia was reconstituted. In 1948 it became a people's republic. In 1968 efforts to liberalise the society were ended by an invasion of Soviet led forces. Popular pressure 21 years later forced the communists to introduce a multi-party system. Nationalist forces in Slovakia called for greater autonomy, resulting in the dissolution of the federation at the end of 1992.

President:

Feb 1993-	Václav Havel (see Czechoslovakia)

Prime Ministers:

Jan-Sept 1969	Stanislav Razl
Sept 1969-Jan 1970	Josef Kempný
Jan 1970-March 1987	Josef Korčák
March 1987-Oct 1988	Ladislav Adamec (see Czechoslovakia)
Oct 1988-Feb 1990	František Pitra
Feb 1990-July 1992	Petr Pithárt
July 1992-Jan 1998	Václav Klaus (CDP)
Jan-July 1998	Josef Tošovský
July 1998-	Miloš Zeman (SDP)

CDP = Civic Democratic Party
SDP = Social Democratic Party

Former Independent States

BOHEMIA

Capital: Prague

Kings:

1198-Dec 1230	Premsyl Otakar I

Dec 1230-1253	Václav I (*son*)
1253-Aug 1278	Premsyl Otakar II (*son*)
Aug 1278-1305	Václav II (*son*) (Wacław I of Poland)
1305-06	Václav III (*son*) (Wacław II of Poland) (assassinated)
(1306-10	interregnum)
1310-Aug 1346	Ján (*son-in-law of Václav II*)
Aug 1346-Nov 1378	Karel (*son*)
Nov 1378-Aug 1419	Václav IV (*son*)
Aug 1419-1437	Sigismund (*son*) (also King of Hungary)
1437-39	Albrekt (Albert of Hungary)
(1439-43	interregnum)
1443-Nov 1457	Vladislav II (Ladislaus of Austria)
(Nov 1457-March 1458	interregnum)
March 1458-March 1471	Jiří
May 1469-May 1471	Matej I (Mátyás of Hungary) (rival king)
May 1471-March 1516	Vladislav III (Ulászló of Hungary)
March 1516-Aug 1526	Ludvik (Lajos II of Hungary)
(Aug-Oct 1526	interregnum)
Oct 1526-July 1564	Ferdinand I (Ferdinand I of Austria)
July 1564-Oct 1576	Maximilian (Maximilian II of Austria)
Oct 1576-May 1611	Rudolf (Rudolf II of Austria)
May 1611-1617	Matej II (Matthias of Austria)
1617-Aug 1619	Ferdinand II (Ferdinand II of Austria) (deposed)
Aug 1619-Nov 1620	Frederik (fled)
(Nov 1620-Oct 1918	Archdukes/Emperors of Austria)

CZECHOSLOVAKIA

Official names: Czechoslovak Republic 1918-39 & 1945-48, Czechoslovak People's Republic 1948-60, Czechoslovak Socialist Republic 1960-90, Czech and Slovak Federative Republic 1990-92
Independence date: 28 October 1918
Dissolution date: 31 December 1992
Capital: Prague

Presidents:

Nov 1918-Dec 1935	Tomás Masaryk
Dec 1935-Oct 1938	Edvard Beneš (1st)
Oct-Nov 1938	Ján Syrový (acting)
Nov 1938-March 1939	Emil Hácha
(1939-45	German occupation)
March 1945-June 1948	Edvard Beneš (2nd) (in Košice March-May 1945)
June 1948-March 1953	Klement Gottwald (†)
March 1953-Nov 1957	Antonín Zápotocký (†)
Nov 1957-March 1968	Antonín Novotný

March 1968-May 1975   Ludvik Svoboda
May 1975-Dec 1989   Gustáv Husak   (see Slovakia)
Dec 1989-July 1992   Václav Havel   (CF)
(July-Dec 1992   post vacant)

Prime Ministers:

Oct 1918-July 1919	Karel Kramář
July 1918-Sept 1920	Vlastimil Tusar (SDP)
Sept 1920-Sept 1921	Ján Černý (1st)
Sept 1921-Oct 1922	Edvard Beneš (NSP)
Oct 1922-March 1926	Antonín Švehla (1st) (CAP)
March-Oct 1926	Ján Černý (2nd)
Oct 1926-Feb 1929	Antonín Švehla (2nd) (CAP)
Feb 1929-Oct 1932	František Udržal (CAP)
Oct 1932-Nov 1935	Ján Malypetr (CPP)
Nov 1935-Sept 1938	Milan Hodža (SAP)
Sept-Dec 1938	Ján Syrový
Dec 1938-March 1939	Rudolf Beran (AP)
(1939-45	German occupation)
March-April 1945	Ján Sramek (in Košice)
April 1945-June 1946	Zdenek Fierlinger (SP) (in Košice April-May 1945)
June 1946-June 1948	Klement Gottwald (CP)
June 1948-March 1953	Antonín Zápotocký (CP)
March 1953-Sept 1963	Vilem Široký (CP)
Sept 1963-April 1968	Jozef Lénart (CP)
April 1968-Jan 1970	Oldřich Černik (CP)
Jan 1970-Oct 1988	Lubomír Štrougal (CP)
Oct 1988-Dec 1989	Ladislav Adamec (see Czech Republic) (CP)
Dec 1989-July 1992	Marián Čalfa (CP,PAV,CDU)
July-Dec 1992	Jan Stráský (CDP)

Communist Party Leaders:

First Secretary 1948-May 1971
General Secretary May 1971-89

Feb 1948-March 1953	Klement Gottwald (†)
March 1953-Jan 1968	Antonín Novotný
Jan 1968-April 1969	Alexander Dubček (see Slovakia)
April 1969-Dec 1987	Gustáv Husák (see Slovakia)
Dec 1987-Nov 1989	Miloš Jakeš
Nov-Dec 1989	Karel Urbánek
(Dec 1989	Party relinquished leading role)

AP = Agrarian Party
CAP = Czech Agrarian Party
CDP = Civic Democratic Party (*f* CF)

CDU = Civic Democratic Union (f PAV)
CF = Civic Forum
CP = Communist Party (dominant role constitutionally defined 1948-89)
CPP = Czech Popular Party
NSP = National Socialist Party
PAV = Public Against Violence
SAP = Slovakian Agrarian Party
SDP = Social Democratic Party
SP = Socialist Party

GOVERNMENT-IN-EXILE 1940-45

Headquarters: London
Operated during German occupation

President:

July 1940-March 1945	Edvard Beneš

Prime Minister:

July 1940-March 1945	Ján Sramek

German Protectorate

BOHEMIA-MORAVIA

Capital: Prague

Commissioners:

March 1939-Sept 1941	Konstantin Neurath
Sept 1941-May 1942	Reinhard Heydrich
May 1942-Sept 1943	Kurt Daluege
Sept 1943-May 1945	Wilhelm Frick

Prime Ministers:

April 1939-Sept 1941	Alois Elíaš
(Sept 1941-Jan 1942	post vacant)
Jan 1942-Jan 1945	Jaroslav Krejči
Jan-May 1945	Rudolf Bienert

Autonomous Regions of Czechoslovakia 1938-39

BOHEMIA

Capital: Prague

Prime Minister:

Dec 1938-March 1939　　　　　Rudolf Beran　(see Czechoslovakia)

CARPATHO-UKRAINE

Former names: Ruthenia until 1938, Carpatho-Russia 1938-39
Capital: Khusht

Prime Ministers:

11-26 Oct 1938	Andreas Brody
Oct 1938-March 1939	Augustin Voloshin
15-16 March 1939	Julius Révay
(1939-45	Occupied by Hungary)
(1945	Transferred to Ukraine)

SLOVAKIA - see separate entry

DENMARK

Official name: Kingdom of Denmark, Kongeriget Danmark
State founded: 10th century
Capital: Roskilde until 1443, Copenhagen (København)

The Kingdom of Denmark emerged during the 10th century. During the 14th and 15th centuries, Denmark, Norway, and Sweden were ruled by the same monarchs, and from 1481 to Sweden shared a sovereign. During World War II Denmark was occupied by Germany, the king and his government were left alone but did not exercise authority between 1943 and 1945.

Kings/Queens:

c900-940	Gorm
940-85	Harald I Blaatland (*son*)
985-1014	Svend I (*son*) (Sweyn of England)
1014-19	Harald II Svendsen (*son*)
1019-35	Knud I (*brother*) (Canute of England)
Nov 1035-June 1042	Hardeknud (*son*) (Hardicanute of England)
June 1042-Oct 1047	Magnus
Oct 1047-April 1074	Svend II Estridsen (*grandson of Svend I*)
April 1074-April 1080	Harald III (*son*)
April 1080-July 1086	Knud II (*brother*)
July 1086-Aug 1095	Olav I (*brother*)
Aug 1095-June 1103	Erik I (*brother*)
1104-34	Niels (*brother*) (assassinated)
1134-Sept 1137	Erik II (*son of Erik I*)
Sept 1137-Aug 1146	Erik III (*grandson of Erik I*)
Aug 1146-1157	Svend III (*son of Erik II*)
1157	Knud III (*grandson of Niels*)
1157-May 1182	Valdemar I (*grandson of Erik I*)
May 1182-Nov 1202	Knud IV Valdemarsen (*son*)
Nov 1202-March 1241	Valdemar II (*brother*)
March 1241-Aug 1250	Erik IV (*son*) (assassinated)
Aug 1250-June 1252	Abel (*brother*)
June 1252-May 1259	Christoffer I (*brother*)
May 1259-Nov 1286	Erik V Klipping (*son*)
Nov 1286-Nov 1319	Erik VI Maendved (*son*)
1320-Aug 1332	Christoffer II (*brother*) (deposed)
(Aug 1332-June 1340	Interregnum)
June 1340-Oct 1375	Valdemar IV (*son*)

1376-Aug 1387	Olav I (*grandson*) (Olav IV of Norway) (Regent: 1376-87 Margrethe)
Aug 1387-89	Margrethe I (*mother*) (also Queen of Norway & Sweden)
1389-Oct 1439	Erik VII (*grand-nephew*) (Erik III of Norway, Erik XIII of Sweden) (deposed)
1439-Jan 1448	Christoffer III (*nephew*) (also King of Norway & Sweden)
Jan 1448-May 1481	Christian I (also King of Sweden)
May 1481-Feb 1513	Hans (Johann II of Sweden)
Feb 1513-April 1523	Christian II (*son*) (Christian I of Sweden) (deposed)
April 1523-April 1533	Frederik I (*uncle*)
(April 1533-April 1536	Interregnum)
April 1536-Jan 1559	Christian III (*son*)
Jan 1559-April 1588	Frederik II (*son*)
April 1588-Feb 1648	Christian IV (*son*)
Feb 1648-Feb 1670	Frederik III (*son*)
Feb 1670-Aug 1699	Christian V (*son*)
Aug 1699-Oct 1730	Frederik IV (*son*)
Oct 1730-Aug 1746	Christian VI (*son*)
Aug 1746-Jan 1766	Frederik V (*son*)
Jan 1766-March 1808	Christian VII (*son*)
March 1808-Dec 1839	Frederik VI (*son*)
Dec 1839-Jan 1848	Christian VIII (*son*)
Jan 1848-Nov 1863	Frederik VII (*son*)
Nov 1863-Jan 1906	Christian IX
Jan 1906-May 1912	Frederik VIII (*son*)
May 1912-April 1947	Christian X (*son*)
April 1947-Feb 1972	Frederik IX (*son*)
Feb 1972-	Margrethe II (*daughter*)

Prime Ministers:

March 1848-Jan 1852	Adam Moltke
Jan 1852-April 1853	Christian Bluhme (1st)
April 1853-Dec 1854	Andreas Orsted
Dec 1854-Oct 1856	Peter Bang
Oct 1856-May 1857	Carl Andrae
May 1857-Dec 1859	Carl Hall (1st)
Dec 1859-Feb 1860	Carl Rotwitt
Feb 1860-Dec 1863	Carl Hall (2nd)
Dec 1863-July 1864	Ditlev Monrad
July 1864-Nov 1865	Christian Bluhme (2nd)
Nov 1865-May 1870	Christian Frijs
May 1870-July 1874	Ludvig Holstein
July 1874-June 1875	Christian Fonnesbeck
June 1875-Aug 1894	Jacob Estrup

Aug 1894-May 1897	Tage Reedtz-Thott
May 1897-April 1900	Hugo Hørring
April 1900-July 1901	Hannibal Sehested
July 1901-Jan 1905	Johan Deuntzer
Jan 1905-Oct 1908	Jens Christensen
Oct 1908-Aug 1909	Niels Neergaard (1st) (LP)
Aug-Oct 1909	Johan Holstein
Oct 1909-July 1910	Carl Zahle (1st) (RP)
July 1910-June 1913	Klaus Bernstein
June 1913-March 1920	Carl Zahle (2nd) (RP)
March-April 1920	Otto Liebe
April-May 1920	Michael Friis
May 1920-April 1924	Niels Neergaard (2nd) (LP)
April 1924-Dec 1926	Thorvald Stauning (1st) (SDP)
Dec 1926-April 1929	Thomas Madsen-Mygdal (LP)
April 1929-May 1942	Thorvald Stauning (2nd) (SDP) (†)
May-Nov 1942	Vilhelm Buhl (1st) (SDP)
Nov 1942-May 1945	Erik Scavenius (SDP) (ceased to exercise authority from Aug 1943)
May-Nov 1945	Vilhelm Buhl (2nd) (SDP)
Nov 1945-Nov 1947	Knud Kristensen (AP)
Nov 1947-Oct 1950	Hans Hedtoft (1st) (SDP)
Oct 1950-Sept 1953	Erik Eriksen (AP)
Sept 1953-Feb 1955	Hans Hedtoft (2nd) (SDP)
Feb 1955-Feb 1960	Hans Hansen (SDP) (†)
Feb 1960-Sept 1962	Viggo Kampmann (SDP)
Sept 1962-Feb 1968	Jens-Otto Krag (1st) (SDP)
Feb 1968-Oct 1971	Hilmar Baunsgaard (RP)
Oct 1971-Oct 1972	Jens-Otto Krag (2nd) (SDP)
Oct 1972-Dec 1973	Anker Jørgensen (1st) (SDP)
Dec 1973-Feb 1975	Poul Hartling (LP)
Feb 1975-Sept 1982	Anker Jørgensen (2nd) (SDP)
Sept 1982-Jan 1993	Poul Schlüter (CP)
Jan 1993-	Poul Nyrup Rasmussen (SDP)

AP = Agrarian Party
CP = Conservative Party
LP = Liberal Party
RP = Radical Party
SDP = Social Democratic Party

Territories

FAROE ISLANDS

Foroyar (Faroese), Faerøerne (Danish)

Capital: Thorshavn

Commissioners:

1972-81	Leif Groth
1981-89	Niels Bentsen
1989-95	Bent Klinte
1995-	Vibeke Larsen

Prime Ministers:

May 1948-Dec 1950	Andreas Samuelsen (UP)
Dec 1950-Jan 1959	Kristian Djurhuus (1st) (UP)
Jan 1959-Jan 1963	Peter Mohr Dam (1st) (SDP)
Jan 1963-Jan 1967	Hakun Djurhuus (PP)
Jan 1967-Nov 1968	Peter Mohr Dam (2nd) (SDP) (†)
Nov 1968-Dec 1970	Kristian Djurhuus (2nd) (UP)
Dec 1970-Jan 1981	Atli Dam (1st) (SDP)
Jan 1981-Dec 1984	Pauli Ellefsen (UP)
Dec 1984-Jan 1989	Atli Dam (2nd) (SDP)
Jan 1989-Nov 1990	Jogvan Sundstein (PP)
Nov 1990-Jan 1993	Atli Dam (3rd) (SDP)
Jan 1993-Sept 1994	Marita Petersen (SDP)
Sept 1994-May 1998	Edmund Joensen (UP)
May 1998-	Anfinn Kallsberg (PP)

PP = People's Party
SDP = Social Democratic Party
UP = Union Party

GREENLAND

Kalâtdlit-Nunat (Greenlandic), Grønland (Danish)
Capital: Nûk (Godthaab)

Governors:

June 1950-Sept 1960	Poul Lundsteen
Sept 1960-June 1963	Finn Nielsen
June 1963-Dec 1972	Niels Christensen
Jan 1973-May 1979	Hans Lassen

Commissioners:

May 1979-92	Torben Pedersen

1992-95	Steen Spore
1995-	Gunnar Martens

Prime Ministers:

May 1979-March 1991	Jonathan Motzfeldt	(1st)	(FP)
March 1991-Sept 1997	Lars Emil Johansen		(FP)
Sept 1997-	Jonathan Motzfeldt	(2nd)	(FP)

FP = Forward Party (Siumut)

DJIBOUTI

Official name: Republic of Djibouti, Jamhuriya Djibouti
Previous names: French Somaliland until 1967, French Territory of the Afars and the Issas 1967-77
Independence date: 27 June 1977
Capital: Djibouti

The French established themselves in the town of Obock in 1862 and a French colony was formed in 1888. French Somaliland became an overseas territory in 1946. Self-government was granted in 1967, and in 1977 Djibouti became an independent republic.

Governors:

1887-99	Antoine Lagarde
1899-1900	Alfred-Albert Martineau
1900-04	Adrien Binhoure (1st)
1904-13	Pierre Pascal
1913-15	Adrien Bonhoure
1915-16	Paul Simoni
1916-18	Victor-Marie Fillon
1918-24	Jules Lauret
1924-34	Pierre Chapon-Baissac
1934-35	Jules-Marcel de Coppet (see Dahomey)
1935-36	Achille Silvestre
1936-37	Armand-Léon Annet
1937-38	Marie-François Alype
1938-40	Hubert-Jules Deschamps
1940	Gaëtan Germain
1940-42	Pierre Nouailhetas
1942	Christian-Raimond Dupont
1942-43	Ange Bayardelle
1943-44	Michel Saller
1944-46	Jean Chalvet
1946-50	Paul-Henri Siriex
1950-54	Numa Sadoul (see French Congo)
1954	Roland Pré (see Upper Volta)
1954-57	Jean Petitbon
1957-58	Maurice Meker
1958-62	Jacques Compain
1962-66	René Tirant (see Dahomey)
Sept 1966-67	Louis Saget (see Comoros)

High Commissioners:

1967-69	Louis Saget
Feb 1969-Aug 1971	Dominique Ponchardier
Aug 1971-Dec 1974	Georges Thiercy
Dec 1974-Feb 1976	Christian Dablanc
Feb 1976-June 1977	Camille d'Ornano

Presidents:

June 1977-May 1999	Hassan Gouled Aptidon (APLI,PRP)
May 1999-	Ismael Omar Gelleh *(nephew)* (PRP)

Prime Ministers:

July 1967-July 1976	Ali Aref Bourhan (ADR)
July 1976-May 1977	Abdullah Kamil (1st)
May-July 1977	Hassan Gouled Aptidon (APLI)
July-Dec 1977	Ahmed Dini Ahmed
Dec 1977-Jan 1978	Hassan Gouled Aptidon (acting)
Jan-Sept 1978	Abdullah Kamil (2nd)
Sept 1978-	Barkhat Gourad Hamadou

ADR = Afar Democratic Regrouping
APLI = African People's League for Independence
PRP = Popular Rally for Progress (*f* APLI, sole legal party 1981-92)

DOMINICA

Official name: Commonwealth of Dominica
Independence date: 3 November 1978
Capital: Roseau

Dominica was discovered by Columbus but the first European settlers were French. In 1763 the island was ceded to Britain, but this remained disputed until 1805, when British control was ratified. In 1960 Dominica was granted a measure of self- government, and from 1958 until 1962 it was a member of the West Indies Federation. In 1967 Dominica became an Associated State of the UK until 1978 when full independence was granted.

Administrators:

1895-99	Philip Templer
1899-1905	Hugh Bell
1905-13	William Young
1914	Edward Drayton
1915-19	Arthur Mahaffy
1919-23	Robert Walter
1923-30	Edward Eliot
1931-33	Walter Bowring
1933-37	Henry Popham
1938-45	James Neill
1946-52	Edwin Arrowsmith (see Turks & Caicos)
1952-59	Henry Lindo
1959-65	Alec Lovelace (see Antigua)
1965-67	Geoffrey Guy (see Turks & Caicos)

Governors:

March-Nov 1967	Geoffrey Guy
Nov 1967-Nov 1978	Louis Cools-Lartigue

Presidents:

Nov-Dec 1978	Louis Cools-Lartigue (acting) (1st)
Dec 1978-June 1979	Frederick Degazon
15-16 June 1979	Louis Cools-Lartigue (acting) (2nd)
June 1979-Feb 1980	Jenner Armour (acting)
Feb 1980-Dec 1983	Aurelius Marie
Dec 1983-Oct 1993	Clarence Seignoret
Oct 1993-Oct 1998	Crispin Sorhaindo

Oct 1998-   Vernon Shaw

Chief Ministers:

Jan 1960-Jan 1961   Frank Barron   (DUPP)
Jan 1961-March 1967   Edward LeBlanc   (DLP)

Prime Ministers:

Premier 1967-78

March 1967-July 1974   Edward LeBlanc   (DLP)
July 1974-June 1979   Patrick John   (DLP)
June 1979-July 1980   Oliver Seraphine   (DLPD)
July 1980-June 1995   M.Eugenia Charles   (DFP)
June 1995-Feb 2000   Edison James   (UWP)
Feb 2000-   Roosevelt (Rosie) Douglas   (DLP)

DLPD = Democratic Labour Party of Dominica
DFP = Dominica Freedom Party
DLP = Dominica Labour Party
DUPP = Dominica United People's Party
UWP = United Workers' Party

DOMINICAN REPUBLIC

Official name: Dominican Republic, República Dominicana
Independence dates: 1 December 1821 and 27 February 1844
Capital: Santo Domingo (known as Ciudad Trujillo 1936-61)

The Dominican Republic occupies the eastern portion of the island of Hispaniola which was discovered by Columbus in 1492. Until 1795 it was a Spanish colony, then it was ceded to France, occupied by Haiti (1801-5) and by France (1805-9) before returning to Spanish rule. In 1821 it declared itself independent, but was soon occupied again by Haiti. Independence was regained in 1844, but the country was briefly occupied by Spain (1861-5). The USA intervened militarily from 1916 to 1924. Recent history was dominated by the Trujillo dictatorship (1930- 61), the civil war of 1965 and the return to democracy in 1966.

Presidents:

Dec 1821-Feb 1822	José Núñez de Cáceres
(Feb 1822-Feb 1844	Haitian occupation)
Feb 1844-Nov 1848	Pedro Santana (1st)
Nov 1848-May 1849	Manuel Jiménez
May-Sept 1849	Pedro Santana (2nd)
Sept 1849-Feb 1853	Buenaventura Baéz (1st)
Feb 1853-June 1856	Pedro Santana (3rd)
June-Oct 1856	Manuel de Regla-Motta
Oct 1856-June 1858	Buenaventura Baéz (2nd) (deposed)
June 1858-Jan 1859	José Valverde
Jan 1859-May 1861	Pedro Santana (4th)
(May 1861-May 1865	Spanish occupation)
May-Nov 1865	Pedro Pimental
Nov 1865	José Cabral (1st)
Nov 1865-June 1866	Buenaventura Baéz (3rd)
June 1866-May 1868	José Cabral (2nd)
May 1868-Dec 1873	Buenaventura Baéz (4th) (deposed)
Jan 1874	Ganier d'Abin (acting)
Jan 1874-Feb 1876	Ignacio González (1st)
Feb-Nov 1876	Ulises Espaillat (acting Feb-June 1876)
Nov-Dec 1876	Ignacio González (2nd)
Dec 1876-Feb 1878	Buenaventura Baéz (5th)
April 1878-Dec 1879	Cesáreo Guillermo
Dec 1879-Oct 1880	Gregorio Luperón
Oct 1880-Sept 1884	Fernando de Merino
Sept 1884-Sept 1885	Ulises Heureaux (1st)
Sept 1885-Sept 1887	Francisco Billini

Sept 1887-July 1889   Ulises Heureaux   (2nd) († assassinated)
1-31 Aug 1889   Juan Figuereo
Aug-Nov 1889   Horacio Vásquez   (1st)
Nov 1889-May 1902   Juan Jiménez   (1st) (deposed)
May 1902-March 1903   Horacio Vásquez   (2nd) (deposed)
April-Nov 1903   Alejandro Wos y Gil   (deposed)
Dec 1903-April 1904   Juan Jiménez   (2nd)
June 1904-Jan 1906   Carlos Morales Lauguasco
Jan 1906-Nov 1911   Ramón Cáceres   († assassinated)
Dec 1911-Nov 1912   Eladio Victoria
Dec 1912-March 1913   Adolfo Nouel y Bobadilla
April 1913-Aug 1914   José Bordas Valdes
Aug-Dec 1914   Ramón Baéz
Dec 1914-May 1916   Juan Jiménez   (3rd)
May 1916-Oct 1922   Francisco Henriquez y Carvajal
Oct 1922-July 1924   Juan Vicini Burgos
July 1924-Feb 1930   Horacio Vásquez   (3rd)
March-Aug 1930   Rafael Estrella Urena
Aug 1930-June 1938   Rafael Trujillo Molina   (1st)
June 1938-March 1940   Jacinto Peynado   (†)
March 1940-May 1942   Manuel Troncoso de la Concha
May 1942-May 1952   Rafael Trujillo Molina   (2nd) (assassinated 1961)
May 1952-Aug 1960   Héctor Trujillo Molina   (*brother*)
Aug 1960-Jan 1962   Joaquín Balaguer   (1st)
Jan 1962-Feb 1963   Rafael Bonelly
Feb-Sept 1963   Juan Bosch Gaviño   (RDP) (deposed)
Sept-Dec 1963   Emilio dos Santos
Dec 1963-April 1965   Donald Reid Cabral   (deposed)
26 April 1965   José Molina Urena
April-May 1965   Pedro Benoit
May-Sept 1965   Francisco Caamaño Deño*
May-Aug 1965   Antonio Imbert Barreras*
   *rival governments during civil war

Sept 1965-Aug 1966   Héctor García-Godoy Cáceres
Aug 1966-Aug 1978   Joaquín Balaguer   (2nd) (SCRP)
Aug 1978-July 1982   Antonio Guzmán Fernández   (RDP) († suicide)
July-Aug 1982   Jacobo Majluta Azar   (RDP)
Aug 1982-Aug 1986   Salvador Jorge Blanco   (RDP)
Aug 1986-Aug 1996   Joaquín Balaguer   (3rd) (SCRP)
Aug 1996-   Leonel Fernández Reyna   (LP)

LP = Liberation Party
SCRP = Social Christian Reform Party
RDP = Revolutionary Democratic Party

EAST TIMOR

Official name: East Timor

Previous names: Portuguese Timor (until 1975), Democratic People's Republic of Timor (1975-79?), Province of East Timor (1976-99)

Independence date: 28 November 1975

Capital: Dili

Portugal began trading for sandalwood in Timor in c1520. In 1613 the Dutch arrived in the south-west and the Portuguese moved to the north and east. Division of the island between the two colonial powers was settled in 1859. Portugese Timor was administered from Macau until 1894. The western half of the island became part of Netherlands East Indies, later Indonesia. As Portugal began decolonisation after the 1974 coup, conflict between different groups in Timor erupted. A pro-independence force gained control of Dili, and in November 1975 declared independence. In December 1975 Indonesia invaded the territory, annexing it in July 1976. The pro-independence forces operated a rival government until 1979, while conducting a guerilla war. Political changes in Indonesia allowed a referendum in East Timor in 1999, which showed overwhelming support for independence. This was followed by widespread violence. Indonesia accepted a United Nations intervention force and the results of the referendum. A United Nations administration was established to prepare for independence in 2001.

Governors:

1894-1908	José da Silva
1908-09	Eduardo Marques
1910	Alfredo Martins (see Portuguese Guinea)
1911-17	Filomeno Cabral
1919-21	Manuel Gentil
1924-26	Raimundo Meira
1926-28	Teofilo Duarte (see Cape Verde)
1929-30	Cesario Viana
1930-33	António Justo
1933-36	Raul Cruz
1937-39	Alvaro de Fontoura
1940-42	Manuel de Carvalho
(1942-45	Japanese occupation)
1946-50	Oscar Ruas
1950-58	César Rosa
1959-63	Filipe Barata
1963-68	José Correira
1968-73	José Pires
1973-74	Fernando Aldeia

Nov 1974-Nov 1975   Mario Pires

Presidents:

Nov 1975-Sept 1977   Francisco do Amaral   (in Dili Nov-Dec 1975)
Sept 1977-Jan 1979   Nicolau Lobato   († killed in battle)
(1975-99   Indonesian rule)

Prime Ministers:

Nov 1975-Sept 1977   Nicolau Lobato   (in Dili Nov-Dec 1975)
Dec 1975-July 1976   Arnaldo Araújo   (pro-Indonesian government in Dili)
(1976-   post abolished)

Administrator:

Oct 1999-   Sergio Vieira de Mello   (see Kosovo)

ECUADOR

Official name: Republic of Ecuador, República del Ecuador
Independence date: 13 May 1830
Capital: Quito

A Spanish colony was founded in present day Ecuador in 1532. In the early 19th century the colony joined in the revolt against Spain and became part of Greater Colombia in 1819. In 1830 Ecuador became a separate republic. There have been a number of military governments during its history; in 1979 the country returned to democratic rule.

Presidents:

May 1830-Aug 1835	Juan Flores (1st) (deposed)
Aug 1835-Jan 1839	Vicente Rocafuerte
Jan 1839-Dec 1845	Juan Flores (2nd)
Dec 1845-Dec 1850	Vicente Ramón Roca
Dec 1850-Sept 1851	Diego Noboa Arteta (deposed)
Sept 1851-Oct 1856	José Urbina
Oct 1856-Aug 1859	Francisco Robles
Aug 1859-Aug 1865	Gabriel García Morena (1st)
Aug 1865-Dec 1867	Geronimo Carrión
Jan 1868-Aug 1869	Javier Espinosa
Aug 1869-Aug 1875	Gabriel García Moreno (2nd) († assassinated)
Aug 1875-Jan 1877	Antonio Borrero y Cortazar
Jan 1877-Feb 1884	Ignacio de Veintemilla (acting Jan-May 1877)
Feb 1884-July 1888	José Plácido Caamaño
Aug 1888-July 1892	Antonio Flores
Aug 1892-Dec 1896	Luis Cordero
Jan 1897-Sept 1901	Eloy Alfaro (1st)
Sept 1901-Aug 1905	Leonidas Plaza Gutiérrez (1st)
Sept 1905-Jan 1906	Lizardo García (deposed)
Jan 1906-Aug 1911	Eloy Alfaro (2nd) († assassinated)
Aug-Dec 1911	Emilio Estrada (†)
Jan-Feb 1912	Carlos Fraile
Feb-March 1912	Julio Andrade Marín
April 1912-Sept 1916	Leonidas Plaza Gutiérrez (2nd)
Sept 1916-Aug 1920	Alfredo Baquerizo Morena (1st)
Sept 1920-Aug 1924	José Tamayo

Sept 1924-July 1925	Gonzalo Hernández Cordoba (deposed)
July 1925-April 1926	Francisco Gómez de la Torre
April 1926-Aug 1931	Isidro Ayora
Aug-Oct 1931	Luis Larrea Alba (deposed)
Oct 1931-Aug 1932	Alfredo Baquerizo Morena (2nd)
Aug-Sept 1932	Naftalio Bonifaz (acting)
Sept-Dec 1932	Alberto Guerrero Martínez
Dec 1932-Oct 1933	Juan Martínez Mera
Oct 1933-Aug 1934	Abelardo Montalva
Sept 1934-Aug 1935	José Velasco Ibarra (1st) (deposed)
Aug-Sept 1935	Antonio Pons (acting)
Sept 1935-Oct 1937	Federico Páez (deposed)
Oct 1937-Aug 1938	Alberto Enríquez
Aug-Dec 1938	Manuel Borrero
Dec 1938-Nov 1939	Aurelio Mosquero Narváez (†)
Nov-Dec 1939	Carlos Arroyo del Rio (acting)
Dec 1939-Aug 1940	Andrés Cordova
10-31 Aug 1940	Julio Moreno (acting)
Sept 1940-May 1944	Carlos Arroyo del Rio (deposed)
May 1944-Aug 1947	José Velasco Ibarra (2nd) (deposed)
Aug-Sept 1947	Carlos Mancheno (deposed)
3-15 Sept 1947	Mariano Suárez Veintemilla
Sept 1947-Aug 1948	Carlos Arosemena Tola
Sept 1948-Aug 1952	Galo Plaza Lasso (see OAS)
Sept 1952-Aug 1956	José Velasco Ibarra (3rd)
Sept 1956-Aug 1960	Camilo Ponce Enríquez (PA)
Sept 1960-Nov 1961	José Velasco Ibarra (4th) (deposed)
Nov 1961-July 1963	Carlos Arosemena Monroy (*son of C.Arosemena Tola*) (deposed)
July 1963-March 1966	Ramón Castro Jijón (deposed)
March-Nov 1966	Clemente Yerovi Indaburu
Nov 1966-Sept 1968	Otto Arosemena Gómez (DIC)
Sept 1968-Feb 1972	José Velasco Ibarra (5th) (deposed)
Feb 1972-Jan 1976	Guillermo Rodríguez Lara (deposed)
Jan 1976-Aug 1979	Alfredo Poveda Burbano
Aug 1979-May 1981	Jaime Roldós Aguillera († air accident) (PD)
May 1981-Aug 1984	Osvaldo Hurtado Larrea (PD)
Aug 1984-Aug 1988	León Febres Cordero (SCP)
Aug 1988-Aug 1992	Rodrigo Borja Cevellos (DL)
Aug 1992-Aug 1996	Sixto Durán Ballén (SCP)
Aug 1996-Feb 1997	Abdalá Bucaram Ortiz (RP)
8-12 Feb 1997	Rosalia Arteaga
Feb 1997-Aug 1998	Fabián Alarcón Rivera (RAF)
Aug 1998-Jan 2000	Jamil Mahuad Witt (PD) (deposed)
21 Jan 2000	Lucio Gutiérrez
21-22 Jan 2000	Junta: Carlos Mendoza/Antonio Vargas/Carlos Solórzano)

Jan 2000-   Gustavo Noboa Bejarano

DIC = Democratic Institutional Coalition
DL = Democratic Left
PA = Popular Alliance
PD = Popular Democracy
RAF = Radical Alfarista Front
RP = Roldosista Party
SCP = Social Christian Party

EGYPT

Official name: Arab Republic of Egypt, Jamhuriyat Misr al-Arabiya
Previous names: Kingdom of Egypt 1922-53, Republic of Egypt 1953-58, United Arab Republic 1958-71 (with Syria 1958-61)
Independence date: 1 March 1922
Capital: Cairo (Al-Qahirah)

The ancient state of Egypt was formed by the union of Lower and Upper Egypt in c3100 BC, and retained its independence until it became a Roman province in 30 BC. It then came under the Byzantine Roman Empire from the fourth to the seventh century, followed by Islamic rule of several dynasties; in 1517 Egypt came under Turkish rule. It was briefly occupied by France (1798-1805), and then returned to Turkey, but this time under an autonomous Viceroy. In 1882 Britain occupied Egypt, and in 1914 proclaimed it a protectorate. An independent kingdom was proclaimed in 1922. A revolution in 1952 toppled King Farouk, a republic being proclaimed a year later. In 1958 Egypt and Syria united under the name United Arab Republic; Syria left the union in 1961 but Egypt retained the name until 1971. A federation formed with Syria and Libya in 1972 was short-lived. After Egypt signed a peace treaty with Israel in 1979 it was expelled from the Arab League, but readmitted in 1989.

Viceroys:

July 1805-Sept 1848	Mohammed Ali
Sept-Nov 1848	Ibrahim *(adopted son)*
Nov 1848-July 1854	Abbas I *(grandson of Mohammed Ali)*
July 1854-June 1863	Mohammed Said *(uncle)*

Khedives:

June 1863-June 1879	Ismail *(son of Ibrahim)*
Aug 1879-Jan 1892	Mohammed Tewfik *(son)*
Jan 1892-Dec 1914	Abbas II *(son)*

Sultans:

Dec 1914-Oct 1917	Hussain *(uncle)*
Oct 1917-March 1922	Fuad I *(brother)*

Kings:

March 1922-April 1936	Fuad I
April 1936-July 1952	Farouk *(son)* (abdicated)
July 1952-June 1953	Ahmad Fuad II *(son)* Regent: Prince Abdul Moneim

Presidents:

June 1953-Nov 1954	Mohammed Naguib
Nov 1954-Sept 1970	Gamal Nasser (ASU) (†)
Sept 1970-Oct 1981	Anwar el-Sadat (acting Sept-Oct 1970) (ASU, NDP) († assassinated)
6-13 Oct 1981	Sufi Talib (acting)
Oct 1981-	Hosni Mubarak (NDP)

Prime Ministers:
Chairman of the Regional Executive Council 1958-61

Sept 1878-March 1879	Nubar Pasha Nubarian (1st)
March-April 1879	Prince Mohammed Tewfik (1st)
April-Aug 1879	Sherif Pasha (1st)
Aug-Sept 1879	Khedive Mohammed Tewfik (2nd)
Sept 1879-Sept 1881	Riaz Pasha (1st)
Sept 1881-Feb 1882	Sherif Pasha (2nd)
Feb-Sept 1882	Mahmud Pasha Sami
Sept 1882-Jan 1884	Sherif Pasha (3rd)
Jan 1884-June 1888	Nubar Pasha Nubarian (2nd)
June 1888-May 1891	Riaz Pasha (2nd)
May 1891-Jan 1893	Mustafa Pasha Fehmi (1st)
15-17 Jan 1893	Fakhri Pasha
Jan 1893-April 1894	Riaz Pasha (3rd)
April 1894-Dec 1895	Nubar Pasha Nubarian (3rd)
Dec 1895-Nov 1908	Mustafa Pasha Fehmi (2nd)
Nov 1908-Feb 1910	Butros Pasha Ghali († assassinated)
Feb 1910-April 1913	Mohammed Said Pasha (1st)
April 1913-April 1919	Hussain Rushdi Pasha
May-Nov 1919	Mohammed Said Pasha (2nd)
Nov 1919-May 1920	Yusuf Wahba Pasha
May 1920-March 1921	Tewfik Nessim Pasha (1st)
March-Dec 1921	Adly Yeghen Pasha (1st)
Dec 1921-Nov 1922	Abdul Sarwat Pasha (1st)
Nov 1922-Feb 1923	Tewfik Nessim Pasha (2nd)
March 1923-Jan 1924	Yehya Ibrahim Pasha
Jan-Nov 1924	Saad Zaghlul Pasha
Nov 1924-June 1926	Ahmed Ziwar
June 1926-April 1927	Adly Yeghen Pasha (2nd)
April 1927-March 1928	Abdul Sarwat Pasha (2nd)
March-June 1928	Mustafa Nahas Pahsa (1st)
June 1928-Oct 1929	Mohammed Mahmud Pasha (1st)
Oct-Dec 1929	Adly Yeghen Pasha (3rd)
Jan-June 1930	Mustafa Nahas Pasha (2nd)
June 1930-Sept 1933	Ismail Sidky Pasha (1st)
Sept 1933-Nov 1934	Abdul Yehya Pasha

Nov 1934-Jan 1936	Tewfik Nessim Pasha (3rd)
Jan-May 1936	Ali Maher Pasha (1st)
May 1936-Dec 1937	Mustafa Nahas Pasha (3rd)
Dec 1937-Aug 1939	Mohammed Mahmud Pasha (2nd)
Aug 1939-June 1940	Ali Maher Pasha (2nd)
June 1940-Feb 1942	Hussein Sirry Pasha (1st)
Feb 1942-Oct 1944	Mustafa Nahas Pasha (4th)
Oct 1944-Feb 1945	Ahmed Maher Pasha
Feb 1945-Feb 1946	Mahmud Nokrashy Pasha (1st)
Feb-Dec 1946	Ismail Sidky Pasha (2nd)
Dec 1946-Dec 1948	Mahmud Nokrashy Pasha (2nd) († assassinated)
Dec 1948-Jan 1950	Ibrahim Hadi Pasha
Jan 1950-Jan 1952	Mustafa Nahas Pasha (5th)
Jan-March 1952	Ali Maher Pasha (3rd)
March-June 1952	Ibrahim al-Hilaly Pasha (1st)
2-22 July 1952	Hussein Sirry Pasha (2nd)
22-23 July 1952	Ibrahim al-Hilaly Pasha (2nd) (deposed)
July-Sept 1952	Ali Maher Pasha (4th)
Sept 1952-Feb 1954	Mohammed Naguib
Feb 1954-June 1956	Gamal Nasser (1st)
(June 1956-Oct 1958	post abolished)
Oct 1958-Sept 1960	Nureddin Tarraf
Sept 1960-Aug 1961	Kamaleddin Hussein
(Aug 1961-Sept 1962	post abolished)
Sept 1962-Sept 1965	Aly Sabry
Oct 1965-Sept 1966	Zakaria Mohieddin
Sept 1966-June 1967	Sedki Solimon
June 1967-Sept 1970	Gamal Nasser (2nd) (†)
Oct 1970-Jan 1972	Mahmud Fawzi
Jan 1972-March 1973	Aziz Sidky
March 1973-Sept 1974	Anwar el-Sadat (1st)
Sept 1974-April 1975	Abdel Hegazy
April 1975-Oct 1978	Mamdouh Salem
Oct 1978-May 1980	Mustafa Khalil
May 1980-Oct 1981	Anwar el-Sadat (2nd) († assassinated)
Oct 1981-Jan 1982	Hosni Mubarak
Jan 1982-June 1984	Fuad Mohieddin (†)
June 1984-Sept 1985	Kamal Hassan Ali (acting June-July 1984)
Sept 1985-Nov 1986	Ali Lutfy
Nov 1986-Jan 1996	Atif Sidky
Jan 1996-Oct 1999	Kamal el-Ganzouri
Oct 1999-	Atif Obeid

ASU = Arab Socialist Union (sole legal party 1962-76)
NDP = National Democratic Party (*f* ASU)

Defunct Federation

FEDERATION OF ARAB REPUBLICS

Date formed: 1 January 1972 (no activity after 1975)
Member states: Egypt, Libya, Syria
Capital: Cairo

President:
President of the Presidential Council

Jan 1972-1975   (?)   Anwar el-Sadat (President of Egypt)

Prime Minister:

Jan 1972-1975   (?)   Ahmed Khatib (*f*President of Syria)

EL SALVADOR

Official name: Republic of El Salvador, República de el Salvador
Independence date: 30 January 1841
Capital: San Salvador

El Salvador was part of Spanish Central America from 1526 until 1821, when Spanish rule was overthrown. From 1823 until 1839 El Salvador formed part of the Central American Confederation, and formally declared independence in 1841. In recent times the country has suffered from civil war between right wing governments and left wing guerillas. A peace settlement was reached in 1993.

Presidents:

Jan 1841-Jan 1842	Juan Lindo
Jan-Feb 1842	Antonio Cañas
Feb 1842	Pedro Arce
Feb-April 1842	Ecolastico Marin
April 1842-Feb 1844	Juan Guzmán (1st)
Feb 1844-Feb 1845	Francisco Malespin (deposed)
Feb 1845-Feb 1846	Juan Guzmán (2nd)
Feb 1846	Francisco Palacio
Feb 1846-Feb 1848	Eugenio Aguilar
Feb 1848-March 1851	Doroteo Vasconcelos
March 1851-Jan 1852	Juan Quiros
Jan 1852-Jan 1854	Francisco Dueñas (acting Jan-March 1852) (1st)
Feb 1854-Feb 1856	José San Martín y Ulloa
Feb 1856-Jan 1858	Rafael Campo
Jan 1858-Jan 1860	Miguel Santin de Castillo
Jan 1860-Oct 1863	Gerardo Barrios (assassinated 1864)
Nov 1863-April 1871	Francisco Dueñas (2nd)
April 1871-Jan 1876	Santiago González
Jan-July 1876	Andrés Valles
July 1876-May 1885	Rafael Zaldívar y Lazo (deposed)
May 1885-June 1890	Francisco Menéndez
June 1890-June 1894	Carlos Ezeta
June 1894-Nov 1898	Ramón Gutiérrez Ezetas
Nov 1898-March 1903	Tomás Regaldo Ezetas (acting Nov 1898-March 1899)
March 1903-Feb 1907	Pedro Escalon
March 1907-Feb 1911	Fernando Figueroa
March 1911-Feb 1913	Manuel Araújo (†)
Feb 1913-Aug 1914	Carlos Meléndez (1st)
Aug 1914-Feb 1915	Alfonso Quiñonez Molina (1st)

March 1915-Feb 1919	Carlos Meléndez (2nd)
March 1919-Feb 1923	Jorge Meléndez (brother)
March 1923-Feb 1927	Alfonso Quiñonez Molina (2nd)
March 1927-Feb 1931	Pio Bosque
March-Dec 1931	Arturo Araújo (deposed)
Dec 1931-May 1944	Maximiliano Hernández Martínez (acting Dec 1931-March 1932)
May-Oct 1944	Andrés Menéndez (deposed)
Oct 1944-March 1945	Osmin Aguirre y Salinas
March 1945-Dec 1948	Salvador Castaneda Castro (deposed)
Dec 1948-Feb 1949	Manuel Córdoba
Feb 1949-Sept 1956	Oscar Osorio (RPDU)
Sept 1956-Oct 1960	José Lemus (RPDU) (deposed)
Oct 1960-Jan 1961	César Yanes Urias (deposed)
Jan-Feb 1961	Anibal Portillo
Feb 1961-Jan 1962	Miguel Castillo
Jan-July 1962	Eusebio Cordón Cea
July 1962-July 1967	Julio Rivera Carballo (NCP)
July 1972-July 1972	Fidel Sánchez Hernández (NCP)
July 1972-July 1977	Arturo Molina Barraza (NCP)
July 1977-Oct 1979	Carlos Romero Mena (NCP) (deposed)
(Oct 1979-Dec 1980	Junta leaders: Adolfo Majano/Jaime Gutiérrez)
Dec 1980-May 1982	José Napoleon Duarte (1st)
May 1982-June 1984	Alvaro Magaña
June 1984-June 1989	José Napoleon Duarte (2nd) (CDP)
June 1989-June 1994	Alfredo Cristiani Burkard (NRA)
June 1994-June 1999	Armando Calderón Sol (NRA)
June 1999-	Francisco Flores (NRA)

CDP = Christian Democratic Party
NCP = National Conciliation Party
NRA = Nationalist Republican Alliance (ARENA)
RPDU = Revolutionary Party of the Democratic Union

EQUATORIAL GUINEA

Official name: Republic of Equatorial Guinea, República de Guinea Ecuatorial
Previous name: Spanish Guinea until 1963, Equatorial Guinea 1963-68
Independence date: 12 October 1968
Capital: Malabo (*f* Santa Isabel)

The island of Fernando Po (now called Bioko) was discovered by Spanish explorers in 1472 and ceded to Spain in 1778. From 1827 to 1844 it was administered by Britain. Together with the mainland territory of Rio Muni (now called Mbini) it formed the colony of Spanish Guinea until 1959, when the territories became overseas provinces. Internal autonomy was granted in 1963, and full independence followed in 1968. The oppressive rule of President Macías was ended by a coup led by his nephew in 1979.

Governors:

1900-01	Francisco Dueñas
1901-05	José de Ibarra Autran
1905-06	José Gómez de la Serna
1906	Diego Saavedra y Magdalena
1906-07	Angel Barrera y Luyando (1st)
1907-08	Luis Ramos Izquierdo
1908-09	José Centeno Anchorena
1910-24	Angel Barrera y Luyando (2nd)
1924-26	Carlos Tovar de Revilla
1926-31	Miguel Núñez de Prado
1931-32	Gustavo de Sostoa y Sthamer
1933-34	Estanislao Lluesma García
1934-35	Angel Manzaneque Feltrer
1935-36	Luis Sánchez Guerra Saéz
1937	Manuel de Mendivil y Elio
1937-41	Juan Fontan y Lobe
1942-43	Mariano Alonso
1943-49	Juan Bonelli Rubio
1949-62	Faustino Ruiz González
1962-63	Francisco Núñez Rodríguez

High Commissioners:

1963-64	Francisco Núñez Rodríguez
1964-66	Pedro Latorre Alcubierre (see Spanish Sahara)
1966-68	Víctor Suances Díaz del Rio

Presidents:

Oct 1968-Aug 1979   Francisco Macías Nguema   (deposed, executed)
Aug 1979-   Teodoro Obiang Nguema   (*nephew*)

Prime Ministers:

Dec 1963-Oct 1968   Bonifacio Ondo Edu
(Oct 1968-Oct 1982   post abolished)
Oct 1982-Jan 1992   Cristino Seriche Bioko
Jan 1992-March 1996   Silvestre Siale Bileka
March 1996-   Angel Seriche Dougan

ERITREA

Official name: State of Eritrea
Independence date: 24 May 1993
Capital: Asmara

Eritrea was linked to Ethiopia from c950 until it fell under Ottoman rule in the 16th century. Control was then disputed between several powers until the 1889 treaty between Italy and Ethiopia established an Italian colony. In 1941 it was occupied by British forces, and in 1952 it was federated with Ethiopia. In 1962, Ethiopia annexed Eritrea, triggering an armed struggle which lasted until 1991 when the Marxist government collapsed, and a provisional government was formed in Asmara. After a referendum in 1993 independence was proclaimed.

Governors:

1889-90	Baldassare Orero
1890-92	Antonio Gandolfi
1892-96	Oreste Baratieri
1896-97	Antonio Baldiserra
1896-1907	Ferdinando Martini
1907-15	Giuseppe Salvago-Raggi
1915-19	Nobile di Martino (see Somalia)
1919-23	Giovanni Cerrina-Feroni (see Somalia)
1923-28	Jacopo Gasparini
1928-30	Corrado Zoli
1930-35	Riccardo di Lucchesi
1936-37	Alfredo Guzzoni
1937	Vincenzo de Feo
1937-40	Giuseppe Daodiace

Chief Administrators:

1941-42	Brian Kennedy-Cooke
1942-44	Stephen Longrigg
1944-45	C.D.McCarthy
1945-46	John Benoy
1946-51	Francis Drew
1951-52	Duncan Cummin

President:

May 1993-	Issais Afewerki

Prime Ministers:
Government Secretary-General 1991-93

Aug 1952-Aug 1955	Tedla Bairu
Aug 1955-Nov 1962	Fitaurari Woldemikael
(Nov 1962	post abolished)
May 1991-May 1993	Issais Afewerki
(May 1993	post abolished)

ESTONIA

Official name: Estonian Republic, Eesti Vabarik
Previous name: Estonian Soviet Socialist Republic 1940-90 (as part of USSR)
Independence dates: 8 November 1917, 20 August 1991
Constituent republic of USSR: 6 August 1940-20 August 1991
Capital: Tallinn

Estonia was autonomous until the 13th century, then ruled by the Teutonic Knights until 1561, Sweden (1561-1721) and Russia. In 1918 it proclaimed its independence, but in 1940 was forcibly incorporated into the USSR. From 1941 to 1944 it was occupied by Germany. Following the brief 1991 coup in Moscow, Estonia again proclaimed its independence.

Presidents:

Chief of State 1920-Jan 1934
President of the Presidium of the Supreme Soviet 1940-90
Chairman of the Supreme Soviet March 1990-Oct 1992

June-Oct 1920	Jaan Tonisson (1st)
Oct 1920-Jan 1921	Ants Piip
Jan 1921-Oct 1922	Konstantin Päts (1st)
Oct 1922-Aug 1923	Johan Kukk
Aug 1923-March 1924	Konstantin Päts (2nd)
March-Dec 1924	Frederik Akel
Dec 1924-Dec 1925	Jüri Jaakson
Dec 1925-Feb 1927	Jaan Teemant (1st)
Feb-Nov 1927	Jüri Uluots
Dec 1927-Nov 1928	Jaan Tonisson (2nd)
Nov 1928-July 1929	August Rei
July 1929-Feb 1931	Otto Strandmann
Feb 1931-Jan 1932	Konstantin Päts (3rd)
Feb-June 1932	Jaan Teemant (2nd)
July-Oct 1932	Karl Einbund (later Kaanel Eenpalu)
Nov 1932-April 1933	Konstantin Päts (4th)
May-Oct 1933	Jaan Tonisson (3rd)
Oct 1933-June 1940	Konstantin Päts (5th)
July 1940-June 1941	Johannes Vares (1st)
(June 1941-Sept 1944	German occupation)
Sept 1944-Nov 1946	Johannes Vares (2nd)
Nov 1946-April 1950	Edvard Paall
May 1950-Feb 1958	August Jakobson
Feb 1958-Oct 1961	Johän Eichfeld

Oct 1961-Oct 1970	Aleksei Müürisepp (†)
Oct-Dec 1970	Aleksandr Ansberg (acting)
Dec 1970-May 1978	Arthur Vader (†)
July 1978-Feb 1984	Johannes Kabin
Feb 1984-Oct 1992	Arnold Rüütel
Oct 1992-	Lenart Meri (FA)

Prime Ministers:

Chairman of the Council of People's Commissars 1940-46
Chairman of the Council of Ministers 1946-92

Oct-Nov 1917	Konstantin Päts (1st)
Nov 1917-Jan 1918	Jaan Anvelt
(Feb-Nov 1918	German occupation)
Nov 1918-May 1919	Konstantin Päts (2nd)
May-Nov 1919	Otto Strandman
Nov 1919-June 1920	Jaan Tonisson
(June 1920-Jan 1934	post held by President)
(Jan 1934-April 1938	post abolished)
April 1938-Oct 1939	Kaanel Eenpalu (f Karl Einbund)
Oct 1939-June 1940	Jüri Uluots
June 1940-June 1941	Johannes Vares
(June 1941-Sept 1944	German occupation)
Sept 1944-March 1951	Arnold Veimar
March 1951-Oct 1961	Aleksei Müürisepp
Oct 1961-Jan 1984	Valther Klausson
Jan 1984-Nov 1988	Bruno Saul
Nov 1988-April 1990	Indrek Toome
April 1990-Jan 1992	Edgar Savisaar
Jan-Oct 1992	Tiit Vähi (1st)
Oct 1992-Oct 1994	Mart Laar (1st) (FA)
Oct 1994-April 1995	Andres Tarand
April 1995-March 1997	Tiit Vähi (2nd) (CPRU)
March 1997-March 1999	Mart Siimann
March 1999-	Mart Laar (2nd) (FA)

CPRU = Coalition Party & Rural Union
FA = Fatherland Alliance

Communist Party Leaders:

First Secretary

Sept 1944-50	Nikolai Karotamm
1950-July 1978	Johannes Kabin
July 1978-June 1988	Karl Vaino
June 1988-1990	Vaino Vyelyas
(April 1990	multi-party system introduced)

ETHIOPIA

Official name: Ethiopian Federal Democratic Republic

Former names: Empire of Ethiopia until 1974, Socialist Ethiopia 1974-87, Democratic People's Republic of Ethiopia 1987-91, Ethiopia 1991-95

State founded: pre-recorded times

Capital: Addis Ababa

Ethiopia is an ancient state which was probably founded at Aksum some 2000 years ago. It retained its independence through the period of colonization of Africa until in 1936 it was occupied by Italy. Independence was restored in 1941. In 1952 the former Italian colony of Eritrea was federated with Ethiopia, but in 1962 the federation was dissolved and a unitary state established - this caused an armed struggle for independence. The revolution of 1974 brought an end to the monarchy and a Marxist state was proclaimed; in 1987 Ethiopia became a republic. Several rebel groups began to operate in the country. In 1991 the government collapsed, and was taken over by rebels.

Emperors:

1270-85	Tasfa Iyasu
1285-94	Solomon I
1294-97	Senfa Asgad/Bahr Asgad
1297-99	Hezba Ared
1299-1314	Jin Asgad
1314-44	Amda Seyon I
1344-72	Newaya Krestos
1372-82	Newaya Mariam
1382-1411	Dawit I
1411-14	Tewodoros I
1414-29	Yeshak
1429-30	Endreyas
1430-33	Takla Mariam
1433	Sarue Iyasu
1433-34	Amda Iyasu
1434-68	Zara Yakob
1468-78	Baeda Mariam I
1478-94	Eskender
1494	Amda Seyon II
1494-1508	Naod
July 1508-Sept 1540	Dawit II
Sept 1540-March 1559	Calawdewos (*son*)
March 1559-Jan 1564	Minas (*brother*)
Jan 1564-Aug 1597	Sarsa Dengel (*son*)

Aug 1597-Sept 1603	Yakob (*son*) (1st)
Sept 1603-Oct 1604	Za-Dengel (*nephew of Sarsa Dengel*)
Oct 1604-March 1607	Yakob (2nd)
March 1607-Sept 1632	Susneyos (*great-grandson of Dawit II*)
Sept 1632-Oct 1667	Fasildas (*son*)
Oct 1667-July 1682	Yohannes I (*son*)
July 1682-March 1706	Iyasu I (*son*)
March 1706-July 1708	Takla Haymanot I (*son*)
July 1708-Oct 1711	Theophilos (*son of Yohannes I*)
Oct 1711-Feb 1716	Yostos (*great-grandson of Yohannes I*)
Feb 1716-May 1721	Dawit III (*son of Iyasu I*)
May 1721-Sept 1730	Bakafa (*brother*)
Sept 1730-June 1755	Iyasu II (*son*)
June 1755-May 1769	Joas (*brother*) (deposed)
May-Oct 1769	Yohannes II (*son of Iyasu I*)
Oct 1769-77	Takla Haymanot II (*son*)
1777	Hayl Sagad
Sept 1777-July 1779	Solomon II
July 1779-Feb 1784	Takla Giyorghis I (*son of Yohannes II*) (1st)
Feb 1784-87	Iyasu III (*great-grandson of Iyasu I*)
1787-April 1788	Baeda Mariam II (1st)
April 1788-July 1789	Takla Giyorghis I (2nd)
July 1789-Jan 1794	Hezkeyas (*son of Iyasu III*)
Jan 1794-April 1795	Takla Giyorghis I (3rd)
April-Dec 1795	Baeda Mariam II (2nd)
Dec 1795-May 1796	Takla Giyorghis I (4th)
July 1796-July 1797	Solomon III (1st)
July 1797-Jan 1798	Yonas
Jan 1798-May 1799	Takla Giyorghis I (5th)
May 1799	Solomon III (2nd)
1799-March 1800	Demetros (1st)
March-July 1800	Takla Giyorghis I (6th)
July 1800-June 1801	Demetros (2nd)
June 1801-June 1818	Eguala Seyon (*son of Hezkeyas*)
June 1818-June 1821	Joas II (*brother*)
June 1821-April 1826	Gigar (1st)
April 1826	Baeda Mariam III
April 1826-June 1830	Gigar (2nd)
June 1830-March 1832	Iyasu IV (*son of Solomon III*)
March-June 1832	Gabre Krestos
June 1832-Aug 1840	Sahla Dengel (1st)
Aug 1840-Oct 1841	Yohannes III (*son of Takla Giyorghis I*)
Oct 1841-Feb 1855	Sahla Dengel (2nd)
Feb 1855-April 1868	Tewodros II (*b* Kassa Haylu) (suicide)
April 1868-Jan 1872	Takla Giyorghis II (*b* Ras Gobaze)

Jan 1872-March 1899	Yohannes IV (*b* Kassa Abba Bezbez)
March 1889-Dec 1913	Menelik II (*son*)
	(Regent: 1909-1911 Tassamma Nadaw)
Dec 1913-Sept 1916	Iyasu V (*grandson*)
Sept 1916-April 1930	Zauditu (Empress) (*aunt*)
	(Regent: 1916-30 Ras Taffari Makonnen)
April 1930-May 1936	Haile Selassie (*b* Ras Taffari Makonnen) (1st)

Viceroys:

May-June 1936	Pietro Badoglio
June 1936-Nov 1937	Rodolfo Graziani (see Somalia)
Nov 1937-Nov 1940	Amadeo, Duke of Aosta

Emperor:

May 1941-Sept 1974	Haile Selassie (2nd) (deposed)

Heads of State:
Chairman of the Provisional Military Administrative Council

Sept-Nov 1974	Aman Andom (deposed, executed)
Nov 1974-Feb 1977	Teferi Benti (deposed, executed)
Feb 1977-Sept 1987	Mengistu Haile Mariam

Presidents:

Sept 1987-May 1991	Mengistu Haile Mariam
21-28 May 1991	Tesfaye Gebre-Kidan (acting) (deposed)
June 1991-Aug 1995	Meles Zinawi (*b* Legesse Zinawi) (acting June-July 1991)
Aug 1995-	Negaso Gidada

Prime Ministers:
Chairman of the Council of Ministers 1976-87

1944-Nov 1957	Bitwadded Makonnen
Nov 1957-Dec 1960	Ras Abebe Aragai († assassinated)
(Dec 1960-March 1961	post vacant)
March 1961-Feb 1974	Aklilu Habte Wold (executed Sept 1974)
Feb-July 1974	Endalkachaw Makonnen (executed Sept 1974)
July-Sept 1974	Mikhail Imru
(Sept 1974-Dec 1976	post abolished)
Dec 1976-Sept 1987	Mengistu Haile Mariam
Sept 1987-Nov 1989	Fikre-Selassie Wogderes
Nov 1989-April 1991	Hailu Yimenu (acting)
April-May 1991	Tesfaye Dinka
June 1991-Aug 1995	Tamirat Laynie (acting June-Aug 1991)
Aug 1995-	Meles Zinawi

FIJI

Official name: Republic of the Fiji Islands
Previous name: Dominion of Fiji 1970-87, Republic of Fiji 1987-98
Independence date: 10 October 1970
Capital: Suva

The first European visitor to Fiji was Tasman in 1643. After a brief attempt to form a united kingdom the islands were ceded by local chiefs to Britain in 1874. Self-government was granted in 1967 and independence in 1970. After the 1987 elections produced a government dominated by people of Indian descent, the army staged a coup to ensure Melanesian control of government; a second coup later the same year was followed by the proclamation of a republic.

King:

June 1871-Oct 1874	Apenisa Cakobau

Governors:

1875-80	Baron Stanmore (Arthur Hamilton-Gordon)
1880-87	George Des Voeux
1887-88	Charles Mitchell
1888-97	John Thurston
1897-1902	George O'Brien
1902-04	Henry Jackson
1904-11	Everard Thurn
1911-12	Francis May
1912-18	Ernest Sweet-Escott (see British Honduras)
1918-25	Cecil Rodwell
1925-29	Eyre Hutson
1929-35	Arthur Fletcher
1936-38	Arthur Richards (see Gambia)
1938-42	Harry Luke
1942-45	Philip Mitchell
1945-48	Alexander Grantham
1948-52	Leslie Freeston
1952-58	Ronald Garvey (see British Honduras)
1958-63	Kenneth Maddocks
1963-68	Francis Jakeway
1968-70	Robert Foster

Governors-General:

Represented monarch who was concurrently British monarch

Oct 1970-Jan 1973	Robert Foster
Jan 1973-Feb 1983	George Cakobau
Feb 1983-Oct 1987	Penaia Ganilau

Head of State:

Oct-Dec 1987	Sitiveni Rabuka

Presidents:

Dec 1987-Dec 1993	Penaia Ganilau	(†)
Dec 1993-	Kamisese Mara	(acting Dec 1993-Jan 1994)

Chief Minister:

Sept 1967-Oct 1970	Kamisese Mara	(AP)

Prime Ministers:

Chairman of the Council of Ministers (May & Sept-Dec 1987)

Oct 1970-April 1987	Kamisese Mara	(AP) (1st)
April-May 1987	Timoci Bavadra	(LP) (deposed)
19-22 May 1987	Sitiveni Rabuka	(1st)
(May-Sept 1987	post abolished)	
Sept-Dec 1987	Sitiveni Rabuka	(2nd)
Dec 1987-June 1992	Kamisese Mara	(2nd)
June 1992-May 1999	Sitiveni Rabuka	(FPP) (3rd)
May 1999-	Mahendra Chaudhry	(LP)

AP = Alliance Party
FPP = Fiji Political Party
LP = Labour Party

FINLAND

Official name: Republic of Finland, Suomen Tasavalta (Finnish), Republiken Finland (Swedish)
Independence date: 6 December 1917
Capital: Helsinki (Helsingfors)

From the Middle ages Finland was part of the kingdom of Sweden. In the 18th century parts of the south-east were conquered by Russia, the remainder being ceded in 1809. In 1917, following the Russian revolution, Finland declared its independence, becoming a republic in 1919. Soviet troops invaded Finland in 1939 after Finland rejected Soviet territorial demands which were acceded to in the peace treaty of 1940. Further territorial concessions were made in 1944.

Regents:

May-Dec 1918	Pehr Svinhufud
Dec 1918-June 1919	Karl Mannerheim

Presidents:

July 1919-Feb 1925	Kaarlo Ståhlberg (PP)
March 1925-Feb 1931	Lauri Relander (AU)
March 1931-Feb 1937	Pehr Svinhufud
March 1937-Nov 1940	Kjösti Kallio (AU) (†)
Nov 1940-Aug 1944	Risto Ryti (acting Nov-Dec 1940) (LP)
Aug 1944-March 1946	Karl Mannerheim
March 1946-Feb 1956	Juho Paasikivi
March 1956-Oct 1981	Urho Kekkonen (AL,CP)
Oct 1981-March 1994	Mauno Koivisto (acting Oct 1981-March 1982) (SDP)
March 1994-March 2000	Martti Ahtisaari (SDP)
March 2000-	Tarja Halonen (SDP)

Prime Ministers:

Nov 1917-May 1918	Pehr Svinhufud (1st)
May-Nov 1918	Juho Paasikivi (1st)
Nov 1918-April 1919	Lauri Ingman (1st)
April-Aug 1919	Kaarlo Castrén
Aug 1919-March 1920	Juho Vennola (1st)
March 1920-April 1921	Rafael Erich
April 1921-June 1922	Juho Vennola (2nd)
June-Nov 1922	Aimo Cajander (1st) (LP)
Nov 1922-Jan 1924	Kjösti Kallio (1st) (AU)

Jan-May 1924	Aimo Cajander (2nd) (LP)
May 1924-March 1925	Lauri Ingman (2nd)
March-Dec 1925	Antti Tulenheimo
Dec 1925-Dec 1926	Kjösti Kallio (2nd) (AU)
Dec 1926-Dec 1927	Väinö Tanner
Dec 1927-Dec 1928	Juho Sunila (1st)
Dec 1928-Aug 1929	Oskari Mantere
Aug 1929-July 1930	Kjösti Kallio (3rd) (AU)
July 1930-Feb 1931	Pehr Svinhufud (2nd)
Feb-March 1931	Juho Vennola (3rd)
March 1931-Dec 1932	Juho Sunila (2nd)
Dec 1932-Oct 1936	Toivo Kivimaki
Oct 1936-March 1937	Kjösti Kallio (4th) (AU)
March 1937-Dec 1939	Aimo Cajander (3rd) (LP)
Dec 1939-Dec 1940	Risto Ryti (LP)
Jan 1941-March 1943	Johann Rangell (PP)
March 1943-Aug 1944	Edwin Linkomies (Cons)
Aug-Sept 1944	Antti Hackzell (Cons)
Sept-Nov 1944	Urho Castrén
Nov 1944-March 1946	Juho Paasikivi (2nd)
March 1946-July 1948	Mauno Pekkala (FDPL)
July 1948-March 1950	Karl Fagerholm (1st) (SDP)
March 1950-Nov 1953	Urho Kekkonen (1st) (AL)
Nov 1953-May 1954	Sakari Tuomioja
May-Oct 1954	Ralf Törngren (SPP)
Oct 1954-March 1956	Urho Kekkonen (2nd) (AL)
March 1956-May 1957	Karl Fagerholm (2nd) (SDP)
May-Nov 1957	Väinö Sukselainen (1st) (AL)
Nov 1957-April 1958	Rainer von Fieandt
April-Aug 1958	Reino Kuuskoski
Aug 1958-Jan 1959	Karl Fagerholm (3rd) (SDP)
Jan 1959-July 1961	Väinö Sukselainen (2nd) (AL)
July 1961-April 1962	Martti Miettunen (1st) (AL)
April 1962-Dec 1963	Ahti Karjalainen (1st(AL)
Dec 1963-Sept 1964	Reino Lehto
Sept 1964-May 1966	Johannes Virolainen (CP)
May 1966-March 1968	Rafael Paasio (1st) (SDP)
March 1968-May 1970	Mauno Koivisto (1st) (SDP)
May-July 1970	Teuvo Aura (1st)
July 1970-Oct 1971	Ahti Karjalainen (2nd) (CP)
Oct 1971-Feb 1972	Teuvo Aura (2nd)
Feb-Sept 1972	Rafael Paasio (2nd) (SDP)
Sept 1972-June 1975	Kalevi Sorsa (1st) (SDP)
June-Nov 1975	Keijo Liinamaa (SDP)
Nov 1975-May 1977	Martti Miettunen (2nd) (CP)

May 1977-May 1979	Kalevi Sorsa (2nd) (SDP)
May 1979-Jan 1982	Mauno Koivisto (2nd) (SDP)
Jan 1982-April 1987	Kalevi Sorsa (3rd) (SDP)
April 1987-May 1991	Harri Holkeri (Cons)
May 1991-April 1995	Esko Aho (CP)
April 1995-	Paavo Lipponen (SDP)

AL = Agrarian League
AU = Agrarian Union
CP = Centre Party (*f* AL)
Cons = Conservative Party
FDPL = Finnish Democratic People's League
LP = Liberal Party
PP = Progressive Party
SDP = Social Democratic Party
SPP = Swedish People's Party

Autonomous province

ÅLAND ISLANDS

Capital: Mariehamn

Governor:

1993-	Henrik Gustafsson

Chairmen of the Executive Council:
Lantrad

June 1922-Dec 1938	Carl Björkman
Dec 1938-54	Victor Strandfeldt
1955-March 1967	Hugo Johansson
March 1967-June 1972	Martin Isaksson
July 1972-Sept 1978	Alarik Häggblom
Sept 1978-April 1988	Folke Woivalin
April 1988-Oct 1991	Sune Eriksson
Oct 1991-Oct 1995	Ragnar Erlandsson
Oct 1995-	Roger Jansson

FRANCE

Official name: French Republic, République Française
Previous names: Kingdom of France until 1792 & 1814-48, French Empire 1804-14, May-June 1815 & 1852-70, French State 1940-44 (Vichy government)
State formed: 8th century
Capital: Paris

The kingdom of the Franks emerged in the 8th century and formed the western part of the empire of Charles the Great (Charlemagne), who was awarded the title of Holy Roman Emperor by the Pope in 800. The French monarchy survived until the revolution of 1792 and the execution of Louis XVI. After a period of republican governments (1792-1804) Napoléon Bonaparte crowned himself emperor, but after his military defeat in 1815 the monarchy was restored. In 1848 the Second Republic was proclaimed, followed in 1852 by the second Bonapartist empire. After France's defeat by Germany in 1870 the Third Republic was established. In 1940 Germany occupied part of France, while a government was allowed to function in unoccupied France from Vichy. After World War II a period of unstable government under the Fourth Republic was followed by a new constitution with a strong presidency.

Kings:

Oct 751-Jan 752	Childerich III (co-ruler)
Oct 751-Sept 768	Pepin III (co-ruler 751-2)
Sept 768-Dec 771	Carloman I (*son*) (co-ruler)
Sept 768-Jan 814	Charles I (Charlemagne) (*brother*) (co-ruler 768-71)
Jan 814-June 840	Louis I (*son*)
June 840-Aug 843	Lothair I (*brother*)
Aug 843-Oct 877	Charles II (*half-brother*)
Oct 877-April 879	Louis II (*son*)
April 879-Aug 882	Louis III/Carloman II (*sons*)
882-7	Charles (III, Holy Roman Emperor) (the Fat) (deposed) (*great grandson of Charles I*)
888-Jan 898	Odo (Eudes)
Jan 898-June 922	Charles III (the Simple) (*son of Louis II*)
June 922-June 923	Robert I (killed in battle) (*brother of Odo*)
July 923-Jan 936	Rudolf (Raoul) (*son-in-law*)
Jan 936-Sept 954	Louis IV (*son of Charles III*)
Sept 954-March 986	Lothair II (*son*)
March 986-May 987	Louis V (*son*)
May 987-Oct 996	Hugues Capet (*grandson of Robert I*)
Oct 996-July 1031	Robert II (*son*)
July 1031-Aug 1060	Henri I (*son*)

Aug 1060-July 1108	Philippe I	(*son*)
July 1108-Aug 1137	Louis VI	(*son*)
Aug 1137-Sept 1180	Louis VII	(*son*)
Sept 1180-July 1223	Philippe II	(*son*)
July 1223-Nov 1226	Louis VIII	(*son*)
Nov 1226-Aug 1270	Louis IX	(*son*)

   (Regent: 1226-42 Blanche de Castile)

Aug 1270-Oct 1285	Philippe III	(*son*)
Oct 1285-Oct 1314	Philippe IV	(*son*)
Oct 1314-June 1316	Louis X	(*son*)
June-Nov 1316	Jean I	(*son*)
Nov 1316-Jan 1332	Philippe V	(*uncle*)
Jan 1322-Feb 1328	Charles IV	(*brother*)
(Feb-May 1328	interregnum)	
May 1328-Aug 1350	Philippe VI	(*brother of Philippe IV*)
Aug 1350-Sept 1356	Jean II	(*son*)
Sept 1356-Sept 1380	Charles V	(*son*)
Sept 1380-Nov 1422	Charles VI	(*son*)

   (Regents: 1380-2 Louis, Duc d'Anjou
   1382-8 Philippe, Duc de Burgundy)

Nov 1442-July 1461	Charles VII	(*son*)
July 1461-Aug 1483	Louis XI	(*son*)
Aug 1483-April 1498	Charles VIII	(*son*)
April 1498-June 1515	Louis XII	(*grand nephew of Charles VI*)
June 1515-March 1547	François I	(*nephew*)
March 1547-July 1559	Henri II	(*son*)
July 1559-Dec 1560	François II	(*son*)
Dec 1560-May 1574	Charles IX	(*brother*)
May 1574-Aug 1589	Henri III	(*brother*) (assassinated)
Aug 1589-May 1610	Henri IV	(assassinated)
May 1610-May 1643	Louis XIII	(*son*)

   (Regent: 1610-14 Queen Marie de Medicis)

May 1643-Sept 1715	Louis XIV	(*son*)

   (Regent: 1643-51 Queen Anne of Austria)

Sept 1715-May 1774	Louis XV	(*great-grandson*)

   (Regent: Philippe d'Orléans)

May 1774-Aug 1792	Louis XVI	(*grandson*) (abdicated, executed 1793)
(28 Jan 1793	Louis XVII	(*son*), proclaimed king by royalists in exile; died in prison in 1795)
(Sept 1792-Oct 1795	rule by National Convention)	
(Oct 1795-Nov 1799	five-member Directory)	

First Consul:

Nov 1799-May 1804	Napoléon Bonaparte

Emperor:

May 1804-April 1814   Napoléon I   (*b* N.Bonaparte) (1st) (deposed)

King:

April 1814-March 1815   Louis XVIII   (*brother of Louis XVI*) (1st)

Emperor:

March-June 1815   Napoléon I   (2nd) (deposed)
(22 June 1815   Napoléon II   (*son*), proclaimed by supporters but did not reign)

Kings:

June 1815-Sept 1824   Louis XVIII   (2nd)
Sept 1824-Aug 1830   Charles X   (*brother*) (abdicated)
2 Aug 1830   Louis XIX   (*son*) (nominal) (abdicated)
2-9 Aug 1830   Henri V   (*nephew*) (nominal) (deposed)
Aug 1830-Feb 1848   Louis-Philippe   (*great-great-great-great grandson of Louis XIII*) (abdicated)

Heads of State:

March-May 1848   Philippe Buchez
May-Dec 1848   Louis Cavaignac

President:

Dec 1848-Dec 1852   Louis Napoléon Bonaparte   (*nephew of Napoleon I*)

Emperor:

Dec 1852-Sept 1870   Napoleon III   (*b* L.N.Bonaparte) (deposed)

Presidents:

Aug 1871-May 1873   Adolphe Thiers
May 1873-Jan 1879   M.Patrice MacMahon
Jan 1879-Dec 1887   Jules Grevy
Dec 1887-June 1894   François Sadi-Carnot   († assassinated)
June 1894-Jan 1895   Jean Casimir-Périer
Jan 1895-Feb 1899   François Faure   (†)
Feb 1899-Feb 1906   Émile Loubet
Feb 1906-Feb 1913   Armand Fallières
Feb 1913-Feb 1920   Raymond Poincaré
Feb-Sept 1920   Paul Deschanel
Sept 1920-June 1924   Alexandre Millerand
June 1924-June 1931   Gaston Doumergue

June 1931-May 1932   Paul Doumer   († assassinated)
May 1932-July 1940   Albert Le Brun
July 1940-Aug 1944   H.Philippe Pétain   (Vichy government; Paris in German occupied France)
(Aug 1944-Jan 1947   provisional government)
Jan 1947-Jan 1954   Vincent Auriol   (SP)
Jan 1954-Jan 1959   René Coty   (IRP)
Jan 1959-April 1969   Charles de Gaulle   (UNR,DUR)
April-June 1969   Alain Poher   (acting) (1st) (CP)
June 1969-April 1974   Georges Pompidou   (†) (DUR)
April-May 1974   Alain Poher   (acting) (2nd) (CP)
May 1974-May 1981   Valéry Giscard d'Estaing   (IRP)
May 1981-May 1995   François Mitterrand   (SP)
May 1995-   Jacques Chirac   (RFR)

Chief Ministers:

April 1624-Dec 1642   Duc de Richelieu   (Armand Jean du Plessis) (†)
Dec 1642-March 1661   Jules Mazarin

Prime Ministers:

May 1814-March 1815   Pierre de Blacas d'Aulps
March-June 1815   Benjamin de Rebeque
June-Sept 1815   Charles de Talleyrand-Peregord
Sept 1815-Dec 1818   Duc de Richelieu   (Armand Emmanuel du Plessis) (1st)
Dec 1818-Nov 1819   Marquis Dessoles   (Jean Dessoles)
Nov 1819-Feb 1820   Comptes de Decazes   (Elie de Decazes)
Feb 1820-Dec 1822   Duc de Richelieu   (Armand Emmanuel du Plessis) (2nd)
Dec 1822-Jan 1828   Joseph Villèle
Jan 1828-Aug 1829   Jean-Baptiste Martignac
Aug 1829-July 1830   Jules de Polignac
July-Aug 1830   Marquis de Lafayette   (Marie Motier)
Aug-Nov 1830   Duc de Broglie   (Achille de Broglie) (1st)
Nov 1830-March 1831   Jacques Laffitte
March 1831-May 1832   Casimir Périer   (†)
(May-Oct 1832   post vacant)
Oct 1832-April 1834   Duc de Broglie   (Achille de Broglie) (2nd)
April-July 1834   Nicolas Soult   (1st)
July-Oct 1834   Étienne Gérard
14-18 Nov 1834   Duc de Bassano   (Hugues Maret)
Nov 1834-Feb 1835   Edouard Mortier
March 1835-Feb 1836   Duc de Broglie   (Achille de Broglie) (3rd)
Feb-Sept 1836   Adolphe Thiers   (1st)
Sept 1836-March 1839   Compte Molé   (Louis Molé)
(March-May 1839   post vacant)
May 1839-Feb 1840   Nicolas Soult   (2nd)

March-Oct 1840	Adolphe Thiers (2nd)
Oct 1840-Sept 1847	Nicolas Soult (3rd)
Sept 1847-Feb 1848	François Guizot
Feb-May 1848	Jacques-Charles Dupont
June-Dec 1848	Louis Cavaignac
Dec 1848-Oct 1849	Odilon Barrot
Oct 1849-April 1851	Alphonse Hautpoul
April 1851-Dec 1852	Léon Faucher

Chief Ministers:

Dec 1852-Feb 1855	Léon Faucher
Feb 1855-July 1869	Eugène Rouher

Prime Ministers:

July-Dec 1869	Jean de Forcade de la Roquette
Jan-Aug 1870	Émile Ollivier
Aug-Sept 1870	Duc de Palikao (Charles Cousin-Montauban)
Sept 1870-Feb 1871	Louis Trochu
Feb 1871-May 1873	Adolphe Thiers (3rd)
May 1873-May 1874	M.Patrice MacMahon
May 1874-March 1875	Ernest de Cissey
March 1875-Feb 1876	Louis Buffet
Feb-Dec 1876	Jules Dufaure (1st)
Dec 1876-May 1877	Jules Simon
May-Nov 1877	Duc de Broglie (Albert de Broglie) (*son of Achille de Broglie*)
Nov-Dec 1877	Gaëtan de Rochebouet
Dec 1877-Feb 1879	Jules Dufaure (2nd)
Feb-Dec 1879	William Waddington
Dec 1879-Sept 1880	Charles de Freycinet (1st)
Sept 1880-Nov 1881	Jules Ferry (1st)
Nov 1881-Jan 1882	Léon Gambetta
Jan-Aug 1882	Charles de Freycinet (2nd)
Aug 1882-Jan 1883	Charles Duclerc
Jan-Feb 1883	Armand Fallières
Feb 1883-April 1885	Jules Ferry (2nd)
April 1885-Jan 1886	Henri Brisson (1st)
Jan-Dec 1886	Charles de Freycinet (3rd)
Dec 1886-May 1887	René Goblet
May-Dec 1887	Maurice Rouvier (1st)
Dec 1887-April 1888	Pierre Tirard (1st)
April 1888-Feb 1889	Charles Floquet
Feb 1889-March 1890	Pierre Tirard (2nd)
March 1890-Feb 1892	Charles de Freycinet (4th)
Feb-Dec 1892	Émile Loubet

Dec 1892-April 1893	Alexandre Ribot (1st)
April-Dec 1893	Charles Dupuy (1st)
Dec 1893-May 1894	Jean Casimir-Périer (*grandson of Casimir Périer*)
May 1894-Jan 1895	Charles Dupuy (2nd)
Jan-Nov 1895	Alexandre Ribot (2nd)
Nov 1895-April 1896	Léon Bourgeois
April 1896-June 1898	Jules Meline
June-Oct 1898	Henri Brisson (2nd)
Oct 1898-June 1899	Charles Dupuy (3rd)
June 1899-June 1902	P.René Waldeck-Rousseau
June 1902-Jan 1905	Émile Combes
Jan 1905-March 1906	Maurice Rouvier (2nd)
March-Oct 1906	Ferdinand Sarrien
Oct 1906-July 1909	Georges Clemenceau (1st)
July 1909-March 1911	Aristide Briand (1st) (SP)
March-June 1911	Ernest Monis
June 1911-Jan 1912	Joseph Caillaux
Jan 1912-Jan 1913	Raymond Poincaré (1st)
Jan-March 1913	Aristide Briand (2nd) (SP)
March-Dec 1913	Louis Barthou
Dec 1913-June 1914	Gaston Doumergue (1st) (RSP)
June 1914-Oct 1915	René Viviani (SP)
Oct 1915-March 1917	Aristide Briand (3rd) (SP)
March-Sept 1917	Alexandre Ribot (3rd)
Sept-Nov 1917	Paul Painlevé (1st)
Nov 1917-Jan 1920	Georges Clemenceau (2nd)
Jan-Sept 1920	Alexandre Millerand
Sept 1920-Jan 1921	Georges Leygues
Jan 1921-Jan 1922	Aristide Briand (4th) (SP)
Jan 1922-June 1924	Raymond Poincaré (2nd)
8-15 June 1924	Frédéric François-Marsal
June 1924-April 1925	Edouard Herriot (1st) (RSP)
April-Oct 1925	Paul Painlevé (2nd)
Nov 1925-July 1926	Aristide Briand (5th) (SP)
19-21 July 1926	Edouard Herriot (2nd) (RSP)
July 1926-July 1929	Raymond Poincaré (3rd)
July-Nov 1929	Aristide Briand (6th) (SP)
Nov 1929-Feb 1930	André Tardieu (1st)
Feb-March 1930	Camille Chautemps (1st) (RSP)
March-Dec 1930	André Tardieu (2nd)
Dec 1930-Jan 1931	Théodore Steeg (RSP)
Jan 1931-Feb 1932	Pierre Laval (1st)
Feb-June 1932	André Tardieu (3rd)
June-Dec 1932	Edouard Herriot (3rd) (RSP)
Dec 1932-Jan 1933	Joseph Paul-Boncour (RSU)

Jan-Oct 1933	Edouard Daladier (1st) (RSP)
Oct-Nov 1933	Albert Sarraut (1st) (RSP)
Nov 1933-Jan 1934	Camille Chautemps (2nd) (RSP)
Jan-Feb 1934	Edouard Daladier (2nd) (RSP)
Feb-Nov 1934	Gaston Doumergue (2nd) (RSP)
Nov 1934-June 1935	Pierre Flandin (DA)
1-4 June 1935	Ferdinand Bouisson (SP)
June 1935-Jan 1936	Pierre Laval (2nd)
Jan-June 1936	Albert Sarraut (2nd) (RSP)
June 1936-June 1937	Léon Blum (1st) (SP)
June 1937-March 1938	Camille Chautemps (3rd) (RSP)
March-April 1938	Léon Blum (2nd) (SP)
April 1938-March 1940	Edouard Daladier (3rd) (RSP)
March-June 1940	Paul Reynaud (RA)
June 1940-April 1942	H.Philippe Pétain (in Vichy from July 1940)
April 1942-Aug 1944	Pierre Laval (3rd) (in Vichy) (executed 1945)
Sept 1944-Jan 1946	Charles de Gaulle (1st)
Jan-June 1946	Félix Gouin (SP)
June-Dec 1946	Georges Bidault (1st) (PRM)
Dec 1946-Jan 1947	Léon Blum (3rd) (SP)
Jan-Nov 1947	Paul Ramadier (SP)
Nov 1947-July 1948	Robert Schuman (1st) (PRM)
July-Aug 1948	André Marie (RSP)
Aug-Sept 1948	Robert Schuman (2nd) (PRM)
Sept-Oct 1948	Henri Queuille (1st) (RSP)
Oct 1948-June 1950	Georges Bidault (2nd) (PRM)
June-July 1950	Henri Queuille (2nd) (RSP)
July 1950-March 1951	René Pleven (1st) (DR)
March-Aug 1951	Henri Queuille (3rd) (RSP)
Aug 1951-Jan 1952	René Pleven (2nd) (DR)
Jan-March 1952	Edgar Faure (1st) (RSP)
March 1952-Jan 1953	Antoine Pinay (IRP)
Jan-June 1953	René Mayer (RSP)
June 1953-June 1954	Joseph Laniel (IRP)
June 1954-Feb 1955	Pierre Mendès-France (RSP)
14-19 Feb 1955	Christian Pineau (SP)
Feb 1955-Jan 1956	Edgar Faure (2nd) (RSP)
Jan 1956-June 1957	Guy Mollet (SP)
June-Nov 1957	Maurice Bourges-Maunoury (RSP)
Nov 1957-May 1958	Félix Gaillard (RSP)
May-June 1958	Pierre Pflimlin (PRM)
June 1958-Jan 1959	Charles de Gaulle (2nd)
Jan 1959-April 1962	Michel Debré (UNR)
April 1962-July 1968	Georges Pompidou (UNR)
July 1968-June 1969	Maurice Couve de Murville (DUR)

June 1969-July 1972	Jacques Chaban-Delmas (DUR)
July 1972-May 1974	Pierre Messmer (DUR)
May 1974-Aug 1976	Jacques Chirac (1st) (DUR)
Aug 1976-May 1981	Raymond Barre
May 1981-July 1984	Pierre Mauroy (SP)
July 1984-March 1986	Laurent Fabius (SP)
March 1986-May 1988	Jacques Chirac (2nd) (RFR)
May 1988-May 1991	Michel Rocard (SP)
May 1991-April 1992	Édith Cresson (*b* É.Campion) (SP)
April 1992-March 1993	Pierre Bérégovoy (SP)
March 1993-May 1995	Edouard Balladur (RFR)
May 1995-June 1997	Alain Juppé (RFR)
June 1997-	Lionel Jospin (SP)

CP = Centre Party
DA = Democratic Alliance
DR = Democratic Resistance
DUR = Democratic Union for the 5th Republic (*f* UNR)
IRP = Independent Republican Party
PRM = People's Revolutionary Movement
RA = Republican Alliance
RFR = Rally for the Republic (*f* DUR)
RSP = Radical Socialist Party
RSU = Radical Socialist Union
SP = Socialist Party
UNR = Union for the New Republic

Regions

ALSACE

Capital: Strasbourg

Council Presidents:

Jan 1974-77	André Bord (DUR,RFR)
1977-80	Pierre Schiele
1980-March 1996	Marcel Rudloff (UDF) (†)
April 1996-	Adrien Zeller (UDF)

UDF = Union pour la Democratie Française

AQUITAINE

Capital: Bordeaux

Council Presidents:

Jan 1974-79	Jacques Chaban-Delmas (1st) (DUR,RFR)

1979-82	André Labarrère (SP)
1982-85	Philippe Madrelle
1985-88	Jacques Chaban-Delmas (2nd) (RFR)
1988-93	Jean Tavernier
1993-98	Jacques Valade (RFR)
March 1998-	Alain Rousset (SP)

AUVERGNE

Capital: Clermont-Ferrand

Council Presidents:

Jan 1974-77	Jean Morellon (IRP)
1977-78	Augustin Chauvet
1978-86	Maurice Pourchon
March 1986-	Valéry Giscard d'Estaing (UDF)

BASSE-NORMANDIE

Capital: Caen

Council Presidents:

Jan 1974-75	Michel d'Ornano (1st) (IRP)
1975-78	Léon Jozeau-Marigne (1st)
1978-82	Paul Germain
1982-83	Léon Jozeau-Marigne (2nd)
1983-86	Michel d'Ornano (2nd) (IRP)
1986-	René Garrec (UDF)

BOURGOGNE
Burgundy

Capital: Dijon

Council Presidents:

Jan 1974-Jan 1978	Jean Chamant (IRP)
Jan 1978-Oct 1979	Marcel Lucotte (1st)
Oct 1979-Oct 1982	Pierre Joxe (SP)
Oct 1982-May 1983	André Billardon
May 1983-April 1985	Frédéric Lescure
April 1985-March 1989	Marcel Lucotte (2nd)
April 1989-March 1992	Raymond Janot
March 1992-March 1993	Jean-Pierre Soisson (1st)

April 1993-March 1998	Jean-François Bazin	(RFR)
March 1998-	Jean-Pierre Soisson (2nd)	(UDF)

BRETAGNE
Brittany

Capital: Rennes

Council Presidents:

Jan 1974-Jan 1976	René Pleven	
Jan 1976-79	André Colin	
1979-86	Raymond Marcellin	
1986-98	Yvon Bourges	(RFR)
March 1998-	Josselin de Rohan	(RFR)

CENTRE

Capital: Orléans

Council Presidents:

Jan 1974-Jan 1976	Raymond Boisdé	(IRP)
Jan 1976-79	Pierre Sudreau	
1979-84	Jean Delaneau	
1984-85	Daniel Bernadet	
1985-98	Maurice Dousset	(UDF)
March-April 1998	Bernard Harang	(UDF)
April 1998-	Michel Sapin	(SP)

CHAMPAGNE-ARDENNES

Capital: Reims

Council Presidents:

Jan 1974-75	Paul Granet	
1975-81	Jacques Sourdille	(DUR,RFR)
1981-88	Bernard Stasi	
1988-98	Jean Kaltenbach	(RFR)
March 1998-	Jean-Claude Étienne	(RFR)

FRANCHE-COMTE

Capital: Besançon

Council Presidents:

Jan 1974-81	Edgar Faure	(1st)
1981-82	Jean-Pierre Chevènement	(SP)
1982-88	Edgar Faure	(2nd)
1988-98	Pierre Chantelat	(UDF)
April 1998-	Jean-François Humbert	(UDF)

HAUT-NORMANDIE

Capital: Rouen

Council Presidents:

Jan 1974-75	Jean Lecanaut	
1975-81	André Bettencourt	
1981-82	Laurent Fabius	(SP)
1982-92	Roger Fosse	
March 1992-March 1998	Antoine Rufenacht	(RFR)
March 1998	Jean-Paul Gauzès	(RFR)
March 1998-	Alain Le Vern	(SP)

ÎLE DE FRANCE

Capital: Paris

Council Presidents:

July 1976-88	Michel Giraud	(1st)
1988-March 1992	Pierre-Charles Krieg	
March 1992-March 1998	Michel Giraud	(2nd)
March 1998-	Jean-Paul Huchon	(SP)

LANGUEDOC-ROUSSILLON

Capital: Montpellier

Council Presidents:

1974-75	Francis Vals	(SP)
1975-83	Edgar Tailhades	(SP)
1983-86	Robert Capdeville	
1986-	Jacques Blanc	(UDF)

LIMOUSIN

Capital: Limoges

Council Presidents:

Jan 1974-81	André Chandernagor
1981-86	Louis Longequeue
1986-	Robert Savy (SP)

LORRAINE

Capital: Nancy

Council Presidents:

Jan 1974-75	Jean Vilmain
1975-78	Jean-Jacques Servan-Schreiber
1978-80	Pierre Messmer (RFR)
1980-82	André Madoux
1982-92	Jean-Marie Rausch
April 1992-	Gérard Longuet (UDF)

MIDI-PYRÈNÉES

Capital: Toulouse

Council Presidents:

Jan 1974-81	Alain Savary (SP)
1981-86	Alex Raymond
1986-88	Dominique Baudis
1988-98	Marc Censi (UDF)
April 1998-	Martin Malvy (SP)

NORD-PAS-DE-CALAIS

Capital: Lille

Council Presidents:

Jan 1974-82	Pierre Mauroy (SP)
1982-92	Noël Josephe
April 1992-March 1998	Marie-Christine Blandin (GP)
March 1998-	Michel Delebarre (SP)

GP = Green Party

PAYS DE LA LOIRE

Capital: Nantes

Council Presidents:

Jan 1974-75	Vincent Ansquer (DUR)
1975-March 1998	Olivier Guichard (RFR)
March 1998-	François Fillon (RFR)

PICARDIE

Capital: Amiens

Council Presidents:

Jan 1974-Jan 1976	Jean Legendre
Jan 1976-78	Charles Baur (1st) (MSDF)
1978-80	Jacques Mossion
1980-81	Raymond Maillet
1981-83	René Dosière
1983-85	Walter Amsallem
1985-	Charles Baur (2nd) (SDP, UDF)

MSDF = Movement of Social Democracy of France
SDP = Social Democratic Party (*f* MSDF)

POITOU-CHARENTES

Capital: Poitiers

Council Presidents:

Jan 1974-Jan 1976	Lucien Grand
Jan 1976-78	Jacques Fourchier
1978-80	Francis Hardy
1980-82	Fernand Chaussebourg
1982-85	Raoul Cartraud
1985-86	René Monory
1986-89	Louis Fruchard
1989-	Jean-Pierre Raffarin (UDF)

PROVENCE-ALPES-CÔTE D'AZUR

Capital: Marseilles

Council Presidents:

Jan 1974-81	Gaston Defferre
1981-86	Michel Pezet
1986-98	Jean-Claude Gaudin (UDF)
March 1998-	Michel Vauzelle (SP)

RHÔNE-ALPES

Capital: Lyon

Council Presidents:

Jan 1974-81	Paul Ribeyre
1981-89	Charles Beraudier
1989-	Charles Millon (UDF)

Territorial Collectivity

CORSICA
La Corse

Capital: Ajaccio

Prefects:

1990-92	Alain Bidou
1992-93	Roger Gros
1993-94	Jean-Paul Frouin
1994-96	Jacques Coeffe
1996-Feb 1998	Claude Erignac († assassinated)
Feb 1998-April 1999	Bernard Bonnet
May 1999-	Jean-Pierre La Croix

Assembly Presidents:

Council President 1974-92

Feb 1974-Feb 1979	François Giacobbi
Feb 1979-Feb 1980	Jean Filippi
Feb 1980-July 1981	Jean-Paul de Rocca-Serra (1st) (RFR)
July 1981-Aug 1984	Prosper Alfonsi (LRM)
Aug 1984-March 1998	Jean-Paul de Rocca-Serra (2nd) (RFR)
March 1998-	José Rossi (UDF)

LRM = Left Radical Movement

Overseas Departments

FRENCH GUIANA
Guyane Française

Capital: Cayenne

Governors:

1899-1903	Émile Merwart

1903-05	Louis-Albert Grodet
1905	Charles Marchal
1905-06	Victor Rey
1906	Louis-Alphonse Bonhoure
1906-07	Edouard Picanon
1907-09	François-Pierre Rodier
1909-10	William-Maurice Fawtier
1910	Fernand-Ernest Thérond
1910-11	Paul Samary
1911	Denis-Joseph Goujon
1911-14	Pierre Didelot (1st)
1914-16	Fernand Lévécque
1916	Pierre Didelot (2nd)
1916-17	Georges Levy
1917	Jules Lauret
1917-18	Antoine Barre
1918-23	Henri Lejeune
1923	Julien-Edgard Cantau
1923-26	Marc Chanel
1926-27	Gabriel Thaly
1927	Frédéric-Adrien Juvanon
1927-28	Émile Buhot-Launay
1928-29	Camille Maillet
1929-31	Bernard Siadous
1931-33	Louis-Joseph Bouge
1933-35	Julien-Georges Lamy
1935-36	Charles de Saint Félix
1936	Pierre Tap
1936-38	René Véber (1st) (see Martinique)
1938-42	Robert-Paul Chot-Plassot
1942-43	René Véber (2nd)
1943-44	Jean Rapenne (see French Soudan)
1944-46	Jules-Eucher Surlemont
1946	Jean Pezet

Prefects:

1947-55	Robert Vignon
1955-57	Pierre Malvy
1957-58	Pierre Voitelier
1958-60	André Dubois-Chabert
1960-63	René Erignac
1963-67	René Letellier
1967-70	Paul Boutellier
1970-72	Jean Monfeix

1972-74   Jacques Delauney
1974-77   Herve Bourseiller
1977-80   Jean Le Direach
1980-81   Désiré Carli
1981-82   Maxime Gonzalvo
1982-84   Claude Silbersahn
1984-86   Bernard Courtois
1986-88   Jacques Dewatre
1988-90   Jean-Pierre Lacroix
1990-93   Jean-François di Chiara
1993-95   Jean-François Cordet
1995-97   Pierre Dartout
Jan 1997-   Dominique Vian

General Council Presidents:

1947-49   Vermont Policarpe
1949-55   Auguste Boudinot
1955-56   Eudoxie Verin
1956-58   Roland Barrat
1958-65   Joseph Symphorien
1965-67   Henri Plenet
1967-70   Jules Harmois
1970-73   Léopold Héder
1973-79   Claude Ho-A-Chuck
1979-82   Emmanuel Bellony
1982-March 1994   Elie Castor   (GSP)
March 1994-March 1998   Stéphan Phinéra-Horth   (GSP)
March 1998-   André Leconte   (DGA)

Regional Council Presidents:

1975-80   Serge Patient
1980-81   Jacques Lony
1981-March 1992   Georges Othily   (GSP)
March 1992-   Antoine Karam   (GSP)

DGA = Democratic Guyanese Action
GSP = Guiana Socialist Party

GUADELOUPE

Capital: Basse-Terre

Governors:

1895-1901   Dauphin Moracchini
1901-03   Martial-Henri Merlin

1903-05	Paul de la Loyere
1905-07	Léon Boulloche
1907-09	Victor Ballot
1909-11	Henri Cor
1911-13	Jean Peuvergne
1913-17	Émile Merwat (see Dahomey)
1917-20	Jules Gourbeil
1920-24	Pierre Duprat
1924	Jocelyn Robert (see French Polynesia)
1924-26	Maurice Beurnier
1926-29	Louis Gerbinis
1929-31	Théophile Tellier
1931-34	Alphonse Choteau (see Niger)
1934-36	Louis-Joseph Bouge
1936-39	Adolphe Eboué (see Martinique)
1939-40	Marie-François Pierre-Alype
1940-44	Constant Sorin
1944-46	Maurice Bertaut
1946-47	Ernest de Nattes

Prefects:

1947-51	Gilbert Philipson
1951-54	Gaston Villéger
1954-55	Jacques Ravaul
1955-58	Guy Malines
1958-60	Jean-Pierre Abeille
1960-65	Albert Bonhomme
1965-67	Pierre Bolotte
1967-69	Jean Deleplanque
1969-73	Pierre Brunon
1973-75	Jacques Le Cornec
1976-78	Jean-Claude Aurousseau
1978-84	Guy Maillard
1984-86	Robert Miguet
1986-87	Maurice Saborin
1987-90	Yves Bonnet
1990-91	Jean-Paul Proust
1991-93	Franck Perriez
1993-95	Alain Froute
1995-96	Michel Diefenbacher
1996-99	Jean Fedini
1999-	Jean-François Carenco

General Council Presidents:

1950-53	Joseph Pitat

1953-55	Adrien Bourgarel (1st)
1955-57	René Toribio
1957-58	Adrien Bourgarel (2nd)
1958-73	Henri Rinaldo
1973-74	Léopold Héder
1974-76	Lucien Bernier (1st)
1976-79	Georges Dagonia
1979-82	Lucien Bernier (2nd)
1982-85	Lucette Michaux-Chevry (RFR)
March 1985-March 1998	Dominique Larifla (SP)
March 1998-	Marcellin Lubeth

Regional Council Presidents:

1976-79	Pierre Mathieu
1979-83	Robert Pentier
Feb 1983-March 1986	José Moustache (RFR)
March 1986-March 1992	Félix Proto (SP)
March-Dec 1992	Lucette Michaux-Chevry (1st) (RFR)
(Dec 1992-Feb 1993	post vacant)
Feb 1993-	Lucette Michaux-Chevry (2nd) (RFR)

MARTINIQUE

Capital: Fort de France

Governors:

1898-1901	Marie-Louis Gabrié
1901-02	Louis Mouttel
1902-04	Jean Lemaire
1904-07	Louis-Alphonse Bonhoure
1907-08	Charles Lepreux
1908-13	Fernand Fourneau
1913-14	Joseph Vacher
1914-15	Georges-Virgile Poulet
1915-20	Camille Guy
1920-21	Jules-Maurice Gourbeil
1921-23	Fernand Levecque (see French Guiana)
1923-26	Henri-Marius Richard
1926-28	Robert de Guise
1928-33	Louis Gerbinis
1933-34	Adolphe Eboué
1934	René Véber
1934-35	Mathieu-Maurice Alfassa
1935-36	Louis Fousset (see French Soudan)

1936	Marie-Marc Pelicier
1936-38	Jean-Baptiste Alberti
1938	Léopold Allys
1938-39	Maurice Dechartre
1939-40	Georges-Aimé Spitz
1940-41	Louis Bressoles
1941-43	Yves-Maurice Nicol
1943-44	Louis Ponton
1944-45	Antoine-Marie Angelini
1945-46	Georges-Hubert Parisot (see Gabon)
1946	Georges Orselli (see French Polynesia)

Prefects:

1946-47	Georges Orselli
1947-50	Pierre Trouillé
1950-54	Christian Laigret
1954-57	Gaston Villéger
1957-59	Jacques Boissier
1959-61	Jean Parsi
1961-63	Michel Grollemund
1963-66	Raphaël Petit
1966-67	Pierre Lambertin
1967-69	Jean Deliau
1970-73	Jean Terrade
1973-75	Christian Orsetti
1975-78	Paul Noirot-Cosson
1978-79	Raymond Heim
1979-84	Marcel Julia
1984-85	Jean Chevance
1985-89	Edouard Croix
1989-91	Jean-Claude Roure (1st)
1991-92	Michel Morin
1992-95	Jean-Claude Roure (2nd)
1995-	Jean-François Cordet

General Council Presidents:

1946	Joseph Lagrosillière
1946-47	Georges Gratiant
1947-48	Paul Symphor
1948-53	François Duval (1st)
1953-57	Alphonse Jean-Joseph
1957-64	Tertullien Robinel
1964-70	François Duval (2nd)
1970-92	Émile Maurice (RFR)

1992-   Claude Lise   (MPP)

Regional Council Presidents:

1972-83	Camille Petit
Feb 1983-June 1988	Aimé Cesaire (MPP)
June 1988-March 1992	Camille Darsières (MPP)
March 1992-March 1998	Émile Capgras
March 1998-	Alfred Marie-Jeanne (MIM)

MIM = Martinique Independence Movement
MPP = Martinique Progress Party

RÉUNION

Capital: Saint Denis

Governors:

1896-1901	Laurent Beauchamp
1901-06	Paul Samary
1906-08	Adrien Bonhoure (see French Somaliland)
1908-10	Camille Guy
1910	Philippe-Émile Jullien
1910-13	François-Pierre Rodier
1913-20	Pierre Duprat
1920-23	Frédéric Estèbe
1923-25	Maurice-Pierre Lapalud
1925-34	Jules-Vincent Repiquet
1934-36	Alphonse Choteau
1936-38	Léon-Hippolyte Truitard
1938-40	Joseph-Urbain Court
1940-42	Pierre-Émile Aubert
1942-46	André Capagorry

Prefects:

1946-47	André Capagorry
1947-50	Paul Demange
1950-53	Roland Bechoff
1953-56	Pierre Philip
1956-62	Jean Perreau-Pradier
1962-66	Alfred Diefenbacher
1966-69	Jean Vaudeville
1969-72	Paul Cousseran (see French Polynesia)
1972-75	Claude Vieillescazes
1975-76	Robert Lamy

1977-80	Bernard Landouzy
1980-81	Jacques Seval
Aug 1981-March 1984	Michel Levallois
March 1984-May 1986	Michel Blangy
May 1986-Sept 1989	Jean Anciaux
Sept 1989-Sept 1991	Daniel Constantin
Sept 1991-1992	Jacques Dewatre (see French Guiana)
1992-94	Hubert Fournier
1994-96	Pierre Steinmetz
1996-99	Robert Pommies (see Wallis and Futuna)
1999-	Jean Daubigny

General Council Presidents:

May 1946	Paul Picard
June-Dec 1946	Léon de Lepervenche
Dec 1946-Oct 1949	Roger Vidot
Oct 1949-Jan 1966	Roger Payet
March-Sept 1966	Marcel Cerneaux
Sept 1969-March 1982	Pierre Lagourgue
March 1982-Oct 1988	Auguste Legros (RFR)
Oct 1988-Aug 1993	Eric Boyer
Aug 1993-April 1994	Joseph Sinimalé (RFR)
April 1994-March 1998	Christophe Payet (SP)
March 1998-	Jean-Luc Poudroux (UDF)

Regional Council Presidents:

Dec 1973-Jan 1978	Marcel Cernaux
Jan 1978-Feb 1983	Yves Barau
Feb 1983-March 1986	Mario Hoareau (CP)
March 1986-March 1992	Pierre Lagourgue (FRA)
March 1992-June 1993	Camille Sudre
June 1993-March 1998	Marguerite Sudre (*wife*)
March 1998-	Paul Vergès (CP)

CP = Communist Party
FRA = France-Réunion-Avenir

Overseas Territorial Collectivities

MAYOTTE

Capital: Dzaoudzi

Prefects:

1976-78	Jean-Marie Coussirou

1978-80	Jean Rigotard
1980-81	Philip Kessler
1981	Pierre Sevellec
1981-83	Christian Pellerin
1983-85	Yves Bonner
1985-87	François Bonnelle
1987-90	Akli Khider
1990-91	Daniel Limodin
1991-Feb 1993	Jean-Paul Costes
Feb 1993-95	Jean-Jacques Debacq
1995-97	Alain Weil
1997-July 1998	Philippe Boisadam
July 1998-	Pierre Bayle

General Council President:

Jan 1983-	Younoussa Bamana (PMM)

PMM = Popular Mahorais Movement

SAINT PIERRE AND MIQUELON

Capital: St Pierre

Governors:

1887-1891	Henri-Félix de la Mothe
1891-95	Paul Feillet
1895-97	Laurent Beauchamp
1897-1900	Paul-Émile Daclin-Sibour
1900-01	Paul Samary
1901-05	Philippe-Émile Jullien
1905-06	Paul Cousturier

Administrators:

1906-09	Raphaël Antonetti
1909-12	Pierre Didelot
1912-15	Charles Marchand
1915-22	Ernest Lachat
1922-23	Jean Bensch

Governors:

1923-28	Jean Bensch
1928-29	François-Adrien Juvanon
1929-32	Henri-Camille Sautot
1932-33	Georges Chanot

Administrators:

1933-37	Georges Barrillot
1937-42	Gilbert de Bournat
1942-43	Alain-François Savary
1943-46	Pierre Garrouste

Governors:

1946-47	Maurice Marchand
1947-49	Jean-Pierre Moisset
1949-50	Guy Clech
1950-52	Eugène Alaniou
1952-55	Irenée Davier
1955-58	Pierre Sicaud
1958-61	René-Louis Pont
1961-62	Pierre Maillard
1962-65	Jacques Herry (see Wallis & Futuna)
1965-67	Georges Poulet
1967-71	Jean-Jacques Buggia
1971-74	Henri Beaux
Aug 1974-June 1975	Jean Cluchard
June 1975-May 1977	Jean Massendes

Prefects:

June 1977-Sept 1979	Pierre Eydoux
Oct 1979-July 1981	Clement Bouhin
Aug 1981-March 1982	Claude Guyon
April 1982-May 1983	Philippe Parant
June 1983-March 1985	Gérard Lefèbre
April 1985-July 1987	Bernard Leurquin
July 1987-Dec 1988	Jean-René Garnier
Jan 1989-June 1991	Jean-Pierre Marquie
June 1991-93	Kamel Khrissate
1993-94	Yves Henry
1994-96	René Maurice
1996-98	Jean-François Carenco
1998-	Rémi Thuau

General Council Presidents:

Jan 1947-Feb 1952	Henri Dagort
Feb 1952-Nov 1956	Alfred-Léon Briand
Nov 1956-Nov 1964	Henri Claireaux
Nov 1964-Oct 1966	Albert Briand
Oct 1966-June 1968	Paul Lebailly

June 1968-Oct 1984	Albert Pen (SP)
Oct 1984-94	Marc Plantegenest (SP)
1994-96	Gérard Grignon (SP)
1996-	Bernard Le Soavec

Overseas Territories

FRENCH POLYNESIA
Polynésie Française

Capital: Papeete

Governors:

1881-83	Frédéric-Jean des Essarts
1883-85	Marie-Nicolas Moran
1885-93	Étienne Lacascade
1893-96	Pierre Papinaud
1896-1901	Gustave Gallet
1901	Victor Rey
1901-04	Edouard Petit
1904	Victor Lanzerac
1904-05	Henri Cox
1905-07	Philippe-Émile Jullien (see St Pierre & Miquelon)
1907-08	Elie Chartier
1908-10	Joseph-Pascal François
1910-12	Adrien Bonhoure
1912	Charles Hostein
1912-13	Baptisie-Léon Geraue
1913-15	William-Maurice Fawtier
1915-19	Gustave Julien
1919-21	Jocelyn Robert
1921-22	Auguste Guédès
1922-27	Louis Rivet
1927-28	Jean Solari
1928-30	Joseph-Louis Bouge
1930-32	Léonce Jore (see Senegal)
1932-33	Alfred-Léon Bouchet
1933-35	Michel-Lucien Montagne
1935-37	Henri-Camille Sautot (see St Pierre & Miquelon)
1937-40	Frédéric de Gery
1940-41	Émile de Curton
1941-45	Georges Orselli
1945-47	Jean-Camille Haumant
1947-49	Pierre-Louis Maestracchi
1949-50	Armand Anziani

1950-54	Jean Petitbon
1954-58	Jean-François Toby
1958	Camille-Victor Bailly (see French Soudan)
1958-61	Pierre Sicaud
1961-65	Aimé Grimald
1965-69	Jean-Charles Sicurani (see French Soudan)
1969-73	Pierre-Louis Angeli
1973-75	Daniel Videau
1975-77	Charles Schmitt

High Commissioners:

1977-81	Paul Cousseran (see Réunion)
1981-82	Paul Noirot-Cossin (see Martinique)
1982-85	Alain Ohrel
1985-88	Bernard Gerard
1988-92	Jean Montpezat
1992-94	Michel Jau
1994-97	Paul Roncière
Nov 1997-	Jean Aribaud

Government Leaders:
Vice-President of the Government Council; the High Commissioner was the non-voting President

June 1977-June 1982	Francis Sanford (UF)
June 1982-Sept 1984	Gaston Flosse (TH)

Prime Ministers:
President of the Council of Ministers

Sept 1984-Feb 1987	Gaston Flosse (1st) (TH)
Feb-Dec 1987	Jacques Teheiura (TH)
Dec 1987-March 1991	Alexandre Leontieff (TH)
March-July 1991	Gaston Flosse (2nd) (TH)
12-19 July 1991	Michel Buillard (acting) (TH)
July 1991-	Gaston Flosse (3rd) (TH)

TH = Tahoeroa Huiraatira (Popular Union Party)
UF = United Front

FRENCH SOUTHERN AND ANTARCTIC LANDS

Terres Australes et Antarctique Françaises

Administrators:
Based in Paris

1954-59	Xavier Richard

1959-71	Pierre Rolland
1971-79	Roger Barberot
1979-82	Francis Jacquemont
1982-89	Claude Pieri
1989-91	Claude Corbier
1991-92	Bernard de Gouttes
1992-97	Christian Dors
1997-98	Pierre Lise
1998-	Brigette Girardin

NEW CALEDONIA
Nouvelle Calédonie

Capital: Nouméa

Governors:

1894-1902	Paul Feillet
1902-05	Edouard Picanon
1906-08	Victor-Théophile Liotard
1909-10	Louis-Alphonse Bonhoure
1910-14	Auguste Brunet
1915-19	Jules-Vincent Repiquet (1st)
1919-20	Joseph Joulia
1921-23	Jules-Vincent Repiquet (2nd)
1923-25	Henri d'Arboussier
1925-32	Marie-Joseph Guyon
1932-33	Léonce Jore (1st) (see French Polynesia)
1933-36	Bernard Siadous
1936-38	Alexandre Machessou
1938-39	Léonce Jore (2nd)
1939	René Barthes
1939-40	Marie-Marc Pelicier
1940-42	Henri-Camille Sautot
1942-43	Marie-Henri Montchamp
1943-44	Christian Laigret
1944-47	Georges-Hubert Parisot
1948-51	Pierre Cournarie
1951-54	Raoul-Eugène Angammare
1954-56	René Hoffherr
1956-59	Aimé Grimald
1959-63	Laurent-Elisée Pechoux
1963-65	Casimir-Marc Biros
1965-69	Jean Risterucci
1969-73	Louis Verger
1973-76	Jean-Gabriel Eriau

High Commissioners:

1976-78	Jean-Gabriel Eriau
1978-81	Claude Charbonniaud
1981-82	Christian Nucci
1982-84	Jacques Roynette
1984	Charles Barbeau
Dec 1984-May 1985	Edgard Pisani
May 1985-88	Félix Wibaux
1988-91	Bernard Grasset
1991-94	Alain Christnacht
1994-95	Didier Cultiaux
Aug 1995-96	Dominique Burr
1996-98	Henri-Michel Comet
1998-	Thierry Lataste

Government Leaders:

Vice-President of the Government Council; the High Commissioner was the non-voting President

Sept 1977-Oct 1978	André Caillard (RCR)
Oct 1978-July 1979	Maurice Lenormand (CU)
July 1979-July 1982	Dick Ukéïwé (RCR)
July 1982-Nov 1984	Jean-Marie Tjibaou (CU) (assassinated 1989)

Prime Minister:

President of the Council of Ministers 1984-86
Chairman of the Executive Council 1986-88

Nov 1984-Nov 1988	Dick Ukéïwé (RCR)

Territorial Assembly Presidents:

July 1989-July 1995	Simon Loueckhote (RCR)
July 1995-June 1997	Pierre Frogier (RCR)
June 1997-May 1999	Harold Martin (RCR)

Prime Minister:

President of the Government

May 1999-	Jean Leques (RCR)

CU = Caledonian Union
RCR = Rally for Caledonia in the Republic

RIVAL GOVERNMENT

Provisional Government of Kanaky

Prime Minister:

Dec 1984-Dec 1985   Jean-Marie Tjibaou

Provinces (f Regions 1985-89)

Centre Region

Council President:

Dec 1985-July 1989   Léopold Jorédié   (CU)
(July 1989   region became part of North Province)

Loyalty Islands

Capital: Wé   (Chépénéhé)

Council Presidents:

Dec 1985-July 1989   Yeiwene Yeiwene   (CU)
July 1989-July 1995   Richard Kaloi   (CU)
July 1995-May 1999   Nidoïsh Naiseline   (KSL)
May 1999-   Robert Xowie

KSL = Kanak Socialist Liberation

North Province

(North and Centre Regions combined in 1989)
Capital: Koné

Council Presidents:

Dec 1985-July 1989   Jean-Marie Tjibaou   (CU)
July 1989-May 1999   Léopold Jorédié   (CU)
May 1999-   Paul Néaoutyine

South Province

Capital: Nouméa

Council Presidents:

Dec 1985-July 1989   Jean Leques   (RCR)
July 1989-   Jacques Lafleur   (RCR)

Wallis and Futuna

Capital: Mata-Utu

Chief Administrators:

1961	Jacques Herry (1st)
Oct 1961-March 1962	Jean Perie
March-Aug 1962	Jacques Herry (2nd)
Aug 1962-Feb 1964	Jean-Marie Bertrand
Feb 1964-July 1966	André Dufayard
July 1966-July 1968	Fernand Lamodière
July 1968-March 1971	Jacques Bach
March 1971-Nov 1976	Guy Boileau
Nov 1976-July 1979	Henri Beaux (see St Pierre & Miquelon)
July 1979-Dec 1980	Pierre Isaac
Dec 1980-Dec 1983	Robert Thill
Jan 1984-April 1985	Michel Kunmunch
Dec 1985-April 1986	Bernard Lesterlin
July 1986-Sept 1987	Jacques Le Hénaff
Nov 1987-Sept 1988	Gerard Lambotte
Sept 1988-Aug 1990	Roger Dumec
Aug-Sept 1990	Philippe Deblonde (acting)
Sept 1990-Aug 1994	Robert Pommies
Aug 1994-97	Léon Legrand
1997-98	Claude Pierret
Oct 1998-	Christian Dors (see Fr. Southern & Antarctic Lands)

Territorial Assembly Presidents:

1961-66	Paino Tuugahala
1966-71	Sosefo Makape Papilio
1971-74	Mikaele Folaumahina
1974-77	Soane Lakina
1977-83	Manuele Lisiahi (1st)
1983-85	Falakiko Gata (1st)
1985-86	Petelo Takatai
Dec 1986-March 1987	Keleto Lakalaka
March-Dec 1987	Falakiko Gata (2nd)
Dec 1987-88	Manuele Lisiahi (2nd)
1988-89	Basile Tui
1989-March 1992	Clovis Logologofolau
March 1992-Dec 1994	Soane Mani Uhita (1st)
Dec 1994-March 1997	Mikaele Tauhavili
March 1997-1999	Victor Brial (RFR)
1999-	Soane Mani Uhita (2nd)

Kingdoms of Wallis & Futuna

Ato

Kings:

1972-73	Petelo Maituku
1973-74	Mikaele Katea
1974-?	Patita Savea
?-78	Petelo Savea
1978-87	Nofeletu Tuikalepa
(1987-90	interregnum)
1990-	Lomano Musulamu

Sigave

Kings:

1929-32	Keletaona Keletaona
1932-?	Fololiano Sui Tamole
1978-79	Alafosio Keletaona
1980-82	Nasalio Keletaona
1983-84	Sagato Keletaona
1985-86	Muni Lagekula
1987-89	Sosepho Vanai
1989-Oct 1994	Lafaele Malau (deposed)
Oct 1994-	Esipio Takasi

Wallis

Kings/Queen:

1895-1904	Vito Lavelua
1904-06	Lusiano Aisake
1906-10	Sosefo Mautamakia (1st)
April 1910-Nov 1916	Soane Patita Vaimua
1917-18	Sosefo Mautamakia (2nd)
1918-24	Vitolio Kulihaapai
Nov 1924-Dec 1928	Tomasi Kulimoetoke I
Dec 1928-July 1931	Mikaele Tufele (1st)
July 1931-March 1933	Sosefo Mautamakia (3rd)
May-Nov 1933	Mikaele Tufele (2nd)
(Nov 1934-March 1941	interregnum)
March 1941-April 1947	Leone Mulikihaamea
June 1947-April 1950	Pelenato Fuluhea

April 1950-Nov 1953	Kapeliele Tufele dit Setu
Nov 1953-Sept 1958	Aloisia Tautuu (Queen)
March 1959-	Tomasi Kulimoetoke II

Prime Ministers:

? -199?	Patelise Alikiagalelei
199?-99	Make Pilioko
1999-	Atelemo Taofifenua

Former independent state

TAHITI

Now part of French Polynesia
Capital: Papeete

Kings/Queen:

c1751-1803	Pomare I (*b* Tu Tinah) (abdicated)
1803-Dec 1821	Pomare II
Dec 1821-24	Pomare III (infant)
1827-77	Pomare IV (Queen) (*b* Aimata)
1877-91	Pomare V (*b* Teri'i Tari'a)

GABON

Official name: Gabonese Republic, République Gabonaise
Independence date: 17 August 1960
Capital: Libreville

Libreville was founded by the French in 1849 and became the administrative centre for the region in 1860. Gabon was annexed to the French Congo in 1888, and in 1908 became part of French Equatorial Africa. In 1946 Gabon became an Overseas Territory. Self-government was granted in 1958, and independence in 1960.

Lieutenant-Governors:

1904-05	Louis Ormières
1905-06	Alfred-Louis Fourneau
1906-07	Fernand-Ernest Thérond
1907-09	Alfred-Albert Martineau
1909-10	Léon-Félix Richaud
1910	Joseph-Pascal François
1910-11	Adolphe-Louis Cureau (see Middle Congo)
1911-13	Georges-Virgile Poulet
1913-18	Marie-Casimir Guyon
1918-19	Maurice-Pierre Lapalud
1919-22	Jean-Henri Marchand
1922-23	Edmond-Emilien Cadier
1923	Jocelyn Robert (see French Polynesia)
1923-24	Louis Cercus
1924-31	Marie-Joseph Bernard
1931-34	Marcel Marchesson
1934-35	Louis Bonvin (1st)
1935-36	Charles Assier de Pompignan (1st)
1936-37	Louis Bonvin (2nd)
1937-38	Georges-Hubert Parisot
1938-40	Georges-Pierre Masson
1941-42	Victor Valentin-Smith
1942-43	Charles Assier de Pompignan (2nd)
1943-44	Paul Vuillaume
1944-46	Numa Sadoul

Governors:

1946-47	Roland Pré
1947-49	Numa Sadoul

1949-51   Pierre-François Pelieu
1951-52   Charles-Émile Hanin
1952-58   Yves-Jean Digo
1958   Louis Samarco

High Commissioner:

1959-60   Jean Risterucci

Presidents:

Aug 1960-Feb 1964   Léon Mba   (1st) (DGB) (deposed)
18-19 Feb 1964   Jean-Hilaire Aubame   (deposed)
Feb 1964-Nov 1967   Léon Mba   (2nd) (DGB) (†)
Nov 1967-   Omar Bongo   (f Albert-Bernard Bongo) (DGB, DPG)

Prime Ministers:

July 1958-Feb 1964   Léon Mba   (1st) (DGB)
(18-19 Feb 1964   post vacant during brief coup)
Feb 1964-Nov 1967   Léon Mba   (2nd) (†)
Nov 1967-April 1975   Omar Bongo
April 1975-May 1990   Léon Mebiame
May 1990-Oct 1994   Casimir Oyé Mba
Oct 1994-Jan 1999   Paulin Obame-Nguema
Jan 1999-   Jean-François Ntoutoume-Emane

DGB = Democratic Gabonese Block
DPG = Democratic Party of Gabon (f DGB) (sole legal party 1968-91)

THE GAMBIA

Official name: Republic of the Gambia
Previous name: Dominion of the Gambia 1965-70
Independence date: 18 February 1965
Capital: Banjul (*f* Bathurst)

During the 17th century English traders established trading settlements on the Gambia River, and from 1803 these were controlled from Sierra Leone. In 1843 Gambia became a Crown Colony and formed part of the West African Settlements from 1866 until 1888. Self-government was granted in 1963 and independence in 1965. In 1970 the Gambia became a republic. From 1982 to 1989 the Gambia and neighbouring Senegal formed the Confederation of Senegambia, each state retaining its sovereign independence.

Governors:

1901-11	George Denton
1911-14	Henry Gallwey
1914-20	Edward Cameron
1920-27	Cecil Armitage
1927-28	John Armitage
1928-30	Edward Denham
1930-33	Herbert Palmer
1933-36	Arthur Richards
1936-42	Wilfred Southorn
1942-47	Hilary Blood (see Grenada)
1947-49	Andrew Wright
1949-58	Percy Wyn-Harris
1958-62	Edward Windley
1962-65	John Paul

Governors-General:
Represented monarch who was concurrently British monarch

Feb 1965-Feb 1966	John Paul
Feb 1966-April 1970	Farimang Singhateh

Presidents:

April 1970-July 1994	Dauda Jawara (PPP) (deposed)
July 1994-	Yahya Jammeh (APRC)

COUNTRIES AND REGIONS

Chief Minister:

March 1961-June 1962   Pierre N'Jie   (UP)

Prime Minister:

June 1962-April 1970   Dauda Jawara   (PPP)
(April 1970   post abolished)

APRC = Alliance for Patriotic Reorientation and Construction
PPP = People's Progressive Party
UP = United Party

GEORGIA

Official name: Georgia, Sakartvelos

Previous names: Kingdom of Georgia until 1800, Georgian Social Democratic Republic 1918-21, Georgian Soviet Socialist Republic 1921-90, Republic of Georgia 1990-95

Independence dates: 26 May 1918; 9 April 1991

Admission to USSR: 30 December 1922 (member of Transcaucasian Federation 1922-36)

Capital: Tbilisi (*f* Tiflis until 1936)

An independent state existed in the second century BC, but was divided until the 11th century. In 1801 the country was annexed by Russia. After the Russian revolution of 1917 Georgia proclaimed itself independent, but in 1921 a soviet government was installed by Russia, and Georgia joined the Soviet Union in 1922 as a member of the Transcaucasian Federation which was dissolved in 1936. In 1990 as communist power in the Soviet Union weakened, a non-communist government came to power in Georgia which proclaimed independence in 1991. The republic has experienced internal conflicts between different power groups and attempts to secede from two regions, Abhazia and South Ossetia.

Kings/Queens:

c1008-14	Bagrat III
1014-27	Giorgi I (*son*)
1027-72	Bagrat IV (*son*)
1072-1112	Giorgi II (*son*) (co-ruler 1089-1112)
1089-1125	Dawith III (*son*) (co-ruler 1089-1112 & 1125)
1125-56	Dmitri I (co-ruler 1125 & 1155) (abdicated)
1155	Dawith IV (*son*) (co-ruler)
1156-79	Giorgi III (*brother*) (co-ruler 1179-84)
1179-1212	Thamar (*daughter*) (co-ruler 1179-84 & 1193-1212)
1193-1207	Dawith Soslan (*cousin*) (co-ruler)
1205-23	Giorgi IV (*son of Thamar*) (co-ruler 1205-12)
1223-45	Rusadan (*sister*) (co-ruler 1234-45)
1234-58	Dawith V (*son*) (co-ruler)
1250-69	Dawith VI (*son of Giorgi IV*) (co-ruler 1250-58)
(1269-73	Mongol occupation)
1274-89	Dmitri II (executed)
1289-92	Vaxtang II (*son of Dawith V*) (co-ruler 1291-92)
1291-1310	Dawith VII (*son of Dmitri*) (co-ruler 1291-92 & 1299-1310)
1301-07	Vaxtang III (*brother*) (co-ruler)
1307-14	Giorgi V (*son of Dawith VII*) (co-ruler)
1299-1346	Giorgi VI (*son of Dmitri II*) (co-ruler 1299-1314)
1346-60	Dawith VII (*son*) (co-ruler 1355-60)

1355-86	Bagrat V	(*son*) (co-ruler 1355-60 & 1369-86) (deposed)
1369-1405	Giorgi VII	(*son*) (co-ruler 1369-86)
1405-12	Konstantin I	(*brother*) (co-ruler 1408-12) (killed in battle)
1408-42	Aleksandr I	(*son*) (co-ruler 1408-12) (abdicated)
c1442-46	Vaxtang IV	(*son*)
c1446-53	Dmitri III	(*brother*) (co-ruler) (deposed)
c1446-65	Giorgi VIII	(*brother*) (co-ruler)
c1460-78	Giorgi IX	(*son*) (co-ruler)
c1460-78	Bagrat VI	(*nephew*) (co-ruler 1465-78)
(1478-1762	country divided)	
1762-98	Irakli II	
1798-Dec 1800	Giorgi XIII	(*son*)
(1801-1918	annexed by Russia)	

Presidents:

Chairman of the Central Executive Committee 1921-38
President of the Presidium of the Supreme Soviet 1938-Nov 1990
Chairman of the Supreme Soviet Nov 1990-May 1991
Chairman of the State Council March-Oct 1992
Chairman of Parliament Oct 1992-Nov 1995

1921-Feb 1922	Mikhail Tskhakaya	(1st)
Feb 1922-Jan 1924	Filipp Makharadze	(1st)
Jan 1924-June 1925	Mikhail Tskhakaya	(2nd)
June 1925-April 1927	Filipp Makharadze	(2nd)
April 1927-28	Lavrenti Kartvelishvili	
1928-29	Filipp Makharadze	(3rd)
1929-30	Mikhail Tskhakaya	(3rd)
1931-41	Filipp Makharadze	(4th) (†)
Dec 1941-March 1948	Georgi Sturua	(see Abhazia)
March 1948-April 1952	Vasili Gogua	
April 1952-53	Zakhari Chkhubianishvili	
1953-55	V. Tskhovrebashvili	
1955-April 1959	Miron Chubinidze	
April 1959-Jan 1976	Georgi Dzotsenidze	(†)
Jan 1976-March 1989	Pavel Gilashvili	(see Abhazia)
March-Nov 1989	Otar Cherkeziya	
Nov 1989-Nov 1990	Givi Gumbaridze	
Nov 1990-Jan 1992	Zviad Gamsakhurdia	(RT) (deposed)
(Jan-March 1992	Military Council Leaders: Tengiz Kitovani/Jaba Ioseliani)	
March 1992-	Eduard Shevardnadze	(CUG)

Prime Ministers:

Chairman of the Council of People's Commissars 1921-46
Chairman of the Council of Ministers 1946-95

May 1918-Feb 1919	Alaki Chkhenkeli

Feb 1919-Feb 1921	Noe Zhordania
Feb 1921-Feb 1922	P.G.(Budu) Mdivani
1922-23	Sergei Kavtaradze
1923	Filipp Makharadze
1923-24	Mikhail Tskhakaya
Jan 1924-30	Shalva Eliava (see Transcaucasia)
1930-Sept 1931	L.Sukhishvili (1st)
Sept 1931-37	G.Mgalobishvili
1937-38	L.Sukhishvili (2nd)
1938-46	Valerin Bakradze (1st)
1946-April 1952	Zakhari Chkhubianishvili
April 1952-April 1953	Z.Ketskhoveli
April-Sept 1953	Valerin Bakradze (2nd)
Sept 1953-Dec 1975	Givi Dzhavakhishvili
Dec 1975-June 1982	Zurab Pataradze († motor accident)
June 1982-April 1986	Dmitri Kartvelishvili
April 1986-March 1989	Otar Cherkeziya
March-April 1989	Zurab Chkheidze
April 1989-Nov 1990	Nodar Chitanava
Nov 1990-Aug 1991	Tengiz Sigua (1st)
Aug 1991-Jan 1992	Vissarion Gugushvili
Jan 1992-Aug 1993	Tengiz Sigua (2nd)
6-20 Aug 1993	Eduard Shevardnadze (acting)
Aug 1993-Dec 1995	Otar Patsatsia

Ministers of State:

Dec 1995-Aug 1998	Nikoloz Lekishvili
Aug 1998-	Vazha Lortkipanidze

CUG = Citizens Union of Georgia
RT = Round Table

Communist Party Leaders:

First Secretary

1920	Ivan (Mamia) Orakelashvili
1921-23	Filipp Makharadze
1923-31	Lavrenti Kartvelishvili
Nov 1931-July 1938	Lavrenti Beria (executed 1953)
July 1938-March 1952	Kandid Charkviani
March 1952-April 1953	Akaki Mgeladze (see Abhazia)
April-Sept 1953	Aleksandr Mirtskulava (see Abhazia)
Sept 1953-Sept 1972	Vasili Mzhavanadze
Sept 1972-July 1985	Eduard Shevardnadze
July 1985-April 1989	Dzhumar Tatiashvili

April 1989-Nov 1990   Givi Gumbaridze
(Nov 1990   non-communist government elected)

Autonomous republics

ABHAZIA

Official name: Abhazian Republic
Previous name: Abhazian Autonomous Soviet Socialist Republic (1921-91)
Republic formed: 4 March 1921
Capital: Sukumi

Attempted secession from Georgia caused a civil war 1992-93. Georgian forces were expelled and Abhazia regards itself as an independent state. The situation remains unresolved.

Presidents:

Chairman of the Central Executive Committee 1922-38
President of the Presidium of the Supreme Soviet 1938-90
Chairman of the Supreme Soviet 1990-Nov 1994

1922-23	Yefrem Eshba
1923-30	Samson Chauba
1930-36	Nestor Lakoba (†)
1937-38	Avksenti Rapava
1938-58	Mikhail Delba
Feb 1958-April 1978	Bagrat Shinkuba
April 1978-Sept 1991	Valerian Kobakhiya
Sept 1991-	Vladislav Ardzinba (in Gadauta 1992-93)

Prime Ministers:

Chairman of the Council of People's Commissars 1922-46
Chairman of the Council of Ministers since 1946

Feb 1922-36	Nestor Lakoba (†)
1937- ?	A.S.Agrba
? -46	Aleksandr Mirtskulava
1946-Feb 1958	Mikhail Bgazhba
Feb 1958-67	Mikhail Chikovani
1967-72	Pavel Gilashvili
May 1973-75	Shota Tatarashvili (†)
Sept 1978-April 1987	Yuza Ubilava
April 1987-July 1989	Otar Zukhbaya
July 1989-Sept 1991	Givi Anchabadze
Sept 1991-92	Zurab Erkvania (1st)
1992-Nov 1994	Sokrat Jinjolia
Jan 1995-96	Zurab Erkvania (2nd)
1996-April 1997	Gennadi Gagulia
April 1997-	Sergei Bagapsh

Communist Party Leaders:

First Secretary

1921	G.Khrishtof
1921-22	Nikolai Svanidze
1922	S.Gubelia-Mezmariashvili
April 1922-Nov 1923	N.N.Akirtava
Nov 1923-24	G.M.Makarov
1924-25	Ye.Asribekov
1925-27	Georgi Sturua
1928	A.Amus
1937	Kiril Bechvaya
? -43	M.Bechvaya
Feb 1943-52	Akaki Mgeladze
1952-53	S.Getiya
Feb 1958-Sept 1965	Mikhail Bgazhba
Sept 1965-April 1978	Valerian Kobakhiya
April 1978-April 1989	Boris Adleyba
April 1989-91	Vladimir Khishby

RIVAL GOVERNMENT

Headquarters: Tiblisi
Set up in opposition to the pro-independence government in Sukhumi

President:

Chairman of the Supreme Council

1993-	Tamaz Nadareishvili

Prime Minister:

1993-	Londer Tsaava

ADJARIA

Official name: Adjarian Republic
Previous name: Adjarian Autonomous Soviet Socialist Republic   (1921-91)
Republic formed: 16 July 1921
Capital: Butumi

Presidents:

Chairman of the Central Executive Committee until 1938
President of the Presidium of the Supreme Soviet 1938-90
Chairman of the Supreme Soviet since 1990

? -37	Zakaria Lortkipanidze	(removed, executed)

1937-41	Ismail Futkaradze
? -55	David Davitadze
April 1955-March 1969	R.Komakidze
March 1969-90	David Diasamidze
1990-91	Tengiz Khakhva
April 1991-	Aslan Abashidze

Prime Ministers:

Chairman of the Council of People's Commissars until 1946
Chairman of the Council of Ministers since 1946

? -28	—— Shimnashvili
1928-41	Levan Gogobaridze
1941- ?	Ismail Futkaradze
1953-54	David Mamuladze
1954-March 1961	Aleksandr Tkhiliashvili
March 1961-Jan 1975	Levan Davitadze
Jan 1975-Jan 1977	Irkali Dzhashi
Jan 1977-90	Yuri Ungiadze
1990-Aug 1993	Guram Chigogidze
Aug 1993	Aslan Abashidze (acting)
Aug 1993-94	Guram Varshalomidze
1994-	Jemal Nakashidze

Communist Party Leaders:

First Secretary

? -27	Nikolai Svanidze
1932-37	Artemi Geurkov
1937	Iosef Kochlamuzaashvili
1938	A.I.Taplashvili
1945-51	Kirill Bechvaya
1951-53	—— Bindsibadze
1953-March 1961	David Mamuladze
March 1961-Jan 1975	Aleksandr Tkhiliashvili
Jan 1975-Aug 1986	Vakhtang Papunidze
Aug 1986-91	G.K.Emiridze
May 1991	Ilya Tsulukidze

Autonomous region

SOUTH OSSETIA
Yugo Ossetiya

Region established: 20 April 1922
Republic proclaimed: September 1990

Capital: Tskhinvali

Attempted secession from Georgia in 1990 effectively ended by 1993

Presidents:
Chairman of the National Assembly (*f* Supreme Soviet)

1990-94	Torez Kolumbegov (jailed by Georgia 1991-92)
May 1994-	Ludvig Chibirov

Prime Ministers:
Chairman of the Executive Committee until 1991

Dec 1959-Feb 1966	V.G.Sanakoyev
Feb 1966-72	K.Dzhioyev
1972-73	Feliks Sanakoyev
Nov 1973-Nov 1981	G.I.Murdanov
Nov 1981-May 1986	Tamara Kablova
May 1986-90	Anatoly Kachmazov
1990-91	Torez Kolumbegov
Nov 1991-92	Znaur Gasiyev
1992-94	Oleg Teziyev
May 1994-96	Feliks Gasiyev
1996-97	Vladislav Gabarayev
1997-May 1998	Valery Khubulov († assassinated)
1998-	Merab Chigoyev

Communist Party Leaders:
First Secretary

Feb 1960-Feb 1965	V.D.Kozayev
Feb 1965-Nov 1973	G.N.Dzhosoyev
Nov 1973-April 1988	Feliks Sanakoyev
April 1988-Nov 1989	Anatoly Chekhoyev
1990-91	Valentin Tskhovrebashvili
1991	Znaur Gasiyev

Defunct federation

TRANSCAUCASIAN FEDERATION

Official name: Transcausian Soviet Federal Socialist Republic
Member states: Armenia, Azerbaijan, Georgia
Federation formed: 15 December 1922
Admitted to USSR: 30 December 1922
Federation dissolved: 5 December 1936
Capital: Tiflis (renamed Tbilisi in 1936)

Presidents:
Chairman of the Central Executive Committee

The Presidents of Armenia, Azerbaijan and Georgia served as co-presidents

Prime Ministers:
Chairman of the Council of People's Commissars

Dec 1922-June 1927	Ivan (Mamia) Orakelashvili (1st)
June 1927-31	Shalva Eliava
1931-32	Ivan (Mamia) Orakelashvili (2nd)
1932-36	Gazanfar Musabekov (executed 1938)

Communist Party Leaders:
First Secretary

1930-31	Vissarion Lominadze
1931-32	Ivan (Mamia) Orakelashvili
1932-36	Lavrenti Beria

GERMANY

Official name: Federal Republic of Germany, Bundesrepublik Deutschland

Previous names: German Realm 1871-1945, Federal Republic of Germany (West Germany) 1949-90, German Democratic Republic (East Germany) 1949-90

State founded: 18 January 1871, West Germany: 21 September 1949, East Germany: 7 October 1949, Reunited: 3 October 1990

Capital: Berlin (Seat of government until 1999: Bonn). W.Germany - Bonn ; E.Germany - East Berlin

In the Middle Ages, Germany was a multitude of small principalities, many of them owing allegiance to the Holy Roman Emperor. In the 18th century the electorate of Brandenburg was transformed into the Kingdom of Prussia and achieved pre-eminence through the military victories of Friedrich II (Frederick the Great). Napoléon abolished the Holy Roman Empire in 1806 and reduced the number of German states. After his defeat in 1815 the 36 German states formed a loose confederation. After Prussian victories against Austria in 1866 and France in 1870 Germany was united as an empire under the kings of Prussia, the states retaining some autonomy. A republic was proclaimed after Germany's defeat in World War II. The rise of the Nazi leader Hitler to power in 1933 was followed by German expansion into Austria, Czechoslovakia and Poland, the latter triggering World War II. After Germany's defeat in 1945 four zones of occupation were established. The Soviet zone became the German Democratic Republic, and the British, French and British zones were merged to form the Federal Republic of Germany in 1949. The communist government in the GDR collapsed in 1989, free elections were held and the two German states united in 1990 under the West German constitution.

Emperors:

Jan 1871-March 1888	Wilhelm I (King Wilhelm I of Prussia)
March-June 1888	Friedrich (*son*) (King Friedrich III of Prussia)
June 1888-Nov 1918	Wilhelm II (*son*) (King Wilhelm II of Prussia) (abdicated)

Presidents:
Führer (Leader) 1934-45
(West Germany 1949-90)

Feb 1919-Feb 1925	Friedrich Ebert (MSP) (†)
Feb-May 1925	Walter Simons (acting)
May 1925-Aug 1934	Paul von Hindenburg (†)
Aug 1934-April 1945	Adolf Hitler (NSP) († suicide)
April-May 1945	Karl Dönitz
(May 1945-Sept 1949	Governed by allied occupation forces)
Sept 1949-July 1959	Theodor Heuss (FDP)
July 1959-July 1969	Heinrich Lübke (CDU)

July 1969-July 1974   Gustav Heinemann   (SDP)
July 1974-July 1979   Walter Scheel   (FDP)
July 1979-July 1984   Karl Carstens   (CDU)
July 1984-July 1994   Richard von Weizsäcker   (CDU) (see Berlin) (*grandson of K. Weizsäcker of Württemberg*)
July 1994-July 1999   Roman Herzog
July 1999-   Johannes Rau   (SDP) (see N.Rhine-Westphalia)

Chancellors:
(West Germany 1949-90)

Jan 1871-March 1890   Otto von Bismarck   (see Prussia)
March 1890-Oct 1894   Leo von Caprivi   (see Prussia)
Oct 1894-Oct 1900   Chlodwig Hohenlohe-Schillingfurst   (see Prussia & Bavaria)
Oct 1900-July 1909   Bernhard von Bülow   (see Prussia)
July 1909-July 1917   Theobald von Bethman-Hollweg   (see Prussia)
July-Oct 1917   Georg Michaelis   (see Prussia)
Oct 1917-Oct 1918   Georg von Hertling   (see Prussia)
Oct-Nov 1918   Prince Max von Baden   (see Prussia)
Nov 1918-Feb 1919   Friedrich Ebert   (MSP)
Feb-June 1919   Philipp Scheidemann   (MSP)
June 1919-March 1920   Gustav Bauer   (MSP)
March-June 1920   Hermann Müller   (1st) (MSP)
June 1920-May 1921   Konstantin Fehrenbach   (CP)
May 1921-Nov 1922   Karl Wirth   (CP)
Nov 1922-Aug 1923   Wilhelm Cuno
Aug-Nov 1923   Gustav Stresemann   (GPP)
Nov 1923-Jan 1925   Wilhelm Marx   (1st) (see Prussia) (CP)
Jan 1925-May 1926   Hans Luther
May 1926-June 1928   Wilhelm Marx   (2nd) (CP)
June 1928-March 1930   Hermann Müller   (2nd) (SDP)
March 1930-June 1932   Heinrich Brüning   (CP)
June-Dec 1932   Franz von Papen   (see Prussia) (CP)
Dec 1932-Jan 1933   Kurt von Schleicher   (see Prussia)
Jan 1933-April 1945   Adolf Hitler   (NSP) († suicide)
30 April-1 May 1945   Joseph Goebbels   (NSP) († suicide)
(May 1945-Sept 1949   Governed by allied occupation forces)
Sept 1949-Oct 1963   Konrad Adenauer   (CDU)
Oct 1963-Dec 1966   Ludwig Erhard   (CDU)
Dec 1966-Oct 1969   Kurt-Georg Kiesinger   (CDU) (see Baden-Württemberg)
Oct 1969-May 1974   Willy Brandt   (*b* Herbert Frahm) (SDP) (see Berlin)
6-16 May 1974   Walter Scheel   (acting) (FDP)
May 1974-Oct 1982   Helmut Schmidt   (SDP)
Oct 1982-Oct 1998   Helmut Kohl   (CDU) (see Rhineland-Palatinate)
Oct 1998-   Gerhard Schröder   (SDP) (see Lower Saxony)

CP = Centre Party
CDU = Christian Democratic Union
FDP = Free Democratic Party
GPP = German People's Party
MSP = Majority Socialist Party
NSP = National Socialist Party (Nazi)
SDP = Social Democratic Party

EAST GERMANY

German Democratic Republic

Presidents:
Chairman of the State Council Sept 1960-April 1990

Oct 1949-Sept 1960	Wilhelm Pieck (†)
Sept 1960-Aug 1973	Walter Ulbricht (†)
(Aug-Oct 1973	post vacant)
Oct 1973-Oct 1976	Willi Stoph
Oct 1976-Oct 1989	Erich Honecker
Oct-Dec 1989	Egon Krenz
Dec 1989-April 1990	Manfred Gerlach (acting)
April-Oct 1990	Sabine Bergmann-Pohl (acting)

Prime Ministers:
Chairman of the Council of Ministers

Oct 1949-Sept 1964	Otto Grotewohl (†)
Sept 1964-Oct 1973	Willi Stoph (1st)
Oct 1973-Oct 1976	Horst Sindermann
Oct 1976-Nov 1989	Willi Stoph (2nd)
Nov 1989-April 1990	Hans Modrow
April-Oct 1990	Lothar de Maiziere (CDU)

Communist Party* Leaders:
*Socialist Unity Party (SUP)
Secretary-General 1950-53
First Secretary 1953-76
General Secretary 1976-89

July 1950-May 1971	Walter Ulbricht
May 1971-Oct 1989	Erich Honecker
Oct-Dec 1989	Egon Krenz
(Dec 1989	Party relinquished leading role)

States

BADEN-WÜRTTEMBERG

Formed by union of Baden, Württemberg-Baden and Württemberg-Hohenzollern
Capital: Stuttgart

Prime Ministers:
Minister-President

Dec 1951-Oct 1953	Reinhold Maier (FDP) (see Württemberg-Baden)
Oct 1953-June 1958	Gebhard Müller (CDU) (see Württemberg-Hohenzollern)
June 1958-Dec 1966	Kurt-Georg Kiesinger (CDU)
Dec 1966-Aug 1978	Hans Filbinger (CDU)
Aug 1978-Jan 1991	Lothar Spaeth (CDU)
Jan 1991-	Erwin Teufel (CDU)

BAVARIA

Bayern
Capital: Munich (München)

Kings:

Jan 1806-Oct 1825	Maximilian I
Oct 1825-March 1848	Ludwig I (*son*) (abdicated)
March 1848-March 1864	Maximilian II (*son*)
March 1864-June 1886	Ludwig II (*son*)
June 1886-Nov 1913	Otto (deposed)
Nov 1913-Nov 1918	Ludwig III (*cousin*)

Prime Ministers:
Minister-President

Feb 1799-Feb 1817	Maximilian Montegelas
Feb 1817-Oct 1825	Heinrich Reigersberg
Oct 1825-Dec 1831	Georg Zentner
Dec 1831-Oct 1837	Friedrich Gise
Oct 1837-Feb 1847	Karl von Abel
Feb-Nov 1847	Friedrich Zu-Rhein
Nov 1847-March 1848	Ludwig Ottingen-Wallerstein
March 1848-March 1849	Otto Bray-Steinburg (1st)
March 1849-March 1859	Ludwig Pfordten (1st)
March 1859-Dec 1864	Karl Schrenk
Dec 1864-Dec 1866	Ludwig Pfordten (2nd)
Dec 1866-March 1870	Chlodwig Hohenlohe-Schillingfurst
March 1870-June 1871	Otto Bray-Steinburg (2nd)

June 1871-June 1872	Friedrich Hegnenburg-Dux
Sept 1872-March 1880	Adolf Pfretzschner
March 1880-May 1890	Johann Lutz
May 1890-Feb 1903	Krafft Crailshein
Feb 1903-Feb 1912	Klemens Podewils-Durniz
Feb 1912-Nov 1917	Georg Hertling
Nov 1917-Nov 1918	Otto von Dandl
Nov 1918-Feb 1919	Kurt Eisner († assassinated)
Feb 1919-Feb 1920	Johannes Hoffmann (SDP)
Feb 1920-Aug 1921	Gustav von Kahr
Aug 1921-June 1922	Hugo von Lerchenfeld
June 1922-Feb 1924	Eugen von Knilling
Feb 1924-March 1933	Heinrich Held (BPP)
March-April 1933	Franz Ritter von Epp (NSP)
April 1933-Nov 1942	Ludwig Siebert (NSP)
Nov 1942-May 1945	Paul Giesler (NSP) († suicide)
May-Sept 1945	Friedrich (Fritz) Schaffer (BPP)
Sept 1945-Dec 1946	Wilhelm Högner (1st) (SDP)
Dec 1946-Dec 1954	Hans Ehard (1st) (CSU)
Dec 1954-Oct 1957	Wilhelm Högner (2nd) (SDP)
Oct 1957-Jan 1960	Hans Siedel (CSU)
Jan 1960-Dec 1962	Hans Ehard (2nd) (CSU)
Dec 1962-Nov 1978	Alfons Goppel (CSU)
Nov 1978-Oct 1988	Franz-Josef Strauss (CSU) (†)
Oct 1988-May 1993	Max Streibl (CSU)
May 1993-	Edmund Stoiber (CSU)

BPP = Bavarian People's Party
CSU = Christian Social Union

BERLIN

West Berlin 1947-91

Governing Mayors:

March-June 1947	Friedrich Ostrowski (SDP)
June-July 1947	Luise Schröder (acting)
July 1947-Sept 1953	Ernst Reuter (SDP) (†)
Sept 1953-Jan 1955	Walter Schreiber (SDP)
Jan 1955-Aug 1957	Otto Suhr (SDP) (†)
Oct 1957-Dec 1966	Willy Brandt (*b* Herbert Frahm) (SDP)
Dec 1966-Oct 1967	Heinrich Albertz (SDP)
Oct 1967-May 1977	Klaus Schutz (SDP)
May 1977-Jan 1981	Dietrich Stobbe (SDP)
Jan-May 1981	Hans-Jochen Vogel (SDP)

May 1981-Feb 1984	Richard von Weizsäcker (CDU)
Feb 1984-March 1989	Eberhard Diepgen (1st) (CDU)
March 1989-Jan 1991	Walter Momper (SDP)
Jan 1991-	Eberhard Diepgen (2nd) (CDU)

BRANDENBURG

Capital: Potsdam

Prime Ministers:
Minister-President

Dec 1946-Dec 1949	Karl Steinhoff (SUP)
Dec 1949-July 1952	Rudi Jahn (SUP)
(1952-90	State abolished)
Oct 1990-	Manfred Stolpe (SDP)

BREMEN

Capital: Bremen

Senate Presidents:

Jan-April 1919	Martin Donandt (1st)
April 1919-July 1920	Karl Deichmann
July 1920-March 1933	Martin Donandt (2nd)
March 1933-Oct 1934	Richard Markert
Oct 1934-June 1937	Otto Heider
June 1937-June 1944	Johann Bohmcker
June 1944-April 1945	Richard Duckwitz
26-30 April 1945	Johannes Schroers (acting)
May-Aug 1945	Erich Vagts
Aug 1945-July 1965	Wilhelm Kaisen (SDP)
July 1965-Nov 1967	Willy Dehnkamp (SDP)
Nov 1967-Sept 1985	Hans Koschnick (SDP)
Sept 1985-July 1995	Klaus Wedemeier (SDP)
July 1995-	Henning Scherf (SDP)

HAMBURG

Capital: Hamburg

Senate Presidents:

1918-Dec 1919	Werner von Melle
Jan-Feb 1920	Gustav Sthamer

Feb 1920-Dec 1923	Arnold Diestel
Jan 1924-Dec 1929	Carl Petersen (1st)
Jan 1930-Dec 1931	Rudolf Ross
Jan 1932-March 1933	Carl Petersen (2nd)
March-May 1933	Carl Krogmann
(May 1933-May 1945	post abolished)
May 1945-Nov 1946	Rudolf Petersen
Nov 1946-Dec 1953	Max Brauer (1st) (SDP)
Dec 1953-Nov 1957	Kurt Sievking (CDU)
Nov 1957-Dec 1960	Max Brauer (2nd) (SDP)
Jan 1961-June 1965	Paul Nevermann (SDP)
June 1965-June 1971	Herbert Weichmann (SDP)
June 1971-Nov 1974	Peter Schulz (SDP)
Nov 1974-June 1981	Hans-Ulrich Klose (SDP)
June 1981-May 1988	Klaus von Dohnanyi (SDP)
May 1988-Nov 1997	Henning Voscherau (SDP)
Nov 1997-	Ortwin Runde (SDP)

HESSE

Capital: Darmstadt (until 1945), Wiesbaden

Grand Dukes:

Aug 1806-April 1830	Ludwig I
April 1830-June 1848	Ludwig II (*son*)
June 1848-June 1877	Ludwig III (*son*)
June 1877-March 1892	Ludwig IV (*nephew*)
March 1892-Nov 1918	Ernst Ludwig (*son*)

Prime Ministers:

Minister-President

1821-Feb 1829	Karl von Grolmann
Feb 1829-March 1848	Karl du Bos du Thil
March-May 1848	Heinrich Gagern
May-July 1848	Carl Zimmermann
July 1848-June 1860	Heinrich Jaup
June 1860-April 1871	Karl Dalwigk
April 1871-Sept 1872	Friedrich Lindelof
Sept 1872-May 1876	Karl von Hofmann
May 1876-May 1884	Julius Rinck
May 1884-1898	Jakob Finger
1898-Jan 1906	Karl Rothe
Feb 1906-Nov 1918	Christian von Ewald
Nov 1918-Feb 1928	Carl Ulrich
Feb 1928-March 1933	Bernhard Adelung

March-Sept 1933	Ferdinand Werner
Sept 1933-March 1935	Philipp Jung
March 1935-March 1945	Jakob Sprenger
(March-Oct 1945	post vacant)
Oct 1945-Jan 1947	Karl Geiler
Jan 1947-Jan 1951	Christian Stock (SDP)
Jan 1951-Oct 1969	Georg-August Zinn (SDP)
Oct 1969-Oct 1976	Albert Osswald (SDP)
Oct 1976-April 1987	Holger Börner (SDP)
April 1987-April 1991	Walter Wallmann (CDU)
April 1991-April 1999	Hans Eichel (SDP)
April 1999-	Roland Koch (CDU)

LOWER SAXONY
Niedersachsen

Capital: Hanover

Prime Ministers:
Minister-President

Oct 1945-May 1955	Heinrich Kopf (1st) (SDP)
May 1955-May 1959	Heinrich Hellwege (CDU)
May 1959-Dec 1961	Heinrich Kopf (2nd) (SDP)
Dec 1961-July 1970	Georg Diederichs (SDP)
July 1970-Feb 1976	Alfred Kubel (SDP) (see Brunswick)
Feb 1976-May 1990	Ernst Albrecht (CDU)
May 1990-Oct 1998	Gerhard Schröder (SDP)
Oct 1998-Dec 1999	Gerhard Glogowski (SDP)
Dec 1999-	Sigmar Gabriel (SDP)

MECKLENBURG-WESTERN POMERANIA
Mecklenburg-Vorpommern

Former name: Mecklenburg 1933-52
Capital: Schwerin

Prime Ministers:
Minister President

Dec 1933-Oct 1934	Hugo Engell (NSP) (see Mecklenburg-Schwerin)
Oct 1934-May 1945	Friedrich Schärf (NSP)
(May 1945-Dec 1946	post vacant)
Dec 1946-July 1951	Wilhelm Höcker (SUP)
19-28 July 1951	Kurt Burger (SUP)
July 1951-July 1952	Bernhard Quandt (SUP)
(1952-90	State abolished)

Oct 1990-March 1992   Alfred Gomolka (CDU)
March 1992-Nov 1998   Berndt Seite (CDU)
Nov 1998-   Harald Ringstorff (SDP)

NORTH RHINE-WESTPHALIA
Nordrhein-Westfalen

Capital: Düsseldorf

Prime Ministers:
Minister-President

Aug 1946-June 1947   Rudolf Amelunxen
June 1947-Feb 1956   Karl Arnold (CDU)
Feb 1956-July 1958   Fritz Steinhoff (SDP)
July 1958-Dec 1966   Franz Meyers (CDU)
Dec 1966-Sept 1978   Heinz Kühn (SDP)
Sept 1978-May 1998   Johannes Rau (SDP)
May 1998-   Wolfgang Clement (SDP)

RHINELAND-PALATINATE
Rheinland-Pfalz

Capital: Mainz

Prime Ministers:
Minister-President

Dec 1946-June 1947   Wilhelm Boden (CDU)
June 1947-May 1969   Peter Altmeier (CDU)
May 1969-Oct 1976   Helmut Kohl (CDU) (later Chancellor)
Oct 1976-Dec 1988   Bernhard Vogel (CDU)
Dec 1988-May 1991   Carl-Ludwig Wagner (CDU)
May 1991-Oct 1994   Rudolf Scharping (SDP)
Oct 1994-   Kurt Beck (SDP)

SAARLAND

Capital: Saarbrücken
Admitted to FRG on 1 January 1957

Prime Ministers:
Minister-President

1946-Dec 1947   Max Müller
Dec 1947-Oct 1955   Johannes Hoffmann (CPP)

Oct 1955-Jan 1956	Heinrich Welsch
Jan 1956-March 1957	Hubert Ney (CDU)
March 1957-April 1959	Egon Reinart (CDU) († motor accident)
April 1959-June 1979	Franz-Josef Röder (CDU) (†)
June 1979-March 1985	Werner Zeyer (CDU)
March 1985-Nov 1998	Oskar Lafontaine (SDP)
Nov 1998-Sept 1999	Reinhard Klimmt (SDP)
Sept 1999-	Peter Müller (CDU)

CPP = Christian People's Party

SAXONY
Sachsen

Capital: Dresden

Kings:

Dec 1806-May 1827	Friedrich August I
May 1827-June 1836	Anton (*brother*)
June 1836-Aug 1854	Friedrich August II (*nephew*)
Aug 1854-Oct 1873	Johann (*brother*)
Oct 1873-June 1902	Albrecht (*son*)
June 1902-Oct 1904	Georg (*brother*)
Oct 1904-Nov 1918	Friedrich August III (*son*) (abdicated)

Prime Ministers:
Minister-President

March 1848-Feb 1849	Alexander Braun
Feb-May 1849	Gustav Held
May 1849-Oct 1858	Ferdinand von Zschinsky
Oct 1858-Aug 1866	Friedrich von Beust
Aug 1866-Oct 1871	Johann Falkenstein
Oct 1871-Nov 1876	Richard Friesen
Nov 1876-March 1891	Alfred von Friesen
March 1891-June 1901	Karl von Gerber
June 1901-April 1906	Georg von Metzsch-Reichenbach
April 1906-Dec 1910	Konrad von Ruger
Dec 1910-July 1912	Viktor von Otto
July 1912-May 1914	Max Hausen
May 1914-Oct 1918	Heinrich Beck
Oct-Nov 1918	Rudolf Heinze (1st)
Nov 1918-Jan 1919	Richard Lipinski (SP)
Jan 1919-May 1920	Georg Gradnauer (MSP)
May 1920-March 1923	Wilhelm Buck (MSP)

March-Oct 1923	Erich Zeigner (SDP)
29-31 Oct 1923	Rudolf Heinze (2nd) (GPP)
Oct 1923-Jan 1924	Karl Fellisch (SDP)
Jan 1924-June 1929	Max Heldt (SDP)
June 1929-Feb 1930	Wilhelm Bünger (GPP)
May 1930-March 1933	Walter Schieck
March 1933-Feb 1935	Manfred von Killinger (NSP)
Feb 1935-May 1945	Martin Mutschmann (NSP)
(May-July 1945	post vacant)
July 1945-June 1947	Rudolf Friedrichs (SDP)
July 1947-July 1952	Max Seydewitz (SUP)
(1952-90	State abolished)
Oct 1990-	Kurt Biedenkopf (CDU)

SAXONY-ANHALT

Sachsen-Anhalt

Capital: Halle

Prime Ministers:
Minister-President

Aug 1945-Nov 1950	Erhard Hubener (LDP)
Nov 1950-July 1952	Werner Bruschke (SUP)
(1952-90	State abolished)
Oct 1990-July 1991	Gerd Gies (CDU)
July 1991-Nov 1993	Werner Münch (CDU)
Dec 1993-July 1994	Christoph Bergner (CDU)
July 1994-	Reinhard Höppner (SDP)

LDP = Liberal Democratic Party

SCHLESWIG-HOLSTEIN

Capital: Kiel

Prime Ministers:
Minister-President

April 1946-April 1947	Theodor Steltzer (CDU)
April 1947-Aug 1949	Hermann Ludemann (SDP)
Aug 1949-Sept 1950	Bruno Diekmann (SDP)
Sept 1950-June 1951	Walter Bartram (CDU)
June 1951-Oct 1954	Friedrich Lübke (CDU)
Oct 1954-Jan 1963	Kai-Uwe von Hassel (CDU)
Jan 1963-May 1971	Helmut Lemke (CDU)
May 1971-Oct 1982	Gerhard Stoltenberg (CDU)

Oct 1982-Sept 1987	Uwe Barschel	(CDU)
Sept 1987-May 1988	Henning Schwarz	(CDU)
May 1988-May 1993	Bjorn Engholm	(SDP)
May 1993-	Heide Simonis	(*b* H.Steinhardt) (SDP)

THURINGIA
Thüringen

Capital: Weimar

Prime Ministers:
Minister-President

Nov 1920-Oct 1921	Arnold Paulssen	(1st) (DP)
Oct 1921-Feb 1924	August Frölich	(MSP,SDP)
Feb 1924-Aug 1928	Richard Leutheusser	(GPP)
Nov 1928-April 1929	K.Riedel	(GPP)
May-Oct 1929	Arnold Paulssen	(2nd) (DP)
Jan 1930-July 1932	Erwin Baum	(CL)
Aug 1932-May 1933	Fritz Sauckel	(NSP)
May 1933-April 1945	Willy Marschler	(NSP)
(April-July 1945	post vacant)	
July 1945-Sept 1947	Rudolf Paul	(SUP)
Sept 1947-July 1952	Werner Eggerath	(SUP)
(1952-90	State abolished)	
Oct 1990-Feb 1992	Josef Duchac	(CDU)
Feb 1992-	Bernhard Vogel	(CDU) (see Rhineland-Palatinate)

CL = Country League

Former states

ANHALT

Capital: Dessau

Dukes:

April 1807-Aug 1817	Leopold III	
Aug 1817-May 1871	Leopold IV	(*grandson*)
May 1871-Jan 1904	Friedrich I	(*son*)
Jan 1904-April 1918	Friedrich II	(*son*)
April-Sept 1918	Eduard	(*brother*)
Sept-Nov 1918	Joachim Ernst	(*son*)
	(Regent: Prince Aribert)	

Prime Ministers:

8-14 Nov 1918	Max Gutknecht
Nov 1918-July 1919	Wolfgang Heine (MSP)
July 1919-July 1924	Heinrich Deist (1st) (MSP,SDP)
July-Nov 1924	R.Willi Knorr (GNP)
Nov 1924-Feb 1932	Heinrich Deist (2nd) (SDP)
May 1932-Jan 1940	Alfred Freyburg (NSP)
Jan 1940-April 1945	Rudolf Jordan (NSP)

GNP = German National Party

Anhalt became part of the state of Saxony-Anhalt.

BADEN

Capital: Karlsruhe (until 1945), Freiburg (1945-52)

Dukes:

Aug 1806-June 1811	Karl Friedrich
June 1811-Dec 1818	Karl (*grandson*)
Dec 1818-March 1830	Ludwig I (*uncle*)
March 1830-April 1852	Leopold (*brother*)
April 1852-Sept 1856	Ludwig II (*son*)
	(Regent: 1852-56 Prince Friedrich)
Sept 1856-Sept 1907	Friedrich I (*brother*) (*f* Regent)
Sept 1907-Nov 1918	Friedrich II (*son*) (abdicated)

Prime Ministers:

1830-38	Georg Winter
1838-39	Karl Nebenius (1st)
1839-Nov 1843	Friedrich Blittersdorf
Nov 1843-March 1845	Christian von Boeckh
March 1845-Dec 1846	Karl Nebenius (2nd)
Dec 1846-March 1848	Johann Bekk
March 1848-June 1849	Karl Hoffmann
July 1849-May 1856	Friedrich Kluber
May 1856-April 1860	Franz Stengel
April 1860-July 1866	Anton von Stabel
July 1866-Feb 1868	Karl Mathy
Feb 1868-Sept 1876	Julius Jolly
Sept 1876-March 1893	Friedrich Turban
March 1893-June 1901	Franz Nokk
June 1901-March 1905	Arthur von Braun
March 1905-Dec 1917	Alexander Dusch

Dec 1917-Nov 1918   Heinrich Bodman
Nov 1918-Aug 1920   Anton Geiss   (MSP)
Aug 1920-Nov 1921   Gustav Trunk   (1st) (CP)
Nov 1921-Nov 1922   Hermann Hummel   (DP)
Nov 1922-Nov 1923   Adam Remmele   (1st) (SDP)
Nov 1923-Nov 1924   Heinrich Köhler   (1st) (CP)
Nov 1924-Nov 1925   Willi Hellpach   (DP)
Nov 1925-Nov 1926   Gustav Trunk   (2nd) (CP)
Nov 1926-Feb 1927   Heinrich Köhler   (2nd) (CP)
Feb-Nov 1927   Gustav Trunk   (3rd) (CP)
Nov 1927-Nov 1928   Adam Remmele   (2nd) (SDP)
Nov 1928-Nov 1930   Josef Schmitt   (1st) (CP)
Nov 1930-Sept 1931   Josef Wittemann   (CP)
Sept 1931-March 1933   Josef Schmitt   (2nd) (CP)
March-May 1933   Robert Wagner   (NSP)
May 1933-April 1945   Walter Köhler   (NSP)
(April 1945-Dec 1946   post vacant)
Dec 1946-April 1952   Leonhard Wohleb   (BCSU, CDU)

BCSU = Baden Christian Social Union
DP = Democratic Party

Baden is now part of Baden-Württemberg

BRUNSWICK
Braunschweig

Capital: Brunswick

Dukes:

Sept 1735-March 1780   Karl I
March 1780-Nov 1806   Karl II   (*son*)
Nov 1806-June 1815   Friedrich Wilhelm   (*son*)
June 1815-Dec 1830   Karl III   (*son*) (deposed)
Dec 1830-Oct 1884   Wilhelm   (*brother*)
1885-Sept 1906   Regent: Albrecht
1907-Nov 1913   Regent: Johann Albrecht
Nov 1913-Nov 1918   Ernst August   (*grandson of Georg V of Hanover*)

Prime Ministers:

Nov 1918-April 1919   Sepp Oerter   (1st) (SP)
April 1919-June 1920   Heinrich Jasper   (1st) (SDP)
June 1920-Nov 1921   Sepp Oerter   (2nd) (SP)
Nov 1921-March 1922   August Junke   (SP)
March-May 1922   Otto Antrick   (SDP)

May 1922-Dec 1924	Heinrich Jasper (2nd) (SDP)
Dec 1924-Dec 1927	Gerhard Marquordt (GPP)
Dec 1927-Oct 1930	Heinrich Jasper (3rd) (SDP)
Oct 1930-March 1933	Werner Kuchenthal (GNPP)
March 1933-April 1945	Dietrich Klagges (NSP)
May 1945-May 1946	Hubert Schlebusch
May-Nov 1946	Alfred Kubel

GNPP = German National People's Party
SP = Socialist Party

Brunswick, Oldenburg & Hanover united in 1946 to form the state of Lower Saxony.

HANOVER

Capital: Hanover

Electors:

1692-Jan 1698	Ernst August
Jan 1698-June 1727	Georg I (George I of England)
June 1727-Oct 1760	Georg II (*son*) (George II of England)
Oct 1760-Oct 1814	Georg III (*son*) (George III of England)

Kings:

Oct 1814-Jan 1820	Georg III
Jan 1820-June 1830	Georg IV (*son*) (George IV of England)
June 1830-June 1837	Wilhelm (William IV of England)
June 1837-Nov 1851	Ernst August (*brother*)
Nov 1851-Sept 1866	Georg V (*son*)

Prime Ministers:

March 1848-Oct 1850	Alexander Benningsen
Oct 1850-Nov 1851	Alexander Münchhausen
Nov 1851-Nov 1853	Eduard Schele
Nov 1853-July 1855	Eduard von Lutcken
Aug 1855-Dec 1862	Eduard Kielmansegg-Gulzow
Dec 1862-Oct 1865	Wilhelm Hammerstein
Oct 1865-June 1866	Georg Bacmeister

In 1866 Hanover was incorporated into Prussia

HESSE-CASSEL

Capital: Cassel

Electors:

Oct 1795-Nov 1808	Wilhelm I (1st)

(Nov 1808-Nov 1813   French occupation)
Nov 1813-Feb 1821   Wilhelm I   (2nd)
Feb 1821-Nov 1847   Wilhelm II   (*son*)
Nov 1847-Aug 1866   Friedrich Wilhelm   (*son*)

Prime Ministers:

Jan 1831-May 1832	Schenk von Schweinsberg
May 1832-July 1837	Hans Hassenpflug (1st)
July 1837-Oct 1841	Carl von Hanstein
Nov 1841-Sept 1847	Hermann Koch
Sept 1847-March 1848	Friedrich Scheffer (1st)
March 1848-Feb 1850	Bernhard Eberhard
Feb 1850-Oct 1855	Hans Hassenpflug (2nd)
Oct 1855-May 1860	Friedrich Scheffer (2nd)
May 1860-June 1866	Carl von Stiernberg

Hesse-Cassel was incorporated into Prussia in 1866

LIPPE

Capital: Detmold

Princes:

Oct 1720-Oct 1734	Simon Heinrich Adolf
Oct 1734-May 1782	Simon August (*son*)
May 1782-April 1802	Leopold I (*son*)
	(Regent: 1782-9 Count Adolf)
April 1802-Jan 1851	Leopold II (*son*)
Jan 1851-Dec 1875	Leopold III (*son*)
Dec 1875-March 1895	Woldemar (*brother*)
March 1895-Oct 1905	Alexander (*brother*)
	Regents: 1895-7 Prince Adolf of Lippe-Bieterfeld
	1897-1904 Count Ernst of Lippe-Bieterfeld
	1904-5 Count Leopold of Lippe-Bieterfeld
Oct 1905-Nov 1918	Leopold IV (*f* Regent)

Prime Ministers:

Nov 1918-March 1933	Heinrich Drake
1933	Ernst Krappe
1933-36	Hans Riecke
1936-April 1945	Alfred Meyer

Lippe is now part of the state of North Rhine-Westphalia.

LÜBECK

Capital: Lübeck

Governing Mayors:

1917-20	Emil Fehling
1920-27	Johann Neumann
1927-May 1933	Paul Nowigt
March 1933-April 1937	Otto-Heinrich Dreschler

In 1937 Lübeck was incorporated into the Prussian province of Schleswig-Holstein

MECKLENBURG-SCHWERIN

Capital: Schwerin

Grand Dukes (Dukes until 1815):

Nov 1747-May 1756	Christian Ludwig II
May 1756-April 1785	Friedrich (*son*)
April 1785-Feb 1837	Friedrich Franz I (*nephew*)
Feb 1837-March 1842	Paul Friedrich (*grandson*)
March 1842-April 1883	Friedrich Franz II (*son*)
April 1883-April 1897	Friedrich Franz III (*son*)
April 1897-Nov 1918	Friedrich Franz IV (*son*)

Prime Ministers:

Nov 1918-July 1920	Hugo Wendorff (DP)
July 1920-April 1921	Hermann Reinicke-Bloch
April 1921-March 1924	Johannes Stelling (MSP)
March 1924-July 1926	Joachim von Brandenstein (GNP)
July 1926-July 1929	Paul Schröder (SDP)
July 1929-June 1932	Karl Eschenburg (MNLP)
June 1932-Aug 1933	Walter Granzow (NSP)
Aug-Dec 1933	Hugo Engell (NSP)

MNLP = Mecklenburg National Labour Party

United with Mecklenburg-Strelitz in 1933 to form Mecklenburg

MECKLENBURG-STRELITZ

Capital: Strelitz

Grand Dukes (Dukes until 1815):

March 1701-May 1708	Adolf Friedrich II

May 1708-Dec 1752	Adolf Friedrich III	*(nephew)*
Dec 1752-June 1794	Adolf Friedrich IV	*(brother)*
June 1794-Nov 1816	Karl	*(son)*
Nov 1816-Sept 1860	Georg	*(son)*
Sept 1860-May 1904	Friedrich Wilhelm	*(son)*
May 1904-June 1914	Adolf Friedrich V	*(son)*
June 1914-Feb 1918	Adolf Friedrich VI	*(son)* († suicide)

Prime Ministers:

Nov 1918-Jan 1919	Peter Stubmann (DP)
Jan-Oct 1919	Hans Kruger (MSP)
Oct 1919-July 1923	Kurt von Reibnitz (1st) (MSP)
July 1923-Feb 1928	Karl Schwabe (GNP)
March 1928-April 1929	Kurt von Reibnitz (2nd) (SDP)
12-16 April 1929	Kurt Häntzschel
April 1929-Dec 1931	Kurt von Reibnitz (3rd) (SDP)
Dec 1931-May 1933	Heinrich von Michael (GNP)
May-Dec 1933	Fritz Stichtenoth (NSP)

United with Mecklenburg-Schwerin in 1933 to form Mecklenburg

NASSAU

Capital: Wiesbaden

Dukes:

1719-Nov 1753	Karl August	
Nov 1753-Nov 1788	Karl	*(son)*
Nov 1788-Jan 1816	Friedrich Wilhelm	*(son)*
Jan 1816-Aug 1839	Wilhelm	*(son)*
Aug 1839-Sept 1866	Adolf	*(son)* (see Luxembourg)

Nassau was annexed to Prussia in 1866 and is now part of the state of Hesse.

OLDENBURG

Capital: Oldenburg

Grand Dukes (Dukes until 1829):

July 1823-May 1829	Peter I	
May 1829-Feb 1853	August	*(son)*
Feb 1853-June 1900	Peter II	*(son)*
June 1900-Nov 1918	Friedrich August	*(son)*

Prime Ministers:

1814-42	Carl von Brandenstein

1843-48	Wilhelm von Beaulieu
1848	Johann Schloifer
1849-51	Christian von Buttel
1851-74	Peter Rossing
1874-76	Carl von Berg
1876-90	Friedrich Andreas Ruhstrat
1890-1900	Gerhard Jansen
1901-08	Friedrich Willich
1908-16	Friedrich Julius Ruhstrat
1916-18	Franz Ruhstrat
Nov 1918-June 1919	Bernhard Kuhut
June 1919-April 1923	Theodor Tantzen (1st)
April 1923-Dec 1930	Eugen von Finckh
Dec 1930-June 1932	Friedrich Cassebohm
June 1932-May 1933	Carl Rover
May 1933-May 1945	Georg Joel
May 1945-Nov 1946	Theodor Tantzen (2nd)

Oldenburg, Brunswick and Hanover merged in 1946 to form the state of Lower Saxony.

PRUSSIA
Preussen

Capital: Berlin

Kings:

Jan 1701-Feb 1713	Friedrich I
Feb 1713-April 1740	Friedrich Wilhelm I (*son*)
April 1740-Aug 1786	Friedrich II (*son*)
Aug 1786-Nov 1797	Friedrich Wilhelm II (*nephew*)
Nov 1797-June 1840	Friedrich Wilhelm III (*son*)
June 1840-Jan 1861	Friedrich Wilhelm IV (*son*)
Jan 1861-March 1888	Wilhelm I (*brother*) (Emperor of Germany from 1871)
March-June 1888	Friedrich III (*son*) (Emperor of Germany)
June 1888-Nov 1918	Wilhelm II (*son*) (Emperor of Germany) (abdicated)

Prime Ministers:

March 1848	Adolf Arnim-Boitzenburg
March-Sept 1848	Ludolf Camphausen
Sept-Oct 1848	Ernst von Pfuel
Nov 1848-Nov 1850	Count Friedrich Wilhelm von Brandenburg
Dec 1850-Nov 1858	Otto Manteuffel
Nov 1858-March 1862	Karl Hohenzollern-Sigmaringen
March-Nov 1862	Adolf Hohenlohe-Ingelfuigen
Nov 1862-Jan 1873	Otto von Bismarck (1st)

Jan-Nov 1873	Albrecht Roon
Nov 1873-March 1890	Otto von Bismarck (2nd) (†) (Chancellor of Germany)
March 1890-March 1892	Leo von Caprivi (Chancellor)
March 1892-Oct 1894	Botho Eulenburg
Oct 1894-Oct 1900	Chlodwig Hohenlowe-Schillingfurst (Chancellor, also see Bavaria)
Oct 1900-July 1909	Bernhard von Bülow (Chancellor)
July 1909-July 1917	Theobald von Bethmann-Hollweg (Chancellor)
July-Oct 1917	Georg Michaelis (Chancellor)
Oct 1917-Oct 1918	Georg von Hertling (Chancellor)
Oct-Nov 1918	Prince Max von Baden (Chancellor)
Nov 1918-March 1920	Paul Hirsch (MSP)
March 1920-April 1921	Otto Braun (1st) (MSP)
April-Nov 1921	Adam Stegerwald (CP)
Nov 1921-Feb 1925	Otto Braun (2nd) (MSP)
18-20 Feb 1925	Wilhelm Marx (CP) (*f* & later Chancellor)
April 1925-June 1932	Otto Braun (3rd) (MSP)
June-July 1932	Heinrich Hirtsiefer (CP)
July-Dec 1932	Franz von Papen (1st) (CP) (Chancellor)
Dec 1932-Jan 1933	Kurt von Schleicher (Chancellor)
Jan-April 1933	Franz von Papen (2nd) (GNP) (Chancellor)
April 1933-April 1945	Hermann Göring (NSP)

The state of Prussia was abolished in 1945 and divided between Poland and Germany.

REUSS-GREIZ

Capital: Greiz

Princes (Counts until 1778):

1714-Nov 1722	Heinrich II
Nov 1722-March 1723	Heinrich IX (*son*)
March 1723-June 1800	Heinrich XI (*son*)
June 1800-Jan 1817	Heinrich XIII (*son*)
Jan 1817-Oct 1836	Heinrich XIX (*son*)
Oct 1836-Nov 1859	Heinrich XX (*brother*)
Nov 1859-April 1902	Heinrich XXII (*son*)
April 1902-Nov 1918	Heinrich XXIV (*son*) (abdicated)

Reuss-Greiz became part of Thuringia in 1920

REUSS-SCHLEIZ

Capital: Gera

Princes (Counts until 1806):

Dec 1744-June 1784	Heinrich XII

June 1784-April 1818	Heinrich XLII	(son)
April 1818-June 1854	Heinrich LXII	(son)
June 1854-July 1867	Heinrich LXVIII	(brother)
July 1867-March 1913	Heinrich XIV	(son)
March 1913-Nov 1918	Heinrich XXVII	(son) (abdicated)

Reuss-Schleiz became part of Thuringia in 1920

SAXE-ALTENBURG

Capital: Altenburg

Dukes:

Nov 1826-Sept 1834	Friedrich	
Sept 1834-Nov 1848	Joseph	(son) (abdicated)
Dec 1848-Aug 1853	Georg	(brother)
Aug 1853-Feb 1908	Ernst I	(son)
Feb 1908-Nov 1918	Ernst II	(nephew) (abdicated)

Prime Ministers:

Nov 1918-March 1919	Wilhelm Tell
March 1919-Nov 1920	August Frolich

Saxe-Altenburg became part of Thuringia in 1920

SAXE-COBURG-GOTHA

Capital: Coburg

Dukes:

Dec 1806-Jan 1844	Ernst I	
Jan 1844-Aug 1893	Ernst II	(son)
Aug 1893-July 1900	Alfred	(nephew, & son of Queen Victoria of UK)
July 1900-Nov 1918	Karl Eduard	(deposed)

Prime Minister:

1919-Nov 1920	Ernst Fritsch

Saxe-Coburg-Gotha was divided between Bavaria and Thuringia

SAXE-MEININGEN

Capital: Meiningen

Dukes:

Jan 1763-July 1782	Carl/Georg I	(brothers)

July 1782-Dec 1803	Georg I
Dec 1803-Sept 1866	Bernhard II (*son*) (abdicated)
Sept 1866-June 1914	Georg II (*son*)
June 1914-Nov 1918	Bernhard III (*son*) (abdicated)

Prime Minister:

Nov 1918-Nov 1920	Ludwig von Turcke

Saxe-Meiningen became part of Thuringia in 1920

SAXE-WEIMAR-EISENSACH

Capital: Weimar

Grand Dukes (Dukes until 1815):

1741-Jan 1748	Ernst August I
Jan 1748-May 1758	Ernst August II (*son*)
May 1758-June 1828	Carl August (*son*)
June 1828-July 1853	Carl Friedrich (*son*)
July 1853-Jan 1901	Carl Alexander (*son*)
Jan 1901-Nov 1918	Wilhelm Ernst (*grandson*) (abdicated)

Saxe-Weimer-Eisensach became part of Thuringia in 1920

SCHAUMBERG-LIPPE

Capital: Bückeburg

Princes:

Aug 1808-Nov 1860	Georg I
Nov 1860-May 1893	Adolf I (*son*)
May 1893-April 1911	Georg II (*son*)
April 1911-Nov 1918	Adolf II (*son*)

Prime Ministers:

1849-71	Eduard von Laur-Munchhofen
(1871-85	post abolished)
1885-95	Heinrich Spring
1895-97	Martin von Wegnern
1898-1918	Friedrich von Feilitzsch
1918-19	Heinrich Lorenz (1st)
1919-22	Otto Bömers
1922-23	Konrad Wippermann
1923-27	Erich Steinbrecher
1927-33	Heinrich Lorenz (2nd)

1933-45   Karl Dreier

Schaumberg-Lippe became part of Lower Saxony in 1946

SCHWARZENBURG-RUDOLSTADT

Capital: Rudolstadt

Princes:

1767-Aug 1790	Ludwig Gunther IV
Aug 1790-April 1793	Friedrich Karl (*son*)
April 1793-April 1807	Ludwig Friedrich II (*son*)
April 1807-June 1867	Friedrich Gunther (*son*)
June 1867-Nov 1869	Albrecht (*brother*)
Nov 1869-Jan 1890	Georg (*son*)
Jan 1890-Nov 1918	Gunther (*cousin*)

Prime Minister:

1919-Nov 1920   Emil Hartmann

Schwarzenburg-Rudolstadt became part of Thuringia in 1920

SCHWARZENBURG-SONDERSHAUSEN

Capital: Sondershausen

Princes:

1740-Nov 1758	Heinrich XXXVIII
Nov 1858-Oct 1794	Christian Gunther III (*nephew*)
Oct 1794-Aug 1835	Gunther Karl I (*son*) (abdicated)
Aug 1835-July 1880	Gunther Karl II (*son*) (abdicated)
July 1880-March 1909	Karl
March 1909-Nov 1918	Gunther (of Schwarzenburg-Rudolstadt)

Prime Minister:

1919-Nov 1920   Theodor Bauer

Schwarzenburg-Sonderhausen became part of Thuringia in 1920

WALDECK

Capital: Arolsen

Princes:

Sept 1813-May 1845   Georg II

May 1845-May 1893	Georg Viktor
	(Regent: 1845-52 Princess Emma, later Regent of the Netherlands)
May 1893-Nov 1918	Friedrich

Prime Ministers:

March-July 1848	Carl von Stockhausen
July 1848-June 1849	Wilhelm Gleisner
June 1849-1851	Wolrad Schumacher
1851-67	Carl Winterberg
Jan 1868-72	Adalbert von Flottwell
1872-81	Hugo von Sommerfeld
1881-84	Jesko von Putkamer
1885-86	Ernst von Saldern
1886-1907	Johannes von Saldern
1907-08	Leo von Lutzow
1908-14	Ernst von Glasenapp
1914-20	Wilhelm von Redern
1920-March 1929	Wilhelm Schmieding

Waldeck was incorporated into Hesse in 1929

WÜRTTEMBERG

Capital: Stuttgart

Kings:

Dec 1805-Oct 1816	Friedrich
Oct 1816-June 1864	Wilhelm I
June 1864-Oct 1891	Karl (*son*)
Oct 1891-Nov 1918	Wilhelm II

Prime Ministers:

March 1848-Oct 1849	Friedrich von Romer
Oct 1849-July 1850	Johannes von Schlayer
July 1950-Sept 1864	Joseph Linden
Sept 1864-Aug 1870	Karl Varnbuler
Aug 1870-July 1876	Johann Wachter
July 1876-Nov 1900	Hermann Mittnacht
Nov 1900-April 1901	Max Schott
April 1901-Dec 1906	Wilhelm von Breitlung
Dec 1906-Nov 1918	Karl Weizsäcker
Nov 1918	Theodor Liesching (PPP)
Nov 1918-June 1920	Wilhelm Blos (MSP)
June 1920-April 1924	Johannes von Heiber (DP)

April-June 1924	Eduard Rau	(acting)
June 1924-June 1928	Wilhelm Bazille	(GNP)
June 1928-March 1933	Eugen Bolz	(CP)
March-May 1933	Wilhelm Murr	(NSP)
May 1933-April 1945	Christian Mergenthaler	(NSP)

PPP = Progressive People's Party

Württemberg is now part of the state of Baden-Württemberg.

WÜRTTEMBERG-BADEN

Capital: Stuttgart

Prime Minister:

Minister-President

Sept 1945-April 1952   Reinhold Maier   (FDP) (later PM of Baden-Württemberg)

Württemberg-Baden is now part of Baden-Württemberg.

WÜRTTEMBERG-HOHENZOLLERN

Capital: Tübingen

Prime Ministers:

Minister-President

July 1947-Aug 1948   Lorenz Bock   (CDU)
Aug 1948-April 1952   Gebhard Müller   (CDU) (later PM of Baden-Württemberg)

Württenberg-Hohenzollern is now part of Baden-Württemberg.

GHANA

Official name: Republic of Ghana
Previous names: Gold Coast until 1957, Dominion of Ghana 1957-60
Independence date: 6 March 1957
Capital: Accra

The Portuguese began trading on the Gold Coast in 1471, but were displaced by the Dutch and English in the 17th century. In 1821 Britain assumed control of the Gold Coast and an administration was established at Accra. The Ashanti kingdom was annexed to the colony in 1901. A measure of self-government was granted in 1951, followed by full self-government the following year. In 1957 Gold Coast became independent, taking the name of the ancient West African state of Ghana. It became a republic in 1960. Ghana has had four periods of military rule; a multi-party democracy was re-instituted in 1993.

Governors:

1900-04	Matthew Nathan
1904-10	John Rodger
1910-12	James Thorburn
1912-19	Hugh Clifford
1919-27	Frederick Guggisberg
1927-32	Alexander Slater
1932-34	Thomas Thomas
1934-41	Arnold Hodson
1941-48	Alan Burns
1948-49	Gerald Creasy
1949-57	Charles Arden-Clarke (see Basutoland)

Governors-General:

Represented monarch who was concurrently British monarch

March-Nov 1957	Charles Arden-Clarke
Nov 1957-July 1960	Lord Listowel (William Hare)

Presidents:

Chairman of the National Liberation Council 1966-9
Chairman of the Presidential Commission 1969-70
Chairman of the National Redemption Council 1972-5
Chairman of the Supreme Military Council 1975-9
Chairman of the Armed Forces Revolutionary Council June-Sept 1979
Chairman of the Provisional National Defence Council 1981-93

July 1960-Feb 1966	Kwame Nkrumah (CPP) (deposed)

Feb 1966-April 1969   Joseph Ankrah
April 1969-Aug 1970   Akwast Afrifa   (executed 1979)
Aug 1970-Jan 1972   Edward Akufo-Addo   (deposed)
Jan 1972-July 1978   Ignatius Acheampong   (deposed, executed 1979)
July 1978-June 1979   Frederick Akuffo   (deposed, executed)
June-Sept 1979   Jerry Rawlings   (1st)
Sept 1979-Dec 1981   Hilla Limann   (PNP) (deposed)
Dec 1981-   Jerry Rawlings   (2nd) (NDC)

Government Leader:

Feb 1951-March 1952   Kwame Nkrumah   (CPP)

Prime Ministers:

Co-ordinating Secretary (1982-88) & Chairman (1988-93) of the Committee of Secretaries

March 1952-Feb 1966   Kwame Nkrumah   (CPP)
(Feb 1966-Sept 1969   post abolished)
Sept 1969-Jan 1972   Kofi Busia   (PP) (deposed)
(Jan 1972   post abolished)
May 1982-March 1993   Paul Obeng
(March 1993   post abolished)

CPP = Convention People's Party
NDC = National Democratic Congress
PNP = People's National Party
PP = Progress Party

GREECE

Official name: Hellenic Republic, Elleniki Dimokratia
Previous name: Kingdom of Hellas 1833-1924, 1935-73
Independence date: 25 March 1821
Capital: Athens (Athenai)

Greece was conquered by the Turks in the 15th century and remained under Ottoman rule until 1821, when independence was declared. After the war of independence a monarchy was established in 1833. Greece became a republic for a second time from 1923-35 when the monarchy was restored. During World War II, Greece was occupied by Germany who set up a puppet government while the king set up a government-in-exile. The war was followed by a civil war caused by an attempt to set up a communist state. In 1967 the military took over the country, and in 1973 a republic was proclaimed. The interference of Greece in Cyprus in 1974 led to the collapse of the military government and the restoration of democracy.

Presidents:

Jan 1822-March 1823	Alexandros Mavrocordatos
March-Dec 1823	Petros Mavromichalis
Dec 1823-1826	Georgios Koundouriotis
March 1827-Oct 1831	Ioannis Kapodistrias († assassinated)
Dec 1831-April 1832	Augustinos Kapodistrias (*brother*)

Kings:

Feb 1833-Oct 1862	Othon (*b* Prince Otto of Bavaria, *son of* Ludwig I of Bavaria), (Regent: Feb 1833-July 1835 Josef von Armansperg) (deposed)
(Oct 1862-March 1863)	Regents: Konstantinos Kanaris/Demetrios Voulgaris/Benizelos Roufos
March 1863-March 1913	Georgios I (*b* Prince William of Denmark, *son of* Christian IX of Denmark) (assassinated)
March 1913-June 1917	Konstantinos I (*son*) (1st) (abdicated)
June 1917-Oct 1920	Alexandros (*son*)
Dec 1920-Sept 1922	Konstantinos I (2nd) (abdicated)
Sept 1922-Dec 1923	Georgios II (*son*) (1st)

Regent:

Dec 1923-March 1924	Paulos Koundouriotis

Presidents:

March 1924-March 1926	Paulos Koundouriotis (1st)

March-Aug 1926   Theodoros Pangalos   (deposed)
Aug 1926-Dec 1929   Paulos Koundouriotis   (2nd)
Dec 1929-Oct 1935   Alexandros Zaimis

Regent:

Oct-Nov 1935   Georgios Kondylis

King:

Nov 1935-April 1941   Georgios II   (2nd) (exiled)
(April 1941-Oct 1944   German occupation)

Regent:

Dec 1944-Sept 1946   Archbishop Damaskinos   (*b* Demetrios Papandreou)

Kings:

Sept 1946-April 1947   Georgios II   (3rd)
April 1947-March 1964   Paulos   (*brother*)
March 1964-April 1967   Konstantinos II   (*son*) (exiled)

Regents:

April 1967-March 1972   Georgios Zoitakis
March 1972-June 1973   Georgios Papadopoulos

Presidents:

June-Nov 1973   Georgios Papadopoulos   (deposed)
Nov 1973-Dec 1974   Phaedon Gizikis
Dec 1974-June 1975   Michael Stassinopoulos
June 1975-May 1980   Konstantinos Tsatsos
May 1980-March 1985   Konstantinos Karamanlis   (1st)
10-29 March 1985   Ioannis Alevras   (acting)
March 1985-May 1990   Christos Sartzetakis
May 1990-March 1995   Konstantinos Karamanlis   (2nd)
March 1995-   Kostas Stephanopoulos

Prime Ministers:

Feb-Oct 1833   Spyridon Trikoupis
Oct 1833-June 1834   Alexandros Mavrokordatos   (1st)
June 1834-July 1835   Ioannis Kolettis   (1st)
July 1835-Feb 1837   Josef von Armansperg
Feb-Dec 1837   Ignaz von Rudhart
Dec 1837-Feb 1841   Konstantinos Zographos

Feb-Aug 1841	Alexandros Mavrokordatos (2nd)
Aug 1841-Sept 1843	Antonios Kriezis (1st)
Sept 1843-Feb 1844	Andreas Metaxas
Feb-April 1844	Konstantinos Kanaris (1st)
April-Aug 1844	Alexandros Mavrokordatos (3rd)
Aug 1844-Sept 1847	Ioannis Kolettis (2nd)
Sept 1847-March 1848	Kitsos Tsavelos
March-Oct 1848	Georgios Koundouriotis
Oct 1848-Dec 1849	Konstantinos Kanaris (2nd)
Dec 1849-May 1854	Antonios Kriezis (2nd)
May 1854-Oct 1855	Alexandros Mavrokordatos (4th)
Oct 1855-Nov 1857	Demetrios Voulgaris (1st)
Nov 1857-Feb 1862	Konstantinos Kanaris (3rd)
Feb-March 1862	Athanasios Miaoulis (acting)
March-June 1862	Konstantinos Kanaris (4th)
June-Oct 1862	Gennaios Kolokotronis
Oct 1862-Feb 1863	Demetrios Voulgaris (2nd)
Feb-April 1863	Zinovios Balbis (1st)
April-May 1863	Demetrios Kriakos
May-Nov 1863	Benizelos Roufos (1st)
Nov 1863-March 1864	Demetrios Voulgaris (3rd)
March-April 1864	Konstantinos Kanaris (5th)
April-Aug 1864	Zinovios Balbis (2nd)
Aug 1864-March 1865	Konstantinos Kanaris (6th)
March-June 1865	Alexandros Koumoundouros (1st)
June-Aug 1865	Demetrios Voulgaris (4th)
Aug-Nov 1865	Alexandros Koumoundouros (2nd)
1-15 Nov 1865	Epaminondas Deligeorgis (1st)
15-18 Nov 1865	Demetrios Voulgaris (5th)
18-25 Nov 1865	Alexandros Koumoundouros (3rd)
Nov 1865-Feb 1866	Epaminondas Deligeorgis (2nd)
Feb-June 1866	Benizelos Roufos (2nd)
June-Dec 1866	Demetrios Voulgaris (6th)
Dec 1866-Jan 1868	Alexandros Koumoundouros (4th)
Jan-Feb 1868	Aristeidis Moraitinis
Feb 1868-Feb 1869	Demetrios Voulgaris (7th)
Feb 1869-July 1870	Thracyvoulos Zaimis (1st)
July 1870-Nov 1871	Epaminondas Deligeorgis (3rd)
Nov-Dec 1871	Thracyvoulos Zaimis (2nd)
Dec 1871-Jan 1872	Alexandros Koumoundouros (5th)
Jan-July 1872	Demetrios Voulgaris (8th)
July 1872-Feb 1874	Epaminondas Deligeorgis (4th)
Feb 1874-May 1875	Demetrios Voulgaris (9th)
May-Oct 1875	Kharilaos Trikoupis (1st) (*son of S.Trikoupis*)
Oct 1875-Dec 1876	Alexandros Koumoundouros (6th)

8-13 Dec 1876	Epaminondas Deligeorgis (5th)
Dec 1876-March 1877	Alexandros Koumoundouros (7th)
March-May 1877	Epaminondas Deligeorgis (6th)
May-June 1877	Alexandros Koumoundouros (8th)
June 1877-Jan 1878	Konstantinos Kanaris (7th)
Jan-Nov 1878	Alexandros Koumoundouros (9th)
2-7 Nov 1878	Kharilaos Trikoupis (2nd)
Nov 1878-March 1880	Alexandros Koumoundouros (10th)
March-Oct 1880	Kharilaos Trikoupis (3rd)
Oct 1880-March 1882	Alexandros Koumoundouros (11th)
March 1882-April 1885	Kharilaos Trikoupis (4th)
April 1885-May 1886	Theodoros Deliyiannis (1st)
12-21 May 1886	Zinovios Balbis (3rd)
May 1886-Nov 1890	Kharilaos Trikoupis (5th)
Nov 1890-Jan 1892	Theodoros Deliyiannis (2nd)
Jan-March 1892	Kharilaos Trikoupis (6th)
March 1892-May 1893	Konstantinos Konstantopoulos
May-Nov 1893	Sotirios Sotiropoulos
Nov 1893-Jan 1895	Kharilaos Trikoupis (7th)
Jan-June 1895	Nikolas Deliyiannis
June 1895-April 1897	Theodoros Deliyiannis (3rd)
April-Oct 1897	Demetrios Rallis (1st)
Oct 1897-April 1899	Alexandros Zaimis (1st)
April 1899-Nov 1901	Georgios Theotokis (1st)
Nov 1901-Dec 1902	Alexandros Zaimis (2nd)
Dec 1902-June 1903	Theodoros Deliyiannis (4th)
June-July 1903	Georgios Theotokis (2nd)
July-Dec 1903	Demetrios Rallis (2nd)
18-28 Dec 1903	Georgios Theotokis (3rd)
Dec 1903-June 1905	Theodoros Deliyiannis (5th)
June 1905-Dec 1906	Demetrios Rallis (3rd)
Dec 1906-July 1909	Georgios Theotokis (4th)
July-Aug 1909	Demetrios Rallis (4th)
Aug 1909-Jan 1910	Kyriakoulis Mavromichalis
Jan-Oct 1910	Stephanos Dragoumis
Oct 1910-March 1915	Eleutherios Venizelos (1st)
March-Aug 1915	Demetrios Gounaris (1st)
Aug-Oct 1915	Eleutherios Venizelos (2nd)
Oct-Nov 1915	Alexandros Zaimis (3rd)
Nov 1915-June 1916	Stephanos Skouloudis
June-Sept 1916	Alexandros Zaimis (4th)
Sept-Oct 1916	Nikolaos Kalogeropoulos (1st)
Oct 1916-May 1917	Spyridon Lambros
May-June 1917	Alexandros Zaimis (5th)
June 1917-Nov 1920	Eleutherios Venizelos (3rd)

Nov 1920-Feb 1921	Demetrios Rallis (5th)
Feb-April 1921	Nikolas Kalogeropoulos (2nd)
April 1921-May 1922	Demetrios Gounaris (2nd) (executed Nov 1922)
16-22 May 1922	Nikolas Stratos (executed Nov 1922)
May-Sept 1922	Petros Protopapadakis (executed Nov 1922)
10-29 Sept 1922	Nikolas Trianthophilakos
Sept-Oct 1922	Sotirios Krokidas
11-22 Oct 1922	Alexandros Zaimis (6th)
Oct-Nov 1922	Nikolas Politis
Nov 1922-Jan 1924	Stylianos Gonatas
Jan-Feb 1924	Eleutherios Venizelos (4th)
Feb-March 1924	Georgios Kafandaris (1st)
March-July 1924	Alexandros Papanastasiou (1st)
July-Oct 1924	Thermistocles Sophoulis (1st)
Oct 1924-June 1925	Andreas Mikalapokoulos
June 1925-Jan 1926	Alexandros Chatzikyriakos
Jan-July 1926	Theodoros Pangalos
July-Aug 1926	Athanasios Eftaxias
Aug-Dec 1926	Georgios Kondylis (1st)
Dec 1926-June 1928	Alexandros Zaimis (7th)
June-July 1928	Georgios Kafandaris (2nd) (PP)
July 1928-May 1932	Eleutherios Venizelos (5th) (LP)
May-July 1932	Alexandros Papanastasiou (2nd)
July-Oct 1932	Eleutherios Venizelos (6th) (LP)
Nov 1932-Jan 1933	Panayotis Tsalderis (1st) (Pop)
Jan-March 1933	Eleutherios Venizelos (7th) (LP)
6-8 March 1933	Alexandros Othonaos
March 1933-Oct 1935	Panayotis Tsalderis (2nd) (Pop)
Oct-Nov 1935	Georgios Kondylis (2nd)
Nov 1935-April 1936	Konstantinos Demerdzis (†) (UP)
April 1936-Jan 1941	Ioannis Metaxas (†)
Jan-April 1941	Alexandros Korizis († suicide)
April-May 1941	Emmanouli Tsouderos
May 1941-Dec 1942	Georgios Tsolokoglu
Dec 1942-April 1943	Konstantinos Logothetopoulos
April 1943-Oct 1944	Ioannis Rallis
Oct-Dec 1944	Georgios Papandreou (1st) (SDP)
Jan-April 1945	Nikolas Plastiras (1st)
April-Oct 1945	Petros Voulgaris
Oct-Nov 1945	Archbishop Damaskinos (*b* Demetrios Papandreou)
1-20 Nov 1945	Panayotis Kanellopoulos (1st)
Nov 1945-April 1946	Thermistocles Sofoulis (2nd) (LP)
4-17 April 1946	Panayotis Poulitsas
April 1946-Jan 1947	Konstantinos Tsalderis (Pop)
Jan-Sept 1947	Demetrios Maximos (Pop)

Sept 1947-June 1949	Thermistocles Sofoulis (3rd) (LP) (†)
June 1949-Jan 1950	Alexandros Diomedes
Jan-March 1950	Ioannis Theotokis
March-April 1950	Sophocles Venizelos (*son of E.Venizelos*) (1st) (LP)
April-Aug 1950	Nikolas Plastiras (2nd) (NPU)
Aug 1950-Nov 1951	Sophocles Venizelos (2nd) (LP)
Nov 1951-Oct 1952	Nikolas Plastiras (3rd) (NPU)
Oct-Nov 1952	Demetrios Kioussopoulos
Nov 1952-Oct 1955	Alexandros Papagos (GR) (†)
4 Oct 1955	Stephanos Stephanopoulos (1st) (GR)
Oct 1955-June 1963	Konstantinos Karamanlis (1st) (GR,NRU)
June-Sept 1963	Panayotis Pipinelis
Sept-Nov 1963	Stylianos Mavromichalis
Nov-Dec 1963	Georgios Papandreou (2nd) (CU)
Dec 1963-Feb 1964	Ioannis Paraskevopoulos (1st)
Feb 1964-July 1965	Georgios Papandreou (3rd) (CU)
July-Aug 1965	Georgios Athanasiadis-Novas (CU)
Aug-Nov 1965	Elias Tsirimokos (CU)
Nov 1965-Dec 1966	Stephanos Stephanopoulos (2nd) (CU)
Dec 1966-March 1967	Ioannis Paraskevopoulos (2nd)
3-21 April 1967	Panayotis Kanellopoulos (2nd) (NRU) (deposed)
April-Dec 1967	Konstantinos Kollias
Dec 1967-Oct 1973	Georgios Papadopoulos
Oct-Nov 1973	Spyros Markezinis
Nov 1973-July 1974	Adamantios Androutsopoulos
July 1974-May 1980	Konstantinos Karamanlis (2nd) (ND)
May 1980-Oct 1981	Georgios Rallis (*son of I.Rallis*) (ND)
Oct 1981-July 1989	Andreas Papandreou (*son of G.Papandreou*) (1st) (PHSM)
July-Oct 1989	Tzanis Tzannetakis (ND)
Oct-Nov 1989	Ioannis Grivas
Nov 1989-April 1990	Xenophon Zolatas
April 1990-Oct 1993	Konstantinos Mitsotakis (ND)
Oct 1993-Jan 1996	Andreas Papandreou (2nd) (PHSM)
Jan 1996-	Kostas Simitis (PHSM)

CU = Centre Union
GR = Greek Rally
LP = Liberal Party
ND = New Democracy
NPU = National Progressive Union
NRU = National Radical Union (*f* GR)
PHSM = Pan-Hellenic Socialist Movement (PASOK)
Pop = Populist Party
PP = Progressive Party

GOVERNMENT-IN-EXILE 1941-44

Headquarters: London 1941-43, Cairo May 1941 and 1943-44
Operated during German occupation

King:

May 1941-Oct 1944	Georgios II

Prime Ministers:

May 1941-April 1944	Emmanouli Tsouderos
13-26 April 1944	Sophocles Venizelos
April-Oct 1944	Georgios Papandreou

RIVAL GOVERNMENT

Communist government formed in northern Greece during civil war.

Prime Minister:

Dec 1947-Aug 1948	Markos Vafiades

GRENADA

Official name: State of Grenada
Independence date: 7 February 1974
Capital: St George's

Grenada was discovered by Colombus in 1498. It was first colonized by France, but was ceded to Britain in 1783. Grenada formed part of the West Indies Federation from 1958 to 1962, and a measure of self-government was granted in 1960. Grenada became a UK associated state in 1967 and fully independent in 1974. In 1983 the left-wing government was overthrown and a radical military regime formed; the US military intervened and restored civilian rule.

Administrators:

1892-1915	Edward Drayton
1915-30	Herbert Ferguson
1930-35	Hilary Blood
1935-40	William Heape
1940-42	Charles Talbot
1942-51	George Green
1951-57	Wallace Macmillan
1957-62	James Lloyd
1962-64	Lionel Pinard
1964-67	Ian Turbott (see Antigua)

Governors:

1967-68	Ian Turbott
1968-Jan 1974	Hilda Bynoe
Jan-Feb 1974	Leo de Gale (acting)

Governors-General:

Represent monarch who is concurrently British monarch

Feb 1974-Sept 1978	Leo de Gale
Sept 1978-Aug 1992	Paul Scoon
Aug 1992-Aug 1996	Reginald Palmer
Aug 1996-	Daniel Williams

Chief Ministers:

Jan 1960-April 1961	Herbert Blaize (1st) (GNP)
April-Aug 1961	George Clyde (GULP)

Aug 1961-June 1962   Eric Gairy   (GULP)
(June 1962-Dec 1965   post abolished)
Dec 1965-March 1967   Herbert Blaize   (2nd) (GNP)

Prime Ministers:
Premier 1967-74
Chairman of the Revolutionary Council Oct 1983
Chairman of the Advisory Council Nov 1983-Dec 1984

March-Aug 1967	Herbert Blaize (1st) (GNP)
Aug 1967-March 1979	Eric Gairy (GULP) (deposed)
March 1979-Oct 1983	Maurice Bishop (NJM) (deposed, executed)
19-25 Oct 1983	Hudson Austin (deposed)
Nov 1983-Dec 1984	Nicholas Braithwaite (1st) (acting Nov-Dec 1983)
Dec 1984-Dec 1989	Herbert Blaize (2nd) (GNP,NNP) (†)
Dec 1989-March 1990	Ben Jones (NNP)
March 1990-Feb 1995	Nicholas Braithwaite (2nd) (NDC)
Feb-June 1995	George Brizan (NDC)
June 1995-	Keith Mitchell (NNP)

GNP = Grenada National Party
GULP = Grenada United Labour Party
NDC = National Democratic Congress
NJM = New Jewel Movement
NNP = New National Party

GUATEMALA

Official name: Republic of Guatemala, República de Guatemala
Independence date: 15 September 1821
Capital: Guatemala City (Ciudad de Guatemala)

Guatemala became a Spanish colony in 1524. In 1821 it declared its independence, and from 1823 until 1839 it formed part of the Central American Confederation. In its recent history, a US backed coup in 1954 ousted a left wing government which was replaced by a series of right wing military backed presidents. The coups of 1982 and 1983 opened the way for a return to democracy in 1986.

Presidents:

April 1839-Dec 1841	Mariano Rivera Paz (1st)
Dec 1841-May 1842	Vernancio López
May 1842-Dec 1844	Mariano Rivera Paz (2nd)
Dec 1844-Oct 1848	Rafael Carrera (1st)
Oct-Nov 1848	Juan Martínez
Nov-Dec 1848	Bernardo Escobar
Jan 1849-Oct 1851	Mariano Paredes
Oct 1851-April 1865	Rafael Carrera (2nd) (†)
April-May 1865	Pedro Aycinena
May 1865-June 1871	Vicente Cerna (deposed)
June 1871-June 1873	Miguel García Granados
June 1873-July 1882	Justo Rufino Barrios (1st)
July 1882-Jan 1883	José Orantes (acting)
Jan 1883-April 1885	Justo Rufino Barrios (2nd) (†)
2-7 April 1885	Alejandro Sinibaldi
April 1885-March 1892	Manuel Barillas (acting April 1885-March 1886)
March 1892-Feb 1898	José Reina Barrios (*nephew of J.Rufino Barrios*) († assassinated)
Feb 1898-April 1920	Manuel Estrada Cabrera (deposed)
April 1920-March 1922	Carlos Herrera y Luna
March 1922-Sept 1926	José Orellana (†)
Sept 1926-Dec 1930	Lazaro Chacon
13-17 Dec 1930	Baudillo Palma
17-31 Dec 1930	Manuel Orellana
Jan-Feb 1931	José Reina Andrade
Feb 1931-July 1944	Jorge Ubico Castañeda (deposed)
July-Oct 1944	Federico Ponce Vaides
Dec 1944-March 1945	Jacobo Arbenz Guzmán (1st)
March 1945-March 1951	Juan Arévalo
March 1951-June 1954	Jacobo Arbenz Guzmán (2nd) (RAP) (deposed)

27-29 June 1954	Carlos Díaz
June-July 1954	Elfego Monzon
July 1954-July 1957	Carlos Castillo Armas († assassinated)
July-Oct 1957	Luiz González López
Oct 1957-March 1958	Guillermo Flores Avendaño
March 1958-March 1963	Miguel Ydígoras Fuentes (NRP) (deposed)
March 1963-July 1966	Enrique Peralta Azurdia
July 1966-July 1970	Julio Méndez Montenegro (RP)
July 1970-July 1974	Carlos Araña Osorio (NLM)
July 1974-July 1978	Kjell Laugerud García (NLM)
July 1978-March 1982	Romeo Lucas García (RP) (deposed)
(1982	Aníbal Guevara Rodríguez, President-elect, deposed)
March 1982-Aug 1983	Efraín Ríos Montt (deposed)
Aug 1983-Jan 1986	Oscar Mejía Victores
Jan 1986-Jan 1991	Vinicio Cerezo Arévalo (CDP)
Jan 1991-June 1993	Jorge Serrano Elías (SAM)
1-6 June 1993	Gustavo Espina Salguero (acting)
June 1993-Jan 1996	Ramiro de León Carpio (UNC)
Jan 1996-Jan 2000	Alvaro Arzú Irigoyen (NAP)
Jan 2000-	Alfonso Portillo Cabrera (RFP)

CDP = Christian Democratic Party
NAP = National Advancement Party
NLM = National Liberation Movement
NRP = National Reconciliation Party
RAP = Revolutionary Action Party
RFP = Republican Front Party
RP = Revolutionary Party
SAM = Solidarity Action Movement
UNC = Union of the National Center

GUINEA

Official name: Republic of Guinea, République de Guinée
Previous names: French Guinea until 1958, People's Revolutionary Republic of Guinea 1979-84
Independence date: 2 October 1958
Capital: Conakry

French merchants were active in the area of present-day Guinea in the 17th century. In 1849 a French protectorate was proclaimed in the Boke district, and by 1882 the rest of the coast and much of the interior was under French control. In 1946 the status of French Guinea was changed from that of a colony to that of overseas territory. Self-government was granted in July 1958. Unlike the rest of French Africa, Guinea voted in favour of immediate independence which was proclaimed in October 1958.

Lieutenant-Governors:

1893-1900	Noël Ballay
1900-04	Paul Cousturier
1904-06	Antoine Frezouls
1906-08	Joost van Vollenhoven
1908-10	Victor-Théophile Liotard (see Dahomey)
1910-13	Camille Guy
1913-16	Jean Peuvergne
1916-29	Jean Poiret
1930-31	Louis-Jean Antonin
1931-32	Robert de Guise (see Martinique)
1932-36	Joseph Vadier

Governors:

1936-40	Louis-Placide Blacher
1940-42	Félix Giacobbi
1942-44	Horace Crocicchia (see Ivory Coast)
1944-46	Jacques-Georges Fourneau
1946-48	Edouard Terrac
1948-50	Roland Pré (see Gabon)
1950-53	Paul-Henri Siriex (see French Somaliland)
1953-55	Jean-Paul Parisot (see Martinique)
1955-56	Charles-Henri Bonfils (see Dahomey)
1956-57	Jean-Paul Ramadier (see Niger)
1958	Jean Mauberna

Presidents:

Oct 1958-March 1984	Ahmed Sékou Touré	(DPG) (†)
March-April 1984	Lansana Beavogui	(acting) (deposed)
April 1984-	Lansana Conté	(PUP)

Prime Ministers:

July 1958-Jan 1961	Ahmed Sékou Touré	(DPG)
(Jan 1961-April 1972	post abolished)	
April 1972-April 1984	Lansana Beavogui	
April-Dec 1984	Diallo Traoré	
(Dec 1984-July 1996	post abolished)	
July 1996-March 1999	Sidia Touré	
March 1999-	Lamine Sidime	

DPG = Democratic Party of Guinea (sole legal party 1958-84)
PUP = Party for Unity and Progress

GUINEA-BISSAU

Official name: Republic of Guinea-Bissau, República de Guiné-Bissau
Previous name: Portuguese Guinea until 1973/74
Independence date: 10 September 1973 (officially granted 10 September 1974)
Capital: Bissau

The area was first visited by the Portuguese in 1446, and they established settlements there. In 1879 it became a separate colony, and in 1851 its status was changed to any overseas province. An armed struggle for independence began in 1963, and by 1973 much of the country was under control of this movement and independence was proclaimed. Following the coup in Portugal in 1974, independence was acknowledged and the Portuguese withdrew.

Governors:

1901-03	Joaquim Biker
1903-04	Alfredo Martins
1904	João Valente
1904-06	Carlos Muzanty
1906-09	Joao Muzanty
1909-10	Francelino Pimental
1910-13	Carlos Pereira
1913	José Sequeira (1st)
1914-15	José Duque (1st)
1915-17	José Sequeira (2nd)
1917	Manuel Coelho
1917-18	Carlos Ferreira
1918-19	José Duque (2nd)
1919	José Marinho
1919-20	Henrique Guerra
1921-26	Jorge Caroco
1927-31	António de Magalhães
1931-32	João Zilhão
1932-40	Luís Viegas
1941-45	Ricardo Monteiro (see São Tomé & Principe)
1945-49	Diogo de Melo e Alvina
1949-53	Álvaro Tavares
1958-62	António Correia (see Cape Verde)
1962-65	Vasco Rodrigues
1965-68	Arnaldo Schultz (1st)
1968-Sept 1972	António de Spinola
1972-74	Bettenco Rodrigues

1974 Arnaldo Schultz (2nd)

Presidents:
President of the Council of State 1973-80 and since 1984
President of the Revolutionary Council 1980-84

Sept 1973-Nov 1980	Luís Cabral (APIGC) (deposed)
Nov 1980-May 1999	João Vieira (APIGC) (deposed)
May 1999-Feb 2000	Malam Bacai Sanha
Feb 2000-	Kumba Yallá (PSR)

Prime Ministers:
Chief State Commissioner 1973-80

Sept 1973-July 1978	Francisco Mendes († motor accident)
July-Oct 1978	Constantino Teixeira (acting)
Oct 1978-Nov 1980	João Vieira
(Nov 1980-May 1982	post abolished)
May 1982-March 1984	Victor Saúde Maria
(March 1984-Dec 1991	post abolished)
Dec 1991-Oct 1994	Carlos Correia (1st)
Oct 1994-June 1997	Manuel Saturnino da Costa
June 1997-Jan 1999	Carlos Correia (2nd
Jan 1997-Feb 2000	Francisco Fadul
Feb 2000-	Caetano N'Tchama

APIGC = African Party for the Independence of Guinea-Bissau and Cape Verde (PAIGC) (sole legal party until 1991)
PSR = Party for Social Renewal

GUYANA

Official name: Co-operative Republic of Guyana
Previous names: British Guiana until 1966, Dominion of Guyana 1966-70
Independence date: 26 May 1966
Capital: Georgetown

The region was settled by the Dutch in the 1620s but was captured by Britain in 1796 and formally ceded in 1814. A measure of self-government was granted in 1957. In 1958 British Guiana became a member state of the West Indies Federation until its dissolution in 1962. Full self government was granted in 1961, with independence following in 1966. A republic was declared in 1970.

Governors:

1898-1901	Walter Sendall
1901-04	James Swettenham
1904-12	Frederick Hodgson
1912-17	Walter Egerton
1918-23	Wilfred Collet (see British Honduras)
1923-25	Graeme Thomson
1925-28	Cecil Rodwell
1928-30	Frederick Guggisberg (see Gold Coast)
1930-35	Edward Denham
1935-37	Geoffrey Northcote
1937-41	Wilfred Jackson
1941-47	Gordon Lethem
1947-53	Charles Woolley (see Cyprus)
1953-55	Alfred Savage
1955-59	Patrick Renison (see British Honduras)
1959-64	Ralph Grey
1964-66	Richard Luyt

Governors-General:
Represented monarch who was concurrently British monarch

May-Oct 1966	Richard Luyt
Oct 1966-Nov 1969	David Rose (see Antigua) (†)
Nov 1969-Feb 1970	Edward Luckhoo (acting)

Presidents:

Feb-May 1970	Edward Luckhoo (acting)
May 1970-Oct 1980	Arthur Chung

Oct 1980-Aug 1985   Forbes Burnham   (PNC) (†)
Aug 1985-Oct 1992   Desmond Hoyte   (PNC)
Oct 1992-March 1997   Cheddi Jagan   (PPP) (†)
March-Dec 1997   Samuel Hinds   (PPP)
Dec 1997-Aug 1999   Janet Jagan   (*b* J.Rosenberg) (*widow of C.Jagan*) (PPP)
Aug 1999-   Bharrat Jagdeo   (PPP)

Chief Minister:

Aug 1957-Aug 1961   Cheddi Jagan   (PPP)

Prime Ministers:

Aug 1961-Dec 1964   Cheddi Jagan   (PPP)
Dec 1964-Oct 1980   Forbes Burnham   (PNC)
Oct 1980-Aug 1984   Ptolemy Reid   (PNC)
Aug 1984-Aug 1985   Desmond Hoyte   (PNC)
Aug 1985-Oct 1992   Hamilton Green   (PNC)
Oct 1992-March 1997   Samuel Hinds   (1st) (PPP)
March-Dec 1997   Janet Jagan   (PPP)
Dec 1997-Aug 1999   Samuel Hinds   (2nd) (PPP)
9-11 Aug 1999   Bharrat Jagdeo   (PPP)
Aug 1999-   Samuel Hinds   (3rd) (PPP)

PNC = People's National Congress
PPP = People's Progressive Party

HAITI

Official name: Republic of Haiti, République d'Haiti
Independence date: 1 January 1804
Capital: Port-au-Prince

Haiti occupies the western third of the island of Hispaniola which was discovered by Columbus in 1492. In 1697 it was ceded to France. In 1801 an unsuccessful attempt to gain independence was made; full sovereignty was achieved in 1804. Haiti soon declared itself an empire, becoming a republic in 1806. During the 19th century it twice reverted to a monarchy. From 1915 to 1934 Haiti was under effective United States occupation. The country has suffered from political instability, lack of development and dictatorships. In 1994 a United Nations force was established to oversee the return of the elected president, but political instability has continued.

Governors:

May 1801-May 1802	François Toussaint L'Ouverture
(May 1802-Nov 1803	French rule)
Nov 1803-Oct 1804	Jean-Jacques Dessalines

Emperor:

Oct 1804-Oct 1806   Jacques I   (Jean-Jacques Dessalines) (assassinated)

President:

Oct 1806-1811   Henri Christophe   (Hayti/North Haiti)

King:

1811-Oct 1820   Henri I   (H.Christophe) (Hayti) (suicide)

Presidents:

Oct 1806-March 1818	Alexandre Pétion (Saint-Domingues/South Haiti) (†)
March 1818-March 1843	Jean-Pierre Boyer (Saint-Domingues 1818-20)
March 1843-May 1844	Charles Hérard
May 1844-April 1845	Philippe Guerrier
April 1845-Feb 1846	Jean-Louis Pierrot
Feb 1846-Feb 1847	Jean-Baptiste Riché (†)
March 1847-Aug 1849	Faustin Soulouque

Emperor:

Aug 1949-Jan 1859   Faustin I   (F.Soulouque) (deposed)

Presidents:

President of the Council of Government 1986-88

Jan 1859-March 1867	N.Fabre Geffrard (deposed)
May 1867-Dec 1869	Sylvain Salnave († assassinated)
Dec 1869-May 1874	Nissage Saget (acting Dec 1869-May 1870)
June 1874-May 1876	Michel Domingue
May 1876-Oct 1879	Boisrand Canal (1st) (deposed)
Oct 1879-Aug 1888	Louis Salomon (†)
Aug-Sept 1888	Seide Télémanque (†)
Sept 1888-Aug 1889	François Legitime
Aug 1889-March 1896	Louis Hyppolyte (acting Aug-Oct 1889) († assassinated)
March 1896-May 1902	T.Simon Sam
May-Dec 1902	Boisrand Canal (2nd)
Dec 1902-Dec 1908	Alexis Nord (deposed)
Dec 1908-Aug 1911	Antoine Simon (deposed)
Aug 1911-Aug 1912	Cincinnatus Leconte (†)
Aug 1912-May 1913	Tancrède Auguste (†)
May 1913-Jan 1914	Michel Oreste
Feb-Oct 1914	Oreste Zamor
Nov 1914-Feb 1915	Davilmar Théodore
March-July 1915	Joseph Vilbrun-Guillaume († assassinated)
July 1915-May 1922	Philippe Dartiguenave
May 1922-April 1930	Louis Borno
May-Nov 1930	Étienne Roy
Nov 1930-April 1941	Sténio Vincent
April 1941-Jan 1946	Elie Lescot (deposed)
Jan-Aug 1946	Frank Lavaud (1st)
Aug 1946-May 1950	Dumarsais Estimé (deposed)
May-Dec 1950	Frank Lavaud (2nd)
Dec 1950-Dec 1956	Paul Magloire
Dec 1956-Feb 1957	Joseph Pierre-Louis (acting)
Feb-April 1957	François Sylvain
April-May 1957	Léon Cantave
May-June 1957	Daniel Fignole (deposed)
June-Oct 1957	Antoine Kebreau
Oct 1957-April 1971	François Duvalier (†)
April 1971-Feb 1986	Jean-Claude Duvalier (son) (deposed)
Feb 1986-Feb 1988	Henri Namphy (1st)
Feb-June 1988	Leslie Manigat (RNDP) (deposed)
June-Sept 1988	Henri Namphy (2nd) (deposed)
Sept 1988-March 1990	Prosper Avril
10-13 March 1990	Hérard Abraham (acting)
March 1990-Feb 1991	Ertha Pascal-Trouillot
(6-7 Jan 1991	Roger Lafontant - proclaimed president during brief coup attempt)

Feb-Sept 1991	Jean-Bertrand Aristide	(1st) (deposed)
Oct 1991-June 1992	Joseph Nerette	
(June 1992-May 1994	post vacant)	
May-Oct 1994	Émile Jonassaint	
Oct 1994-Feb 1996	Jean-Bertrand Aristide	(2nd)
Feb 1996-	René Preval (L)	

Prime Ministers:

Feb-June 1988	Martial Celestin	
(June 1988-Feb 1991	post abolished)	
Feb-Sept 1991	René Preval	
Oct 1991-June 1992	Jean-Jacques Honourat	
June 1992-June 1993	Marc Bazin	
(June-Sept 1993	post vacant)	
Sept 1993-May 1994	Robert Malval	(1st)
May-Oct 1994	Émile Jonassaint	
Oct-Nov 1994	Robert Malval	(2nd)
Nov 1994-Nov 1995	Smarck Michel	
Nov 1995-March 1996	Claudette Werleigh	
March 1996-Oct 1997	Rosny Smarth	
(Oct 1997-March 1999	post vacant)	
March 1999-	Jacques Alexis	

L = Lavalas
RNDP = Rally of Democratic National Progressives

Military Leader:

Sept 1991-Oct 1994	Raoul Cedras
(Oct 1994	civilan rule restored)

HONDURAS

Official name: Republic of Honduras, República de Honduras
Independence date: 15 September 1821
Capital: Tegucigalpa

Honduras was occupied by Spain in 1526, and along with other Central American states overthrew Spanish rule in 1821. Until 1838 Honduras formed part of the Central American Confederation. For many years, Honduras experienced political instability, with several military rulers. Since 1982, the country has had democratically elected presidents.

Presidents:

Sept 1839-Dec 1840	Francisco Zelaya y Ayes
Jan 1841-Jan 1845	Francisco Ferrer
Jan 1845-Jan 1847	Coronado Chávez
Jan 1847-March 1852	Juan Lindo y Zelaya
March 1852-Oct 1855	José Trinidad Cabañas
Oct 1855-Feb 1856	Francisco Aguilar
Feb 1856-Jan 1862	José Santos Guardiola († assassinated)
Jan-Feb 1862	José Montes (acting) (1st)
Feb-Oct 1862	Victoriano Castellanos (†)
Oct 1862-June 1863	José Montes (acting) (2nd)
June-Dec 1863	José Medina (1st)
Dec 1863-March 1864	Francisco Inestrona
March 1864-July 1872	José Medina (2nd)
July 1872-Jan 1874	Carlos Arias
Jan 1874-June 1876	Pariano Leiva (1st)
8-13 June 1876	Marcelino Mejía
June-Aug 1876	Crescencio Gómez
Aug 1876-Oct 1883	Marco Aurelio Soto
Nov 1883-March 1885	Luis Bogrond (1st)
March-June 1885	Pariano Leiva (2nd)
June 1885-April 1886	Luis Bogrond (2nd)
April-Aug 1886	Pariano Leiva (3rd)
Aug 1886-Nov 1891	Luis Bogrond (3rd)
Nov 1891-Feb 1893	Pariano Leiva (4th)
Feb-April 1893	Rosendo Agüero
April 1893-Feb 1894	Domingo Vasquez
Feb 1894-Feb 1899	Policarpo Bonilla
Feb 1899-Jan 1903	Terencio Sierra
Feb-April 1903	Juan Arias

April 1903-April 1907	Manuel Bonilla
Aug 1907-March 1911	Miguel Dávila
March 1911-Feb 1912	Francisco Bertran (1st)
Feb 1912-March 1913	Miguel Bonilla (†)
March 1913-Sept 1919	Francisco Bertran (2nd)
Nov 1919-March 1924	Rafael López Gutiérrez (†)
March-April 1924	Fausto Dávila (acting)
April 1924-Feb 1925	Vicente Tosta
Feb 1925-Feb 1929	Miguel Paz Barahona
Feb 1929-Feb 1933	Vicente Colindres
Feb 1933-Jan 1949	Tiburcio Carías Andino (NP)
Jan 1949-Dec 1954	Juan Gálvez (NP)
Dec 1954-Oct 1955	Julio Lozano Díaz (deposed)
Oct 1955-Dec 1957	Roque Rodríguez/Hector Caraccioli (junta leaders)
Dec 1957-Oct 1963	Ramón Villeda Morales (LP) (deposed)
Oct 1963-June 1971	Osvaldo López Arellano (1st)
June 1971-Dec 1972	Ramón Cruz Uclés (NP) (deposed)
Dec 1972-April 1975	Osvaldo López Arellano (2nd) (deposed)
April 1975-Aug 1978	Juan Melgar Castro (deposed)
Aug 1978-Jan 1982	Policarpo Paz García
Jan 1982-Jan 1986	Roberto Suazo Córdova (LP)
Jan 1986-Jan 1990	José Azcona del Hoyo (LP)
Jan 1990-Jan 1994	Rafael Callejas (NP)
Jan 1994-Jan 1998	Carlos Reina Idiaquez (LP)
Jan 1998-	Carlos Flores Facusse (LP)

LP = Liberal Party
NP = National Party

HUNGARY

Official name: Republic of Hungary, Magyar Köztársaság

Previous names: Kingdom of Hungary until 1946 except for two short periods, in 1849 and in 1919, Republic of Hungary April-Aug 1849, Jan-March 1919 & 1946-49, Hungarian Soviet Republic March-July 1919, Hungarian People's Republic 1949-89

Independence dates: Dec 1000 & 14 April 1848

Capital: Budapest

The Kingdom of Hungary was founded in 1000. In the 16th century a large part of the country was conquered by the Turks; when the Turks were driven out in the 17th century, Hungary came under Austrian rule. An attempt to secure independence in 1848-9 was crushed, but in 1867 the Austrian Empire was transformed into the Dual Monarchy of Austro-Hungary and Hungary became self-governing. After World War I Hungary was separated from Austria. A communist republic was briefly established in 1919, followed by a conservative regime headed by a regent. After World War II a republic was proclaimed (1946), which in 1949 was changed into a people's republic. An attempt in 1956 to break away from the Soviet bloc was crushed by a Soviet invasion. In 1989 the ruling communist party transformed itself into a socialist party in preparation for multi-party elections in 1990 which were won by non-communists.

Kings/Queen:

Dec 1000-Aug 1038	István I (St Stephen)
Aug 1038-41	Péter (*nephew*) (1st) (deposed)
1041-44	Samuel (*brother-in-law of István I*) (executed)
1044-46	Péter (2nd)
(1046-47	interregnum)
1047-60	András I (murdered)
1060-63	Béla I (*brother*)
1063-74	Salamon (*nephew*) (deposed)
1074-77	Géza I (*son of Béla I*)
1077-June 1095	László I (*brother*)
June 1095-Feb 1116	Kálmán (*nephew*)
Feb 1116-31	István II (*son*)
1131-41	Béla II (*nephew of Kálmán*)
1141-61	Géza II (*son*)
1161-62	István III (*son*) (1st) (deposed)
1162-63	László II (*uncle*) (deposed)
1163	István III (2nd) (deposed)
1163-65	István IV (*uncle*)

1165-73	István III (3rd)
1173-96	Béla III (*son of Géza II*)
1196-1204	Imre (*son*)
1204-05	László III (*son*)
1205-35	András II (*brother*)
1235-54	Béla IV (*son*)
1254-May 1270	Béla IV/István V (*son*)
May 1270-72	István V
1272-July 1290	László IV (*son*) (assassinated)
July 1290-1301	András III (*grandson of András II*)
(1301-08	interregnum - claims by László and Otto not recognized)
1308-July 1342	Károlyi I (*great grandson of István V*)
July 1342-Sept 1382	Lajos I (*son*)
Sept 1382-85	Maria (*daughter*) (1st) (deposed)
1385-Feb 1386	Károlyi II (assassinated)
Feb 1386-95	Maria (2nd)/Sigismund (*husband*)
1395-1437	Sigismund
Jan 1438-Oct 1439	Albrecht I
Oct 1439-Nov 1444	Ulászló I (also Władysław III of Poland)
Nov 1444-Nov 1457	László V (*son of Albrecht I*)
Jan 1458-May 1490	Matyas I
May 1490-June 1508	Ulászló II (*son of Kazimierz IV of Poland*)
June 1508-March 1516	Ulászló II/Lajos II (*son*)
March 1516-Aug 1526	Lajos II
(1526-1848	Austrian rule)

Governors:

April-Aug 1848	Lajos Kossuth
Aug 1848	Artur Görgey

Kings:

Feb 1867-Oct 1918	Emperors of Austria

Presidents:

Jan-March 1919	Mihály Károlyi
March-July 1919	Sándor Garbai (deposed)

Regents:

July-Aug 1919	Archduke Joseph
(Aug 1919-May 1920	post vacant)
May 1920-Oct 1944	Miklós Horthy de Nagybánya (deposed)

(Oct 1944-April 1945) Regency council: Károly Beregfay/Ferenc Rajniss/Sándor Csia)
Nov 1945-Feb 1946 Béla Zsedenyi (acting)

Presidents:
Chairman of the Presidential Council Aug 1949-Oct 1989

Feb 1946-July 1948	Zoltán Tildy
July 1948-April 1950	Árpád Szakasits
April 1950-Aug 1952	Sándor Ronai
Aug 1952-April 1967	István Dobi
April 1967-June 1987	Pál Losonczi
June 1987-June 1988	Károlyi Nemeth
June 1988-Oct 1989	Bruno Straub
Oct 1989-May 1990	Mátyás Szüros (acting)
May 1990-	Árpád Göncz

Prime Ministers:

March-Sept 1848	Lajos Batthyany
Sept 1848-April 1849	Lajos Kossuth
April-Aug 1849	Bertalan Szermere
(Aug 1849-Feb 1867	post abolished)
Feb 1867-Nov 1871	Gyula Andrassy
Nov 1871-Dec 1872	Menyhért Lóngay
Dec 1872-March 1874	József Szlávy
March 1874-Feb 1875	István Bitto
March-Oct 1875	Béla Wenckheim
Oct 1875-March 1890	Kálmán Tisza
March 1890-Nov 1892	Gyula Szarpáry
Nov 1892-Jan 1895	Sándor Wekerle (1st)
Jan 1895-Feb 1899	Deszö Banffy
Feb 1899-June 1903	Kálmán Szell
June-Nov 1903	Károlyi Khuen-Héderváry (1st)
Nov 1903-June 1905	István Tisza (*son of K.Tisza*) (1st)
June 1905-April 1906	Géza Fejervary
April 1906-Jan 1910	Sándor Wekerle (2nd)
Jan 1910-April 1912	Károlyi Khuen-Héderváry (2nd)
April 1912-June 1913	László Lukacs
June 1913-June 1917	István Tisza (2nd)
June-Aug 1917	Móric Esterházy
Aug 1917-Oct 1918	Sándor Wekerle (3rd)
30-31 Oct 1918	János Hadik
Oct 1918-Jan 1919	Mihály Károlyi
Jan-March 1919	Dénes Berinkey
March-June 1919	Sándor Garbai

June-Aug 1919   Antal Dovcsak
1-6 Aug 1919   Gyula Peidl
Aug-Nov 1919   István Friedrich
Nov 1919-March 1920   Károlyi Huszár
March-July 1920   Sándor Simonyi-Semadam
July 1920-April 1921   Pál Teleki (1st)
April 1921-Aug 1931   István Bethlen
Aug 1931-Sept 1932   Gyula Károlyi
Sept 1932-Oct 1936   Gyula Gömbös (†)
Oct 1936-May 1938   Kálmán Dárányi
May 1938-Feb 1939   Béla Imrédy (executed 1946)
Feb 1939-April 1941   Pál Teleki (2nd) († suicide)
April 1941-March 1942   László Bardossy (executed 1946)
March 1942-March 1944   Miklós Kállai (deposed)
March-Aug 1944   Döme Szótjay (executed 1946)
Aug-Oct 1944   Géza Lakatos (deposed)
Oct 1944-April 1945   Ferenc Szálasi (executed 1946)
April-Nov 1945   Béla Dálnoki-Miklós
Nov 1945-Feb 1946   Zoltán Tildy (SP)
Feb 1946-May 1947   Ferenc Nagy (SP)
May 1947-Dec 1948   Lajos Dinnyés (SP)
Dec 1948-Aug 1952   István Dobi (SP)
Aug 1952-July 1953   Mátyás Rákosi (HWPP)
July 1953-April 1955   Imre Nagy (1st) (HWPP)
April 1955-Oct 1956   András Hegedus (HWPP)
Oct-Nov 1956   Imre Nagy (2nd) (HWPP) (deposed, executed)
Nov 1956-Jan 1958   János Kádár (1st) (HSWP)
Jan 1958-Sept 1961   Ferenc Münnich (HSWP)
Sept 1961-June 1965   János Kádár (2nd) (HSWP)
June 1965-April 1967   Gyula Kállai (HSWP)
April 1967-May 1975   Jenö Fock (HSWP)
May 1975-June 1987   György Lázár (HSWP)
June 1987-Nov 1988   Károlyi Grosz (HSWP)
Nov 1988-May 1990   Miklós Németh (HSWP,HSP)
May 1990-Dec 1993   József Antall (DF) (†)
Dec 1993-June 1994   Péter Boross
June 1994-July 1998   Gyula Horn (HSP)
July 1998-   Viktor Orban (FYD)

DF = Democratic Forum
FYD = Federation of Young Democrats
HSP = Hungarian Socialist Party (*f* HSWP)
HSWP = Hungarian Socialist Workers' Party (*f* HWPP) (sole legal party 1956-89)
HWPP = Hungarian Working People's Party
SP = Smallholders' Party

Communist Party* Leaders:

*Hungarian Working People's Party (1949-56), Hungarian Socialist Workers' Party (1956-89)
Secretary-General 1949-June 1953
First Secretary June 1953-Nov 1985
General Secretary Nov 1985-Oct 1989

Aug 1949-July 1953	Mátyás Rákosi (1st)
(July-Nov 1953	Triumvirate: Mátyás Rákosi/Lajos Acz/Béla Veg)
Nov 1953-July 1956	Mátyás Rákosi (2nd)
July-Nov 1956	Ernö Gerö (*b* E.Singer)
Nov 1956-May 1988	János Kádár
May 1988-Oct 1989	Károlyi Grosz
(April-Oct 1989	De facto leader as party president: Reszö Nyers)
(Oct 1989	multi-party system introduced)

ICELAND

Official name: Republic of Iceland, Lyðveldid Ísland
Previous name: Kingdom of Iceland 1918-44
Independence date: 1 December 1918
Capital: Reykjavík

Iceland was first settled by Norsemen in 874. From 930 it was an independent state until in 1264 when it came under Norwegian rule. In 1381 Norway passed to the Danish crown, and when Denmark and Norway separated in 1814 Iceland remained Danish territory. In 1918 Iceland was granted independence, and a republic was proclaimed in 1944.

Regent:

June 1941-June 1944   Sveinn Björnsson

Presidents:

June 1944-Jan 1952	Sveinn Björnsson (†)
(Jan-Aug 1952	Presidential Council: Jón Pálmason/Jón Asbjörnsson/Streingrímur Steinthórsson)
Aug 1952-Aug 1968	Ásgeir Ásgeirsson
Aug 1968-Aug 1980	Kristján Eldjárn
Aug 1980-Aug 1996	Vigdís Finnbogadóttir
Aug 1996-	Ólafur Grímsson

Prime Ministers:

March 1914-March 1922	Jón Magnusson (1st)
March 1922-March 1924	Sigurdur Eggerz
March 1924-June 1926	Jón Magnusson (2nd) (†)
July 1926-Aug 1927	Jón Thorlaksson
Aug 1927-June 1932	Tryggvi Thorhallsson
June 1932-March 1934	Ásgeir Ásgeirsson (SDP)
March 1934-May 1942	Hermann Jónasson (1st) (PP)
May-Dec 1942	Ólafur Thors (1st) (IP)
Dec 1942-Dec 1944	Björn Thordarson
Dec 1944-Feb 1947	Ólafur Thors (2nd) (IP)
Feb 1947-Dec 1949	Stefan Stefansson (SDP)
Dec 1949-March 1950	Ólafur Thors (3rd) (IP)
March 1950-Sept 1953	Steingrímur Steinthórsson (PP)
Sept 1953-July 1956	Ólafur Thors (4th) (IP)

July 1956-Dec 1958	Hermann Jónasson (2nd) (PP)
Dec 1958-Nov 1959	Emil Jónsson (SDP)
Nov 1959-Nov 1963	Ólafur Thors (5th) (IP)
Nov 1963-July 1970	Bjarni Benediktsson (IP) (†)
July 1970-July 1971	Jóhann Hafstein (IP)
July 1971-Aug 1974	Ólafur Jóhannesson (1st) (PP)
Aug 1974-Aug 1978	Geir Hallgrimsson (IP)
Aug 1978-Oct 1979	Ólafur Jóhannesson (2nd) (PP)
Oct 1979-Feb 1980	Benedikt Groendal (SDP)
Feb 1980-May 1983	Gunnar Thoroddsen (IP)
May 1983-July 1987	Steingrímur Hermannsson (1st) (PP)
July 1987-Sept 1988	Thorsteinn Pálsson (IP)
Sept 1988-April 1991	Steingrímur Hermannsson (2nd) (PP)
April 1991-	Davið Oddsson (IP)

IP = Independence Party
PP = Progressive Party
SDP = Social Democratic Party

INDIA

Official name: Republic of India, Bharat Janarajya (Hindi)
Previous names: Empire of Hind 1526-1857, Empire of India 1857-1947, Dominion of India 1947-50
Independence date: 15 August 1947
Capital: Delhi (until 1757), Calcutta (1857-1912), New Delhi (since 1912)

India was ruled by the Moghul dynasty from the 16th century but as their power declined in the 18th century that of the English East India Company increased, and gradually developed into political control of the entire subcontinent. The first British governor-general was appointed in 1774 and with the abolition of the East India Company in 1858 the government of India came under the Crown and the governors-general were henceforth known as viceroys. In 1947 British India was partitioned into two independent states, the predominantly Moslem areas becoming Pakistan, and the predominantly Hindu areas becoming India. A republic was proclaimed in 1950. India is the world's most populous democratic country, with the Congress Party dominating politics for most of the country's independent existence.

Moghul Emperors:

April 1526-30	Babur
1530-39	Humayan (*son*) (1st)
1539-May 1545	Sher Shah (usurper)
May 1545-53	Islam Shah (*son*)
1553	Firuz (murdered)
1553-July 1555	Mohammed Adil Shah (deposed)
July 1555-Jan 1556	Humayan (2nd)
Jan 1556-Oct 1605	Akbar (*son*)
Oct 1605-Nov 1627	Jahangir (*son*)
Nov 1627-Feb 1628	Dawar Bakhsh (*grandson*)
Feb 1628-July 1658	Shah Jahan I (*son of Jahangir*) (deposed)
July 1658-March 1707	Auranzeb Alamgir I (*b* Muhiuddin Mohammed) (*son*)
March 1707-Feb 1712	Bahadur Shah I (Shah Alam I) (*son*)
Feb 1712-Feb 1713	Jahandar Shah (*son*) (assassinated)
Feb 1713-Feb 1719	Farrukhsiyar (*nephew*) (assassinated)
Feb-June 1719	Rafi Ud-Daulat (*nephew of Jahandar Shah*) (deposed)
June-Aug 1719	Shah Jahan II (*brother*) (deposed)
Aug-Sept 1719	Nikusiyar (*grandson of Auranzeb Alamgir I*) (deposed, assassinated)
Sept 1719-Oct 1720	Mohammed Shah (*nephew of Jahandar Shah*) (1st) (deposed)
Oct-Nov 1720	Mohammed Ibrahim (*brother of Shah Jahan II*)
Nov 1720-April 1748	Mohammed Shah (2nd)
April 1748-June 1754	Ahmad Shah (*son*) (abdicated)

June 1754-Nov 1779	Alamgir II (*son of Jahandar Shah*)
Nov 1779-Nov 1806	Shah Alam II (*son*)
Nov 1806-Sept 37	Akbar Shah II (*son*)
1837-Sept 1857	Bahadur Shah II (*son*) (deposed)

Viceroys:

1858-62	Earl Canning (Charles Canning)
1862-63	Earl of Elgin and Kincardine (James Bruce)
1864-69	Baron Lawrence (John Lawrence)
1869-72	Earl of Mayo (Richard Bourke)
1872-76	Earl of Northbrook (Thomas Baring)
1876-80	Earl of Lytton (Edward Bulwer-Lytton)
1880-84	Marquess of Ripon (George Robinson)
1884-88	Marquess of Dufferin (Frederick Hamilton-Temple-Blackwood) (see Canada)
1888-94	Marquess of Lansdowne (Henry Petty-Fitzmaurice) (see Canada)
1894-99	Earl of Elgin and Kincardine (Victor Bruce)
1899-1905	Marquess Curzon (George Curzon)
1905-10	Earl of Minto (Gilbert Elliot-Murray-Kynynmound) (see Canada)
1910-16	Baron Hardinge (Charles Hardinge)
1916-21	Baron Chelmsford (Frederick Thesiger)
1921-26	Marquess of Reading (Rufus Isaacs)
1926-31	Baron Irwin (Edward Wood-Halifax)
1931-36	Viscount of Willingdon (Freeman Freeman-Thomas) (see Canada)
1936-43	Marquess of Linlithgow (Victor Hope)
1943-47	Viscount Wavell (Archibald Wavell)
1947	Lord Louis Mountbatten (*b* L.Battenberg)

Governors-General:

Represented monarch who was concurrently British monarch

Aug 1947-June 1948	Lord Louis Mountbatten (assassinated 1979)
June 1948-Jan 1950	Chakravarti Rajagopalachari (see Madras)

Presidents:

Jan 1950-May 1962	Rajendra Prasad
May 1962-May 1967	Sarvepalli Radhakrishnan
May 1967-May 1969	Zakir Hussain (†) (see Bihar)
May-July 1969	Varahagiri Giri (acting) (see Mysore and Kerala)
July-Aug 1969	Mohammed Hidayatullah (acting)
Aug 1969-Aug 1974	Varahagiri Giri
Aug 1974-Feb 1977	Fakhruddin Ali Ahmed (†)
Feb-July 1977	Basappa Jatti (acting) (see Mysore)
July 1977-July 1982	N.Sanjiva Reddy (see Andhra Pradesh)

July 1982-July 1987   G.Zail Singh   (see Punjab)
July 1987-July 1992   Ramaswami Venkataraman
July 1992-July 1997   Shankar Sharma   (see Maharashtra and Punjab)
July 1997-   Kocheril Narayanan

Prime Ministers:

Aug 1947-May 1964   Jawaharlal Nehru   (CP) (†)
May-June 1964   Gulzarilal Nanda   (acting) (1st) (CP)
June 1964-Jan 1966   Lal Bahadur Shastri   (CP) (†)
Jan-Feb 1966   Gulzarilal Nanda   (acting) (2nd) (CP)
Feb 1966-March 1977   Indira Gandhi   (*b* I.Nehru) (*daughter of J.Nehru*) (1st) (CP)
March 1977-July 1979   Morarji Desai   (JP) (see Bombay)
July 1979-Jan 1980   Charan Singh   (JSP,LD) (see Uttar Pradesh)
Jan 1980-Oct 1984   Indira Gandhi   (2nd) (CIP) († assassinated)
Oct 1984-Dec 1989   Rajiv Gandhi   (*son*) (CIP) (assassinated 1991)
Dec 1989-Nov 1990   Vishwanath Pratap Singh   (JD) (see Uttar Pradesh)
Nov 1990-June 1991   Chandra Shekhar   (JDS)
June 1991-May 1996   P.V.Narasimha Rao   (CIP) (see Andhra Pradesh)
May-June 1996   Atal Bihari Vajpayee   (1st) (BJP)
June 1996-April 1997   Haradanahalli Deve Gowda   (JD) (see Karnataka)
April 1997-March 1998   Inder Gujral   (JD)
March 1998-   Atal Bihari Vajpayee   (2nd) (BJP)

BJP = Bharatiya Janata Party
CP = Congress Party
CIP = Congress I (Indira) Party
LD = Lok Dal
JD = Janata Dal
JDS = Janata Dal (S)
JP = Janata Party
JSP = Janata Secular Party (later LD)

States

ANDHRA PRADESH

Statehood: 1 October 1953 (*f* part of Madras)
Capital: Hyderabad

Governors:

Oct 1953-June 1957   Chandulal Trivedi
June 1957-Aug 1962   Bhim Sen Sachar
Aug 1962-May 1964   Satyavant Shrinagesh
May 1964-April 1968   Pattom Pillai   (see Punjab)
April 1968-Jan 75   Khandubhai Desai
Jan 1975-June 76   Moham Sukhadia

June 1976	Obul Reddy (acting)
June 1976-Feb 77	R.D.Bhandare
Feb-April 1977	B.J. Diwan
April 1977-Aug 1978	Sharada Mukherjee (acting)
Aug 1978-July 1983	Kochakkan Abraham
July 1983-Aug 1984	Thakur Ram Lal
Aug 1984-Nov 1985	Shankar Sharma
Nov 1985-Jan 1990	Kumudben Joshi
Jan 1990-Aug 1997	Krishna Kant
Nov 1997-	Chakravarty Rangarajan

Chief Ministers:

Oct 1953-Nov 1954	Tanguturi Prakasam (see Madras) (CP)
(Nov 1954-March 1955	President's rule)
March 1955-Oct 1956	Gopala Reddy (CP)
Nov 1956-Jan 1960	N.Sanjiva Reddy (1st) (CP)
Jan 1960-March 1962	Damodaran Sanjiviah (CP)
March 1962-Feb 1964	N.Sanjiva Reddy (2nd) (CP)
Feb 1964-Sept 1971	K.Brahmananda Reddy (CP)
Sept 1971-Jan 1973	P.V.Narasimha Rao (CP)
(Jan-Dec 1973	President's rule)
Dec 1973-Feb 1980	J.Vengal Rao (CP)
March-Oct 1980	Marri Chenna Reddy (1st) (CIP)
Oct 1980-Feb 1982	T.Anjaiala (CIP)
Feb-Sept 1982	Bhavanam Reddy (CIP)
Sept 1982-Jan 1983	Vijaya Reddy (CIP)
Jan 1983-Aug 1984	Nandmuri Rama Rao (1st) (TDP)
Aug-Sept 1984	N.Bhaskara Rao
Sept 1984-Dec 1989	Nandmuri Rama Rao (2nd) (TDP)
Dec 1989-Dec 1990	Marri Chenna Reddy (2nd) (CIP)
Dec 1990-Oct 1992	N.Janarhan Reddy
Oct 1992-Dec 1994	Kotla Vijayabhaskara Reddy
Dec 1994-Aug 1995	Nandmuri Rama Rao (3rd) (TDP)
Sept 1995-	Chandrababu Naidu (TDP)

TDP = Telegu Dasam Party

ARUNACHAL PRADESH

Statehood: February 1987
Capital: Itanagar

Chief Commissioners:

1972-73	K.A.A.Raja

1974-75	M.L.Kampani
1976-77	K.Raja
1977-78	Braj Nehru (see Assam)
1978-80	R.N.Haldipur (see Sikkim)
1980-81	S.N.Krishnatry (1st) (see Andaman & Nicobar)
1981	H.S.Dubey (acting)
1981-83	S.N.Krishnatry (2nd)

Lieutenant-Governors:

1983-85	Thangavelu Rajeshwar
1985-86	Shiva Swaroop
1986-87	Bhishma Narain Singh

Governors:

Feb-March 1987	Bhishma Narain Singh (Gov of Assam)
March 1987-Jan 1990	R.D.Pradhan
1990-March 1991	D.D.Thakur (Gov of Assam)
March 1991-June 1993	Surendra Nath Dwiwedi
1993-May 1999	Mata Prasad
May-July 1999	S.K. Sinha (acting) (Gov of Assam)
July 1999-	Arvind Dave

Chief Ministers:

Aug 1975-Sept 1979	Prem Thungon (JP)
Sept-Oct 1979	Tomo Riba (UPP)
(Nov 1979-Jan 1980	President's rule)
Jan 1980-Jan 1999	Gagong Apang (CIP,CA)
Jan 1999-	Mukut Mithi

CA = Congress Arunachal
UPP = United People's Party

ASSAM

Capital: Shillong until 1972, Dispur since 1972

Governors:

Aug 1947-Dec 1948	Mohammed Akbar Hydari (†)
Dec 1948-Feb 1949	Ronald Lodge (acting)
Feb 1949-May 1950	Sri Prakasa
May 1950-May 1956	Jairamdas Daulataram (see Bihar)
May 1956-Aug 1960	Saiyid Fazl Ali (†)
Oct 1960-Aug 1961	Vishnu Sahay (1st)
Aug 1961-Aug 1962	Satyavant Shrinagesh

Aug 1962-April 1968   Vishnu Sahay   (2nd)
April 1968-Sept 1973 Braj Nehru
Sept 1973-Aug 1980   Lallan Prasad Singh
Aug 1980-1984   Prakash Mehotra
1985-April 1989   Bhishma Narain Singh   (see Sikkim)
April-Dec 1989   Harideo Joshi   (see Rajasthan)
1990-March 1991   D.D.Thakur
March 1991-97   Loknath Mishra
1997-   S.K.Sinha

Prime Ministers:

1937-March 1942   Mohammed Saadulla   (1st)
(March-Dec 1942   Governor's rule)
Dec 1942-46   Mohammed Saadulla   (2nd)
1946-50   Gopinath Bardoloi

Chief Ministers:

1950-Dec 1957   Bishnuram Mehdi   (CP)
Dec 1957-Oct 1970   Bimala Chaliha   (CP)
Nov 1970-Jan 1972   Mahendra Choudhury   (CP)
Jan 1972-March 1978   Sarat Sinha   (CP)
March 1978-Sept 1979 Golap Borbora   (JP)
Sept-Dec 1979   Jogendra Hazarika   (JP)
(Dec 1979-Dec 1980   President's rule)
Dec 1980-June 1981   Syeda Taimur   (CIP)
(June 1981-Jan 1982   President's rule)
Jan-March 1982   Keshab Gogoi   (CIP)
(March 1982-Feb 1983 President's rule)
Feb 1983-Dec 1985   Hiteswar Saikia   (1st) (CIP)
Dec 1985-Nov 1990   Prafulla Mahanta   (1st) (APC)
(Nov 1990-June 1991   President's rule)
June 1991-April 1996 Hiteswar Saikia   (2nd) (CIP) (†)
April-May 1996   Bhumidhar Barman   (CIP)
May 1996-   Prafulla Mahanta   (2nd) (APC)

APC = Assam People's Conference

BIHAR

Capital: Patna

Governors:

Aug 1947-Jan 1948   Jairamdas Daulataram
Jan 1948-April 1952   Madhavrao Aney

April 1952-May 1957	Ranganath Diwakar
May 1957-May 1962	Zakir Hussain
May 1962-Dec 1967	Ananthasayanam Ayyangar
Dec 1967-Feb 1971	Sityanand Kanungo (see Gujarat)
Feb 1971-73	Deva Borooah
1974-76	R.D.Bhandare
June 1976-Sept 1979	Jagan Kanshal
Sept 1979-85	Akhlaq Kidwai (1st)
1985-Feb 1988	Pondakainti Venkatasubbiah
Feb 1988-Feb 1989	Govind Narain Singh (see Madhya Pradesh)
Feb 1989-Jan 1990	Jagannath Paghadia
Jan 1990-Feb 1991	Yunus Saleem
Feb-March 1991	Satya Narain Reddy (acting) (Gov of Uttar Pradesh)
March 1991-Aug 1993	Mohammed Qureshi
Aug 1993-April 1998	Akhlaq Kidwai (2nd)
April 1998-March 1999	Sunder Singh Bhandari
March-Oct 1999	Brij Mohan Lal (acting)
Oct-Nov 1999	Suraj Bhan
Nov 1999-	Vinod Chandra Pandey

Prime Ministers:

1937-Oct 1939	Sri Krishna Sinha (1st) (CP)
(Oct 1939-April 1946	Governor's rule)
April 1946-Jan 1950	Sri Krishna Sinha (2nd) (CP)

Chief Ministers:

Jan 1950-Jan 1961	Sri Krishna Sinha (CP) (†)
1-18 Feb 1961	Dip Narain Sinha (CP)
Feb 1961-Oct 1963	Binodanand Jha (CP)
Oct 1963-March 1967	Krishna Sahay (CP)
March 1967-Jan 1968	Mahamaya Sinha (JKD)
Jan-March 1968	Bindeshwari Mandal (SD)
March-June 1968	Bhola Shastri (1st) (DCP)
(June 1968-March 1969	President's rule)
March-June 1969	Harihar Prasad Singh (CP)
June-July 1969	Bhola Shastri (2nd) (DCP)
(July 1969-Feb 1970	President's rule)
Feb-Dec 1970	Daroga Rai (CP)
Dec 1970-June 1971	Karpoori Thakur (1st) (SSP)
June-Dec 1971	Bhola Shastri (3rd) (PLF)
(Jan-March 1972	President's rule)
March 1972-June 1973	Kedar Pandey (CP)
July 1973-April 1975	Abdul Ghafoor (CP)
April 1975-June 1977	Jagannath Mishra (1st) (CP)

June 1977-April 1979	Karpoori Thakur (2nd) (CIP)
April 1979-June 1980	Ram Sunder Das (JP)
June 1980-Aug 1983	Jagannath Mishra (2nd) (CIP)
Aug 1983-March 1985	Chandra Sekhar Singh (CIP)
March 1985-Feb 1988	Bindeshwari Dubey (CIP)
Feb 1988-March 1989	Bhagwat Azad (CIP)
March-Dec 1989	Satyendra Sinha (CIP)
Dec 1989-March 1990	Jagannath Mishra (3rd) (CIP)
March 1990-March 1995	Lallu Prasad Yadav (1st) (JD)
(March-April 1995	President's rule)
April 1995-July 1997	Lallu Prasad Yadav (2nd) (JD, RJD)
July 1997-Feb 1999	Rabri Devi (1st) (*wife*) (RJD)
(Feb-March 1999	President's rule)
March 1999-March 2000	Rabri Devi (2nd) (RJD)
3-12 March 2000	Nitish Kumar (SP)
March 2000-	Rabri Devi (3rd) (RJD)

DCP = Democratic Congress Party
JKD = Jana Kranti Dal
PLF = Progressive Legislative Front
RJD = Rashtriya Janata Dal
SD = Soshit Dal
SP = Samatra Party
SSP = Samyutka Socialist Party

GOA

Statehood: June 1987 (*f* part of Portuguese India until 1961, and of the Territory of Goa, Daman and Diu 1961-87)
Capital: Panaji (*f* Nova Goa)

Governors:

1897-1900	Joaquim Machado
1900-05	Eduardo Galhardo
1905-07	Arnaldo Rebelo
1907-10	José Horta e Costa
1910-17	Francisco da Costa
1917-19	José Ribeiro
1919	Augusto Mota
1919-25	Jaime Morais
1925-26	Mariano Martins
1926-29	Pedro de Amorim
1929	Artur de Almeida
1929-36	João Lopes
1936-38	Francisco Lopes

1938-45	José Cabral
1945-46	Paulo Guedes (1st)
1946-48	José Bossa
1948-52	Fernando Mendoça e Dias
1952-58	Paulo Guedes (2nd)
1958-61	Manuel Vasalo e Silva (deposed by Indian forces)
1961-62	Kenneth Candeth

Lieutenant-Governors:

1962-63	Tumkur Sivasankar
1963-65	Kashinath Damle
1965-67	Hari Sharma
1967-72	Nakul Sen
1972-76	Shishir Banerjee
1976-77	B.K.Goshwami
1977-79	Partal Singh Gill
(1979-81	post vacant)
1981-82	Jagmohan (see Delhi)
1982-83	Idris Latif (see Maharashtra)
1983-84	K.T.Satarawala
1984-87	Gopal Singh

Governors:

March 1987-89	Gopal Singh
1989-March 1991	Khurshid Alam Khan
March 1991-April 1994	Bhanu Pratap Singh (see Karnataka)
April-July 1994	Basavaiah Rachaiah (see Kerala)
July 1994-June 1995	Gopala Ramanujan
June 1995-July 1996	Romesh Bhandari (see Tripura)
July 1996-Feb 1998	P.Cherian Alexander (see Maharashtra)
Feb-April 1998	Tumkur Satish Chaudran
April 1998-Nov 1999	Jack Jacob
Nov 1999-	Mohammed Fuzal

Chief Ministers:

Dec 1963-Dec 1966	Dayanand Bandodkar (1st) (MG)
(Dec 1966-April 1967	President's rule)
April 1967-Aug 1973	Dayanand Bandodkar (2nd) (MG) (†)
Aug 1973-April 1979	Shashikala Kakodkar (*daughter*) (MG)
(April 1979-Jan 1980	President's rule)
Jan 1980-April 1990	Pratap Singh Rane (1st) (CSP,CIP)
April-Dec 1990	Churchill Alemao (PDF)
(Dec 1990-Jan 1991	President's rule)

Jan 1991-May 1993   Ravi Naik   (1st) (MG)
May 1993-April 1994   Wilfred D'Souza   (1st) (MG)
2-8 April 1994   Ravi Naik   (2nd) (MG)
April-Dec 1994   Wilfred D'Souza   (2nd) (MG)
Dec 1994-July 1998   Pratap Singh Rane   (2nd) (CIP)
July-Nov 1998   Wilfred D'Souza   (3rd) (MG)
Nov 1998-Feb 1999   Luizinho Faleiro   (1st) (CIP)
(Feb-June 1999   President's rule)
June-Nov1999   Luizinho Faleiro   (2nd) (CIP)
Nov 1999-   Francisco Sardinha

CSP = Congress S (Socialist) Party
MG = Maharashtrawi Gomantak
PDF = People's Democratic Front

GUJARAT

Statehood: 1 May 1960 (f part of Bombay)
Capital: Ahmedabad until 1970, Gandhiagar since 1970

Governors:

May 1960-Aug 1965   Nawab Mehdi Nawaz Jang
Aug 1965-Dec 1967   Sityanand Kanungo
Dec 1967-73   Shriman Narayan
1973-78   Kambanthodath Vishwanatham
1978-July 1983   Sharada Mukherjee
July 1983-85   Kizhekethil Chandy
1985-88   Braj Nehru   (see Assam)
1988-Jan 1990   Ram Trivedi
Jan-Dec 1990   M.Shastri
Dec 1990-June 1995   Sarap Singh   (see Kerala)
June 1995-Feb 1996   Naresh Chandra
Feb 1996-April 1998   Krishna Pal Singh
April 1998-Feb 1999   Anshuman Singh
March 1999-   Sunder Singh Bhandari   (see Bihar)

Chief Ministers:

April 1960-Sept 1963   Jivraj Mehta   (CP)
Sept 1963-Sept 1965   Balwantrai Mehta   (CP)
Sept 1965-May 1971   Hitendra Desai   (CP)
(May 1971-March 1972   President's rule)
March 1972-June 1973   Ghanshyam Oza   (CP)
July 1973-Feb 1974   Chimanbhai Patel   (1st) (CP)
(Feb 1974-Jan 1975   President's rule)

Jan 1975-March 1976   Babubhai Patel   (1st) (JP)
(March-Dec 1976   President's rule)
Dec 1976-April 1977   Madhavsinh Solanki   (1st) (CP)
April 1977-Feb 1980   Babubhai Patel   (2nd) (JP)
(Feb-June 1980   President's rule)
June 1980-July 1985   Madhavsinh Solanki   (2nd) (CIP)
July 1985-Dec 1989   Amarsinh Chaudhary   (CIP)
Dec 1989-March 1990   Madhavsinh Solanki   (3rd) (CIP)
March 1990-Feb 1994   Chimanbhai Patel   (2nd) (†) (JD,CIP)
Feb 1994-March 1995   Chhabildas Mehta   (acting Feb-April 1994) (CIP)
March-Oct 1995   Keshubhai Patel   (1st) (BJP)
Oct 1995-Sept 1996   Sureshchandra Mehta   (BJP)
(Sept-Oct 1996   President's rule)
Oct 1996-April 1998   Shankarsingh Vaghela   (MJP)
April 1998-   Keshubhai Patel   (2nd) (BJP)

MJP = Mahagujarat Janata Party

HARYANA

Statehood: 1 November 1966 (*f* part of Punjab)
Capital: Chandigarh (shared with Punjab)

Governors:

Nov 1966-Sept 1967   Dharma Veera   (Gov of Punjab)
Sept 1967-Aug 1976   Birendra Chakravarti   (1st)
Aug 1976-July 1977   Jaisukh Lal Hathi
July 1977-78   Harcharan Singh Brar
1978-Feb 1980   Birendra Chakravarti   (2nd)
Feb 1980-84   Sri Ganpatrao Tapase
1984-Feb 1988   S.M.H.Burney
Feb 1988-Jan 1990   Hari Barari
Jan 1990-June 1995   Dhanik Lal Mandal
June 1995-   Mahabir Prasad

Chief Ministers:

Nov 1966-March 1967   Bhagwat Sharma   (CP)
March-Nov 1967   Pao Birendra Singh   (CP)
(Nov 1967-May 1968   President's rule)
May 1968-Dec 1975   Bansi Lal   (1st) (CP)
Dec 1975-June 1977   Banarasi Gupta   (1st) (CP)
June 1977-June 1979   Devi Lal   (1st) (JP)
June 1979-June 1986   Bhajan Lal   (1st) (CIP)
June 1986-June 1987   Bansi Lal   (2nd) (CIP)

June 1987-Dec 1989	Devi Lal (2nd) (LD,JD)
Dec 1989-May 1990	Om Prakash Chautala (*son*) (1st) (JD)
May-July 1990	Banarasi Gupta (2nd) (JD)
12-16 July 1990	Om Prakash Chautala (2nd) (JD)
July 1990-March 1991	Hukam Singh
March-April 1991	Om Prakash Chautala (3rd) (JDS)
(April-June 1991	President's rule)
June 1991-May 1996	Bhajan Lal (2nd) (CIP)
May 1996-July 1999	Bansi Lal (3rd) (HVP)
July 1999-	Om Prakash Chautala (4th)

HVP = Haryana Vikas Party

HIMACHAL PRADESH

Statehood: 25 January 1971
Capital: Simla

Chief Commissioners:

1948-51	E.P.Menon
1951-52	Bhagwan Sahay
1952-54	M.S.Himmatsinhji
1954-66	Bajrang Bhadri

Lieutenant-Governors:

1966-67	Venkata Vishwanathan
1967-71	Kanwar Bahadur Singh

Governors:

Jan 1971-77	Subramaniam Chakravarti
Feb 1977-Aug 1981	Amin Ahmad Khan
Aug 1981-April 1983	Asoka Banerjee
April 1983-April 86	Hokishe Sema (see Nagaland)
April 1986-Jan 1990	Rustom Gandhi
Jan-Dec 1990	Basavaiah Rachaiah
Dec 1990-Feb 1993	Virendra Varma (see Punjab)
Feb-June 1993	Bali Ram Bhagat
June-Nov 1993	Gulsher Ahmed
Nov 1993-July 1994	Surendra Nath (Gov of Punjab) († air crash)
July 1994-Sept 1995	Sudhakarrao Naik
Nov 1995-April 1996	Sheila Kaul
April 1996-July 1997	Mahabir Prasad (Gov of Haryana)
July 1997-Dec 1999	V.S.Rama Devi
Dec 1999-	Prem Kumar Dhamal

Chief Ministers:

July 1963-Jan 1977	Yeshwant Parmar	(CP)
Jan-June 1977	Ram Lal Chauhan	(CP)
June 1977-Feb 1980	Shanta Kumar	(1st) (JP)
Feb 1980-April 1983	Ram Lal	(CIP)
April 1983-March 1990	Virabhadra Singh	(1st) (CIP)
March 1990-Dec 1992	Shanta Kumar	(2nd) (BJP)
(Dec 1992-Dec 1993	President's rule)	
Dec 1993-March 1998	Virabhadra Singh	(2nd) (CIP)
March 1998-	Prem Kumar Dhamal	(BJP)

JAMMU AND KASHMIR

Statehood: March 1965
Capitals: Jammu (winter), Srinagar (summer)

Head of State:

Oct 1952-March 1965	Yuvraj Karan Singh

Governors:

March 1965-May 1967	Yuvraj Karan Singh	
May 1967-July 1973	Bhagwan Sahay	(see Himachal Pradesh)
July 1973-81	Lakshmi Kanth Jha	
1981-March 1984	Braj Nehru	(see Assam)
March 1984-Nov 1988	Jagmohan	(1st) (see Delhi)
Nov 1988-Jan 1990	K.V.Krishna Rao	(1st) (see Manipur)
Jan-May 1990	Jagmohan	(2nd)
May 1990-March 1993	Girish Saxena	(1st)
March 1993-April 1998	K.V.Krishna Rao	(2nd)
April 1998-	Girish Saxena	(2nd)

Prime Ministers:

1937-July 1943	B.Gopalaswami Ayyangar	
July 1943-Feb 1944	Kailas Haksar	
Feb 1944-June 1945	Bengal Rau	
June 1945-Aug 1947	Ram Chandra Kak	
Aug-Oct 1947	Janak Singh	(acting)
Oct 1947-March 1948	Mehr Mahajan	
March 1948-Aug 1953	Mohammed Abdullah	(1st) (NCP)
Aug 1953-Aug 1963	Bakshi Ghulam Mohammed	(NCP)
Oct 1963-Feb 1964	Khwaja Shamsuddin	(NCP)
Feb 1964-March 1965	Ghulam Sadiq	(CP)

Chief Ministers:

March 1965-Dec 1971	Ghulam Sadiq (CP) (†)
Dec 1971-Feb 1975	Syed Mir Qasim (CP)
Feb 1975-March 1977	Mohammed Abdullah (2nd) (NCP)
(March-July 1977	Governor's rule)
July 1977-Sept 1982	Mohammed Abdullah (3rd) (NCP) (†)
Sept 1982-July 1984	Farooq Abdullah (*son*) (1st) (NCP)
July 1984-March 1986	Ghulam Mohammed Shah (*brother-in-law*)
(March-Nov 1986	Governor's rule)
Nov 1986-Jan 1990	Farooq Abdullah (2nd) (NCP)
(Jan-July 1990	Governor's rule)
(July 1990-Oct 1996	President's rule)
Oct 1996-	Farooq Abdullah (3rd) (NCP)

NCP = National Conference Party

KARNATAKA

Previous name: Mysore until 1973
Capital: Bangalore

Governors:

Aug 1947-March 1964	Sri Jaya Chamraya Wadiyar Bahadur (Maharaja of Mysore)
March 1964-April 1965	Satyavant Shrinagesh (see Andhra Pradesh)
April 1965-March 1967	Varahagiri Giri (see Kerala)
March 1967-Oct 1969	Gopal Pathak
Oct 1969-Feb 1972	Dharma Veera (see Haryana & Punjab)
Feb 1972-75	Mohan Lal Sukhadia
1975-77	Umarshankar Dikshit
1977-83	Govind Narain Singh (see Madhya Pradesh)
1983-Feb 1988	A.N.Banerjee (see Himachal Pradesh)
Feb 1988-Jan 1990	Pondakainti Venkatasubbiah (see Bihar)
1990-Jan 1991	Bhanu Pratap Singh
Jan 1991-Dec 1999	Khurshid Alam Khan (see Goa)
Dec 1999	V.S. Rama Devi (see Himachal Pradesh)

Chief Ministers:

Oct 1947-April 1952	Kyasambally Reddy (CP)
April 1952-Aug 1956	Kengal Hanumanthaiya (CP)
Aug-Nov 1956	Kadilal Manjappa (CP)
Nov 1956-May 1958	Siddavanahalli Nijalingappa (1st) (CP)
May 1958-March 1962	Basappa Jatti (CP)
March-June 1962	Shivalingappa Kanthi (CP)
June 1962-May 1968	Siddavanahalli Nijalingappa (2nd) (CP)

May 1968-March 1971	Veerebdral Patil (CP)
(March 1971-March 1972	President's rule)
March 1972-Dec 1977	D.Devaraj Urs (1st) (CP)
(Dec 1977-Feb 1978	President's rule)
Feb 1978-Jan 1980	D.Devaraj Urs (2nd) (CIP)
Jan 1980-Jan 1983	R.Gundu Rao (CIP)
Jan 1983-Aug 1988	Ramakrishna Hegde (JP)
Aug 1988-April 1989	Somappa Bommai (JP)
(April-Dec 1989	President's rule)
Dec 1989-Oct 1990	Veerendra Patil (CIP)
(Oct 1990	President's rule)
Oct 1990-Nov 1992	S.Bangarappa
Nov 1992-Dec 1994	M.Veerappa Moily
Dec 1994-May 1996	Haradanahalli Deve Gowda (JD)
May 1996-Oct 1999	J.H.Patel (JD)
Oct 1999-	S.M. Khrishna (CIP)

KERALA

Previous names: Travancore until 1949, Travancore-Cochin 1949-56
Capital: Thiruvananthapuram (Trivandrum)

Governors:

Aug 1949-Dec 1956	Raja Bahadur Shamshir Jang (Maharaja of Travancore)
Dec 1956-60	B.Ramakrishna Rao (see Hyderabad)
1961-65	Varahagiri Giri
April 1965-Feb 1966	Ajit Jain
Feb 1966-April 1967	Bhagwan Sahay
April 1967-73	Venkata Viswanathan
1973-Oct 1977	Niranjan Wanchoo
Oct 1977-Oct 1982	Jyoti Venkatachalam
Oct 1982-Feb 1988	Parthasarathy Ramachandran
Feb 1988-Jan 1990	Rama Dulari Sinha
Jan-Dec 1990	Sarap Singh
Dec 1990-Nov 1995	Basavaiah Rachaiah (see Himachal Pradesh)
Nov 1995-May 1996	Shiv Shankar (see Sikkim)
May 1996-Jan 1997	Khurshid Alam Khan (see Karnataka)
Jan 1997-	Sukhdev Singh Kang

Chief Ministers:

March-Oct 1948	Pattom Pillai (1st) (CP)
Oct 1948-March 1952	T.K.Narayana Pillai (CP)
March 1952-March 1954	Anapparambal John (CP)
March 1954-Feb 1955	Pattom Pillai (2nd) (PSP)

Feb 1955-March 1956	Govinda Menon (CP)
(March 1956-April 1957	President's rule)
April 1957-July 1959	Sankaran Nambudiripad (1st) (CPI)
(July 1959-Feb 1960	President's rule)
Feb 1960-Sept 1962	Pattom Pillai (3rd) (PSP)
Sept 1962-Sept 1964	R.Shankar (CP)
(Sept 1964-March 1967	President's rule)
March 1967-Nov 1969	Sankaran Nambudiripad (2nd) (CPI)
Nov 1969-March 1977	C.Achutha Menon (CPI)
March-April 1977	Kannoth Karunakaran (1st) (CP)
April 1977-Oct 1978	A.K.Anthony (1st) (CP)
Oct 1978-Oct 1979	P.Vasudevan Nair (CPI)
Oct-Dec 1979	C.Mohammed Koya (ML)
(Dec 1979-Jan 1980	President's rule)
Jan 1980-Oct 1981	Ezhambala Nayanar (1st) (CPM)
(Oct-Dec 1981	President's rule)
Dec 1981-March 1982	Kannoth Karunakaran (2nd) (CIP)
(March-May 1982	President's rule)
May 1982-March 1987	Kannoth Karunakaran (3rd) (CIP)
March 1987-June 1991	Ezhambala Nayanar (2nd) (CPM)
June 1991-March 1995	Kannoth Karunakaran (4th) (CIP)
March 1995-May 1996	A.K.Anthony (2nd) (CIP)
May 1996-	Ezhambala Nayanar (3rd) (CPM)

CPI = Communist Party of India
CPM = Communist Party-Marxist
ML = Moslem League
PSP = Praja Socialist Party

MADHYA PRADESH

Previous name: Central Provinces until 1950
Capital: Bhopal

Governors:

Aug 1947-June 1952	Mangaldas Pakvasa
June 1952-June 1957	B.Pattabhi Sitarammaya
June 1957-Nov 1964	Hari Pataskar
Nov 1964-March 1971	Kyasambally Reddy
March 1971-77	Satya Narain Sinha
1977-78	Niranjan Wanchoo (see Kerala)
1978-80	Cheppudira Poonacha
1980-85	Bhagwat Sharma (see Haryana & Orissa)
Nov 1985-March 1989	Kizheketil Chandy (see Gujarat)
March 1989-Jan 1990	Sarla Grewal

Jan 1990-June 1993   Mahmood Ali
June 1993-April 1998   Mohammed Qureshi   (see Bihar)
April 1998-   Bhai Mahavir

Prime Ministers:

Aug 1937-July 1938   N.B.Khare   (CP)
(July 1938-April 1946   Governor's rule)
April 1946-Jan 1950   Ravishankar Shukla   (CP)

Chief Ministers:

Jan 1950-Jan 1957   Ravishankar Shukla   (CP)
Jan 1957-March 1962   Kailas Katju   (CP)
March 1962-Sept 1963   Bhagwantrao Mandloi   (CP)
Sept 1963-July 1967   Dwarka Mishra   (CP)
July 1967-March 1969   Govind Narain Singh   (CP)
March 1969-Jan 1972   Shyam Shukla   (1st) (CP)
Jan 1972-Dec 1975   Prakash Sethi   (CP)
Dec 1975-June 1977   Shyam Shukla   (2nd) (CP)
June 1977-Jan 1979   Kailash Joshi   (JP)
Jan 1979-Feb 1980   Virendra Saklecha   (JP)
(Feb-June 1980   President's rule)
June 1980-March 1985   Arjun Singh   (1st) (CIP)
March 1985-Feb 1988   Motilal Vora   (1st) (CIP)
Feb 1988-Jan 1989   Arjun Singh   (2nd) (CIP)
Jan-Dec 1989   Motilal Vora   (2nd) (CIP)
Dec 1989-March 1990   Shyam Shukla   (3rd) (CIP)
March 1990-Dec 1992   Sunderlal Patwa   (BJP)
(Dec 1992-Dec 1993   President's rule)
Dec 1993-   Digvijay Singh   (CIP)

MAHARASHTRA

Statehood: 1 May 1960
Capital: Bombay (Mumbai)

Governors:

May 1960-April 1962   Sri Prakasa   (see Assam, Bombay & Madras)
April 1962-Oct 1963   P.Subbarayan   (†)
Nov 1963-Nov 1964   Vijaya Lakshmi Pandit   (*sister of J.Nehru*)
Nov 1964-69   P.V.Cherian   (†)
Feb 1970-Dec 1976   Ali Yavar Jung   (Nawab Jung Bahadur) (†)
April 1977-Nov 80   Sadiq Ali   (1st)
Nov 1980-Feb 82   Idris Latif

Feb 1982-May 1985   Sadiq Ali   (2nd)
May 1985-April 1986   Kona Prabhakara Rao
April 1986-Aug 1987   Shankar Sharma
(Aug 1987-Feb 1988   post vacant)
Feb 1988-Jan 1990   K.Brahmanandu Reddy
Jan 1990-92   C.Subramaniam
1992   Sarup Singh   (acting)
1992-   P.Cherian Alexander   (see Tamil Nadu)

Chief Ministers:

May 1960-Nov 1962   Yashwantrao Chavan   (see Bombay) (CP)
Nov 1962-Nov 1963   Marotrao Kannamwar   (CP)
Dec 1963-Feb 1975   Vasantrao Naik   (CP)
Feb 1975-April 1977   Shankarrao Chavan   (1st) (CP)
April 1977-July 1978   Vasantrao Patil   (1st) (CP)
July 1978-Feb 1980   Sharad Pawar   (1st) (PCP)
(Feb-June 1980   President's rule)
June 1980-Jan 1982   Abdur Rehman Antulay   (CIP)
Jan 1982-Feb 1983   Babasaher Bhosale   (CIP)
Feb 1983-June 1985   Vasantrao Patil   (2nd) (CIP)
June 1985-March 1986   Shivajirao Nilangerkar   (CIP)
March 1986-June 1988   Shankarrao Chavan   (2nd) (CIP)
June 1988-June 1991   Sharad Pawar   (2nd) (CIP)
June 1991-Feb 1993   Sudhakarrao Naik   (CIP)
March 1993-March 1995   Sharad Pawar   (3rd) (CIP)
March 1995-Feb 1999   Manohar Joshi   (SS)
Feb-Oct 1999   Narayan Rane   (SS)
Oct 1999-   Vilasrao Deshmukh   (CIP)

PCP = Progressive Congress Party
SS = Shiv Sena

MANIPUR

Statehood: 21 January 1972
Capital: Imphal

Chief Commissioners:

1949-51   Himmat Singh Maheswari
1952-53   R.B.Bharqawa
1954-58   P.C.Mathews
1958-63   Jagat Mohan Raina
1963-69   Baleshwar Prasad

Lieutenant-Governors:

Feb 1969-70	Baleshwar Prasad
1970-72	Dalip Kohli

Governors:

Jan 1972-82	Governors of Assam
1982-83	Lallan Prasad Singh
1983-84	S.M.H.Burney
1984-Nov 1988	K.V.Krishna Rao
April 1989-March 1993	Chintamani Panigrahi
March 1993-Dec 1994	K.V.Raghunath Reddy (Gov of Tripura)
Dec 1994-Dec 1999	Oudh Narain Srivastava (Gov of Nagaland)
Dec 1999-	Ved Prakash Marwah

Chief Ministers:

July 1963-Oct 1967	Mairebam Koireng Singh (1st) (CP)
5-24 Oct 1967	Longjam Thambou Singh (CP)
(Oct 1967-Feb 1968	President's rule)
Feb 1968-Sept 1969	Mairebam Koireng Singh (2nd) (CP)
(Sept 1969-March 1972	President's rule)
March 1972-March 1973	Mohammed Alimuddin (1st) (MPP)
(March 1973-March 1974	President's rule)
March-July 1974	Mohammed Alimuddin (2nd) (MPP)
July-Dec 1974	Yangmasho Shaiza (1st) (MHU)
Dec 1974-May 1977	Rajkumar Dorendra Singh (1st) (CP)
(May-June 1977	President's rule)
June 1977-Nov 1979	Yangmasho Shaiza (2nd) (JP) (assassinated 1984)
(Nov 1979-Jan 1980	President's rule)
Jan-Nov 1980	Rajkumar Dorendra Singh (2nd) (CIP)
Nov 1980-March 1988	Rishang Keishang (1st) (CIP)
March 1988-Feb 1990	Jaichandra Singh (CIP)
Feb 1990-Jan 1992	Rajkumar Ranbir (MPP)
(Jan-April 1992	President's rule)
April 1992-Dec 1993	Rajkumar Dorendra Singh (3rd) (CIP)
(Dec 1993-Dec 1994	President's rule)
Dec 1994-Dec 1997	Rishang Keishang (2nd) (CIP)
Dec 1997-	Wahengbam Nipamacha Singh (CIP)

MPP = Manipur People's Party
MHU = Manipur Hills Union

MEGHALAYA

Statehood: 21 January 1972
Capital: Shillong

Governors:

1972-82	Governors of Assam
1982-89	Governors of Manipur
July 1989-Jan 1990	Abubaker Abdul Rahim
Jan 1990-June 1995	Madhukar Dighe
June 1995-	M.M.Jacob

Chief Ministers:

April 1970-March 1978	Williamson Sangma (1st) (APHLC)
March 1978-May 1979	Darwin Dohpugh (APHLC)
May 1979-May 1981	Brington Lyngdoh (1st) (APHLC)
May 1981-Feb 1988	Williamson Sangma (2nd) (APHLC)
Feb 1988-March 1990	Purno Sangma (CIP)
March 1990-Oct 1991	Brington Lyngdoh (2nd) (MUPP)
(Oct 1991-Feb 1992	President's rule)
Feb 1992-Feb 1993	D.D.Lapang (CIP)
Feb 1993-March 1998	Selsang Marak (CIP)
March 1998-March 2000	Brington Lyngdoh (3rd) (UDP)
March 2000-	E.K. Mawlong

APHLC = All People's Hill Leaders Conference
MUPP = Meghalaya United Parliamentary Party
UDP = United Democratic Party

MIZORAM

Statehood: February 1987
Capital: Aizawi

Lieutenant-Governors:

1972-75	Shanti Priya Mukherjee (see Tripura)
1975-77	S.K.Chhibbar
1978-80	N.P.Mathur
1980-81	K.A.A.Raja (see Arunachal Pradesh)
1981-83	S.N.Kohli
1983-87	Hari Dhube

Governors:

Feb 1987-July 1989	Hiteswar Saikia (see Assam)

July 1989-Jan 1990   Williamson Sangma   (see Meghalaya)
Jan 1990-Feb 1992   Swaraj Kaushal
Feb 1992-Feb 1998   P.R.Kyndiah
Feb-April 1998   Arun Mukherjee
April 1998-   A.Padmanabhan

Chief Ministers:

April 1972-May 1977   Chal Chhunga   (MU)
(May 1977-June 1978   President's rule)
June-Nov 1978   Thenphunga Sailo   (1st) (PC)
(Nov 1978-May 1979   President's rule)
May 1979-May 1984   Thenphunga Sailo   (2nd) (PC)
May 1984-June 1986   Lal Thanhawla   (1st) (CIP)
June 1986-Jan 1989   Laldenga   (MNF)
Jan 1989-Dec 1998   Lal Thanhawla   (2nd) (MNF-D)
Dec 1998-   Zoramthanga

MNF = Mizo National Front
MNF-D = Mizo National Front-Democrat
MU = Mizo Union
PC = People's Conference

NAGALAND

Statehood: 1 December 1963
Capital: Kohima

Chief Commissioners:

1957-60   Luthva
1960-61   M.Ramunay
1961-62   G.S.Puri
1962-63   Udit Sharma

Governors:

Dec 1963-82   Governors of Assam
1982-July 1989   Governors of Manipur
July 1989-Jan 1990   Gopal Singh   (see Goa)
1990-April 1992   M.M.Thomas
April 1992-July 1994   Loknath Mishra   (acting) (Gov of Assam)
July 1994-96   Oudh Narain Srivastava
1996-   Om Prakash Sharma

Chief Ministers:

Dec 1963-Aug 1966   P.Shilu Ao   (NPC,NNP)

Aug 1966-Feb 1969	T.N.Angami (NNP)
Feb 1969-Feb 1974	Hokishe Sema (1st) (NNP)
Feb 1974-March 1975	Vizol (1st) (UDF)
10-22 March 1975	John Jasokie (1st) (NNDP)
(March 1975-Nov 1977	President's rule)
Nov 1977-April 1980	Vizol (2nd) (UDF)
April-June 1980	S.Chubatoshi Jamir (1st) (UDF-P)
June 1980-Nov 1982	John Jasokie (2nd) (NNDP)
Nov 1982-Oct 1986	S.Chubatoshi Jamir (2nd) (CIP)
Oct 1986-Aug 1988	Hokishe Sema (2nd) (CIP)
(Aug 1988-Jan 1989	President's rule)
Jan 1989-May 1990	S.Chubatoshi Jamir (3rd) (CIP)
May-June 1990	K.L.Chisi (NPCo)
June 1990-April 1992	S.Vamuzo (JLP)
(April 1992-Feb 1993	President's rule)
Feb 1993-	S.Chubatoshi Jamir (4th) (CIP)

JLP = Joint Legislature Party
NPC = Naga People's Convention
NPCo = Naga People's Council
NNP = Naga National Party (f NPC)
NNDP = Naga National Democratic Party
UDF = United Democratic Front
UDF-P = United Democratic Front-Progressive

ORISSA

Capital: Bhubaneswar

Governors:

May 1946-Aug 1947	Chandulal Trivedi
Aug 1947-June 1948	Kailash Katju
June 1948-May 1951	Janab Asaf Ali
May 1951-May 1952	Vapal Menon (acting)
May 1952-Feb 1954	Saiyad Fazl Ali
Feb 1954-Sept 1956	Poosapati Kumaraswamy Raj
Sept 1956-July 1957	Bhimsen Sachar (see Punjab)
July 1957-62	Yeshwant Sukhthankar
1962-68	Ayudhia Khosla
1968-71	S.S.Ansari
1971-72	Sardar Jogendra Singh
1972-74	Basappa Jatti
1974-76	Akbar Ali Khan (see Uttar Pradesh)
1976-80	Bhagwat Sharma
1980-83	Cheppudira Poonacha (see Coorg)
1983-Nov 1988	Bishambhar Pande

Nov 1988-Jan 1990	Syed Nurul Hasan (see West Bengal)
Jan 1990-92	Yagya Dutt Sharma
May 1993-June 1995	Satya Narain Reddy (see Uttar Pradesh)
June 1995-April 1998	Gopala Ramanujan (see Goa)
April 1998-Nov 1999	Chakravarty Rangarajan (Gov of Andhra Pradesh)
Nov 1999-	M. Rajendran

Prime Ministers:

1937-39	Biswanath Das (1st)
(1939-Nov 1941	Governor's rule)
Nov 1941-June 1944	Maharajah of Parlakimedi
(June 1944-April 1946	Governor's rule)
April 1946-Jan 1950	Harekrushna Mahatab (CP)

Chief Ministers:

Jan-May 1950	Harekrushna Mahatab (1st) (CP)
May 1950-Oct 1956	Nabakrushna Chaudhuri (CP)
Oct 1956-Feb 1961	Harekrushna Mahatab (2nd) (CP)
(Feb-June 1961	President's rule)
June 1961-Aug 1963	Bijayanand Patnaik (CP)
Aug 1963-Feb 1965	Biren Mitra (CP)
Feb 1965-March 1967	Sadasiba Tripathy (CP)
March 1967-Jan 1971	Rajendra Singh Deo (SP)
(Jan-April 1971	President's rule)
April 1971-June 1972	Biswanath Das (2nd)
June 1972-March 1973	Nandini Satpathy (1st) (CP)
(March 1973-March 1974	President's rule)
March 1974-Dec 1976	Nandini Satpathy (2nd) (CP)
(16-29 Dec 1976	President's rule)
Dec 1976-June 1977	Binayak Acharya (CP)
June 1977-Feb 1980	Nilamani Routray (JP)
(Feb-June 1980	President's rule)
June 1980-Dec 1989	Janaki Patnaik (1st) (CIP)
Dec 1989-March 1990	Hemananda Biswal (1st) (CIP)
March 1990-March 1995	Biju Patnaik (JD)
March 1995-Feb 1999	Janaki Patnaik (2nd) (CIP)
Feb-Dec 1999	Giridhari Gomang (CIP)
Dec 1999-March 2000	Hemananda Biswal (2nd) (CIP)
March 2000-	Naveen Patnaik (BJD)

BJD = Biju Janata Dal
SP = Swatantra Party

PUNJAB

Capital: Chandigarh (shared with Haryana)

Governors:

Aug 1947-March 1953	Chandulal Trivedi (see Orissa)
March 1953-Sept 1958	Chanewesvar Narain Singh
Sept 1958-Aug 1962	Narhar Gadgil
Aug 1962-Oct 1963	K.C.Reddy
Oct 1963-May 1964	Pattom Pillai (see Kerala)
May 1964-Aug 1966	Hafiz Ibrahim
Aug 1966-Sept 1967	Dharma Veera (also Gov of Haryana)
Oct 1967-73	Dadasaheb Pavate
1973-Sept 1977	Mahendra Choudhury
Sept 1977-Feb 82	Jaisukh Hathi
Feb-April 1982	Amin Ahmed Khan
April 1982-Feb 1983	Marri Chenna Reddy (see Uttar Pradesh)
Feb-Oct 1983	A.P.Sharma
Oct 1983-June 1984	Bhairab Pandey (see West Bengal)
June 1984-March 1985	K.T.Satarwala
March-Nov 1985	Arjun Singh (see Madhya Pradesh)
Nov 1985-April 1986	Shankar Sharma (see Maharashtra)
April 1986-Dec 1989	Siddharta Ray (see West Bengal)
Dec 1989-June 1990	Nirmal Mukarji
June-Dec 1990	Virendra Varma
Dec 1990-June 1991	O.P.Malhotra
Aug 1991-July 1994	Surendra Nath († air crash)
July-Sept 1994	Sidharkar Kurdukar (acting)
Sept 1994-Nov 1999	Bakshi Chhibber
Nov 1999-	Jack Jacob (see Goa)

Chief Ministers:

Aug 1947-April 1949	Gopichand Bhargava (1st) (CP)
April-Oct 1949	Bhimsen Sachar (1st) (CP)
Oct 1949-June 1951	Gopichand Bhargava (2nd) (CP)
(June 1951-March 1952	President's rule)
March 1952-Nov 1956	Bhimsen Sachar (2nd) (CP)
Nov 1956-June 1964	Partap Singh Kairon (CP)
June-July 1964	Gopichand Bhargava (3rd) (CP)
July 1964-June 1966	Ram Kishan (CP)
(July-Oct 1966	President's rule)
Nov 1966-March 1967	Gurmukh Singh Musafir (1st) (CP)
March-Nov 1967	Gurnam Singh (1st) (AD)
Nov 1967-Aug 1968	Lachman Singh Gill (JP)

(Aug 1968-Feb 1969	President's rule)
Feb 1969-March 1970	Gurnam Singh (2nd) (AD)
March 1970-June 1971	Prakash Singh Badal (1st) (AD)
(June 1971-March 1972	President's rule)
March 1972-June 1977	G.Zail Singh (CP) (later President)
June 1977-Feb 1980	Prakash Singh Badal (2nd) (AD)
(Feb-June 1980	President's rule)
June 1980-Oct 1983	Darbara Singh (CIP)
(Oct 1983-Sept 1985	President's rule)
Sept 1985-May 1987	Surjit Singh Barnala (AD)
(May 1987-Feb 1992	President's rule)
Feb 1992-Aug 1995	Beant Singh (CIP) († assassinated)
Aug 1995-Nov 1996	Harcharan Singh Brar (acting Aug-Sept 1995) (CIP)
Nov 1996-Feb 1997	Rajinder Kaul Bhattal (CIP)
Feb 1997-	Prakash Singh Badal (3rd) (AD)

AD = Akali Dal

RAJASTHAN

Capital: Jaipur

Governors:

April 1948-Dec 1956	Bupal Singh Bahadur (Maharaja of Udaipur)
Dec 1956-April 1962	Gurmukh Nihal Singh (see Delhi)
April 1962-May 1967	Sampurnanand (see Uttar Pradesh)
May 1967-July 1972	Sardar Hukam Singh
July 1972-May 1977	Sardar Jogendra Singh
May 1977-March 1982	Raghukul Tilak
March 1982-83	O.P.Mehra
1983-Nov 1985	K.D.Sharma
Nov 1985-Feb 1988	Vasantrao Patil (see Maharashtra)
Feb 1988-Jan 1990	Sukhdev Prasad
Jan 1990-Aug 1991	Debi Chattopadhyay
Aug 1991-Feb 92	Swarap Singh
Feb 1992-May 1993	Marri Chenna Reddy
May-June 1993	Dhanik Lal Madal (Governor of Haryana)
June 1993-Feb 1998	Bali Ram Bhagat (see Himachal Pradesh)
April 1998-Jan 1999	Darbara Singh (see Punjab)
Jan 1999-	Anshuman Singh (see Gujarat)

Chief Ministers:

April 1948-April 1951	Manik Lal Verma
April 1951-March 1952	Jainarain Vyas (1st) (CP)

March 1952-53	T.Palliwal (CP)
1953-Nov 1954	Jainarain Vyas (2nd) (CP)
Nov 1954-March 1967	Mohahlal Sukhadia (1st) (CP)
(March-April 1967	President's rule)
April 1967-July 1971	Mohanlal Sukhadia (2nd) (CP)
July 1971-Oct 1973	Barkatullah Khan (CP) (†)
Oct 1973-June 1977	Harideo Joshi (1st) (CP)
June 1977-Feb 1980	Bhairon Shekhawat (1st) (JP)
(Feb-June 1980	President's rule)
June 1980-July 1981	Jagannath Pahadia (CIP)
July 1981-Feb 1985	Shiv Mathur (1st) (CIP)
Feb-March 1985	Heera Devpura (CIP)
March 1985-Jan 1988	Harideo Joshi (2nd) (CIP)
Jan 1988-Dec 1989	Shiv Mathur (2nd) (CIP)
Dec 1989-March 1990	Harideo Joshi (3rd) (CIP)
March 1990-Dec 1992	Bhairon Shekhawat (2nd) (BJP)
(Dec 1992-Dec 1993	President's rule)
Dec 1993-Dec 1998	Bhairon Shekhawat (3rd) (BJP)
Dec 1998-	Ashok Gehlot (CIP)

SIKKIM

Statehood: May 1975
Capital: Gangtok

Until 1975 Sikkim was a monarchy under British (until 1947) and Indian protection

Kings:

1641-79	Penchoo Namgyal I
1670-1700	Tensung Namgyal
1700-17	Chakdon Namgyal
1717-34	Gyurme Namgyal
1734-80	Penchoo Namgyal II
1780-90	Tenzing Namgyal
1790-1861	Chopoe Namgyal
1861-74	Sikhyong Namgyal
1874-Feb 1914	Thotub Namgyal
Feb-Dec 1914	Tulku Namgyal (*son*)
Dec 1914-Dec 1963	Tashi Namgyal (*brother*)
Dec 1963-May 1975	Palden Thondup Namgyal (*son*) (abdicated)

Governors:

May 1975-Dec 80	Bipen Behari Lal
Jan 1981-March 84	Homi Taleyarkhan
1984-85	Bhishma Narain Singh

1985	Kona Prabhakara Rao
Nov 1985-Nov 1988	Thangavelu Rajeshwar (see Arunachal Pradesh)
Feb 1989-Jan 1990	S.K.Bhatnagar
Jan 1990-Sept 1994	Radhakrishnan Tahiliani
Sept 1994-Nov 1995	Shiv Shankar
Nov 1995-March 1996	K.V.Raghunath Reddy (see West Bengal)
March 1996-	Chaudhury Randkir Singh

Chief Administrative Officers:

Dewan

1949-54	J.S.Lall
1954-59	Nari Rustomji
1959-63	Baleshwar Prasad
1963-68	R.N.Haldipur (1st)
April-Nov 1968	Netuk Tshering
1968-70	R.N.Haldipur (2nd)
1970-73	Inder Chopra
1973-74	B.S.Das

Chief Ministers:

July 1974-Aug 1979	Kazi Lhendup Dorji (CP)
(Aug-Oct 1979	President's rule)
Oct 1979-May 1984	Nar Bahadur Bhandari (1st) (JPP,SSP)
11-25 May 1984	B.B.Gurung
(May 1984-March 1985	President's rule)
March 1985-May 1994	Nar Bahadur Bhandari (2nd) (SSP)
May-Dec 1994	Sanchman Limboo (SSP)
Dec 1994-	Pawan Kumar Chamling (SDF)

JPP = Janata Parishad Party
SDF = Sikkim Democratic Front
SSP = Sikkim Samgram Parishad (f JPP)

TAMIL NADU

Previous name: Madras until 1968
Capital: Chennai (f Madras)

Governors:

Aug 1947-Sept 1948	Archibald Nye
Sept 1948-Feb 1952	Krishna Kumar Singhji Bhavsinghji (Maharaja of Bhavnagar)
Feb 1952-Nov 1956	Sri Prakasa (see Assam)
Nov 1956-Jan 1958	Anapparambil John
Jan 1958-May 1964	Bishnuram Mehdi

May 1964-May 1971   Sri Jaya Chamaraja Wadiyar Bahadur   (Maharajah of Mysore) (see Mysore)
May 1971-75   Sardar Ujjal Singh
1975-76   Kardardas Shah
1976-77   Mohanlal Sukhadia   (see Rajasthan)
April 1977-78   Prabhudas Patwari
1978-80   Chandresvar Narain Singh
May 1980-83   Sadiq Ali
1983-88   Sundar Khurana
Feb 1988-Jan 1990   P.Cherian Alexander
May 1990-Feb 1991   Surjit Singh Barnala   (see Punjab)
Feb 1991-May 1993   Bhishma Narain Singh
May 1993-Dec 1996   Marri Chenna Reddy   (†) (see Rajasthan)
Dec 1996-Jan 1997   Khrishna Kant   (acting) (Governor of Andhra Pradesh)
Jan 1997-   M.S.Fathima Beevi

Prime Ministers:

1937-Oct 1939   Chakravarti Rajagopalachari   (CP) (later Governor-General)
(Oct 1939-April 1946   Governor's rule)
April 1946-April 1947   Tanguturi Prakasam   (see Andhra Pradesh) (CP)
April 1947-March 1949   O.P.Ramaswami Reddiar   (CP)
March 1949-Jan 1950   P.S.Kumaraswami Raja   (CP)

Chief Ministers:

Jan 1950-April 1952   P.S.Kumaraswami Raja   (CP)
April 1952-April 1954   Chakravarti Rajagopalachari   (CP)
April 1954-Sept 1963   Kumaraswami Kamaraj Nadar   (CP)
Oct 1963-March 1967   M.Bhaktavatsalam   (CP)
March 1967-Feb 1969   Conjeevaram Annadurai   (DMK) (†)
3-10 Feb 1969   V.Nedunchezhian   (acting) (1st)
Feb 1969-Jan 1976   Muthuvel Karunanidhi   (1st) (DMK)
(Jan 1976-June 1977   President's rule)
June 1977-Feb 1980   Marudar Ramachandran   (1st) (ADMK)
(Feb-June 1980   President's rule)
June 1980-Dec 1987   Marudar Ramachandran   (2nd) (ADMK) (†)
Dec 1987-Jan 1988   V.Nedunchezhian   (acting) (2nd)
7-30 Jan 1988   Janika Ramachandran   (*widow of M.Ramachandran*) (ADMK)
(Jan 1988-Jan 1989   President's rule)
Jan 1989-Jan 1991   Muthuvel Karunanidhi   (2nd) (DMK)
(Jan-June 1991   President's rule)
June 1991-May 1996   Jayalalitha Jayaram   (A-IADMK)
May 1996-   Muthuvel Karunanidhi   (3rd) (DMK)

A-IADMK = All-India Anna Dravida Munnetra Kazhagam
ADMK = Anna Dravida Munnetra Kazhagam
DMK = Dravida Munnetra Kazhagam (Dravida Progress Movement)

TRIPURA

Statehood: 21 January 1972
Capital: Agartala

Chief Commissioners:

1949-51	R.K.Ray
1951-55	Venkatasubrami Nanjappa
1955-56	H.L.Atal
1956-58	Kalka Bhargawa
1958-62	N.M.Patnaik
1962-67	Shanti Priya Mukherjee
1967-68	Udit Sharma (see Nagaland)
1968-71	Anthony Dias
1971-72	Braj Nehru (Governor of Assam)

Governors:

Jan 1972-82	Governors of Assam
1982-July 1989	Governors of Manipur
July 1989-Jan 1990	Sultan Singh
Jan 1990-Aug 1993	K.V.Raghunath Reddy
Aug 1993-June 1995	Romesh Bhandari
June 1995-	Siddheshwar Prasad

Chief Ministers:

July 1963-Nov 1971	Sachinda Lal Singh (CP)
(Nov 1971-March 1972	President's rule)
March 1972-April 1977	Sukhamoy Sengupta (CP)
April-July 1977	Prafulla Kumar Das (CD)
July-Nov 1977	Radhika Gupta (JP)
(Nov 1977-Jan 1978	President's rule)
Jan 1978-Jan 1988	Nripen Chakravorty (CPM)
Jan 1988-Feb 1992	Sudhir Majumber (CIP)
Feb 1992-March 1993	Samir Burman (CIP)
(March-April 1993	President's rule)
April 1993-March 1998	Dasarath Deb (CPM)
March 1998-	Manik Sarkar (CPM)

CD = Congress for Democracy

UTTAR PRADESH

Previous name: United Provinces until 1950
Capital: Lucknow

Governors:

Aug 1947-March 49	Sarojini Naidu (†)
March-May 1949	Bidhubhusan Malik (acting)
May 1949-May 1952	Hormasji Mody
May 1952-May 1957	Kanaiyalal Munshi
May 1957-July 60	Varahagiri Giri
July 1960-April 62	B.Ramakrishna Rao
April 1962-March 1967	Biswanath Das
March 1967-Nov 72	Bezwada Gopala Reddy
Nov 1972-Oct 74	Akbar Ali Khan
Oct 1974-Oct 77	Marri Chenna Reddy
Oct 1977-Feb 1980	Ganpatrao Tapase
Feb 1980-March 1985	Chandresvar Narain Singh
March 1985-Jan 1990	Mohammed Usman Arif
Jan 1990-May 1993	Satya Narain Reddy
May 1993-May 1996	Motilal Vohra
May-July 1996	Mohammed Qureshi (Governor of Madhya Pradesh) (1st)
July 1996-March 1998	Romesh Bhandari (see Goa)
March-April 1998	Mohammed Qureshi (2nd)
April 1998-	Suraj Bhan

Prime Minister:

June 1946-Jan 1950	Govind Ballabh Pant (CP)

Chief Ministers:

Jan 1950-Dec 1955	Govind Ballabh Pant (CP)
Dec 1955-Dec 1960	Sampurnanand (CP)
Dec 1960-Aug 1963	Chandra Gupta (1st) (CP)
Aug 1963-March 1967	Sucheta Kripalani (CP)
March-April 1967	Chandra Gupta (2nd) (CP)
April 1967-April 1968	Charan Singh (1st) (JCP)
(April 1968-Feb 1969	President's rule)
Feb 1969-Feb 1970	Chandra Gupta (3rd) (CP)
Feb-Oct 1970	Charan Singh (2nd) (BKD) (later PM of India)
(2-17 Oct 1970	President's rule)
Oct 1970-April 1971	Tribhuvan Narayan Singh (OCP)
April 1971-June 1973	Kamlapati Tripathi (CP)
(June-Nov 1973	President's rule)
Nov 1973-Nov 1975	Hemavati Bahuguna (CP)

(Nov 1975-Jan 1976	President's rule)
Jan 1976-June 1977	Narain Tiwari (1st) (CP)
June 1977-Feb 1979	Ram Naresh Yadav (JP)
Feb 1979-Feb 1980	Banarasi Das (CP)
(Feb-June 1980	President's rule)
June 1980-July 1982	Vishwanath Pratap Singh (CIP) (later PM of India)
July 1982-Aug 1984	Shripati Mishra (CIP)
Aug 1984-Sept 1985	Narain Tiwari (2nd) (CIP)
Sept 1985-June 1988	Vir Bahadur Singh (CIP)
June 1988-Dec 1989	Narain Tiwari (3rd) (CIP)
Dec 1989-June 1991	Mulayam Singh Yadav (1st) (JD)
June 1991-Dec 1992	Kalyan Singh (1st) (BJP)
(Dec 1992-Dec 1993	President's rule)
Dec 1993-June 1995	Mulayam Singh Yadav (2nd) (SP)
June-Oct 1995	Mayawati (1st) (BSP)
(Oct 1995-March 1997	President's rule)
March-Sept 1997	Mayawati (2nd) (BSP)
Sept 1997-Feb 1998	Kalyan Singh (2nd) (BJP)
21-26 Feb 1998	Jagdambika Pal (LC)
Feb 1998-Nov 1999	Kalyan Singh (3rd) (BJP)
Nov 1999-	Ram Prakash Gupta (BJP)

BKD = Bharatiya Kranti Dal
BSP = Bahujan Samaj Party
JCP = Jana Congress Party
LC = Loktantrik Congress
OCP = Opposition Congress Party
SP = Samajwadi Party

WEST BENGAL

Capital: Calcutta

Governors:

Aug 1947-June 1948	Chakravarti Rajagopalachari (later Governor-General)
June 1948-Nov 1951	Kailish Katju
Nov 1951-56	Harendra Mukherjee
1956-June 1967	Padmaja Naidu
June 1967-Nov 1969	Dharma Veera (see Haryana & Punjab)
Nov 1969-Aug 1971	Shanti Dhavan
Aug 1971-March 1977	Anthony Dias (see Tripura)
March 1977-Sept 1981	Trihuvana Narayana Singh
Sept 1981-Oct 1983	Bhairub Pandey
Oct 1983-84	Anand Sharma
1984-Aug 1986	Umashankar Dikshit (see Karnataka)
Aug 1986-Nov 1988	Syed Nurul Hasan (1st)

March 1989-Jan 1990   Thangavelu Rajeshwar   (see Sikkim)
Jan 1990-July 1993   Syed Nurul Hasan   (2nd) (†)
July-Aug 1993   Satya Narain Reddy   (acting) (Gov of Orissa)
Aug 1993-April 1998   K.V.Raghunath Reddy   (see Tripura)
April 1998-May 1999   Akhlaq Kidwai   (see Bihar)
May-Dec 1999   Shyamal Kumar Sen   (acting)
Dec 1999-   Viren Shah

Prime Ministers:

Aug 1947-Jan 1948   Prafulla Ghosh   (1st)
Feb 1948-Jan 1950   Bidhan Roy   (CP)

Chief Ministers:

Jan 1950-July 1962   Bidhan Roy   (CP) (†)
July 1962-March 1967   Prafulla Sen   (CP)
March-Nov 1967   Ajoy Mukherjee   (1st) (BCP)
Dec 1967-Feb 1968   Prafulla Ghosh   (2nd)
(Feb 1968-Feb 1969   President's rule)
Feb 1969-March 1970   Ajoy Mukherjee   (2nd) (BCP)
(March 1970-April 1971   President's rule)
April-June 1971   Ajoy Mukherjee   (3rd) (BCP)
(June 1971-March 1972   President's rule)
March 1972-June 1977   Siddharta Ray   (CP)
June 1977-   Jyoti Basu   (CPM)

BCP = Bangla Congress Party

Union Territories

ANDAMAN AND NICOBAR ISLANDS

Capital: Port Blair

Chief Commissioners:

1949-53   Ajoy Kumar Ghosh
1953-56   Sankar Maitra
1956-57   S.G.N.Ayyar
1958-60   M.V.Rajvade
1961-66   Mahabir Singh
1966-71   H.S.Butalia
1971-73   Har Mande Singh
1976   S.M.Krishnatry   (1st)

1977-78	H.Singh
1978-80	S.M.Krishnatry (2nd)

Lieutenant-Governors:

1980-85	M.L.Kampani (see Arunachal Pradesh)
Dec 1985-Dec 1989	Tirath Oberoi
Dec 1989-Jan 1990	Romesh Bhandari
Jan-Dec 1990	R.S.Dyal (see Pondicherry)
Dec 1990-March 1993	Surjit Singh Barnala (Gov of Tamil Nadu)
March 1993-96	Vakkom Parushothaman
1996-98	Rajendra Bajpai
April 1998-	I.P.Gupta

CHANDIGARH

Joint capital of Haryana and Punjab

Chief Commissioners:

1966-69	M.S.Randhavi
1969-73	B.P.Bagchi
1974-77	Mohan Mathur
1977-78	T.N.Chaturvedi
1978-80	J.C.Agrawal
1980-85	Khrishna Banerji

Administrators:

1985-93	Governors of Punjab
1993-95	Ramesh Chandra
1995-	B.K.N.Chhiber

DADRA AND NAGAR HAVELI

Capital: Silvassa

Administrators:

1961-66	Lieutenant-Governors of Goa
1966-72	H.K.Khan
1972-76	Shishir Banerji (Lieut-Gov of Goa)
1976-77	K.G.Badlani
1977-87	Lieutenant-Governors of Goa
1987-93	Governors of Goa
1993-95	K.S.Baidwan
1995-	S.P.Aggarwal

DAMAN AND DIU

Part of Goa, Daman and Diu until 1987
Capital: Daman

Administrators:

1987-93	Governors of Goa
1993-95	K.S.Baidwan
1995-98	S.P.Aggarwal
1998-	Ramesh Negi

DELHI

State until 1956
Capital: New Delhi

Commissioners:

1948-54	Shankar Prasada
1954-59	Anand Pandit
1959-63	Bhagwan Sahay
1963-66	Venkata Vishvanathan

Lieutenant-Governors:

1966-70	Adity Jha
1970-71	M.C.Pimputkar
1971-74	Baleshwar Prasad (see Manipur)
1974-78	Krishan Chand
1978-79	Dalip Kohli
Feb 1980-81	Jagmohan (1st)
1981-82	Sundar Khurana
1982-84	Jagmohan (2nd)
March-Nov 1984	Padmakar Gavai
Nov 1984-Nov 1985	Maumohan Wali
Nov 1985-87	Hari Krishnan Kapur
1987-89	Romesh Bhandari
1989-Dec 1990	Arjun Singh
Dec 1990-92	Markendaya Singh
1992-96	Prasannabhai Dave
1996-April 1998	Tejendra Khanna
April 1998-	Vijay Kapour

Chief Ministers:

March 1952-Feb 1955	Chaudhary Brahim Prakash (CP)

Feb 1955-Nov 1956   Gurmukh Nihal Singh   (CP)
(Nov 1956   post abolished)

Chief Executive Councillors:

1980-85   Kidar Sahan
1985-Jan 1990   J.Pravash Chandra
(Jan 1990   post abolished)

Chief Ministers:

Dec 1993-Feb 1996   Madan Lal Khurana   (BJP)
Feb 1996-Oct 1998   Sahib Singh Verma   (BJP)
Oct-Dec 1998   Sushma Swaraj   (BJP)
Dec 1998-   Sheila Dixit   (CIP)

LAKSHADWEEP

Previous name: Laccadive, Minicoy & Amindivi Islands
Capital: Kavaratti Island

Administrators:

1956-58   S.Moni
1958-62   C.K.Balakrishna Nair
1962-66   M.Ramnuny
1966-73   C.H.Naire
1973-76   W.Shaiza
1976-78   M.C.Verma
1978-83   P.M.Nair
1983-85   O.Saigal
1985-89   J.Sagar
1989-90   Wajahat Habidullah
1990-93   Pradeep Singh
1993-95   S.P.Aggarwal
1995-96   G.S.Chima
1996-   Rajeev Talwar

PONDICHERRY

Previous name: French India until 1954
Capital: Pondicherry

Governors:

1898-1902   François-Pierre Rodier

1902-04	Victor Lanrezac
1904-05	Jean Lemaire
1905-06	Joseph-Pascal François
1906-08	Gabriel-Louis Angoulvant
1908-09	Adrien Bonhoure (see Reunion)
1909-10	Fernand Lévécque
1910-12	Pierre Duprat
1912-18	Alfred-Albert Martineau (see Gabon)
1918-26	Louis Gerbinis
1926-28	Pierre Didelot (see Senegal)
1928-31	Robert de Guise (see Martinique)
1931-34	François-Adrien Jaivanon
1934-36	Léon Solomiac
1936-45	Louis Bonvin
1945-47	Nicolas Jeandrin
1947-48	Charles Baron

Commissioners:

1948-49	Charles Baron
1949-50	Charles Chambon
1950-54	André Menard

Chief Commissioners:

1954-57	Kewal Singh
1957-58	M.K.Kripalani
1958-60	L.R.S.Singh
1960	A.S.Bam
1961-63	Sarat Dutta

Lieutenant-Governors:

1963-64	Sarat Dutta
1964-68	S.L.Sailain
1968-72	Basappa Jatti
1972-76	Cheddy Lal
1976-79	Bidesh Kulkarni (1st)
1979-80	Ram Vyan
1980-82	R.N.Haldipur (see Arunachal Pradesh & Sikkim)
1982-83	Kizhekethil Chandy
1983-84	Bidesh Kulkarni (2nd)
1984	Sundar Khurana (acting)
1984-85	K.Prabhakara Rao
1985-88	Tribhuvan Tewary
1988-90	R.S Dyal
Jan-Dec 1990	Chandravati

Dec 1990-92　　　　　　　　Har Swarup Singh
1993-95　　　　　　　　　　Marri Chenna Reddy　(see Tamil Nadu)
April 1995-April 1998　　　　Rajendra Bajpai
April 1998-　　　　　　　　Rajni Roy

Chief Ministers:

July 1963-Sept 1964　　　　Edouard Goubert　(CP)
Sept 1964-April 1967　　　　V.Venkatasurba Reddiar　(1st) (CP)
April 1967-March 1968　　　M.O.Hasan Farook Maricar　(1st) (CP)
March-Sept 1968　　　　　　V.Venkatasurba Reddiar　(2nd) (CP)
(Sept 1968-March 1969　　　President's rule)
March 1969-Dec 1973　　　　M.O.Hasan Farook Maricar　(2nd) (DMK)
(Jan-March 1974　　　　　　President's rule)
March 1974　　　　　　　　Subramanyan Ramaswamy　(1st) (ADMK)
(March 1974-July 1977　　　　President's rule)
July 1977-Nov 1978　　　　　Subramanyan Ramaswamy　(2nd) (ADMK)
(Nov 1978-Jan 1980　　　　　President's rule)
Jan 1980-June 1983　　　　　D.Ramachandran　(1st) (DMK)
(June 1983-March 1985　　　　President's rule)
March 1985-March 1990　　　M.O.Hasan Farook Maricar　(3rd) (CIP)
March-Dec 1990　　　　　　D.Ramachandran　(2nd) (DMK)
(Dec 1990-June 1991　　　　　President's rule)
June 1991-May 1996　　　　　V.Vaithilingam　(CIP)
May 1996-March 2000　　　　R.V.Janakiraman　(DMK)
March 2000-　　　　　　　　P. Shanmughan

Former States

AJMER

Capital: Ajmer

Chief Minister:

March 1952-Nov 1956　　　　Hari Upadhayaya　(CP)

In 1956 Ajmer became part of Rajasthan

BARODA

Capital: Baroda

Prime Minister:

May 1948-May 1949　　　　　Jivraj Mehta

Baroda was incorporated into Bombay in 1949 and is now part of Gujarat

BHOPAL

Capital: Bhopal

Prime Ministers:

April 1948-Jan 1949	Oudhnarain Bisatya
Jan-May 1949	Chaturnarain Malaviya

In 1949 Bhopal became part of Madhya Pradesh

BOMBAY

Capital: Bombay

Governors:

Aug 1947-Jan 1948	David Colville
Jan 1948-May 1952	Maharaj Singh
May 1952-Dec 1954	Girijashankar Bajpai (†)
Jan 1955-Oct 1956	Harekrushna Mahatab (see Orissa)
Oct-Dec 1956	Mahomed Chagla
Dec 1956-May 1960	Sri Prakasa (see Assam & Madras)

Prime Minister:

1937-Oct 1939	B.G.Kher (1st) (CP)
(Oct 1939-April 1946	Governor's rule)
April 1946-Jan 1950	B.G.Kher (2nd) (CP)

Chief Ministers:

Jan 1950-April 1952	B.G.Kher (CP)
April 1952-Oct 1956	Morarji Desai (CP) (later PM of India)
Oct 1956-May 1960	Yashwantrao Chavan (CP) (later CM of Maharashtra)

In 1960 Bombay was divided into Gujarat and Maharashtra

COORG

Capital: Mercara

Chief Minister:

March 1952-Nov 1956	Cheppudira Poonacha (CP)

In 1956 Coorg was incorporated into Mysore (now Karnataka)

HYDERABAD

Capital: Hyderabad

Governor:

Dec 1949-Nov 1956   Osman Ali Khan

Chief Ministers:

Dec 1949-March 1952   M.K.Vellodi   (CP)
March 1952-Nov 1956   B.Ramakrishna Rao

In 1956 Hyderabad was divided between Andhra Pradesh, Bombay and Maharashtra

MADHYA BHARAT

Capital: Gwalior (winter), Indore (summer)

Governor:

May 1948-Nov 1956   George Jivaji Rao Sindhia   (Maharaja of Gwalior)

Chief Ministers:

Jan 1948-May 1949   Liladhar Joshi   (CP)
May 1949-51   Gopikrishan Vijayavargiya   (CP)
1951-March 1952   Takhatmal Jain   (1st) (CP)
March 1952-April 1955   Mishrilal Gangwal   (CP)
April 1955-Nov 1956   Takhatmal Jain   (2nd) (CP)

In 1956 Madhya Bharat was incorporated into Madhya Pradesh

MATSYA UNION

Prime Minister:

March 1948-May 1949   Shobaram

Matsya Union was incorporated into Rajasthan in 1949

PATIALA AND EAST PUNJAB STATE UNION (PEPSU)

Capital: Patiala

Governor:

July 1948-Nov 1956   Yadavendra Singh Mahendra Bahadur   (Maharajah of Patiala)

Chief Ministers:

May 1951-April 1952	Raghbir Singh	(1st) (CP)
April 1952-March 1953	Sardar Rarewala	(UF)
(March 1953-March 1954	President's rule)	
March 1954-Jan 1955	Raghbir Singh	(2nd) (CP)
Jan 1955-Nov 1956	Brish Bhan	(CP)

UF = United Front

In 1956 PEPSU became part of Punjab

SAURASHTRA

Capital: Rajkot

Governors:

1948	Krishna Kumar Singh (Maharaja of Bhavnagar) (acting)
1948-Nov 1956	Digvijayasinhji Ranjit Singh Jadeya (Maharaja of Nawanagar)

Chief Ministers:

Feb 1948-Dec 1954	Uchharangarai Dhebar (CP)
Dec 1954-Nov 1956	Rasiklal Parikh (CP)

In 1956 Saurashtra became part of Bombay and is now part of Gujarat

VINDHYA PRADESH

Capital: Rewa

Governor:

1948-49	Martand Singh Bahadur (Maharaja of Rewa)
(1949	post abolished)

Chief Ministers:

April 1948-April 1949	K.P.Saksena (CP)
(April 1949-March 1952	Governor's & President's rule)
March 1952-Nov 1956	Sambhu Shukla (CP)

In 1956 Vindhya Pradesh became part of Madhya Pradesh

INDONESIA

Official name: Republic of Indonesia, Republik Indonesia (Bahasa Indonesia)
Previous names: Netherlands East Indies until 1945/49, United States of Indonesia 1949-50
Independence date: 17 August 1945
Capital: Jakarta

The Portuguese and British traders who were active in the East Indies in the 16th century were ousted by the Dutch in 1595. From 1602 until 1798 the East Indies were ruled by the Netherlands East India Company. In 1816 the area was proclaimed a Dutch colony. In 1941 the islands were occupied by Japan. After the Japanese surrender an independent republic was proclaimed in Jakarta. The Dutch regained control of the outer islands and an autonomous East Indonesia government was established in 1946. In 1949 agreement was reached between the Jakarta government and the Netherlands for the transfer of sovereignty to an independent federal Indonesia, but the federation was abolished in 1950 in favour of a unitary state. An attempted communist coup in 1965 was violently suppressed, and led to the handover of power to President Suharto who oversaw significant economic growth during three decades of strong centralised rule. His resignation in1998 paved the way to multi-party democracy.

Governors-General:

1899-1904	Willem Rooseboom
1904-09	Johannes van Heutsz
1909-16	Alexander van Idenburg
1916-21	Johannes van Limburg-Stirum
1921-26	Dirk Fock
1926-31	Andries de Graeff
1931-36	Bonifacius de Jonge
1936-42	Alidius van Starckenbrogh-Stachower
(1942-45	Japanese occupation)
1946-48	Hubertus van Mook

Presidents:

Aug 1945-Feb 1967	Ahmed Sukarno
Feb 1967-May 1998	Suharto (acting Feb 1967-March 1968) (SGK)
May 1998-Oct 1999	Bacharuddin Habibie (SGK)
Oct 1999-	Abdurrahman Wahid (NAP)

Prime Ministers:

Nov 1945-June 1947	Sutan Sjahrir
July 1947-Jan 1948	Amir Sjarifuddin
Jan-Dec 1948	Mohammed Hatta (1st)

Dec 1948-May 1949	Sjarifuddin Prawiraranegara
May-July 1949	Susanto Tirtoprodjo
July 1949-Jan 1950	Mohammed Hatta (2nd)
Jan-Aug 1950	Halim
Sept 1950-March 1951	Mohammed Natsir
April 1951-Feb 1952	Wirjosandjojo Sukiman
April 1952-June 1953	Wilopo
July 1953-June 1955	Ali Sastroamidjoyo (1st)
Aug 1955-March 1956	Burhanuddin Harahap
March 1956-March 1957	Ali Sastroamidjoyo (2nd)
April 1957-Nov 1963	Djuanda Kartawidjaja (†)
Nov 1963-March 1966	Ahmed Sukarno
March 1966-Feb 1967	Suharto
(Feb 1967	post abolished)

NAP = National Awakening Party
SGK = Sekber Golongan Karya (Golkar)

RIVAL GOVERNMENT

Formed in Bukittingi (Central Sumatra); rebellion put down by the Jakarta government.

Prime Minister:

Feb-May 1958	Sjarifuddin Prawiraranegara

Former Autonomous States

EAST INDONESIA

Capital: Macassar

President:

Dec 1946-Aug 1950	Tjokordo Sukawali

Prime Ministers:

Jan-Oct 1947	Najamuddin Daeng Malewa
Oct 1947-48	S.J.Warouw
1948-Jan 1950	Anak Agung Nadjmuddin
Jan-April 1950	Diapari
April-Aug 1950	Putuhena

EAST JAVA

Capital: Surabaya

President:

Dec 1948-March 1950   Ahmed Kusumonegoro

EAST SUMATRA

Capital: Medan

President:

1948-50   T. Mansur

GREAT SIAK (East Borneo)

Capital: Samarinda

Prime Minister:

May 1947-Feb 1948   Mohamed Parikesit   (Sultan of Kutai)

KALIMANTAN (West Borneo)

Capital: Banjermassin

Prime Minister:

March 1947-Feb 1948   Abdul Hamid II   (Sultan of Pontianak)

MADURA

Capital: Pamekasan

President:

Feb 1948-March 1950   Tjakraningrat

SOUTH SUMATRA

Capital: Palembang

President:

Aug 1948-March 1950   Abdul Malik

WEST JAVA (Pasundan)

Capital: Bandung

Presidents:

Feb 1948-49   Ario Wiranatukusamah
1949-50   Anwar Tjokroaminoto

Prime Ministers:

April-Dec 1948   Adil Puradiredja
Jan 1949-50   R.Djumhana

Former Netherlands Colony

NETHERLANDS NEW GUINEA

Known as West New Guinea (1962-63), and as Irian Jaya after incorporation into Indonesia in 1963 (also see West Papua New Guinea below).

Capital: Hollandia   (renamed Kotabaru in 1963)

Governors:

1949-53   Simon van Waardenburg
1953-58   Jan van Baal
1958-62   Pieter Platteel

Administrators:

1-22 Oct 1962   José Rolz-Bennett
Oct 1962-May 1963   Djalal Abdoh

Secessionist States

SOUTH MOLUCCAS

Republic of the South Moluccas
Capital: Ambon (1950), Ceram (1950-56)

Presidents:

April-May 1950   J.H.Manukutu   (acting)
May 1950-56   Christiaan Sumokil   (executed 1956)
1956   Johannes Manusama   (later in exile in the Netherlands)

Prime Ministers:

April-Oct 1950   Albert Wairisal
Nov 1950-56   Christiaan Sumokil

WEST PAPUA NEW GUINEA

Secessionist government proclaimed in Irian Jaya, but did not control any significant area and did not function for long.

President:

1971   Seth Runkorem

IRAN

Official name: Islamic Republic of Iran, Jomhori-e-Islame-e-Iran (Farsi)
Previous name: Empire of Iran (until 1979) (also known as Persia until 1935)
State founded: c550 BC
Capital: Teheran

The ancient Persian Empire was founded by Cyrus the Great in about 550 BC. Persia was conquered by the Arabs in 637, by the Turks in 1029, and by the Mongols in the 13th century. The kingdom was reunited by the Safavid dynasty in 1501. The revolution of 1925 brought the Pahlavi family to power. In 1979 the monarchy was overthrown and an Islamic republic proclaimed.

Shahs:

(From the Safavid dynasty)

1501-24	Ismail I
1524-76	Tahmasp I (*son*)
1576-7	Ismail II (*son*)
1577-86	Mohammed (*brother*)
1587-Jan 1629	Abbas I (*son*)
Jan 1629-42	Safi I (*grandson*)
1642-67	Abbas II (*son*)
1667-94	Safi II Suleiman (*nephew*)
1694-1726	Soltan Hosein (*son*) (assassinated)
1726-32	Tahmasp II (*son*) (deposed)
1732-36	Abbas III (*son*) (deposed)
1736-June 1747	Nader Shah (*f* Nadi Qoli Beg) (assassinated)
June 1747-1796	Rokh (*grandson*) (assassinated)
1796-June 1797	Aga Mohammed Khan (assassinated)
June 1797-Oct 1834	Fath Ali Khan (*nephew*)
Oct 1834-Sept 1848	Mohammed Shah (*grandson*)
Sept 1848-June 1896	Nasir Ad-din (*son*)
June 1896-Jan 1907	Muzaffar Ad-din (*son*)
Jan 1907-July 1909	Mohammed Ali (*son*) (deposed)
July 1909-Oct 1925	Ahmed Mirza Shah (*son*) (deposed)
	Regents: 1909-11 Asad al-Mulk
	1911-14 Abolqassem Nasser ol-Molk
Oct 1925-Sept 1941	Reza Shah Pahlavi (*b* Mohammed Reza Khan) (abdicated)
Sept 1941-Feb 1979	Mohammed Reza Pahlavi (*son*) (deposed)
(Feb 1979-Feb 1980	Provisional government)

Presidents:

Feb 1980-June 1981	Abolhassan Bani-Sadr
(June-Aug 1981	Presidential council: Mohammed Ali Raja'i/ Ali Akhbar Hashemi Rafsanjani/ Mohammed Beheshti († assassinated June)/Abdulkarim Moussawi-Ardebili)
2-30 Aug 1981	Mohammed Ali Raja'i († assassinated)
(Aug-Oct 1981	Presidential council: Ali Akhbar Hashemi Rafsanjani/ Abdulkarim Moussawi-Ardebili)
Oct 1981-Aug 1989	Ali Khamene'i
Aug 1989-Aug 1997	Ali Akhbar Hashemi Rafsanjani
Aug 1997-	Mohammed Khatami

Prime Ministers:

1884-Nov 1896	Ali Asghar Amin os-Soltan (1st)
(Nov 1896-Feb 1897	post vacant)
Feb 1897-June 1898	Ali Khan Amin od-Dowleh
June 1898-Jan 1907	Ali Asghar Amin os-Soltan (2nd)
Jan-March 1907	Nasrollah Moshir od-Dowleh
March-May 1907	Lotfali Khan Vazir Afkham
May-Sept 1907	Ali Asghar Amin os-Soltan (3rd) († assassinated)
Sept-Oct 1907	Ahmed Khan Moshir od-Dowleh (1st)
Oct-Dec 1907	Abolqassem Nasser ol-Molk (1st)
Dec 1907-June 1908	Hosseinali Khan Nezam os-Saltaneh Mafi
June 1908-May 1909	Ahmed Khan Moshir od-Dowleh (2nd)
May-July 1909	Abolqassem Nasser ol-Molk (2nd)
July-Oct 1909	Javad Khan Sa'ad od-Dowleh (acting)
Oct 1909-July 1910	Mohammed Vali Khan Sepahdar Azam (1st)
July 1910-March 1911	Hassan Khan Mostowfi al-Mamalek (1st)
March-July 1911	Mohammed Vali Khan Sepahdar Azam (2nd)
July 1911-Jan 1913	Najafqoli Khan Samsam os-Saltaneh (1st)
Jan 1913-Aug 1914	Mohammed Khan Ala os-Saltaneh
Aug 1914-March 1915	Hassan Khan Mostowfi al-Mamalek (2nd)
March-May 1915	Hassan Khan Moshir od-Dowleh (1st)
May-Aug 1915	Abdul-Majid Mirza Ayn od-Dowleh (1st)
Aug-Dec 1915	Hassan Khan Mostowfi al-Mamalek (3rd)
Dec 1915-March 1916	Abdul-Hossein Mirza Farman Farma
March-Aug 1916	Mohammed Vali Khan Sepahdar Azam (3rd)
Aug 1916-June 1917	Hassan Khan Vossuq od-Dowleh (1st)
June-Nov 1917	Mohammed Ali Khan Ala os-Saltaneh
Nov 1917-Jan 1918	Abdul-Majid Mirza Ayn od-Dowleh (2nd)
Jan-April 1918	Hassan Khan Mostowfi al-Mamalek (4th)
April-Aug 1918	Najafqoli Khan Samsam os-Saltaneh (2nd)
April 1918-July 1920	Hassan Khan Vossuq od-Dowleh (2nd)
July-Oct 1920	Hassan Khan Moshir od-Dowleh (2nd)

Oct 1920-Feb 1921	Fathollah Khan Sardar Mansur Sepahdar Azam
Feb-June 1921	Seyyid Zia Ed-Din Tabataba'i
June 1921-Jan 1922	Ahmed Qavam os-Soltaneh (*brother of Vossuq od-Dowleh*) (1st)
Jan-June 1922	Hassan Khan Moshir od-Dowleh (3rd)
June 1922-Feb 1923	Ahmed Qavam os-Saltaneh (2nd)
Feb-June 1923	Hassan Khan Mostowfi al-Mamalek (5th)
June-Oct 1923	Hassan Khan Moshir od-Dowleh (3rd)
Oct 1923-Oct 1925	Mohammed Reza Khan (later Shah Reza ShahPahlavi)
Nov 1925-July 1926	Mohammed Ali Forughi (1st)
July 1926-July 1927	Hassan Mostowfi (*f Hassan Khan Mostowfial-Mamalek*) (6th)
July 1927-Sept 1933	Mehdiqoli Hedayat
Sept 1933-Dec 1935	Mohammed Ali Forughi (2nd)
Dec 1935-Oct 1939	Mahmud Jam
Nov 1939-July 1940	Ahmad Matin-Daftari
July 1940-Aug 1941	Ali Mansur (1st)
Aug 1941-Feb 1942	Mohammed Ali Forughi (3rd)
March 1942-March 1944	Ali Soheily
March-Nov 1944	Mohammed Sa'ed (1st)
Nov 1944-April 1945	Mortezaqoli Bayat
May-June 1945	Ibrahim Hakimi (1st)
June-Oct 1945	Muhsin Sadr
Nov 1945-Jan 1946	Ibrahim Hakimi (2nd)
Jan 1946-Dec 1947	Ahmed Qavam os-Saltaneh (3rd)
10-21 Dec 1947	Fakhar Hekmat
Dec 1947-June 1948	Ibrahim Hakimi (3rd)
June-Nov 1948	Abdul-Hossein Hajir (assassinated 1949)
Nov 1948-March 1950	Mohammed Sa'ed (2nd)
April-June 1950	Ali Mansur (2nd)
June 1950-March 1951	Ali Razmara († assassinated)
March-April 1951	Hossein Ala (1st)
April 1951-July 1952	Mohammed Mossadegh (1st)
17-22 July 1952	Ahmed Qavam os-Saltaneh (4th)
July 1952-Aug 1953	Mohammed Mossadegh (2nd) (deposed)
Aug 1953-April 1955	Fazlollah Zahedi
April 1955-April 1957	Hossein Ala (2nd)
April 1957-Aug 1960	Manuchehr Ikbal
Aug 1960-May 1961	Jaffar Sharif-Emami (1st)
May 1961-July 1962	Ali Amini
July 1962-March 1964	Asadollah Alam
March 1964-Jan 1965	Hassan Mansur (*son of Ali Mansur*) († assassinated)
Jan 1965-Aug 1977	Amir-Abbas Hoveida (executed 1979)
Aug 1977-Aug 1978	Jamshid Amouzegar
Aug-Nov 1978	Jaffar Sharif-Emami (2nd)
Nov 1978-Jan 1979	Gholam Azhari
Jan-Feb 1979	Shapour Bakhtiar (deposed)

Feb-Nov 1979	Mehdi Barzagan
(Nov 1979-Aug 1980	post vacant)
Aug 1980-Aug 1981	Mohammed Ali Raja'i
5-30 Aug 1981	Mohammed Bahonar († assassinated)
Sept-Oct 1981	Mohammed Mahdavi-Kani
Oct 1981-Aug 1989	Hossein Mousavi
(Aug 1989	post abolished)

Religious Leaders:

Feb 1979-June 1989	Ruhollah Khomeini (†)
June 1989-	Ali Khamene'i

Secessionist States

AZERBAIJAN

Capital: Tabriz

Prime Minister:

Dec 1945-Dec 1946	Jaafar Pishevari

KURDISTAN

Mahabad Peoples Republic
Capital: Sinandaj   (Sinneh)

Prime Minister:

1945-Dec 1946	Mohammed Ghazi

IRAQ

Official name: Republic of Iraq, Al-Jamhuriyah al-Iraqia
Previous name: Kingdom of Iraq 1921-58
State founded: 23 August 1921
Independence date: 3 October 1932
Capital: Baghdad

Iraq has its origins in the ancient kingdoms of Mesopotamia. In 633 it was conquered by the Arabs and thereafter was ruled by the Mongols, Persians and Turks. The last period of Turkish rule began in 1638. During the second half of the 19th century British influence in the area increased, and during World War I Britain occupied the area, ending Turkish rule. In 1921 Iraq became a League of Nations mandated territory under British administration. Full independence was granted in 1932. In February 1958 Iraq and Jordan formed a federation, but a coup in Iraq in July of that year ended the monarchy and the federation, and a republic was declared. Since 1968 the country has been dominated by the Baath Party. In 1990 Iraq invaded and occupied Kuwait, but was forced out by an international armed force six months later in the Gulf War.

Kings:

Aug 1921-Sept 1933	Faisal I (*son of King Hussein of Hejaz*) (*f* King of Syria)
Sept 1933-April 1939	Ghazi (*son*) († motor accident)
April 1939-July 1958	Faisal II (*son*) (deposed, assassinated)
	Regent: April 1939-May 1953
	Prince Abdul-Illah (assassinated 1958)

Presidents:
Chairman of the Sovereignty Council 1958-63

July 1958-Feb 1963	Najib el-Rubai (deposed)
Feb 1963-April 1966	Abdul Salam Arif († air accident)
April 1966-July 1968	Abdul Rahman Arif (*brother*) (deposed)
July 1968-July 1979	Ahmed al-Bakr (ABSP)
July 1979-	Saddam Hussein (ABSP)

Prime Ministers:

Oct 1920-Nov 1922	Abdur al-Gailani
Nov 1922-Nov 1923	Abdul es-Saadun (1st)
Nov 1923-Aug 1924	Jaafar al-Askari (1st)
Aug 1924-June 1925	Yasin al-Hashimi (1st)
June 1925-Nov 1926	Abdul es-Saadun (2nd)
Nov 1926-Dec 1927	Jaafar al-Askari (2nd)

Jan 1928-Jan 1929	Abdul es-Saadun (3rd)
April-Aug 1929	Tewfiq el-Suweidi (1st)
Sept-Nov 1929	Abdul es-Saadun (4th)
Nov 1929-March 1930	Naji as-Suweidi
March 1930-Nov 1932	Nuri es-Said (1st)
Nov 1932-March 1933	Naji Shaukat
March-Nov 1933	Rashid al-Gailani (1st)
Nov 1933-Aug 1934	Jamil al-Midfai (1st)
Aug 1934-March 1935	Ali al-Ayoubi (1st)
5-16 March 1935	Jamil al-Midfai (2nd)
March 1935-Oct 1936	Yasin al-Hashimi (2nd)
Oct 1936-Aug 1937	Hikmat Suleiman
Aug 1937-Dec 1938	Jamil al-Midfai (3rd)
Dec 1938-March 1940	Nuri es-Said (2nd)
March 1940-Feb 1941	Rashid al-Gailani (2nd)
Feb-April 1941	Taha al-Hashimi
April-July 1941	Rashid al-Gailani (3rd)
July-Sept 1941	Jamil al-Midfai (4th)
Sept 1941-June 1944	Nuri es-Said (3rd)
June 1944-Feb 1946	Hamdi Pachachi
Feb-May 1946	Tewfiq el-Suweidi (2nd)
June-Nov 1946	Arshad al-Umari
Nov 1946-March 1947	Nuri es-Said (4th)
March 1947-Jan 1948	Salih Jabr
Jan-June 1948	Mohammed el-Sadri
June 1948-Jan 1949	Muzahim al-Pachachi
Jan-Dec 1949	Nuri es-Said (5th)
Dec 1949-Feb 1950	Ali al-Ayoubi (2nd)
Feb-Sept 1950	Tewfiq el-Suweidi (3rd)
Sept 1950-July 1952	Nuri es-Said (6th)
July-Nov 1952	Mustafa al-Umari (1st)
Nov-Dec 1952	Nureddin Mahmud
Jan-May 1953	Jamil al-Midfai (5th)
May 1953-March 1954	Fadil Jamali
April-Aug 1954	Mustafa al-Umari (2nd)
Aug 1954-June 1957	Nuri es-Said (7th)
June-Dec 1957	Ali al-Ayoubi (3rd)
Dec 1957-March 1958	Abdul Mirjan
March-May 1958	Nuri es-Said (8th) (assassinated July 1958)
May-July 1958	Ahmed Baban (deposed)
July 1958-Feb 1963	Abdul Kassem (deposed, executed)
Feb-Nov 1963	Ahmed al-Bakr (1st)
Nov 1963-Sept 1965	Taher Yahya (1st)
3-16 Sept 1965	Arif Razzak
Sept 1965-Aug 1966	Abdul al-Bazzaz

Aug 1966-May 1967	Naji Talib
May-July 1967	Abdul Rahman Arif
July 1967-July 1968	Taher Yahya (2nd) (deposed)
19-30 July 1968	Abdel al-Nayef
July 1968-July 1979	Ahmed al-Bakr (2nd)
July 1979-March 1991	Saddam Hussein (1st)
March-Sept 1991	Sa'adoun Hammadi
Sept 1991-Sept 1993	Mohammed al-Zubaydi
Sept 1993-May 1994	Ahmed Khudayer
May 1994-	Saddam Hussein (2nd)

ABSP = Arab Baath Socialist Party (constitutionally dominant)

Autonomous Region

KURDISTAN

After the Gulf War, most of Kurdistan came under United Nations protection, and in 1992 a regional government was elected without the approval of Baghdad.

Capital: Irbil

Prime Ministers:

Chairman of the Executive Council 1980-91

1980-91	Mohammed Amin Mohammed
July 1992-March 1993	Fuad Maasum (PUK)
April 1993-Sept 1996	Kosrat Rasul (PUK)
Sept 1996-	Roz Nuri Shawez (KDP)

KDP = Kurdistan Democratic Party
PUK = Patriotic Union of Kurdistan

Defunct Federation

FEDERATION OF ARAB STATES

Date formed: 14 February 1958
Date dissolved: 1 August 1958
Member states: Iraq, Jordan
Capital: Baghdad

Heads of State:

Feb-July 1958	King Faisal II (Iraq) (deposed, assassinated)
July-Aug 1958	King Hussein (Jordan)

Prime Minister:

Feb-July 1958	Nuri es-Said (deposed, assassinated)

IRELAND

Official name: Republic of Ireland, Poblacht na h'Éireann (Gaelic)
Previous names: Irish Free State 1922-37, Ireland (Eire) 1937-49
Independence date: 6 December 1922
Capital: Dublin

Ireland consisted of five kingdoms until the English invasion of 1171. The country was formally united with Great Britain in 1801. In 1916 there was an uprising against British rule, followed by an armed struggle in 1919. A measure of autonomy was then granted, and in 1922 the Irish Free State was proclaimed, but the six counties of Ulster (Northern Ireland) remained part of the United Kingdom. In 1937 Ireland adopted a republican constitution, and formally left the Commonwealth in 1949.

Lord-Lieutenants:

July 1895-Aug 1902	Earl Cadogan (George Cadogan)
Aug 1902-Dec 1905	Earl of Dudley (William Ward)
Dec 1905-Dec 1915	Earl of Aberdeen (John Gordon)
Dec 1915-May 1916	Viscount Wimborne (Ivor Guest) (1st)
May-Aug 1916	Viscount French of Ypras (John French)
Aug 1916-May 1918	Viscount Wimborne (Ivor Guest) (2nd)
May 1918-Oct 1922	Edmund Howard

Presidents:

Dec 1918-Jan 1922	Éamon de Valéra (1st)
Jan-Aug 1922	Arthur Griffith (†)
12-22 Aug 1922	Michael Collins († assassinated)
Aug-Dec 1922	William Cosgrave (acting Aug-Sept)

Governors-General:
Represented monarch who was concurrently British monarch

Dec 1922-Feb 1928	Timothy Healy
Feb 1928-Nov 1932	James McNeill
Nov 1932-Dec 1936	Donal Buckley
(Dec 1936	post abolished)

Presidents:

(Dec 1937-June 1938	Presidential commission: FrankFahy/Timothy Sullivan/Conor Maguire)
June 1938-June 1945	Douglas Hyde
June 1945-June 1959	Seán O'Kelly

June 1959-June 1973	Éamon de Valéra (2nd)
June 1973-Nov 1974	Erskine Childers (†)
(Nov-Dec 1974	Presidential commission: Thomas O'Higgins/SeánTreacy/James Dooge)
Dec 1974-Oct 1976	Cearbhall O'Dalaigh
(Oct-Dec 1976	Presidential commission: Thomas O'Higgins/SeánTreacy/James Dooge)
Dec 1976-Dec 1990	Patrick Hillery
Dec 1990-Sept 1997	Mary Robinson (*b* M.Bourke)
(Sept-Nov 1997	Presidential commission: Liam Hamilton/SéamusPattison/Liam Cosgrave 12-17 Sept; Brian Mullooly)
Nov 1997-	Mary McAleese (*b* M. Leneghan)

Prime Ministers:

President of the Executive Council 1922-37
Taoiseach since 1937

Jan-Aug 1922	Michael Collins
Aug 1922-March 1932	William Cosgrave (acting Aug-Sept 1922) (UIP)
March 1932-Feb 1948	Éamon de Valéra (1st) (FF)
Feb 1948-June 1951	John Costello (1st) (FG)
June 1951-June 1954	Éamon de Valéra (2nd) (FF)
June 1954-March 1957	John Costello (2nd) (FG)
March 1957-June 1959	Éamon de Valéra (3rd) (FF)
June 1959-Nov 1966	Seán Lemass (FF)
Nov 1966-March 1973	John Lynch (1st) (FF)
March 1973-July 1977	Liam Cosgrave (*son of W.Cosgrave*) (FG)
July 1977-Dec 1979	John Lynch (2nd) (FF)
Dec 1979-June 1981	Charles Haughey (1st) (FF)
June 1981-March 1982	Garret Fitzgerald (1st) (FG)
March-Dec 1982	Charles Haughey (2nd) (FF)
Dec 1982-March 1987	Garret Fitzgerald (2nd) (FG)
March 1987-Feb 1992	Charles Haughey (3rd) (FF)
Feb 1992-Dec 1994	Albert Reynolds (FF)
Dec 1994-June 1997	John Bruton (FG)
June 1997-	Bertie Ahern (FF)

FF = Fianna Fail
FG = Fine Gael
UIP = United Ireland Party

ISRAEL

Official name: State of Israel, Medinat Israel
Independence date: 14 May 1948
Capital: Jerusalem (Yerushalayim)

Present-day Israel consists of most of the former territory of Palestine, which was ruled by the Turks from 1517 until 1917, when it was occupied by British forces. In 1922 Palestine became a League of Nations mandated territory under British rule. In 1947 the United Nations approved a resolution partitioning Palestine into a Jewish and an Arab state. The State of Israel was proclaimed in May 1948 in the Jewish area, and the surrounding Arab states then invaded Palestine. After the hostilities Israel was left in control of 75% of the former territory of Palestine. There were further Arab-Israeli wars in 1956, 1967 and 1973. During the 1967 conflict Israel occupied the remaining parts of Palestine. Peace talks with the PLO (see below) led to the establishment of Palestinian autonomy in some areas in 1994.

Presidents:
President of the Provisional State Council May 1948-Feb 1949

May 1948-Nov 1952	Chaim Weizmann (†)
Nov-Dec 1952	Joseph Springzak (acting)
Dec 1952-April 1963	Izhak Ben-Zvi (*b* I.Shimshelewitz) (†)
April-May 1963	Kadish Luz (acting)
May 1963-May 1973	Zalman Shazar (*b* Z.Rubashov)
May 1973-May 1978	Ephraim Katzir (*b* E.Katchalsky)
May 1978-May 1983	Yitzhak Navon
May 1983-May 1993	Chaim Herzog
May 1993-	Ezer Weizman (*nephew of C.Weizmann*)

Prime Ministers:

May 1948-Dec 1953	David Ben-Gurion (*b* D.Grün) (1st) (MP)
Dec 1953-Nov 1955	Moshe Sharett (*b* M.Shartok) (MP)
Nov 1955-June 1963	David Ben-Gurion (2nd) (MP)
June 1963-Feb 1969	Levi Eshkol (*b* L.Shkolnik) (MP,LP) (†)
Feb-March 1969	Yigal Allon (acting) (LP)
March 1969-May 1974	Golda Meir (*f* Meyerson, *b* G.Mabtovich) (LP)
May 1974-June 1977	Yitzhak Rabin (1st) (LP)
June 1977-Oct 1983	Menachem Begin (L)
Oct 1983-Sept 1984	Yitzhak Shamir (*b* Y.Yezernitzky) (1st) (L)
Sept 1984-Oct 1986	Shimon Peres (*b* S.Persky) (1st) (LP)
Oct 1986-July 1992	Yitzhak Shamir (2nd) (L)
July 1992-Nov 1995	Yitzhak Rabin (2nd) (LP) († assassinated)

Nov 1995-June 1996	Shimon Peres (acting 5-22 Nov 1995) (2nd) (LP)
June 1996-July 1999	Binyamin Netanyahu (L)
July 1999-	Ehud Barak (LP)

L = Likud
LP = Labour Party (*f* MP)
MP = Mapai Party

PALESTINE

After the proclamation of the State of Israel, an Arab government was formed in Gaza, but it soon went into exile in Egypt; it was dissolved in 1952. In 1964 various Palestinian groups formed an umbrella organization, the Palestine Liberation Organization. In 1980 the PLO proclaimed the State of Palestine from its base in Tunisia. In 1993 peace talks between Israel and the PLO led to the establishment of Palestinian autonomy in Jericho and Gaza in 1994. Control of other areas was transferred later.

Capital: Jerusalem

High Commissioners:

1920-25	Herbert Samuel
1925-28	Herbert Plumer
1928-31	John Chancellor (see Southern Rhodesia)
1931-38	Arthur Wauchope
1938-44	Harold MacMichael
1944-46	Viscount Gort (John Vereker) (see Malta)
1946-48	Alan Cunningham

GOVERNMENTS-IN-EXILE

Headquarters: Cairo (1948-52); Tunis (1989-94)

Presidents:

President of the Supreme Council 1948-52

Oct 1948-52	Amin el-Husseini
(1952	Government dissolved)
April 1989-July 1994	Yasser Arafat

Prime Minister:

Sept 1948-52	Ahmed Hilmi
(1952	Government dissolved)

PALESTINE LIBERATION ORGANIZATION

Headquarters: Beirut (1964-82), Tunis (1982-)

Chairmen:

June 1964-Dec 1967	Ahmed Shukairy
Dec 1967-Feb 1969	Yehia Hammouda
Feb 1969-	Yasser Arafat

PALESTINIAN AUTONOMOUS AREAS

Headquarters: Gaza City

President of the National Authority:

July 1994-	Yasser Arafat

ITALY

Official name: Italian Republic, Repubblica Italiana
Previous name: Kingdom of Italy 1861-1946
State founded: 18 February 1861
Capital: Turin (1861-65), Florence (1865-71), Rome (Roma) (since 1871)

Before the middle of the 19th century Italy consisted of a number of states. In the 1850s the Kingdom of Sardinia (Piedmont-Sardinia) assumed the leading role in the movement towards unification. Austria was driven out of Lombardy, the duchy of Tuscany was annexed, the Bourbon rulers of Naples and Sicily were deposed, and a united Kingdom of Italy was established in 1861. The Papal States became part of the kingdom, but the city of Rome was only incorporated in 1871. The Vatican City was recognized as a sovereign state in 1929. During World War II the Italian dictator, Mussolini, sided with Germany. After the war the monarchy was abolished and a republic proclaimed. The republic has suffered from unstable governments, with a succession of mostly Christian Democratic led coalitions. Electoral reforms and new party alignments in the 1990s led to some changes in the political landscape, with pressures for more devolution to regions.

Kings:

Feb 1861-Jan 1878	Vittorio Emanuele II (*f* King of Piedmont-Sardinia)
Jan 1878-July 1900	Umberto I (*son*) (assassinated)
July 1900-May 1946	Vittorio Emanuele III (*son*) (abdicated)
May-June 1946	Umberto II (*son*)

Presidents:

June 1947-May 1948	Enrico de Nicola
May 1948-May 1955	Luigi Einadi
May 1955-May 1962	Giovanni Gronchi (CDP)
May 1962-Dec 1964	Antonio Segni (CDP)
6-29 Dec 1964	Cesare Merzagora (acting)
Dec 1964-Dec 1971	Giuseppe Saragat (CDP)
Dec 1971-June 1978	Giovanni Leone (CDP)
June-July 1978	Amintore Fanfani (acting)
July 1978-June 1985	Alessandro Pertini (ISP)
June 1985-April 1992	Francesco Cossiga (CDP)
April-May 1992	Giovanni Spadolini (acting)
May 1992-May 1999	Oscar Scalfaro (CDP,IPP)
15-18 May 1999	Nicola Mancino (acting)
May 1999-	Carlo Azeglio Ciampi

Prime Ministers:

Feb-June 1861	Camille Cavour (see Piedmont-Sardinia) (†)
June 1861-March 1862	Bettino Ricasoli (Count of Brolio) (see Tuscany) (1st)
March-Dec 1862	Urbano Rattazzi (1st)
Dec 1862-March 1863	Luigi Farina
March 1863-Sept 1864	Marco Minghetti (1st)
Sept 1864-June 1866	Alfonso la Marmora (see Piedmont-Sardinia)
June 1866-April 1867	Bettino Ricasoli (Count Brolio) (2nd)
April-Oct 1867	Urbano Rattazzi (2nd)
Oct 1867-Dec 1869	Luigi Menabrea
Dec 1869-June 1873	Giovanni Lanza
June 1873-March 1876	Marco Minghetti (2nd)
March 1876-March 1878	Agostino Depretis (1st)
March-Dec 1878	Benedetto Cairoli (1st)
Dec 1878-July 1879	Agostino Depretis (2nd)
Aug 1879-May 1881	Benedetto Cairoli (2nd)
May 1881-July 1887	Agostino Depretis (3rd) (†)
July 1887-Feb 1891	Francesco Crispi (1st)
Feb 1891-May 1892	Marchese di Rudini (Antonio Starabba) (1st)
May 1892-Dec 1893	Giovanni Giolitti (1st)
Dec 1893-March 1896	Francesco Crispi (2nd)
March 1896-June 1898	Marchese di Rudini (Antonio Starabba) (2nd)
June 1898-June 1900	Luigi Pelloux
June 1900-Feb 1901	Giuseppe Saracco
Feb 1901-Oct 1903	Giuseppe Zanardelli
Oct 1903-March 1905	Giovanni Giolitti (2nd)
March 1905-Feb 1906	Alessandro Fortis
Feb-May 1906	Sidney Sonnino (1st)
May 1906-Dec 1909	Giovanni Giolitti (3rd)
Dec 1909-March 1910	Sidney Sonnino (2nd)
March 1910-March 1911	Luigi Luzzatti
March 1911-March 1914	Giovanni Giolitti (4th)
March 1914-June 1916	Antonio Salandra
June 1916-Oct 1917	Paolo Boselli
Oct 1917-June 1919	Vittorio Orlando
June 1919-June 1920	Francesco Nitti
June 1920-June 1921	Giovanni Giolitti (5th)
July 1921-Feb 1922	Ivanoe Bonomi (1st)
Feb-Oct 1922	Luigi Facta
Oct 1922-July 1943	Benito Mussolini (executed 1945)
July 1943-Nov 1944	Pietro Badoglio
Dec 1944-June 1945	Ivanoe Bonomi (2nd) (LDP)
June-Nov 1945	Ferruccio Parri (AP)
Dec 1945-Aug 1953	Alcide de Gasperi (CDP)
Aug 1953-Jan 1954	Giuseppe Pella (CDP)
Jan-Feb 1954	Amintore Fanfani (1st) (CDP)

Feb 1954-July 1955	Mario Scelba (CDP)
July 1955-May 1957	Antonio Segni (1st) (CDP)
May 1957-July 1958	Adone Zoli (CDP)
July 1958-Feb 1959	Amintore Fanfani (2nd) (CDP)
Feb 1959-March 1960	Antonio Segni (2nd) (CDP)
March-July 1960	Fernando Tambroni (CDP)
July 1960-June 1963	Amintore Fanfani (3rd) (CDP)
June-Nov 1963	Giovanni Leone (1st) (CDP)
Nov 1963-June 1968	Aldo Moro (1st) (CDP)
June-Dec 1968	Giovanni Leone (2nd) (CDP)
Dec 1968-Aug 1970	Mariano Rumor (1st) (CDP)
Aug 1970-Feb 1972	Emilio Colombo (CDP)
Feb 1972-July 1973	Giulio Andreotti (1st) (CDP)
July 1973-Nov 1974	Mariano Rumor (2nd) (CDP)
Nov 1974-July 1976	Aldo Moro (2nd) (CDP) (assassinated 1978)
July 1976-Aug 1979	Giulio Andreotti (2nd) (CDP)
Aug 1979-Oct 1980	Francesco Cossiga (CDP)
Oct 1980-June 1981	Arnaldo Forlani (CDP)
June 1981-Dec 1982	Giovanni Spadolini (RP)
Dec 1982-Aug 1983	Amintore Fanfani (4th) (CDP)
Aug 1983-April 1987	Benedetto (Bettino) Craxi (ISP)
April-July 1987	Amintore Fanfani (5th) (CDP)
July 1987-April 1988	Giovanni Goria (CDP)
April 1988-July 1989	Ciriaco de Mita (CDP)
July 1989-June 1992	Giulio Andreotti (3rd) (CDP)
June 1992-April 1993	Giuliano Amato (1st) (ISP)
April 1993-May 1994	Carlo Azeglio Ciampi
May 1994-Jan 1995	Silvio Berlusconi (FI)
Jan 1995-May 1996	Lamberto Dini
May 1996-Oct 1998	Romano Prodi (IPP)
Oct 1998-April 2000	Massimo D'Alema (DPL)
April 2000-	Giuliano Amato (2nd) (ISP)

AP = Action Party
FI = Forza Italia
CDP = Christian Democratic Party
DPL = Democratic Party of the Left
IPP = Italian Popular Party (f CDP)
ISP = Italian Socialist Party
LDP = Labour Democratic Party
RP = Republican Party

RIVAL GOVERNMENT

Italian Social Republic (Pro-German government which operated in northern Italy during the latter part of World War II)
Headquarters: Salo

Prime Minister:

Sept 1943-April 1945   Benito Mussolini   (executed)

Autonomous Regions
Five regions have special statute (*) (greater autonomy)

ABRUZZO

Capital: L'Aquila

Government Presidents:

Sept 1970-March 1972	Ugo Crescenzi (1st) (CDP)
March 1972-July 1973	Giustino De Cecco (1st) (CDP)
July 1973-May 1974	Ugo Crescenzi (2nd) (CDP)
May 1974-Oct 1975	Giustino De Cecco (2nd) (CDP)
Oct 1975-March 1977	Felice Spadaccini (1st) (CDP)
March 1977-Nov 1981	Romeo Ricciuti (CDP)
Dec 1981-May 1983	Anna Nenna D'Antonio (CDP)
May 1983-Oct 1985	Felice Spadaccini (2nd) (CDP)
Oct 1985-Aug 1990	Emilio Matucci (CDP)
Aug 1990-Sept 1992	Rocco Salini (CDP)
Oct 1992-June 1995	Vincenzo Del Colle (CDP,IPP)
June 1995-April 2000	Antonio Falconio (IPP)
April 2000-	Giovanni Pace

BASILICATA

Capital: Potenza

Government Presidents:

June 1970-March 1983	Vincenzo Verrastro (CDP)
March 1983-June 1985	Carmelo Azzara (CDP)
June 1985-May 1990	Gaetano Michetti (CDP)
May 1990-April 1995	Antonio Boccia (CDP)
April 1995-April 2000	Raffaele Dinardo (IPP)
April 2000	Filippo Bubbico

CALABRIA

Capital: Catanzaro

Government Presidents:

Oct 1970-Oct 1974   Antonio Guarasci   (CDP)

Oct 1974-Aug 1975	Aldo Ferrara (1st) (CDP)
Aug 1975-Oct 1976	Pasquale Perugini (CDP)
Oct 1976-Dec 1980	Aldo Ferrara (2nd) (CDP)
Dec 1980-Nov 1985	Bruno Dominijanni (ISP)
Nov 1985-Dec 1987	Francesco Principe (ISP)
Dec 1987-Nov 1991	Rosario Olivo (ISP)
Feb 1992-June 1994	Guido Rhodio (CDP)
Aug 1994-April 1995	Donato Veraldi (IPP)
June 1995-Feb 1999	Giuseppe Nistico (FI)
Feb 1999-April 2000	Luigi Meduri
April 2000-	Giuseppe Chiararalloti

CAMPANIA

Capital: Naples

Government Presidents:

Nov 1970-Oct 1971	Carlo Leone (CDP)
Nov 1971-Sept 1972	Nicola Mancino (1st) (CDP)
Sept 1972-July 1973	Alberto Servidio (CDP)
July 1973-Aug 1975	Vittorio Cascetta (CDP)
Aug 1975-Aug 1976	Nicola Mancino (2nd) (CDP)
Aug 1976-Sept 1979	Gaspare Russo (CDP)
Sept 1979-Aug 1980	Ciro Cirillo (CDP)
Aug 1980-March 1983	Emilio de Feo (CDP)
March 1983-May 1989	Antonio Fantini (CDP)
May 1989-April 1993	Ferdinando Clemente di San Luca (CDP)
April 1993-June 1995	Giovanni Grasso (CDP)
June 1995-99	Antonio Rastrelli (NA)
1999-April 2000	Andrea Losco
April 2000-	Antonio Bassolini

NA = National Alliance

EMILIA-ROMAGNA

Capital: Bologna

Government Presidents:

July 1970-May 1976	Guido Fanti (ICP)
May 1976-Jan 1978	Sergio Cavina (ICP)
Jan 1978-April 1987	Lanfranco Turci (ICP)
April 1987-May 1990	Luciano Guerzoni (ICP)
July 1990-June 1993	Enrico Boselli (ISP)
July 1993-May 1996	Pier Luigi Bersani (DPL)

June 1996-March 1999	Antonio La Forgia (DPL)
March 1999-	Vasco Errani (DPL)

DPL = Democratic Party of the Left (*f* ICP)
ICP = Italian Communist Party

FRIULI-VENEZIA GIULIA*

Capital: Trieste

Government Presidents:

June 1964-July 1973	Alfredo Berzanti (CDP)
July 1973-Oct 1984	Antonio Comelli (CDP)
Oct 1984-Jan 1992	Adriano Biasutti (CDP)
Jan 1992-July 1993	Vinicio Turello (CDP)
Aug 1993-Jan 1994	Pietro Fontanini (NL)
Jan-July 1994	Renzo Travanut (DPL)
July 1994-Nov 1995	Alessandra Guerra (NL)
Nov 1995-Dec 1996	Sergio Cecotti (NL)
Dec 1996-June 1998	Giancarlo Cruder (IPP)
June 1998-	Roberto Antonione (FI)

NL = Northern League

LAZIO

Capital: Rome

Government Presidents:

Sept 1970-Jan 1972	Girolamo Mechelli (CDP)
Jan 1972-Oct 1973	Luigi Cipriani (CDP)
Oct 1973-Sept 1975	Rinaldo Santini (CDP)
Sept 1975-March 1976	Roberto Palleschi (ISP)
March 1976-Aug 1977	Maurizio Ferrara (ICP)
Aug 1977-May 1983	Giulio Santarelli (ISP)
May 1983-April 1984	Bruno Landi (1st) (ISP)
April 1984-Aug 1985	Gabriele Panizzi (ISP)
Aug 1985-May 1987	Sebastiano Montali (ISP)
May 1987-July 1990	Bruno Landi (2nd) (ISP)
July 1990-Aug 1992	Rodolfo Gigli (CDP)
Aug 1992-Feb 1994	Giorgio Pasetto (CDP)
Feb 1994-Jan 1995	Carlo Proietti
Jan-June 1995	Arturo Osio
June 1995-April 2000	Piero Badaloni
April 2000-	Francesco Storace

LIGURIA

Capital: Genoa

Government Presidents:

July 1970-April 1975	Gianni Dagnino (CDP)
April-July 1975	Giorgio Verda (CDP)
July 1975-June 1979	Angelo Carossino (ICP)
June 1979-Oct 1980	Armando Magliotto (ICP)
Oct 1980-Sept 1981	Giovanni Persico (RP)
Sept 1981-May 1983	Alberto Teardo (ISP)
Aug 1983-March 1990	Rinaldo Magnani (ISP)
March-Sept 1990	Renzo Muratore (ISP)
Sept 1990-Jan 1992	Giacomo Gualco (CDP)
Jan 1992-March 1995	Edmondo Ferrero (CDP, IPP)
March 1995-April 2000	Giancarlo Mori (IPP)
April 2000-	Sandro Biasotti

LOMBARDY

Lombardia

Capital: Milan

Government Presidents:

July 1970-74	Piero Bassetti (CDP)
1974-79	Cesare Golfari (CDP)
1979-87	Giuseppe Guzzetti (CDP)
1987-Jan 1989	Bruno Tabacci (CDP)
Jan 1989-Dec 1992	Giuseppe Giovenzana (CDP)
Dec 1992-June 1994	Fiorella Ghilardotti (DPL)
June 1994-June 1995	Paolo Arrigoni (LL)
June 1995-	Roberto Formigoni (UDC)

LL = Lombardy League
UDC = United Democratic Christians

MARCHE

Capital: Ancona

Government Presidents:

Aug 1970-Dec 1972	Giuseppe Serrini (CDP)
Dec 1972-Sept 1975	Dino Tiberi (CDP)

Sept 1975-Sept 1978   Adriano Ciaffi   (CDP)
Sept 1978-July 1990   Emidio Massi   (ISP)
July 1990-July 1993   Rodolfo Giampaoli   (CDP)
July 1993-July 1995   Gaetano Recchi   (ISP)
July 1995-   Vito D'Ambrosio   (DPL)

MOLISE

Capital: Campobasso

Government Presidents:

Aug 1970-Jan 1973   Carlo Vitale   (CDP)
Jan 1973-July 1976   Giustino D'Uva   (1st) (CDP)
July 1976-Feb 1982   Florindo D'Aimmo   (CDP)
March 1982-Oct 1984   Giustino D'Uva   (2nd) (CDP)
Nov 1984-May 1985   Ulderico Colagiovanni   (CDP)
Oct 1985-Jan 1988   Paolo Nuvoli   (CDP)
Jan 1988-July 1990   Ferdinando Di Laura Frattura   (CDP)
July 1990-Aug 1992   Enrico Santoro   (CDP)
Aug 1992-March 1994   Luigi Di Bartolomeo   (CDP)
March 1994-June 1995   Giovanni Di Giandomenico   (CDP)
June 1995-Feb 1998   Marcello Veneziale   (1st) (MDP)
Feb 1998-Feb 1999   A.Michele Iorio   (IPP)
Feb 1999-April 2000   Marcello Veneziale   (2nd)
April 2000-   Giovanni Di Stasi

MDP = Molise Democratico Popolare

PIEMONTE

Capital: Turin

Government Presidents:

July 1970-Dec 1973   Edoardo Calleri di Sala   (CDP)
Dec 1973-Aug 1975   Giovanni Oberto   (CDP)
Aug 1975-July 1980   Aldo Viglione   (1st) (ISP)
July 1980-July 1983   Ezio Enrietti   (ISP)
July 1983-Aug 1985   Aldo Viglione   (2nd) (ISP)
Aug 1985-July 1990   Vittorio Beltrami   (CDP)
July 1990-June 1995   Gian Paolo Brizio   (CDP, IPP)
June 1995-   Enzo Ghigo   (FI)

PUGLIA

Capital: Bari

Government Presidents:

1970-75	Gennaro Liuzzi (1st) (CDP)
1976-78	Nicola Rotolo (CDP)
1979-82	Nicola Quarta (CDP)
1983-84	Gennaro Liuzzi (2nd) (CDP)
1985-88	Salvatore Fitto (CDP) († motor accident)
1988-89	Francesco Borgia (acting) (ISP)
Jan 1989-Oct 1990	Giuseppe Colasanto (CDP)
Oct 1990-Oct 1992	Michele Bellomo (CDP)
Oct-Dec 1992	Cosimo Convertino (ISP)
Dec 1992-Sept 1993	Giovanni Copertino (CDP)
Sept 1993-Feb 1994	Vito Savino (CDP)
March 1994-June 1995	Giuseppe Martellotta (CDP)
June 1995-April 2000	Salvatore Distaso (IPP)
April 2000-	Raffaele Fitto

SARDINIA*
Sardegna

Capital: Cagliari

Government Presidents:

June 1949-Jan 1954	Luigi Crespellani (CDP)
Jan 1954-June 1955	Alfredo Corrias (CDP)
June 1955-Nov 1958	Giuseppe Brotzu (CDP)
Nov 1958-March 1966	Efisio Corrias (CDP)
March 1966-Feb 1967	Paolo Dettori (CDP)
Feb 1967-Feb 1970	Giovanni del Rio (1st) (CDP)
Feb-Nov 1970	Lucio Abis (CDP)
Nov 1970-Feb 1972	Antonio Giagu de Martini (CDP)
Feb-March 1972	Pietro Soddu (1st) (CDP)
March-Dec 1972	Salvatorangelo Spano (CDP)
Dec 1972-Dec 1973	Nino Giagu (CDP)
Dec 1973-May 1976	Giovanni del Rio (2nd) (CDP)
May 1976-Aug 1979	Pietro Soddu (2nd) (CDP)
Aug-Sept 1979	Mario Puddu (1st) (CDP)
Sept 1979-Oct 1980	Alessandro Ghinami (ISDP)
Oct-Nov 1980	Pietro Soddu (3rd) (CDP)
Nov-Dec 1980	Mario Puddu (2nd) (CDP)
Dec 1980-May 1982	Francesco Rais (ISP)
May-June 1982	Mario Melis (1st) (SAP)

June 1982-Aug 1984	Angelo Roych (CDP)
Aug 1984-Aug 1989	Mario Melis (2nd) (SAP)
Aug 1989-Nov 1991	Mario Florias (CDP)
Nov 1991-Aug 1994	Antonello Cabras (ISP)
Aug 1994-	Federico Palomba (SCP)

SAP = Sardinian Action Party
SCP = Social Christian Party

SICILY*
Sicilia

Capital: Palermo

Government Presidents:

May 1947-Jan 1949	Giuseppe Alessi (1st) (CDP)
Jan 1949-July 1955	Franco Restivo (CDP)
July 1955-Sept 1956	Giuseppe Alessi (2nd) (CDP)
Sept 1956-Oct 1958	Giuseppe La Loggia (CDP)
Oct 1958-Feb 1960	Silvio Milazzo (CDP)
Feb 1960-Jan 1961	Benedetto Majorana della Nicchiara (MP)
June-Sept 1961	Salvatore Corallo (SP)
Sept 1961-Aug 1964	Giuseppe D'Angelo (CDP)
Aug 1964-Aug 1967	Francesco Coniglio (CDP)
Aug-Sept 1967	Vincenzo Giumarra (1st) (CDP)
Sept 1967-Feb 1969	Vincenzo Carollo (CDP)
Feb 1969-Dec 1972	Mario Fasino (CDP)
Dec 1972-March 1974	Vincenzo Giumarra (2nd) (CDP)
March 1974-March 1978	Angelo Bonfiglio (CDP)
March 1978-May 1980	Piersanti Mattarella (CDP)
May 1980-Dec 1982	Mario D'Acquisto (CDP)
Dec 1982-Oct 1983	Calogero Lo Giudice (CDP)
Oct 1983-April 1984	Santi Nicita (CDP)
April 1984-Feb 1985	Modesto Sardo (CDP)
Feb 1985-Aug 1991	Rino Nicolosi (CDP)
Aug 1991-July 1992	Vincenzo Leanza
July 1992-Dec 1993	Giuseppe Campione (CDP)
Dec 1993-May 1995	Francesco Di Martino (CDP)
May 1995-July 1996	Matteo Graziano (CDP)
July 1996-Jan 1998	Giuseppe Provenzano (FI)
Jan-Nov 1998	Giuseppe Drago (DCC)
Nov 1998-	Angelo Capodicasa (DPL)

DCC = Democratic Christian Centre
MP = Monarchist Party

TRENTINO-ALTO ADIGE*

Capitals: Bolzano and Trento

Government Presidents:

Jan 1949-Dec 1960	Tullio Odorozzi (CDP)
Jan 1961-Nov 1967	Luigi Dalvit (CDP)
Nov 1967-Dec 1973	Giorgio Grigolli (CDP)
March 1974-May 1976	Bruno Kessler (CDP)
May 1976-Jan 1977	Flavio Mengoni (CDP)
Jan 1977-April 1979	Spartaco Marziani (CDP)
April 1979-May 1984	Enrico Pancheri (CDP)
May 1984-Nov 1987	Pierluigi Angeli (CDP)
Nov 1987-Nov 1992	Gianni Bazzanella (CDP)
Nov 1992-Nov 1993	Tarcisio Andreolli (CDP)
Nov 1993-Feb 1999	Tarcisio Grandi (IPP)
Feb 1999-	Margherita Cogo

Autonomous provinces of Trentino-Alto Adige

South Tyrol

Capital: Bolzano

Government Presidents:

1948-56	Karl Erckert (STPP)
1956-60	Alois Pupp (STPP)
1960-89	Silvius Magnago (STPP)
1989-	Luis Durnwalder (STPP)

STPP = South Tyrol People's Party

Trento

Capital: Trento

Government Presidents:

1948-52	Giuseppe Balista (CDP)
1952-56	Remo Albertini (CDP)
1956-60	Riccardo Rosa (CDP)
1960-73	Bruno Kessler (CDP)
1973-78	Giorgio Grigolli (CDP)
1978-85	Flavio Mengoni (CDP)
Oct 1985-Feb 1989	Pierluigi Angeli (CDP)
Feb 1989-June 1992	Mario Malossini (CDP)

June 1992-93	Gianni Bazzanella	(CDP)
1993-98	Carlo Andreotti	(ATTP)
1998-	Lorenzo Dellai	(M)

ATTP = Autonomist Trentino-Tyrol Party
M = Margherita

TUSCANY
Toscana

Capital: Florence (Firenze)

Government Presidents:

July 1970-Sept 1978	Lelio Lagorio	(ISP)
Sept 1978-May 1983	Mario Leone	(ISP)
May 1983-July 1990	Gianfranco Bartolini	(ICP)
July 1990-Dec 1991	Marco Marcucci	
Feb 1992-April 2000	Vannino Chiti	(ICP, DPL)
April 2000-	Claudio Martini	

UMBRIA

Capital: Perugia

Government Presidents:

July 1970-May 1976	Pietro Conti	(ICP)
May 1976-May 1987	Germano Morri	(ICP)
May 1987-June 1992	Francesco Mandarini	(ICP)
June 1992-93	Francesco Ghirelli	(ICP,DPL)
1993-95	Claudio Carnieri	(DPL)
June 1995-April 2000	Bruno Bracalente	(DPL)
April 2000-	Maria Rita Lorenzetti	

VALLE D'AOSTA*

Capital: Aosta

Government Presidents:

May 1949-Dec 1954	Severino Caveri	(1st) (UV)
Dec 1954-June 1956	Vittorino Bondaz	(UV)
June 1956-Nov 1963	Oreste Marcoz	(UV)
Nov 1963-May 1966	Severino Caveri	(2nd) (UV)
May 1966-Sept 1969	Cesare Bionaz	(CDP) (†)
Sept 1969-May 1970	Mauro Bordon	(CDP)

May 1970-Dec 1974	Cesare Dujany (CDP)
Dec 1974-Jan 1984	Mario Andrione (UV)
Jan 1984-June 1990	Augusto Rollandin (UV)
June 1990-June 1992	Gianni Bondaz (CDP)
June 1992-June 1993	Ilario Lahivi (GM)
June 1993-	Dino Vierin (UV)

GM = Gruppo Misto
UV = Unione Valdotain

VENETO

Capital: Venice

Government Presidents:

Aug 1970-April 1972	Angelo Tomelleri (1st) (CDP)
April-May 1972	Luigi Tartari (CDP)
May 1972-March 1973	Pietro Feltrin (CDP)
March 1973-Aug 1980	Angelo Tomelleri (2nd) (CDP)
Aug 1980-July 1989	Carlo Bernini (CDP)
July 1989-July 1992	Gianfranco Cremonese (CDP)
July 1992-May 1993	Franco Frigo (CDP)
May 1993-May 1994	Giuseppe Pupillo (ICP)
May 1994-June 1995	Aldo Bottin (CDP)
June 1995-	Giancarlo Galan (FI)

Pre-unification States

LUCCA

Capital: Lucca

Leaders:

(1397-1797	Collective leadership with a 2-month rotating head)
(1797-1805	French rule)

Dukes/Duchesses:

March 1805-March 1814	Elisa (*sister of Napoléon I*) (co-ruler June 1805-March 1814) (deposed)
June 1805-March 1814	Felice (*b* Felix Bacciochi) (*husband*) (deposed)
Nov 1817-March 1824	Maria Luisa
March 1824-Oct 1847	Carlo Lodovico (Carlo II of Parma & Piacenza & Carlo Luigi of Etruria) (*son*) (abdicated)

Lucca became part of Tuscany in 1847

MODENA

Capital: Modena

Dukes:

1452-71	Borso	
1471-1505	Ercole I	
1505-35	Alfonso I	*(son)*
1535-59	Ercole II	*(son)*
1559-97	Alfonso II	*(son)*
1597-1628	Cesare	*(grandson)*
1628-29	Alfonso III	*(son)* (abdicated)
1629-58	Francesco I	*(brother)*
1658-62	Alfonso IV	*(son)*
1662-Sept 1694	Francesco II	*(son)*
Sept 1694-Oct 1737	Rinaldo	*(uncle)*
Oct 1737-Feb 1780	Francesco III	*(son)*
Feb 1780-Feb 1797	Ercole III	*(brother)*
(Feb 1797-1803	French occupation)	
1803-06	Ferdinand	*(son-in-law of Ercole III)*
April 1814-Jan 1846	Francesco IV	*(son)*
Jan 1846-March 1860	Francesco V	*(son)*

Annexed by Piedmont-Sardinia in March 1860

NAPLES AND SICILY

Kingdom of Naples

Capital: Naples

Kings/Queens:

1266-85	Carlo I	(Charles of Anjou) (also of Sicily) *(son of Louis VIII of France)*
1285-1309	Carlo II	*(son)*
1309-43	Roberto	*(son)*
1343-82	Giovanna I	*(granddaughter)* (deposed, murdered)
May 1382-Feb 1386	Carlo III	*(great grandson of Carlo II)* (Karolyi I of Hungary)
Feb 1386-Aug 1414	Laslo	*(son)*
Aug 1414-Feb 1435	Giovanna II	*(sister)*
Feb 1435-July 1442	Rinaldo	(deposed)
July 1442-June 1458	Alfonso I	(Alfonso I of Aragon)
June 1458-Jan 1494	Ferrante I	(Ferdinando) *(son)*
Jan 1494-Jan 1495	Alfonso II	*(son)* (abdicated)
Jan 1495-Oct 1496	Ferrante II	*(son)*
Oct 1496-1501	Federigo	*(uncle)* (deposed)

(1501-4	interregnum)
1504-Jan 1516	Ferdinando III (Ferdinando II of Sicily; Ferdinand V of Spain)
Jan 1516-Jan 1556	Carlo IV (Carlo I of Sicily; Carlos I of Spain)
Jan 1556-Sept 1598	Filippo I (Felipe II of Spain)
Sept 1598-March 1621	Filippo II (Felipe III of Spain)
March 1621-Sept 1665	Filippo III (Felipe IV of Spain)
Sept 1665-Nov 1700	Carlo V (Carlo II of Sicily; Carlos II of Spain)
Nov 1700-July 1707	Filippo IV (Felipe V of Spain)
July 1707-April 1711	Giuseppe (Josef I of Austria)
April 1711-May 1735	Carlo VI (Carlo III of Sicily; Karl II of Austria)
May 1735-Oct 1759	Carlo VII (Carlo IV of Sicily; Carlos III of Spain) (abdicated)
Oct 1759-March 1806	Ferdinando IV (*son*) (1st) (Ferdinando III of Sicily) (deposed)
March 1806-June 1808	Giuseppe (Joseph Bonaparte) (José of Spain) (*brother of Napoléon I of France*)
June 1808-June 1815	Gioacchino (Joachim Murat) (executed Oct 1815)
June 1815-Dec 1816	Ferdinando IV (2nd)

Viceroys:

July-Oct 1707	Georg von Martinitz
1707-8	Wierich von Daun (1st)
1708-10	Vincenzo Grimani
1710-13	Carlo Borromeo
1713-19	Wierich von Daun (2nd)
1719	Johann Gallas
1719-21	Wolfgang von Schrattenbach
1721-22	Marcantonio Borghese
1722-28	Michael von Althann
July-Dec 1728	Marchese d'Almahara
1728-33	Aloys Harrach
1733-34	Giulio Borromeo

Kingdom of Sicily

Capital: Palermo

Kings/Queens:

1130-Feb 1154	Ruggiero II
Feb 1154-May 1166	Guglielmo I (*son*)
May 1166-Nov 1189	Guglielmo II (*son*)
Nov 1189-Feb 1194	Tancrede (*grandson of Ruggiero II*)
Feb-Dec 1194	Guglielmo III (*son*) (murdered?)
Dec 1194-Nov 1198	Constanza (*daughter of Ruggiero II*) (co-ruler)
Dec 1194-Sept 1197	Enrico (*husband*) (co-ruler)
April 1198-Dec 1250	Federico I Ruggiero (*son*)

Dec 1250-May 1254	Corrado I (*son*)
May 1254-58	Corrado II (*son*) (1st)
1258-66	Manfred (*son of Federico I*)
1266-68	Corrado II (2nd)
1268-82	Carlo (Charles of Anjou) (Carlo I of Naples) (*son of Louis VIII of France*)
1282-85	Pietro I (Pedro III of Aragon) (*son-in-law of Manfred*)
1285-95	Giacomo (Jaime II of Aragon)
1295-June 1337	Federico III (*brother*)
June 1337-1342	Pietro II (*son*)
1342-55	Lodovico (*son*)
1355-77	Federico IV
1377-1402	Maria (*daughter*) (co-ruler 1391-1402)
1391-1409	Martino I (*husband*) (co-ruler 1391-1402)
1409-10	Martino II (*father*) (Martin I of Aragon)
(1410-12	interregnum)
1412-April 1416	Ferdinando I (Fernando I of Aragon)
April 1416-June 1458	Alfonso I (Alfonso I of Aragon and of Naples)
June 1458-60	Giovanni (Juan II of Aragon)
1460-Jan 1516	Ferdinando II (Ferdinando III of Naples; Ferdinand V of Spain)
Jan 1516-April 1555	Giovanna (Giovanna III of Naples; Juana of Spain) (nominal)
Jan 1516-Jan 1556	Carlo I (Carlo IV of Naples; Carlos I of Spain)
Jan 1556-Sept 1598	Filippo I (Filippo I of Naples; Felipe II of Spain)
Sept 1598-March 1621	Filippo II (Filippo II of Naples; Felipe III of Spain)
March 1621-Sept 1665	Filippo III (Filippo III of Naples; Felipe IV of Spain)
Sept 1665-Nov 1700	Carlo II (Carlo V of Naples; Carlos II of Spain)
Nov 1700-July 1707	Filippo IV (Filippo IV of Naples; Felipe V of Spain)
July 1707-April 1711	Giuseppe (also of Naples; Josef I of Austria)
April 1711-Sept 1713	Carlo III (1st) (Carlo VI of Naples; Karl II of Austria)
Sept 1713-Aug 1718	Vittorio Amedeo (Vittorio Amedeo II of Sardinia)
Aug 1718-May 1735	Carlo III (2nd) (Carlo VI of Naples)
May 1735-Oct 1759	Carlo IV (Carlo VII of Naples; Carlos III of Spain)
Oct 1759-Dec 1816	Ferdinando III (Ferdinando IV of Naples)

Kingdom of Two Sicilies

Naples and Sicily were formally united in 1816

Capital: Naples

Kings:

Dec 1816-Jan 1825	Ferdinando I (*f* Ferdinando III of Sicily & IV of Naples)
Jan 1825-Nov 1830	Francesco I (*son*)
Nov 1830-May 1859	Ferdinando II
May 1859-Feb 1861	Francesco II (*son*) (abdicated)

Prime Ministers:

Jan-April 1848	Niccolo Maresca
April-May 1848	Carlo Troya
May 1848-49	Gennaro Spinelli
1849-Jan 1852	Giustino Fortunato
Jan 1852-May 1859	Fernando di Troya
May 1859-June 1860	Carlo Filangieri
June 1860-Feb 1861	Antonio Spinelli

PAPAL STATES

Capital: Rome

Incorporated into the kingdom of Italy in 1861; for list of Popes see Vatican City State.

PARMA AND PIACENZA

Part of Papal States until 1545
Capital: Parma

Dukes/Duchesses:

1545-47	Pier-Luigi (*son of Pope Paul III*) (assassinated)
1547-86	Ottavio (*son*)
1586-92	Alessandro (*son*)
1592-1622	Ranuccio I (*son*)
1622-46	Odoardo (*son*)
1646-94	Ranuccio II (*son*)
1694-1727	Francesco (*son*)
1727-Jan 1731	Antonio (*brother*)
Jan 1731-Oct 1735	Carlo I (Carlos III of Spain)
Oct 1735-Oct 1740	Carlo (II) (Karl II of Austria)
Oct 1740-Oct 1748	Maria Teresa (Archduchess of Austria)
Oct 1748-July 1765	Filippo (brother of Carlo I)
July 1765-Oct 1802	Ferdinando (*son*)
(Oct 1802-April 1814	French annexation)
April 1814-Dec 1847	Maria Luisa (*2nd wife of Napoléon I*)
Dec 1847-March 1849	Carlo II (*grandson of Ferdinando*) (*f* Carlo Ludovico of Lucca & Lodovico II of Etruria)
March 1849-March 1854	Carlo III (*son*) (assassinated)
March 1854-June 1859	Roberto (*son*)

In 1859 Parma and Piacenza was annexed by Piedmont-Sardinia

PIEDMONT-SARDINIA

Previous name until the acquisition of Sardinia in 1718: Savoy and Piedmont
Capital: Turin

Dukes:

Feb 1417-34	Amedeo VIII (abdicated)
1434-65	Lodovico (*son*)
1465-72	Amedeo IX (*son*)
1472-82	Filiberto I (*son*)
1482-90	Carlo I (*brother*)
1490-96	Carlo II (*son*)
1496-97	Filippo II (*son of Lodovico*)
1497-1504	Filiberto II (*son*)
1504-Aug 1553	Carlo III (*brother*)
Aug 1553-Aug 1580	Emanuele Filiberto (*son*)
Aug 1580-July 1630	Carlo Emanuele I (*son*)
July 1630-Oct 1637	Vittorio Amedeo I (*son*)
Oct 1637-Oct 1638	Francesco Giacinto (*son*)
Oct 1638-June 1675	Carlo Emanuele II (*brother*)
June 1675-Aug 1718	Vittorio Amedeo II (*son*)

Kings:

Aug 1718-Sept 1730	Vittorio Amedeo II
Sept 1730-Feb 1773	Carlo Emanuele III (*son*)
Feb 1773-Oct 1796	Vittorio Amedeo III (*son*)
Oct 1796-June 1802	Carlo Emanuele IV (*son*) (abdicated)
June 1802-March 1821	Vittorio Emanuele I (*brother*) (abdicated)
March 1821-April 1831	Carlo Felice (*brother*)
April 1831-March 1849	Carlo Alberto (abdicated)
March 1849-Feb 1861	Vittorio Emanuele II (*son*) (King of Italy 1861-78)

Prime Ministers:

March 1815-March 1848	Clemente della Margherita
March-July 1848	Cesare Balbo
July-Aug 1848	Gabrio Casati
Aug-Sept 1848	Marchese di Sostegno (Cesare Alfieri)
Sept-Oct 1848	Ettore Perrone
Oct-Dec 1848	Pierdionigi Pinelli
Dec 1848-Feb 1849	Vincenzo Gioberti
Feb-March 1849	Agostino Chiodo
March-May 1849	Claudio Delaunay
May 1849-Nov 1852	Marchese di d'Azeglio (Massimo Tapparelli)
Nov 1852-July 1859	Camillo Cavour (1st)

July 1859-March 1860   Alfonso la Marmora   (later PM of Italy)
March 1860-March 1861   Camillo Cavour   (2nd) (PM of Italy from Feb 1861)

TUSCANY

Republic of Florence 1208-1569, Grand Duchy of Tuscany 1569-1860, Kingdom of Etruria 1801-1807
Capital: Florence

Leaders:

1434-64	Cosimo de 'Medici
1464-69	Piero I de 'Medici (*son*)
1469-78	Giuliano I de 'Medici (*son*) (co-ruler) (assassinated)
1469-92	Lorenzo I de 'Medici (*brother*)
1492-Nov 1494	Piero II de 'Medici (deposed)
Nov 1494-98	Girolamo Savonarola (deposed, executed)
1502-12	Piero Soderini
1512-14	Giuliano II de 'Medici
1514-19	Lorenzo II de 'Medici (*son of Piero II*)
1519-23	Giulio de 'Medici (*later Pope Clement VII*)
1523-27	Ippolito de 'Medici (*grandson of Piero II*)

Dukes:

1531-37	Alessandro de 'Medici (assassinated)
1537-69	Cosimo de 'Medici

Grand Dukes/Duchess:

1569-74	Cosimo I (*f Duke of Florence*)
1574-87	Francesco I (*son*)
1587-1609	Ferrante I (*brother*)
1609-21	Cosimo II (*son*)
1621-May 1670	Ferrante II (*son*)
May 1670-1723	Cosimo III (*son*)
1723-July 1737	Gian Gastone (*son*)
July 1737-Aug 1765	Francesco II (*f François III of Lorraine*)
Aug 1765-July 1790	Leopoldo I (Leopold II of Austria) (*son*)
July 1790-March 1799	Fernando III (*son*) (1st) (deposed)
(March-June 1799	Civil Commissioner: Carl Reinhard)
June 1799-Oct 1800	Fernando III (2nd)
(Oct 1800- Feb 1801	provisional government)
Feb 1801-3	Luigi (*son of Ferdinando of Parma*)
1803-Dec 1807	Carlo Luigi (*son*) (later Carlo II of Parma & Piacenzo)
	Regent: 1803-7 Marie Louise
(Dec 1807-March 1809	French annexation)
March 1809-Feb 1814	Elisa Baciocchi (*sister of Napoléon I of France*)

Sept 1814-July 1824	Fernando III (3rd)
July 1824-Feb 1849	Leopold II (*son*) (1st) (deposed)
(Feb-March 1849	republican triumvirate)
March 1849-July 1859	Leopold II (2nd)
July-Aug 1859	Fernando IV (*son*) (abdicated)

Prime Ministers:

1815-April 1844	Vittorio Fossombroni
April 1844-Oct 1845	Prince Neri III Corsini
(Oct 1845-Sept 1847	post vacant)
Sept 1847-June 1848	Prince Neri IV Corsini (*nephew*)
June-July 1848	Cosimo Ridolfi
Aug-Oct 1848	Gino Capponi
Oct 1848-Feb 1849	Francesco Guerrazzi (1st)
Feb-March 1849	Giuseppe Montanelli (Triumvirate Chairman)
March-April 1849	Francesco Guerrazzi (2nd)
May 1849-April 1959	Giovanni Baldasseroni
April-May 1859	Ubaldino Peruzzi
May 1859	Carlo di Mombello
May-Aug 1859	Bettino Ricasoli (Count Brolio) (later PM of Italy)

Tuscany became part of Piedmont-Sardinia in 1859

VENICE

Most Serene Republic of Venice

Capital: Venice

Doges:

Jan 1401-13	Michele Steno
Jan 1414-23	Tommase Mocenigo
1423-57	Francesco Foscanni (abdicated)
1457-62	Pasquale Malipiero
May 1462-Nov 1471	Cristoforo Moro
Nov 1471-Aug 1473	Niccolo Tron
Aug 1473-Dec 1474	Niccolo Marcello
Dec 1474-May 1478	Pietro Mocenigo (*nephew of T.Mocenigo*)
May 1478-Nov 1485	Giovanni Mocenigo (*brother*)
Nov 1485-Aug 1486	Marco Barbarigo
Aug 1486-Nov 1501	Agostino Barbarigo
Nov 1501-July 1521	Leonardo Loredano
July 1521-May 1523	Antonio Grimani
May 1523-Jan 1539	Andrea Gritti
Jan 1539-Nov 1545	Pietro Lando
Nov 1545-June 1553	Francesco Donato
June 1553-June 1554	Marcantonio Trevisano

June 1554-June 1556	Francesco Venier
June 1556-Sept 1559	Lorenzo Priuli
Sept 1559-Nov 1567	Girolamo Priuli
Nov 1567-May 1570	Pietro Loredano
May 1570-June 1577	Alviso Mocenigo I
June 1577-March 1578	Sebastiano Venier
March 1578-Aug 1585	Nicolo da Ponte
Aug 1585-April 1595	Pasquale Cicogna
April 1595-Jan 1606	Marino Grimani
Jan 1606-July 1612	Leonardo Donato
July 1612-Dec 1615	Marcantonio Memo
Dec 1615-March 1618	Giovanni Bembo
March-April 1618	Nicolo Dona
May 1618-Sept 1623	Antonio Priuli
Sept 1623-Jan 1625	Francesco Centurioni
Jan 1625-Jan 1630	Giovanni Cornari I
Jan 1630-April 1631	Nicolo Centurioni
April 1631-Jan 1646	Francesco Erizzo
Jan 1646-March 1655	Francesco Molin
March 1655-May 1656	Carlo Contarini
June 1656-April 1658	Bertuccio Valier
April 1658-Oct 1659	Giovanni Pesaro
Oct 1659-Feb 1675	Domenico Contarini
Feb 1675-Aug 1676	Nicolo Sagredo
Aug 1676-Jan 1684	Alviso Contarini
Jan 1684-April 1688	Marcantonio Giustiniani
April 1688-Feb 1694	Francesco Morosini
Feb 1694-July 1700	Silvestro Valier
July 1700-May 1709	Alviso Mocenigo II (*great grandnephew of Alviso I*)
May 1709-Aug 1722	Giovanni Cornari II
Aug 1722-June 1732	Alviso Mocenigo III
June 1732-Jan 1735	Carlo Ruzzini
Jan 1735-April 1741	Alviso Pisani
April 1741-March 1752	Pietro Grimani
March 1752-May 1762	Francesco Loredano
May 1762-April 1763	Marco Foscarini
April 1763-Dec 1778	Alviso Mocenigo IV
Jan 1779-March 1789	Paolo Renier
March 1789-May 1797	Lodovico Manin (deposed)
(1797-1848	Austrian rule)

President:

March 1848-Aug 1849	Daniele Manin (deposed)
(1849-66	Austrian rule; then incorporated into Italy)

JAMAICA

Official name: Jamaica
Independence date: 6 August 1962
Capital: Kingston

Jamaica was visited by Colombus in 1494 and was Spanish territory until it was occupied by Britain in 1655. In 1944 a measure of self-government was granted. Full self-government followed in 1959, followed by independence in 1962.

Governors:

1898-1904	Augustus Hemming
1904-07	James Swettenham
1907-13	Sydney Olivier
1913-18	William Manning
1918-24	Leslie Probyn (see Barbados)
1924-26	Samuel Wilson
1926-32	Reginald Stubbs
1932-34	Alexander Slater
1934-38	Edward Denham
1938-43	Arthur Richards (see Fiji)
1943-51	John Huggins
1951-57	Hugh Foot
1957-62	Kenneth Blackburne

Governors-General:

Represents monarch who is concurrently British monarch

Aug-Oct 1962	Kenneth Blackburne
Oct 1962-Feb 1973	Clifford Campbell
Feb-June 1973	Herbert Dufus (acting)
June 1973-March 1991	Florizel Glasspole
March-Aug 1991	Edward Zacca (acting)
Aug 1991-	Howard Cooke

Chief Ministers:

Dec 1944-Jan 1955	Alexander Bustamante (*b* W.A.Clarke) (JLP)
Jan 1955-July 1959	Norman Manley (PNP)

Prime Ministers:

July 1959-April 1962	Norman Manley (PNP)

April 1962-Feb 1967	Alexander Bustamante (JLP)
Feb-April 1967	Donald Sangster (JLP) (†)
April 1967-March 1972	Hugh Shearer (JLP)
March 1972-Nov 1980	Michael Manley (*son of N.Manley*) (1st) (PNP)
Nov 1980-Feb 1989	Edward Seaga (JLP)
Feb 1989-March 1992	Michael Manley (2nd) (PNP)
March 1992-	Percival Patterson (PNP)

JLP = Jamaican Labour Party
PNP = People's National Party

JAPAN

Official name: Japan, Nippon
State founded: c200
Capital: Kyoto (until 1868), Tokyo (since 1868)

Japan consisted of numerous small kingdoms until the kingdom of Yamamoto gained primacy in about AD 200 and united the nation. Through the centuries Japan has remained an independent state; in the 13th century attempted invasions by the Mongols were repulsed, and until the 19th century Japan isolated itself from European influence. With the resignation of the last Shogun in 1867 and the accession of Emperor Mutsuhito in 1868, the modernization of Japan began. During the 1930s Japan pursued an expansionist policy, occupying parts of China, and during World War II joined the Axis and occupied many parts of South-East Asia. After atom bombs were dropped on Hiroshima and Nagasaki by the USA in 1945 Japan surrendered. The country was under US military occupation until 1952, although a Japanese government was allowed to function. Japan has developed into one of the world's major economic powers, with its politics dominated by the Liberal Democratic Party.

Emperors/Empresses (from 1392):

May 1392-Aug 1412	Komatsu (abdicated)
Dec 1412-28	Shoku (Mihito)
Dec 1429-July 1464	Hanazono (Fusahito)
Dec 1465-1500	Tsuchi-Mikado II (Hikohito)
1500-26	Kashiwabara II (Katsuhito) (*son*)
1526-57	Nara II (Tomohito) (*son*)
1557-Nov 1586	Ogimachi (Shigeahito) (*son*) (abdicated)
Nov 1586-March 1611	Yozei II (Katahito) (*grandson*) (abdicated)
April 1611-Nov 1629	Mizuno II (Kotohito) (*son*) (abdicated)
Nov 1629-Oct 1643	Meisho (Oki-ko) (*daughter*) (abdicated)
Oct 1643-54	Komyo II (Tsuguhito) (*brother*)
1654-Jan 1663	Saiin (Nagahito) (*brother*) (abdicated)
April 1663-86	Reigen (Satohito) (*brother*) (abdicated)
April 1686-1709	Higashiyama (Asahito) (*son*)
1709-March 1735	Naka-No-Mikado (Yasuhito) (*son*) (abdicated)
Nov 1735-May 1747	Sakuramachi I (Akihito) (*son*) (abdicated)
Sept 1747-62	Momozono I (Tohito) (*son*)
(1762-63	interregnum)
Nov 1763-71	Sakuramachi (Toshi-ko) (abdicated)
April 1771-Nov 1779	Momozono II (Hidehito)
Dec 1779-March 1817	Kokaku (Kanehito) (abdicated)
Sept 1817-Sept 1847	Ninko (Ayahito) (*son*)
Sept 1847-Oct 1868	Osahito (Komei) (*son*)

Oct 1868-July 1912   Mutsuhito   (Mejei) (*son*)
July 1912-Dec 1926   Yoshihito   (*son*)
Dec 1926-Jan 1989   Hirohito   (*son*)
Jan 1989-   Akihito   (*son*)

Shoguns:

Feb 1603-April 1605   Ieyasu Tokugawa
April 1605-July 1623   Hidetada Tokugawa
July 1623-Aug 1651   Iemitsu Tokugawa
Aug 1651-Aug 1680   Ietsuna Tokugawa
Aug 1680-May 1709   Tsunayoshi Tokugawa
May 1709-April 1713   Ienobu Tokugawa
April 1713-Aug 1716   Ietsugu Tokugawa
Aug 1716-Nov 1745   Yoshimune Tokugawa
Nov 1745-Sept 1761   Ieshige Tokugawa
Sept 1761-Sept 1786   Iehara Tokugawa
April 1787-1838   Ienari Tokugawa
April 1838-Oct 1853   Ieyoshi Tokugawa
Oct 1853-Feb 1858   Iesada Tokugawa
Feb 1858-Dec 1866   Iemochi Tokugawa
Dec 1866-Nov 1867   Keika   (Yoshinobu) Tokugawa
(Nov 1867   post abolished)

Supreme Administrators:

Jan-June 1868   Taruhito Arisugawa
June 1868-Feb 1869   Tomomi Iwakura   (co-Administrator)
June 1869-Dec 1885   Sanjo Sanetomi   (co-Administrator 1868-69)

Prime Ministers:

Dec 1885-April 1888   Hirobumi Ito   (1st)
April 1888-Dec 1889   Kiyotaka Kuroda   (1st)
Dec 1889-May 1891   Aritomo Yamagata   (1st)
May 1891-Aug 1892   Masayoshi Matsukata   (1st)
Aug 1892-Sept 1896   Hirobumi Ito   (2nd)
Sept 1896-April 1897   Masayoshi Matsukata   (2nd)
April-June 1897   Kiyotaka Kuroda   (2nd)
June 1897-Jan 1898   Masayoshi Matsukata   (3rd)
Jan-June 1898   Hirobumi Ito   (3rd)
June-Nov 1898   Shigenobu Okuma   (1st)
Nov 1898-Oct 1900   Arotomo Yamagata   (2nd)
Oct 1900-May 1901   Hirobumi Ito   (4th)
May-June 1901   Kimmochi Saionji   (1st)
June 1901-Jan 1906   Taro Katsura   (1st)

Jan 1906-July 1908	Kimmochi Saionji (2nd)
July 1908-Aug 1911	Taro Katsura (2nd)
Aug 1911-Dec 1912	Kimmochi Saionji (3rd)
Dec 1912-Feb 1913	Taro Katsura (3rd)
Feb 1913-April 1914	Gonnohyoe Yamamoto (1st)
April 1914-Oct 1916	Shigenobu Okuma (2nd)
Oct 1916-Sept 1918	Matsakate Terauchi
Sept 1918-Nov 1921	Takashi Hara († assassinated)
4-13 Nov 1921	Yasuya Uchida
Nov 1921-June 1922	Korekiyo Takahashi (1st)
June 1922-Aug 1923	Tomosabura Kato (†)
Sept 1923-Jan 1924	Gonnohyoe Yamamoto (2nd)
Jan-June 1924	Keigo Kiyoura
June 1924-Jan 1926	Takaaki Kato
Jan 1926-April 1927	Reijiro Wakatsuki (1st)
April 1927-July 1929	Giichi Tanaka
July 1929-April 1931	Osachi Hamaguchi
June-Dec 1931	Reijiro Wakatsuki (2nd)
Dec 1931-May 1932	Takashi Inukai († assassinated)
16-26 May 1932	Korekiyo Takahashi (2nd)
May 1932-July 1934	Makoto Saito (assassinated 1936)
July 1934-Feb 1936	Keisuke Okada (1st)
26-29 Feb 1936	Fumio Goto
Feb-March 1936	Keisuke Okada (2nd)
March 1936-Feb 1937	Koki Hirota
Feb-May 1937	Senjuro Hayashi
May 1937-Jan 1939	Fumimaro Konoye (1st)
Jan-Aug 1939	Kiichiro Hironuma
Aug 1939-Jan 1940	Nobuyaki Abe
Jan-July 1940	Mitsumasa Yonai
July 1940-Oct 1941	Fumimaro Konoye (2nd)
Oct 1941-July 1944	Hideki Tojo (executed 1948)
July 1944-April 1945	Kuniaki Koiso
April-Aug 1945	Kantaro Suzuki
Aug-Oct 1945	Higashikini Naruhiko
Oct 1945-May 1945	Kijuro Shidehara
May 1946-May 1947	Shigeru Yoshida (1st) (LP)
May 1947-Feb 1948	Tetsu Katayama (SP)
Feb-Oct 1948	Hitoshi Ashida (DP)
Oct 1948-Dec 1954	Shigeru Yoshida (2nd) (LP)
Dec 1954-Dec 1956	Ichiro Hatoyama (DP,LDP)
Dec 1956-Feb 1957	Tanzan Ishibashi (LDP)
Feb 1957-July 1960	Nobusuke Kishi (*b* N.Sato) (LDP)
July 1960-Nov 1964	Hayato Ikeda (LDP)
Nov 1964-July 1972	Eisaku Sato (*brother of N.Kishi*) (LDP)

July 1972-Dec 1974	Kakuei Tanaka (LDP)
Dec 1974-Dec 1976	Takeo Miki (LDP)
Dec 1976-Nov 1978	Takeo Fukuda (LDP)
Nov 1978-June 1980	Masayoshi Ohira (LDP) (†)
June-July 1980	Masayoshi Ito (acting) (LDP)
July 1980-Nov 1982	Zenko Suzuki (LDP)
Nov 1982-Nov 1987	Yasuhiro Nakasone (LDP)
Nov 1987-June 1989	Nobaru Takeshita (LDP)
June-Aug 1989	Sosuke Uno (LDP)
Aug 1989-Nov 1991	Toshiki Kaifu (LDP)
Nov 1991-Aug 1993	Kiichi Miyazawa (LDP)
Aug 1993-April 1994	Morihito Hosokawa (*grandson of F.Konoye*) (JNP)
April-June 1994	Tsutomu Hata (JRP)
June 1994-Jan 1996	Tomiichi Murayama (SP)
Jan 1996-July 1998	Ryutaro Hashimoto (LDP)
July 1998-April 2000	Keizo Obuchi (LDP)
April 2000-	Yoshiro Mori (LDP)

DP = Democratic Party
JNP = Japan New Party
JRP = Japan Renewal Party (Shinseito)
LDP = Liberal Democratic Party (*f*DP)
LP = Liberal Party
SP = Socialist Party

Former US Administered Territory

RYUKYU ISLANDS

Capital: Naha City

The Ryukyu Islands were administered by the United States from 1945 until 1972 when they were returned to Japan.

Chief Executives:

April 1952-Oct 1956	Shuhei Higa
Nov 1956-Nov 1959	Jugo Toma
Nov 1959-Oct 1964	Seisaku Ota (LDP)
Oct 1964-Nov 1968	Seiho Matsuoka (LDP)
Nov 1968-May 1972	Chobyo Yara (LDP)

JORDAN

Official name: Hashemite Kingdom of Jordan, Al-Mamlaka al-Urduniya al-Hashemiyah
Previous name: Transjordan until 1949
Independence date: 22 March 1946
Capital: Amman

The area of present-day Jordan was under Turkish rule until the end of World War I. It was part of the independent state of Syria proclaimed in May 1920, but when Damascus was occupied by the French two months later, Transjordan came under British rule from Palestine. In 1921 the British installed Emir Abdullah as the ruler, and in 1922 Transjordan became a League of Nations territory under British control. In 1946 it became fully independent. Jordan administered the West Bank area of Palestine from 1948 until its occupation by Israel in 1967. In 1958 Jordan was briefly federated with Iraq. Jordan signed a peace agreement with Israel in 1994, only the second Arab country to do so.

Emir:

March 1921-May 1946	Abdullah I bin Hussein	(*son of King Hussein of Hejaz*)

Kings:

May 1946-July 1951	Abdullah I bin Hussein	(assassinated)
July-Sept 1951	Regent: Emir Nayef	
Sept 1951-Aug 1952	Talal bin Abdullah	(*son*) (abdicated)
Aug 1952-Feb 1999	Hussein bin Talal	(*son*)
Feb 1999-	Abdullah II bin Hussein	(*son*)

Chief Ministers:

March-April 1921	Rashid al-Tali	
April 1921	Muzhir al-Raslan	(1st)
April 1921-Jan 1923	Rida al-Rikabi	(1st)
Feb-Sept 1923	Muzhir al-Raslan	(2nd)
Sept 1923-Jan 1924	Hassan Khalid Abulhuda	(1st)
Jan 1924-June 1926	Rida al-Rikabi	(2nd)
June 1926-Nov 1931	Hassan Khalid Abulhuda	(2nd)
Nov 1931-Sept 1938	Ibrahim Hashim	
Sept 1938-Aug 1939	Tewfik Abulhuda	

Prime Ministers:

Aug 1939-April 1950	Tewfik Abulhuda	(1st)
April-Dec 1950	Said el-Mufti	(1st)
Dec 1950-July 1951	Samir el-Rifai	(1st)

July 1951-May 1953	Tewfik Abulhuda (2nd)
May 1953-May 1954	Fawzi al-Mulki
May 1954-May 1955	Tewfik Abulhuda (3rd)
May-Dec 1955	Said el-Mufti (2nd)
14-19 Dec 1955	Hazzaa el-Majali (1st)
Dec 1955-Jan 1956	Ibrahim Hashim (1st)
Jan-May 1956	Samir el-Rifai (2nd)
May-July 1956	Said el-Mufti (3rd)
July 1956-Oct 1956	Ibrahim Hashim (3rd)
Oct 1956-April 1957	Suliman Nabulsi
11-13 April 1957	Hussein Khalidi
April 1957-May 1958	Ibrahim Hashim (4th)
May 1958-May 1959	Samir el-Rifai (3rd)
May 1959-Aug 1960	Hazzaa el-Majali (2nd) (†)
Aug 1960-Jan 1962	Bahjat al-Talhouni (1st)
Jan 1962-March 1963	Wasfi Tell (1st)
March-April 1963	Samir el-Rifai (4th)
April 1963-July 1964	Sherif Hussein bin Nasser (*uncle of King Hussein*)
July 1964-Feb 1965	Bahjat al-Talhouni (2nd)
Feb 1965-March 1967	Wasfi Tell (2nd)
March-Oct 1967	Saad Jumaa
Oct 1967-March 1969	Bahjat al-Talhouni (3rd)
March-Aug 1969	Abdul el-Rifai (*brother of Samir el-Rifai*) (1st)
Aug 1969-June 1970	Bahjat al-Talhouni (4th)
June-Sept 1970	Abdul el-Rifai (2nd)
16-26 Sept 1970	Mohammed Daoud
Sept-Oct 1970	Ahmed Toukan
Oct 1970-Nov 1971	Wasfi Tell (3rd) († assassinated)
Nov 1971-May 1973	Ahmed Lawzi
May 1973-July 1976	Zaid el-Rifai (*son of Samir el-Rifai*) (1st)
July 1976-Dec 1979	Mudar Badran (1st)
Dec 1979-July 1980	Sherif Abdul Sharaf (†)
July-Aug 1980	Kassem Rimawi
Aug 1980-Jan 1984	Mudar Badran (2nd)
Jan 1984-April 1985	Ahmed Ubeidat
April 1985-April 1989	Zaid el-Rifai (2nd)
April-Dec 1989	Zaid bin Shaker (1st) (*cousin of King Hussein*)
Dec 1989-June 1991	Mudar Badran (3rd)
June-Nov 1991	Taher Masri
Nov 1991-May 1993	Zaid bin Shaker (2nd)
May 1993-Jan 1995	Abdul Salam al-Majali (1st)
Jan 1995-Feb 1996	Zaid bin Shaker (3rd)
Feb 1996-March 1997	Abdel Karim Kabariti
March 1997-Aug 1998	Abdul Salam al-Majali (2nd)
Aug 1998-March 1999	Fayez al-Tarawneh
March 1999-	Abdul-Raouf Rawabdeh

KAZAKHSTAN

Official name:	Republic of Kazakhstan, Kazak Respublikasy
Previous names:	Kirghiz Autonomous Soviet Socialist Republic 1920-25, Kazakh Autonomous Soviet Socialist Republic 1925-36, Kazakh Soviet Socialist Republic 1936-91
State formed:	26 August 1920
Admission to USSR:	5 December 1936
Independence date:	16 December 1991
Capital:	Astana (*f* Akmola), Orenburg 1920-25, Kyzyl-Orda 1925-29, Almaty (Alma-Ata, *f* Verny) 1929-97

In 1920 a number of central Asian provinces of Russia combined to form an autonomous republic. Some areas of Turkistan were also added. In 1936 Kazakhstan was admitted to the Soviet Union as a constituent republic. As the Soviet Union collapsed in 1991 full independence was declared.

Presidents:
Chairman of the Central Executive Committee 1920-38
President of the Presidium of the Supreme Soviet 1938-90
Chairman of the Supreme Soviet 1990-Dec 1991

1920-25	Seitgali Mendeshev
1925-28	Zhalau Munbayev
1928-30	Ye.Ernazarov
Oct 1930-June 1937	Uzakbay Kulumbetov
June-July 1937	Ismail Salvafeka (acting)
July-Oct 1937	Ali Dzhangildin (acting)
Oct 1937-April 1938	Nurbapa Umurzakov
April 1938-Jan 1947	Abdisamat Kazakpayev
Jan-March 1947	I.K.Lukyanets (acting)
March 1947-Jan 1952	Daniyal Kerimbayev
Jan 1952-April 1955	Murtas Undasynov
April 1955-Jan 1960	Zhumabek Tashenev
Jan-Aug 1960	Fazyl Karibzhanov
Aug 1960-April 1965	Isagali Sharipov
April 1965-Dec 1978	Sabir Niyazbekov
Dec 1978-Dec 1979	Isatai Abdukarimov
Dec 1979-Feb 1984	Sattar Imashev (†)
March 1984-Sept 1985	Baiken Ashimov
Sept 1985-Feb 1988	Salamat Mukashev
Feb-Dec 1988	Zakash Kamalidenov
March 1989-Feb 1990	Makhtay Sagdiyev

Feb 1990- Nursultan Nazarbayev

Prime Ministers:
Chairman of the Council of People's Commissars 1920-46
Chairman of the Council of Ministers 1946-93

Oct 1920-22	Viktor Radus-Zenkovich
1922-24	Saken Seyfullin
1924-25	Nigmet Nurmakov
1926-28	Ismail Waqqas
1928-37	Uraz Isayev
1937-38	Ibrahim Tazhiev (acting)
July 1938-Jan 1952	Murtas Undasynov
Jan 1952-Feb 1955	Yelubai Taibekov
Feb 1955-Jan 1960	Dinmuhammed Kunayev (1st)
Jan 1960-Jan 1961	Zhumabek Tashenev
Jan 1961-Sept 1962	Salken Daulenov
Sept-Dec 1962	Massimkhan Beisebayev (1st)
Dec 1962-Dec 1964	Dinmuhammed Kunayev (2nd)
Dec 1964-April 1970	Massimkhan Beisebayev (2nd)
April 1970-March 1984	Baiken Ashimov
March 1984-June 1989	Nursultan Nazarbayev
July 1989-Dec 1991	Uzabakay Karamanov
Dec 1991-Oct 1994	Sergei Tereshchenko
Oct 1994-Oct 1997	Akezhan Kazhageldin
Oct 1997-Oct 1999	Nurlan Balgynbayev
Oct 1999-	Kasymzhomart Tokayev (acting 1-12 Oct 1999)

Communist Party Leaders:
First Secretary

1921-22	M.Musagaliev
1922-25	Sultan Khodzhan
1925-33	Filipp Goloshchokin
1933-38	Levon Mirzoyan
1938-45	Nikolai Skvortsov
1945-Feb 1954	Zhumabay Shayakhmetov
Feb 1954-May 1955	Panteleimon Ponomarenko (see Belorussia)
May 1955-May 1956	Leonid Brezhnev (see USSR)
May 1956-Dec 1957	Ivan Yakovlev
Dec 1957-Jan 1960	Nikolai Beliayev
Jan 1960-Dec 1962	Dinmuhammed Kunayev (1st)
Dec 1962-Dec 1964	Ismail Yusupov
Dec 1964-Dec 1986	Dinmuhammed Kunayev (2nd)
Dec 1986-June 1989	Gennadi Kolbin
June 1989-Aug 1991	Nursultan Nazarbayev
(Aug 1991	party dissolved)

KENYA

Official name: Republic of Kenya, Jamhuri wa Kenya   (Swahili)
Independence date: 12 December 1963
Capital: Nairobi

A British protectorate was declared in Kenya in 1895 and in 1906 a Governor was appointed, although the coastal area remained part of the Sultan of Zanzibar's dominion. In 1920 the protectorate was proclaimed a colony. In June 1963 self-government was granted. Zanzibar then ceded the coastal strip to Kenya and in December 1963 full independence was attained. A year later Kenya became a republic.

Governors:

1920-22	Edward Northey
1922-25	Robert Coryndon
1925-31	Edward Grigg
1931-37	Joseph Byrne
1937-40	Henry Brooke-Popham
1940-44	Henry Moore
1944-52	Philip Mitchell
1952-59	Evelyn Baring (see Southern Rhodesia)
1959-63	Patrick Renison
Jan-Dec 1963	Malcolm MacDonald (*son of Ramsay MacDonald, UK PM*)

Governor-General:

Represented monarch who was concurrently British monarch

Dec 1963-Dec 1964	Malcolm MacDonald

Presidents:

Dec 1964-Aug 1978	Jomo Kenyatta (*b* Kamau wa Ngenge) (†) (KANU)
Aug 1978-	Daniel Arap Moi (KANU)

Leader of Government Business:

April 1961-April 1962	Ronald Ngala (KADU)
(April 1962	post abolished)

Prime Minister:

June 1963-Dec 1964	Jomo Kenyatta (KANU)
(Dec 1964	post abolished)

KADU = Kenya African Democratic Union
KANU = Kenya African National Union (sole legal party 1964-91)

KIRIBATI

Official name: Republic of Kiribati, Ribaberikiri Kiribati
Previous name: Gilbert Islands until 1979
Independence date: 12 July 1979
Capital: Bairiki

The Gilbert Islands were first visited by Europeans in the 16th century. In 1892 a British protectorate was proclaimed in the Gilbert and Ellice Islands, and in 1916 the territory became a colony. From 1942 to 1943 the islands were occupied by Japan. A measure of autonomy was granted in 1972. In 1975 the Ellice Islands were separated and re-named Tuvalu. The Gilbert Islands became fully self-governing in 1977, and were granted independence in 1979 under the name Kiribati.

Commissioners:

1892-1901	Charles Swayne
1901-09	W. Telfer Campbell
1909-13	John Dickson
1913-21	Edward Eliot
1921-26	Herbert McClure
1926-33	Arthur Grimble
1933-41	Jack Barley
1941-42	Vivian Fox-Strangeways (1st)
(1942-43	Japanese occupation)
1943-46	Vivian Fox-Strangeways (2nd)
1946-49	Henry Maude
1949-52	William Peel
1952-61	Michael Bernacchi
1962-70	Valdemar Andersen
1970-72	John Field (see St Helena)

Governors:

1972-73	John Field
1973-78	John Smith
1978-79	Reginald Wallace

Presidents:

July 1979-Dec 1982	Ieremia Tabai (1st)
Dec 1982-Feb 1983	Rota Onario (acting)
Feb 1983-July 1991	Ieremia Tabai (2nd)
July 1991-May 1994	Teatao Teannaki (NPP)

May-June 1994   Tekire Tameura   (acting)
June-Oct 1994   Ata Teaotai   (acting)
Oct 1994-   Teburoro Tito   (CDP)

Government Leader:

Jan 1972-May 1974   Reuben Uatioa

Chief Ministers:

May 1974-March 1978   Naboua Ratieta
March 1978-July 1979   Ieremia Tabai
(July 1979   post abolished)

CDP = Christian Democratic Party
NPP = National Progressive Party

KOREA

State founded: 2nd century BC
Capital: Seoul

Korea is an ancient state. After periods of division it was united in 1392 under the Yi dynasty. China claimed suzerainty over Korea, but was militarily defeated by Japan in 1895. Korea became increasingly under Japanese influence until it formally annexed the country in 1910. After the Japanese defeat in World War II Korea was divided into two occupation zones, a Soviet zone in the north and an American zone in the south. (See North Korea and South Korea below).

Kings:

1392-99	T'aejo (Yi Songgye)
1399-1400	Chongjong (abdicated)
1400-18	T'aejong (abdicated)
1418-50	Sejong
1450-52	Munjong
1452-55	Tanjong (abdicated)
1455-68	Sejo (abdicated)
1468-69	Yejong
1469-94	Songjong
	(Regent: 1469-77 Chong-hui)
1494-1506	Yonsan-gun (deposed)
1506-44	Chungjong
1544-45	Injong
1545-67	Myongjong
	(Regent: 1545-52 Munjong)
1567-1608	Sonjo I
	(Regent: 1867-68 In-sun)
1608-22	Kwanghae-gun (deposed)
1623-49	Injo
1649-59	Hyojong
1659-74	Hyonjong
1674-1720	Sukchong
1720-24	Kyongjong
1724-76	Yongjo (abdicated)
1776-1800	Chongjo
1800-34	Sonjo II
	(Regent: 1800-04 Chong-sun)
1834-49	Honjong
	(Regent: 1834 Kim Sun-won Whang ho)

1849-63   Ch'oljong
          (Regent: 1849-50 Kim Sun-won Whang ho)
1864-97   Kojong
          (Regent: 1864-73 Yi Han-gun   (Taewon-gun))

Emperors:

1897-July 1907   Kwangmu   (*f* King Kojong) (abdicated)
July 1907-Aug 1910 Sunjong   (*son*) (abdicated)

Governors-General:

1910-16   Terauchi Masakata
1916-19   Hasagawa Yoshimichi
1919-27   Saito Makoto   (1st)
1927   Ugaki Kazushige   (1st)
1927-29   Yamanashi Hanzo
1929-31   Saito Makoto   (2nd)
1931-36   Ugaki Kazushige   (2nd)
1936-42   Minami Jiro
1942-44   Koiso Kuniteru
1944-45   Abe Nobuyuki

Prime Ministers:

1873-76   Li Choe Ung
1876-81   Pak Kyu Su
1881-84   Shih Hun
Dec 1884   Hong Yon Sik
Dec 1884-88   Kim Hong Jip   (1st)
1888-July 1894   Shum Sun Tek
July 1894-April 1895 Kim Hong Jip   (2nd)
April-June 1895   Pak Yong Hyo
June-Oct 1895   Pak Che Sun   (1st)
Oct 1895-Feb 1896   Kim Hong Jip   (3rd)
1896   Han Kyu Sol   (1st)
1896-97   Li Won Yong   (1st)
1897-98   Yong Yong Son   (1st)
1898   Yu Kui Hwai   (acting)
1899-1901   Shin Ki Sun
1901-03   Yong Yong Sun   (2nd)
1904-05   Li Kum Myong
1905   Han Kyu Sol   (2nd)
1905-07   Pak Che Sun   (2nd)
1907-09   Li Won Yong   (2nd)
1909-July 1910   Pak Che Son   (3rd)

July-Aug 1910   Li Won Yong   (3rd)
(Aug 1910-45   Japanese occupation)
Sept 1945   Lyuh Woon Hung   (not recognised by occupation forces)

GOVERNMENT-IN-EXILE (1919-45)

Headquarters: Shanghai (1919-37), Chungking (1937-45)
Operated during Japanese occupation

Presidents:

Sept 1919-March 1925   Syngman Rhee   (Lee Syn Man)
March-July 1925   Park Eun Sik
(July 1925   post abolished)

Prime Ministers:

April-Sept 1919   Syngman Rhee   (Lee Syn Man)
Sept 1919-Jan 1921   Lee Tong Hui
Jan-May 1921   Lee Tong Yong   (1st)
May 1921-Sept 1922   Shin Kyu Sik
Sept 1922-April 1924   Lho Bak Rin   (1st)
April-Dec 1924   Lee Tong Yong   (2nd)
Dec 1924-March 1925   Park Eun Sik
March-July 1925   Lho Bak Rin   (2nd)
1925   Lee Sang Yong
1925   Yang Ki Suk
Dec 1925-Dec 1926   Hong Ji
Dec 1926-April 1927   Kim Gu
(April 1927   post abolished)

Chairmen:

Aug 1927-March 1933   Lee Tong Yong   (1st)
March 1933-Jan 1934   Song Pyung Jo
Jan 1934-Oct 1935   Yang Ki Suk
Oct-Nov 1935   Lee Tong Yong   (2nd)
Nov 1935-Nov 1936   Lee Si Yong
Nov 1936-Oct 1940   Lee Tong Yong   (3rd)
Oct 1940-Aug 1945   Kim Gu   (assassinated 1949)

NORTH KOREA

Official name: Democratic People's Republic of Korea, Chosun Minchu-chui Inmin Konghwa-guk

Independence date: 8 September 1948

Capital: Pyongyang

After World War II, attempts by the Soviet and American governments to unite Korea were unsuccessful. In 1946 a pro-Soviet provisional government was formed in the north, and in 1948 it proclaimed a people's republic. During the Korean War (1950-53) North Korean forces took over large areas of the south but were pushed back north of the 38th parallel by United Nations forces. For 46 years the country was dominated by Kim Il Sung who established a personality cult, and after his death was succeeded by his son, Kim Jong Il, the first such succession in a communist state.

Presidents:
Chairman/President of the Presidium of the Supreme People's Assembly 1948-72 & since 1998

Sept 1948-Sept 1957	Kim Du Bon
Sept 1957-Dec 1972	Choi Yong Kun
Dec 1972-July 1994	Kim Il Sung (*b* Kim Sung Choo) (†)
(July 1994-Sept 1998	post vacant - Ceremonial duties performed by Vice-Presidents Kim Yong Ju/Pak Sung Chul/Li Jong Ok/Kim Pyong Sik)
Sept 1998-	Kim Yong Nam

Chairmen of the Executive Committee:

Nov-Dec 1945	Cho Man Sik
Dec 1945-Jan 1946	Kim Il Sung

Chairman of the People's Committee:

Feb 1946-Sept 1948	Kim Il Sung

Prime Ministers:

Sept 1948-Dec 1972	Kim Il Sung
Dec 1972-April 1976	Kim Il
April 1976-Dec 1977	Pak Sung Chul
Dec 1977-Jan 1984	Li Jong Ok
Jan 1984-Dec 1986	Kang Song San (1st)
Dec 1986-Dec 1988	Li Gun Mo
Dec 1988-Dec 1992	Yon Hyong Muk
Dec 1992-Feb 1997	Kang Song San (2nd)

Feb 1997- Hong Song Nam (acting Feb 1997-Sept 1998)

Communist Party* Leaders:
*Korean Workers' Party
Chairman of the Central Committee until 1966
General Secretary since 1966

Sept 1948-July 1994	Kim Il Sung (†)
(July 1994-Oct 1997	post vacant)
Oct 1997-	Kim Jong Il (*son*)

National Defence Committee Chairman:
(Defined as the supreme state post in 1998)

April 1993- Kim Jong Il

SOUTH KOREA

Official name: Republic of Korea, Daehan Minkuk
Independence date: 15 August 1948
Capital: Seoul

In 1948 an independent republic was proclaimed in the American zone south of the 38th parallel. South Korea was invaded by North Korea in 1950, but United Nations forces intervened and pushed them back across the dividing line. The military assumed power in 1962 and again in 1980. The military leaders transformed themselves into elected presidents, but it was only in 1993 that a civilian president was elected.

Presidents:

Aug 1948-April 1960	Syngman Rhee (Lee Syn Man) (LP)
April-Aug 1960	Huh Chung (acting)
Aug 1960-March 1962	Yun Bo Sun (DP)
March 1962-Oct 1979	Park Chung Hee (acting March 1962-Oct 1963) (DRP) († assassinated)
Oct 1979-Aug 1980	Choi Kyu Hah (acting Aug-Dec 1979) (DRP)
Aug-Sept 1980	Park Choong Hoon (acting)
Sept 1980-Feb 1988	Chun Doo Hwan (DJP)
Feb 1988-Feb 1993	Roh Tae Woo (DJP,DLP)
Feb 1993-Feb 1998	Kim Young Sam (DLP,NKP)
Feb 1998-	Kim Dae Jung (NCNP)

Prime Ministers:

Aug 1948-Nov 1950	Lee Bum Suk
Nov 1950-April 1952	Chang Myun (John Chang) (1st)
April-Oct 1952	Chang Taik Sang
(Oct 1952-April 1953	post vacant)
April 1953-June 1954	Paik Too Chin (1st)
June-Dec 1954	Pyun Yung Tai
(Dec 1954-Aug 1960	post abolished)
Aug 1960-May 1961	Chang Myun (2nd) (DP) (deposed)
May-July 1961	Chang Do Yun
July 1961-June 1962	Song Yo Chang
June 1962-Dec 1963	Kim Hyun Chul
Dec 1963-May 1964	Choi Too Sun
May 1964-Dec 1970	Chung Il Kwun
Dec 1970-June 1971	Paik Too Chin (2nd)
June 1971-Dec 1975	Kim Chong Pil (1st)
Dec 1975-Dec 1979	Choi Kyu Hah

Dec 1979-May 1980	Shin Hyon Hwack
May-Sept 1980	Park Choong Hoon
Sept 1980-Jan 1982	Nam Duck Woo
Jan-June 1982	Yoo Chang Soon
June 1982-Oct 1983	Kim Sang Hyup
Oct 1983-Feb 1985	Chin Iee Chong
Feb 1985-May 1987	Lho Shin Yong
May-July 1987	Lee Han Key
July 1987-Feb 1988	Kim Chong Yul
Feb-Dec 1988	Lee Hyun Jae
Dec 1988-Dec 1990	Kang Young Hoon
Dec 1990-May 1991	Ro Jai Bong
May 1991-Oct 1992	Chung Won Shik
Oct 1992-Feb 1993	Hyun Soong Jong
Feb-Dec 1993	Hwang In Sung
Dec 1993-April 1994	Lee Hoi Chang
April-Dec 1994	Lee Young Duck
Dec 1994-Dec 1995	Lee Hong Koo
Dec 1995-March 1997	Lee Soo Sung
March 1997-March 1998	Koh Kun
March 1998-Jan 2000	Kim Chong Pil (acting March-Aug 1998) (2nd)
Jan 2000-	Park Tae Joon

DP = Democratic Party
DJP = Democratic Justice Party
DLP = Democratic Liberal Party (formed by merger of DJP and two other parties)
DRP = Democratic Republican Party
LP = Liberal Party
NCNP = National Congress for New Policies
NKP = New Korea Party (*f* DLP)

KUWAIT

Official name: State of Kuwait, Dowlat al Kuwait
State founded: 1756
Independence date: 19 June 1961
Capital: Kuwait

Kuwait was founded in 1756 by the Sabah family, which still rules the country. In 1899 the ruler concluded a treaty with Great Britain which made the state a British protectorate. This lasted until 1961 when Kuwait became fully independent. In 1990 it was occupied by Iraq, who installed a puppet regime, followed by annexation. A multinational force led by the USA ejected the Iraqis seven months later.

Heads of State:
Emir since 1961

1756-62	Shaikh Sabah Abu Abdullah bin Jabir as-Sabah
1762-Feb 1814	Shaikh Abdullah I bin Sabah as-Sabah (*son*)
Feb 1814-59	Shaikh Jabir bin Abdullah as-Sabah (*son*)
1859-Nov 1866	Shaikh Sabah bin Jabir as-Sabah (*son*)
Nov 1866-May 1892	Shaikh Abdullah II bin Sabah as-Sabah (*son*)
May 1892-May 1896	Shaikh Mohammed bin Sabah as-Sabah (*brother*)
May 1896-Jan 1915	Shaikh Mubarak bin Sabah as-Sabah (*half-brother*)
Jan 1915-June 1917	Shaikh Jabir bin Mubarak as-Sabah (*son*)
June 1917-Feb 1921	Shaikh Salem bin Mubarak as-Sabah (*brother*)
Feb 1921-Jan 1950	Shaikh Ahmed bin Jabir as-Salem as-Sabah (*nephew*)
Jan 1950-Nov 1965	Shaikh Abdullah as-Salem as-Sabah (*cousin*)
Nov 1965-Dec 1977	Shaikh Sabah as-Salem as-Sabah (*brother*)
Dec 1977-Aug 1990	Shaikh Jabir al-Ahmed as-Sabah (*son of Shaikh Ahmed*) (1st) (deposed)
(Aug 1990-Feb 1991	Iraqi occupation and annexation)
March 1991-	Shaikh Jabir al-Ahmed as-Sabah (2nd)

Prime Ministers:

Jan 1962-Jan 1963	Shaikh Abdullah as-Salem as-Sabah
Jan 1963-Nov 1965	Shaikh Sabah as-Salem as-Sabah
Nov 1965-Feb 1978	Shaikh Jabir al-Ahmed as-Sabah
Feb 1978-Aug 1990	Shaikh Saad al-Abdullah as-Sabah (1st)
4-8 Aug 1990	Ala Hussain Ali
(Aug 1990-Feb 1991	Iraqi annexation)
March 1991-	Shaikh Saad al-Abdullah as-Sabah (2nd)

GOVERNMENT-IN-EXILE 1990-91

Headquarters: Taif (Saudi Arabia)
Operated during Iraqi occupation

Emir:

Aug 1990-March 1991   Shaikh Jabir al-Ahmed as-Sabah

Prime Minister:

Aug 1990-March 1991   Shaikh Saad al-Abdullah as-Sabah

KYRGYZSTAN

Official name: Republic of Kyrgyzstan, Kyrgyz Respublikasy

Previous names: Kara-Kirghiz Autonomous Region 1924-26, Kirghiz Autonomous Soviet Socialist Republic 1926-36, Kirghiz Soviet Socialist Republic 1936-90

State formed (autonomous republic): 1 February 1926

Admission to USSR: 5 December 1936

Independence date: 31 August 1991

Capital: Bishkek (known as Frunze 1926-91)

The area of Kyrgyzstan (Kirghizia) was part of Turkistan until 1924 when it was proclaimed an autonomous region of Russia in 1924. Two years later it was elevated to autonomous republic level, and in 1936 it became a constituent republic of the Soviet Union. It became independent in 1991 with the end of the Soviet Union.

Presidents:
Chairman of the Central Executive Committee 1926-38
President of the Presidium of the Supreme Soviet 1938-90
Chairman of the Supreme Soviet April-Oct 1990

1926-37	Abdulkadyv Urazbekov
1937	Sultankul Shamurzin (acting)
1937-38	Murad Salikhov
July 1938-43	Asanali Tolubayev
1943-45	Moldogazi Tokobayev
1945-Aug 1978	Turabay Kulatov
Aug 1978-Jan 1979	Sultan Ibraimov
Jan 1979-Jan 1981	Arstanbek Duyshenev
Jan 1981-Aug 1987	Temirbek Koshoyev
Aug 1987-April 1990	Tashtambek Akhmatov
April-Oct 1990	Absamat Masaliyev
Oct 1990-	Askar Akayev

Prime Ministers:
Chairman of the Council of People's Commissars 1926-46
Chairman of the Council of Ministers 1946-91

1926-27	Turar Reptenlov
March 1927-31	Abdulkadyv Urazbekov
1931-37	Yusup Abdurakhmanov
1937	Bayab Isakayev

Oct 1937-Jan 1938	Murad Salikhov
Jan 1938-45	Turabay Kulatov
1945-50	Ishak Razzakov
July 1950-March 1958	Abdy Suyerkulov
March 1958-May 1961	Kazy Dikambayev
May 1961-Jan 1968	Bolot Mambetov
Jan 1968-Dec 1978	Akhmatbek Suyumbayev
Dec 1978-Dec 1980	Sultan Ibraimov († assassinated)
Jan 1981-May 1986	Arstanbek Duysheyev
May 1986-Jan 1991	Apas Jumagulov (1st)
Jan-Nov 1991	Nasirdin Isanov († motor accident)
Nov 1991-Feb 1992	Tursunbek Chyngyshev (acting)
Feb-Nov 1992	Askar Akayev
Nov 1992-Dec 1993	Tursunbek Chyngyshev
Dec 1993-March 1998	Apas Jumagulov (2nd)
March-Dec 1998	Kabanychbek Jumaliyev
23-25 Dec 1998	Boris Silayev (acting) (1st)
Dec 1998-April 1999	Jumabek Ibraimov (†)
4-12 April 1999	Boris Silayev (acting) (2nd)
April 1999-	Amangeldy Muraliyev

Communist Party Leaders:

First Secretary

1924	Grigori Korostelev
1924-26	Mikhail Kamensky
1926	— — Babakhanov
1929-30	Mikhail Kulkov
1933	A.S.Sakhai
1936-37	M.I.Belotsky
March 1937-July 1938	Maksim Ammosov
July 1938-July 1945	Aleksei Vagov
July 1945-51	Nikolai Bogolyubov
1951-May 1961	Ishak Razzakov
May 1961-Nov 1985	Turdakun Usubaliev
Nov 1985-April 1991	Absamat Masaliyev
April-Aug 1991	Jumgalbek Amanbayev
(Aug 1991	party suspended)

LAOS

Official name: Lao People's Democratic Republic, Sataranalat Pasetepatay Pasason Lao
Previous names: Kingdom of Luang Prabang 1894-1949, Kingdom of Laos 1949-75
State founded: 14th century
Independence date: 23 October 1953
Capital: Vientiane

The kingdom of Lan Xang controlled large areas of south-east Asia in the 14th century, but crumbled during invasions from Annam and Burma. In 1707 Laos split into three kingdoms. Thailand invaded the area and occupied Vientiane in 1827. The Thais were expelled in 1893 by French forces, who established a French protectorate. In 1945 the French were driven out by the Japanese, but returned in 1946. In 1949 Laos became a French associated state, and in 1953 full sovereignty was recognized. There was armed conflict between left and right-wing forces until 1975, when communist forces took over the country and proclaimed a people's republic.

Kings:

1894-March 1904	Sakarinthone
March 1904-Oct 1959	Sisavang Vong (*son*)
Oct 1959-Dec 1975	Savang Vatthana (*son*) (abdicated)

Presidents:

Dec 1975-Aug 1991	Souphanouvong (nominal Oct 1986-Aug 1991)
(Oct 1986-Aug 1991	Phoumi Vongvichit (acting))
Aug 1991-Nov 1992	Kaysone Phomvihan (†)
Nov 1992-Feb 1998	Nouhak Phounsavanh
Feb 1998-	Khamtai Siphandon

Prime Ministers:
Chairman of the Council of Ministers since 1982

Sept-Oct 1945	Prince Phetsarath
Oct 1945-April 1946	Phaya Khammao
April 1946-March 1947	Prince Kindavong
March 1947-Oct 1949	Prince Souvannarath
Oct 1949-Feb 1950	Prince Boun Oum (1st)
Feb 1950-Aug 1951	Phoui Sananikone (1st)
Aug 1951-Nov 1954	Prince Souvanna Phouma (*half-brother of Souphanouvong*) (1st)
Nov 1954-March 1956	Katay Sasorith
March 1956-Aug 1958	Prince Souvanna Phouma (2nd)

Aug 1958-Dec 1959	Phoui Sananikone (2nd)
Jan-June 1960	Kou Abhay Og Long
June-Aug 1960	Prince Somsanith (deposed)
Aug-Dec 1960	Prince Souvanna Phouma (3rd) (deposed)
Dec 1960-June 1962	Prince Boun Oum (2nd)
June 1962-Dec 1975	Prince Souvanna Phouma (4th)
Dec 1975-Aug 1991	Kaysone Phomvihan
Aug 1991-Feb 1998	Khamtai Siphandon
Feb 1998-	Sisavat Keobounphan

Communist Party* Leaders:

*Lao People's Revolutionary Party
General Secretary 1975-91
President since 1991

Dec 1975-Nov 1992	Kaysone Phomvihan (†)
Nov 1992-	Khamtai Siphandon

LATVIA

Official name: Republic of Latvia, Latvijas Republika
Previous name: Latvian Soviet Socialist Republic 1940-90
Independence dates: 18 November 1918, 21 August 1991
Constituent republic of USSR: 5 August 1940-August 1991
Capital: Riga

After being ruled by the Teutonic Knights from the 13th century until 1561, Latvia came under Polish rule. In 1629 it was divided between Poland and Sweden until the 18th century when it passed to Russia. In 1917 an autonomous government was formed, with independence being declared in 1918. In 1940 Latvia was forcibly incorporated into the USSR. After the failed hardline communist coup in the USSR in 1991, Latvia again declared independence.

Presidents:
President of the Presidium of the Supreme Soviet 1940-90
Chairman of the Supreme Council March 1990-July 1993

Nov 1918-March 1927	Janis Tchakste (†)
April 1927-April 1930	Gustavs Zemgals
April 1930-April 1936	Alberts Kviesis
April 1936-June 1940	Karlis Ulmanis
June 1940-July 1941	August Kirchensteins (1st)
(July 1941-Sept 1944	German occupation)
Oct 1944-April 1952	August Kirchensteins (2nd)
April 1952-Nov 1959	Karlis Ozolins
Nov 1959-May 1970	Janis Kalnberzin
May 1970-Aug 1974	Vitaly Ruben
Aug 1974-June 1985	Peteris Strautmanis
June 1985-Oct 1988	Janis Vagris
Oct 1988-July 1993	Anatolys Gurbanovs
July 1993-July 1999	Guntis Ulmanis (*grand nephew of K.Ulmanis*) (LPU)
July 1999-	Vaira Vike-Freiberga

Prime Ministers:
Chairman of the Council of People's Commissars 1940-46
Chairman of the Council of Ministers 1946-92

Nov 1917-Nov 1918	Voldemars Samuels (1st)
Dec 1917-Feb 1918	F.Rozins (rival government)
Nov 1918-Jan 1919	Karlis Ulmanis (1st)
Jan-April 1919	Peteris Stucka

April-July 1919   Andrievs Niedra
July 1919-June 1921   Karlis Ulmanis   (2nd)
June 1921-Jan 1923   Zigfrids Meierovics
Jan 1923-Jan 1924   Janis Pauluks
Jan-Dec 1924   Voldemars Samuels   (2nd)
Dec 1924-Dec 1925   Hugo Celmans   (1st)
Dec 1925-April 1926   Karlis Ulmanis   (3rd)
May-Dec 1926   Artur Alberlings
Dec 1926-Jan 1928   Margers Skujenieks   (1st)
Jan-Nov 1928   Peteris Jurasevskid
Dec 1928-March 1931   Hugo Celmans   (2nd)
March-Nov 1931   Karlis Ulmanis   (4th)
Dec 1931-Feb 1933   Margers Skujenieks   (2nd)
March 1933-March 1934   Adolfs Blodnieks
March 1934-June 1940   Karlis Ulmanis   (5th)
June 1940-July 1941   August Kirchensteins
(July 1941-Sept 1944   German occupation)
Oct 1944-Nov 1959   Villis Latsis
Nov 1959-April 1962   Janis Peive
April 1962-May 1970   Vitaly Ruben
May 1970-Oct 1988   Yury Ruben
Oct 1988-May 1990   Vilnis Bresis
May 1990-July 1993   Ivar Godmanis
July 1993-Sept 1994   Valdis Birkavs   (LW)
Sept 1994-Dec 1995   Maris Gailis   (LW)
Dec 1995-Aug 1997   Andris Shkele
Aug 1997-Nov 1998   Guntars Krasts   (FF)
Nov 1998-July 1999   Vilis Krishtopans   (LW)
July 1999-April 2000   Andris Shkele   (2nd) (PP)
April 2000-   Andris Berzins

Communist Party Leaders:

First Secretary

Oct 1944-Nov 1959   Janis Kalnberzin
Nov 1959-April 1966   Arvids Pelse
April 1966-April 1984   August Voss
April 1984-Oct 1988   Boriss Pugo
Oct 1988-April 1990   Janis Vagris
April-May 1990   Alfreds Rubiks
(May 1990   multi-party system introduced)

FF = Fatherland & Freedom
LPU = Latvian Peasants' Union
LW = Latvian Way
PP = People's Party

LEBANON

Official name: Republic of Lebanon, Jamhuriya al-Lubnaniya
Independence date: 26 November 1941
Capital: Beirut (Bayrut)

Lebanon was under Turkish suzerainty from the 16th century until 1918 when it was occupied by French and British troops. The latter withdrew in 1919 and Lebanon became a mandated territory under French control. In 1926 a republic was established, and complete independence was proclaimed in 1941. The presence of Palestinian guerilla groups and Israeli reprisals led to clashes between various armed groups in 1975. Civil war brought about Syrian intervention in 1976 and Israeli occupation of southern Lebanon in 1982. Israel subsequently withdrew, but the internal divisions remained until 1989 when moves towards reconciliation brought internal peace.

Presidents:

May 1926-Jan 1934	Charles Debbas
Jan 1934-Jan 1936	Habib Pasha el-Saad
Jan 1936-April 1941	Emile Eddeh
April 1941-May 1943	Alfred Nakkache
May-July 1943	Ayub Thabit (acting)
July-Sept 1943	Petro Trad
Sept 1943-Sept 1952	Beshara al-Khuri
18-24 Sept 1952	Fuad Chehab (acting)
Sept 1952-Sept 1958	Camille Chamoun
Sept 1958-Sept 1964	Fuad Chehab
Sept 1964-Sept 1970	Charles Helou
Sept 1970-Sept 1976	Suleiman Franjieh
Sept 1976-Sept 1982	Elias Sarkis
(Sept 1982	Bashir Gemayel, President-elect, assassinated)
Sept 1982-Sept 1988	Amin Gemayel (*brother*)
(Sept 1988-Nov 1989	post vacant)
5-22 Nov 1989	René Moawad († assassinated)
Nov 1989-Nov 1998	Elias Hrawi
Nov 1998-	Emile Lahoud

Prime Ministers:

May 1926-May 1927	Auguste Adib Pasha (1st)
May 1927-Aug 1928	Beshara al-Khuri (1st)
Aug 1928-May 1929	Habib Pasha el-Saad
May-Oct 1929	Beshara al-Khuri (2nd)

Oct 1929-March 1930	Emile Eddeh
March 1930-March 1932	Auguste Adib Pasha (2nd)
March 1932-Jan 1934	Charles Debbas
Jan 1934-Jan 1936	Abd Abdullah Baihum (1st)
Jan 1936-Jan 1937	Ayub Thabit (1st)
Jan 1937-March 1938	Khair al-Ahdab
March-Oct 1938	Khalid Chebab (1st)
Nov 1938-Sept 1939	Abdullah al-Yafi (1st)
Sept 1939-April 1941	Abd Abdullah Baihum (2nd)
April-Dec 1941	Alfred Nakkache
Dec 1941-July 1942	Ahmed Daouk (1st)
July 1942-March 1943	Sanni es-Solh (1st)
March-July 1943	Ayub Thabit (2nd)
July-Sept 1943	Petro Trad
Sept-Nov 1943	Riad es-Sulh (1st)
Nov 1943-July 1944	Henri Pharaon
July 1944-Jan 1945	Riad es-Sulh (2nd)
Jan-Aug 1945	Abdul Karami
Aug 1945-May 1946	Sanni es-Solh (2nd)
May-Dec 1946	Saadi Munlah
Dec 1946-Feb 1951	Riad es-Sulh (3rd)
Feb-April 1951	Hussain al-Oweini (1st)
April 1951-Feb 1952	Abdullah al-Yafi (2nd)
Feb-Sept 1952	Sanni es-Solh (3rd)
9-15 Sept 1952	Nazim Akkari
15-18 Sept 1952	Saeb Salam (1st)
Sept-Oct 1952	Fuad Chehab
Oct 1952-April 1953	Khalid Chebab (2nd)
April-Aug 1953	Saeb Salam (2nd)
Aug 1953-July 1955	Abdullah al-Yafi (3rd)
July-Sept 1955	Sanni es-Solh (4th)
Sept 1955-March 1956	Rashid Karami (*son of A.Karami*) (1st)
March-Nov 1956	Abdullah al-Yafi (4th)
Nov 1956-Sept 1958	Sanni es-Solh (5th)
Sept 1958-May 1960	Rashid Karami (2nd)
May-July 1960	Ahmed Daouk (2nd)
Aug 1960-Oct 1961	Saeb Salam (3rd)
Oct 1961-Feb 1964	Rashid Karami (3rd)
Feb 1964-July 1965	Hussain al-Oweini (2nd)
July 1965-March 1966	Rashid Karami (4th)
April-Dec 1966	Abdullah al-Yafi (5th)
Dec 1966-Feb 1968	Rashid Karami (5th)
Feb 1968-Jan 1969	Abdullah al-Yafi (6th)
Jan 1969-Sept 1970	Rashid Karami (6th)
Oct 1970-April 1973	Saeb Salam (4th)

April-July 1973	Amin Hafez
July 1973-Oct 1974	Takieddine Solh
Oct 1974-May 1975	Rashid al-Solh (1st)
23-26 May 1975	Nureddine Rifai
May 1975-Dec 1976	Rashid Karami (7th)
Dec 1976-Oct 1980	Selim Hoss (1st)
Oct 1980-May 1984	Shafik al-Wazzan
May 1984-June 1987	Rashid Karami (8th) († assassinated)
June 1987-Dec 1990	Selim Hoss (2nd) (acting June 1987-Nov 1989)
Dec 1990-May 1992	Omar Karami *brother of R.Karami*
May-Oct 1992	Rashid al-Solh (2nd)
Oct 1992-Dec 1998	Rafik Hariri
Dec 1998-	Selim Hoss (3rd)

RIVAL GOVERNMENT

Christian-led government based in east Beirut

Prime Minister:

Sept 1988-Oct 1990   Michel Aoun

LESOTHO

Official name: Kingdom of Lesotho, Muso oa Lesotho
Previous name: Basutoland until 1966
Independence date: 4 October 1966
Capital: Maseru

The Basotho nation was founded in the early 19th century by Moshoeshoe I. Because of continued conflict with the Boers he requested the British to assume direct control of the country in 1868. Soon after, control was handed over to the Cape Colony, but in 1884 direct British rule was restored. In 1965 the country became self-governing, and full independence was granted in 1966.

Commissioners:

1884-93	Marshall Clarke
1893-1901	Godfrey Lagden
1901-15	Herbert Sloley
1916-17	Robert Coryndon
1917-26	Edward Garraway (see Bechuanaland)
1926-35	John Sturrock
1935-42	Edmund Richards
1942-46	Charles Arden-Clarke (see Bechuanaland)
1947-51	Aubrey Thompson (see Bechuanaland)
1952-55	Edwin Arrowsmith (see Dominica)
1955-61	Alan Chaplin
1961-66	Alexander Giles

Kings:

Oct 1966-Nov 1990	Moshoeshoe II (*b* Constantine Bereng Seeiso) (1st) (dethroned)
Nov 1990-Jan 1995	Letsie III (*b* David Mohato Seeiso) (*son*) (1st) (abdicated)
Jan 1995-Jan 1996	Moshoeshoe II (2nd) († motor accident)
Jan-Feb 1996	Regent: Queen Mamohato (*widow*)
Feb 1996-	Letsie III (2nd)

Prime Ministers:

May-June 1965	Sekhonyana Maseribane (BNP)
June 1965-Jan 1986	Leabua Jonathan (BNP) (deposed)

Chairmen of the Military Council:

Jan 1986-April 1991	Justin Lekhanya (deposed)

COUNTRIES AND REGIONS

May 1991-April 1993   Elias Ramaema

Prime Ministers:
Chairman of the Provisional Council Aug-Sept 1994

April 1993-Aug 1994	Ntsu Mokhehle (1st) (BCP)
Aug-Sept 1994	Hae Phoofolo
Sept 1994-June 1998	Ntsu Mokhehle (2nd) (BCP, LCD)
June 1998-	Pakalitha Mosisili (LCD)

BCP = Basotho Congress Party
BNP = Basotho National Party
LCD = Lesotho Congress of Democrats

LIBERIA

Official name: Republic of Liberia
Independence date: 26 July 1847
Capital: Monrovia

In 1821 the first group of freed black slaves from the southern United States arrived in what is now Liberia. In 1847 an independent republic was proclaimed with a constitution based on that of the USA. Descendants of the original settlers dominated the political life of Liberia until the coup of 1980. From 1990 until 1994 a state of civil war existed. A West African intervention force helped enforce a cease-fire and oversaw elections in 1997.

Governors:

1836-41	Thomas Buchanan	(†)
1841-47	Joseph Roberts	

Presidents:

Chairman of the National Redemption Council April 1980-January 1986
Chairman of the State Council March 1994-August 1997

Jan 1848-Dec 1856	Joseph Roberts	(1st)
Dec 1856-Dec 1864	Stephen Benson	
Dec 1864-Dec 1868	Daniel Warner	
Dec 1868-Dec 1870	James Payne	(1st)
Dec 1870-Oct 1871	Edward Roye	
Oct 1871-Dec 1872	James Smith	
Dec 1872-Dec 1876	Joseph Roberts	(2nd)
Dec 1876-Dec 1878	James Payne	(2nd)
Dec 1878-Jan 1883	Anthony Gardiner	(TWP)
Jan 1883-Dec 1884	Alfred Russell	(TWP)
Dec 1884-Dec 1892	Hilary Johnson	(TWP)
Dec 1892-Nov 1896	Joseph Cheeseman	(TWP)
Nov 1896-Dec 1900	William Coleman	(TWP)
Dec 1900-Dec 1904	Garretson Gibson	(TWP)
Dec 1904-Jan 1912	Arthur Barclay	(TWP)
Jan 1912-Jan 1920	Daniel Howard	(TWP)
Jan 1920-Dec 1930	Charles King	(TWP)
Dec 1930-Jan 1944	Edwin Barclay	(TWP)
Jan 1944-July 1971	William Tubman	(†) (TWP)
July 1971-April 1980	William Tolbert	(TWP) (deposed, assassinated)
April 1980-Sept 1990	Samuel Doe	(NDPL) (deposed, assassinated)
Sept-Nov 1990	David Nimley	

(Sept-Nov 1990	Prince Johnson-rival president in Monrovia)
(Aug 1990-March 1994	Charles Taylor-rival president in Gbarnga)
Nov 1990-March 1994	Amos Sawyer
March 1994-Sept 1995	David Kpomakpor
Sept 1995-Sept 1996	Wilton Sankawulo
Sept 1996-Aug 1997	Ruth Perry
Aug 1997-	Charles Taylor (NPP)

NDPL = National Democratic Party of Liberia
NPP = National Patriotic Party
TWP = True Whig Party

LIBYA

Official name: Great Socialist People's Libyan Arab Jamahiriyah, Al-Jamahiriyah al-Arabiya al-Libya as-Shabiya al-Ishtirakiya al-Uzma

Previous names: Kingdom of Libya 1951-69, Libyan Arab Republic 1969-77, Socialist People's Libyan Arab Jamahiriyah 1977-86

Independence date: 24 December 1951

Capital: Tripoli (Tarabulus)

Tripoli was conquered by the Turks in the 16th century and remained under Turkish rule until occupied by Italy in 1911. During World War II Italian and German forces were expelled, and Tripolitania and Cyrenaica were placed under British control, while Fezzan came under French rule. The three territories were joined in a federation and the independent kingdom of Libya came into being in 1951. The federal arrangement was abolished in 1951. In 1969 the king was deposed and a republic proclaimed. In 1977 a people's masses state was established.

Governors-General:

1928-33	Pietro Badoglio
1933-40	Italo Balbo
1940-41	Marchese di Neghelli (Rodolfo Graziani)
1941	Italo Gariboldi
1941-43	Ettore Bastico
(1943-51	British & French occupation)

King:

Dec 1951-Sept 1969   Idris   (see Cyrenaica) (deposed)

Head of State:

Chairman of the Revolutionary Command Council 1969-77
Leader of the Revolution since 1977 (not a formal state post, but functions as de facto head of state)

Sept 1969-   Muammar Gaddafi

General People's Congress Secretaries-General:

This position has some of the features of a head of state

March 1977-March 1979	Muammar Gaddafi
March 1979-Jan 1981	Abdul al-Obeidi
Jan 1981-Feb 1984	Mohammed Ragab
Feb 1984-Oct 1991	Miftah Omar

Oct 1991-Nov 1992 Abdar-Raziq Sawsa
Nov 1992- Zentani Mohammed al-Zentani

Prime Ministers:
Secretary of the General People's Council since 1977

March 1951-Feb 1954	Mahmud Muntasir (see Tripolitania) (1st)
Feb-April 1954	Mohammed Sakizly (see Cyrenaica)
April 1954-May 1957	Mustafa Ben Halim
May 1957-Oct 1960	Abdul Kubar
Oct 1960-March 1963	Mohammed bin Othman es-Said
March 1963-Jan 1964	Mohieddine Fekini
Jan 1964-Oct 1965	Mahmud Muntasir (2nd)
Oct 1965-July 1967	Hussain Maziq (see Cyrenaica)
July-Oct 1967	Abdel al-Badri
Oct 1967-Sept 1968	Abdul Bakkush
Sept 1968-Sept 1969	Wanis al-Geddafi (see Cyrenaica) (deposed)
Sept 1969-Jan 1970	Mahmud al-Maghreby
Jan 1970-July 1972	Muammar Gaddafi
July 1972-March 1977	Abdul Jalloud
March 1977-March 1979	Abdul al-Obeidi
March 1979-Feb 1984	Jadallah at-Talhi (1st)
Feb 1984-March 1986	Mohammed Ragab
March 1986-March 1987	Jadallah at-Talhi (2nd)
March 1987-Oct 1990	Umar al-Muntasir
Oct 1990-Jan 1994	Abu Zaid Durda
Jan 1994-Dec 1997	Abd al-Majid al-Qa'ud
Dec 1997-March 2000	Mohammed al-Mangoush
March 2000-	Mubarak al-Shamikh

Former Provinces

The federal system was abolished in 1963

CYRENAICA

Capital: Benghazi

Emir:

1916-23	Idris (1st)
(1923-Oct 1946	post abolished)
Oct 1946-Dec 1951	Idris (2nd) (later King of Libya)

Governors:

Dec 1951-Aug 1953	Mohammed Sakizly
Aug 1953-1960	Hussain Maziq
1960-63	Mahmud Buhadma

Prime Ministers:

Sept 1949-March 1951	Omar Mansur al-Kikiya
1952-62	Wanis al-Geddafi
1962-63	Hamid Abbar

FEZZAN

Capital: Sebha

Governors:

Dec 1951-1956	Ahmed Saif an-Nasr
1956-1963	Omar Saif an-Nasr

Prime Minister:

195?-63	Abdul Jalil Saif an-Nasr

TRIPOLITANIA

Capital: Tripoli

Governors:

Dec 1951-1955	Fadhil bin Zikri (1st)
1955	Abdessalam Bussairy
1955-1958	Jamal Bashaga
1958-1960	Taher Bekir
1960-1963	Fadhil bin Zikri (2nd)

Prime Ministers:

March-Dec 1951	Mahmud Muntasir
? -58	Mahmud el-Bishti
1958-61	A. Dansouf
1961-63	Ali Adib

LIECHTENSTEIN

Official name: Principality of Liechtenstein, Fürstentum Liechtenstein
State founded: 23 January 1719
Capital: Vaduz

The history of the Principality dates back to the 14th century and its present boundaries were recognized by the Emperor Charles VI (Karl II of Austria) in 1719. The first seven ruling princes never visited the country, and the first to take up residence there was Franz Joseph II, who became head of state in 1938.

Princes:

Jan 1719-Oct 1721	Anton Florian
Oct 1721-Dec 1732	Joseph Johann Adam (*son*)
Dec 1732-Dec 1748	Johann Nepomuk Karl (*son*)
Dec 1748-Feb 1772	Josef Wenzel (*cousin of Joseph Johann Adam*)
Feb 1772-Aug 1781	Franz Joseph I (*nephew*)
Aug 1781-March 1805	Alois I (*son*)
March 1805-April 1836	Johannes I (*brother*)
April 1836-Nov 1858	Alois II (*son*)
Nov 1858-Feb 1929	Johannes II (*son*)
Feb 1929-July 1938	Franz (*brother*)
July 1938-Nov 1989	Franz Joseph II (*grand-nephew*)
Nov 1989-	Hans Adam (*son*) (executive authority since Aug 1984)

Prime Ministers:
Head of Government

June 1922-Aug 1928	Gustav Schädler (PP)
Aug 1928-Sept 1945	Joseph Hoop (PCP)
Sept 1945-July 1962	Alexander Frick (PCP)
July 1962-Feb 1970	Gerard Batliner (PCP)
Feb 1970-March 1974	Alfred Hilbe (FU)
March 1974-Feb 1978	Walter Kieber (PCP)
Feb 1978-May 1993	Hans Brunhart (FU)
May-Dec 1993	Markus Büchel (PCP)
Dec 1993-	Mario Frick (FU)

FU-Fatherland Union
PCP = Progressive Citizens' Party
PP = People's Party

LITHUANIA

Official name: Republic of Lithuania, Lietuvos Respublika
Previous name: Lithuanian Soviet Socialist Republic 1940-90
Independence date: 16 February 1918, 11 March 1990
Constituent republic of USSR: 5 August 1940-1990/91
Capital: Káunas (1920-44), Vilnius (since 1944)

Lithuania was founded in the thirteenth century, and later entered into a personal union with Poland after the marriage of Duke Jogaila to the Polish queen. In 1569 the two countries were formally united. When Poland was partitioned in 1795, Lithuania came under Russian rule until it declared independence in 1918. In 1940 it was incorporated into the USSR. As reforms began to develop in the USSR, Lithuanians elected a non-communist government in 1990 which proclaimed independence, although this had little effect until after the failed 1991 coup in Moscow.

Dukes:

1236-63	Mindaugas
(1263-90	period of anarchy)
1290-1316	Vytenis
1316-41	Gediminas (*brother*)
1341-45	Jaunutis (*son*) (deposed)
1347-77	Algirdas (*brother*)
1377-81	Jogaila (*son*) (1st) (deposed)
1381-82	Kestutis (*son of Gediminas*) (deposed,killed)
1382-87	Jogaila (2nd) (became King Władysław II of Poland)
1387-1430	Vytautas
1430-40	Władysław (Władysław III of Poland)
1440-92	Kazimierz (Kazimierz IV of Poland)
(1492-1569	Polish kings concurrently Dukes)
(1569-1795	united with Poland)
(1795-1918	Russian rule)

Presidents:

President of the Presidium of the Supreme Soviet 1940-90
Chairman of the Supreme Soviet Jan-March 1990
Chairman of the Supreme Council March 1990-Nov 1992

April 1919-June 1920	Antanas Smetona	(1st)
June 1920-June 1926	Aleksandras Stulginskis	
June-Dec 1926	Kazys Grinius	(deposed)
Dec 1926-June 1940	Antanas Smetona	(2nd)

July 1940-July 1941   Justas Paleckis   (1st)
(July 1941-Sept 1944   German occupation)
Oct 1944-April 1967   Justas Paleckis   (2nd)
April 1967-Dec 1975   Matejas Sumauskas
Dec 1975-Nov 1985   Antanas Barkauskas
Nov 1985-Nov 1987   Ringaudas Songaila
Dec 1987-Jan 1990   Vytautas Astraukas
Jan-March 1990   Algirdas Brazauskas   (1st)
March 1990-Nov 1992   Vytautas Landsbergis
Nov 1992-Feb 1998   Algirdas Brazauskas   (acting Nov 1992-Feb 1993) (2nd) (DLP)
Feb 1998-   Valdas Adamkus

Prime Ministers:
Chairman of the Council of People's Commissars 1940-46
Chairman of the Council of Ministers 1946-92

Nov-Dec 1918   Augustinius Voldemaras   (1st)
Dec 1918-March 1919   Mykolas Sleževičius   (1st)
Dec 1918-June 1919   Vikenti Mitskevich-Kapsukas   (rival government; also PM of Belorussia)
March-April 1919   Pranas Dovydaitis
April-Oct 1919   Mykolas Sleževičius   (2nd)
Oct 1919-June 1920   Ernst Galvanauskas   (1st)
June 1920-Feb 1923   Kazys Grinius
Feb 1923-June 1924   Ernst Galvanauskas   (2nd)
June 1924-Feb 1925   Antanas Tumenas
Feb-Sept 1925   Vytautas Petrulis
Sept 1925-June 1926   Leones Bistras
June-Dec 1926   Mykolas Sleževičius   (3rd)
Dec 1926-Sept 1929   Augustinius Voldemaras   (2nd)
Sept 1929-March 1938   Juozas Tubelis
March 1938-March 1939   Vladislovas Mironas
March-Nov 1939   Jonas Černius
Nov 1939-June 1940   Antanas Merkys
June 1940-July 1941   Justas Paleckis
(July 1941-Sept 1944   German occupation)
Oct 1944-Jan 1956   Mečislovas Gedvilas
Jan 1956-April 1967   Matejas Šumauskas
April 1967-Jan 1981   Juuzas Maniusis
Jan 1981-Nov 1985   Ringaudas Songaila
Nov 1985-March 1990   Vytautas Sakalauskas
March 1990-Jan 1991   Kazimiera Prunskiene
10-13 Jan 1991   Albertas Shiminas
Jan 1991-July 1992   Gediminas Vagnorius   (1st)
July-Dec 1992   Alexandras Abisala
Dec 1992-March 1993   Bronislovas Lubys

March 1993-Feb 1996	Adolfas Sleževičius	(DLP)
Feb-Nov 1996	Laurynas Mindaugas Stankevičius	
Nov 1996-May 1999	Gediminas Vagnorius (2nd)	
4-18 May 1999	Irena Degutiene (acting) (1st)	
May-Oct 1999	Rolandas Paksas	
Oct-Nov 1999	Irena Degutiene (acting) (2nd)	
Nov 1999-	Andrius Kubilis	

DLP = Democratic Labour Party

Communist Party Leaders:
First Secretary

Oct 1944-Feb 1974	Antanas Šnieckus
Feb 1974-Nov 1987	Piatras Griskevičius (†)
Nov 1987-Oct 1988	Ringaudas Songaila
Oct 1988-March 1990	Algirdas Brazauskas
(March 1990	multi-party system introduced)

Former Autonomous Region

MEMEL

Memel was an autonomous region of independent Lithuania from 1923 to 1939 when it was incorporated into Germany. It is now part of Lithuania.

Governors:

Feb 1923-Oct 1924	Antanas Smetona
Oct 1924-Nov 1925	Jonas Budrys
Nov 1925-Aug 1927	Jonas Zilius
Aug-Nov 1927	K. Zalkauskas
Nov 1927-May 1932	Antanas Merkys
May 1932-Nov 1933	Vytautas Gylys
Nov 1933-Feb 1935	J. Navaka
Feb 1935-Oct 1936	V. Kurkauskas
Oct 1936-Dec 1938	J. Kubilius
Dec 1938-March 1939	Viktoras Gailius

Prime Ministers:
Directors

Jan-Feb 1923	Erdmonas Simonaitis	(1st)
Feb 1923-Feb 1925	Viktoras Gailius	
Feb 1925-Jan 1926	Endrias Borchetas	
Jan-Nov 1926	Erdmonas Simonaitis	(2nd)

Nov 1926-Jan 1927	V. Falkas
Jan-Oct 1927	V. Švelnys
Dec 1927-May 1930	O. Kadgiehn (O. Kadgienas)
Aug-Oct 1930	Martynas Reisgys (1st)
Jan 1931-Feb 1932	Otto Bottcher (Otonas Betcheris)
Feb-May 1932	Eduard Samaitis (Simmat)
June 1932-March 1934	Ottomar Schreibar (Otomaras Streibens)
March-Dec 1934	Martynas Reisgys (2nd)
Dec 1934-Nov 1935	Juergis Bruvelaitis
Nov 1935-Jan 1939	August Baldschus (Augustas Baldzius)
Jan-March 1939	Wilhelm Bertuleit (Vilius Bertulitis)

LUXEMBOURG

Official name: Grand Duchy of Luxembourg, Grand-Duché de Luxembourg (Letzeburgisch)

Independence date: 16 March 1815

Capital: Luxembourg-Ville

The County of Luxembourg came into existence in the 11th century, and in 1354 it became a duchy. Annexed by France in the 17th century, the duchy passed into Spanish hands, became part of Austrian Netherlands in 1713, and returned to French control in 1795. By the treaty of Vienna in 1815 Luxembourg became an independent grand duchy, linked in personal union to the Netherlands. In 1890 the grand duchy was inherited by Adolf of Nassau. During World War II Luxembourg was occupied by Germany.

Grand Dukes/Duchesses:

March 1815-Oct 1840	Guillaume I (Willem I of the Netherlands) (abdicated)
Oct 1840-March 1849	Guillaume II (Willem II of the Netherlands) (*son*)
March 1949-Nov 1890	Guillaume III (Willem III of the Netherlands) (*son*)
Nov 1890-Nov 1905	Adolphe (*f* Adolf, Duke of Nassau)
Nov 1905-Feb 1912	Guillaume IV (*son*)
Feb 1912-Jan 1919	Marie Adelaide (*daughter*) (abdicated)
Jan 1919-May 1940	Charlotte (*sister*) (1st) (exiled)
(May 1940-Sept 1944	German occupation)
Sept 1944-Nov 1964	Charlotte (2nd) (abdicated)
Nov 1964-	Jean (*son*) (scheduled to abdicate Sept 2000)
(Sept 2000-	Henri (*son*) (heir apparent))

Prime Ministers:

Aug-Dec 1848	J.-T.-I.de la Fontaine
Dec 1848-Sept 1853	Jean-Jacques Willmar
Sept 1853-Sept 1860	Mathias Simons
Sept 1860-Dec 1867	Victor de Tornaco
Dec 1867-Dec 1874	Emmanuel Servais
Dec 1874-Feb 1885	Félix de Blochausen
Feb 1885-Sept 1888	Edouard Thilges
Sept 1888-Oct 1915	Paul Eyschen (†)
Oct-Nov 1915	Mathias Mongenast
Nov 1915-Feb 1916	Hubert Loutsch
Feb 1916-June 1917	Victor Thorn
June 1917-Sept 1918	Léon Kauffmann

Sept 1918-March 1925	Émile Reuter (RP)
March 1925-July 1926	Pierre Prum (NIP)
July 1926-Nov 1937	Joseph Bech (1st) (RP)
Nov 1937-May 1940	Pierre Dupong (1st) (RP)
(May 1940-Sept 1944	German occupation)
Sept 1944-Dec 1953	Pierre Dupong (2nd) (CSP) (†)
Dec 1953-March 1958	Joseph Bech (2nd) (CSP)
March 1958-March 1959	Pierre Frieden (CSP)
March 1959-June 1974	Pierre Werner (1st) (CSP)
June 1974-June 1979	Gaston Thorn (LP)
June 1979-July 1984	Pierre Werner (2nd) (CSP)
July 1984-Jan 1995	Jacques Santer (CSP)
Jan 1995-	Jean-Claude Juncker (CSP)

CSP = Christian Social Party
LP = Liberal Party
NIP = National Independent Party
RP = Right Party

GOVERNMENT-IN-EXILE 1940-44

Headquarters: London
Operated during German occupation

Grand Duchess:

May 1940-Sept 1944   Charlotte

Prime Minister:

May 1940-Sept 1944   Pierre Dupong

MACEDONIA

Official name: Republic of Macedonia, Republika Makedonija
Previous name: Socialist Republic of Macedonia 1945-91 (as part of Yugoslavia)
Independence date: 20 November 1992
Capital: Skopje

Macedonia was conquered by Bulgars in the 7th century. In the nineth century it became part of a Macedo-Bulgar empire until it was conquered by the Byzantines in 1014. In the fourteenth century it fell to Serbia, but was soon taken over by the Turks. After the Balkan Wars (1912-13) the Turks were ousted, Serbia receiving most of it with the remainder going to Bulgaria and Greece. In 1945 it became a republic within Yugoslavia. As other republics seceded from Yugoslavia, Macedonia also declared independence, but international acceptance was complicated by Greece's objections to the use of the name Macedonia since it is the same as one of the Greek provinces - this was overcome by referring to the country as the Former Yugoslav Republic of Macedonia.

Presidents:
President of the People's Assembly 1951-74
President of the State Presidency 1974-91

1951-53	Vidoje Smilevski (1st)
1953-62	Lazar Koliševski
1962-63	Ljupco Arsov (1st)
1963-67	Vidoje Smilevski (2nd)
1967-68	Mito Hadzivasilev
1968-74	Nikola Minčev
May 1974-Oct 1979	Vidoje Smilevski (3rd)
Oct 1979-May 1982	Ljupco Arsov (2nd)
May 1982-May 1983	Angel Cemerski
May 1983-May 1984	Blagoje Taleski
May 1984-May 1985	Tome Bukleski
May 1985-May 1986	Vanco Apostolski
May 1986-May 1988	Dragoljub Stavrev
May 1988-April 1990	Jezdimir Bogdanski
April 1990-Jan 1991	Vladimir Mitkov
Jan 1991-Nov 1999	Kiro Gligorov (LCM, SDLM)
Nov-Dec 1999	Savo Klimovski (acting)
Dec 1999-	Boris Trajkovski (IMRO)

Prime Ministers:
President of the Executive Council 1945-91

April 1945-Dec 1953	Lazar Koliševski

Dec 1953-61   Ljupco Arsov
1961-63   Aleksandar Grlichkov   (1st)
1963-64   Vidoje Smilevski
1964-66   Aleksandar Grlichkov   (2nd)
1966-68   Nikola Mincev
1968-May 1974   Ksente Bogoev
May 1974-April 1982   Blagoje Popov
April 1982-April 1986 Dragoljub Stravrev
April 1986-March 1991 Gligorije Gogovski
March 1991-Aug 1992   Nikola Kljusev
Aug 1992-Nov 1998   Branko Crvenkovski   (SDLM)
Nov 1998-   Ljubcho Georgievski   (IMRO)

IMRO = Internal Macedonian Revolutionary Organisation
LCM = League of Communists of Macedonia
SDLM = Social Democratic League of Macedonia

Communist Party Leaders:

1945-July 1963   Lazar Koliševski
July 1963-March 1969 Krste Crvenkovski
March 1969-May 1982   Angel Cemerski
May 1982-May 1984   Krste Markovski
May 1984-May 1986   Milan Pančevski
May 1986-Jan 1991   Jakov Lazarovski
(Jan 1991   multi-party government elected)

MADAGASCAR

Official name: Republic of Madagascar, République du Madagascar, Repoblika n'i Madagaskar
Previous names: Malagasy Republic 1958-75, Democratic Republic of Madagascar 1975-93
Independence date: 26 June 1960
Capital: Tananarive

Madagascar was united into a single kingdom at the end of the 18th century. In 1896 France established a protectorate there and the following year annexed Madagascar as a colony. In 1946 it became an Overseas Territory, and self-government was granted in 1958, followed by full independence in 1960. The military came to power in 1972, but a multi-party system was introduced in 1993.

Kings/Queens:

1787-1810	Andriananampoinimerina (*b* Prince Ramboasalama)
1810-July 1828	Radama I (*son*)
July 1828-Aug 1861	Ranavalona I (*b* Princess Ramavo) (*widow*)
Aug 1861-May 1863	Radama II (*b* Prince Rakoto) (*son*) (assassinated)
May 1863-April 1868	Rasoherina (*b* Princess Rabodo) (*widow*)
April 1868-July 1883	Ranavalona II (*b* Princess Ramona) (*cousin*)
July 1883-Feb 1897	Ranavalona III (*b* Princess Razafindrahety)

Governors-General:

1897-1905	Joseph-Simon Gallieni
1905-10	Jean-Victor Augagneur
1910-14	Albert Picquie
1914-17	Hubert-Auguste Garbit (1st)
1917-18	Martial-Henri Merlin (see French Equatorial Africa)
1918-19	Abraham Schrameck
1919-20	Marie-Casimir Guyon
1920-24	Hubert-Auguste Garbit (2nd)
1924-30	Marcel Olivier
1930-39	Léon Caylon (1st)
1939-40	Jules-Marcel de Coppet (see Mauritania)
1940-41	Léon Caylon (2nd) (see French West Africa)
1941-42	Armand-Léon Annet
1942-43	Paul-Louis de Gentilhomme
1943-44	Pierre de Saint-Mart (see Ubangui-Chari)
1944-46	Paul de Saint-Mart

High Commissioners:

1946-48	Jules-Marcel de Coppet
1948-50	Pierre de Chevigne
1950-54	Isaac-Robert Bargues
1954-60	Jean Souçadaux

Presidents:

Head of State Oct 1972-Feb 1975
Chairman of the National Military Directorate Feb-June 1975
President of the Supreme Revolutionary Council June-Dec 1975

May 1959-Oct 1972	Philibert Tsiranana (SDP)
Oct 1972-Feb 1975	Gabriel Ramanantsoa
5-11 Feb 1975	Richard Ratsimandrava († assassinated)
Feb-June 1975	Gilles Andriamahazo
June 1975-March 1993	Didier Ratsiraka (1st) (VMR)
March 1993-Sept 1996	Albert Zafy (NUDD)
Sept 1996-Feb 1997	Norbert Ratsirahonana (acting)
Feb 1997-	Didier Ratsiraka (2nd)

Chief Ministers:

1828-Sept 1830	Andriamihaja
Sept 1830-Feb 1852	Rainiharo
Feb 1852-1861	Rainijohary
1861-65	Raharo

Prime Ministers:

1865-Oct 1895	Rainilaiarivony
Oct 1895-Sept 1896	Rainitsimbazafy
Sept 1896-Feb 1897	Rasanjy
(Feb 1897-July 1958	post abolished)
July 1958-May 1959	Philibert Tsiranana (SDP)
(May 1959-May 1972	post abolished)
May 1972-Feb 1975	Gabriel Ramanantsoa
5-11 Feb 1975	Richard Ratsimandrava († assassinated)
(Feb-June 1975	post vacant)
June 1975-Jan 1976	Didier Ratsiraka
Jan-July 1976	Joël Rakotomalala († air accident)
July 1976-Aug 1977	Justin Rakotoniaina
Aug 1977-Feb 1988	Desiré Rakotoarijaona
Feb 1988-July 1991	Victor Ramahatra
Aug 1991-Aug 1993	Guy Razanamasy
Aug 1993-Oct 1995	Francisque Ravony
Oct 1995-June 1996	Emmanuel Rakotovahiny

June 1996-Feb 1997   Norbert Ratsirahonana
Feb 1997-July 1998   Pascal Rakotomavo
July 1998-   Tantely Andrianarivo

NUDD = National Union for Democracy and Development
SDP = Social Democratic Party
VMR = Vanguard of the Malagasy Revolution (AREMA)

MALAWI

Official name: Republic of Malawi, Dziko La Malawi
Previous names: Nyasaland until 1964, Malawi 1964-66
Independence date: 6 July 1964
Capital: Zomba until 1975, Lilongwe since 1975

In 1891 the territory of present-day Malawi was proclaimed a British protectorate under the name Nyasaland. In 1953 it became part of the Federation of Rhodesia and Nyasaland. Ten years later Nyasaland became self-governing, shortly before the dissolution of the federation. Independence was granted in 1964 as Malawi, and in 1966 a republic was proclaimed. The country was ruled by Kamuzu Banda for over 30 years until he agreed to renounce the Life Presidency and hold multi-party elections in 1994.

Governors:

1907-10	Alfred Sharpe
1911-13	William Manning (see Ceylon)
1913-23	George Smith
1923-29	Charles Bowring
1929-32	Thomas Thomas
1932-34	Hubert Young
1934-39	Harold Kittermaster
1939-42	Henry Mackenzie-Kennedy
1942-47	Edmund Richards
1948-56	Geoffrey Colby
1956-61	Robert Armitage
1961-64	Glyn Jones

Governor-General:

Represented monarch who was concurrently British monarch

July 1964-July 1966	Glyn Jones

Presidents:

July 1966-May 1994	Hastings Kamuzu Banda (MCP)
May 1994-	Bakili Muluzi (UDF)

Prime Minister:

Feb 1963-July 1966	Hastings Kamuzu Banda (MCP)
(July 1966	post abolished)

MCP = Malawi Congress Party (sole legal party 1966-93)
UDF = United Democratic Front

MALAYSIA

Official name: Federation of Malaysia, Persekutuan tanah Malaysia
State formed: 16 September 1963
Independence date (Malaya): 31 August 1957
Capital: Kuala Lumpur

In the 14th century the kingdom of Malacca dominated the Malay peninsula, but in 1511 it was conquered by Portugal. In 1641 the area fell under Dutch control, the British (1719-1818), Dutch again in 1818, and back to British control in 1824. In 1826 Malacca, Penang and Singapore were combined as the Straits Settlements colony. British residents were appointed to some of the Malay states and in 1895 four states (Perak, Selangor, Negri Sembilan and Pahang) formed the Federated Malay States. During World War II Malaya was occupied by Japan, with Thailand annexing the northern states. After liberation, a union of all the states was formed in 1946, and became the Federation of Malaya in 1948. In 1955 Malaya became self-governing, and in 1957 Britain granted full independence. In 1963 Malaya, Singapore, Sabah and Sarawak formed the Federation of Malaysia. Singapore left the federation in 1965.

Information prior to 1963 refers to Malaya only

High Commissioners:

1946-48	Gerald Gent
1948-51	Henry Gurney
1952-54	Gerald Templer
1954-57	Donald McGillivry

Heads of State:

Aug 1957-April 1960	Tuanku Abdul Rahman	(Ruler of Negri Sembilan) (†)
April-Sept 1960	Sultan Hisamuddin Alam Shah	(Sultan of Selangor) (†)
Sept 1960-Sept 1965	Tuanku Syed Putra	(Raja of Perlis)
Sept 1965-Sept 1970	Tuanku Ismail Nasiruddin Shah	(Sultan of Trengganu)
Sept 1970-Sept 1975	Sultan Abdul Halim Muadzam Shah	(Sultan of Kedah)
Sept 1975-March 1979	Sultan Yahya Petra	(Sultan of Kelantan) (†)
March 1979-April 1984	Sultan Ahmad Shah	(Sultan of Pahang)
April 1984-April 1989	Sultan Mahmud Iskander	(Sultan of Johore)
April 1989-April 1994	Sultan Azlan Shah	(Sultan of Perak)
April 1994-April 1999	Tuanku Jaafar Abdul Rahman	(Ruler of Negri Sembilan)
April 1999-	Sultan Salahuddin Abdul Aziz Shah	(Sultan of Selangor)

Chief Minister:

July 1955-Aug 1957   Tunku Abdul Rahman Putra   (*uncle of Abdul Halim Muadzam Shah*) (UMNO)

Prime Ministers:

Aug 1957-Feb 1959	Tunku Abdul Rahman Putra (1st) (UMNO)
Feb-Aug 1959	Tun Abdul Razak bin Hussein (1st) (UMNO)
Aug 1959-Sept 1970	Tunku Abdul Rahman Putra (2nd) (UMNO)
Sept 1970-Jan 1976	Tun Abdul Razak bin Hussein (2nd) (UMNO) (†)
Jan 1976-July 1981	Hussein bin Onn (UMNO)
July 1981-	Mahathir bin Mohamed (UMNO)

UMNO = United Malay National Organization

States

JOHORE

Capital: Johore Bahru

Sultans:

1812-19	Abdul Rahman Muadzam Shah
1819-25	Abdul Rahman
1825-62	Ibrahim
1862-Sept 1895	Abubakar
Sept 1895-May 1959	Ibrahim Shah
May 1959-May 1981	Ismail Shah
May 1981-	Mahmud Iskander (Regent 1984-89 Ibrahim Ismail)

Chief Ministers:

1886-1919	Jaafar bin Mohamed
1920-22	Mohamed bin Mahbob
1922-26	Abdullah bin Jaafar
(1926-28	post vacant)
1928-31	Mustaffa bin Jaafar
1931-34	Abdul Mahid bin Yusof
1935-47	Ungku Abdul Aziz bin Abdul Majid
1947-50	Onn bin Jaafar
(1950-52	post vacant)
1952-55	Syed Abdul Kadir bin Mohamed
1955-59	Wan Idris bin Ibrahim
1959-67	Hassan bin Yunus
1967-82	Othman bin Mohamed Saat

1982-86	Abdul Ajib bin Ahmad
1986-95	Muhyiddin Yassin
April 1995-	Abdul Ghani Othman

KEDAH

Capital: Alor Star

Sultans:

1798-1803	Zia-Ud-Din Muadzam Shah
1803-21	Ahmad Tajuddin Halim Shah (1st)
(1821-43	Interregnum)
1843	Ahmad Tajuddin Halim Shah (2nd)
1843-54	Zain-Ul-Rashid Muadzam Shah I
1854-79	Ahmad Tajuddin Mukarram Shah
1879-81	Zain-Ul-Rashid Muadzam Shah II
1881-May 1943	Abdul Hamid Halim Shah
May 1943-July 1958	Badlishah (*brother of Tunku Abdul Rahman*)
July 1958-	Abdul Halim Muadzam Shah (*son*)
	(Regent: 1970-75 Tunku Abdul Malik)

Chief Ministers:

Feb 1948-Jan 1954	Mohamed Shariff bin Osman
Feb 1954-May 1959	Tunku Ismail bin Tunku Yahya
May 1959-Dec 1967	Syed Omar bin Syed Abdullah Shahabudin
Dec 1967-July 1978	Syed Ahmad bin Syed Mahmud Shahabudin
July 1978-Jan 1985	Syed Nahar bin Sheh Shahabudin
Jan 1985-June 1996	Osman bin Aroff
June 1996-Dec 1999	Sanusi Junid
Dec 1999-	Razak bin Zain

KELANTAN

Capital: Kota Bahru

Sultans:

c1800-38	Mohamed Shah I
1838-86	Mohamed Shah II
1886-89	Ahmad Shah
1889-91	Mohamed Shah III
1891-99	Mansur Shah
1899-1919	Mohamed Shah IV
1919-42	Ismail Shah

(1942-45 Thai rule)
Dec 1945-July 1960 Ibrahim Shah
July 1960-March 1979 Yahya Petra
   (Regent: 1975-79 Ismail Petra)
March 1979- Ismail Petra

Chief Ministers:

1886-90	Nik Yusof bin Nik Abdul Majid (1st)
1890-94	Said bin Ngah
1894-1900	Nik Yusof bin Nik Abdul Majid (2nd)
1900-20	Hassan bin Mohamed Salleh
1921-44	Nik Mahmud bin Ismail
1944-53	Nik Ahmed Kamil bin Nik Mahmud
1953-59	Mohamed Hamzah bin Zainal Abidin
1959-64	Ishak bin Lofti Omar (PMIP)
1964-74	Mohamed Asri bin Muda (PMIP)
1974-Nov 1977	Mohamed bin Nasir (1st) (FMIC)
(Nov 1977-Feb 1978	post vacant)
Feb-March 1978	Mohamed bin Nasir (2nd) (FMIC)
March 1978-Nov 1990	Mohamed bin Yaacob (UMNO)
Nov 1990-	Nik Abdul Aziz bin Nik Mamat (S46)

FMIC = Front Malaysian Islamic Council (BERJASA)
PMIP = Pan-Malaya Islamic Party
S46 = Semangat 46

MALACCA
Melaku

Capital: Malacca

Heads of State:

Aug 1957-Aug 1959	Leong Yew Koh
Aug 1959-Aug 1971	Abdul Malek bin Yusuf
Aug 1971-May 1975	Abdul Aziz bin Abdul Majid
May 1975-Dec 1984	Syed Zahiruddin bin Syed Hassain
Dec 1984-	Utama Syed Ahmed bin Syed Mahmud Shahabuddin

Chief Ministers:

Aug 1957-May 1959	Kurnia Jasa Othman bin Talib
June 1959-Oct 1967	Abdul Ghafar bin Baba
Oct 1967-Aug 1972	Abdul Talib bin Abdul Karim
Aug 1972-July 1978	Abdul Ghani bin Ali
July 1978-April 1982	Mohamed Abid bin Mohamed Adam

April 1982-Oct 1994	Abdul Rahim bin Tamby Chik
Oct 1994-May 1997	Mohamed Zin Abdul Ghani (acting 1994-95)
May 1997-Dec 1999	Abu Zahar Isnin
Dec 1999-	Mohamed Ali Rustam

NEGRI SEMBILAN

Capital: Seremban

Heads of State:

1808-24	Raja Lenggang
1824-26	Raja Kerjan
1826-30	Raja Laboh
1830-61	Raja Radin
1861-69	Raja Ulin
(1869-72	post vacant)
1872-88	Tuanku Antah
1888-1933	Tuanku Mohamed
1933-April 1960	Tuanku Abdul Rahman (Regent: 1957-60 Tuanku Munawir)
April 1960-April 1968	Tuanku Munawir
April 1968-	Tuanku Jaafar Abdul Rahman (Regent 1994-99 Tengku Nadzaruddin)

Chief Ministers:

1948-53	Abdul Malik bin Yusof
1953-59	Shamsuddin bin Nain (1st)
1959-64	Mohamed Said bin Mohamed
1964-69	Shamsuddin bin Nain (2nd)
1969-78	Mansor bin Othman
1978-82	Rais Yatim bin Yatim
April 1982-	Mohamed Isa bin Abdul Samad

PAHANG

Capital: Kuantan

Sultans:

1806-57	Ali
1857-63	Wan Mutahir
1864-1914	Ahmad Muadzam Shah
1914-17	Mahmud Shah II
1917-32	Abdullah Muktasim Billah Shah
June 1932-May 1974	Abubakar Riayatuddin Muadzam Shah

May 1974- Ahmad Shah
(Regent: 1979-84 Tengku Abdulla)

Chief Ministers:

Feb 1948-Feb 1951	Mahmud bin Mat
Feb 1951-Feb 1955	Mohamed ibni al-Marhum Sultan Ahmed (1st)
Feb-June 1955	Abdul Razak bin Hussein
June 1956-Jan 1957	Mohamed ibni al-Marhum Sultan Ahmed (2nd)
Jan 1957-July 1959	Abdullah bin Tok Muda Ibrahim
July 1959-May 1964	Wan Abdul Aziz bin Ungku Abdullah
May 1964-Aug 1972	Yahya bin Mohamed Seh
Sept 1972-Aug 1974	Abdul Aziz bin Ahmad
Sept 1974-July 1978	Mohamed bin Jusoh
July 1978-Nov 1981	Abdul Rahim bin Abubakar
Nov 1981-Aug 1986	Mohamed Najib bin Abdul Razak
Aug 1986-	Mohamed Khalil bin Yaacob

PENANG
Pulau Pinang

Capital: George Town

Heads of State:

Aug 1957-Aug 1967	Uda bin Mohamed (see Selangor)
Aug 1967-Feb 1975	Seyed Sheh bin Syed Abdullah
Feb 1975-May 1981	Sardon bin Jubir
May 1981-May 1989	Awang bin Hassan
May 1989-	Hamdan Shaikh Tahir

Chief Ministers:

June 1959-March 1969	Wong Pow Nee
May 1969-Nov 1990	Lim Chong Eu
Nov 1990-	Koh Tsu Koon

PERAK

Capital: Ipoh

Sultans:

1806-25	Abdul Malik Mansur Shah
1825-31	Abdullah Muadzam Shah
1831-51	Shihabuddin Riayat Shah
1851-57	Abdullah Mohamed Shah I

1857-65	Jafar Muadzam Shah
1865-71	Ali al-Kamil Riayat Shah
1871-74	Ismail Muabidin Shah
1874-77	Abdullah Mohamed Shah II
1877-87	Yusuf Sharifuddin Mufzal Shah
1887-1916	Idris Murshid ul-Azam Shah
1916-18	Abdul Jalil Shah
1918-38	Iskander Shah
1938-48	Abdul Aziz Shah
March 1948-Jan 1963	Yusuf Izzidin Shah
Jan 1963-Jan 1984	Idris al-Mutawakil Allahi Shah
Jan 1984-	Azlan Shah
	(Regent: 1989-94 Raja Nazrin)

Chief Ministers:

Feb 1948-July 1957	Abdul Wahab bin Toh Muda Abdul Aziz
Aug 1957-April 1960	Mohamed Ghazali bin Jawi (1st)
April 1960-May 1964	Shaari bin Shafi
May 1964-March 1970	Ahmad bin Said
March 1970-Sept 1974	Kamaruddin bin Mat Isa
Sept 1974-Sept 1977	Mohamed Ghazali bin Jawi (2nd)
Sept 1977-March 1983	Wan Mohamed bin Wan Teh
March 1983-	Ramli bin Ngali Talib

PERLIS

Capital: Kangar

Rajas:

1843-73	Tuanku Syed Husain
1873-97	Tuanku Syed Ahmad
1897-1905	Tuanku Syed Safi
Dec 1905-43	Tuanku Syed Alwi
(1943-45	Thai rule)
Dec 1945-April 2000	Tuanku Syed Putra
	(Regent: 1960-65 Tunku Sulaiman)
April 2000-	Tuanku Syed Sirajuddin

Chief Ministers:

Feb 1948-Jan 1957	Raja Ahmad bin Raja Endut
Feb-May 1957	Mohamed Razali bin Mohamed Ali Wasi
1-28 May 1957	Mohamed Shamsuddin bin Mohamed Yaakub (acting)
May 1957-Dec 1971	Ahmad bin Mohamed Hashim
Dec 1971-Jan 1981	Jaafar bin Hassan

Jan 1981-March 1986	Ali bin Ahmad
March 1986-April 1995	Abdul Hamid bin Pawanteh
April 1995-	Sahidan Kassim

SABAH

Previous name: North Borneo (until 1963)
Capital: Kota Kinabalu (*f* Jesselton)

Governors:

1881-87	William Treacher
1888-95	Charles Creagh
1895-1900	Leicester Beaufort
1900-01	Hugh Clifford
1901-04	Ernest Birch
1904-12	Edward Gueritz
1912-15	Cecil Parr
1915-22	Aylmer Pearson (1st)
1922-25	William Rycroft
1925-26	Aylmer Pearson (2nd)
1926-29	John Humphreys
1929-33	Arthur Richards
1933-37	Douglas Jardine
1937-42	Charles Smith
(1942-45	Japanese occupation)
1946-49	Edward Twining (see St Lucia)
1949-54	Herbert Hone
1954-60	Roland Turnbull
1960-63	William Goode (see Singapore)

Heads of State:

Sept 1963-Sept 1965	Mustapha bin Harun
Sept 1965-74	Ahmad Raffae bin Omar
1974-July 1975	Mohamed Fuad (*f* Donald Stephens)
July 1975-77	Mohammed Indan bin Kari
1977	Mohamed Hamdan bin Abdallah
Oct 1977-June 1978	Ahmad Koroh
June 1978-Jan 1987	Mohamed Adnan Robert
Jan 1987-Dec 1994	Mohammed Said bin Keruak
Dec 1994-	Sakaran bin Dandai

Chief Ministers:

Sept 1963-Jan 1965	Donald Stephens (later Mohamed Fuad) (1st)

Jan 1965-June 1967	Peter Lo Sun Yin
June 1967-Oct 1975	Mustapha bin Harun
Oct 1975-April 1976	Mohamed Said bin Keruak
April-June 1976	Mohamed Fuad (2nd) († air accident)
June 1976-April 1985	Harris bin Mohamed Salleh (UMNO)
April 1985-March 1994	Joseph Pairin Kitingan (SUP)
March-Dec 1994	Sakaran bin Dandai (UMNO)
Dec 1994-May 1996	Mohamed Salleh Said Keruak (UMNO)
May 1996-Dec 1997	Yong Teck Lee (SPP)
Dec 1997-March 1999	Bernard Dompok (SDP)
March 1999-	Osu Sukam

SDP = Sabah Democratic Party
SPP = Sabah Progress Party
SUP = Sabah United Party

SARAWAK

Capital: Kuching

Rajas:

Sept 1841-June 1868	James Brooke
June 1868-May 1917	Charles Brooke (*b* C.Johnson) (*nephew*)
May 1917-July 1946	Charles Vyner Brooke (*son*)

Governors:

1946-49	Charles Arden-Clarke (see Basutoland)
1949	Duncan Stewart
1949-59	Anthony Abell
1959-63	Alexander Waddell

Heads of State:

Sept 1963-April 1969	Openg bin Sapi'ee
April 1969-April 1973	Bujang bin Othman
April 1973-April 1977	Louis Bereng bin Anyut
April 1977-April 1981	Mohamed Salahuddin
April 1981-April 1985	Abdul Rahman bin Ya'akob
April 1985-	Ahmed Mohamed Noor

Chief Ministers:

Sept 1963-June 1966	Stephen Ningkan
June 1966-July 1970	Tawa Sli
July 1970-March 1981	Abdul Rahman bin Ya'acob
March 1981-	Abdul Taib Mahmood (*nephew*)

SELANGOR

Capital: Kuala Lumpur (until 1977), Shah Alam (since 1977)

Sultans:

1778-1826	Ibrahim Shah
1826-57	Mohamed Shah
(1857-59	Interregnum)
1859-98	Abdul Samad Shah
1898-April 1938	Suleiman Shah
April 1938-42	Hisamuddin Alam Shah (1st)
1942-45	Musa Ghiyatuddin Riayat Shah
1945-Sept 1960	Hisamuddin Alam Shah (2nd)
	(Regent: April-Sept 1960 Salahuddin Abdul Aziz Shah)
Sept 1960-	Salahuddin Abdul Aziz Shah
	(Regent: 1999- Idris Shah)

Chief Ministers:

1948-July 1949	Hamzah bin Abdullah
July 1949-March 1953	Uda bin Mohamed (1st)
March 1953-Nov 1954	Osman bin Mohamed
Nov 1954-Aug 1955	Uda bin Mohamed (2nd)
Sept 1955-56	Abdul Aziz bin Abdul Majid
1957-58	Mohamed Ismail bin Abdul Latiff
1958-59	Abdul Jamil bin Rais
June 1959-March 1964	Abu Bakar bin Baginda
March 1964-March 1976	Harun bin Idris
March 1976-May 1982	Hormat bin Rafei (acting March-April 1976)
May 1982-Aug 1986	Ahmad Razali bin Mohamed Ali
Aug 1986-April 1997	Mohamed bin Mohamed Taib
May 1997-	Abu Hassan Omar

TRENGGANU

Capital: Kuala Trengganu

Sultans:

1808-27	Ahmad Shah
1827-31	Abdul Rahman Shah
1831	Daud Shah
1831-36	Mansur Shah II
1836-76	Omar Shah
1876-81	Ahmad Muadzam Shah
1881-1918	Zainal Abdin Muadzam Shah

1918-20	Mohamed Shah II
1920-43	Suleiman Badrul-Alam Shah
(1943-45	Thai rule)
Dec 1945-Sept 1979	Ismail Nasiruddin Shah
	(Regent: 1965-70 Mahmud)
Sept 1979-May 1998	Mahmud
May 1998-	Mirzan Zainal Abidin (*son*)

Chief Ministers:

1949-59	Kamruddin bin Idris
1959-64	Ibrahim Fikri bin Mohamed
1964-68	Mohamed Daud bin Abdul Samad
1968-70	Nik Hassan bin Nik Abdul Rahman
1970-74	Mahmud bin Suleiman
1974-Dec 1999	Wan Mokhtar bin Ahmad
Dec 1999-	Abdul Hadi Awang

MALDIVES

Official name: Republic of Maldives, Divehi Jumhuriya   (Divehi)
Previous name: Sultanate of the Maldives until 1953 & 1954-68
Independence date: 26 July 1965
Capital: Malé

From 1518 until 1528 the Maldives were under the control of the Portuguese, and in 1645 they came under the protection of the Dutch in Ceylon. When the British took over Ceylon in 1795 this protecting role passed to them, and was formalized in 1887. The Maldives became a republic in 1953, but reverted to a sultanate a year later. In 1965 full independence was granted, and in 1968 a second republic was declared.

Sultans (from 1799):

1799-1835	Mohammed Muin-ud-din I
1835-82	Mohammed Imad-ud-din IV
1882-86	Ibrahim Nur-ud-din (1st)
1886-88	Mohammed Muin-ud-din II
1888-92	Ibrahim Nur-ud-din (2nd)
1892-93	Mohammed Imad-ud-din V
1893	Mohammed Shams-ud-din II
1893-1903	Mohammed Imad-ud-din VI
1903-34	Mohammed Shams-ud-din III
Feb 1935-45	Hassan Nur-ud-din Iskander II
1945-Jan 1953	Abdul Majid Didi

Presidents:

Jan-Sept 1953	Amin Didi (deposed)
Sept 1953-March 1954	Ibrahim Ali Didi/Ibrahim Mohammed Didi

Sultan:

March 1954-Nov 1968	Mohammed Farid Didi

Presidents:

Nov 1968-Nov 1978	Ibrahim Nasir
Nov 1978-	Maumon Gayoom

Prime Ministers:

1883-1925	Ibrahim Didi

1926-32	Abdul Majid Didi
1932-Jan 1953	Mohammed Farid Didi
Jan-Sept 1953	Amin Didi (deposed)
Sept 1953-March 1954	Ibrahim Mohammed Didi (co-PM)
Sept 1953-Dec 1957	Ibrahim Ali Didi (co-PM 1953-54)
Dec 1957-Nov 1968	Ibrahim Nasir
(Nov 1968-Sept 1972	post abolished)
Sept 1972-March 1975	Ahmed Zaki
(March 1975	post abolished)

MALI

Official name: Republic of Mali, République du Mali
Previous name: French Soudan until 1960
Independence date: 22 September 1960
Capital: Bamako

French Soudan was proclaimed a French colony in 1893 and became part of French West Africa. In 1946 the Soudan became a French Overseas Territory, and self-government was granted in 1958. From 1959 until 1960 it was part of the Federation of Mali, together with Senegal. With the break-up of the federation the Soudan declared itself independent, taking the name Mali. The military seized power in 1968, and later ruled through a one-party system. A second coup in 1991 paved the way for multi-party elections in 1992.

Lieutenant-Governors:

1904-08	Amédée-Guillaume Merlaud-Ponty
1908-15	Marie-François Clozel
Aug 1916-Feb 1918	Raphaël Antonetti (see Senegal)
Feb 1918-Aug 1919	Auguste Brunet
Aug 1919-24	Marcel Olivier
1924-31	Jean-Henri Terrason de Fougères
June 1931-Nov 1935	Louis Fousset
Nov 1935-Nov 1936	Matthieu-Maurice Alfassa (see Martinique)
Nov 1936-37	Ferdinand Rougier

Governors:

1937-38	Ferdinand Rougier
March 1938-Nov 1940	Jean-Hyacinthe Desanti
Nov 1940-April 1942	Jean Rapenne
April 1942-May 1946	Auguste Calvel
May 1946-April 1952	Edmond-Jean Louveau
April-July 1952	Camille-Victor Bailly (see Senegal)
July 1952-Feb 1953	Salvador-Jean Etcheber
Feb-Dec 1953	Albert-Jean Mouragues
Dec 1953-Nov 1956	Lucien-Eugène Geay (see Senegal)
Nov 1956-Dec 1958	Henri Gipoulon

High Commissioner:

Jan 1959-Sept 1960	Jean-Charles Sicurani

Presidents:

Sept 1960-Nov 1968	Modibo Keita (SU) (deposed)
Nov 1968-March 1991	Moussa Traoré (DUMP) (deposed)
March 1991-June 1992	Amadou Toumani Touré
June 1992-	Alpha Konaré (DAM)

Prime Ministers:

July 1958-April 1959	Jean-Marie Koné
April 1959-Nov 1968	Modibo Keita (SU)
Nov 1968-Sept 1969	Yoro Diakité
Sept 1969-June 1986	Moussa Traoré
June 1986-June 1988	Mamadou Dembelé
(June 1988-April 1991	post abolished)
April 1991-June 1992	Soumana Sacko
June 1992-April 1993	Younoussi Touré
April 1993-Feb 1994	Abdoulaye Sékou Sow
Feb 1994-Feb 2000	Ibrahim Keita
Feb 2000-	Mande Sidibe

DAM = Democratic Alliance of Mali (ADEMA)
DUMP = Democratic Union of the Malian People (sole party 1979-91)
SU = Soudanese Union

MALTA

Official name: Republic of Malta, Repubblika ta Malta
Previous name: Dominion of Malta 1964-74
Independence date: 22 September 1964
Capital: Valletta

The island of Malta was handed over to the Knights of St John in 1530. In 1798 they were dispersed by Napoleon and in 1802 the islanders requested British protection. Malta was formally annexed in 1814. In 1921 self-government was granted, but the constitution was suspended three times (1930-32, 1933-47 and 1958-62). In 1964 Malta became independent, assuming republican status in 1974.

Governors:

1899-1903	Baron Grenfell (Francis Grenfell)
1903-07	Charles Clarke
1907-09	Henry Grant
1909-15	Henry Rundle
1915-19	Baron Methuen (Paul Methuen)
1919-24	Baron Plumer (Herbert Plumer)
1924-27	Walter Congreve
1927-31	John Du Cane
1931-36	David Campbell
1936-40	Charles Bonham-Carter
1940-42	William Dobbie
1942-44	Viscount Gort (John Vereker) (see Gibraltar)
1944-46	Edmond Screiber
1946-49	Francis Douglas
1949-54	Gerald Creasy (see Gold Coast)
1954-59	Robert Laycock
1959-62	Guy Grantham
1962-64	Maurice Dorman (see Sierra Leone)

Governors-General:

Represented monarch who was concurrently British monarch

Sept 1964-June 1971	Maurice Dorman
June 1971-Dec 1974	Anthony Mamo

Presidents:

Dec 1974-Dec 1976	Anthony Mamo
Dec 1976-Dec 1981	Anton Buttigieg

Dec 1981-Feb 1982   Albert Hyzler   (acting)
Feb 1982-Feb 1987   Agatha Barbara
Feb 1987-April 1989   Paul Xuereb   (acting)
April 1989-April 1994   Censu   (Vincent) Tabone
April 1994-April 1999   Ugo Mifsud Bonnici
April 1999-   Guido de Marco

Prime Ministers:

Nov 1921-Nov 1923   Joseph Howard
Nov 1923-Sept 1924   Francesco Buhagiar
Sept 1924-Aug 1927   Ugo Mifsud   (1st) (NP)
Aug 1927-April 1930   Lord Strickland   (Gerald Strickland) (CP)
(April 1930-Oct 1932   post abolished)
Oct 1932-Nov 1933   Ugo Mifsud   (2nd) (NP)
(Nov 1933-Nov 1947   post abolished)
Nov 1947-Sept 1950   Paul Boffa   (LP)
Sept-Dec 1950   Enrico Mizzi   (NP) (†)
Dec 1950-March 1955   George Borg Olivier   (1st) (NP)
March 1955-April 1958   Dominic Mintoff   (1st) (LP)
(April 1958-March 1962   post abolished)
March 1962-April 1971   George Borg Olivier   (2nd) (NP)
April 1971-Dec 1984   Dominic Mintoff   (2nd) (LP)
Dec 1984-May 1987   Carmelo Mifsud-Bonnici   (LP)
May 1987-Oct 1996   Edward Fenech-Adami   (1st) (NP)
Oct 1996-Sept 1998   Alfred Sant   (LP)
Sept 1998-   Edward Fenech-Adami   (2nd) (NP)

CP = Constitutional Party
LP = Labour Party
NP = National Party

MARSHALL ISLANDS

Official name: Republic of the Marshall Islands
Independence date: 22 December 1990
Capital: Dalap-Uliga-Darrit (on Majuro)

The Marshall Islands became a German protectorate in 1886. In 1914 they were occupied by Japan, and after World War I they became a League of Nations trusteeship territory under Japanese administration. They were captured by Allied forces in 1944, and in 1947 became part of the United Nations Trust Territory of the Pacific under US administration. In 1979 they were granted self-government and signed a Compact of Free Association with the US in October 1986. The trusteeship was ended in 1990.

Presidents:

May 1979-Dec 1996	Amata Kabua	(†)
Dec 1996-Jan 1997	Kunio Lemari	(acting)
Jan 1997-Jan 2000	Imata Kabua	*(cousin of A.Kabua)*
Jan 2000-	Kessai Note	

MAURITANIA

Official name: Arab and African Islamic Republic of Mauritania, République Islamique Arabe et Africaine de Mauritanie

Previous name: Islamic Republic of Mauritania 1958-91

Independence date: 28 November 1960

Capital: Nouakchott

A French protectorate was proclaimed in Mauritania in 1903 and in 1920 the territory became a colony, forming part of French West Africa. In 1946 its status was changed to that of an overseas territory. Mauritania was granted self-government in 1958, and in 1960 it became an independent republic.

Governors:

1920-27	Nicolas Gaden
1928-29	Alphonse Choteau
1929-31	René Chazal
1931-34	Gabriel-Omer Descemet
1934-35	Jean-Victor Chazelas
1935-36	Jules-Marcel de Coppet (see French Somaliland)
1936-42	Jean-Louis Beyries
1942-44	Jean Chalvet
1944-46	Christian Laigret
1947-48	Lucien-Eugène Geay
1948-49	Henri de Mauduit
1949-50	Edouard Terrac (see French Guinea)
1950-51	Jacques Rogue (see Chad)
1951-54	Pierre Messmer
1954-55	Albert-Jean Mouragues (1st) (see French Soudan)
1955-56	Jean-Paul Parisot
1956-58	Albert-Jean Mouragues (2nd)

High Commissioner:

1959-60	Pierre Anthonioz (see New Hebrides)

Presidents:

Nov 1960-July 1978	Moktar Ould Daddah (MPP) (deposed)
July 1978-June 1979	Mustapha Ould Salek
June 1979-Jan 1980	Mahmed Ould Louly
Jan 1980-Dec 1984	Mohammed Khouna Ould Haydalla (deposed)
Dec 1984-	Moaouya Ould Sidi Ahmed Taya (RDSP)

Prime Ministers:

July 1958-July 1978	Moktar Ould Daddah (PRM,MPP) (deposed)
July 1978-April 1979	Mustapha Ould Salek
April-May 1979	Ahmed Ould Bousseif († air accident)
28-31 May 1979	Ahmed Ould Sidi (acting)
May 1979-Dec 1980	Mohammed Khouna Ould Haydalla (1st)
Dec 1980-April 1981	Sidi Ahmed Ould Bneijara
April 1981-March 1984	Moaouya Ould Sidi Ahmed Taya (1st)
March-Dec 1984	Mohammed Khouna Ould Haydalla (2nd)
Dec 1984-April 1992	Moaouya Ould Sidi Ahmed Taya (2nd)
April 1992-Jan 1996	Sidi Mohammed Ould Boubaker
Jan 1996-Dec 1997	Cheikh el-Avia Ould Mohammed Khouna (1st)
Dec 1997-Nov 1998	Mohammed Lemine Ould Guig
Nov 1998-	Cheikh el-Avia Ould Mohammed Khouna (2nd)

MPP = Mauritanian People's Party (*f* PRM) (sole legal party 1960-78)
PRM = Party of Mauritanian Regrouping
RDSP = Republican Democratic and Social Party

MAURITIUS

Official name: Republic of Mauritius
Previous name: Mauritius until 1992
Independence date: 12 March 1968
Capital: Port Louis

The island of Mauritius was settled by the Dutch in 1598, but abandoned in 1710. The French occupied the island from 1715 until 1810, when it became British. A measure of self-government was granted by Britain in 1961, followed by full self-government in 1964 and independence in 1968. In 1992 Mauritius became a republic.

Governors:

1897-1903	Charles Bruce
1904-11	Cavendish Boyle
1911-16	John Chancellor
1916-25	Henry Bell
1925-30	Herbert Read
1930-37	Wilfred Jackson
1937-42	Bede Clifford (see Bahamas)
1942-49	Henry Mackenzie-Kennedy
1949-53	Hilary Blood (see Barbados)
1953-59	Robert Scott
1959-62	Colville Deverell
1962-68	John Rennie

Governors-General:
Represented monarch who was concurrently British monarch

March-Sept 1968	John Rennie
Sept 1968-Dec 1972	A.Leonard Williams (†)
Dec 1972-Oct 1977	Abdul Rahman Osman (acting Dec 1972-March 1973)
Oct 1977-March 1978	Henry Garrioch (acting)
March 1978-Dec 1983	Dayendranath Burrenchobay (acting March 1978-Oct 1979)
Dec 1983-Dec 1985	Seewoosagur Ramgoolam (†)
Dec 1985-Jan 1986	Cassam Moolam (acting)
Jan 1986-March 1992	Veersamy Ringadoo

Presidents:

March-June 1992	Veersamy Ringadoo
June 1992-	Cassam Uteem

Chief Minister:

Sept 1961-March 1964   Seewoosagur Ramgoolam   (LP)

Prime Ministers:

March 1964-June 1982   Seewoosagur Ramgoolam   (LP)
June 1982-Dec 1995   Aneerood Jugnauth   (MMM,MSM)
Dec 1995-   Navinchandra Ramgoolam   (*son of S.Ramgoolam*) (LP)

LP = Labour Party
MMM = Mauritius Militant Movement
MSM = Mauritius Socialist Movement (split from MMM)

MEXICO

Official name: United Mexican States, Estados Unidos Mexicanos
Previous name: Mexican Empire 1822-23, 1864-67
Independence date: 16 September 1810
Capital: Mexico City (Ciudad de México)

The Aztec empire of Mexico, founded in the 14th century, was overthrown by Spain in 1521, and Mexico remained a Spanish colony until 1810, when independence was declared. Independence was only completely achieved with military victory in 1821. During the 19th century the country suffered from considerable instability with revolutions and frequent changes of leaders; there were two brief periods when Mexico had an Imperial form of government. The long rule of President Díaz was ended by the revolution of 1911, leading to the present constitution. From the late 1920s until the 1990s the government was totally dominated by the Institutional Revolutionary Party, but democratic reforms allowed other parties freer access to political institutions.

President:

Aug 1821-May 1822   Augustin de Iturbide

Emperor:

May 1822-March 1823   Augustin   (*b* A.de Iturbide) (abdicated, assassinated 1824)

Presidents:

March 1823-Jan 1828	Manuel Guadelupe Victoria (*b* Félix Fernández)
Jan-Dec 1828	Manuel Gómez Pedraza (1st)
Dec 1828-June 1829	Vicente Guerrero (deposed, executed 1831)
June-Dec 1829	José de Bocanegra (acting)
Jan 1830-Aug 1832	Anastasio Bustamente (1st)
Aug-Dec 1832	Melchor Múzquiz (acting)
Dec 1832-April 1833	Manuel Gómez Pedraza (2nd)
April 1833-Jan 1835	Antonio López de Santa Anna (acting April 1833-April 1834) (1st)
Jan 1835-Feb 1836	Miguel de Barraga
Feb 1836-April 1837	José Caro
April 1837-March 1839	Anastasio Bustamente (2nd)
March-July 1839	Antonio López de Santa Anna (2nd)
July 1839-July 1840	Anastasio Bustamente (3rd)
July 1840-Sept 1841	Nicolás Bravo (acting)
Sept 1841	Xavier Echeverría (acting)
Sept-Oct 1841	Valentin Gómez Farías (acting) (1st)

Oct 1841-March 1844	Antonio López de Santa Anna (3rd)
March-Sept 1844	José Herrera (1st)
Sept-Dec 1844	Valentín Canalizo (2nd)
Jan-Dec 1845	José Herrera (2nd)
Jan 1846	Mariano Paredes y Arrillaga (acting)
Jan-July 1846	José de Salas
Aug 1846	Antonio López de Santa Anna (4th)
Aug 1846	Valentin Gómez Farías (acting) (2nd)
Aug 1846-Sept 1847	Antonio López de Santa Anna (5th)
Sept 1847-Jan 1848	Pedro Anaya (acting)
Jan-June 1848	Manuel de la Peña y Peña (acting)
June 1848-June 1851	José Herrera (3rd)
June 1851-Jan 1853	Mariano Arista
Jan-Feb 1853	Juan Bautista Ceballos (acting)
Feb-March 1853	Manuel Lombardini (acting)
March 1853-Aug 1855	Antonio López de Santa Anna (acting March-April 1853) (6th)
Aug-Sept 1855	Martin Carrera
Sept-Oct 1855	Romulo Díaz de la Vega
Oct-Dec 1855	Juan Alvarez
Dec 1855-Dec 1857	Ignacio Comonfort
Dec 1857-Jan 1858	Benito Juárez (acting)
Jan 1858-Feb 1859	Félix Zuloaga
Feb-Dec 1859	Miguel Miramón (deposed)
Dec 1859-April 1864	Benito Juárez (1st) (deposed)

Emperor:

April 1864-May 1867	Maximilian (*brother of Franz Josef of Austria*) (deposed, executed)

Presidents:

May 1867-July 1872	Benito Juárez (2nd) (†)
July 1872-Nov 1876	Sebastian Lerdo de Tejada (acting July-Sept 1872)
Nov 1876-Feb 1877	Juan Méndez (acting)
Feb 1877-Nov 1880	Porfirio Díaz (1st)
Nov 1880-Nov 1884	Manuel González
Nov 1884-May 1911	Porfirio Díaz (2nd) (deposed)
May-Nov 1911	Francisco de la Barra (acting)
Nov 1911-Feb 1913	Francisco Indalecio Madero († assassinated)
18 Feb 1913	Pedro Lascurain
Feb 1913-July 1914	Victoriano Huerta
July-Aug 1914	Francisco Carbajal (acting)
Aug-Nov 1914	Venustiano Carranza (1st)
Nov 1914-April 1915	Eulalio Gutiérrez
April 1915-May 1920	Venustiano Carranza (2nd) († assassinated)
May-Dec 1920	Adolfo de la Huerta (acting)

Dec 1920-Nov 1924	Alvaro Obregón
Dec 1924-Nov 1928	Plutarco Calles
(1928	Alvaro Obregón, President-elect, assassinated)
Dec 1928-Feb 1930	Emilio Portes Gil (acting)
Feb 1930-Sept 1932	Pascual Ortiz Rubio (NRP)
Sept 1932-Dec 1934	Abelardo Rodríguez (acting) (NRP)
Dec 1934-Dec 1940	Lazaro Cárdenas (NRP,MRP)
Dec 1940-Dec 1946	Manuel Avila Camacho (MRP)
Dec 1946-Dec 1952	Miguel Alemán Valdés (IRP)
Dec 1952-Dec 1958	Adolfo Ruiz Cortines (IRP)
Dec 1958-Dec 1964	Adolfo López Mateos (IRP)
Dec 1964-Dec 1970	Gustavo Díaz Ordaz (see Puebla) (IRP)
Dec 1970-Dec 1976	Luis Echeverría Alvarez (IRP)
Dec 1976-Dec 1982	José López Portillo y Pacheco (IRP)
Dec 1982-Dec 1988	Miguel de la Madrid Hurtado (IRP)
Dec 1988-Dec 1994	Carlos Salinas de Gortari (IRP)
Dec 1994-	Ernesto Zedillo Ponce de León (IRP)

NRP = National Revolutionary Party
MRP = Mexican Revolutionary Party (*f* NRP)
IRP = Institutional Revolutionary Party (*f* MRP)

Presidents of Government

June 1864-Oct 1866	José de Lacunza
Oct 1866-March 1867	Teodosro Lares
March-May 1867	Santiago Vidaurri
(May 1867-	post abolished)

Former independent state

TENOCHTITLAN (AZTEC EMPIRE)

Emperors:

1345-c1372	Tenoch
c1372-91	Acamapichtli
1391-1415	Huitzilhuitl (*son*)
1415-26	Chimalpopoca (*son*) (executed 1428)
1426-40	Itzcóatl (*son*)
1440-68	Moctezuma I Ilhuicamina (*son of Huitzilhuitl*)
1468-81	Axayácatl (*grandson of Itzcóatl*)
1481-86	Tizoc (*brother*) (murdered ?)
1486-1502	Anhuitzotl (*brother*)
1502-June 1520	Moctezuma II Xocoyotzin (*brother*) (deposed)

June-Sept 1520	Cuitáhuac (*brother*)
Sept 1520-Aug 1521	Cuauhtémoc (*son of Anhuitzotl*) (deposed, executed)
1525-26	Tlactozin (Diego Velasquez) (*great-great-grandson of Huitzilhuitl*) (installed by Spanish)
(1526-1821	Spanish rule)

States

Governors from the 1930s are listed. Unless otherwise stated, they belong to the IRP.

AGUASCALIENTES

Capital: Aguascalientes

Governors:

Dec 1932-Nov 1936	Enrique Osornio Camarena
Dec 1936-Nov 1940	Juan Alvarado Lavallade
Dec 1940-Nov 1944	Alberto del Valle
Dec 1944-Nov 1950	Jesús Rodríguez Flores
Dec 1950-July 1953	Edmundo Games Orozco (†)
July-Sept 1953	Joaquín Cruz Ramirez (acting)
Sept 1953-Nov 1956	Benito Palomino Dena
Dec 1956-Nov 1962	Luis Ortega Douglas
Dec 1962-Nov 1968	Enrique Olivares Santana
Dec 1968-Nov 1974	Francisco Guel Jiménez
Dec 1974-Nov 1980	J.Refugio Esparza Reyes
Dec 1980-Nov 1986	Rodolfo Landeros Gallegos
Dec 1986-Nov 1992	Miguel Barberena Vega
Dec 1992-Nov 1998	Otto Granados Roldán
Dec 1998-	Felipe González

BAJA CALIFORNIA NORTE

Statehood: 21 November 1952
Capital: Mexicali

Governors:

Oct 1947-Nov 1953	Alfonso García González
Dec 1953-Nov 1959	Braulio Maldonaldo Sánchez
Dec 1959-Dec 1964	Eligio Esquivel Méndez (†)
Dec 1964-Oct 1965	Gustavo Aubanel Vallejo
Nov 1965-Oct 1971	Raúl Sánchez Díaz
Nov 1971-Nov 1977	Milton Castellanos Gerardo
Dec 1977-Oct 1983	Roberto de la Madrid Romandia

Nov 1983-Jan 1989	Xicotencatl Leyra Mortera
Jan-Oct 1989	Oscar Baylon Chacón (acting)
Nov 1989-Oct 1995	Ernesto Ruffo Appel (NAP)
Nov 1995-Oct 1998	Héctor Terán Terán (NAP) (†)
Oct 1998-	Alejandro González Alocer

NAP = National Action Party

BAJA CALIFORNIA SUR

Statehood: 1975
Capital: La Paz

Governors:

Feb 1975-Feb 1981	Angel Mendoza Aramburu
Feb 1981-Feb 1987	Alberto Alvaredo Aramburu
Feb 1987-Feb 1993	Víctor Liceaga Ruibal
Feb 1993-Feb 1999	Guillermo Mercado Romero
Feb 1999-	Leonel Cota Montaño (PDR)

PDR = Party of the Democratic Revolution

CAMPECHE

Statehood: 1857
Capital: Campeche

Governors:

Sept 1931-Sept 1935	Benjamin Romero Esquivel
Sept 1935-Sept 1939	Eduardo Mena Cordova
Sept 1939-Sept 1943	Héctor Pérez Martínez
Sept 1943-Sept 1949	Eduardo Lavalle Urbina
Sept 1949-Sept 1955	Manuel López Hernández
Sept 1955-Sept 1961	Alberto Trueba Urbina
Sept 1961-Sept 1967	José Ortiz Avila
Sept 1967-March 1973	Carlos Sansores Pérez
March-Sept 1973	Carlos Pérez Camara
Sept 1973-Sept 1979	Rafael Rodríguez Barrera
Sept 1979-Sept 1985	Eugenio Echeverría Castellot
Sept 1985-Sept 1991	Abelardo Carillo Zavala
Sept 1991-Sept 1997	Salomon Aznar García
Sept 1997-	José González Curi

CHIAPAS

Statehood: 1824
Capital: Tuxtla Gutiérrez

Governors:

1932-Sept 1936	Victorio Grajales Reynosa
Sept-Dec 1936	Amador Coutino Coss
Dec 1936-Nov 1940	Efraín Gutiérrez Rincon
Dec 1940-Nov 1944	Rafael Gamboa
Dec 1944-Jan 1947	Juan Esponda
Jan 1947-Nov 1948	César Lara Ramos
Dec 1948-Nov 1952	Francisco Grajales
Dec 1952-Nov 1958	Efraín Aranda Osorio
Dec 1958-Nov 1964	Samuel León Brindis
Dec 1964-Nov 1970	José Castillo Tielemans
Dec 1970-Nov 1976	Manuel Velasco Suárez
Dec 1976-Dec 1977	Jorge de la Vega Dominguez
Dec 1977-Jan 1980	Salomon González Blanco
Jan 1980-Nov 1982	Juan Sabines Gutiérrez
Dec 1982	Gustavo Armendariz Ruiz
Dec 1982-Dec 1988	Absalon Castellanos Dominguez
Dec 1988-Jan 1993	José Patrocinio González Garrido
Jan 1993-Jan 1994	Elmar Seltzer Marseille
Jan-Dec 1994	Javier López
Dec 1994-Feb 1995	Eduardo Robledo Rincon
Feb 1995-Jan 1998	Julio Ruiz Ferro
Jan 1998-Nov 1999	Roberto Albores Guillén
Nov 1999-	Enrique Martínez

CHIHUAHUA

Statehood: 1823
Capital: Chihuahua

Governors:

1932-Oct 1936	Rodrigo Quevedo Moreno
Oct 1936-39	Gustavo Talamantes
1939-Oct 1940	Eugenio Prado Proano
Oct 1940-Oct 1944	Alfredo Chaves
Oct 1944-Oct 1950	Fernando Folgio Miramontes
Oct 1950-Aug 1955	Oscar Soto Maynes
Aug-Oct 1955	Jesús Lozoya Solis
Oct 1955-Oct 1962	Teofilo Borunda Ortiz

Oct 1962-Oct 1968	Praxedes Giner Durán
Oct 1968-Oct 1974	Oscar Flores Sánchez
Oct 1974-Oct 1980	Manuel Aguirre Samaniego
Oct 1980-Sept 1985	Oscar Ornelas Kuchle
Sept 1985-Oct 1986	Saul González Herrera
Oct 1986-Oct 1992	Fernando Baeza Meléndez
Oct 1992-Oct 1998	Francisco Barrio Terrazas (NAP)
Oct 1998-	Patricio Martínez

COAHUILA

Statehood: 1868
Capital: Saltillo

Governors:

Dec 1933-Nov 1937	Jesús Valdéz Sánchez
Dec 1937-Nov 1941	Pedro Rodríguez Triana
15-30 Nov 1941	Gabriel Cevera
Dec 1941-Nov 1945	Benecio López Padilla
Dec 1945-July 1947	Ignacio Cepeda Dávila († suicide)
July 1947-March 1948	Vicente Valerio
March-June 1948	Paz Faz Riza
June 1948-Nov 1951	Raúl López Sánchez
Dec 1951-Nov 1957	Ramón Cepeda Flores
Dec 1957-Nov 1963	Raúl Madero González
Dec 1963-Nov 1969	Braulio Madero González
Dec 1969-Nov 1975	Eulalio Gutiérrez Treviño
Dec 1975-Nov 1981	Oscar Flores Tapia
Dec 1981-Nov 1987	José de la Fuente Rodríguez
Dec 1987-Nov 1993	Eliseo Mendoza Berrueto
Nov 1993-Nov 1999	Rogelio Montemayor Seguy
Nov 1999-	Enrique Martínez

COLIMA

Capital: Colima

Governors:

Nov 1931-Aug 1935	Salvador Saucedo
Aug-Nov 1935	José Campero
Nov 1935-Oct 1939	Miguel Santana
Nov 1939-Oct 1943	Pedro Torres Ortiz
Nov 1943-Oct 1949	Manuel Gudino Díaz
Nov 1949-Oct 1955	Jesús González Lugo
Nov 1955-Oct 1961	Rodolfo Chavez Carrillo

Nov 1961-Oct 1967	Francisco Velasco Curiel
Nov 1967-Oct 1973	Pablo Silva García
Nov-Dec 1973	Leonel Ramirez García
Jan 1974-Dec 1979	Arturo Noriega Pizano
Jan 1980-Dec 1985	Griselda Alvarez Ponce de León
Jan 1986-Dec 1991	Elías Zamora Verduzio
Jan 1992-Dec 1997	Carlos de la Madrid Virgen
Jan 1998-	Fernando Morena Peña

DURANGO

Statehood: 1863
Capital: Victoria de Durango

Governors:

Sept 1932-Dec 1935	Carlos Real
Jan-Aug 1936	Severino Ceniceros
Aug 1936-40	Enrique Calderón Rodríguez
1940-Sept 1944	Elpidio Velazquez Perdomo
Sept 1944-April 1947	Blas Corral Martínez (†)
April-Sept 1947	Francisco Celis
Sept 1947-Sept 1950	José Ramón Valdes
Sept 1950-Sept 1956	Enrique Torres Sánchez
Sept 1956-July 1962	Francisco González de la Vega
July-Sept 1962	Rafael Hernández Piedra
Sept 1962-Aug 1966	Enrique Dupre Ceniceros
Aug 1966-Sept 1968	Angel Rodríguez Solorzano
Sept 1968-Sept 1974	Alejandro Páez Urquidi
Sept 1974-Dec 1979	Héctor Mayagoitia Dominguez
Dec 1979-Sept 1980	Salvador Gamiz Fernández
Sept 1980-Sept 1986	Armando Castillo Franco
Sept 1986-Sept 1992	José Ramirez Guerrero
Sept 1992-Sept 1998	Maximiliano Silerio Esparza
Sept 1998-	Angel Guerrero Mier

GUANAJUATO

Statehood: 1824
Capital: Guanajuato

Governors:

June-Sept 1932	José Reynoso
Sept 1932-Sept 1935	Melchor Ortega
Sept-Dec 1935	J.Jesús Yañez Maya

Dec 1935-April 1937	Enrique Fernández Martínez (1st)
April 1937-April 1938	Luis Rodríguez
April 1938-Sept 1939	Rafael Rangel
Sept 1939-Sept 1943	Enrique Fernández Martínez (2nd)
Sept 1943-Jan 1946	Ernesto Hidalgo
8-10 Jan 1946	Daniel Velasco
Jan 1946-Sept 1947	Niceforo Guerrero Mendoza
Sept 1947-Oct 1948	J.Jesús Castorena
Oct 1948-Sept 1949	Luis Díaz Infante
Sept 1949-Sept 1955	José Aguilar y Maya
Sept 1955-Sept 1961	Jesús Rodríguez Gaona
Sept 1961-Sept 1967	Juan Torres Landa
Sept 1967-Sept 1973	Manuel Moreno
Sept 1973-Sept 1979	Luis Ducoing Gamba
Sept 1979-84	Enrique Velasco Ibarra
1984-Sept 1985	Agustín Tellez Cruces
Sept 1985-Sept 1991	Rafael Corrales Ayala
(1991	Ramón Aguirre - Governor-elect; did not assume office)
Sept 1991-June 1995	Carlos Medina Plasencia (NAP)
June 1995-Aug 1999	Vicente Fox Quesada (NAP)
Aug 1999-	Ramón Martín Huerta

GUERRERO

Statehood: 1849
Capital: Chilpacingo

Governors:

1929-33	Gabriel Guevara
March 1933-Nov 1935	José Lugo
Nov 1935-March 1937	Alberto Berber
April 1937-Feb 1941	Carlos Carraco Cardoso
Feb-June 1941	Rafael Catalan Calvo
June 1941-March 1945	Gabriel Leyva Mancilla
April 1945-March 1951	Alejandro Gómez Maganda
April 1951-May 1954	Dario Arrieta
May 1954-March 1957	Raúl Caballero Aburto
April 1957-Jan 1961	Arturo Martínez Adame
Jan 1961-March 1963	Raimundo Abarca Alarcon
April 1963-Jan 1969	Caritino Maldonado Pérez (†)
Jan 1969-March 1971	Roberto Rodríguez Mercado
April 1971-Jan 1975	Israel Nogueda Otero
Feb-April 1975	Javier Olea Muñoz
April 1975-March 1981	Rubén Figueroa Figueroa

April 1981-March 1987	Alejandro Cervantes Delgado
April 1987-Feb 1993	José Ruiz Massieu (assassinated 1994)
Feb 1993-March 1996	Rubén Figueroa Alcocer (*son of R.Figueroa Figueroa*)
March 1996-April 1999	Angel Aguirre Rivero
April 1999-	René Juárez Cisneros

HIDALGO

Statehood: 1869
Capital: Pachuca de Soto

Governors:

1929-33	Bartolomé Vargas Lugo
1933-37	Ernesto Viveros
1937-40	Javier Rojo Gómez
1940-41	Ofilio Villegas
1941-45	José Lugo Guerrero
1945-March 1951	Vicente Aguirre
April 1951-March 1957	Quintin Rueda Villagran
April 1957-Dec 1958	Alfonso Corona del Rosal
Dec 1958-March 1963	Oswaldo Cravioto Cisneros
April 1963-March 1969	Carlos Ramirez Guerrero
April 1969-Dec 1970	Manuel Sánchez Vite (1st)
Dec 1970-May 1972	Donaciano Serna
May 1972-March 1975	Manuel Sánchez Vite (2nd)
1-29 April 1975	Otoniel Miranda Andrade
May-Aug 1975	Raúl Lozano Ramirez
Aug 1975-Dec 1976	Jorge Rojo Lugo (1st)
Dec 1976-June 1978	José Suárez Molina
June 1978-March 1981	Jorge Rojo Lugo (2nd)
April 1981-March 1987	Guillermo Rossell de la Lama
April 1987-March 1993	Adolfo Lugo Verduzco
April 1993-March 1999	Jesús Murillo Karam
March 1999-	Miguel Nuñez

JALISCO

Capital: Guadalajara

Governors:

April 1932-Feb 1935	Sebastian Allende
March 1935-39	Everardo Topete
1939-43	Silvano Barba González
1943-Feb 1947	Marcelina García Barragan

Feb 1947-Nov 1949   Saturnino Coronado
Nov 1949-Feb 1953   Carlos Guzmán
March 1953-Feb 1959   Agustín Yañez
March 1959-Dec 1964   Juan Gil Preciado
Dec 1964-Feb 1965   José de Jesús Liman
March 1965-Feb 1971   Francisco Medina Asencio
March 1971-Feb 1977   Alberto Orozco Romero
March 1977-Feb 1983   Flavio Romero de Velasco
March 1983-Feb 1989   Enrique Alvarez del Castillo
Feb 1989-May 1992   Guillermo Cossío Vidaurrin
May 1992-Feb 1995   Carlos Rivera Aceves
March 1995-   Alberto Cárdenas   (NAP)

MÉXICO

Capital: Toluca de Lerdo

Governors:

Sept 1933-June 1936   José Solorzano
July 1936-Sept 1937   Eucario López
Sept 1937-Sept 1941   Wenceslao Labra García
Sept 1941-March 1942   Alfredo Zárate Albarran   († assassinated)
8-15 March 1942   José Gutiérrez   (acting)
March 1942-Sept 1945   Isidro Fabela
Sept 1945-Sept 1951   Alfredo del Mazo Velez
Sept 1951-Sept 1957   Salvador Sánchez Colin
Sept 1957-Sept 1963   Gustavo Baz
Sept 1963-Sept 1969   Juan Fernández Albarrán
Sept 1969-Sept 1975   Carlos Hank González
Sept 1975-Sept 1981   Jorge Jiménez Cantú
Sept 1981-April 1986   Alfredo del Mazo González
April 1986-Sept 1987   Alfredo Baranda García
Sept 1987-Sept 1989   Mario Ramón Beteta
Sept 1989-Sept 1993   Ignacio Pichardo Pagaza
Sept 1993-June 1995   Emilio Chuayffet Chemor
July 1995-Sept 1999   César Camacho Quiroz
Sept 1999-   Arturo Montiel

MICHOACÁN

Capital: Morelia

Governors:

June 1935-Sept 1936   Rafael Ordorico Villamar

Sept 1936-Dec 1939	Gildardo Magaña (†)
Sept 1940-Sept 1944	Félix Ireta Viveros
Sept 1944-Aug 1949	José Mendoza Pardo
Aug 1949-Sept 1950	Daniel Renteria
Sept 1950-Sept 1956	Damasco Cárdenas del Rio
Sept 1956-Sept 1962	David Franco Rodríguez
Sept 1962-Sept 1968	Agustín Arriaga Rivera
Sept 1968-Sept 1971	Carlos Galvez Betancourt
Sept 1971-Sept 1974	José Chavez Hernández
Sept 1974-Sept 1980	Carlos Torres Manzo
Sept 1980-Sept 1986	Cuauhtémoc Cárdenas Solorzano (*son of Pres L.Cárdenas*)
Sept 1986-Dec 1988	Luis Martínez Villicaña
Dec 1988-Sept 1992	Genovevo Figueroa
Sept-Oct 1992	Eduardo Villaseñor Peña
Oct 1992-Dec 1995	Ausencio Chavez Hernández
Dec 1995-	Víctor Tinoco Rubi

MORELOS

Capital: Cuernavaca

Governors:

1934-May 1938	José Bustamante
6-16 May 1938	Alfonso Sámano Torres
May 1938-May 1942	Elpidio Perdomo
May 1942-May 1946	Jesús Castillo López
May 1946-May 1952	Ernesto Escobar Muñoz
May 1952-May 1958	Rodolfo López de Nava
May 1958-May 1964	Norberto López Avelar
May 1964-May 1970	Emilio Riva Palacio
May 1970-May 1976	Felipe Rivera Crespo
May 1976-May 1982	Armando León Bejarana
May 1982-May 1988	Lauro Ortega Martínez
May 1988-May 1994	Antonio Riva Palacio López
May 1994-May 1998	Jorge Carillo Olea
May 1998-	Jorge Morales Barud

NAYARIT

Statehood: 1917
Capital: Tepic

Governors:

Jan 1930-Aug 1931	Luis Castillo Ledón

Aug 1931-32	Juventino Espinosa Sánchez (1st)
1932-Dec 1933	Gustavo Azcárraga
Jan 1934-Dec 1937	Francisco Parra
Jan 1938-Dec 1941	Juventino Espinosa Sánchez (2nd)
Jan 1942-Dec 1945	Candelario Miramontes
Jan 1946-Dec 1951	Gilberto Flores Muñoz
Jan 1952-Dec 1957	José Limon Gutiérrez
Jan 1958-Dec 1963	Francisco García Mercado
Jan 1964-Dec 1969	Julian Gascón Mercado
Jan 1970-Dec 1975	Roberto Gómez Reyes
Jan 1976-Dec 1981	Rogelio Flores Cunel
Jan 1982-Dec 1987	Emilio González Parra
Jan 1988-Dec 1993	Celso Delgado Ramirez
Jan 1994-Dec 1999	Rigoberto Ochoa Zaragoza
Jan 2000-	Antonio Echeverria (NAP)

NUEVO LEÓN

Statehood: 1824
Capital: Monterrey

Governors:

1931-33	Francsico Cárdenas
1933-Sept 1935	Pablo Quiroga
Sept 1935-36	Gregorio Morales Sánchez
1936-39	Anacleto Guerrero
1939-43	Bonifacio Salinas Leal
1943-44	Armando Arteaga y Santoyo
1944-Oct 1949	Arturo de la Garza
Oct 1949-Dec 1952	Ignacio Morones Prieto
Dec 1952-Oct 1955	José Vivanco
Oct 1955-Oct 1961	Raúl Rangel Frias
Oct 1961-Oct 1967	Eduardo Livas Villarreal
Oct 1967-June 1971	Eduardo Elizondo
June 1971-Oct 1973	Luis Farrias
Oct 1973-Oct 1979	Pedro Zorilla Martínez
Oct 1979-Oct 1985	Alfonso Martínez Dominguez
Oct 1985-Oct 1991	Jorge Treviño Martínez
Oct 1991-April 1996	Socrates Rizzo
April 1996-Oct 1997	Benjamin Clarion Reyes
Oct 1997-	Fernando Canales Clarion (NAP)

OAXACA

Capital: Oaxaca de Juárez

Governors:

Dec 1932-Nov 1936	Anastasio García Toledo
Dec 1936-Nov 1940	Constantino Chapital
Dec 1940-Nov 1944	Vicente González Fernández
Dec 1944-Jan 1947	Edmundo Sánchez Cano
Jan 1947-Nov 1950	Eduardo Vasconcelos
Dec 1950-July 1952	Manuel Mayoral Heredia
Aug 1952-Oct 1955	Manuel Cabrera Carrasquedo
Oct 1955-Nov 1956	José Pacheco Iturribarria
Dec 1956-Nov 1962	Alfonso Pérez García
Dec 1962-Nov 1968	Rodolfo Brena Torres
Dec 1968-Nov 1970	Víctor Bravo Ahuja
Dec 1970-Nov 1974	Fernando Gómez Sandoval
Dec 1974-March 1977	Manuel Zárate Aquino
March 1977-Nov 1980	Eliseo Jiménez Ruiz
Dec 1980-1985	Pedro Vázquez Colmenares
1985-86	Jesús Martínez Alvarez
Dec 1986-Nov 1992	Heladio Ramirez López
Dec 1992-Nov 1998	Diodoro Carrasco Altamirano
Dec 1998-	José Murat Casab

PUEBLA

Capital: Puebla de Zaragoza

Governors:

1933-Jan 1937	José Mijares Palencio
Feb 1937-Jan 1941	Maximino Avila Camacho
Feb 1941-42	Gonzalo Bautista Castillo
1942-Jan 1945	Gustavo Díaz Ordaz (later President)
Feb 1945-Jan 1951	Carlos Betancourt
Feb 1951-Jan 1957	Rafael Avila Camacho
Feb 1957-Jan 1963	Fausto Ortega
Feb 1963-Oct 1964	Antonio Nava Castillo
Nov 1964-Jan 1969	Aaron Merino Fernández
Feb 1969-April 1972	Rafael Moreno Valle
April 1972-March 1973	Gonzalo Bautista O'Farrill
March 1973-Jan 1975	Guillermo Morales Blumenkron
Feb 1975-Jan 1981	Alfredo Toxqui Fernández
Feb 1981-Jan 1987	Guillermo Jiménez Morales

Feb 1987-Jan 1993	Mariano Piña Olaya
Jan 1993-Jan 1999	Manuel Bartlett Díaz
Jan 1999-	Melquiades Morales

QUERÉTARO

Statehood: 1824
Capital: Querétaro

Governors:

Oct 1931-Sept 1935	Saturnino Osornio
Oct 1935-Sept 1939	Ramón Rodríguez Familiar
Oct 1939-Sept 1943	Noradino Rubio Ortiz
Oct 1943-April 1949	Agapito Pozo
April-Sept 1949	Eduardo Luque Loyola
Oct 1949-Sept 1955	Octavio Mondragon Guerra
Oct 1955-Sept 1961	Juan Gorraez
Oct 1961-Sept 1967	Manuel González Cosío
Oct 1967-Sept 1973	Juventino Castro Sánchez
Oct 1973-Sept 1979	Antonio Calzada Urquiza
Oct 1979-Sept 1985	Rafael Camacho Guzmán
Oct 1985-Sept 1991	Mariano Palacios Alcocer
Sept 1991-Sept 1997	Enrique Burgos García
Sept 1997-	Ignacio Loyola Vera (NAP)

QUINTANA ROO

Statehood: October 1974
Capital: Chetumal

Governors:

Jan 1971-April 1975	David Gutiérrez Ruiz
April 1975-April 1981	Jesús Martínez Ross
April 1981-April 1987	Pedro Coldwell
April 1987-April 1993	Miguel Borje
April 1993-April 1999	Mario Villanueva Madrid
April 1999-	Joaquin Hendricks Díaz

SAN LUIS POTOSI

Capital: San Luis Potosi

Governors:

1931-35	Ildefonso Turrubiartes
1935-36	Aurelio Anaya
Sept 1936-May 1938	Mateo Hernández Netro
May 1938-39	Genovevo Rivas Guillen
1939-Aug 1941	Reynaldo Pérez Gallardo
Aug 1941-Sept 1943	Ramón Jiménez Delgado
Sept 1943-Sept 1949	Gonzalo Santos
Sept 1949-Sept 1955	Ismael Salas
Sept 1955-Jan 1959	Manuel Alvarez López
April 1969-Sept 1961	Francisco Martínez de la Vega
Sept 1961-Sept 1967	Manuel López Dávila
Sept 1967-Sept 1973	Antonio Rocha Cordero
Sept 1973-Sept 1979	Guillermo Fonseca Alvarez
Sept 1979-Sept 1985	Carlos Jonguitud Barrios
Sept 1985-May 1987	Florencio Salazar Martínez
May 1987-Sept 1991	Leopoldino Ortiz Santos
Sept-Oct 1991	Fausto Zapata
Oct 1991-Sept 1992	Gonzalo Martínez Corbala
Sept 1992-April 1993	Teofilo Torres Corzo
April 1993-Sept 1997	Horacio Sánchez Unzueta
Sept 1997-	Fernando Silva Nieto

SINALOA

Capital: Culiacán Rosales

Governors:

1933-Dec 1935	Manuel Páez
Dec 1935-Sept 1936	Gabriel Leyva Velazquez (1st)
Sept 1936-Sept 1940	Alfredo Delgado
Sept 1940-Feb 1944	Rodolfo Loaiza († assassinated)
Feb-Dec 1944	Ricardo Cruz
Jan 1945-Dec 1950	Pablo Macías Valenzuela
Jan 1951-Feb 1953	Enrique Pérez Arce
Aug 1953-Dec 1956	Rigoberto Aguilar Pico
Jan 1957-Dec 1962	Gabriel Leyva Velazquez (2nd)
Jan 1963-Dec 1968	Leopoldo Sánchez Celis
Jan 1969-Dec 1974	Alfredo Valdez Montoya
Jan 1975-Dec 1980	Alfonso Calderón Velarde
Jan 1981-Dec 1986	Antonio Toledo Corro
Jan 1987-Dec 1992	Francisco Labastida Ochoa
Jan 1993-Dec 1998	Renato Vega Alvarado
Jan 1999-	Juan Millán Lizárraga

SONORA

Statehood: 1830
Capital: Hermosillo

Governors:

Sept-Dec 1935	Ramón Ramos
Dec 1935-Jan 1937	Jesús Gutiérrez Cazares
Jan 1937-Aug 1939	Roman Yocupicio
Sept 1939-Aug 1943	Anselmo Macías Valenzuela
Sept 1943-April 1948	Abelardo Rodríguez
April 1948-Aug 1949	Horacio Sobarzo
Sept 1949-Aug 1955	Ignacio Soto
Sept 1955-Aug 1961	Alvaro Obregón
Sept 1961-Aug 1967	Luis Encinas Johnson
Sept 1967-Aug 1973	Faustino Felix Serna
Sept 1973-Oct 1975	Carlos Biebrich Torres
Oct 1975-Aug 1979	Alejandro Carrillo Marcor
Sept 1979-Aug 1985	Samuel Ocana García
Sept 1985-Aug 1991	Rodolfo Valdes
Sept 1991-Aug 1997	Manlio Beltrones Tapia
Sept 1997-	Armando López Nogales

TABASCO

Statehood: 1824
Capital: Villahermosa

Governors:

1935	Manuel Lastra Ortiz
July 1935-36	Aureo Calles
1936-Dec 1938	Víctor Fernández Manero
Jan 1939-Dec 1943	Francisco Trujillo Gurria
Jan 1944-Dec 1947	Noe de la Flor Casanova
Jan 1948-Dec 1952	Francisco Santamaria
Jan 1953-March 1955	Manuel Bartlett Bautista
March 1955-Dec 1958	Miguel Orrico de los Llanos
Jan 1959-Dec 1964	Carlos Madrazo
Jan 1965-Dec 1970	Manuel Mora
Jan 1971-Dec 1976	Mario Trujillo García
Jan 1977-Dec 1982	Leandro Rovirosa Wade
Jan 1983-87	Enrique González Pedreo
1987-Dec 1988	José Peralta López
Jan 1989-Jan 1992	Salvador Neme Castillo

Jan 1992-Dec 1994 — Manuel Gurria Ordoñez
Dec 1994- — Roberto Madrazo Pintado

TAMAULIPAS

Capital: Ciudad Victoria

Governors:

Feb 1933-Nov 1935	Rafael Villareal
Nov 1935-Feb 1937	Enrique Canseco
Feb 1937-Feb 1941	Marte Gómez
Feb 1941-Feb 1945	Magdaleno Aguilar Castillo
Feb 1945-April 1947	Hugo González
April 1947-Feb 1951	Raúl Garate Legleu
Feb 1951-Feb 1957	Horacio Terán
Feb 1957-Feb 1963	Norberto Treviño Zapata
Feb 1963-Feb 1969	Praxedis Balboa Gojon
Feb 1969-Feb 1975	Manuel Ravize
Feb 1975-Feb 1981	Enrique Cárdenas González
Feb 1981-Feb 1987	Emilio Martínez Manatou
Feb 1987-Feb 1993	Americo Villarreal Guerra
Feb 1993-Feb 1999	Manuel Cavazos Lerma
Feb 1999-	Tomás Yarrington Ruvalcaba

TLAXCALA

Capital: Tlaxcala

Governors:

1933-37	Adolfo Bonilla
1937-41	Isidro Candia
1941	Joaquín Cisneros Molina (acting)
1941-Aug 1944	Manuel Santillan
Aug 1944-Jan 1945	Mauro Angulo
Jan 1945-Jan 1951	Rafael Avila Bretón
Jan 1951-Jan 1957	Felipe Mazarrasa
Jan 1957-Jan 1963	Joaquín Cisneros Molina
Jan 1963-Jan 1969	Anselmo Cervantes Hernández
Jan 1969-Jan 1970	Ignacio Bonilla Vázquez (†)
Jan 1970	Enrique Delgado Ortega (acting)
Jan-April 1970	Cristano Cuéllar Abaroa
April 1970-Jan 1975	Luciano Huerta Sánchez
Jan 1975-Jan 1981	Emilio Sánchez Piedras
Jan 1981-Jan 1987	Tulio Hernández Gómez

Jan 1987-Jan 1993	Beatriz Paredes
Jan 1993-Jan 1999	José Alvarez Lima
Jan 1999-	Alfonso Sánchez Anaya (PDR)

PDR = Party of the Democratic Revolution

VERACRUZ

Statehood: 1824
Capital: Jalapa Enriquez

Governors:

Dec 1932-July 1935	Gonzalo Vázquez Vela
July 1935-Nov 1936	Guillermo Rebolledo
Dec 1936-39	Miguel Alemán
1939-Nov 1940	Francisco Casas Alemán
Dec 1940-Nov 1944	Jorge Cerdan
Dec 1944-48	Adolfo Ruiz Cortines (later President)
1948-Nov 1950	Angel Carvajal
Dec 1950-Nov 1956	Marco Muñoz
Dec 1956-Nov 1962	Antonio Quirasco
Dec 1962-Nov 1968	Fernando López Arias
Dec 1968-Nov 1974	Rafael Murillo Vidal
Dec 1974-Nov 1980	Rafael Hernández Ochoa
Dec 1980-Nov 1986	Agustín Acosta Lagunes
Dec 1986-89	Fernando Gutiérrez Barrios
1989-Nov 1992	Dante Delgado Rannauro
Dec 1992-Nov 1998	Patricio Chirinos Calero
Dec 1998-	Miguel Alemán Velasco

YUCATAN

Statehood: 1824
Capital: Mérida

Governors:

Feb 1930-Feb 1934	Bartolome García Corres
Feb 1934-Oct 1935	César Alayola Barrera
Oct 1935-July 1936	Fernando López Cardena
July 1936-July 1938	Florencio Polamo Valencia
July 1938-Feb 1942	Humberto Canto Echeverría
Feb 1942-Feb 1946	Ernesto Novelo Torres
Feb 1946-Sept 1951	José González Beytia
Sept 1951-Feb 1952	Humberto Esquivel Medina
Feb 1952-June 1953	Tomás Marentes Miranda

June 1953-Feb 1958	Víctor Mena Palomo
Feb 1958-Feb 1964	Agustín Franco Aguilar
Feb 1964-Feb 1970	Luis Torres Mesias
Feb 1970-Feb 1976	Carlos Loret de Mola Medíz
Feb 1976-Feb 1982	Francisco Luna Kan
Feb 1982-Feb 1988	Víctor Cervera Pacheco (1st)
Feb 1988-Feb 1991	Víctor Manzanilla Shaffer
Feb 1991-Dec 1993	Dulce María Isauri Riancho (1st)
Dec 1993-Jan 1994	Ricardo Avila Heredia
Jan 1994-95	Dulce María Isauri Riancho (2nd)
1995-	Víctor Cervera Pacheco (2nd)

ZACATECAS

Capital: Zacatecas

Governors:

Sept 1932-Sept 1936	Matías Ramos Santos
Sept 1936-Sept 1940	J.Félix Banuelos
Sept 1940-Sept 1944	Panfilo Natera
Sept 1944-Sept 1950	Leobardo Reynosos
Sept 1950-Sept 1956	José Minero Roque
Sept 1956-Sept 1962	Francisco García
Sept 1962-Sept 1968	José Rodríguez Elías
Sept 1968-Sept 1974	Pedro Ruiz González
Sept 1974-Sept 1980	Fernando Pámanes Escobedo
Sept 1980-Sept 1986	José Cervantes Corona
Sept 1986-Sept 1992	Genaro Borrego Estrada
Sept 1992-Sept 1998	Arturo Romo Gutiérrez
Sept 1998-	Ricardo Monreal Avila (PDR)

MICRONESIA

Official name: Federated States of Micronesia
Independence date: 22 December 1990
Capital: Palikir

Spain acquired sovereignty over the Caroline Islands, which now constitute Micronesia, in 1885-86, but sold them to Germany in 1899. They were occupied by Japan in 1914, and after World War I they remained under Japanese rule under a League of Nations trusteeship. In 1994 allied forces occupied the islands, and in 1947 they became part of the United Nations Trusteeship Territory of the Pacific under US administration. In 1979 the federation of four island groups was formed, becoming a free associated state with the US in November 1986. The trusteeship was ended in December 1990.

Presidents:

May 1979-May 1987	Tosiwo Nakayama
May 1987-May 1991	John Haglelgam
May 1991-May 1997	Bailey Olter (incapacitated July 1996)
May 1997-May 1999	Jacob Nena (acting July 1996-May 1997) (see Kosrae)
May 1999-	Leo Falcam (see Pohnpei)

States

CHUUK

Previous name: Truk until 1990
Capital: Weno

Governors:

May 1979-89	Erhart Aten
1989-June 1996	Sasao Gouland
June 1996-Feb 1997	Marcellino Umwech
Feb 1997-	Ansito Walter

KOSRAE

Capital: Tofol

Governors:

May 1979-May 1983	Jacob Nena
May 1983-May 1995	Yosiwo George

May 1995-98   Moses Mackwelung
1998-   Rensley Sigrah

POHNPEI

Previous name: Ponape until 1984
Capital: Kolonia

Governors:

May 1979-Dec 1981   Leo Falcam
Jan 1982-Dec 1990   Resio Moses
Jan 1991-Dec 1995   Johnny David   (1st)
Jan 1996-Dec 1999   Del Pangelinan
Jan 2000-   Johnny David   (2nd)

YAP

Capital: Colonia

Governors:

1979-90   John Mangefel
1990-97   Petrus Tun
1997-   Vincent Figir

MOLDOVA

Official name: Republic of Moldova, Republica Moldovenească
Previous names: Moldavian Autonomous Soviet Socialist Republic 1924-40, Moldavian Soviet Socialist Republic 1940-91
State formed: 12 October 1924
Admission to USSR: 2 August 1940
Independence date: 27 August 1991
Capital: Balta (1924-29), Tiraspol (1929-40), Chisanau (Kishenev) since 1940

The Moldavian Autonomous Republic was formed in 1924 within the Ukraine. In 1940 this was combined with the areas of Bessarabia ceded by Romania to the USSR to form a constituent republic of the Soviet Union. In 1991, as the Union collapsed, the republic declared itself independent.

Presidents:
Chairman of the Central Executive Committee 1925-38
President of the Presidium of the Supreme Soviet 1938-90
Chairman of the Supreme Soviet May-Sept 1990

April 1925-May 1926	Grigory Staryi
May 1926-May 1937	Yefstafi Voronovich
May 1937-July 1938	N.P.Stresny (acting)
July 1938-Aug 1940	Tikhon Konstantinov
Aug 1940-June 1941	Feodor Brovko (1st)
(June 1941-Aug 1944	Romanian occupation)
Aug 1944-51	Feodor Brovko (2nd)
1951-April 1963	Ivan Koditsa
April 1963-April 1980	Kirill Ilyashenko
April 1980-Dec 1985	Ivan Kalin
Dec 1985-July 1989	Aleksandr Mokanu
July 1989-Jan 1997	Mircea Snegur
Jan 1997-	Petru Lucinschi

Prime Ministers:
Chairman of the Council of People's Commissars 1925-46
Chairman of the Council of Ministers 1946-94

1925-May 1926	Aleksandr Stroev
May 1926-28	Grigory Staryi (1st)
1928-32	Sergei Dimitriu
1932-37	Grigory Staryi (2nd)
1940-June 1941	Tikhon Konstantinov (1st)

(June 1941-Aug 1944   Romanian occupation)
Aug 1944-45   Tikhon Konstantinov   (2nd)
1945-May 1947   Nikolai Koval
May 1947-Jan 1958   Gerasim Rud
Jan 1958-April 1970   Aleksandr Diorditsa
April 1970-Sept 1976   Pyotr Paskar   (1st)
Sept 1976-Dec 1980   Semyon Grossu
Dec 1980-Dec 1985   Ivan Ustiyanu
Dec 1985-Jan 1990   Ivan Kalin
Jan-May 1990   Pyotr Paskar   (2nd)
May 1990-May 1991   Mircea Druk
May 1991-June 1992   Valery Muravsky
July 1992-Jan 1997   Andrei Sangheli
Jan 1997-March 1999   Ion Cebuc
March-Dec 1999   Ion Sturza
Dec 1999-   Dumitru Braghis

Communist Party Leaders:

First Secretary

1929-?   Ilya Ilin
1934   — — Bulat
1937   N.I.Golub
1938-40   Stepan Zelencuk
1940-41   Petr Borodin
(June 1941-Aug 1944   Romanian occupation)
Aug 1944-Feb 1946   Nikita Salogor
Feb 1946-July 1950   Nikolai Koval
July 1950-Oct 1952   Leonid Brezhnev   (see Kazakhstan & USSR)
Oct 1952-54   Dmitri Gladky
1954-May 1961   Zinovi Serdyuk
May 1961-Dec 1980   Ivan Bodyul
Dec 1980-Nov 1989   Semyon Grossu
Nov 1989-Feb 1991   Pyotr Luchinsky   (Petru Lucinschi)
Feb-Aug 1991   Grigory Yeremey
(Aug 1991   party banned)

Autonomous Regions (f Secessionist states)

GAGAUZ-ERI

Previous name: Gagauz Soviet Socialist Republic 1990-95
Capital: Komrat

The Turkic-speaking minority attempted to secede from Moldova in 1990. The 1994 Moldovan constitution established an autonomous region.

President:

Oct 1990-June 1995   Stepan Topal

Governors:

June 1995-Sept 1999   Gheorghe Tabunshchik
Sept 1999-   Dumitru Croitoru

TRANSDNESTRIA

Official name: Tansdnestrian Moldovan Soviet Socialist Republic
Secession declared: 2 September 1990
Capital: Tiraspol

Russian inhabitants of this region declared secession from Moldova in 1990. This is not recognised by Moldova, but the 1994 constitution allows for an autonomous region.

President:
Chairman of the Supreme Soviet 1990-95

Oct 1990-   Igor Smirnov

MONACO

Official name: Principality of Monaco, Principauté de Monaco
State formed: 10th century
Capital: Monaco

The Principality of Monaco was probably formed in the 10th century, but a more significant date is 1297, the year the Grimaldi family, who still rule there, took possession. In 1612 the ruling Seigneur was proclaimed Prince of Monaco. Monaco was annexed by France from 1793 to 1814.

Princes/Princess:

1612-Jan 1662	Honoré II
Jan 1662-Jan 1701	Louis I (*grandson*)
Jan 1701-Feb 1731	Antoine (*son*)
Feb-Dec 1731	Louise-Hippolyte (*daughter*) (co-ruler)
Feb 1731-Nov 1733	Jacques (*b* J.Matignon) (husband) (co-ruler 1731) (abdicated)
Nov 1733-March 1793	Honoré III (*son*) (deposed)
(March 1793-May 1814	French annexation)
May 1814-Feb 1819	Honoré IV (*son*)
Feb 1819-Oct 1841	Honoré V (*son*)
Oct 1841-June 1856	Florestan (*brother*)
June 1856-Sept 1889	Charles III (*son*)
Sept 1889-June 1922	Albert I (*son*)
June 1922-May 1949	Louis II (*son*)
May 1949-	Rainier III (*grandson*)

Ministers of State:

Feb 1911-Dec 1917	Émile Flach
Jan 1918-Feb 1919	Georges Jaloustre
Feb 1919-Aug 1923	Raymond Le Bourdon
Aug 1923-Jan 1932	Maurice Piette
Jan-June 1932	Henri Mauran (acting) (1st)
June 1932-May 1937	Maurice Bouilloux-Lafont
June-Aug 1937	Henri Mauran (acting) (2nd)
Aug 1937-Nov 1944	Émile Roblot
Nov 1944-Dec 1948	Pierre de Witasse
Jan-June 1949	Pierre Blanchy (acting) (1st)
June 1949-July 1950	Jacques Rueff
July 1950-Oct 1953	Pierre Voizard
Oct 1953-Jan 1959	Henri Soum

Jan 1959-Jan 1962	Émile Pelletier
Jan 1962-Aug 1963	Pierre Blanchy (acting) (2nd)
Aug 1963-Dec 1966	Jean-Émile Reymond
Dec 1966-March 1969	Paul Demange
March 1969-May 1972	François-Didier Gregh
May 1972-July 1981	André Saint-Mleux
July 1981-Sept 1985	Jean Herly
Sept 1985-April 1991	Jean Ausseil
April 1991-Dec 1994	Jacques Dupont
Dec 1994-Feb 1997	Paul Dijoud
Feb 1997-	Michel Lévéque

MONGOLIA

Official name: State of Mongolia, Mongol Uls
Previous name: Mongolian People's Republic 1924-92
Independence date: 11 July 1921
Capital: Ulan Bator (*f* Urga or Niyslel Huree)

Mongolia was a Chinese province from 1686 until 1911, when it became an autonomous state under Russian protection. From 1919 until 1921 it was occupied by China. In July 1921 an independent state was established and in 1924 Mongolia became a people's republic. Following political changes in the USSR and eastern Europe, multi-party elections were held in 1990 which were won by the communists.

Head of State:

Dec 1911-Nov 1919	Bogdo Gegen Khan	(8th Jebtsen Damba Khutukhtu) (1st)
(Nov 1919-Feb 1921	Chinese occupation)	
July 1921-May 1924	Bogdo Gegen Khan	(8th Jebtsen Damba Khutukhtu) (2nd) (†)

Presidents:
Chairman of the Presidium of the People's Khural until Sept 1990

Nov 1924-Feb 1928	Peljidiyn Gendun	
Feb-Dec 1928	Jamtsangiyn Damdinsuren	
Dec 1928-April 1930	Kharlogiyn Choibalsan	
April 1930-July 1934	Losolyn Langone	
July 1934-March 1936	Anandyn Amor	
March 1936-March 1939	Damsranbelegiyn Doksom	(removed, executed)
(March 1939-July 1940	post vacant)	
July 1940-Sept 1953	Gonchigiyn Bumatsende	(†)
Sept 1953-July 1954	Suhbaataryn Yanjmaa	(acting)
July 1954-May 1972	Jamsarangiyn Sambu	(†)
May 1972-June 1974	Sonomyn Luvsan	(acting)
June 1974-Aug 1984	Yumjagiyn Tsedenbal	
Aug-Dec 1984	Nyamyn Jagvaral	(acting)
Dec 1984-March 1990	Jambyn Batmounkh	
March 1990-June 1997	Punsalmaagiyn Ochirbat	
June 1997-	Natsagiyn Bagabandi	(MPRP)

Prime Ministers:
Chairman of the Council of Ministers 1924-90

Jan-Nov 1912	Tserenchimit	
Nov 1912-Oct 1915	Shirindambyn Namnansuren	(Sain Noyan Khan)

Oct 1915-Nov 1919	Da Lama Shanzav Badamdorji
(Nov 1919-Feb 1921	Chinese occupation)
Feb-July 1921	Dambinbadzar (Jalhansa Khutukhtu) (1st)
July 1921-Jan 1922	Dogsomyn Bodo (deposed, executed)
Aug 1922-July 1923	Dambinbadzar (Jalhansa Khutukhtu) (2nd) (†)
1923-Feb 1928	Balingiyn Tserendorji (†)
Feb 1928-July 1932	Anandyn Amor (1st)
July 1932-March 1936	Peljidiyn Gendun (deposed, executed 1937)
March 1936-March 1939	Anandyn Amor (2nd) (effectively deposed 1938, executed 1939)
April 1939-Jan 1952	Kharlogiyn Choibalsan (†)
Jan 1952-June 1974	Yumjagiyn Tsedenbal (acting Jan-May 1952)
June 1974-Dec 1984	Jambyn Batmounkh
Dec 1984-March 1990	Dumaagiyn Sodnom
March-Sept 1990	Sharavyn Gungaadorj
Sept 1990-July 1992	Dashiyn Byambasuren
July 1992-July 1996	Punsagiyn Jasray (MPRP)
July 1996-April 1998	Mendsayhany Enhsayhan (SDP)
April-Dec 1998	Tsakhiagiyn Elbegdorj (MNDP)
Dec 1998-July 1999	Janlaviyn Narantsatsralt (MNDP)
22-30 July 1999	Nyam-Osoriyn Tuyaa (acting)
July 1999-	Rinchinnyamiyn Amarjargal

MNDP = Mongolian National Democratic Party
MPRP = Mongolian People's Revolutionary Party
SDP = Social Democratic Party

Communist Party* Leaders:

*Mongolian People's Party 1921-24
 Mongolian People's Revolutionary Party since 1924
Chairman of the Central Committee 1921-40
General Secretary 1940-54 and Sept 1981-March 1991
First Secretary 1954-Sept 1981

March 1921-Aug 1924	Khorloogiyn Danzan (deposed, executed)
Aug 1924-Oct 1928	Tserenvacharyn Dambadorji
Oct 1928-39	Darzavyn Losol
April 1940-April 1954	Yumjagiyn Tsedenbal (1st)
April 1954-Nov 1958	Dashiyn Damba
Nov 1958-Aug 1984	Yumjagiyn Tsedenbal (2nd)
Aug 1984-March 1990	Jambyn Batmounkh
March 1990-March 1991	Gombojavyn Ochirbat
(1990	multi-party system introduced)

RIVAL GOVERNMENT

Formed in opposition to Chinese installed government. Took over the government in Urga in July 1921.
Headquarters: Kyakhta (Russia)

Prime Ministers:

March 1921	Chakdorjab
March-July 1921	Dogsomyn Bodo

Autonomous State

WESTERN MONGOLIA

A Russian puppet state which existed briefly in 1921.
Capital: Kobdo

Prime Minister:

July-? 1921   Durdet Khan Tumen Delgerjab

MOROCCO

Official name: Kingdom of Morocco, Al-Mamlaka al-Maghrebia
Previous name: Sultanate of Morocco until 1957
State founded: 8th century
Independence date: 2 March 1956
Capital: Rabat (Ribat)

The area of present-day Morocco was conquered by the Arabs in the 8th century. In 1912 the country was divided into French and Spanish protectorates. The French area gained independence in March 1956, with the Spanish region joining it the following month. In 1957 its status was changed from a sultanate to a kingdom. King Hassan II introduced gradual democratic reforms in the mid 1990s resulting in a greater role for political parties.

Sultans:

1757-90	Mohammed III
1790-92	Yasid (*son*)
1792-Nov 1822	Suleiman (*brother*)
Nov 1822-Aug 1859	Abderrahman (*nephew*)
Aug 1859-Sept 1873	Mohammed IV (*son*)
Sept 1873-June 1894	Hassan I (*son*)
June 1894-Jan 1908	Abdel Aziz (*son*) (deposed)
Jan 1908-Aug 1912	Abdel Hafidh (*brother*) (abdicated)
Aug 1912-Nov 1927	Yusuf (*brother*)
Nov 1927-Aug 1953	Mohammed V (*son*) (1st) (deposed)
Aug 1953-Oct 1955	Mohammed (VI) bin Arafa (*uncle*)
Oct 1955-Aug 1957	Mohammed V (2nd)

Kings:

Aug 1957-Feb 1961	Mohammed V
Feb 1961-July 1999	Hassan II (*son*)
July 1999-	Mohammed VI (*son*)

Prime Ministers:

Oct-Nov 1955	Fatmi Ben Slimane
Dec 1955-April 1958	M'Bareka el-Bekai
May-Dec 1958	Ahmed Balafrej
Dec 1958-May 1960	Abdullah Ibrahim
May 1960-Feb 1961	King Mohammed V (†)

Feb 1961-Nov 1963	King Hassan II (1st)
Nov 1963-June 1965	Ahmed Bahnini
June 1965-July 1967	King Hassan II (2nd)
July 1967-Oct 1969	Mohammed Benhima
Oct 1969-Aug 1971	Ahmed Laraki
Aug 1971-Nov 1972	Mohammed Karim Lamrani (1st)
Nov 1972-March 1979	Ahmed Osman (*brother-in-law of Hassan II*)
March 1979-Nov 1983	Maati Bouabid
Nov 1983-Sept 1986	Mohammed Karim Lamrani (2nd)
Sept 1986-Aug 1992	Azzedine Laraki
Aug 1992-May 1994	Mohammed Karim Lamrani (3rd)
May 1994-Feb 1998	Abdellatif Filali
Feb 1998-	Abdarrahman Yousifi (SUPF)

SUPF = Socialist Union of Popular Forces

Secessionist State

RIF REPUBLIC

Set up to oppose Spanish authorities in north Morocco.
Capital: Ajdir

Head of State:

Feb 1923-May 1926	Mohammed Abd-el-Krim al-Khattabi

Former Spanish Territory

IFNI

Capital: Sidi Ifni

Governors-General:

1958-61	Gómez Zamalloq
1961-64	Joaquín Agulla Jiménez-Coronado
1964-69	Adolfo Artelejo Campos
June 1969-	Returned to Morocco

MOZAMBIQUE

Official name: Republic of Mozambique, República de Moçambique
Previous name: People's Republic of Mozambique 1975-90
Independence date: 25 June 1975
Capital: Maputo (*f* Lourenço Marques)

Mozambique was colonized by the Portuguese in 1505. In 1951 its status was changed from colony to overseas territory. An armed struggle for independence began in 1964. Following the military coup in Portugal in 1974, agreement to grant independence was achieved. An interim government was formed in September 1974 and independence was granted in June 1975. Initially a Marxist state, rivals launched a civil war backed first by Rhodesia and then South Africa which caused widespread damage. Peace was brokered in 1992, leading to multi-party elections in 1994.

Governors-General:

1900-02	Manuel Gorjão
1902-05	Tomás Rosado
1905-06	João de Sequeira
1906-10	Alfredo de Andrade
1910-11	José Ribeiro
1911-12	José de Azevedo e Silva
1912-13	José de Magalhães
1913-14	Augusto dos Santos
1914-15	Joaquim Machado (3rd)
1915	Alfredo Coelho
1915-18	Alvaro de Castro
1918-19	Pedro do Amorim
1919-21	Manuel da Fonseca (1st)
1921-23	Manuel Camacho
1923-24	Manuel da Fonseca (2nd)
1924-26	Vitor Coutinho
1926-38	José Cabral
1937-40	José de Oliveira
1940-47	José de Bettencourt
1947-58	Gabriel Teixeira
1958-61	Pedro de Barros
1961-64	José da Costa
1964-68	Baltasar Almeida
1968-70	Eduardo de Oliveira
1971-74	Manuel dos Santos

High Commissioner:

1974-75 Vitor Crespo

Presidents:

June 1975-Oct 1986 Samora Machel (MLF) († air accident)
Nov 1986- Joaquim Chissano (MLF)

Prime Ministers:

Sept 1974-June 1975 Joaquim Chissano
(June 1975-July 1986 post abolished)
July 1986-Dec 1994 Mario Machungo
Dec 1994- Pascoal Mocumbi

MLF = Mozambique Liberation Front (Frelimo) (sole legal party 1975-92)

MYANMAR

Official name: Union of Myanmar, Myanma Nainggan-daw
Previous names: Union of Burma 1948-74, Socialist Republic of the Union of Burma 1974-89
Independence date: 4 January 1948
Capital: Rangoon (Yangon)

The ancient kingdom of Burma was reunited in 1757 after two centuries of divison. In 1885 it was annexed by Britain, becoming a province of British India in 1886. In 1937 Burma was separated from India and granted self government. During World War II the country was occupied by Japan who set up a nominally independent administration. After the war Britiah rule was restored, and in 1948 independence outside the Commonwealth was granted. In 1962 the military government transformed Burma into a one party socialist state, but its isolationist policies led to economic decline, and in 1988 widespread unrest and another military coup. Elections were held in 1989, but the military annulled the results and retained power.

Kings:

1757-60	Alaungpaya
1760-82	Hsinbyushin (*son*)
1782-1819	Bayinnaung
1819-37	Bagyidaw
1837-46	Tharrawaddy Min
1846-53	Pagan Min
1853-78	Mindon Min
1878-85	Thibaw (*son*)

Lieutenant-Governors:

1897-1903	Frederick Fryer
1903-05	Hugh Barnes
1905-10	Herbert White
1910-15	Harvey Adamson
1915-18	Spencer Butler
1918-23	Reginald Craddock

Governors:

1923-27	Spencer Butler
1927-33	Charles Innes
1933-36	Hugh Stephenson
1936-41	Archibald Douglas

1941-42   Reginald Dorman-Smith   (1st)
(1942-45   Japanese occupation)
1945-46   Reginald Dorman-Smith   (2nd)
1946   Henry Knight
1946-48   Hubert Rance

Presidents:

Chairman of the Revolutionary Council 1962-74
Chairman of the State Law & Order Restoration Committee Sept 1988-Nov 1997
Chairman of the State Peace & Development Council since Nov 1997

Jan 1948-March 1952   Sao Shwe Thaike
March 1952-March 1957   Ba U
March 1957-March 1962   U Win Maung   (deposed)
March 1962-Nov 1981   U Ne Win   (*b* Shu Maung)
Nov 1981-July 1988   U San Yu
July-Aug 1988   U Sein Lwin
Aug-Sept 1988   Maung Maung   (deposed)
Sept 1988-April 1992   Saw Maung
April 1992-   Than Shwe

Prime Ministers:

April 1937-Feb 1939   Ba Maw   (1st)
Feb 1939-Oct 1940   U Pu Yamethin   (UP)
Oct 1940-Jan 1942   U Saw   (NP)
Jan-May 1942   Paw Tun   (PP)
(May-Aug 1942   post vacant)
Aug 1942-May 1945   Ba Maw   (2nd)
(May-Nov 1945   post vacant)
Nov 1945-July 1947   Aung San   († assassinated) (AFPFL)
July 1947-June 1956   U Nu   (1st) (AFPFL)
June 1956-Feb 1957   U Ba Swe   (AFPFL)
Feb 1957-Oct 1958   U Nu   (2nd) (AFPFL) (deposed)
Oct 1958-Feb 1960   Ne Win   (later U Ne Win) (1st)
Feb 1960-March 1962   U Nu   (3rd) (UnP) (deposed)
March 1962-March 1974   U Ne Win   (2nd)
March 1974-March 1977   U Sein Win
March 1977-July 1988   U Maung Maung Kha
July-Sept 1988   U Tun Tin
Sept 1988-April 1992   Saw Maung
April 1992-   Than Shwe

AFPFL = Anti-Fascist People's Freedom League
NP = National Party
PP = Patriotic Party
UP = United Party
UnP = Union Party

Party Leaders:

Chairman of the Burma Socialist Programme Party

July 1962-July 1988	U Ne Win
July-Aug 1988	U Sein Lwin
Aug-Sept 1988	Maung Maung
(Sept 1988	BSPP rule ended)

RIVAL GOVERNMENT 1990-95

Headquarters: Manerplaw (captured by government forces Jan 1995)

Prime Minister:

Dec 1990-Jan 1995	Sein Winn

States

Until 1974 the states had a degree of autonomy

CHIN

Capital: Haka

Ministers of State:

1947-54	Vam Thu Maung
1954-56	U Shein Htang
1956-62	U Za Hre Lian

Chairman of the Supreme State Council:

March 1962-March 1974	U San Kho Lian

KACHIN

Capital: Myitkyina

Ministers of State:

1947-56	Sama Duwa Sinwa Nawng	(1st)
1956-60	U Zan Hta Sin	
1960-62	Sama Duwa Sinwa Nawng	(2nd)

Chairman of the Supreme State Council:

March 1962-March 1974	U Ding Ratang

KAREN

Previous name: Kawthule 1964-74
Statehood: 1 June 1954
Capital: Pa-an

Ministers of State:

June 1954-June 1955	U Aung Pa
June 1955-March 1962	Saw Hla Tun

Chairman of the Supreme State Council:

March 1962-March 1974   Saw Hla Tun

KAYAH

Previous name: Karenni 1947-52
Capital: Loi-kaw

Minister of State:

1947-62   Saw Wunna

Chairman of the State Supreme Council:

March 1962-March 1974   U A Mya Lay

SHAN

Capital: Taunggyi

Minister of State:

1947-62   Sao Hkun Hkio

Chairman of the State Supreme Council:

March 1962-March 1974   U Tun Aye

NAMIBIA

Official name: Republic of Namibia

Previous name: South-West Africa until 1990 (The name Namibia was adopted by the United Nations in 1968)

Independence date: 21 March 1990

Capital: Windhoek

The territory of South-West Africa was proclaimed a German protectorate in 1884. In 1915, during World War I, it was occupied by South African Forces, and in 1919 it became a League of Nations mandated territory under South African administration. After the formation in 1945 of the United Nations South Africa refused to transfer South-West Africa to it, and during the 1950s and 1960s plans were made to incorporate it into South Africa and form black homelands. In 1966 an armed campaign led by the South-West African People's Organization (SWAPO) began, and in 1971 the World Court declared the South African presence illegal. South Africa continued its administration, and in 1978 introduced a form of self-government with the aim of eventual independence. Various international efforts to resolve the country's future were made, and agreement was reached in 1988 to grant independence. Elections held in 1989 were won by SWAPO, and in March 1990 Namibia became independent.

Governors:

April 1898-1905	Theodor Leutwein
1905	Lothar von Trotha (acting)
Nov 1905-07	Friedrich von Lindequist
1907-10	Bruno von Scuckmann
Nov 1910-14	Theodor Seitz

Administrators:

1915-20	Howard Gorges
1920-26	Gys Hofmeyer
1926-33	Albert Werth
1933-43	David Conradie
1943-51	Petrus Hoogenhout
1951-53	Albertus van Rhijn
1953-63	Daniel Viljoen
1963-68	Wentzel du Plessis
1968-71	Johannes van der Wath
1971-77	Barend van der Walt

Administrators-General:

Sept 1977-Aug 1979	Marthinus Steyn

Aug 1979-Sept 1980	Gerrit Viljoen
Sept 1980-Feb 1983	Daniel Hough
Feb 1983-July 1985	Willem van Niekerk
July 1985-March 1990	Louis Pienaar

President:

March 1990-	Samuel Nujoma (SWAPO)

Prime Minister:
Chairman of the Ministers' Council

July 1980-Jan 1983	Dirk Mudge (DTA)
(Jan 1983	post abolished)

Cabinet Chairmen:
(post held in rotation by ministers)

June-Sept 1985	David Bezuidenhout (1st) (LP)
Sept-Dec 1985	Johannes Diergaardt (RFP)
Dec 1985-March 1986	Moses Katjiuongua (1st) (SWANU)
March-June 1986	Fanuel Kozonguizi (DTA)
June-Sept 1986	Andrew Matjila (1st) (DTA)
Sept-Dec 1986	Dirk Mudge (1st) (DTA)
Dec 1986-Jan 1987	Ebenzei van Zijl (NP)
Feb-April 1987	Andreas Shipanga (1st) (SWAPO-D)
May-July 1987	David Bezuidenhout (2nd) (LP)
Aug 1987-Jan 1988	Johannes (Jan) de Wet (NP)
Jan-April 1988	Moses Katjiuongua (2nd) (SWANU)
April-July 1988	Andrew Matjila (2nd) (DTA)
July-Oct 1988	Dirk Mudge (2nd) (DTA)
Oct-Dec 1988	Andreas Shipanga (2nd) (SWAPO-D)
Dec 1988-Jan 1989	Andrew Matjila (3rd) (DTA)
Jan-Feb 1989	Harry Booysen (LP)
(Feb 1989	post abolished)

Prime Minister:

March 1990-	Hage Geingob (SWAPO)

DTA = Democratic Turnhalle Alliance
LP = Labour Party
NP = National Party
RFP = Rehoboth Freedom Party
SWANU = South West African National Union
SWAPO = South West African People's Organization
SWAPO-D = South West African People's Organization-Democrats

Self-governing Regions/Ethnic Authorities

South Africa planned to create homelands for the different groups in Namibia, and three areas, Caprivi, Owambo and Kavango, were granted self-government. In 1980 the system was changed to one of separate governments on the basis of ethnicity only, and not geography. These governments were abolished in 1989 at the start of the transition to independence.

CAPRIVI

Headquarters: Katima Mulilo

Chief Councillor:

March 1972-March 1976	Josiah Moraliswane

Chief Ministers:

March-Sept 1976	Josiah Moraliswane
Sept 1976-March 1981	Richard Muhinda Mamili (DTA)

Chairman of the Executive Committee:

March 1981-June 1984	Josiah Moraliswane
(June 1984-May 1989	central rule)

COLOURED

Headquarters: Windhoek

Chairmen of the Executive Committee:

Nov 1980-March 1984	Leonard Barnes (LP)
March 1984-June 1985	David Bezuidenhout (LP)
June 1985-Feb 1988	William Phillips (LP)
Feb 1988-May 1989	Reginald Diergaardt (LP)

DAMARA

Headquarters: Khorixas

Chairman of the Executive Committee:

Dec 1980-May 1989	Justus Garoëb (DC)

DC = Damara Council

HERERO

Headquarters: Okahandja

Chairmen of the Executive Committee:

Dec 1980-Sept 1984	Thimoteus Tjamuaha	
Sept 1984-Aug 1987	Erastus Tjejamba	(1st)
Aug-Oct 1987	Gottlob Mbaukua	(1st)
Oct 1987-Feb 1988	Erastus Tjejamba	(2nd)
Feb 1988-May 1989	Gottlob Mbaukua	(2nd)

KAVANGO

Headquarters: Rundu

Chief Councillor:

Oct 1970-May 1973	Linus Shashipapo

Chief Ministers:

May-Sept 1973	Linus Shashipapo
Sept 1973-Jan 1981	Alfons Mayavero

Chairman of the Executive Committee:

Jan 1981-May 1989	Sebastiaan Kamwanga	(DTA)

NAMA

Headquarters: Keetmanshoop

Chairmen of the Executive Committee:

July 1980-March 1985	Cornelius Cloete	(DTA)
March 1985-May 1989	Daniel Luipert	(DTA)

OWAMBO

Headquarters: Ondangua

Chief Councillors:

Oct 1968-Jan 1972	Ushona Shiimi	(† motor accident)
Jan 1972-May 1973	Filemon Elifas	

Chief Ministers:

May 1973-Aug 1975	Filemon Elifas	(† assassinated)
Aug 1975-July 1980	Cornelius Ndjoba	

Chairmen of the Executive Committee:

July 1980-Oct 1981   Cornelius Ndjoba   (assassinated 1982)
Oct 1981-May 1989   Peter Kalangula   (CDA)

CDA = Christian Democratic Action

REHOBOTH (BASTER)

Headquarters: Rehoboth

Chairman of the Executive Committee:

July 1979-June 1989   Johannes Diergaardt   (RFP)

TSWANA

Headquarters: Aminuis

Chairman of the Executive Committee:

Dec 1980-May 1989   Constance Kgosiemang   (DTA)

WHITE

Headquarters: Windhoek

Chairmen of the Executive Committee:

1977-May 1980   Abraham du Plessis   (NP)
June 1980-April 1988   Jacobus   (Kosie) Pretorius   (NP)
May 1988-May 1989   Johannes   (Jan) de Wet   (NP)

Former independent state

UPINGTONIA

State declared: 20 October 1885
Ceased to exist: 1887
Formed by white settlers from South Africa

President:

1885-87   G.D.P.Prinsloo

NAURU

Official name: Republic of Nauru
Independence date: 31 January 1968
Capital: Yaren

The island of Nauru was annexed by Germany in 1888. In 1914 it was taken by Australian forces, and after World War I it became a League of Nations trust territory, jointly administered by Britain, Australia and New Zealand, but governed by Australia. Nauru was granted independence in 1968.

Administrators:

1921-27	Thomas Griffiths
1927-33	William Newman
1933-38	Rupert Garsia
1938-42	Frederick Chalmers
(1942-45	Japanese occupation)
1945-49	Mark Ridgway
1949	Harold Reeve
1949-53	Robert Richards
1953-54	John Lawrence
1954-58	Reginald Leydin (1st)
1958-62	John White
1962-66	Reginald Leydin (2nd)
1966-68	Leslie King

Presidents:

Chairman of the Council of State Jan-May 1968

Jan 1968-Dec 1976	Hammer de Roburt (1st)
Dec 1976-April 1978	Bernard Dowiyogo (1st)
April-May 1978	Lagumot Harris (1st)
May 1978-Sept 1986	Hammer de Roburt (2nd)
Sept-Oct 1986	Kennan Adeang (1st)
Oct 1986-Aug 1989	Hammer de Roburt (3rd)
Aug-Dec 1989	Kenas Aroi
Dec 1989-Nov 1995	Bernard Dowiyogo (2nd)
Nov 1995-Nov 1996	Lagumot Harris (2nd)
12-26 Nov 1996	Bernard Dowiyogo (3rd)
Nov-Dec 1996	Kennan Adeang (2nd)
Dec 1996-Feb 1997	Reuben Kun
Feb 1997-June 1998	Kinza Clodumar
June 1998-April 1999	Bernard Dowiyogo (4th)
April 1999-April 2000	René Harris
April 2000-	Bernard Dowiyogo (5th)

NEPAL

Official name: Kingdom of Nepal, Nepál Alhirajya
State founded: 29 September 1768
Capital: Katmandu

Present-day Nepal was formed by the unification of the country into a single kingdom by King Prithwi Narayana in 1768. In the 19th century real power passed into the hands of the prime minister, which was a hereditary appointment until 1951. After a brief period of party political government (1959-60), the king re-established his authority, ruling through nominated councils. Pro-democracy demonstrations in 1990 led to the establishment of a constitutional monarchy and an elected government.

Kings:

Sept 1768-74	Prithwi Narayana
1774-78	Pratadasinha Sah (*son*)
1778-March 1799	Rana Bahadur Sah (*son*) (1st) (abdicated)
	Regents: 1778-85 Queen Rajendra Lakshmi
	1785-94 Bahadur Sah
March 1799-1804	Girvan (*son*) (1st)
	Regents: 1799-1800 Queen Raj Rajeshvari Devi
	1800-03 Survana Prabha
	1803-04 Queen Raj Rajeshvari Devi
1804-06	Rana Bahadur Sah (2nd) (assassinated)
1806-Nov 1816	Girvan (2nd)
	Regent: 1806-12 Queen Lalit Tripura Sundari
Nov 1816-47	Rajendra (*son*) (deposed)
	Regent: 1816-39 Bhimsena Thapa
1847-Dec 1881	Surendra (*son*)
Dec 1881-Dec 1911	Prithwi (*grandson*)
Dec 1911-March 1955	Tribhuwan (*son*)
March 1955-Feb 1972	Mahendra (*son*)
Feb 1972-	Birendra (*son*)

Prime Ministers:

1799-04	Damodar Pande († assassinated)
1804-06	King Rana Bahadur Sah
April 1806-37	Bhimsena Thapa
1837-Nov 1840	Rana Jung Pande
Nov 1840-Jan 1843	Fateh Jung Chautaria (1st)
Nov 1843-May 1845	Mathabur Singh Thapa (*nephew*) († assassinated)

Sept 1845-46	Fateh Jung Chautaria (2nd)
Sept 1846-Feb 1877	Jung Bahadur (†)
Feb 1877-Nov 1885	Ranadip Singh Bahadur (*brother*) († assassinated)
Nov 1885-March 1901	Shumshere Jung (*nephew*) (†)
March-June 1901	Deb Shumshere Jung (*son*)
June 1901-Nov 1929	Chandra Shumshere Jung (*brother*) (†)
Nov 1929-31	Bhim Shumshere Jung (*brother*) (†)
1931-March 1946	Juddha Shumshere Jung (*brother*)
March 1946-June 1948	Padma Shumshere Jung (*nephew*)
June 1948-Nov 1951	Mohan Shumshere Jung (*son of Chandra Shumshere Jung*)
Nov 1951-Aug 1952	Matrika Koirala (1st)
Aug 1952-Feb 1954	King Tribhuwan
Feb 1954-March 1955	Matrika Koirala (2nd)
March 1955-Jan 1956	King Mahendra (1st)
Jan 1956-July 1957	Tanka Achariya
July-Nov 1957	Kunvar Singh
Nov 1957-May 1958	King Mahendra (2nd)
May 1958-May 1959	Subarna Shumshere
May 1959-Dec 1960	Bishewar Koirala (*brother of M.Koirala*) (NCP)
Dec 1960-April 1963	King Mahendra (3rd)
April 1963-Jan 1965	Tulsi Giri (1st)
Jan 1965-April 1969	Surya Bahadur Thapa (1st)
April 1969-April 1970	Kirtinidhi Bista (1st)
April 1970-April 1971	King Mahendra (4th)
April 1971-July 1973	Kirtinidhi Bista (2nd)
July 1973-Dec 1975	Nagendra Rijal
Dec 1975-Sept 1977	Tulsi Giri (2nd)
Sept 1977-May 1979	Kirtinidhi Bista (2nd)
May 1979-July 1983	Surya Bahadur Thapa (2nd)
July 1983-March 1986	Lokendra Chand (1st)
March 1986-April 1990	Marich Man Singh Shrestha
6-19 April 1990	Lokendra Chand (2nd)
April 1990-May 1991	Krishna Bhattarai (1st) (NCP)
May 1991-Nov 1994	Girija Koirala (1st) (NCP) (*brother of B.Koirala*)
Nov 1994-Sept 1995	Man Mohan Adhikari (UCPN)
Sept 1995-March 1997	Sher Bahadur Deupa (NCP)
March-Oct 1997	Lokendra Chand (3rd) (RPP)
Oct 1997-April 1998	Surya Bahadur Thapa (3rd) (RPP)
April 1998-May 1999	Girija Koirala (2nd) (NCP)
May 1999-March 2000	Krishna Bhattarai (2nd) (NCP)
March 2000-	Girija Koirala (3rd) (NCP)

NCP = Nepal Congress Party
RPP = Rashtriya Prajatantra Party
UCPN = United Communist Party of Nepal

NETHERLANDS

Official name: Kingdom of the Netherlands, Koninkrijk van der Nederlanden
Previous names: United Provinces of the Netherlands 1579-1795, Batavian Republic 1795-1806, Kingdom of Holland 1806-13
Independence date: 26 July 1581
Capital: The Hague ('s-Gravenhage)

The Netherlands was part of the duchy of Burgundy and became part of the Habsburg domains with the marriage of Mary of Burgundy to the Emperor Maximilian I in 1477. The struggle for independence culminated in the establishment of a Dutch republic in 1579 with Prince Willem of Orange as the first Stadhouder. Ties with the Austrian crown were formally ended in 1581. France invaded the Netherlands in 1795 and the country remained under French control until 1813, first as the Batavian Republic and then as a monarchy under the rule of one of Napoleon Bonaparte's brothers. In 1815 the independent kingdom of the Netherlands was proclaimed. The southern provinces became the independent kingdom of Belgium in 1830. The Netherlands were occupied by Germany during World War II, during which time a government-in-exile operated from London.

Stadhouders:

Jan 1579-July 1584	Willem I (assassinated)
July 1584-April 1625	Maurits (*son*)
April 1625-March 1647	Frederick Hendrik (*half-brother*)
March 1647-Nov 1650	Willem II (*son*)
(Nov 1650-July 1672	post vacant)
July 1672-March 1702	Willem III (William III of England)
(March 1702-May 1747	post vacant)
May 1747-Oct 1751	Willem IV (*great-grandnephew of Willem II*) (*son*)
Oct 1751-May 1795	Willem V (deposed)
(May 1795-June 1806	French occupation)

Kings/Queens:

June 1806-July 1810	Lodewijk I (Louis Bonaparte, *brother of Napoléon I of France*) (abdicated)
4-9 July 1810	Lodewijk II (Napoléon-Louis Bonaparte) (*son*)
(July 1810-Nov 1813	French annexation)
(Nov 1813-March 1815	provisional government)
March 1815-Oct 1840	Willem I (*son of Willem V*) (also Guillaume I of Luxembourg) (abdicated)
Oct 1840-March 1849	Willem II (*son*) (also Guillaume II of Luxembourg)
March 1849-Nov 1890	Willem III (*son*) (also Guillaume III of Luxembourg)

NETHERLANDS

Nov 1890-May 1940 — Wilhelmina   (*daughter*) (1st) (exiled)
Regent: Nov 1890-Aug 1898 Queen Emma

Commissioner:

May 1940-May 1945 — Artur Seyss-Inquart   (see Austria)

Queens:

May 1945-Sept 1948 — Wilhelmina   (2nd) (abdicated)
Sept 1948-April 1980 — Juliana   (*daughter*) (abdicated)
April 1980- — Beatrix   (*daughter*)

Prime Ministers:

March-Nov 1848	Gerrit Schimmelpenninck
Nov 1848-Nov 1849	Jacob de Kempenaer/Dirk Donker Curtius (1st)
Nov 1849-April 1853	Jan Thorbecke (1st)
April 1853-July 1856	Floris van Hall (1st)/Dirk Donker Curtius (2nd)
July 1856-March 1858	Justinius van der Brugghen
March 1858-Feb 1860	Jacob Rochussen/Pieter van Bosse (1st)
Feb 1860-March 1861	Floris van Hall (2nd)/Schelte van Heemstra
March 1861-Jan 1862	Julius van Zuylen van Nijevelt (1st)/James Louden
Feb 1862-Feb 1866	Jan Thorbecke (2nd)
Feb-June 1866	Isaac Fransen van de Putte (1st)
June 1866-June 1868	Julius van Zuylen van Nijevelt (2nd)/Jan Heemskerk (1st)
June 1868-Jan 1871	Pieter van Bosse (2nd)
Jan 1871-Aug 1872	Jan Thorbecke (3rd)
Aug 1872-Aug 1874	Isaac Fransen van de Putte (2nd)/Gerrit de Vries
Aug 1874-Nov 1877	Constantinius van Lynden van Sandenburg (1st)/Jan Heemskerk (2nd)
Nov 1877-Aug 1879	Johannes Kappeyne van de Coppello
Aug 1879-April 1883	Constantinius van Lynden van Sandenburg (2nd)
April 1883-April 1888	Jan Heemskerk (3rd)
April 1888-Aug 1891	Aeneas Mackay
Aug 1891-May 1894	Cornelius van Tienhoven (Lib)
May 1894-July 1897	Johan Roell (Lib)
July 1897-Aug 1901	Nicolaas Pierson (Lib)
Aug 1901-Aug 1905	Abraham Kuyper
Aug 1905-Dec 1908	Theodoor de Meester (Lib)
Dec 1908-Aug 1913	Theodoor Heemskerk (*son of J.Heemskerk*) (ARP)
Aug 1913-Sept 1918	Pieter Cort van der Linden (Lib)
Sept 1918-Aug 1925	Charles Ruys de Beerenbrouck (1st) (CP)
Aug 1925-May 1929	Hendrickus Colijn (1st) (ARP)
May-Aug 1929	Dirk de Geer (1st)
Aug 1929-May 1933	Charles Ruys de Beerenbrouck (2nd) (CP)
May 1933-Aug 1939	Hendrickus Colijn (2nd)
Aug 1939-May 1940	Dirk de Geer (2nd)

COUNTRIES AND REGIONS

(May 1940-May 1945	German occupation)
May-July 1945	Pieter Gerbrandy (ARP)
July 1945-July 1946	Willem Schermerhorn (SP)
July 1946-Aug 1948	Louis Beel (1st) (CP)
Aug 1948-Dec 1958	Willem Drees (SP)
Dec 1958-May 1959	Louis Beel (2nd) (CP)
May 1959-July 1963	Jan de Quay (CP)
July 1963-April 1965	Victor Marijnen (CP)
April 1965-Nov 1966	Joseph Cals (CP)
Nov 1966-April 1967	Jelle Zijlstra (ARP)
April 1967-July 1971	Petrus de Jong (CP)
July 1971-May 1973	Barend Biesheuvel (ARP)
May 1973-Dec 1977	Johannes (Joop) den Uyl (Lab)
Dec 1977-Nov 1982	Andreas van Agt (CDA)
Nov 1982-Aug 1994	Rudolphus (Ruud) Lubbers (CDA)
Aug 1994-	Wim Kok (Lab)

ARP = Anti-Revolutionary Party
CDA = Christian Democratic Appeal
CP = Catholic Party
Lab = Labour Party
Lib = Liberal Party
SP = Socialist Party

GOVERNMENT-IN-EXILE 1940-45

Headquarters: London
Operated during German occupation

Queen:

May 1940-May 1945	Wilhelmina

Prime Ministers:

May-Sept 1940	Dirk de Geer
Sept 1940-May 1945	Pieter Gerbrandy

Overseas Territories

ARUBA

Part of the Netherlands Antilles until 1986
Capital: Oranjestad

Lieutenant-Governors:

1901-09	Gerard Zeppenfeldt

1911-20	Hendrik Beaujon
1920-28	Jan Quast
1928-45	Isaac Wagemaker
1945-57	Lindoro Kwartsz
1957	P.Croes (acting)
1957-58	K.H.de Boer
1958-59	E.Arends
1959	Oscar Henriquez (acting)
1959-64	F.J.C.Beaujon
1964-73	Oscar Henriquez
1973-79	F.J.(Jossy) Tromp
1979-82	Francisco de Figaroa
1982	Remy Zaandam (acting)
1982-83	E.Nicolaas (acting)
1983-86	Pedro Bislip

Governors:

Jan 1986-Jan 1992	Felipe Tromp
Jan 1992-	Lindo Koolman

Prime Ministers:

Jan 1986-Feb 1989	Hendrik (Henny) Eman (1st) (APP)
Feb 1989-Aug 1994	Nelson Oduber (PEM)
Aug 1994-	Hendrik (Henny) Eman (2nd) (APP)

APP = Aruba People's Party
PEM = People's Electoral Movement

NETHERLANDS ANTILLES

Capital: Willemstad

Governors:

1890-1901	Charles Barge
1901-09	Jan de Jong Beek en Donk
1909-19	Theodorus Nuyens
1919-21	Oscar Helfrich
1921-28	Nicolaas Brantjes
1928-29	Marinus van Dijk (acting)
1929	Leonard Fruytier
1929-30	Herman Schotborgh
1930-36	Bartholomaeus van Slobbe
1936-42	Gielliam Wonters
1942-48	Petrus Kasteel
1948-51	Leonard Peters

1951	Frans Jas (acting)
1951-56	Anton Struycken
1956-57	Frans van der Valk (acting)
1957-62	Antonius Speekenbrink
1962-63	Christiaan Winkel (acting)
1963-71	Nicolaas Debrot
1971-83	Bernardito (Ben) Leito
1983	Julius Beaujon (acting)
1983-90	René Römer
1990-	Jaime Saleh

Prime Ministers:

April 1951-Nov 1954	Moises da Costa Gomez (NPP)
Nov 1954-Feb 1968	Ephraim Jonckheer (CDP)
Feb 1968-Sept 1969	Ciro Kroon (CDP)
Sept-Dec 1969	C.G.Sprockel
Dec 1969-Feb 1971	Ernesto Petronia
Feb-June 1971	Ramez Isa
June 1971-Dec 1973	Otto Beaujon
Dec 1973-Oct 1977	Juancho Evertsz (NPP)
Oct 1977-July 1979	Silvio (Boy) Rozendal (DP)
July-Dec 1979	Miguel Pourier (1st) (BPU)
Dec 1979-Sept 1984	Dominico Martina (1st) (NAM)
Sept 1984-Jan 1986	Maria Liberia Peters (1st) (NPP)
Jan 1986-May 1988	Dominico Martina (2nd) (NAM)
May 1988-Nov 1993	Maria Liberia Peters (2nd) (NPP)
Nov-Dec 1993	Susanne Camelia-Römer (acting)
Dec 1993-March 1994	Alejandro (Jandi) Paula
March 1994-May 1998	Miguel Pourier (2nd) (ARP)
May 1998-	Susanne Camelia-Römer (NPP)

ARP = Antilles Restructuring Party
BPU = Bonaire Patriotic Union
CDP = Curacao Democratic Party
DP = Democratic Party
NAM = New Antilles Movement
NPP = National People's Party

Constitutive Islands of Netherlands Antilles

Bonaire

Capital: Kralendijk

Lieutenant-Governors:

1905-07	Herman Müller (acting)

1910-20	Jacob Thielen (acting 1910-11)
1920-21	Carl de Haseth
1921-23	Richard Beaujon
1923-27	Johan Gentil
1927-28	William Plantz
1928-35	Herman Schotborgh (acting 1928-29)
1935-39	Johan van Eps
1929-43	Pieter van Leeuwen
1943-52	Johan Meiners
1952-56	Xavier Krugers
1952-56	Willem de Haseth (1st)
1956-57	Antonius van Hesteren
1957-58	Willem de Haseth (2nd)
1958-63	Antonius van Hesteren
1963-69	Elias Morkos
1969-73	Raymundo Saleh
1973-84	Alfred Sint Jago
1984-86	A.J.Cecilia (acting)
1986-91	George Soleano
1991-	Fritz Goedgedrag

Curaçao

Capital: Willemstad

Lieutenant-Governors:

(Post held by Governors of Netherlands Antilles until 1951)

1951-67	Michael Gorsira
1967-68	Willem de Haseth (acting)
1968-69	Oscar Beaujon
1969-70	Elias Morkos (see Bonaire)
1970-76	Anno Kibbelaar
1976-82	Ornelio Martina
1982-88	Ronald Casseres
1988-94	Elmer Wilsoe
Sept 1994-	Stanley Betrian

Windward Islands

Capital: Philipsburg

Lieutenant-Governors:

1894-1901	Joseph Moller
1901-18	Abraham Brouwer
1918-19	Frits Thielen (acting)

1919-20	G.J.Tijmstra (acting)
1920	A.W.de Haseth (acting)
1920-23	J.van der Zee (acting)
1923-27	Richard Beaujon (see Bonaire)
1927	C.F.Boskaljon (acting)
1927-30	Willem Lampe
1930-43	Johan Meiners
1943-47	Pieter van Leeuwen
1947-48	M.J.Huith (acting)
1948-57	Johannes Paap
1957	Walter Buncamper (acting) (1st)
1957-58	Hendrik Hessling (acting)
1958-59	Walter Buncamper (acting) (2nd)
1959-68	Jan Beaujon
1968-75	Reinier van Delden (acting 1968-69)
1975-81	Th.M.Pandt
1981-83	Ralph Richardson

The three Windward Islands, Saba, Saint Eustatius and Saint Maarten, obtained separate administrations in 1983.

Saba

Capital: Leverock (*f* The Bottom)

Lieutenant-Governors:

1983-90	Wycliffe Smith
1990-	Sydney Sorton

Saint Eustatius

Capital: Oranjestadt

Lieutenant-Governors:

1983-90	George Sleeswijk
1990-	Irvin Temmer

Saint Maarten

Capital: Philipsburg

Lieutenant-Governors:

1983-91	Ralph Richardson (see Windward Is)
1991-94	Russel Voges
Sept 1994-	Dennis Richardson

NEW ZEALAND

Official name: Dominion of New Zealand, Aotearoa (Maori)
Independence date: 26 September 1907
Capital: Wellington

New Zealand was settled by the Maoris, a Polynesian people, many centuries before the arrival of Europeans. The first European visitor was the Dutch explorer Tasman in 1643, followed by Cook in the eighteenth century. In 1840 the Treaty of Waitangi between Britain and the Maoris made the country a British colony. Self-government was granted in 1856, and Dominion status was accorded in 1907.

Governors:

Aug 1897-June 1904	Earl of Ranfurly (Uchter Knox)
June 1904-June 1910	Baron Plunkett (William Plunkett)
8-27 June 1910	Robert Stoutt (acting) (1st)
June 1910-Dec 1912	Baron Islington (John Dickson-Poynder)
2-19 Dec 1912	Robert Stoutt (acting) (2nd)
Dec 1912-June 1917	Earl of Liverpool (Arthur Foljambe)

Governors-General:
Represents monarch who is concurrently British monarch

June 1917-July 1920	Earl of Liverpool (Arthur Foljambe)
July-Sept 1920	Robert Stoutt (acting) (1st)
Sept 1920-Nov 1924	Viscount Jellicoe (John Jellicoe)
Nov-Dec 1924	Robert Stoutt (acting) (2nd)
Dec 1924-Feb 1930	Charles Fergusson
Feb-March 1930	Michael Myers (acting) (1st)
March 1930-March 1935	Viscount Bledisloe (Charles Bathurst)
March-April 1935	Michael Myers (acting) (2nd)
April 1935-Feb 1941	Viscount Galway (George Monckton-Arundell)
3-22 Feb 1941	Michael Myers (acting) (3rd)
Feb 1941-April 1946	Baron Newall (Cyril Newall)
April-June 1946	Michael Myers (acting) (4th)
June 1946-Aug 1952	Baron Freyburg (Bernard Freyburg)
Aug-Dec 1952	Humphrey O'Leary (acting)
Dec 1952-July 1957	Baron Norrie (Willoughby Norrie)
July-Sept 1957	Harold Barrowclough (acting) (1st)
Sept 1957-Sept 1962	Viscount Cobham (Charles Lyttleton)
Sept-Nov 1962	Harold Barrowclough (acting) (2nd)
Nov 1962-Oct 1967	Bernard Fergusson (*son of Charles Fergusson*)

Oct-Nov 1967	Richard Wild (acting) (1st)
Nov 1967-Sept 1972	Arthur Porritt
6-27 Sept 1972	Richard Wild (acting) (2nd)
Sept 1972-Oct 1977	Denis Blundell
5-26 Oct 1977	Richard Wild (acting) (3rd)
Oct 1977-Oct 1980	Keith Holyoake
Oct-Nov 1980	Ronald Davison (acting)
Nov 1980-Nov 1985	David Beattie
Nov 1985-Nov 1990	Paul Reeves
Nov 1990-March 1996	Catherine Tizard (*b* C.Maclean)
March 1996-	Michael Hardie Boys

Prime Ministers:

7-20 May 1856	Henry Sewell
May-June 1856	William Fox (1st)
June 1856-July 1861	Edward Stafford (1st)
July 1861-Aug 1862	William Fox (2nd)
Aug 1862-Oct 1863	Alfred Domett
Oct 1863-Nov 1864	Frederick Whitaker (1st)
Nov 1864-Oct 1865	Frederick Weld
Oct 1865-June 1869	Edward Stafford (2nd)
June 1869-Sept 1872	William Fox (3rd)
Sept-Oct 1872	Edward Stafford (3rd)
Oct 1872-March 1873	George Waterhouse
March-April 1873	William Fox (4th)
April 1873-July 1875	Julius Vogel (1st)
July 1875-Feb 1876	Daniel Pollen
Feb-Sept 1876	Julius Vogel (2nd)
Sept 1876-Oct 1877	Harry Atkinson (1st)
Oct 1877-Oct 1879	George Grey
Oct 1879-April 1882	John Hall
April 1882-Sept 1883	Frederick Whitaker (2nd)
Sept 1883-Aug 1884	Harry Atkinson (2nd)
16-28 Aug 1884	Robert Stout (1st)
Aug-Sept 1884	Harry Atkinson (3rd)
Sept 1884-Oct 1887	Robert Stout (2nd)
Oct 1887-Jan 1891	Harry Atkinson (4th)
Jan 1891-April 1893	John Ballance (Lib) (†)
May 1893-June 1906	Richard Seddon (Lib) (†)
June-Aug 1906	William Hall-Jones (Lib)
Aug 1906-March 1912	Joseph Ward (1st) (Lib)
March-July 1912	Thomas MacKenzie (Lib)
July 1912-May 1925	William Massey (RP) (†)
14-30 May 1925	Francis Bell (RP)

May 1925-Dec 1928	Joseph Coates (RP)
Dec 1928-May 1930	Joseph Ward (2nd) (UP)
May 1930-Dec 1935	George Forbes (UP)
Dec 1935-March 1940	Michael Savage (Lab) (†)
March 1940-Dec 1949	Peter Fraser (acting March-April 1940) (Lab)
Dec 1949-Sept 1957	Sidney Holland (NP)
Sept-Dec 1957	Keith Holyoake (1st) (NP)
Dec 1957-Dec 1960	Walter Nash (Lab)
Dec 1960-Feb 1972	Keith Holyoake (2nd) (NP)
Feb-Dec 1972	John Marshall (NP)
Dec 1972-Aug 1974	Norman Kirk (Lab) (†)
1-6 Sept 1974	Hugh Watt (acting) (Lab)
Sept 1974-Dec 1975	Wallace (Bill) Rowling (Lab)
Dec 1975-July 1984	Robert Muldoon (NP)
July 1984-Aug 1989	David Lange (Lab)
Aug 1989-Sept 1990	Geoffrey Palmer (Lab)
Sept-Oct 1990	Michael Moore (Lab)
Oct 1990-Dec 1997	James (Jim) Bolger (NP)
Dec 1997-Dec 1999	Jenny Shipley (NP)
Dec 1999-	Helen Clark (Lab)

Lab = Labour Party
Lib = Liberal Party
NP = National Party
RP = Reform Party
UP = United Party

Territories

COOK ISLANDS

Capital: Avarua

Queen:

1874-1901	Makea Takau
(1888-1901	British protectorate)

Commissioners:

1901-09	Walter Gudgeon
1909-13	James Eman Smith
1913-16	Henry Northcote
1916-21	Frederick Platts
1921-23	John Hewitt
1923-37	Hugh Ayson (1st)

1937-38	Stephen Smith
1938-43	Hugh Ayson (2nd)
1943-51	William Tailby
1951-60	Geoffrey Nevill
1960-65	Albert Dare (see Niue)

High Commissioners:

1965	Albert Dare
1965-73	Leslie Davis
1973-75	G.J.Brocklehurst

Queen's Representatives:

1975-85	Gavin Donne (acting 1975-82)
1985-90	Tangaroa Tangaroa
1990-	Apenera Short

Prime Ministers:

Aug 1965-June 1978	Albert Henry (CIP)
June 1978-April 1983	Thomas Davis (1st) (DP)
April-Nov 1983	Geoffrey Henry (1st) (*cousin of A.Henry*) (CIP)
Nov 1983-July 1987	Thomas Davis (2nd) (DP)
July 1987-Jan 1989	Pupuke Robati (DP)
Jan 1989-Aug 1999	Geoffrey Henry (2nd) (CIP)
Aug-Nov 1999	Joseph Williams
Nov 1999-	Terepai Moate (DA)

CIP = Cook Islands Party
DP = Democratic Party
DA = Democratic Alliance

NIUE

Capital: Alofi

Kings:

March 1875-87	Mataio Tuitoga
Nov 1888-96	Fata'a-iki
June 1897-Oct 1900	Tongia
(Oct 1900-June 1901	British protectorate)

Resident Commissioners:

1901-02	Stephenson Smith
1902-07	Christopher Maxwell

1907-18	Henry Cornwall
1918-20	Guy Morris (1st)
1920-22	John Evison
1922-26	Guy Morris (2nd)
1926-31	Albert Luckham
1931-42	William Bell
1942-43	Joseph McMahon-Box
1943-53	Cecil Larson
1953-56	Jock McEwen
1956-58	Albert Dare
1958-62	David Heatley
1962-68	Lyle Shanks
1968-73	Selwyn Wilson
1973-74	C.A.Roberts
(1974	post abolished)

High Commissioners:

Aug 1973-96	Warren Searell
Feb 1997-May 2000	Mike Pointer
May 2000-	John Bryant

Government Leader:

Nov 1968-Oct 1974	Robert Rex

Prime Ministers:

Oct 1974-Dec 1992	Robert Rex (†)
Dec 1992-March 1993	Young Vivian
March 1993-March 1999	Frank Lui
March 1999-	Sani Lakatami

TOKELAU

Administrators:

1967-71	R.O.Gabites
1971-73	R.B.Taylor
1973-75	W.G.Thorpe
1975-84	Frank Corner
1984-Feb 1988	H.Francis
Feb 1988-July 1990	Neil Walter
July 1990-March 1993	Graham Ansell
March 1993-94	Lindsay Watt
1994-	Brian Absolum

Heads:

Ulu-o-Tokelau

Jan-Dec 1992	Kuresa Nasau (1st)
Jan-Dec 1993	Salesio Lui
Jan-Dec 1994	Peniuto Semisi
Jan-Dec 1995	Lepaio Simi
Jan-Dec 1996	Pio Tuia (1st)
Jan-Dec 1997	Falima Teao
Jan-Dec 1998	Kuresa Nasau (2nd)
Jan-Dec 1999	Pio Tuia (2nd)
Jan-Dec 2000	Kolouei O'Brien

Atolls of Tokelau

Atafu

Faipules:

Jan 1987-Jan 1993	Kuresa Nasau (1st)
Jan 1993-Jan 1996	Lepaio Simi
Jan 1996-	Kuresa Nasau (2nd)

Fakaofo

Faipules:

Jan 1987-Jan 1996	Peniuto Semisi
Jan 1996-Jan 1999	Falima Teao
Jan 1999-	Kolouei O'Brien

Nukunonu

Faipules:

Jan 1990-Jan 1996	Salesio Lui
Jan 1996-	Pio Tuia

NICARAGUA

Official name: Republic of Nicaragua, República de Nicaragua
Independence date: 15 September 1821
Capital: Managua

Nicaragua was colonized by Spain in 1526. Independence was declared in 1821, and from 1823 until 1838 Nicaragua formed part of the Central American Confederation. The coup of 1936 marked the start of 43 years of dictatorship dominated by the Somoza family which was ended in 1979 with the establishment of the left-wing Sandanista government. Democratic elections were held in 1990.

Presidents:

April 1825-Nov 1828	Manuel de la Cerda
May 1830-March 1833	Dionisio Herrera
Feb 1835-Jan 1837	José Zepeda (†)
Jan 1837-June 1839	José Núñez
June-July 1839	Patricio Rivas (1st)
July-Nov 1839	Joaquín Cosio
Nov 1839-Sept 1840	Tomás Valladares
Sept 1840-March 1841	Patricio Rivas (2nd)
March-April 1841	Pablo Buitrago
April 1841-April 1845	Juan de Dios Orozco
April 1845-April 1847	José Sandoval
April 1847-April 1848	José Guerrero
April 1848-May 1851	Norberto Ramirez
May 1851-April 1853	Laureano Pineda
April 1853-March 1854	Frutos Chamorro (†)
June 1854-May 1855	Francisco Castellon (†)
May 1855-July 1856	José Estrada (deposed)
July 1856-Jan 1857	William Walker
Jan-June 1857	Patricio Rivas (3rd)
June 1857-March 1867	Tomás Martínez
March 1867-Feb 1871	Fernando Guzmán
March 1871-Feb 1875	Vicente Cuandra
March 1875-Feb 1879	Pedro Chamorro
March 1879-Feb 1883	Joaquín Zavala
March 1883-Feb 1885	Adan Cárdenas
March 1885-Feb 1887	Pedro Chamorro
March 1887-Aug 1889	Evaristo Carazo (†)
Aug 1889-June 1893	Roberto Sacasa
June 1893-Dec 1909	José Santos Zelaya (acting June 1893-Feb 1894)

Dec 1909-Aug 1910	José Madriz (acting)
Aug 1910-Jan 1911	José D.Estrada (†)
Jan-May 1911	José J.Estrada (*brother*)
May 1911-Dec 1916	Adolfo Díaz (1st)
Jan 1917-Dec 1920	Emiliano Chamorro Vargas (1st)
Jan 1921-Oct 1923	Diego Chamorro (*nephew*) (†)
Oct 1923-Dec 1924	Bartolomé Martínez Bartolo (acting)
Dec 1924-Jan 1926	Carlos Solórzano
Jan-Nov 1926	Emiliano Chamorro Vargas (2nd)
Nov 1926-Jan 1928	Adolfo Díaz (2nd)
Jan 1928-Dec 1932	José Moncada
Jan 1933-June 1936	Juan Bautista Sacasa (deposed)
June-Dec 1936	Carlos Brenes Jarquin
Dec 1936-May 1947	Anastasio Somoza García (1st)
1-25 May 1947	Leonardo Argüello (deposed)
May-Aug 1947	Benjamin Lacayo Sacasa (deposed)
Aug 1947-May 1950	Víctor Roman y Reyes (*uncle of A.Somoza García*) (†)
May 1950-Sept 1956	Anastasio Somoza García (NLP) (2nd) († assassinated)
Sept 1956-May 1963	Luis Somoza Debayle (*son*) (NLP)
May 1963-Aug 1966	René Shick Gutiérrez (NLP) (†)
Aug 1966-May 1967	Lorenzo Guerrero Gutiérrez (NLP)
May 1967-May 1972	Anastasio Somoza Debayle (*son of A.Somoza García*) (NLP) (1st)
(May 1972-Dec 1974	Triumvirate:
May 1972-Dec 1974	Roberto Martínez Laclaya (NLP)
May 1972-Dec 1974	Alfonso Lobo Cordero (NLP)
May 1972-Jan 1973	Fernando Agüero Rocha (CP)
Jan 1973-Dec 1974	Edmundo Paguaga Irias (CP))
Dec 1974-July 1979	Anastasio Somoza Debayle (NLP) (2nd) (assassinated 1980)
17-19 July 1979	Francisco Urcuyo Maliaño (deposed)
(July 1979-March 1981	Five-member junta)
March 1981-April 1990	Daniel Ortega Saavedra (Junta co-ordinator March 1981-Jan 1985) (SNLF)
April 1990-Jan 1997	Violeta Barrios de Chamorro (UNO)
Jan 1997-	Arnaldo Alemán (LCP)

CP = Conservative Party
LCP = Liberal Constitutionalist Party
NLP = National Liberal Party
SNLF = Sandanista National Liberation Front
UNO = United National Opposition

NIGER

Official name: Republic of Niger, République du Niger
Independence date: 3 August 1960
Capital: Niamey

Niger was proclaimed a French colony in 1891, and later became part of French West Africa. In 1946 its status was changed to Overseas Territory, and in 1958 self-government was granted. In 1960 Niger became an independent republic.

Lieutenant-Governors:

1922-29	Jules Brevie
1930	Alphonse Choteau (see Mauritania)
1931	Louis-Placide Blacher
1932-33	Théophile Tellier (see Dahomey)
1933-34	Maurice-Léon Bourgine
1934-35	Léon Petre (see Togo)
1936-37	Joseph-Urbain Court

Governors:

1937-38	Joseph-Urbain Court
1939-40	Jean Rapenne
1941-42	Maurice-Émile Falvy
1942-54	Jean-François Toby
1955-56	Jean-Paul Ramadier
1956-58	Paul-Camille Bordier
1958	Louis-Félix Rollet
1958	Don-Jean Colombani (see Senegal)

High Commissioner:

1959-60	Don-Jean Colombani

Presidents:

Aug 1960-April 1974	Hamani Diori (deposed)
April 1974-Nov 1987	Seyni Kountché (†)
Nov 1987-April 1993	Ali Saibou
April 1993-Jan 1996	Mahamane Ousmane (DSC) (deposed)
Jan 1996-April 1999	Ibrahim Barry Mainassara († assassinated)
April 1999-Dec 1999	Douda Mallam Wanké
Dec 1999-	Tandja Mamadou (NMDS)

Prime Ministers:

July-Dec 1958	Djibo Bakary	(NDU)
Dec 1958-Aug 1960	Hamani Diori	(NPP)
(Aug 1960-Jan 1983	post abolished)	
Jan-Nov 1983	Oumarou Mamane	(1st)
Nov 1983-July 1988	Hamid Algabid	
July 1988-Dec 1989	Oumarou Mamane	(2nd)
(Dec 1989-March 1990	post abolished)	
March 1990-Oct 1991	Aliou Mahamidou	
Oct 1991-April 1993	Amadou Cheffou	
April 1993-Sept 1994	Mahamadou Issoufou	(NPDS)
Sept 1994-Feb 1995	Abdoulaye Souley	
8-21 Feb 1995	Amadou Boubacar Cisse	(1st)
Feb 1995-Jan 1996	Hama Amadou	(1st)
Jan 1996-June 1997	Boukary Adji	
June-Nov 1997	Amadou Boubacar Cisse	(2nd)
Nov 1997-Jan 2000	Ibrahim Maiyaki	
Jan 2000-	Hama Amadou	(2nd) (NMDS)

DSC = Democratic and Social Convention
NDU = Niger Democratic Union
NMDS = National Movement for Development of Society
NPDS = Niger Party for Democracy and Socialism
NPP = Niger Progress Party

NIGERIA

Official name: Federal Republic of Nigeria
Previous names: Federation of Nigeria 1954-63, Republic of Nigeria Jan-July 1966
Independence date: 1 October 1960
Capital: Lagos (until 1991), Abuja (since 1991)

Lagos was ceded to Great Britain by the local ruler in 1861, and in 1886 it was made a separate colony. Southern Nigeria became a British protectorate in 1885, and Northern Nigeria was transferred to the British crown in 1899, having been ruled by the Royal Niger Company since 1886. In 1906 Lagos and Southern Nigeria were united, and in 1914 were joined by Northern Nigeria to form the colony and protectorate of Nigeria. In 1954 Nigeria became a federation, with full self-government being granted in 1957 and independence in 1960. In 1963 Nigeria became a republic. From 1967 to 1970 the secession of the eastern region as Biafra, led to civil war. Except for the periods 1960-66 and 1979-83, the country has been ruled by the military.

Governors:

1914-19	Frederick Lugard
1919-25	Hugh Clifford
1925-31	Graeme Thomson
1931-35	Donald Cameron
1935-42	Bernard Bourdillon
1942-43	Alan Burns
1943-48	Arthur Richards
1948-54	John MacPherson

Governors-General:
Represented monarch who was concurrently British monarch

1954-55	John MacPherson
1955-Nov 1960	James Robertson
Nov 1960-Sept 1963	Nnamdi Azikiwe (see Eastern Nigeria)

Presidents:
Chairman of the Supreme Military Council 1966-79, 1983-85
Chairman of the Interim Government Aug-Nov 1993
Chairman of the Provisional Ruling Council 1993-99

Oct 1963-Jan 1966	Nnamdi Azikiwe (deposed)
Jan-July 1966	Johnson Aguiyi-Ironsi (deposed, assassinated)
Aug 1966-July 1975	Yakubu Gowon (deposed)
July 1975-Feb 1976	Murtala Mohammed († assassinated)

Feb 1976-Oct 1979	Olusegun Obasanjo (1st)
Oct 1979-Dec 1983	Shehu Shagari (NPN) (deposed)
Dec 1983-Aug 1985	Mohammed Buhari (see North Eastern State) (deposed)
Aug 1985-Aug 1993	Ibrahim Babangida
Aug-Nov 1993	Ernest Shonekan
Nov 1993-June 1998	Sani Abacha (†)
June 1998-May 1999	Abdulsalam Abubakar
May 1999-	Olusegun Obasanjo (2nd) (PDP)

Prime Minister:

Aug 1957-Jan 1966	Abubakar Tafawa Balewa (NPC) (deposed, assassinated)
(Jan 1966	post abolished)

Head of Government:

Chairman of the Transitional Council

Jan-Aug 1993	Ernest Shonekan

NPC = Northern People's Congress
NPN = National Party of Nigeria
PDP = People's Democratic Party

Regions 1954-67

EASTERN NIGERIA

Capital: Port Harcourt

Lieutenant-Governors:

1951-52	James Pyke-Nott
1952-54	Clement Pleass

Governors:

1954-56	Clement Pleass
1956-60	Robert Stapleton
Oct 1960-Jan 1966	Francis Ibiam
Jan 1966-May 1967	C. Odemegwu Ojukwu

Premiers:

Oct 1954-Dec 1959	Nnamdi Azikiwe (NCP)
Dec 1959-Jan 1966	Michael Okpara (NCP)
(Jan 1966	post abolished)

NCP = National Council Party

In 1967 the Eastern Region seceded as the state of Biafra

MID-WESTERN NIGERIA

Capital: Benin

Governors:

1963-Jan 1966	J.S.Mariere
Jan 1966-Aug 1967	D.A.Ejoor
(Aug-Sept 1967	Seceded as Benin - see below)
Sept 1967-March 1968	Samuel Ogbemudia

Premier:

Aug 1963-Jan 1966	Dennis Osadebay (deposed)
(Jan 1966	post abolished)

NORTHERN NIGERIA

Capital: Kano

Lieutenant-Governors:

1951-52	Eric Thompson
1952-54	Bryan Sharwood-Smith

Governors:

1954-57	Bryan Sharwood-Smith
1957-62	Gawain Bell
1962-Jan 1966	Kashim Ibrahim
Jan 1966-March 1968	Hassan Katsina

Premier:

Oct 1954-Jan 1966	Ahmadu Bello (NPC) (deposed, assassinated)
(Jan 1966	post abolished)

WESTERN NIGERIA

Capital: Ibadan

Lieutenant-Governors:

1951	Theodore Hoskyns-Abrahall
1951-54	Hugo Marshall

Governors:

1954-60	John Rankine

Oct 1960-Dec 1962   Adesogi Aderemi (Oni of Ife)
Dec 1962-Jan 1966   Joseph Fadahunsi
Jan-July 1966   Francis Fajuyi († assassinated)
July 1966-March 1968 Robert Adebayo

Premiers:

Oct 1954-Dec 1959   Obafemi Awolowo   (AG)
Dec 1959-May 1962   Samuel Akintola   (1st) (AG)
(May 1962-Jan 1963 post vacant)
Jan 1963-Jan 1966   Samuel Akintola   (2nd) (UPP) (deposed)
(Jan 1966   post abolished)

AG = Action Group
UPP = United People's Party

Secessionist States

BENIN
Republic of Benin

Previous name: Mid-Western Nigeria
Independence date: 18 August 1967
Secession ended: September 1967
Capital: Benin

Administrator:

Aug-Sept 1967   George Okonkwo

BIAFRA
Republic of Biafra

Previous name: Eastern Nigeria
Independence date: 30 May 1967
Secession ended: 15 January 1970
Capital: Port Harcourt

Heads of State:

May 1967-Jan 1970   C.Odemegwu Ojukwu
12-15 Jan 1970   Phillip Effiong

States
In 1968 the four regions were organized into 12 states. In 1976 these were re-organized into 19 states, with two more being created in 1987. Nine new states were created in 1991 and six more in 1996.

ABIA

Part of Imo until 1991
Capital: Umuahia

Administrator:

Aug 1991-Jan 1992   Frank Ajobena

Governor:

Jan 1992-Nov 1993   Ogbonnaya Onu   (NRC)

Administrators:

Dec 1993-Sept 1994   Ike Nwosu
Sept 1994-Aug 1996   Temi Ejoor   (see Enugu)
Aug 1996-Aug 1998   Moses Fasanya
Aug 1998-May 1999   Anthony Obi   (see Osun)

Governor:

May 1999-   Oriji Kalu   (PDP)

NRC = National Republican Convention

ADAMAWA

Part of North Eastern State 1968-76
Previous name: Gongola 1976-91
Capital: Yola

Governors:

March 1976-July 1978   Mohammed Jega   (1st)
July 1978-Oct 1979   A.Mamadu
Oct 1979-Oct 1983   Abubakar Barde   (GNPP)
Oct-Dec 1983   B.Turkur   (NPN)
Jan 1984-Aug 1985   Mohammed Jega   (2nd)
Aug 1985-Aug 1986   Yohanna Madaki
Aug 1986-Dec 1987   Honah Jang
Dec 1987-Dec 1989   Isah Mohammed
Dec 1989-Jan 1992   Abubakr Salihu
Jan 1992-Nov 1993   Saleh Michika

Administrators:

Dec 1993-Sept 1994   G.Agboneni
Sept 1994-Aug 1996   Mustapha Ismail   (see Kwara)

Aug 1996-Aug 1998	J.A.Kalu-Igboama
Aug 1998-May 1999	A.G.Husseni

Governor:

(1999	Abubakar Atiku (PDP) Governor-elect; became Vice-President)
May 1999-	Haruna Bonnie (PDP)

GNPP = Greater Nigerian People's Party

AKWA-IBOM

Part of Cross River until 1987
Capital: Uyo

Governors:

Sept 1987-July 1988	Jonathan Ogbeha
July 1988-Aug 1990	Godwin Abbe
Aug 1990-Jan 1992	I.O.Nkanga
Jan 1992-Nov 1993	Akpan Isemin (NRC)

Administrators:

Dec 1993-Aug 1996	Y.Bako
Aug 1996-Aug 1998	J.A.Adewusi
Aug 1998-May 1999	John Ebiye

Governor:

May 1999-	Victor Attah (PDP)

ANAMBRA

Part of Enugu (*f* Anambra) until 1991
Capital: Awka

Administrator:

Aug 1991-Jan 1992	Joseph Abula

Governor:

Jan 1992-Nov 1993	Chukwuemeka Ezeife

Administrators:

Dec 1993-Aug 1996	M.E.Atta
Aug 1996-Aug 1998	Rufai Garba

Aug 1998-May 1999   Emmanuel Ukaegbu

Governor:

May 1999-   Chinwoke Mbadinuju   (PDP)

BAUCHI

Part of North Eastern State 1968-76
Capital: Bauchi

Governors:

March 1976-July 1978   B.Kaliel
July 1978-Oct 1979   Garba Duba
Oct 1979-Dec 1983   Tatari Ali   (NPN)
Jan 1984-Aug 1985   M.S.Sani
Aug 1985-Dec 1987   Chris Gabuka
Dec 1987-Aug 1990   Joshua Madaki
Aug 1990-Jan 1992   Abu Ali
Jan 1992-Nov 1993   Dahiru Mohammed   (NRC)

Administrators:

Dec 1993-Sept 1994   James Kalau
Sept 1994-Aug 1996   R.A.Raji
Aug 1996-Aug 1998   Theophilus Bamigboye
Aug 1998-May 1999   Abdul Mshelia

Governor:

May 1999-   Ahmadu Muazu   (PDP)

BAYELSA

Part of Rivers until 1996
Capital: Yenogoa

Administrators:

Oct 1996-Aug 1998   Oladipo Phillips
Aug 1998-May 1999   Paul Obi

Governor:

May 1999-   Diepreye Alameyseigha   (PDP)

BENUE

Part of Benue-Plateau 1968-76
Capital: Makurdi

Governors:

March 1976-July 1978	Abdullahi Shelleng
July 1978-Oct 1979	Bayo Lawal
Oct 1979-Dec 1983	Aper Aku (NPN)
Jan 1984-Aug 1985	John Kpera (see Enugu)
Aug 1985-Aug 1986	David Jang
Aug-Sept 1986	Yohanna Madaki (see Gongola)
Sept 1986-87	Ishaya Bakul
1987	Idris Garba
Dec 1987-Jan 1992	Fidelis Makka
Jan 1992-Nov 1993	Moses Adesu

Administrators:

Dec 1993-Aug 1996	J.O.Obademi
Aug 1996-Aug 1998	Aminu Kontagora
Aug 1998-May 1999	Dominic Oneya (see Kano)

Governor:

May 1999-	George Akum (PDP)

BORNO

Part of North Eastern State 1968-76
Capital: Maiduguri

Governors:

March 1976-July 1978	M.A Amin
July 1978-Oct 1979	Tunde Idiagbon
Oct 1979-Oct 1983	Mohammed Goni (GNPP)
Oct-Dec 1983	S.Jarma (NPP)
Jan 1984-Aug 1985	A.Waziri (see Bendel)
Aug 1985-Dec 1987	Abdul Momin Aminu
Dec 1987-Dec 1989	Abduwan Mohammed
Dec 1989-June 1990	Mohammed Maina
June 1990-Jan 1992	Mohammed Murwa
Jan 1992-Nov 1993	Abba Gana Terab

Administrators:

Dec 1993-Aug 1996	I.Dada

Aug 1996-Aug 1998   V.A.Ozodunobi
Aug 1998-May 1999   Lawal Haruna

Governor:

May 1999-   Marla Kachalla   (APP)

APP = All People's Party

CROSS RIVER

Previous name: South Eastern State 1968-76
Capital: Calabar

Governors:

April 1968-July 1975   Uduokaha Esuene
July 1975-July 1978   Paul Omu
July 1978-Oct 1979   M.Elegbede
Oct 1979-Oct 1983   Clement Isong   (NPN)
Oct-Dec 1983   Donald Etiebet   (NPN)
Jan 1984-86   Daniel Archibong
1986-Dec 1989   Ibim Princewell
Dec 1989-Jan 1992   Ernest Atta
Jan 1992-Nov 1993   Clement Ebri   (NRC)

Administrators:

Dec 1993-Sept 1994   I.Kephas
Sept 1994-Aug 1996   G.Agboneni   (see Adamawa)
Aug 1996-Aug 1998   Umar Farouk Ahmed
Aug 1998-May 1999   Christopher Osundu

Governor:

May 1999-   Donald Duke   (PDP)

DELTA

Part of Edo (*f* Bendel) until 1991
Capital: Asaba

Administrator:

Aug 1991-Jan 1992   S.C.Ochulor

Governor:

Jan 1992-Nov 1993   Felix Ibru   (SDP)

Administrators:

Dec 1993-Sept 1994	Bassey Asuquo
Sept 1994-Aug 1996	I.Kephas (see Cross River)
Aug 1996-Aug 1998	John Dung
Aug 1998-May 1999	Walter Feghabo

Governor:

May 1999-	James Ibori (PDP)

SDP = Social Democratic Party

EBONYI

Part of Abia and Enya until 1996
Capital: Abakaliki

Administrators:

Oct 1996-Aug 1998	Ayu Fegahabor
Aug 1998-May 1999	Simeon Oduoye (see Niger)

Governor:

May 1999-	Sam Egwu (PDP)

EDO

Previous names: Mid-Western State 1968-76, Bendel 1976-91
Capital: Benin City

Governors:

March 1968-July 1975	Samuel Ogbemudia (1st)
July 1975-March 1976	George Innih
March 1976-July 1978	Hussaini Abdullahi
July 1978-Oct 1979	A.Waziri
Oct 1979-Oct 1983	Ambrose Ali (UPN)
Oct-Dec 1983	Samuel Ogbemudia (2nd) (NPN)
Jan 1984-Aug 1985	J.T.Useni
Aug 1985-Dec 1987	John Inienger
Dec 1987-Aug 1990	Jonathan Ogbeha (see Akwa-Ibom)
Aug 1990-Jan 1992	J.Yeri
Jan 1992-Nov 1993	John Oyegun (SDP)

Administrators:

Dec 1993-Sept 1994	M.A.S.Oluka

Sept 1994-Aug 1996   Bassey Asuquo   (see Delta)
Aug 1996-Aug 1998   B.A.Iyam
Aug 1998-May 1999   Anthony Onyearugbulem   (see Ondo)

Governor:

May 1999-   Lucky Igbinedion   (PDP)

UPN = Unity Party of Nigeria

EKITI

Part of Ondo until 1996
Capital: Ado-Ekiti

Administrators:

Oct 1996-Aug 1998   Mohammed Bawa
Aug 1998-May 1999   M.Atanda Yussuf

Governor:

May 1999-   Niyi Adebayo   (AD)

AD = Alliance for Democracy

ENUGU

Part of East Central State 1968-76
Previous name: Anambra 1976-91
Capital: Enugu

Governors:

March 1976-July 1978   John Kpera
July 1978-Oct 1979   D.S.Abubakar
Oct 1979-Oct 1983   Jim Nwobodo   (NPP)
Oct-Dec 1983   Christian Onoh   (NPN)
Jan 1984-Aug 1985   Allison Madueke
Aug 1985-Dec 1987   Samson Omeruah
Dec 1987-Aug 1990   Robert Akonobi
Aug 1990-Jan 1992   Herbert Eze
Jan 1992-Nov 1993   Okwesilieze Nwodo   (NRC)

Administrators:

Dec 1993-Sept 1994   Temi Ejoor
Sept 1994-Aug 1996   L.Mike Torey   (see Ondo)
Aug 1996-Aug 1998   S.Ahman

Aug 1998-May 1999   Adewumi Agbaje

Governor:

May 1999-   Chimaroke Nnamani   (PDP)

NPP = Nigerian People's Party

GOMBE

Part of Bauchi until 1996
Capital: Gombe

Administrators:

Oct 1996-Aug 1998   J.I.Oriji
Aug 1998-May 1999   Mohammed Bawa   (see Ekiti)

Governor:

May 1999-   Abubakar Abu Hasheed   (APP)

IMO

Part of East Central State 1968-76
Capital: Owerri

Governors:

March 1976-77   G.Kanu
1977-July 1978   Adekunle Lawal   (see Lagos)
July 1978-Oct 1979   S.A.Adenihun
Oct 1979-Dec 1983   Samuel Mbakwe   (1st) (NPN)
Jan 1984-Aug 1985   I.Nwachukwu
Aug 1985-86   Allison Madueke   (see Enugu)
1986-89   Amedi Ikwechegh
1989-Aug 1990   Samuel Mbakwe   (2nd)
Aug 1990-Jan 1992   A.E.Oguguo
Jan 1992-Nov 1993   Evan Enwerem   (NRC)

Administrators:

Dec 1993-Aug 1996   J.J.Aneke
Aug 1996-May 1999   Tanko Zubairu

Governor:

May 1999-   Achike Udenwa   (PDP)

JIGAWA

Part of Kano until 1991
Capital: Dutse

Administrator:

Aug 1991-Jan 1992   Olayinka Sule

Governor:

Jan 1992-Nov 1993   A.S.Birni-Kudu   (SDP)

Administrators:

Dec 1993-Aug 1996   J.Aliyu
Aug 1996-Aug 1998   R.A.Shekani
Aug 1998-May 1999   Abubakar Maimalari

Governor:

May 1999-   Ibrahim Turaki   (APP)

KADUNA

Previous name: North Central State 1968-76
Capital: Kaduna

Governors:

April 1968-July 1975   Abba Kyari
July 1975-77   Usman Jibrin
1977-July 1978   Muktar Muhammed
July 1978-Oct 1979   I.Alfa
Oct 1979-Oct 1981   Balarabe Musa   (PRP)
Oct 1981-Oct 1983   Abba Musa Rimi   (PRP)
Oct-Dec 1983   Lawal Kaita   (NPN)
Jan 1984-Aug 1985   U.Muaza
Aug 1985-June 1988   Abubakar Umar
July 1988-Aug 1990   Abdullahi Mukhtar   (see Katsina)
Aug 1990-Jan 1992   Tanko Ayuba
Jan 1992-Nov 1993   Mohammed Lere   (NRC)

Administrators:

Dec 1993-Aug 1996   L.J.Isa
Aug 1996-Aug 1998   Hamed Ali
Aug 1998-May 1999   Umar Farouk Ahmed   (see Cross River)

Governor:

May 1999-   Ahmed Markarfi   (PDP)

PRP = People's Redemption Party

KANO

Capital: Kano

Governors:

April 1968-July 1975	Abdu Bako
July 1975-July 1978	Sani Bello
July 1978-Oct 1979	A.Shekari
Oct 1979-Oct 1983	Abubakar Rimi (PRP)
Oct-Dec 1983	Sabo Bakinzuwo (PRP)
Jan 1984-Aug 1985	Hussaini Abdullahi (see Bendel)
Aug 1985-87	Ahmed Daku
1987-July 1988	Mohammed Umaru (see Kwara)
July 1988-Jan 1992	Idris Garba (see Benue)
Jan 1992-Nov 1993	Kabiru Gaya (NRC)

Administrators:

Dec 1993-Aug 1996	M.Wase
Aug 1996-Aug 1998	Domenic Oneya
Aug 1998-May 1999	Aminu Kontagora (see Benue)

Governor:

May 1999-   Rabiu Kwankwaso   (PDP)

KATSINA

Part of Kaduna until 1987
Capital: Katsina

Governors:

Sept 1987-July 1988	Abdullahi Mukhtar
July 1988-Dec 1989	Lawrence Onoja (see Plateau)
Dec 1989-Jan 1992	John Madaki
Jan 1992-Nov 1993	Sa'idu Barda (NRC)

Administrators:

Dec 1993-Aug 1996   E.Acholonu

Aug 1996-Aug 1998   Samaila Chama
Aug 1998-May 1999   Joseph Akaagerger

Governor:

May 1999-   Umar Musa Yar'adua   (PDP)

KEBBI

Part of Sokoto until 1991
Capital: Birnin Kebbi

Administrator:

Aug 1991-Jan 1992   Patrick Aziza

Governor:

Jan 1992-Nov 1993   Abubakr Musa   (NRC)

Administrators:

Dec 1993-Aug 1996   S.T.Bello
Aug 1996-Aug 1998   J.I.P.Ubah
Aug 1998-May 1999   Samaila Chamah   (see Katsina)

Governor:

May 1999-   Adamu Aliero   (APP)

KOGI

Part of Kwara until 1991
Capital: Lokoja

Administrator:

Aug 1991-Jan 1992   Dauladi Zakari

Governor:

Jan 1992-Nov 1993   Abubakar Audu   (1st) (NRC)

Administrators:

Dec 1993-Aug 1996   T.U.N.Omeruo
Aug 1996-Aug 1998   B.L.Afakirye
Aug 1998-May 1999   Augustine Aniebo

Governor:

May 1999-   Abubakar Audu   (2nd) (APP)

KWARA

Capital: Ilorin

Governors:

April 1968-July 1975	David Bamigboye
July 1975-March 1976	Ibrahim Taiwo
March 1976-July 1978	George Innih (see Mid-Western State)
July 1978-Oct 1979	S.O.Iferle
Oct 1979-Oct 1983	Adamu Atta (NPN)
Oct-Dec 1983	Cornelius Adebayo (NPN)
Jan 1984-Aug 1985	B.Latinwo
Aug 1985-Dec 1987	Mohammed Umaru
Dec 1987-July 1988	Ahmed Abdullahi
July 1988-Dec 1989	Ibrahim Alkali
Dec 1989-Jan 1992	Awali Kazir
Jan 1992-Nov 1993	Shaba Lafiaji (SDP)

Administrators:

Dec 1993-Sept 1994	Mustapha Ismail
Sept 1994-Aug 1996	B.A.Iyam
Aug 1996-Aug 1998	P.A.M.Ogar
Aug 1998-May 1999	Rasheed Shekoni

Governor:

May 1999-   Mohammed Lawal   (APP)

LAGOS

Capital: Ikeja

Governors:

April 1968-July 1975	Mobolaji Johnson
July 1975-77	Adekunle Lawal
1977-July 1978	Godwin Nkanu
July 1978-Oct 1979	O.E.Ukiwe (see Niger)
Oct 1979-Dec 1983	Lateef Jakande (NPN)
Jan 1984-86	Gbolahan Mudashiru
1986-July 1988	Michael Akhigbe (see Ondo)

| July 1988-Jan 1992 | Raji Rasabi   (see Ogun and Ondo) |
| Jan 1992-Nov 1993 | Michael Otedolo   (NRC) |

Administrators:

| Dec 1993-Aug 1996 | O.Oyinlola |
| Aug 1996-May 1999 | Mohammed Marwa |

Governor:

| May 1999- | Bola Tinubu   (AD) |

NASSARAWA

Part of Plateau until 1996
Capital: Lafia

Administrators:

| Oct 1996-Aug 1998 | A.Ibrahim |
| Aug 1998-May 1999 | Bala Mohammed Mande |

Governor:

| May 1999- | Abullahi Adamu   (PDP) |

NIGER

Part of North Western State 1968-76
Capital: Minna

Governors:

March 1976-77	Murtala Myako
1977-July 1978	O.E.Ukiwe
July 1978-Oct 1979	G.O.Oni
Oct 1979-Dec 1983	Muhamadu Ibrahim (NPN)
Jan 1984-86	David Mark
1986-Dec 1987	Garula Mohammed
Dec 1987-Jan 1992	Lawrence Gwadabe
Jan 1992-Nov 1993	Musa Inuwa (NRC)

Administrators:

Dec 1993-Aug 1996	C.K.Emein
Aug 1996-Aug 1998	Simeon Oduoye
Aug 1998-May 1999	Habibu Shuaibu (see Plateau)

Governor:

May 1999-   Abdulkadri Kure   (PP)

OGUN

Part of Western State 1968-76
Capital: Abeokuta

Governors:

March 1976-July 1978	S.A.Balogun
July 1978-Oct 1979	H.Eghagha
Oct 1979-Dec 1983	Bisa Onabajo (UPN)
Jan 1984-Aug 1985	Oladipo Diya
Aug 1985-86	Dayo Popoola (see Oyo)
1986-Dec 1987	Raji Rasabi
Dec 1987-Aug 1990	M.A.Lawal
Aug 1990-Jan 1992	Oladeinde Joseph
Jan 1992-Nov 1993	Olusegun Osoba (1st) (SDP)

Administrators:

Dec 1993-Aug 1996	Daniel Akintonde
Aug 1996-Aug 1998	Sam Ewang
Aug 1998-May 1999	Kayode Olukimo

Governor:

May 1999-   Olusegun Osoba   (2nd) (AD)

ONDO

Part of Western State 1968-76
Capital: Akure

Governors:

March 1976-July 1978	I.D.Ikpeme
July 1978-Oct 1979	S.Tuoyo
Oct 1979-Oct 1983	Michael Ajasin (UPN)
Oct-Dec 1983	A.Omoboriowo (NPN)
Jan 1984-Aug 1985	M.B.Otika
Aug 1985-86	Michael Akhigbe
1986-Dec 1987	Ekundayo Opaleye
Dec 1987-July 1988	Raji Rasabi (see Ogun)
July 1988-Aug 1990	Bode George

Aug 1990-Jan 1992   S.Abiodun Olukoya
Jan 1992-Nov 1993   Dele Olumilua   (SDP)

Administrators:

Dec 1993-Sept 1994   L.Mike Torey
Sept 1994-Aug 1996   Ahmed Usman
Aug 1996-Aug 1998   Anthony Onyearugbulem
Aug 1998-May 1999   Moses Fasanya   (see Abia)

Governor:

May 1999-   Ade Adefarati   (AD)

OSUN

Part of Oyo until 1991
Capital: Oshogbo

Administrator:

Aug 1991-Jan 1992   Lapade Ajiborisha

Governor:

Jan 1992-Nov 1993   Isiaka Adeleka   (SDP)

Administrators:

Dec 1993-Aug 1996   A.Udofia
Aug 1996-Aug 1998   Anthony Obi
Aug 1998-May 1999   Theophilus Bamigboye   (see Bauchi)

Governor:

May 1999-   Bisi Akande   (AD)

OYO

Part of Western State 1968-76
Capital: Ibadan

Governors:

March 1976-July 1978   David Jembibewon
July 1978-Oct 1979   P.C.Tarfa
Oct 1979-Oct 1983   Bola Ige   (UPN)
Oct-Dec 1983   Victor Olunloyo   (NPN)

Jan 1984-Aug 1985	Dayo Popoola
Aug 1985-Dec 1987	Adebunji Olurin
Dec 1987-Aug 1990	S.Oresanya
Aug 1990-Jan 1992	Abdul Adisa
Jan 1992-Nov 1993	Kolapa Oshola (SDP)

Administrators:

Dec 1993-Sept 1994	Adetoye Sode
Sept 1994-Aug 1996	Ike Nwosu (see Abia)
Aug 1996-Aug 1998	Ahmed Usman (see Ondo)
Aug 1998-May 1999	A.Edorhe Oyakhire (see Taraba)

Governor:

May 1999-	Lam Adesina (AD)

PLATEAU

Part of Benue-Plateau 1968-76
Capital: Jos

Governors:

March 1976-July 1978	Dan Suleiman
July 1978-Oct 1979	J.U.Anaja
Oct 1979-Dec 1983	Solomon Lar (NPP)
Jan 1984-Aug 1985	S.B.Aluku
Aug 1985-July 1988	Lawrence Onoja
July 1988-Aug 1990	Aliyu Karma
Aug 1990-Jan 1992	Joshua Madaki (see Bauchi)
Jan 1992-Nov 1993	Fidelas Tapgun (SDP)

Administrators:

Dec 1993-Aug 1996	M.Mana
Aug 1996-Aug 1998	Habibu Shuaibu
Aug 1998-May 1999	Musa Shehu (see Rivers)

Governor:

May 1999-	Joshua Dariye (PDP)

RIVERS

Capital: Port Harcourt

Governors:

April 1968-July 1975	Alfred Diete-Spiff
July 1975-July 1978	Zamani Lekwot
July 1978-Oct 1979	S.Saida
Oct 1979-Dec 1983	Melford Okilo (NPN)
Jan 1984-Aug 1985	B.L.Letimah
Aug 1985-87	Fidelis Oyakilome
1987-July 1988	Anthony Ukpo
July 1988-Aug 1990	E.O.Adelaye
Aug 1990-Jan 1992	Godwin Abbe (see Akwa-Ibom)
Jan 1992-Nov 1993	Rufus Ada-George (NRC)

Administrators:

Dec 1993-Aug 1996	D.M.Komo
Aug 1996-Aug 1998	Musa Shehu
Aug 1998-May 1999	Sam Ewang (see Ogun)

Governor:

May 1999-	Peter Odili (PDP)

SOKOTO

Part of North Western State 1968-76
Capital: Sokoto

Governors:

March 1976-July 1978	Umaru Muhammed (see North Western State)
July 1978-Oct 1979	M.G.Nasko
Oct 1979-82	Shehu Kangiwa (NPN)
1982-Dec 1983	Garba Nadama (NPN)
Jan 1984-Aug 1985	Garba Duba (see Bauchi)
Aug 1985-Dec 1987	Garba Mohammed
Dec 1987-Aug 1990	Ahmed Daku (see Kano)
Aug 1990-Jan 1992	Bashir Magashi
Jan 1992-Nov 1993	Yahya Abdulkarim (NRC)

Administrators:

Dec 1993-Aug 1996	Yakubu Muazu

Aug 1996-Aug 1998   Rasheed Raji   (see Bauchi)
Aug 1998-May 1999   Rufai Garba   (see Anambra)

Governor:

May 1999-   Atahiru Bafarwa   (PDP)

TARABA

Part of Adamawa (Gongola) until 1991
Capital: Jalingo

Administrator:

Aug 1991-Jan 1992   Adeyemi Afolahan

Governor:

Jan 1992-Nov 1993   Jolly Nyame   (1st)

Administrators:

Dec 1993-Aug 1996   Y.Dickson
Aug 1996-Aug 1998   A.Edorhe Oyakhire
Aug 1998-May 1999   Aina Owoniyi

Governor:

May 1999-   Jolly Nyame   (2nd) (PDP)

YOBE

Part of Borno until 1991
Capital: Damaturu

Administrator:

Aug 1991-Jan 1992   Sanni Daura Ahmed

Governor:

Jan 1992-Nov 1993   Bukar Ibrahim   (1st) (SDP)

Administrators:

Dec 1993-Aug 1996   Dabo Aliyu
Aug 1996-Aug 1998   John Kamio
Aug 1998-May 1999   Musa Mohammed

Governor:

May 1999- Bukar Ibrahim (2nd) (APP)

ZAMFARA

Part of Sokoto until 1996
Capital: Gusau

Administrator:

Oct 1996-May 1999 Jibril Yakubu

Governor:

May 1999- Ahmed Sani (APP)

Former States

BENUE-PLATEAU

Capital: Jos

Governors:

April 1968-July 1975 Joseph Gomwalk (executed 1976)
July 1975-March 1976 Abdullahi Mohammed

State divided into Benue and Plateau

EAST CENTRAL STATE

Capital: Enugu

Governors:

April 1968-July 1975 A.Ukbabi Asiki
July 1975-March 1976 Anthony Ochefu

State divided into Anambra and Imo

NORTH EASTERN STATE

Capital: Maiduguri

Governors:

April 1968-July 1975 Musa Usman

July 1975-March 1976   Mohammed Buhari   (later President)

State divided into Borno, Bauchi and Gongola

NORTH WESTERN STATE

Capital: Sokoto

Governors:

April 1968-July 1975   Usman Faruk
July 1975-March 1976   Umaru Muhammed

State divided between Niger and Sokoto

WESTERN STATE

Capital: Ibadan

Governors:

April 1968-71   Robert Adebayo
1971-July 1975   Christopher Rotimi
July 1975-March 1976   Akintunde Aduwo

State divided into Ogun, Ondo and Oyo

NORWAY

Official name: Kingdom of Norway, Kongeriket Norge
State founded: 9th century
Capital: Bergen (12th-13th century), Oslo (*f* Christiania 1624-1877, Kristiania 1877-1925)

Norway was united into a single kingdom in the 9th century. It became part of Denmark from 1450 until 1814. After a brief reign by an independent monarch, Norway shared the Swedish crown until 1905, when an independent monarchy was re-established. During World War II Norway was occupied by Germany.

Kings/Queen:

c870-940	Harald I
940-945	Erik I (*son*) (deposed)/Haakon I (*son*)
945-960	Haakon I (killed in battle)
960-970	Harald II (*son of Erik I*) (assassinated)
(970-95	Interregnum. Ruler:Haarkon Jarl)
995-1000	Olav I (*great-grandson of Harald I*) (killed in battle)
(1000-16	Interregnum: country divided between Erik and Sweyn, sons of Haakon Jarl)
1016-28	Olav II (*nephew of Olav I*) (deposed, assassinated 1030)
1028-35	Sweyn Knutson (*son of Knut of Denmark and England*)
Nov 1035-Oct 1047	Magnus I (*son of Olav II*) (killed in battle)
Oct 1047-Sept 1066	Harald III (*half-brother of Olav II*) (killed in battle)
Sept 1066-April 1069	Magnus II (*son*) (co-ruler)
Sept 1066-Sept 1093	Olav III (*brother*) (co-ruler 1066-69)
Sept 1093-Aug 1103	Magnus III (*son*)
Aug 1103-22	Øystein I (*son*) (co-ruler)
Aug 1103-March 1130	Sigurd I (co-ruler 1103-22)
March 1130-35	Magnus IV (deposed) (*son of Sigurd I*) (co-ruler)
March 1130-Dec 1136	Harald IV (*brother*) (co-ruler 1135-36) (assassinated)
Dec 1136-Feb 1161	Inge I (*son*) (co-ruler 1136-57)
Dec 1136-June 1155	Sigurd II (*brother*) (co-ruler)
1142-Aug 1157	Øystein II (*brother*) (co-ruler)
Feb 1161-62	Haakon II (son of Sigurd II)
1162-July 1184	Magnus V (*grandson of Sigurd II*) (killed in battle)
July 1884-March 1202	Sverre (*son of Sigurd II*)
March 1202-Jan 1204	Haakon III (*son*) (assassinated?)
Jan-Aug 1204	Gutorm
Aug 1204-April 1217	Inge II (*nephew of Sverre*)

April 1217-Dec 1263	Haakon IV (*son of Haakon III*)
Dec 1263-May 1280	Magnus VI (*son*)
May 1280-June 1299	Erik II (*son*)
June 1299-May 1319	Haakon V (*brother*)
May 1319-55	Magnus VII (Magnus II of Sweden) (*grandson*)
1355-May 1380	Haakon VI (*son*)
May 1380-87	Olav IV (*son*)
	Regent: 1380-87 Margrete
1387-89	Margrete (Margrete I of Denmark & Sweden) (*mother*)
1389-June 1442	Erik III (Erik VII of Denmark, Erik XIII of Sweden) (*grandnephew*)
June 1442-Jan 1448	Kristofer (Christopher III of Denmark, Christopher of Sweden) (*nephew*)
Jan 1448-1450	Karl (Carl VIII of Sweden)
(1450-Jan 1814	Danish rule)
Jan-Nov 1814	Kristian Frederik (later Christian VIII of Denmark)
Nov 1814-Feb 1818	Karl I (Carl XIII of Sweden)
Feb 1818-March 1844	Karl II (Carl XIV Johan of Sweden)
March 1844-July 1859	Oskar I (Oscar I of Sweden)
July 1859-Aug 1872	Karl III (Carl XV of Sweden)
Aug 1872-June 1905	Oskar II (Oscar II of Sweden) (renounced throne)
Nov 1905-April 1940	Haakon VII (*b* Prince Carl of Denmark, son of Frederik VII) (1st) (exiled)

Commissioner:

April 1940-May 1945	Josef Terboven

Kings:

May 1945-Sept 1957	Haakon VII (2nd)
Sept 1957-Jan 1991	Olav V (*b* Prince Alexander) (*son*)
Jan 1991-	Harald V (*son*)

Prime Ministers:

Aug 1873-June 1880	Frederik Stang (1st)
June 1880-March 1884	Christian Selmer
March-April 1884	Christian Schweigaard
April 1884-July 1889	Johan Sverdrup
July 1889-Feb 1892	Emil Stang
Feb 1892-April 1893	Johannes Steen (1st)
April 1893-Oct 1895	Frederik Stang (2nd)
Oct 1895-Feb 1898	Georg Hagerup (1st)
Feb 1898-April 1902	Johannes Steen (2nd)
April 1902-Oct 1903	Otto Blehr (1st)
Oct 1903-March 1905	Georg Hagerup (2nd)
March 1905-Oct 1907	Christian Michelsen

Oct 1907-March 1908	Jorgen Lovland
March 1908-Feb 1910	Gunnar Knudsen (1st) (Lib)
Feb 1910-Feb 1912	Wollert Konow (Cons)
Feb 1912-Jan 1913	Jens Bratlie (Cons)
Jan 1913-June 1920	Gunnar Knudsen (2nd) (Lib)
June 1920-June 1921	Otto Halvorsen (1st) (Cons)
June 1921-March 1923	Otto Blehr (2nd) (Lib)
March-May 1923	Otto Halvorsen (2nd) (Cons) (†)
May 1923-June 1924	Abraham Berge (Cons)
June 1924-March 1926	Johan Mowinckel (1st) (Lib)
March 1926-Jan 1928	Ivar Lykke (Cons)
Jan-Feb 1928	Christopher Hornsrud (Lab)
Feb 1928-May 1931	Johan Mowinckel (2nd) (Lib)
May 1931-March 1932	Peder Kolstad (AP) (†)
March 1932-Feb 1933	Jens Hundseid (AP)
March 1933-March 1935	Johan Mowinckel (3rd) (Lib)
March 1935-April 1940	Johan Nygaardsvold (Lab)
25-30 April 1940	Vidkun Quisling (1st)
(April 1940-Feb 1942	post abolished)
Feb 1942-May 1945	Vidkun Quisling (2nd) (executed 1945)
May 1945-Nov 1951	Einar Gerhardsen (1st) (Lab)
Nov 1951-Jan 1955	Oscar Torp (Lab)
Jan 1955-Aug 1963	Einar Gerhardsen (2nd) (Lab)
Aug-Sept 1963	John Lyng (Cons)
Sept 1963-Oct 1965	Einar Gerhardsen (3rd) (Lab)
Oct 1965-March 1971	Per Borten (CP)
March 1971-Oct 1972	Trygve Bratteli (1st) (Lab)
Oct 1972-Oct 1973	Lars Korvald (CPP)
Oct 1973-Jan 1976	Trygve Bratteli (2nd) (Lab)
Jan 1976-Feb 1981	Odvar Nordli (Lab)
Feb-Oct 1981	Gro Harlem Brundtland (*b* G.Harlem) (1st) (Lab)
Oct 1981-May 1986	Kaare Willoch (Cons)
May 1986-Oct 1989	Gro Harlem Brundtland (2nd) (Lab)
Oct 1989-Nov 1990	Jan Syse (Cons)
Nov 1990-Oct 1996	Gro Harlem Brundtland (3rd Lab)
Oct 1996-Oct 1997	Thorbjørn Jagland (Lab)
Oct 1997-March 2000	Kjell Magne Bondevik (CPP)
March 2000-	Jens Stoltenberg (Lab)

AP = Agrarian Party
Cons = Conservative Party
CP = Centre Party
CPP = Christian People's Party
Lab = Labour Party
Lib = Liberal Party

GOVERNMENT-IN-EXILE 1940-45

Headquarters: London
Operated during German occupation

King:

June 1940-May 1945   Haakon VII

Prime Minister:

June 1940-May 1945   Johan Nygaardsvold

Territory

SVALBARD

Capital: Longyearbyen

Governors:

1925-33	Johannes Bassoe
1933-35	Helge Ingstad
1935-41	Wolmar Marlow
(1941-45	post vacant)
1945-56	Hakon Balstad
1956-60	Odd Birketvedt
1960-63	Finn Midtboe
1963-67	Tollef Landsverk
1967-70	Stephen Stephensen
1970-74	Frederik Beichmann
1974-78	Leif Eldring (1st)
1978-82	Jan Grondahl
1982-86	Carl Wendt
1986-91	Leif Eldring (2nd)
1991-95	Odd Blomdal
1995-May 1998	Ann-Kristin Olsen
May 1998-	Morten Ruud

OMAN

Official name: Sultanate of Oman, Saltanat Oman
Previous name: Sultanate of Muscat and Oman until 1970
State founded: 1749
Capital: Muscat (Masqat)

The ancient state of Muscat was occupied by the Portuguese in the 16th century, and then by the Persians in the 18th century. An independent united state was founded in 1749 by Ahmed bin Said, the founder of the Al Bu Said dynasty which still rules. In 1832 the sultan moved his capital to Zanzibar which was part of the sultanate, but in 1856 the two states separated. The country remained backward until after the overthrow of Sultan Said in 1970 when his son, Qaboos initiated major development programmes.

Sultans:

1749-75	Ahmed bin Said	
1775-79	Said bin Ahmed	*(son)*
1779-92	Hamad bin Said	*(son)*
1792-Nov 1804	Sultan bin Ahmed	*(son of Ahmed bin Said)* (assassinated)
Nov 1804-July 1806	Badar bin Seif	*(nephew)* (assassinated)
July 1806-Oct 1856	Said bin Sultan	*(son of Sultan bin Said)* (also Sultan of Zanzibar)
Oct 1856-Feb 1866	Thwaini bin Said	*(son)* (assassinated)
Feb 1866-Oct 186	Salim bin Thwaini	*(son)* (deposed)
Oct 1868-Jan 1871	Azzan bin Qais	*(great-great-grandson of Ahmed bin Said)* (deposed, assassinated)
Jan 1871-June 1888	Turki bin Said	*(son of Said bin Sultan)*
June 1888-Oct 1913	Faisal bin Turki	*(son)*
Oct 1913-Feb 1932	Taimur bin Faisal	*(son)*
Feb 1932-July 1970	Said bin Taimur	*(son)* (deposed)
July 1970-	Qaboos bin Said	*(son)*

Prime Ministers:

July 1970-Jan 1972	Tarik bin Taimur	*(son of Taimur bin Faisal)*
Jan 1972-	Qaboos bin Said	

PAKISTAN

Official name: Islamic Republic of Pakistan, Islami Jamhuria-e-Pakistan
Previous name: Dominion of Pakistan 1947-56
Independence date: 14 August 1947
Capital: Karachi 1947-59, Rawalpindi (interim) 1959-69, Islamabad since 1969

In 1947 British India was partitioned into two states, the predominantly Hindu areas becoming India and the predominantly Moslem areas Pakistan. Kashmir is a disputed territory and India and Pakistan have been to war over it on three occasions (1947-49, 1965 and 1971) with no final resolution - the Pakistan-controlled part is called Azad Kashmir. In 1956 Pakistan became a republic. East Pakistan seceded in 1971 to become Bangladesh. The armed forces have overthrown the civilian authorities four times; the most recent return to democracy was in 1988.

Governors-General:
Represented monarch who was concurrently British monarch

Aug 1947-Sept 1948	Mohammed Jinnah (†)
Sept 1948-Oct 1951	Khawaja Nazimuddin (see Bengal & East Bengal)
Oct 1951-Aug 1955	Ghulam Mohammed
Aug 1955-March 1956	Iskander Mirza

Presidents:

March 1956-Oct 1958	Iskander Mirza
Oct 1958-March 1969	Mohammed Ayub Khan
March 1969-Dec 1971	Agha Mohammed Yahya Khan
Dec 1971-Aug 1973	Zulfikar Bhutto
Aug 1973-Sept 1978	Fazal Elahi Chaudri
Sept 1978-Aug 1988	Mohammed Zia ul-Haq († air accident)
Aug 1988-July 1993	Ghulam Ishaq Khan (acting Aug-Dec 1988)
July-Nov 1993	Wasim Sajjad (acting) (1st)
Nov 1993-Dec 1997	Farooq Laghari
Dec 1997-Jan 1998	Wasim Sajjad (acting) (2nd)
Jan 1998-	Mohammed Rafiq Tarar

Prime Ministers:

Aug 1947-Oct 1951	Liaquat Ali Khan (PML) († assassinated)
Oct 1951-April 1953	Khawaja Nazimuddin (PML)
April 1953-Aug 1955	Mohammed Ali (PML)
Aug 1955-Sept 1956	Chaudri Mohammed Ali (PML)
Sept 1956-Oct 1957	Hussein Suhrawardy (AL) (see Bengal)

Oct-Dec 1957   Ismail Chundrigar   (PML) (see NWF & Punjab)
Dec 1957-Oct 1958   Firoz Khan Noon   (RP) (see Punjab)
7-28 Oct 1958   Mohammed Ayub Khan
(Oct 1958-Dec 1971   post abolished)
7-20 Dec 1971   Nurul Amin   (see East Pakistan)
(Dec 1971-Aug 1973   post abolished)
Aug 1973-July 1977   Zulfikar Bhutto   (PPP) (deposed, executed 1979)
(July 1977-March 1985 post abolished)
March 1985-May 1988   Mohammed Khan Junejo   (PML)
(May-Dec 1988   post vacant)
Dec 1988-Aug 1990   Benazir Bhutto   (*daughter of Z.Bhutto*) (1st) (PPP)
Aug-Nov 1990   Ghulam Mustafa Jatoi   (see Sindh)
Nov 1990-April 1993   Nawaz Sharif   (1st) (PML-IDA) (see Punjab)
April-May 1993   Balkh Sher Mazari
May-July 1993   Nawaz Sharif   (2nd) (PML-IDA)
July-Oct 1993   Moeen Qureshi
Oct 1993-Nov 1996   Benazir Bhutto   (2nd) (PPP)
Nov 1996-Feb 1997   Malik Meraj Khalid
Feb 1997-Oct 1999   Nawaz Sharif   (3rd) (PML) (deposed)

Chief Executive:

Oct 1999-   Pervez Mushahraf

Chief Martial Law Administrators:

Oct 1958-June 1962   Mohammed Ayub Khan
(June 1962-March 1969 martial law lifted)
March 1969-Dec 1971   Agha Mohammed Yahya Khan
Dec 1971-April 1972   Zulfikar Bhutto
(April 1972-July 1977 martial law lifted)
July 1977-Dec 1985   Mohammed Zia ul-Haq
(Dec 1985   martial law lifted)

AL = Awami League
IDA = Islamic Democratic Alliance
PML = Pakistan Moslem League (part of IDA)
PPP = Pakistan People's Party
RP = Republican Party

Provinces

BALUCHISTAN

Capital: Quetta

President of the Council of Rulers:

April 1948-Oct 1955   Ahmed Yar Khan   (Ruler of Kalat)

(Oct 1955   post abolished)

Governors:

Feb 1970-April 1972	Gaus Ralsani (assassinated 1987)
April 1972-Feb 1973	Gaus Bizenjo
Feb 1973-Jan 1974	Akbar Bugti
Jan 1974-Sept 1977	Ahmed Yar Khan
Sept 1977-78	Khuda Bux Marri (acting)
1978-March 1984	Rahimuddin Khan
March-July 1984	Farooq Khan Lodi
July 1984-Dec 1985	K.K.Afridi (acting July-Dec 1984)
Dec 1985-March 1991	Mohammed Musa Khan (†)
March-July 1991	Hazar Khan Khoso (acting)
July 1991-94	Gul Mohammed Khan Jogezai
1994-96	Abdul Rahim Durrani
1996-April 1997	Imranullah Khan
April-July 1997	Amirul Mengal (acting)
July 1997-Oct 1999	Gul Aurangzeb
Oct 1999-	Amirul Mengal

Prime Ministers:

1948-52	Arthur Dring
1952-55	A.R.Khan
(1955	post abolished)

Chief Ministers:

May 1972-Feb 1973	Ataullah Mengal (NAP)
(Feb-April 1973	President's rule)
April 1973-Dec 1975	Jam Ghulam Qadir (1st) (NAP)
(Dec 1975-Dec 1976	President's rule)
Dec 1976-July 1977	Mohammed Khan Barozai
(July 1977-April 1985	post abolished)
April 1985-May 1988	Jam Ghulam Qadir (2nd)
May-Dec 1988	Zafarullah Khan Jamali (1st)
Dec 1988-Jan 1989	Khuda Bux Marri (acting)
Jan 1989-Aug 1990	Akbar Bugti
Aug-Nov 1990	Humayan Mari
Nov 1990-92	Taj Mohammed Jamali (1st)
1992-Nov 1996	Nawab Zulfikar Ali Magsi
Nov 1996-Feb 1997	Zafarullah Khan Jamali (2nd)
Feb 1997-98	Mohammed Akhtar Mengal
1998-99	Taj Mohammed Jamali (2nd)
(Oct 1999-	post abolished)

NAP = National Awami Party

BENGAL

See Bangladesh

EAST PAKISTAN

See Bangladesh

NORTH WEST FRONTIER

Capital: Peshawar

Governors:

Aug 1947-48	George Cunningham
1948-July 1949	Ambrose Dudas
July 1949-Feb 1950	Sahibzada Mohammed Khurshid (†)
Feb 1950-Nov 1951	Ismail Chundrigar
Nov 1951-Nov 1954	Khawaja Shahabuddin (*brother of Khawaja Nazimuddin*)
Nov 1954-Oct 1955	Qarban Ali Khan
(Oct 1955-Feb 1970	post abolished)
Feb 1970-71	Khawaja Mohammed Azhar Khan
1971-April 1972	Hayat Sherpar
April 1972-Feb 1973	Arbab Sikandar Khan
Feb 1973-May 1974	Aslam Khattak
May 1974-May 1976	Said Ghawas
May 1976-Sept 1977	Nasrullah Khan Babar
Sept 1977-78	Abdul Hakim Khan (acting)
1978-Dec 1985	Fazle Haq
Dec 1985-88	Fida Mohammed Khan
1988-94	Amir Gulistan Janjua
1994-Nov 1996	Khurshid Ali Khan
Nov 1996-Oct 1999	Mohammed Arif Bargash
Oct 1999-	Mohammed Shafiq

Chief Ministers:

Oct 1947-April 1953	Khan Abdul Qayum Khan
April 1953-July 1955	Abdul Rashid Khan
July-Oct 1955	Sardar Bahadur Khan
(Oct 1955-May 1972	post abolished)
May 1972-April 1973	Maulana Mufti Mahmood (NAP)
April 1973-Feb 1975	Inayatullah Gandapore
(Feb-May 1975	President's rule)
May 1975-March 1977	Nasrullah Khan Khuttak (PPP)
March-Sept 1977	Iqbal Khan Jadoon (PPP)
(Sept 1977-April 1985	post abolished)

April 1985-May 1988 Arbab Mohammed Jehangir Khan
May-Dec 1988 Fazle Haq   (assassinated 1991)
Dec 1988-Aug 1990 Aftab Ahmad Sherpao   (1st) (PPP)
Aug 1990-Oct 1993 Mir Afzal Khan
Oct 1993-Feb 1994 Mohammed Sabir Shah
(Feb-April 1994 Federal rule)
April 1994-Nov 1996 Aftab Ahmad Sherpao   (2nd) (PPP)
Nov 1996-Feb 1997 Raja Sikander Zaman
Feb 1997-Oct 1999 Mehtab Ahmad Khan Abbasi
(Oct 1999- post abolished)

PUNJAB

Capital: Lahore
In 1947 Punjab was partitioned between India and Pakistan

Governors:

Aug 1947-July 1949 Francis Moodie
Aug 1949-Nov 1951 Sardar Nishtar
Nov 1951-April 1953 Ismail Chundrigar   (see NWF)
July 1953-June 1954 Mian Aminuddin   (see Sind)
June-Nov 1954 Habib Rahimtoola   (see Sind)
Nov 1954-Oct 1955 Mushtaq Gurmani
(Oct 1955-Feb 1970 post abolished)
Feb 1970-71 Mohammed Attiqur Rahman
1971-Feb 1973 Ghulam Mustafa Khar   (1st)
Feb 1973-March 1974 Mohammed Haneef Ramay
March 1974-March 1975 Saddiq Hussein Qureshi
March-July 1975 Ghulam Mustafa Khar   (2nd)
July 1975-Sept 1977 Mohammed Abbasi
Sept 1977-78 Aslan Riaz Hussain
1978-March 1980 Sawar Khan
March 1980-Dec 1985 Ghulam Gilani Khan
Dec 1985-Dec 1988 Makhdoom Quraishi
Dec 1988-Aug 1990 Tikka Khan
Aug 1990-92 Mian Mohammed Azhar
1992-May 1995 Chaudhary Altaf Hussain   (†)
June 1995-Nov 1996 Saroop Khan
Nov 1996-97 Khwaja Ahmed Tariq Rahman
1997-Oct 1999 Shahib Hamid
Oct 1999- Mohammed Safdar

Prime Ministers:

1937-Dec 1942 Sikander Hyat Khan   (†)

Dec 1942-Feb 1945   Malik Khiazar Hyat Khan   (1st)
(Feb 1945-April 1946   Governor's rule)
April 1946-Aug 1947   Malik Khiazar Hyat Khan   (2nd)

Chief Ministers:

Aug 1947-Jan 1949   Khan Iftikhar Hussein
(Jan 1949-April 1952   Governor's rule)
April 1952-April 1953   Mian Mumtaz Daultana   (PML)
April 1953-May 1955   Firoz Khan Noon   (PML)
May-Oct 1955   Abdul Hamid Khan Dasti
(Oct 1955-May 1972   post abolished)
May 1972-Feb 1973   Malik Meraj Khalid   (PPP) († assassinated)
Feb 1973-March 1974   Ghulam Mustafa Khar   (PPP)
March 1974-July 1975   Mohammed Haneef Ramay   (PPP)
July 1975-July 1977   Sadiq Hussein Qureshi   (PPP)
(July 1977-April 1985   post abolished)
April 1985-Aug 1990   Nawaz Sharif   (PML-IDA)
Aug 1990-April 1993   Ghulam Hyder Wyne   (assassinated Sept 1993)
April-June 1993   Manzoor Wattoo   (1st)
(June-Oct 1993   Federal rule)
Oct 1993-Sept 1995   Manzoor Wattoo   (2nd)
Sept 1995-Nov 1996   Mohammed Arif Nakai   (PML-J)
3-18 Nov 1996   Manzoor Wattoo   (3rd)
Nov 1996-Feb 1997   Mian Mohammed Afzal Hayat
Feb 1997-Oct 1999   Shahbaz Sharif   (PML) (*brother of N.Sharif*)
(Oct 1999-   post abolished)

PML-J = Pakistan Muslim League-Junejo

SINDH

Capital: Karachi

Governors:

Aug 1947-Oct 1948   Ghulam Hidayatullah   (†)
Oct 1948-50   Din Mohammed
1950-July 1953   Mian Aminuddin
July 1953-June 1954   Habib Rahimtoola
June 1954-Oct 1955   Khan Iftikar Hussein   (see Punjab)
(Oct 1955-Feb 1970   post abolished)
Feb 1970-71   Rakhman Gul
1971-Feb 1973   Rasul Baksh Talpur
Feb 1973-March 1976   Ra'ana Liaquat Ali Khan   (*widow of Liaquat Ali Khan*)
March 1976-Sept 1977   Dilawar Khan of Junagadh
Sept 1977-78   Abdul Kadir Sheikh   (acting)
1978-84   S.M.Abbasi

1984-June 1986   Jahan Dad Khan
June 1986-June 1988   Ashraf Tabbani
June-Sept 1988   Rahimuddin Khan   (see Baluchistan)
Sept-Dec 1988   Qadiruddin Ahmed
Dec 1988-Aug 1990   Fakhruddin Ebrahim
Aug 1990-May 1995   Mahmood Haroon
May 1995-97   Kamal Azfar
1997-Oct 1999   Moinuddin Haider
Oct 1999-   Azim Daudpota

Prime Ministers:

1937-38   Ghulam Hidayatullah   (1st)
1938-42   Khan Bahadur Allah Baksh
1942-47   Ghulam Hidayatullah   (2nd)

Chief Ministers:

Aug 1947-April 1948   Mohammed Ayub Khuhro   (1st) (PML)
May 1948-Feb 1949   Pir Allahi Baksh   (PML)
Feb 1949-March 1951   Yusuf Haroon
March-Dec 1951   Mohammed Ayub Khuhro   (2nd) (PML)
(Dec 1951-May 1953   Federal rule)
May 1953-Nov 1954   Pirzada Abdus Sattar   (PML)
Nov 1954-Oct 1955   Mohammed Ayub Khuhro   (3rd) (PML)
(Oct 1955-May 1972   post abolished)
May 1972-Dec 1973   Mumtaz Bhutto   (1st) (*cousin of Z.Bhutto*) (PPP)
Dec 1973-July 1977   Ghulam Mustafa Jatoi   (PPP)
(July 1977-April 1985   post abolished)
April 1985-April 1988   Gaus Ali Shah
May-Dec 1988   Akhtar Ali Qazi
Dec 1988-Feb 1990   Syed Qaim Ali Shah   (PPP)
Feb-Aug 1990   Aftab Shahban Mirani   (PPP)
Aug 1990-March 1992   Jam Sadiq Ali   (†)
March 1992-Oct 1993   Muzaffar Hussain Shah
Oct 1993-Nov 1996   Said Abdullah Shah   (PPP)
Nov 1996-Feb 1997   Mumtaz Bhutto   (2nd)
Feb 1997-Oct 1998   Liaquat Ali Khan Jatoi
(Oct 1998-Oct 1999   Federal rule)
(Oct 1999-   post abolished)

WEST PAKISTAN

From 1955 until 1972 the provinces of Baluchistan, North West Frontier, Punjab and Sindh were united into the single province of West Pakistan

Capital: Lahore

Governors:

Oct 1955-Aug 1957   Mushtaq Gurmani   (see Punjab)
Aug 1957-April 1960   Akthar Hussain
April 1960-Sept 1966   Malik Amir Mohammed Khan
Sept 1966-March 1969   Mohammed Musa
March-Sept 1969   Yusuf Haroon   (see Sindh)
Sept 1969-April 1972   M.Nur Khan

Chief Ministers:

Oct 1955-March 1957   Khan Saheb   (ML, RP)
(March-July 1957   President's rule)
July 1957-March 1958   Abdur Rashid Khan   (RP)
March-Oct 1958   Muzaffar Qizilbashi   (RP)
(Oct 1958   post abolished)

Territories

AZAD KASHMIR

Capital: Muzaffarabad

Presidents:

Oct 1947-May 1950   Mohammed Ibrahim Khan   (1st)
May 1950-June 1952   Mohammed Yusuf Shah
June 1952-May 1956   Sher Ahmed
May 1956   Mohammed Yusuf Shah   (acting)
May 1956-April 1957   Sardar Abdul Qayyum Khan   (1st)
April 1957-May 1959   Mohammed Ibrahim Khan   (2nd)
May 1959-Aug 1964   Khurshid Hasan Khurshid
Aug 1964-Nov 1968   Khan Hamidullah Khan
Nov 1968-Oct 1969   Abdul Hamid Khan
Oct 1969-Oct 1970   Abdul Rahman Khan   (1st)
Oct 1970-April 1975   Sardar Abdul Qayyum Khan   (2nd)
April-June 1975   Manzur Masud   (acting)
June 1975-Oct 1978   Mohammed Ibrahim Khan   (3rd)
Oct 1978-Feb 1983   Mohammed Hayat Khan
Feb 1983-Aug 1985   Abdul Rahman Khan   (2nd)
Aug 1985-July 1991   Sardar Abdul Qayyum Khan   (3rd)
July 1991-Aug 1996   Sardar Sikandar Hayat
Aug 1996-   Mohammed Ibrahim Khan   (4th)

Prime Ministers:

June 1975-Aug 1977   Abdul Hamid Khan

Aug 1977-Oct 1978	Abdul Rahman Khan (acting)
(Oct 1978-May 1985	post abolished)
May 1985-July 1990	Sardar Sikandar Hayat
July 1990-July 1991	Mumtaz Rathore (AKPP)
5-11 July 1991	Sardar Mohammed Ashrad (acting)
July 1991-96	Sardar Abdul Qayyum Khan
1996-Aug 1996	Sultan Mahmud Chaudhary
Aug 1996-	Sultan Mahmud Chaudhary

AKPP = Azad Kashmir People's Party

NORTHERN AREAS

Gilgit, Diamur and Baltistan

Government headed by a federally appointed commissioner

PALAU

Official name: Republic of Palau, Belu'u era Belau
Independence date: 1 October 1994
Capital: Koror

The Palau group of islands were under nominal Spanish ownership from 1543, when they were visited by Spanish explorers, until 1899 when together with the Mariana and Caroline Islands they were sold to Germany. In 1914 Palau was occupied by Japan, and remained so until the islands fell to American forces in 1944 during World War II. In 1947 it became part of the United Nations Trust Territory of the Pacific under US administration. Internal self-government was introduced in 1981, and full independence was granted in 1994.

Presidents:

Jan 1981-June 1985	Haruo Remeliik († assassinated)
June-Oct 1985	Alfonso Oiterong (acting)
Oct 1985-Aug 1988	Lazarus Salii († suicide)
Aug 1988-Jan 1989	Thomas Remengesau (acting)
Jan 1989-Jan 1993	Ngiratkel Etpison
Jan 1993-	Kuniwo Nakamura

PANAMA

Official name: Republic of Panama, República de Panama
Independence dates: February 1855 and 3 November 1903
Capital: Panama City

Panama was ruled by Spain from 1510 until 1819, when it became part of the independent state of Greater Colombia. In 1830 it became part of New Granada (Colombia) when Greater Colombia split up. From 1855 until 1863 Panama was an independent republic, but then joined Colombia again until 1903 when it seceded and regained its independence. From 1968 to 1989 Panama was under effective military rule; this was ended by US military intervention, and a civilian government was subsequently installed.

Presidents:

Feb 1855-Oct 1856	Justa Arosemena
Oct 1856-Sept 1858	Bartolomeo Calvo
Sept 1858-62	José de Obaldia
1862	Santiago de la Guardia (deposed, assassinated)
Sept 1862-June 1863	Manuel Díaz
(June 1863-Nov 1903	Union with Colombia)
Nov 1903-Feb 1904	José Arango (acting)
Feb 1904-Oct 1908	Manuel Amador Guerrero
Oct 1908-March 1910	José Domingo de Obaldia (†)
March-Oct 1910	Carlos Mendoza (acting)
Oct 1910-Oct 1912	Pablo Arosemena
Oct 1912-Oct 1916	Belisario Porras (1st)
Oct 1916-June 1918	Ramón Valdes (†)
June-Oct 1918	Ciro Urriola (acting)
Oct 1918-Oct 1924	Belisario Porras (2nd)
Oct 1924-Oct 1928	Rudolfo Chiari
Oct 1928-Jan 1931	Florencio Arosemena (deposed)
3-16 Jan 1931	Harmodio Arias (acting)
Jan 1931-June 1932	Ricardo Alfaro
June 1932-June 1936	Harmodio Arias
June 1936-Dec 1939	Juan Arosemena (†)
Dec 1939-Oct 1940	Augusto Boyd
Oct 1940-Oct 1941	Arnulfo Arias Madrid (1st) (deposed)
Oct 1941-Oct 1945	Ricardo de la Guardia
Oct 1945-Oct 1948	Enrique Jiménez
Oct 1948-Aug 1949	Domingo Díaz Arosemena (†)
Aug-Nov 1949	Daniel Chanis Pinzon (acting)

20-24 Nov 1949	Roberto Chiari (acting) (*son of Rudolfo Chiari*)
Nov 1949-May 1951	Arnulfo Arias Madrid (2nd) (deposed)
May 1951-Oct 1952	Alcibíades Arosemena
Oct 1952-Jan 1955	José Remón Cantero († assassinated)
2-15 Jan 1955	José Guizado (deposed)
Jan 1955-Oct 1956	Ricardo Arias Espinosa
Oct 1956-Oct 1960	Ernesto de la Guardia
Oct 1960-Oct 1964	Roberto Chiari
Oct 1964-Oct 1968	Marco Robles
1-13 Oct 1968	Arnulfo Arias Madrid (3rd) (APP) (deposed)
Oct 1968-Dec 1969	José Pinilla Fábrega
Dec 1969-Oct 1978	Demetrio Lakas Bahas
Oct 1978-July 1982	Arístides Royo
July 1982-Feb 1984	Ricardo de la Espriella
Feb-Oct 1984	Jorge Illueca
Oct 1984-Sept 1985	Nicolás Ardito Barleta (RDP)
Sept 1985-Feb 1988	Eric Arturo del Valle (RDP)
Feb 1988-Sept 1989	Manuel Solís Palma (acting)
Sept-Dec 1989	Francisco Rodríguez (deposed)
Dec 1989-Sept 1994	Guillermo Endara Gallimany (DACO)
Sept 1994-Sept 1999	Ernesto Pérez Balladares (RDP)
Sept 1999-	Mireya Moscoso de Gruber (*widow of A.Arias*) (AP)

AP = Arnulfist Party
APP = Authentic Panamanian Party
DACO = Democratic Alliance of Civil Opposition
RDP = Revolutionary Democratic Party

Chiefs of Government:

Oct 1972-Oct 1978	Omar Torrijos Herrera
(Oct 1978-Dec 1989	post abolished)
15-20 Dec 1989	Manuel Noriega Morena
(Dec 1989	post abolished)

Military Rulers:
Commander of the National Guard

Oct 1968-July 1981	Omar Torrijos Herrera († air accident)
July 1981-March 1982	Florencio Flores
March 1982-June 1983	Rubén Paredes
June 1983-Dec 1989	Manuel Noriega Morena (deposed)
(Dec 1989	civilian rule restored)

PAPUA NEW GUINEA

Official name: Independent State of Papua New Guinea
Independence date: 16 September 1975
Capital: Port Moresby

In 1883 Queensland annexed Papua, which in 1884 was proclaimed a British protectorate. In 1901 the territory's administration was taken over by Australia. New Guinea became a German colony in 1884. It was captured by Australian forces in 1914, and in 1921 became a trust territory under Australian control. In 1949 Papua and New Guinea were placed under a united administration. The country obtained ministerial government in 1972, self-government in 1973 and independence in 1975. The island of Bougainville has twice attempted to secede, resulting in an armed conflict. A peace agreement was reached in 1998.

Administrators:

1949-52	Jack Murray
1952-67	Donald Cleland
1967-70	David Hay
1970-73	Leslie Johnson

High Commissioner:

Dec 1973-Sept 1975   T.K.Critchley

Governors-General:
Represent monarch who is concurrently British monarch

Sept 1975-March 1977	John Guise
March 1977-March 1983	Tore Lokoloko
March 1983-Feb 1989	Kingsford Dibela
Feb 1989-Feb 1990	Ignatius Kilage
Feb 1990-Oct 1991	Vincent Serei Eri
Oct-Nov 1991	Dennis Young (acting)
Nov 1991-Nov 1997	Wiwa Korowi
Nov 1997-	Silas Atopare

Chief Minister:

April 1972-Sept 1975   Michael Somare

Prime Ministers:

Sept 1975-March 1980   Michael Somare   (1st) (PP)

March 1980-Aug 1982	Julius Chan (1st) (PPP)
Aug 1982-Nov 1985	Michael Somare (2nd) (PP)
Nov 1985-July 1988	Paias Wingti (1st) (PDM)
July 1988-July 1992	Rabbie Namaliu (PP)
July 1992-Aug 1994	Paias Wingti (2nd) (PDM)
Aug 1994-March 1997	Julius Chan (2nd) (PPP)
March-June 1997	John Giheno (PP)
June-July 1997	Julius Chan (3rd) (PPP)
July 1997-July 1999	Bill Skate (PNC, PFP)
July 1999-	Mekere Morauta (PDM)

PDM = People's Democratic Movement
PFP = PNG First Party (includes PNC)
PNC = People's National Congress
PP = Pangu Pati
PPP = People's Progressive Party

Provinces

In August 1995 the elected provincial governments were abolished and replaced with appointed Governors; North Solomons (Bougainville) retained a Premier of a provisional government until 1999.

CENTRAL PROVINCE

Capital: Port Moresby

Premiers:

1976-78	Gau Heno
1978-82	Rina Nau
1983	Kone Vanuawaru (1st)
1983-84	Reuben Taureka
1984-87	Kone Vanuawaru (2nd)
1988-91	Emmanuel Ume
1991-93	Isaiah Oda
1993-95	Paul Kipo

Governors:

Aug 1995-97	John Orea
1997-99	Ted Diro
Aug-Nov 1999	Ajax Bia
Nov 1999-	Opa Taureka

EASTERN HIGHLANDS

Capital: Goroka

Premiers:

1976-86	James Yanepa
1986-91	Walter Nombe
1991-95	Robert Atiyafa

Governors:

Aug 1995-Aug 1997	Aita Ivarato
Aug 1997-Aug 1998	Peter Lafanama
Aug 1998-	Damson Lafana

EAST NEW BRITAIN

Capital: Rabaul

Premiers:

1977-78	Koniel Alar
1978-80	Ereman Tobaining
1980-81	Jacob Timele
1981-89	Ronald ToVue
1989-95	Sinai Brown

Governor:

Aug 1995-	Francis Koimanrea

EAST SEPIK

Capital: Wewak

Premiers:

1976-83	Cherobim Dambui
1983-87	Jonathan Sengi
1987-91	Bruce Samban
(March 1991-June 1993	government suspended)
June 1993-Aug 1995	Alex Anisi

Governors:

Aug 1995-Aug 1999	Michael Somare
Aug 1999-	Arthur Somare

ENGA

Part of Western Highlands until 1978

Capital: Wabag

Premiers:

1978-80	Don Kapi
1980-84	Danley Tindiwi (1st)
(Feb 1984-March 1986	government suspended)
1986-90	Ned Laina
1990-93	Danley Tindiwi (2nd)
(March 1993-Aug 1995	government suspended)

Governors:

Aug 1995-97	Jeffery Balakau
1997-	Peter Ipatas

GULF

Capital: Kerema

Premiers:

1978-79	Ope Oeake
1980-85	Sepoe Karava (1st)
1985-87	Francis Malaisa
1987-89	Thomas Koraea
1990-92	Sepoe Karava (2nd)
1992-93	Paul Apio
(Jan 1993-Aug 1995	government suspended)

Governors:

Aug 1995-	Thomas Koraea
1997-98	Chris Havieta
1998-	Riddler Kimave

MADANG

Capital: Madang

Premiers:

1978-84	Bato Bultin
1985-86	Max Moeder

1986-93   Andrew Ariako
(March 1993-Aug 1995   government suspended)

Governors:

Aug 1995-97   Peter Barter
1997-   Jim Kas

MANUS

Capital: Lorengau

Premiers:

1977-78   Papi Rasahei
1979-82   Banabas Kombil
1982-84   Joel Maiah
1984-95   Stephen Pokawin

Governors:

Aug 1995-98   Martin Thompson
Aug 1998-   Stephen Pokawin

MILNE BAY

Capital: Alotau

Premiers:

1978-81   Patrick Paulisbo
1981-82   John Tubira
1983-86   Lepani Watson
1987-89   Navy Aule
1989-91   Elliot Kaidama
1991-Oct 1992   Jeffrey Toloube   (1st)
(Oct 1992-Nov 1993   government suspended)
Nov 1993-94   Jeffrey Toloube   (2nd)
1994-95   Jones Liosi

Governors:

Aug 1995-97   Tim Neville
1997-Dec 1999   Josephine Abaijah   (1st)
Dec 1999-Feb 2000   Titus Philemon
Feb 2000-   Josephine Abaijah   (2nd)

MOROBE

Capital: Lae

Premiers:

1978-80	Pama Anio
1980-87	Utula Samana
1987-88	Enny Moaitz
1988-89	Haggai Joshua
(Sept 1989-Dec 1990	government suspended)
1991-92	Jerry Nalau
1992	Titi Christian (1st)
(Nov 1992-Feb 1994	government suspended)
Feb 1994-Aug 1995	Titi Christian (2nd)

Governor:

Aug 1995-	Jerry Nalau

NEW IRELAND

Capital: Kavieng

Premiers:

1977-86	Robert Seeto
1987-90	Pedi Anis
1990-93	Demas Kavuvu
1993-95	Samson Gila

Governors:

Aug 1995-97	Wilson Peni
1997-	Paul Tohian

NORTH SOLOMON (BOUGAINVILLE)

Attempted to secede from Papua New Guinea as the Republic of Northern Solomons 1985-86 and again as the Republic of Bougainville   (Mekanui) in 1990-93. Unrest continued until 1998.

Capital: Kieta 1975-76, Arawa since 1976

President:

May 1990-Feb 1993	Francis Ona (rebel government)

(Feb 1993   Arawa recaptured by central government)

Prime Minister:

Sept 1975-Aug 1976   Alexis Sarei   (rebel government)

Premiers:

1976-80   Alexis Sarei   (1st)
1980-84   Leo Hannett
1984-87   Alexis Sarei   (2nd)
1987-Aug 1990   Joseph Kabui   (1st)

Administrator:

Aug 1990-April 1995   Sam Tulo

Premiers:

April 1995-Oct 1996   Theodore Miriung   († assassinated)
Nov 1996-May 1999   Gerard Sinato   (co-PM Dec 1998-May 1999)
Dec 1998-May 1999   Jospeh Kabui   (2nd) (co-PM)
(May 1999   Government suspended)

Governor:

Dec 1999-   John Momis

ORO

Previous name: Northern Province
Capital: Popondetta

Premiers:

1977   Edric Eupu
1977-83   Mark Taua
1983-85   Conway Ihova
1985-87   Dennis Kageni
1987-88   Bensen Ariembo
1988-89   Newman Mongagi
1989   Lionel Handu
1990   Kingsley Gegeyo
1991   Parminus Cuthbert
1991-92   Benstead Atoto
1992-95   Douglas Garawa

Governor:

Aug 1995-Sept 1998	Sylvanus Siembo	(1st)
(Sept-Nov	post vacant)	
Nov 1998-	Sylvanus Siembo	(2nd)

SANDAUN

Previous name: West Sepik
Capital: Vanimo

Premiers:

1978-80	Jacob Talis
1980-82	Adam Amod
1982-84	Andrew Komboni
1984-87	Paul Langro
(May 1987-Aug 1988	government suspended)
1988-92	Egbert Yalu
1993-95	Aloitch Peien

Governor:

Aug 1995-	John Tekwie

SIMBU

Capital: Kundiawa

Premiers:

1976-78	Siwi Kurondo
1978-84	Mathew Siune
(1984-86	government suspended)
1986-88	Peter Gul
1988-92	David Mai
1992-93	Edward Bare
1993-95	Edward Aba

Governors:

Aug 1995-Aug 1997	Yauwe Riyong	
Aug 1997-June 1998	Louis Ambane	(1st)
June 1998-April 1999	Simeon Wai	
April 1999-	Louis Ambane	(2nd)

SOUTHERN HIGHLANDS

Capital: Mendi

Premiers:

1978-80	Andrew Andaija
1980-85	Tegi Ebeial
1985-90	Yaungtine Koromba
1990-92	Albert Mokai
(Oct 1992-Aug 1995	government suspended)

Governors:

Aug 1995-1997	Dick Mune
1997-	Anderson Agiru

WESTERN HIGHLANDS

Capital: Mount Hagen

Premiers:

1978-84	Nambuga Mara
1984	Kagel Koroka
1984-87	Philip Kapal (1st)
(March-Dec 1987	government suspended)
1987-90	Philip Kapal (2nd)
1990-92	Lukas Roika
(Dec 1992-Aug 1995	government suspended)

Governors:

Aug 1995-Aug 1997	Paias Wingti
Aug 1997-	Robert Lak

WESTERN PROVINCE (FLY RIVER)

Capital: Daru

Premiers:

1977-83	Tatie Olewale
1983-85	Semai Aitowai
(1985-88	government suspended)
1988-91	Norbert Makmop
1992-95	Isidore Kaseng

Governor:

Aug 1995-   Dere Wamaro

WEST NEW BRITAIN

Capital: Kimbe

Premiers:

1978-87	Bernard Vogae	(1st)
1987-88	Joseph Lehen	
1988-93	Robert Lawrence	
1993-95	Bernard Vogae	(2nd)

Governors:

Aug 1995-1997	Lukas Waka	
1997-March 2000	Bernard Vogae	(†)
March 2000-	Isidore Teli	

PARAGUAY

Official name: Republic of Paraguay, República del Paraguay
Independence date: 14 May 1811
Capital: Asunción

Paraguay became Spanish territory in the 16th century and was governed as part of the Vice-Royalty of Rio de la Plata. In 1811 it declared itself independent. For the first six decades the country was dominated by members of one family whose rule ended with the devasting war of 1865-70 against Brazil, Argentina and Uruguay. From 1954 to 1989 Paraguay was ruled by Alfred Stroessner, the longest serving president on record. Following his removal a more democratic system was put in place.

Duumvirate:

June 1811-Oct 1814   José Rodríguez de Francia/Fulgencio Yegros

Presidents:

Oct 1814-Sept 1840	José Rodríguez de Francia (†)
(Sept 1840-May 1841	junta)
May 1841-March 1844	Consuls: Carlos López (*nephew of J.Rodríguez de Francia*)/Mariano Roque Alonso
March 1844-Sept 1862	Carlos López (†)
Sept 1862-March 1870	Francisco López (*son*) (†)
March 1870-Dec 1871	Cirilio Rivarola
Dec 1871-Nov 1874	Salvador Jovellanos
Nov 1874-April 1877	Juan Bautista Gil († assassinated)
April 1877-Nov 1878	Higinio Uriarte
Nov 1878-Sept 1880	Candido Barreiro (†)
Sept 1880-Nov 1881	Adolfo Saguier
Nov 1881-Nov 1886	Bernardino Caballero
Nov 1886-Sept 1890	Patricio Escobar
Sept 1890-June 1894	Juan González
June-Nov 1894	Marcos Morínigo
Nov 1894-Nov 1898	Juan Bautista Egusquiza
Nov 1898-Jan 1902	Emilio Aceval (†)
Jan-Nov 1902	Héctor Carvallo
Nov 1902-Aug 1904	Juan Bautista Ezcurra
Aug 1904-Dec 1905	Juan Gaona
Dec 1905-Nov 1906	Cecilio Báez
Nov 1906-July 1908	Benigno Ferreira
July 1908-Nov 1910	Emiliano González Navero (1st)

Nov 1910-Jan 1911	Manuel Gondra
Jan-July 1911	Albino Jara (acting)
July-Dec 1911	Liberato Rojas
Jan-March 1912	Pedro Peña
March-Aug 1912	Emiliano González Navero (2nd)
Aug 1912-Aug 1916	Eduardo Schaerer
Aug 1916-June 1919	Manuel Franco (†)
June 1919-Aug 1920	José Montero (acting)
Aug 1920-Oct 1921	Manuel Gondra
Oct-Nov 1921	Félix Paeva (acting)
Nov 1921-April 1923	Eusebio Ayala (1st)
April 1923-April 1924	Eligio Ayala (*brother*) (1st)
April-Aug 1924	Luis Riart
Aug 1924-Aug 1928	Eligio Ayala (2nd)
Aug 1928-Oct 1931	José Guggiari
Oct 1931-Jan 1932	Emiliano González Navero (3rd)
Jan 1932-Feb 1936	Eusebio Ayala (2nd) (deposed)
Feb 1936-Aug 1937	Rafael Franco (deposed)
Aug 1937-Aug 1939	Félix Paeva
Aug 1939-Sept 1940	José Estigarribia († air accident)
Sept 1940-June 1948	Higinio Morínigo (deposed)
June-Aug 1948	Juan Frutos
Aug 1948-Jan 1949	Juan Natalicio González (deposed)
Jan-Feb 1949	Raimundo Rolón (deposed)
Feb 1949-July 1950	Felipe Molas López
July 1950-May 1954	Federico Chavéz (deposed)
May-Aug 1954	Tomás Romero Pereira
Aug 1954-Feb 1989	Alfredo Stroessner (CP) (deposed)
Feb 1989-Aug 1993	Andrés Rodríguez (CP)
Aug 1993-Aug 1998	Juan Carlos Wasmosy (CP)
Aug 1998-March 1999	Raúl Cubás Grau (CP)
March 1999-	Luis González Macchi (CP)

CP = Colorado Party

PERU

Official name: Republic of Peru, República del Perú
Independence date: 28 July 1821
Capital: Lima

Present-day Peru was the centre of the Inca Empire, founded in the 12th century, until it was conquered by Spain in 1533. The Vice-Royalty of Peru was organized in 1544, Spanish rule continued until 1821 when Peru declared itself independent. Peru has experienced political instability and several coups - the last period of military rule was from 1968 to 1980. Since the late 1970s governments have faced insurgencies from left-wing guerilla movements which have become less active after the capture of several leaders.

Presidents:

July 1821-Sept 1822	José de San Martin
Sept 1822-Feb 1823	José de Tagle (1st)
Feb-July 1823	José de la Riva Agüero
July 1823-Feb 1824	José de Tagle (2nd)
Feb 1824-April 1825	Simón Bolívar (1st) (also President of Bolivia, Colombia & Venezuela)
April 1825-Jan 1826	Hipolito Unánue
Jan-Feb 1826	José de la Mar (1st)
Feb 1826-Jan 1827	Simón Bolívar (2nd)
Jan-June 1827	Andrés Santa Cruz (1st)
June-Aug 1827	Manuel Salazar y Baquíjano (1st)
Aug 1827-Aug 1829	José de la Mar (2nd)
Aug 1829-Dec 1833	Agustín Gamarra (1st)
Dec 1833-March 1834	Luis Orbegoso (1st)
March 1834-Feb 1835	Manuel Salazar y Baquíjano (2nd)
Feb 1835-Jan 1836	Felipe Santiago Salaverry († assassinated)
Jan-Aug 1836	Luis Orbegoso (2nd)
Aug 1836-Feb 1839	Andrés Santa Cruz (2nd) (also President of Bolivia)
Feb 1839-June 1841	Agustín Gamarra (2nd) (†)
June 1841-April 1845	Manuel Menéndez
April 1845-April 1851	Ramón Castilla (1st)
April 1851-Jan 1855	José Echenique (deposed)
Jan 1855-Oct 1862	Ramón Castilla (2nd)
Oct 1862-April 1863	Miguel San Román (†)
April 1863	Ramón Castilla (acting)
April-Aug 1863	Pedro Díez Conseco (acting)
April 1863-Nov 1865	Juan Pezet
Nov 1865	Pedro Díez Conseco

Nov 1865-Oct 1867	Mariano Prado (1st)
Oct 1867-Aug 1868	Luis la Puerta (acting)
Aug 1868-July 1872	José Balta († assassinated)
July-Aug 1872	Mariano Herencia Zevallos (acting)
Aug 1872-Aug 1876	Manuel Pardo
Aug 1876-Dec 1879	Mariano Prado (2nd)
Dec 1879-March 1881	Nicolás de Pierola (1st)
March-July 1881	Francisco García Calderón
July 1881-Oct 1883	Lizardo Montero
Oct 1883-June 1886	Miguel Iglesias
June 1886-Aug 1890	Andrés Cáceres (1st)
Aug 1890-April 1894	Remigio Morales Bermudez (†)
April-Aug 1894	Justiniano Borgoño
Aug 1894-March 1895	Andrés Cáceres (2nd)
March-Sept 1895	Manuel Candamo (1st)
Sept 1895-Sept 1899	Nicolás de Pierola (2nd)
Sept 1899-Sept 1903	Eduardo de López de Romana
Sept 1903-April 1904	Manuel Candamo (2nd) (†)
April-Sept 1904	Serapio Calderón
Sept 1904-Sept 1908	José Pardo y Barreja (*son of Manuel Pardo*) (1st)
Sept 1908-Sept 1912	Augusto Leguía y Salcedo (1st)
Sept 1912-Feb 1914	Guillermo Billinghurst (deposed)
Feb 1914-Aug 1915	Oscar Benavides (acting)
Aug 1915-July 1919	José Pardo y Barreja (2nd)
July 1919-Aug 1930	Augusto Leguía y Salcedo (2nd) (deposed)
24-28 Aug 1930	Manuel Ponce (acting)
Aug 1930-March 1931	Luis Sánchez Cerro (acting)
1-5 March 1931	Ricardo Leonicio Elías (acting)
5-10 March 1931	Gustavo Jiménez (acting)
March-Dec 1931	David Samanez Ocampo (acting)
Dec 1931-April 1933	Luis Sánchez Cerro († assassinated)
April 1933-Dec 1939	Oscar Benavides
Dec 1939-July 1945	Manuel Prado y Ugarteche (*son of Mariano Prado*) (1st)
July 1945-Oct 1948	José Bustamente y Rivero (deposed)
Oct 1948-June 1950	Manuel Odría (acting)
June-July 1950	Zenón Noriega (acting)
July 1950-July 1956	Manuel Odría
July 1956-July 1962	Manuel Prado y Ugarteche (2nd) (DM) (deposed)
July 1962-March 1963	Ricardo Pérez Godoy (deposed)
March-July 1963	Nicolás Lindley López
July 1963-Oct 1968	Fernando Belaunde Terry (1st) (AP) (deposed)
Oct 1968-Aug 1975	Juan Velasco Alvaredo (deposed)
Aug 1975-July 1980	Francisco Morales Bermudez (*grandson of R.Morales Bermudez*)
July 1980-July 1985	Fernando Belaunde Terry (2nd) (AP)
July 1985-July 1990	Alan García Pérez (APRA)

July 1990-   Alberto Fujimori   (C 90)

Prime Ministers:

Dec 1885-June 1896	Antonio Arenas
June-Oct 1886	Pedro Solar (1st)
Oct-Nov 1886	José Aranibar
Nov 1886-Aug 1887	Pedro Solar (2nd)
Aug-Sept 1887	Mariano Alvarez
Sept-Oct 1887	Carlos Elías (1st)
Oct-Nov 1887	Raimundo Morales
Nov 1887-March 1889	Aurelio Denegrí
March-April 1889	José Jiménez (1st)
April 1889-Feb 1890	Pedro Solar (3rd)
Feb-Aug 1890	Manuel Irigoyen
Aug 1890-July 1891	Mariano Válcarcel
July-Aug 1891	Alberto Elmore (1st)
Aug-Oct 1891	Justiniano Borgoño
Oct-Nov 1891	Federico Herrera
Nov 1891-April 1892	Juan Ibarra
June 1892-Feb 1893	Carlos Elías (2nd)
March-May 1893	Manuel Velarde
May 1893-March 1894	José Jiménez (2nd)
April-Aug 1894	Baltasar García Urrutia
Aug-Nov 1894	Cesáreo Chacaltana (1st)
Nov 1894-March 1895	Manuel Irigoyen
March-Sept 1895	Manuel Candamo
Sept-Nov 1895	Antonio Bentín
Nov 1895-July 1896	Manuel Barinaga
Aug 1896-Oct 1897	Manuel Olaechea
Nov-Dec 1897	Alejandro López de Romaña
Dec 1897-May 1898	Enrique de la Riva Agüero (1st)
May 1898-Sept 1899	José Loayza
Sept-Dec 1899	Manuel Galves
Dec 1899-Aug 1900	Enrique de la Riva Agüero (2nd)
Aug-Oct 1900	Enrique Zegarra
Oct 1900-Aug 1901	Domingo Almenara
Sept 1901-July 1902	Cesáreo Chacaltana (2nd)
Aug-Oct 1902	Alejandro Deustua
Nov 1902-Sept 1903	Eugenio Larrabure y Unanue
Sept 1903-May 1904	José Pardo
May-Sept 1904	Alberto Elmore (2nd)
Sept 1904-Aug 1907	Augusto Leguía y Salcedo
Aug-Oct 1907	Agustín Tovar
Oct 1907-Sept 1908	Carlos Washburn

Sept 1908-May 1909	Eulogio Romero
June 1909-March 1910	Rafael Villanueva
March-July 1910	Javier Prado Ugarteche
Aug-Oct 1910	Germán Schreiber (1st)
Nov-Dec 1910	José Cavero
Dec 1910-Aug 1911	Enrique Basadre
Aug 1911-Sept 1912	Agustín Ganoza
Sept-Dec 1912	Elías Malpartida
Dec 1912-Feb 1913	Enrique Varela (1st)
Feb-June 1913	Federico Luna y Peralta
June-July 1913	Aurelio Sousa (1st)
July 1913-Feb 1914	Enrique Varela (2nd)
May-Aug 1914	Pedro Muñiz
Aug 1914	Meliton Carvajal
Aug-Nov 1914	Aurelio Sousa (2nd)
Nov 1914-Feb 1915	Germán Schreiber (2nd)
Feb-Aug 1915	Carlos Abrill
Aug 1915-July 1917	Enrique de la Riva Agüero (3rd)
July 1917-Nov 1918	Francisco Tudela y Varela
Dec 1918-April 1919	Germán Arenas (1st)
April-July 1919	Juan Zuloaga
July-Dec 1919	Meliton Porras
Dec 1919-Oct 1922	Germán Leguía y Martínez
Oct 1922-23	Alberto Salomon
1923	Benjamin Huaman de los Heros (1st)
Dec 1923-May 1924	Julio Ego Aguirre
May 1924-Dec 1926	Alejandrino Maguina
Dec 1926-Dec 1929	José Rada y Gamio
Dec 1929-Dec 1931	Benjamin Huaman de los Heros (2nd)
Dec 1931-Jan 1932	Germán Arenas (2nd)
Jan-April 1932	Francisco Lanatta
April 1932-April 1933	Luis Flores
April 1933-Sept 1934	Jorge Prado y Ugarteche
Sept 1934-Oct 1935	Alberto Rey de Castro
Oct 1935-April 1939	Ernesto Montagne Markolz
April-Dec 1939	Manuel Ugarteche
Dec 1939-Dec 1944	Alfredo Solf Muro
Dec 1944-July 1945	Julio East
July 1945-Jan 1946	Rafael Belaunde
Jan 1946-June 1948	José Alzamora
June-Oct 1948	Armando Revoredo
Oct 1948-Aug 1954	Zenón Noriega
Aug 1954-June 1956	Roque Saldias
June-July 1956	Juan Mendoza Gutiérrez
July 1956-June 1958	Manuel Cisneros Sánchez

June 1958-July 1959	Luis Gallo Porras
July 1959-Nov 1961	Pedro Beltrán Espantoso
Nov 1961-July 1962	Carlos Paz Soldan
18-24 July 1962	Ricardo Pérez Godoy
July 1962-July 1963	Nicolás Lindley López
July-Dec 1963	Oscar Trelles Montes
Jan 1964-Sept 1965	Fernando Schwalb López (1st)
Sept 1965-Sept 1967	Daniel Becerra de la Flor
Sept-Nov 1967	Edgardo Seoane Corrales
Nov 1967-May 1968	Raúl Ferrero Rebagliati
May-Oct 1968	Oswaldo Hercelles
2-3 Oct 1968	Miguel Mujica Gallo
Oct 1968-Jan 1973	Ernesto Montagne Sánchez
Jan 1973-Feb 1975	Edgardo Mercado Jarrín
Feb-Sept 1975	Francisco Morales Bermudez
Sept 1975-Feb 1976	Oscar Vargas Prieto
Feb-July 1976	Jorge Fernández Maldonado
July 1976-Jan 1978	Guillermo Arbulú Galliani
Jan 1978-Feb 1979	Omar Molina Pallochia
Feb 1979-July 1980	Pedro Richter Prada
July 1980-Jan 1983	Manuel Ulloa Elías
Jan 1983-April 1984	Fernando Schwalb López (2nd)
April-Oct 1984	Sanfro Mariátegui
Oct 1984-July 1985	Luis Pércovich Roca
July 1985-July 1987	Luis Alva Castro
July 1987-May 1988	Guillermo Larco Cox (1st)
May 1988-May 1989	Armando Villanueva del Campo
May-Oct 1989	Luis Sánchez Sánchez
Oct 1989-July 1990	Guillermo Larco Cox (2nd)
July 1990-Feb 1991	Juan Carlos Hurtado Miller
Feb-Nov 1991	Carlos Torres y Torres Lara
Nov 1991-April 1992	Alfonso de los Heros
April 1992-Aug 1993	Oscar de la Puente Raygada
Aug 1993-Feb 1994	Alfonso Bustamante y Bustamante
Feb 1994-July 1995	Efraín Goldenberg Schreiber
July 1995-April 1996	Dante Córdoba Blanco
April 1996-June 1998	Alberto Pandolfi Arbulú (1st)
June-Aug 1998	Javier Valle Riestra
Aug 1998-Jan 1999	Alberto Pandolfi Arbulú (2nd)
Jan 1999-Oct 1999	Víctor Joy Way Rojas
Oct 1999-	Alberto Bustamente Belaunde

AP = Accion Popular
APRA = Alianza Popular Revolucionaria Americana
C 90 = Cambio 90
DM = Democratic Movement

Former independent state

TAHUANTINSUYU (INCA EMPIRE)

Capital: Cuzco

Emperors:

12th century	Manco Capac
12th/13th century	Sinchi Roca (*son*)
13th century	Lloque Yupanqui (*son*)
13th century	Mayta Capac (*son*)
13th/14th century	Capac Yupanqui (*son*)
14th century	Inca Roca (*son*)
14th century	Yahuar Huacac (*son*) (assassinated)
14th cent-c1440	Viracocha I (*b* Huatan Tupac) (*son*)
c1440-41	Urco (*son*)
1438-71	Pachacuti Inca Yupanqui (*b* Casi Yupanqui) (*brother*) (rival emperor 1438-41) (abdicated)
1471-93	Topa Inca (*son*)
1493-1525	Huayna Capac (*b* Tito Cusi Huallpa) (*son*)
1525	Ninan Cuyucho (*son*)
1525-April 1532	Huascar Inca (*b* Tupac Cusi Huallpa) (*brother*) (murdered)
April-Nov 1532	Atahuallpa (*brother*) (deposed by Spanish, executed)
1533	Topa Huallpa (*brother*) (murdered)
1533-45	Manco Inca Yupanqui (*brother*) (Spanish puppet in Cuzco 1533-35, independent ruler in east 1535-45)
1545-72	Topa Amaru (based in eastern areas) (*son*)

PHILIPPINES

Official name: Republic of the Philippines, República de Filipinas, Republika ñg Pilipinas (Tagalog)

Previous name: Commonwealth of the Philippines (1935-42, 1945-46)

Independence dates: 12 June 1898, 4 July 1946

Capital: Manila (until 1948 & since 1976), Quezon City (1948-76)

Magellan landed in the Philippines in 1521, and were conquered by Spain in 1565. The islands remained in Spanish hands until 1898, when they were ceded to the United States after the Spanish-American war, but local leaders declared independence and were only defeated by the US in 1901. In 1935 the Philippines became a US commonwealth territory with full self-government. During World War II the country was occupied by Japan who established a puppet government. After liberation, full independence was granted in 1946. The long rule of President Marcos ended in 1996 when peaceful civil disturbances organized by the opposition forced him to leave the country, after which democracy was restored. The island of Mindanao has experienced a rebellion by Muslim guerrillas, which ended with the peace agreement of 1996.

Presidents:

Jan 1899-March 1901	Emilio Aguinaldo
(March 1901-Sept 1935	US rule)
Sept 1935-Jan 1942	Manuel Quezon (exiled)
Jan 1942-Oct 1943	Jorge Vargas
Oct 1943-Feb 1945	José Laurel
Feb 1945-April 1946	Sergio Osmeña (NP)
April 1946-April 1948	Manuel Roxas y Acuna (LP) (†)
April 1948-Jan 1954	Elpidio Quirino (LP)
Jan 1954-March 1957	Ramon Magsaysay (NP) († air accident)
March 1957-Dec 1961	Carlos Garcia (NP)
Dec 1961-Dec 1965	Diosdado Macapagal (LP)
Dec 1965-Feb 1986	Ferdinand Marcos (NP,NSM) (deposed)
Feb 1986-June 1992	Corazon Aquino (*b* C.Cojuangco) (UNDO)
June 1992-June 1998	Fidel Ramos (L-NUCD)
June 1998-	Joseph Estrada (SNFM)

Prime Ministers:

Jan 1973-July 1981	Ferdinand Marcos
July 1981-Feb 1986	Cesar Virata
Feb-March 1986	Salvador Laurel (*son of J.Laurel*)
(March 1986	post abolished)

L-NUCD = Lakas-National Union of Christian Democrats
LP = Liberal Party
NP = National Party
NSM = New Society Movement
SNFM = Struggle of the Nationalist Filipino Masses
UNDO = United Nationalist Democratic Organization

GOVERNMENT-IN-EXILE 1942-45

Headquarters: Washington DC
Operated during Japanese occupation

Presidents:

Jan 1942-Aug 1944	Manuel Quezon	(†)
Aug 1944-Feb 1945	Sergio Osmeña	

Autonomous Region

MUSLIM MINDANAO

Capital: Cotabato City

Governors:

Feb 1990-March 1993	Zacaria Candao
March 1993-Sept 1996	Lininding Pangandaman
Sept 1996-	Nur Misuari

POLAND

Official name: Polish Republic, Polska Ludowa
Previous names: Kingdom of Poland until 1795, Polish People's Republic 1945-89
Independence date: 10 November 1918
Capital: Warsaw (Warszawa)

Poland became an independent kingdom in the 10th century, but its independence was extinguished in the 18th century when Poland became a Russian protectorate. In the three partitions of 1772, 1793 and 1795 Poland was divided between Russia, Austria and Prussia. In 1807 Napoleon established a puppet Grand Duchy of Warsaw, and in 1815 a republic was set up in Cracow. The rest of the country came under Russian rule. An independent state was reconstituted in 1918. Poland was occupied by Germany between 1939 and 1945, and after the war it became a people's republic. In 1989 the government allowed partially free elections in which the formerly illegal trade union Solidarity won decisively and then formed a coalition government with the communists and others; the communist party was later transformed into a social democratic party. Free presidential elections were held in 1990.

Kings/Queen:

(Some referred to as Dukes before 14th century)

966-92	Mieczysław I
992-June 1025	Bolesław I (*son*)
1025-34	Mieczysław II (*brother*)
1034-Nov 1058	Kazimierz I (*son*) (deposed during period of anarchy 1037-39)
Nov 1058-79	Bolesław II (*son*) (deposed)
1079-1102	Władysław I Herman (*son of Kazimierz I*) (abdicated)
1102-Oct 1138	Bolesław III (*son*)
Oct 1138-46	Władysław II (*son*) (deposed)
1146-73	Bolesław IV (*brother*)
1173-77	Mieczysław III (*brother*) (1st) (deposed)
1177-94	Kazimierz II (*brother*)
1194-98	Leszek I (*son*) (1st) (deposed)
1198-1202	Mieczysław III (2nd)
1202-27	Leszek I (2nd) (assassinated)
1227-79	Bolesław V (*son*)
1279-89	Leszek II
1289-90	Władysław I (*son of Kazimierz II*) (1st)
1290-96	Przemsyl (usurper) (assassinated)
1296-1305	Wacław I (Václav II of Bohemia)
1305-06	Wacław II (Václav III of Bohemia)
1306-33	Władysław I (2nd)

1333-Nov 1370	Kazimierz III (*son*)
Nov 1370-Sept 1382	Lajos I (*nephew*) (also King of Hungary)
(Sept 1382-Oct 1384	interregnum)
Oct 1384-July 1399	Jadwiga (*daughter*) (co-ruler 1386-99)
Feb 1386-June 1434	Władysław II Jagiello (*husband*) (co-ruler 1386-99)
June 1434-Nov 1444	Władysław III (son) (Ulászló I of Hungary)
(Nov 1444-June 1447	interregnum)
June 1447-June 1492	Kazimierz IV (*brother*)
June 1492-June 1501	Jan I Olbracht (*son*)
June 1501-Aug 1506	Aleksander (*brother*)
Aug 1506-April 1548	Zygmunt I (*brother*) (co-ruler 1530-48)
1530-July 1572	Zygmunt II August (*son*) (co-ruler 1530-48)
(July 1572-May 1573	interregnum)
May 1573-May 1574	Henryk (Henri III of France)
(May 1574-May 1576	interregnum)
May 1576-Dec 1586	Stefan I (*son-in-law of Zygmunt II August*)
(Dec 1586-Aug 1587	interregnum)
Aug 1587-April 1632	Zygmunt III (Sigismund of Sweden)
May 1632-May 1648	Władysław IV (*son*)
May 1648-Aug 1668	Jan II Kazimierz (*brother*) (abdicated)
(Aug 1668-69	interregnum)
1669-Nov 1773	Michał
Nov 1673-May 1674	interregnum)
May 1674-June 1696	Jan III
(June 1696-Sept 1697	interregnum)
Sept 1697-July 1704	August II (1st) (deposed) (Elector Friedrich August I of Saxony)
July 1704-09	Stanisław I (1st) (deposed)
1709-Feb 1733	August II (2nd)
Feb-Oct 1733	Stanisław I (2nd)
Oct 1733-Oct 1763	August III (Elector Friedrich August II of Saxony)
(Oct 1763-Sept 1764	interregnum)
Sept 1764-Nov 1795	Stanisław II August (abdicated)
(1795-1918	Poland partitioned between Austria, Prussia and Russia)

Presidents:

Nov 1918-Dec 1922	Józef Piłsudski
9-16 Dec 1922	Gabriel Narutowicz († assassinated)
Dec 1922-May 1926	Stanisław Wojciechowski
May-June 1926	Maciej Rataj (acting)
June 1926-Sept 1939	Ignacy Móscicki

Governor-General:

Sept 1939-Jan 1945	Hans Frank (executed 1946)

Presidents:
Chairman of the Council of State Nov 1952-July 1989

Jan 1945-Nov 1952	Bolesław Bierut
Nov 1952-Aug 1964	Aleksander Zawadski (†)
Aug 1964-April 1968	Edward Ochab
April 1968-Dec 1970	Marian Spychalski
Dec 1970-May 1972	Józef Cyrankiewicz
May 1972-Nov 1985	Henryk Jabloński
Nov 1985-Dec 1990	Wojciech Jaruzelski
Dec 1990-Dec 1995	Lech Wałęsa (S)
Dec 1995-	Aleksander Kwaśniewski (DLA)

Prime Ministers:
Chairman of the Council of Ministers 1952-92

Nov 1917-Feb 1918	Jan Kucharzewski (1st)
Feb-Aug 1918	Antoni Ponikowski (1st)
Aug-Sept 1918	Jan Steczkowski
Sept-Oct 1918	Jan Kucharzewski (2nd)
Oct-Nov 1918	Józef Swierzyński
5-11 Nov 1918	Władysław Wroblewski
14-18 Nov 1918	Ignacy Daszyński
Nov 1918-Jan 1919	Jędrzej Moraczewski
Jan-Dec 1919	Ignacy Paderewski
Dec 1919-June 1920	Leopold Skulski
June-July 1920	Władysław Grabski (1st)
July 1920-Sept 1921	Wincenty Witos (1st)
Sept 1921-June 1922	Antoni Ponikowski (2nd)
June-July 1922	Stanisław Śliwiński
14-29 July 1922	Wojciech Korfanty
July-Dec 1922	Julian Nowack
Dec 1922-May 1923	Władysław Sikorski
May-Dec 1923	Wincenty Witos (2nd)
Dec 1923-Nov 1925	Władysław Grabski (2nd)
Nov 1925-May 1926	Aleksander Skrzyński
10-15 May 1926	Wincenty Witos (3rd)
May-Oct 1926	Kazimierz Bartel (1st)
Oct 1926-June 1928	Józef Piłsudski
June 1928-April 1929	Kazimierz Bartel (2nd)
April-Dec 1929	Kazimierz Świtalski
Dec 1929-March 1930	Kazimierz Bartel (3rd)
March 1930-May 1931	Walery Sławek (1st)
May 1931-May 1933	Aleksander Prystor
May 1933-May 1934	Janusz Jędrzejewicz
May 1934-March 1935	Leon Kozlowski

March-Oct 1935	Walery Sławek (2nd)
Oct 1935-May 1936	Marian Zyndram-Kościałkowski
May 1936-Sept 1939	Felician Sławej-Składkowski
(Sept 1939-Jan 1945	German occupation)
Jan 1945-Feb 1947	Edward Osóbka-Morawski
Feb 1947-Nov 1952	Józef Cyrankiewicz (1st)
Nov 1952-March 1954	Bolesław Bierut
March 1954-Dec 1970	Józef Cyrankiewicz (2nd)
Dec 1970-Feb 1980	Piotr Jaroszewicz
Feb-Aug 1980	Edward Babiuch
Aug 1980-Feb 1981	Józef Pinkowski
Feb 1981-Nov 1985	Wojciech Jaruzelski
Nov 1985-Sept 1988	Zbigniew Messner
Sept 1988-Aug 1989	Mieczysław Rakowski
2-20 Aug 1989	Czesław Kiszczak
Aug 1989-Jan 1991	Tadeusz Mazowiecki (S)
Jan-Dec 1991	Jan Bielecki (LDC)
Dec 1991-June 1992	Jan Olszewski
June-July 1992	Waldemar Pawlak (1st) (PPP)
July 1992-Oct 1993	Hanna Suchocka (DU)
Oct 1993-March 1995	Waldemar Pawlak (2nd) (PPP)
March 1995-Feb 1996	Józef Oleksy (DLA)
Feb 1996-Oct 1997	Włodzimierz Cimoszewicz (DLA)
Oct 1997-	Jerzy Buzek

DLA = Democratic Left Alliance
DU = Democratic Union
LDC = Liberal Democratic Congress
PPP = Polish Peasant's Party
S = Solidarity

Communist Party* Leaders:

*Polish United Workers' Party
Secretary-General 1945-March 1954
First Secretary March 1954-90

Jan 1945-Sept 1948	Władysław Gomulka (1st)
Sept 1948-March 1956	Boleslaw Bierut (†)
March-Oct 1956	Edward Ochab
Oct 1956-Dec 1970	Władysław Gomulka (2nd)
Dec 1970-Sept 1980	Edward Gierek
Sept 1980-Oct 1981	Stanisław Kania
Oct 1981-July 1989	Wojciech Jaruzelski
July 1989-Jan 1990	Mieczysław Rakowski
(Jan 1990	party dissolved)

GOVERNMENT-IN-EXILE 1939-90

Headquarters: Paris (1939-40), London (1940-90)

Operated initially during German occupation, and after 1945 in opposition to the communist government in Warsaw. During the 1950's it was recognised by Cuba, Ireland, Lebanon, Spain and the Vatican City. It was dissolved in 1990 after the free presidential elections.

Presidents:

Sept 1939-June 1947	Władysław Raczkiewicz (†)
June 1947-April 1972	August Zaleski (†)
April 1972-April 1979	Stanisław Ostrowski
April 1979-April 1986	Edward Raczyński
April 1986-July 1989	Kazimierz Sabbat (†)
July 1989-Dec 1990	Ryszard Kaczorowski

Prime Ministers:

Sept 1939-July 1943	Władysław Sikorski († air accident)
July 1943-Nov 1944	Stanisław Mikołajczyk
Nov 1944-June 1947	Tomasz Arciszewski
July 1947-Feb 1949	Tadeusz Bór-Komorowski
Sept 1949-Aug 1950	Tadeusz Tomaszewski
Sept 1950-Dec 1953	Roman Odzierzyński
Jan-May 1954	Jerzy Dolanowski-Hryniewski
June 1954-June 1955	Stanisław Mackiewicz
Aug-Sept 1955	Hugon Nanke
Sept 1955-June 1965	Antoni Pajak
June 1965-June 1970	Aleksander Zawisza
July 1970-July 1972	Zygmunt Muchniewski
July 1972-July 1976	Alfred Urbański
Aug 1976-April 1986	Kazimierz Sabbat
April 1986-Dec 1990	Edward Szczepanik

Former Independent States

CRACOW

Republic of Cracow

Senate Presidents:

1815-31	Stanisław Wodzicki
1833-36	Gaspar Wieloglowski
1836-39	Józef Haller von Hallenburg
1839-41	—— Bystrzonowski

1841-46   Jan Szindler   (*b* Johann Schindler)
1846   Jan Tyssowski

WARSAW

Grand Duchy of Warsaw

Grand Duke:

July 1807-Feb 1813   Friedrich August I   (King of Saxony)

Former Free City

DANZIG

The free city was created in June 1919. On 30 September 1939 it was incorporated into Germany, but in 1945 was returned to Poland under its Polish name, Gdansk.

Senate Presidents:

June 1919-Jan 1931   Heinrich Sahm
June 1931-June 1933   Ernst Ziehm
June 1933-Nov 1934   Herman Rauschning
Nov 1934-Aug 1939   Arthur Greiser   (executed 1946)
Aug-Sept 1939   Albert Forster   (executed 1948)

PORTUGAL

Official name: Portuguese Republic, República Portuguesa
Previous name: Kingdom of Portugal until 1910
State founded: October 1143
Capital: Lisbon (Lisboa)

Portugal was ruled by the Romans, the Suevi, the Visigoths and the Arabs before the 9th century when it became independent. In the 11th century it fell under the rule of Castile but regained independence in the 12th century. Spain ruled Portugal from 1580 until 1640. The monarchy was abolished in 1910 and a republic was proclaimed. A coup in 1926 brought to power a right-wing government which was led for 36 years by António Salazar. In 1974 it was overthrown and democratic government was introduced two years later. One of the contributing factors to the 1974 coup was the independence wars in some of the Portuguese African colonies, and the new order soon granted independence to all of them.

Kings/Queens:

Oct 1143-Dec 1185	Alfonso I
Dec 1185-March 1211	Sancho I (*son*)
March 1211-March 1223	Alfonso II (*son*)
March 1223-Jan 1248	Sancho II (*son*) (expelled)
Jan 1248-Feb 1279	Alfonso III (*brother*)
Feb 1279-Jan 1325	Denis (*son*)
Jan 1325-May 1357	Alfonso IV (*son*)
May 1357-Jan 1367	Pedro I (*son*)
Jan 1367-Oct 1383	Fernando (*son*)
Oct 1383-March 1385	Regent: Leonor Teles (*widow*)
March 1385-Aug 1433	João I (*son of Pedro I*)
Aug 1433-Sept 1438	Duarte (*son*)
Sept 1438-Aug 1481	Alfonso V (*nephew of Pedro I*)
	Regents: 1438-40 Leonor
	1440-49 Pedro, Duc de Coimbra
Aug 1481-Oct 1495	João II (*son*)
Oct 1495-Dec 1521	Manuel I (*cousin*)
Dec 1521-June 1557	João III (*son*)
June 1557-Aug 1578	Sebastião (*grandson*)
	Regents: 1557-68 Queen Catarina/Prince Henrique
Aug 1578-Jan 1580	Henrique (*f Regent*) (*son of Manuel I*)
June-Aug 1580	António (*son*)
Aug 1580-Sept 1598	Felipe I (Felipe II of Spain)
Sept 1598-March 1621	Felipe II (Felipe III of Spain)
March 1621-Dec 1640	Felipe III (Felipe IV of Spain)

Dec 1640-Nov 1656   João IV   (*great-grandson of Manuel I*)
Nov 1656-Nov 1667   Alfonso VI   (*son*) (deposed)
Nov 1667-Dec 1706   Pedro II   (*brother*)
Dec 1706-July 1750   João V   (*son*)
July 1750-Feb 1777   José   (*son*)
Feb 1777-March 1816 Maria I   (*daughter*) (co-ruler 1777-86)
Feb 1777-March 1786 Pedro III   (*uncle & husband of Maria*) (co-ruler)
March 1816-March 1826 João VI   (*son*)
March-May 1826   Pedro IV   (Pedro I of Brazil) (abdicated)
May 1826-June 1828   Maria II   (*daughter*) (1st)
                     Regents: 1826-28 Princess Isabella Maria
                              1828 Prince Miguel
June 1828-Sept 1833 Miguel   (*f* Regent) (*uncle*) (deposed)
Sept 1833-Nov 1853   Maria II   (2nd)
Nov 1853-Nov 1861   Pedro V   (*son*)
                     Regent: 1853-55 Prince Fernando
Nov 1861-Oct 1889   Luis I   (*brother*)
Oct 1889-Feb 1908   Carlos   (*son*) (assassinated)
(1 Feb 1908   Luis II   (*son*) (technically king for 20 min, assassinated))
Feb 1908-Oct 1910   Manuel II   (*brother*) (deposed)

Presidents:

Oct 1910-Aug 1911   Joaquim Braga   (1st)
Aug 1911-May 1915   Manuel de Arriaga
May-Oct 1915   Joaquim Braga   (2nd)
Oct 1915-Dec 1917   Bernardino Guimarães   (1st) (deposed)
Dec 1917-Dec 1918   Sidinio Pais   († assassinated)
Dec 1918-Oct 1919   João Antunes
Oct 1919-Oct 1923   António de Almeida
Oct 1923-Dec 1925   Manuel Gomes
Dec 1925-June 1926   Bernardino Guimarães   (2nd) (deposed)
(June-Nov 1926   post vacant)
Nov 1926-April 1951 António Carmona   (†)
April-Aug 1951   António Salazar   (acting)
Aug 1951-Aug 1958   Francisco Lopes
Aug 1958-April 1974 Américo Tomás   (deposed)
April-Sept 1974   António de Spínola
Sept 1974-July 1976 Francisco da Costa Gomes
July 1976-March 1986 António Eanes
March 1986-March 1996 Mario Soares   (SP)
March 1996-   Jorge Sampaio   (SP)

Prime Ministers:

May-Nov 1835   Duc de Saldanha   (João Saldanha) (1st)

Nov 1835-April 1836	José Loureiro
April-Sept 1836	Duc de Terceira (António de Noronha) (1st)
Sept-Nov 1836	Conde de Linhares (Vitorio de Sousa Coutinho)
Nov 1836-Sept 1839	Visconde Sá da Bandeira (Bernardo de Sá Nogueira) (1st)
Sept 1839-Dec 1841	Conde de Bonfim (José Valdez)
Jan-Feb 1842	Marquês de Thomar (António da Costa-Cabral) (1st)
Feb 1842-May 1846	Duc de Terceira (António de Noronha) (2nd)
May-Oct 1846	Duc de Palmella (Pedro de Sousa-Holstein)
Oct 1846-April 1851	Marquês de Thomar (António da Costa-Cabral) (2nd)
May 1851-June 1856	Duc de Saldanha (João Saldanha) (2nd)
June 1856-March 1859	Marquês de Loulé (Nuno de Mendoça) (1st)
March 1859-April 1860	Duc de Terceira (António de Noronha) (3rd)
May-July 1860	Joaquim de Aguiar (1st)
July 1860-April 1865	Marquês de Loulé (Nuno de Mendoça) (2nd)
April-Sept 1865	Visconde Sá da Bandeira (Bernardo de Sá Nogueira) (2nd)
Sept 1865-Sept 1866	José Gomes de Castro
Sept 1866-Jan 1868	Joaquim de Aguiar (2nd)
Jan-July 1868	Duc de Avila (António de Avila) (1st)
July 1868-Aug 1869	Visconde Sá da Bandeira (Bernardo de Sá Nogueira) (3rd)
Aug 1869-May 1870	Marquês de Loulé (Nuno de Mendoça) (3rd)
May-Aug 1870	Duc de Saldanha (João Saldanha) (3rd)
Aug-Oct 1870	Visconde Sá da Bandeira (Bernardo de Sá Nogueira (4th)
Oct 1870-Sept 1871	Duc de Avila (António de Avila) (2nd)
Sept 1871-March 1877	António Fontes de Melo (1st)
March 1877-Jan 1878	Duc de Avila (António de Avila) (3rd)
Jan 1878-May 1879	António Fontes de Melo (2nd)
May 1879-March 1881	Anselmo Braamcamp
March-Nov 1881	António Sampaio
Nov 1881-Feb 1886	António Fontes de Melo (3rd)
Feb 1886-Jan 1890	José Luciano de Castro (1st)
Jan-Sept 1890	António Pimental
Oct 1890-Jan 1892	José Abreu e Sousa
Jan 1892-Feb 1893	José Ferreira
Feb 1893-Feb 1897	Ernesto Hintze-Ribeiro (1st)
Feb 1897-June 1900	José Luciano de Castro (2nd)
June 1900-Oct 1904	Ernesto Hintze-Ribeiro (2nd)
Oct 1904-March 1906	José Luciano de Castro (3rd)
March-May 1906	Ernesto Hintze-Ribeiro (3rd)
May 1906-Feb 1908	João Franco
Feb-Dec 1908	Francisco do Amaral
Dec 1908-March 1909	Arturo Henriques
April-May 1909	Sebastião Teles
May-Dec 1909	Venceslau de Lima
Dec 1909-June 1910	Francisco Beirão
June-Oct 1910	António de Sousa

Oct 1910-Sept 1911	Joaquim Braga
Sept-Nov 1911	João Chagas (1st)
Nov 1911-June 1912	Augusto de Vasconcelos
June 1912-Jan 1913	Duarte Leite
Jan 1913-Feb 1914	Afonso Costa (1st)
Feb-Dec 1914	Bernardino Guimarães (1st)
Dec 1914-Jan 1915	Vitor de Coutinho
Jan-May 1915	Joaquim de Castro
15-19 May 1915	João Chagas (2nd)
May-June 1915	Afonso Costa (2nd)
June-Nov 1915	José de Castro
Nov 1915-March 1916	Afonso Costa (3rd)
March 1916-April 1917	António de Almeida
April-Dec 1917	Afonso Costa (4th)
Dec 1917-Dec 1918	Sidinio Pais († assassinated)
Dec 1918-Jan 1919	João Barbosa
Jan-March 1919	José Relvas
March-July 1919	Domingos Pereira (1st)
July 1919-Jan 1920	Alfredo de Sá Cardoso
Jan-March 1920	Domingos Pereira (2nd)
March-June 1920	António Baptista
6-26 June 1920	José Preto (acting)
June-July 1920	António da Silva (1st)
July-Nov 1920	António Granjo (1st)
Nov-Dec 1920	Alvaro de Castro
Dec 1920-Feb 1921	Abel Hipolito
March-May 1921	Bernardino Guimarães (2nd)
May-Aug 1921	Barros Queiros
Aug-Oct 1921	António Granjo (2nd)
Oct-Nov 1921	Manuel Coelho
Nov-Dec 1921	Liberato Pinto
Dec 1921-Feb 1922	Francisco Leal
Feb 1922-June 1924	António da Silva (2nd)
June-Nov 1924	Alfredo Gaspar
Nov 1924-Feb 1925	José dos Santos
Feb-June 1925	Vitorino Guimarães
June-Aug 1925	António da Silva (3rd)
Aug-Dec 1925	João Bastos
Dec 1925-May 1926	António da Silva (4th) (deposed)
May-June 1926	Joaquim Cabeçades
June-July 1926	Manuel da Costa
July 1926-April 1928	António Carmona
April 1928-July 1929	José Freitas
July 1929-Jan 1930	Arturo Ferraz
Jan 1930-June 1932	Domingos Oliveira

July 1932-Sept 1968	António Salazar
Sept 1968-April 1974	Marcello Caetano (deposed)
May-July 1974	Adelino de Palma Carlos
July 1974-Aug 1975	Vasco Gonçalves
Aug 1975-July 1976	José de Azevedo
July 1976-Aug 1978	Mario Soares (1st) (SP)
Aug-Nov 1978	Alfredo da Costa
Nov 1978-Aug 1979	Carlos Mota Pinto
Aug 1979-Jan 1980	Maria Pintasilgo
Jan-Dec 1980	Francisco Sá Carneiro (SDP) († air accident)
Dec 1980-Jan 1981	Diogo do Amaral (acting) (CDP)
Jan 1981-June 1983	Francisco Balsemão (SDP)
June 1983-Nov 1985	Mario Soares (2nd) (SP)
Nov 1985-Oct 1995	Anibal Cavaco Silva (SDP)
Oct 1995-	António Guterres (SP)

CDP = Centre Democratic Party
SDP = Social Democratic Party
SP = Socialist Party

Autonomous Regions

AZORES

Açores
Capital: Angra do Heroísmo

Presidents:

Sept 1976-Oct 1995	João Amaral (SDP)
Oct 1995-Nov 1996	Alberto da Costa
Nov 1996-	Carlos César

MADEIRA

Capital: Funchal

Presidents:

July 1976-March 1978	Jaime Camacho
March 1978-	Alberto Jardim (CDP)

QATAR

Official name: State of Qatar, Dowlat al Qatar
Independence date: 1 September 1971
Capital: Doha

The state of Qatar was founded in 1868 by the al-Thani family, but continued to be part of the Ottoman Empire until 1916 when it became a British protectorate. In 1971 Qatar gained independence.

Heads of State:
Emir since 1971

Sept 1868-78	Shaikh Mohammed bin Thani al-Thani
1878-July 1913	Shaikh Jasim bin Mohammed al-Thani (*son*)
July 1913-Aug 1949	Shaikh Abdullah bin Jasim al-Thani (*son*)
Aug 1949-Oct 1960	Shaikh Ali bin Adbullah al-Thani (*son*) (abdicated)
Oct 1960-Feb 1972	Shaikh Ahmad bin Ali al-Thani (*son*) (deposed)
Feb 1972-June 1995	Shaikh Khalifa bin Hamad al-Thani (*cousin*) (deposed)
June 1995-	Shaikh Hamad bin Khalifa al-Thani (*son*)

Prime Ministers:

May 1971-June 1995	Shaikh Khalifa bin Hamad al-Thani
July 1995-Oct 1996	Shaikh Hamad bin Khalifa al-Thani (*son*)
Oct 1996-	Shaikh Abdullah bin Khalifa al-Thani (*brother*)

ROMANIA

Official name: Romania, România
Previous names: Principality of Romania 1859-81, Kingdom of Romania 1881-1947, People's Republic of Romania 1947-65, Socialist Republic of Romania 1965-89
Independence date: 17 January 1859
Capital: Bucharest (București)

The two principalities of Moldavia and Wallachia lost their independence in the Middle Ages when they were captured by the Turks. In 1829 they were granted autonomy within the Ottoman Empire and in 1859 they were united to form the independent principality of Romania. A kingdom was proclaimed in 1881. In 1947 the king was forced to abdicate and a people's republic was proclaimed. The communist government was overthrown in a popular revolution in 1989, and multi-party elections were held in 1990.

Princes:

Feb 1859-May 1866	Alexandru Cuza (abdicated)
May 1866-March 1881	Carol I (*b* Prince Karl of Hohenzollern)

Kings:

March 1881-Oct 1914	Carol I
Oct 1914-July 1927	Ferdinand (*nephew*)
July 1927-June 1930	Mihai (*grandson*) (1st)
	Regents: Miron Cristea/Gheorghe Buzdugan/Prince Nicolae
June 1930-Oct 1940	Carol II (*father*) (abdicated)
Oct 1940-Dec 1947	Mihai (2nd) (abdicated)

Presidents:

President of the State Council April 1948-March 1974

Dec 1947-April 1948	Mihai Sadoveanu (acting)
April 1948-June 1952	Constantine Parhon
June 1952-Jan 1958	Petru Groza (†)
Jan 1958-March 1961	Ion Maurer
March 1961-March 1965	Gheorghe Gheorghiu-Dej (†)
March 1965-Dec 1967	Chivu Stoica
Dec 1967-Dec 1989	Nicolae Ceaușescu (deposed, executed)
Dec 1989-Nov 1996	Ion Iliescu
Nov 1996-	Emil Constantinescu

Prime Ministers:
Chairman of the Council of Ministers 1948-91

1861-62	Alexandru Moruzi
Feb 1862	Barbu Catargiu
Feb-June 1862	Apostol Arsache
June 1862-Oct 1863	Nicolae Cretulescu (1st)
Oct 1863-Jan 1865	Mihai Kogălniceanu
Jan-Feb 1865	Constantine Bosianu
Feb 1865-May 1866	Nicolae Cretulescu (2nd)
May-July 1866	Lascar Catargiu (1st)
July 1866-March 1867	Ion Ghica (1st)
March-Nov 1867	Nicolae Cretulescu (3rd)
Nov 1867-May 1868	Stefan Golescu
May-Nov 1868	Nicolae Golescu (*brother*)
Nov 1868-Feb 1870	Dimitrie Ghica
Feb-May 1870	Alexandru Golescu
May-Dec 1870	Manolache Epureanu (1st)
Dec 1870-March 1871	Ion Ghica (2nd)
March 1871-April 1876	Lascar Catargiu (2nd)
April-May 1876	Ion Florescu (1st)
May-Aug 1876	Manolache Epureanu (2nd)
Aug 1876-April 1881	Ion Brătianu (1st)
April-June 1881	Dimitrie Brătianu (*brother*)
June 1881-April 1888	Ion Brătianu (2nd)
April 1888-April 1889	Teodor Rosetti
April-Nov 1889	Lascar Catargiu (3rd)
Nov 1889-March 1891	Gheorghe Manu
March-Dec 1891	Ion Florescu (2nd)
Dec 1891-Oct 1895	Lascar Catargiu (4th)
Oct 1895-Dec 1896	Dimitrie Sturdza (1st) (LP)
Dec 1896-April 1897	Petru Aurelian
April 1897-April 1899	Dimitrie Sturdza (2nd) (LP)
April 1899-July 1900	Gheorghe Cantacuzino (1st)
July 1900-Feb 1901	Petru Carp (1st) (CP)
Feb 1901-Jan 1906	Dimitrie Sturdza (3rd) (LP)
Jan 1906-March 1907	Gheorghe Cantacuzino (2nd)
March 1907-Jan 1909	Dimitrie Sturdza (4th) (LP)
Jan-Dec 1909	Ionel Brătianu (*son of Ion Brătianu*) (1st) (LP)
Dec 1909-Jan 1910	Mihai Pherekyde (acting)
Jan 1910-Jan 1911	Ionel Brătianu (2nd) (LP)
Jan 1911-April 1912	Petru Carp (2nd) (CP)
April 1912-Jan 1914	Titu Maiorescu
Jan 1914-Feb 1918	Ionel Brătianu (3rd) (LP)
Feb-March 1918	Alexandru Averescu (1st)

March-Nov 1918	Alexandru Marghilman
Nov-Dec 1918	Constantine Coandă
Dec 1918-Sept 1919	Ionel Brătianu (4th) (LP)
Sept-Dec 1919	Arthur Vaitoianu
Dec 1919-March 1920	Alexandru Vaida-Voevod (1st) (NPoP)
March 1920-Dec 1921	Alexandru Averescu (2nd) (PP)
Dec 1921-Jan 1922	Take Ionescu
Jan 1922-March 1926	Ionel Brătianu (5th) (LP)
March 1926-June 1927	Alexandru Averescu (3rd) (LP)
7-22 June 1927	Barbu Ştirbai
June-Nov 1927	Ionel Brătianu (6th) (LP) (†)
Nov 1927-Nov 1928	Vintilla Brătianu (LP)
Nov 1928-June 1930	Iuliu Maniu (1st) (NPP)
7-8 June 1930	Gheorghe Mironescu (1st)
June-Oct 1930	Iuliu Maniu (2nd) (NPP)
Oct 1930-April 1931	Gheorghe Mironescu (2nd)
April 1931-June 1932	Nicolae Iorga
June-Aug 1932	Alexandru Vaida-Voevod (2nd) (NPP)
Aug 1932-Jan 1933	Iuliu Maniu (3rd) (NPP)
Jan-Nov 1933	Alexandru Vaida-Voevod (3rd) (NPP)
Nov-Dec 1933	Ion Duca (LP) († assassinated)
Dec 1933-Jan 1934	Constantine Angelescu (LP)
Jan 1934-Dec 1937	Gheorghe Tătărescu (1st) (LP)
Dec 1937-Feb 1938	Octavian Goga (NCP)
Feb 1938-March 1939	Miron Cristea (†)
March-Sept 1939	Armand Călineşcu († assassinated)
21-28 Sept 1939	Gheorghe Arteşanu
Sept-Nov 1939	Constantine Argetoianu
Nov 1939-July 1940	Gheorghe Tătărescu (2nd)
July-Sept 1940	Ion Gigurtu
Sept 1940-Aug 1944	Ion Antonescu (deposed, executed 1946)
Aug-Dec 1944	Constantine Sanătescu
Dec 1944-Feb 1945	Nicolae Radescu
March 1945-June 1952	Petru Groza
June 1952-Oct 1955	Gheorghe Gheorghiu-Dej
Oct 1955-March 1961	Chivu Stoica
March 1961-March 1974	Ion Maurer
March 1974-March 1979	Manea Mănescu
March 1979-May 1982	Ilie Verdeţ
May 1982-Dec 1989	Constantine Dăscălescu
Dec 1989-Oct 1991	Petre Roman (NSF)
Oct 1991-Nov 1992	Teodor Stolojan
Nov 1992-Dec 1996	Nicolae Vacaroiu
Dec 1996-March 1998	Victor Ciorba (DCR)
March-April 1998	Gavril Dejeu (acting)

April 1998-Dec 1999	Radu Vasile	
14-21 Dec 1999	Alexandru Athanasiu	(acting)
Dec 1999-	Mugur Isarescu	

CP = Conservative Party
DCR = Democratic Convergence of Romania
LP = Liberal Party
NCP = National Christian Party
NPP = National Peasant's Party
NPoP = National Popular Party
NSF = National Salvation Front
PP = People's Party

Communist Party* Leaders:

*Romanian Workers' Party 1947-65
First Secretary 1947-July 1965
General Secretary July 1965-Dec 1989

Dec 1947-April 1954	Gheorghe Gheorghiu-Dej	(1st)
April 1954-Oct 1955	Gheorghe Apostol	
Oct 1955-March 1965	Gheorghe Gheorghiu-Dej	(2nd) (†)
March 1965-Dec 1989	Nicolae Ceaușescu	
(Dec 1989	communist rule ended)	

GOVERNMENT-IN-EXILE 1944-45

Pro-German government set up after the 1944 coup.
Headquarters: Berlin

Prime Minister:

Aug 1944-May 1945   Horia Sima

RUSSIA

Official name: Russian Federation, Rossiiskaya Federatsiya

Previous names: Grand Duchy of Muscovy 1328-1547, Tsardom of Muscovy 1547-1721, Empire of All Russia 1547-1917, Russian Soviet Federal Socialist Republic 1917-91

State founded: 1328

Capital: Moscow (Moskva) (until 1703 & since 1917), St Petersburg (1703-1917)

The Grand Duchy of Muscovy was formed in the 14th century and became the dominant power in Russia. In 1547 Grand Duke Ivan IV took the title Tsar; Pyotr I declared himself Emperor in 1721, although he and his successors are often referred to as Tsars. The monarchy was overthrown in March 1917, and in November 1917 the Bolshevik revolution established a soviet republic. Some of the non-Russian areas which had been under Russian rule declared their independence, but soviet republics were soon set up in the Ukraine, Belorussia, the Caucasus and Central Asia. In 1922 these states united to form the USSR, but the top leadership was dominated by those ruling in Russia. In 1940 the Baltic states of Estonia, Latvia and Lithuania, which had been independent since 1918, were incorporated into the USSR. During World War II parts of the western USSR were occupied by Germany and Romania. The brief attempted coup in 1991 resulted in the weakening of central government, the suspension of the communist party and the granting of independence to the Baltic states. The central Soviet control then rapidly declined, the republics declared their independence, and the USSR was formally dissolved.

Grand Dukes:

1328-March 1341	Ivan I
March 1341-April 1353	Simeon *(son)*
April 1353-Nov 1359	Ivan II *(brother)*
Nov 1359-May 1389	Dmitry I *(son)*
May 1389-Feb 1425	Vasily I *(son)*
Feb 1425-34	Vasily II *(son)* (1st) (deposed)
1434	Yury *(brother)*
1434-46	Vasily II (2nd) (deposed)
1446-47	Dmitry II *(usurper)*
1447-March 1462	Vasily II (3rd)
March 1462-Oct 1505	Ivan III *(son)*
Oct 1505-Dec 1533	Vasily III *(son)*
Dec 1533-Jan 1547	Ivan IV *(son)* Regent: 1533-38 Yelena

Tsars/Tsarita:

Jan 1547-March 1584	Ivan IV
March 1584-Jan 1598	Fyodor I (*son*)
	Regent: 1584-98 Boris Gudunov
7-17 Jan 1598	Irina (*widow*) (abdicated)
Feb 1598-April 1605	Boris (B.Gudunov) (*brother*)
April-June 1605	Fyodor II (*son*) (deposed, assassinated)
June 1605-May 1606	Dmitry III (usurper) (assassinated)
June 1606-July 1610	Vasily IV (deposed)
(July 1610-Feb 1613	interregnum)
Feb 1613-July 1645	Mikhail
July 1645-Feb 1676	Aleksei (*son*)
Feb 1676-April 1682	Fyodor III (*son*)
April 1682-Jan 1696	Pyotr I/Ivan V (*brothers*)
	Regents: 1682-89 Sophia Aleksevna
	1689-96 Natalia Naryshkina
Jan 1696-Nov 1721	Pyotr I

Emperors/Empresses:

Nov 1721-Feb 1725	Pyotr I
Feb 1725-May 1727	Ekaterina I (*b* Marta Skrowronska) (*widow*)
May 1727-June 1730	Pyotr II (*grandson of Pyotr I*)
June 1730-Oct 1740	Anna (*daughter of Ivan V*)
Oct 1740-Dec 1741	Ivan VI (*grand-nephew*) (deposed, assassinated 1764)
	Regents: Oct-Nov 1740 Ernst Biron
	Nov 1740-Dec 1741 Anna Leopoldovna
Dec 1741-Jan 1762	Eliseveta (*daughter of Pyotr I & Ekaterina I*)
Jan-July 1762	Pyotr III (*b* Prince Karl of Holstein-Gottorp) (*nephew*) (assassinated)
July 1762-Nov 1796	Ekaterina II (*b* Princess Sophie of Anhalt-Zerbst) (*widow*)
Nov 1796-March 1801	Pavel (*son*) (assassinated)
March 1801-Nov 1825	Aleksandr I (*son*)
Nov 1825-March 1855	Nikolai I (*brother*)
March 1855-March 1881	Aleksandr II (*son*) (assassinated)
March 1881-Nov 1894	Aleksandr III (*son*)
Nov 1894-March 1917	Nikolai II (*son*) (abdicated, executed 1918)
(March-Nov 1917	Provisional Government)

Presidents:

Chairman of the Central Executive Committee 1917-38
President of the Presidium of the Supreme Soviet 1938-90
Chairman of the Supreme Soviet March 1990-July 1991

8-20 Nov 1917	Lev Kamenev (*b* L.Rosenfeld) (executed 1937)
Nov 1917-March 1919	Yakov Sverdlov (†)

16-30 March 1919	Mikhail Vladiminsky (acting)
March 1919-July 1938	Mikhail Kalinin
July 1938-Dec 1943	Aleksei Badayev
Dec 1943-March 1946	Nikolai Shvernik
March 1946-Oct 1950	Ivan Vlasov
Oct 1950-April 1959	Mikhail Tarasov
April-Nov 1959	Nikolai Ignatov (1st)
Nov 1959-Dec 1962	Nikolai Organov
Dec 1962-Dec 1966	Nikolai Ignatov (2nd)
Dec 1966-March 1985	Mikhail Yasnov
March 1985-Oct 1988	Vladimir Orlov
Oct 1988-May 1990	Vitaly Vorotnikov
May 1990-Dec 1999	Boris Yeltsin
Dec 1999-	Vladimir Putin (acting Dec 1999-May 2000)

Prime Ministers:

President of the State Council 1812-65
President of the Committee of Ministers 1865-1905
Chairman of the Council of People's Commissars 1917-46
Chairman of the Council of Ministers Jan 1946-Nov 1991
Chairman of the Government since 1991

March 1812-June 1816	Nikolai Saltykov (†)
June 1816-May 1827	Pyotr Lopukhin (†)
May 1827-June 1834	Viktor Kochubei (†)
June 1834-April 1938	Nikolai Novosiltsev (†)
April 1838-March 1947	Ilarion Vasilchikov (†)
March 1847-Oct 1948	Vasily Levashov (†)
Oct 1848-April 1856	Aleksandr Chernyshev
April 1856-Jan 1861	Aleksei Orlov
Jan 1861-March 1864	Dmitry Bludov (†)
March 1864-72	Pavel Gagarin
1872-Dec 1879	Pavel Ignatev
Dec 1879-Oct 1881	Pyotr Valuyev
Oct 1881-Jan 1887	Mikhail Reutern
Jan 1887-June 1895	Nikolai Bunge (†)
June 1895-June 1903	Ivan Durnovo (†)
June 1903-May 1906	Sergei Witte
May-July 1906	Ivan Goremykin (1st)
July 1906-Sept 1911	Pyotr Stolypin (†)
Sept 1911-Feb 1914	Vladimir Kokovtsev
Feb 1914-Feb 1916	Ivan Goremykin (2nd)
Feb-Nov 1916	Boris Sturmer
Nov 1916-Jan 1917	Fyodor Trepov
Jan-March 1917	Nikolai Golitsyn (deposed)
March-July 1917	Georgy Lvov

July-Nov 1917	Aleksandr Kerensky (deposed)
Nov 1917-Jan 1924	Vladimir Lenin (*b* V.Ulyanov) (†)
Feb 1924-May 1928	Aleksei Rykov
May 1928-Dec 1930	Sergei Syrtsov
Dec 1930-July 1937	Daniil Sulimov
July 1937-July 1938	Nikolai Bulganin
July 1938-June 1940	Vasily Vakrushev
June 1940-May 1942	Ivan Khokhlov
May 1942-May 1943	Konstantin Pamfilov (†)
June 1943-March 1946	Aleksei Kosygin
March 1946-March 1949	Mikhail Rodionov
March 1949-Nov 1952	Boris Chernousov
Nov 1952-Jan 1956	Aleksandr Puzanov
Jan 1956-Jan 1958	Mikhail Yasnov
Jan-March 1958	Frol Koslov
March 1958-Nov 1962	Dmitry Polyansky
Nov 1962-July 1971	Gennady Voronov
July 1971-June 1983	Mikhail Solomentsev
June 1983-Oct 1988	Vitaly Vorotnikov
Oct 1988-June 1990	Aleksandr Vlasov
June 1990-Nov 1991	Ivan Silayev
Nov 1991-Dec 1992	Boris Yeltsin
(June-Dec 1992	Yegor Gaidar (acting))
Dec 1992-March 1998	Viktor Chernomyrdin
March-Aug 1998	Sergei Kiriyenko (acting March-April 1998)
Aug-Sept 1998	Viktor Chernomyrdin (acting)
Sept 1998-May 1999	Yevgeny Primakov
May 1999-Aug 1999	Sergei Stepashin (acting 13-19 May 1999)
Aug 1999-May 2000	Vladimir Putin (acting 9-16 Aug 1999)
May 2000-	Mikhail Kasyanov

Communist Party Leaders:

First Secretary

June 1990-Aug 1991	Ivan Polozkov
6-29 Aug 1991	Valentin Kuptsov
(Aug 1991	party suspended)

Former Union

UNION OF SOVIET SOCIALIST REPUBLICS (USSR - SOVIET UNION)

Union formed: 30 December 1922
Union dissolved: 26 December 1991

Member states: Armenia, Azerbaijan, Belorussia, Estonia (1940-91), Georgia, Karelo-Finnish Republic (1940-56), Kazakhstan, Kirghizia, Latvia (1940-91), Lithuania (1940-90), Moldavia, Russia, Tajikistan, Turkmenistan, Ukraine, Uzbekistan.
Capital: Moscow

Presidents:
Chairman of the Central Executive Committee Dec 1922-Jan 1938
President of the Presidium of the Supreme Soviet Jan 1938-May 1989
Chairman of the Supreme Soviet May 1989-March 1990

Dec 1922-March 1946	Mikhail Kalinin (President of Russia until 1938)
March 1946-March 1953	Nikolai Shvernik (see Russia)
March 1953-May 1960	Kliment Voroshilov
May 1960-July 1964	Leonid Brezhnev (1st) (see Moldavia & Kazakhstan)
July 1964-Dec 1965	Anastas Mikoyan (see Azerbaijan)
Dec 1965-June 1977	Nikolai Podgorny (see Ukraine)
June 1977-Nov 1982	Leonid Brezhnev (2nd) (†)
Nov 1982-June 1983	Vasily Kuznetsov (acting) (1st)
June 1983-Feb 1984	Yury Andropov (†)
Feb-April 1984	Vasily Kuznetsov (acting) (2nd)
April 1984-March 1985	Konstantin Chernenko (†)
March-July 1985	Vasily Kuznetsov (acting) (3rd)
July 1985-Oct 1988	Andrei Gromyko
Oct 1988-Aug 1991	Mikhail Gorbachev (1st) (deposed)
19-21 Aug 1991	Gennady Yanayev (acting)
Aug-Dec 1991	Mikhail Gorbachev (2nd)

Prime Ministers:
Chairman of the Council of People's Commissars Dec 1922-March 1946
Chairman of the Council of Ministers March 1946-Aug 1991
Chairman of the Interim Management Committee Aug-Dec 1991

Dec 1922-Jan 1924	Vladimir Lenin (†) (PM of Russia)
Feb 1924-Dec 1930	Aleksei Rykov (PM of Russia 1924-28) (executed 1938)
Dec 1930-May 1941	Vyacheslav Molotov (*b* V.Skryabin)
May 1941-March 1953	Iosef Stalin (*b* I.Dzhugashvili) (†)
March 1953-Feb 1955	Georgy Malenkov
Feb 1955-March 1958	Nikolai Bulganin (see Russia)
March 1958-Oct 1964	Nikita Khrushchev (see Ukraine)
Oct 1964-Oct 1980	Aleksei Kosygin (see Russia)
Oct 1980-Sept 1985	Nikolai Tikhonov
Sept 1985-Jan 1991	Nikolai Ryzhkov
Jan-Aug 1991	Valentin Pavlov
Aug-Dec 1991	Ivan Silayev (PM of Russia)

Communist Party* Leaders:

*All-Russian Communist Party 1918-25
All-Union Communist Party 1925-52
Communist Party of the Soviet Union 1952-91
General Secretary March 1922-Sept 1953 and April 1966-Aug 1991
First Secretary Sept 1953-April 1966

March 1922-March 1953	Iosef Stalin (†)
6-14 March 1953	Georgy Malenkov
March 1953-Oct 1964	Nikita Khrushchev
Oct 1964-Nov 1982	Leonid Brezhnev (†)
Nov 1982-Feb 1984	Yury Andropov (†)
Feb 1984-March 1985	Konstantin Chernenko (†)
March 1985-Aug 1991	Mikhail Gorbachev
(Aug 1991	party suspended)

Republics

ADYGEIA

Official name: Adygeia Republic
Previous name: Adygei Autonomous Region 1922-91
Region established: 27 July 1922
Republic established: 28 June 1991
Capital: Maikop

President:

March 1992-	Aslan Djarimov

Prime Ministers:

Chairman of the Executive Committee until 1992

Sept 1956-April 1970	S.T.Nepshekuyev
April 1970-Feb 1980	Malich Khut
Feb 1980-March 1992	Mugdin Tlekhas
March 1992-March 1995	Aslan Djarimov
March 1995-98	Nikolai Pedan
1998-	Mukharby Tkharkakhov

Communist Party Leaders:

First Secretary

Dec 1955-60	I.S.Chundokov
1960-Jan 1984	Nukh Berzegov
Jan 1984-Jan 1989	Malich Khut
Jan 1989-Aug 1991	Aslan Djarimov

ALTAI REPUBLIC

Official name: Altai Republic
Previous names: Oirot Autonomous Region 1922-48, Gorno-Altai Autonomous Region 1948-91, Gorno-Altai Republic 1991-92
Region established: 1 June 1922
Republic established: 31 March 1992
Capital: Gorno-Altaisk (f Oirot-Altuish)

President:
Chairman of the State Assembly (Supreme Soviet until 1993)

March 1992-Jan 1997	Valery Chaptynov	(†)
Jan-Aug 1997	Vladilen Volkov	(1st)
Aug 1997-Jan 1998-	Daniil Tabayev	
Jan 1998-	Vladilen Volkov	(2nd)

Prime Ministers:
Chairman of the Executive Committee until 1992
Chairman of the Government since October 1993

Dec 1959-June 1972	Ch.K.Kydrashev	
June 1972-March 1990	Mikhail Karamayev	
March 1990-Jan 1997	Vladimir Petrov	
Jan-Aug 1997	Valery Chaptynov	(†)
Aug 1997-Jan 1998	Vladilen Volkov	
Jan 1998-	Semen Zubakin	

Communist Party Leaders:
First Secretary

June 1959-March 1966	N.M.Kiselyev	
March 1966-Dec 1975	N.S.Lazebny	
Dec 1975-Oct 1978	Valery Chaptynov	(1st)
Oct 1978-87	Yury Znamensky	
1987-Oct 1988	Dmitri Nartov	(†)
Oct 1988-89	F.V.Popov	
1989-April 1990	Vladimir Gusev	
April 1990-Aug 1991	Valery Chaptynov	(2nd)

BASHKORTOSTAN

Official name: Republic of Bashkortostan
Previous name: Bashkir Autonomous Soviet Socialist Republic 1919-91
Republic formed: 23 March 1919
Capital: Ufa

Presidents:

Chairman of the Revolutionary Committee 1919-20
Chairman of the Central Executive Committee 1921-38
President of the Presidium of the Supreme Soviet 1938-90
Chairman of the Supreme Soviet March 1990-Dec 1993

Feb 1919-Jan 1920	Kh.Yumagalov
Jan-June 1920	G.Samigulov
1921-Dec 1924	Shagit Khudayberdin (†)
Dec 1924-30	Khafiz Kushayev
1931-36	Afzal Tagirov
1937-45	Rakhim Ibragimov
1945-50	Gilman Nigmadzhanov
1950-63	Fairakhamany Zagafuranov
1963-Sept 1967	M.S.Karimov
Sept 1967-March 1990	Faizulla Sultanov
March 1990-	Murtaza Rakhimov

Prime Ministers:

Chairman of the Council of People's Commissars 1919-46
Chairman of the Council of Ministers 1946-94
Chairman of the Government since March 1994

1919	Mstislav Kulayev
1919-20	Ahmed Zaki-Validov
1920-23	Mirza Galiev
1923-24	Khafiz Kushayev
1925-30	M.Khalikov
1930-37	Zinatulla Bulashev (removed, executed)
1937-43	Fazil Shagimardanov
1943-46	Sabir Vagapov
June 1946-51	Nasir Urazbayev
1951-Feb 1962	Valei Nabiullin
Feb 1962-May 1983	Zekeriya Aknazarov
May 1983-89	Marat Mirgazyamov
1989-94	Anatoly Kopsov
1994-Jan 1999	Rim Bakiyev
Jan 1999-	Rafael Baidevletov

Communist Party Leaders:

First Secretary

1921-Dec 1924	Shagit Khudayberdin (†)
? -37	Ya.B.Bykin
1937- ?	Aleksandr Zalikin
1943-46	Semen Ignatov (1st)
1946-50	Semen Zadionchenko

1950-54	Sabir Vagapov
1954-June 1957	Semen Ignatov (2nd)
June 1957-June 1969	Ziya Nuriyev
June 1969-June 1987	Midkhat Shakirov
June 1987-April 1990	Ravmer Khabibullin
April 1990-Aug 1991	Igor Gorbunov

BURYATIA

Official name: Republic of Buryatia
Previous names: Buryat-Mongol Autonomous Soviet Socialist Republic 1920-58, Buryat Autonomous Soviet Socialist Republic 1958-91, Buryat Soviet Socialist Republic 1991-92
Republic formed: 1 March 1920
Capital: Ulan-Ude

Presidents:

Chairman of the Central Executive Committee 1923-38
President of the Presidium of the Supreme Soviet 1938-90
Chairman of the Supreme Soviet 1990-94

1923-25	— — Amagayev
1925-27	Mikhail Erbanov
1927-30	K.S.Ilin
1931-33	B.D.Dabain
1933-35	D.D.Dorzhiev (1st)
1935-37	I.D.Dampilon
1937	D.D.Dorzhiev (2nd)
1937-40	Gambozh Belgayev
1940-46	I.Borsoyev
1946-60	Dorzhu Tsyrempilon
1960-Dec 1970	Aleksandr Khakholov
Dec 1970-85	Bato Semenov
1985-90	Aleksandr Badiev
1990-91	Sergei Buldayev
Oct 1991-	Leonid Potapov

Prime Ministers:

Chairman of the Council of People's Commissars 1923-46
Chairman of the Council of Ministers since 1946

1923-27	Mikhail Erbanov
1927-30	K.S.Elim
1931-33	B.D.Dabain
1934-35	D.D.Dorzhiev (1st)
1935-37	I.D.Dampilon

1937	D.D.Dorzhiev (2nd)
1937-5?	Solomon Ivanov
1958-60	Vasily Filippov
1960-62	Andrei Mogodayev
1962-March 1967	Konstantin Baryadayev
March 1967-July 1978	Nikolai Pivovarov
July 1978-June 1994	Vladimir Saganov
June 1994-	Leonid Potapov

Communist Party Leaders:
First Secretary

Dec 1921-Sept 1937	Mikhail Erbanov
Sept 1937-April 1953	Semen Ignatov (1st)
1953-54	Aleksandr Khakholov (1st)
1954-57	Semen Ignatov (2nd)
March 1957-June 1961	Aleksandr Khakholov (2nd)
June 1961-June 1962	Vasily Filippov
June 1962-Jan 1984	Andrei Mogodayev
Jan 1984-April 1990	Anatoly Balyakov
April 1990-Aug 1991	Leonid Potapov

CHECHNYA

Official name: Chechen Republic of Ichkeria
Previous name: Checheno-Ingush Autonomous Soviet Republic 1936-44 & 1957-91, Chechen Republic 1991-94 & 1995-98
Republic formed: 5 December 1936, abolished 1944, re-constituted 9 January 1957
Independence date: November 1991 (not recognized by Russia)
Capital: Dzhokhar (*f* Grozny)

Ingushetia separated from the republic in 1992. Chechnya's declaration of independence led to armed conflict with Russia, which captured Grozny in 1995. Conflict continued until 1996 when a coalition government was formed, followed in 1997 by elections which were won by the pro-independence candidate. After Chechen-backed attacks, Russia invaded in late 1998, capturing Grozny in February 2000.

Presidents:
Chairman of the Central Executive Committee 1936-38
President of the Presidium of the Supreme Soviet 1938-44 & 1957-90
Chairman of the Supreme Soviet 1990-91 & Oct-Nov 1995
Chairman of the Interim Council March-Oct 1995
Head of State Nov 1995-Oct 1996

1937-44	Yusup Tambiev
(1944-57	republic abolished)

1957-73   I.A.Almazov
1973-July 1975   Kureis Ozdoev
July 1975-1990   Khazhbikar Bokov
1990-Sept 1991   Doku Zavgayev   (1st)
Sept-Oct 1991   Ahmed Arsanov   (acting)
Oct 1991-March 1995   Dzhokhar Dudayev   (fled to southern Chechenia)
March-Oct 1995   Umar Avturkhanov
Oct-Nov 1995   Amin Osmayev
Nov 1995-Oct 1996 Doku Zavgayev   (2nd)
Oct 1996-Feb 1997 Zelimkhan Yandarbayev
Feb 1997-   Aslan Maskhadov

Prime Ministers:

Chairman of the Council of People's Commissars 1947-44
Chairman of the Council of Ministers 1957-91
Chairman of the Government Dec 1995-Oct 1996

1937-44   S.K.Mollayev
(1944-57   republic abolished)
1957-July 1971   Muslim Gayrbekov
July 1971-Sept 1978   Ramazan Vakhayev
Sept 1978-Sept 1991   Musa Kerimov
Sept-Nov 1991   Sergei Bekov
Nov 1991-92   Dzhokhar Dudayev
1992-93   Yaragi Mamudayev
April 1993-March 1995   Mahirbek Mugadayev
March-Oct 1995   Salambek Khadzhiyev
Oct-Dec 1995   Doku Zavgayev
Dec 1995-Oct 1996 Nikolai Koshman
Oct-Dec 1996   Aslan Maskhadov   (1st)
Dec 1996-Feb 1997 Movladi Udugov   (acting)
Feb 1997-Jan 1998 Aslan Maskhadov   (2nd)
Jan-July 1998   Shamil Basayev   (acting)
July-Aug 1998   Aslan Maskhadov   (acting)
Aug-Oct 1998   Turpal Atgeriyev   (acting)
Oct 1998-   Aslan Maskhadov   (3rd)

Communist Party Leaders:

First Secretary

1937-42   Fedor Bykov
1942-44   — — Ivanov
(1944-57   republic abolished)
1957-59   Aleksandr Yakovlev
Jan 1959-63   Aleksandr Trofimov
1963-65   Fedor Titov

Jan 1966-Dec 1975   Semen Apryatkin
Dec 1975-Aug 1984   Aleksandr Vlasov
Aug 1984-July 1989   Vladimir Foteyev
July 1989-Aug 1991   Doku Zavgayev

RIVAL GOVERNMENTS

1. Pro-Moscow government opposing pro-independence government in Grozny. Installed in Grozny in March 1995 after Russian capture of the city.

President:
Chairman of the Interim Council

July 1994-March 1995   Umar Avturkhanov

2. Pro-independence government fled to southern Chechnya after Russian capture of Grozny in March 1995 and operated until the formation of a coalition government in Oct 1996.

Headquarters: Galanchezh

Presidents:

March 1995-April 1996   Dzhokar Dudayev   († assassinated)
April-Oct 1996   Zelimkhan Yandarbayev

3. Pro-Moscow government set up after Russian invasion in 1999.

President:
Chairman of the Interim Council

Oct 1999-   Malik Saidullayev

CHUVASHIA

Official name: Chuvash Republic
Previous names: Chuvash Autonomous Region 1920-25, Chuvash Autonomous Soviet Socialist Republic 1925-91
Republic formed: 21 April 1925
Capital: Cheboksary

Presidents:
Chairman of the Central Executive Committee 1925-38
President of the Presidium of the Supreme Soviet 1938-90
Chairman of the Supreme Soviet 1990-93

1925-30   N.L.Yushunev
1931-37   A.N.Nikitin
1937-57   Zoya Andreeva

Sept 1957-Jan 1968   Timofey Akhazov
Jan 1968-84   Semen Isliukov
1984-Oct 1988   Aleksandr Petrov
Dec 1988-Aug 1991   Anatoly Leontyev
Aug 1991-Dec 1993   Eduard Kubarev
Dec 1993-   Nikolai Fedorov

Prime Ministers:

Chairman of the Council of People's Commissars 1925-46
Chairman of the Council of Ministers since 1946

1925-31   D.S.Elim
1931-32   Luka Spasov (1st)
1932-37   Vasily Toksin
1937-38   Luka Spasov (2nd)
1938- ?   A.V.Somov
? -41   A.M.Matveev
1941-55   Semen Isliukov
April 1956-March 1963   A.S.Yerlakov
March 1963-Jan 1974   Mikhail Zatysev
Jan 1974-89   Leonid Prokopyev
1989-92   Nikolai Zaitsev
Feb 1992-95   Valerian Viktorov
1995-99   Enver Ablyakimov
1999-   Lev Kurakov

Communist Party Leaders:

First Secretary

1927-42   Sergei Petrov
1942-48   N.M.Charykov
1949-50   Timofey Akhazov
1950-55   Yakov Pavlov
May 1955-Jan 1968   Semen Isliukov
Jan 1968-Nov 1973   Nikolai Voronovski (†)
Jan 1974-Oct 1988   Ilya Prokopyev
Oct 1988-May 1990   Aleksandr Petrov
May 1990-Aug 1991   Valentin Shurchanov

DAGESTAN

Official name: Republic of Dagestan
Previous name: Dagestan Autonomous Soviet Socialist Republic 1920-91
Republic formed: 20 January 1920
Capital: Mahachkala

Presidents:

Chairman of the Central Executive Committee 1921-38
President of the Presidium of the Supreme Soviet 1938-90
Chairman of the Supreme Soviet 1990-94
Chairman of the State Council since 1994

1921-23	Nazhmuddin Samurski
1923-37	Magomet Dalgat
1937-53	Adil-Girei Takhtarov
1953-56	Gusein Mamedov
1956-59	Shakhruddin Shamkholov (1st)
1959-62	Gadsi-Kasum Aliyev
1962-69	Roza Eldarova
1969-July 1971	Kh.I.Amirkhanov
July 1971-78	Shakhruddin Shamkholov (2nd)
1978-Nov 1980	Suleyman Tatliev
Nov 1980-Sept 1985	Alipasha Umalatov
Sept 1985-April 1990	Tatyana Ivanova
April 1990-	Magomedali Magomedov

Prime Ministers:

Chairman of the Council of People's Commissars 1921-46
Chairman of the Council of Ministers 1946-94
Chairman of the Government since 1994

1921-32	D.E.Korkmasov
1932-37	Kerim Mamedbekov
1937-40	Dzhemalutdin Magomedov
1940-48	Abdurakhman Daniyalov
1948-5?	S.M.Aidinbekov
Jan 1957-Nov 1967	Magomed-Salam Umakhanov
Nov 1967-Nov 1980	Alipasha Umalatov
Nov 1980-May 1983	Magomed Usupov
May 1983-April 1990	Magomedali Magomedov
April 1990-Aug 1997	Abdurazak Mirzabekov
Aug 1997-	Khizri Shikhsaidov

Communist Party Leaders:

First Secretary

1920-23	Boris Sheboldayev
1923-27	Nazhmuddin Samurski (1st)
1927-28	Nikolai Oganesov
1928-35	?
1935-37	Nazhmuddin Samurski (2nd)
1937	Maksum Sorokin
? -42	—— Linkun

1942- ?	— — Agababov
1948-Nov 1967	Abdurakhman Daniyalov
Nov 1967-May 1983	Magomed-Salam Umakhanov
May 1983-March 1990	Magomed Usupov
March 1990-Aug 1991	Mukhu Aliev

INGUSHETIA

Official name: Republic of Ingushetia
Republic created: June 1992 (f part of Chechen-Ingushetia)
Capital: Nazran

President:

March 1993-	Ruslan Aushev

Administrator:

Nov 1992-March 1993	Ruslan Aushev

Prime Ministers:
Chairman of the Council of Ministers

March 1993-95	Tamerlan Didigov
1995-98	Mukharbek Didigov
1998	Belan Khamchiyev
1998-99	Magomed-Bashir Darsigov
Nov 1999-	Akhmed Malsagov

KABARDINO-BALKARIA

Official name: Kabardino-Balkar Republic
Previous name: Kabardino-Balkar Autonomous Soviet Socialist Republic until 1991
Republic formed: 5 December 1936, abolished 1944, reconstituted 1957
Capital: Nalchik

Presidents:
Chairman of the Central Executive Committee 1936-38
President of the Presidium of the Supreme Soviet 1938-90
Chairman of the Supreme Soviet 1990-92

1936-38	Ishu Cherkasov
1938-44	Masha Kankulov
(1944-57	republic abolished)
1957-Dec 1959	K.Tlostanov
Dec 1959-April 1967	Chomai Uyanayev

April 1967-78	Magomet Gettuyev
1978-90	Boris Chabdarov
March 1990-	Valery Kokov

Prime Ministers:
Chairman of the Council of People's Commissars 1937-44
Chairman of the Council of Ministers 1957-91

1937- ?	B.I.Antonov
? -44	Kh.Akhokhov
(1944-57	republic abolished)
July 1957-June 1970	Aslanbi Akhokhov
June 1970-90	Kishkuka Kushkhov
1990-Aug 1991	Mikhail Mamkhegov
Sept 1991-98	Georgy Cherkesov
1998-	Khusein Chechenov

Communist Party Leaders:
First Secretary

1938-44	— — Kumekhanov
(1944-57	republic abolished)
1957-Oct 1985	Timbora Malbakhov
Oct 1985-90	Yevgeny Yeliseyev
1990	Valery Kokov
Sept 1990-Aug 1991	Boris Zumakulov

KALMYKIA

Official name: Republic of Kalmykia
Previous names: Kalmyk Autonomous Region 1920-35 & 1957-58, Kalmyk Autonomous Soviet Socialist Republic 1935-43 & 1958-90, Kalmyk Soviet Socialist Republic 1990-91
Republic formed: 22 October 1935, abolished 27 December 1943, reconstituted 29 July 1958
Capital: Elista

Presidents:
Chairman of the Central Executive Committee 1935-38
President of the Presidium of the Supreme Soviet 1938-90
Chairman of the Supreme Soviet 1990-April 1993

1935-38	Vasily Khomutnikov
1938-43	Dorzhi Pyurveyev
(1943-57	republic abolished)
1958-62	L.K.Kilganov
1962-July 1975	Erenzhen Sangayev
July 1975-85	Ilya Namsinov

1985-87   Gennady Sakirov
1987-90   A.B.Aldayev
1990-92   Vladimir Basanov
Nov 1992-April 1993   Ilya Bugdayev
April 1993-   Kirsan Ilyumzhinov

Prime Ministers:

Chairman of the Council of People's Commissars 1935-43
Chairman of the Executive Committee 1957-58
Chairman of the Council of Ministers 1958-91
Chairman of the Government since 1994

1935-37   Dorzhi Pyrurveyev
1937-43   Naldzhi Garyayev
(1943-57   republic abolished)
1957-58   N.I.Zhezlov
1958-March 1962   Erenzhen Sangayev
March 1962-67   Grigory Bembinov
1967-March 1974   Erdmi Mandzhiev   (†)
March 1974-Aug 1989   Lag Badmakhalgayev
Aug 1989-Oct 1992   Batyr Mikhailov
Oct 1992-1995   Maxim Mukubenov
1995-98   Valery Bogdanov
1998-   Viktor Baturin

Communist Party Leaders:

First Secretary

1935-37   A.P.Pyrurveyev
1937- ?   Ivan Karpov
1943   — — Likoinidov
(1943-57   republic abolished)
1958-Aug 1959   N.I.Zhezlov
Aug 1959-Aug 1961   Mikhail Ponomarev
Aug 1961-Dec 1978   Basan Gorodovikov
Dec 1978-Dec 1985   Vladimir Nikulin
Dec 1985-Oct 1990   Vladimir Zakharov
Oct 1990-Aug 1991   Boris Muyev

KARACHAYEVO-CHERKESSIA

Official name: Republic of Karachayevo-Cherkessia
Previous names: Karachayevo-Cherkess Autonomous Region 1957-90, Karachayevo-Cherkess Soviet Socialist Republic 1990-92
Region established: 1922. Divided into Karachai & Cherkess Regions (1926-43); re-established 9 January 1957

Republic established: December 1990
Capital: Cherkessk

Presidents:
Chairman of the Supreme Soviet 1991-95

Aug 1991-94	Viktor Savelyev
1994-May 1999	Vladimir Khubayev (acting 1994-95)
May-July 1999	Igor Ivanov (acting)
July-Sept 1999-	Valentin Vlasov (acting) (see Archangel)
Sept 1999-	Vladimir Semenov

Prime Ministers:
Chairman of the Executive Committee until 1990

June 1957-March 1966	Z.K.Kardanov
March 1966-March 1979	Magomet Botashev
March 1979-95	Vladimir Khubayev
1995-	Anatoly Ozov

Communist Party Leaders:
First Secretary

July 1958-61	V.I.Antonov
1961-75	N.M.Lyzhin
June 1975-Dec 1978	Vsevolod Murakhovsky
Dec 1978-May 1988	Aleksei Inzhiyevsky
May 1988-91	—— Lisnichenko

KARELIA

Official name: Republic of Karelia
Previous names: Karelo-Finnish Soviet Socialist Republic 1940-56, Karelian Autonomous Soviet Socialist Republic 1923-40 and 1956-91
Republic formed: 25 July 1923 (Constituent republic of USSR 31 March 1940-16 July 1956)
Capital: Petrozavodsk

Presidents:
Chairman of the Central Executive Committee 1923-38
President of the Presidium of the Supreme Soviet 1938-90
Chairman of the Supreme Soviet 1990-94
Chairman of the Chamber of the Republic since 1994

July 1923-24	Aleksandr Shotman
1924-28	A.F.Nuorteva
1929-34	N.A.Yushchiev
1934-35	V.P.Averkiev

Feb 1935-Nov 1937   N.V.Arkhipov
Nov 1937-July 1940   Mark Gorbachev
July 1940-May 1956   Otto Kuusinen
May 1956-78   Pavel Prokkonen
1978-Dec 1982   Ivan Mankin
Dec 1982-84   Nikolai Pershin
1984-90   Ivan Senkin
April 1990-April 1994   Viktor Stepanov
April 1994-May 1998 Ivan Aleksandrov
May 1998-   Natalya Kotsuba

Prime Ministers:

Chairman of the Council of People's Commissars 1923-46
Chairman of the Council of Ministers 1946-94
Chairman of the Government since April 1994

1923-34   Edvard Gylling
1934-35   N.V.Arkhipov
1935-37   P.I.Bushuev
1937-40   Petr Solyakov
1941   I.P.Babkin
1941-47   Pavel Prokkonen   (1st)
1947-50   V.Virolainen
1950-56   Pavel Prokkonen   (2nd)
Aug 1956-June 1967   Ivan Belyayev
June 1967-June 1985 Andrei Kochetov
June 1985-April 1990 Yury Ivanov
April 1990-April 1994   Sergei Blinnikov
April 1994-May 1998 Viktor Stepanov
May 1998-   Sergei Katanandov

Communist Party Leaders:

First Secretary

1923-29   I.A.Yarvisalo
1929-35   G.S.Rovio
1935   I.S.Petrov
Aug 1935-37   P.A.Irklis
1937-38   Nikolai Ivanov   (acting)
1938-49   G.N.Kuprianov
1950-51   Aleksandr Kondakov
1951-55   A.Yegorov
Nov 1955-Sept 1958   Leonid Lubennikov
Sept 1958-April 1984 Ivan Senkin
April 1984-Nov 1989 Viktor Stepanov
Nov 1989-Aug 1991   Nikolai Kirzhanov

KHAKASSIA

Official name: Republic of Khakassia
Previous name: Khakass Autonomous Region 1930-92
Region established: 20 October 1930
Republic established: 31 March 1992
Capital: Abakan

President:
Chairman of the Supreme Soviet

March 1992-	Vladimir Shtygashev

Prime Ministers:
Chairman of the Executive Committee until 1992
Chairman of the Council of Ministers 1992-96
Chairman of the Government since 1996

Dec 1958-Oct 1961	V.I.Kolpakov
Oct 1961-Sept 1969	A.G.Oreshkov
Sept 1969-Feb 1992	Vasily Uguzhakov
Feb 1992-Dec 1996	Yevgeny Smirnov
Dec 1996-	Aleksei Lebed

Communist Party Leaders:
First Secretary

Nov 1959-61	I.K.Strakhov
1961-71	A.G.Dankovtsev
Nov 1971-86	Aleksei Krylov
Aug 1990-Aug 1991	Valery Abramenko

KOMI REPUBLIC

Official name: Komi Republic
Previous names: Komi Autonomous Region 1921-36, Komi Autonomous Soviet Socialist Republic 1936-90, Komi Soviet Socialist Republic 1990-91
Republic formed: 5 December 1936
Capital: Syktyvkar

Presidents:
Chairman of the Central Executive Committee 1936-38
President of the Presidium of the Supreme Soviet 1938-90
Chairman of the Supreme Soviet 1990-94
Chairman of the State Council since 1994

1936-46	Gennady Vetoshkin
1946- ?	Ivan Rochev

Aug 1954-63	Nikolai Vakhnin
1963-Dec 1971	Yevgeny Katayev
Dec 1971-85	Zosima Panev
1985-90	Albert Syutkin
April 1990-Feb 1994	Yury Spiridonov
Feb 1994-	Vladimir Torlopov

Prime Ministers:
Chairman of the Council of People's Commissars 1936-46
Chairman of the Council of Ministers 1946-94
Chairman of the Government since 1994

1938- ?	I.I.Oplesnin
1942- ?	— — Turyshev
1946-50	G.Vetoshkin
1950-Dec 1963	Zosima Panev
Dec 1963-Oct 1985	Pavel Beznosov
Oct 1985-March 1987	Vladimir Melnikov
March 1987-Feb 1994	Vyacheslav Khudyayev
Feb 1994-	Yury Spiridonov

Communist Party Leaders:
First Secretary

1937	Ibad Dyakonov
1950-57	Georgi Osipov
Feb 1958-Oct 1965	Aleksandr Dmitrin
Oct 1965-March 1987	Ivan Morozov
March 1987-89	Vladimir Melnikov
1989-Oct 1990	Yury Spiridonov
Oct 1990-Aug 1991	Aleksei Batmanov

MARI-EL

Official name: Mari-El Republic
Previous names: Mari Autonomous Region 1920-36, Mari Autonomous Soviet Socialist Republic 1936-90, Mari Soviet Socialist Republic 1990-91
Republic formed: 5 December 1936
Capital: Yoshkar-Ola

Presidents:
Chairman of the Central Executive Committee 1937-38
President of the Presidium of the Supreme Soviet 1938-90
Chairman of the Supreme Soviet April 1990-Dec 1991

1937-38	I.P.Petrov
1938- ?	Timofei Kavalerov

194?-46	Grigory Kondratyev
1946-5?	Nikolai Ryabchikov
195?-59	P.V.Scherbakov
1959-Dec 1966	Ivan Moskvichev
Dec 1966-March 1980	Petr Almakayev
March 1980-April 1990	Vitaly Romanov
April 1990-Jan 1997	Vladislav Zotin
Jan 1997-	Vyacheslav Kislitsyn

Prime Ministers:

Chairman of the Council of People's Commissars 1937-46
Chairman of the Council of Ministers 1946-91

1937-38	Petr Andreyev
1938-43	Ya.I.Abramov
1943-46	—— Mamayev
1946-March 1963	Grigory Kondratyev
March 1963-Jan 1980	Trofim Gorinov
Jan 1980-90	Arklady Vasilyev
1990-91	Gennady Petrov
Dec 1991-Jan 1997	Vladislav Zotin
Jan 1997-	Vyacheslav Kislitsyn

Communist Party Leaders:

First Secretary

1937	Zinovi Zhdanov
1943	—— Navozov
1950-51	Balysh Ovezov
1951-55	Grigory Kondratyev
1955-58	?
Feb 1958-61	Georgy Pavlov
1961-Nov 1963	Petr Almakayev
Nov 1963-Aug 1967	Petr Urayev
Aug 1967-Sept 1979	Viktor Nikonov
Sept 1979-Jan 1981	I.S.Gusev
Jan 1981-84	Grigory Posibeyev (1st)
1984-March 1985	Ata Akgayev
March 1985-86	Ch.Gedzhenov
1986-91	Grigory Posibeyev (2nd)

MORDOVIA

Official name: Mordovian Republic
Previous names: Mordovian Autonomous Region 1920-34, Mordovian Autonomous Soviet Socialist Republic 1934-91, Mordovian Soviet Socialist Republic 1991-94

Republic formed: 20 December 1934
Capital: Saransk

Presidents:

Chairman of the Central Executive Committee 1934-38
President of the Presidium of the Supreme Soviet 1938-90
Chairman of the Supreme Soviet April 1990-Dec 1991

1934-37	N.G.Surdin
1937-44?	Mikhail Chembulatov
? -47	I.Ya.Tingayev
1947-49	Vera Lemonoza
1949- ?	M.Selyukin
March 1959-62	Stepan Nikolayev
1962-71	Yefimya Yaskina
1971-March 1980	Ivan Astaykin
March 1980-April 1990	Aleksandr Piksayev
April-Dec 1990	Anatoly Berezin
Dec 1990-Dec 1991	Nikolai Biryukov (1st)
Dec 1991-April 1993	Vasily Guslyannikov
April 1993-Sept 1995	Nikolai Biryukov (2nd)
Sept 1995-	Nikolai Merkushkin

Prime Ministers:

Chairman of the Council of People's Commissars 1935-46
Chairman of the Council of Ministers 1946-91
Chairman of the Government since 1995

1935-38	A.Ya.Kozikov
July 1938-44	V.V.Verendyakin
1944- ?	I.Ya.Tingayev
1954-71	Ivan Astaykin
June 1971-May 1979	Aleksandr Piksayev
May 1979-91	Vasily Uchaykin
Dec 1991-April 1993	Vasily Guslyannikov
April 1993-94	Valery Shvetsov
1994-	Vladimir Volkov

Communist Party Leaders:

First Secretary

1937	Ivan Kuznetsov
1943	—— Petrushkov
1946	S.M.Vidayev
? -51	Ivan Piksin
May 1951-March 1958	Vasily Zakhurdayev
March 1958-May 1968	Georgy Osipov
May 1968-June 1971	Petr Elistratov

June 1971-Oct 1990   Anatoly Berezin
Oct 1990-Aug 1991   Viktor Skoptsov

NORTH OSSETIA-ALANIA

Official name: Republic of North Ossetia-Alania
Previous names: North Ossetian Autonomous Region 1924-36, North Ossetian Autonomous Soviet Socialist Republic 1938-91, North Ossetian Republic 1991-94
Republic formed: 5 December 1936
Capital: Vladikavkaz (*f* Ordzhonikidze until 1991)

Presidents:
Chairman of the Central Executive Committee 1937-38
President of the Presidium of the Supreme Soviet 1938-90
Chairman of the Supreme Soviet April 1990-Jan 1994

1937-42	Solomon Abayev
1942-44	Georgy Gugloev
1944-56	?
Jan 1956-63	Vladimir Dzanagov
1963-July 1975	Tamara Khetagurova
July 1975-April 1978	Oleg Basiev
April 1978-Oct 1985	Olga Kolchina
Oct 1985-April 1990	Tobaz Sabanov
April 1990-Feb 1998	Akhsarbek Galazov
Feb 1998-	Aleksandr Dzasokhov

Prime Ministers:
Chairman of the Council of People's Commissars 1937-46
Chairman of the Council of Ministers 1946-94
Chairman of the Government since 1994

1937-39	S.Z.Mirkin
1939-4?	Kubadi Kulov
194?-56	?
Feb 1956-59	B.D.Zangiyev
1959-March 1962	Tamara Khetagurova
March 1962-July 1975	Oleg Basiev
July 1975-April 1990	Mikhail Tsagarayev
April 1990-95	Sergei Khetagurov
1995-98	Yury Biragov
1998-	Taymuraz Mamsurov

Communist Party Leaders:
First Secretary

1936-37   Kasbek Butayev

July-Nov 1937	—— Kokov
Nov 1937-42	Dzhibut Dzugayev
1942-44	—— Mazin
1944-54	?
Feb 1954-Aug 1961	V.M.Agkatsev
Aug 1961-Jan 1982	Bilar Kabaloyev
Jan 1982-Feb 1990	Vladimir Odintsev
Feb 1990-Aug 1991	Akhsarbek Galazov

SAKHA REPUBLIC

Official name: Sakha Republic
Previous names: Yakut Autonomous Soviet Socialist Republic 1922-90, Yakutia-Sakha Soviet Socialist Republic 1990-92
Republic formed: 27 April 1922
Capital: Yakutsk

Presidents:

Chairman of the Central Executive Committee 1922-38
Presidents of the Presidium of the Supreme Soviet 1938-90
Chairman of the Supreme Soviet 1990-Dec 1991

1922-26	Platon Oyansky (*b* P.Sleptsov)
1926-27	M.V.Megezhevsky
1927-28	M.K.Ammosov
June 1928-Jan 1929	N.V.Bubyakin
Jan 1929-Feb 1931	A.K.Andreyev
Feb 1931-Dec 1934	N.S.Yemelyanov
Dec 1934-42	Aleksandr Gabyseb
1942-45	P.V.Ammosov
1945-5?	S.P.Sidorov
Dec 1957-April 1963	Mariya Nartakhova
April 1963-March 1980	Aleksandra Ovchinnikova
March 1980-85	Yevdokiya Gorokhova
1985-89	Lyuliya Grigoreva
Dec 1989-	Mikhail Nikolayev

Prime Ministers:

Chairman of the Council of People's Commissars 1922-46
Chairman of the Council of Ministers 1946-91
Chairman of the Government since 1994

1922-24	I.N.Barakhov
1924-25	I.N.Vinokurov
1925-28	M.K.Ammosov
1928-29	N.V.Bubyakin

1929-31	A.K.Andreyev
1931-37	Kh.P.Sharaborin
1937-38	Stepan Arzhakov
1938-42	— — Fatkulov
1942-43	— — Muratov
1943	Semen Borisov (1st)
1943-46	Ilya Vinokurov
1946-51	Semen Borisov (2nd)
1951-Dec 1965	Vasily Kucherov
Dec 1965-Nov 1966	A.Ye.Lelikov
Nov 1966-Feb 1980	Ivan Petrov
Feb 1980-1990	Sergei Markin
1990-91	Vladislav Shamshin
1991-94	Mikhail Nikolayev
1994-96	Vyacheslav Shtyrov
1996-98	Yury Kaidyshev
1998-	Vasily Vlasov

Communist Party Leaders:

First Secretary

1922-25	M.K.Ammosov
1925- ?	E.G.Pestun
? -37	P.M.Pevznyak
? -46	— — Stepanenko
1946	G.M.Maslennikov
1946-51	Ilya Vinokurov
Nov 1951-Oct 1965	Semen Borisov
Oct 1965-June 1982	Gavriil Chiryayev
June 1982-Aug 1991	Yury Prokopyev

TATARSTAN

Official name: Republic of Tatarstan
Previous name: Tatar Autonomous Soviet Socialist Republic 1920-91
Republic formed: 27 May 1920
Capital: Kazan

Presidents:

Chairman of the Central Executive Committee 1920-38
President of the Presidium of the Supreme Soviet 1938-90
Chairman of the Supreme Soviet 1990-91

1920- ?	Burkhan Mansurov
? -25	— — Khachmandanov
1925-30	— — Shaimardanov

1930	Kh.I.Mratkhazin
1931	Kiyam Abramov
1932-34	M.Yagudin
1934-37	G.G.Baichurin
1937-50	Galei Dinmukhametov
1950-57	S.N.Nizamov
1957-Jan 1960	Kamil Faseyev
Jan 1960-Jan 1984	Salikh Batyev
Jan 1984-April 1990	Anvar Bagautdinov
April 1990-	Mintimer Shaimiyev

Prime Ministers:

Chairman of the Council of People's Commissars 1920-46
Chairman of the Council of Ministers since 1946

1920-21	Sakhibgarey Said-Galiyev
1921-25	—— Mukhtarov
1925-29	Zaki Gabidullin
1929-37	Kiyam Abramov
1937-38	Akhmetsafa Davletyarov
July 1938-39	A.Kh.Tyncherov
1939-43	Sulaiman Gafyatullin
1943-50	Said Sharafeyev (1st)
1950- ?	M.Azivov
? -59	Said Sharafeyev (2nd)
March 1959-March 1966	Abdulkhak Abdrazyakov
March 1966-Oct 1982	Gumer Usmanov
Oct 1982-84	Anvar Bagautdinov
1985-89	Mintimer Shaimiyev
1989-July 1991	I.Kh.Sadykov
July 1991-96	Mukhammat Sabirov
1996-March 1998	Farid Mukhametshin
March 1998-	Rustam Minnikhanov

Communist Party Leaders:

First Secretary

1920-21	Semen Kanatchikov
1923	D.Zhivov
1925-28	Mendel Khatayevich
1931	—— Abdulin
1933-37	A.K.Lepa
1937- ?	Aleksandr Alemasov
? -46	—— Kolybanov
1946-57	Zinnyat Muratov
June 1957-Oct 1960	Semen Ignatyev

Oct 1960-Nov 1979   Fikryat Tabeyev
Nov 1979-Oct 1982   Rashid Musin
Oct 1982-89   Gumer Usmanov
1989-Sept 1990   Mintimer Shaimiyev
Sept 1990-Aug 1991   Revo Idiatullin

TYVA

Official name: Tyva Republic
Previous names: Tannu-Tuva People's Republic 1921-26, Tuva People's Republic 1926-44, Tuva Autonomous Region 1944-61, Tuva Autonomous Soviet Socialist Republic 1961-91, Tuva Republic 1991-93
Independence date: 14 August 1921
Independence abolished: 13 October 1944
Republic formed: 10 October 1961
Capital: Kyzyl (*f* Belotsarsk)

Presidents:
Chairman of the Presidium of the Great Khural 1924-44
President of the Presidium of the Supreme Soviet 1962-90
Chairman of the Supreme Soviet 1990-92

1924-31	Nimazhap
1931-36	Chulydym Lopsakovi
1936-40	Kemchik-ool
1940-42	Polat
1942-44	Khortek Anchim
(1944-62	post abolished)
1962-March 1980	Bai-Kara Dolchanmaa
March 1980-March 1985	Mikhail Mendume
March 1985-Sept 1991	Chimit-Dorzhu Ondar
Oct 1991-March 1992	Kaadyr-ool Bicheldey
March 1992-	Cherik-ool Oorzhak

Prime Ministers:
Chairman of the Council of Ministers 1921-44 & 1961-92
Chairman of the Executive Committee 1944-61

1921-22	Sodnom Balyjir-Beili (S.Bakhir)
1922-23	Lopsan-Osur (later Idam-Syuryun)
1923-24	Buyan Badarakho
1924-28	Donduk
1929-36	Kemchik-ool
1936-40	Curmit-Tayishi (Gyrmittazi)
1940-61	Aleksandr (Saryg) Chimba

March 1961-Feb 1980   Mikhail Mendume
Feb 1980-85   Chimit-Dorzhu Ondar
1985-90   Vladimir Seryakov
April 1990-March 1992   Cherik-ool Oorzhak
(March 1992-   post abolished)

Communist Party Leaders:
General Secretary 1921-44
First Secretary 1944-91

1921-23   Nimazhap
1923   Lopsan-Osur
1923-24   Kyrsedi Oyun Kenden
1924-25   Shardyr
1924-26   Buyan Badarakho
1926-29   Sodnom
1929-32   Irgit Shapdyrzhap
1932-May 1973   Salchak Toka   (†)
June 1973-Aug 1991   Grigory Shirshin

UDMURTIA

Official name: Udmurt Republic
Previous names: Votyak Autonomous Region 1920-32, Udmurt Autonomous Region 1932-36, Udmurt Autonomous Soviet Socialist Republic 1936-91
Republic formed: 28 December 1936
Capital: Izhevsk

Presidents:
Chairman of the Central Executive Committee 1936-38
President of the Presidium of the Supreme Soviet 1938-90
Chairman of the Supreme Soviet 1990-94
Chairman of the State Council since 1994

Dec 1936-July 1937   G.A.Ivanov
July-Nov 1937   — — Reshetnikov
Nov 1937-July 1938   Semen Maksinov
July 1938-43   I.T.Voronchikhin
1943-47   Artem Pavlov
1947-54   Vikenty Chiskov
Feb 1954-April 1963   A.V.Karavayev
April 1963-March 1980   Petr Sysoev
March 1980-April 1990   Afanasy Tubylov
April 1990-Dec 1994   Valentin Tubylov
Dec 1994-   Aleksandr Volkov

Prime Ministers:

Chairman of the Council of People's Commissars 1936-46
Chairman of the Council of Ministers since 1946

Dec 1936-37	G.A.Ivanov
1937-45	Andrei Tronin
1945-54	Petr Sysoev
1954-Oct 1967	Stepan Yefremov
Oct 1967-Feb 1980	Arklady Markov
Feb 1980-89	Yury Kudyshev
1989-90	Gennady Dmitriyev
April 1990-93	Nikolai Mironov
1993-Dec 1994	Aleksandr Volkov
Dec 1994-	Pavel Vershinin

Communist Party Leaders:

First Secretary

1937- ?	Aleksei Voronin
? -50	Anatoly Tserkinov
1950-57	Mikhail Svetin
1957-59	Georgy Vorobev
Dec 1959-Dec 1963	Igor Skulkov
Dec 1963-Dec 1985	Valery Marisov
Dec 1985-June 1990	Pyotr Grishchenko
June 1990-Aug 1991	Nikolai Sapozhnikov

Former Autonomous Republic

GERMAN VOLGA REPUBLIC

Official name: German Volga Autonomous Soviet Socialist Republic
Republic formed: 20 February 1924
Republic abolished: 24 September 1941
Capital: Engels (*f* Pokrovsk)

Presidents:

Chairman of the Central Executive Committee 1924-38
President of the Presidium of the Supreme Soviet 1938-41

1924-30	Ivan Shvab (Johannes Schwab)
1930-34	A.Ya.Gleim
1934	A.N.Fuks (Fuchs)
1935-37	A.A.Velsh (Welsch)
1937	G.A.Luft
Nov 1937-June 1938	David Rozenberger
June 1938-Sept 1941	Konrad Gofman

Prime Ministers:
Chairman of the Council of People's Commissars

1924-26	Vilgelm Kurts (Wilhelm Kurz)
March 1926-29	Ivan Shvab (Johannes Schwab)
1929-30	A.Ya.Gleim
1931	G.M.Fuks (Fuchs)
1933-34	A.N.Fuks (Fuchs)
1935-37	A.A.Velsh (Welsch)
Nov 1937-June 1938	Vladimir Dalinger
June 1938-Sept 1941	I.Gekman

Communist Party Leaders:
First Secretary

? -37	A.A.Velsh (Welsch)
Nov 1937-Sept 1941	Yakov Popok (see Turkmenistan)

Autonomous Region

JEWISH AUTONOMOUS REGION

Region established: 7 May 1934
Capital: Birobidyan

Prime Ministers:
Chairman of the Executive Committee

April 1959-Nov 1962	F.T.Klimenko
Nov 1962-Nov 1971	A.I.Akavitov
Nov 1971-Nov 1990	Sergei Duvakin
Nov 1990-Dec 1991	Boris Karsunsky

Governor:

Dec 1991-	Nikolai Volkov

Communist Party Leaders:
First Secretary

March 1959-Nov 1962	V.I.Cherny
Nov 1962-July 1970	G.Ye.Podgayev
July 1970-July 1987	Lev Shapiro
July 1987-Nov 1990	Boris Karsunsky
Nov 1990-Aug 1991	Anatoly Kapeistov

Krays (Provinces)

ALTAY

Capital: Barnaul

Governors:

Oct 1991-93	Vladimir Raifikesht
1993-Dec 1996	Lev Korshunov
Dec 1996-	Aleksandr Surikov

KHABAROVSK

Capital: Khabarovsk

Governor:

Oct 1991-	Viktor Ishayev

KRASNODAR

Capital: Krasnodar

Governors:

Dec 1992-93	Nikolai Yegorov
1993-Dec 1996	Yevgeny Kharitonov
Dec 1996-	Nikolai Kondratenko

KRASNOYARSK

Capital: Krasnoyarsk

Governors:

1991-93	A.F. Veprev
Jan 1993-June 1998	Valery Zubov
June 1998-	Aleksandr Lebed

MARITIME (PRIMORYE)

Capital: Vladivostok

Governors:

Oct 1991-93	Vladimir Kuznetsov
1993-	Yevgeny Nazdratenko

STRAVROPOL

Capital: Stravropol

Governors:

Oct 1991-93	Yevgeny Kuznetsov
1993-Nov 1996	Petr Marchenko
Nov 1996-	Aleksandr Chernogorov

Oblasts (Regions)

AMUR

Capital: Blagoveschensk

Governors:

Oct 1991-93	Albert Krivchenko
1993-Oct 1994	Aleksandr Surat
Oct 1994-96	Vladimir Polevanov
1996-March 1997	Yury Lyashko
March 1997-	Anatoly Belonogov

ARCHANGEL

Capital: Archangel

Governors:

Sept 1991-93	Pavel Balakshin
1993-96	Pavel Pozdeyev
Feb-March 1996	Valentin Vlasov
March 1996-	Anatoly Yefremov

ASTRAKHAN

Capital: Astrakhan

Governor:

Aug 1991-	Anatoly Guzhvin

BELGOROD

Capital: Belgorod

Governors:

Dec 1991-Oct 1993	Viktor Berestovoy
Oct 1993-	Yevgeny Savchenko

BRYANSK

Capital: Bryansk

Governors:

Dec 1991-Dec 1992	Vladimir Barabanov	(acting Dec 1991-Jan 1992)
Dec 1992-Oct 1993	Yury Lodkin (1st)	
Oct 1993-95	Vladimir Karpov	
1995-Dec 1996	Aleksandr Semernov	
Dec 1996-	Yury Lodkin (2nd)	

CHELYABINSK

Capital: Chelyabinsk

Governors:

Oct 1991-Dec 1996	Vadim Solovev
Dec 1996-	Petr Sumin

CHITA

Capital: Chita

Governors:

Nov 1991-95	Boris Ivanov
1995-	Ravil Genyatulin

IRKUTSK

Capital: Irkutsk

Governors:

Aug 1991-Aug 1997	Yury Nozhikov
Aug 1997-	Boris Govorin

IVANOVO

Capital: Ivanovo

Governors:

Dec 1991-95	Adolf Laptev
1995-	Vladislav Tikhomirov

KALININGRAD

Capital: Kaliningrad

Governors:

Sept 1991-Oct 1996	Yury Matochkin
Oct 1996-	Leonid Gorbenko

KALUGA

Capital: Kaluga

Governors:

Sept 1991-93	Aleksandr Deryagin
1993-Nov 1996	Oleg Savchenko
Nov 1996-	Valery Sudarenko

KAMCHATKA

Capital: Petropavlovsk-Kamchatsky

Governor:

Nov 1991-	Vladimir Biryukov

KEMOROVO

Capital: Kemorovo

Governor:

Aug 1991-July 1997	Mikhail Kislyuk
July 1997-	Aman Tuleyev

KIROV (VYATKA)

Capital: Kirov

Governors:

Nov 1991-Oct 1996	Vasily Desyatnikov
Oct 1996-	Vladimir Sergeyenkov

KOSTROMA

Capital: Kostroma

Governors:

Dec 1991-Dec 1996	Valery Arbuzov
Dec 1996-	Viktor Shershunov

KURGAN

Capital: Kurgan

Governors:

Nov 1991-93	Valentin Gerasimov
1993-Dec 1996	Anatoly Sobolev
Dec 1996-	Oleg Bogombov

KURSK

Capital: Kursk

Governors:

Dec 1991-95	Vasily Shuteyev
1995-Oct 1996	Viktor Surzhikov
Oct 1996-	Aleksandr Rutskoi

LENINGRAD

Capital: St Petersburg

Governors:

Oct 1991-Sept 1996	Aleksandr Belyakov
Sept 1996-Sept 1998	Vadim Gustov
Sept 1998-	Valery Serfyukov (acting Sept 1998-Oct 1989)

LIPETSK

Capital: Lipetsk

Governors:

Dec 1992-April 1993	Vladimir Zaitsev
April 1993-April 1998	Mikhail Narolin
April 1998-Sept 1998	Oleg Korolyov
Sept 1998-	Valery Serdyukov (acting Sept 1998-Oct 1989)

MAGADAN

Capital: Magadan

Governors:

Oct 1991-Nov 1996	Viktor Mikhailov
Nov 1996-	Valentin Tsvetkov

MOSCOW

Capital: Moscow

Governors:

Aug 1991-Jan 2000	Anatoly Tyazhlov
Jan 2000-	Boris Gromov

MURMANSK

Capital: Murmansk

Governors:

Nov 1991-Dec 1996	Yevgeny Komarov
Dec 1996-	Yury Yevdokimov

NIZHNY-NOVGOROD

Capital: Nizhny-Novgorod

Governors:

Nov 1991-April 1997	Boris Nemtsov
July 1997-	Ivan Sklyarov

NOVGOROD

Capital: Novgorod

Governor:

Oct 1991-   Mikhail Prusak

NOVISIBIRSK

Capital: Novisibirsk

Governors:

Nov 1991-Oct 1993   Vitaly Mukha   (1st)
Oct 1993-Dec 1995   Ivan Indinok
Dec 1995-Jan 2000   Vitaly Mukha   (2nd)
Jan 2000-   Viktor Tolkonsky

OMSK

Capital: Omsk

Governor:

Nov 1991-   Leonid Polezhayev

OREL

Capital: Orel

Governors:

Dec 1991-April 1993   Nikolai Yudin
April 1993-   Yegor Stroyev

ORENBURG

Capital: Orenburg

Governors:

Oct 1991-Jan 2000   Vladimir Yelagin
Jan 2000-   Aleksei Chernyshev

PENZA

Capital: Penza

Governors:

Oct 1991-April 1993	Aleksandr Kondratev
April 1993-April 1998	Anatoly Kovlyagin
April 1998-	Vasili Bochkaryov

PERM

Capital: Perm

Governors:

Dec 1991-95	Boris Kuznetsov
1995-	Gennady Igumnov

PSKOV

Capital: Pskov

Governors:

Oct 1991-May 1992	A.Dobryatov
May 1992-Nov 1996	Vladislav Tumanov
Nov 1996-	Yevgeny Mikhailov

ROSTOV

Capital: Rostov-on-Don

Governor:

Sept 1991-	Vladimir Chub

RYAZAN

Capital: Ryazan

Governors:

Sept 1991-93	Lev Bashmakov
1993-Dec 1996	Gennady Merkulov
Dec 1996-	Vyacheslav Lyubimov

SAKHALIN

Capital: Yuzhno-Sakhalin

Governors:

Aug 1991-April 1993	Valentin Fedorov
April 1993-95	Yevgeny Krasnoyarov
1995-	Igor Farkhutdinov

SAMARA

Capital: Samara

Governor:

Aug 1991-April 2000	Konstantin Titov

SARATOV

Capital: Saratov

Governors:

Feb 1992-95	Yury Belykh
1995-	Dmitry Ayatskov

SMOLENSK

Capital: Smolensk

Governors:

Nov 1991-Dec 1995	Valery Fateyev
Dec 1995-May 1998	Anatoly Glushenkov
May 1998-	Aleksandr Prokhorov

SVERDLOSK

Capital: Yekaterinburg

Governors:

Aug 1991-Nov 1993	Eduard Rossel	(1st)
Nov 1993-Aug 1995	Aleksei Strakhov	
Aug 1995-	Eduard Rossel	(2nd)

TAMBOV

Capital: Tambov

Governors:

Dec 1992-Dec 1995	Vladimir Babenko
Dec 1995-Jan 2000	Aleksandr Ryabov
Jan 2000-	Oleg Betin

TOMSK

Capital: Tomsk

Governor:

Oct 1991-	Viktor Kress

TULA

Capital: Tula

Governors:

Oct 1991-March 1997	Nikolai Sevryugin
March 1997-	Vasily Starodabtsev

TVER

Capital: Tver

Governors:

Oct 1991-Dec 1995	Vladimir Suslov
Dec 1995-	Vladimir Platov

TYUMEN

Capital: Tyumen

Governors:

Nov 1991-Feb 1992	Yury Shafranik
Feb 1992-	Leonid Roketsky

ULYANOVSK

Capital: Ulyanovsk

Governors:

Oct 1991-Jan 1992	V.Malafeyev
Jan 1992-	Yury Goryachev

VLADIMIR

Capital: Vladimir

Governors:

Sept 1991-Dec 1996	Yury Vlasov
Dec 1996-	Nikolai Vinogradov

VOLGOGRAD

Capital: Volgograd

Governors:

Sept 1991-Dec 1996	Ivan Shabunin
Dec 1996-	Nikolai Maksyuta

VOLOGDA

Capital: Vologa

Governors:

Oct 1991-95	Nikolai Podgornov
1995-	Vyacheslav Pozgalev

VORONEZH

Capital: Voronezh

Governors:

April 1992-Dec 1996	Aleksandr Kovalev
Dec 1996-	Ivan Shabanov

YAROSLAVL

Capital: Yaroslavl

Governors:

Aug 1991-Dec 1992	V.Kovalev
Dec 1992-	Anatoly Listisyn

Federal Cities

MOSCOW

Mayors:

June 1991-June 1992	Gavriil Popov
June 1992-	Yury Luzhkov

Premier:

June 1991-	Yury Luzhkov

ST PETERSBURG

Mayors:

June 1991-June 1996	Anatoly Sobchak
June 1996-	Vladimir Yakovlev

Autonomous Okrugs (Districts)

AGA-BURYAT

Part of Chita Oblast
Capital: Aga

Governors:

Dec 1991-93	Gurodarma Tsedashiev
1993-Feb 1997	Bolot Ayushyev
Feb 1997-	Bair Zhamsuyev

CHUKCHI

Part of Magadan Oblast
Capital: Anadyr

Governor:

1991-   Aleksandr Nazarov

EVENK

Part of Krasnoyarsk Kray
Capital: Tura

Governors:

Oct 1991-March 1997   Anatoly Yakimov
March 1997-   Aleksandr Bokovikov

KHANTY-MANSI

Part of Tyumen Oblast
Capital: Khanty-Mansiisk

Governor:

Dec 1991-   Aleksandr Filipenko

KOMI-PERMYAK

Part of Perm Oblast
Capital: Kudymkar

Governor:

Dec 1991-   Nikolai Poluyanov

KORYAK

Part of Kamchatka Oblast
Capital: Palana

Governors:

Nov 1991-Nov 1996   Sergei Leushkin
Nov 1996-   Valentina Bronevich

NENETS

Part of Archangel Oblast
Capital: Naryan-Mar

Governors:

Nov 1991-93	Yury Komarovsky
1993-Dec 1996	Vladimir Khabarov
Dec 1996-	Vladimir Butov

TAIMYR (DOLGAN-NENETS)

Part of Krasnoyarsk Kray
Capital: Dudinka

Governor:

Dec 1991-   Gennady Nedelin

UST-ORDA BURYAT

Part of Irkutsk Oblast
Capital: Ust-Ordinsky

Governors:

Dec 1991-96	Aleksei Batagayev
1996-	Valery Maleyev

YAMAL-NENETS

Part of Tyumen Oblast
Capital: Salekhard

Governors:

Oct 1991-93	Lev Bayandin
1993-	Yury Neyelov

Former Soviet Republics

GORTSY REPUBLIC

Mountain Republic

Republic formed: 17 November 1920 (Terek Republic plus adjacent territory)
Republic abolished: 7 July 1924 (divided and incorporated into Chechen-Ingushetia, North & South

Ossetia, Kabardino-Balkaria and Karachai)
Capital: Vladikavkaz

President:
Chairman of the Central Executive Committee

1921-24	—— Syabikov

Prime Ministers:
Chairman of the Council of People's Commissars

1920-22	—— Takoyev
1922-24	S.Mansurov

KUBAN-BLACK SEA REPUBLIC

Republic formed: 30 May 1918
Republic abolished: 6 July 1918 (incorporated into North Caucasus Republic)
Capital: Ekaterinodar (now Krasnodar)

President:
Chairman of the Central Executive Committee

June-July 1918	Abram Rubin	(later President of North Caucasus)

Prime Minister:
Chairman of the Council of People's Commissars

May-July 1918	Yan Poliuan

NORTH CAUCASUS REPUBLIC

Republic formed: 7 July 1918
Republic abolished: December 1918
Capital: Ekaterinodar (now Krasnodar)

Presidents:
Chairman of the Central Executive Committee

July-Oct 1918	Abram Rubin	(† assassinated)
Oct-Dec 1918	Tapa Chermoyev	

STAVROPOL REPUBLIC

Republic formed: January 1918
Republic abolished: 6 July 1918 (incorporated into North Caucasus Republic)
Capital: Stavropol

President:

Chairman of the Central Executive Committee

Jan-July 1918   G.I.Mescheriakov

Prime Minister:

Chairman of the Council of People's Commissars

Jan-July 1918   Aleksandr Ponomarev

TEREK REPUBLIC

Republic formed: 16 March 1918
Republic abolished: 17 November 1920 (incorporated into Gortsy Republic)
Capital: Piatigorsk

President:

Chairman of the Central Executive Committee

March 1918- ?   E.S.Bogdanov

Prime Ministers:

Chairman of the Council of People's Commissars

March-July 1918	Samuil Buachidze	(†)
July 1918	Yu.G.Pashkovski	
July 1918-Nov 1920	F.K.Bulle	

Former independent state

FAR EASTERN REPUBLIC

State formed: March 1920
Incorporated into Russia: November 1922
Capital: Verkhneudinsk (now Ulan-Ude) (March-Sept 1920), Chita (1920-22)

President:

Oct 1920-Nov 1922   Aleksandr Krasnoshchekov

Prime Ministers:

April-Oct 1920   Boris Shumyatsky
Oct 1920-Dec 1921   Petr Nikiferov
Dec 1921-Nov 1922   Nikolai Matveyev

RWANDA

Official name: Republic of Rwanda, République du Rwanda, Republika Y'U Rwanda (Kinyarwanda)
Previous name: Ruanda until 1962
Independence date: 1 July 1962
Capital: Kigali

A kingdom in Rwanda was formed in the 16th century. In 1890 the country became a province of German East Africa, and after World War I it was administered along with Burundi by Belgium as the trust territory of Ruanda-Urundi. During the colonial period the kings retained their position. In 1961 the monarchy was overthrown and a republic proclaimed. Full independence was granted in 1962. In 1994 an outbreak of ethnic fighting led to a civil war with many hundreds of thousands of deaths.

Kings:

1696-1720	Yuhi II
1720-44	Karemera
1744-68	Cyilima II
1768-92	Kigeri III
1792-97	Mibambwe III
1797-1830	Yuhi III
1830-60	Matari II
1860-95	Kigeri IV
1895-96	Mibambwe IV (*son*)
1896-1931	Yuhi IV (*half-brother*)
1931-July 1959	Matari III (*son*)
July 1959-Jan 1961	Kigeri V (*half-brother*) (deposed)

Presidents:

Jan-Oct 1961	Dominique Mbonyumutwa
Oct 1961-July 1973	Gregoire Kayibanda (PEHP) (deposed)
July 1973-April 1994	Juvenal Habyalimana (NRMD) († air crash)
April-July 1994	Théodore Sindikubwabo (acting) (deposed)
July 1994-March 2000	Pasteur Bizimungu
March 2000-	Paul Kagame (acting March-April 2000)

Prime Ministers:

Oct 1960-Oct 1961	Gregoire Kayibanda
(Oct 1961-Oct 1991	post abolished)

Oct 1991-April 1992   Sylvestre Nsanzimana   (NRMD)
April 1992-July 1993   Dismas Nsengiyaremye   (RDP)
July 1993-April 1994   Agathe Uwilingiyimana   († assassinated)
April-July 1994   Jean Kambanda
July 1994-Aug 1995   Faustin Twagiramungu
Aug 1995-March 2000   Pierre-Celestin Rwigema
March 2000-   Bernard Makuza

NRMD = National Revolutionary Movement for Democracy (sole legal party 1975-91)
PEHP = Party of Emancipation of the Hutu People (Parmehutu) (sole legal party 1965-73)
RDP = Republican Democratic Party

SAHARWI REPUBLIC
(Western Sahara)

Official name: Saharwi Arab Democratic Republic
Previous name: Spanish Sahara until 1976
Independence date: 28 February 1976
Capital: Layyoune (El Aaiun) (under Moroccan control)

In 1884 a Spanish protectorate was proclaimed along the Saharan coast, and the area remained a colony until 1958 when it became an overseas province. In 1975 the territory was placed under joint Spanish, Moroccan and Mauritanian control until February 1976 when Spain withdrew. The pro-independence movement POLISARIO then declared an independent republic which has been recognised by over 70 countries. In 1979 Mauritania withdrew from the Sahara and Morocco extended its claim to the whole country, controlling the economically important areas despite the continuing armed struggle. The government of the republic operates from Algeria.

Governors-General:

1958	José Vazquez
1958-61	Mariano Alonso
1961-64	Pedro Latorre Alcubierre
1964-65	Joaquín Jiménez Coronado
1965-67	Angel Enriquez Larrondo
1967-71	José Pérez de Lema Tejero
1971-74	Fernando de Santiago y Díaz de Mendevil
1974-76	Federico Gómez de Salazar y Nieto

President:

Oct 1982-	Mohamed Abdulaziz

Prime Ministers:

March 1976-Nov 1982	Mohamed Lamine ould Ahmed	(1st)
Nov 1982-Dec 1985	Mahfoud Beida	(1st)
Dec 1985-Aug 1988	Mohamed Lamine ould Ahmed	(2nd)
Aug 1988-Sept 1993	Mahfoud Beida	(2nd)
Sept 1993-Sept 1995	Bouchraya Bayoune	(1st)
Sept 1995-Feb 1999	Mahfoud Beida	(3rd)
Feb 1999-	Bouchraya Bayoune	(2nd)

SAINT CHRISTOPHER (ST KITTS) AND NEVIS

Official name: Federation of Saint Christopher and Nevis
Independence date: 19 September 1983
Capital: Basseterre

St Kitts was the first English colony in the West Indies, the first settlements being established there in 1623. In 1958 it became a member of the West Indies Federation which was dissolved in 1962. A measure of autonomy was granted in 1960 and associated statehood followed in 1967. In the same year the island of Anguilla, which had been administered along with St Kitts and Nevis, declared itself independent. After its secession was ended by Britain in 1969, it was formally separated from the other islands in 1980. Full independence was granted to St Kitts and Nevis in 1983.

Administrators:

1895-99	Thomas Griffith
1899-1904	Charles Cox
1904-06	Robert Bromley
1906-16	Thomas Roxburgh
1916-25	John Burdon
1925-29	Thomas St Johnston
1929-31	Terence MacNaughton
1931-40	Douglas Stewart
1940-47	James Harford
1947-49	Leslie Greening
1949	Frederick Noad
1949-56	Hugh Burrowes
1956-66	Henry Howard
1966-67	Frederick Phillips

Governors:

1967-69	Frederick Phillips
1969-75	Milton Allen (acting 1969-72)
1975-81	Probyn Inniss
1981-83	Clement Arrindell

Governors-General:

Represent monarch who is concurrently British monarch

Sept 1983-Jan 1996	Clement Arrindell
Jan 1996-	Cuthbert Sebastian

Chief Ministers:

Jan 1960-July 1966	C.A.Paul Southwell	(LP)
July 1966-Feb 1967	Robert Bradshaw	(LP)

Prime Ministers:

Premier 1967-83

Feb 1967-May 1978	Robert Bradshaw	(LP) (†)
May 1978-May 1979	C.A.Paul Southwell	(LP) (†)
May 1979-Feb 1980	Lee Moore	(LP)
Feb 1980-July 1995	Kennedy Simmonds	(PAM)
July 1995-	Denzil Douglas	(LP)

LP = Labour Party
PAM = People's Action Movement

Federal State

NEVIS

Capital: Charlestown

Premiers:

Sept 1983-May 1992	Simeon Daniel	(NRP)
May 1992-	Vance Amory	(CCM)

CCM = Concerned Citizens Movement
NRP = Nevis Reformation Party

SAINT LUCIA

Official name: Saint Lucia
Independence date: 22 February 1979
Capital: Castries

The island of St Lucia was discovered in about 1500, and the first attempts at settlement were made by the English in 1605 and 1639. In 1650 French settlements were established, but the island was ceded to Britain in 1814. From 1958 until 1962 St Lucia was part of the West Indies Federation. Some autonomy was granted in 1960, and in 1967 it became an Associated State. Full independence followed in 1979.

Commissioners:

1889-1891	Robert Llewelyn (see St Vincent)
1891-97	Valesius Gouldsbury
1897-99	Charles King-Harman
1900-02	Harry Thompson (see St Vincent)
1902-05	George Melville
1905-09	Philip Cork
1909-14	Edward Cameron (see St Vincent)
1914-15	William Young
1915-18	Charles Murray
1918-27	Wilfred Davidson-Houston
1928-35	Charles Doorly
1935-38	Edward Baynes
1938-44	Arthur Wright
1944-46	Edward Twining
1947-53	John Stow
1953-58	John Thorpe

Administrators:

1958-62	Earl of Oxford and Asquith (Julian Asquith)
1962-67	Gerald Bryan

Governors:

1967-74	Frederick Clarke
1974-79	Allen Lewis

Governors-General:

Represent monarch who is concurrently British monarch

Feb 1979-Feb 1980   Allen Lewis   (1st)

Feb 1980-Jan 1983	Boswell Williams (acting)
Jan 1983-April 1987	Allen Lewis (2nd)
April 1987-Oct 1988	Vincent Floissac (acting) (1st)
Oct 1988-June 1996	Stanislaus James (acting Oct 1988-Feb 1992)
June 1996-Aug 1997	George Mallet
Aug-Sept 1997	Vincent Floissac (acting) (2nd)
Sept 1997-	Perlette Louisy

Chief Ministers:

Jan 1960-Oct 1964	George Charles (SLLP)
Oct 1964-March 1967	John Compton (UWP)

Prime Ministers:

Premier 1967-79

March 1967-July 1979	John Compton (1st) (UWP)
July 1979-May 1981	Allan Louisy (SLLP)
May 1981-Jan 1982	Winston Cenac (SLLP)
Jan-May 1982	Michael Pilgrim (SLLP)
May 1982-April 1996	John Compton (2nd) (UWP)
April 1996-May 1997	Vaughan Lewis (UWP)
May 1997-	Kenny Anthony (SLLP)

SLLP = St Lucia Labour Party
UWP = United Workers' Party

SAINT VINCENT AND THE GRENADINES

Official name: Saint Vincent and the Grenadines
Independence date: 27 October 1979
Capital: Kingstown

St Vincent became a British colony in 1763. In 1958 it joined the West Indies Federation, and in 1960 a degree of self-government was granted. St Vincent became an Associated State in 1969 and fully independent in 1979.

Administrators:

1888-89	Robert Llewelyn
1889-93	Irwin Maling
1893-95	John Sandwith
1895-1901	Harry Thompson
1901-09	Edward Cameron
1909-15	Charles Murray
1915-23	Reginald Lobb
1923-29	Herbert Peebles
1933-36	Arthur Grimble
1936-38	Arthur Wright
1938-41	William Gray
1941-44	Alexander Beattie
1944-48	Ronald Garvey
1948-55	Walter Coutts
1955-61	Alexander Giles
1961-66	Samuel Graham
1966-67	John Chapman
1967-69	Hywel George

Governors:

1969-70	Hywel George
1970-77	Rupert John
1977-79	Sydney Gun-Munro

Governors-General:

Represent monarch who is concurrently British monarch

Oct 1979-Feb 1985	Sydney Gun-Munro
Feb 1985-Feb 1988	Joseph Eustace
Feb 1988-Sept 1989	Henry Williams (acting)

Sept 1989-June 1996   David Jack
June 1996-   Charles Antrobus

Chief Ministers:

Jan 1960-May 1967   Ebenezer Joshua   (PPP)
May 1967-Oct 1969   Milton Cato   (SVLP)

Prime Ministers:

Premier 1969-79

Oct 1969-April 1972   Milton Cato   (1st) (SVLP)
April 1972-Dec 1974   James Mitchell   (1st) (NDP)
Dec 1974-July 1984   Milton Cato   (2nd) (SVLP)
July 1984-   James Mitchell   (2nd) (NDP)

NDP = New Democratic Party
PPP = People's Political Party
SVLP = St Vincent Labour Party

SAMOA

Official name: Independent State of Samoa, Malotutu'atasi o Samoa
Previous names: Kingdom of Samoa 1889-1900, Samoa 1900-35, Western Samoa 1935-62, Independent State of Western Samoa 1962-97
Independence date: 1 January 1962
Capital: Apia

In 1889 Samoa was proclaimed neutral territory under a four-power government comprising USA, Germany, Britain and a local administration. In 1899 Germany and Britain renounced all rights over the eastern islands, now American Samoa. The western islands became a German protectorate in 1900 and local autonomy was abolished. After World War I Western Samoa was administered by New Zealand under a League of Nations mandate and later a United Nations Trusteeship. Self-government was granted in 1959, with independence following in 1962.

Kings:

1841-68	Malietoa Moli
1868-69	Regent: Pea Talavou
1869-79	Malietoa Laupepa (1st)
1879-80	Malietoa Talavou
1881-87	Malietoa Laupepa (2nd)
1886-88	Tui A'ana Tamasese
Sept 1888-93	Malietoa Mata'afa (1st)
Nov 1888-Nov 1898	Malietoa Laupepa (3rd) (rival king 1888-93)
Nov 1898-99	Malietoa Mata'afa (2nd)
Nov 1898-1900	Malietoa Tanumafili I (rival King 1898-99)

Governors:

1900-11	Wilhelm Solf
1911-14	Erich Schultz-Ewerth

Administrators:

1914-19	Robert Logan
1920-23	Robert Tate
1923-28	George Richardson
1928-31	Stephen Allen
1931-35	Herbert Hart
1935-46	Alfred Turnbull
1946-48	Francis Voelcker

High Commissioners:

1948-49	Francis Voelcker
1949-60	Guy Powles
1960-61	John Wright

Heads of State:

Jan 1962-April 1963	Tupua Tamasese Mea'ole (†) (joint head)
Jan 1962-	Malietoa Tanumafili II (joint head 1962-63)

Premier:

1873-76	A.B.Steinberger
(1876	post abolished)

Prime Ministers:

Oct 1959-March 1970	Fiame Mata'afa F.M.II (1st)
March 1970-March 1973	Tupua Tamasese Leolofi IV (1st)
March 1973-May 1975	Fiame Mata'afa F.M.II (2nd)
May 1975-March 1976	Tupua Tamasese Leolofi IV (2nd)
March 1976-Feb 1982	Tupuola Taisi Efi (1st) (son of Tupua Tamasese Mea'ole)
Feb-Sept 1982	Va'ai Kolone (1st) (HRPP)
Sept-Dec 1982	Tupuola Taisi Efi (2nd)
Dec 1982-Jan 1986	Tofilau Eti Alesana (1st) (HRPP)
Jan 1986-April 1988	Va'ai Kolone (2nd) (HRPP)
April 1988-Nov 1998	Tofilau Eti Alesana (2nd) (HRPP)
Nov 1998-	Tuile'epa Sailele Malielegaoi (HRPP)

HRPP = Human Rights Protection Party

SAN MARINO

Official name: Most Serene Republic of San Marino, Serenissima Repubblica di San Marino
State founded: 351
Capital: San Marino

San Marino is said to have been founded by St Marinus in the 4th century, and is the oldest republic in the world. It has retained its independence except for a brief period in 1503, when it was occupied on behalf of Rome. In 1957 an attempted communist coup was put down.

Capitani Reggenti (Captains Regents) (since 1899):

Post in existence since at least 1243

Oct 1899-March 1900	Federico Gozi (6th)/Silvestro Vita (2nd)
April-Sept 1900	Domenico Fattori (10th)/Antonio Righi (3rd)
Oct 1900-March 1901	Giovanni Bonelli (2nd)/Pietro Ugolini (5th)
April-Sept 1901	Luigi Tonnini (2nd)/Marino Nicolini (4th)
Oct 1901-March 1902	Antonio Belluzzi (3rd)/Pasquale Busignani (5th)
April-Sept 1902	Onofrio Fattori (2nd)/Egidio Ceccoli
Oct 1902-March 1903	Gernino Gozi (3rd)/Giacomo Marcucci (4th)
April-Sept 1903	Federico Gozi (7th)/Nullo Balducci
Oct 1903-March 1904	Marino Borbiconi (3rd)/Francesco Marcucci (6th)
April-Sept 1904	Menetto Bonelli (4th)/Vincenzo Mulatoni (2nd)
Oct 1904-March 1905	Luigi Tonnini (3rd)/Gustavo Babboni (1st)
April-Sept 1905	Antonio Belluzzi (4th)/Pasquale Busignani (6th)
Oct 1905-March 1906	Onofrio Fattori (3rd)/Piermatteo Carattoni
April-Sept 1906	Giovanni Belluzzi (1st)/Pietro Francini (2nd)
Oct 1906-March 1907	Alfredo Reffi (1st)/Giovanni Arzilli (1st)
April-Sept 1907	Ciro Belluzzi (1st)/Francesco Pasquali (1st)
Oct 1907-March 1908	Giuseppe Angeli (1st)/Francesco Valli
April-Sept 1908	Menetto Bonelli (5th)/Gustavo Babboni (2nd)
Oct 1908-March 1909	Olinto Amati (1st)/Raffaele Minchetti
April-Sept 1909	Luigi Tonnini (3rd)/Domenico Suzzi-Valli (1st)
Oct 1909-March 1910	Marino Borbiconi (4th)/Giacomo Marcucci (5th)
April-Sept 1910	Alfredo Reffi (2nd)/Giovanni Arzilli (2nd)
Oct 1910-March 1911	Giovanni Belluzzi (2nd)/Luigi Lonfernini (1st)
April-Sept 1911	Moro Morri (1st)/Cesare Staccini (1st)
Oct 1911-March 1912	Onofrio Fattori (4th)/Angelo Manzoni-Borghesi (1st)
April-Sept 1912	Gustavo Babboni (3rd)/Francesco Pasquali (2nd)
Oct 1912-March 1913	Menetto Bonelli (6th)/Vincenzo Marcucci (1st)
April-Sept 1913	Giuseppe Angeli (2nd)/Ignazio Grazia
Oct 1913-March 1914	Cirro Belluzzi (2nd)/Domenico Suzzi-Valli (2nd)

April-Sept 1914	Domenico Fattori (11th)/Ferruccio Martelli
Oct 1914-March 1915	Olinto Amati (2nd)/Cesare Stacchini (2nd)
April-Sept 1915	Moro Morri (2nd)/Antonio Burgagni
Oct 1915-March 1916	Alfredo Reffi (3rd)/Luigi Lonfernini (2nd)
April-Sept 1916	Onofrio Fattori (5th)/Ciro Francini (1st)
Oct 1916-March 1917	Gustavo Babboni (4th)/Giovanni Arzilli (3rd)
April-Sept 1917	Egisto Morri (1st)/Vincenzo Marcucci (3rd)
Oct 1917-March 1918	Angelo Manzoni-Borghesi (2nd)/Giuseppe Balducci (1st)
April-Sept 1918	Ferruccio Marlette/Ermenegildo Mularoni
Oct 1918-March 1919	Protogene Belloni/Francesco Morri (1st)
April-Sept 1919	Domenico Vicini/Pietro Suzzi-Valli
Oct 1919-March 1920	Moro Morri (3rd)/Francesco Pasquali (3rd)
April-Sept 1920	Marino Rossi (1st)/Ciro Francini (2nd)
Oct 1920-March 1921	Carlo Balsimelli (1st)/Simone Micheloti
April-Sept 1921	Marino della Balda (1st)/Vincenzo Francini
Oct 1921-March 1922	Egisto Morri (2nd)/Giuseppe Lanci
April-Sept 1922	Eugenio Reffi/Giuseppe Arzilli
Oct 1922-March 1923	Onofrio Fattori (6th)/Giuseppe Balducci (2nd)
April-Sept 1923	Giuliani Gozi (1st)/Filippo Mularoni (1st)
Oct 1923-March 1924	Marino Borbiconi (5th)/Mario Michetti
April-Sept 1924	Angelo Borghesi (1st)/Francesco Mularoni (1st)
Oct 1924-March 1925	Francesco Morri (1st)/Girolami Gozi (1st)
April-Sept 1925	Marino Fattori/Augusto Mularoni
Oct 1925-March 1926	Valerio Pasquali (1st)/Marco Marcucci
April-Sept 1926	Manlio Gozi (1st)/Giuseppe Mularoni
Oct 1926-March 1927	Giuliano Gozi (2nd)/Ruggero Morri (1st)
April-Sept 1927	Gino Gozi (1st)/Marino Morri (1st)
Oct 1927-March 1928	Marino Rossi (2nd)/Nelson Burgagni
April-Sept 1928	Domenico Suzzi-Valli (3rd)/Francesco Pasquali (4th)
Oct 1928-March 1929	Francesco Morri (2nd)/Melchiorre Filippi (1st)
April-Sept 1929	Girolami Gozi (2nd)/Filippo Mularoni (2nd)
Oct 1929-March 1930	Ezio Balducci/Aldo Busignani
April-Sept 1930	Manlio Gozi (2nd)/Marino Lonfernini
Oct 1930-March 1931	Valerio Pasquali (2nd)/Gino Ceccoli (1st)
April-Sept 1931	Angelo Borghesi (1st)/Francesco Mularoni (2nd)
Oct 1931-March 1932	Domenico Suzzi-Valli (4th)/Marino Rossi (2nd)
April-Sept 1932	Giuliani Gozi (3rd)/Pompeo Righi (1st)
Oct 1932-March 1933	Gino Gozi (2nd)/Ruggero Morri (2nd)
April-Sept 1933	Francesco Morri (3rd)/Settimio Belluzzi (1st)
Oct 1933-March 1934	Carlo Balsimelli (2nd)/Melchiorre Filippi (2nd)
April-Sept 1934	Marino Rossi (3rd)/Giovanni Lonfernini (1st)
Oct 1934-March 1935	Angelo Borghesi (3rd)/Marino Michelotti (1st)
April-Sept 1935	Federico Gozi (1st)/Salvatore Foschi (1st)
Oct 1935-March 1936	Pompeo Righi (2nd)/Marino Morri (3rd)
April-Sept 1936	Gino Gozi (3rd)/Ruggero Morri (3rd)

Oct 1936-March 1937	Francesco Morri (4th)/Gino Ceccoli (2nd)
April-Sept 1937	Gino Gozi (4th)/Settimio Belluzzi (2nd)
Oct 1937-March 1938	Marino Rossi (4th)/Giovanni Lonfernini (2nd)
April-Sept 1938	Manlio Gozi (3rd)/Luigi Mularoni
Oct 1938-March 1939	Carlo Balsimelli (3rd)/Celio Gozi (1st)
April-Sept 1939	Pompeo Righi (3rd)/Marino Morri (4th)
Oct 1939-March 1940	Marino Michelotti (2nd)/Orlando Reffi
April-Sept 1940	Angelo Borghesi (4th)/Filippo Mularoni (3rd)
Oct 1940-March 1941	Federico Gozi (2nd)/Salvatore Foschi (2nd)
April-Sept 1941	Gino Gozi (5th)/Secondo Menicucci
Oct 1941-March 1942	Giuliani Gozi (4th)/Giovanni Lonfernini (3rd)
April-Sept 1942	Settimio Belluzzi (3rd)/Celio Gozi (2nd)
Oct 1942-March 1943	Carlo Balsimelli (4th)/Renato Martelli
April-Sept 1943	Marino Michelotti (3rd)/Bartolomeo Borghesi
Oct 1943-March 1944	Marino della Balda (2nd)/Sante Lonfernini
April-Sept 1944	Francesco Balsimelli/Sanzio Valentini
Oct 1944-March 1945	Teodoro Lonfernini/Leonido Suzzi-Valli (1st)
April-Sept 1945	Alvaro Casali (1st)/Vittorio Valentini
Oct 1945-March 1946	Feruccio Martelli (1st)/Secondo Fiorini (1st)
April-Sept 1946	Giuseppe Forcellini (1st)/Vincenzo Pedini (1st)
Oct 1946-March 1947	Filippo Martelli/Luigi Montironi (1st)
April-Sept 1947	Marino della Balda (3rd)/Luigi Zafferani
Oct 1947-March 1948	Domenico Forcellini (1st)/Mariano Ceccoli (1st)
April-Sept 1948	Arnaldo Para (1st)/Giuseppe Renzi (1st)
Oct 1948-March 1949	Giordano Giacomini (1st)/Domenico Tomassoni
April-Sept 1949	Feruccio Martelli (2nd)/Primo Bugli (1st)
Oct 1949-March 1950	Vincenzo Pedini (2nd)/Agostini Biordi (1st)
April-Sept 1950	Giuseppe Forcellini (2nd)/Primo Taddei
Oct 1950-March 1951	Marino della Balda (4th)/Luigi Montironi (2nd)
April-Sept 1951	Alvaro Casali (2nd)/Romolo Giacomini
Oct 1951-March 1952	Domenico Forcellini (2nd)/Giovanni Terenzi
April-Sept 1952	Domenico Morganti/Mariano Ceccoli (2nd)
Oct 1952-March 1953	Arnaldo Para (2nd)/Eugenio Bernardini (1st)
April-Sept 1953	Vincenzo Pedini (3rd)/Alberto Reffi
Oct 1953-March 1954	Giordani Giacomini (2nd)/Giuseppe Renzi (2nd)
April-Sept 1954	Giuseppe Forcellini (3rd)/Secondo Fiorini (2nd)
Oct 1954-March 1955	Agostini Giacomini/Luigi Montironi (3rd)
April-Sept 1955	Domenico Forcellini (3rd)/Vittorio Meloni
Oct 1955-March 1956	Primo Bugli (2nd)/Giuseppe Maiani
April-Sept 1956	Mario Nanni/Enrico Andreoli
Oct 1956-March 1957	Mariano Ceccoli (3rd)/Eugenio Bernardini (2nd)
April-Oct 1957	Giordano Giacomini (3rd)/Primo Marani (deposed)
Oct 1957-March 1958	Marino Franciosi/Federico Micheloni (1st)
April-Sept 1958	Zaccaria Savoretti/Stelio Montironi (1st)
Oct 1958-March 1959	Domenico Forcellini (4th)/Pietro Reffi (1st)

April-Sept 1959	Marino Belluzzi (1st)/Agostini Biordi (2nd)
Oct 1959-March 1960	Giuseppe Forcellini (4th)/Ferruccio Piva (1st)
April-Sept 1960	Alvaro Casali (3rd)/Gino Vannucci
Oct 1960-March 1961	Eugenio Reffi (1st)/Pietro Gianecchi
April-Sept 1961	Federico Micheloni (2nd)/Giancarlo Ghironzi (1st)
Oct 1961-March 1962	G.Vito Marcucci (1st)/Pio Galassi
April-Sept 1962	Domenico Forcellini (5th)/Francesco Valli (1st)
Oct 1962-March 1963	Antonio Morganti/Agostino Biordi (3rd)
April-Sept 1963	Leonido Suzzi-Valli (2nd)/Stelio Montironi (2nd)
Oct 1963-March 1964	Giovan Franciosi (1st)/Domenico Bollini
April-Sept 1964	Marino Belluzzi (2nd)/Eusebio Reffi (2nd)
Oct 1964-March 1965	Giuseppe Micheloni (1st)/Pier Mularoni
April-Sept 1965	Ferruccio Piva (2nd)/Federici Carattoni (1st)
Oct 1965-March 1966	Alvaro Casali (4th)/Pietro Reffi (2nd)
April-Sept 1966	Francesco Valli (2nd)/Emilio della Balda
Oct 1966-March 1967	G.Vito Marcucci (2nd)/Francesco Francini (1st)
April-Sept 1967	Vittorio Rossini/Alberto Lonfernini (1st)
Oct 1967-March 1968	Domenico Forcellini (6th)/Romano Michelotti
April-Sept 1968	M.Benedetto Belluzzi (1st)/Dante Rossi
Oct 1968-March 1969	Pietro Giancecchi/Aldo Zavoli
April-Sept 1969	Ferruccio Piva (3rd)/Stelio Montironi (3rd)
Oct 1969-March 1970	Alvaro Casali (5th)/Giancarlo Ghironzi (2nd)
April-Sept 1970	Francesco Valli (3rd)/Eusebio Reffi (3rd)
Oct 1970-March 1971	Giuseppe Lonfernini/Simone Rossini
April-Sept 1971	Luigi Lonfernini/Attilio Montanari
Oct 1971-March 1972	Federico Carattoni (2nd)/Marino Vagnetti
April-Sept 1972	M.Benedetto Belluzzi (2nd)/Giuseppe Micheloni (2nd)
Oct 1972-March 1973	Rosolino Martelli/Bruno Casali
April-Sept 1973	Francesco Francini (2nd)/Primo Bugli (3rd)
Oct 1973-March 1974	Antonio Volpinari (1st)/Giovan Franciosi (2nd)
April-Sept 1974	Ferruccio Piva (4th)/Giordano Reffi (1st)
Oct 1974-March 1975	Francesco Valli (4th)/Enrico Andreoli (1st)
April-Sept 1975	Alberto Cecchetti (1st)/Michele Righi
Oct 1975-March 1976	Giovannito Marcucci/Giuseppe della Balda
April-Sept 1976	Primo Bugli (4th)/Virgilio Cardelli
Oct 1976-March 1977	Clelio Galassi/Marino Venturini (1st)
April-Sept 1977	Alberto Lonfernini (2nd)/Antonio Volpinari (2nd)
Oct 1977-March 1978	Tito Masi/Giordano Reffi (2nd)
April-Sept 1979	Marino Bollini (1st)/Lino Celli
Oct 1979-March 1980	Giuseppe Amici (1st)/Germano de Biagi (1st)
April-Sept 1980	Pietro Chiaruzzi/Primo Marani
Oct 1980-March 1981	Giancarlo Berardi/Rossano Zafferani (1st)
April-Sept 1981	Maria Pedini-Angellini/Gastone Pasolini
Oct 1981-March 1982	Mario Rossi/Ubaldo Biordi (1st)
April-Sept 1982	Giuseppe Maiani/Marino Venturini (2nd)

Oct 1982-March 1983   Libero Barulli/Maurizio Gobbi
April-Sept 1983   Adriano Reffi   (2nd)/Massino Rossini
Oct 1983-March 1984   Germano de Biagi   (2nd)/Renzo Renzi (1st)
April-Sept 1984   Giorgio Crescentini/Gloriana Ranocchini   (1st)
Oct 1984-March 1985   Marino Bollini   (2nd)/Giuseppe Amici (2nd)
April-Sept 1985   Enzo Colombini/Severino Tura
Sept 1985-March 1986   Pier-Paulo Gasperoni(1st)/Ubaldo Biordi   (2nd)
April-Sept 1986   Marino Venturni   (3rd)/Ariosti Maiani
Oct 1986-March 1987   Giuseppe Arzilli/Maurizio Tomassoni
April-Sept 1987   Renzo Renzi   (2nd)/Carlo Franciosi
Oct 1987-March 1988   Rossano Zafferani   (2nd)/Gian Terenzi
April-Sept 1988   Umberto Barulli/Rosolino Martelli
Oct 1988-March 1989   Luciano Cardelli/Reves Salvatori
April-Sept 1989   Mauro Fiorini/Marino Vagnetti
Oct 1989-March 1990   Leo Achilli/Gloriana Ranocchini   (2nd)
April-Sept 1990   Aldomiro Bartolini/Ottaviano Rossi
Oct 1990-March 1991   Cesare Gasperoni/Roberto Bucci
April-Sept 1991   Claudio Podeschi/Domenico Bernardini
Oct 1991-March 1992   Edda Ceccoli/Marino Riccardi
April-Sept 1992   Ernesto Benedettini/Germano de Biagi
Oct 1992-March 1993   Romeo Morri/Marino Zanotti
April-Sept 1993   Patricia Busignani/Salvatore Tonelli
Oct 1993-March 1994   Gian Berti/Paride Andreoli
April-Sept 1994   Alberto Cecchetti   (2nd)/Fausto Mularoni
Oct 1994-March 1995   Renzo Ghiotti/Luciana Ciavatta
April-Sept 1995   Settimio Lonfernini/Marino Bollini   (3rd)
Oct 1995-March 1996   Piero Mularino/Marino Venturini   (4th)
April-Sept 1996   Pietro Bugli/Pier-Paolo Gasperoni   (2nd)
Oct 1996-March 1997   Maurizio Rattani/Gian Carlo Venturini
April-Sept 1997   Pier Marino Mularino/Barise Andreoli
Oct 1997-March 1998   Luigi Mazza/Marino Zanotti
April-Sept 1998   Loris Francini/Alberto Cecchetti   (3rd)
Oct 1998-March 1999   Pietro Berti/Paolo Bollini
April-Sept 1999   Antonello Baciocchi/Rosa Zafferani
Oct 1999-March 2000   Marino Bollini   (3rd)/Giuseppe Arzilli
April-Sept 2000   Maria Dominica Michelotti/Gian Marco Marcucci

Secretaries of State for Foreign Affairs:

The post of Prime Minister does not exist in San Marino, but the holders of the above office are often regarded as the most senior member of the government and are therefore listed here.

1860-1908   Domenico Fattori
1908-17   Menetto Bonelli
1917-Aug 1943   Giuliano Gozi
Aug 1943-45   Gustavo Babboni

1945-Oct 1957	Giordano Giacomini (CP) (deposed)
Oct 1957-Jan 1972	Federico Bigi (CDP)
Jan 1972-March 1973	Giancarlo Ghironzi (1st) (CDP)
March 1973-Nov 1975	Gian Berti (CDP)
(Nov 1975-March 1976	post vacant)
March 1976-July 1978	Giancarlo Ghironzi (2nd) (CDP)
July 1978-July 1986	Giordano Reffi (SP)
July 1986-	Gabriele Gatti (CDP)

CDP = Christian Democratic Party
CP = Communist Party
SP = Socialist Party

SÃO TOMÉ AND PRINCIPE

Official name: Democratic Republic of São Tomé and Principe, República Democratia de São Tomé e Principe
Independence date: 12 July 1975
Capital: São Tomé

São Tomé and Principe were discovered by the Portuguese in 1471 and proclaimed a Portuguese colony in 1522. In 1951 the status of the colony was changed to an overseas territory. The 1974 coup in Portugal began moves towards independence. A provisional government was formed at the end of 1974, and independence followed in 1975. A multi-party system was introduced in 1991.

Governors:

1899-1901	Amancio Cabral
1901-02	Joaquim de Brito
1902-03	João Guimarães
1903	José Ferreira (1st)
1903-07	Francisco de Paulo Cid (see Cape Verde)
1907-08	Pedro Berquo
1909-10	José da Fonseca
1910	Jaime do Rego (1st)
1910	Henrique de Oliveira
1910	Carlos Pimental e Melo
1910-11	António Guedes
1911	Jaime do Rego (2nd)
1911-13	Mariano Martins
1913-17	Pedro Machado
1917-18	Rafael Oliveira
1918-19	José Ferreira (2nd)
1919-20	Avelino Leite
1920-21	Eduardo de Lemos
1921-24	António Pereira
1924-26	Eugenio Branco
1926-28	José Rato
1928-29	Sebastião Barbosa
1929-33	Luis Fernandes
1933-41	Ricardo Monteiro
1941-45	Amadeu de Figueiredo (see Cape Verde)
1945-53	Carlos Gorgulho
1953-57	Francisco Barata
1957-63	Manuel Amaral (see Cape Verde)

1963-71   António Sebastião
1972-74   João Gonçalves
1974-75   António Veloso

Presidents:

July 1975-April 1991   Manuel Pinto da Costa   (MLSTP)
April 1991-Aug 1995   Miguel Trouvoada   (1st) (deposed)
15-17 April 1995   Manuel de Almeida   (junta leader)
17-22 Aug 1995   Francisco Pires   (acting)
Aug 1995-   Miguel Trouvoada   (2nd)

Prime Ministers:

Dec 1974-July 1975   Leonel d'Alva   (MLSTP)
July 1975-Feb 1979   Miguel Trouvoada   (MLSTP)
(Feb 1979-March 1980   post abolished)
March 1980-Jan 1988   Manuel Pinto da Costa   (MLSTP)
Jan 1988-Feb 1991   Celestina Rochas da Costa   (MLSTP)
Feb 1991-April 1992   Daniel Daio   (DCP)
May 1992-July 1994   Norberto Costa Alegre   (DCP)
July-Oct 1994   Evaristo Carvalho
Oct 1994-Aug 1995   Carlos da Graça   (1st) (MLSTP-SDP)
(15-22 Aug 1995   post vacant during coup attempt)
Aug-Dec 1995   Carlos da Graça   (2nd) (MLSTP-SDP)
Dec 1995-Nov 1996   Armindo Vaz de Almeida   (MLSTP-SDP)
Nov 1996-Jan 1999   Raul Bragança Neto   (MLSTP-SDP)
Jan 1999-   Guilherme Posser da Costa   (MLSTP-SDP)

DCP = Democratic Convergence Party
MLSTP = Movement for the Liberation of São Tomé and Principe (sole legal party until 1991)
MLSTP-SDP = MLSTP-Social Democractic Party (*f* MLSTP)

Autonomous Region

PRINCIPE

Capital: Santo António

President of Government:

April 1995-   Damião Vaz d'Almeida

SAUDI ARABIA

Official name: Kingdom of Saudi Arabia, Al-Mamlaka al-Arabiya as-Saudiya
State formed: 18 September 1932
Capital: Riyadh (Ar-Riyad)

The tribal domains of Nejd were united by the Wahhabis at the beginning of the 19th century. Neighbouring Hejaz was under the nominal rule of the Sharifan rulers of Mecca until the beginning of the 19th century when it came under the control of the Egyptian viceroy. From 1845 until the revolt of 1916 it was under Turkish rule. In 1925 Hejaz was taken over by Emir Abdul-Aziz of Nejd, who formally united the two states in 1932 to form Saudi Arabia.

Kings:

Sept 1932-Nov 1953	Abdul-Aziz bin Abdur-Rahman
Nov 1953-Nov 1964	Saud bin Abdul-Aziz (*son*) (abdicated)
Nov 1964-March 1975	Faisal bin Abdul-Aziz (*brother*) (assassinated)
March 1975-June 1982	Khalid bin Abdul-Aziz (*brother*)
June 1982-	Fahd bin Abdul-Aziz (*brother*)

Prime Ministers:

Oct 1953-Aug 1954	Saud bin Abdul-Aziz (1st)
Aug 1954-Dec 1960	Faisal bin Abdul-Aziz (1st)
Dec 1960-Oct 1962	Saud bin Abdul-Aziz (2nd)
Oct 1962-March 1975	Faisal bin Abdul-Aziz (2nd) (assassinated)
March 1975-June 1982	Khalid bin Abdul-Aziz
June 1982-	Fahd bin Abdul-Aziz

Pre-unification states

HEJAZ

Capital: Mecca

Kings:

June 1916-Oct 1924	Hussain bin Ali
Oct 1924-Dec 1925	Ali bin Hussain (*son*)
Dec 1925-Sept 1932	Abdul-Aziz bin Abdur-Rahman (Emir of Nejd)

NEJD

Capital: Riyadh

Emirs:

1803-14	Saud bin Abdul-Aziz
1814-18	Abdullah bin Saud (*son*)
1818-20	Mishari bin Saud (*brother*)
1821-34	Turki bin Abdullah (*nephew*)
1834-38	Faisal bin Turki (*son*) (1st)
1838-41	Khalid bin Saud
1841-43	Abdullah bin Thunaian
1843-65	Faisal bin Turki (2nd)
1865-April 1871	Abdullah bin Faisal (*son*) (1st)
April-Aug 1871	Saud bin Faisal (*brother*) (1st)
Aug 1871-Jan 1873	Abdullah bin Faisal (2nd)
Jan 1873-Jan 1875	Saud bin Faisal (2nd)
Jan 1875-86	Abdullah bin Faisal (3rd)
1886-97	Mohammed bin Rashid
1897-1901	Abdul-Aziz bin Mitab
1901-Sept 1932	Abdul-Aziz bin Abdur-Rahman

SENEGAL

Official name: Republic of Senegal, République du Sénégal
Independence date: 29 August 1960
Capital: Dakar

In 1659 the French established a trading town at St Louis at the mouth of the Senegal River. It was captured by the British during the Napoleonic Wars but returned to France in 1817. In 1854 the first French governor in Senegal was appointed and by 1890 the entire area was under French control. In 1895 all French territories in West Africa were combined into French West Africa, which had its headquarters in Senegal. Self-government was granted in 1958 and the following year Senegal and French Soudan formed the Federation of Mali. Senegal withdrew from the federation in 1960 and became independent. From 1982 until 1989 Senegal and the Gambia formed a confederation with each country retaining its sovereignty.

Lieutenant-Governors:

1902-08	Camille Guy
1908-09	Jules Gourbeil
1909-11	Jean Peuvergne
1911-14	Henri Cor
1914-16	Raphaël Antonetti (see St Pierre & Miquelon)
1916-21	Fernand Lévecque (see French Guiana)
1921-24	Pierre Didelot
1924-26	Camille Maillet
1926-29	Léonce Jore
1929-36	Maurice Beurnier
1936-37	Louis-Charles Lefèbre

Governors:

1937-38	Louis-Charles Lefèbre
1938-41	Georges-Hubert Parisot (see Gabon)
1941-43	Georges-Pierre Rey
1943-44	Hubert-Jules Deschamps
1944-45	Charles Dagain
1945-46	Pierre-Louis Maestracci
1946-47	Oswald Durand
1947-50	Laurent-Marcel Wiltord
1950-52	Camille-Victor Bailly (see French Somaliland)
1952-53	Lucien-Eugène Geay
1953-54	Daniel Goujon

1954-55	Maxime Jourdain
1955-57	Don-Jean Colombani
1957-58	Pierre Lami (see Ivory Coast)

High Commissioner:

1959-60	Pierre Lami

Presidents:

Aug 1960-Dec 1980	Léopold Senghor (SPU, SP)
Jan 1981-April 2000	Abdou Diouf (SP)
April 2000-	Abdoulaye Wade (SDP)

Prime Ministers:

July 1958-Dec 1962	Mamadou Dia
Dec 1962-March 1963	Léopold Senghor (SPU)
(March 1963-Feb 1970	post abolished)
Feb 1970-Jan 1981	Abdou Diouf
Jan 1981-April 1983	Habib Thiam (1st)
3-29 April 1983	Moustapha Niasse (1st)
(April 1983-April 1991	post abolished)
April 1991-July 1998	Habib Thiam (2nd)
July 1998-April 2000	Mamadou Lamine Loum
April 2000-	Moustapha Niasse (2nd)

SDP = Senegalese Democratic Party
SP = Socialist Party (f SPU)
SPU = Senegal Progressive Union

Former Federations

FRENCH WEST AFRICA

Capital: Dakar
Member states: Dahomey, French Guinea, French Soudan, Ivory Coast, Mauritania, Niger, Senegal, Upper Volta

Governors-General:

1895-1900	Jean Chaudie
1900-02	Noël Ballay
1902-08	Ernest-Nestor Roume
1908-16	Amédée Merlaud-Ponty
1916-17	Marie-François Clozel (see Ivory Coast)
1917-18	Joost van Vollenhoven (see French Guinea)

1918-19	Gabriel-Louis Angoulvant (see Ivory Coast)
1919-23	Martial-Henri Merlin (see Madagascar)
1923-30	Jules-Gaston Carde
1930-36	Jules Brevie (see Ivory Coast)
1936-40	Jules-Marcel de Coppet (see Mauritania)
1940	Léon Cayla (see Madagascar)

High Commissioners:

1940-43	Pierre-François Boisson (see French Equatorial Africa)
1943-46	Pierre Cournarie
1946-48	René Barthes
1948-51	Paul Bechard
1951-56	Bernard Cornut-Gentille (see French Equatorial Africa)
1956-58	Gaston Cusin

High Commissioner-General:

1958-60	Pierre Messmer (see French Equatorial Africa)

FEDERATION OF MALI

Capital: Dakar
Member states: French Soudan, Senegal

President:

April 1959-Aug 1960	Léopold Senghor

Prime Minister:

April 1959-Aug 1960	Modibo Keita

CONFEDERATION OF SENEGAMBIA

Capital: Dakar

President:

Nov 1982-Sept 1989	Abdou Diouf

SEYCHELLES

Official name: Republic of Seychelles
Independence date: 29 June 1976
Capital: Victoria

The Seychelles were visited by Arab and Persian traders in the Middle Ages and sighted by the Portuguese explorer Vasco da Gama in 1502. In 1742 they were explored by the French and claimed by them in 1756. In 1794 the islands were surrendered to Britain. British possession was confirmed in 1814, and the islands were administered from Mauritius. In 1903 Seychelles became a separate colony. Ministerial government was introduced in 1970, full self-government in 1975 and in 1976 Seychelles became independent.

Administrators:

1889-95	Thomas Griffith
1895-99	Henry Stewart
1899-1903	Ernest Sweet-Escott

Governors:

1903-04	Ernest Sweet-Escott
1904-12	Walter Davidson
1912-18	Charles O'Brien
1918-21	Eustace Twistleton-Wykeham-Fiennes
1922-27	Joseph Byrne
1927	Malcolm Stevenson
1928-34	DeSymons Honey
1934-36	Gordon Lethem
1936-42	Arthur Grimble (see St Vincent)
1942-47	William Logan
1947-51	Percy Selwyn-Clarke
1951-53	Frederick Crawford
1953-58	William Addis
1958-61	John Thorpe (see St Lucia)
1962-67	Earl of Oxford and Asquith (Julian Asquith) (see St Vincent)
1967-69	Hugh Norman-Walker (see Bechuanaland)
1969-73	Bruce Greatbach
1973-76	Colin Allan

Presidents:

June 1976-June 1977	James Mancham (SDP) (deposed)
June 1977-	F. Albert René (SPPF)

Chief Minister:

Nov 1970-June 1975   James Mancham   (SDP)

Prime Ministers:

June 1975-June 1976   James Mancham   (SDP)
June 1976-June 1977   F. Albert René   (SPUP)
(June 1977   post abolished)

SDP = Seychelles Democratic Party
SPPF = Seychelles People's Progressive Front (f SPUP) (sole legal party 1978-92)
SPUP = Seychelles People's United Party

SIERRA LEONE

Official name: Republic of Sierra Leone
Previous name: Dominion of Sierra Leone 1961-71
Independence date: 27 April 1961
Capital: Freetown

The coastal area of present-day Sierra Leone became British territory in 1787 as a home for freed African slaves. In 1896 a British protectorate was proclaimed over the hinterland. In 1958 self-government was granted and in 1961 Sierre Leone became independent. Ten years later a republic was proclaimed. Sierra Leone has experienced three periods of military rule, the most recent (1997-98) was ended by a Nigerian-led intervention force.

Governors:

1888-92	James Hay
1892-94	Francis Fleming
1894-1900	Frederick Carlew
1900-04	Charles King-Harman
1904-11	Leslie Probyn
1911-16	Edward Merewether
1916-22	Richard Wilkinson
1922-27	Alexander Slater
1927-31	Joseph Byrne
1931-34	Arnold Hodson
1934-37	Henry Moore
1937-41	Douglas Jardine
1941-48	Hubert Stevenson
1948-53	George Stooke
1953-56	Robert Hall
1956-61	Maurice Dorman

Governors-General:
Represented monarch who was concurrently British monarch

April 1961-May 1962	Maurice Dorman
May 1962-March 1967	Henry Boston
(March 1967-April 1968	post vacant during military rule)
April 1968-March 1971	Banja Tajan-Sie (acting)
March-April 1971	Christopher Okoro Cole (acting)

Presidents:
Chairman of the National Provisional Ruling Council May 1992-March 1996

Chairman of the Armed Forces Revolutionary Council May 1997-Feb 1998

19-21 April 1971	Christopher Okoro Cole (acting)
April 1971-Nov 1985	Siaka Stevens (APC)
Nov 1985-April 1992	Joseph Momoh (APC) (deposed)
May 1992-Jan 1996	Valentine Strasser (deposed)
Jan-March 1996	Julius Maada Bio
March 1996-May 1997	Ahmed Tejan Kabbah (1st) (SLPP) (deposed)
May 1997-Feb 1998	Johnny-Paul Koroma (deposed)
March 1998-	Ahmed Tejan Kabbah (2nd) (SLPP)

Chief Minister:

July 1954-July 1958	Milton Margai (SLPP)

Prime Ministers:

July 1958-April 1964	Milton Margai (SLPP) (†)
April 1964-March 1967	Albert Margai (*brother*) (SLPP)
21 March 1967	Siaka Stevens (1st) (APC) (deposed)

Military Rulers:

Chairman of the National Redemption Council March 1967-April 1968
Chairman of the National Interim Council April 1968

21-23 March 1967	David Lansana (deposed)
23-27 March 1967	Ambrose Genda (nominal, overseas)
March 1967-April 1968	Andrew Juxon-Smith (deposed)
18-26 April 1968	Patrick Conteh

Prime Ministers:

April 1968-April 1971	Siaka Stevens (2nd) (APC)
April 1971-July 1975	Sorie Koroma
July 1975-June 1978	Christian Kamara-Taylor
(June 1978	post abolished)

Chief Secretaries of State:

July-Dec 1992	John Benjamin
Dec 1992-July 1993	Solomon Musa (1st)
July 1993-March 1995	Julius Maada Bio
March 1995-March 1996	Akim Gibril
(March 1996-July 1997	post abolished)
July 1997-Feb 1998	Solomon Musa (2nd)
(Feb 1998	post abolished)

APC = All People's Congress (sole legal party 1978-91)
SLPP = Sierra Leone People's Party

SINGAPORE

Official name: Republic of Singapore, Republik Singapura (Malay), Sing-ka-poh Kung-woh-kwok (Chinese)

Previous name: State of Singapore 1959-65

Independence date: 9 August 1965

Capital: Singapore

The original town on the island of Singapore was destroyed in the 14th century by the Javanese Hindu empire. Singapore later became the property of the Sultan of Johore, who gave it to the British scholar Alexander Hamilton in 1703. In 1819 Thomas Raffles established a port for British trade, and in 1824 the island formally became British, forming part of the Straits Settlements from 1826. Singapore was occupied by Japan from 1942 until 1945. In 1946 it became a separate colony; ministerial government was introduced in 1955 and full self-government was granted in 1959. In 1963 Singapore joined the Federation of Malaysia, but left in 1965 to become a sovereign republic.

Governors:

1946-52	Franklin Gimson
1952-55	John Nicoll
1955-57	Robert (Robin) Black
1957-59	William Goode

Heads of State:

June-Dec 1959	William Goode
Dec 1959-Aug 1965	Yusof bin Ishak

Presidents:

Aug 1965-Nov 1970	Yusof bin Ishak (†)
Nov 1970-Jan 1971	Yeoh Ghim Seng (acting) (1st)
Jan 1971-May 1981	Benjamin Sheares (†)
May-Oct 1981	Yeoh Ghim Seng (acting) (2nd)
Oct 1981-March 1985	C.V.Devan Nair
28-30 March 1985	Wee Chong Jin (acting)
March-Sept 1985	Yeoh Ghim Seng (acting) (3rd)
Sept 1985-Sept 1993	Wee Kim Wee
Sept 1993-Sept 1999	Ong Tong Cheong
Sept 1999-	Sellapan Nathan

Chief Ministers:

April 1955-June 1956	David Marshall	(LF)
June 1956-June 1959	Lim Yew Hock	(LF)

Prime Ministers:

June 1959-Nov 1990	Lee Kuan Yew	(PAP)
Nov 1990-	Goh Chok Tong	(PAP)

LF = Labour Front
PAP = People's Action Party

SLOVAKIA

Official name: Slovak Republic, Slovenská Republika
Previous names: Slovak Autonomous Region (1945-60), Slovak Socialist Republic (1969-90)
Independence dates: 14 March 1939, 1 January 1993
Capital: Bratislava

Slovakia was part of the Austro-Hungarian Empire until 1918 when it became part of the new nation of Czechoslovakia. During the Second World War, it was an independent puppet state of Germany, but after liberation again formed part of Czechoslovakia. Under the communist regime there, it was given a measure of autonomy, and in 1969 gained republic status in the new federal arrangement. After the fall of communism in 1989, differences between the Czech and Slovak republics led to the dissolution of the federation at the end of 1992, and the birth of an independent Slovakia.

Presidents:

March 1939-April 1945	Jozef Tiso (executed 1947)
(April 1945	post abolished)
March 1993-March 1998	Michal Kovač
(March 1998-June 1999	post vacant)
June 1999-	Rudolf Schuster

Prime Ministers:

Chairman of the Board of Commissioners 1945-60

Dec 1938-March 1939	Jozef Tiso (1st)
12-13 March 1939	Karol Sidor
March-Oct 1939	Jozef Tiso (2nd)
Oct 1939-Sept 1944	Vojtech Tuka (executed 1946)
Sept 1944-March 1945	Stefan Tiso (*nephew of J.Tiso*)
April 1945-Nov 1947	Karel Šmidke
Nov 1947-May 1950	Gustáv Husák
May 1950-Jan 1953	Karel Bačilek
Jan 1953-April 1960	Rudolf Strechaj
(April 1960	post abolished)
Jan-May 1969	Stefan Sadovsky
May 1969-Oct 1988	Peter Colotka
Oct 1988-June 1989	Iván Knolek
June-Dec 1989	Pavel Hrivnak
Dec 1989-June 1990	Milán Čič
June 1990-April 1991	Vladimir Mečiar (1st) (PAV)
April 1991-June 1992	Ján Čarnogurský (CDM)

June 1992-March 1994	Vladimir Mečiar	(2nd) (MDS)
March-Dec 1994	Jozef Moravčik	
Dec 1994-Oct 1998	Vladimir Mečiar	(3rd) (MDS)
Oct 1998-	Mikulas Dzurinda	(SDC)

CDM = Christian Democratic Movement
MDS = Movement for a Democratic Slovakia
PAV = Public Against Violence
SDC = Social Democratic Coalition

Communist Party Leaders:
First Secretary

Sept 1953-63	Karel Bačilek
1963-Aug 1968	Alexander Dubček
Aug 1968-May 1969	Gustav Husák
May 1969-Jan 1970	Stefan Sadovsky
Jan 1970-April 1988	Jozef Lénart (see Czechoslovakia)
April 1988-Dec 1989	Ignac Janak
(Dec 1989	Party relinquished leading role)

SLOVENIA

Official name: Republic of Slovenia, Republika Slovenija
Previous name: Socialist Republic of Slovenia 1945-90 (as part of Yugoslavia)
Independence date: 25 June 1991
Capital: Ljubljana

Slovenia was part of the Austria-Hungary Empire until 1918 when it became part of the new state of Yugoslavia. In 1945 when a communist republic was proclaimed Slovenia gained autonomy as a republic within the federation. In 1990 multi-party elections were held and a non-communist government took office. Slovenia declared itself independent the following year.

Presidents:
President of the People's Assembly 1945-74
President of the State Presidency since 1974

1945-53	Josep Vidmar
1953-62	Miha Marinho
1962-63	Vida Tomsić
1963-65	Viktor Avbelj (1st)
1965-67	Ivan Maček
1967-73	Sergij Krajgher (1st)
1973-74	Tone Krapušek
May 1974-May 1979	Sergej Krajgher (2nd)
May 1979-May 1984	Viktor Avbelj (2nd)
May 1984-May 1988	France Popit
May 1988-Dec 1989	Janez Stanovnik
Dec 1989-	Milan Kučan

Prime Ministers:
President of the Executive Council

May 1945-46	Boris Kidrić
1946-53	Miha Marinko
1953-62	Boris Krajgher
1962-65	Viktor Avbelj
1965-67	Janko Smole
1967-Oct 1972	Stane Kavčić
Nov 1972-April 1978	Andrej Marinć
April 1982-July 1980	Anton Vratusa
July 1980-May 1984	Janez Zemljarić
May 1984-May 1990	Dušan Sinigoj

May 1990-April 1992   Lojze Peterle   (CDP)
April 1992-   Janez Drnovsek   (LDP) (see Yugoslavia)

CDP = Christian Democratic Party
LDP = Liberal Democratic Party

Communist Party Leaders:

1945-46	Boris Kidrić
1946-66	Miha Marinko
1966-68	Albert Jakopič
1968-April 1982	France Popit
April 1982-May 1986	Andrej Marinč
May 1986-Dec 1989	Milan Kučan
Dec 1989-May 1990	Ciril Ribičić
(May 1990	non-communist government elected)

SOLOMON ISLANDS

Official name: Solomon Islands
Previous name: British Solomon Islands 1893-1978
Independence date: 7 July 1978
Capital: Honiara

The Solomon Islands were visited by the Portuguese in 1568, and by the French in the 18th century. However they were not colonized until the late 19th century, when Britain and Germany delimited spheres of influence. The northern islands became German and most are now part of Papua New Guinea; the southern islands were proclaimed a British protectorate in 1893. The islands were occupied by Japan from 1942 to 1944. In 1974 the territory's first chief minister was appointed, with full self-government following in 1976. In 1978 independence was granted.

Commissioners:
(Also High Commissioner for the Western Pacific from 1953)

1886-1915	Charles Woodford
1915-17	Frederick Barnett
1917-21	Charles Workman
1921-29	Richard Kane
1929-39	Francis Ashley
1939-42	William Marchant
(1942-45	Japanese occupation)
1945-50	Owen Noel
1950-53	Henry Gregory-Smith
1953-55	Robert Stanley
1955-61	John Gutch
1961-64	David Trench
1964-68	Robert Foster
1969-73	Michael Gass

Governors:

1973-76	Donald Luddington
1976-78	Colin Allen

Governors-General:
Represent monarch who is concurrently British monarch

July 1978-July 1988	Baddeley Devesi
July 1988-June 1994	George Lepping
June 1994-July 1999	Moses Pitakaka

July 1999-   John Lapli

Chief Ministers:

Aug 1974-July 1976   Solomon Mamaloni
July 1976-July 1978   Peter Kenilorea   (SIUP)

Prime Ministers:

July 1978-Sept 1981   Peter Kenilorea   (1st) (SIUP)
Sept 1981-Nov 1984   Solomon Mamaloni   (1st) (PAP)
Nov 1984-Dec 1986   Peter Kenilorea   (2nd) (SIUP)
Dec 1986-March 1989   Ezekial Alebua   (SIUP)
March 1989-June 1993   Solomon Mamaloni   (2nd) (PAP)
June 1993-Nov 1994   Francis Billy Hilly
Nov 1994-Aug 1997   Solomon Mamaloni   (3rd) (SINURPP)
Aug 1997-   Bartholomew Ulufa'alu   (LP)

LP = Liberal Party
PAP = People's Alliance Party
SINURPP = Solomon Islands National Unity, Reconciliation and Progress Party
SIUP = Solomon Islands United Party

Provinces

At the time of going to press, only one complete list and the names of other current **Premiers** and some immediate predecessors were available. Capitals are given in brackets.

CENTRAL PROVINCE

Capital: Tulagi

 ? -1998   Peter Manetiva
1998-   Mark Kemakeza

CHOISEUL

Capital: Taro

 ? -1999   Clement Kengava
1999-   Jackson Kiloe

GUADALCANAL

Capital: Honiara

 ? -1998   Siriako Usa
1998-   Ezekial Alebua

ISABEL

Capital: Buala

1981-84	Culwick Vahia
1985-88	Jason Leguhavi
1989-90	Clement Rojumana
1990-92	Philip Manehatha
1993-94	Stanley Vunagi
1994-96	Amos Gigini
1997-98	Joseph Hiro
1998-	Jacob Pitu

MAKIRA & ULAWA

Capital: KiraKira

?-?	Daniel Nahusu

MALAITA

Capital: Auki

?-?	David Oeta

RENNELL & BELLONA

Capital: Tigoa

? -1999	Ajalan Nasiu
1999-	Francia Taupongi

TEMOTU

Capital: Lata

? -1999	John Lapli
1999-	Gabriel Teao

WESTERN PROVINCE

Capital: Gizo

? -1999	Clement Base
1999-	Ruben Lilo

SOMALIA

Official name: Somali Democratic Republic, Al-Jamhuriya as-Somaliya al-Democradia
Previous names: Italian Somalia until 1943, Somalia 1943-60, Somali Republic 1960-69
Independence date: 1 July 1960
Capital: Mogadishu

Italian interest in Somalia began in 1885 and in 1905 it became a colony. In 1940 Italian forces occupied British Somaliland, but a year later they were driven out and Britain occupied all of Somalia. In 1950 the occupied area was returned to Italy under United Nations trusteeship. In 1956 Italy granted self-government, and in 1960 both the Italian and British areas were granted independence and they united into a single state. During the 1980s various rebel groups began fighting the government culminating in its collapse in 1991. This was followed soon after by the proclamation of an independent state in the former British colony. After the 1991 coup, the country entered a period of anarchy with the government in Mogadishu exerting very little authority. United Nations forces entered the country to restore order, but withdrew in 1994. No effective government was in place.

Governors:

1893-97	Vincenzo Filonardi
1897-1903	Emilio Dulio
1903-05	Alessandro Sapelli (1st)
1905-06	Luigi Mercatelli
1906	Alessandro Sapelli (2nd)
1906-07	Giovanni Cerrina-Feroni (1st)
1907-08	Tommaso Carletti
1908-10	Gino Macchioro
1910-16	Nobile de Martino
1916-20	Giovanni Cerrina-Feroni (2nd)
1920-23	Carlo Riveri
1923-28	Cesare de Val Cismon
1928-31	Guido Corni
1931-35	Maurizio Rava
1935-36	Rodolfo Graziani
1936-37	Ruggiero Sanlini
1937-40	Francesco Caroselli
1940-41	Carlo De Simone
1941	Reginald Smith
1941-43	William Scupham
1943-48	Denis Wickham
1948	Eric de Candole

1948-50   Geoffrey Gamble

Administrators:

1950-53   Giovanni Fornani
1953-55   Enrico Martino
1955-58   Enrico Anzilotti
1958-60   Mario de Stefani

Presidents:
President of the Supreme Revolutionary Council 1969-76

July 1960-June 1967   Aden Abdullah Osman
June 1967-Oct 1969   Abdirashid Shermarke   († assassinated)
15-21 Oct 1969   Mukhtar Hussain   (acting) (deposed)
Oct 1969-Jan 1991   Mohammed Siyad Barreh   (SRSP) (deposed)
Jan 1991-   Ali Mahdi Mohammed   (*after late 1991 authority limited to north Mogadishu*)
June 1995-Aug 1996   Mohammed Farrah Aideed   (*rival president in south Mogadishu*) (†)
Aug 1996-   Hussein Mohammed Aideed   (*son*) (*in south Mogadishu*)

Prime Ministers:
Chairman of the Council of Ministers 1976-87

March 1956-July 1960   Abdullah Issa
July 1960-July 1964   Abdirashid Shermarke   (SYL)
July 1964-July 1967   Abdirizak Hussain   (SYL)
July 1967-Oct 1969   Mohammed Egal   (see Somaliland) (deposed)
(Oct 1969-July 1976   post abolished)
July 1976-Feb 1987   Mohammed Siyad Barreh
Feb 1987-Sept 1990   Mohammed Ali Samatar
Sept 1990-Jan 1991   Mohammed Hawadle Madar
Jan 1991-May 1993   Omar Arteh Ghalib   (*no effective role from late 1991*)
(May 1993-   post vacant)

SRSP = Somali Revolutionary Socialist Party (sole legal party 1976-91)
SYL = Somali Youth League

Self-declared Autonomous States

BAY

Capital: Baidoa

Governor:

Dec 1999-   Mohammed Ali Aden Qalineh

PUNTLAND

Capital: Garoe

President:

July 1998-   Ahmed Abdullahi Yusuf

Secessionist state

SOMALILAND

Official name: Republic of Somaliland
Previous name: Somaliland Protectorate (British Somaliland) until 1960
Independence dates: 26 June 1960, 21 May 1991 (not internationally recognised)
Capital: Hargeisa

Governors:

1919-22	Geoffrey Archer
1922-26	Gerald Summers
1926-32	Harold Kittermaster
1932-39	Arthur Lawrance
1939-41	Vincent Glenday
1941-43	Arthur Chater
1943-48	Gerald Fisher
1948-54	Gerald Reece
1954-59	Theodore Pike
1959-60	Douglas Hall
(1960-91	part of Somalia)

Presidents:

May 1991-May 1993	Abdul-Rahman Ahmed Ali Tur
May 1993-	Mohammed Egal

Prime Minister:

Jan-July 1960	Mohammed Egal
(July 1960	post abolished)

SOUTH AFRICA

Official name: Republic of South Africa
Previous name: Union of South Africa 1910-61
Independence date: 31 May 1910
Capitals: Pretoria (administrative), Cape Town (legislative)

In 1652 the Dutch established a settlement at the Cape. This was surrendered to the British in 1795. After a brief return to Dutch rule the Cape was again occupied by Britain, and formally became a colony in 1814. European settlements spread out from the Cape and southern black tribes were brought under British rule. In the east the Zulu kingdom emerged in the early part of the 19th century. Descendents of the Dutch settlers established a republic in Natal in 1839, but this was occupied by Britain in 1843, becoming a colony in 1856. The Dutch-speaking Boers then moved north and founded republics in the Transvaal and Orange Free State. In 1887 Zululand was annexed by Britain and incorporated into Natal in 1897. Hostilities between Britain and the two republics broke out twice and after the second war the republics became British colonies in 1902. In 1910 the four colonies joined to form the Union of South Africa, which became a republic in 1961. Government remained in the hands of the whites through the policy of apartheid, with designated black areas called national states (homelands) obtaining self-government. Moves away from apartheid began in 1990 and led to democratic elections in 1994.

Governors-General:
Represented monarch who was concurrently British monarch

May 1910-Sept 1914	Viscount Gladstone (Herbert Gladstone)
Sept 1914-June 1920	Viscount Buxton (Sydney Buxton)
June-Nov 1920	James Rose Innes (acting)
Nov 1920-Jan 1924	Prince Arthur, Duke of Connaught (see Canada)
Jan 1924-Nov 1930	Prince Alexander of Teck, Earl of Athlone (see Canada)
Nov 1930-Jan 1931	Jacob de Villiers (acting)
Jan 1931-March 1937	Earl of Clarendon (George Hyde)
March-April 1937	John Curlewis (acting)
April 1937-July 1943	Patrick Duncan (†)
July 1943-Dec 1945	Nicolaas de Wet (acting)
Dec 1945-Dec 1950	Gideon Brand van Zyl (see Cape Province)
Jan 1951-Nov 1959	Ernest Jansen (†)
Nov 1959-Jan 1960	Lucas Steyn (acting) (1st)
Jan 1960-May 1961	Charles Swart
1-31 May 1961	Lucas Steyn (acting) (2nd)

Presidents:

State President

May 1961-May 1967	Charles Swart
(1967	T.Ebenhezer Dönges, President-elect; did not assume office due to illness)
May 1967-April 1968	Jozua (Tom) Naudé (acting)
April 1968-April 1975	Jacobus (Jim) Fouché (see Orange Free State)
10-19 April 1975	Jan de Klerk (acting)
April 1975-Aug 1978	Nicolaas Diederichs (†)
Aug-Oct 1978	Marais Viljoen (acting)
Oct 1978-June 1979	B.Johannes Vorster
June 1979-Sept 1984	Marais Viljoen (acting 4-19 June 1979)
Sept 1984-Aug 1989	Pieter Botha (acting 5-14 Sept 1984) (NP)
Aug 1989-May 1994	Frederik de Klerk (*son of J.de Klerk*) (acting Aug-Sept 1989) (NP)
May 1994-June 1999	Nelson Mandela (ANC)
June 1999-	Thabo Mbeki (ANC)

Prime Ministers:

May 1910-Aug 1919	Louis Botha (see Transvaal) (SAP) (†)
Aug 1919-April 1924	Jan Smuts (1st) (SAP)
April 1924-Sept 1939	James Barry Hertzog (NP,UP)
Sept 1939-June 1948	Jan Smuts (2nd) (UP)
June 1948-Nov 1954	Daniel Malan (NP)
Nov 1954-Aug 1958	Johannes Strijdom (NP) (†)
Aug-Sept 1958	Charles Swart (acting)
Sept 1958-Sept 1966	Hendrik Verwoerd (NP) († assassinated)
6-13 Sept 1966	T.Ebenhezer Dönges (acting)
Sept 1966-Sept 1978	B.Johannes Vorster (NP)
Sept 1978-Sept 1984	Pieter Botha (NP)
(Sept 1984	post abolished)

Chairmen of Ministers' Councils:

a. White

Sept-Dec 1984	Sarel Hayward (acting) (1st)
Dec 1984-April 1985	Cornelius (Nak) van der Merwe (NP) (†)
April-July 1985	Sarel Hayward (acting) (2nd)
July 1985-Sept 1989	Frederik de Klerk (NP)
Sept 1989-Jan 1992	Jacobus (Kobie) Coetsee (NP)
Jan 1992-March 1993	Magnus Malan (NP)
March 1993-March 1994	Adriaan Vlok (NP)
(March 1994	post abolished)

b. Coloured

Sept 1984-Feb 1992	Helenand (Allan) Hendrickse (LP)
Feb 1992-March 1994	Jakobus (Jac) Rabie (NP)
(March 1994	post abolished)

c. Indian

Sept 1984-Jan 1989	Amichand Rajbansi (NPP)
Jan-March 1989	Kassipershad Ramduth (acting)
March 1989-Feb 1993	Jayaram Reddy (S)
Feb 1993-March 1994	Bhadra Ramchod (NP)
(March 1994	post abolished)

ANC = African National Congress
LP = Labour Party
NP = National Party
NPP = National People's Party
SAP = South African Party
S = Solidarity
UP = United Party

Provinces until 1994

CAPE PROVINCE

Previous name: Cape of Good Hope (until 1910)
Capital: Cape Town

Governors:

1900-01	Viscount Milner (Alfred Milner)
1901-10	Walter Hely-Hutchinson (see Natal)

Prime Ministers:

Dec 1871-Feb 1878	John Molteno
Feb 1878-May 1881	Gordon Sprigg (1st)
May 1881-May 1884	Thomas Scanlen
May 1884-Nov 1886	Thomas Upington
Nov 1886-July 1890	Gordon Sprigg (2nd)
July 1890-Jan 1896	Cecil Rhodes
Jan 1896-Oct 1898	Gordon Sprigg (3rd)
Oct 1898-June 1900	William Schreiner
June 1900-Feb 1904	Gordon Sprigg (4th)
Feb 1904-Feb 1908	Leander Starr Jameson (PP)
Feb 1908-May 1910	John X. Merriman

PP = Progressive Party

Administrators:

May 1910-Dec 1925	N.Frederik de Waal
Jan 1926-Aug 1929	Adriaan Fourie
Sept 1929-Sept 1939	Johannes Conradie
Sept 1939-Sept 1942	François Joubert (†)
Oct 1942-Dec 1945	Gideon Brand van Zyl
Jan-July 1946	Philippus Myburgh (†)
July 1946-July 1951	Johan Carinus
Aug 1951-March 1958	Philippus Olivier (†)
March-May 1958	Jan Terblanche (acting)
May 1958-April 1960	Josias du Plessis (†)
April 1960-May 1970	J.Nicolaas Malan (acting April-May 1960)
June 1970-May 1975	Andries Vosloo
June 1975-June 1979	Lourens Munnik
June 1979-July 1989	Eugene Louw
July 1989-May 1994	Jacobus Meiring

(Divided between Eastern Cape, Northern Cape, Western Cape and North West Provinces)

NATAL

Capital: Pietermaritzburg

Governors:

1880-81	George Colley
1881-82	Charles Mitchell (1st)
1881-85	Henry Bulwer
1885-89	Arthur Havelock
1889-93	Charles Mitchell (2nd)
1893-1901	Walter Hely-Hutchinson
1901-07	Henry McCallum
1907-09	Matthew Nathan
1909-10	Baron Methuen (Paul Methuen)

Prime Ministers:

Oct 1893-Feb 1897	John Robinson
Feb-Oct 1897	Harry Escombe
Oct 1897-June 1899	Henry Binns (†)
June 1899-Aug 1903	Albert Hime
Aug 1903-May 1905	George Sutton
May 1905-Nov 1906	Charles Smythe
Nov 1906-May 1910	Frederick Moor

Administrators:

May 1910-Jan 1918	Charles Smythe
Feb 1918-Jan 1928	George Plowman
Feb 1928-Jan 1943	Herbert Watson
Feb 1943-Nov 1944	George Nicholls
Nov 1944-Feb 1948	Douglas Mitchell
Feb 1948-May 1958	Denis Shepstone
June 1958-Nov 1961	Alfred Trollip
Nov 1961-Aug 1970	Theodor Gerdener
Aug 1970-June 1979	Benjamin Havemann
June-Aug 1979	Frank Martin (acting) (1st)
Aug 1979-Sept 1984	J.Christoffel Botha
Sept-Nov 1984	Frank Martin (acting) (2nd)
Nov 1984-April 1990	Radclyffe Cadman
April 1990-May 1994	Cornelius (Con) Botha

Recombined with KwaZulu to form KwaZulu-Natal

ORANGE FREE STATE

Previous name: Orange River Colony 1902-10
Capital: Bloemfontein

Presidents:

Feb 1854-Feb 1855	Josias Hoffman (acting Feb-Aug 1854)
Feb-Aug 1855	Jacobus Venter (acting) (1st)
Aug 1855-June 1859	Jacobus Boshof
June 1859-Feb 1860	Esaias Snyman (acting)
Feb 1860-April 1863	Marthinus Pretorius (also President of Transvaal)
April 1863-Feb 1864	Jacobus Venter (acting) (2nd)
Feb 1864-July 1888	Johannes Brand (†)
Aug 1888-Jan 1889	Pieter Blignaut (acting)
Jan 1889-Feb 1896	Francis Reitz
Feb 1896-May 1902	Marthinus Steyn
29-31 May 1902	Christian de Wet (acting)

Governors:

1902-05	Viscount Milner (Alfred Milner) (see Cape of Good Hope)
1905-07	Earl of Selborne (William Palmer)
1907-10	Hamilton Goold-Adams

Prime Minister:

Nov 1907-May 1910	Abraham Fischer (OU)

OU = Orangia Unie

Administrators:

May 1910-May 1915	Alfred Ramsbottom
May 1915-March 1924	Cornelis Wessels (†)
March 1924-March 1929	Esaias Grobler
March 1929-Nov 1936	Carl Wilcocks (†)
Nov-Dec 1936	Johannes Buys (acting)
Dec 1936-Dec 1940	Johannes van Rensburg
Dec 1940-Dec 1950	Stephanus Barnard
Jan 1951-Dec 1959	Jacobus (Jim) Fouché
Dec 1959-Dec 1969	Johannes du Plessis
Dec 1969-Dec 1974	Gabriel Froneman
Dec 1974-Nov 1980	Abraham van Wyk
Nov 1980-Aug 1991	Louis Botha
Aug 1991-May 1994	Louis van der Watt

TRANSVAAL

Previous name: South African Republic (1857-77 & 1880-1902)
Capital: Potchefstroom (1857-60), Pretoria (after 1867)

Presidents:

Jan 1857-Sept 1860	Marthinus Pretorius (1st) (also President of Orange Free State)
Sept-Oct 1860	J.H.Grobbelaar (acting)
Oct 1860-April 1862	Stephanus Schoeman (acting)
April 1862-May 1864	Willem Janse van Rensburg (acting April 1862-Oct 1863)
May 1864-Nov 1871	Marthinus Pretorius (2nd)
Nov 1871-July 1872	Daniel Erasmus (acting)
July 1872-April 1877	Thomas Burgers
(April 1877-Dec 1880	British occupation)
(Dec 1880-April 1883	Presidential council: Marthinus Pretorius/S.J.Paulus Kruger/Petrus Joubert)
April 1883-Oct 1900	S.J.Paulus Kruger
Oct 1900-May 1902	Schalk Burger (acting)

Governors:

1902-05	Viscount Milner (Alfred Milner) (Gov of Orange River Colony)
1905-10	Earl of Selborne (William Palmer) (Gov of Orange River Colony)

Prime Minister:

Feb 1907-May 1910	Louis Botha (HV)

HV = Het Volk

Administrators:

May 1910-July 1917	Johann Rissik
July 1917-Feb 1924	Alfred Robinson
March 1924-Feb 1929	Jan Hofmeyr
March 1929-Feb 1934	Jacobus Smit
March 1934-July 1938	Simon Bekker (†)
Sept 1938-Aug 1948	J.Jacobus Pienaar
Nov 1948-Oct 1958	Willem Nicol
Nov 1958-Feb 1966	Frans Odendaal (†)
Feb 1966-July 1979	Sybrand van Niekerk
July 1979-May 1988	Willem Cruywagen
June 1988-May 1994	Daniel Hough (see South West Africa)

Divided between Gauteng, Mpumalanga, Northern Province, and North West Province

Former independent states

GOSHEN REPUBLIC

Capital: Rooigrond

Head of State:

Chairman of the Executive Council 1882-84
Administrator 1884-85

Jan 1882-Jan 1885   Nicolaas Gey van Pittius

In March 1885 Goshen became part of the Cape of Good Hope

NEW REPUBLIC

Capital: Vryheid

President:

Aug 1884-July 1888   Lucas Meyer

In 1888 the New Republic joined the Transvaal, but was incorporated into Natal in 1900.

STELLALAND

Capital: Vryburg

Administrator:

Aug 1883-Feb 1885   Gerrit van Niekerk

In 1885 Stellaland was incorporated into Bechuanaland, but it was transferred to the Cape of Good Hope in 1895.

ZULULAND
KwaZulu

Kings:

1816-Sept 1828	Shaka (assassinated)
Dec 1828-Feb 1840	Dingane (*half-brother*) (deposed, assassinated)
Feb 1840-Oct 1872	Mpande (*half-brother*)
Sept 1873-July 1879	Cetshwayo (*son*) (1st) (deposed)
(July 1879-Jan 1883	British occupation)
Jan 1883-Feb 1884	Cetshwayo (2nd)
(Feb-May 1884	Regents: Mnyamana/Ndabuko
May 1884-June 1887	Dinuzulu (*son*) (deposed)

Prime Ministers:
Chief in Duna

1816-28	Ngomane
(Sept-Dec 1828	Mbopha - in charge of administration)
June 1829-Jan 1840	Ndhlela (executed)
1840-Aug 1873	Masipula
1873-July 1879	Mnyamana (1st)
(July 1879-Jan 1883	British occupation)
Jan 1883-Feb 1884	Mnyamana (2nd)
1884-87	Mankulumana

In 1887 Zululand was annexed by Britain and incorporated into Natal in Dec 1897.

Former National States (Homelands)

Ten self-governing territories for different black ethnic groups were established as part of the policy of apartheid. Four of these were granted independence, but they did not receive international recognition. In 1994 these four states were re-incorporated into South Africa, and all were absorbed into the new provinces.

BOPHUTHATSWANA

Republic of Bophuthatswana 1977-94
Independence date: 6 December 1977
Capital: Mmabatho

President:

Dec 1977-March 1994	Lucas Mangope (BDP, CDP) (deposed)
(10 Feb 1988	Rocky Malebane-Metsing – self-declared president during brief coup attempt)

Administrators:

March-April 1994　　　　　Tjaart van der Walt/Job Mokgoro

Chief Councillor:

Dec 1968-June 1972　　　　Lucas Mangope

Chief Minister:

June 1972-Dec 1977　　　　Lucas Mangope　　(BNP, BDP)
(Dec 1977　　　　　　　　post abolished)

CDP = Christian Democratic Party (f BDP)
BDP = Bophuthatswana Democratic Party (f BNP)
BNP = Bophuthatswana National Party

Mostly incorporated into North West Province, with smaller areas joining Free State and Northern Cape

CISKEI

Republic of Ciskei 1981-94
Independence date: 4 December 1981
Capital: Zwelitsha (until 1981), Bisho

Presidents:

Chairman of the Council of State 1990-94

Dec 1981-March 1990　　　Lennox Sebe　　(CNP) (deposed)
March 1990-March 1994　　Oupa Gqozo

Administrators:

March-April 1994　　　　　Pieter Goosen/Bongani Finca

Chief Councillor:

Nov 1968-Oct 1972　　　　Justice Mabandla

Chief Ministers:

Oct 1972-May 1973　　　　Justice Mabandla　　(CNP)
May 1973-Dec 1981　　　　Lennox Sebe　　(CNIP)
(Dec 1981　　　　　　　　post abolished)

CNIP = Ciskei National Independence Party
CNP = Ciskei National Party

Became part of Eastern Cape

GAZANKULU

Capital: Giyani

Chief Councillor:

Oct 1969-Feb 1973   Hudson Ntsanwise

Chief Ministers:

Feb 1973-March 1993   Hudson Ntsanwise   (XPP) (†)
March-April 1993   Edward Mhinga   (acting)
April 1993-April 1994   Samuel Nxumalo   (XPP)

XPP = Ximoko Progressive Party

Became part of Northern Province

KANGWANE

Capital: Louieville

Chief Councillor:

Oct 1977-June 1982   Enos Mabuza   (1st)
(June-Dec 1982   post abolished)
Dec 1982-Aug 1984   Enos Mabuza   (2nd)

Chief Ministers:

Aug 1984-April 1991   Enos Mabuza
April 1991-April 1994   M.Cephas Zitha

Became part of Mpumalanga

KWANDEBELE

Capital: Siyabuswa (until 1986), KwaMhlanga

Chief Councillor:

Nov 1977-April 1981   Simon Skosana

Chief Ministers:

April 1981-Nov 1986   Simon Skosana   (†)
17-27 Nov 1986   Klaas Mtshweni   (acting)
Nov 1986-Feb 1989   G.Majozi Mahlangu
Feb 1989-April 1990   Jonas Mabhena

| April 1990-April 1994 | Prince James Mahlangu |

Became part of Mpumalanga

KWAZULU

Capital: Ulundi

Chief Councillor:

| April 1972-Feb 1977 | Mangosuthu Buthelezi | (*grandson of Mnyamana, Zululand PM*) |

Chief Minister:

| Feb 1977-April 1994 | Mangosuthu Buthelezi | (IFP) |

IFP = Inkatha Freedom Party

Became part of KwaZulu-Natal

LEBOWA

Capital: Lebowakgomo

Chief Councillor:

| Aug 1969-Oct 1972 | Makgoma Matlala |

Chief Ministers:

Oct 1972-May 1973	Makgoma Matlala	(LNP)
May 1973-Oct 1987	Cedric Phatudi	(LPP) (†)
7-21 Oct 1987	Z.T.Seleki	(acting)
Oct 1987-April 1994	Nelson Ramodike	(LPP)

LNP = Lebowa National Party
LPP = Lebowa People's Party

Became part of Northern Province

QWAQWA

Capital: Phuthaditjhaba

Chief Councillor:

| April 1969-Nov 1974 | Wessels Mota |

Chief Ministers:

| Nov 1974-March 1975 | Wessels Mota | (BUP) |

March 1975-April 1994   T.Kenneth Mopeli   (DP)

BUP = Basuto Unity Party
DP = Dikwankwetla Party

Became part of Free State

TRANSKEI

Republic of Transkei 1976-94
Independence date: 26 October 1976
Capital: Umtata

Presidents:

Oct 1976-Dec 1978	Botha Sigcau (†)
Dec 1978-Feb 1979	Zwelibanzi Mabandla (acting)
Feb 1979-Feb 1986	Kaiser Matanzima
Feb 1986-April 1994	Tutor Ndamase

Chief Councillor:

1961-Nov 1963   Kaiser Matanzima

Chief Minister:

Nov 1963-Oct 1976   Kaiser Matanzima   (TNIP)

Prime Ministers:

Oct 1976-Feb 1979	Kaiser Matanzima (TNIP)
Feb 1979-Oct 1987	George Matanzima (*brother*) (TNIP)
2-5 Oct 1987	Dumisani Gwadiso (acting)
Oct-Dec 1987	Stella Sigcau (*daughter of B.Sigcau*) (TNIP) (deposed)

Chairman of the Military Council:

Jan 1988-April 1994   Bantu Holomisa

TNIP = Transkei National Independence Party

Became part of Eastern Cape

VENDA

Republic of Venda 1979-94
Independence date: 13 September 1979
Capital: Thohoyandhou

Presidents:

Chairman of the Council of National Unity 1990-94

Sept 1979-April 1988	Patrick Mphephu (VNP) (†)
April 1988-April 1990	Frank Ravele (acting April-May 1988) (VNP) (deposed)
April 1990-Feb 1994	Gabriel Ramushwana
Feb-April 1994	Tshamano Ramabulana

Chief Councillor:

Oct 1969-Feb 1973   Patrick Mphephu

Chief Minister:

Feb 1973-Sept 1979   Patrick Mphephu   (VNP)
(Sept 1979   post abolished)

VNP = Venda National Party
Became part of Northern Province

Provinces since 1994

EASTERN CAPE

Capital: Bisho

Premiers:

May 1994-Feb 1997	Raymond Mhlaba (ANC)
Feb 1997-	Makhenkosi Stofile (ANC)

FREE STATE

Previous name: Orange Free State until 1995
Capital: Bloemfontein

Premiers:

May 1994-Dec 1996	Patrick Lekota (ANC)
Dec 1996-June 1999	Ivy Matsepa-Casaburri (ANC)
June 1999-	Winkie Direko (ANC)

GAUTENG

Previous name: Pretoria-Witwatersrand-Vereeniging (PWV) until 1995
Capital: Johannesburg

Premiers:

May 1994-Jan 1998	Tokyo Sexwale	(ANC)
Jan 1998-June 1999	Mathole Motshekga	(ANC)
June 1999-	Mbhazima Shilowa	(ANC)

KWAZULU-NATAL

Capitals: Pietermaritzburg and Ulundi

Premiers:

May 1994-Feb 1997	Frank Mdlalose	(IFP)
March 1997-Feb 1999	Baldwin (Ben) Ngubane	(IFP) (acting 1-19 March 1997)
5-10 Feb 1999	Nyanga Ngubane	(acting)
Feb 1999-	Lionel Mtshali	(IFP)

MPUMALANGA

Previous name: Eastern Transvaal until 1995
Capital: Nelspruit

Premiers:

May 1994-June 1999	Mathews Phosa	(ANC)
June 1999-	J. Ndaweni	(ANC)

NORTHERN CAPE

Capital: Kimberley

Premier:

May 1994-	E.Manne Dipico	(ANC)

NORTHERN PROVINCE

Previous name: Northern Transvaal until 1995
Capital: Pietersburg

Premier:

May 1994-	Ngoako Ramatlhodi	(ANC)

NORTH WEST PROVINCE

Capital: Mafikeng

Premier:

May 1994-   Popo Molefe   (ANC)

WESTERN CAPE

Capital: Cape Town

Premiers:

May 1994-May 1998   J.Hermanus (Hernus) Kriel   (NP)
May 1998-   Gerald Morkel   (NP)

SPAIN

Official name: Kingdom of Spain, Reino de España
Previous names: Spanish Republic 1873-74 and 1931-39, Spanish State 1939-78
State founded (de facto): January 1479
Capital: Burgos until 1561, Madrid since 1561 (officially 1607)

Most of the Iberian peninsular was conquered by the Moors in the 6th century, but Christian kingdoms were formed in the north and northwest. The marriage of Isabella of Castile to Fernando of Aragon in 1479 united the two most powerful kingdoms, and the Moors were finally expelled from Spain in 1492. The Spanish crown passed to the Habsburg dynasty in 1516 and to a branch of the Bourbon family in 1700. A republic was briefly established in 1873-4. In 1931 a republic was again proclaimed, but the victory of General Franco's forces in the civil war (1936-39) led to the nominal restoration of the monarchy, with Franco as head of state. After his death in 1975 the monarchy was fully restored and democratic government was established in 1977.

Kings/Queens:

1479-Nov 1504	Isabella I (co-ruler)
Nov 1504-Jan 1516	Fernando II of Aragon/V of Castile (*husband*) (co-ruler)
Nov 1504-Jan 1516	Juanita (*daughter*) (nominal Queen of Castile) (co-ruler)
	Regent: 1510-16 Fernando V
Nov 1504-Sept 1506	Felipe I (*husband*)
Jan 1516-Jan 1555	Carlos I (Karl I of Austria) (*son*) (abdicated)
	Regent 1516-18 Francisco Jiménez de Cisneros
Jan 1555-Sept 1598	Felipe II (*son*)
Sept 1598-March 1621	Felipe III (*son*)
March 1621-Sept 1665	Felipe IV (*son*)
Sept 1665-Nov 1700	Carlos II (*son*)
Nov 1700-Jan 1724	Felipe V (*grandson of Louis XIV of France*) (1st) (abdicated)
Jan-March 1724	Luis (*son*)
March 1724-July 1746	Felipe V (2nd)
July 1746-March 1759	Fernando VI (*son*)
March 1759-Dec 1788	Carlos III (Carlo VII of Naples & Sicily) (*brother*)
Dec 1788-March 1808	Carlos IV (*son*) (abdicated)
March-May 1808	Fernando VII (*son*) (1st) (deposed)
June 1808-Dec 1813	Joseph Bonaparte (also King of Naples &Sicily) (*brother of Napoléon I of France*)
March 1814-Sept 1833	Fernando VII (2nd)
Sept 1833-Feb 1869	Isabella II (*daughter*) (exiled)
	Regents: 1833-40 Queen María Cristina I

                            1840-43 Joaquín Baldomero Espartero
Feb 1869-Nov 1870   Regent: Francisco Serrano y Dominguez
Nov 1870-Feb 1873   Amadeo   (*son of Vittorio Emanuele II of Italy*)

Presidents:
Chief of Executive Power

Feb-June 1873   Estanislao Figueras y Moracas
June-July 1873   Francisco Pi y Margall
July-Sept 1873   Nicolás Salmeron y Alonso
Sept 1873-Jan 1874   Emilio Castelar y Ripoll
Jan-Dec 1874   Francisco Serrano y Dominguez

Kings:

Dec 1874-Nov 1885   Alfonso XII   (*son of Isabella II*)
Nov 1885-May 1886   Regent: María Cristina II
May 1886-April 1931   Alfonso XIII   (*son*) (deposed)
                            Regent: 1886-1902 María Cristina II

Presidents:

Dec 1931-April 1936   Niceto Alcala Zamora
April-May 1936   Diego Martínez Barrio   (acting)
May 1936-April 1939   Manuel Azaña y Diéz   (deposed)

Chief of State:

April 1939-Nov 1975   Francisco Franco Bahamonde   (†)

King:

Nov 1975-   Juan Carlos   (*grandson of Alfonso XIII*)

Prime Ministers:
President of the Government

Oct 1833-Jan 1834   Francisco Cea Bermudez
Jan 1834-June 1835   Francisco Martínez de la Rosa
June-Sept 1835   Conde de Toreno   (José Ruiz de Saravia)
Sept 1835-May 1836   Juan Alvarez Mendizábal
May-Aug 1836   Manuel Isturiz y Montero
Aug 1836-Aug 1837   José Calatrava
Aug-Dec 1837   Eusebio Bardaji y Azara
Dec 1837-Sept 1838   Conde de Ofalia   (Narciso de Heredia)
Sept-Dec 1838   Duc de Frias   (Bernardino Fernández Velasco)
6-9 Dec 1838   Evaristo Pérez de Castro

Dec 1838-July 1840	Isidro Alaix
July-Aug 1840	Antonio González y González (1st)
12-29 Aug 1840	Valentin Ferraz
Aug-Sept 1840	Modesto Cortazar
Sept 1840-May 1841	Duc de Vitoria (Joaquín Baldomero Espartero) (1st)
May 1841-June 1842	Antonio González y González (2nd)
June 1842-May 1843	José Rodil y Gallaso
9-19 May 1843	Joaquín López (1st)
May-July 1843	Alvaro Gómez Becera
July-Nov 1843	Joaquín López (2nd)
Nov-Dec 1843	Salustiano de Olozaga
Dec 1843-May 1844	Luiz González Bravo (1st)
May 1844-Feb 1846	Duc de Valencia (Ramón Narváez) (1st)
Feb-April 1846	Marqués de Miraflores (Manuel Macea y Dávila) (1st)
April 1846-Jan 1847	Francisco Isturiz y Montero (1st)
Jan-March 1847	Duc de Sotomayor (Juan Ramirez de Avellano)
March-Sept 1847	Joaquín Pacheco y Gutiérrez
Sept-Oct 1847	Florencio García Gómez
Oct 1847-Jan 1850	Duc de Valencia (Ramón Narváez) (2nd)
Jan 1850-Dec 1852	Juan Bravo Murillo
Dec 1852-April 1853	Federico Roncali
April-Sept 1853	Francisco de Lersundi Ormaechea
Sept 1853-July 1854	Luiz Sartorius
17-18 July 1854	Fernando Fernández de Córdoba
July 1854-July 1855	Angel de Saavedra
July 1855-July 1856	Duc de Vitoria (Joaquín Baldomero Espartero) (2nd)
July-Oct 1856	Leopoldo O'Donnell y Joria (1st)
Oct 1856-Oct 1857	Duc de Valencia (Ramón Narváez) (3rd)
Oct 1857-Jan 1858	Francisco Armero y Peñaranda
Jan-June 1858	Francisco Isturiz y Montero (2nd)
Jan 1858-May 1863	Leopoldo O'Donnell y Joria (2nd)
May 1863-Jan 1864	Marqués de Miraflores (Manuel Macea y Dávila) (2nd)
Jan-March 1864	Lorenzo Arrazola
March-Sept 1864	Alejandro Mon
Sept 1864-June 1865	Duc de Valencia (Ramón Narváez) (4th)
June 1865-June 1866	Leopoldo O'Donnell y Joris (3rd)
June 1866-April 1868	Duc de Valencia (Ramón Narváez) (5th) (†)
April-Sept 1868	Luiz González Bravo (2nd)
Sept-Oct 1868	José Gutiérrez de la Concha
Oct 1868-June 1869	Francisco Serrano y Dominguez (1st)
June 1869-Dec 1870	Juan Prim y Prets
Dec 1870-Jan 1871	Juan Topete y Carballa (acting)
Jan-July 1871	Francisco Serrano y Dominguez (2nd)
July-Oct 1871	Manuel Ruiz Zorilla (1st)
Oct-Dec 1871	José Malcampo y Monge

Dec 1871-May 1872	Praxedes Sagasta (1st)
May-June 1872	Juan Topete y Carballa
June 1872-Feb 1873	Manuel Ruiz Zorilla (2nd)
(Feb 1873-Feb 1874	post abolished)
Feb-June 1874	Marqués de Sierra Bullones (Juan Zabala y de la Puente)
June-Dec 1874	Praxedes Sagasta (2nd)
Dec 1874-Sept 1875	Antonio Cánovas del Castillo (1st)
Sept-Dec 1875	Joaquín Jovellar
Dec 1875-March 1879	Antonio Cánovas del Castillo (2nd)
March-Dec 1879	Arsenio Martínez-Campos
Dec 1879-Feb 1881	Antonio Cánovas del Castillo (3rd)
Feb 1881-Oct 1883	Praxedes Sagasta (3rd)
Oct 1883-Jan 1884	José de Posada Herrera
Jan 1884-Nov 1885	Antonio Cánovas del Castillo (4th)
Nov 1885-July 1890	Praxedes Sagasta (4th)
July 1890-Dec 1892	Antonio Cánovas del Castillo (5th)
Dec 1892-March 1895	Praxedes Sagasta (5th)
March 1895-Aug 1897	Antonio Cánovas del Castillo (6th)
Aug-Oct 1897	Marcelo de Azcarraga y Palmero (1st)
Oct 1897-March 1899	Praxedes Sagasta (6th)
March 1899-Oct 1900	Francisco Silvela y Le-Vielleuze (1st)
Oct 1900-Feb 1901	Marcelo de Azcarraga y Palmero (2nd)
Feb 1901-Dec 1902	Praxedes Sagasta (7th)
Dec 1902-July 1903	Francisco Silvela y Le-Vielleuze (2nd)
July-Dec 1903	Raimundo Fernández de Villaverde (1st) (CP)
Dec 1903-Dec 1904	Antonio Maura y Montaner (1st) (CP)
Dec 1904-Jan 1905	Marcelo de Azcarraga y Palmero (3rd)
Jan-June 1905	Raimundo Fernández de Villaverde (2nd) (CP)
June-Dec 1905	Eugene Montero Ríos
Dec 1905-July 1906	Segismundo Moret y Prendergast (1st) (LP)
July-Nov 1906	José López Dominguez (LP)
Nov-Dec 1906	Segismundo Moret y Prendergast (2nd) (LP)
Dec 1906-Jan 1907	Marqués de la Vega de Armijo (Antonio de Aguilar y Correa) (LP)
Jan 1907-Oct 1909	Antonio Maura y Montaner (2nd) (CP)
Oct 1909-Feb 1910	Segismundo Moret y Prendergast (3rd) (LP)
Feb 1910-Nov 1912	José Canalejas y Mendez (LP) († assassinated)
12-15 Nov 1912	Conde de Romanones (Alvaro de Figueroa y Torres) (1st) (LP)
Nov 1912-Oct 1913	Marqués de Alhucemas (Manuel García Prieto) (1st) (LP)
Oct 1913-Dec 1915	Eduardo Dato y Iradier (1st) (CP)
Dec 1915-April 1916	Conde de Romanones (Alvaro de Figueroa y Torres) (2nd) (LP)
April 1916-June 1917	Marqués de Alhucemas (Manuel García Prieto) (2nd) (LP)
June-Nov 1917	Eduardo Dato y Iradier (2nd) (CP)
Nov 1917-March 1918	Marqués de Alhucemas (Manuel García Prieto) (3rd) (LP)
March-Nov 1918	Antonio Maura y Montaner (3rd) (CP)
Nov-Dec 1918	Marqués de Alhucemas (Manuel García Prieto) (4th) (LP)

Dec 1918-April 1919	Conde de Romanones (Alvaro de Figueroa y Torres) (3rd) (LP)
April-July 1919	Antonio Maura y Montaner (4th) (CP)
July-Dec 1919	Joaquín Sánchez de Toca
Dec 1919-May 1920	Manuel Allende Salazar (1st)
May 1920-March 1921	Eduardo Dato y Iradier (3rd) (CP) († assassinated)
8-13 March 1921	Gabino Bugallal Araújo (acting)
March-Aug 1921	Manuel Allende Salazar (2nd)
Aug 1921-March 1922	Antonio Maura y Montaner (5th) (CP)
March-Dec 1922	José Sánchez Guerra (CP)
Dec 1922-Sept 1923	Marqués de Alhucemas (Manuel García Prieto) (5th) (LP) (deposed)
Sept 1923-Jan 1930	Miguel Primo de Rivera y Orbaneja
Jan 1930-Feb 1931	Damaso Berenguer y Fuste
Feb-April 1931	Juan Bautista Azmar-Cabanas (deposed)
April-Oct 1931	Niceto Alcala Zamora
Oct 1931-Sept 1933	Manuel Azaña y Diéz (1st) (LRP)
Sept-Oct 1933	Alejandro Lerroux y García (1st) (RP)
Oct-Dec 1933	Diego Martínez Barrio (1st) (RP)
Dec 1933-April 1934	Alejandro Lerroux y García (2nd) (RP)
April-Oct 1934	Ricardo Samper Ibáñez
Oct 1934-Oct 1935	Alejandro Lerroux y García (3rd) (RP)
Oct-Dec 1935	Joaquín Chapaprieta y Terragosa
Dec 1935-Feb 1936	Manuel Portela Valladares
Feb-May 1936	Manuel Azaña y Diéz (2nd) (LRP)
May-July 1936	Santiago Cásares Quiroga
18 July 1936	Diego Martínez Barrio (2nd)
July-Sept 1936	José Giral y Pereira
Sept 1936-March 1937	Francisco Largo Caballero (SP)
March 1937-March 1939	Juan Negrín (SP) (deposed)
April 1939-June 1973	Francisco Franco Bahamonde
June-Dec 1973	Luis Carrero Blanco († assassinated)
Dec 1973-Jan 1974	Torcuato Fernández Miranda (acting)
Jan 1974-July 1976	Carlos Arias Navarro
1-5 July 1976	Fernando de Santiago y Díaz (acting)
July 1976-Feb 1981	Adolfo Suárez González (UDC)
Feb 1981-Dec 1982	Leopoldo Calvo-Sotelo y Bustelo (UDC)
Dec 1982-May 1996	Felipe González Marquez (SSWP)
May 1996-	José María Aznar López (PP) (see Castile y León)

CP = Conservative Party
LP = Liberal Party
LRP = Left Republican Party
PP = Popular Party
RP = Radical Party
SP = Socialist Party
SSWP = Spanish Socialist Workers' Party
UDC = Union of the Democratic Centre

RIVAL GOVERNMENT 1936-39

Formed by General Franco during the civil war against the republican government in Madrid, taking control of the capital in 1939.
Headquarters: Salamanca

Chief of State:

Oct 1936-April 1939   Francisco Franco Bahamonde

Prime Ministers:
Junta Chairman 1936-38

July-Sept 1936	Miguel Cabanellas Ferrer
Oct 1936-Feb 1938	Fidel Dávila Arrondo
Feb 1938-April 1939	Francisco Franco Bahamonde

GOVERNMENT-IN-EXILE 1945-77

A republican government-in-exile was proclaimed in Mexico in 1945 to oppose General Franco. It soon moved to France. It was dissolved in 1977 after democracy was re-established in Spain.
Headquarters: Paris

Presidents:

Aug 1945-Jan 1962	Diego Martínez Barrio (†)
1962-70	Luis Jiménez de Ashua
1970-June 1977	José Maldonado

Prime Ministers:

Aug 1945-Feb 1947	José Giral y Pereira
Feb-Sept 1947	Rodolfo Llopis Ferrandiz
Sept 1947-Nov 1951	Alvaro de Albornoz
Nov 1951-58	Felix Gordon Ordas
March 1959-70	Claudio Sánchez Albornoz
1970-June 1977	Fernando Valera Aparacio

Pre-unification Kingdoms

ARAGON

Formerly part of Navarre
Capital: Jaca (until 1118), Zaragoza (after 1118)

Kings/Queen:

1035-63   Ramiro I   (*son of Sáncho III of Navarre*)

1063-June 1094	Sáncho I Ramirez
June 1094-1104	Pedro I
1104-34	Alfonso I
1134-37	Ramiro II (*brother*) (abdicated)
1137-62	Petronilla (*daughter*)
1162-96	Alfonso II Ramón (*son*)
1196-1213	Pedro II (*son*) (killed in battle)
1215-July 1276	Jaime I (*son*)
July 1276-85	Pedro III (*son*)
1285-91	Alfonso III (*son*)
1291-1327	Jaime II (*brother*)
1327-Jan 1336	Alfonso IV (*son*)
Jan 1336-87	Pedro IV (*son*)
1387-95	Juan I (*son*)
1395-1410	Martin I (*brother*)
(1410-12	interregnum)
1412-April 1416	Fernando I (*nephew of Pedro IV*)
April 1416-June 1458	Alfonso V (*son*)
June 1458-Jan 1479	Juan II (*brother*)
Jan 1479-Jan 1516	Fernando II (*son*) (Fernando V of Castile)

The marriage of Fernando to Isabella I of Castile led to the union of the two states.

ASTURIAS

León and Asturias after 910
Capital: Cangas de Onís (until 780), Pravia (until c820), Oviedo

Kings:

718-c737	Pelayo
c737-c739	Fávila (*son*)
c739-757	Alfonso I (*son-in-law of Pelayo*)
757-c768	Froíla I (*son*) (assassinated)
c768-c774	Aurelio (*nephew*)
c774-783	Silo (*brother-in-law*)
783-788	Mauregato (*son of Alfonso I*)
788-791	Vermudo I (*nephew of Alfonso I*) (abdicated)
791-842	Alfonso II (*son of Froíla I*)
842-850	Ramiro I (*son of Vermudo I*)
850-866	Ordoño I (*son*)
866-Dec 910	Alfonso III (*son*)
Dec 910-914	García I (*son*)
914-c925	Ordoño II (*brother*)
c925	Froíla II (*brother*)
c925	Alfonso Froílaz (*son*) (deposed)

c925-931	Alfonso IV (*son of Ordoño II*) (deposed)
931-951	Ramiro II (*brother*) (abdicated)
951-956	Ordoño III (*son*)
956-c958	Sáncho I (*brother*) (1st) (deposed)
c958-960	Ordoño IV (*cousin*) (deposed)
960-966	Sáncho I (2nd) (assassinated)
966-984	Ramiro III (*son*) (assassinated)
984-999	Vermudo II (*grandson of Froíla II*)
999-1027	Alfonso V (*son*) (assassinated)
1027-37	Vermudo III (*son*) (killed in battle)

In 1037 León and Asturias was conquered by Castile

CASTILE

Formerly part of Navarre
Capital: Burgos

Kings/Queens:

1035-Dec 1065	Fernando I (also of León 1037-65) (*son of Sáncho III of Navarre*)
Dec 1065-Oct 1072	Sáncho II (*son*)
Oct 1072-1109	Alfonso VI (*brother*) (also of León 1065-1109)
1109-1126	Urraca (*daughter*)
1126-Aug 1157	Alfonso VII (*son*)
Aug 1157-58	Sáncho III (*son*)
1158-Oct 1214	Alfonso VIII (*son*)
Oct 1214-17	Enrique (*son*)
1217-52	Fernando III (*son of Alfonso IX of León*) (also of León 1230-52)
1252-April 1284	Alfonso X (*son*)
April 1284-95	Sancho IV (*son*)
1295-1312	Fernando IV (*son*)
1312-March 1350	Alfonso XI (*son*)
March 1350-66	Pedro I (*son*) (1st) (deposed)
1366-67	Enrique II (*son of Alfonso XI*) (1st) (deposed)
1367-March 1369	Pedro I (2nd) (assassinated)
March 1369-May 1379	Enrique II
May 1379-90	Juan I (*son*)
1390-1406	Enrique III (*son*)
1406-July 1454	Juan II (*son*)
July 1454-Dec 1474	Enrique IV (*son*)
Dec 1474-Nov 1504	Isabella I (*daughter*) (co-ruler)
Dec 1474-Nov 1504	Fernando V (*husband*) (Fernando II of Aragon)
Nov 1504-Jan 1516	Juanita (*daughter*) (nominal)

The marriage of Isabella I to Fernando effectively united Spain.

CÓRDOBA

In 756 the Moors established an emirate in Córdoba nominally subject to the Caliph in Baghdad. In 929 these ties were broken.

Emirs:

756-788	Abd-ar-Rahman I
788-796	Hisham I (*son*)
796-822	Al-Hakam I (*son*)
822-852	Abd-ar-Rahman II (*son*)
852-886	Mohammed I (*son*)
886-888	Al-Mundhir (*son*)
888-912	Abdullah (*brother*)
912-929	Abd-ar-Rahman III (*grandson*)

Caliphs:

929-961	An-Nasir (Abd-ar-Rahman III)
961-976	Al-Mustanir (Al-Hakim II) (*son*)
976-1016	Al-Muayyad (Hisham II) (*son*)

Arab Spain split into numerous weak entities which were gradually reconquered by Christian rulers.

LEÓN

After the conquest of León and Asturias by Castile, the crown of León was sometimes separated from that of Castile.

Kings/Queen:

1037-Dec 1065	Fernando I (also of Castile)
1065-1109	Alfonso VI (also of Castile)
1109-26	Urraca (also of Castile)
1126-Aug 1157	Alfonso VII (also of Castile)
Aug 1157-88	Fernando II (*son*)
1188-1230	Alfonso IX (*son*)
1230-52	Fernando III (*son*)

Castile and León were completely united after 1230

NAVARRE

Pamplona until 1150
Capital: Pamplona

Kings/Queens:

905-925	Sáncho I Garces
925-970	García I Sánchez
970-c994	Sáncho II Garces
c994-1000	García II
1000-35	Sáncho III Garces
1035-54	García III (*son*)
1054-76	Sáncho IV (*son*) (deposed)
1076-June 1094	Sáncho V Ramirez (Sáncho I Ramirez of Aragon)
June 1094-1104	Pedro I (Pedro I of Aragon)
1104-34	Alfonso I (Alfonso I of Aragon)
1134-50	García IV Ramirez
1150-94	Sáncho VI
1194-1234	Sáncho VII
1234-53	Thibaut (Teobaldo) I (*nephew*)
1253-70	Thibaut (Teobaldo) II
1270-74	Henri (Enrique) I
1274-1305	Jeanne (Juana) I (co-ruler 1284-1305)
1284-Nov 1314	Philippe (Felipe) I (Philippe IV of France) (*husband*)
Nov 1314-June 1316	Louis (Luis) I (Louis X of France)
(June-Nov 1316	interregnum)
Nov 1316	Jean (Juan) I (Jean I of France)
Nov 1316-Jan 1322	Philippe (Felipe) II (Philippe V of France)
Jan 1322-Feb 1328	Charles (Carlos) I (Charles IV of France)
Feb 1328-49	Jeanne (Juana) II (co-ruler) (*daughter of Louis I*)
Feb 1328-49	Philippe (Felipe) III (co-ruler) (*husband*)
1349-87	Charles (Carlos) II (*son*)
1387-1425	Charles (Carlos) III (*son*)
1425-41	Blanche (Blanca) (co-ruler) (*daughter*)
1425-79	Jean (Juan) II (co-ruler 1425-41) (*husband*)
1479	Eleonore (Leonor) (*daughter*)
1479-83	François (Francisco) (*grandson*)
1483-Feb 1512	Catherine (Catarina) (*sister*) (co-ruler 1484-1512)
1484-1516	Jean (Juan) III (*husband*) (co-ruler 1484-1512)
1516-55	Henri II (*son*)
1555-72	Jeanne III (*daughter*)
1572-May 1610	Henri III (*son*)
May 1610-Oct 1620	Louis II (Louis XII of France)

At the beginning of the 16th century most of Navarre was seized by Aragon. The remainder was annexed by France in 1620

Autonomous Regions

ANDALUCIA

Capital: Sevilla

Presidents:
Presidents of the Junta

May 1978-July 1982	Plácido Fernández Viagas (SSWP)
July 1982-March 1984	Rafael Escuredo Rodríguez (SSWP)
March 1984-June 1990	José Rodríguez de la Borbolla (SSWP)
June 1990-	Manuel Chaves González (SSWP)

ARAGON

Capital: Zaragoza

Presidents:
President of the General Delegation 1978-82

April 1978-Sept 1981	Juan Bolea Foradoda (UDC)
May 1981-Nov 1982	Gaspar Castellano
Nov-Dec 1982	José Maria Hernández de la Torre (acting)
Dec 1982-June 1983	Juan de Andres Rodriguez
June 1983-May 1987	Santiago Marraco (SSWP)
May 1987-May 1991	Hipólito Gómez de las Roces (SSWP)
May 1991-Sept 1993	Emilio Eiroa García (ARP)
Sept 1993-Jan 1995	José Marco Bergós (SSWP)
Jan-July 1995	Ramón Tejedor Sanz (acting)
July 1995-Aug 1999	Santiago Lanzuela Marina (PP)
Aug 1999-	Marcolino Iglesias Ricou

ARP = Aragon Regional Party

ASTURIAS

Capital: Oviedo

Presidents:
President of the Council Nov 1978-May 1982

Nov 1978-June 1983	Rafael Fernández Alvarez (SSWP)
June 1983-May 1991	Pedro de Silva Cienfuegos-Jovellanos (SSWP)
May 1991-July 1993	Juan Rodríguez-Vigil Rubo (SSWP)
July 1993-July 1995	Antonio Trevín Lomban (SSWP)
July 1995-July 1999	Sergio Marqués (PP)
July 1999-	Vicente Alvarez Areces (SWP)

BALEARIC ISLANDS
Baleares

Capital: Palma

Presidents:
President of the Council 1978-83

July 1978-June 1983	Jerónimo Albertí Picornell (UDC)
June 1983-July 1995	Gabriel Cañellas Fons (PA,PP)
July 1995-June 1996	Cristófol Soler i Clodera (PP)
June 1996-July 1999	Jaume Matas Palou (PP)
July 1999-	Francesc Antich (SSWP)

BASQUE COUNTRY
Euzkadi

Capital: Vitoria

Presidents:

Oct 1936-June 1937	José Aguirre (deposed) (in exile in Barcelona 1937-39)
(June 1937-Feb 1978	post abolished)
Feb 1978-April 1980	Ramón Rubial (SSWP)
April 1980-Jan 1985	Carlos Garaicoetxea (BNP)
Jan 1985-Dec 1998	José Ardanza (BNP)
Dec 1998-	Juan José Ibarretxe (BNP)

BNP = Basque National Party

CANARY ISLANDS

Capitals: Las Palmas and Santa Cruz de Tenerife

Presidents:

April 1978-May 1983	Alfonso Benítez de Lugo
May 1983-June 1987	Jerónimo Saavedra Acevedo (1st) (SSWP)
June 1987-Jan 1989	Fernando Fernández Martín (DSC)
Jan 1989-91	Lorenzo Olarte Cullén (DSC)
1991-93	Jerónimo Saavedra Acevedo (2nd) (SWP)
1993-July 1999	Manuel Hermoso Rojas (CC)
July 1999-	Román Rodríguez Rodríguez (CC)

CC = Canarias Coalition
DSC = Democratic & Social Centre

CANTABRIA

Capital: Santander

Presidents:

April 1982-March 1984	José Rodríguez Martínez
March 1984-May 1987	Angel Díaz de Entresotos
May 1987-Dec 1990	Juan Hormaechea Cazón (1st) (PA, PP)
Dec 1990-May 1991	Jaime Blanco García (SSWP)
May 1991-Nov 1994	Juan Hormaechea Cazón (2nd) (PP)
Nov 1994-	José Martínez Sieso (PP)

CASTILE-LA MANCHA

Capital: Toledo

Presidents:

President of the Junta

1978-83	Antonio Fernández-Galiano
June 1983-	José Bono Martínez (SSWP)

CASTILE Y LEÓN

Capital: Valladolid

Presidents:

July 1978-June 1983	Juan Reol Tejada (UDC)
June 1983-Nov 1986	Demetrio Madrid López (SSWP)
Nov 1986-May 1987	José Naldo García (SSWP)
May 1987-Sept 1989	José María Aznar López (PA,PP)
Sept 1989-May 1991	Jesús Posada Moreno (PP)
May 1991-	Juan Lucas Jiménez (PP)

CATALONIA
Cataluña

Capital: Barcelona

Presidents:

President of the Generalitat

Dec 1932-Dec 1933	Francesco Maciá (†)
Dec 1933-Oct 1934	Lluis Campanys (1st)

(Oct 1934-March 1936   post abolished)
March 1936-Feb 1939   Lluis Campanys   (2nd) (deposed, executed 1940)
(Feb 1939-Oct 1977   post abolished)
Oct 1977-May 1980   Josep Tarrandellas   (CRL)
May 1980-   Jordi Pujol Soley   (DCC)

CRL = Catalonian Republican Left
DCC = Democratic Convergence of Catalonia

EXTREMADURA

Capital: Mérida

Presidents:

President of the Junta

Sept 1978-June 1983   Luis Ramallo García
June 1983-   Juan Rodríguez Ibarra   (SSWP)

GALICIA
Galiza

Capital: Santiago de Compostela

Presidents:

President of the Xunta

April 1978-Jan 1982   Antonio Rosón   (UDC)
Jan 1982-Oct 1987   Gerardo Fernández Albor   (PA)
Oct 1987-Feb 1990   Fernando González Laxe   (SSWP)
Feb 1990-   Manuel Fraga Iribarne   (PP)

LA RIOJA

Capital: Logroño

Presidents:

Sept 1982-May 1983   Adolfo Agudo   (UDC)
May 1983-May 1987   José de Miguel Gil   (SSWP)
May 1987-May 1991   Joaquín Espert Pérez-Caballero   (PA,PP)
May 1991-July 1995   José Pérez Saénz   (SSWP)
July 1995-   Pedro Sanz Alonso   (PP)

MADRID

Capital: Madrid

Presidents:

June 1983-July 1995	Joaquín Leguina Herrán (SSWP)
July 1995-	Alberto Ruiz-Gallardon Jiménez (PP)

MURCIA

Capital: Murcia

Presidents:

Nov 1978-June 1983	Antonio Pérez Crespo (UDC)
June 1983-April 1984	Andrés Hernández Ros (SSWP)
April 1984-May 1993	Carlos Collado Mena (SSWP)
May 1993-July 1995	María Antonia Martínez (SSWP)
July 1995-	Ramón Valcárcel Siso (PP)

NAVARRE

Capital: Pamplona

Presidents:

May 1984-May 1991	Gabriel Urralburu Taínta (SSWP)
May 1991-July 1995	Juan Alli Aranguren (UNP)
July 1995-June 1996	Javier Otano Cid (SSWP)
June-Sept 1996	Juan Alli Aranguren (acting) (CDN)
Sept 1996-	Miguel Sanz Sesma (UNP)

CDN = Convergence of Democratic Navarre
UNP = Union of Navarre People

VALENCIA

Capital: Valencia

Presidents:

President of the Generalitat

April 1978-Aug 1982	José Albiñana Olmos (SSWP)
Aug 1982-July 1995	Joan Lerma Blasco (SSWP)
July 1995-	Eduardo Zaplana (PP)

Autonomous Enclaves in North Africa

CEUTA

Mayors/Presidents:

June 1995-July 1996	Basileo Fernández López
July 1996-Aug 1999	Jesús Cayetano Fortes Ramos (PP)
Aug 1999-	Antonio Samprieto Casamarrona

MELILLA

Mayors/Presidents:

June 1995-Feb 1998	Ignacio Velasquez
Feb 1998-1999	Enrique Palacios (PP)
1999-	Mustafa Hamed Mon Aberchán

SRI LANKA

Official name: Democratic Socialist Republic of Sri Lanka, Sri Lanka Prajatantrika Samajawadi Janarajaya

Previous names: Dominion of Ceylon 1948-72, Republic of Sri Lanka 1972-78

Independence date: 4 February 1948

Capital: Colombo

Various Sinhalese kingdoms flourished in Sri Lanka from the 5th century BC until 1505, when Portugal occupied the island. In 1658 control passed to the Dutch who ruled until 1796, when Britain took over. Independence was granted in 1948, and in 1972 a republic was declared. In 1983 an armed struggle by Tamil secessionists in the north and east of the country began, and still continues.

Governors:

1895-1903	Joseph Ridgeway
1903-07	Henry Blake
1907-13	Henry McCallum
1913-16	Robert Chalmers
1916-18	John Anderson
1918-25	William Manning
1925-27	Hugh Clifford
1927-31	Herbert Stanley (see Northern Rhodesia)
1931-33	Graeme Thomson (see British Guiana)
1933-37	Reginald Stubbs
1937-44	Andrew Caldecott
1944-48	Henry Moore

Governors-General:

Represented monarch who was concurrently British monarch

Feb 1948-July 1949	Henry Moore
July 1949-July 1954	Lord Soulbury (Herwald Ramsbotham)
July 1954-March 1962	Oliver Goonetilleke
March 1962-May 1972	William Gopallawa

Presidents:

May 1972-Feb 1978	William Gopallawa
Feb 1978-Jan 1989	Junius Jayawardene (UNP)
Jan 1989-May 1993	Ranasinghe Premadasa (UNP) († assassinated)
May 1993-Nov 1994	Dingiri Wijetunge (UNP) (acting 1-7 May 1993)

Nov 1994- Chandrika Kumaratunga (PA)

Prime Ministers:

Feb 1948-March 1952	Donald Senanayake (UNP) (†)
March 1952-Oct 1953	Dudley Senanayake (*son*) (1st) (UNP)
Oct 1953-April 1956	John Kotalawala (UNP)
April 1956-Sept 1959	Solomon Bandaranaike (SLFP) († assassinated)
Sept 1959-March 1960	Wijeyananda Dahanayake (SLFP)
March-July 1960	Dudley Senanayake (2nd) (UNP)
July 1960-March 1965	Sirimavo Bandaranaike (*b* S.Ratwatte) (*widow of Solomon Bandaranaike*) (1st) (SLFP)
March 1965-May 1970	Dudley Senanayake (3rd) (UNP)
May 1970-July 1977	Sirimavo Bandaranaike (2nd) (SLFP)
July 1977-Feb 1978	Junius Jayawardene (UNP)
Feb 1978-March 1989	Ranasinghe Premadasa (UNP)
March 1989-May 1993	Dingiri Wijetunge (UNP) (see North Western Province)
May 1993-Aug 1994	Ranil Wickremasinghe (UNP)
Aug-Nov 1994	Chandrika Kumaratunga (*daughter of S.Bandaranaike*) (SLFP) (see Western Province)
Nov 1994-	Sirimavo Bandaranaike (3rd) (SLFP)

PA = Peoples' Alliance (includes SLFP)
SLFP = Sri Lanka Freedom Party
UNP = United National Party

Provinces

CENTRAL PROVINCE

Capital: Kandy

Governors:

June 1988-Feb 1990	E.Hurulle
Feb 1990-May 1994	P.C.Imbulana (see Uva)
May 1994-98	E.L. Senanayake (see North Central Province)
May 1998-	Stanley Tilekeratne

Chief Ministers:

June 1988-June 1998	W.Dissanayake (UNP)
(June 1998-April 1999	post vacant)
April 1999-	Nandimithra Ekanayake (PA)

NORTH CENTRAL PROVINCE

Capital: Aruradhapura

Governors:

May 1988-May 1989	D.B.Welagedera
May 1989-May 1994	E.L.Senanayake
May-Sept 1994	E.Hurulle (see Central Province)
Sept 1994-98	Maithripala Senanayeke
1998-	G. Samaraweera

Chief Ministers:

May 1988-May 1996	G.D.Mahindasoma (UNP)
May 1996-June 1998	Jayasena Dissanayake (UNP)
(June 1998-April 1999	post vacant)
April 1999-	Berty Premalal Dissanayake (PA)

NORTH EASTERN PROVINCE

Capital: Trincomalee

Governors:

Dec 1988-93	Nalin Senevitatne
1993-Nov 1998	Gamini Fonseka
Nov 1998-	Asoka Jayawardene

Chief Minister:

Dec 1988-March 1990	Annamalai Perumal (EPRLF)
(March 1990-	post vacant)

EPRLF = Eelam People's Revolutionary Liberation Front

NORTH WESTERN PROVINCE (WAYAMBA)

Capital: Kurunegala

Governors:

May 1988-Feb 1989	Dingiri Wijetunge
Feb 1989-Oct 1993	Montague Jayawickrema
Oct 1993-July 1994	Karunasena Kodituwakku
July 1994-Jan 1995	Ananda De Alwis
Jan 1995-98	H.G.Arawwawala
1998-	Siripala Jayaweera

Chief Ministers:

May 1988-Oct 1993	Gamini Jayawickrema Perera	(UNP)
Oct 1993-Aug 1994	G.M.Premachandra	(DUNF)
Aug 1994-Feb 1999	R.Nimal Bandara	(UNP)
Feb 1999-	S.B.Nawinna	(PA)

DUNF = Democratic United National Front

SABARAGAMUWA

Capital: Ratnapura

Governors:

May 1988-93	Noel Wimalasena
1993-	C.N. Saliya Mathew

Chief Ministers:

April 1988-April 1989	G.V.Punchinilame	(UNP)
May 1989-March 1993	Abeyratne Pilapitiya	(UNP)
March 1993-June 1998	H. Jayathilaka Podinilame	(UNP)
(June 1998-April 1999	post vacant)	
April 1999-	Athanda Senevitatne	(PA)

SOUTHERN PROVINCE

Capital: Galle

Governors:

June 1988-Dec 1993	M.Bakeer Marker
Dec 1993-Dec 1994	Lesley Jayaratne
Jan 1995-	Neville Kanakarratne

Chief Ministers:

June 1988-Oct 1993	M.S.Amarasiri	(UNP)
Oct 1993-Jan 1994	Amarasiri Dodangoda	(1st) (PA)
(Jan-March 1994	post vacant)	
March-Sept 1994	Amarasiri Dodangoda	(2nd) (PA)
Sept 1994-	Mahinda Abeyawardena	(PA)

UVA

Capital: Badulla

Governors:

May 1988-Jan 1990	P.C.Imbulana
Feb 1990-March 1993	Tilak Ratnayake
March 1993-Dec 1994	Abeyratne Pilapitiya (see Sabaragamuwa)
Jan 1995-	Ananda Dassanayaka

Chief Ministers:

May 1988-June 1998	Percy Samaraweera (UNP)
(June 1998-April 1999	post vacant)
April 1999-	Samaraweera Weerawani (PA)

WESTERN PROVINCE

Capital: Colombo

Governors:

June 1988-July 1994	S.Sharvananda
July-Dec 1994	D.M.Swaminathan
March 1995-	K.Vignarajah

Chief Ministers:

June 1988-June 1993	Susil Munasinghe (UNP)
June 1993-Aug 1994	Chandrika Kumaratunga (PA)
Aug 1994-July 1995	Morris Rajapakse (PA) (†)
July 1995-June 1998	Susil Premajayantha (1st) (PA)
(June 1998-April 1999	post vacant)
April 1999-	Susil Premajayantha (2nd) (PA)

SUDAN

Official name: Republic of Sudan, Jamhuriyat es-Sudan

Previous names: Republic of the Sudan 1956-69, Democratic Republic of the Sudan 1969-75, Democratic Republic of Sudan 1975-85

Independence date: 1 January 1956

Capital: Khartoum

Most of present-day Sudan was ruled by the Egyptians until the 8th century BC. For the next 1000 years it formed part of the kingdom of Cush, and was then divided into three Nuba kingdoms. Following the introduction of Islam various sultanates were established. In 1821 Sudan was taken over by Egypt, initially as a province. In 1899 an Anglo-Egyptian condominium was established. Self-government was granted in 1954 and independence in 1956. The military has seized power four times since then. In the 1960s armed rebellion in the non-Arab south for independence or autonomy began, and ended with the 1972 agreement for autonomy. However, it resumed in 1983 with the introduction of Shari'a law.

Governors-General:

1899	Lord Kitchener (Horatio Kitchener)
1899-1916	Francis Wingate
1916-24	Lee Stack
1924-26	Geoffrey Archer (see Uganda)
1926-34	John Maffey
1934-40	George Symes
1940-47	Hubert Huddleston
1947-54	Robert Howe
1954-Dec 1955	Alexander Helm

Presidents:

President of the Supreme Council 1958-64, 1965-69
Chairman of the Revolutionary Command Council May 1969-Oct 1971
Chairman of the Transitional Military Council April 1985-April 1986
President of the Council of State April 1986-June 1989
President of the Revolutionary Council June 1989-Oct 1993

(Jan 1956-Nov 1958	Five-member Council of Sovereignty)
Nov 1958-Nov 1964	Ibrahim Abboud
(Nov 1964-July 1965	Five-member Council of Sovereignty)
July 1965-May 1969	Ismail el-Azhari (deposed)
May 1969-July 1971	Jaafar el-Nemery (1st) (deposed)
19-20 July 1971	Hashem el-Atta (later executed)
20-22 July 1971	Babiker al-Nur Osman (nominal, deposed, executed)

July 1971-April 1985   Jaafar el-Nemery   (2nd) (SSU) (deposed)
April 1985-April 1986   Abdul Rahman Swareddahab
April 1986-June 1989   Ahmed el-Mirghani
June 1989-   Omar al-Bashir

Prime Ministers:

Jan 1954-July 1956   Ismail el-Azhari   (NUP)
July 1956-Nov 1958   Abdullah Khalil   (UP) (deposed)
Nov 1958-Oct 1964   Ibrahim Abboud
Oct 1964-June 1965   Al-Khatim al-Khalifa
June 1965-July 1966   Mohammed Mahgoub   (1st) (UP)
July 1966-May 1967   Sadiq el-Mahdi   (1st) (UP)
May 1967-May 1969   Mohammed Mahgoub   (2nd) (UP) (deposed)
May-Oct 1969   Abubakr Awadallah
Oct 1969-July 1971   Jaafar el-Nemery   (1st)
20-22 July 1971   Farouk Hamadalla   (nominal, later executed)
July 1971-Aug 1976   Jaafar el-Nemery   (2nd)
Aug 1976-Aug 1977   El-Rashid Bakr
Aug 1977-April 1985   Jaafar el-Nemery   (3rd)
April 1985-April 1986   Al-Jazouli Dafallah
May 1986-June 1989   Sadiq el-Mahdi   (2nd) (UP) (deposed)
June 1989-   Omar al-Bashir

NUP = National Unionist Party
SSU = Sudanese Socialist Union (sole legal party 1971-85)
UP = Umma Party

Former Autonomous Region

SOUTHERN SUDAN

Comprised the provinces (later states) of Bahr el-Ghazal, Equatoria and Upper Nile
Capital: Juba

Presidents:

President of the High Executive Council

April 1972-Feb 1978   Abel Alier   (1st)
Feb 1978-Feb 1980   Joseph Lago
Feb 1980-Oct 1981   Abel Alier   (2nd)
Oct 1981-June 1982   Gasmallah Rassas
June 1982-June 1983   Joseph Tombura
(June 1983-April 1985   post abolished)
April 1985-May 1986   James Loro
(May 1986   post abolished)

Prime Ministers:

Cabinet Chairman 1985-87
Council Chairman 1987-88

April 1985-Jan 1987	James Cirisio
May 1987-Jan 1988	Matthew Abor Ayang
Jan 1988-June 1989	Angelo Beda
(June 1989	post abolished)

Chairman of the Consultative Council:

Aug 1997-	Riek Mashar

States

BAHR AL-JABAL

Capital: Juba

Governors:

Feb 1994-Dec 1997	Agnes Lukodi
Dec 1997-Jan 2000	Christopher Loki
Jan 2000-	Henri Jada Zakariya

BLUE NILE

Capital: Damazin

Governors:

Feb 1994-Dec 1997	Abdalla Abu-Fatma Abdalla
Dec 1997-Jan 2000	Abd ar-Rahman Abu Madyani
Jan 2000-	Al-Hadi Bushra

AL-BUHAIRAT (LAKES)

Capital: Rumbek

Governors:

Feb-May 1994	Mong Geng Shir
May 1994-Dec 1997	Ramzi Badri Shir
Dec 1997-Jan 2000	Nektora Ashik
Jan 2000-	Gabriel Shol Yak

EASTERN EQUATORIA

Capital: Kaboita

Governors:

Feb-June 1994	Caesar Paia (1st)
June-Nov 1994	Marboz Konda
June 1994-Dec 1997	Caesar Paia (2nd)
Dec 1997-Jan 2000	Abdullah Amiri
Jan 2000-	Abdullah Allajabo

GADAREF

Capital: Gadaref

Governors:

Feb 1994-Dec 1997	Al-Sharif Badr (see former Northern State)
Dec 1997-Jan 2000	Ibrahim Ubaydullah (see Al-Gezira)
Jan 2000-	Al-Amin Dafa'alla

AL-GEZIRA

Capital: Wad Medani

Governors:

Feb 1994-Dec 1997	Ibrahim Ubaydullah
Dec 1997-	Sharif Ahmad Umar Badr

JONGLEI

Capital: Bor

Governors:

Feb 1994-Dec 1997	Al-Shaikh Bish Akor
Dec 1997-	Riak Gai Kok

KASSALA

Capital: Kassala

Governors:

1994	Abdul-Qasim Ibrahim

1994	Abdullah Siahmed (acting)
1994	Al-Amin Daffala
Aug 1994-Dec 1997	Abu Mohammed
Dec 1997-	Ibrahim Hamid

KHARTOUM

Capital: Khartoum

Governors:

Feb 1991-Feb 1994	Mohammed Saeed
Feb 1994-Dec 1997	Badr al-Din Taha
Dec 1997-	Majzoub al-Khalifa

NORTHERN BAHR EL-GHAZAL

Capital: Aweel

Governors:

Feb 1994-Dec 1997	Joseph Ajaung
Dec 1997-	Kuaj Miar Makwai

NORTHERN DARFUR

Capital: Fashir

Governors:

Feb 1994-Dec 1997	Al-Tijani Hassan al-Amin
Dec 1997-Jan 2000	Abd as-Sayyar Ali Safar
Jan 2000-	Abdullah Safi-al-Nur

NORTHERN KORDOFAN

Capital: Obeid

Governors:

Feb-Sept 1994	Mohammed al-Amu
Sept 1994-Dec 1997	Al-Awad al-Hassan (see former Northern State)
Dec 1997-Jan 2000	Ibrahim as-Sanussi
Jan 2000-	Osman al-Itadi Ibrahim

NORTHERN STATE

Capital: Dongola

Governors:

Feb-Sept 1994	Al-Awad al-Hassan
Sept 1994-Dec 1997	Adam Yusuf
Dec 1997-Jan 2000	Badwei al-Khair (see Red Sea)
Jan 2000-	Muttasim Abdul-Rahim

RED SEA

Capital: Port Sudan

Governors:

Feb 1994-Feb 1995	Badwei al-Khair
Feb-Aug 1995	Awad Khier Allah
Aug 1995-Dec 1997	Mohammed Osman
Dec 1997-	Abu Ali Majdhub Abu Ali

RIVER NILE

Capital: Damar

Governors:

Feb 1994-95	Al-Jayli as-Sharif
1995-Dec 1997	Abd al-Rahman al-Khatim
Dec 1997-Jan 2000	Ahmed Ali Qunayf
Jan 2000-	Hassan Sa'ad Ahmed

SENNAR

Capital: Singa

Governors:

Feb-June 1994	Mohammed Said
June-Aug 1994	Ali Mohammed
Aug 1994-May 1995	Mohammed Sidahmed
May 1995-Jan 2000	Ya'qub Shura
Jan 2000-	Younis al-Hussein

SOUTHERN DARFUR

Capital: Nyala

Governors:

Feb 1994-Dec 1997	Babikir Jabir Kabalo
Dec 1997-Jan 2000	Adam Yusuf (see Northern State)
Jan 2000-	Heraika Izz-Eddin

SOUTHERN KORDOFAN

Capital: Kadogli

Governors:

Feb 1994-Dec 1997	Habib Makhtoum
Dec 1997-Jan 2000	Abdullah Ubaydullah
Jan 2000-	Majzoub Babiker

UPPER NILE

Capital: Malakal

Governors:

Feb 1994-Dec 1997	Musa al-Mak Kor
Dec 1997-Feb 1998	Timothy Taban († air accident)
Feb 1998-Jan 2000	Timothy Tonfik
Jan 2000-	Peter Charlman

WAHDA (UNITY)

Capital: Bantio

Governors:

May 1995-Dec 1997	Michael Maein Chol
Dec 1997-	Taban Deng Gai

WARAP

Capital: Warap

Governors:

1994-2000	Arop Achur Akol
Jan 2000-	Moses Machar

WESTERN BAHR EL-GHAZAL

Capital: Wau

Governors:

Feb 1994-Dec 1997	Ali Fartak
Dec 1997-	Charles Jolo Boba

WESTERN DARFUR

Capital: Geneina

Governors:

Feb 1994-Sept 1995	Mohammed al-Fadul
Sept 1995-Dec 1997	Hassan Suleiman
Dec 1997-Jan 2000	Ibrahim Abd ar-Rahman
Jan 2000-	Omar Haroun Abdullah

WESTERN EQUATORIA

Capital: Yambio

Governor:

Feb 1994-	Isaiah Bol Riyani

WESTERN KORDOFAN

Capital: Fula

Governors:

Feb 1994-Dec 1997	Salah Ali al-Ghali
Dec 1997-Jan 2000	Bashir Rahmal
Jan 2000-	Al-Jaili Ahmed al-Sharif

WHITE NILE

Capital: Rabak

Governors:

Feb 1994-May 1995	Abdullah Deng Nial
May 1995-Dec 1997	Abdullah Said Ahmad
Dec 1997-Jan 2000	Abd al-Halim al-Mutu'afi
Jan 2000-	Badwai al-Kahir Idris (see Norther State)

Former States

BAHR EL-GHAZAL

Capital: Wau

Governors:

1991-92	George Kongor
1992-Feb 1994	Joseph Lasu

Divided into Buhairat, Northern Bahr el-Ghazal and Western Bahr el-Ghazal.

CENTRAL STATE

Capital: Wad Medani

Governor:

Feb 1991-Feb 1994	Suleiman Mohammed Suleiman

Divided into Blue Nile, al-Gezira, Sennar and White Nile.

DARFUR

Capital: Fashir

Governor:

Aug 1991-Feb 1994	El-Tayib Khayr

Divided into Northern, Southern and Western Darfur.

EASTERN STATE

Capital: Kassala

Governor:

Feb 1991-Feb 1994	El-Awad el-Hassan

Divided into Gadaref, Kassala, Red Sea and Warap.

EQUATORIA

Capital: Juba

Governors:

Aug 1991-Sept 1993	Satorlino Afika
Sept 1993-Feb 1994	Angelo Beda (see Southern Sudan)

Divided into Bahr al-Jabal, Eastern Equatoria and Western Equatoria.

KORDOFAN

Capital: Obeid

Governors:

1991	Faisal Mukhtar
1991-Feb 1994	El-Saeed el-Husseni

Divided into Northern, Southern and Western Kordofan.

NORTHERN STATE

Capital: Damar

Governors:

Feb 1991-Sept 1993	Mussad el-Nuweirri
Sept 1993-Feb 1994	Al-Sherif Badr

Divided into Northern State and River Nile

UPPER NILE

Capital: Malakal

Governor:

Feb 1991-Sept 1993   Gatluak Deng   († air accident)

Divided into Jonglei, Upper Nile and Wahda.

SURINAM

Official name: Republic of Surinam, Republiek Suriname
Independence date: 25 November 1975
Capital: Paramaribo

In 1667 Surinam became a Dutch colony in return for British occupation of New Netherlands in North America. Surinam was briefly occupied by Britain during the Napoleonic wars - 1799-1802 and 1804-16 - but returned to the Netherlands. In 1949 self- government was granted and in 1954 Surinam became part of the Dutch kingdom. Full independence was granted in 1975.

Governors:

1896-1902	Warmolt Tonckens
1902-05	Cornelis Lely
1905-08	Alexander Idenburg
1908-11	Dirk Fock
1911-16	Willem van Asbeck
1916-21	Gerard Staal
1921-28	Arnoud Heemstra
1928-33	Abrahaam Rutgers
1933-44	Johannes Kielstra
1944-48	Johannes Brons
1948-49	Willem Huender
1949-Feb 1956	Jan Klaasesz
Feb 1956-March 1963	Jan van Tilburg
March 1963-Feb 1965	Archibald Currie
Feb 1965-70	H.de Fries
1970-Nov 1975	Johan Ferrier

Presidents:

Nov 1975-Aug 1980	Johan Ferrier
Aug 1980-Feb 1982	Henk Chin A Sen
Feb 1982-Jan 1988	Fred Misier (acting Feb 1982-Feb 1984)
Jan 1988-Dec 1990	Ramsewak Shankar (deposed)
Dec 1990-Sept 1991	Johan Kraag
Sept 1991-Sept 1996	Ronald Venetiaan
Sept 1996-	Jules Wijdenbosch (NDP)

Prime Ministers:

June 1949-Jan 1951	Julius de Miranda (PSPP)

Jan 1951-Sept 1954	Johannes Buiskool
Sept 1954-May 1955	Archibald Currie
May 1955-June 1958	Johan Ferrier
June 1958-June 1963	Serverinus Emanuels
June 1963-Feb 1969	Johan-Adolf Pengel (NP)
Feb-Oct 1969	A.J.May
Oct 1969-Dec 1973	Jules Sedney (PNP)
Dec 1973-Feb 1980	Henck Arron (1st) (NP) (deposed)
March-Dec 1980	Henk Chin A Sen
(Dec 1980-March 1982	post abolished)
March-Dec 1982	Henry Neyhorst
Dec 1982-Feb 1983	Desiré (Desi) Bouterse (de facto)
Feb 1983-Jan 1984	Errol Alibux
Feb 1984-July 1986	Wim Udenhout
July 1986-Feb 1987	Pretaapnarain Radhakishun (1st)
Feb 1987-Jan 1988	Jules Wijdenbosch (1st)
Jan 1988-Dec 1990	Henck Arron (2nd) (NP)
Dec 1990-Sept 1991	Jules Wijdenbosch (2nd)
Sept 1991-Oct 1996	Jules Ajodhia
Oct 1996-	Pretaapnarain Radhakishun (MRC) (2nd)

MRC = Movement for Renewal and Change
NDP = National Democratic Party
NP = National Party
PNP = Progressive National Party
PSPP = Progressive Surinam People's Party

Military Leaders:

Chairman of the National Military Council

Feb-July 1980	Badresein Sital
July-Oct 1980	Charles Mijnals
Oct 1980-Jan 1988	Desiré (Desi) Bouterse
(Jan 1988	military rule ended)

SWAZILAND

Official name: Kingdom of Swaziland, Umbuso we Swatini
Independence date: 6 September 1968
Capital: Mbabane

The Swazi people moved into the area of present-day Swaziland in the latter half of the 17th century, and the Swazi kingdom was founded by Sobhuza I in about 1815. An agreement between the governments of Swaziland, Britain and the South African Republic (Transvaal) gave protective powers to the Transvaal. In 1902 these powers were taken over by Britain, and in 1910 Swaziland became a High Commission territory. In 1967 self-government was granted and Swaziland became a protectorate; full independence followed in 1968.

Kings:

c1750-c1780	Ngwane III
c1780-c1815	Nduvungunye (son)
c1815-c1836	Sobhuza I (Ngwane IV) (son)
1836-68	Mswati II (son)
1868-72	Ludvonga II (son)
	Regent: Sisile
1872-June 1875	Regent: Sisile
June 1875-Oct 1889	Mbandzeni (Dlamini IV) (half-brother of Ludvonga)
Oct 1889-Sept 1890	Regent: Labotsibeni (1st)
Sept 1890-Dec 1899	Bhunu (Ngwane) (son of Mbandzeni)
Dec 1899-Dec 1921	Regent: Labotsibeni (2nd)
Dec 1921-Aug 1982	Sobhuza II (b Nkhotfotjeni)
Aug 1982-Aug 1983	Regent: Dzeliwe Shongwe
Aug 1983-April 1986	Regent: Ntombi Thawala
April 1986-	Mswati III (b Makhosetive) (son of Sobhuza II & Ntombi)

Prime Ministers:

April 1967-May 1976	Prince Makhosini Dlamini (INM)
May 1976-Oct 1979	Maphevu Dlamini (†)
Oct-Nov 1979	Benjamin Nsibandze (acting)
Nov 1979-March 1983	Prince Mabandla Dlamini
March 1983-Oct 1986	Prince Bhekimpi Dlamini
Oct 1986-July 1989	Sotsha Dlamini
July 1989-Oct 1993	Obed Dlamini
Oct-Nov 1993	Andreas Fakudze (acting)
Nov 1993-May 1996	Prince Mbilini Dlamini

May-Aug 1996   Sishayi Nxumalo (acting)
Aug 1996-   B. Sibusiso Dlamini

INM = Imbokodvo National Movement

Resident Commissioners:

1907-16	Robert Coryndon
1917-28	DeSymons Honey
1928-35	Thomas Dickson
1935-37	Allan Marwick
1937-42	Charles Bruton
1942-46	Eric Featherstone
1946-50	Edward Beetham
1950-56	David Morgan
1956-63	Brian Marwick
1963-68	Francis Lloyd

SWEDEN

Official name: Kingdom of Sweden, Konungariket Sverige
State formed: 10th century
Capital: Stockholm

Sweden became a united country at the end of the 10th century when the Swedes and the Goths were united by Olof. The country has remained an independent monarchy, sometimes sharing monarchs with Norway and Denmark. Sweden has maintained a policy of neutrality through the conflicts which occurred in Europe in the twentieth century. In 1974, the functions of appointing the prime minister and signing laws was removed from the monarch, reducing the role to a purely ceremonial one.

Kings/Queens:

950-95	Erik VIII
995-1022	Olof (*son*)
1022-50	Anund Jakob (*son*)
1050-60	Edmund (*half-brother*)
1060-80	Stenkil (*son-in-law*)
1080-1110	Inge I/Halsten (*sons*)
1110-18	Filip (*son of Halsten*)
1118-22	Inge II (*brother*)
1130-56	Sverker I (assassinated)
1156-60	Erik IX (*cousin*)
1161-67	Carl VII Sverkersson (*son of Sverker I*) (assassinated)
1167-96	Knut I Eriksson (*son of Erik XII*)
1196-1208	Sverker II Carlsson (*son of Carl VII*) (deposed)
1208-April 1216	Erik X Knutsson (*son of Knut I*)
1216-22	Johan I Sverkersson (*son of Sverker II*) (deposed)
1222-29	Erik XI Eriksson (*son of Erik X*) (1st) (deposed)
1229-34	Knud II (*usurper*)
1234-50	Erik XI Eriksson (2nd)
Feb 1250-75	Valdemar (*nephew of Erik XI*) (deposed) (Regent 1250-66 Birgir)
1275-90	Magnus I Ladulas (*brother*)
1290-1318	Birgir Magnusson (*son*) (deposed) (Regent 1290-98 Torgils Knutsson)
1319-64	Magnus II Eriksson (*nephew*) (Magnus VII of Norway) (co-ruler 1356-64) (deposed)
1356-59	Erik XII (*son*) (co-ruler)
1362-64	Haakon (*son*) (Haakon VI of Norway) (deposed)
1364-89	Albrekt (*nephew of Magnus II*) (deposed)

1380-97	Margrethe (Margrethe I of Denmark & Norway)
1397-1434	Erik XIII (*great-nephew*) (Erik VII of Denmark & III of Norway)
1434-36	Regent: Engelbrekt Engelbrektsson
1436-40	Regent: Carl Knutsson
Oct 1440-Jan 1448	Christoffer (Christoffer III of Denmark & Norway) (*nephew of Erik XIII*)
Jan 1448-49	Regent: Bengt Jonsson Oxenstiorna
1449-57	Carl VIII Knutsson (*fRegent*) (1st) (deposed)
April 1457-64	Christian I (Christian I of Denmark)
1464-65	Carl VIII Knutsson (2nd)
(1465-67	interregnum)
1467-May 1470	Carl VIII Knutsson (3rd)
May 1470-97	Regent: Sten Sture the Elder
1497-Jan 1501	Johan II (Hans of Denmark)
Jan 1501-03	Regent: Sten Sture the Elder
1503-Jan 1512	Regent: Svante Sture
Jan-Aug 1512	Regent: Erik Trolle
Aug 1512-Feb 1520	Regent: Sten Sture the Younger
Feb 1520-June 1523	Christian II (Christian II of Denmark)
June 1523-Sept 1560	Gustaf I
Sept 1560-April 1568	Erik XIV (*son*) (deposed)
April 1568-May 1592	Johan III (*brother*)
May 1592-99	Sigismund (*son*) (deposed)
1599-Oct 1611	Carl IX (*uncle*)
Oct 1611-Nov 1632	Gustaf II Adolf (*son*) (killed in battle)
Nov 1632-June 1654	Christina (*daughter*) (abdicated)
June 1654-Feb 1660	Carl X Gustaf (*grandson of Carl IX*)
Feb 1660-April 1697	Carl XI (*son*)
April 1697-Dec 1718	Carl XII (*son*) (killed in battle)
Dec 1718-March 1720	Ulrica Eleonora (*sister*) (abdicated)
March 1720-April 1751	Fredrik (*husband*) (*b* Friedrich of Hesse)
April 1751-Feb 1771	Adolf Fredrik
Feb 1771-March 1792	Gustaf III (*son*) (assassinated)
March 1792-June 1809	Gustaf IV Adolf (*son*) (deposed)
June 1809-Feb 1818	Carl XIII (*uncle*)
Feb 1818-March 1844	Carl XIV Johan (*b* Jean-Baptiste Bernadotte) (*adopted son*)
March 1844-July 1859	Oscar I (*son*)
July 1859-Aug 1872	Carl XV (*son*)
Aug 1872-Dec 1907	Oscar II (*brother*)
Dec 1907-Oct 1950	Gustaf V (*son*)
Oct 1950-Sept 1973	Gustaf VI Adolf (*son*)
Sept 1973-	Carl XVI Gustaf (*grandson*)

Chancellors:

April 1858-June 1870	Ludwig Gerhard de Geer (1st)
June 1870-March 1874	Axel Adlercreutz
March 1874-May 1875	Edvard Carleson
May 1875-Feb 1876	Ludwig Gerhard de Geer (2nd)

Prime Ministers:

Feb 1876-April 1880	Ludwig Gerhard de Geer
April 1880-June 1883	Arvid Posse
June 1883-May 1884	Carl Thyselius
May 1884-Feb 1885	Oscar Themtander
Feb 1885-Oct 1889	Didrik Bildt
Oct 1889-July 1891	Johannes Akerhielm
July 1891-Sept 1900	Erik Bostrom (1st) (CP)
Sept 1900-July 1902	Frederik von Otter
July 1902-April 1905	Erik Bostrom (2nd) (CP)
April-Aug 1905	Johan Ramstedt
Aug-Nov 1905	Christian Lundeberg
Nov 1905-May 1906	Karl Staaf (1st) (LP)
May 1906-Sept 1911	Salomon Lindman (1st) (CP)
Oct 1911-Feb 1914	Karl Staaf (2nd) (LP)
Feb 1914-March 1917	Hjalmar Hammerskjold (CP)
March-Oct 1917	Carl Swartz (CP)
Oct 1917-March 1920	Nils Eden (LP)
March-Oct 1920	Hjalmar Branting (1st) (SDP)
Oct 1920-Feb 1921	Ludwig de Geer (CP)
Feb-Oct 1921	Oscar von Sydow (CP)
Oct 1921-April 1923	Hjalmar Branting (2nd) (SDP)
April 1923-Oct 1924	Ernst Trygger (LP)
Oct 1924-Jan 1925	Hjalmar Branting (3rd) (SDP)
Jan 1925-June 1926	Richard Sandlar
June 1926-Oct 1928	Carl Ekman (1st) (LP)
Oct 1928-June 1930	Salomon Lindman (2nd) (LP)
June 1930-Aug 1932	Carl Ekman (2nd) (LP)
Aug-Sept 1932	Felix Hamrin (LP)
Sept 1932-June 1936	Per Hansson (1st) (SDP)
June-Sept 1936	Axel Pehrsson-Bramstorp (AP)
Sept 1936-Oct 1946	Per Hansson (2nd) (SDP) (†)
Oct 1946-Oct 1969	Tage Erlander (SDP)
Oct 1969-Oct 1976	Olof Palme (1st) (SDP)
Oct 1976-Oct 1978	Thorbjörn Fälldin (1st) (CP)
Oct 1978-Oct 1979	Ola Ullsten (LP)
Oct 1979-Oct 1982	Thorbjörn Fälldin (2nd) (CP)
Oct 1982-Feb 1986	Olof Palme (2nd) (SDP) († assassinated)

Feb 1986-Oct 1991	Ingvar Carlsson (1st) (SDP)
Oct 1991-Oct 1994	Carl Bildt (CP)
Oct 1994-March 1996	Ingvar Carlsson (2nd) (SDP)
March 1996-	Göran Persson (SDP)

AP = Agrarian Party
CP = Conservative Party
LP = Liberal Party
SDP = Social Democratic Party

SWITZERLAND

Official name: Swiss Confederation, Schweizerische Eidgenossenschaft, Confederation Suisse, Confederazione Svizzera, Confederaziun Svizzra

State formed: 1 August 1291

Capital: Bern (Berne)

In 1291 three cantons, Uri, Unterwalden and Schwyz, formed the League of Helvetia. Other areas later joined forming a confederation which was recognised as an independent state by the Peace of Westphalia in 1648. France invaded Switzerland in 1798 and proclaimed the Helvetic Republic which lasted until 1813. In 1845 an attempt by seven cantons to secede led to virtual civil war. Agreement to end the dispute was followed by the formation of a central government in 1848. Switzerland has maintained a policy of neutrality throughout its existence.

Presidents:

Nov 1848-Dec 1849	Jonas Furrer (1st)
Jan-Dec 1850	Daniel-Henri Druery
Jan-Dec 1851	Martin Munzinger
Jan-Dec 1852	Jonas Furrer (2nd)
Jan-Dec 1853	Wilhelm Naeff
Jan-Dec 1854	Friedrich Frey-Herosee (1st)
Jan-Dec 1855	Jonas Furrer (3rd)
Jan-Dec 1856	Jakob Stämpfli (1st) (*f* Pres.of Bern)
Jan-Dec 1857	Charles Fornerod (1st) (*f* Pres.of Vaud)
Jan-Dec 1858	Jonas Furrer (4th)
Jan-Dec 1859	Jakob Stämpfli (2nd)
Jan-Dec 1860	Friedrich Frey-Herosee (2nd)
Jan-Dec 1861	Melchior Knüsel (1st)
Jan-Dec 1862	Jakob Stämpfli (3rd)
Jan-Dec 1863	Charles Fornerod (2nd)
Jan-Dec 1864	Jakob Dubs (1st) (*f* Pres.of Zurich)
Jan-Dec 1865	Karl Schenk (1st) (*f* Pres.of Berne)
Jan-Dec 1866	Melchior Knüsel (2nd)
Jan-Dec 1867	Charles Fornerod (3rd)
Jan-Dec 1868	Jakob Dubs (2nd)
Jan-Dec 1869	Emil Welti (1st) (*f* Pres.of Aargau)
Jan-Dec 1870	Jakob Dubs (3rd)
Jan-Dec 1871	Karl Schenk (2nd)
Jan-Dec 1872	Emil Welti (2nd)
Jan-Dec 1873	Paul Ceresole
Jan-Dec 1874	Karl Schenk (3rd)

Jan-Dec 1875	Jakob Scherer
Jan-Dec 1876	Emil Welti (3rd)
Jan-Dec 1877	Joachim Heer
Jan-Dec 1878	Karl Schenk (4th)
Jan-Dec 1879	Bernhard Hammer (1st)
Jan-Dec 1880	Emil Welti (4th)
Jan-Dec 1881	Numa Droz (1st)
Jan-Dec 1882	Simeon Bavier
Jan-Dec 1883	Louis Ruchonnet (1st) (*f* Pres.of Vaud)
Jan-Dec 1884	Emil Welti (5th)
Jan-Dec 1885	Karl Schenk (5th)
Jan-Dec 1886	Adolf Deucher (1st)
Jan-Dec 1887	Numa Droz (2nd)
Jan-Nov 1888	Wilhelm Hertenstein (†)
Nov 1888-Dec 1889	Bernhard Hammer (acting Nov-Dec 1888) (2nd)
Jan-Dec 1890	Louis Ruchonnet (2nd)
Jan-Dec 1891	Emil Welti (6th)
Jan-Dec 1892	Walter Hauser (1st)
Jan-Dec 1893	Karl Schenk (6th)
Jan-Dec 1894	Emil Frey
Jan-Dec 1895	Joseph Zemp (1st)
Jan-Dec 1896	Adrien Lachenal
Jan-Dec 1897	Adolf Deucher (2nd)
Jan-Dec 1898	Eugène Ruffy (*f* Pres.of Vaud)
Jan-Dec 1899	Eduard Müller (1st)
Jan-Dec 1900	Walter Hauser (2nd)
Jan-Dec 1901	Ernst Brenner (1st)
Jan-Dec 1902	Joseph Zemp (2nd)
Jan-Dec 1903	Adolf Deucher (3rd)
Jan-Dec 1904	Robert Complesse (1st)
Jan-Dec 1905	Marc-Émile Ruchet (1st)
Jan-Dec 1906	Ludwig Forrer (1st)
Jan-Dec 1907	Eduard Müller (2nd)
Jan-Dec 1908	Ernst Brenner (2nd)
Jan-Dec 1909	Adolf Deucher (4th)
Jan-Dec 1910	Robert Complesse (2nd)
Jan-Dec 1911	Marc-Émile Ruchet (2nd)
Jan-Dec 1912	Ludwig Forrer (2nd)
Jan-Dec 1913	Eduard Müller (3rd)
Jan-Dec 1914	Arthur Hoffman
Jan-Dec 1915	Giuseppe Motta (1st)
Jan-Dec 1916	Camille Decoppet (see Vaud)
Jan-Dec 1917	Edmund Schulthess (1st)
Jan-Dec 1918	Felix Calonder
Jan-Dec 1919	Gustave Ador

Jan-Dec 1920	Giuseppe Motta (2nd)
Jan-Dec 1921	Edmund Schulthess (2nd)
Jan-Dec 1922	Robert Haab (1st)
Jan-Dec 1923	Karl Scheurer
Jan-Dec 1924	Ernst Chuard (see Vaud)
Jan-Dec 1925	Jean-Marie Musy (1st)
Jan-Dec 1926	Heinrich Häberlin (1st)
Jan-Dec 1927	Giuseppe Motta (3rd)
Jan-Dec 1928	Edmund Schulthess (3rd)
Jan-Dec 1929	Robert Haab (2nd)
Jan-Dec 1930	Jean-Marie Musy (2nd)
Jan-Dec 1931	Heinrich Häberlin (2nd)
Jan-Dec 1932	Giuseppe Motta (4th)
Jan-Dec 1933	Edmund Schulthess (4th)
Jan-Dec 1934	Marcel Pilet-Golaz (1st)
Jan-Dec 1935	Rudolf Minger
Jan-Dec 1936	Albert Meyer (see Zug)
Jan-Dec 1937	Giuseppe Motta (5th)
Jan-Dec 1938	Johannes Baumann
Jan-Dec 1939	Philipp Etter (1st) (CCP) (see Zug)
Jan-Dec 1940	Marcel Pilet-Golaz (2nd)
Jan-Dec 1941	Ernst Wetter
Jan-Dec 1942	Philipp Etter (2nd) (CCP)
Jan-Dec 1943	Enrico Celio (1st) (CCP)
Jan-Dec 1944	Walter Stämpfli (RP)
Jan-Dec 1945	Eduard von Steiger (1st) (PMCP)
Jan-Dec 1946	Karl Kobelt (1st) (RP)
Jan-Dec 1947	Philipp Etter (3rd) (CCP)
Jan-Dec 1948	Enrico Celio (2nd) (CCP)
Jan-Dec 1949	Ernst Nobs (SP) (see Zurich)
Jan-Dec 1950	Max Petitpierre (1st) (RP)
Jan-Dec 1951	Eduard von Steiger (2nd) (PMCP)
Jan-Dec 1952	Karl Kobelt (2nd) (RP)
Jan-Dec 1953	Philipp Etter (4th) (CCP)
Jan-Dec 1954	Rodolphe Rubattel (RP) (see Vaud)
Jan-Dec 1955	Max Petitpierre (2nd) (RP)
Jan-Dec 1956	Markus Feldmann (PMCP) (see Bern)
Jan-Dec 1957	Hans Streuli (RP) (see Zurich)
Jan-Dec 1958	Thomas Holenstein (CCP)
Jan-Dec 1959	Paul Chaudet (1st) (RP) (see Vaud)
Jan-Dec 1960	Max Petitpierre (3rd) (RP)
Jan-Dec 1961	Friedrich Wahlen (PMCP)
Jan-Dec 1962	Paul Chaudet (2nd) (RP)
Jan-Dec 1963	Willy Spühler (1st) (SDP)
Jan-Dec 1964	Ludwig von Moos (1st) (CCP) (see Obwalden)

Jan-Dec 1965   Hans-Peter Tschudi   (1st) (SDP) (see Basel-Stadt)
Jan-Dec 1966   Hans Schaffner   (RP)
Jan-Dec 1967   Roger Bonvin   (1st) (CCP)
Jan-Dec 1968   Willy Spühler   (2nd) (SDP)
Jan-Dec 1969   Ludwig von Moos   (2nd) (CCP)
Jan-Dec 1970   Hans-Peter Tschudi   (2nd) (SDP)
Jan-Dec 1971   Rudolf Gnägi   (1st) (PMCP) (see Bern)
Jan-Dec 1972   Nello Celio   (RP) (see Ticino)
Jan-Dec 1973   Roger Bonvin   (2nd) (CCP)
Jan-Dec 1974   Ernst Brugger   (RP)
Jan-Dec 1975   Pierre Graber   (SDP) (see Vaud)
Jan-Dec 1976   Rudolf Gnägi   (2nd) (PMCP)
Jan-Dec 1977   Kurt Furgler   (1st) (CDPP)
Jan-Dec 1978   Willi Ritschard   (SDP) (see Solothurn)
Jan-Dec 1979   Hans Hürlimann   (CDPP) (see Zug)
Jan-Dec 1980   George-André Chevallez   (RDP)
Jan-Dec 1981   Kurt Furgler   (2nd) (CDPP)
Jan-Dec 1982   Fritz Honegger   (RDP)
Jan-Dec 1983   Pierre Aubert   (1st) (SDP) (see Vaud)
Jan-Dec 1984   Leon Schlumpf   (CDPP) (see Graubünden)
Jan-Dec 1985   Kurt Furgler   (3rd) (CDPP)
Jan-Dec 1986   Alphons Egli   (CDPP)
Jan-Dec 1987   Pierre Aubert   (2nd) (SDP)
Jan-Dec 1988   Otto Stich   (1st) (SDP)
Jan-Dec 1989   Jean-Pascal Delamuraz   (1st) (RDP)
Jan-Dec 1990   Arnold Koller   (1st) (CDPP)
Jan-Dec 1991   Flavio Cotti   (1st) (CDPP) (see Ticino)
Jan-Dec 1992   René Felber   (SDP)
Jan-Dec 1993   Adolf Ogi   (1st) (SPP)
Jan-Dec 1994   Otto Stich   (2nd) (SDP)
Jan-Dec 1995   Kaspar Villiger   (RDP)
Jan-Dec 1996   Jean-Pascal Delamuraz   (2nd) (RDP)
Jan-Dec 1997   Arnold Koller   (2nd) (CDPP)
Jan-Dec 1998   Flavio Cotti   (2nd) (CDPP)
Jan-Dec 1999   Ruth Dreifuss   (SP)
Jan-Dec 2000   Adolf Ogi   (2nd) (SPP)

CCP = Catholic Conservative Party
CDPP = Christian Democratic People's Party
PMCP = Peasant & Middle Class Party
RDP = Radical Democratic Party (fRP)
RP = Radical Party
SDP = Social Democratic Party
SP = Socialist Party
SPP = Swiss People's Party

Cantons and Half-Cantons (latter designated by *)

In most cases government leaders since 1900 are listed

AARGAU

Entry into confederation: 1803
Capital: Aarau

Presidents:

Landammann

April 1900-March 1901	Karl Fahrländer (4th)
April 1901-March 1902	Arnold Ringier (4th)
April 1902-March 1903	Gottlieb Käppeli (6th)
April 1903-March 1904	Hans Müri (1st)
April 1904-March 1905	Peter Conrad (3rd)
April 1905-March 1906	Karl Fahrländer (5th)
April 1906-March 1907	Arnold Ringier (5th)
April 1907-March 1908	Hans Müri (2nd)
April 1908-March 1909	Hermann Huber
April 1909-March 1910	Peter Conrad (4th)
April 1910-March 1911	Max Schmidt (1st)
April 1911-March 1912	Arnold Ringier (6th)
April 1912-March 1913	Emil Keller (1st)
April 1913-March 1914	Peter Conrad (5th)
April 1914-March 1915	Max Schmidt (2nd)
April 1915-March 1916	Oskar Schibler (1st)
April 1916-March 1917	Arnold Ringier (7th)
April 1917-March 1918	Xaver Stalder (1st)
April 1918-March 1919	Emil Keller (2nd)
April 1919-March 1920	Max Schmidt (3rd)
April 1920-March 1921	Oskar Schibler (2nd)
April 1921-March 1922	Xaver Stalder (2nd)
April 1922-March 1923	Albert Studler (1st)
April 1923-March 1924	Emil Keller (3rd)
April 1924-March 1925	Max Schmidt (4th)
April 1925-March 1926	Oskar Schibler (3rd)
April 1926-March 1927	Xaver Stalder (3rd)
April 1927-March 1928	Albert Studler (2nd)
April 1928-March 1929	Emil Keller (4th)
April 1929-March 1930	Oskar Schibler (4th)
April 1930-March 1931	Xaver Stalder (4th)
April 1931-March 1932	Fritz Zaugg (1st)
April 1932-March 1933	Albert Studler (3rd)

April 1933-March 1934	Emil Keller (5th)
April 1934-March 1935	Xaver Stalder (5th)
April 1935-March 1936	Rudolf Siegrist (1st)
April 1936-March 1937	Fritz Zaugg (2nd)
April 1937-March 1938	Albert Studler (4th)
April 1938-March 1939	Josef Rüttimann (1st)
April 1939-March 1940	Emil Keller (6th)
April 1940-March 1941	Rudolf Siegrist (2nd)
April 1941-March 1942	Fritz Zaugg (3rd)
April 1942-March 1943	Albert Studler (5th)
April 1943-March 1944	Josef Rüttimann (2nd)
April 1944-March 1945	Emil Keller (7th)
April 1945-March 1946	Rudolf Siegrist (3rd)
April 1946-March 1947	Fritz Zaugg (4th)
April 1947-March 1948	Albert Studler (6th)
April 1948-March 1949	Ernst Bachmann (1st)
April 1949-March 1950	Josef Rüttimann (3rd)
April 1950-March 1951	Rudolf Siegrist (4th)
April 1951-March 1952	Fritz Zaugg (5th)
April 1952-March 1953	Kurt Kim (1st)
April 1953-March 1954	Ernst Bachmann (2nd)
April 1954-March 1955	Rudolf Siegrist (5th)
April 1955-March 1956	Paul Hausherr (1st)
April 1956-March 1957	Ernst Schwarz (1st)
April 1957-March 1958	Kurt Kim (2nd)
April 1958-March 1959	Adolf Richner (1st)
April 1959-March 1960	Ernst Bachmann (3rd)
April 1960-March 1961	Paul Hausherr (2nd)
April 1961-March 1962	Ernst Schwarz (2nd)
April 1962-March 1963	Kurt Kim (3rd)
April 1963-March 1964	Adolf Richner (2nd)
April 1964-March 1965	Ernst Bachmann (4th)
April 1965-March 1966	Ernst Schwarz (3rd)
April 1966-March 1967	Kurt Kim (4th)
April 1967-March 1968	Adolf Richner (3rd)
April 1968-March 1969	Leo Weber (1st)
April 1969-March 1970	Arthur Schmid (1st)
April 1970-March 1971	Bruno Hunziker (1st)
April 1971-March 1972	Leo Weber (2nd)
April 1972-March 1973	Louis Lang (1st)
April 1973-March 1974	Jorg Ursprung (1st)
April 1974-March 1975	Arthur Schmid (2nd)
April 1975-March 1976	Bruno Hunziker (2nd)
April 1976-March 1977	Louis Lang (2nd)
April 1977-March 1978	Jorg Ursprung (2nd)

April 1978-March 1979	Arthur Schmid (3rd)
April 1979-March 1980	Kurt Lareida (1st)
April 1980-March 1981	Hans Huber (1st)
April 1981-March 1982	Louis Lang (3rd)
April 1982-March 1983	Jorg Ursprung (3rd)
April 1983-March 1984	Arthur Schmid (4th)
April 1984-March 1985	Kurt Lareida (2nd)
April 1985-March 1986	Hans Huber (2nd)
April 1986-March 1987	Ulrich Siegrist (1st)
April 1987-March 1988	Arthur Schmid (5th)
April 1988-March 1989	Kurt Lareida (3rd)
April 1989-March 1990	Victor Rickenbach
April 1990-March 1991	Ulrich Siegrist (2nd)
April 1991-March 1992	Arthur Schmid (6th)
April 1992-March 1993	Peter Wertli (1st)
April 1993-March 1994	Ulrich Siegrist (3rd)
April 1994-March 1995	Thomas Pfisterer (1st)
April 1995-March 1996	Peter Wertli (2nd)
April 1996-March 1997	Silvio Bircher
April 1997-March 1998	Stéphanie Mörikofer-Zwez
April 1998-March 1999	Ulrich Siegrist (3rd)
April 1999-March 2000	Thomas Pfisterer (2nd)
April 2000-	Peter Wertli (3rd)

APPENZELL-AUSSER RHODEN*

Half-canton created: 1597; Appenzell entered confederation in 1513
Capital: Herisau

Presidents:

Landammann

April 1898-April 1901	Jakob Lutz (1st)
April 1901-April 1904	Arthur Eugster (1st)
April 1904-April 1907	Jakob Lutz (2nd)
April 1907-April 1910	Arthur Eugster (2nd)
April 1910-April 1913	Johannes Baumann (1st)
April 1913-April 1916	Johann Tobler
April 1916-April 1919	Johannes Baumann (2nd)
April 1919-April 1921	Hans Ruckstuhl
April 1921-April 1924	Johannes Baumann (3rd)
April 1924-April 1927	Gustav Altherr (1st)
April 1927-April 1930	Johannes Baumann (4th)
April 1930-April 1933	Gustav Altherr (2nd)
April 1933-April 1936	Walter Ackermann (1st)

April 1936-April 1939	Gustav Altherr (3rd)
April 1939-April 1942	Walter Ackermann (2nd)
April 1942-April 1945	Alfred Hofstetter
April 1945-April 1948	Walter Ackermann (3rd)
April 1948-April 1951	Jakob Bruderer (1st)
April 1951-April 1954	Adolf Bodmer (1st)
April 1954-April 1956	Jakob Bruderer (2nd)
April 1956-April 1959	Adolf Bodmer (2nd)
April 1959-April 1962	Jakob Langenauer (1st)
April 1962-April 1965	Hermann Kündig
April 1965-April 1968	Jakob Langenauer (2nd)
April 1968-April 1971	Otto Bruderer (1st)
April 1971-April 1972	Jakob Langenauer (2nd)
April 1972-April 1975	Otto Bruderer (2nd)
April 1975-April 1978	Willi Walser (1st)
April 1978-April 1980	Otto Bruderer (3rd)
April 1980-April 1981	Willi Walser (2nd)
April 1981-April 1984	Rudolf Reutlinger
April 1984-April 1987	Hans Höhener (1st)
April 1987-April 1990	Hans Hohl (1st)
April 1990-April 1993	Hans Höhener (2nd)
April 1993-April 1994	Hans Hohl (2nd)
April 1994-June 1997	Hans Höhener (3rd)
June 1997-June 2000	Marianne Kleiner

APPENZELL-INNER RHODEN*

Half canton created: 1597; Appenzell entered confederation in 1513
Capital: Appenzell

Presidents:

Landammann

April 1899-April 1901	Karl Sonderegger (2nd)
April 1901-April 1903	Johann Dähler (5th)
April 1903-April 1905	Karl Sonderegger (3rd)
April 1905-April 1907	Johann Dähler (6th)
April 1907-April 1909	Adolf Steuble (1st)
April 1909-April 1911	Johann Dähler (7th)
April 1911-April 1913	Adolf Steuble (2nd)
April 1913-April 1915	Johann Dähler (8th)
April 1915-April 1917	Adolf Steuble (3rd)
April 1917-April 1919	Johann Dähler (9th)
April 1919-April 1921	Adolf Steuble (4th)

April 1921-April 1923	Johann Dähler (10th)
April 1923-April 1925	Adolf Steuble (5th)
April 1925-April 1927	Carl Rusch (1st)
April 1927-April 1929	Edmund Dähler (1st)
April 1929-April 1931	Carl Rusch (2nd)
April 1931-April 1933	Edmund Dähler (2nd)
April 1933-April 1935	Carl Rusch (3rd)
April 1935-April 1937	Edmund Dähler (3rd)
April 1937-April 1939	Carl Rusch (4th)
April 1939-April 1941	Armin Locher (1st)
April 1941-April 1943	Carl Rusch (5th)
April 1943-April 1945	Armin Locher (2nd)
April 1945-April 1946	Carl Rusch (6th) (†)
April 1946-April 1949	Armin Locher (3rd)
April 1949-April 1951	Albert Broger (1st)
April 1951-April 1953	Armin Locher (4th)
April 1953-April 1955	Albert Broger (2nd)
April 1955-April 1957	Armin Locher (5th)
April 1957-April 1959	Albert Broger (3rd)
April 1959-Oct 1960	Beat Dorig (†)
Oct 1960-April 1963	Albert Broger (4th)
April 1963-April 1965	Karl Dobler
April 1965-April 1967	Leo Mittelholzer (1st)
April 1967-April 1969	Raymund Broger (1st)
April 1969-April 1971	Leo Mittelholzer (2nd)
April 1971-April 1973	Raymund Broger (2nd)
April 1973-April 1974	Leo Mittelholzer (3rd)
April 1974-April 1976	Raymund Broger (3rd)
April 1976-April 1978	Johann Fritsche (1st)
April 1978-Feb 1980	Raymund Broger (4th) (†)
Feb 1980-April 1982	Johann Fritsche (2nd)
April 1982-April 1984	Franz Breitenmoser
April 1984-April 1986	Carlo Schmid (1st)
April 1986-April 1988	Beat Graf (1st)
April 1988-April 1990	Carlo Schmid (2nd)
April 1990-April 1992	Beat Graf (2nd)
April 1992-April 1994	Carlo Schmid (3rd)
April 1994-April 1996	Arthur Loepfe (1st)
April 1996-April 1998	Carlo Schmid (4th)
April 1998-April 2000	Arthur Loepfe (2nd)

BASEL-LANDSCHAFT*

Entry into confederation: 1501 as part of Basel which was divided into two half-cantons in 1833
Capital: Liestal

Presidents:

July 1900-June 1901	Adolf Brodbeck (1st)
July 1901-June 1902	Albert Grieder (2nd)
July 1902-June 1903	Heinrich Glaser (5th)
July 1903-June 1904	Gustav Rebmann (5th)
July 1904-June 1905	Albert Grieder (3rd)
July 1905-June 1906	Adolf Brodbeck (2nd)
July 1906-June 1907	Gustav Rebmann (6th)
July 1907-June 1908	Gustav Bay (2nd)
July 1908-June 1909	Heinrich Glaser (6th)
July 1909-June 1910	Albert Grieder (4th)
July 1910-June 1911	Adolf Brodbeck (3rd)
July 1911-June 1912	Gustav Rebmann (7th)
July 1912-June 1913	Gustav Bay (3rd)
July 1913-June 1914	Heinrich Glaser (7th)
July 1914-June 1915	Albert Grieder (5th)
July 1915-June 1916	Adolf Brodbeck (4th)
July 1916-June 1917	Gustav Bay (4th)
July 1917-June 1918	Albert Schwander
July 1918-June 1919	Albert Grieder (6th)
July 1919-June 1920	Adolf Brodbeck (5th)
July 1920-June 1921	Gustav Bay (5th)
July 1921-June 1922	Carl Tanner
July 1922-June 1923	Albert Grieder (7th)
July 1923-June 1924	Gustav Bay (6th)
July 1924-June 1925	Carl Spinnler
July 1925-June 1926	Julius Frei (1st)
July 1926-June 1927	Adolf Seiler (1st)
July 1927-June 1928	Albert Grieder (8th)
July 1928-June 1929	Gustav Bay (7th)
July 1929-June 1930	Jakob Mosimann (1st)
July 1930-June 1931	Julius Frei (2nd)
July 1931-June 1932	Adolf Seiler (2nd)
July 1932-June 1933	Jakob Mosimann (2nd)
July 1933-June 1934	Julius Frei (3rd)
July 1934-June 1935	Walter Hilfiker (1st)
July 1935-June 1936	Ernst Erny (1st)
July 1936-June 1937	Adolf Seiler (3rd)
July 1937-June 1938	Jakob Mosimann (3rd)
July 1938-June 1939	Walter Hilfiker (2nd)
July 1939-June 1940	Ernst Erny (2nd)
July 1940-June 1941	Hugo Gschwind (1st)
July 1941-June 1942	Jakob Mosimann (4th)
July 1942-June 1943	Walter Hilfiker (3rd)

July 1943-June 1944	Ernst Erny (3rd)
July 1944-June 1945	Hugo Gschwind (2nd)
July 1945-June 1946	Jakob Mosimann (5th)
July 1946-June 1947	Hans Leupin
July 1947-June 1948	Leo Mann
July 1948-June 1949	Ernst Erny (4th)
July 1949-June 1950	Heinrich Abegg (1st)
July 1950-June 1951	Otto Kopp (1st)
July 1951-June 1952	Max Kaufmann (1st)
July 1952-June 1953	Heinrich Abegg (2nd)
July 1953-June 1954	Ernst Börlin (1st)
July 1954-June 1955	Paul Gurtler (1st)
July 1955-June 1956	Otto Kopp (2nd)
July 1956-June 1957	Max Kaufmann (2nd)
July 1957-June 1958	Heinrich Abegg (3rd)
July 1958-June 1959	Ernst Börlin (2nd)
July 1959-June 1960	Paul Gurtler (2nd)
July 1960-June 1961	Max Kaufmann (3rd)
July 1961-June 1962	Heinrich Abegg (4th)
July 1962-June 1963	Ernst Börlin (3rd)
July 1963-June 1964	Leo Lejeune (1st)
July 1964-June 1965	Paul Gurtler (3rd)
July 1965-June 1966	Max Kaufmann (4th)
July 1966-June 1967	Ernst Börlin (4th)
July 1967-June 1968	Ernst Löliger (1st)
July 1968-June 1969	Leo Lejeune (2nd)
July 1969-June 1970	Karl Zeltner
July 1970-June 1971	Theo Meier (1st)
July 1971-June 1972	Paul Manz (1st)
July 1972-June 1973	Ernst Löliger (2nd)
July 1973-June 1974	Leo Lejeune (3rd)
July 1974-June 1975	Theo Meier (2nd)
July 1975-June 1976	Clemens Stöckli (1st)
July 1976-June 1977	Paul Manz (2nd)
July 1977-June 1978	Theo Meier (3rd)
July 1978-June 1979	Paul Jenni (1st)
July 1979-June 1980	Paul Nyffeler (1st)
July 1980-June 1981	Clemens Stöckli (2nd)
July 1981-June 1982	Paul Manz (3rd)
July 1982-June 1983	Theo Meier (4th)
July 1983-June 1984	Paul Jenni (2nd)
July 1984-June 1985	Paul Nyffeler (2nd)
July 1985-June 1986	Clemens Stöckli (3rd)
July 1986-June 1987	Werner Spitteler (1st)
July 1987-June 1988	Paul Nyffeler (3rd)

July 1988-June 1989	Clemens Stöckli (4th)
July 1989-June 1990	Werner Spitteler (2nd)
July 1990-June 1991	Hans Fünfschilling (1st)
July 1991-June 1992	Eduard Belser (1st)
July 1992-June 1993	Peter Schmid (1st)
July 1993-June 1994	Werner Spitteler (3rd)
July 1994-June 1995	Hans Fünfschilling (2nd)
July 1995-June 1996	Andreas Koellreuter
July 1996-June 1997	Eduard Belser (2nd)
July 1997-June 1998	Peter Schmid (2nd)
July 1998-June 1999	Elisabeth Schneider
July 1999-June 2000	Hans Fünfschilling (3rd)

BASEL-STADT*

Entry into confederation: 1501 as part of Basel which was divided into two half-cantons in 1833
Capital: Basel

Presidents:

May 1900-May 1901	Heinrich Reese (1st)
May 1901-May 1902	Heinrich David
May 1902-May 1903	Paul Speiser (3rd)
May 1903-May 1904	Richard Zutt (3rd)
May 1904-May 1905	Eugen Wullschleger (1st)
May 1905-May 1906	Albert Burckhardt-Finsler
May 1906-May 1907	Heinrich Reese (2nd)
May 1907-May 1908	Hans Burckhardt
May 1908-May 1909	Christian Burckhardt-Schazmann
May 1909-May 1910	Richard Zutt (4th)
May 1910-May 1911	Eugen Wullschleger (2nd)
May 1911-May 1912	Armin Stöcklin (1st)
May 1912-May 1913	Paul Speiser (4th)
May 1913-May 1914	Hermann Blocher
May 1914-May 1915	Friedrich Aemmer (1st)
May 1915-May 1916	Eugen Wullschleger (3rd)
May 1916-May 1917	Rudolf Miescher (1st)
May 1917-May 1918	Armin Stöcklin (2nd)
May 1918-May 1919	Adolf Im Hof (1st)
May 1919-May 1920	Friedrich Aemmer (2nd)
May 1920-May 1921	Fritz Hauser (1st)
May 1921-May 1922	August Brenner (1st)
May 1922-May 1923	Friedrich Schneider
May 1923-May 1924	Rudolf Niederhauser (1st)
May 1924-May 1925	Rudolf Miescher (2nd)

May 1925-May 1926	Adolf Im Hof (2nd)
May 1926-May 1927	Friedrich Aemmer (3rd)
May 1927-May 1928	Gustav Wenk (1st)
May 1928-May 1929	Fritz Hauser (2nd)
May 1929-May 1930	August Brenner (2nd)
May 1930-May 1931	Rudolf Niederhauser (2nd)
May 1931-May 1932	Adolf Im Hof (3rd)
May 1932-May 1933	Carl Ludwig (1st)
May 1933-May 1934	Friedrich Aemmer (4th)
May 1934-May 1935	Gustav Wenk (2nd)
May 1935-May 1936	Fritz Hauser (3rd)
May 1936-May 1937	Edwin Zweifel (1st)
May 1937-May 1938	Fritz Brechbühl (1st)
May 1938-May 1939	Fritz Ebi (1st)
May 1939-May 1940	Adolf Im Hof (4th)
May 1940-May 1941	Carl Ludwig (2nd)
May 1941-May 1942	Gustav Wenk (3rd)
May 1942-May 1943	Edwin Zweifel (2nd)
May 1943-May 1944	Carl Miville
May 1944-May 1945	Fritz Brechbühl (2nd)
May 1945-May 1946	Fritz Ebi (2nd)
May 1946-May 1947	Carl Peter (1st)
May 1947-May 1948	Gustav Wenk (4th)
May 1948-May 1949	Peter Zschokke (1st)
May 1949-May 1950	Edwin Zweifel (1st)
May 1950-May 1951	Fritz Brechbühl (3rd)
May 1951-May 1952	Fritz Ebi (3rd)
May 1952-May 1953	Alfred Schaller (1st)
May 1953-May 1954	Carl Peter (2nd)
May 1954-May 1955	Peter Zschokke (2nd)
May 1955-May 1956	Hans-Peter Tschudi
May 1956-May 1957	Edwin Zweifel (2nd)
May 1957-May 1958	Fritz Brechbühl (4th)
May 1958-May 1959	Max Wullschleger (1st)
May 1959-May 1960	Alfred Schaller (2nd)
May 1960-May 1961	Carl Peter (3rd)
May 1961-May 1962	Peter Zschokke (3rd)
May 1962-May 1963	Edmund Wyss (1st)
May 1963-May 1964	Fritz Brechbühl (5th)
May 1964-May 1965	Max Wullschleger (2nd)
May 1965-May 1966	Alfred Ab Egg
May 1966-May 1967	Franz Hauser (1st)
May 1967-May 1968	Edmund Wyss (2nd)
May 1968-May 1969	Lukas Burckhardt (1st)
May 1969-May 1970	Arnold Schneider (1st)

May 1970-May 1971	Otto Miescher
May 1971-May 1972	Max Wullschleger (3rd)
May 1972-May 1973	Franz Hauser (2nd)
May 1973-May 1974	Edmund Wyss (3rd)
May 1974-May 1975	Eugen Keller (1st)
May 1975-May 1976	Kurt Jenny (1st)
May 1976-May 1977	Lukas Burckhardt (2nd)
May 1977-May 1978	Arnold Schneider (2nd)
May 1978-May 1979	Karl Schnyder (1st)
May 1979-May 1980	Hansruedi Schmid
May 1980-May 1981	Edmund Wyss (4th)
May 1981-May 1982	Eugen Keller (2nd)
May 1982-May 1983	Peter Facklam (1st)
May 1983-May 1984	Kurt Jenny (2nd)
May 1984-May 1985	Karl Schnyder (2nd)
May 1985-May 1986	Eugen Keller (3rd)
May 1986-May 1987	Hans-Rudolf Striebel (1st)
May 1987-May 1988	Mathias Feldges (1st)
May 1988-May 1989	Remo Gysin
May 1989-May 1990	Peter Facklam (2nd)
May 1990-May 1991	Kurt Jenny (3rd)
May 1991-May 1992	Karl Schnyder (3rd)
May 1992-May 1993	Hans-Rudolf Striebel (2nd)
May 1993-May 1994	Mathias Feldges (2nd)
May 1994-May 1995	Christoph Stutz
May 1995-Jan 1997	Jörg Schild
Feb 1997-Jan 1998	Ueli Vischer
Feb 1998-Jan 1999	Veronica Schaller
Feb 1999-Jan 2000	Hans-Martin Tschudi
Feb 2000-	Stefan Cornaz

BERN

Entry into confederation: 1353
Capital: Bern (Berne)

Presidents:

June 1900-May 1901	Johann Minder
June 1901-May 1902	Louis Joliat
June 1902-May 1903	Edmund von Steiger (2nd)
June 1903-May 1904	Albert Gobat (3rd)
June 1904-May 1905	Friedrich von Wattenwyl (2nd)
June 1905-May 1906	Johann Ritschard (2nd)
June 1906-May 1907	Gottfried Kunz

June 1907-May 1908	Alfred Kläy (2nd)
June 1908-May 1909	Henri Simonin (1st)
June 1909-May 1910	Karl Könitzer
June 1910-May 1911	Karl Moser (1st)
June 1911-May 1912	Fritz Burren (1st)
June 1912-May 1913	Emil Lohner (1st)
June 1913-May 1914	Karl Schreuer
June 1914-May 1915	Rudolf von Erlach
June 1915-May 1916	Albert Locher
June 1916-May 1917	Hans Tschumi (1st)
June 1917-May 1918	Leo Merz (1st)
June 1918-May 1919	Henri Simonin (2nd)
June 1919-May 1920	Karl Moser (2nd)
June 1920-May 1921	Alfred Stauffer
June 1921-May 1922	Fritz Burren (2nd)
June 1922-May 1923	Friedrich Volmar
June 1923-May 1924	Hans Tschumi (2nd)
June 1924-May 1925	Emil Lohner (2nd)
June 1925-May 1926	Leo Merz (2nd)
June 1926-May 1927	Walter Bösiger (1st)
June 1927-May 1928	Karl Moser (3rd)
June 1928-May 1929	Fritz Joss (1st)
June 1929-May 1930	Paul Guggisberg (1st)
June 1930-May 1931	Hugo Dürrenmatt (1st)
June 1931-May 1932	Alfred Rudolf (1st)
June 1932-May 1933	Henri Mouttet (1st)
June 1933-May 1934	Hans Stähli (1st)
June 1934-May 1935	Alfred Stauffer (2nd)
June 1935-May 1936	Walter Bösiger (2nd)
June 1936-May 1937	Arnold Seematter (1st)
June 1937-May 1938	Fritz Joss (2nd)
June 1938-May 1939	Paul Guggisberg (2nd)
June 1939-May 1940	Hugo Dürrenmatt (2nd)
June 1940-May 1941	Robert Grimm
June 1941-May 1942	Georges Moeckli (1st)
June 1942-May 1943	Max Gagner (1st)
June 1943-May 1944	Alfred Rudolf (2nd)
June 1944-May 1945	Henri Mouttet (2nd)
June 1945-May 1946	Hans Stähli (2nd)
June 1946-May 1947	Arnold Seematter (2nd)
June 1947-May 1948	Markus Feldmann
June 1948-May 1949	Walter Siegenthaler (1st)
June 1949-May 1950	Fritz Giovanoli (1st)
June 1950-May 1951	Samuel Brawand (1st)
June 1951-May 1952	Virgile Moine (1st)

June 1952-May 1953	Dewet Buri (1st)
June 1953-May 1954	Georges Moeckli (2nd)
June 1954-May 1955	Rudolf Gnägi
June 1955-May 1956	Max Gagner (2nd)
June 1956-May 1957	Robert Bauder (1st)
June 1957-May 1958	Henri Huber (1st)
June 1958-May 1959	Walter Siegenthaler (2nd)
June 1959-May 1960	Fritz Giovanoli (2nd)
June 1960-May 1961	Fritz Moser (1st)
June 1961-May 1962	Samuel Brawand (2nd)
June 1962-May 1963	Hans Tschumi (1st)
June 1963-May 1964	Virgile Moine (2nd)
June 1964-May 1965	Erwin Schneider (1st)
June 1965-May 1966	Dewet Buri (2nd)
June 1966-May 1967	Adolf Blaser
June 1967-May 1968	Robert Bauder (2nd)
June 1968-May 1969	Henri Huber (2nd)
June 1969-May 1970	Fritz Moser (2nd)
June 1970-May 1971	Hans Tschumi (2nd)
June 1971-May 1972	Erwin Schneider (2nd)
June 1972-May 1973	Simon Kohler
June 1973-May 1974	Ernst Jaberg
June 1974-May 1975	Ernst Blaser (1st)
June 1975-May 1976	Robert Bauder (3rd)
June 1976-May 1977	Werner Martignoni (1st)
June 1977-May 1978	Bernhard Müller (1st)
June 1978-May 1979	Kurt Meyer
June 1979-May 1980	Ernst Blaser (3rd)
June 1980-May 1981	Nehri-Louis Favre
June 1981-May 1982	Gotthelf Bürki
June 1982-May 1983	Henri Sommer
June 1983-May 1984	Peter Schmid (1st)
June 1984-May 1985	Hans Krähenbuhl
June 1985-May 1986	Werner Martignoni (2nd)
June 1986-May 1987	René Bärtschi (1st)
June 1987-May 1988	Bernhard Müller (2nd)
June 1988-May 1989	Peter Siegenthaler
June 1989-May 1990	Ueli Augsburger
June 1990-May 1991	Peter Schmid (2nd)
June 1991-May 1992	René Bärtschi (2nd)
June 1992-May 1993	Peter Widmer
June 1993-May 1994	Hermann Fehr
June 1994-May 1995	Mario Annoni (1st)
June 1995-May 1996	Dori Schaer-Born
June 1996-May 1997	Hans Lauri

COUNTRIES AND REGIONS

June 1997-May 1998   Elisabeth Zölch-Balmer
June 1998-May 1999   Mario Annoni   (2nd)
June 1999-May 2000   Samuel Bhend

FRIBOURG

Entry into confederation: 1481
Capital: Fribourg

Presidents of the Council of State:

Jan-Dec 1900	Aloys Bossy (1st)
Jan-Dec 1901	Charles Weck (1st)
Jan-Dec 1902	Stanislas Aeby (1st)
Jan-Dec 1903	Georges Python (1st)
Jan-Dec 1904	Louis Cardinaux (1st)
Jan-Dec 1905	Alphonse Theraulaz (1st)
Jan- ? 1906	Aloys Bossy (2nd)
? -Dec 1906	Charles Weck (2nd)
Jan-Dec 1907	Alphonse Theraulaz (2nd)
Jan-Dec 1908	Georges Python (2nd)
Jan-Dec 1909	Louis Weck
Jan-Dec 1910	Stanislas Aeby (2nd)
Jan-Dec 1911	Louis Cardinaux (2nd)
Jan-Dec 1912	Eugène Deschenaux
Jan-Dec 1913	Fernand Torche
Jan-Dec 1914	Georges Python (3rd)
Jan-Dec 1915	Jean Musy
Jan-Dec 1916	Émile Savoy (1st)
Jan-Dec 1917	Marcel Vonderweid (1st)
Jan-Dec 1918	Joseph Chuard
Jan-Dec 1919	Ernest Perrier (1st)
Jan-Dec 1920	Émile Savoy (2nd)
Jan-Dec 1921	Marcel Vonderweid (2nd)
Jan-Dec 1922	Victor Buchs (1st)
Jan-Dec 1923	Romain Chatton (1st)
Jan-Dec 1924	Bernard Weck (1st)
Jan-Dec 1925	Ernest Perrier (2nd)
Jan-Dec 1926	Émile Savoy (3rd)
Jan-Dec 1927	Marcel Vonderweid (3rd)
Jan-Dec 1928	Victor Buchs (2nd)
Jan-Dec 1929	Romain Chatton (2nd)
Jan-Dec 1930	Bernard Weck (2nd)
Jan-Dec 1931	Jules Bovet (1st)

Jan-Dec 1932	Ernest Perrier (3rd)
Jan-Dec 1933	Émile Savoy (4th)
Jan-Dec 1934	Marcel Vonderweid (4th)
Jan-Dec 1935	Victor Buchs (3rd)
Jan-Dec 1936	Romain Chatton (3rd)
Jan-Dec 1937	Bernard Weck (3rd)
Jan-Dec 1938	Jules Bovet (2nd)
Jan-Dec 1939	Joseph Piller (1st)
Jan-Dec 1940	Maxime Quartenoud (1st)
Jan-Dec 1941	Aloys Baeriswyl (1st)
Jan-Dec 1942	Richard Corboz
Jan-Dec 1943	Bernard Weck (4th)
Jan-Dec 1944	Jules Bovet (3rd)
Jan-Dec 1945	Joseph Piller (2nd)
Jan-Dec 1946	Maxime Quarternoud (2nd)
Jan-Dec 1947	Joseph Ackermann
Jan-Dec 1948	Aloys Baeriswyl (2nd)
Jan-Dec 1949	Jules Bovet (4th)
Jan-Dec 1950	Maxime Quartenoud (3rd)
Jan-Dec 1951	Paul Torche (1st)
Jan-Dec 1952	Pierre Glasson (1st)
Jan-Dec 1953	Aloys Baeriswyl (3rd)
Jan-Dec 1954	Maxime Quartenoud (4th)
Jan-Dec 1955	Paul Torche (2nd)
Jan-Dec 1956	José Python (1st)
Jan-Dec 1957	Théodore Ayer (1st)
Jan-Dec 1958	Georges Ducotterd (1st)
Jan-Dec 1959	Pierre Glasson (2nd)
Jan-Dec 1960	Paul Torche (3rd)
Jan-Dec 1961	Claud Genoud (1st)
Jan-Dec 1962	José Python (2nd)
Jan-Dec 1963	Alphonse Roggo
Jan-Dec 1964	Théodore Ayer (2nd)
Jan-Dec 1965	Georges Ducotterd (3rd)
Jan-Dec 1966	Émile Zehnder (1st)
Jan-Dec 1967	Claude Genoud (2nd)
Jan-Dec 1968	Georges Ducotterd (2nd)
Jan-Dec 1969	Paul Genoud
Jan-Dec 1970	Émile Zehnder (2nd)
Jan-Dec 1971	Max Aebischer (1st)
Jan-Dec 1972	Arnold Waeber (1st)
Jan-Dec 1973	Pierre Dreyer (1st)
Jan-Dec 1974	Max Aebischer (2nd)
Jan-Dec 1975	Jean Riesen
Jan-Dec 1976	Joseph Cottet (1st)

Jan-Dec 1977   Remi Brodard   (1st)
Jan-Dec 1978   Arnold Waeber   (2nd)
Jan-Dec 1979   Pierre Dreyer   (2nd)
Jan-Dec 1980   Joseph Cottet   (2nd)
Jan-Dec 1981   Ferdinand Masset   (1st)
Jan-Dec 1982   Hans Bächler   (1st)
Jan-Dec 1983   Marius Cottier   (1st)
Jan-Dec 1984   Remi Brodard   (2nd)
Jan-Dec 1985   Ferdinand Masset   (2nd)
Jan-Dec 1986   Edouard Gremaud   (1st)
Jan-Dec 1987   Félicien Morel   (1st)
Jan-Dec 1988   Denis Clerc
Jan-Dec 1989   Hans Bächler   (2nd)
Jan-Dec 1990   Marius Cottier   (2nd)
Jan-Dec 1991   Edouard Gremaud   (2nd)
Jan-Dec 1992   Raphaël Rimaz
Jan-Dec 1993   Félicien Morel   (2nd)
Jan-Dec 1994   Augustin Macheret   (1st)
Jan-Dec 1995   Michel Pittet   (1st)
Jan-Dec 1996   Ruth Lüthi   (1st)
Jan-Dec 1997   Urs Schwaller
Jan-Dec 1998   Augustin Macheret   (2nd)
Jan-Dec 1999   Michel Pittet   (2nd)
Jan-Dec 2000   Ruth Lüthi   (2nd)

GENÈVE

Canton formed: 1815
Capital: Geneva

Presidents of the Council of State:

Nov 1899-Nov 1900   Alfred Vincent   (1st)
Nov 1900-Nov 1901   Georges Favon
Nov 1901-Nov 1902   Henri Fazy   (1st)
Nov 1902-June 1903   Alfred Didier   (2nd) (†)
July-Nov 1903   Alfred Vincent   (2nd)
Nov 1903-Nov 1904   Henri Fazy   (2nd)
Nov 1904-Nov 1905   Alfred Vincent   (3rd)
Nov 1905-Nov 1906   Henri Fazy   (3rd)
Nov 1906-Nov 1907   François Besson
Dec 1907-Nov 1908   Henri Fazy   (4th)
Dec 1908-Nov 1909   Victor Charbonnet
Nov 1909-Nov 1910   Henri Fazy   (5th)

Nov 1910-Nov 1911	Jules Perréard
Dec 1911-Nov 1912	Henri Fazy (6th)
Nov 1912-Nov 1913	William Rosier (1st)
Dec 1913-Nov 1914	Henri Fazy (7th)
Dec 1914-Nov 1915	William Rosier (2nd)
Nov 1915-Nov 1916	Henri Fazy (8th)
Dec 1916-Nov 1917	John Rochaix (1st)
Dec 1917-Nov 1918	Henri Fazy (9th)
Nov 1918-Nov 1919	John Gignoux (1st)
Dec 1919-Nov 1920	Jules Mussard
Nov 1920-Nov 1921	John Gignoux (2nd)
Nov 1921-Nov 1922	Jacques Rutty
Nov 1922-Nov 1923	Jacques Gavard
Nov 1923-Nov 1924	John Gignoux (3rd)
Nov 1924-Nov 1925	John Rochaix (2nd)
Dec 1925-Nov 1926	Alexandre Moriaud (1st)
Nov 1926-Dec 1927	Antoine Bron
Dec 1927-Nov 1928	Alexandre Moriaud (2nd)
Dec 1928-Nov 1929	Jean Boissonnas
Dec 1929-Dec 1930	Alexandre Moriaud (3rd)
Dec 1930-Nov 1931	Alfred Desbaillets
Dec 1931-Nov 1932	Frédéric Martin
Dec 1932-Dec 1933	Paul Lachenal
Dec 1933-Dec 1934	Léon Nicole (1st)
Dec 1934-Nov 1935	Albert Naine
Dec 1935-Dec 1936	Léon Nicole (2nd)
Dec 1936-Nov 1937	Adrien Lachenal (1st)
Nov 1937-Nov 1938	Albert Picot (1st)
Nov 1938-Dec 1939	Adrien Lachenal (2nd)
Dec 1939-Nov 1940	Louis Casai (1st)
Nov 1940-Nov 1941	Paul Balmer
Nov 1941-Dec 1942	François Perréard (1st)
Dec 1942-Nov 1943	Adrien Lachenal (3rd)
Dec 1943-Nov 1944	Albert Picot (2nd)
Dec 1944-Nov 1946	François Perréard (2nd)
Dec 1946-Nov 1947	Albert Picot (3rd)
Dec 1947-Dec 1948	Louis Casai (2nd)
Dec 1948-Nov 1949	Charles Duboule (1st)
Dec 1949-Nov 1950	Aymon de Senarclens (1st)
Dec 1950-Dec 1951	François Perréard (3rd)
Dec 1951-Nov 1952	Louis Casai (3rd)
Dec 1952-Nov 1953	Antoine Pugin
Dec 1953-Nov 1954	Charles Duboule (2nd)
Dec 1954-Nov 1955	François Perréard (4th)
Dec 1955-Nov 1956	Aymon de Senarclens (2nd)

Dec 1956-Dec 1957	Alfred Borel
Dec 1957-Nov 1958	Jean Dutoit
Dec 1958-Nov 1959	Émile Dupont (1st)
Dec 1959-Nov 1960	Jean Treina (1st)
Dec 1960-Dec 1961	Edouard Chamay
Dec 1961-Nov 1962	Émile Dupont (2nd)
Dec 1962-Nov 1963	Charles Duchemin
Dec 1963-Nov 1964	René Helg
Dec 1964-Dec 1965	Jean Treina (2nd)
Dec 1965-Nov 1966	André Ruffieux
Dec 1966-Nov 1967	André Chavanne (1st)
Dec 1967-Nov 1968	François Peyrot
Dec 1968-Dec 1969	Gilbert Duboule (1st)
Dec 1969-Nov 1970	Jean Babel (1st)
Dec 1970-Nov 1971	Willy Donzé (1st)
Dec 1971-Nov 1972	Henri Schmitt (1st)
Dec 1972-Dec 1973	François Picot
Dec 1973-Nov 1974	Gilbert Duboule (2nd)
Dec 1974-Nov 1975	André Chavanne (2nd)
Dec 1975-Nov 1976	Jean Babel (2nd)
Dec 1976-Dec 1977	Henri Schmitt (2nd)
Dec 1977-Nov 1978	Willy Donzé (2nd)
Dec 1978-Nov 1979	Jaques Vernet (1st)
Dec 1979-Nov 1980	Guy Fontanet
Dec 1980-Dec 1981	André Chavanne (3rd)
Dec 1981-Nov 1982	Robert Ducret (1st)
Dec 1982-Nov 1983	Pierre Wellhauser (1st)
Dec 1983-Nov 1984	Alain Borner
Dec 1984-Nov 1985	Jaques Vernet (2nd)
Nov 1985-Nov 1986	Aloys Werner
Dec 1986-Nov 1987	Robert Ducret (2nd)
Dec 1987-Nov 1988	Pierre Wellhauser (2nd)
Dec 1988-Nov 1989	Jaques Vernet (3rd)
Dec 1989-Nov 1990	Dominique Föllmi
Dec 1990-Nov 1991	Bernard Ziegler
Dec 1991-Nov 1992	Jean-Philippe Maitre (1st)
Dec 1992-Nov 1993	Christian Grobet
Dec 1993-Nov 1994	Claude Haegi
Dec 1994-Nov 1995	Olivier Vodoz
Dec 1995-Nov 1996	Guy-Olivier Segond (1st)
Dec 1996-Nov 1997	Jean-Philippe Maitre (2nd)
Dec 1997-Nov 1998	Gérard Ramseyer
Dec 1998-Nov 1999	Martine Brunschwig Graf
Dec 1999-	Guy-Olivier Segond (2nd)

GLARUS

Entry into confederation: 1352
Capital: Glarus

Presidents:

Landammann

1837-40	Dietrich Schindler
1840-48	Cosmos Blumer
1848-57	Caspar Jenny
1857-75	Joachim Heer
1876-87	Esajas Zweifel
1887-1925	Eduard Blumer
1926-32	Edwin Hauser
1932-38	Melchior Hefti
1938-42	Rudolf Gallati
1942-45	Joseph Müller
1945-50	Hans Hefti
1950-56	Heinrich Heer
1956-62	Franz Landolt
1962-68	Hermann Feusi
1968-73	Fridolin Stucki
1973-78	Hans Meier
1978-82	Kaspar Rhyner
1982-86	Martin Brunner
1986-90	Fritz Weber
1990-94	Jules Landolt
1994-98	Christoph Stüssi
1998-	Rudolf Gisler

GRAUBÜNDEN

Canton formed: 1803
Capital: Chur

Presidents:

Jan-Dec 1900	Johann Schmid	(2nd)
Jan-Dec 1901	Andreas Vital	(2nd)
Jan-Dec 1902	Anton Caflisch	(1st)
Jan-Dec 1903	Friedrich Brugger	
Jan-Dec 1904	Johann Stiffler	(1st)
Jan-Dec 1905	Rudolf Ganzoni	(1st)
Jan-Dec 1906	Balthazar Vieli	
Jan-Dec 1907	Anton Caflisch	(2nd)
Jan-Dec 1908	Johann Stiffler	(2nd)

Jan-Dec 1909	Rudolf Ganzoni (2nd)
Jan-Dec 1910	Paul Raschein
Jan-Dec 1911	Julius Dedual (1st)
Jan-Dec 1912	Andreas Laely (1st)
Jan-Dec 1913	A. Steinhauser
Jan-Dec 1914	Oreste Olgiati (1st)
Jan-Dec 1915	Julius Dedual (2nd)
Jan-Dec 1916	Johann Vonmoos (1st)
Jan-Dec 1917	Andreas Laely (2nd)
Jan-Dec 1918	Johann Bossi
Jan-Dec 1919	Oreste Olgiati (2nd)
Jan-March 1920	Johann Vonmoos (2nd)
April-Dec 1920	Eduard Walser (1st)
Jan-Dec 1921	Wilhelm Plattner (1st)
Jan-Dec 1922	Domenic Bezzola
Jan-Dec 1923	Georg Willi
Jan-Dec 1924	Christian Michel
Jan-Dec 1925	Eduard Walser (2nd)
Jan-Dec 1926	Wilhelm Plattner (2nd)
Jan-Dec 1927	Robert Ganzoni (1st)
Jan-Dec 1928	Josef Vieli (1st)
Jan-Dec 1929	Georg Fromm (1st)
Jan-Dec 1930	Johann Huonder (1st)
Jan-Dec 1931	Georg Hartmann
Jan-Dec 1932	Robert Ganzoni (2nd)
Jan-Dec 1933	Josef Vieli (2nd)
Jan-Dec 1934	Georg Fromm (2nd)
Jan-May 1935	Johann Huonder (2nd) (†)
May-Dec 1935	Albert Lardelli
Jan-Dec 1936	Sebastian Capaul (1st)
Jan-Dec 1937	Peter Liver
Jan-Dec 1938	Luigi Albrecht (1st)
Jan-Dec 1939	Adolf Nadig
Jan-Dec 1940	Sebastian Capaul (2nd)
Jan-Dec 1941	Andreas Gadient (1st)
Jan-Dec 1942	Luigi Albrecht (2nd)
Jan-Dec 1943	Joos Regi (1st)
Jan-Dec 1944	Rudolf Planta (1st)
Jan-Dec 1945	Walter Liesch (1st)
Jan-Dec 1946	Andreas Gadient (2nd)
Jan-Dec 1947	Joos Regi (2nd)
Jan-Dec 1948	Gion Darms
Jan-Dec 1949	Rudolf Planta (2nd)
Jan-Dec 1950	Walter Liesch (2nd)
Jan-Dec 1951	Christian Margadant (1st)

Jan-Dec 1952	Konrad Bärtsch
Jan-Dec 1953	Ettore Tenchio (1st)
Jan-Dec 1954	Arno Theus
Jan-Dec 1955	Augustin Cahannes (1st)
Jan-Dec 1956	Christian Margadant (2nd)
Jan-Dec 1957	Ettore Tenchio (2nd)
Jan-Dec 1958	Augustin Cahannes (2nd)
Jan-Dec 1959	Andrea Bezzola (1st)
Jan-Dec 1960	Renzo Lardelli (1st)
Jan-Dec 1961	Georg Brosi
Jan-Dec 1962	Andrea Bezzola (2nd)
Jan-Dec 1963	Gion Willi (1st)
Jan-Dec 1964	Emmanuel Huonder (1st)
Jan-Dec 1965	Renzo Lardelli (2nd)
Jan-Dec 1966	Hans Stiffler (1st)
Jan-Dec 1967	Gion Willi (2nd)
Jan-May 1968	Emmanuel Huonder (2nd) (†)
May 1968-Dec 1969	Leon Schlumpf (1st)
Jan-Dec 1970	Hans Stiffker (2nd)
Jan-Dec 1971	Georg Velli (1st)
Jan-Dec 1972	Giachen Casaulta (1st)
Jan-Dec 1973	Jakob Schutz (1st)
Jan-Dec 1974	Leon Schlumpf (2nd)
Jan-Dec 1975	Georg Velli (2nd)
Jan-Dec 1976	Tobias Kuoni (1st)
Jan-Dec 1977	Giachen Casaulta (2nd)
Jan-Dec 1978	Jakob Schutz (2nd)
Jan-Dec 1979	Otto Largiadèr (1st)
Jan-Dec 1980	Tobias Kuoni (2nd)
Jan-Dec 1981	Donat Cadruvi (1st)
Jan-Dec 1982	Reto Mengiardi (1st)
Jan-Dec 1983	Bernardo Lardi
Jan-Dec 1984	Otto Largiadèr (2nd)
Jan-Dec 1985	Donat Cadruvi (2nd)
Jan-Dec 1986	Reto Mengiardi (2nd)
Jan-Dec 1987	Christoffel Brandli (1st)
Jan-Dec 1988	Donat Cadruvi (3rd)
Jan-Dec 1989	Reto Mengiardi (3rd)
Jan-Dec 1990	Luzi Bärtsch (1st)
Jan-Dec 1991	Joachim Caluori (1st)
Jan-Dec 1992	Christoffel Brandli (2nd)
Jan-Dec 1993	Aluis Maissen (1st)
Jan-Dec 1994	Luzi Bärtsch (2nd)
Jan-Dec 1995	Peter Aliesch (1st)
Jan-Dec 1996	Joachim Caluori (2nd)

Jan-Dec 1997	Aluis Maissen (2nd)
Jan-Dec 1998	Luzi Bärtsch (3rd)
Jan-Dec 1999	Claus Huber
Jan-Dec 2000	Peter Aliesch (2nd)

JURA

Canton created: 1 January 1979 (*f* part of Berne)
Capital: Delemont

Presidents:

Jan-Dec 1979	François Lachat (1st)
Jan-Dec 1980	Jean-Pierre Beuret (1st)
Jan-Dec 1981	François Mertenat (1st)
Jan-Dec 1982	Pierre Boillat (1st)
Jan-Dec 1983	Roger Jardin
Jan-Dec 1984	François Lachat (2nd)
Jan-Dec 1985	Jean-Pierre Beuret (2nd)
Jan-Dec 1986	François Mertenat (2nd)
Jan-Dec 1987	Pierre Boillat (2nd)
Jan-Dec 1988	François Lachat (3rd)
Jan-Dec 1989	Jean-Pierre Beuret (3rd)
Jan-Dec 1990	François Mertenat (3rd)
Jan-Dec 1991	Gaston Brahier
Jan-Dec 1992	Pierre Boillat (3rd)
Jan-Dec 1993	François Lachat (4th)
Jan-Dec 1994	Jean-Pierre Beuret (4th)
Jan-Dec 1995	Pierre Kohler (1st)
Jan-Dec 1996	Claude Hache
Jan-Dec 1997	Anita Rion
Jan-Dec 1998	Gérald Schaller
Jan-Dec 1999	Jean-François Roth
Jan-Dec 2000	Pierre Kohler (2nd)

LUZERN

Entry into confederation: 1332
Capital: Luzern

Presidents:

Schultheiss

Jan-Dec 1900	Josef Schobinger (3rd)
Jan-Dec 1901	Josef Schmid (2nd)
Jan-Dec 1902	Sebastian Vogel (2nd)

Jan-Dec 1903	Josef Düring (2nd)
Jan-Dec 1904	Heinrich Walther (2nd)
Jan-Dec 1905	Josef Schobinger (4th)
Jan-Dec 1906	Edmund von Schumacher (3rd)
Jan-Dec 1907	Josef Schmid (3rd)
Jan-Dec 1908	Josef Düring (3rd)
Jan-Dec 1909	Heinrich Walther (3rd)
Jan-Dec 1910	Theodor Schmid (1st)
Jan-Dec 1911	Hans Steinmann (1st)
Jan-Dec 1912	Jakob Sigrist (1st)
Jan-Dec 1913	Feli von Schumacher
Jan-Dec 1914	Arthur Oswald
Jan-Dec 1915	Josef During (4th)
Jan-Dec 1916	Heinrich Walther (4th)
Jan-Dec 1917	Theodor Schmid (2nd)
Jan-Dec 1918	Hans Steinmann (2nd)
Jan-Dec 1919	Jakob Sigrist (2nd)
Jan-Dec 1920	Anton Erni (1st)
Jan-Dec 1921	Heinrich Walther (5th)
Jan-Dec 1922	Xaver Schnieper (1st)
Jan-Dec 1923	Albert Zust
Jan-Dec 1924	Josef Frey (1st)
Jan-Dec 1925	Max Wey
Jan-Dec 1926	Jakob Sigrist (3rd)
Jan-Dec 1927	Anton Erni (2nd)
Jan-Dec 1928	Heinrich Walther (6th)
Jan-Dec 1929	Xaver Schnieper (2nd)
Jan-Dec 1930	Josef Frey (2nd)
Jan-Dec 1931	Arnold Ott
Jan-Dec 1932	Jakob Sigrist (4th)
Jan-Dec 1933	Anton Erni (3rd)
Jan-Dec 1934	Jakob Renggli (1st)
Jan-Dec 1935	Xaver Schnieper (3rd)
Jan-Dec 1936	Josef Frey (3rd)
Jan-Dec 1937	Vinzenz Winiker (1st)
Jan-Dec 1938	Josef Wismer (1st)
Jan-Dec 1939	Gotthard Egli (1st)
Jan-Dec 1940	Jakob Renggli (2nd)
Jan-April 1941	Xaver Schnieper (4th)
April-Dec 1941	Josef Frey (4th)
Jan-Dec 1942	Vinzenz Winiker (2nd)
Jan-Dec 1943	Hans Felber (1st)
Jan-Dec 1944	Josef Wismer (2nd)
Jan-Dec 1945	Gotthard Egli (2nd)
Jan-Dec 1946	Franz Leu (1st)

Jan-Dec 1947	Josef Frey (5th)
Jan-Dec 1948	Emil Emmenegger (1st)
Jan-Dec 1949	Vinzenz Winiker (3rd)
Jan-Dec 1950	Hans Felber (2nd)
Jan-Dec 1951	Josef Wismer (3rd)
Jan-Dec 1952	Gotthard Egli (3rd)
Jan-Dec 1953	Franz Leu (2nd)
Jan-Dec 1954	Emil Emmenegger (2nd)
Jan-Dec 1955	Adolf Käch (1st)
Jan-Dec 1956	Hans Rogger (1st)
Jan-Dec 1957	Werner Kurzmeyer (1st)
Jan-Dec 1958	Franz Leu (3rd)
Jan-Dec 1959	Werner Bühlmann (1st)
Jan-Dec 1960	Josef Isenschmid (1st)
Jan-Dec 1961	Adolf Käch (2nd)
Jan-Dec 1962	Hans Rogger (2nd)
Jan-Dec 1963	Werner Kurzmeyer (2nd)
Jan-Dec 1964	Franz Leu (4th)
Jan-Dec 1965	Anton Muheim (1st)
Jan-Dec 1966	Werner Bühlmann (2nd)
Jan-Dec 1967	Josef Isenschmid (2nd)
Jan-Dec 1968	Adolf Käch (3rd)
Jan-Dec 1969	Hans Rogger (3rd)
Jan-Dec 1970	Werner Kurzmeyer (3rd)
Jan-Dec 1971	Anton Muheim (2nd)
Jan-Dec 1972	Felix Wili (1st)
Jan-Dec 1973	Peter Knüsel (1st)
Jan-Dec 1974	Carl Mugglin (1st)
Jan-Dec 1975	Karl Kennel (1st)
Jan-Dec 1976	Walter Gut (1st)
Jan-Dec 1977	Anton Muheim (3rd)
Jan-Dec 1978	Felix Wili (2nd)
Jan-Dec 1979	Peter Knüsel (2nd)
Jan-Dec 1980	Carl Mugglin (2nd)
Jan-Dec 1981	Karl Kennel (2nd)
Jan-Dec 1982	Walter Gut (2nd)
Jan-Dec 1983	Robert Bühler (1st)
Jan-Dec 1984	Hans-Ernst Balsiger
Jan-Dec 1985	Karl Kennel (3rd)
Jan-Dec 1986	Erwin Muff (1st)
Jan-Dec 1987	Josef Egli (1st)
Jan-Dec 1988	Heinrich Zemp
Jan-Dec 1989	Robert Bühler (2nd)
Jan-Dec 1990	Erwin Muff (2nd)
Jan-Dec 1991	Klaus Fellmann (1st)

Jan-Dec 1992   Brigitte Mürner-Gilli   (1st)
Jan-Dec 1993   Paul Huber   (1st)
Jan-Dec 1994   Josef Egli   (2nd)
Jan-Dec 1995   Ulrich Fässler
Jan-Dec 1996   Klaus Fellmann   (2nd)
Jan-Dec 1997   Brigitte Mürner-Gilli   (2nd)
Jan-Dec 1998   Paul Huber   (2nd)
Jan-Dec 1999   Kurt Meyer
Jan-Dec 2000   Max Pfister

NEUCHÂTEL

Canton created: 1815
Capital: Neuchâtel

Presidents of the Council of State:

June 1900-May 1901   Frédéric Soguel
June 1901-May 1902   Edouard Droz   (1st)
June 1902-May 1903   Edouard Quartier-la-Tente   (1st)
June 1903-May 1904   Louis-Auguste Pettavel   (1st)
June 1904-May 1905   Jean Berthoud   (2nd)
June 1905-May 1906   Louis Perrier   (1st)
June 1906-May 1907   Edouard Droz   (2nd)
June 1907-May 1908   Edouard Quartier-la-Tente   (2nd)
June 1908-May 1909   Louis-Auguste Pettavel   (2nd)
June 1909-May 1910   Louis Perrier   (2nd)
June 1910-May 1911   Edouard Droz   (3rd)
June 1911-May 1912   Edouard Quartier-la-Tente   (3rd)
June 1912-May 1913   Louis-Auguste Pettavel   (3rd)
June 1913-May 1914   Albert Calame   (1st)
June 1914-May 1915   Henri Calame   (1st)
June 1915-May 1916   Edouard Quartier-la-Tente   (4th)
June 1916-May 1917   Louis-Auguste Pettavel   (4th)
June 1917-May 1918   Albert Calame   (2nd)
June 1918-May 1919   Alfred Clottu   (1st)
June 1919-May 1920   Henri Calame   (2nd)
June 1920-May 1921   Edouard Quartier-la-Tente   (5th)
June 1921-May 1922   Ernest Béguin   (1st)
June 1922-May 1923   Edgar Renaud   (1st)
June 1923-May 1924   Alfred Clottu   (2nd)
June 1924-May 1925   Henri Calame   (3rd)
June 1925-May 1926   Ernest Béguin   (2nd)
June 1926-May 1927   Edgar Renaud   (2nd)
June 1927-May 1928   Alfred Clottu   (3rd)

June 1928-May 1929	Henri Calame (4th)
June 1929-May 1930	Antoine Borel (1st)
June 1930-May 1931	Ernest Béguin (3rd)
June 1931-May 1932	Edgar Renaud (3rd)
June 1932-May 1933	Alfred Clottu (4th)
June 1933-May 1934	Antoine Borel (2nd)
June 1934-May 1935	Ernest Béguin (4th)
June 1935-May 1936	Alfred Guinchard (1st)
June 1936-May 1937	Edgar Renaud (4th)
June 1937-May 1938	Jean Humbert (1st)
June 1938-May 1939	Antoine Borel (3rd)
June 1939-May 1940	Ernest Béguin (5th)
June 1940-May 1941	Alfred Guinchard (2nd)
June 1941-May 1942	Edgar Renaud (5th)
June 1942-May 1943	Jean Humbert (2nd)
June 1943-May 1944	Jean-Louis Barrelet (1st)
June 1944-May 1945	Camille Brandt (1st)
June 1945-May 1946	Léo DuPasquier
June 1946-May 1947	Jean Humbert (3rd)
June 1947-May 1948	Jean-Louis Barrelet (2nd)
June 1948-May 1949	Camille Brandt (2nd)
June 1949-May 1950	Pierre-Auguste Leuba (1st)
June 1950-May 1951	Jean Humbert (4th)
June 1951-May 1952	Jean-Louis Barrelet (3rd)
June 1952-May 1953	Edmond Guinand (1st)
June 1953-May 1954	Pierre-Auguste Leuba (2nd)
June 1954-May 1955	Jean-Louis Barrelet (4th)
June 1955-May 1956	Edmond Guinand (2nd)
June 1956-May 1957	Gaston Clottu (1st)
June 1957-May 1958	André Sandoz
June 1958-May 1959	Pierre-Auguste Leuba (3rd)
June 1959-May 1960	Jean-Louis Barrelet (5th)
June 1960-May 1961	Edmond Guinand (3rd)
June 1961-May 1962	Gaston Clottu (2nd)
June 1962-May 1963	Pierre-Auguste Leuba (4th)
June 1963-May 1964	Jean-Louis Barrelet (6th)
June 1964-May 1965	Fritz Bourquin (1st)
June 1965-May 1966	Gaston Clottu (3rd)
June 1966-May 1967	Jean-Louis Barrelet (7th)
June 1967-May 1968	Fritz Bourquin (2nd)
June 1968-May 1969	Carlos Grosjean (1st)
June 1969-May 1970	Rémy Schläppy (1st)
June 1970-May 1971	Carlos Grosjean (2nd)
June 1971-May 1972	Jacques Béguin (1st)
June 1972-May 1973	François Jeanneret (1st)

June 1973-May 1974	René Meylan (1st)
June 1974-May 1975	Carlos Grosjean (3rd)
June 1975-May 1976	Rémy Schläppy (2nd)
June 1976-May 1977	Jacques Béguin (2nd)
June 1977-May 1978	François Jeanneret (2nd)
June 1978-May 1979	René Meylan (2nd)
June 1979-May 1980	Rémy Schläppy (3rd)
June 1980-May 1981	Jacques Béguin (3rd)
June 1981-May 1982	André Brandt (1st)
June 1982-May 1983	Pierre Dubois (1st)
June 1983-May 1984	Jacques Béguin (4th)
June 1984-May 1985	René Felber
June 1985-May 1986	Jean Cavadini (1st)
June 1986-May 1987	André Brandt (2nd)
June 1987-May 1988	Pierre Dubois (2nd)
June 1988-May 1989	Jean-Claude Jaggi
May 1989-May 1990	Jean Cavadini (2nd)
June 1990-May 1991	Francis Matthey (1st)
June 1991-May 1992	Pierre Dubois (3rd)
June 1992-May 1993	Michel von Wyss
May 1993-May 1994	Francis Matthey (2nd)
June 1994-May 1995	Pierre Hirschy (1st)
June 1995-May 1996	Pierre Dubois (4th)
June 1996-May 1997	Maurice Jacot
May 1997-May 1998	Jean Guinand
June 1998-May 1999	Francis Matthey (3rd)
May 1999-May 2000	Pierre Hirschy (2nd)
May 2000	Thierry Béguin

NIDWALDEN*

Half-canton formed: 1803 (*f* part of Unterwalden)
Capital: Stans

Presidents:

Landammann

Jan-Dec 1900	Jakob B.Wyrsch (7th)
Jan-Dec 1901	Ferdinand Businger (6th)
Jan-Dec 1902	Jakob B.Wyrsch (8th)
Jan-Dec 1903	Ferdinand Businger (7th)
Jan-Dec 1904	Jakob B.Wyrsch (9th)
Jan-Dec 1905	Ferdinand Businger (8th)
Jan-Dec 1906	Jakob B.Wyrsch (10th)
Jan-Dec 1907	Ferdinand Businger (9th)

Jan-Dec 1908	Jakob B.Wyrsch	(11th)
Jan-June 1909	Ferdinand Businger	(10th)
June 1909-Dec 1910	Jakob B.Wyrsch	(12th) (acting June-Dec 1909)
Jan-Dec 1911	Jakob S.Wyrsch	(1st)
Jan-Dec 1912	Jakob B.Wyrsch	(13th)
Jan-Dec 1913	Jakob S.Wyrsch	(2nd)
Jan-Dec 1914	Jakob B.Wyrsch	(14th)
Jan-Dec 1915	Jakob S.Wyrsch	(3rd)
Jan-Dec 1916	Jakob B.Wyrsch	(15th)
Jan-Dec 1917	Jakob S.Wyrsch	(4th)
Jan-Dec 1918	Jakob B.Wyrsch	(16th)
Jan-Dec 1919	Jakob S.Wyrsch	(5th)
Jan-Dec 1920	Hans von Matt	(1st)
Jan-Dec 1921	Jakob S.Wyrsch	(6th)
Jan-Dec 1922	Hans von Matt	(2nd)
Jan-Dec 1923	Jakob S.Wyrsch	(7th)
Jan-Dec 1924	Hans von Matt	(3rd)
Jan-Dec 1925	Jakob S.Wyrsch	(8th)
Jan-Dec 1926	Hans von Matt	(4th)
Jan-Dec 1927	Anton Zgraggen	(1st)
Jan-Dec 1928	Hans von Matt	(5th)
Jan-Dec 1929	Anton Zgraggen	(2nd)
Jan-Dec 1930	Hans von Matt	(6th)
Jan-Dec 1931	Anton Zgraggen	(3rd)
Jan-Dec 1932	Theodor Gabriel	(1st)
Jan-Sept 1933	Anton Zgraggen	(4th)
Sept 1933-Dec 1934	Theodor Gabriel	(2nd) (acting Sept-Dec 1933)
Jan-Dec 1935	Werner Christen	(1st)
Jan-Dec 1936	Remigi Joller	(1st)
Jan-Dec 1937	Werner Christen	(2nd)
Jan-Dec 1938	Remigi Joller	(2nd)
Jan-Dec 1939	Werner Christen	(3rd)
Jan-Dec 1940	Remigi Joller	(3rd)
Jan-Dec 1941	Werner Christen	(4th)
Jan-Dec 1942	Remigi Joller	(4th)
Jan-Dec 1943	Werner Christen	(5th)
Jan-Dec 1944	Remigi Joller	(5th)
Jan-Dec 1945	Werner Christen	(6th)
Jan-Dec 1946	Remigi Joller	(6th)
Jan-Dec 1947	Otto Wymann	(1st)
Jan-Dec 1948	Remigi Joller	(7th)
Jan-Dec 1949	Otto Wymann	(2nd)
Jan-Dec 1950	Josef Odermatt	(1st)
Jan-Dec 1951	Otto Wymann	(3rd)
Jan-Dec 1952	Josef Odermatt	(2nd)

Jan-Dec 1953	Ernst Zgraggen	(1st)
Jan-Dec 1954	Josef Odermatt	(3rd)
Jan-Dec 1955	Ernst Zgraggen	(2nd)
Jan-Dec 1956	Josef Odermatt	(4th)
Jan-Dec 1957	Ernst Zgraggen	(3rd)
Jan-Dec 1958	Josef Odermatt	(5th)
Jan-Dec 1959	Remigi Blattler	(1st)
Jan-Dec 1960	Josef Odermatt	(6th)
Jan-Dec 1961	Remigi Blattler	(2nd)
Jan-Dec 1962	Alfred Gräni	(1st)
Jan-Dec 1963	Remigi Blattler	(3rd)
Jan-Dec 1964	Alfred Gräni	(2nd)
Jan-Dec 1965	Walter Vokinger	(1st)
Jan-Dec 1966	Alfred Gräni	(3rd)
Jan-Dec 1967	Walter Vokinger	(2nd)
Jan-Dec 1968	Alfred Gräni	(4th)
Jan-Dec 1969	Walter Vokinger	(3rd)
Jan-Dec 1970	Adolf von Matt	(1st)
Jan-Dec 1971	Walter Vokinger	(4th)
Jan-Dec 1972	Adolf von Matt	(2nd)
Jan-Dec 1973	Walter Vokinger	(5th)
Jan-Dec 1974	Norbert Zumbuhl	(1st)
Jan-Dec 1975	German Murer	(1st)
Jan-Dec 1976	Norbert Zumbuhl	(2nd)
Jan-Dec 1977	German Murer	(2nd)
Jan-Dec 1978	Paul Niederberger	(1st)
Jan-Dec 1979	German Murer	(3rd)
Jan-Dec 1980	Paul Niederberger	(2nd)
Jan-Dec 1981	German Murer	(4th)
Jan-Dec 1982	Paul Niederberger	(3rd)
Jan-Dec 1983	Remigi Blättler	(1st)
Jan-Dec 1984	Paul Niederberger	(4th)
Jan-Dec 1985	Remigi Blättler	(2nd)
Jan-Dec 1986	Bruno Leuthold	(1st)
Jan-Dec 1987	Remigi Blättler	(3rd)
Jan-Dec 1988	Bruno Leuthold	(2nd)
Jan-Dec 1989	Remigi Blättler	(4th)
Jan-Dec 1990	Hans-Peter Käslin	(1st)
Jan-Dec 1991	Eduard Engelberger	(1st)
Jan-Dec 1992	Hans-Peter Käslin	(2nd)
Jan-Dec 1993	Eduard Engelberger	(2nd)
Jan-Dec 1994	Hans-Peter Käslin	(3rd)
Jan-Dec 1995	Eduard Engelberger	(3rd)
Jan-Dec 1996	Hans-Peter Käslin	(4th)
Jan-Dec 1997	Werner Keller	(1st)

Jan-Dec 1998	Meinrad Hofmann
Jan-Dec 1999	Viktor Furrer
Jan-Dec 2000	Werner Keller (2nd)

OBWALDEN*

Half-canton formed: 1803 (*f* part of Unterwalden)
Capital: Sarnen

Presidents:

Landammann

Jan-Dec 1900	Theodor Wirz (11th)
Jan-Dec 1901	Josef Omlin (2nd)
Jan-Dec 1902	Adalbert Wirz (1st)
Jan-Dec 1903	Paul von Moos (1st)
Jan-Dec 1904	Adalbert Wirz (2nd)
Jan-Dec 1905	Paul von Moos (2nd)
Jan-Dec 1906	Adalbert Wirz (3rd)
Jan-Dec 1907	Paul von Moos (3rd)
Jan-Dec 1908	Adalbert Wirz (4th)
Jan-Dec 1909	Paul von Moos (4th)
Jan-Dec 1910	Peter Ming (1st)
Jan-Dec 1911	Josef Businger (1st)
Jan-Dec 1912	Peter Ming (2nd)
Jan-Dec 1913	Josef Businger (2nd)
Jan-Dec 1914	Peter Ming (3rd)
Jan-Dec 1915	Josef Businger (3rd)
Jan-Dec 1916	Peter Ming (4th)
Jan-Dec 1917	Josef Businger (4th)
Jan-Dec 1918	Peter Ming (5th)
Jan-Dec 1919	Josef Businger (5th)
Jan-Dec 1920	Peter Ming (6th)
Jan-Dec 1921	Josef Businger (6th)
Jan-Dec 1922	Peter Ming (7th)
Jan-Dec 1923	Josef Businger (7th)
Jan-Dec 1924	Maria Odermatt
Jan-Dec 1925	Josef Businger (8th)
Jan-Dec 1926	Karl Stockmann (1st)
Jan-Dec 1927	Josef Businger (9th)
Jan-Dec 1928	Karl Stockmann (2nd)
Jan-Dec 1929	Josef Businger (10th)
Jan-Dec 1930	Karl Stockmann (3rd)
Jan-Dec 1931	Walter Amstalden (1st)
Jan-Dec 1932	Karl Stockmann (4th)

Jan-Dec 1933	Walter Amstalden (4th)
Jan-Dec 1934	Arnold Röthlin (1st)
Jan-Dec 1935	Walter Amstalden (5th)
Jan-Dec 1936	Arnold Röthlin (2nd)
Jan-Dec 1937	Walter Amstalden (6th)
Jan-Dec 1938	Josef Stockmann (†)
Jan-Dec 1939	Walter Amstalden (7th)
Jan-Dec 1940	Eduard Infanger (1st)
Jan-Dec 1941	Walter Amstalden (8th)
Jan-Dec 1942	Eduard Infanger (2nd)
Jan-Dec 1943	Walter Amstalden (9th)
Jan-Dec 1944	Eduard Infanger (3rd)
Jan-Dec 1945	Alois Abächerli (1st)
Jan-Dec 1946	Gotthard Odermatt (1st)
Jan-Dec 1947	Alois Abächerli (2nd)
Jan-Dec 1948	Gotthard Odermatt (2nd)
Jan-Dec 1949	Arnold Ming (1st)
Jan-Dec 1950	Gotthard Odermatt (3rd)
Jan-Dec 1951	Arnold Ming (2nd)
Jan-Dec 1952	Gotthard Obermatt (4th)
Jan-Dec 1953	Ludwig von Moos (1st)
Jan-Dec 1954	Gotthard Odermatt (5th)
Jan-Dec 1955	Ludwig von Moos (2nd)
Jan-Dec 1956	Gotthard Odermatt (6th)
Jan-Dec 1957	Ludwig von Moos (3rd)
Jan-Dec 1958	Gotthard Odermatt (7th)
Jan-Dec 1959	Ludwig von Moos (4th)
Jan-Dec 1960	Hans Gasser (1st)
Jan-Dec 1961	Christian Dillier (1st)
Jan-Dec 1962	Hans Gasser (2nd)
Jan-Dec 1963	Christian Dillier (2nd)
Jan-Dec 1964	Leo von Wyl (1st)
Jan-Dec 1965	Christian Dillier (3rd)
Jan-Dec 1966	Leo von Wyl (2nd)
Jan-Dec 1967	Christian Dillier (4th)
Jan-Dec 1968	Leo von Wyl (3rd)
Jan-Dec 1969	Arnold Durrer (1st)
Jan-Dec 1970	Leo von Wyl (4th)
Jan-Dec 1971	Arnold Durrer (2nd)
Jan-Dec 1972	Oskar Imfeld
Jan-Dec 1973	Hermann Walliman (1st)
Jan-Dec 1974	Willy Hophan (1st)
Jan-Dec 1975	Hermann Walliman (2nd)
Jan-Dec 1976	Willy Hophan (2nd)

Jan-Dec 1977	Alfred von Ah (1st)
Jan-Dec 1978	Willy Hophan (3rd)
Jan-Dec 1979	Alfred von Ah (2nd)
Jan-Dec 1980	Willy Hophan (4th)
Jan-Dec 1981	Beat Amgarten (1st)
Jan-Dec 1982	Anton Wolfisberg (1st)
Jan-Dec 1983	Beat Amgarten (2nd)
Jan-Dec 1984	Anton Wolfisberg (2nd)
Jan-Dec 1985	Beat Amgarten (3rd)
Jan-Dec 1986	Anton Wolfisberg (3rd)
Jan-Dec 1987	Alexander Höchli (1st)
Jan-Dec 1988	Anton Wolfisberg (4th)
Jan-Dec 1989	Alexander Höchli (2nd)
Jan-Dec 1990	Anton Röthlin (1st)
Jan-Dec 1991	Alexander Höchli (3rd)
Jan-Dec 1992	Anton Röthlin (2nd)
Jan-Dec 1993	Adalbert Durrer (1st)
Jan-Dec 1994	Anton Röthlin (3rd)
Jan-Dec 1995	Adalbert Durrer (2nd)
Jan-Dec 1996	Anton Röthlin (4th)
Jan-Dec 1997	Josef Nigg (1st)
Jan-Dec 1998	Hans Hofer (1st)
Jan-Dec 1999	Josef Nigg (2nd)
Jan-Dec 2000	Hans Hofer (2nd)

SANKT GALLEN

Canton created: 1803
Capital: Sankt Gallen

Presidents:

Landammann

July 1900-July 1901	Eduard Scherrer (2nd)
July 1901-July 1902	Johann Schubiger (2nd)
July 1902-July 1903	Adolf Kaiser (2nd)
July 1903-July 1904	Ludwig Zollikofer (2nd)
July 1904-July 1905	Johann Rukstuhl (2nd)
July 1905-July 1906	Albert Mächler (1st)
July 1906-July 1907	Heinrich Scherrer (1st)
July 1907-July 1908	Anton Messmer
July 1908-July 1909	Alfred Riegg (1st)
July 1909-July 1910	Adolf Kaiser (3rd)

July 1910-July 1911	Edwin Rukstuhl (1st)
July 1911-July 1912	Albert Mächler (2nd)
July 1912-July 1913	Heinrich Scherrer (2nd)
July 1913-July 1914	Johann Schubiger
July 1914-July 1915	Alfred Riegg (2nd)
July 1915-July 1916	Johann Hauser
July 1916-July 1917	Gottlieb Baumgartner (1st)
July 1917-July 1918	Edwin Rukstuhl (2nd)
July 1918-July 1919	Albert Mächler (3rd)
July 1919-July 1920	Heinrich Scherrer (3rd)
July 1920-July 1921	Alfred Riegg (3rd)
July 1921-July 1922	Edwin Rukstuhl (3rd)
July 1922-July 1923	Otto Weber
July 1923-July 1924	Gottlieb Baumgartner (2nd)
July 1924-July 1925	Emil Mäder (1st)
July 1925-July 1926	Albert Mächler (4th)
July 1926-July 1927	Emil Grünenfelder (1st)
July 1927-July 1928	Alfred Riegg (4th)
July 1928-July 1929	Edwin Rukstuhl (4th)
July 1929-July 1930	Gottlieb Baumgartner (3rd)
July 1930-July 1931	Emil Mäder (2nd)
July 1931-July 1932	Albert Mächler (5th)
July 1932-July 1933	Emil Grünenfelder (2nd)
July 1933-July 1934	Valentin Keel (1st)
July 1934-July 1935	Gottlieb Baumgartner (4th)
July 1935-July 1936	Edwin Rukstuhl (5th)
July 1936-July 1937	Karl Kobelt
July 1937-July 1938	Emil Grünenfelder (3rd)
July 1938-July 1939	Valentin Keel (2nd)
July 1939-July 1940	Adolf Roemer (1st)
July 1940-July 1941	Josef Riedener (1st)
July 1941-July 1942	Johann Gabathuler (1st)
July 1942-July 1943	Albert Gemperli (1st)
July 1943-July 1944	Ernst Graf
July 1944-July 1945	Josef Riedener (2nd)
July 1945-July 1946	Adolf Roemer (2nd)
July 1946-July 1947	Alfred Kessler
July 1947-July 1948	Paul Müller (1st)
July 1948-July 1949	Johann Gabathuler (2nd)
July 1949-July 1950	Albert Gemperli (2nd)
July 1950-July 1951	Adolf Roemer (3rd)
July 1951-July 1952	Josef Riedener (3rd)
July 1952-July 1953	Simon Frick (1st)
July 1953-July 1954	Paul Müller (2nd)
July 1954-July 1955	Mathias Eggenberger (1st)

July 1955-July 1956	Walter Clavadetscher
July 1956-July 1957	Albert Gemperli (3rd)
July 1957-July 1958	Adolf Roemer (4th)
July 1958-July 1959	Josef Riedener (4th)
July 1959-July 1960	Simon Frick (2nd)
July 1960-July 1961	Paul Müller (3rd)
July 1961-July 1962	Mathias Eggenberger (2nd)
July 1962-July 1963	Hans Schneider (1st)
July 1963-July 1964	Gottfried Hoby (1st)
July 1964-July 1965	Guido Eigenmann
July 1965-July 1966	Albert Scherrer
July 1966-July 1967	Simon Frick (3rd)
July 1967-July 1968	Edwin Koller (1st)
July 1968-July 1969	Mathias Eggenberger (3rd)
July 1969-July 1970	Hans Schneider (2nd)
July 1970-July 1971	Gottfried Hoby (2nd)
July 1971-July 1972	Willy Hermann (1st)
July 1972-July 1973	August Schmuki
July 1973-July 1974	Willi Geiger (1st)
July 1974-July 1975	Edwin Koller (2nd)
July 1975-July 1976	Florian Schlegel (1st)
July 1976-July 1977	Ernst Rüesch (1st)
July 1977-July 1978	Gottfried Hoby (3rd)
July 1978-July 1979	Willy Hermann (2nd)
July 1979-July 1980	Edwin Koller (3rd)
July 1980-July 1981	Willi Geiger (2nd)
July 1981-July 1982	Paul Gemperli (1st)
July 1982-July 1983	Florian Schlegel (2nd)
July 1983-July 1984	Ernst Rüesch (2nd)
July 1984-July 1985	Karl Mätzler (1st)
July 1985-July 1986	Willi Geiger (3rd)
July 1986-July 1987	Edwin Koller (4th)
July 1987-July 1988	Burkhard Vetsch (1st)
July 1988-July 1989	Paul Gemperli (2nd)
July 1989-July 1990	Hans Rohrer (1st)
July 1990-July 1991	Hans Stöckling (1st)
July 1991-July 1992	Karl Mätzler (2nd)
July 1992-July 1993	Burkhard Vetsch (2nd)
July 1993-July 1994	Alex Oberholzer
July 1994-July 1995	Walter Kägi (1st)
July 1995-July 1996	Peter Schönenberger
July 1996-July 1997	Hans Rohrer (2nd)
July 1997-July 1998	Hans Stöckling (2nd)
July 1998-July 2000	Rita Roos-Niedermann
July 2000-	Walter Kägi (2nd)

SCHAFFHAUSEN

Entry into confederation: 1501
Capital: Schaffhausen

Presidents:

Jan-Dec 1900	Gottlob Hug (3rd)
Jan-Dec 1901	Karl Rahm (4th)
Jan-Dec 1902	Christoph Moser-Ott (6th)
Jan-Dec 1903	Jakob Keller (2nd)
Jan-Dec 1904	Robert Grieshaber (7th)
Jan-Dec 1905	Gottlob Hug (4th)
Jan-Dec 1906	Karl Rahm (5th)
Jan-Dec 1907	Jakob Keller (3rd)
Jan-Dec 1908	Robert Grieshaber (8th)
Jan-Dec 1909	Traugott Waldvogel (1st)
Jan-Dec 1910	Fritz Sturzenegger (1st)
Jan-Dec 1911	Jakob Keller (4th)
Jan-Dec 1912	Robert Grieshaber (9th)
Jan-Dec 1913	Traugott Waldvogel (2nd)
Jan-Dec 1914	Fritz Sturzenegger (2nd)
Jan-Dec 1915	Robert Grieshaber (10th)
Jan-Dec 1916	Traugott Waldvogel (2nd)
Jan-Dec 1917	Fritz Sturzenegger (3rd)
Jan-Dec 1918	Gottfried Altorfer (1st)
Jan-Dec 1919	Albert Moser-Tobler
Jan-Dec 1920	Robert Grieshaber (11th)
Jan-Dec 1921	Traugott Waldvogel (3rd)
Jan-Dec 1922	Fritz Sturzenegger (4th)
Jan-Dec 1923	Gottfried Altorfer (2nd)
Jan-Dec 1924	Jakob Schlatter (1st)
Jan-Dec 1925	Traugott Waldvogel (4th)
Jan-Dec 1926	Fritz Sturzenegger (5th)
Jan-Dec 1927	Gottfried Altorfer (3rd)
Jan-Dec 1928	Jakob Schlatter (2nd)
Jan-Dec 1929	Jakob Ruh (1st)
Jan-Dec 1930	Traugott Waldvogel (5th)
Jan-Dec 1931	Fritz Sturzenegger (6th)
Jan-Dec 1932	Gottfried Altorfer (4th)
Jan-Dec 1933	Otto Schärrer (1st)
Jan-Dec 1934	Jakob Ruh (2nd)
Jan-Dec 1935	Ernst Lieb (1st)
Jan-Dec 1936	Gottfried Altorfer (5th)
Jan-Dec 1937	Otto Schärrer (2nd)
Jan-Dec 1938	Ernst Lieb (2nd)

Jan-Dec 1939	Traugott Wanner (1st)
Jan-Dec 1940	Gottfried Altorfer (5th)
Jan-Dec 1941	Ernst Lieb (3rd)
Jan-Dec 1942	Theodor Scherrer
Jan-Dec 1943	Gustav Schoch
Jan-Dec 1944	Traugott Wanner (2nd)
Jan-Dec 1945	Walther Brühlmann (1st)
Jan-Dec 1946	Ernst Lieb (4th)
Jan-Dec 1947	Traugott Wanner (3rd)
Jan-Dec 1948	Walther Brühlmann (2nd)
Jan-Dec 1949	Ernst Lieb (5th)
Jan-Dec 1950	Georg Leu (1st)
Jan-Dec 1951	Theo Wanner (1st)
Jan-Dec 1952	Walther Brühlmann (3rd)
Jan-Dec 1953	Karl Waldvogel
Jan-Dec 1954	Ernst Lieb (6th)
Jan-Dec 1955	Georg Leu (2nd)
Jan-Dec 1956	Theo Wanner (2nd)
Jan-Dec 1957	Robert Schärrer (1st)
Jan-Dec 1958	Ernst Lieb (7th)
Jan-Dec 1959	Georg Leu (3rd)
Jan-Dec 1960	Franz Fischer (2nd)
Jan-Dec 1961	Robert Schärrer (2nd)
Jan-Dec 1962	Ernst Lieb (8th)
Jan-Dec 1963	Franz Fischer (2nd)
Jan-Dec 1964	Erwin Hofer (1st)
Jan-Dec 1965	Hermann Wanner
Jan-Dec 1966	Robert Schärrer (3rd)
Jan-Dec 1967	Ernst Lieb (9th)
Jan-Dec 1968	Franz Fischer (3rd)
Jan-Dec 1969	Erwin Hofer (2nd)
Jan-Dec 1970	Robert Schärrer (4th)
Jan-Dec 1971	Franz Fischer (4th)
Jan-Dec 1972	Ernst Neukomm (1st)
Jan-Dec 1973	Erwin Hofer (3rd)
Jan-Dec 1974	Bernhard Stamm (1st)
Jan-Dec 1975	Kurt Waldvogel (1st)
Jan-Dec 1976	Ernst Neukomm (2nd)
Jan-Dec 1977	Kurt Amsler (1st)
Jan-Dec 1978	Paul Harnisch (1st)
Jan-Dec 1979	Bernhard Stamm (2nd)
Jan-Dec 1980	Kurt Waldvogel (2nd)
Jan-Dec 1981	Ernst Neukomm (3rd)
Jan-Dec 1982	Kurt Amsler (2nd)
Jan-Dec 1983	Paul Harnisch (2nd)

Jan-Dec 1984   Bernhard Stamm   (3rd)
Jan-Dec 1985   Kurt Waldvogel   (3rd)
Jan-Dec 1986   Ernst Neukomm   (4th)
Jan-Dec 1987   Ernst Leu   (1st)
Jan-Dec 1988   Hermann Keller   (1st)
Jan-Dec 1989   Ernst Neukomm   (5th)
Jan-Dec 1990   Peter Briner   (1st)
Jan-Dec 1991   Ernst Leu   (2nd)
Jan-Dec 1992   Hermann Keller   (2nd)
Jan-Dec 1993   Hans-Jörg Kunz   (1st)
Jan-Dec 1994   Ernst Neukomm   (6th)
Jan-Dec 1995   Peter Briner   (2nd)
Jan-Dec 1996   Hans Peter Lenherr
Jan-Dec 1997   Hermann Keller   (3rd)
Jan-Dec 1998   Han-Jörg Kunz   (2nd)
Jan-Dec 1999   Ernst Neukomm   (7th)
Jan-Dec 2000   Peter Briner   (3rd)

SCHWYZ

One of the original three confederation members
Capital: Schwyz

Presidents:

Landammann

July 1900-June 1902   Vital Schwander   (3rd)
July 1902-June 1904   Karl Reichlin   (4th)
July 1904-June 1906   Heinrich Wyss
July 1906-June 1908   Josef Schuler
July 1908-June 1910   Josef Räber
July 1910-June 1912   Joseph Fassbind
July 1912-June 1914   Martin Ochsner
July 1914-June 1916   Anton Büeler
July 1916-June 1918   Kaspar Bamert
July 1918-June 1920   Josef Camenzind
July 1920-June 1922   Alois ab Yberg
July 1922-June 1924   Meinrad Ziltener
July 1924-June 1926   Karl von Weber
July 1926-June 1928   Karl Kälin
July 1928-June 1930   Josef Bösch   (1st)
July 1930-June 1932   Anton Ruoss
July 1932-June 1934   Rudolf Sidler
July 1934-June 1936   Mathe Theiler
July 1936-June 1938   August Bettschart

July 1938-June 1940	Vital Schwander (1st)
July 1940-June 1942	Josef Bürgi
July 1942-June 1944	Alois Knüsel
July 1944-June 1946	Josef Bösch (2nd)
July 1946-June 1948	Casar Bachmann
July 1948-June 1950	Klemens Dober
July 1950-June 1952	Josef Heinzer
July 1952-June 1954	Rudolf Sidler
July 1954-June 1956	Stephan Oechslin
July 1956-June 1958	Vital Schwander (2nd)
July 1958-June 1960	Fritz Husi
July 1960-June 1962	Meinrad Schuler
July 1962-June 1964	Balz Feusi
July 1964-June 1966	Josef Diethelm
July 1966-June 1968	Josef Ulrich
July 1968-June 1970	Alois ab Yberg
July 1970-June 1972	Georges Leimbachner
July 1972-June 1974	Hans Fuchs
July 1974-June 1976	Xaver Reichmuth
July 1976-June 1978	Karl Bolfing
July 1978-June 1980	Rudolf Sidler
July 1980-June 1982	Josef Feusi
July 1982-June 1984	Heinrich Kistler
July 1984-June 1986	Walter Gisler
July 1986-June 1988	Paul Brandenberg
July 1988-June 1990	Marcel Kürzi
July 1990-June 1992	Franz Marty
July 1992-June 1994	Margrit Röllin-Weber
July 1994-June 1996	Egon Bruhin
July 1996-June 1998	Richard Wyrsch
July 1998-June 1999	Richard Camenzind

SOLOTHURN

Entry into confederation: 1481
Capital: Solothurn

Presidents:

Landammann

Jan-Dec 1900	Franz Hänggi (3rd)
Jan-Dec 1901	Eugen Büttiker (1st)
Jan-Dec 1902	Oskar Munzinger (4th)
Jan-Dec 1903	Rudolf Kyburz (5th)
Jan-Dec 1904	Rudolf von Arx (5th)

Jan-Dec 1905	Franz Hänggi (4th)
Jan-Dec 1906	Eugen Büttiker (2nd)
Jan-Dec 1907	Rudolf Kyburz (6th)
Jan-Dec 1908	Rudolf von Arx (6th)
Jan-Dec 1909	Werner Kaiser
Jan-Dec 1910	Eugen Büttiker (3rd)
Jan-Dec 1911	Rudolf Kyburz (7th)
Jan-Dec 1912	Siegfried Hartmann (1st)
Jan-Dec 1913	Franz Obrecht (1st)
Jan-Dec 1914	Hans Kaufmann (1st)
Jan-Dec 1915	Robert Schöpfer (1st)
Jan-Dec 1916	Siegfried Hartmann (2nd)
Jan-Aug 1917	Franz Obrecht (2nd)
Aug-Dec 1917	Ferdinand von Arx (1st)
Jan-Dec 1918	Hans Kaufmann (2nd)
Jan-Dec 1919	Robert Schöpfer (2nd)
Jan-Dec 1920	Siegfried Hartmann (3rd)
Jan-Dec 1921	Hans Affolter (1st)
Jan-Dec 1922	Ferdinand von Arx (2nd)
Jan-Dec 1923	Hans Kaufmann (3rd)
Jan-Dec 1924	Robert Schöpfer (3rd)
Jan-Dec 1925	Siegfried Hartmann (3rd)
Jan-Dec 1926	Hans Affolter (2nd)
Jan-Dec 1927	Ferdinand von Arx (3rd)
Jan-Dec 1928	Hans Kaufmann (4th)
Jan-Dec 1929	Franz Obrecht (3rd)
Jan-Dec 1930	Siegfried Hartmann (4th)
Jan-Dec 1931	Ferdinand von Arx (4th)
Jan-Dec 1932	Hans Kaufmann (5th)
Jan-Aug 1933	Robert Schöpfer (4th)
Aug-Dec 1933	Max Obrecht (1st)
Jan-Dec 1934	Jacques Schmid (1st)
Jan-Dec 1935	Ferdinand von Arx (5th)
Jan-Dec 1936	Hans Kaufmann (6th)
Jan-Dec 1937	Oskar Stampfli (1st)
Jan-Dec 1938	Max Obrecht (2nd)
Jan-Dec 1939	Jacques Schmid (2nd)
Jan-Dec 1940	Otto Stampfli (1st)
Jan-Dec 1941	Urs Dietschi (1st)
Jan-Dec 1942	Oskar Stampfli (1st)
Jan-Dec 1943	Max Obrecht (3rd)
Jan-Dec 1944	Jacques Schmid (3rd)
Jan-Dec 1945	Otto Stampfli (2nd)
Jan-Dec 1946	Urs Dietschi (2nd)
Jan-Dec 1947	Oskar Stampfli (3rd)

Jan-Dec 1948	Max Obrecht (4th)
Jan-Dec 1949	Otto Stampfli (3rd)
Jan-Dec 1950	Urs Dietschi (3rd)
Jan-Dec 1951	Oskar Stampfli (4th)
Jan-Dec 1952	Max Obrecht (5th)
Jan-Dec 1953	Gottfried Klaus (1st)
Jan-Dec 1954	Otto Stampfli (4th)
Jan-Dec 1955	Urs Dietschi (4th)
Jan-Dec 1956	Werner Vogt (1st)
Jan-Dec 1957	Max Obrecht (6th)
Jan-Dec 1958	Gottfried Klaus (2nd)
Jan-Dec 1959	Otto Stampfli (5th)
Jan-Dec 1960	Urs Dietschi (5th)
Jan-Dec 1961	Werner Vogt (2nd)
Jan-Dec 1962	Gottfried Klaus (3rd)
Jan-Dec 1963	Urs Dietschi (6th)
Jan-Dec 1964	Franz Jeger (1st)
Jan-Dec 1965	Hans Erzer (1st)
Jan-Dec 1966	Werner Vogt (3rd)
Jan-Dec 1967	Willi Ritschard (1st)
Jan-Dec 1968	Franz Jeger (2nd)
Jan-Dec 1969	Hans Erzer (2nd)
Jan-Dec 1970	Alfred Wyser (1st)
Jan-Dec 1971	Willi Ritschard (2nd)
Jan-Dec 1972	Franz Jeger (3rd)
Jan-Dec 1973	Rudolf Bachmann (1st)
Jan-Dec 1974	Hans Erzer (3rd)
Jan-Dec 1975	Alfred Wyser (2nd)
Jan-Dec 1976	Alfred Rotheli (1st)
Jan-Dec 1977	Rudolf Bachmann (2nd)
Jan-Dec 1978	Gottfried Wyss (1st)
Jan-Dec 1979	Hans Erzer (4th)
Jan-Dec 1980	Alfred Rotheli (2nd)
Jan-Dec 1981	Rudolf Bachmann (3rd)
Jan-Dec 1982	Gottfried Wyss (2nd)
Jan-Dec 1983	Walter Burgi (1st)
Jan-Dec 1984	Alfred Rotheli (3rd)
Jan-Dec 1985	Fritz Schneider (1st)
Jan-Dec 1986	Gottfried Wyss (3rd)
Jan-Dec 1987	Walter Burgi (2nd)
Jan-Dec 1988	Rolf Ritschard (1st)
Jan-Dec 1989	Frits Schneider (2nd)
Jan-Dec 1990	Peter Hänggi (1st)
Jan-Dec 1991	Cornelia Füeg-Hitz (1st)
Jan-Dec 1992	Rolf Ritschard (2nd)

Jan-Dec 1993   Fritz Schneider (3rd)
Jan-Dec 1994   Peter Hänggi (2nd)
Jan-Dec 1995   Cornelia Füeg-Hitz (2nd)
Jan-Dec 1996   Thomas Wallner (1st)
Jan-Dec 1997   Rolf Ritschard (3rd)
Jan-Dec 1998   Christian Wanner
Jan-Dec 1999   Thomas Wallner (2nd)
Jan-Dec 2000   Ruth Gisi-Willisegger

THURGAU

Entry into confederation: 1803
Capital: Frauenfeld

Presidents:

June 1900-May 1901   Friedrich Braun (2nd)
June 1901-May 1902   Alfred Kreis (2nd)
June 1902-May 1903   Johann Egloff (3rd)
June 1903-May 1904   August Wild (1st)
June 1904-May 1905   Albert Bohi (2nd)
June 1905-May 1906   Alfred Kreis (3rd)
June 1906-May 1907   August Wild (2nd)
June 1907-May 1908   Emil Hofman (1st)
June 1908-May 1909   Alexander Aepli (1st)
June 1909-May 1910   Alfred Kreis (4th)
June 1910-May 1911   Eugen Schmid
June 1911-May 1912   Alexander Aepli (2nd)
June 1912-May 1913   Emil Hofmann (1st)
June 1913-May 1914   Alfred Kreis (5th)
June 1914-May 1915   Alois Wiesli (1st)
June 1915-May 1916   Alexander Aepli (3rd)
June 1916-May 1917   Emil Hofmann (2nd)
June 1917-May 1918   Alfred Kreis (6th)
June 1918-May 1919   Alois Wiesli (2nd)
June 1919-May 1920   Emil Hofmann (3rd)
June 1921-May 1922   Paul Altwegg (1st)
June 1922-May 1923   Alfred Kreis (7th)
June 1923-May 1924   Emil Hofmann (4th)
June 1924-May 1925   Anton Schmid (1st)
June 1925-May 1926   Adolf Koch (1st)
June 1926-May 1927   Paul Altwegg (2nd)
June 1927-May 1928   Albert Leutenegger (1st)
June 1928-May 1929   Anton Schmid (2nd)
June 1929-May 1930   Robert Freyenmuth (1st)

June 1930-May 1931	Adolf Koch (2nd)
June 1931-May 1932	Paul Altwegg (3rd)
June 1932-May 1933	Albert Leutenegger (2nd)
June 1933-May 1934	Anton Schmid (3rd)
June 1934-May 1935	Robert Freyenmuth (2nd)
June 1935-May 1936	Paul Altwegg (4th)
June 1936-May 1937	Anton Schmid (4th)
June 1937-May 1938	Jakob Müller (1st)
June 1938-May 1939	Willi Stähelin (1st)
June 1939-May 1940	Robert Freyenmuth (3rd)
June 1940-May 1941	Paul Altwegg (5th)
June 1941-May 1942	Anton Schmid (5th)
June 1942-May 1943	Jakob Müller (2nd)
June 1943-May 1944	Willi Stähelin (2nd)
June 1944-May 1945	August Roth
June 1945-May 1946	Paul Altwegg (6th)
June 1946-May 1947	Hans Reutlinger (1st)
June 1947-May 1948	Jakob Müller (3rd)
June 1948-May 1949	Willi Stähelin (3rd)
June 1949-May 1950	August Roth (2nd)
June 1950-May 1951	Hans Reutlinger (2nd)
June 1951-May 1952	Ernst Reiber (1st)
June 1952-May 1953	Jakob Müller (4th)
June 1953-May 1954	Willi Stähelin (4th)
June 1954-May 1955	Hans Reutlinger (3rd)
June 1955-May 1956	Ernst Reiber (2nd)
June 1956-May 1957	Jakob Müller (5th)
June 1957-May 1958	Willi Stähelin (5th)
June 1958-May 1959	Rudolf Schümperli (1st)
June 1959-May 1960	Ernst Reiber (3rd)
June 1960-May 1961	Jakob Müller (6th)
June 1961-May 1962	Willi Stähelin (6th)
June 1962-May 1963	Rudolf Schümperli (2nd)
June 1963-May 1964	Walter Ballmoos (1st)
June 1964-May 1965	Jakob Müller (7th)
June 1965-May 1966	Willi Stähelin (7th)
June 1966-May 1967	Rudolf Schümperli (3rd)
June 1967-May 1968	Walter Ballmoos (2nd)
June 1968-May 1969	Albert Schläpfer (1st)
June 1969-May 1970	Erich Böckli (1st)
June 1970-May 1971	Rudolf Schümperli (4th)
June 1971-May 1972	Walter Ballmoos (3rd)
June 1972-May 1973	Josef Harder
June 1973-May 1974	Albert Schläpfer (2nd)
June 1974-May 1975	Erich Böckli (2nd)

June 1975-May 1976	Alfred Abegg
June 1976-May 1977	Felix Rosenberg (1st)
June 1977-May 1978	Erich Böckli (3rd)
June 1978-May 1979	Arthur Haffter (1st)
June 1979-May 1980	Hanspeter Fischer (1st)
June 1980-May 1981	Felix Rosenberg (2nd)
June 1981-May 1982	Erich Böckli (4th)
June 1982-May 1983	Arthur Haffter (2nd)
June 1983-May 1984	Hanspeter Fischer (2nd)
June 1984-May 1985	Ulrich Schmidli (1st)
June 1985-May 1986	Felix Rosenberg (3rd)
June 1986-May 1987	Arthur Haffter (3rd)
June 1987-May 1988	Hanspeter Fischer (3rd)
June 1988-May 1989	Ulrich Schmidli (2nd)
June-Sept 1989	Felix Rosenberg (4th)
Sept 1989-May 1990	Hermann Bürgi (1st)
June 1990-May 1991	Arthur Haffter (4th)
June 1991-May 1992	Hanspeter Fischer (4th)
June 1992-May 1993	Ulrich Schmidli (3rd)
June 1993-May 1994	Philipp Stähelin (1st)
June 1994-May 1995	Hermann Bürgi (2nd)
June 1995-May 1996	Hermann Lei (1st)
June 1996-May 1997	Philipp Stähelin (2nd)
June 1997-May 1998	Roland Eberle
June 1998-May 1999	Hermann Lei (2nd)
May 1999-May 2000	Hans Peter Ruprecht

TICINO

Canton created: 1803
Capital: Bellinzona

Presidents of the Council of State:

Jan-Dec 1900	Curzio Curti
Jan-Dec 1901	Rinaldo Simen (1st)
Jan-Dec 1902	Antonio Battaglini
Jan-Dec 1903	Luigi Colombi
Jan-Dec 1904	Rinaldo Simen (2nd)
Jan-Dec 1905	Achille Borella (1st)
Jan-Dec 1906	Stefano Gabuzzi (1st)
Jan-Dec 1907	Evaristo Garbani-Nerini (1st)
Jan-Dec 1908	Gaetano Donini
Jan-Dec 1909	Achille Borella (2nd)
Jan- ? 1910	Stefano Gabuzzi (2nd)
? -Dec 1910	Achille Borella (3rd)

Jan-Dec 1911	Evaristo Garbani-Nerini (2nd)
Jan-Dec 1912	Giovanni Rossi (1st)
Jan-Dec 1913	Achille Borella (4th)
Jan-Dec 1914	Emilio Bossi
Jan-Dec 1915	Giovanni Rossi (2nd)
Jan-Dec 1916	Carlo Maggini (1st)
Jan-Dec 1917	Evaristo Garbani-Nerini (3rd)
Jan-Dec 1918	Giovanni Rossi (3rd)
Jan-Dec 1919	Carlo Maggini (2nd)
Jan-Dec 1920	Sebastiano Martinoli
Jan-Dec 1921	Evaristo Garbani-Nerini (4th)
Jan-Dec 1922	Giuseppe Cattori (1st)
Jan-Dec 1923	Raimondo Rossi (1st)
Jan-Dec 1924	Guglielmo Canevascini (1st)
Jan-Dec 1925	Giuseppe Cattori (2nd)
Jan-Dec 1926	Raimondo Rossi (2nd)
Jan-Dec 1927	Giuseppe Cattori (3rd)
Jan-Dec 1928	Guglielmo Canevascini (2nd)
Jan-Dec 1929	Angiolo Martignoni (1st)
Jan-Dec 1930	Giuseppe Cattori (4th)
Jan-Dec 1931	Guglielmo Canevascini (3rd)
Jan-Dec 1932	Angiolo Martignoni (2nd)
Jan-Dec 1933	Guglielmo Canevascini (4th)
Jan-Dec 1934	Enrico Celio (1st)
Jan-Dec 1935	Angiolo Martignoni (3rd)
Jan-Dec 1936	Isidoro Antognini (1st)
Jan-Dec 1937	Enrico Celio (2nd)
Jan-Dec 1938	Emilio Forni (1st)
Jan-Dec 1939	Angiolo Martignoni (4th)
Jan-Dec 1940	Isidoro Antognini (2nd)
Jan-Dec 1941	Giuseppe Lepori (1st)
Jan-Dec 1942	Guglielmo Canevascini (5th)
Jan-Dec 1943	Emilio Forni (2nd)
Jan-Dec 1944	Angiolo Martignoni (5th)
Jan-Dec 1945	Fulvio Bolla
Jan-Dec 1946	Giuseppe Lepori (2nd)
Jan-Dec 1947	Guglielmo Canevascini (6th)
Jan-Dec 1948	Nello Celio (1st)
Jan-Dec 1949	Agostino Bernasconi
Jan-Dec 1950	Brenno Galli (1st)
Jan-Dec 1951	Giuseppe Lepori (3rd)
Jan-Dec 1952	Guglielmo Canevascini (7th)
Jan-Dec 1953	Nello Celio (2nd)
Jan-Dec 1954	Adolfo Janner (1st)
Jan-Dec 1955	Brenno Galli (2nd)

Jan- ? 1956	Mario Soldini
? -Dec 1956	Guglielmo Canevascini (8th)
Jan-Dec 1957	Nello Celio
Jan-Dec 1958	Adolfo Janner (2nd)
Jan- ? 1959	Guglielmo Canevascini (9th)
? -Dec 1959	Albert Stefani (1st)
Jan-Dec 1960	Franco Zorzi
Jan-Dec 1961	Alberto Stefani (2nd)
Jan-Dec 1962	Plinio Cioccari
Jan-Dec 1963	Federico Ghisletta (1st)
Jan-Dec 1964	Angelo Pellegrini
Jan-Dec 1965	Arturo Lafranchi (1st)
Jan-Dec 1966	Federico Ghisletta (2nd)
Jan-Dec 1967	Argante Righetti (1st)
Jan-Dec 1968	Bixio Celio
Jan-Dec 1969	Arturo Lafranchi (2nd)
Jan-Dec 1970	Federico Ghisletta (3rd)
Jan-Dec 1971	Alberto Lepori
Jan-Dec 1972	Argante Righetti (2nd)
Jan-Dec 1973	Arturo Lafranchi (3rd)
Jan-Dec 1974	Ugo Sadis (1st)
Jan-Dec 1975	Benito Bernasconi (1st)
Jan-Dec 1976	Argante Righetti (3rd)
Jan-Dec 1977	Flavio Cotti (1st)
Jan-Dec 1978	Ugo Sadis (2nd)
Jan-Dec 1979	Benito Bernasconi (2nd)
Jan-Dec 1980	Fulvio Caccia (1st)
Jan-Dec 1981	Flavio Cotti (2nd)
Jan-Dec 1982	Carlo Speziali (1st)
Jan-Dec 1983	Fulvio Caccia (2nd)
Jan-Dec 1984	Carlo Speziali (2nd)
Jan-Dec 1985	Claudio Generali (1st)
Jan-Dec 1986	Renzo Respini (1st)
Jan-Dec 1987	Rossano Bervini
Jan-Dec 1988	Claudio Generali (2nd)
Jan-Dec 1989	Giuseppe Buffi (1st)
Jan-Dec 1990	Renzo Respini (2nd)
Jan-Dec 1991	Pietro Martinelli (1st)
Jan-Dec 1992	Dick Marty
Jan-Dec 1993	Giuseppe Buffi (2nd)
Jan-Dec 1994	Renzo Respini (3rd)
Jan-Dec 1995	Alex Pedrazzini (1st)
Jan-Dec 1996	Pietro Martinelli (2nd)
Jan-Dec 1997	Giuseppe Buffi (3rd)
Jan-Dec 1998	Marina Masoni

Jan-April 1999   Alex Pedrazzini (2nd)
April-Dec 1999   Marco Borradori
Jan-Dec 2000   Giuseppe Buffi (4th)

URI

One of the original confederation members
Capital: Altdorf

Presidents:

Landammann

1898-1902	Gustav Muheim (3rd)
1902-04	Florian Lusser (2nd)
1904-05	Franz Schmid
1905-07	Florian Lusser (3rd)
1907-09	Josef Furrer (1st)
1909-11	Alois Huber (1st)
1911-13	Josef Furrer (2nd)
1913-15	Josef Wipfli
1915-20	Martin Gamma
1920-22	Isidor Meyer (1st)
1922-24	Josef Lusser (1st)
1924-26	Karl Huber (1st)
1926-28	Josef Lusser (2nd)
1928-30	Isidor Meyer (2nd)
1930-32	Josef Lusser (3rd)
1932-34	Karl Huber (2nd)
1934-36	Josef Lusser (4th)
1936-38	Ludwig Walker (1st)
1938-40	Rudolf Huber (1st)
1940-42	Ludwig Walker (2nd)
1942-44	Rudolf Huber (2nd)
1944-46	Franz Arnold (1st)
1946-48	Josef Indergand (1st)
1948-50	Franz Arnold (2nd)
1950-52	Josef Indergand (2nd)
1952-54	Ludwig Danioth (1st)
1954-56	Peter Tresch
1956-60	Ludwig Danioth (2nd)
1960-62	Hans Villiger
1962-64	Josef Müller
1964-66	Alfred Weber (1st)
1966-68	Ludwig Danioth (3rd)
1968-70	Alfred Weber (2nd)
1970-72	Werner Huber

1972-74	Josef Brücker (1st)
1974-76	Raymund Gamma
1976-78	Anton Arnold
1978-80	Josef Brücker (2nd)
1980-82	Hans Danioth
1982-84	Hansheiri Dahinden
1984-86	Josef Brücker (3rd)
1986-88	Hans Zurfluh
1988-90	Carlo Dittli
1990-92	Ambros Gisler
1992-94	Hansruedi Stadler (1st)
1994-96	Alberik Ziegler
1996-98	Hansrudei Stadler (2nd)
1998-	Peter Mattli

VALAIS

Canton created: 1815
Capital: Sion

Presidents of the Council of State:

May 1900-April 1901	Achille Chappaz
May 1901-April 1902	Ignace Zen-Ruffinen
May 1902-April 1903	Henri Ducrey
May 1903-April 1904	Henri de Torrenté
May 1904-April 1905	Charles de Preux
May 1905-April 1906	Henri Bioley (1st)
May 1906-April 1907	Joseph Burgener (1st)
May 1907-April 1908	Arthur Couchepin (1st)
May 1908-April 1909	Joseph Kuntschen (1st)
May 1909-April 1910	Raphaël von Werra
May 1910-April 1911	Henri Bioley (2nd)
May 1911-April 1912	Joseph Burgener (2nd)
May 1912-April 1913	Arthur Couchepin (2nd)
May 1913-April 1914	Joseph Kuntschen (2nd)
May 1914-April 1915	Hermann Seiler (1st)
May 1915-April 1916	Maurice Troillet (1st)
May 1916-April 1917	Joseph Burgener (3rd)
May 1917-April 1918	Joseph Kuntschen (3rd)
May 1918-April 1919	Hermann Seiler (2nd)
May 1919-April 1920	Edmond Delacoste (1st)
May 1920-April 1921	Maurice Troillet (2nd)
May 1921-April 1922	Joseph Burgener (4th)
May 1922-April 1923	Joseph Kuntschen (4th)
May 1923-April 1924	Joseph de Chastoney

May 1924-April 1925	Edmond Delacoste (2nd)
May 1925-April 1926	Maurice Troillet (3rd)
May 1926-April 1927	Joseph Kuntschen (5th)
May 1927-April 1928	Oscar Walpen
May 1928-April 1929	Paul de Cocatrix (1st)
May 1929-April 1930	Maurice Troillet (4th)
May 1930-April 1931	Raymond Loretan (1st)
May 1931-April 1932	Cyrille Pitteloud (1st)
May 1932-April 1933	Paul de Cocatrix (2nd)
May 1933-April 1934	Maurice Troillet (5th)
May 1934-April 1935	Joseph Escher
May 1935-April 1936	Raymond Loretan (2nd)
May 1936-April 1937	Cyrille Pitteloud (2nd)
May 1937-April 1938	Maurice Troillet (6th)
May 1938-April 1939	Albano Fama (1st)
May 1939-April 1940	Oscar de Chastonay
May 1940-April 1941	Karl Anthamatten (1st)
May 1941-April 1942	Cyrille Pitteloud (3rd)
May 1942-April 1943	Maurice Troillet (7th)
May 1943-April 1944	Albano Fana (2nd)
May 1944-April 1945	Karl Anthamatten (2nd)
May 1945-April 1946	Cyrille Pitteloud (4th)
May 1946-April 1947	Jean Coquoz
May 1947-April 1948	Maurice Troillet (8th)
May 1948-April 1949	Karl Anthamatten (3rd)
May 1949-April 1950	Marcel Gard (1st)
May 1950-April 1951	Cyrille Pitteloud (5th)
May 1951-April 1952	Maurice Troillet (9th)
May 1952-April 1953	Oskar Schnyder (1st)
May 1953-April 1954	Karl Anthamatten (4th)
May 1954-April 1955	Marcel Gard (2nd)
May 1955-April 1956	Oskar Schnyder (2nd)
May 1956-April 1957	Marius Lampert (1st)
May 1957-April 1958	Marcel Gross (1st)
May 1958-April 1959	Marcel Gard (3rd)
May 1959-April 1960	Oskar Schnyder (3rd)
May 1960-April 1961	Marius Lampert (2nd)
May 1961-April 1962	Ernst von Roten (1st)
May 1962-April 1963	Marcel Gross (2nd)
May 1963-April 1964	Marcel Gard (4th)
May 1964-April 1965	Oskar Schnyder (4th)
May 1965-April 1966	Marius Lampert (3rd)
May 1966-April 1967	Ernst von Roten (2nd)
May 1967-April 1968	Marcel Gross (3rd)
May 1968-April 1969	Wolfgang Loretan (1st)

May 1969-April 1970	Arthur Bender (1st)
May 1970-April 1971	Ernst von Roten (3rd)
May 1971-April 1972	Wolfgang Loretan (2nd)
May 1972-April 1973	Antoine Zufferey (1st)
May 1973-April 1974	Guy Genoud (1st)
May 1974-April 1975	Arthur Bender (2nd)
May 1975-April 1976	Wolfgang Loretan (3rd)
May 1976-April 1977	Antoine Zufferey (2nd)
May 1977-April 1978	Franz Steiner (1st)
May 1978-April 1979	Guy Genoud (2nd)
May 1979-April 1980	Antoine Zufferey (3rd)
May 1980-April 1981	Hans Wyer (1st)
May 1981-April 1982	Franz Steiner (2nd)
May 1982-April 1983	Guy Genoud (3rd)
May 1983-April 1984	Bernard Comby (1st)
May 1984-April 1985	Hans Wyer (2nd)
May 1985-April 1986	Bernard Bornet (1st)
May 1986-April 1987	Bernard Comby (2nd)
May 1987-April 1988	Hans Wyer (3rd)
May 1988-April 1989	Raymond Deferr (1st)
May 1989-April 1990	Richard Gertschen (1st)
May 1990-April 1991	Bernard Bornet (2nd)
May 1991-April 1992	Bernard Comby (3rd)
May 1992-April 1993	Hans Wyer (4th)
May 1993-April 1994	Raymond Deferr (2nd)
May 1994-April 1995	Richard Gertschen (2nd)
May 1995-April 1996	Bernard Bornet (3rd)
May 1996-April 1997	Serge Sierro (1st)
May 1997-April 1998	Wilhelm Schnyder
May 1998-April 1999	Serge Sierro (2nd)
May 1999-April 2000	Jean-Jacques Rey-Bellet
April 2000-	Jean-René Fournier

VAUD

Canton created: 1803
Capital: Lausanne

Presidents of the Council of State:

Jan-Dec 1900	A.Jordan-Martin (2nd)
Jan-Dec 1901	F.Virieux (2nd)
Jan-Dec 1902	R.Cossy (2nd)
Jan-Dec 1903	Adrien Thélin (1st)
Jan-Dec 1904	Isaac Oyez-Ponnaz (1st)

Jan-Dec 1905	V.Duboux
Jan-Dec 1906	Camille Décoppet (1st)
Jan-Dec 1907	Paul Etier (1st)
Jan-Dec 1908	F.Virieux (3rd)
Jan-Dec 1909	R.Cossy (3rd)
Jan-Dec 1910	Adrien Thélin (2nd)
Jan-Dec 1911	Isaac Oyez-Ponnaz (2nd)
Jan-Dec 1912	Camille Décoppet (2nd)
Jan-Dec 1913	Paul Etier (2nd)
Jan-Dec 1914	Eugène Fonjallaz
Jan-Dec 1915	Ernest Chuard (1st)
Jan-Dec 1916	Alphonse Dubuis (1st)
Jan-Dec 1917	R.Cossy (4th)
Jan-Dec 1918	Adrien Thélin (3rd)
Jan-Aug 1919	Paul Etier (3rd)
Aug-Dec 1919	Ernest Chuard (2nd)
Jan-Dec 1920	Alphonse Dubuis (2nd)
Jan-Dec 1921	Charles Fricker
Jan-Dec 1922	M.Bujard (1st)
Jan-Dec 1923	Henri Simon (1st)
Jan-Dec 1924	F.Porchet (1st)
Jan-Dec 1925	J.Dufour (1st)
Jan-Dec 1926	Norbert Bosset (1st)
Jan-Dec 1927	E.Fazan (1st)
Jan-Dec 1928	Alphonse Dubuis (3rd)
Jan-Dec 1929	M.Bujard (2nd)
Jan-Dec 1930	Henri Simon (2nd)
Jan-Dec 1931	F.Porchet (2nd)
Jan-Dec 1932	J.Dufour (2nd)
Jan-Dec 1933	Norbert Bosset (2nd)
Jan-Dec 1934	E.Fazan (2nd)
Jan-Dec 1935	P.Perret (1st)
Jan-Dec 1936	E.Fischer (1st)
Jan-Dec 1937	J.Baup
Jan-Dec 1938	M.Bujard (3rd)
Jan-Dec 1939	F.Porchet (3rd)
Jan-Dec 1940	Norbert Bosset (3rd)
Jan-Dec 1941	E.Fazan (3rd)
Jan-Dec 1942	P.Perret (2nd)
Jan-Dec 1943	E.Fischer (2nd)
Jan-Dec 1944	A.Vodoz
Jan-Dec 1945	L.Rubattel (1st)
Jan-April 1946	Norbert Bosset (4th)
April-Dec 1946	Rodolphe Rubattel (1st)
Jan-Dec 1947	Gabriel Despland (1st)

Jan-Dec 1948	Edouard Jaquet (1st)
Jan-Dec 1949	Paul Chaudet
Jan-Dec 1950	Paul Nerfin
Jan-Dec 1951	Arthur Maret (1st)
Jan-Dec 1952	Pierre Oguey (1st)
Jan-Dec 1953	A.Oulevay (1st)
Jan-March 1954	L.Rubattel (2nd)
March-Dec 1954	Gabriel Despland (2nd)
Jan-Dec 1955	Edouard Jaquet (2nd)
Jan-Dec 1956	Arthur Maret (2nd)
Jan-Dec 1957	Pierre Oguey (2nd)
Jan-Dec 1958	A.Oulevay (2nd)
Jan-Dec 1959	Lucien Guisan (1st)
Jan-Dec 1960	Gabriel Despland (3rd)
Jan-Dec 1961	Charles Sollberger
Jan-April 1962	Arthur Maret (3rd)
April-Dec 1962	Pierre Oguey (3rd)
Jan-Dec 1963	R.Villard
Jan-Dec 1964	Lucien Guisan (2nd)
Jan-Dec 1965	P.Schumacher (1st)
Jan-Dec 1966	Edouard Debétaz (1st)
Jan-Dec 1967	Marc-Henri Ravussin (1st)
Jan-Dec 1968	Pierre Graber
Jan-Dec 1969	P.Schumacher (2nd)
Jan-Dec 1970	J.-P.Pradervand
Jan-Dec 1971	Claude Bonnard (1st)
Jan-Dec 1972	Edouard Debétaz (2nd)
Jan-Dec 1973	Marc-Henri Ravussin (2nd)
Jan-Dec 1974	Pierre Aubert (1st)
Jan-Dec 1975	A.Gavillet
Jan-Dec 1976	Edouard Debétaz (3rd)
Jan-Dec 1977	Marc-Henri Ravussin (3rd)
Jan-April 1978	Claude Bonnard (2nd)
April-Dec 1978	Raymond Junod (1st)
Jan-Dec 1979	Claude Perey (1st)
Jan-Dec 1980	Edouard Debétaz (4th)
Jan-Dec 1981	Pierre Aubert (2nd)
Jan-Dec 1982	Marcel Blanc (1st)
Jan-Dec 1983	Jean-François Leuba (1st)
Jan-Dec 1984	Raymond Junod (2nd)
Jan-Dec 1985	Claude Perey (2nd)
Jan-Dec 1986	Daniel Schmutz (1st)
Jan-Dec 1987	Pierre Duvoisin (1st)
Jan-Dec 1988	Marcel Blanc (2nd)
Jan-Dec 1989	Jean-François Leuba (2nd)

Jan-Dec 1990	Pierre Cevey
Jan-Dec 1991	Philippe Pidoux
Jan-Dec 1992	Daniel Schmutz (2nd)
Jan-Dec 1993	Pierre Duvoisin (2nd)
Jan-Dec 1994	Jacques Martin
Jan-Dec 1995	Claude Ruey (1st)
Jan-March 1996	Pierre-François Veillon
March-Dec 1996	Daniel Schmutz (3rd)
Jan-Dec 1997	Charles Favre
Jan-Dec 1998	Philippe Biéler
Jan-Dec 1999	Claude Ruey (2nd)
Jan-Dec 2000	Jacqueline Maurer-Mayor

ZUG

Entry into confederation: 1352
Capital: Zug

Presidents:

Landammann

Jan 1899-Dec 1900	Philipp Meyer (1st)
Jan 1901-Dec 1902	Josef Schmid
Jan 1903-Dec 1904	Philipp Meyer (2nd)
Jan 1905-Dec 1906	Fritz Spillmann
Jan 1907-Dec 1908	Alois Herrmann (1st)
Jan 1909-Dec 1910	Josef Knusel (1st)
Jan 1911-Dec 1912	Karl Merz
Jan 1913-Dec 1914	Josef Steiner
Jan 1915-Dec 1916	Hermann Stadlin
Jan 1917-Dec 1918	Josef Hildebrand (1st)
Jan 1919-Dec 1920	Alois Herrmann (2nd)
Jan 1921-Dec 1922	Josef Knusel (2nd)
Jan 1923-Dec 1924	Josef Hildebrand (2nd)
Jan 1925-Dec 1926	Otto Henggeler (1st)
Jan 1927-Dec 1928	Philipp Etter
Jan 1929-Dec 1930	Albert Meyer (1st)
Jan 1931-Dec 1932	Alois Müller
Jan 1933-Dec 1934	Heinrich Gallmann
Jan 1935-Dec 1936	Josef Knusel (3rd)
Jan 1937-Dec 1938	Karl Staub (1st)
Jan 1939-Dec 1940	Otto Henggeler (2nd)
Jan 1941-Dec 1942	Emil Steimer (1st)
Jan 1943-Dec 1944	Albert Meyer (2nd)
Jan 1945-Dec 1946	Karl Staub (2nd)
Jan 1947-Dec 1948	Johann Wyss

Jan 1949-Dec 1950	Rudolf Schmid
Jan 1951-Dec 1952	Emil Steimer (2nd)
Jan 1953-Dec 1954	Leo Iten
Jan 1954-Dec 1956	Josef Burkart
Jan 1957-Dec 1958	Klemenz Meienberg (1st)
Jan 1959-Dec 1960	Emil Steimer (3rd)
Jan 1961-Dec 1962	Bonaventura Iten (1st)
Jan 1963-Dec 1964	Alois Hürlimann
Jan 1965-Dec 1966	Hans Hürlimann
Jan 1967-Dec 1968	Silvan Nussbaumer (1st)
Jan 1969-Dec 1970	Klemenz Meienberg (2nd)
Jan 1971-Dec 1972	Hans Straub
Jan 1973-Dec 1974	Bonaventura Iten (2nd)
Jan 1975-Dec 1976	Carl Staub
Jan 1977-Dec 1978	Silvan Nussbaumer (2nd)
Jan 1979-Dec 1980	Thomas Fraefel
Jan 1981-Dec 1982	Anton Scherer (1st)
Jan 1983-Dec 1984	Georg Stucky
Jan 1985-Dec 1986	Andreas Iten (1st)
Jan 1987-Dec 1988	Anton Scherer (2nd)
Jan 1989-Dec 1990	Urs Kohler
Jan 1991-Dec 1992	Andreas Iten (2nd)
Jan 1993-Dec 1994	Paul Twerenbold
Jan 1995-Dec 1996	Urs Birchler
Jan 1997-Dec 1998	Robert Bisig
Jan 1999-	Walter Suter

ZURICH

Entry into confederation: 1351
Capital: Zurich

Presidents:

May 1900-April 1901	Heinrich Kern (1st)
May 1901-April 1902	Heinrich Ernst (1st)
May 1902-April 1903	Konrad Bleuler-Huni (2nd)
May 1903-April 1904	Albert Locher (2nd)
May 1904-April 1905	Jakob Lutz (1st)
May 1905-April 1906	Heinrich Nägeli (3rd)
May 1906-April 1907	Johann Stössel (1st)
May 1907-April 1908	Heinrich Kern (2nd)
May 1908-April 1909	Heinrich Ernst (2nd)
May 1909-April 1910	Konrad Bleuler-Huni (3rd)
May 1910-April 1911	Albert Locher (3rd)

May 1911-April 1912	Jakob Lutz (2nd)
May 1912-April 1913	Heinrich Nägeli (4th)
May 1913-April 1914	Johann Stössel (2nd)
May 1914-April 1915	Gustav Keller (1st)
May 1915-April 1916	Heinrich Ernst (3rd)
May 1916-April 1917	Heinrich Mousson (1st)
May 1917-April 1918	Oskar Wettstein (1st)
May 1918-April 1919	Gustav Keller (2nd)
May 1919-April 1920	Heinrich Ernst (4th)
May 1920-April 1921	Fritz Ottiker (1st)
May 1921-April 1922	Heinrich Mousson (2nd)
May 1922-April 1923	Ernst Tobler
May 1923-April 1925	Oskar Wettstein (2nd)
May 1924-April 1925	Rudolf Maurer (1st)
May 1925-April 1926	Emil Walter
May 1926-April 1929	Adolf Streuli (1st)
May 1927-April 1928	Fritz Ottiker (2nd)
May 1928-April 1929	Heinrich Mousson (3rd)
May 1929-April 1930	Oskar Wettstein (3rd)
May 1930-April 1931	Rudolf Streuli (1st)
May 1931-April 1932	Rudolf Maurer (2nd)
May 1932-April 1933	Adolf Streuli (2nd)
May 1933-April 1934	Otto Pfister (1st)
May 1934-April 1935	Karl Hafner (1st)
May 1935-April 1936	Rudolf Streuli (2nd)
May 1936-April 1937	Rudolf Maurer (3rd)
May 1937-April 1938	Otto Pfister (2nd)
May 1938-April 1939	Karl Hafner (2nd)
May 1939-April 1940	Robert Briner (1st)
May 1940-April 1941	Ernst Nobs
May 1941-April 1942	Hans Streuli (1st)
May 1942-April 1943	Josef Henggeler (1st)
May 1943-April 1944	Jakob Kägi (1st)
May 1944-April 1945	Paul Corrodi
May 1945-April 1946	Robert Briner (2nd)
May 1946-April 1947	Hans Streuli (2nd)
May 1947-April 1948	Josef Henggeler (2nd)
May 1948-April 1949	Jakob Heusser (1st)
May 1949-April 1950	Jakob Kägi (2nd)
May 1950-April 1951	Ernst Vaterlaus (1st)
May 1951-April 1952	Hans Streuli (3rd)
May 1952-April 1953	Rudolf Meier (1st)
May 1953-April 1954	Jakob Heusser (2nd)
May 1954-April 1955	Paul Meierhans (1st)
May 1955-April 1956	Franz Egger (1st)

May 1956-April 1957	Ernst Vaterlaus (2nd)
May 1957-April 1958	Walter König (1st)
May 1958-April 1959	Rudolf Meier (2nd)
May 1959-April 1960	Jakob Heusser (3rd)
May 1960-April 1961	Paul Meierhans (2nd)
May 1961-April 1962	Franz Egger (2nd)
May 1962-April 1963	Walter König (2nd)
May 1963-April 1964	Rudolf Meier (3rd)
May 1964-April 1965	Ernst Brugger
May 1965-April 1966	Robert Zumbuhl
May 1966-April 1967	Franz Egger (3rd)
May 1967-April 1968	Walter König (3rd)
May 1968-April 1969	Urs Bürgi
May 1969-April 1970	Alois Gunthard (1st)
May 1970-April 1971	Rudolf Meier (4th)
May 1971-April 1972	Albert Mossdorf (1st)
May 1972-April 1973	Arthur Bachmann (1st)
May 1973-April 1974	Hans Künzi (1st)
May 1974-April 1975	Jakob Stucki (1st)
May 1975-April 1976	Alfred Gilgen (1st)
May 1976-April 1977	Alois Gunthard (2nd)
May 1977-April 1978	Albert Mossdorf (2nd)
May 1978-April 1979	Arthur Bachmann (2nd)
May 1979-April 1980	Hans Künzi (2nd)
May 1980-April 1981	Jakob Stucki (2nd)
May 1981-April 1983	Peter Wiederkehr (1st)
May 1983-April 1984	Alfred Gilgen (2nd)
May 1983-April 1985	Konrad Gisler
May 1984-April 1986	Albert Sigrist
May 1985-April 1987	Hans Künzi (3rd)
May 1986-April 1987	Jakob Stucki (3rd)
May 1987-April 1988	Alfred Gilgen (3rd)
May 1988-April 1989	Peter Wiederkehr (2nd)
May 1989-April 1990	Hedi Lang (1st)
May 1990-April 1991	Hans Künzi (4th)
May 1991-April 1992	Alfred Gilgen (4th)
May 1992-April 1993	Hans Hofmann (1st)
May 1993-April 1994	Eric Honegger (1st)
May 1994-April 1995	Hedi Lang (2nd)
May 1995-April 1996	Ernst Homberger
May 1996-April 1997	Hans Hofmann (2nd)
May 1997-April 1998	Ernst Buschor
May 1998-April 1999	Eric Honegger (2nd)
May 1999-April 2000	Verena Diener
May 2000-	Rita Fuhrer

SYRIA

Official name: Syrian Arab Republic, Al-Jamhuriyah al-Arabiya as-Suriya

Previous names: Kingdom of Syria 1918-20; Syrian Republic 1934-58; part of United Arab Republic 1958-61

Independence dates: September 1918 & 27 September 1941

Capital: Damascus (Dimashq)

Syria was part of the Ottoman Empire until World War I. A brief period of independence (1918-20) was followed by French occupation. Syria then became a League of Nations mandated territory under French administration. France gradually granted autonomy, with full independence being declared in 1941. In 1958 Syria and Egypt united to form the United Arab Republic, but Syria seceded in 1961. Since 1963 the country has been ruled by the Baath Party.

King:

Sept 1918-July 1920	Faisal	(*son of Hussein of Hejaz*) (later King of Iraq)
(July 1920	French occupation)	

Presidents:

President of the Revolutionary Council 1963-64
President of the Presidential Council 1964-66

April 1926-Feb 1928	Damad Ahmad Nami
Feb 1928-Nov 1931	Taj Addin el-Husni (1st)
(Nov 1931-June 1932	post vacant)
June 1932-Dec 1936	Mohammed al-Adib
Dec 1936-July 1939	Hashim al-Atassi (1st)
(July 1939-Sept 1941	post vacant)
Sept 1941-Jan 1943	Taj Addin el-Husni (2nd) (†)
Jan-March 1943	Jamil al-Ushi (acting)
March-July 1943	Ata al-Ayoubi (acting)
July 1943-March 1949	Shukri al-Kuwatli (1st) (deposed)
(March-June 1949	post vacant)
June-Aug 1949	Husni el-Zaim (deposed, executed)
(Aug-Dec 1949	post vacant)
Dec 1949-Dec 1951	Hashim al-Atassi (2nd) (deposed)
2-3 Dec 1951	Adib es-Shishakli (1st)
Dec 1951-July 1953	Fawzi Silo
July 1953-Feb 1954	Adib es-Shishakli (2nd) (deposed) (assassinated 1964)
Feb 1954-Sept 1955	Hashim al-Atassi (3rd)
Sept 1955-Feb 1958	Shukri al-Kuwatli (2nd)
(Feb 1958-Sept 1961	united with Egypt)

(Sept-Dec 1961) post vacant)
Dec 1961-March 1963 Nazim Kudsi   (deposed)
March-July 1963 Loay Atassi
July 1963-Feb 1966 Amin al-Hafez   (ABSP) (deposed)
Feb 1966-Nov 1970 Nureddin al-Atassi   (ABSP) (deposed)
Nov 1970-March 1971 Ahmed Khatib
March 1971- Hafez al-Assad   (ABSP)

Prime Ministers:

Chairman of the Regional Executive Council Oct 1958-Sept 1961

Oct 1918-Dec 1919	Ali Rida Pasha ar-Rikabi (1st)
14-? Dec 1919	Abdul Hamad Pasha
Dec 1919-April 1920	Ali Rida Pasha ar-Rikabi (2nd)
May-June 1920	Hashim al-Atassi (1st)
June-Aug 1920	Ala Addin ar-Rubi
(Aug 1920-Jan 1925	post abolished)
Jan-Dec 1925	Subhi Bey Barakat
Dec 1925-Jan 1926	Hashim al-Atassi (2nd)
(Jan-April 1926	post vacant)
April 1926-Feb 1928	Damad Ahmad Nami
Feb 1928-Nov 1931	Taj Addin el-Husni (1st)
(Nov 1931-June 1932	post vacant)
June 1932-March 1934	Haqqi al-Azm
March 1934-Feb 1935	Taj Addin el-Husni (2nd)
Feb 1935-Dec 1936	Ata al-Ayoubi (1st)
Dec 1936-Feb 1939	Jamil Mardam Bey (1st)
Feb-April 1939	Lutfi al-Haffar
April-May 1939	Nasuhi al-Bukhari
July 1939-April 1941	Bahij al-Khatib
April-Sept 1941	Khalid al-Azm (1st)
Sept 1941-April 1942	Hassan al-Hakim (1st)
April 1942-Jan 1943	Husni al-Berazi
Jan-March 1943	Jamil al-Ulshi
March-Aug 1943	Ata al-Ayoubi (2nd)
Aug 1943-Oct 1944	Saadullah al-Jabiri (1st)
Oct 1944-April 1945	Ata al-Ayoubi (3rd)
April-Oct 1945	Fayez el-Khoury
Oct 1945-Dec 1946	Saadullah al-Jabiri (2nd)
Dec 1946-Dec 1948	Jamil Mardam Bey (2nd)
Dec 1948-April 1949	Khalid al-Azm (2nd) (deposed)
April-June 1949	Husni el-Zaim (executed Aug 1949)
June-Aug 1949	Mohsen Berazi (deposed, executed)
14-15 Aug 1949	Sami Hinnawi (acting)
Aug-Dec 1949	Hashim al-Atassi (3rd) (deposed)

24-28 Dec 1949	Nazim Kudsi (1st)
Dec 1949-May 1950	Khalid al-Azm (3rd)
June 1950-March 1951	Nazim Kudsi (2nd)
March-July 1951	Khalid al-Azm (4th)
Aug-Nov 1951	Hassan al-Hakim (2nd) (deposed)
Nov-Dec 1951	Maaruf Dawalibi (1st)
1-4 Dec 1951	Hamid Khoja
Dec 1951-June 1953	Fawzi Silo
July 1953-Feb 1954	Adib es-Shishakli (deposed)
March-June 1954	Sabri el-Assali (1st)
June-Oct 1954	Said el-Ghazzi (1st)
Oct 1954-Feb 1955	Faris al-Khuri
Feb-Sept 1955	Sabri el-Assali (2nd)
Sept 1955-June 1956	Said el-Ghazzi (2nd)
June 1956-Feb 1958	Sabri el-Assali (3rd)
(Feb-Oct 1958	post abolished)
Oct 1958-Aug 1961	Nureddin Kuhala
Aug-Sept 1961	Abdul el-Sarraj
Sept-Nov 1961	Mamoun Kuzbari
Nov-Dec 1961	Izzat en-Noss
Dec 1961-March 1962	Maaruf Dawalibi (2nd)
April-Sept 1962	Bashir Azmah
Sept 1962-March 1963	Khalid al-Azm (5th) (deposed)
March-May 1963	Salah Bitar (1st)
11-13 May 1963	Sami al-Jundi
May-Nov 1963	Salah Bitar (2nd)
Nov 1963-May 1964	Amin al-Hafez (1st)
May-Oct 1964	Salah Bitar (3rd)
Oct 1964-Sept 1965	Amin al-Hafez (2nd)
Sept-Dec 1965	Yussif Zeayan (1st)
Dec 1965-Jan 1966	Amin al-Hafez (3rd)
Jan-Feb 1966	Salah Bitar (4th) (deposed) (assassinated 1980)
Feb 1966-Oct 1968	Yussif Zeayan (2nd)
Oct 1968-Nov 1970	Nureddin al-Atassi (deposed)
Nov 1970-April 1971	Hafez al-Assad
April 1971-Dec 1972	Abdel Khleifawi (1st)
Dec 1972-Aug 1976	Mahmud al-Ayoubi
Aug 1976-Jan 1978	Abdel Khleifawi (2nd)
Jan 1978-Jan 1980	Mohammed al-Halabi
Jan 1980-Oct 1987	Abdel al-Kasm
Oct 1987-March 2000	Mahmud al-Zubi
March 2000-	Mohammed Mustafa Miro

ABSP = Arab Baath Socialist Party

TAJIKISTAN

Official name: Republic of Tajikistan, Jumhurii Tojikiston
Previous names: Tajik Autonomous Soviet Socialist Republic 1924-29, Tajik Soviet Socialist Republic 1929-91
State formed: 14 October 1924
Admission to USSR: 5 December 1929
Independence date: 9 September 1991
Capital: Dushanbe (Stalinabad 1929-61)

In 1924 the central Asian areas of the Soviet Union were reorganized. Tajikistan was formed as an autonomous republic within Russia from areas of Turkistan and Bokhara with mainly Tajik populations. In 1929 it became a constituent republic of the Soviet Union. When the Union began to collapse in 1991 Tajikistan declared itself independent. Armed conflict between Islamic groups and the government began soon after independence, and lasted until the 1997 peace agreement.

Presidents:
Chairman of the Central Executive Committee 1924-38
President of the Presidium of the Supreme Soviet 1938-90
Chairman of the Supreme Soviet April-Nov 1990

Nov 1924-Dec 1933	Nasratollah Maksum
Dec 1933-37	Shirinsho Shotemor
1937-July 1950	Minovar Shagadayev
July 1950-May 1956	Nazarsho Dodkhudoyev
May 1956-March 1963	Mirzo Rakhmatov
March 1963-Jan 1984	Makhmadullo Kholov
Jan 1984-April 1990	Gaibnazar Pallayev
April 1990-Aug 1991	Kakhar Makhkamov
Aug-Sept 1991	Kadreddin Aslonov (acting)
Sept-Oct 1991	Rakhman Nabiyev (1st)
Oct-Nov 1991	Akbarsho Iskanderov (acting) (1st)
Nov 1991-Sept 1992	Rakhman Nabiyev (2nd)
Sept-Nov 1992	Akbarsho Iskanderov (acting) (2nd)
Nov 1992-	Imamali Rakhmanov (acting Nov 1992-Nov 1994)

Prime Ministers:
Chairman of the Council of People's Commissars 1926-46
Chairman of the Council of Ministers 1946-94

1925-26	Nasratollah Maksum

Dec 1926-28	Usman Pulatkhodzhayev (Mukhitdinov) (see Bokhara)
1928-29	Mumin Khodzhayev
1929-Dec 1933	Abdurrahim Hodzhibayev (removed, executed)
Dec 1933-37	Abdullah Rahimbayev (see Turkistan)
1937	U. Amurov
1937-46	Mamdali Kurbanov
1946-March 1955	Djabar Rasulov
March 1955-May 1956	Tursunbai Uldzhabayev
May 1956-April 1961	Nazarsho Dodkhudoyev
April 1961-July 1973	Abdulakhad Kakharov
July 1973-April 1982	Rakhman Nabiyev
April 1982-Dec 1985	Kakhar Makhkamov
Dec 1985-Jan 1992	Izatullo Khayayev (see Gorno-Badakhshan)
Jan-Aug 1992	Akbar Mirzoyev
Aug-Sept 1992	Jamshed Karimov (acting)
Sept 1992-Dec 1993	Abdulmalik Abdullojanov (acting Sept-Dec 1992)
Dec 1993-Dec 1994	Abduljalil Samadov
Dec 1994-Feb 1996	Jamshed Karimov
Feb 1996-Dec 1999	Yahya Azimov
Dec 1999-	Akil Akilov

Communist Party Leaders:

First Secretary

1926	— — Imamov
1926-27	— — Tadzhiev
1927-28	Mumin Khodzhayev
1928-30	Boris Goldayev
1930-33	Mirza Guseinov (see Azerbaijan)
Nov 1933-34	Grigory Broido
1934-37	S. K. Sadunts
1937-46	Dmitri Protopopov
1946-May 1956	Bodozhan Gafurov
May 1956-April 1961	Tursunbai Uldzhabayev
April 1961-April 1982	Djabar Rasulov (†)
April 1982-Dec 1985	Rakhman Nabiyev
Dec 1985-Sept 1991	Kakhar Makhkamov

Autonomous Region

GORNO-BADAKHSHAN

Established: 2 January 1925
Capital: Khorog

Prime Ministers:
Chairman of the Executive Committee

Aug 1961-July 1963	M.Shirindzhanov
July 1963-March 1978	Izatullo Khayeyev
March 1978-1990	Muminsho Abdulvasiyev
1990-92	Akbarsho Iskanderov
1992-	Garibsho Shabozov

Communist Party Leaders:
First Secretary

July 1963-April 1970	M.Nazarshoyev
April 1970-June 1982	Khushkadam Davlyatkadamov
June 1982-April 1987	Mukhitdin Zairov
April 1987-Aug 1991	Soibnazar Beknazarov

TANZANIA

Official name:	United Republic of Tanzania, Jamhuri ya Muungano wa Tanzania
Previous names:	German East Africa 1891-1918, Tanganyika 1916/18-61, Dominion of Tanganyika 1961-62, Republic of Tanganyika 1962-64, United Republic of Tanganyika and Zanzibar April-Oct 1964
State founded (Tanzania):	27 April 1964
Independence date (Tanganyika):	9 December 1961
Capital:	Dodoma (*f* capital: Dar es Salaam, still serves as seat of government)

Tanganyika was a German colony from 1884, forming part of German East Africa until World War I. After the German defeat it became a mandated territory under British administration. In 1960 ministerial government was introduced, followed in May 1961 by full self-government. In December 1961 Tanganyika became independent, and in 1962 a republic was proclaimed. Zanzibar was a Portuguese trading station that was taken over by Oman at the end of the 17th century. In 1832 the Sultan of Oman established his capital there, but in 1856 Zanzibar and Oman separated. In 1890 Zanzibar became a British protectorate until 1963 when independence was granted. In 1964 the sultanate was overthrown and a republic proclaimed, and three months later Tanganyika and Zanzibar united, although Zanzibar retained its own government.

Information for 1891-1918 refers to German East Africa, and for 1916-1964 Tanganyika

Governors:

German East Africa
1891-93	Julius von Soden
1893-95	Friedrich von Schele
1895-96	Hermann von Wissmann
1896-1901	Eduard von Liebert
1901-06	Adolf von Gotzen
1906-12	Albrecht von Rechenberg
1912-18	Heinrich Schnee

Tanganyika
1916-24	Horace Byatt
1924-31	Donald Cameron
1931-33	George Symes
1933-38	Harold MacMichael
1938-42	Mark Young

1942-45	Wilfred Jackson
1945-49	William Battershill
1949-58	Edward Twining
1958-61	Richard Turnbull

Governor-General:

Represented monarch who was concurrently British monarch

Dec 1961-Dec 1962	Richard Turnbull

Presidents:

Dec 1962-Nov 1985	Julius Nyerere (TANU, CCM)
Nov 1985-Nov 1995	Ali Hassan Mwinyi (see Zanzibar) (CCM)
Nov 1995-	Benjamin Mkapa (CCM)

Chief Minister:

Sept 1960-May 1961	Julius Nyerere (TANU)

Prime Ministers:

May 1961-June 1962	Julius Nyerere (TANU)
June 1962-April 1964	Rashidi Kawawa (TANU) (1st)
(April 1964-Feb 1972	post abolished)
Feb 1972-Feb 1977	Rashidi Kawawa (2nd)
Feb 1977-Nov 1980	Edward Sokoine (1st)
Nov 1980-Feb 1983	Cleopa Msuya (1st)
Feb 1983-April 1984	Edward Sokoine (2nd) († motor accident)
April 1984-Nov 1985	Salim Ahmed Salim
Nov 1985-Nov 1990	Joseph Warioba
Nov 1990-Dec 1994	John Malecela
Dec 1994-Nov 1995	Cleopa Msuya (2nd)
Nov 1995-	Frederick Sumaye

CCM = Chama Cha Mapinduzi (Revolutionary Party) (formed by merger of ASP and TANU) (sole legal party 1977-92)
TANU = Tanganyika African National Union (sole legal party 1965-77)

Autonomous Region & former independent state

ZANZIBAR

Sultanate of Zanzibar until 1964, People's Republic of Zanzibar Jan-April 1964
Independence date: 9 December 1963
Capital: Zanzibar

Sultans:

1832-Oct 1856	Said bin Sultan	(also Sultan of Muscat & Oman)
Oct 1856-Oct 1870	Majid bin Said	(*son*)
Oct 1870-March 1888	Barghash bin Said	(*brother*)
March 1888-Feb 1890	Khalifa bin Barghash	(*son*)
Feb 1890-March 1893	Ali bin Said	(*uncle*)
March 1893-Aug 1896	Hamed bin Thwain	(*nephew*)
25-27 Aug 1896	Khalid	
Aug 1896-July 1902	Hamoud bin Mohammed	(*nephew of Khalifa bin Barghash*)
July 1902-Dec 1911	Ali bin Hamoud	(*son*)
Dec 1911-Oct 1960	Khalifa bin Harub	(*nephew of Hamed bin Thwain*)
Oct 1960-July 1963	Abdullah bin Khalifa	(*son*)
July 1963-Jan 1964	Jamshid bin Abdullah	(*son*) (deposed)

Presidents:

Jan 1964-April 1972	Abeid Karume (ASP) († assassinated)
April 1972-Jan 1984	Aboud Jumbe (ASP)
Jan 1984-Oct 1985	Ali Hassan Mwinyi (acting Jan-April 1984) (ASP,CCM) (later President of Tanzania)
Oct 1985-Oct 1990	Idris Wakil (CCM)
Oct 1990-	Salmin Amur Juma (CCM)

Chief Ministers:

Feb-June 1961	G.C.Lawrence (acting)
June 1961-June 1963	Mohammed Hamadi

Prime Ministers:

June 1963-Jan 1964	Mohammed Hamadi (deposed)
Jan-April 1964	Abdullah Hanga
(April 1964	post abolished)

Chief Ministers:

Feb 1983-Feb 1984	Ramadhani Saki
Feb 1984-Jan 1988	Seif Sharif Hamad
Jan 1988-Nov 1995	Omar Ali Juma
Nov 1995-	Mohammed Gharib Bilal

ASP = Afro-Shirazi Party (sole legal party 1964-77)

THAILAND

Official name: Kingdom of Thailand, Prathet Thai
Previous name: Kingdom of Siam until 1939
State founded: 1767
Capital: Ayutthaya (until c1770), Bangkok (Krung Thep)

From the 14th to the 18th century the area of Thailand was the state of Ayutthaya. In 1767 the country was invaded by the Burmese, but they were expelled in the same year and a united Thai state was founded. The present royal family came to power in 1782. Until 1932 Siam was an absolute monarchy. A coup was followed by the promulgation of a provisional constitution. Since then there have been several military takeovers.

Kings:

1767-April 1782	Phraya Taksin (deposed, executed)
April 1782-Sept 1809	Chao Phraya Chakkri (Phuttha Yot Fa) (Rama I)
Sept 1809-July 1824	Loet La Nabhalai (Rama II) *(son)*
July 1824-April 1851	Nang Klao (Rama III) *(son)*
April 1851-Oct 1868	Maha Mongkut (Rama IV) *(half-brother)*
Oct 1868-Oct 1910	Chulalongkorn (Rama V) *(son)*
Oct 1910-Nov 1925	Vajiravudh (Rama VI) *(son)*
Nov 1925-March 1935	Prajadhipok (Rama VII) *(brother)* *(abdicated)*
March 1935-June 1946	Ananda Mahidol (Rama VIII) *(nephew)*
June 1946-	Bhumibol Adulyadej (Rama IX) *(brother)*
	(Regent: Prince Rangsit 1946-50)

Prime Ministers:

June 1932-Nov 1933	Manopakorn
Nov 1933-Dec 1938	Bhanon Bhonphahuyasena (deposed)
Dec 1938-July 1944	Pibul Songgram (1st)
July 1944-Aug 1945	Kovid Aphaiwongse (1st)
Aug-Sept 1945	Thawi Bunyakat
Sept 1945-Jan 1946	Seni Pramoj (1st)
Jan-March 1946	Kovid Aphaiwongse (2nd)
March-Aug 1946	Pridi Phanomjong
Aug 1946-Dec 1947	Dhamrong Nawasasat (deposed)
Dec 1947-April 1948	Kovid Aphaiwongse (3rd)
April 1948-Sept 1947	Pibul Songgram (2nd) (SMP)
Sept 1957-Jan 1958	Pote Sarasin
Jan-Oct 1958	Thanom Kitticachorn (1st) (deposed)

Oct 1958-Dec 1963	Sarit Thanarat (†)
Dec 1973-Oct 1973	Thanom Kitticachorn (2nd)
Oct 1973-Feb 1975	Sanya Dharmasaki
Feb-March 1975	Seni Pramoj (2nd) (DP)
March 1975-April 1976	Kukrit Pramoj (*brother*) (SAP)
April-Oct 1976	Seni Pramoj (3rd) (DP) (deposed)
(6-22 Oct 1976	Sa'ngad Chaloryoo - military ruler (1st))
Oct 1976-Oct 1977	Thanin Kraivichien (deposed)
(Oct-Nov 1977	Sa'ngad Chaloryoo - military ruler (2nd))
Nov 1977-Feb 1980	Kriangsak Chamanand
Feb 1980-Aug 1988	Prem Tinsulanond
Aug 1988-Feb 1991	Chatichai Choonhavan (CT) (deposed)
(Feb-March 1991	Sunthorn Kompongsong - military ruler)
March 1991-April 1992	Anand Panyarachun (1st)
April-May 1992	Suchinda Kraprayoon
May-June 1992	Meechai Ruchupan (acting)
June-Oct 1992	Anand Panyarachun (2nd)
Oct 1992-July 1995	Chuan Leekpai (1st) (DP)
July 1995-Nov 1996	Banharn Silapaarcha (CT)
Nov 1996-Nov 1997	Chavalit Yongchaiyudh (NAP)
Nov 1997-	Chuan Leekpai (2nd) (DP)

NAP = New Assimilation Party
CT = Chart Thai (Thai Nation)
DP = Democratic Party
SAP = Social Action Party
SMP = Seri Manangasila Party

TOGO

Official name: Togolese Republic, République Togolaise
Previous name: Autonomous Togolese Republic 1956-58
Independence date: 27 April 1960
Capital: Lomé

Togo was a German protectorate from 1894 until 1914 when it was occupied by French and British forces. After World War I it was divided into two League of Nations trust territories. The British-administered area became part of Ghana in 1957. The French-administered area was granted self-government in 1956, and in 1960 became the independent Togolese Republic.

Governors:

1898-1902	August Köhler
1902-03	Waldemar Horn
1903-10	Julius Zech
1910-12	Edmund Bruckner
1912-14	Adolf Herzog zu Mecklenburg
1916-17	Gaston Fourn
1917-21	Adolf-Louis Woelfel

High Commissioners:

1921-22	Adolf-Louis Woelfel
1922-31	Auguste-François Bonnecarrère
1931-33	Robert de Guise (see Martinique)
1933-34	Léon Pêtre
1934-35	Maurice-Léon Bourgine (see Niger)
1935-36	Léon Geismar
1936-41	Michel-Lucien Montagné
1941	Léonce-Joseph Delpech
1941-42	Jean de Saint-Alary
1942-43	Pierre-Jean Saliceli
1943-44	Albert Mercadier
1944-48	Jean Noutary
1948-51	Jean Cédile
1951-52	Yves-Jean Digo
1952-54	Laurent-Elisée Péchoux
1955-57	Jean Bérard
1957-60	Georges-Léon Spénale

Presidents:

Head of State 1960-61
Chairman of the Insurrectionary Committee Jan 1963
President of the Committee for National Reconciliation Jan-April 1967

April 1960-Jan 1963	Sylvanus Olympio (CTU) († assassinated)
13-16 Jan 1963	Emmanuel Bodjollé
Jan 1963-Jan 1967	Nicholas Grunitzky (*brother-in-law of S.Olympio*) (deposed)
Jan-April 1967	Kléber Dadjo
April 1967-	Gnassingbé Eyadéma (*f* Étienne Eyadéma) (RTP)

Prime Ministers:

Sept 1956-April 1958	Nicholas Grunitzky (PTU)
April 1958-April 1961	Sylvanus Olympio (CTU)
(April 1961-Aug 1991	post abolished)
Aug 1991-April 1994	J.Kokou Koffigoh
April 1994-Aug 1996	Edem Kodjo (TUD)
Aug 1996-May 1999	Kwassi Klutsé (RTP)
May 1999-	Koffi Adoboli

CTU = Committee of Togolese Unity
PTU = Party of Togolese Unity
RTP = Rally of the Togolese People (sole party 1969-91)
TUD = Togolese Union for Democracy

TONGA

Official name: Kingdom of Tonga, Pule'anga Fakatu'i'o Tonga
State founded: 4 June 1845
Independence date: 4 June 1970
Capital: Nuku'alofa

In 1845 the ruler of the island of Ha'apai, Taufa'ahau, united all the islands of the Tonga group into a single kingdom. In 1900 the country became a British protectorate, and in 1970 full independence was restored.

Kings/Queen:

June 1845-Feb 1893	George Tupou I	(f Taufa'ahau)
Feb 1893-April 1918	George Tupou II	(great-grandson)
April 1918-Dec 1965	Salote Tupou III	(daughter)
Dec 1965-	Taufa'ahau Tupou IV	(f Tupouto'a Tungi) (son)

Prime Ministers:

Premier 1876-1970

1876-80	Prince Tevita Unga	(son of George Tupou I) (†)
1880-July 1890	Shirley Baker	
July 1890-93	Siaosi Uiliame Tuku'aho	
1893-1904	Siosateki Veikune	
1904-Jan 1905	Siaosi Tu'ipelehake	
Jan 1905-Sept 1912	Sione Mateialona	
Sept 1912-June 1922	Tevita Tu'ivakano	
June 1922-July 1941	Prince Uiliame Tungi	(husband of Queen Salote) (†)
Aug 1941-Dec 1949	Solomone Ata	
Dec 1949-Dec 1965	Prince Tupouto'a Tungi	(later King Taufa'ahau Tupou IV)
Dec 1965-July 1991	Prince Fatafehi Tu'ipelehake	(brother)
July 1991-Jan 2000	Baron Vaea of Houma	
Jan 2000-	Prince Ulukalala Lavaka Ata	(son of King Taufa'ahau Tupou IV)

TRINIDAD AND TOBAGO

Official name: Republic of Trinidad and Tobago
Previous name: Dominion of Trinidad and Tobago 1962-76
Independence date: 31 August 1962
Capital: Port of Spain

Trinidad was discovered by Columbus in 1498 and was colonized by Spain in the 16th century. In 1797 it was occupied by Britain and formally ceded in 1802. Tobago was initially colonized by the Dutch in 1632, and then became French in 1677. It was controlled by Britain from 1763 to 1783 and by France 1783 to 1815, when it became British again. In 1889 Trinidad and Tobago were united into a single colony, which became self-governing in 1956. From 1958 to 1962 it was a member of the West Indies Federation, which had its headquarters in Trinidad. After its dissolution, Trinidad and Tobago became independent, and in 1976 a republic was proclaimed.

Governors:

1900-04	Cornelius Moloney (see British Honduras)
1904-09	Henry Jackson
1909-16	George LeHunte
1916-22	John Chancellor (see Mauritius)
1922-24	Samuel Wilson
1924-30	Horace Byatt
1930-36	Alfred Hollis
1936-38	Arthur Fletcher
1938-42	Hubert Young
1942-47	Bede Clifford (see Bahamas)
1947-50	John Shaw
1950-55	Hubert Rance (see Burma)
1955-60	Edward Beetham
1960-62	Solomon Hochoy

Governors-General:
Represented monarch who was concurrently British monarch

Aug 1962-Sept 1972	Solomon Hochoy
Sept 1972-July 1976	Ellis Clarke

Presidents:

July 1976-March 1987	Ellis Clarke
March 1987-March 1997	Noor Hassanali
March 1997-	Arthur Robinson

Chief Minister:

Oct 1956-July 1959   Eric Williams   (PNM)

Prime Ministers:

July 1959-March 1981	Eric Williams (PNM) (†)
March 1981-Dec 1986	George Chambers (PNM)
Dec 1986-Dec 1991	Arthur Robinson (NAR)
Dec 1991-Nov 1995	Patrick Manning (PNM)
Nov 1995-	Basdeo Panday (UNC)

NAR = National Alliance for Reconstruction
PNM = People's National Movement
UNC = United National Congress

Autonomous region

TOBAGO

Capital: Scarborough

Assembly Chairmen:

1980-86	Arthur Robinson
1986-92	Jefferson Davis
1992-98	Lennox Denoon
1998-	Hochoi Charles

Defunct Federation

WEST INDIES FEDERATION

Date formed: 3 January 1958
Date dissolved: May 1962
Capital: Port of Spain
Member states: Antigua, Barbados, Dominica, Grenada, Jamaica, Montserrat, St Christopher-Nevis-Anguilla, St Lucia, St Vincent, Trinidad & Tobago

Governor-General:

Aug 1958-May 1962   Lord Hailes   (Patrick Buchan-Hepburn)

Prime Minister:

Aug 1958-May 1962   Grantley Adams   (see Barbados) (FLP)

FLP = Federal Labour Party

TUNISIA

Official name: Republic of Tunisia, Al-Jamhuriya at-Tunisiya
Previous name: Tunisian State 1956-57
State formed: July 1705
Independence date: 20 March 1956
Capital: Tunis

Present-day Tunisia became part of the Turkish Empire in 1574. In 1705 a Tunisian state was formed under nominal Turkish sovereignty, but in 1883 it became a French protectorate. Self- government was introduced in 1943, and in 1956 Tunisia became an independent monarchy. A year later a republic was proclaimed.

Beys:

July 1705-Sept 1735	Hussein I	(deposed)
Sept 1735-Sept 1756	Ali I	(*nephew*) (assassinated)
Sept 1756-March 1759	Mohammed I	(*cousin*)
March 1759-Feb 1782	Ali II	(*brother*)
Feb 1782-Sept 1814	Hammuda	(*son*)
Sept-Dec 1814	Othman	(*brother*)
Dec 1814-March 1824	Mahmud	(*son of Mohammed I*)
March 1824-May 1835	Hussein II	(*son*)
May 1835-Oct 1837	Mustafa	(*brother*)
Oct 1837-May 1855	Ahmed I	(*son*)
May 1855-Sept 1859	Mohammed II	(*cousin*)
Sept 1859-Oct 1882	Mohammed III al-Sadiq	(*brother*)
Oct 1882-June 1902	Ali III Muddat	(*brother*)
June 1902-May 1906	Mohammed IV al-Hadji	(*son*)
May 1906-July 1922	Mohammed V al-Nasir	(*cousin*)
July 1922-Feb 1929	Mohammed VI al-Habib	(*cousin*)
Feb 1929-July 1942	Ahmad II	(*cousin*)
July 1942-May 1943	Mohammed VII al-Munsif	(*son of Mohammed V*) (abdicated)
May 1943-July 1957	Mohammed VIII al-Amin	(*son of Mohammed VI*) (deposed)

Presidents:

July 1957-Nov 1987	Habib Bourguiba
Nov 1987-	Zine el-Abidine Ben Ali

Prime Ministers:

1943-Nov 1946	Salaheddin Baccouche	(1st)

Nov 1946-Aug 1950	Mohammed Kaak
Aug 1950-April 1952	Mohammed Chenik
April 1952-March 1954	Salaheddin Baccouche (2nd)
May-July 1954	Mohammed Salah Mzali
July 1954-April 1956	Tahar Ben Ammar
April 1956-Nov 1969	Habib Bourguiba
Nov 1969-Nov 1970	Bahi Ladgham
Nov 1970-April 1980	Hedi Nouira
April 1980-July 1986	Mohammed Mzali
July 1986-Oct 1987	Rashid Sfar
Oct-Nov 1987	Zine el-Abidine Ben Ali
Nov 1987-Sept 1989	Hedi Baccouche
Sept 1989-Nov 1999	Hamad Karoui
Nov 1999-	Mohammed Ghannouchi

TURKEY

Official name: Republic of Turkey, Türkiye Cumhuriyeti

Previous names: Sultanate of Turkey until 1922 (the name Ottoman Empire was applied to all the lands under Turkish rule), Turkey 1922-23

State founded: 13th century

Capital: Edirne (until 1453), Istanbul (1453-1923), Ankara (since 1923)

In the 13th century the kingdom of Othman I became the dominant power in Asia Minor. In 1453 the Turks captured Constantinople (renamed Istanbul) and established an empire that extended from Morocco to Persia and westwards into the Balkans reaching the gates of Vienna in 1683. In the 19th century the Ottoman Empire declined, and Turkey's defeat in World War I was followed by the loss of all non-Turkish territories. In 1920 Mustafa Kemal Ataturk, the founder of modern Turkey, established an opposing government in Ankara, and in 1923 the monarchy was abolished and a republic proclaimed. The military has staged two coups, in 1960 and in 1980, and continues to influence policies even though democracy was restored in 1983.

Sultans:

1281-1324	Othman I (abdicated)
1324-60	Orkhan (*son*) (abdicated)
1360-89	Murad I (*son*) (abdicated)
June 1389-July 1402	Bayezid I (*son*) (deposed)
(July 1402-July 1413	interregnum)
July 1413-May 1421	Mohammed I (*son*)
May 1421-Dec 1444	Murad II (*son*) (1st) (abdicated)
Dec 1444-Sept 1446	Mohammed II (*son*) (1st) (deposed)
Sept 1446-Feb 1451	Murad II (2nd)
Feb 1451-May 1481	Mohammed II (2nd)
May 1481-April 1512	Bayezid II (*son*) (deposed)
April 1512-Sept 1520	Selim I (*brother*)
Sept 1520-Sept 1566	Suleiman I (*son*)
Sept 1566-Dec 1574	Selim II (*son*)
Dec 1574-Jan 1595	Murad III (*son*)
Jan 1595-Dec 1603	Mohammed III (*son*)
Dec 1603-Nov 1617	Ahmed I (*son*)
Nov 1617-Feb 1618	Mustafa I (*brother*) (1st) (deposed)
Feb 1618-May 1622	Othman II (*nephew*) (deposed, assassinated)
May 1622-Sept 1623	Mustafa I (2nd) (deposed)
Sept 1623-Feb 1640	Murad IV (*nephew*)
Feb 1640-Aug 1648	Ibrahim (*brother*) (deposed, assassinated)

Aug 1648-Nov 1687	Mohammed IV (*son*) (abdicated)
Nov 1687-June 1691	Suleiman II (*brother*)
June 1691-Feb 1695	Ahmed II (*brother*) (deposed)
Feb 1695-Aug 1703	Mustafa II (*nephew*) (deposed)
Aug 1703-Oct 1730	Ahmed III (*brother*) (deposed)
Oct 1730-Dec 1754	Mahmud I (*son of Mustafa II*)
Dec 1754-Oct 1757	Othman III (*brother*)
Oct 1757-Jan 1774	Mustafa III (*son of Ahmed III*)
Jan 1774-April 1789	Abdul Hamid I (*brother*)
April 1789-May 1807	Selim III (*nephew*) (deposed, assassinated 1808)
May 1807-July 1808	Mustafa IV (*son of Abdul Hamid I*) (deposed)
July 1808-July 1839	Mahmud II (*brother*)
July 1839-June 1861	Abdul Majid (*son*)
June 1861-May 1876	Abdul Aziz (*brother*) (deposed)
May-Aug 1876	Murad V (*son of Abdul Mejid*) (deposed)
Aug 1876-April 1909	Abdul Hamid II (*brother*) (deposed)
April 1909-July 1918	Mohammed V (*brother*)
July 1918-Nov 1922	Mohammed VI Vahideddin (*brother*) (deposed)

Caliph:

Nov 1922-Oct 1923	Abdul Mejid (*son of Abdul Aziz*)

Presidents:

Oct 1923-Nov 1938	Mustafa Kemal Atatürk (*f* Mustafa Kemal Paşa) (†)
Nov 1938-May 1950	İsmet İnönü (*f* Mustafa İsmet Paşa)
May 1950-May 1960	Celâl Bayar (deposed)
May 1960-March 1966	Cemal Gürsel
March 1966-March 1973	Cevdet Sunay
March-April 1973	Tekin Ariburun (acting)
April 1973-April 1980	Fahri Korutürk
April-Sept 1980	Ihsan Çağlayangil (acting)
Sept 1980-Nov 1989	Kenan Evren
Nov 1989-April 1993	Turgut Özal (†)
April-May 1993	Hüsamettin Çindoruk (acting)
May 1993-	Süleyman Demirel

Grand Viziers:

Post in existence since 14th century; names from the 1876 constitution listed. (In Istanbul)

Dec 1876-Feb 1877	Ali Haydar Midhat Paşa (2nd)
Feb 1877-Jan 1878	Ibrahim Edhem Paşa
Jan-Feb 1878	Ahmed Hamdi Paşa (acting)
Feb-April 1878	Ahmed Vefik Paşa (acting)

April-May 1878	Mehmed Sadik Paşa (acting)
May-June 1878	Mehmed Rüsdü Paşa (acting)
June-Oct 1878	Mehmed Esad Saffek Paşa (acting)
Oct 1878-Aug 1879	Tunuslu Hayreddin Paşa
Aug-Oct 1879	Ahmed Arifi Paşa
Oct 1879-June 1880	Mehmed Said Paşa (1st)
June-Sept 1880	Kadri Paşa
Sept 1880-May 1882	Mehmed Said Paşa (2nd)
May-June 1882	Abdürrahman Nureddin Paşa
June-Nov 1882	Mehmed Said Paşa (3rd)
Nov-Dec 1882	Ahmed Vefik Paşa
Dec 1882-Oct 1885	Mehmed Said Paşa (4th)
Oct 1885-Sept 1891	Mehmed Kamil Paşa (1st)
Sept 1891-June 1895	Ahmed Cevad Paşa
Oct-Nov 1895	Mehmed Kamil Paşa (2nd)
Nov 1895-Nov 1901	Halil Rifat Paşa
Nov 1901-Jan 1903	Mehmed Said Paşa (5th)
Jan 1903-July 1908	Mehmed Ferid Paşa (1st)
July-Aug 1908	Mehmed Said Paşa (6th)
Aug 1908-Feb 1909	Mehmed Kamil Paşa (3rd)
Feb-April 1909	Hüseyin Hilmi Paşa (1st)
April-May 1909	Ahmed Tevfik Paşa (1st)
May 1909-Jan 1910	Hüseyin Hilmi Paşa (2nd)
Jan 1910-Oct 1911	Ibrahim Hakki Paşa
Oct 1911-July 1912	Mehmed Said Paşa (7th)
17-21 July 1912	Ahmed Tevfik Paşa (2nd)
July-Oct 1912	Gazi Ahmed Mukhtar Paşa
Oct 1912-Jan 1913	Mahmud Şevket Paşa
Jan 1913-Feb 1917	Said Halim Paşa
Feb 1917-April 1918	Mehmed Talat Paşa
April-Nov 1918	Ahmed Izzet Paşa
Nov 1918-March 1918	Ahmed Tevfik Paşa (3rd)
March-Oct 1919	Damad Ferid Paşa (1st)
Oct 1919-March 1920	Ali Riza Paşa
March-April 1920	Salih Paşa
April-Oct 1920	Damad Ferid Paşa (2nd)
Oct 1920-Nov 1922	Ahmed Tevfik Paşa (4th)

Prime Ministers:

(In Ankara)

May 1920-Jan 1921	Mustafa Kemal Paşa (later Atatürk)
Jan 1921-July 1922	Fevzi Paşa (later Cakmak)
July 1922-Aug 1923	Hüseyin Rauf (later Orbay)
Aug-Oct 1923	Fethi Okyar

Oct 1923-Oct 1937	İsmet İnönü (f Mustafa İsmet Paşa) (1st) (RPP)
Oct 1937-Jan 1939	Celal Bâyar (RPP)
Jan 1939-July 1942	Refik Saydam (RPP) (†)
July 1942-Aug 1946	Şükrü Sarajoğlu (RPP)
Aug 1946-Sept 1947	Recep Peker (RPP)
Sept 1947-Jan 1949	Hasan Saka (RPP)
Jan 1949-May 1950	Şenseddin Günaltay (RPP)
May 1950-May 1960	Adnan Menderes (DP) (deposed, executed 1961)
May 1960-Oct 1961	Cemal Gürsel
Oct-Nov 1961	Fahri Özdilek (acting)
Nov 1961-Feb 1965	İsmet İnönü (2nd) (RPP)
Feb-Oct 1965	Suat Ürgüplü
Oct 1965-March 1971	Süleyman Demirel (1st) (JP)
March 1971-May 1972	Nihat Erim (assassinated 1980)
May 1972-April 1973	Ferit Melen (RPP)
April 1973-Jan 1974	Naim Talû
Jan-Nov 1974	Bülent Eçevit (1st) (RPP)
Nov 1974-March 1975	Sadi Irmak
March 1975-June 1977	Süleyman Demirel (2nd) (JP)
June-July 1977	Bülent Eçevit (2nd) (RPP)
July 1977-Jan 1978	Süleyman Demirel (3rd) (JP)
Jan 1978-Nov 1979	Bülent Eçevit (3rd) (RPP)
Nov 1979-Sept 1980	Süleyman Demirel (4th) (JP) (deposed)
Sept 1980-Dec 1983	Bülent Ülüsü
Dec 1983-Nov 1989	Turgut Özal (MP)
Nov 1989-June 1991	Yildirim Akbulut (MP)
June-Nov 1991	Mesut Yilmaz (1st) (MP)
Nov 1991-May 1993	Süleyman Demirel (5th) (TPP)
May-June 1993	Erdal İnönü (acting)
June 1993-March 1996	Tansu Çiller (TPP)
March-June 1996	Mesut Yilmaz (2nd) (MP)
June 1996-June 1997	Neçmettin Erbakan (WP)
June 1997-Jan 1999	Mesut Yilmaz (3rd) (MP)
Jan 1999-	Bülent Eçevit (4th) (DLP)

DLP = Democratic Left Party
DP = Democratic Party
JP = Justice Party
MP = Motherland Party
RPP = Republican People's Party
TPP = True Path Party
WP = Welfare Party

Former Autonomous State

HATAY

Capital: Antioch

Administered as part of Syria until 1938; united with Turkey in 1939

President:

Sept 1938-July 1939   Tayfur Sökman

TURKMENISTAN

Official name: Republic of Turkmenistan, Turkmenistan Jumhuriyëti
Previous name: Turkmenistan Soviet Socialist Republic 1924-91
State formed: 27 October 1924
Admission to USSR: 13 May 1925
Independence date: 27 October 1991
Capital: Ashgabat (Ashkhabad)

Turkmenistan was formed in 1924 from parts of Turkistan, Bokhara and Khiva during the reorganization of Soviet Central Asia, and in 1925 it was admitted to the Soviet Union as a constituent republic. With the collapse of the Union in 1991 it became an independent state.

Presidents:
Chairman of the Central Executive Committee 1925-38
President of the Presidium of the Supreme Soviet 1938-90
Chairman of the Supreme Soviet Jan-Oct 1990

Feb 1925-37	Nedirbai Aitakov	(see Turkistan)
1937-42	Khivali Babayev	
1942-47	Alla Berdiev	
1947-March 1959	Akmamed Saryev	
March 1959-March 1963	Nurberdi Bairamov	
March 1963-Dec 1978	Annamuchamed Klychev	
Dec 1978-Aug 1988	Bally Iazkuliev	
Aug 1988-Jan 1990	Roza Bazarova	
Jan 1990-	Saparmurad Niyazov	(DP)

Prime Ministers:
Chairman of the Council of People's Commissars 1925-46
Chairman of the Council of Ministers 1946-92

Feb 1925-37	Kaigisyz Atabayev	(see Turkistan)
1937-45	Aitbay Khudaibergenov	
Oct 1945-51	Sukhan Babayev	
1951-Jan 1958	Balysh Ovezov	(1st)
Jan-Dec 1958	Djuma Karayev	
Jan 1959-May 1960	Balysh Ovezov	(2nd)
June 1960-March 1963	Abdy Annaliev	
March 1963-Dec 1969	Mukhamednazar Gapurov	
Dec 1969-Dec 1975	Oraz Orazmukhamedov	

Dec 1975-Dec 1978   Bally Iazkuliev
Dec 1978-Feb 1985   Chary Karryev
March-Dec 1985   Saparmurad Niyazov   (1st)
Dec 1985-Nov 1989   Annamurad Khodzhamuradov
Dec 1989-May 1992   Khan Akhmedov
May 1992-   Saparmurad Niyazov   (2nd)

DP = Democratic Party

Communist Party Leaders:

First Secretary

1925-28   Halmurad Sakhatmuradov
1928-30   — — Aronshtam
Aug 1930-July 1937   Yakov Popok
1937-39   Yakov Chubin
1939-47   M. Fonin
1947-50   Shadzha Batryov
1950-51   Balysh Ovezov   (1st) (see Mari Republic)
1951-Dec 1958   Sukhan Babayev
Dec 1958-May 1960   Djuma Karayev   (†)
May 1960-Dec 1969   Balysh Ovezov   (2nd)
Dec 1969-Dec 1985   Mukhamednazar Gapurov
Dec 1985-Aug 1991   Saparmurad Niyazov
(Aug 1991   party transformed into Democratic Party)

TUVALU

Official name: Constitutional Monarchy of Tuvalu, Fakavae Aliki-malo i Tuvalu
Previous name: Ellice Islands until 1975
Independence date: 1 October 1978
Capital: Fongafale (on Funafuti)

The Ellice Islands became a British protectorate in 1892 together with the Gilbert Islands. In 1975 the Ellice Islands were separated from the Gilbert Islands, taking the name Tuvalu. In 1978 Tuvalu became independent.

Commissioner:

Oct 1975-Oct 1978   Thomas Layng

Governors-General:
Represent monarch who is concurrently British monarch

Oct 1978-March 1986	Penitala Fiatau Teo
March 1986-Oct 1990	Tupua Leupena
Oct 1990-Dec 1993	Toaripi Lauti
Dec 1993-July 1994	Tomu Malaefono Sione
July 1994-June 1998	Tulaga Manuella
June 1998-	Tomasi Puapua

Chief Minister:

Oct 1975-Oct 1978   Toaripi Lauti

Prime Ministers:

Oct 1978-Sept 1981	Toaripi Lauti	
Sept 1981-Oct 1989	Tomasi Puapua	
Oct 1989-Dec 1993	Bikenibeu Paeniu	(1st)
Dec 1993-Dec 1996	Kamuta Laatasi	
Dec 1996-April 1999	Bikenibeu Paeniu	(2nd)
April 1999-	Ionatana Ionatana	

UGANDA

Official name: Republic of Uganda, Jamhuri wa Uganda
Previous names: Dominion of Uganda 1962-63, Commonwealth of Uganda 1963-67
Independence date: 9 October 1962
Capital: Kampala

By the 19th century the kingdom of Buganda had become dominant in the area of present-day Uganda. In 1893 a British protectorate was established over Buganda and three other kingdoms, Ankole, Bunyoro and Toro. In 1961 Uganda was granted some autonomy, extended to full self-government and independence in 1962. In 1963 links with the British monarchy were abolished, and in 1967 the monarchies of the four constitutive kingdoms were abolished and a republic proclaimed. Their restitution began in 1993 for ceremonial purposes. Uganda has suffered from periods of instability and civil conflict. The dictatorial rule of Idi Amin was ended with the aid of Tanzanian forces in 1979, but the elected government established was deposed in 1985. Further instability continued until 1986 when the National Resistance Army captured Kampala; the country has since recovered economically, although some conflicts still occur in the north.

Governors:

1905-10	Henry Bell
1910-11	Harry Cordeaux
1911-18	Frederick Jackson
1918-22	Robert Coryndon
1922-25	Geoffrey Archer (see British Honduras)
1925-32	William Gowers
1932-35	Bernard Bourdillon
1935-40	Philip Mitchell
1940-44	Charles Dundas (see Bahamas)
1944-52	John Hall
1952-57	Andrew Cohen
1957-61	Frederick Crawford
1961-62	Walter Coutts (see St Vincent)

Governor-General:

Represented monarch who was concurrently British monarch

Oct 1962-Oct 1963   Walter Coutts

Presidents:

Chairman of the National Military Council May-Dec 1980

Oct 1963-April 1966   Edward Mutesa II   (King of Buganda)

April 1966-Jan 1971	Milton Obote (1st) (UPC) (deposed)
Jan 1971-April 1979	Idi Amin Dada (deposed)
April-June 1979	Yusufu Lule
June 1979-May 1980	Godfrey Binaisa (deposed)
May-Dec 1980	Paulo Muwanga
Dec 1980-July 1985	Milton Obote (2nd) (UPC) (deposed)
July 1985-Jan 1986	Tito Okello (deposed)
Jan 1986-	Yoweri Museveni

Chief Minister:

July 1961-March 1962	Benedicto Kiwanuka (DP)

Prime Ministers:

March-April 1962	Benedicto Kiwanuka (DP)
April 1962-Sept 1967	Milton Obote (UPC)
(Sept 1967-Dec 1980	post abolished)
Dec 1980-July 1985	Otema Alimadi
1-25 Aug 1985	Paulo Muwanga
Aug 1985-Jan 1986	Abraham Waligo
Jan 1986-Jan 1991	Samson Kisseka
Jan 1991-Nov 1994	George Adyebo
Nov 1994-April 1999	Kintu Musoke
April 1999-	Apolo Nsibambi

DP = Democratic Party
UPC = Uganda People's Congress (sole legal party 1969-71)

Constitutive Kingdoms

Rulers up to 1967 are listed. The re-instated kingdoms are not included.

ANKOLE

Kings:

1863-73	Mutambuka
1875-95	Ntare V (*grandson*)
1897-1944	Kahaya II (*nephew*)
1944-Sept 1967	Charles Gasyonga II (deposed)

BUGANDA

Kings:

1825-57	Suna II

1857-84	Mukabya Mutesa I (*son*)
1884-88	Danieri Mwanga II (*son*) (1st) (deposed)
1888-89	Kiwewa Mutebi II (*half-brother*)
June-Oct 1889	Kalema (*half-brother*) (deposed)
1892-97	Danieri Mwanga II (2nd)
1897-1939	Daudi Chwa II (*son*)
1939-April 1966	Edward Mutesa II (*son*) (deposed)

Prime Ministers:

Sept 1955-Nov 1964	Michael Kintu
Nov 1964-April 1966	Joshua Mayanja-Nkangi

BUNYORO

Kings:

c1825-c1855	Nyabongo II
c1855-c1856	Olimi V (*son*)
c1856-c1870	Kyemambe IV
c1870-1898	Chwa II (*son*)
1898-Oct 1902	Kithahimbwa (*son*) (deposed)
Oct 1902-March 1924	Duhaga II (*half-brother*)
March 1924-Sept 1967	Winyi IV (*half-brother*) (deposed)

TORO

Kings:

1891-1928	Daudi Kasagama
1928-65	George Rukidi III (*son*)
1965-Sept 1967	Patrick Olimi (*son*) (deposed)

UKRAINE

Official name: Ukraine, Ukraina

Previous names: Ukrainian People's Republic 1918-19, Ukrainian Soviet Socialist Republic 1919-91

Independence dates: 22 January 1918; 24 August 1991

Admission to USSR: 30 December 1922

Capital: Kiev (Capital 1920-34: Kharkov)

Various states existed around Kiev over the centuries. Kievan-Rus lasted from the 9th to the 13th century when it was conquered by the Mongols. The western region remained an independent principality until the 14th century. Ukraine was then annexed by Lithuania and Poland, but in 1569 the whole country was transferred to Poland. It was briefly a quasi-independent Cossack state from 1648 to 1654 when Muscovy suzereignty was imposed. Towards the end of the 18th century the last vestiges of autonomy were abolished by Russia. In 1917 Ukraine declared independence, but in 1919 a Soviet government took over and Ukraine became a founding member of the USSR. During World War II Germany occupied the country. As the Soviet Union collapsed in 1991, independence was again declared.

Presidents:

Chairman of the Central Executive Committee 1919-38
President of the Presidium of the Supreme Soviet 1938-90
Chairman of the Supreme Soviet 1990-Dec 1991

In Kiev:
March 1917-April 1918	Myhaylo Hrushevsky
April-Dec 1918	Pavilo Skoropadsky
Dec 1918-Feb 1919	Volodymir Vinnichenko
Feb-Dec 1919	Simon Petliura

In Kharkov 1917-34; in Kiev after 1934:
Dec 1917-March 1918	Ye.Medvedev
March 1918-March 1919	Vladimir Zatonsky
March 1919-March 1938	Grigory Petrovsky
March 1938-July 1939	Leonid Korniets
July 1939-June 1941	Mikhail Grechukha (1st)
(June 1941-Nov 1943	German occupation -Commissioner: Erich Koch)
Nov 1943-Jan 1954	Mikhail Grechukha (2nd)
Jan 1954-April 1969	Demyan Korotchenko (†)
April 1969-June 1972	Aleksandr Lyashko
July 1972-June 1976	Ivan Grushetsky
June 1976-Nov 1984	Alexis Vatchenko (†)
Nov 1984-June 1990	Valentina Shevchenko (acting Nov 1984-March 1985)

June-July 1990	Vladimir Ivashko
July 1990-July 1994	Leonid Kravchuk
July 1994-	Leonid Kuchma

Prime Ministers:

Chairman of the Council of People's Commissars 1919-46
Chairman of the Council of Ministers since 1946

In Kiev:

July 1917-Jan 1918	Volodymir Vinnichenko
Jan-April 1918	Vsevolod Holubovich
29-30 April 1918	Mykola Ustymovich
April-May 1918	Mykola Vasylenko
May-Nov 1918	Fedir Lyzohub
Nov-Dec 1918	Serhy Gerbel
Dec 1918-Feb 1919	Volodymir Chekhishky
Feb-April 1919	Serhy Ostapenko
April-June 1919	Boris Martos
April-June 1919	Isaak Mazepa
July-Oct 1919	Viacheslav Prokopovich
Oct-Dec 1919	Andry Livytsky

In Kharkov 1919-34; in Kiev after 1934:

Jan 1919	Georgy Piatakov
Jan-Dec 1919	Khristian Rakovsky (1st)
Dec 1919-Feb 1920	Grigory Petrovsky
Feb 1920-23	Khristian Rakovsky (2nd)
1923-33	Vlas Chubar (1st)
1933-Aug 1937	Panas Lyubchenko († suicide)
Sept-Oct 1937	Mikhail Bondarenko
Oct 1937-Feb 1938	Vlas Chubar (2nd) (executed 1939)
Feb 1938-July 1939	Demyan Korotchenko (1st)
July 1939-June 1941	Leonid Korniets (1st)
(June 1941-Nov 1943	German occupation)
Nov 1943-March 1944	Leonid Korniets (2nd)
March 1944-Dec 1947	Nikita Khrushchev
Dec 1947-Jan 1954	Demyan Korotchenko (2nd)
Jan 1954-Feb 1961	Nikifor Kalchenko
Feb 1961-June 1963	Vladimir Shcherbitsky (1st)
June 1963-Oct 1965	Ivan Kazanets
Oct 1965-June 1972	Vladimir Shcherbitsky (2nd)
June 1972-July 1987	Aleksandr Lyashko
July 1987-Oct 1990	Vitaly Masol (1st)
Nov 1990-Sept 1992	Vitold Fokin
Sept-Oct 1992	Valentin Simonenko (acting)
Oct 1992-Sept 1993	Leonid Kuchma

Sept 1993-June 1994	Yukhim Zvyagilsky (acting)
June 1994-March 1995	Vitaly Masol (2nd)
March 1995-May 1996	Yevheny Marchuk (acting March-June 1995)
May 1996-June 1997	Pavlo Lazarenko
June-July 1997	Vasyl Durdynets (acting)
July 1997-Dec 1999	Valery Pustovoitenko
Dec 1999-	Viktor Yushchenko

Communist Party Leaders:

First Secretary

March 1921-May 1925	Emmanuil Kvirning
May 1925-28	Lazar Kaganovich (1st)
1928-Jan 1938	Stanislav Kossior
Jan 1938-June 1941	Nikita Khrushchev (1st)
(June 1941-Nov 1943	German occupation)
Nov 1943-March 1947	Nikita Khrushchev (2nd)
March-Dec 1947	Lazar Kaganovich (2nd)
Dec 1947-Dec 1949	Nikita Khrushchev (3rd)
Dec 1949-June 1953	Leonid Melnikov
June 1953-Dec 1957	Aleksei Kirichenko
Dec 1957-June 1963	Nikolai Podgorny
June 1963-May 1972	Pyotr Shelest
May 1972-Sept 1989	Vladimir Shcherbitsky
Sept 1989-June 1990	Vladimir Ivashko
June 1990-Aug 1991	Stanislav Gurenko
(Aug 1991	party suspended)

Autonomous Republic

CRIMEA

Official name: Crimean Republic
Previous names: Crimean Democratic Republic 1917-18, Crimean Autonomous Soviet Socialist Republic 1921-46 & 1991-92
Republic formed: 18 October 1921 (within Russia)
Republic abolished: 25 June 1946 (transferred to Ukraine in 1954)
Re-established: 12 February 1991
Capital: Simferopol

Presidents:

Chairman of the Central Executive Committee 1921-38
President of the Presidium of the Supreme Soviet 1938-46
Chairman of the Supreme Council (*f* Soviet) 1991-94 & since 1995

Oct 1917-Feb 1918	Chelebi Chelebiev (deposed, executed)

(Feb 1918-Nov 1921   post abolished)
Nov 1921-23   Juris Gavenis
1923-28   Veli Ibrahimov
1928-31   Mehmet Kubey
1931-37   Ilias Tarhan
1937-41   Abdulla Manbariev   (1st)
(1941-44   German occupation)
1944-46   Abdulla Manbariev   (2nd)
(June 1946-Feb 1991   republic abolished)
Feb 1991-Feb 1994   Nikolai Bagrov
Feb 1994-March 1995   Yury Meshkov
March-July 1995   Sergei Tsekov
July 1995-Oct 1996   Evgeny Suprunyuk
Oct 1996-Feb 1997   Vasyl Kyselyov
Feb 1997-May 1998   Anatoly Hrytsenko
May 1998-   Leonid Hrach

Prime Ministers:

Chairman of the Provisional Government 1918-19
Chairman of the Council of People's Commissars 1919-46
Chairman of the Council of Ministers since 1991

Jan-May 1918   Anton Slutsky
May-June 1918   Jafar Seydahmet Kirimer
June-Nov 1918   Suleyman Sulkevich
Nov 1918-April 1919   Salomon Krym
(1919-21   post abolished)
1921-24   Sakhibgarey Said-Galiyev   (see Tatarstan)
1924-26   O.Deren-Ayerlei   (1st)
1926   —— Shugur
1926-27   Veli Ibrahimov
1927-31   O.Deren-Ayerlei   (2nd)
1931-37   Ibrahim Samedin
1937- ?   Mehmet Ibrahimov
(1941-44   German occupation)
 ? -46   A.Kabanov
(1946-91   republic abolished)
Feb 1991-Feb 1994   Boris Samsonov
Feb-Sept 1994   Evgeny Saburov
Sept 1994-March 1995   Anatoly Franchuk   (1st)
March-April 1995   Anatoly Drobotov
April 1995-Jan 1996   Anatoly Franchuk   (2nd)
Jan 1996-June 1997   Arkady Demydenko   (acting Jan-Feb 1996)
June 1997-May 1998   Anatoly Franchuk   (3rd)
May 1998-   Serhy Kunitsyn

Communist Party Leaders:
First Secretary

1919-21	Juris Gavenis
1921-22	Ivan Akulov
1922-24	?
1924-28	Ivan Nosov
1928-37	?
1937	Lavrenti Kartelishvili (see Georgia)
1937	Nikolai Shchukin
1937	Ion Dyakonov (acting)
1937-41	V.S.Bulatov
(1941-44	German occupation)

UNITED ARAB EMIRATES

Official name: State of the United Arab Emirates (UAE), Dowlat Al-Imaarat al-Arabiya al-Muttahida
State formed: 2 December 1971
Capital: Abu Dhabi

In 1820 the rulers of the seven states now constituting the United Arab Emirates signed a treaty with Britain, effectively becoming protectorates under the collective name of the Trucial States. In December 1971 six of the emirates joined to form the UAE, ending their protectorate status. The seventh, Ras al-Khaimah, joined in early 1972.

President:

Dec 1971-	Shaikh Zaid bin Sultan al-Nahayan	(Ruler of Abu Dhabi)

Prime Ministers:

Dec 1971-July 1979	Shaikh Maktum bin Rashid al-Maktum	(1st)
July 1979-Oct 1990	Shaikh Rashid bin Said al-Maktum	(*father*) (Ruler of Dubai) (†)
Nov 1990-	Shaikh Maktum bin Rashid al-Maktum	(2nd) (Ruler of Dubai)

Emirates

ABU DHABI

Rulers:

1761-93	Shaikh Dhiyab bin Isa al-Nahayan	(assassinated)
1793-1816	Shaikh Shakbut bin Dhiyab al-Nahayan	
1816-18	Shaikh Mohammed bin Shakbut al-Nahayan	(deposed)
1818-33	Shaikh Tahnun bin Shakbut al-Nahayan	(assassinated)
1833-45	Shaikh Khalifa bin Shakbut al-Nahayan	(assassinated)
1845-55	Shaikh Said bin Tahnun al-Nahayan	(deposed)
1855-May 1909	Shaikh Zaid bin Khalifa al-Nahayan	
May 1909-Oct 1912	Shaikh Tahnun bin Zaid al-Nahayan	
Oct 1912-Aug 1922	Shaikh Hamdan bin Zaid al-Nahayan	(assassinated)
Aug 1922-Aug 1926	Shaikh Sultan bin Zaid al-Nahayan	(assassinated)
Aug 1926-April 1928	Shaikh Saqr bin Zaid al-Nahayan	(assassinated)
April 1928-Aug 1966	Shaikh Shakbut bin Sultan al-Nahayan	(deposed)
Aug 1966-	Shaikh Zaid bin Sultan al-Nahayan	(President of UAE)

Prime Minister:

Chairman of the Executive Council

July 1971-   Shaikh Khalifa bin Zaid al-Nahayan

AJMAN

Rulers:

pre-1820-38	Shaikh Rashid bin Humaid al-Naimi	(I)
1838-41	Shaikh Humaid bin Rashid al-Naimi	(I) (1st)
1841-48	Shaikh Abdel-Aziz bin Rashid al-Naimi	
1848-72	Shaikh Humaid bin Rashid al-Naimi	(I) (1st)
1872-91	Shaikh Rashid bin Humaid al-Naimi	(II)
1891-July 1900	Shaikh Humaid bin Rashid al-Naimi	(II) (assassinated)
July 1900-Feb 1910	Shaikh Abdel-Aziz bin Humaid al-Naimi	
Feb 1910-Jan 1928	Shaikh Humaid bin Abdel-Aziz al-Naimi	
Jan 1928-Sept 1981	Shaikh Rashid bin Humaid al-Naimi	(III)
Sept 1981-	Shaikh Humaid bin Rashid al-Naimi	(III)

DUBAI

Rulers:

1833-52	Shaikh Maktum bin Bhutti al-Maktum
1852-59	Shaikh Said bin Bhutti al-Maktum
1859-86	Shaikh Hashar bin Maktum al-Maktum
1886-94	Shaikh Rashid bin Maktum al-Maktum
1894-Feb 1906	Shaikh Maktum bin Hashar al-Maktum
Feb 1906-Nov 1912	Shaikh Bhutti bin Suhail al-Maktum
Nov 1912-Oct 1958	Shaikh Said bin Maktum al-Maktum
Oct 1958-Oct 1990	Shaikh Rashid bin Said al-Maktum
Oct 1990-	Shaikh Maktum bin Rashid al-Maktum

FUJEIRA

Rulers:

1940-74	Shaikh Mohammed bin Hamad al-Sharqi
1974-	Shaikh Hamad bin Mohammed al-Sharqi

KALBA

Incorporated into Sharjah in 1951

Ruler:

1937-51   Shaikh Hamad bin Said

RAS AL-KHAIMA

Rulers:

1803-66	Shaikh Sultan bin Saqr al-Qasimi (Ruler of Sharjah)
1866-April 1868	Shaikh Khalid bin Sultan al-Qasimi (Ruler of Sharjah)
April 1868-69	Shaikh Salim bin Sultan al-Qasimi (Ruler of Sharjah)
1869-1900	Shaikh Humaid bin Abdullah al-Qasimi
1900-14	Shaikh Saqr bin Khalid al-Qasimi (Ruler of Sharjah)
1914-19	Shaikh Khalid bin Ahmed al-Qasimi (Ruler of Sharjah)
1919-Feb 1948	Shaikh Sultan bin Salim al-Qasimi (deposed)
Feb 1948-	Shaikh Saqr bin Mohammed al-Qasimi

SHARJAH

Rulers:

1803-66	Shaikh Sultan bin Saqr al-Qasimi (I)
1866-April 1868	Shaikh Khalid bin Sultan al-Qasimi
April 1868-83	Shaikh Salim bin Sultan al-Qasimi
1883-April 1914	Shaikh Saqr bin Khalid al-Qasimi
April 1914-24	Shaikh Khalid bin Ahmed al-Qasimi (abdicated)
1924-May 1951	Shaikh Sultan bin Saqr al-Qasimi (II)
May 1951-June 1965	Shaikh Saqr bin Sultan al-Qasimi (deposed)
June 1965-Jan 1972	Shaikh Khalid bin Mohammed al-Qasimi (assassinated)
Jan 1972-June 1987	Shaikh Sultan bin Mohammed al-Qasimi (1st) (deposed)
16-24 June 1987	Shaikh Abdul-Aziz bin Mohammed al-Qasim (abdicated)
June 1987-	Shaikh Sultan bin Mohammed al-Qasimi (2nd)

Executive Council Chairman:

July 1987-   Shaikh Sultan bin Mohammed al-Qasimi

UMM AL QIWAIN

Rulers:

1775- ?	Shaikh Majid al-Ali al-Mualla
? -pre-1820	Shaikh Rashid bin Majid al-Qasimi
pre-1820-54	Shaikh Abdullah bin Rashid al-Mualla (I)
1854-72	Shaikh Ali bin Abdullah al-Mualla

1872-June 1904	Shaikh Ahmed bin Abdullah al-Mualla
June 1904-Aug 1922	Shaikh Rashid bin Ahmed al-Mualla (I)
Aug 1922-Oct 1923	Shaikh Abdullah bin Rashid al-Mualla (II)
Oct 1923-Feb 1929	Shaikh Hamad bin Rashid al-Mualla
Feb 1929-Feb 1981	Shaikh Ahmed bin Rashid al-Mualla
Feb 1981-	Shaikh Rashid bin Ahmed al-Mualla (II)

UNITED KINGDOM

Official name: United Kingdom of Great Britain and Northern Ireland (UK)
Previous name: United Kingdom of Great Britain and Ireland 1801-1922
State formed: England unified 827, Scotland unified 843, Union of England and Scotland 1 May 1707
Capital: London

The English monarchy extends back to the 9th century, with the emergence of the kings of Wessex as rulers of a unified kingdom. The monarchy was strengthened by the Norman conquest of 1066. On the death of Elizabeth I in 1603 the crown passed to James VI of Scotland, though England and Scotland were not formally united until the Act of Union in 1707. Ireland, which had been under English rule since the 12th century, was incorporated into the United Kingdom in 1801; following the rebellion of 1916 the independence of the southern counties was recognised in 1922. The six counties of Ulster comprise the province of Northern Ireland, which, because of conflict between the Protestant and Catholic communities, was under direct British rule 1974-98; a peace agreement was reached in 1998. In 1999, constitutional changes devolved some powers to Scotland and Wales.

Kings/Queens:
Information up to 1603 refers to England only

827-39	Egbert
839-56	Ethelwulf (*son*) (abdicated)
856-60	Ethelbald (*son*)
860-66	Ethelbert (*brother*)
866-April 871	Ethelred I (*brother*)
April 871-Oct 899	Alfred the Great (*brother*)
Oct 899-July 924	Edward the Elder (*son*)
July 924-Oct 939	Athelstan (*son*)
Oct 939-May 946	Edmund I (*half-brother*)
May 946-Nov 955	Edred (*brother*)
Nov 955-Oct 959	Edwy (*son of Edmund I*)
Oct 959-July 975	Edgar I (*brother*)
July 975-March 978	Edward the Martyr (*son*) (assassinated)
March 978-1013	Ethelred II the Unready (*half-brother*) (1st) (deposed)
1013-Feb 1014	Sweyn (Svend I of Denmark)
Feb 1014-April 1016	Ethelred II the Unready (2nd)
April-Nov 1016	Edmund II (*son*)
Nov 1016-Nov 1035	Canute (Knud of Denmark) (*son of Sweyn*)
Nov 1035-37	Regent: Harold Harefoot
1037-March 1040	Harold I Harefoot (*son*)
March 1040-June 1042	Hardicanute (Hardeknud of Denmark) (*half-brother*)

June 1042-Jan 1066	Edward the Confessor (*son of Ethelred II*)
Jan-Oct 1066	Harold II (*brother-in-law*) (killed in battle)
Oct-Dec 1066	Edgar II (*grandson of Edmund II*)
Dec 1066-Sept 1097	William I (Duke of Normandy)
Sept 1097-Aug 1100	William II (*son*)
Aug 1100-Dec 1135	Henry I (*brother*)
Dec 1135-April 1141	Stephen (*nephew*) (1st) (deposed)
April-Nov 1141	Matilda (*daughter of Henry I*)
Nov 1141-Oct 1154	Stephen (2nd)
Dec 1154-July 1189	Henry II (*son of Matilda*)
July 1189-April 1199	Richard I (*son*)
May 1199-Oct 1216	John (*brother*)
Oct 1216-Nov 1272	Henry III (*son*)
Nov 1272-July 1307	Edward I (*son*)
July 1307-Jan 1327	Edward II (*son*) (deposed)
Jan 1327-June 1377	Edward III (*son*)
	Regents: 1327-30 Queen Isabella/Roger Mortimer
June 1377-Sept 1399	Richard II (*grandson*) (deposed, executed)
Sept 1399-March 1413	Henry IV (*grandson of Edward III*)
March 1413-Sept 1422	Henry V (*son*)
Sept 1422-March 1461	Henry VI (*son*) (1st) (deposed)
	Regent: 1422-29 Prince John, Duke of Bedford
March 1461-Oct 1470	Edward IV (1st)
Oct 1470-May 1471	Henry VI (2nd)
May 1471-April 1483	Edward IV (2nd)
April 1483-Aug 1485	Edward V (*son*) (murdered)
Aug 1485-April 1509	Richard III (*brother of Edward IV*)
April 1509-Jan 1547	Henry VII
April 1509-Jan 1547	Henry VIII (*son*)
Jan 1547-July 1553	Edward VI (*son*)
	Protectors: 1547-52 Edward Seymour, Duke of Somerset
	1552-53 John Dudley, Duke of Northumberland
10-19 July 1553	Jane (*great-granddaughter of Henry VII*) (deposed, executed)
July 1553-Nov 1558	Mary I (*daughter of Henry VIII*)
Nov 1558-March 1603	Elizabeth I (*sister*)
March 1603-March 1625	James I (James VI of Scotland) (*great-great-grandson of Henry VII*)
March 1625-Jan 1649	Charles I (*son*) (deposed, executed)

Lord Protectors:

March 1649-Sept 1658	Oliver Cromwell (†)
Sept 1658-May 1659	Richard Cromwell (*son*)

Kings/Queens:

May 1660-Feb 1685	Charles II (*son of Charles I*)

Feb 1685-Dec 1688	James II (*brother*) (deposed)
Feb 1689-Dec 1694	Mary II (*daughter*) (co-ruler)
Feb 1689-March 1702	William III (Willem III of the Netherlands) (*husband*) (co-ruler 1689-94)
March 1702-Aug 1714	Anne (*sister of Mary II*)
Aug 1714-June 1727	George I (Georg I of Hanover) (*great-grandson of James I*)
June 1727-Oct 1760	George II (Georg II of Hanover) (*son*)
Oct 1760-Jan 1820	George III (Georg III of Hanover) (*grandson*)
Jan 1820-June 1830	George IV (Georg IV of Hanover) (*son*)
June 1830-June 1837	William IV (Wilhelm IV of Hanover) (*brother*)
June 1837-Jan 1901	Victoria (*niece, granddaughter of George III*)
Jan 1901-May 1910	Edward VII (*son*)
May 1910-Jan 1936	George V (*son*)
Jan-Dec 1936	Edward VIII (*son*) (abdicated)
Dec 1936-Feb 1952	George VI (*f* Prince Albert) (*brother*)
Feb 1952-	Elizabeth II (*daughter*)

Prime Ministers:

April 1721-Feb 1742	Robert Walpole
Feb 1742-July 1743	Earl of Wilmington (Spencer Compton) (†)
Aug 1743-Feb 1746	Henry Pelham (1st)
10-12 Feb 1746	Earl of Bath (William Pulteney)
Feb 1746-March 1754	Henry Pelham (2nd(†))
March 1754-Oct 1756	Duke of Newcastle (Thomas Pelham-Holles) (1st) (*brother*)
Nov 1756-May 1757	Duke of Devonshire (William Cavendish)
8-12 June 1757	Earl of Waldegrave (James Waldegrave)
July 1757-May 1762	Duke of Newcastle (Thomas Pelham-Holles) (2nd)
May 1762-April 1763	Earl of Bute (John Stuart)
April 1763-July 1765	George Grenville
July 1765-July 1766	Marquis of Rockingham (Charles Wentworth) (1st)
July 1766-Oct 1768	Earl of Chatham (William Pitt the Elder)
Oct 1768-Jan 1770	Duke of Grafton (Augustus Fitzroy)
Jan 1770-March 1782	Baron North (Frederick North)
March-July 1782	Marquis of Rockingham (Charles Wentworth) (2nd) (†)
July 1782-April 1783	Earl of Shelburne (William Petty-Fitzmaurice)
April-Dec 1783	Duke of Portland (William Cavendish-Bentinck) (1st)
Dec 1783-March 1801	William Pitt (*son of William Pitt, Earl of Chatham*) (1st)
March 1801-April 1804	Henry Addington
May 1804-Jan 1806	William Pitt (2nd)
Jan 1806-March 1807	Lord Grenville (William Grenville) (*son of George Grenville*)
March 1807-Sept 1809	Duke of Portland (William Cavendish-Bentinck) (2nd)
Oct 1809-May 1812	Spencer Perceval († assassinated)
June 1812-Feb 1827	Earl of Liverpool (Robert Jenkinson)
Feb-Aug 1827	George Canning (†)
Aug 1827-Jan 1828	Viscount Goderich (Frederick Robinson)

Jan 1828-Nov 1830	Duke of Wellington (Arthur Wellesley) (1st)
Nov 1830-June 1834	Lord Grey (Charles Grey) (WP)
July-Nov 1834	Viscount Melbourne (William Lamb) (1st) (WP)
Nov-Dec 1834	Duke of Wellington (Arthur Wellesley) (2nd)
Dec 1834-April 1835	Robert Peel (1st) (CP)
April 1835-Aug 1841	Viscount Melbourne (William Lamb) (2nd) (WP)
Sept 1841-June 1846	Robert Peel (2nd) (CP)
July 1846-Feb 1852	Lord John Russell (1st) (WP)
Feb-Dec 1852	Earl of Derby (Edward Stanley) (1st) (CP)
Dec 1852-Jan 1855	Earl of Aberdeen (George Hamilton-Gordon) (WP)
Feb 1855-Feb 1858	Viscount Palmerston (Henry Temple) (1st) (WP)
Feb 1858-June 1859	Earl of Derby (Edward Stanley) (2nd) (CP)
June 1859-Oct 1865	Viscount Palmerston (Henry Temple) (2nd) (WP) (†)
Oct 1865-June 1866	Lord John Russell (2nd) (WP)
June 1866-Feb 1868	Earl of Derby (Edward Stanley) (3rd) (CP)
Feb-Dec 1868	Benjamin Disraeli (1st) (CP)
Dec 1868-Feb 1874	William Gladstone (1st) (Lib)
Feb 1874-April 1880	Benjamin Disraeli (2nd) (CP)
April 1880-June 1885	William Gladstone (2nd) (Lib)
June 1885-Jan 1886	Marquis of Salisbury (Robert Cecil) (1st) (CP)
Jan-July 1886	William Gladstone (3rd) (Lib)
Aug 1886-Aug 1892	Marquis of Salisbury (Robert Cecil) (2nd) (CP)
Aug 1892-March 1894	William Gladstone (4th) (Lib)
March 1894-June 1895	Earl of Rosebery (Archibald Primrose) (Lib)
June 1895-July 1902	Marquis of Salisbury (Robert Cecil) (3rd) (CP)
July 1902-Dec 1905	Arthur Balfour (CP)
Dec 1905-April 1908	Henry Campbell-Bannerman (Lib)
April 1908-Dec 1916	Herbert Asquith (Lib)
Dec 1916-Oct 1922	David Lloyd George (Lib)
Oct 1922-May 1923	Andrew Bonar Law (CP)
May 1923-Jan 1924	Stanley Baldwin (1st) (CP)
Jan-Nov 1924	Ramsay MacDonald (1st) (Lab)
Nov 1924-June 1929	Stanley Baldwin (2nd) (CP)
June 1929-June 1935	Ramsay MacDonald (2nd) (Lab)
June 1935-May 1937	Stanley Baldwin (3rd) (CP)
May 1937-May 1940	Neville Chamberlain (CP)
May 1940-July 1945	Winston Churchill (1st) (CP)
July 1945-Oct 1951	Clement Attlee (Lab)
Oct 1951-April 1955	Winston Churchill (2nd) (CP)
April 1955-Jan 1957	Anthony Eden (CP)
Jan 1957-Oct 1963	Harold MacMillan (CP)
Oct 1963-Oct 1964	Alexander Douglas-Home (CP)
Oct 1964-June 1970	Harold Wilson (1st) (Lab)
June 1970-March 1974	Edward Heath (CP)
March 1974-April 1976	Harold Wilson (2nd) (Lab)

April 1976-May 1979	James Callaghan (Lab)
May 1979-Nov 1990	Margaret Thatcher (*b* M.Roberts) (CP)
Nov 1990-May 1997	John Major (CP)
May 1997-	Anthony Blair (Lab)

CP = Conservative Party
Lab = Labour Party
Lib = Liberal Party
WP = Whig Party

Former independent kingdom

SCOTLAND

Capital: Perth until 1437, Edinburgh since 1437

Kings/Queens:

843-60	Kenneth I MacAlpin
860-63	Donald I (*brother*)
863-77	Constantine II (*son of Kenneth I*)
877-78	Aedh (*brother*)
878-89	Eocha (*nephew*) (co-ruler)
878-89	Giric (co-ruler)
889-900	Donald II (*son of Constantine II*)
900-42	Constantine III (*son of Aedh*) (abdicated)
942-54	Malcolm I (*son of Donald II*) (assassinated)
954-62	Indulf (*son of Constantine III*) (assassinated)
962-67	Duff (*son of Malcolm I*) (assassinated)
967-71	Colin (*son of Indulf*) (assassinated)
971-95	Kenneth II (*son of Malcolm I*) (assassinated)
995-97	Constantine IV (*son of Colin*) (assassinated)
997-March 1005	Kenneth III (*son of Duff*) (assassinated)
March 1005-Nov 1034	Malcolm II (*son of Kenneth II*)
Nov 1034-Aug 1040	Duncan I (*grandson*) (assassinated)
Aug 1040-Aug 1057	Macbeth (assassinated)
Aug 1057-March 1058	Lulach (*stepson*) (assassinated)
March 1058-Nov 1093	Malcolm III (*son of Duncan I*)
Nov 1093-May 1094	Donald III Bane (*brother*) (1st) (deposed)
May-Nov 1094	Donald II (*son of Malcolm III*) (assassinated)
Nov 1094-Oct 1097	Edmund (*half-brother*) (co-ruler) (deposed)
Nov 1094-Oct 1097	Donald III Bane (2nd) (co-ruler) (deposed)
Oct 1097-Jan 1107	Edgar (*son of Malcolm III*)
Jan 1107-April 1124	Alexander I (*brother*)
April 1124-May 1153	David I (*brother*)
May 1153-Dec 1165	Malcolm IV (*grandson*)

Dec 1165-Dec 1214	William I (*brother*)
Dec 1214-July 1249	Alexander II (*son*)
July 1249-March 1286	Alexander III (*son*)
March 1286-Nov 1290	Margaret (*grand-daughter*) (Regency council)
(Nov 1290-Nov 1292	interregnum)
Nov 1292-July 1296	John Balliol (abdicated) (*great-great-great-grandson of David I*)
(July 1296-March 1306	interregnum)
March 1306-June 1329	Robert I the Bruce (*great-great-great-great-grandson of David I*)
June 1329-Feb 1371	David II (*son*)
(1332-38	Edward (*son of John Balliol*)- rival king)
Feb 1371-April 1390	Robert II (*grandson of Robert I*)
April 1390-April 1406	Robert III (*son*)
April 1406-Feb 1437	James I (*son*)
	Regents: 1406-20 Robert Stewart
	1420-24 Murdoch Stewart (assassinated)
Feb 1437-Aug 1460	James II (*son*) (died in battle)
	Regents: 1437-9 Joan Beaufort/Archibald Douglas
Aug 1460-June 1488	James III (*son*)
June 1488-Sept 1513	James IV (*son*)
Sept 1513-Dec 1542	James V (*son*)
	Regent: 1513-24 John Stewart
Dec 1542-July 1567	Mary (*daughter*) (abdicated, executed 1587)
	Regents: 1542-54 James Hamilton, Earl of Arran
	1554-59 Mary of Guise
July 1567-March 1625	James VI (James I of England) (*son*)
	Regents: 1567-70 James Stewart,Earl of Moray
	1570-71 Matthew Stewart,Earl Lennox
	1571-72 John Erskine,Earl of Mar
	1572-80 James Douglas,Earl of Morton

Regions

SCOTLAND

Capital: Edinburgh

First Minister :

July 1999-	Donald Dewar (Lab)

WALES

Capital: Cardiff

First Secretaries:

July 1999-Feb 2000	Alun Michael (Lab)
Feb 2000-	Rhodi Morgan (Lab)

Province

NORTHERN IRELAND

Capital: Belfast

Governors:

Dec 1922-Sept 1945	Duke of Abercorn (James Hamilton)
Sept 1945-Dec 1952	Earl Granville (William Leveson-Gower) (see Isle of Man)
Dec 1952-Dec 1964	Lord Wakehurst (John Loder)
Dec 1964-Dec 1968	Baron Erskine of Rerrick (John Erskine)
Dec 1968-March 1972	Lord Grey of Naunton (Ralph Grey) (see Bahamas)
(March 1972	post abolished)

Prime Ministers:

June 1921-Nov 1940	Viscount Craigavon (James Craig) (†) (UUP)
Nov 1940-May 1943	John Andrews (UUP)
May 1943-March 1963	Viscount Brookebrough (Basil Brooke) (UUP)
March 1963-May 1969	Terence O'Neill (UUP)
May 1969-March 1971	James Chichester-Clark (UUP)
March 1971-March 1972	Brian Faulkner (UUP)
(March 1972	post abolished)

Chief Executive:

Nov 1973-May 1974	Brian Faulkner
(May 1974	post abolished)

First Minister:

July 1998-	David Trimble (UUP)

UUP = Ulster Unionist Party

Crown Dependencies

GUERNSEY

Official name: Bailiwick of Guernsey
Capital: St Peter Port

Lieutenant-Governors:

1899-1903	M.H.Saward
1903-08	Barrington Campbell
1908-11	Robert Auld (†)

1911-14	Edward Hamilton
1914	— — Lawson
1914-18	Reginald Hart
1918-20	Launcelot Kiggell
1920-25	John Capper
1925-29	Lord Sackville (Charles Sackville-West)
1929-34	Lord Ruthven (Walter Hore-Ruthven)
1934-39	Edward Broadbent
1939-40	Alexander Telfer-Smollett
(1940-45	German occupation)
Aug 1945-53	Philip Neame
1953-58	Thomas Elmhirst
1958-63	W.Geoffrey Robson
1963-69	Charles Coleman
1969-74	Charles Mills
1974-80	John Loveridge
1980-85	Peter Le Cheminant
1985-90	Alexander Boswell
1990-94	Michael Wilkins
1994-	John Coward

Bailiffs:

The office of Bailiff dates from at least the 13th century

1808-10	Robert Le Marchant
1810-21	Peter De Havilland
1821-43	Daniel De Lisle Brock
1843-45	John Guille
1845-83	Peter Carey
1883-84	John Utermarck
1884-95	Edgar MacCulloch
1895-1902	T.Godfrey Carey
1902-08	Henry Giffard
1908-15	William Carey
1915-22	Edward Chepmell Ozanne
1922-29	Havilland de Sausmarez
1929-35	Arthur Bell
1935-40	Victor Carey (1st)
(1940-45	German occupation)
1945-46	Victor Carey (2nd)
1946-60	Ambrose Sherwell
1960-73	William Arnold
1973-83	John Loveridge
1983-92	Charles Frossard
1992-99	Graham Dorey

1999-   D Vic Carey

Dependencies of Guernsey

Alderney

Capital: St Anne's

Presidents of the States:

1949-70	Sydney Herivel
1970-75	George Baron (1st)
1975-94	Jon Kay-Mouat
1994-	George Baron (2nd)

Sark

Seigneurs/Dame:

1852-82	William T.Collings
1882-1927	William F.Collings
1927-July 1974	Sibyl Hathaway
July 1974-	J.Michael Beaumont

ISLE OF MAN
Ellan Vannin

Capital: Douglas

Lieutenant-Governors:

1895-1902	Lord Henniker (John Henniker-Major)
1902-18	Lord Raglan (George Somerset)
1918-25	William Fry
1925-32	Clause Hill
1933-37	Montagu Butler
1937-45	Earl Granville (William Leveson-Gower)
1945-52	Geoffrey Bromet
Sept 1952-59	Ambrose Dundas
Sept 1959-Sept 1966	Ronald Garvey (see British Honduras)
Sept 1966-74	Peter Stallard (see British Honduras)
1974-80	John Paul (see Bahamas)
1980-85	Nigel Cecil
1985-90	Laurence New
1990-95	Lawrence Jones
1995-	Timothy Daunt

Chief Ministers:

Chairman of the Executive Council 1967-90

Feb 1967-Jan 1971	E.N.Crowe
Jan 1971-Jan 1977	Percy Radcliffe (1st)
Jan 1977-Nov 1981	Clifford Irving
Nov 1981-85	Percy Radcliffe (2nd)
1985-Nov 1986	Edgar Mann
Nov 1986-Nov 1996	Miles Walker
Nov 1996-	Donald Gelling

JERSEY

Official name: Bailiwick of Jersey
Capital: St Helier

Lieutenant-Governors:

1900-04	Henry Abadie
1904-10	Hugh Gough
1910-16	Alexander Rochfort
1916-20	Alexander Wilson
1920-24	W.Douglas-Smith
1924-29	Francis Bingham
1929-34	Edward Willis
1934-39	Horace Martelli
1939-40	James Harrison
(1940-45	German occupation)
Aug 1945-53	Edward Grassett
1953-58	Gresham Nicholson
1958-64	George Erskine
Jan 1964-69	Michael Villiers
1969-74	John Davis
1974-79	Desmond Fitzpatrick
1979-84	Peter Whiteley
1985-90	William Pillar
1990-95	John Sutton
1995-	Michael Wilkes

Bailiffs:

The office of Bailiff dates from at least the 13th century

1826-31	Thomas Le Baron (1st)
1831-48	John De Veulle
1848-58	Thomas Le Baron (2nd)
1858-80	John Hammond

1880-84	Robert Marett
1884-99	George Bertram
1899-1931	William Venables-Vernon
1931-35	Charles Malet de Carteret
1935-40	Lord Coutanche (Alexander Coutanche) (1st)
(1940-45	German occupation)
1945-62	Lord Coutanche (Alexander Coutanche) (2nd)
1962	C.S.Harrison (acting)
1962-75	Robert Le Masurier
1975-86	Frank Ereaut
1986-95	Peter Crill
1995-96	Philip Bailhache
1996-	Francis Hamon

British Overseas Territories

ANGUILLA

Independence declared: 11 July 1967
Independence ended by British intervention: 19 March 1969
Capital: The Valley

Presidents:

July-Aug 1967	Peter Adams
Aug 1967-March 1969	Ronald Webster
(March 1969	post abolished)

Commissioners:

1969	Anthony Lee
1969	John Cumber
July 1969-71	Willoughby Thompson
1971-74	Arthur Watson
1974-78	David LeBreton
1978-80	Charles Godden

Governors:

1980-83	Charles Godden
1983-87	Alastair Baillie
1987-89	Geoffrey Whittaker
Nov 1989-Aug 1992	Brian Canty
Aug 1992-May 1997	Alan Shave
May 1997-2000	Robert Harris
Feb 2000-	Peter Johnston

Chief Ministers:

Feb 1976-Feb 1977	Ronald Webster (1st) (AUP)
Feb 1977-May 1980	Emile Gumbs (1st) (ANA)
May 1980-March 1984	Ronald Webster (2nd) (APP)
March 1984-March 1994	Emile Gumbs (2nd) (ANA)
March 1994-March 2000	Hubert Hughes (AUP)
March 2000-	Osbourne Fleming (ANA)

ANA = Anguilla National Alliance
APP = Anguilla People's Party
AUP = Anguilla United Party

BERMUDA

Capital: Hamilton

Governors:

1896-1902	George Barker
1902-04	Henry Geary
1904-07	Robert Stewart
1907-08	Joscelyn Wodehouse
1908-12	Frederick Kitchener
1912-17	George Bullock
1917-22	James Willocks
1922-27	Joseph Asser
1927-31	Louis Bols
1931-36	Thomas Astley-Cubitt
1936-39	Reginald Hildyard
1939-41	Denis Bernard
1941-43	Francis Knollys
1943-46	Marquess of Exeter (David Cecil)
1946-49	Ralph Leatham
1949-55	Alexander Hood
1955-59	John Woodall
1959-64	Julian Gascoine
1964-Oct 1972	Baron Martonmere (John Robinson)
Oct 1972-March 1973	Richard Sharples († assassinated)
March-May 1973	Ian Kinnear (acting)
May 1973-77	Edwin Leather
1977-80	Peter Ramsbotham
1980-83	Richard Posnette
July 1983-Oct 1988	Viscount Dunrossil (John Morrison)
Oct 1988-April 1992	Desmond Langley
April 1992-May 1997	Lord Waddington (David Waddington)
June 1997-	J.Thorold Masefield

Government Leaders:

June 1968-Dec 1971   Henry Tucker   (UBP)
Dec 1971-April 1973   Edward Richards   (UBP)

Prime Ministers:

April 1973-Dec 1975   Edward Richards   (UBP)
Dec 1975-Aug 1977   John Sharpe   (UBP)
Aug 1977-Jan 1982   David Gibbons   (UBP)
Jan 1982-Aug 1995   John Swan   (UBP)
Aug 1995-March 1997   David Saul   (UBP)
March 1997-Nov 1998   Pamela Gordon   (UBP)
Nov 1998-   Jennifer Smith   (PLP)

PLP = Progressive Labour Party
UBP = United Bermuda Party

BRITISH ANTARCTIC TERRITORY

Commissioners:

(Based in Falkland Islands)

1962-89   Governors of Falkland Islands
1989   C.L de Chassiron
Oct 1989-91   M.Baker-Bates
1991-95   Peter Newton
1995-99   Anthony Longrigg
1999-   John White

Administrators:

1989-92   John Heap
1992-   M.G.Richardson

BRITISH INDIAN OCEAN TERRITORY

Commissioners:

(based in London from 1976)

1965-76   Governors of Seychelles
1976   Norman Aspin
1976-79   Philip Mansfield
1979-82   John Robson
1982-85   W.Nigel Wenban-Smith
1985-89   William Marsden

1989-91	Richard Edis
1991-94	Thomas Harris
1994-96	David MacLennan
1996-	Bruce Dinwiddy

Administrators:

(Based in Seychelles 1965-76 and London since 1976)

1965-74	J.R.Todd
1974-75	David Dale
1975-76	F.R.Williams
1976-77	M.K.Ewans
1977-78	Alan Munro
1978-79	John Robson
1979-80	J.G.Wallace
1980-82	P.A.Raftery
1982-84	Denis Doble
1984-85	T.Stitt
1985-89	Peter Gregory-Hood
1989-91	M.Robin Compton
1991-92	Roger Wells
1992-95	Don Cairns
1995-96	David Smith
1996-	Louise Savill

BRITISH VIRGIN ISLANDS

Capital: Road Town

Administrators:

1887-94	Edward Cameron
1894-96	Alexander Mackay
1896-1903	Nathaniel Cookman
1903-10	Robert Earl
1910-19	Thomas Jarvis
1919-22	Herbert Peebles
1922-23	R.Hargrove
1923-26	Otho Hancock
1926-34	Frank Clarkson
1934-46	Donald Wailling
1946-54	John Cruikshank
1954-56	Henry Howard
1956-59	Geoffrey Allesbrook
1959-62	Gerald Bryan

1962-67	Martin Staveley
1967-71	John Thomson
1971	Hywell George (see St Vincent)
1971-72	Derek Cudmore

Governors:

1972-74	Derek Cudmore
1974-78	Walter Wallace
1978-81	James Davidson
1982-86	David Barwick
1986-92	J.Mark Herdman
1992-95	Peter Penfold
June 1995-May 1998	David Mackilligin
May 1998-	Frank Savage (see Montserrat)

Chief Ministers:

April 1967-June 1971	H.Lavity Stoutt (1st)
June 1971-Nov 1979	Willard Wheatley
Nov 1979-Nov 1983	H.Lavity Stoutt (2nd) (VIP)
Nov 1983-Oct 1986	Cyril Romney (UP)
Oct 1986-May 1995	H.Lavity Stoutt (3rd) (VIP) (†)
May 1995-	Ralph O'Neal (acting May-June 1995) (VIP)

UP = United Party
VIP = Virgin Islands Party

CAYMAN ISLANDS

Capital: Georgetown

Administrators:

1958-60	Alan Donald
1960-64	Jack Rose
1964-68	John Cumber
1968-71	Athelstan Long
1971-74	Kenneth Crook

Governors:

1974-81	Thomas Russell
1982-87	G.Peter Lloyd
June 1987-Sept 1992	Alan Scott
Sept 1992-Sept 1995	Michael Gore
Sept 1995-May 1999	John Owen
May 1999-	Peter Smith

FALKLAND ISLANDS

Capital: Port Stanley

Governors:

1897-1904	William Grey-Wilson
1904-15	William Allardyce
1915-20	William Young (see Dominica)
1920-27	John Middleton
1927-31	Arnold Hodson
1931-35	James O'Grady
1935-41	Herbert Heaton
1941-46	Allan Cardinall
1946-54	George Clifford
1954-57	Oswald Arthur
1957-64	Edwin Arrowsmith (see Basutoland)
1964-70	Cosmo Haskard
1970-75	Ernest Lewis
1975-77	Neville French
1977-80	James Parker
1980-April 1982	Rex Hunt (1st)
April-June 1982	Mario Menéndez (during Argentinian occupation)
June 1982-Sept 1985	Rex Hunt (2nd)
Oct 1985-Nov 1988	Gordon Jewkes
Nov 1988-Aug 1992	William Fullerton
Aug 1992-Jan 1996	David Tatham
Jan 1996-May 1999	Richard Ralph
May 1999-	Donald Lamont

Chief Executives:

Nov 1983-89	David Taylor
1989-95	Ronald Sampson
1995-	Andrew Gurr

GIBRALTAR

Governors:

1900-05	George White
1905-10	Frederick Forester-Walker
1910-13	Archibald Hunter
1913-18	Herbert Miles
1918-23	Herbert Smith-Dorrien

1923-28	Charles Monro
1928-33	Alexander Godley
1933-38	Charles Harington
1938-39	Edmund Ironside
1939-41	Clive Liddell
1941-42	Viscount Gort (John Vereker)
1942-44	Noel Mason-MacFarlane
1944-47	Ralph Eastwood
1947-52	Kenneth Anderson
1952-55	Gordon MacMillan
1955-58	Harold Redman
1958-62	Charles Keightley
1962-65	Alfred Ward
1965-69	Gerald Lathbury
1969-73	Varyl Begg
1973-78	John Grandy
1978-82	William Jackson
1982-85	David Williams
1985-89	Peter Terry
1989-93	Derek Reffell
April 1993-Dec 1995	John Chapple
Dec 1995-Feb 1997	Hugo White
Feb 1997-April 2000	Richard Luce
April 2000-	David Durie

Chief Ministers:

April 1964-Aug 1969	Joshua Hassan (1st) (GLP)
Aug 1969-June 1972	Robert Peliza (IBP)
June 1972-Dec 1987	Joshua Hassan (2nd) (GLP)
Dec 1987-March 1988	Adolfo Canepa (GLP)
March 1988-May 1996	José (Joe) Bossano (SLP)
May 1996-	Peter Caruana (GSD)

GLP = Gibraltar Labour Party
GSD = Gibraltar Social Democrats
IBP = Integration with Britain Party
SLP = Socialist Labour Party

MONTSERRAT

Capital: Plymouth (abandoned because of volcanic eruption 1996); Olveston

Commissioners:

1900-06	Frederick Watkins
1906-18	Wilfred Davidson-Houston

1918-22	Claude Condell
1922-29	Herbert Peebles
1929-32	Hugh Hutchings
1932-46	Thomas Haynes
1946-49	Hugh Burrowes
1949-56	Charlesworth Ross

Administrators:

1956-60	Arthur Dawkins
1960-64	Donald Wiles
1964-71	Dennis Gibbs

Governors:

1971-74	Willoughby Thompson (see Anguilla)
1974-77	Norman Matthews
1977-80	Gwilym Jones
1980-85	David Dale
1985-87	Arthur Watson (see Turks & Caicos)
1987-90	Christopher Turner (see Turks & Caicos)
May 1990-June 1993	David Taylor
June 1993-Sept 1997	Frank Savage
Sept 1997-	Anthony Abbot

Chief Ministers:

Jan 1960-Dec 1970	Wilfred Bramble (MLP)
Dec 1970-Nov 1978	P.Austin Bramble (*son*) (PDP)
Nov 1978-Oct 1991	John Osborne (PLM)
Oct 1991-Nov 1996	Reuben Meade (NPP)
Nov 1996-Aug 1997	Bertrand Osborne (NDP)
Aug 1997-	David Brandt (NPP)

NDP = National Development Party
NPP = National Progressive Party
MLP = Montserrat Labour Party
PDP = Progressive Democratic Party
PLM = People's Liberation Movement

PITCAIRN ISLAND

Capital: Adamstown

Governors:

(President in New Zealand since 1970)

(1952-70   Governors of Fiji)

1970-73	Arthur Galsworthy
1973-75	David Scott
1976-80	Harold Smedley
1980-84	Richard Stratton
1984-87	Terence O'Leary
1987-90	Robin Byatt
July 1990-June 1994	David Moss
June 1994-Aug 1997	Robert Alston
Aug 1997-	Martin Williams

Island Magistrates:

1904-06	James McCoy
1906-07	Albert Young (1st)
1907-08	William Young
1908-09	Edmond McCoy
1909-19	Gerard Christian
1919-20	Charles Parkin Christian (1st)
1920-21	Fred Christian
1921-22	Charles Parkin Christian (2nd)
1922-24	Edgar Christian (1st)
1924-25	Charles Parkin Christian (3rd)
1925-29	Edgar Christian (2nd)
1929-31	Albert Young (2nd)
1931-32	Edgar Christian (3rd)
1932-34	Charles Parkin Christian (4th)
1934-39	Edgar Christian (4th)
1939-40	Andrew Young
1940-41	Frederick Christian (1st)
1941-42	Charles Parkin Christian (5th)
1942-43	Frederick Christian (2nd)
1943-44	Charles Parkin Christian (6th)
1944-48	H. Norris Young
1948-49	Charles Parkin Christian (7th)
1949-51	Warren Christian (1st)
1951-Dec 1954	John Christian (1st)
Dec 1954-Dec 1957	Charles Parkin Christian (8th)
Dec 1957-Dec 1960	Warren Christian (2nd)
Dec 1960-Dec 1966	John Christian (2nd)
Dec 1966-Dec 1975	Pervis Young
Dec 1975-Dec 1984	Ivan Christian
Dec 1984-Dec 1990	Brian Young
Dec 1990-	Jay Warren

SAINT HELENA

Capital: Jamestown

Governors:

1897-1903	Robert Sterndale
1903-11	Henry Gallwey
1912-20	Harry Cordeaux
1920-25	Robert Peel
1925-32	Charles Harper
1932-38	Steuart Davis
1938-41	Henry Pilling
1941-47	William Gray
May 1947-54	George Joy
1954-58	James Harford
Feb 1958-62	Robert Alford
1962-68	John Field
1968-71	Dermot Murphy
1971-76	Thomas Oates
1976-80	Geoffrey Guy (see Dominica)
1981-83	John Massingham
1983-88	Francis Baker
April 1988-91	Robert Stimson
1991-95	Alan Hoole
1995-99	David Smallman
June 1999-	David Hollamby

Dependencies of St. Helena

Ascension

Capital: Georgetown

Administrators:

1965-70	J.Wainwright
1970-72	H.McDonald
1972-75	Geoffrey Guy
1975-78	G.McDonald
1978-80	C.B.Kendall
1980-82	Bernard Pauncefort
1982-84	Ian Thow
1984-89	M.Blick
1989-90	John Beale
1990-95	Brian Connelly
1995-	Roger Huxley

Tristan da Cunha

Capital: Edinburgh

Administrators:

1949-53	H.Elliot
1953-56	P.Forsythe Thompson
1956-58	Godfrey Harris
1958-59	P.A.Day (1st)
1959-61	P.Wheeler
(1961-63	island evacuated - volcanic eruption)
1963-65	P.A.Day (2nd)
1965-70	Brian Watkins
1970-75	J.Fleming
1975-79	S.G.Trees
1979-81	E.C.Brooks
Nov 1981-Sept 1984	C.F.Redstom
Sept-Oct 1984	E.Alexander (acting)
Oct 1984-Feb 1989	Roger Perry
Feb 1989-Jan 1992	Bernard Pauncefort (see Ascension)
Jan 1992-April 1994	Philip Johnson
May-Sept 1994	Lewis Glass (acting)
Sept 1994-Nov 1997	Brendan Dalley
Nov 1997-Jan 1998	B.W.Money (acting)
Jan 1998-	Brian Baldwin

Chief Islanders:

1817-53	William Glass
1856-65	Alexander Cotton
1865-1902	Peter Green (Pieter Groen)
(1902-32	post abolished)
1932-70	William Repetto
1970-73	Harold Green (1st)
1973-79	Albert Glass (1st)
1979-82	Harold Green (2nd)
1982-85	Albert Glass (2nd)
1985-88	Harold Green (3rd)
1988-91	Anne Green
1991-94	Lewis Glass
1994-	James Glass

SOUTH GEORGIA & SOUTH SANDWICH ISLANDS

Commissioners:

1985-   Governors of Falkland Islands

TURKS AND CAICOS

Capital: Cockburn Town

Commissioners:

1899-1901	Geoffrey St Aubyn
1901-05	William Young
1905-14	Frederick Watkins
1914-23	George Smith
1923-32	Harold Phillips
1932-34	Hugh Hutchings
1934-36	Frank Clarkson
1936-40	Hugh Hill
1940-46	Edwin Arrowsmith
1947-52	Cyril Wool-Lewis
1952-55	Peter Bleackley
1955-58	Ernest Lewis
1958-59	Geoffrey Guy

Administrators:

1959-65	Geoffrey Guy
1965	Robert Wainwright (1st)
1965-67	John Golding
1967-71	Robert Wainwright (2nd)
1971-73	Alexander Mitchell

Governors:

1973-75	Alexander Mitchell
1975-78	Arthur Watson (see Anguilla)
1978-82	John Strong
1982-87	Christopher Turner
March 1987-Feb 1993	Michael Bradley
Feb 1993-June 1996	Martin Bourke
June 1996-Jan 2000	John Kelly
Jan 2000-	Mervyn Jones

Chief Ministers:

Sept 1976-May 1980   James McCartney   (PDM) († air accident)

June-Nov 1980　　　　　　　　Oswald Skippings　(1st) (PDM)
Nov 1980-March 1985　　　　　Norman Saunders　(PNP)
March 1985-July 1986　　　　　Nathaniel Francis　(PNP)
(July 1986-March 1988　　　　 post abolished)
March 1988-April 1991　　　　 Oswald Skippings　(2nd) (PDM)
April 1991-Feb 1995　　　　　 Washington Misick　(PNP)
Feb 1995-　　　　　　　　　　Derek Taylor　(PDM)

PDM = People's Democratic Movement
PNP = Progressive National Party

UNITED STATES OF AMERICA

Official name: United States of America (USA)
Independence date: 4 July 1776
Capital: Philadelphia 1776-1800, Washington DC since 1800

In the 16th century European maritime exploration opened up the eastern seaboard of America, and Spanish missions penetrated the southwest. The first British colony was established in Virginia in 1607. By the 18th century the 13 British colonies were strong enough to demand self-government and achieve it in the War of Independence of 1779-83. The former colonies formed the United States of America in 1789, and settlements spread westwards forming new territories and later states. In the civil war of 1861-65 the attempt of the southern states to form a Confederacy and secede from the Union was defeated. By 1912 forty-eight states had been formed; Alaska became the 49th in 1959 and Hawaii the 50th in 1960.

Presidents:

April 1789-March 1797	George Washington	(FP)
March 1797-March 1801	John Adams	(FP)
March 1801-March 1809	Thomas Jefferson	(see Virginia) (DRP)
March 1809-March 1817	James Madison	(DRP)
March 1817-March 1825	James Monroe	(see Virginia) (DRP)
March 1825-March 1829	John Quincy Adams	(*son of John Adams*) (DRP)
March 1829-March 1837	Andrew Jackson	(see Florida) (DP)
March 1837-March 1841	Martin Van Buren	(see New York) (DP)
March-April 1841	William Harrison	(WP) (†)
April 1841-March 1845	John Tyler	(see Virginia) (WP)
March 1845-March 1849	James Polk	(see Tennessee) (DP)
March 1849-July 1850	Zachary Taylor	(WP) (†)
July 1850-March 1853	Millard Fillmore	(WP)
March 1853-March 1857	Franklin Pierce	(DP)
March 1857-March 1861	James Buchanan	(DP)
March 1861-April 1865	Abraham Lincoln	(RP) († assassinated)
April 1865-March 1869	Andrew Johnson	(see Tennessee) (RP)
March 1869-March 1877	Ulysses Grant	(RP)
March 1877-March 1881	Rutherford Hayes	(see Ohio) (RP)
March-Sept 1881	James Garfield	(RP) († assassinated)
Sept 1881-March 1885	Chester Arthur	(RP)
March 1885-March 1889	Grover Cleveland	(see New York) (1st) (DP)
March 1889-March 1893	Benjamin Harrison	(RP)
March 1893-March 1897	Grover Cleveland	(2nd) (DP)
March 1897-Sept 1901	William McKinley	(see Ohio) (RP) († assassinated)

Sept 1901-March 1909	Theodore Roosevelt (see New York) (RP)
March 1909-March 1913	William Taft (RP)
March 1913-March 1921	Woodrow Wilson (see New Jersey) (DP)
March 1921-Aug 1923	Warren Harding (RP) (†)
Aug 1923-March 1929	Calvin Coolidge (see Massachusetts) (RP)
March 1929-March 1933	Herbert Hoover (RP)
March 1933-April 1945	Franklin Roosevelt (see New York) (DP) (†)
April 1945-Jan 1953	Harry Truman (DP)
Jan 1953-Jan 1961	Dwight Eisenhower (RP)
Jan 1961-Nov 1963	John Kennedy (DP) († assassinated)
Nov 1963-Jan 1969	Lyndon Johnson (DP)
Jan 1969-Aug 1974	Richard Nixon (RP)
Aug 1974-Jan 1977	Gerald Ford (*b* Leslie King) (RP)
Jan 1977-Jan 1981	James (Jimmy) Carter (see Georgia) (DP)
Jan 1981-Jan 1989	Ronald Reagan (see California) (RP)
Jan 1989-Jan 1993	George Bush (RP)
Jan 1993-	William Clinton (*b* W.Blythe) (see Arkansas) (DP)

FP = Federal Party
DP = Democratic Party (*f* DRP)
DRP = Democratic Republican Party
RP = Republican Party
WP = Whig Party

Secessionist State

CONFEDERATE STATES OF AMERICA

Member states: Alabama, Arkansas, Florida, Georgia, Louisiana, Mississippi, North Carolina, South Carolina, Tennessee, Texas, Virginia
State formed: 4 February 1861
Capital: Richmond

President:

Feb 1861-May 1865	Jefferson Davis

States

Note: Additional parties for state Governors -

AJDP = Anti-Jackson Democratic Party
AP = American Party
ARP = American Republican Party
CP = Conservative Party
CRP = Conservative Republican Party
DFLP = Democratic Farmer-Labor Party
DPP = Democratic Populist Party

FLP = Farmer-Labor Party
ID-Independent Democrat
IR = Independent Republican
KNP = Know-Nothing Party
LR = Liberal Republican
NPL = Non-partisan League
NRP = National Republican Party
Pop = Populist Party
PP = Progressive Party
Ref = Reform Party
SP = Silver Party
TP = Toleration Party
UDP = Union Democratic Party
UP = Unionist Party

ALABAMA

Statehood: 14 December 1819
Capital: Montgomery

Governors:

Sept 1817-July 1820	William Bibb	(DRP) (†)
July 1820-Nov 1821	Thomas Bibb	(*son*) (DRP)
Nov 1821-Nov 1825	Israel Pickens	(DRP)
Nov 1825-Nov 1829	John Murphy	(DP)
Nov 1829-March 1831	Gabriel Moore	(DP)
March-Nov 1831	Samuel Moore	(*brother*) (DP)
Nov 1831-Nov 1835	John Gayle	(DP)
Nov 1835-July 1837	Clement Clay	(DP)
July-Nov 1837	Hugh McVay	(DP)
Nov 1837-Nov 1841	Arthur Bagby	(DP)
Nov 1841-Dec 1845	Benjamin Fitzpatrick	(DP)
Dec 1845-Dec 1847	Joshua Martin	(DP)
Dec 1847-Dec 1849	Reuben Chapman	(DP)
Dec 1849-Dec 1853	Henry Collier	(DP)
Dec 1853-Dec 1857	John Winston	(DP)
Dec 1857-Dec 1861	Andrew Moore	(DP)
Dec 1861-Dec 1863	John Shorter	(DP)
Dec 1863-April 1865	Thomas Watts	(DP)
June-Dec 1865	Lewis Parsons	
Dec 1865-July 1868	Robert Patton	
July 1868-Nov 1870	William H.Smith	(RP)
Nov 1870-Nov 1872	Robert Lindsay	(DP)
Nov 1872-Nov 1874	David Lewis	(RP)
Nov 1874-Nov 1878	George Houston	(DP)
Nov 1878-Dec 1882	Rufus Cobb	(DP)

Dec 1882-Dec 1886	Edward O'Neal (DP)
Dec 1886-Dec 1890	Thomas Seay (DP)
Dec 1890-Dec 1894	Thomas Jones (DP)
Dec 1894-Dec 1896	William Oates (DP)
Dec 1896-Dec 1900	Joseph Johnston (DP)
1-26 Dec 1900	William Jelks (acting) (DP)
Dec 1900-June 1901	William Samford (DP) (†)
June 1901-Jan 1907	William Jelks (DP)
Jan 1907-Jan 1911	Braxton Comer (DP)
Jan 1911-Jan 1915	Emmett O'Neal (*son of Edward O'Neal*) (DP)
Jan 1915-Jan 1919	Charles Henderson (DP)
Jan 1919-Jan 1923	Thomas Kilby (DP)
Jan 1923-Jan 1927	William Brandon (DP)
Jan 1927-Jan 1931	D.Bibb Graves (1st) (DP)
Jan 1931-Jan 1935	Benjamin Miller (DP)
Jan 1935-Jan 1939	D.Bibb Graves (2nd) (DP)
Jan 1939-Jan 1943	Frank Dixon (DP)
Jan 1943-Jan 1947	Chauncey Sparks (DP)
Jan 1947-Jan 1951	James Folsom (1st) (DP)
Jan 1951-Jan 1955	Gordon Persons (DP)
Jan 1955-Jan 1959	James Folsom (2nd) (DP)
Jan 1959-Jan 1963	John Patterson (DP)
Jan 1963-Jan 1967	George Wallace (1st) (DP)
Jan 1967-May 1968	Lurleen Wallace (*wife*) (*b* L.Morgan) (DP) (†)
May 1968-Jan 1971	Albert Brewer (DP)
Jan 1971-Jan 1979	George Wallace (2nd) (DP)
Jan 1979-Jan 1983	Forrest James (1st) (DP)
Jan 1983-Jan 1987	George Wallace (3rd) (DP)
Jan 1987-April 1993	Guy Hunt (RP)
April 1993-Jan 1995	James Folsom Jnr (DP) (*son of J.Folsom*)
Jan 1995-Jan 1999	Forrest James (2nd) (RP)
Jan 1999-	Don Siegelman (DP)

ALASKA

Statehood: 3 January 1959
Capital: Juneau

Governors:

April 1913-April 1918	John Strong
April 1918-June 1921	Thomas Riggs
June 1921-Aug 1925	Scott Bone
Aug 1925-April 1933	George Parks
April 1933-Dec 1939	John Troy

Dec 1939-Oct 1953	Ernest Gruening
Oct 1953-Jan 1957	B.Frank Heintzleman
Jan-Aug 1957	Waino Hendrickson (acting) (1st)
Aug 1957-Sept 1958	Michael Stepovich
Sept 1958-Jan 1959	Waino Hendrickson (acting) (2nd)
Jan 1959-Dec 1966	William Egan (1st) (DP)
Dec 1966-Jan 1969	Walter Hickel (1st) (RP)
Jan 1969-Dec 1970	Keith Miller (RP)
Dec 1970-Dec 1974	William Egan (2nd) (DP)
Dec 1974-Dec 1982	Jay Hammond (RP)
Dec 1982-Dec 1986	William Sheffield (DP)
Dec 1986-Dec 1990	Steve Cowper (DP)
Dec 1990-Dec 1994	Walter Hickel (2nd) (Ind)
Dec 1994-	Tony Knowles (DP)

ARIZONA

Statehood: 14 February 1912
Capital: Phoenix

Governors:

March 1864-April 1866	John Goodwin (RP)
April 1866-March 1869	Richard McCormick (RP)
April 1869-April 1877	Anson Safford (RP)
April 1877-June 1878	John Hoyt (RP)
June 1878-Nov 1881	John Fremont (RP)
Nov 1881-March 1882	John Gosper (acting)
March 1882-Oct 1885	Frederick Tritle (RP)
Oct 1885-April 1889	C.Meyer Zulick (DP)
April 1889-Oct 1890	Lewis Wolfley (RP)
Oct 1890-May 1892	John Irwin (RP)
May 1892-March 1893	Nathan Murphy (1st) (RP)
March 1893-March 1896	Louis Hughes (DP)
March 1896-July 1897	Benjamin Franklin (DP)
July 1897-July 1898	Myron McCord (RP)
July 1898-July 1902	Nathan Murphy (2nd) (RP)
July 1902-Feb 1905	Alexander Brodie (RP)
March 1905-May 1909	Joseph Kibbey (RP)
May 1909-Jan 1912	Richard Sloan (RP)
Jan 1912-Jan 1916	George Hunt (1st) (DP)
Jan 1916-Jan 1918	Thomas Campbell (1st) (DP)
Jan 1918-Jan 1919	George Hunt (2nd) (DP)
Jan 1919-Jan 1923	Thomas Campbell (2nd) (DP)
Jan 1923-Jan 1929	George Hunt (3rd) (DP)

Jan 1929-Jan 1931	John Phillips (RP)
Jan 1931-Jan 1933	George Hunt (4th) (DP)
Jan 1933-Jan 1937	Benjamin Moeur (DP)
Jan 1937-Jan 1939	Rawghlie Stanford (DP)
Jan 1939-Jan 1941	Robert Jones (DP)
Jan 1941-May 1948	Sidney Osborne (DP)
May 1948-Jan 1951	Dan Garvey (DP)
Jan 1951-Jan 1955	Howard Pyle (RP)
Jan 1955-Jan 1959	Ernest McFarland (DP)
Jan 1959-Jan 1965	Paul Fannin (RP)
Jan 1965-Jan 1967	Samuel Goddard (DP)
Jan 1967-Jan 1975	John (Jack) Williams (RP)
Jan 1975-Oct 1977	Raul Castro (DP)
Oct 1977-March 1978	Wesley Bolin (DP) (†)
March 1978-Jan 1987	Bruce Babbit (DP)
Jan 1987-April 1988	Evan Mecham (RP)
April 1988-Jan 1991	Rose Mofford (DP)
Jan 1991-Sept 1997	Fife Symington (RP)
Sept 1997-	Jane Dee Hull (*b* J.D.Bowersock) (RP)

ARKANSAS

Statehood: 15 June 1836
Capital: Little Rock

Governors:

March 1819-March 1825	James Miller
March 1825-March 1829	George Izzard
March 1829-March 1835	John Pope
March 1835-Sept 1836	William Fulton
Sept 1836-Nov 1840	James Conway (DP)
Nov 1840-April 1844	Archibald Yell (DP)
April-Nov 1844	Samuel Adams (acting) (DP)
Nov 1844-Jan 1849	Thomas Drew (DP)
Jan 1849-Nov 1852	John Roane (DP)
Nov 1852-Nov 1860	Elias Conway (DP)
Nov 1860-Nov 1862	Henry Rector (DP)
Nov 1862-Jan 1864	Harris Flanagin (DP)
Jan 1864-July 1868	Isaac Murphy (UP)
July 1868-March 1871	Powell Clayton (RP)
March 1871-Jan 1873	Ozra Hadley (acting) (RP)
Jan 1873-Nov 1874	Elisha Baxter (RP)
Nov 1874-Jan 1877	Augustus Garland (DP)
Jan 1877-Jan 1881	William Miller (DP)

Jan 1881-Jan 1883	Thomas Churchill (DP)
Jan 1883-Jan 1885	James Berry (DP)
Jan 1885-Jan 1889	Simon Hughes (DP)
Jan 1889-Jan 1893	James Eagles (DP)
Jan 1893-Jan 1895	James Fishback (DP)
Jan 1895-Jan 1897	James Clarke (DP)
Jan 1897-Jan 1901	Daniel Jones (DP)
Jan 1901-Jan 1907	Jeff Davis (DP)
Jan-Feb 1907	John Little (DP)
Feb-May 1907	John Moore (acting) (DP)
May 1907-Jan 1909	Xenophon Pindall (acting) (DP)
Jan 1909-March 1913	George Donaghey (DP)
March 1913	Joseph Robinson (DP)
March-Aug 1913	Junius Futrell (acting) (DP)
Aug 1913-Jan 1917	George Hays (DP)
Jan 1917-Jan 1921	Charles Brough (DP)
Jan 1921-Jan 1925	Thomas McCrae (DP)
Jan 1925-Jan 1927	Thomas Terral (DP)
Jan 1927-March 1928	John Martineau (DP)
March 1926-Jan 1933	Harvey Parnell (DP)
Jan 1933-Jan 1937	Junius Futrell (DP)
Jan 1937-Jan 1941	Carl Bailey (DP)
Jan 1941-Jan 1945	Homer Adkins (DP)
Jan 1945-Jan 1949	Ben Laney (DP)
Jan 1949-Jan 1953	Sidney McMath (DP)
Jan 1953-Jan 1955	Francis Cherry (DP)
Jan 1955-Jan 1967	Orval Faubus (DP)
Jan 1967-Jan 1971	Winthrop Rockefeller (RP)
Jan 1971-Jan 1975	Dale Bumpers (DP)
Jan 1975-Jan 1979	David Pryor (DP)
Jan 1979-Jan 1981	William Clinton (*b* W.Blythe) (1st) (DP)
Jan 1981-Jan 1983	Frank White (RP)
Jan 1983-Dec 1992	William Clinton (2nd) (DP) (later President)
Dec 1992-May 1996	Jim Guy Tucker (DP)
May 1996-	Mike Huckabee (RP)

CALIFORNIA

Statehood: 9 September 1850
Capital: Sacramento

Governors:

Dec 1849-Jan 1851	Peter Burnett (ID)
Jan 1851-Jan 1852	John McDougal (acting) (ID)

Jan 1852-Jan 1856	John Bigler (DP)
Jan 1856-Jan 1858	John Johnson (KNP)
Jan 1858-Jan 1860	John Weller (DP)
9-14 Jan 1860	Milton Latham (DP)
Jan 1860-Jan 1861	John Downey (acting) (DP)
Jan 1861-Dec 1863	Leland Stanford (RP)
Dec 1863-Dec 1867	Frederick Low (UP)
Dec 1867-Dec 1871	Henry Haight (DP)
Dec 1871-Feb 1875	Newton Booth (RP)
Feb-Dec 1875	Romualdo Pacheco (acting) (RP)
Dec 1875-Jan 1880	William Irwin (DP)
Jan 1880-Jan 1883	George Perkins (RP)
Jan 1883-Jan 1887	George Stoneman (DP)
Jan-Sept 1887	Washington Bartlett (DP)
Sept 1887-Jan 1891	Robert Waterman (acting) (RP)
Jan 1891-Jan 1895	Henry Markham (RP)
Jan 1895-Jan 1899	James Budd (DP)
Jan 1899-Jan 1903	Henry Gage (RP)
Jan 1903-Jan 1907	George Pardee (RP)
Jan 1907-Jan 1911	James Gillett (RP)
Jan 1911-March 1917	Hiram Johnson (PP)
March 1917-Jan 1923	William Stephens (RP)
Jan 1923-Jan 1927	Friend Richardson (RP)
Jan 1927-Jan 1931	Clement Young (RP)
Jan 1931-June 1934	James Rolph (RP)
June 1934-Jan 1939	Frank Merriman (RP)
Jan 1939-Jan 1943	Culbert Olson (DP)
Jan 1943-Oct 1953	Earl Warren (RP)
Oct 1953-Jan 1959	Goodwin Knight (RP)
Jan 1959-Jan 1967	Edmund (Pat) Brown (DP)
Jan 1967-Jan 1975	Ronald Reagan (later President) (RP)
Jan 1975-Jan 1983	Edmund (Jerry) Brown Jr (*son of Pat Brown*) (DP)
Jan 1983-Jan 1991	George Deukemejian (RP)
Jan 1991-Jan 1999	Peter Wilson (RP)
Jan 1999-	Gray Davis (DP)

COLORADO

Statehood: 1 August 1876
Capital: Denver

Governors:

March 1861-March 1862	William Gilpin
March 1862-Aug 1865	John Evans

Aug 1865-May 1867	Alexander Cummings
May 1867-April 1869	A. Cameron Hunt
April 1869-April 1873	Edward McCook (1st)
April 1873-June 1874	Samuel Elbert
June 1874-Feb 1875	Edward McCook (2nd)
Feb 1875-Jan 1879	John Routt (1st) (RP)
Jan 1879-Jan 1883	Frederick Pitkin (RP)
Jan 1883-Jan 1885	James Grant (DP)
Jan 1885-Jan 1887	Benjamin Eaton (RP)
Jan 1887-Jan 1889	Alva Adams (1st) (DP)
Jan 1889-Jan 1891	Job Cooper (RP)
Jan 1891-Jan 1893	John Routt (2nd) (RP)
Jan 1893-Jan 1895	Davis Waite (Pop)
Jan 1895-Jan 1897	Albert McIntyre (RP)
Jan 1897-Jan 1899	Alva Adams (2nd) (DP)
Jan 1899-Jan 1901	Charles Thomas (DP)
Jan 1901-March 1903	James Orman (DP)
March 1903-Jan 1905	James Peabody (1st) (DP)
Jan-March 1905	Alva Adams (3rd) (DP)
18 March 1905	James Peabody (2nd) (DP)
March 1905-Jan 1907	Jesse McDonald (RP)
Jan 1907-Jan 1909	Henry Buchtel (RP)
Jan 1909-Jan 1913	John Shafroth (DP)
Jan 1913-Jan 1915	Elias Ammons (DP)
Jan 1915-Jan 1917	George Carlson (RP)
Jan 1917-Jan 1919	Julius Gunter (DP)
Jan 1919-Jan 1923	Oliver Shoup (RP)
Jan 1923-Jan 1925	William Sweet (DP)
Jan 1925-Jan 1927	Clarence Morley (RP)
Jan 1927-Jan 1933	William Adams (*brother of A. Adams*) (DP)
Jan 1933-Jan 1937	Edwin Johnson (1st) (DP)
1-12 Jan 1937	Ray Talbot (DP)
Jan 1937-Jan 1939	Tellor Ammons (*son of E. Ammons*) (DP)
Jan 1939-Jan 1943	Ralph Carr (RP)
Jan 1943-Jan 1947	John Vivian (RP)
Jan 1947-April 1950	William Knous (DP)
April 1950-Jan 1951	Walter Johnson (acting) (DP)
Jan 1951-Jan 1955	Dan Thornton (RP)
Jan 1955-Jan 1957	Edwin Johnson (2nd) (DP)
Jan 1957-Jan 1963	Stephen McNichols (DP)
Jan 1963-July 1973	John Love (RP)
July 1973-Jan 1975	John Vanderhoof (RP)
Jan 1975-Jan 1987	Richard Lamb (DP)
Jan 1987-Jan 1999	Roy Romer (DP)
Jan 1999-	Bill Owens (RP)

CONNECTICUTT

One of the original 13 states
Capital: Hartford

Governors:

June 1776-May 1784	Jonathan Trumbull Sr
May 1784-May 1786	Matthew Griswold
May 1786-Jan 1796	Samuel Huntingdon (FP) (†)
Jan 1796-Dec 1797	Oliver Wolcott (FP) (†)
Dec 1797-Aug 1809	Jonathan Trumbull Jr (*son of J.Trumbull Sr*) (FP) (†)
Aug 1809-May 1811	John Treadwell (FP)
May 1811-Oct 1812	Roger Griswold (*son of M.Griswold*) (FP) (†)
Oct 1812-May 1817	John Cotton Smith (FP)
May 1817-May 1827	Oliver Wolcott Jr (*son of O.Wolcott*) (TP)
May 1827-May 1831	Gideon Tomlinson (DRP)
May 1831-May 1833	John Peters (NRP)
May 1833-May 1834	Henry Edwards (1st) (DP)
May 1834-May 1835	Samuel Foot (WP)
May 1835-May 1838	Henry Edwards (2nd) (DP)
May 1838-May 1842	William Ellsworth (WP)
May 1842-May 1844	Chauncey Cleveland (DP)
May 1844-May 1846	Roger Baldwin (WP)
May 1846-May 1847	Isaac Toucey (DP)
May 1847-May 1849	Clark Bissell (WP)
May 1849-May 1850	Joseph Trumbull (*grandson of J.Trumbull Sr*) (WP)
May 1850-Oct 1853	Thomas Seymour (DP)
Oct 1853-May 1854	Charles Pond (DP)
May 1854-May 1855	Henry Dutton (WP)
May 1855-May 1857	William Minor (KNP)
May 1857-May 1858	Alexander Holley (WP)
May 1858-May 1866	William Buckingham (RP)
May 1866-May 1867	Joseph Hawley (RP)
May 1867-May 1869	James English (1st) (DP)
May 1869-May 1870	Marshall Jewell (1st) (RP)
May 1870-May 1871	James English (2nd) (DP)
May 1871-May 1873	Marshall Jewell (2nd) (RP)
May 1873-Jan 1877	Charles Ingersoll (DP)
Jan 1877-Jan 1881	Charles Andrews (RP)
Jan 1881-Jan 1883	Hobart Bigelow (RP)
Jan 1883-Jan 1885	Thomas Waller (DP)
Jan 1885-Jan 1887	Henry Harrison (RP)
Jan 1887-Jan 1889	Phineas Lounsbury (RP)
Jan 1889-Jan 1893	Morgan Bulkeley (RP)
Jan 1893-Jan 1895	Luzon Morris (DP)

Jan 1895-Jan 1897	O.Vincent Coffin (RP)
Jan 1897-Jan 1899	Lorrin Cooke (RP)
Jan 1899-Jan 1901	George Lounsbury (*brother of P.Lounsbury*) (RP)
Jan 1901-Jan 1903	George McLean (RP)
Jan 1903-Jan 1905	Abiram Chamberlain (RP)
Jan 1905-Jan 1907	Henry Roberts (RP)
Jan 1907-Jan 1909	Rollin Woodruff (RP)
Jan-April 1909	George Lilley (RP) (†)
April 1909-Jan 1911	Frank Weeks (RP)
Jan 1911-Jan 1915	Simeon Baldwin (DP)
Jan 1915-Jan 1921	Marcus Holcomb (RP)
Jan 1921-Jan 1923	Everett Lake (RP)
Jan 1923-Jan 1925	Charles Templeton (RP)
7-8 Jan 1925	Hiram Bingham (RP)
Jan 1925-Jan 1931	John Trumbull (RP)
Jan 1931-Jan 1939	Wilbur Cross (DP)
Jan 1939-Jan 1941	Raymond Baldwin (1st) (RP)
Jan 1941-Jan 1943	Robert Hurley (DP)
Jan 1943-Feb 1946	Raymond Baldwin (2nd) (RP)
Feb 1946-Jan 1947	Wilbur Snow (DP)
Jan 1947-March 1948	James McConaughty (RP) (†)
March 1948-Jan 1949	John Shannon (RP)
Jan 1949-Jan 1951	Chester Bowles (DP)
Jan 1951-Jan 1955	John Davis Lodge (RP)
Jan 1955-Jan 1961	Abraham Ribicoff (DP)
Jan 1961-Jan 1971	John Dempsey (DP)
Jan 1971-Jan 1975	Thomas Meskill (RP)
Jan 1975-Dec 1981	Ella Grasso (*b* E.Tambussi) (DP)
Dec 1981-Jan 1991	William O'Neill (DP)
Jan 1991-Jan 1995	Lowell Weicker (Ind)
Jan 1995-	John Rowland (RP)

DELAWARE

One of the original 13 states
Capital: Dover

Presidents:

Feb-Sept 1777	John McKinly
Sept-Oct 1777	Thomas McKean (acting)
Oct 1777-March 1778	George Read (acting)
March 1778-Nov 1781	Caesar Rodney
Nov 1781-Nov 1782	John Dickinson
Nov 1782-Feb 1783	John Cook (acting)

Feb 1783-Oct 1786   Nicholas Van Dyke
Oct 1786-March 1789   Thomas Collins
March-May 1789   Jehu Davis (acting)
May 1789-Jan 1793   Joshua Clayton

Governors:

Period	Governor
Jan 1793-Jan 1796	Joshua Clayton (FP)
Jan 1796-Sept 1797	Gunning Bedford (FP)
Sept 1797-Jan 1799	Daniel Rogers (acting) (FP)
Jan 1799-March 1801	Richard Bassett (FP)
March 1801-Jan 1802	James Sykes (acting) (FP)
Jan 1802-Jan 1805	David Hall (DRP)
Jan 1805-Jan 1808	Nathaniel Mitchell (FP)
Jan 1808-Jan 1811	George Truitt (FP)
Jan 1811-Jan 1814	Joseph Haslett (1st) (DRP)
Jan 1814-Jan 1817	Daniel Rodney (FP)
Jan 1817-Jan 1820	John Clark (FP)
Jan 1820-Jan 1821	Jacob Stoutt (acting) (FP)
Jan 1821-April 1822	John Collins (DRP)
April 1822-Jan 1823	Caleb Rodney (acting) (FP)
Jan-June 1823	Joseph Haslett (2nd) (DRP)
June 1823-Jan 1824	Charles Thomas (acting) (DRP)
Jan 1824-Jan 1827	Samuel Paynter (FP)
Jan 1827-Jan 1830	Charles Polk (FP)
Jan 1830-Jan 1833	David Hazzard (ARP)
Jan 1833-April 1836	Caleb Bennett (DP)
April 1836-Jan 1837	Charles Polk (acting) (WP)
Jan 1837-Jan 1841	Cornelius Comegys (WP)
Jan 1841-Jan 1845	William Cooper (WP)
Jan 1845-March 1846	Thomas Stockton (WP)
March-May 1846	Joseph Maull (acting) (WP)
May 1846-Jan 1847	William Temple (acting) (WP)
Jan 1847-Jan 1851	William Tharp (DP)
Jan 1851-Jan 1855	William Ross (DP)
Jan 1855-Jan 1859	Peter Causey (KNP)
Jan 1859-Jan 1863	William Burton (DP)
Jan 1863-March 1865	William Cannon (UP)
March 1865-Jan 1871	Gove Saulsbury (acting 1865-67) (DP)
Jan 1871-Jan 1875	James Ponder (DP)
Jan 1875-Jan 1879	John Cochran (DP)
Jan 1879-Jan 1883	John Hall (DP)
Jan 1883-Jan 1887	Charles Stockley (DP)
Jan 1887-Jan 1891	Benjamin Biggs (DP)
Jan 1891-Jan 1895	Robert Reynolds (DP)

Jan-April 1895	Joshua Marvel (RP)
April 1895-Jan 1897	William Watson (acting) (DP)
Jan 1897-Jan 1901	Ebe Tunnell (DP)
Jan 1901-Jan 1905	John Hunn (RP)
Jan 1905-Jan 1909	Preston Lea (RP)
Jan 1909-Jan 1913	Simeon Pennewill (RP)
Jan 1913-Jan 1917	Charles Miller (RP)
Jan 1917-Jan 1921	John Townsend (RP)
Jan 1921-Jan 1925	William Denney (RP)
Jan 1925-Jan 1929	Robert Robinson (RP)
Jan 1929-Jan 1937	C. Douglass Buck (RP)
Jan 1937-Jan 1941	Richard McMullen (DP)
Jan 1941-Jan 1949	Walter Bacon (RP)
Jan 1949-Jan 1953	Elbert Carvel (1st) (DP)
Jan 1953-Dec 1960	James Boggs (RP)
Dec 1960-Jan 1961	David Buckson (acting) (RP)
Jan 1961-Jan 1965	Elbert Carvel (2nd) (DP)
Jan 1965-Jan 1969	Charles Terry (DP)
Jan 1969-Jan 1973	Russell Peterson (RP)
Jan 1973-Jan 1977	Sherman Tribbit (DP)
Jan 1977-Jan 1985	Pierre Dupont (RP)
Jan 1985-Jan 1993	Michael Castle (RP)
Jan 1993-	Thomas Carper (DP)

FLORIDA

Statehood: 3 March 1845
Capital: Tallahassee

Governors:

March-Dec 1821	Andrew Jackson (later President)
June 1822-34	William Duvall
1834-36	John Eaton
1836-39	Richard Call (1st)
1839-41	Robert Reid
1841-44	Richard Call (2nd)
1844-June 1845	John Branch
June 1845-Oct 1849	William Moseley (DP)
Oct 1849-Oct 1853	Thomas Brown (WP)
Oct 1853-Oct 1857	James Broome (DP)
Oct 1857-Oct 1861	Madison Perry (DP)
Oct 1861-April 1865	John Milton (DP) (†)
April-May 1865	Abraham Allison (acting) (DP)
July-Dec 1865	William Marvin

Dec 1865-June 1868	David Walker (DP)
June 1868-Jan 1873	Harrison Reed (RP)
Jan 1873-March 1874	Ossian Hart (RP) (†)
March 1874-Jan 1877	Marcellus Stearns (acting) (RP)
Jan 1877-Jan 1881	George Drew (DP)
Jan 1881-Jan 1885	William Bloxham (1st) (DP)
Jan 1885-Jan 1889	Edward Perry (DP)
Jan 1889-Jan 1893	Francis Fleming (DP)
Jan 1893-Jan 1897	Henry Mitchell (DP)
Jan 1897-Jan 1901	William Bloxham (2nd) (DP)
Jan 1901-Jan 1905	William Jennings (DP)
Jan 1905-Jan 1909	Napoleon Broward (DP)
Jan 1909-Jan 1913	Albert Gilchrist (DP)
Jan 1913-Jan 1917	Park Trammell (DP)
Jan 1917-Jan 1921	Sidney Catts (DP)
Jan 1921-Jan 1925	Carey Hardee (DP)
Jan 1925-Jan 1929	John W. Martin (DP)
Jan 1929-Jan 1933	Doyle Carton (DP)
Jan 1933-Jan 1937	David Sholtz (DP)
Jan 1937-Jan 1941	Frederick Cone (DP)
Jan 1941-Jan 1945	Spessard Holland (DP)
Jan 1945-Jan 1949	Millard Caldwell (DP)
Jan 1949-Jan 1953	Fuller Warren (DP)
Jan-Sept 1953	Daniel McCarthy (DP) (†)
Sept 1953-Jan 1955	Charles Johns (DP)
Jan 1955-Jan 1961	Leroy Collins (DP)
Jan 1961-Jan 1965	C. Farris Bryant (DP)
Jan 1965-Jan 1967	Haydon Burns (DP)
Jan 1967-Jan 1971	Claude Kirk (RP)
Jan 1971-Jan 1979	Reubin Askew (DP)
Jan 1979-Jan 1987	Robert Graham (DP)
3-7 Jan 1987	Wayne Mixson (DP)
Jan 1987-Jan 1991	Robert Martinez (RP)
Jan 1991-Dec 1998	Lawton Chiles (†) (DP)
Dec 1998-Jan 1999	Kenneth (Buddy) MacKay (DP)
Jan 1999-	John (Jeb) Bush (RP) (*son of President G. Bush*)

GEORGIA

One of the original 13 states
Capital: Atlanta

Chief Executives:

Jan-June 1775	Archibald Bulloch (1st)

June-July 1775	William Ewen (1st)
July-Dec 1775	Archibald Bulloch (2nd)
Dec 1775-Jan 1776	William Ewen (2nd)
Jan 1776-Feb 1777	Archibald Bulloch (3rd)
Feb-May 1777	Button Gwinnett

Governors:

May 1777-Jan 1778	John Treutlen
Jan-Dec 1778	John Houston (1st)
Dec 1778-Nov 1779	John Wereat
Nov 1779-Jan 1780	George Walton (1st)
Jan 1780-Jan 1781	Richard Howley
Jan-Aug 1781	Stephen Heard
Aug 1781	Myrick Davies
Aug 1781-Jan 1782	Nathan Brownson
Jan 1782-Jan 1783	John Martin
Jan 1783-Jan 1784	Lyman Hall
Jan 1784-Jan 1785	John Houston (2nd)
Jan 1785-Jan 1786	Samuel Elbert
Jan 1786-Jan 1787	Edward Telfair (1st)
Jan 1787-Jan 1788	George Matthews (1st)
Jan 1788-Nov 1789	George Handley
Nov 1789-Nov 1790	George Walton (2nd) (DRP)
Nov 1790-Nov 1793	Edward Telfair (2nd) (DRP)
Nov 1793-Jan 1796	George Matthews (2nd) (DRP)
Jan 1796-Jan 1798	Jared Irwin (1st) (DRP)
Jan 1798-March 1801	James Jackson (DRP)
March-Nov 1801	David Emmanuel (DRP)
Nov 1801-Jan 1802	Josiah Tattnall (DRP)
Jan 1802-Sept 1806	John Milledge (DRP)
Sept 1806-Nov 1809	Jared Irwin (2nd) (DRP)
Nov 1809-Nov 1813	David Mitchell (1st) (DRP)
Nov 1813-Nov 1815	Peter Early (DRP)
Nov 1815-March 1817	David Mitchell (2nd) (DRP)
March 1817-Oct 1819	William Rabun (DRP)
Oct-Nov 1819	Matthew Talbot (DRP)
Nov 1819-Nov 1823	John Clark (DRP)
Nov 1823-Nov 1827	George Troup (DRP)
Nov 1827-Nov 1829	John Forsyth (DRP)
Nov 1829-Nov 1831	George Gilmer (1st) (NRP)
Nov 1831-Nov 1835	Wilson Lumpkin (UDP)
Nov 1835-Nov 1837	William Schley (UDP)
Nov 1837-Nov 1839	George Gilmer (2nd) (WP)
Nov 1839-Nov 1843	Charles Macdonald (DP)
Nov 1843-Nov 1847	George Crawford (WP)

Nov 1847-Nov 1851	George Towns (DP)
Nov 1851-Nov 1853	Howell Cobb (DP)
Nov 1853-Nov 1857	Herschel Johnson (DP)
Nov 1857-May 1865	Joseph E.Brown (DP)
June-Dec 1865	James Johnson (DP)
Dec 1865-Jan 1868	Charles Jenkins (DP)
Jan-June 1868	Thomas Ruger
June 1868-Nov 1871	Rufus Bullock (RP)
Nov 1871-Jan 1872	Benjamin Conley (acting) (RP)
Jan 1872-Jan 1877	James M.Smith (DP)
Jan 1877-Nov 1882	Alfred Colquitt (DP)
Nov 1882-March 1883	Alexander Stephen (DP)
March-May 1883	James Boynton (acting) (DP)
May 1883-Nov 1886	Henry McDaniel (DP)
Nov 1886-Oct 1890	John Gordon (DP)
Oct 1890-Oct 1894	William Northen (DP)
Oct 1894-Oct 1898	William Atkinson (DP)
Oct 1898-Oct 1902	Allen Candler (DP)
Oct 1902-June 1907	Joseph Terrell (DP)
June 1907-June 1909	Hoke Smith (1st) (DP)
June 1909-July 1911	Joseph M.Brown (*son of J.E.Brown*) (1st) (DP)
July-Nov 1911	Hoke Smith (2nd) (DP)
Nov 1911-June 1913	Joseph M.Brown (2nd) (DP)
June 1913-June 1915	John Slaton (DP)
June 1915-June 1917	Nathaniel Harris (DP)
June 1917-June 1921	Hugh Dorsey (DP)
June 1921-June 1923	Thomas Hardwick (DP)
June 1923-June 1927	Clifford Walker (DP)
June 1927-June 1931	Lamartine Hardman (DP)
June 1931-Jan 1933	Richard Russell (DP)
Jan 1933-Jan 1937	Eugene Talmadge (1st) (DP)
Jan 1937-Jan 1941	Eurith Rivers (DP)
Jan 1941-Jan 1943	Eugene Talmadge (2nd) (DP)
Jan 1943-March 1947	Ellis Arnall (DP)
March 1947-Nov 1948	Melvin Thompson (DP)
Nov 1948-Jan 1955	Herman Talmadge (*son of E.Talmadge*) (DP)
Jan 1955-Jan 1959	Marvin Griffin (DP)
Jan 1959-Jan 1963	Ernest Vandiver (DP)
Jan 1963-Jan 1967	Carl Sander (DP)
Jan 1967-Jan 1971	Lester Maddox (DP)
Jan 1971-Jan 1975	James (Jimmy) Carter (later President) (DP)
Jan 1975-Jan 1983	George Busbee (DP)
Jan 1983-Jan 1991	Joe Frank Harris (DP)
Jan 1991-Jan 1999	Zell Miller (DP)
Jan 1999-	Roy Barnes (DP)

HAWAII

Independent state formed: 1810
Statehood: 18 March 1959   (US Territory 1900-59)
Capital: Honolulu

Kings/Queen:

1810-May 1819	Kamehameha I (*b* Paiea)
May 1819-July 1824	Kamehameha II (*b* Liholiho) (*son*)
	Regent: Kaahumanu
June 1825-Dec 1854	Kamehameha III (*b* Kauikeaouli) (*brother*)
	Regents: 1825-32 Kaahumanu
	1832-33 Kinau
Dec 1854-Nov 1863	Kamehameha IV (*b* Alexander Liholiho) (*nephew*)
Nov 1863-Dec 1872	Kamehameha V (*b* Lot Kamehameha) (*brother*)
Jan 1873-Feb 1874	Lunalino (*b* William Charles)
Feb 1874-Jan 1891	Kalakaua (*b* David)
Jan 1891-Jan 1893	Liliuokalani (*b* Lydia) (*sister*)

Prime Ministers:

Kuhina nui

May 1819-June 1832	Kaahumanu (†)
June 1832-April 1839	Kinau (*daughter of Kamehameha I*) (†)
April 1839-June 1845	M.A.Kekaulouhi (*mother of Lunalino*)
June 1845-Sept 1853	John Young (1st)
Sept 1853	Lot Kamehameha (later King)
Sept 1853-Jan 1855	John Young (2nd)
Jan 1855-Dec 1863	Victoria Kamamalu
Dec 1863-Aug 1864	Mataio Kekuanaoa
(Aug 1864	post abolished)

President:

Jan 1893-June 1900	Sanford Dole

Governors:

June 1900-Nov 1903	Sanford Dole (RP)
Nov 1903-Aug 1907	George Carter (RP)
Aug 1907-Nov 1913	Walter Frear (RP)
Nov 1913-June 1918	Lucius Pinkham (DP)
June 1918-July 1921	Charles McCarthy (DP)
July 1921-July 1929	Wallace Farrington (RP)
July 1929-March 1934	Lawrence Judd (RP)
March 1934-Aug 1942	Joseph Poindexter (DP)

Aug 1942-April 1951	Ingram Stainback (DP)
May 1951-Feb 1953	Oren Long (DP)
Feb 1953-July 1957	Samuel King (RP)
July-Sept 1957	Farrant Turner (acting)
Sept 1957-Dec 1962	William Quinn (RP)
Dec 1962-Dec 1974	John Burns (DP)
Dec 1974-Dec 1986	George Ariyoshi (DP)
Dec 1986-Dec 1994	John Waihee (DP)
Dec 1994-	Benjamin Cayetano (DP)

IDAHO

Statehood: 3 July 1890
Capital: Boise

Governors:

1863	William Wallace (RP)
1863-64	William Daniels (acting) (RP)
1864-65	Caleb Lyon (RP)
1865	C.de Witt Smith (acting) (RP)
1866	Horace Gilson (acting) (RP)
1866-70	David Ballard (RP)
1870-71	Edward Curtis (acting) (1st) (RP)
1871	Thomas Bowen (RP)
1871	Edward Curtis (acting) (2nd) (RP)
1871-75	Thomas Bennett (RP)
1875	Edward Curtis (acting) (3rd)
1875-76	David Thompson (RP)
1876-78	Mason Brayman (RP)
1878-80	R.A.Sidebottom (acting) (RP)
1880-83	John Neil (RP)
1883	Edward Curtis (acting) (4th) (RP)
1883	John Irwin (RP)
1883-84	Edward Curtis (acting) (5th) (RP)
1884-85	William Bunn (RP)
1885-89	Edward Stephenson (DP)
Jan 1889-Dec 1890	George Shoup (RP)
Dec 1890-Jan 1893	Norman Willey (RP)
Jan 1893-Jan 1897	William McConnell (RP)
Jan 1897-Jan 1901	Frank Steunenberg (DP) (assassinated 1905)
Jan 1901-Jan 1903	Frank Hunt (DP)
Jan 1903-Jan 1905	John Morrison (RP)
Jan 1905-Jan 1909	Frank Gooding (RP)
Jan 1909-Jan 1911	James Brady (RP)

Jan 1911-Jan 1913	James Hawley (DP)
Jan 1913-Jan 1915	John Haines (RP)
Jan 1915-Jan 1919	Moses Alexander (DP)
Jan 1919-Jan 1923	David Davis (RP)
Jan 1923-Jan 1927	Charles Moore (RP)
Jan 1927-Jan 1931	H.Clarence Baldridge (RP)
Jan 1931-Jan 1937	C.Ben Ross (DP)
Jan 1937-Jan 1939	Barzilla Clark (DP)
Jan 1939-Jan 1941	Clarence Bottolfsen (1st) (RP)
Jan 1941-Jan 1943	Chase Clark (*brother of B.Clark*) (DP)
Jan 1943-Jan 1945	Clarence Bottolfsen (2nd) (RP)
Jan-Nov 1945	Charles Gossett (DP)
Nov 1945-Jan 1947	Arnold Williams (DP)
Jan 1947-Jan 1951	Charles Robins (RP)
Jan 1951-Jan 1955	Len Jordan (RP)
Jan 1955-Jan 1967	Robert Smylie (RP)
Jan 1967-Jan 1971	Don Samuelson (RP)
Jan 1971-Jan 1977	Cecil Andrus (1st) (DP)
Jan 1977-Jan 1987	John V.Evans (DP)
Jan 1987-Jan 1995	Cecil Andrus (2nd) (DP)
Jan 1995-Jan 1999	Phil Batt (RP)
Jan 1999-	Dirk Kempthorne (RP)

ILLINOIS

Statehood: 3 December 1818
Capital: Springfield

Governors:

1809-Oct 1818	Ninian Edwards (1st)
Oct 1818-Dec 1822	Shadrach Bond (DRP)
Dec 1822-Dec 1826	Edward Coles (DRP)
Dec 1826-Dec 1830	Ninian Edwards (2nd) (DRP)
Dec 1830-Nov 1834	John Reynolds (DP)
Nov-Dec 1834	William Ewing (DP)
Dec 1834-Dec 1838	Joseph Duncan (DP)
Dec 1838-Dec 1842	Thomas Carlin (DP)
Dec 1842-Dec 1846	Thomas Ford (DP)
Dec 1846-Jan 1853	Augustus French (DP)
Jan 1853-Jan 1857	Joel Matteson (DP)
Jan 1857-March 1860	William Bissel (RP)
March 1860-Jan 1861	John Wood (RP)
Jan 1861-Jan 1865	Richard Yates (RP)
Jan 1865-Jan 1869	Richard Oglesby (1st) (RP)

Jan 1869-Jan 1873	John Palmer (RP)
13-23 Jan 1873	Richard Oglesby (2nd) (RP)
Jan 1873-Jan 1877	John Beveridge (RP)
Jan 1877-Feb 1883	Shelby Cullom (RP)
Feb 1883-Jan 1885	John Hamilton (RP)
Jan 1885-Jan 1889	Richard Oglesby (3rd) (RP)
Jan 1889-Jan 1893	Joseph Fifer (RP)
Jan 1893-Jan 1897	John Altgeld (DP)
Jan 1897-Jan 1901	John Tanner (RP)
Jan 1901-Jan 1905	Richard Yates (RP)
Jan 1905-Feb 1913	Charles Deneen (RP)
Feb 1913-Jan 1917	Edward Dunne (DP)
Jan 1917-Jan 1921	Frank Lowden (RP)
Jan 1921-Jan 1929	Len Small (RP)
Jan 1929-Jan 1933	Louis Emmerson (RP)
Jan 1933-Oct 1940	Henry Horner (DP)
Oct 1940-Jan 1941	John Steele (DP)
Jan 1941-Jan 1949	Dwight Green (RP)
Jan 1949-Jan 1953	Adlai Stevenson (DP)
Jan 1953-Jan 1961	William Stratton (RP)
Jan 1961-May 1968	Otto Kerner (DP)
May 1968-Jan 1973	Richard Ogilvie (RP)
Jan 1973-Jan 1977	Daniel Walker (DP)
Jan 1977-Jan 1991	James Thompson (RP)
Jan 1991-Jan 1999	Jim Edgar (RP)
Jan 1999-	George Ryan (RP)

INDIANA

Statehood: 11 December 1816
Capital: Indianapolis

Governors:

1800-01	John Gibson (acting) (1st)
1801-12	William Harrison
1812-13	John Gibson (acting) (2nd)
1813-16	Thomas Posey
Nov 1816-Sept 1822	Jonathan Jennings (DRP)
Sept-Dec 1822	Ratliff Boon (DRP)
Dec 1822-Feb 1825	William Hendricks (DRP)
Feb 1825-Dec 1831	James Ray (DRP)
Dec 1831-Dec 1837	Noah Noble (NRP)
Dec 1837-Dec 1840	David Wallace (WP)
Dec 1840-Dec 1843	Samuel Bigger (WP)

Dec 1843-Dec 1848   James Whitcomb   (DP)
Dec 1848-Dec 1849   Paris Dunning   (DP)
Dec 1849-Jan 1857   Joseph Wright   (DP)
Jan 1857-Oct 1860   Ashbel Willard   (DP)
Oct 1860-Jan 1861   Abram Hammond   (DP)
14-16 Jan 1861   Henry Lane   (RP)
Jan 1861-Jan 1867   Oliver Morton   (RP)
Jan 1867-Jan 1873   Conrad Baker   (RP)
Jan 1873-Jan 1877   Thomas Hendricks   (DP)
Jan 1877-Nov 1880   James Williams   (DP)
Nov 1880-Jan 1881   Isaac Gray   (acting) (DP)
Jan 1881-Jan 1885   Albert Porter   (RP)
Jan 1885-Jan 1889   Isaac Gray   (DP)
Jan 1889-Nov 1891   Alvin Hovey   (RP)
Nov 1891-Jan 1893   Ira Chase   (RP)
Jan 1893-Jan 1897   Claude Matthews   (DP)
Jan 1897-Jan 1901   James Mount   (RP)
Jan 1901-Jan 1905   Winfield Durbin   (RP)
Jan 1905-Jan 1909   J.Frank Hanley   (RP)
Jan 1909-Jan 1913   Thomas Marshall   (DP)
Jan 1913-Jan 1917   Samuel Ralston   (DP)
Jan 1917-Jan 1921   James Goodrich   (RP)
Jan 1921-April 1924   Warren McCray   (RP)
April 1924-Jan 1925   Emmet Branch   (RP)
Jan 1925-Jan 1929   Ed Jackson   (RP)
Jan 1929-Jan 1933   Harry Leslie   (RP)
Jan 1933-Jan 1937   Paul McNutt   (DP)
Jan 1937-Jan 1941   Clifford Townsend   (DP)
Jan 1941-Jan 1945   Henry Shricker   (1st) (DP)
Jan 1945-Jan 1949   Ralph Gates   (RP)
Jan 1949-Jan 1953   Henry Shricker   (2nd) (DP)
Jan 1953-Jan 1957   George Craig   (RP)
Jan 1957-Jan 1961   Harold Handley   (RP)
Jan 1961-Jan 1965   Matthew Welsh   (DP)
Jan 1965-Jan 1969   Roger Branigan   (DP)
Jan 1969-Jan 1973   Edgar Whitcomb   (RP)
Jan 1973-Jan 1981   Otis Bowen   (RP)
Jan 1981-Jan 1989   Robert Orr   (RP)
Jan 1989-Jan 1997   Evan Bayh   (DP)
Jan 1997-   Frank O'Bannon   (DP)

IOWA

Statehood: 28 December 1846
Capital: Des Moines

Governors:

1838-41	Robert Lucas
1841-45	John Chambers
1845-46	James Clark
Dec 1846-Dec 1850	Ansel Biggs (DP)
Dec 1850-Dec 1854	Stephen Hempstead (DP)
Dec 1854-Jan 1858	James Grimes (WP)
Jan 1858-Jan 1860	Ralph Lowe (RP)
Jan 1860-Jan 1864	Samuel Kirkwood (1st) (RP)
Jan 1864-Jan 1868	William Stone (RP)
Jan 1868-Jan 1872	Samuel Merrill (RP)
Jan 1872-Jan 1876	Cyrus Carpenter (RP)
Jan 1876-Feb 1877	Samuel Kirkwood (2nd) (RP)
Feb 1877-Jan 1878	Joshua Newbold (RP)
Jan 1878-Jan 1882	John Gear (RP)
Jan 1882-Jan 1886	Buren Sherman (RP)
Jan 1886-Feb 1890	William Larrabee (RP)
Feb 1890-Jan 1894	Horace Boies (DP)
Jan 1894-Jan 1896	Frank Jackson (RP)
Jan 1896-Jan 1898	Francis Drake (RP)
Jan 1898-Jan 1902	Leslie Shaw (RP)
Jan 1902-Nov 1908	Albert Cummins (RP)
Nov 1908-Jan 1909	Warren Garst (RP)
Jan 1909-Jan 1913	Beryl Carroll (RP)
Jan 1913-Jan 1917	George Clarke (RP)
Jan 1917-Jan 1921	William Harding (RP)
Jan 1921-Jan 1925	Nathan Kendall (RP)
Jan 1925-Jan 1931	John Hammill (RP)
Jan 1931-Jan 1933	Daniel Turner (RP)
Jan 1933-Jan 1937	Clyde Herring (DP)
Jan 1937-Jan 1939	Nelson Kraschel (DP)
Jan 1939-Jan 1943	George Wilson (RP)
Jan 1943-Jan 1945	Bourke Hickenlooper (RP)
Jan 1945-Jan 1949	Robert Blue (RP)
Jan 1949-Nov 1954	William Beards (RP) († motor accident)
Nov 1954-Jan 1955	Leo Elthon (RP)
Jan 1955-Jan 1957	Leo Hoegh (RP)
Jan 1957-Jan 1961	Herschel Loveless (DP)
Jan 1961-Jan 1963	Norman Erbe (RP)
Jan 1963-Jan 1969	Harold Hughes (DP)
1-16 Jan 1969	Robert Fulton
Jan 1969-Jan 1983	Robert Ray (RP)
Jan 1983-Jan 1999	Terry Branstad (RP)
Jan 1999-	Tom Vilsack (DP)

KANSAS

Statehood: 29 January 1861
Capital: Topeka

Governors:

1854-55	Andrew Reeder
1855-56	Wilson Shannon
1856-57	John Geary
1857	Robert Walker
1857-58	James Denver
1858-60	Samuel Medary
1860-61	George Beebe (acting)
Feb 1861-Jan 1863	Charles Robinson (RP)
Jan 1863-Jan 1865	Thomas Carney (RP)
Jan 1865-Nov 1868	Samuel Crawford (RP)
Nov 1868-Jan 1869	Nehemiah Green (acting) (RP)
Jan 1869-Jan 1973	James Harvey (RP)
Jan 1873-Jan 1877	Thomas Osborn (RP)
Jan 1877-Jan 1879	George Anthony (RP)
Jan 1879-Jan 1883	John St John (RP)
Jan 1883-Jan 1885	George Glick (DP)
Jan 1885-Jan 1889	John A.Martin (RP)
Jan 1889-Jan 1893	Lyman Humphrey (RP)
Jan 1893-Jan 1895	Lorenzo Lewelling (PP)
Jan 1895-Jan 1897	Edmund Morrill (RP)
Jan 1897-Jan 1899	John Leedy (PP)
Jan 1899-Jan 1903	William Stanley (RP)
Jan 1903-Jan 1905	William Bailey (RP)
Jan 1905-Jan 1909	Edward Hoch (RP)
Jan 1909-Jan 1913	Walter Stubbs (RP)
Jan 1913-Jan 1915	George Hodges (DP)
Jan 1915-Jan 1919	Arthur Capper (RP)
Jan 1919-Jan 1923	Henry Allen (RP)
Jan 1923-Jan 1925	Jonathan Davis (DP)
Jan 1925-Jan 1929	Ben Paulen (RP)
Jan 1929-Jan 1931	Clyde Reed (RP)
Jan 1931-Jan 1933	Harry Woodring (DP)
Jan 1933-Jan 1937	Alfred Landon (RP)
Jan 1937-Jan 1939	Walter Huxman (DP)
Jan 1939-Jan 1943	Payne Ratner (RP)
Jan 1943-Jan 1947	Andrew Schoeppel (RP)
Jan 1947-Nov 1950	Frank Carlson (RP)
Nov 1950-Jan 1951	Frank Hagaman (RP)
Jan 1951-Jan 1955	Edward Arn (RP)

Jan 1955-Jan 1957	Fred Hall (RP)
3-14 Jan 1957	John McCuish (RP)
Jan 1957-Jan 1961	George Docking (DP)
Jan 1961-Jan 1965	John Anderson (RP)
Jan 1965-Jan 1967	William Avery (RP)
Jan 1967-Jan 1975	Robert Docking (*son of G.Docking*) (DP)
Jan 1975-Jan 1979	Robert Bennett (RP)
Jan 1979-Jan 1987	John Carlin (DP)
Jan 1987-Jan 1991	John (Mike) Hayden (RP)
Jan 1991-Jan 1995	Joan Finney (*b* J. McInroy) (DP)
Jan 1995-	Bill Graves (RP)

KENTUCKY

Statehood: 1 June 1792
Capital: Frankfort

Governors:

June 1792-June 1796	Isaac Shelby (1st) (DRP)
June 1796-June 1804	James Garrard (DRP)
June 1804-June 1808	Christopher Greeneys (DRP)
June 1808-June 1812	Charles Scott (DRP)
June 1812-June 1816	Isaac Shelby (2nd) (DRP)
June-Oct 1816	George Madison (DRP)
Oct 1816-June 1820	Gabriel Slaughter (DRP)
June 1820-June 1824	John Adair (DRP)
June 1824-June 1828	Joseph Desha (DRP)
June 1828-June 1832	Thomas Metcalf (NRP)
June 1832-Feb 1834	John Breathitt (DP)
Feb 1834-June 1836	James Moorehead (NRP)
June 1836-Sept 1839	James Clark (WP)
Sept 1839-June 1840	Charles Wickliffe (WP)
June 1840-June 1844	Robert Lecher (WP)
June 1844-June 1848	William Owsley (WP)
June 1848-July 1850	John Crittenden (WP)
July 1850-Sept 1851	John Helm (1st) (WP)
Sept 1851-Sept 1855	Lazarus Powell (DP)
Sept 1855-Sept 1859	Charles Moorehead (KNP)
Sept 1859-Aug 1862	Beriah Magoffin (DP)
Aug 1862-Sept 1863	James Robinson (UP)
Sept 1863-Sept 1867	Thomas Bramlette (UP)
3-8 Sept 1867	John Helm (†) (2nd) (DP)
Sept 1867-Feb 1871	John Stevenson (DP)
Feb 1871-Sept 1875	Preston Leslie (DP)

Sept 1875-Sept 1879	James McCreary	(DP)
Sept 1879-Sept 1883	Luke Blackburn	(DP)
Sept 1883-Sept 1887	J.Proctor Knott	(DP)
Sept 1887-Sept 1891	Simon Buckner	(DP)
Sept 1891-Dec 1895	John Y.Brown	(DP)
Dec 1895-Dec 1899	William Bradley	(RP)
Dec 1899-Jan 1900	William Taylor	(RP)
Jan-Feb 1900	William Goebel	(DP)
Feb 1900-Dec 1907	John Beckham	(DP)
Dec 1907-Dec 1911	Augustus Wilson	(RP)
Dec 1911-Dec 1915	James McCreary	(DP)
Dec 1915-Dec 1919	Augustus Wilson	(RP)
Dec 1919-Jan 1924	Edwin Morrow	(RP)
Jan 1924-Dec 1927	William Fields	(DP)
Dec 1927-Dec 1931	Flem Sampson	(RP)
Dec 1931-Dec 1935	Ruby Lafoon	(DP)
Dec 1935-Dec 1939	Albert Chandler (1st)	(DP)
Dec 1939-Dec 1943	Keen Johnson	(DP)
Dec 1943-Dec 1947	Simeon Willis	(RP)
Dec 1947-Dec 1951	Earle Clements	(DP)
Dec 1951-Dec 1955	Lawrence Weatherby	(DP)
Dec 1955-Dec 1959	Albert Chandler (2nd)	(DP)
Dec 1959-Dec 1963	Bert Combs	(DP)
Dec 1963-Dec 1967	Edward Breathitt	(DP)
Dec 1967-Dec 1971	Louie Nunn	(RP)
Dec 1971-Dec 1974	Wendell Ford	(DP)
Dec 1974-Dec 1979	Julian Carroll	(DP)
Dec 1979-Dec 1983	John Y.Brown Jr	(DP)
Dec 1983-Dec 1987	Martha Layne Collins (*b* M.Hall)	(DP)
Dec 1987-Dec 1991	Wallace Wilkinson	(DP)
Dec 1991-Dec 1995	Brereton Jones	(DP)
Dec 1995-	Paul Patten	(DP)

LOUISIANA

Previous name: New Orleans until 1816
Statehood: 30 April 1812
Capital: Baton Rouge

Governors:

Dec 1804-Dec 1816	William Claiborne	(DRP)
Dec 1816-Dec 1820	Jacques Villere	(DRP)
Dec 1820-Nov 1824	Thomas Robertson	(DRP)
Nov-Dec 1824	Henry Thibodeaux (acting)	(DRP)

Dec 1824-Dec 1828	Henry Johnson (AP)
Dec 1828-June 1829	Pierre Derbigny (AP)
June 1829-Jan 1830	Armand Beauvais (acting) (NRP)
Jan 1830-Jan 1831	Jacques Dupre (acting) (NRP)
Jan 1831-Feb 1835	André Roman (1st) (NRP)
Feb 1835-Feb 1839	Edward White (WP)
Feb 1839-Jan 1843	André Roman (2nd) (WP)
Jan 1843-Feb 1846	Alexander Mouton (DP)
Feb 1846-Jan 1850	Isaac Johnson (DP)
Jan 1850-Jan 1853	Joseph Walker (DP)
Jan 1853-Jan 1856	Paul Hebert (DP)
Jan 1856-Jan 1860	Robert Wickliffe (DP)
Jan 1860-March 1864	Thomas Moore (DP)
March-April 1864	Henry Allen (DP)
April 1864-March 1865	Michael Hahn (acting April-June 1864) (UP)
March 1865-June 1867	James Wells (acting March-Dec 1865)
June 1867-Jan 1868	Benjamin Flanders (acting)
Jan-June 1868	James Baker
June 1868-Sept 1872	Henry Warmoth (acting) (RP)
Sept 1872-Jan 1873	Pinckney Pinchback (acting) (RP)
Jan 1873-Jan 1877	William Kellogg (RP)
Jan 1877-Jan 1880	Francis Nicholls (1st) (DP)
Jan 1880-Oct 1881	Louis Wiltz (DP) (†)
Oct 1881-May 1888	Samuel McEnery (acting Oct 1881-May 1884) (DP)
May 1888-May 1892	Francis Nicholls (2nd) (DP)
May 1892-May 1900	Murphy Foster (DP)
May 1900-May 1904	William Heard (DP)
May 1904-May 1908	Newton Blanchard (DP)
May 1908-May 1912	Jared Sanders (DP)
May 1912-May 1916	Luther Hall (DP)
May 1916-May 1920	Ruffin Pleasant (DP)
May 1920-May 1924	John Parker (DP)
May 1924-Oct 1926	Henry Fuqua (DP) (†)
Oct 1926-May 1928	Oramel Simpson (acting) (DP)
May 1928-Jan 1932	Huey Long (DP) (assassinated 1935)
Jan-May 1932	Alvin King (acting) (DP)
May 1932-Jan 1936	Oscar Allen (DP) (†)
Jan-May 1936	James Noe (acting) (DP)
May 1936-June 1939	Richard Leche (DP)
June 1939-May 1940	Earl Long (acting) (*brother of H.Long*) (DP)
May 1940-May 1944	Sam Jones (DP)
May 1944-May 1948	James Davies (1st) (DP)
May 1948-May 1952	Earl Long (1st) (DP)
May 1952-May 1956	Robert Kennon (DP)
May 1956-May 1960	Earl Long (2nd) (DP)

May 1960-May 1964	James Davies (2nd) (DP)
May 1964-May 1972	John McKeithen (DP)
May 1972-May 1980	Edwin Edwards (1st) (DP)
May 1980-May 1984	David Treen (RP)
May 1984-May 1988	Edwin Edwards (2nd) (DP)
May 1988-May 1992	Charles (Buddy) Roemer (DP,RP)
Jan 1992- Jan 1996	Edwin Edwards (3rd) (DP)
Jan 1996-	Murphy (Mike) Foster (*grandson of M. Foster*) (RP)

MAINE

Statehood: 15 March 1820
Capital: Augusta

Governors:

March 1820-May 1821	William King (DRP)
May-Dec 1821	William Williamson (acting) (DRP)
Dec 1821-Jan 1822	Benjamin Ames (acting) (DRP)
2-5 Jan 1822	Daniel Rose
Jan 1822-Jan 1827	Albion Parris (DRP)
Jan 1827-Oct 1829	Enoch Lincoln (DRP)
Oct 1829-Feb 1830	Nathan Cutler (acting) (DP)
3 Feb 1830	Joshua Hall (acting) (DP)
Feb 1830-Jan 1831	Jonathan Hunton (DP)
Jan 1831-Jan 1834	Samuel Smith (DP)
Jan 1834-Jan 1838	Robert Dunlap (DP)
Jan 1838-Jan 1839	Edward Kent (1st) (WP)
Jan 1839-Jan 1840	John Fairfield (1st) (DP)
Jan 1840-Jan 1841	Edward Kent (2nd) (WP)
Jan 1841-March 1843	John Fairfield (2nd) (DP)
March 1843-Jan 1844	Edward Kavanaugh (acting) (DP)
Jan 1844-May 1847	Hugh Anderson (DP)
May 1847-May 1850	John Dana (DP)
May 1850-Jan 1853	John Hubbard (DP)
Jan 1853-Jan 1855	William Crosby (WP)
Jan 1855-Jan 1856	Anson Morrill (RP)
Jan 1856-Jan 1857	Samuel Wells (DP)
Jan-Feb 1857	Hannibal Hamlin (RP)
Feb 1857-Jan 1858	Joseph Williams (acting) (RP)
Jan 1858-Jan 1861	Lot Morrill (*brother of A.Morrill*) (RP)
Jan 1861-Jan 1863	Israel Washburn (RP)
Jan 1863-Jan 1864	Abner Coburn (RP)
Jan 1864-Jan 1867	Samuel Cony (DP)
Jan 1867-Jan 1871	Joshua Chamberlain (RP)
Jan 1871-Jan 1874	Sidney Perham (RP)

Jan 1874-Jan 1876   Nelson Dingley   (RP)
Jan 1876-Jan 1879   Seldon Connor   (RP)
Jan 1879-Jan 1880   Alonzo Garcelon   (DP)
Jan 1880-Jan 1881   Daniel Davis   (RP)
Jan 1881-Jan 1883   Harris Plaisted   (DP)
Jan 1883-Jan 1887   Frederick Robie   (RP)
Jan-Dec 1887   Joseph Bodwell   (RP)
Dec 1887-Jan 1889   Sebastian Marble   (acting) (RP)
Jan 1889-Jan 1893   Edwin Burleigh   (RP)
Jan 1893-Jan 1897   Henry Cleaves   (RP)
Jan 1897-Jan 1901   Llewellyn Powers   (RP)
Jan 1901-Jan 1905   John Hill   (RP)
Jan 1905-Jan 1909   William Cobb   (RP)
Jan 1909-Jan 1911   Bert Fernald   (RP)
Jan 1911-Jan 1913   Frederick Plaisted   (*son of H.Plaisted*) (DP)
Jan 1913-Jan 1915   William Haines   (RP)
Jan 1915-Jan 1917   Oakley Curtis   (DP)
Jan 1917-Jan 1921   Carl Milliken   (RP)
5-31 Jan 1921   Frederick Parkhurst   (RP)
Jan 1921-Jan 1925   Percival Baxter   (RP)
Jan 1925-Jan 1929   Owen Brewster   (RP)
Jan 1929-Jan 1933   William Gardiner   (RP)
Jan 1933-Jan 1937   Louis Brann   (DP)
Jan 1937-Jan 1941   Lewis Barrows   (RP)
Jan 1941-Jan 1945   Sumner Sewall   (RP)
Jan 1945-Jan 1949   Horace Hildreth   (RP)
Jan 1949-Dec 1952   Frederick Payne   (RP)
Dec 1952-Dec 1955   Burton Cross   (RP)
Dec 1955-Jan 1959   Edmund Muskie   (DP)
2-7 Jan 1959   Robert Haskell
Jan-Dec 1959   Clinton Clauson   (DP)
Dec 1959-Jan 1967   John Reed   (RP)
Jan 1967-Jan 1975   Kenneth Curtis   (DP)
Jan 1975-Jan 1979   James Longley   (Ind)
Jan 1979-Jan 1987   Joseph Brennan   (DP)
Jan 1987-Jan 1995   John McKernan   (RP)
Jan 1995-   Angus King   (Ind)

MARYLAND

One of the original 13 states
Capital: Annapolis

Governors:

March 1777-Nov 1779   Thomas Johnson

Nov 1779-Nov 1782	Thomas Sim Lee (1st)
Nov 1782-Nov 1785	William Paca
Nov 1785-Nov 1788	William Smallwood
Nov 1788-Nov 1791	John Howard (FP)
Nov 1791-Feb 1792	George Plater (FP)
Feb-April 1792	James Brice (acting) (FP)
April 1792-Nov 1794	Thomas Sim Lee (2nd) (FP)
Nov 1794-Nov 1797	John Stone (FP)
Nov 1797-Nov 1798	John Henry (FP)
Nov 1798-Nov 1801	Benjamin Ogle (FP)
Nov 1801-Nov 1803	John Mercer (DRP)
Nov 1803-Nov 1806	Robert Bowie (1st) (DRP)
Nov 1806-May 1809	Robert Wright (DRP)
May-June 1809	James Butcher (acting) (DRP)
June 1809-Nov 1811	Edward Lloyd (DRP)
Nov 1811-Nov 1812	Robert Bowie (2nd) (DRP)
Nov 1812-Jan 1816	Levin Winder (FP)
Jan 1816-Jan 1819	Charles Ridgely (FP)
Jan-Dec 1819	Charles Goldsborough (FP)
Dec 1819-Dec 1822	Samuel Sprigg (DRP)
Dec 1822-Jan 1826	Samuel Stevens (DRP)
Jan 1826-Jan 1829	Joseph Kent (DRP)
Jan 1829-Jan 1830	Daniel Martin (1st) (A-JD)
Jan 1830-Jan 1831	Thomas Carroll (DP)
Jan-July 1831	Daniel Martin (2nd) (A-JD)
July 1831-Jan 1833	George Howard (WP)
Jan 1833-Jan 1836	James Thomas (WP)
Jan 1836-Jan 1839	Thomas Veazey (WP)
Jan 1839-Jan 1842	William Grayson (DP)
Jan 1842-Jan 1845	Francis Thomas (DP)
Jan 1845-Jan 1848	Thomas Pratt (WP)
Jan 1848-Jan 1851	Philip Thomas (DP)
Jan 1851-Jan 1854	Enoch Lowe (DP)
Jan 1854-Jan 1858	Thomas Ligon (DP)
Jan 1858-Jan 1862	Thomas Hicks (KNP)
Jan 1862-Jan 1866	August Bradford (UP)
Jan 1866-Jan 1869	Thomas Swann (UP,DP)
Jan 1869-Jan 1872	Oden Bowie (DP)
Jan 1872-March 1874	William Whyte (DP)
March 1874-Jan 1876	James Groome (DP)
Jan 1876-Jan 1880	John Carroll (DP)
Jan 1880-Jan 1884	William Hamilton (DP)
Jan 1884-March 1885	Robert McLane (DP)
March 1885-Jan 1888	Henry Lloyd (acting March 1885-Jan 1886) (DP)
Jan 1888-Jan 1892	Eliha Jackson (DP)

Jan 1892-Jan 1896	Frank Brown (DP)
Jan 1896-Jan 1900	Lloyd Lownes (RP)
Jan 1900-Jan 1904	John W.Smith (DP)
Jan 1904-Jan 1908	Edwin Warfield (DP)
Jan 1908-Jan 1912	Austin Crothers (DP)
Jan 1912-Jan 1916	Philips Goldsborough (RP)
Jan 1916-Jan 1920	Emerson Harrington (DP)
Jan 1920-Jan 1935	Albert Ritchie (DP)
Jan 1935-Jan 1939	Harry Nice (RP)
Jan 1939-Jan 1947	Herbert O'Connor (DP)
Jan 1947-Jan 1951	William Lane (DP)
Jan 1951-Jan 1959	Theodore McKeldin (RP)
Jan 1959-Jan 1967	J.Millard Tawes (DP)
Jan 1967-Jan 1969	Spiro Agnew (RP)
Jan 1969-June 1977	Marvin Mandel (DP)
June 1977-Jan 1979	Blair Lee (DP)
Jan 1979-Jan 1987	Harry Hughes (DP)
Jan 1987-Jan 1995	William Schaefer (DP)
Jan 1995-	Parris Glendening (DP)

MASSACHUSETTS

One of the original 13 states
Capital: Boston

Governors:

Jan 1780-Jan 1785	John Hancock (1st)
Jan 1785-Jan 1787	James Bodwin
Jan 1787-Oct 1793	John Hancock (2nd) (†)
Oct 1793-Jan 1797	Samuel Adams (acting 1793-94)
Jan 1797-June 1799	Increase Sumner (FP)
June 1799-May 1800	Moses Gill (acting) (FP) (†)
May 1800-Jan 1807	Caleb Strong (1st) (FP)
Jan 1807-Dec 1808	James Sullivan (DRP) (†)
Dec 1808-Jan 1809	Levi Lincoln (acting) (DRP)
Jan 1809-Jan 1810	Christopher Gore (FP)
Jan 1810-Jan 1812	Elbridge Gerry (DRP)
Jan 1812-Jan 1816	Caleb Strong (2nd) (FP)
Jan 1816-Jan 1823	John Brookes (FP)
Jan 1823-Feb 1825	William Eustis (DRP) (†)
Feb-July 1825	Marcus Morton (acting) (DRP)
July 1825-Jan 1834	Levi Lincoln (DRP)
Jan 1834-March 1835	John Davis (1st) (WP)
March 1835-Jan 1836	Samuel Armstrong (acting) (WP)

Jan 1836-Jan 1840	Edward Everett (WP)
Jan 1840-Jan 1841	Marcus Morton (DP)
Jan 1841-Jan 1843	John Davis (2nd) (WP)
Jan 1843-Jan 1851	George Briggs (WP)
Jan 1851-Jan 1853	George Boutwell (DP)
Jan 1853-Jan 1854	John Clifford (WP)
Jan 1854-Jan 1855	Emory Washburn (WP)
Jan 1855-Jan 1858	Henry Gardner (KNP)
Jan 1858-Jan 1861	Nathaniel Banks (RP)
Jan 1861-Jan 1866	John Andrew (RP)
Jan 1866-Jan 1869	Alexander Bullock (RP)
Jan 1869-Jan 1872	William Claflin (RP)
Jan 1872-April 1874	William Washburn (RP)
May 1874-Jan 1875	Thomas Talbot (acting) (RP)
Jan 1875-Jan 1876	William Gaston (DP)
Jan 1876-Jan 1879	Alexander Rice (RP)
Jan 1879-Jan 1880	Thomas Talbot (RP)
Jan 1880-Jan 1883	John Long (RP)
Jan 1883-Jan 1884	Benjamin Butler (DP,Ind)
Jan 1884-Jan 1887	George Robinson (RP)
Jan 1887-Jan 1890	Oliver Ames (RP)
Jan 1890-Jan 1891	John Brackett (RP)
Jan 1891-Jan 1894	William Russell (DP)
Jan 1894-March 1896	Frederic Greenhalge (RP) (†)
March 1896-Jan 1900	Roger Wolcott (acting 1896-97) (RP)
Jan 1900-Jan 1903	W.Murray Crane (RP)
Jan 1903-Jan 1905	John Bates (RP)
Jan 1905-Jan 1906	William Douglas (DP)
Jan 1906-Jan 1909	Curtis Guild (RP)
Jan 1909-Jan 1911	Eben Draper (RP)
Jan 1911-Jan 1914	Eugene Foss (PDP)
Jan 1914-Jan 1916	David Walsh (DP)
Jan 1916-Jan 1919	Samuel McCall (RP)
Jan 1919-March 1921	Calvin Coolidge (later President) (RP)
March 1921-Jan 1925	Channing Fox (RP)
Jan 1925-Jan 1929	Alvin Fuller (RP)
Jan 1929-Jan 1931	Frank Allen (RP)
Jan 1931-Jan 1935	Joseph Ely (DP)
Jan 1935-Jan 1937	James Curley (DP)
Jan 1937-Jan 1939	Charles Hurley (DP)
Jan 1939-Jan 1945	Leverett Saltonstall (RP)
Jan 1945-Jan 1947	Maurice Tobin (DP)
Jan 1947-Jan 1949	Robert Bradford (RP)
Jan 1949-Jan 1953	Paul Dever (DP)
Jan 1953-Jan 1957	Christian Herter (RP)

Jan 1957-Jan 1961	Foster Furcolo (DP)
Jan 1961-Jan 1963	John Volpe (1st) (RP)
Jan 1963-Jan 1965	Endicott Peabody (DP)
Jan 1965-Jan 1969	John Volpe (2nd) (RP)
Jan 1969-Jan 1975	Francis Sargent (acting 1969-71) (RP)
Jan 1975-Jan 1979	Michael Dukakis (1st) (DP)
Jan 1979-Jan 1983	Edward King (DP)
Jan 1983-Jan 1991	Michael Dukakis (2nd) (DP)
Jan 1991-July 1997	William Weld (RP)
July 1997-	Paul Cellucci (RP)

MICHIGAN

Statehood: 26 January 1837
Capital: Lansing

Governors:

Jan 1805-Oct 1813	William Hull
Oct 1813-Aug 1831	Lewis Cass
Aug 1831-July 1834	George Potter
July 1834-Sept 1835	Stevens Mason (1st)
Sept-Nov 1835	John Horner (acting)
Nov 1835-Jan 1840	Stevens Mason (2nd) (DP)
Jan 1840-Feb 1841	William Woodbridge (WP)
Feb 1841-Jan 1842	James Gordon (acting) (WP)
Jan 1842-Jan 1846	John Barry (1st) (DP)
Jan 1846-March 1847	Alpheus Felch (DP)
March 1847-Jan 1848	William Greenly (acting) (DP)
Jan 1848-Jan 1850	Ephaphroditus Ransom (DP)
Jan 1850-Jan 1851	John Barry (2nd) (DP)
Jan 1851-March 1853	Robert McClelland (DP)
March 1853-March 1855	Andrew Parsons (acting) (DP)
March 1855-March 1859	Kinsley Bingham (RP)
March 1859-March 1861	Moses Wisner (RP)
March 1861-March 1865	Austin Blair (RP)
March 1865-March 1869	Henry Crapo (RP)
March 1869-March 1873	Henry Baldwin (RP)
March 1873-March 1877	John Bagley (RP)
March 1877-March 1881	Charles Croswell (RP)
March 1881-March 1883	David Jerome (RP)
March 1883-March 1885	Josiah Begole (DP)
March 1885-March 1887	Russell Alger (RP)
March 1887-March 1891	Cyrus Luce (RP)
March 1891-March 1893	Edwin Winans (DP)

March 1893-March 1897	John Rich (RP)
March 1897-March 1901	Hazen Pingree (RP)
March 1901-March 1905	Aaron Bliss (RP)
March 1905-March 1911	Fred Warner (RP)
March 1911-March 1913	Chase Osborn (RP)
March 1913-March 1917	Woodbridge Ferris (DP)
March 1917-March 1921	Albert Sleeper (RP)
March 1921-March 1925	Alexander Groesbeck (RP)
March 1925-March 1931	Fred Green (RP)
March 1931-March 1933	Wilber Brucker (RP)
March 1933-March 1935	William Comstock (DP)
March 1935-March 1937	Frank Fitzgerald (1st) (RP)
March 1937-March 1938	Frank Murphy (DP)
March 1938-March 1939	Frank Fitzgerald (2nd) (RP)
March 1939-Jan 1941	Luren Dickinson (RP)
Jan 1941-Jan 1943	Murray Van Wagoner (DP)
Jan 1943-Jan 1947	Harry Kelly (RP)
Jan 1947-Jan 1949	Kim Sigler (RP)
Jan 1949-Jan 1961	G.Mennen Williams (DP)
Jan 1961-Jan 1963	John Swainson (DP)
Jan 1963-Jan 1969	George Romney (RP)
Jan 1969-Jan 1983	William Milliken (RP)
Jan 1983-Jan 1991	James Blanchard (DP)
Jan 1991-	John Engler (RP)

MINNESOTA

Statehood: 11 May 1858
Capital: St Paul

Governors:

June 1849-May 1853	Alexander Ramsey (1st) (WP)
May 1853-April 1857	Willis Gorman (DP)
April 1857-May 1858	Samuel Medary (DP)
May 1858-Jan 1860	Henry Sibley (DP)
Jan 1860-July 1863	Alexander Ramsey (2nd) (RP)
July 1863-Jan 1864	Henry Swift (RP)
Jan 1864-Jan 1866	Stephen Miller (RP)
Jan 1866-Jan 1870	William Marshall (RP)
Jan 1870-Jan 1974	Horace Austin (RP)
Jan 1874-Jan 1876	Cushman Davis (RP)
Jan 1876-Jan 1882	John Pillsbury (RP)
Jan 1882-Jan 1887	Lucius Hubbard (RP)
Jan 1887-Jan 1889	Andrew McGill (RP)

Jan 1889-Jan 1893	William Merriam (RP)
Jan 1893-Jan 1895	Knute Nelson (RP)
Jan 1895-Jan 1899	David Clough (RP)
Jan 1899-Jan 1901	John Lind (DPP)
Jan 1901-Jan 1905	Samuel Van Sant (RP)
Jan 1905-Sept 1909	John Johnson (DP) (†)
Sept 1909-Jan 1915	Adolph Eberhart (RP)
Jan 1915-Dec 1917	William Hammond (DP) (†)
Dec 1917-Jan 1921	Joseph Burnquist (RP)
Jan 1921-Jan 1925	Jacob Preus (RP)
Jan 1925-Jan 1931	Thomas Christianson (RP)
Jan 1931-Aug 1936	Floyd Olson (FLP) (†)
Aug 1936-Jan 1937	Hjalmar Petersen (FLP)
Jan 1937-Jan 1939	Elmer Benson (FLP)
Jan 1939-April 1943	Harold Stassen (RP)
April 1943-Jan 1947	Edward Thye (RP)
Jan 1947-Sept 1951	Luther Youngdahl (RP)
Sept 1951-Jan 1955	C.Elmer Anderson (RP)
Jan 1955-Jan 1961	Orville Freeman (DFLP)
Jan 1961-March 1963	Elmer L.Anderson (RP)
March 1963-Jan 1967	Karl Rolvaag (DFLP)
Jan 1967-Jan 1971	Harold LeVander (RP)
Jan 1971-Dec 1976	Wendell Anderson (DFLP)
Dec 1976-Jan 1979	Rudolph Perpich (1st) (DFLP)
Jan 1979-Jan 1983	Albert Quie (IR)
Jan 1983-Jan 1991	Rudolph Perpich (2nd) (DFLP)
Jan 1991-Jan 1999	Arne Carlson (RP)
Jan 1999-	Jesse Ventura (Ref)

MISSISSIPPI

Statehood: 10 December 1817
Capital: Jackson

Governors:

May 1798-May 1801	Winthrop Sargent
May 1801-March 1805	William Claiborne
March 1805-March 1809	Robert Williams
March 1809-Jan 1820	David Holmes (1st) (DRP)
Jan 1820-Jan 1822	George Poindexter (DRP)
Jan 1822-Nov 1825	Walter Leake (DRP) (†)
Nov 1825-Jan 1826	Gerard Brandon (1st) (DRP)
Jan-July 1826	David Holmes (2nd) (DRP)
July 1826-Jan 1832	Gerard Brandon (2nd) (DRP)

Jan 1832-June 1833   Abram Scott   (DP) (†)
June-Nov 1833   Charles Lynch   (1st) (DP)
Nov 1833-Dec 1835   Hiram Runnels   (DP)
Dec 1835-Jan 1836   John Quitman   (1st) (WP)
Jan 1836-Jan 1838   Charles Lynch   (2nd) (DP)
Jan 1838-Jan 1842   Alexander McNutt   (DP)
Jan 1842-Jan 1844   Tilghman Tucker   (DP)
Jan 1844-Jan 1848   Albert G. Brown   (DP)
Jan 1848-Jan 1850   Joseph Matthews   (DP)
Jan 1850-Feb 1851   John Quitman   (2nd) (DP)
Feb-Nov 1851   John Guion   (DP)
Nov 1851-Jan 1852   James Whitfield   (DP)
Jan 1852-Jan 1854   Henry Foote   (UDP)
5-10 Jan 1854   John Pettus   (1st) (DP)
Jan 1854-Nov 1857   John McCrae   (DP)
Nov 1857-Nov 1859   William McWillie   (DP)
Nov 1859-Nov 1864   John Pettus   (2nd) (DP)
Nov 1864-June 1865   Charles Clark   (DP)
June-Oct 1865   William Sharkey
Oct 1865-June 1868   Benjamin Humphreys   (DP)
June 1868-March 1870   Adelbert Ames   (1st)
March 1870-Nov 1871   James Alcorn   (RP)
Nov 1871-Jan 1874   Ridgely Powers   (RP)
Jan 1874-March 1876   Adelbert Ames   (2nd) (RP)
March 1876-Jan 1882   John Stone   (1st) (DP)
Jan 1882-Jan 1890   Robert Lowry   (DP)
Jan 1890-Jan 1896   John Stone   (2nd) (DP)
Jan 1896-Jan 1900   Anselm McLaurin   (DP)
Jan 1900-Jan 1904   Andrew Longino   (DP)
Jan 1904-Jan 1908   James Vardaman   (DP)
Jan 1908-Jan 1912   Edmond Noel   (DP)
Jan 1912-Jan 1916   Earl Brewer   (DP)
Jan 1916-Jan 1920   Theodore Bilbo   (1st) (DP)
Jan 1920-Jan 1924   Lee Russell   (DP)
Jan 1924-Jan 1928   Henry Whitfield   (DP)
Jan 1928-Jan 1932   Theodore Bilbo   (2nd) (DP)
Jan 1932-Jan 1936   Martin Connor   (DP)
Jan 1936-Jan 1940   Hugh White   (1st) (DP)
Jan 1940-Jan 1943   Paul Johnson   (DP)
Jan 1943-Jan 1944   Dennis Murphee   (DP)
Jan 1944-Nov 1946   Thomas Bailey   (DP) (†)
Nov 1946-Jan 1952   Fielding Wright   (DP)
Jan 1952-Jan 1956   Hugh White   (2nd) (DP)
Jan 1956-Jan 1960   James Coleman   (DP)
Jan 1960-Jan 1964   Ross Barnett   (DP)

Jan 1964-Jan 1968	Paul Johnson Jr (*son of P.Johnson*) (DP)
Jan 1968-Jan 1972	John Bell Williams (DP)
Jan 1972-Jan 1976	William Waller (DP)
Jan 1976-Jan 1980	Cliff Finch (DP)
Jan 1980-Jan 1984	William Winter (DP)
Jan 1984-Jan 1988	William Allain (DP)
Jan 1988-Jan 1992	Ray Mabus (DP)
Jan 1992-Jan 2000	Kirk Fordyce (RP)
Jan 2000-	Ronnie Musgrove (DP)

MISSOURI

Statehood: 10 August 1821
Capital: Jefferson City

Governors:

March 1805-March 1807	James Wilkinson
1807	Joseph Browne (acting)
1807	Frederick Bates (acting) (1st)
1807-09	Meriweather Lewis
Oct 1809-April 1810	Frederick Bates (acting) (2nd)
April 1810-Feb 1812	Benjamin Howard
Feb 1812-June 1813	Frederick Bates (acting) (3rd)
June 1813-Sept 1820	William Clark
Sept 1820-Nov 1824	Alexander McNair (DRP)
Nov 1824-Aug 1825	Frederick Bates (DRP)
Aug 1825-Jan 1826	Abraham Williams (acting) (DRP)
Jan 1826-Nov 1832	John Miller (DRP)
Nov 1832-Sept 1836	Daniel Dunklin (DP)
Sept 1836-Nov 1840	Lilburn Boggs (DP)
Nov 1840-Feb 1844	Thomas Reynolds (DP)
Feb-Nov 1844	Meredith Marmaduke (acting) (DP)
Nov 1844-Dec 1848	John Edwards (DP)
Dec 1848-Jan 1853	Austin King (DP)
Jan 1853-Jan 1857	Sterling Price (DP)
Jan-Feb 1857	Trusten Polk (DP)
Feb-Oct 1857	Hancock Jackson (DP)
Oct 1857-Jan 1861	Robert Stewart (DP)
Jan-July 1861	Claiborne Jackson (DP)
July 1861-Jan 1864	Hamilton Gamble (UP)
Jan 1864-Jan 1865	Willard Hall (acting) (UP)
Jan 1865-Jan 1869	Thomas Fletcher (RP)
Jan 1869-Jan 1871	Joseph McClurg (RP)
Jan 1871-Jan 1873	Benjamin Gratz Brown (LRP)
Jan 1873-Jan 1875	Silas Woodson (LRP)

Jan 1875-Jan 1877	Charles Hardin (DP)
Jan 1877-Jan 1881	John Phelps (DP)
Jan 1881-Jan 1885	Thomas Crittenden (DP)
Jan 1885-Dec 1887	John Marmaduke (*son of M.Marmaduke*) (DP)
Dec 1887-Jan 1889	Albert Moorehouse (DP)
Jan 1889-Jan 1893	David Francis (DP)
Jan 1893-Jan 1897	William Stone (DP)
Jan 1897-Jan 1901	Lon Stephens (DP)
Jan 1901-Jan 1905	Alexander Dockery (DP)
Jan 1905-Jan 1909	Joseph Folk (DP)
Jan 1909-Jan 1913	Herbert Hadley (RP)
Jan 1913-Jan 1917	Elliott Major (DP)
Jan 1917-Jan 1921	Frederick Gardner (DP)
Jan 1921-Jan 1925	Arthur Hyde (RP)
Jan 1925-Jan 1929	Sam Baker (RP)
Jan 1929-Jan 1933	Henry Caulfield (RP)
Jan 1933-Jan 1937	Guy Park (DP)
Jan 1937-Feb 1941	Lloyd Stark (DP)
Feb 1941-Jan 1945	Forrest Donnell (RP)
Jan 1945-Jan 1949	Phil Donnelly (1st) (DP)
Jan 1949-Jan 1953	Forrest Smith (DP)
Jan 1953-Jan 1957	Phil Donnelly (2nd) (DP)
Jan 1957-Jan 1961	James Blair (DP)
Jan 1961-Jan 1965	John Dalton (DP)
Jan 1965-Jan 1973	Warren Hearnes (DP)
Jan 1973-Jan 1977	Christopher Bond (1st) (RP)
Jan 1977-Jan 1981	Joseph Teakle (DP)
Jan 1981-Jan 1985	Christopher Bond (2nd) (RP)
Jan 1985-Jan 1989	John Ashcroft (RP)
Jan 1989-	Mel Carnahan (DP)

MONTANA

Statehood: 8 November 1889
Capital: Helena

Governors:

June 1864-July 1866	Sidney Edgerton (RP)
July 1866-April 1869	Green Smith (RP)
April 1869-July 1870	James Ashley (RP)
July 1870-Jan 1883	Benjamin Potts (RP)
Jan 1883-Dec 1884	J.Schluyer Crosby (DP)
Dec 1884-July 1885	B.Platt Carpenter (RP)
July 1885-Feb 1887	Samuel Hauser (DP)

Feb 1887-April 1889	Preston Leslie (DP)
April-Nov 1889	Benjamin White (RP)
Nov 1889-Jan 1893	Joseph Toole (1st) (DP)
Jan 1893-Jan 1897	John Rickards (RP)
Jan 1897-Jan 1901	Robert Smith (DP)
Jan 1901-April 1908	Joseph Toole (2nd) (DP)
April 1908-Jan 1913	Edwin Norris (DP)
Jan 1913-Jan 1921	Sam Stewart (DP)
Jan 1921-Jan 1925	Joseph Dixon (RP)
Jan 1925-May 1933	John Erikson (DP)
May 1933-Dec 1935	Frank Cooney (DP) (†)
Dec 1935-Jan 1937	W.Elmer Holt (DP)
Jan 1937-Jan 1941	Roy Ayres (DP)
Jan 1941-Jan 1949	Sam Ford (RP)
Jan 1949-Jan 1953	John Bonner (DP)
Jan 1953-Jan 1961	J.Hugo Anderson (RP)
Jan 1961-Jan 1962	Donald Nutter (RP) († air accident)
Jan 1962-Jan 1969	Tim Babcock (RP)
Jan 1969-Jan 1973	Forrest Anderson (DP)
Jan 1973-Jan 1981	Thomas Judge (DP)
Jan 1981-Jan 1989	Edward Schwinden (DP)
Jan 1989-Jan 1993	Stanley Stephens (RP)
Jan 1993-	Marc Racicot (RP)

NEBRASKA

Statehood: 1 March 1867
Capital: Lincoln

Governors:

Oct 1854	Francis Burt (DP) (†)
Oct 1854-Feb 1855	Thomas Cuming (acting) (1st) (DP)
Feb 1855-Oct 1857	Mark Izard (DP)
Oct 1857-Jan 1858	Thomas Cuming (acting) (2nd) (DP)
Jan-Dec 1858	William Richardson (DP)
Dec 1858-May 1859	Julius Morton (acting) (1st) (DP)
May 1859-Feb 1861	Samuel Black (DP)
Feb-May 1861	Julius Morton (acting) (2nd) (DP)
May 1861	Algenon Paddock (acting) (RP)
May 1861-March 1867	Alvin Saunders (RP)
March 1867-June 1871	David Butler (RP)
June 1871-Jan 1873	William James (acting) (RP)
Jan 1873-Jan 1875	Robert Furnas (RP)
Jan 1875-Jan 1879	Silas Garber (RP)

Jan 1879-Jan 1883   Albinus Nance   (RP)
Jan 1883-Jan 1887   James Dawes   (RP)
Jan 1887-Jan 1891   John Thayer   (1st) (RP)
Jan-May 1891   James Boyd   (1st) (DP)
May 1891-Feb 1892   John Thayer   (2nd) (RP)
Feb 1892-Jan 1893   James Boyd   (2nd) (DP)
Jan 1893-Jan 1895   Lorenzo Crounse   (RP)
Jan 1895-Jan 1899   Silas Holcomb   (DPP)
Jan 1899-Jan 1901   William Poynter   (DPP)
Jan-May 1901   Charles Dietrich   (RP)
May 1901-Jan 1903   Ezra Savage   (acting) (RP)
Jan 1903-Jan 1907   John Mickey   (RP)
Jan 1907-Jan 1909   George Sheldon   (RP)
Jan 1909-Jan 1911   Ashton Shallenberger   (DP)
Jan 1911-Jan 1913   Chester Aldrich   (RP)
Jan 1913-Jan 1917   John Morehead   (DP)
Jan 1917-Jan 1919   Keith Neville   (DP)
Jan 1919-Jan 1923   Samuel McKelvie   (RP)
Jan 1923-Jan 1925   Charles Bryan   (1st) (DP)
Jan 1925-Jan 1929   Adam McMullen   (RP)
Jan 1929-Jan 1931   Arthur Weaver   (RP)
Jan 1931-Jan 1935   Charles Bryan   (2nd) (DP)
Jan 1935-Jan 1941   Robert Cochran   (DP)
Jan 1941-Jan 1947   Dwight Griswold   (RP)
Jan 1947-Jan 1953   Val Peterson   (RP)
Jan 1953-Jan 1955   Robert Crosby   (RP)
Jan 1955-Jan 1959   Victor Anderson   (RP)
Jan 1959-Sept 1960   Ralph Brooks   (DP) (†)
Sept 1960-Jan 1961   Dwight Burney   (acting) (RP)
Jan 1961-Jan 1967   Frank Morrison   (DP)
Jan 1967-Jan 1971   Norbert Tiemann   (RP)
Jan 1971-Jan 1979   James Exon   (DP)
Jan 1979-Jan 1983   Charles Thone   (RP)
Jan 1983-Jan 1987   Robert Kerrey   (DP)
Jan 1987-Jan 1991   Kay Orr   (RP)
Jan 1991-Jan 1999   Benjamin Nelson   (DP)
Jan 1999-   Mike Johanns   (RP)

NEVADA

Statehood: 31 October 1864
Capital: Carson City

Governors:

March 1861-Dec 1864   James Nye   (RP)

Dec 1864-Jan 1871	Henry Bladsel	(RP)
Jan 1871-Jan 1879	Lewis Bradley	(DP)
Jan 1879-Dec 1882	John Kinkead	(RP)
Jan 1883-Dec 1886	Jewett Adams	(DP)
Jan 1887-Sept 1890	Charles Stephenson	(RP) (†)
Sept-Dec 1890	Frank Bell	(acting) (RP)
Jan 1891-Dec 1894	Roswell Colcord	(RP)
Jan 1895-April 1896	John Jones	(SP) (†)
April 1896-Jan 1903	Reinhold Sadler	(acting 1896-99) (SP)
Jan 1903-May 1908	John Sparks	(DP)
May 1908-Dec 1910	Denver Dichinson	(acting) (DP)
Jan 1911-Dec 1914	Tasker Oddie	(RP)
Jan 1915-Dec 1922	Emmet Boyle	(DP)
Jan 1923-Jan 1927	James Scrugham	(DP)
Jan 1927-March 1934	Frederick Balzar	(RP)
March 1934-Jan 1935	Morley Griswold	(acting) (RP)
Jan 1935-Jan 1939	Richard Kirman	(DP)
Jan 1939-July 1945	Edward Carville	(DP)
July 1945-Jan 1951	Vail Pittman	(acting 1945-47) (DP)
Jan 1951-Jan 1959	Charles Russell	(RP)
Jan 1959-Jan 1967	Grant Sawyer	(DP)
Jan 1967-Jan 1971	Paul Laxalt	(RP)
Jan 1971-Jan 1979	Donal O'Callaghan	(DP)
Jan 1979-Jan 1983	Robert List	(RP)
Jan 1983-Jan 1989	Richard Bryan	(DP)
Jan 1989-Jan 1999	Robert Miller	(DP)
Jan 1999-	Kenny Guinn	(RP)

NEW HAMPSHIRE

One of the original 13 states
Capital: Concord

Presidents:

1775-76	Matthew Thornton	
1776-85	Meshech Weare	
1785-86	John Langton	(1st)
1786-88	John Sullivan	(1st)
1788-89	John Langton	(2nd)
1789-90	John Sullivan	(2nd)
1790-94	Josiah Bartlett	

Governors:

1794-Jan 1805	John Gilman	(1st) (FP)

Jan 1805-Jan 1809	John Langton (1st) (DRP)
Jan 1809-Jan 1810	Jeremiah Smith (FP)
Jan 1810-Jan 1812	John Langton (2nd) (DRP)
Jan 1812-Jan 1813	William Plumer (1st) (DRP)
Jan 1813-Jan 1816	John Gilman (2nd) (FP)
Jan 1816-Jan 1819	William Plumer (2nd) (DRP)
Jan 1819-Jan 1823	Samuel Bell (DRP)
Jan 1823-Jan 1824	Levi Woodbury (DRP)
Jan 1824-Jan 1827	David Morrill (DRP)
Jan 1827-Jan 1828	Benjamin Pierce (1st) (DRP)
Jan 1828-Jan 1829	John Bell (*brother of S.Bell*) (DRP)
Jan 1829-Jan 1830	Benjamin Pierce (2nd) (DP)
Jan 1830-Jan 1831	Matthew Harvey (DP)
Jan-Feb 1831	Josiah Harper (acting) (DP)
Feb 1831-Jan 1834	Samuel Dinsmoor (1st) (DP)
Jan 1834-Jan 1836	William Badger (DP)
Jan 1836-Jan 1839	Isaac Hill (DP)
Jan 1839-Jan 1842	John Page (DP)
Jan 1842-Jan 1844	Henry Hubbard (DP)
Jan 1844-Jan 1846	John Steele (DP)
Jan 1846-Jan 1847	Anthony Colby (WP)
Jan 1847-Jan 1849	Jared Williams (DP)
Jan 1849-Jan 1852	Samuel Dinsmoor (2nd) (DP)
Jan 1852-Jan 1854	Noah Martin (DP)
Jan 1854-Jan 1855	Nathaniel Baker (DP)
Jan 1855-Jan 1857	Ralph Metcalf (KNP)
Jan 1857-Jan 1859	William Haile (RP)
Jan 1859-Jan 1861	Ichabod Goodwin (RP)
Jan 1861-Jan 1863	Nathaniel Berry (RP)
Jan 1863-Jan 1865	Joseph Gilmore (RP)
Jan 1865-Jan 1867	Frederick Smyth (RP)
Jan 1867-Jan 1869	Walter Harriman (RP)
Jan 1869-Jan 1871	Onslow Stearns (RP)
Jan 1871-Jan 1872	James Weston (1st) (DP)
Jan 1872-Jan 1874	Ezekiel Straw (RP)
Jan 1874-Jan 1875	James Weston (2nd) (DP)
Jan 1875-Jan 1877	Person Cheney (RP)
Jan 1877-Jan 1879	Benjamin Prescott (RP)
Jan 1879-Jan 1881	Natt Head (RP)
Jan 1881-Jan 1883	Charles Bell (RP)
Jan 1883-Jan 1885	Samuel Hale (RP)
Jan 1885-Jan 1887	Moody Currier (RP)
Jan 1887-Jan 1889	Charles Sawyer (RP)
Jan 1889-Jan 1891	David Goodell (RP)
Jan 1891-Jan 1893	Hiram Tuttle (RP)

Jan 1893-Jan 1895	John B. Smith (RP)
Jan 1895-Jan 1897	Charles Busiel (RP)
Jan 1897-Jan 1899	George Ramsdell (RP)
Jan 1899-Jan 1901	Frank Rollins (RP)
Jan 1901-Jan 1903	Chester Jordan (RP)
Jan 1903-Jan 1907	Nahum Bachelder (RP)
Jan 1907-Jan 1909	John McLane (RP)
Jan 1909-Jan 1911	Henry Quinby (RP)
Jan 1911-Jan 1913	Robert Bass (RP)
Jan 1913-Jan 1915	Samuel Felker (DP)
Jan 1915-Jan 1917	Roland Spaulding (RP)
Jan 1917-Jan 1919	Henry Keyes (RP)
Jan 1919-Jan 1921	John Bartlett (RP)
Jan 1921-Jan 1923	Albert O. Brown (RP)
Jan 1923-Jan 1925	Fred Brown (DP)
Jan 1925-Jan 1927	John Winant (1st) (RP)
Jan 1927-Jan 1929	Huntley Spaulding (RP)
Jan 1929-Jan 1931	Charles Tobey (RP)
Jan 1931-Jan 1935	John Winant (2nd) (RP)
Jan 1935-Jan 1937	H. Styles Bridges (RP)
Jan 1937-Jan 1941	Francis Murphy (RP)
Jan 1941-Jan 1945	Robert Blood (RP)
Jan 1945-Jan 1949	Charles Dale (RP)
Jan 1949-Jan 1953	Sherman Adams (RP)
Jan 1953-Jan 1955	Hugh Gregg (RP)
Jan 1955-Jan 1959	Lane Dwinell (RP)
Jan 1959-Jan 1963	Wesley Powell (RP)
Jan 1963-Jan 1969	John King (DP)
Jan 1969-Jan 1973	Walter Peterson (RP)
Jan 1973-Jan 1979	Meldrim Thompson (RP)
Jan 1979-Dec 1982	Hugh Gallen (DP) (†)
Dec 1982-Jan 1983	Vesta Roy (acting)
Jan 1983-Jan 1989	John Sununu (RP)
Jan 1989-Jan 1993	Judd Gregg (*son of H. Gregg*) (RP)
Jan 1993-Jan 1997	Steve Merrill (RP)
Jan 1997-	Jeanne Shaheen (DP)

NEW JERSEY

One of the original 13 states
Capital: Trenton

Governors:

Sept 1776-July 1790	William Livingston (FP)

July 1790-92	William Paterson (FP)
1792-Oct 1801	Richard Howell (FP)
Oct 1801-Oct 1802	Joseph Bloomfield (1st) (DRP)
Oct 1802-Oct 1803	John Lambert (acting) (DRP)
Oct 1803-Dec 1812	Joseph Bloomfield (2nd) (DRP)
Jan-Oct 1813	Aaron Ogden (FP)
Oct 1813-June 1815	William S.Pennington (DRP)
June 1815-Feb 1817	Mahlon Dickerson (DRP)
Feb 1817-Nov 1829	Isaac Williamson (FP)
Nov 1829-Oct 1832	Peter Broom (1st) (DP)
Oct 1832-Feb 1833	Samuel Southard (WP)
Feb-Oct 1833	Elias Seeley (WP)
Oct 1833-Nov 1836	Peter Broom (2nd) (DP)
Nov 1836-Oct 1837	Philemon Dickerson (*brother of M.Dickerson*) (DP)
Oct 1837-Oct 1843	William Pennington (*son of W.S.Pennington*) (WP)
Oct 1843-Jan 1845	Daniel Haines (1st) (DP)
Jan 1845-Jan 1848	Charles Stratton (WP)
Jan 1848-Jan 1851	Daniel Haines (2nd) (DP)
Jan 1851-Jan 1954	George Forte (DP)
Jan 1854-Jan 1857	Rodman Price (DP)
Jan 1857-Jan 1860	William Newell (RP)
Jan 1860-Jan 1863	Charles Olden (RP)
Jan 1863-Jan 1866	Joel Parker (1st) (DP)
Jan 1866-Jan 1869	Marcus Ward (RP)
Jan 1869-Jan 1872	Theodore Randolph (DP)
Jan 1872-Jan 1875	Joel Parker (2nd) (DP)
Jan 1875-Jan 1878	Joseph Bedle (DP)
Jan 1878-Jan 1881	George McClelland (DP)
Jan 1881-Jan 1884	George Ludlow (DP)
Jan 1884-Jan 1887	Leon Abbett (1st) (DP)
Jan 1887-Jan 1890	Robert Green (DP)
Jan 1890-Jan 1893	Leon Abbett (2nd) (DP)
Jan 1893-Jan 1896	George Werts (DP)
Jan 1896-Jan 1898	John Griggs (RP)
Jan-Oct 1898	Foster Voorhees (acting) (RP)
Oct 1898-Jan 1899	David Watkins (acting) (RP)
Jan 1899-Jan 1902	Foster Voorhees (RP)
Jan 1902-Jan 1905	Franklin Murphy (RP)
Jan 1905-Jan 1908	Edward Stokes (RP)
Jan 1908-Jan 1911	John Fort (RP)
Jan 1911-March 1913	Woodrow Wilson (DP) (later President)
March-Oct 1913	James Fielder (acting) (DP)
Oct 1913-Jan 1914	Leon Taylor (acting) (DP)
Jan 1914-Jan 1917	James Fielder (DP)
Jan 1917-Jan 1919	Walter Edge (1st) (RP)

Jan-May 1919	William Runyon	(RP)
May 1919-Jan 1922	Edward Edwards	(DP)
Jan 1922-Jan 1926	George Silzer	(DP)
Jan 1926-Jan 1929	A.Harry Moore	(1st) (DP)
Jan 1929-Jan 1932	Morgan Larson	(RP)
Jan 1932-Jan 1935	A.Harry Moore	(2nd) (DP)
Jan 1935-Jan 1938	Harold Hoffmann	(RP)
Jan 1938-Jan 1941	A.Harry Moore	(3rd) (DP)
Jan 1941-Jan 1944	Charles Edison	(DP)
Jan 1944-Jan 1947	Walter Edge	(2nd) (RP)
Jan 1947-Jan 1954	Alfred Driscoll	(RP)
Jan 1954-Jan 1962	Robert Mayner	(DP)
Jan 1962-Jan 1970	Richard Hughes	(DP)
Jan 1970-Jan 1974	William Cahill	(RP)
Jan 1974-Jan 1982	Brendan Byrne	(DP)
Jan 1982-Jan 1990	Thomas Kean	(RP)
Jan 1990-Jan 1994	James Florio	(DP)
Jan 1994-	Christine Todd Whitman	(RP)

NEW MEXICO

Statehood: 5 January 1912
Capital: Santa Fé

Governors:

Jan 1851-June 1852	James Calhoun
June-July 1852	John Greiner (acting)
July 1852-53	William Lane
1853	W.S.Messervy (acting)
May 1853-Aug 1856	David Meriwether
Aug 1856-Aug 1857	W.Davis (acting)
Aug 1857-May 1861	Abraham Rencher
May 1861-Jan 1866	Henry Connelley
Jan 1866	W.Arny (acting)
Jan 1866-May 1869	Robert Mitchell
May 1869-July 1871	William Pile
July 1871-June 1875	Marsh Giddings
June-July 1875	William Ritch (acting)
July 1875-Sept 1878	Samuel Axtell
Sept 1878-May 1881	Lewis Wallace
May 1881-May 1885	Lionel Sheldon
May 1885-April 1889	Edmund Ross
April 1889-April 1893	L.Bradford Prince
April 1893-June 1897	William Thornton

June 1897-Jan 1906	Miguel Otero
Jan 1906-Jan 1907	Herbert Hagerman
Jan-April 1907	J.W.Reynolds (acting)
April 1907-Oct 1910	George Curry
Oct 1910-Jan 1912	William Mills
Jan 1912-Jan 1917	William McDonald (DP)
Jan-Feb 1917	Ezequiel de Baca (DP)
Feb 1917-Jan 1919	Washington Lindsey (RP)
Jan 1919-Jan 1921	Octaviano Larrazolo (RP)
Jan 1921-Jan 1923	Merritt Mechem (RP)
Jan 1923-Jan 1925	James Hinkle (DP)
Jan 1925-Jan 1927	Arthur Hannett (DP)
Jan 1927-Jan 1931	Richard Dillon (RP)
Jan 1931-Sept 1933	Arthur Seligman (DP)
Sept 1933-Jan 1935	Andrew Hockenhull (DP)
Jan 1935-Jan 1939	Clyde Tingley (DP)
Jan 1939-Jan 1943	John Miles (DP)
Jan 1943-Jan 1947	John Dempsey (DP)
Jan 1947-Jan 1951	Thomas Mabry (DP)
Jan 1951-Jan 1955	Edwin Mechem (*nephew of M.Mechem*) (1st) (RP)
Jan 1955-Jan 1957	John Simms (DP)
Jan 1957-Jan 1959	Edwin Mechem (2nd) (RP)
Jan 1959-Jan 1961	John Burroughs (DP)
Jan 1961-Nov 1962	Edwin Mechem (3rd) (RP)
Nov 1962-Jan 1963	Tom Bolack (acting) (RP)
Jan 1963-Jan 1967	Jack Campbell (DP)
Jan 1967-Jan 1971	David Cargo (RP)
Jan 1971-Jan 1975	Bruce King (1st) (DP)
Jan 1975-Jan 1979	Jerry Apodaca (DP)
Jan 1979-Jan 1983	Bruce King (2nd) (DP)
Jan 1983-Jan 1987	Toney Anaya (DP)
Jan 1987-Jan 1991	Garrey Carruthers (RP)
Jan 1991-Jan 1995	Bruce King (3rd) (DP)
Jan 1995-	Gary Johnson (RP)

NEW YORK

One of the original states
Capital: Albany

Governors:

July 1777-July 1795	George Clinton (1st)
July 1795-July 1801	John Jay
July 1801-July 1804	George Clinton (2nd) (DRP)

July 1804-July 1807	Morgan Lewis (DRP)
July 1807-Feb 1817	Daniel Tompkins (DRP)
Feb-July 1817	John Tayler (acting) (DRP)
July 1817-Dec 1822	De Witt Clinton (1st) (DRP)
Jan 1823-Dec 1824	Joseph Yates (DRP)
Jan 1825-Feb 1828	De Witt Clinton (2nd) (DRP) (†)
Feb-Dec 1828	Nathaniel Pitcher (acting) (DRP)
Jan-March 1829	Martin Van Buren (DP) (later President)
March 1829-Dec 1832	Enos Throop (acting 1929-30) (DP)
Jan 1833-Dec 1838	William Marcey (DP)
Jan 1839-Dec 1842	William Seward (WP)
Jan 1843-Dec 1844	William Bouch (DP)
Jan 1845-Dec 1846	Silas Wright (DP)
Jan 1847-Dec 1848	John Young (WP)
Jan 1849-Dec 1850	Hamilton Fish (WP)
Jan 1851-Dec 1852	Washington Hunt (WP)
Jan 1853-Dec 1854	Horatio Seymour (1st) (DP)
Jan 1855-Dec 1856	Myron Clark (WP)
Jan 1857-Dec 1858	John King (RP)
Jan 1859-Dec 1862	Edwin Morgan (RP)
Jan 1863-Dec 1864	Horatio Seymour (2nd) (DP)
Jan 1865-Dec 1868	Reuben Fenton (RP)
Jan 1869-Dec 1872	John Hoffman (DP)
Jan 1873-Dec 1874	John Adams Dix (RP)
Jan 1875-Dec 1876	Samuel Tilden (DP)
Jan 1877-Dec 1979	Lucius Robinson (DP)
Jan 1880-Dec 1882	Alonzo Cornell (RP)
Jan 1883-Jan 1885	Grover Cleveland (DP) (later President)
Jan 1885-Dec 1891	David Hill (acting 1885) (DP)
Jan 1892-Dec 1894	Roswell Flower (DP)
Jan 1895-Dec 1896	Levi Morton (RP)
Jan 1897-Dec 1898	Frank Black (RP)
Jan 1899-Dec 1900	Theodore Roosevelt (RP) (later President)
Jan 1901-Dec 1904	Benjamin Odell (RP)
Jan 1905-Dec 1906	Frank Higgins (RP)
Jan 1907-Dec 1910	Charles Hughes (RP)
Jan 1911-Dec 1912	John Alden Dix (DP)
Jan-Oct 1913	William Sulzer (DP)
Oct 1913-Dec 1914	Martin Glynn (acting) (DP)
Jan 1915-Dec 1918	Charles Whitman (RP)
Jan 1919-Dec 1920	Alfred Smith (1st) (DP)
Jan 1921-Dec 1922	Nathan Miller (RP)
Jan 1923-Dec 1928	Alfred Smith (2nd) (DP)
Jan 1929-Jan 1933	Franklin Roosevelt (DP) (later President)
Jan 1933-Dec 1942	Herbert Lehman (DP)

3-31 Dec 1942	Charles Poletti (acting) (DP)
Jan 1943-Dec 1954	Thomas Dewey (RP)
Jan 1955-Dec 1958	Averell Harriman (DP)
Jan 1959-Dec 1973	Nelson Rockefeller (RP)
Dec 1973-Dec 1974	Malcolm Wilson (RP)
Jan 1975-Dec 1982	Hugh Carey (DP)
Jan 1983-Dec 1994	Mario Cuomo (DP)
Jan 1995-	George Pataki (RP)

NORTH CAROLINA

One of the original 13 states
Capital: Raleigh

Governors:

Nov 1776-April 1780	Richard Caswell (1st)
April 1780-June 1781	Abner Nash
June 1781-April 1782	Thomas Burke
April 1782-April 1785	Alexander Martin (1st)
April 1785-Dec 1787	Richard Caswell (2nd)
Dec 1787-Dec 1789	Samuel Johnston
Dec 1789-Dec 1792	Alexander Martin (2nd) (FP)
Dec 1792-Nov 1795	Richard Spraight Sr (DRP)
Nov 1795-Dec 1798	Samuel Ashe (DRP)
Dec 1798-Nov 1799	William Davie (FP)
Nov 1799-Dec 1802	Benjamin Williams (1st) (DRP)
(1802	John Ashe - Governor-elect, (died before assuming office)
Dec 1802-Dec 1805	James Turner (DRP)
Dec 1805-Dec 1807	Nathaniel Alexander (DRP)
Dec 1807-Dec 1808	Benjamin Williams (2nd) (DRP)
Dec 1808-Dec 1810	David Stone (DRP)
Dec 1810-Dec 1811	Benjamin Smith (DRP)
Dec 1811-Nov 1814	William Hawkins (DRP)
Nov 1814-Dec 1817	William Miller (DRP)
Dec 1817-Dec 1820	John Branch (DRP)
Dec 1820-Dec 1821	Jesse Franklin (DRP)
Dec 1821-Dec 1824	Gabriel Holmes (DRP)
Dec 1824-Dec 1827	Hutchins Burton (DRP)
Dec 1827-Dec 1828	James Iredell (DRP)
Dec 1828-Dec 1830	John Owen (DP)
Dec 1830-Dec 1832	Montford Stokes (DP)
Dec 1832-Dec 1835	David Swain (DP)
Dec 1835-Dec 1837	Richard Spraight Jr (*son of R.Spraight Sr*) (DP)

Dec 1837-Jan 1841	Edward Dudley (WP)
Jan 1841-Jan 1845	John Morehead (WP)
Jan 1845-Jan 1849	William Graham (WP)
Jan 1849-Jan 1851	Charles Manly (WP)
Jan 1851-Dec 1854	David Reid (DP)
Dec 1854-Jan 1855	Warren Winslow (acting) (DP)
Jan 1855-Jan 1859	Thomas Bragg (DP)
Jan 1859-July 1861	John Ellis (DP) (†)
July 1861-Sept 1862	Henry Clark (acting) (DP)
Sept 1862-Feb 1865	Zebulon Vance (1st) (CP)
Feb-Dec 1865	William Holden (acting)
Dec 1865-Jan 1868	Jonathan Worth (CP)
Jan 1868-Dec 1870	William Holden (RP)
Dec 1870-July 1874	Tod Caswell (acting 1870-Jan 1873) (RP) (†)
July 1874-Jan 1877	Curtis Bogden (acting) (RP)
Jan 1877-Feb 1879	Zebulon Vance (2nd) (DP)
Feb 1879-Jan 1885	Thomas Jarvie (acting 1879-Jan 1881) (DP)
Jan 1885-Jan 1889	Alfred Scales (DP)
Jan 1889-April 1891	Daniel Fowle (DP)
April 1891-Jan 1893	Thomas Holt (acting) (DP)
Jan 1893-Jan 1897	Elias Carr (DP)
Jan 1897-Jan 1901	Daniel Russell (RP)
Jan 1901-Jan 1905	Charles Aycock (DP)
Jan 1905-Jan 1909	Robert Glenn (DP)
Jan 1909-Jan 1913	William Kitchin (DP)
Jan 1913-Jan 1917	Locke Craig (DP)
Jan 1917-Jan 1921	Thomas Bickett (DP)
Jan 1921-Jan 1925	Cameron Morrison (DP)
Jan 1925-Jan 1929	Angus McLean (DP)
Jan 1929-Jan 1933	O.Max Gardner (DP)
Jan 1933-Jan 1937	John Ehringhaus (DP)
Jan 1937-Jan 1941	Clyde Hoey (DP)
Jan 1941-Jan 1945	J.Melville Broughton (DP)
Jan 1945-Jan 1949	R.Gregg Cherry (DP)
Jan 1949-Jan 1953	W.Kerr Scott (DP)
Jan 1953-Nov 1954	William Unstead (DP) (†)
Nov 1954-Jan 1961	Luther Hodges (acting Nov 1954-Jan 1957) (DP)
Jan 1961-Jan 1965	Terry Sanford (DP)
Jan 1965-Jan 1969	Daniel Moore (DP)
Jan 1969-Jan 1973	Robert Scott (DP)
Jan 1973-Jan 1977	James Holshouser (RP)
Jan 1977-Jan 1985	James Hunt (1st) (DP)
Jan 1985-Jan 1993	James Martin (DP)
Jan 1993-	James Hunt (2nd) (DP)

NORTH DAKOTA

Statehood: 2 November 1889
Capital: Bismarck

Governors:

Nov 1889-Jan 1891	John Miller (RP)
Jan 1891-Jan 1893	Andrew Burke (RP)
Jan 1893-Jan 1895	Eli Shortridge (PP)
Jan 1895-Jan 1897	Roger Allin (RP)
Jan 1897-Aug 1898	Frank Biggs (RP)
Aug 1898-Jan 1899	Joseph Devine (acting) (RP)
Jan 1899-Jan 1901	Frederick Francher (RP)
Jan 1901-Jan 1905	Frank White (RP)
Jan 1905-Jan 1907	Elmore Sarles (RP)
Jan 1907-Jan 1913	John Burke (DP)
Jan 1913-Jan 1917	Louis Hanna (RP)
Jan 1917-Oct 1921	Lynn Frazier (NPL)
Oct 1921-Jan 1925	Ragnvald Nestos (RP)
Jan 1925-Aug 1928	Arthur Sorbie (RP) (†)
Aug 1928-Jan 1929	Walter Maddock (acting) (NPL)
Jan 1929-Jan 1933	George Shafer (RP)
Jan 1933-July 1934	William Langer (1st) (NPL)
July 1934-Jan 1935	Ole Olson (RP)
Jan-Feb 1935	Thomas Moodie (DP)
Feb 1935-Jan 1937	Walter Welford (RP)
Jan 1937-Jan 1939	William Langer (2nd) (Ind)
Jan 1939-Jan 1945	John Moses (DP)
Jan 1945-Jan 1951	Fred Aandahl (RP)
Jan 1951-Jan 1957	Norman Brunsdale (RP)
Jan 1957-Jan 1961	John Davis (RP)
Jan 1961-Jan 1973	William Guy (DP)
Jan 1973-Jan 1981	Arthur Link (DP)
Jan 1981-Jan 1985	Allen Olson (RP)
Jan 1985-Jan 1993	George Sinner (RP)
Jan 1993-	Edward Schafer (RP)

Dakota Territory

Governors:

1861-63	William Jayne
1863-66	Newton Edmunds
1866-69	Andrew Faulk
1869-74	John Burbank
1874-78	John Pennington

1878-80	William Howard (†)
1880-84	Nehemiah Ordway
1884-87	Gilbert Pierce
1887-89	Louis Church
1889	Arthur Mellette (see South Dakota)

OHIO

Statehood: 19 February 1803
Capital: Columbus

Governors:

July 1788-Dec 1802	Arthur St Clair
Dec 1802-March 1803	Charles Byrd (acting)
March 1803-Jan 1807	Edward Tiffin (DRP)
Jan 1807-Dec 1808	Thomas Kirker (acting) (DRP)
Dec 1808-Dec 1810	Samuel Huntington (DRP)
Dec 1810-March 1814	Return Meigs (DRP)
March-Dec 1814	Othniel Looker (acting) (DRP)
Dec 1814-Dec 1818	Thomas Worthington (DRP)
Dec 1818-Jan 1822	Ethan Brown (DRP)
Jan-Dec 1822	Allen Trimble (acting) (FP)
Dec 1822-Dec 1826	Jeremiah Morrow (DRP)
Dec 1826-Dec 1830	Allen Trimble (FP)
Dec 1830-Dec 1832	Duncan McArthur (FP)
Dec 1832-Dec 1836	Robert Lucas (DP)
Dec 1836-Dec 1838	Joseph Vance (WP)
Dec 1838-Dec 1840	Wilson Shannon (1st) (DP)
Dec 1840-Dec 1842	Thomas Corwin (WP)
Dec 1842-April 1844	Wilson Shannon (2nd) (DP)
April-Dec 1844	Thomas Bartley (acting) (DP)
Dec 1844-Dec 1846	Mordecai Bartley (*father*) (WP)
Dec 1846-Jan 1849	William Bebb (WP)
Jan 1849-Dec 1850	Seabury Ford (WP)
Dec 1850-July 1853	Reuben Wood (DP)
July 1853-Jan 1856	William Medill (acting) (DP)
Jan 1856-Jan 1860	Salmon Chase (RP)
Jan 1860-Jan 1862	William Dennison (RP)
Jan 1862-Jan 1864	David Tod (RP)
Jan 1864-Aug 1865	John Brough (RP)
Aug 1865-Jan 1866	Charles Anderson (acting) (RP)
Jan 1866-Jan 1868	Jacob Cox (RP)
Jan 1868-Jan 1872	Rutherford Hayes (1st) (RP)
Jan 1872-Jan 1874	Edward Noyes (RP)

Jan 1874-Jan 1876	William Allen (DP)
Jan 1876-March 1877	Rutherford Hayes (2nd) (RP) (later President)
March 1877-Jan 1878	Thomas Young (acting) (RP)
Jan 1878-Jan 1880	Richard Bishop (DP)
Jan 1880-Jan 1884	Charles Foster (RP)
Jan 1884-Jan 1886	George Hoadley (DP)
Jan 1886-Jan 1890	Joseph Foraker (RP)
Jan 1890-Jan 1892	James Campbell (DP)
Jan 1892-Jan 1896	William McKinley (RP) (later President)
Jan 1896-Jan 1900	Asa Bushnell (RP)
Jan 1900-Jan 1904	George Nash (RP)
Jan 1904-Jan 1906	Myron Herrick (RP)
Jan-June 1906	John Pattison (DP)
June 1906-Jan 1909	Andrew Harris (acting) (RP)
Jan 1909-Jan 1913	Judson Harmon (DP)
Jan 1913-Jan 1915	James Cox (1st) (DP)
Jan 1915-Jan 1917	Frank Willis (RP)
Jan 1917-Jan 1921	James Cox (2nd) (DP)
Jan 1921-Jan 1923	Harry Davis (RP)
Jan 1923-Jan 1929	Alvin Donahey (DP)
Jan 1929-Jan 1931	Myers Cooper (RP)
Jan 1931-Jan 1935	George White (DP)
Jan 1935-Jan 1939	Martin Davey (DP)
Jan 1939-Jan 1945	John Bricker (RP)
Jan 1945-Jan 1947	Frank Lausche (1st) (DP)
Jan 1947-Jan 1949	Thomas Herbert (RP)
Jan 1949-Jan 1957	Frank Lausche (2nd) (DP)
3-14 Jan 1957	John W.Brown (RP)
Jan 1957-Jan 1959	C.William O'Neill (RP)
Jan 1959-Jan 1963	Michael DiSalle (DP)
Jan 1963-Jan 1971	James Rhodes (1st) (RP)
Jan 1971-Jan 1975	John Gilligan (DP)
Jan 1975-Jan 1983	James Rhodes (2nd) (RP)
Jan 1983-Jan 1991	Richard Celeste (DP)
Jan 1991-Dec 1998	George Voinovich (RP)
Dec 1998-Jan 1999	Nancy Hollister (RP)
Jan 1999-	Bob Taft (RP)

OKLAHOMA

Statehood: 16 November 1907
Capital: Oklahoma City

Governors:

May 1890-Oct 1891	George Steele (RP)

Oct 1891-Feb 1892	Robert Martin (acting) (RP)
Feb 1892-May 1893	Abraham Seay (RP)
May 1893-May 1897	William Renfrow (DP)
May 1897-May 1901	Cassius Barnes (RP)
May-Nov 1901	William Jenkins (RP)
Nov-Dec 1901	William Grimes (acting) (RP)
Dec 1901-Jan 1906	Thompson Ferguson (RP)
Jan 1906-Nov 1907	Frank Frantz (RP)
Nov 1907-Jan 1911	Charles Haskell (DP)
Jan 1911-Jan 1915	Lee Cruce (DP)
Jan 1915-Jan 1919	Robert Williams (DP)
Jan 1919-Jan 1923	James Robertson (DP)
Jan-Nov 1923	John Walton (DP)
Nov 1923-Jan 1927	Martin Trapp (DP)
Jan 1927-March 1929	Henry Johnston (DP)
March 1929-Jan 1931	William Holloway (DP)
Jan 1931-Jan 1935	William Murray (DP)
Jan 1935-Jan 1939	Ernest Marland (DP)
Jan 1939-Jan 1943	Leon Phillips (DP)
Jan 1943-Jan 1947	Robert Kerr (DP)
Jan 1947-Jan 1951	Roy Turner (DP)
Jan 1951-Jan 1955	Johnston Murray (*son of W.Murray*) (DP)
Jan 1955-Jan 1959	Raymond Gary (DP)
Jan 1959-Jan 1963	J.Howard Edmondson (DP)
6-14 Jan 1963	George Nigh (1st) (DP)
Jan 1963-Jan 1967	Henry Bellmon (1st) (RP)
Jan 1967-Jan 1971	Dewey Bartlett (RP)
Jan 1971-Jan 1975	David Hall (DP)
Jan 1975-Jan 1979	David Boren (DP)
Jan 1979-Jan 1987	George Nigh (2nd) (DP)
Jan 1987-Jan 1991	Henry Bellmon (2nd) (RP)
Jan 1991-Jan 1995	David Walters (DP)
Jan 1995-	Frank Keating (RP)

OREGON

Statehood: 14 February 1859
Capital: Salem

Governors:

July 1845-May 1849	George Abernethey
May 1849-June 1850	Joseph Lane (1st)
June-Aug 1850	Kintzing Pritchett (acting)
Aug 1850-May 1853	John Gaines

May 1853	Joseph Lane (2nd)
May-Dec 1853	George Curry (1st)
Dec 1853-Aug 1854	John W. Davis
Aug 1854-March 1859	George Curry (2nd)
March 1859-Sept 1862	John Whiteaker (DP)
Sept 1862-Sept 1866	Addison Gibbs (RP)
Sept 1866-Sept 1870	George Woods (RP)
Sept 1870-Feb 1877	Lafayette Grover (DP)
Feb 1877-Sept 1878	Stephen Chadwick (acting) (DP)
Sept 1878-Sept 1882	William Thayer (DP)
Sept 1882-Jan 1887	Zenas Moody (RP)
Jan 1887-Jan 1895	Sylvester Pennoyer (DPP)
Jan 1895-Jan 1899	William Lord (RP)
Jan 1899-Jan 1903	Theodore Geer (RP)
Jan 1903-March 1909	George Chamberlain (DP)
March 1909-June 1910	Frank Benson (RP)
June 1910-Jan 1911	Jay Bowerman (acting) (RP)
Jan 1911-Jan 1915	Oswald West (DP)
Jan 1915-March 1919	James Withycombe (RP)
March 1919-Jan 1923	Benjamin Olcott (RP)
Jan 1923-Jan 1927	Walter Pierce (DP)
Jan 1927-Dec 1929	Isaac Patterson (RP) (†)
Dec 1929-Jan 1931	Albin Norblad (acting) (RP)
Jan 1931-Jan 1935	Julius Meier (Ind)
Jan 1935-Jan 1939	Charles Martin (DP)
Jan 1939-Jan 1943	Charles Sprague (RP)
Jan 1943-Oct 1947	Earl Snell (RP) († air accident)
Oct 1947-Jan 1949	John Hall (acting) (RP)
Jan 1949-Dec 1952	Douglas McKay (RP)
Dec 1952-Feb 1956	Paul Patterson (acting 1952-55) (RP) (†)
Feb 1956-Jan 1957	Elmo Smith (acting) (RP)
Jan 1957-Jan 1959	Robert Holmes (DP)
Jan 1959-Jan 1967	Mark Hatfield (RP)
Jan 1967-Jan 1975	Thomas McCall (RP)
Jan 1975-Jan 1979	Robert Straub (DP)
Jan 1979-Jan 1987	Victor Atiyeh (RP)
Jan 1987-Jan 1991	Neil Goldschmidt (DP)
Jan 1991-Jan 1995	Barbara Roberts (*b* B. Hughey) (DP)
Jan 1995-	John Kitzhaber (DP)

PENNSYLVANIA

One of the original 13 states
Capital: Harrisburg

Presidents:

Sept 1776-March 1777	Benjamin Franklin	(1st)
March 1777-May 1778	Thomas Warton	(†)
May-Dec 1778	George Bryan	
Dec 1778-Oct 1781	Joseph Reed	
Oct 1781-Oct 1782	William Moore	
Nov 1782-Oct 1785	John Dickinson	
Oct 1785-Oct 1788	Benjamin Franklin	(2nd)
Oct 1788-Dec 1790	Thomas Mifflin	

Governors:

Dec 1790-Dec 1799	Thomas Mifflin	(DRP)
Dec 1799-Dec 1808	Thomas McKean	(DRP)
Dec 1808-Dec 1817	Simon Snyder	(DRP)
Dec 1817-Dec 1820	William Findlay	(DRP)
Dec 1820-Dec 1823	Joseph Hiester	(DRP)
Dec 1823-Dec 1829	John Shulze	(DRP)
Dec 1829-Dec 1835	George Wolfe	(DRP)
Dec 1835-Jan 1839	Joseph Ritner	(AMP)
Jan 1839-Jan 1845	David Porter	(DP)
Jan 1845-July 1848	Francis Shunk	(DP)
July 1848-Jan 1852	William Johnston	(WP)
Jan 1852-Jan 1855	William Bigler	(DP)
Jan 1855-Jan 1858	James Pollock	(WP)
Jan 1858-Jan 1861	William Packer	(DP)
Jan 1861-Jan 1867	Andrew Curtin	(RP)
Jan 1867-Jan 1873	John Geary	(RP)
Jan 1873-Jan 1879	John Hartranft	(RP)
Jan 1879-Jan 1883	Henry Hoyt	(RP)
Jan 1883-Jan 1887	Robert Pattison	(1st) (DP)
Jan 1887-Jan 1891	James Beaver	(RP)
Jan 1891-Jan 1895	Robert Pattison	(2nd) (DP)
Jan 1895-Jan 1899	Daniel Hastings	(RP)
Jan 1899-Jan 1903	William Stone	(RP)
Jan 1903-Jan 1907	Samuel Pennypacker	(RP)
Jan 1907-Jan 1911	Edwin Stewart	(RP)
Jan 1911-Jan 1915	John Tener	(RP)
Jan 1915-Jan 1919	Martin Brumbaugh	(RP)
Jan 1919-Jan 1923	William Sproul	(RP)
Jan 1923-Jan 1927	Gifford Pinchot	(1st) (RP)
Jan 1927-Jan 1931	John Fisher	(RP)
Jan 1931-Jan 1935	Gifford Pinchot	(2nd) (RP)
Jan 1935-Jan 1939	George Earle	(DP)
Jan 1939-Jan 1943	Arthur James	(RP)

Jan 1943-Jan 1947	Edward Martin (RP)
Jan 1947	John Bell (RP)
Jan 1947-Jan 1951	James Duff (RP)
Jan 1951-Jan 1955	John Fine (RP)
Jan 1955-Jan 1959	George Leader (DP)
Jan 1959-Jan 1963	David Lawrence (DP)
Jan 1963-Jan 1967	William Scranton (RP)
Jan 1967-Jan 1971	Raymond Shafer (RP)
Jan 1971-Jan 1979	Milton Shapp (DP)
Jan 1979-Jan 1987	Richard Thornburgh (RP)
Jan 1987-Jan 1995	Robert Casey (DP)
Jan 1995-	Thomas Ridge (RP)

RHODE ISLAND

One of the original 13 states
Capital: Providence

Governors:

Nov 1775-May 1778	Nicholas Cooke
May 1778-May 1786	William Greene
May 1786-May 1790	John Collins
May 1790-Oct 1805	Arthur Fenner (AF,DRP)
Oct 1805-May 1806	Henry Smith (DRP)
May 1806-Jan 1807	Isaac Wilbur (DRP)
Jan 1807-May 1811	James Fenner (1st) (*son of A.Fenner*) (DRP)
May 1811-May 1817	William Jones (FP)
May 1817-May 1824	Nehemiah Knight (DRP)
May 1824-May 1831	William Gibbs (DRP)
May 1824-May 1831	James Fenner (2nd) (DRP)
May 1831-May 1833	Lemuel Arnold (DP)
May 1833-May 1838	John Francis (DP)
May 1838-May 1839	William Sprague (1st) (WP)
May 1839-May 1843	Samuel King (acting 1839-40) (WP)
May 1843-May 1845	James Fenner (3rd) (WP)
May 1845-May 1846	Charles Jackson (DP)
May 1846-May 1847	Byron Diman (WP)
May 1847-May 1849	Elisha Harris (WP)
May 1849-May 1851	Henry Anthony (WP)
May 1851-July 1853	Philip Allen (DP)
July 1853-May 1854	Francis Dimond (acting) (DP)
May 1854-May 1857	William Hoppin (KNP)
May 1857-May 1859	Elisha Dyer (RP)
May 1859-May 1860	Thomas Turner (RP)

May 1860-March 1863	William Sprague (2nd) (UDP)
March-May 1863	William Cozzens (UDP)
May 1863-May 1866	James Y.Smith (RP)
May 1866-May 1869	Ambrose Burnside (RP)
May 1869-May 1873	Seth Padelford (RP)
May 1873-May 1875	Henry Howard (RP)
May 1875-May 1877	Henry Lippitt (RP)
May 1877-May 1880	Charles Van Zandt (RP)
May 1880-May 1883	Alfred Littlefield (RP)
May 1883-May 1885	Augustus Bourn (RP)
May 1885-May 1887	George Wetmore (RP)
May 1887-May 1888	John Davis (1st) (DP)
May 1888-May 1889	Royal Taft (RP)
May 1889-May 1890	Herbert Ladd (1st) (RP)
May 1890-May 1891	John Davis (2nd) (DP)
May 1891-May 1892	Herbert Ladd (2nd) (RP)
May 1892-May 1895	D.Russell Brown (RP)
May 1895-May 1897	Charles Lippitt (*son of H.Lippitt*) (RP)
May 1897-May 1900	Elisha Dyer Jr (*son of E.Dyer*) (RP)
May 1900-Dec 1901	William Gregory (RP) (†)
Dec 1901-Jan 1903	Charles Kimball (RP)
Jan 1903-Jan 1905	Lucius Garvin (DP)
Jan 1905-Jan 1907	George Utter (RP)
Jan 1907-Jan 1909	James Higgins (DP)
Jan 1909-Jan 1915	Aram Pothier (1st) (RP)
Jan 1915-Jan 1921	R.Livingston Beeckman (RP)
Jan 1921-Jan 1923	Emery San Souci (RP)
Jan 1923-Jan 1925	William Flynn (DP)
Jan 1925-Jan 1929	Aram Pothier (2nd) (RP)
Jan 1929-Jan 1933	Norman Case (RP)
Jan 1933-Jan 1937	Theodore Green (DP)
Jan 1937-Jan 1939	Robert Quinn (DP)
Jan 1939-Jan 1941	William Vanderbilt (RP)
Jan 1941-Oct 1945	J.Howard McGrath (DP)
Oct 1945-Jan 1951	John Pastore (DP)
Jan 1951-Jan 1961	Christopher Del Sesto (RP)
Jan 1961-Jan 1963	John Notte (DP)
Jan 1963-Jan 1969	John Chafee (RP)
Jan 1969-Jan 1973	Frank Licht (DP)
Jan 1973-Jan 1977	Philip Noel (DP)
Jan 1977-Jan 1985	Joseph Garrahy (DP)
Jan 1985-Jan 1991	Edward DiPrete (RP)
Jan 1991-Jan 1995	Bruce Sundlun (DP)
Jan 1995-	Lincoln Almond (RP)

SOUTH CAROLINA

One of the original 13 states
Capital: Columbia

Presidents:

March 1776-March 1777	John Rutledge
March 1777-Jan 1779	Rawlins Lowndes

Governors:

Jan 1779-Jan 1782	John Rutledge
Jan 1782-Feb 1783	John Mathewes
Feb 1783-Feb 1785	Benjamin Guerard
Feb 1785-Aug 1787	William Moultrie (1st)
Aug 1787-Jan 1789	Thomas Pinckney
Jan 1787-Dec 1792	Charles Pinckney (1st)
Dec 1792-Dec 1794	William Moultrie (2nd) (FP)
Dec 1794-Dec 1796	Arnoldus Vander-Horst (FP)
Dec 1796-Dec 1798	Charles Pinckney (2nd) (DRP)
Dec 1798-Jan 1800	Edward Rutledge (*brother of J.Rutledge*) (FP)
Jan 1800-Dec 1802	John Drayton (1st) (DRP)
Dec 1802-Dec 1804	James Richardson (DRP)
Dec 1804-Dec 1806	Paul Hamilton (DRP)
Dec 1806-Dec 1808	Charles Pinckney (3rd) (DRP)
Dec 1808-Dec 1810	John Drayton (2nd) (DRP)
Dec 1810-Dec 1812	Henry Middleton (DRP)
Dec 1812-Dec 1814	Joseph Alston (DRP)
Dec 1814-Dec 1816	David Williams (DRP)
Dec 1816-Dec 1818	Andrew Pickens (DRP)
Dec 1818-Dec 1820	John Geddes (DRP)
Dec 1820-Dec 1822	Thomas Bennett (DRP)
Dec 1822-Dec 1824	John Wilson (DRP)
Dec 1824-Dec 1826	Richard Manning (DRP)
Dec 1826-Dec 1828	John Taylor (DRP)
Dec 1828-Dec 1830	Stephen Miller (DRP)
Dec 1830-Dec 1832	James Hamilton (DP)
Dec 1832-Dec 1834	Robert Hayne (DP)
Dec 1834-Dec 1836	George McDuffie (DP)
Dec 1836-Dec 1838	Pierce Butler (DP)
Dec 1838-April 1840	Patrick Noble (DP)
April-Dec 1840	Barnabus Henegan (acting) (DP)
Dec 1840-Dec 1842	John Richardson (DP)
Dec 1842-Dec 1844	James Hammond (DP)
Dec 1844-Dec 1846	William Aiken (DP)

Dec 1846-Dec 1848	David Johnson (DP)
Dec 1848-Dec 1850	Whitemarsh Seabrook (DP)
Dec 1850-Dec 1852	John Means (DP)
Dec 1852-Dec 1854	John Manning (*son of R.Manning*) (DP)
Dec 1854-Dec 1856	James Adams (DP)
Dec 1856-Dec 1858	Robert Allston (DP)
Dec 1858-Dec 1860	William Gist (DP)
Dec 1860-Dec 1862	Francis Pickens (*son of A.Pickens*) (DP)
Dec 1862-Dec 1864	Milledge Bonham (DP)
Dec 1864-May 1865	Andrew McGrath (DP)
June-Dec 1865	Benjamin Perry (DP)
Dec 1865-July 1868	James Orr
July 1868-Dec 1872	Robert Scott (CP)
Dec 1872-Dec 1874	Franklin Moses (RP)
Dec 1874-Dec 1876	Daniel Chamberlain (RP)
Dec 1876-Feb 1879	Wade Hampton (RP)
Feb 1879-Sept 1880	William Simpson (acting) (DP)
Sept-Dec 1880	Thomas Jeter (DP)
Dec 1880-Dec 1882	Johnson Hagood (DP)
Dec 1882-Jan 1886	Hugh Thompson (DP)
Jan-Nov 1886	John Sheppard (acting) (DP)
Nov 1886-Dec 1890	John Richardson Jr (*son of J.Richardson*) (DP)
Dec 1890-Dec 1894	Benjamin Tillman (DP)
Dec 1894-Jan 1897	John G.Evans (DP)
Jan 1897-June 1899	William Ellerbe (DP)
June 1899-Jan 1903	Miles McSweeney (DP)
Jan 1903-Jan 1907	Duncan Heyward (DP)
Jan 1907-Jan 1911	Martin Ansel (DP)
Jan 1911-Jan 1915	Coleman Blease (DP)
14-19 Jan 1915	Charles Smith (acting) (DP)
Jan 1915-Jan 1919	Richard Manning III (*grandson of R.Manning*) (DP)
Jan 1919-May 1922	Robert Cooper (DP)
May 1922-Jan 1923	Wilson Harvey (DP)
Jan 1923-Jan 1927	Thomas McLeod (DP)
Jan 1927-Jan 1931	John Richards (DP)
Jan 1931-Jan 1935	Ibra Blackwood (DP)
Jan 1935-Jan 1939	Olin Johnston (1st) (DP)
Jan 1939-Nov 1941	Burnet Maybank (DP)
Nov 1941-March 1942	Joseph Harley (DP)
March 1942-Jan 1943	Richard Jeffries (DP)
Jan 1943-Jan 1945	Olin Johnston (2nd) (DP)
Jan 1945-Jan 1947	Ransome Williams (DP)
Jan 1947-Jan 1951	J.Strom Thurmond (DP)
Jan 1951-Jan 1955	James Byrnes (DP)
Jan 1955-Jan 1959	George Timmerman (DP)

Jan 1959-Jan 1963	Ernest Hollings (DP)
Jan 1963-April 1965	Donald Russell (DP)
April 1965-Jan 1971	Robert McNair (DP)
Jan 1971-Jan 1975	John West (DP)
Jan 1975-Jan 1979	James Edwards (RP)
Jan 1979-Jan 1987	Richard Riley (DP)
Jan 1987-Jan 1995	Carroll Campbell (RP)
Jan 1995-Jan 1999	David Beasley (RP)
Jan 1999-	Jim Hodges (DP)

SOUTH DAKOTA

Statehood: 2 November 1889
Capital: Pierre

Governors:

Nov 1889-Jan 1893	Arthur Mellette (see Dakota Territory) (RP)
Jan 1893-Jan 1897	Charles Sheldon (RP)
Jan 1897-Jan 1901	Andrew Lee (DPP)
Jan 1901-Jan 1905	Charles Herreid (RP)
Jan 1905-Jan 1907	Samuel Elrod (RP)
Jan 1907-Jan 1909	Coe Crawford (RP)
Jan 1909-Jan 1913	Robert Vessey (RP)
Jan 1913-Jan 1917	Frank Byrne (RP)
Jan 1917-Jan 1921	Peter Norbeck (RP)
Jan 1921-Jan 1925	William McMaster (RP)
Jan 1925-Jan 1927	Carl Gunderson (RP)
Jan 1927-Jan 1931	William Bulow (DP)
Jan 1931-Jan 1933	Warren Green (RP)
Jan 1933-Jan 1937	Thomas Berry (DP)
Jan 1937-Jan 1939	Leslie Jensen (RP)
Jan 1939-Jan 1943	Harlan Bushfield (RP)
Jan 1943-Jan 1947	Merrell Sharpe (RP)
Jan 1947-Jan 1951	George T.Mickelson (DP)
Jan 1951-Jan 1955	Sigurd Anderson (RP)
Jan 1955-Jan 1959	Joseph Foss (RP)
Jan 1959-Jan 1961	Ralph Herseth (DP)
Jan 1961-Jan 1965	Archie Gubbrud (RP)
Jan 1965-Jan 1969	Nils Boe (RP)
Jan 1969-Jan 1971	Frank Farrar (RP)
Jan 1971-July 1978	Richard Kniep (DP)
July 1978-Jan 1979	Harvey Wollman (DP)
Jan 1979-Jan 1987	William Janklow (1st) (RP)
Jan 1987-April 1993	George S.Mickelson (*son of G.T.Mickelson*) (DP) († air accident)

April 1993-Jan 1995 Walter Miller
Jan 1995- William Janklow   (2nd) (RP)

TENNESSEE

Statehood: 1 June 1796
Capital: Nashville

Governors:

Sept 1790-March 1796	William Blount (DRP)
March 1796-Sept 1801	John Sevier (1st) (DRP)
Sept 1801-Sept 1803	Archibald Roan (DRP)
Sept 1803-Sept 1809	John Sevier (2nd) (DRP)
Sept 1809-Sept 1815	Willie Blount (*half-brother of W.Blount*) (DRP)
Sept 1815-Oct 1821	Joseph McMinn (DRP)
Oct 1821-Oct 1827	William Carroll (1st) (DRP)
Oct 1827-April 1829	Sam Houston (see Texas) (DRP)
April-Oct 1829	William Hall (acting) (DRP)
Oct 1829-Oct 1835	William Carroll (2nd) (DP)
Oct 1835-Oct 1839	Newton Channon (WP)
Oct 1839-Oct 1841	James Polk (DP) (later President)
Oct 1841-Oct 1845	James Jones (WP)
Oct 1845-Oct 1847	Aaron Brown (DP)
Oct 1847-Oct 1849	Neil Brown (WP)
Oct 1849-Oct 1851	William Trousdale (DP)
Oct 1851-Oct 1853	William Campbell (WP)
Oct 1853-Nov 1857	Andrew Johnson (1st) (RP)
Nov 1857-May 1862	Ishan Harris (DP)
May 1862-April 1865	Andrew Johnson (2nd) (RP) (later President)
April 1865-Feb 1869	William Brownlow (RP)
Feb 1869-Oct 1871	De Witt Senter (CRP)
Oct 1871-Jan 1875	John C.Brown (*brother of N.Brown*) (DP)
Jan 1875-Feb 1879	James Porter (DP)
Feb 1879-Jan 1881	Albert Marks (DP)
Jan 1881-Jan 1883	Alvin Hawkins (RP)
Jan 1883-Jan 1887	William Bate (DP)
Jan 1887-Jan 1891	Robert Taylor (1st) (DP)
Jan 1891-Jan 1893	John Buchanan (DP)
Jan 1893-Jan 1897	Peter Turney (DP)
Jan 1897-Jan 1899	Robert Taylor (2nd) (DP)
Jan 1899-Jan 1903	Benton McMillin (DP)
Jan 1903-March 1905	James Frazier (DP)
March 1905-Jan 1907	John Cox (DP)
Jan 1907-Jan 1911	Malcolm Patterson (DP)

Jan 1911-Jan 1915	Ben Hooper (RP)
Jan 1915-Jan 1919	Thomas Rye (DP)
Jan 1919-Jan 1921	Albert Roberts (DP)
Jan 1921-Jan 1923	Alfred Taylor (*brother of R.Taylor*) (RP)
Jan 1923-Oct 1927	Austin Peay (DP) (†)
Oct 1927-Jan 1933	Henry Horton (DP)
Jan 1933-Jan 1937	Hill McAlister (DP)
Jan 1937-Jan 1939	Gordon Browning (1st) (DP)
Jan 1939-Jan 1945	Prentice Cooper (DP)
Jan 1945-Jan 1949	Jim McCord (DP)
Jan 1949-Jan 1953	Gordon Browning (2nd) (DP)
Jan 1953-Jan 1959	Frank Clement (1st) (DP)
Jan 1959-Jan 1963	Buford Ellington (1st) (DP)
Jan 1963-Jan 1967	Frank Clement (2nd) (DP)
Jan 1967-Jan 1971	Buford Ellington (2nd) (DP)
Jan 1971-Jan 1975	Winfield Dunn (RP)
Jan 1975-Jan 1979	Ray Blanton (DP)
Jan 1979-Jan 1987	Lamar Alexander (RP)
Jan 1987-Jan 1995	Ned McWherter (DP)
Jan 1995-	Don Sundquist (RP)

TEXAS

Independence date: 2 March 1836
Statehood: 29 December 1845
Capital: Austin

Governor:

Nov 1835-March 1836	Henry Smith

Presidents:

March-Oct 1836	David Burnett
Oct 1836-Dec 1838	Sam Houston (1st) (see Tennessee)
Dec 1838-Dec 1841	Mirabeau Lamar
Dec 1841-Dec 1844	Sam Houston (2nd)
Dec 1844-Feb 1846	Anson Jones

Governors:

Feb 1846-Dec 1847	J.Pinckney Henderson (DP)
Dec 1847-Dec 1849	George Wood (DP)
Dec 1849-Nov 1853	P.Hansborough Bell (DP)
Nov-Dec 1853	James Henderson (acting) (DP)

Dec 1853-Dec 1857	Elisha Pease (1st) (DP)
Dec 1857-Dec 1859	Hardin Runnels (DP)
Dec 1859-March 1861	Sam Houston (Ind)
March-Nov 1861	Edward Clark (acting) (DP)
Nov 1861-Nov 1863	Francis Lubbock (DP)
Nov 1863-June 1865	Pendleton Murrah (DP)
June-Aug 1865	Fletcher Stockdale (acting)
Aug 1865-Aug 1866	Andrew Hamilton (CP)
Aug 1866-July 1867	James Throckmorton (CP)
July 1867-Sept 1869	Elisha Pease (2nd) (DP)
(Sept 1869-Jan 1870	post vacant)
Jan 1870-April 1874	Edmund Davis (RP)
April 1874-Dec 1876	Richard Coke (DP)
Dec 1876-Jan 1879	Richard Hubbard (DP)
Jan 1879-Jan 1883	Oran Roberts (DP)
Jan 1883-Jan 1887	John Ireland (DP)
Jan 1887-Jan 1891	Lawrence Ross (DP)
Jan 1891-Jan 1895	James Hogg (DP)
Jan 1895-Jan 1899	Charles Culberson (DP)
Jan 1899-Jan 1903	Joseph Sayers (DP)
Jan 1903-Jan 1907	Samuel Lanham (DP)
Jan 1907-Jan 1911	Thomas Campbell (DP)
Jan 1911-Jan 1915	Oscar Colquitt (DP)
Jan 1915-Aug 1917	James Ferguson (DP)
Aug 1917-Jan 1921	William Hobby (DP)
Jan 1921-Jan 1925	Pat Neff (DP)
Jan 1925-Jan 1927	Miriam Ferguson (*b* M.Wallace) (*wife of J.Ferguson*) (1st) (DP)
Jan 1927-Jan 1931	Dan Moody (DP)
Jan 1931-Jan 1933	Ross Sterling (DP)
Jan 1933-Jan 1935	Miriam Ferguson (2nd) (DP)
Jan 1935-Jan 1939	James Alfred (DP)
Jan 1939-Aug 1941	W.Lee O'Daniel (DP)
Aug 1941-Jan 1947	Coke Stevenson (DP)
Jan 1947-July 1949	Beauford Jester (DP) (†)
July 1949-Jan 1957	Allan Shivers (DP)
Jan 1957-Jan 1963	Price Daniel (DP)
Jan 1963-Jan 1969	John Connally (DP)
Jan 1969-Jan 1973	Preston Smith (DP)
Jan 1973-Jan 1979	Dolph Briscoe (DP)
Jan 1979-Jan 1983	William Clements (1st) (RP)
Jan 1983-Jan 1987	Mark White (DP)
Jan 1987-Jan 1991	William Clements (2nd) (RP)
Jan 1991-Jan 1995	Ann Richards (DP)
Jan 1995-	George W.Bush (RP) (*son of President G. Bush*)

UTAH

Previous name: Deseret until 1851
Statehood: 4 June 1896
Capital: Salt Lake City

Governors:

Sept 1850-July 1857	Brigham Young
July 1857-May 1861	Alfred Cumming
May-July 1861	Francis Wootten (acting)
July-Oct 1861	John Dawson
Oct 1861-March 1862	Frank Fuller (acting)
March 1862-June 1863	Stephen Harding
June 1863-June 1865	James Doty
June-July 1865	Amos Reed (acting)
July 1865-Dec 1869	Charles Durkee
Dec 1869-Jan 1870	Edward Higgins (acting)
Jan-Oct 1870	S.A.Mann (acting)
Oct 1870	J.Wilson Shaffer
1870-71	Vernon Vaughan (acting)
1871	George Black (acting)
Feb 1871-74	George Woods
1874-Feb 1875	S.B.Axtell
Feb 1875-Jan 1880	George Emery
Jan 1880-April 1886	Eli Murray
April 1886-May 1889	Caleb West (1st)
May 1889-April 1893	Arthur Thomas
April 1893-Jan 1896	Caleb West (2nd)
Jan 1896-Jan 1905	Heber Wells (RP)
Jan 1905-Jan 1909	John Cutler (RP)
Jan 1909-Jan 1917	William Spry (RP)
Jan 1917-Jan 1921	Simon Bamberger (DP)
Jan 1921-Jan 1925	Charles Mabey (RP)
Jan 1925-Jan 1933	George Dern (DP)
Jan 1933-Jan 1941	Henry Blood (DP)
Jan 1941-Jan 1949	Herbert Maw (DP)
Jan 1949-Jan 1957	J.Bracken Lee (RP)
Jan 1957-Jan 1965	George Clyde (RP)
Jan 1965-Jan 1977	Calvin Rampton (DP)
Jan 1977-Jan 1985	Scott Matheson (DP)
Jan 1985-Jan 1993	Norman Bangerter (RP)
Jan 1993-	Michael Leavitt (RP)

VERMONT

Statehood: 4 March 1791
Capital: Montpelier

Governors:

1778-Oct 1789	Thomas Chittenden (1st)
Oct 1789-Oct 1790	Moses Robinson
Oct 1790-Aug 1797	Thomas Chittenden (2nd)
Aug-Oct 1797	Paul Brigham (acting)
Oct 1797-Oct 1807	Isaac Techenor (1st) (FP)
Oct 1807-Oct 1808	Israel Smith (DRP)
Oct 1808-Oct 1809	Isaac Techenor (2nd) (FP)
Oct 1809-Oct 1813	Jonas Galusha (1st) (DRP)
Oct 1813-Oct 1815	Martin Chittenden (*son of T.Chittenden*) (FP)
Oct 1815-Oct 1820	Jonas Galusha (2nd) (DRP)
Oct 1820-Oct 1823	Richard Skinner (DRP)
Oct 1823-Oct 1826	Cornelius Van Ness (DRP)
Oct 1826-Oct 1828	Ezra Butler (NRP)
Oct 1828-Oct 1831	Samuel Crafts (NRP)
Oct 1831-Oct 1835	William Palmer (AMP)
Oct 1835-Oct 1841	Silas Jennison (WP)
Oct 1841-Oct 1843	Charles Paine (WP)
Oct 1843-Oct 1844	John Mattocks (WP)
Oct 1844-Oct 1846	William Slade (WP)
Oct 1846-Oct 1848	Horace Eaton (WP)
Oct 1848-Oct 1850	Carlos Coolidge (WP)
Oct 1850-Oct 1852	Charles Williams (WP)
Oct 1852-Nov 1853	Erastus Fairbanks (1st) (WP)
Nov 1853-Oct 1854	John Robinson (DP)
Oct 1854-Oct 1856	Stephen Royce (RP)
Oct 1856-Oct 1858	Ryland Fletcher (RP)
Oct 1858-Oct 1860	Hiland Hall (RP)
Oct 1860-Oct 1861	Erastus Fairbanks (2nd) (RP)
Oct 1861-Oct 1863	Frederick Holbrook (RP)
Oct 1863-Oct 1865	John Gregory Smith (RP)
Oct 1865-Oct 1867	Paul Dillingham (RP)
Oct 1867-Oct 1869	John Page (RP)
Oct 1869-Feb 1870	Paul Washburn (RP) (†)
Feb-Oct 1870	George Hendee (RP)
Oct 1870-Oct 1872	John Stewart (RP)
Oct 1872-Oct 1874	Julius Converse (RP)
Oct 1874-Oct 1876	Ashael Peck (RP)
Oct 1876-Oct 1878	Horace Fairbanks (*son of E.Fairbanks*) (RP)
Oct 1878-Oct 1880	Redfield Proctor (RP)

Oct 1880-Oct 1882	Roswell Farnham (RP)
Oct 1882-Oct 1884	John Barstow (RP)
Oct 1884-Oct 1886	Samuel Pingree (RP)
Oct 1886-Oct 1888	Ebenezer Ormsbee (RP)
Oct 1888-Oct 1890	William Dillingham (RP)
Oct 1890-Oct 1892	Carroll Page (RP)
Oct 1892-Oct 1894	Levi Fuller (RP)
Oct 1894-Oct 1896	Urban Woodbury (RP)
Oct 1896-Oct 1898	Josiah Grout (RP)
Oct 1898-Oct 1900	Edward Smith (RP)
Oct 1900-Oct 1902	William Stickney (RP)
Oct 1902-Oct 1904	John McCullough (RP)
Oct 1904-Oct 1906	Charles Bell (RP)
Oct 1906-Oct 1908	Fletcher Proctor (*son of R.Proctor*) (RP)
Oct 1908-Oct 1910	George Prouty (RP)
Oct 1910-Oct 1912	John Mead (RP)
Oct 1912-Jan 1915	Allen Fletcher (RP)
Jan 1915-Jan 1917	Charles Gates (RP)
Jan 1917-Jan 1919	Horace Graham (RP)
Jan 1919-Jan 1921	Percival Clement (RP)
Jan 1921-Jan 1923	James Hartness (RP)
Jan 1923-Jan 1925	Redfield Proctor Jr (*brother of F.Proctor*) (RP)
Jan 1925-Jan 1927	Franklin Billings (RP)
Jan 1927-Jan 1931	John Weeks (RP)
Jan 1931-Jan 1935	Stanley Wilson (RP)
Jan 1935-Jan 1937	Charles Smith (RP)
Jan 1937-Jan 1941	George Aiken (RP)
Jan 1941-Jan 1945	William Wills (RP)
Jan 1945-Jan 1947	Mortimor Proctor (*son of F.Proctor*) (RP)
Jan 1947-Jan 1950	Ernest Gibson (RP)
Jan 1950-Jan 1951	Harold Arthur (RP)
Jan 1951-Jan 1955	Lee Emerson (RP)
Jan 1955-Jan 1959	Joseph Johnson (RP)
Jan 1959-Jan 1961	Robert Stafford (RP)
Jan 1961-Jan 1963	F.Ray Keyser (RP)
Jan 1963-Jan 1969	Philip Hoff (DP)
Jan 1969-Jan 1973	Deane Davis (RP)
Jan 1973-Jan 1977	Thomas Salmon (DP)
Jan 1977-Jan 1985	Richard Snelling (1st) (RP)
Jan 1985-Jan 1991	Madeleine Kunin (*b* M.May) (RP)
Jan-Aug 1991	Richard Snelling (2nd) (RP) (†)
Aug 1991-	Howard Dean (DP)

VIRGINIA

One of the original 13 states
Capital: Richmond

Governors:

July 1776-June 1779	Patrick Henry (1st)
June 1779-Jan 1781	Thomas Jefferson (later President)
Jan-June 1781	William Fleming (acting)
June-Dec 1781	Thomas Nelson
Dec 1781-Dec 1784	Benjamin Harrison
Dec 1784-Dec 1786	Patrick Henry (2nd)
Dec 1786-Dec 1788	Edmund Randolph
Dec 1788-Dec 1791	Beverley Randolph
Dec 1791-Dec 1794	Henry Lee
Dec 1794-Dec 1796	Robert Brooke (DRP)
Dec 1796-Dec 1799	James Wood (DRP)
Dec 1799-Dec 1802	James Monroe (1st) (DRP)
Dec 1802-Dec 1805	John Page (DRP)
Dec 1805-Dec 1808	William Cabell (DRP)
Dec 1808-Jan 1811	John Tyler Sr (DRP)
Jan-Nov 1811	James Monroe (2nd) (DRP) (later President)
Nov-Dec 1811	George Smith (acting) (DRP)
Dec 1811-Jan 1812	Peyton Randolph (acting) (*son of E.Randolph*) (DRP)
Jan 1812-Dec 1814	James Barbour (DRP)
Dec 1814-Dec 1816	Wilson Nicholas (DRP)
Dec 1816-Dec 1819	James Preston (DRP)
Dec 1819-Dec 1822	Thomas Randolph (DRP)
Dec 1822-Dec 1825	James Pleasants (DRP)
Dec 1825-March 1827	John Tyler (DRP) (later President)
March 1827-March 1830	William Giles (DRP)
March 1830-March 1834	John Floyd (DP)
March 1834-March 1836	Littleton Tazewell (DP)
March 1836-March 1837	Wyndham Robertson (acting) (DP)
March 1837-March 1840	David Campbell (WP)
March 1840-March 1841	Thomas Gilmer (WP)
20-31 March 1841	John Patton (acting) (WP)
March 1841-March 1842	John Rutherfoord (acting) (WP)
March 1842-Jan 1843	John Gregory (acting) (WP)
Jan 1843-Jan 1846	James McDowell (DP)
Jan 1846-Jan 1849	William Smith (1st) (DP)
Jan 1849-Jan 1852	John Buchanan Floyd (*son of J.Floyd*) (DP)
Jan 1852-Jan 1856	Joseph Johnson (DP)
Jan 1856-Jan 1860	Henry Wise (DP)
Jan 1860-Jan 1864	John Letcher (DP)

Jan 1864-May 1865	William Smith (2nd) (DP)
May 1865-April 1868	Francis Pierpont (RP)
April 1868-Sept 1869	Henry Wells (acting) (RP)
Sept 1869-Jan 1874	Gilbert Walker (acting Sept 1869-Jan 1870) (RP)
Jan 1874-Jan 1878	James Kemper (DP)
Jan 1878-Jan 1882	Frederick Holliday (CP)
Jan 1882-Jan 1886	William Cameron (RP)
Jan 1886-Jan 1890	Fitzhugh Lee (DP)
Jan 1890-Jan 1894	Philip McKinney (DP)
Jan 1894-Jan 1898	Charles O'Ferrall
Jan 1898-Jan 1902	J.Hoge Tyler (DP)
Jan 1902-Feb 1906	Andrew Montague (DP)
Feb 1906-Feb 1910	Claude Swanson (DP)
Feb 1910-Feb 1914	William Mann (DP)
Feb 1914-Feb 1918	Henry Stuart (DP)
Feb 1918-Feb 1922	Westmoreland Davis (DP)
Feb 1922-Feb 1926	E.Lee Trinkle (DP)
Feb 1926-Jan 1930	Harry Byrd (DP)
Jan 1930-Jan 1934	John Pollard (DP)
Jan 1934-Jan 1938	George Peery (DP)
Jan 1938-Jan 1942	James Price (DP)
Jan 1942-Jan 1946	Colgate Darden (DP)
Jan 1946-Jan 1950	William Tuck (DP)
Jan 1950-Jan 1954	John Battle (DP)
Jan 1954-Jan 1958	Thomas Stanley (DP)
Jan 1958-Jan 1962	J.Lindsay Almond (DP)
Jan 1962-Jan 1966	Albertis Harrison (DP)
Jan 1966-Jan 1970	Mills Godwin (1st) (DP)
Jan 1970-Jan 1974	Linwood Holton (RP)
Jan 1974-Jan 1978	Mills Godwin (2nd) (DP)
Jan 1978-Jan 1982	John Dalton (RP)
Jan 1982-Jan 1986	Charles Robb (*son-in-law of President L.Johnson*) (DP)
Jan 1986-Jan 1990	Gerald Baliles (DP)
Jan 1990-Jan 1994	Douglas Wilder (DP)
Jan 1994-Jan 1998	George Allen (RP)
Jan 1998-	James Gilmore (RP)

WASHINGTON

Statehood: 11 November 1889
Capital: Olympia

Governors:

March 1853-1857	Isaac Stevens (DP)

1857	J.Patton Anderson (DP)
Sept 1857-July 1859	Fayette McMullin (DP)
July 1859-April 1861	Richard Gholson (DP)
April 1861	William Wallace (RP)
1861-June 1862	L.Jay Turner (acting)
June 1862-Nov 1866	William Pickering (RP)
Nov 1866-March 1867	George Cole (DP)
March 1867-1869	Marshall Moore (RP)
1869-April 1870	Alvan Flanders (RP)
April 1870-April 1872	Edward Saloman (RP)
April 1872-April 1880	Elisha Ferry (1st) (RP)
April 1880-April 1884	William Newell (RP)
April 1884-April 1887	Watson Squire (RP)
April 1887-March 1889	Eugene Semple (DP)
March-Nov 1889	Miles Moore (RP)
Nov 1889-Jan 1893	Elisha Ferry (2nd) (RP)
Jan 1893-Jan 1897	John McGraw (RP)
Jan 1897-Dec 1901	John Rogers (DPP)
Dec 1901-Jan 1905	Henry McBride (RP)
Jan 1905-Jan 1909	Albert Mead (RP)
Jan-March 1909	Samuel Cosgrove (RP)
March 1909-Jan 1913	Marion Hay (RP)
Jan 1913-Feb 1919	Ernest Lister (DP(†))
Feb 1919-Jan 1925	Louis Hart (RP)
Jan 1925-Jan 1933	Roland Hartley (RP)
Jan 1933-Jan 1941	Clarence Martin (DP)
Jan 1941-Jan 1945	Arthur Langlie (1st) (RP)
Jan 1945-Jan 1949	Monrad Wallgren (DP)
Jan 1949-Jan 1957	Arthur Langlie (2nd) (RP)
Jan 1957-Jan 1965	Albert Rosellini (DP)
Jan 1965-Jan 1977	Daniel Evans (RP)
Jan 1977-Jan 1981	Dixy Ray Lee (DP)
Jan 1981-Jan 1985	John Spellman (RP)
Jan 1985-Jan 1993	Booth Gardner (RP)
Jan 1993-Jan 1997	Mike Lowry (DP)
Jan 1997-	Gary Locke (DP)

WEST VIRGINIA

Part of Virginia until 1863
Statehood: 20 June 1863
Capital: Charleston

Governors:

June 1863-Feb 1869	Arthur Boreman (RP)

Feb-March 1869	Daniel Farnsworth (RP)
March 1869-March 1871	William Stevenson (RP)
March 1871-March 1877	John Jacob (DP)
March 1877-March 1881	Henry Mathews (DP)
March 1881-March 1885	Jacob Jackson (DP)
March 1885-Feb 1890	E.Willis Wilson (DP)
Feb 1890-March 1893	A.Brooks Fleming (DP)
March 1893-March 1897	William MacCorkle (DP)
March 1897-March 1901	George Atkinson (RP)
March 1901-March 1905	Albert White (RP)
March 1905-March 1909	William Dawson (RP)
March 1909-March 1913	William Glasscock (RP)
March 1913-March 1917	Henry Hatfield (RP)
March 1917-March 1921	John Cornwell (DP)
March 1921-March 1925	Ephraim Morgan (RP)
March 1925-March 1929	Howard Gore (RP)
March 1929-March 1933	William Conley (RP)
March 1933-Jan 1937	H.Guy Kump (DP)
Jan 1937-Jan 1941	Homer Holt (DP)
Jan 1941-Jan 1945	M.Mansfield Neely (DP)
Jan 1945-Jan 1949	Clarence Meadows (DP)
Jan 1949-Jan 1953	Okev Patteson (DP)
Jan 1953-Jan 1957	William Marland (DP)
Jan 1957-Jan 1961	Cecil Underwood (1st) (RP)
Jan 1961-Jan 1965	William Barron (DP)
Jan 1965-Jan 1969	Hulett Smith (DP)
Jan 1969-Jan 1977	Arch Moore (1st) (RP)
Jan 1977-Jan 1985	John Rockefeller IV (DP)
Jan 1985-Jan 1989	Arch Moore (2nd) (RP)
Jan 1989-Jan 1997	Gaston Caperton (DP)
Jan 1997-	Cecil Underwood (2nd) (RP)

WISCONSIN

Statehood: 29 May 1848
Capital: Madison

Governors:

July 1836-Oct 1841	Henry Dodge (1st) (DP)
Oct 1841-Sept 1844	James Doty (DP)
Sept 1844-May 1845	Nathaniel Tallmadge (DP)
May 1845-June 1848	Henry Dodge (2nd) (DP)
June 1848-Jan 1852	Nelson Dewey (DP)
Jan 1852-Jan 1854	Leonard Farwell (WP)

Jan 1854-March 1856	William Barstow (DP)
March 1856	Arthur MacArthur (acting) (DP)
March 1856-Jan 1858	Coles Bashford (RP)
Jan 1858-Jan 1862	Alexander Randall (RP)
Jan-April 1862	Louis Harvey (RP) (†)
April 1862-Jan 1864	Edward Fairchild (RP)
Jan 1864-Jan 1866	James Lewis (RP)
Jan 1866-Jan 1872	Lucius Fairchild (RP)
Jan 1872-Jan 1874	Cadwallader Washburn (RP)
Jan 1874-Jan 1876	William Taylor (DP)
Jan 1876-Jan 1878	Harrison Ludington (RP)
Jan 1878-Jan 1882	William E. Smith (RP)
Jan 1882-Jan 1889	Jeremiah Ruck (RP)
Jan 1889-Jan 1891	William Hoard (RP)
Jan 1891-Jan 1895	George Peck (DP)
Jan 1895-Jan 1897	William Upham (RP)
Jan 1897-Jan 1901	Edward Scofield (RP)
Jan 1901-Jan 1906	Robert La Follette (RP)
Jan 1906-Jan 1911	James Davidson (RP)
Jan 1911-Jan 1915	Francis McGovern (RP)
Jan 1915-Jan 1921	Emmanuel Philipp (RP)
Jan 1921-Jan 1927	John Blaine (RP)
Jan 1927-Jan 1929	Fred Zimmerman (RP)
Jan 1929-Jan 1931	Walter Kohler Sr (RP)
Jan 1931-Jan 1933	Philip La Follette (*son of R.La Follette*) (1st) (RP)
Jan 1933-Jan 1935	Albert Schmedeman (DP)
Jan 1935-Jan 1939	Philip La Follette (2nd) (PP)
Jan 1939-Jan 1943	Julius Heil (RP)
(1943	Orland Loomis - Governor-elect, died before assuming office)
Jan 1943-March 1947	Walter Goodland (RP) (†)
March 1947-Jan 1951	Walter Kohler Jr (RP)
Jan 1951-Jan 1959	Vernon Thomson (RP)
Jan 1959-Jan 1963	Gaylord Nelson (DP)
Jan 1963-Jan 1965	John Reynolds (DP)
Jan 1965-Jan 1971	Warren Knowles (RP)
Jan 1971-July 1977	Patrick Lucey (DP)
July 1977-Jan 1979	Martin Schreiber (DP)
Jan 1979-Jan 1983	Lee Dreyfus (RP)
Jan 1983-Jan 1987	Anthony Earl (DP)
Jan 1987-	Tommy Thompson (RP)

WYOMING

Statehood: 10 July 1890
Capital: Cheyenne

Governors:

April 1869-Feb 1875	John Campbell (RP)
Feb 1875-April 1878	John Thayer (RP)
April 1878-Aug 1882	John Hoyt (RP)
Aug 1882-Jan 1885	William Hale (RP)
Jan 1885-Nov 1886	Francis Warren (1st) (RP)
Nov-Dec 1886	George Baxter (DP)
Dec 1886-March 1889	Thomas Moonlight (DP)
March 1889-Nov 1890	Francis Warren (2nd) (RP)
Nov 1890-Jan 1893	Amos Barber (acting) (RP)
Jan 1893-Jan 1895	John Osborne (DP)
Jan 1895-Jan 1899	William Richards (RP)
Jan 1899-April 1903	De Forest Richards (RP) (†)
April 1903-Jan 1905	Fenimore Chatterton (acting) (RP)
Jan 1905-Jan 1911	Bryant Brooks (RP)
Jan 1911-Jan 1915	Joseph Carey (DP)
Jan 1915-Feb 1917	John Kendrick (DP)
Feb 1917-Jan 1919	Frank Houx (acting) (DP)
Jan 1919-Jan 1923	Robert Carey (RP)
Jan 1923-Oct 1924	William Ross (DP) (†)
Oct 1924-Jan 1925	Frank Lucas (acting) (RP)
Jan 1925-Jan 1927	Nellie Ross (*b* N.Wynns) (*widow of W.Ross*) (DP)
Jan 1927-Feb 1931	Frank Emerson (RP)
Feb 1931-Jan 1933	Alonzo Clark (acting) (RP)
Jan 1933-Oct 1939	Leslie Miller (DP)
Oct 1939-Jan 1943	Nels Smith (RP)
Jan 1943-Jan 1949	Lester Hunt (DP)
Jan 1949-Feb 1951	Arthur Crane (acting) (RP)
Feb 1951-Jan 1953	Frank Barrett (RP)
Jan 1953-Jan 1955	Clifford Roger (acting) (RP)
Jan 1955-Jan 1959	Milward Simpson (RP)
Jan 1959-Jan 1961	John Hickey (DP)
Jan 1961-Jan 1963	Jack Gage (acting) (DP)
Jan 1963-Jan 1967	Clifford Hansen (RP)
Jan 1967-Jan 1975	Stanley Hathaway (RP)
Jan 1975-Jan 1987	Edward Herschler (DP)
Jan 1987-Jan 1995	Michael Sullivan (DP)
Jan 1995-	Jim Geringer (RP)

United States Territories

AMERICAN SAMOA

Capital: Fagatoga

Governors:

Elected from 1978

1900-01	Benjamin Tilley
1901-02	Uriel Sebree
1903-05	Edmund Underwood
1905-08	Charles Moore
1908-10	John Parker
1910-13	William Crose
1913-14	Clark Stevens
1915-19	John Poyer
1919-20	Warren Terhune
1920-22	Waldo Evans
1922-23	Edwin Pollock
1923-25	Edward Kellogg
1925-27	Henry Bryan
1927-32	Stephen Graham
1932-34	Gatewood Lincoln
1934-36	Otto Dowling
1936-38	MacGillivray Milne
1938-40	Edward Hanson
1940-42	Laurence Wild
1942-44	John Moyer
1944-45	Allen Hobbs
1945	Ralph Hungerford
1945-47	Harold Houser
1947-49	Vernon Huber
1949-51	Thomas Darden Jr
1951-52	Phelps Phelps
1952-53	James Owing
1953	Lawrence Judd
1953-56	Richard Lowe
1956-60	Peter Tali Coleman (1st)
1961-67	H.Rex Lee
1967-69	Owen Aspinall
1969-76	John Haydon
1976-78	Earl Ruth
Jan 1978-Jan 1985	Peter Tali Coleman (2nd)
Jan 1985-Jan 1989	Aifili Lutali (1st)
Jan 1989-Jan 1993	Peter Tali Coleman (3rd)
Jan 1993-Jan 1997	Aifili Lutali (2nd)
Jan 1997-	Tauese Sunia

GUAM

Capital: Agaña (Hagåtña)

Governors:

Elected from 1971

1898	José Sisto (1st)
1898-99	Francisco Portusach
1899	José Sisto (2nd)
1899	Joaquín Pérez
1899	William Coe
1899-1900	Richard Leary
1900-01	Seaton Schroeder (1st)
1901	William Swift
1901-03	Seaton Schroeder (2nd)
1903-04	William Sewell
1904-06	George Dyer
1906-07	Temphin Potts
1907	Luke McNamee
1907-11	Edward Dorn
1911-12	George Salisbury
1912-13	Robert Coontz
1913-16	William Maxwell
1916-18	Roy Smith
1918-20	William Gilmer
1920-22	Ivan Wettengel
1922-23	Adelbert Althouse
1923-26	Henry Price
1926-29	Lloyd Shapley
1929-31	Willis Bradley
1931-33	Edmund Root
1933-36	George Alexander
1936-38	Benjamin McCandlish
1938-40	James Alexander
1940-41	George McMillin
(1941-44	Japanese occupation)
1944-46	Chester Nimitz
1946-50	Charles Pownall
1950-53	Carlton Skinner
1953-56	Ford Elvidge
1956-60	Richard Lowe
1960-62	Joseph Flores
1962-63	William Daniel
1963-69	Manuel Guerrero
1969-Jan 1975	Carlos García Camacho (RP)
Jan 1975-Jan 1979	Ricardo Bordallo (1st) (RP)
Jan 1979-Jan 1983	Paul McDonald Calvo (RP)
Jan 1983-Jan 1987	Ricardo Bordallo (2nd) (RP)

Jan 1987-Feb 1995   Joseph Ada   (RP)
March 1995-   Carl Gutiérrez   (DP)

NORTHERN MARIANAS

Commonwealth of the Northern Marianas
Capital: Saipan

Governors:

Jan 1978-Jan 1982   Carlos Camacho
Jan 1982-Jan 1990   Pedro P.Tenorio   (1st) (RP)
Jan 1990-Jan 1994   Lorenzo   (Larry) Guerrero   (RP)
Jan 1994-Jan 1998   Froilan Tenorio   (DP)
Jan 1998-   Pedro P.Tenorio   (2nd) (RP)

PUERTO RICO

Commonwealth of Puerto Rico
Capital: San Juan

Governor-General:

24-28 July 1898   Luis Muñoz Rivera

Governors:
Elected from 1949

1898   John Brooke
1898-99   Guy Henry
1899-1900   George Davis
1900-02   Charles Allen
1902-04   William Hunt
1904-07   Beekman Winthrop
1907-09   Regis Post
1909-13   George Colton
1913-21   Arthur Yager
1921-23   Edward Reily
1923-29   Horace Towner
1929-32   Theodore Roosevelt II
1932-33   James Beverley
1933-34   Robert Gore
1934-39   Blanton Winship
1939-41   William Leahy
1941-46   Rexford Tugwell
1946-49   Jesús Piñero

Jan 1949-Jan 1965	Luis Muñoz Marín (*son of L.Muñoz Rivera*) (PDP)
Jan 1965-Jan 1969	Robert Sánchez Vilella (PDP)
Jan 1969-Jan 1973	Luis Ferré (NPP)
Jan 1973-Jan 1977	Rafael Hernández Colon (1st) (PDP)
Jan 1977-Jan 1985	Carlos Romero Barceló (NPP)
Jan 1985-Jan 1993	Rafael Hernández Colon (2nd) (PDP)
Jan 1993-	Pedro Rosselló (NPP)

NPP = New Progressive Party
PDP = Popular Democratic Party

UNITED STATES VIRGIN ISLANDS

Previous name until 1917: Danish West Indies
Capital: Charlotte Amalie

Governors:

Elected from 1971

1893-1903	Carl Hedemann
1903-05	Frederik Nordlien
1905-08	Christian Cold
1908-12	Peter Limpricht
1912-16	Lars Helweg-Larsen
1916-17	Henrik Konow
1917-19	James Oliver
1919-21	Joseph Oman
1921-22	Sumner Kitbelle
1922-23	Henry Hough
1923-25	Philip Williams
1925-27	Martin Trench
1927-31	Waldo Evans
1931-35	Paul Pearson
1935-41	Lawrence Cramer
1941-46	Charles Harwood
May 1946-49	William Hastie
1949-54	Morris de Castro
1954-55	Archibald Alexander
1955-58	Walter Gordon
1958-61	John Merwin
1961-69	Ralph Paiewonsky
1969-Jan 1975	Melvin Evans (RP)
Jan 1975-Feb 1978	Cyril King (ICM) (†)
Feb 1978-Jan 1987	Juan Luis (ICM)
Jan 1987-Jan 1995	Alexander Farrely (DP)
Jan 1995-Jan 1999	Roy Schneider (DP)

Jan 1999-   Charles Turnbull   (DP)

DP = Democratic Party
ICM = Independent Citizens' Movement
RP = Republican Party

Other Territories

The United States administers several islands in the Pacific Ocean, namely WAKE ISLAND, MIDWAY ISLAND and JOHNSTONE ATOLL, all administered by the US military, and HOWLAND, JARUIS and BAKER ISLANDS, and PALMYRA administered by the Interior Department.

URUGUAY

Official name: Oriental Republic of Uruguay, República Oriental del Uruguay
Previous name: Banda Oriental until 1825
Independence date: 25 May 1825
Capital: Montevideo

Uruguay was ruled by Spain from 1516, apart for a brief period of Portuguese rule in the 18th century. Attempts to win independence began in 1813 and in 1820 Uruguay became a province of Brazil. In 1825 Uruguay declared itself independent; Brazil and Argentina fought for its control but in 1828 recognized its independence. In 1952 Uruguay introduced a system of government based on the Swiss model, but in 1967 the presidential system was restored.

Protector:

1813-Sept 1820	José Artigas (deposed)
(1820-25	Brazilian rule)
(1825-28	war between Brazil and Argentina)

Governors:

Aug-Dec 1828	Joaquín Suárez del Rondelo (1st)
Dec 1828-April 1830	José Rondeau
April-Oct 1830	Joaquín Suárez del Rondelo (2nd)

Presidents:
President of the Council of Government May 1952-Feb 1967

Oct 1830-Oct 1834	José Fructuoso Rivera (1st)
Oct 1834-March 1835	Carlos Anaya (acting)
March 1835-Oct 1838	Manuel Oribe
Oct-Nov 1838	Gabriel Pereira (acting)
Nov 1838-March 1843	José Fructuoso Rivera (2nd)
March 1843-March 1852	Joaquín Suárez del Rondelo
March 1852-March 1854	Juan Giró
March 1854-Oct 1855	Venancio Flores (1st)
Oct 1855-March 1856	Manuel Bustamente (acting)
March 1856-March 1860	Gabriel Pereira
March 1860-March 1864	Bernardo Berro
March 1864-Feb 1865	Anastasio Cruz Aguirre
Feb 1865-March 1866	Venancio Flores (acting) (assassinated 1868)
March 1866-Feb 1868	Francisco Vidal (1st)

16-19 Feb 1868	Pedro Varela (acting)
19-22 Feb 1868	Manuel Flores (*brother of V.Flores*)
Feb 1868-March 1872	Lorenzo Batlle y Grau
March 1872-March 1873	Tomás Gomensoro
March 1873-March 1875	José Ellauri
March 1875-March 1876	Pedro Varela (deposed)
March 1876-March 1880	Lorenzo Latorre
March 1880-March 1882	Francsico Vidal (2nd)
March 1882-Nov 1886	Máximo Santos
Nov 1886-March 1890	Máximo Tajes
March 1890-March 1894	Julio Herrera y Obes
March 1894-Aug 1897	Juan Borda (†)
Aug 1897-Feb 1903	Juan Cuestas
Feb 1903-Feb 1907	José Batlle y Ordoñez (*son of L.Batlle y Grau*) (1st) (CP)
Feb 1907-March 1911	Claudio Williman (CP)
March 1911-March 1915	José Batlle y Ordoñez (2nd) (CP)
March 1915-March 1919	Feliciano Viera (CP)
March 1919-March 1923	Baltasar Brum (CP)
March 1923-March 1927	José Serrato (CP)
March 1927-March 1931	Juan Campestiguy (CP)
March 1931-March 1938	Gabriel Terra (CP)
March 1938-March 1943	Alfredo Baldomir (*brother-in-law*) (CP)
March 1943-March 1947	Juan Amézaga (CP)
March-Aug 1947	Tomás Berreta (CP) (†)
Aug 1947-March 1951	Luis Batlle Berres (*nephew of J.Batlle y Ordoñez*) (1st) (CP)
March 1951-Feb 1955	Andrés Martínez Trueba (CP)
March 1955-Feb 1956	Luis Batlle Berres (2nd) (CP)
March 1955-Feb 1957	Alberto Fermin Zubiria (CP)
March 1955-Feb 1958	Arturo Lezama (CP)
March 1958-Feb 1959	Carlos Fischer (CP)
March 1959-Feb 1960	Martin Etchegoyen (NP)
March 1960-Feb 1961	Benito Nardone (NP)
March 1961-Feb 1962	Eduardo Haedo (NP)
March 1962-Feb 1963	Faustino Harrison (NP)
March 1963-Feb 1964	Daniel Fernández Crespo (NP)
March 1964-Feb 1965	Luis Giannatasio (NP) (†)
Feb 1965-Feb 1966	Washington Beltrán (acting Feb-March 1965) (NP)
March 1966-Feb 1967	Alberto Héber Usher (NP)
March-Dec 1967	Oscar Gestido (CP) (†)
Dec 1967-March 1972	Jorge Pacheco Arego (CP)
March 1972-June 1976	Juan Bordaberry Arocena (CP)
June-Sept 1976	Alberto Demichelli Lizaso
Sept 1976-Sept 1981	Aparisio Méndez
Sept 1981-Feb 1985	Gregorio Alvarez Armelino
Feb-March 1985	Rafael Addiego (acting)

March 1985-March 1990	Julio Sanguinetti (1st) (CP)
March 1990-March 1995	Luis Lacalle Herrera (NP)
March 1995-March 2000	Julio Sanguinetti (2nd) (CP)
March 2000-	Jorge Batlle (*son of L. Batlle*) (CP)

CP = Colorado Party
NP = National Party

UZBEKISTAN

Official name: Republic of Uzbekistan, Ozbekistan Respublikasy
Previous name: Uzbek Soviet Socialist Republic 1924-91
State formed: 5 December 1924
Admission to USSR: 13 May 1925
Independence date: 31 August 1991
Capital: Tashkent

The area of central Asia which included present-day Uzbekistan was conquered by Russia in the 1860s. From Russian Turkistan the states of Bokhara and Khiva were subjugated in 1873. Following the Russian revolution, Soviet republics were established in the three countries. In 1924 the area was reorganized and Uzbekistan, Turkmenistan and Tajikistan were created. Uzbekistan became a constituent republic of the USSR in 1925. In 1991 it declared itself independent as the Soviet Union collapsed.

Presidents:
Chairman of the Central Executive Committee 1925-38
President of the Presidium of the Supreme Soviet 1938-90
Chairman of the Supreme Soviet March-Nov 1990

Feb 1925-March 1943	Yuldash Akhunbabayev (†)
March 1943-March 1947	Abdulvali Muminov
March 1947-Aug 1950	Amin Niyazov
Aug 1950-March 1959	Sharaf Rashidov
March 1959-Sept 1970	Yadgar Nasriddinova
Sept 1970-Dec 1978	Nazar Matchanov
Dec 1978-Feb 1984	Inamzhon Usmankhodzayev
Feb 1984-Dec 1986	Akil Salimov
Dec 1986-Jan 1988	Rafik Nishanov
April 1988-March 1989	Pulat Khabibullayev
March 1989-March 1990	Mirzoalim Ibragimov
March 1990-	Islam Karimov

Prime Ministers:
Chairman of the Council of People's Commissars 1925-46
Chairman of the Council of Ministers 1946-92

Feb 1925-June 1937	Fayzulla Khodzhayev	(see Bokhara) (removed, executed)
July-Oct 1937	Abdullah Karimov	
Oct 1937-July 1938	Sultan Segizbayev	

July 1938-Aug 1950   Abdudzhar Abdurakhmanov
Aug 1950-51   Abdurrazak Mavlyanov
1951-53   Nuritdin Mukhitdinov   (1st)
1953-54   Usman Yusupov
1954-Dec 1955   Nuritdin Mukhitdinov   (2nd)
Dec 1955-Dec 1957   Sabir Kamalov   (see Kara-Kalpakstan)
Dec 1957-March 1959   Mansur Mirza-Akhmedov
March 1959-Sept 1961   Arif Alimov
Sept 1961-Feb 1971   Rakhankul Kurbanov
Feb 1971-Nov 1984   Narmakhonmadi Khudaiberdyov
Nov 1984-Oct 1989   Gayrat Kadyrov
Oct 1989-March 1990   Irakhmat Mirkasymov
March-Nov 1990   Shakurulla Mirsaidov
(Nov 1990-Dec 1991   post abolished)
Dec 1991-Dec 1995   Abdulkhashim Mutalov
Dec 1995-   Utkir Sultanov

Communist Party Leaders:

First Secretary

Feb 1925-Sept 1937   Akmal Ikramov   (removed, executed)
1937-50   Usman Yusupov
1950-Dec 1955   Amin Niyazov
Dec 1955-Dec 1957   Nuritdin Mukhitdinov
Dec 1957-March 1959   Sabir Kamalov
March 1959-Feb 1984   Sharaf Rashidov   (†)
Feb 1984-Jan 1988   Inamzhon Usmankhodzayev
Jan 1988-June 1989   Rafik Nishanov
June 1989-Aug 1991   Islam Karimov
(Aug 1991   party dissolved)

Autonomous republic

KARA-KALPAKSTAN

Official name: Republic of Kara-Kalpakstan
Previous names: Kara-Kalpak Autonomous Region 1925-32, Kara-Kalpak Autonomous Soviet Socialist Republic 1932-91
Republic formed: 20 March 1932
Capital: Nukus

Presidents:

Chairman of the Central Executive Committee 1932-38
President of the Presidium of the Supreme Soviet 1938-90
Chairman of the Supreme Soviet since 1990

1932-34   Kopleon Mukhamedov

1934-37 Kasym Avezov
1937-47 V.A.Khomutnikov
1947-Nov 1960 Mateke Dzhumanazarov
Nov 1960-1978 Davlet Yeshimbetov
1978-85 Kamal Rzayev
1985-91 Tursyn Eshimbetova
March 1991-92 Dauletbai Shamshetov
1992-97 Ubbiniyaz Ashirbekov
1997- Timur Kamalov

Prime Ministers:

Chairman of the Council of People's Commissars 1932-46
Chairman of the Council of Ministers since 1946

May 1932-34 Kasym Avezov
1934-44 Dzhumbay Kurbanov
1945 Mateke Dzhumanazarov
1946-50 P.Seitov
1950-55 D.Seitniyazev
1955-57 Sabir Kamalov
Dec 1957-March 1959 Naruz Zhapakov
March 1959-March 1963 Kalibek Kamalov
March 1963-Feb 1981 Yerezhep Aytmuratov
Feb 1981-Oct 1985 Marat Yusupov
Oct 1985-89 Damir Yadgarov
1989-92 Amin Tojiev   (1st)
1992-95 Rajapbay Yuldashev
1995 Bahram Jumaniyazov
1995-98 Saparbay Avezmatov
1998- Amin Tojiev   (2nd)

Communist Party Leaders:

First Secretary

1925- ? A.Kudabayev
193?-37 — — Aliev
1937-39 K.B.Baltayev
1941-46 Sabir Kamalov
1949-50 Tursun Kambarov
1950-54 P.Seitov
1954-56 Arzi Makhmudov
1956-March 1963 Nazir Makhmudov
March 1963-Aug 1984 Kalibek Kamalov
Aug 1984-89 Kakimbek Salykov
1989-91 Sagyndyk Niyetullayev

Former states

BOKHARA

Official names: Emirate of Bokhara until 1920, Soviet Republic of Bokhara 1920-24
Divided between Tajikistan, Turkmenistan & Uzbekistan in 1924
Capital: Bokhara (in present-day Uzbekistan)

Emirs:

1799-1826	Sayid Ameer Hyder
1826	Mir Hussein
1826-27	Mir Omir
1827-60	Mir Nasrulla
1860-Nov 1895	Muzaffer-ed-Din
Nov 1895-1911	Sayid Abdul Ahad
1911-Aug 1920	Said Mir Alim Khan (deposed)

Presidents:
Chairman of the Central Executive Committee

1921	Mirza Muhiddin
Sept 1921-April 1922	Usman Pulatkodzhayev (Mukhitdinov) (see Tajikistan)
April-Aug 1922	Muin Gan bin Amin (Aminov)
Aug 1922-Dec 1924	Fayzulla Khodzhayev (see Uzbekistan)

Prime Ministers:
Chairman of the Council of People's Commissars

Oct 1920-Sept 1921	Usman Pulatkodzhayev (Mukhitdinov)
Sept 1921-Dec 1924	Fayzulla Khodzhayev

KHOREZM (KHIVA)

Official names: Khanate of Khiva until 1920, Soviet Republic of Khorezm 1920-24
Divided between Turkmenistan & Uzbekistan in 1924
Capital: Khiva (in present-day Uzbekistan)

Khans:

1806-25	Mohammed Rahim Khan
1825-42	Alla Kuli Khan
1842-45	Rahim Kuli Khan
1845-55	Mohammed Arnin Khan
1855-56	Abdullah Khan
1856	Kutlugh Murad Khan
1856-65	Seyid Mohammed Khan

1865-1910	Sajid Mohammed Rahim Khan
1910-Feb 1920	Said Asfendiar (deposed)

Presidents:
Chairman of the Central Executive Committee

April 1920-May 1920	Yusuf Pahlawan Niyaz (Yusupov)
May-Nov 1921	Ata Mahdum
Nov 1921-22	Alim Gan Akchurin
1922	— — Makhmudov
1922-24	N.I.Petrushkov

Prime Ministers:
Chairman of the Council of People's Commissars

Feb 1920-March 1921	Mohammed Salimoglu
March-Sept 1921	Koch Karaglu (Kochakar)
Sept-Nov 1921	Temur Khodzha
Nov 1921-Dec 1924	Sultanmurad Kany

TURKISTAN

Official names: Turkistan Autonomous Soviet Republic 1918-21, Turkistan Soviet Republic 1921-24
Republic formed: 16 March 1918 (in Russia)
Republic abolished: 27 October 1924. Divided between Tajikistan, Turkmenistan, Uzbekistan & Kirghizia.
Capital: Tashkent

Presidents:
Chairman of the Central Executive Committee

April-May 1918	Petr Kobozev
May-Oct 1918	A.F.Solkin
1918-19	V.D.Votintsev
1919	Arishtarkh Kazakov
1919-20	Nazir Tyuryakulov (1st)
1920	Turar Ryskulov
1920-21	Nazir Tyuryakulov (2nd)
Feb-April 1921	Nizam Khodzhayev
April 1921-22	Abdullah Rahimbayev (see Tajikistan)
1922-Oct 1924	Nedirbai Aitakov (see Turkmenistan)

Prime Ministers:
Chairman of the Council of People's Commissars

April-Nov 1918	F.I.Kolisev

Nov 1918-Jan 1919	Vladislav Figelski (deposed, executed)
1919	Karp Sorokin
1919	Isidor Lyubimov (1st)
March-April 1920	Yan Rudzutak
1920	Nizam Khodzhayev
1920	Isidor Lyubimov (2nd)
1920-22	Kaigisyz Atabayev (see Turkmenistan)
1922-24	Turar Ryskulov
Jan-Oct 1924	Ahmed Islamov

Communist Party Leaders:

First Secretary

1921-22	Yan Rudzutak
1922-23	Nazir Tyuryakulov
1923-24	Abdullah Rahimbayev

VANUATU

Official name: Republic of Vanuatu, République du Vanuatu, Ripablik blong Vanuatu (Bislama)
Previous name: New Hebrides until 1980
Independence date: 30 July 1980
Capital: Port Vila

British and French settlements were established in the New Hebrides during the 19th century and in 1906 an Anglo-French condominium was set up to administer the islands. Ministerial government was introduced in 1977, and in 1980 the islands became the independent state of Vanuatu.

Resident Commissioners:

British:
1902-07	Ernest Rason
1907-24	Merton King
1924-27	Geoffrey Smith-Rewse
1927-40	George Joy
1940-50	Richard Blandy
1950-55	Hubert Flaxman
1955-62	John Rennie
1962-66	Alexander Wilkie
1966-73	Colin Allan
1973-75	Roger du Boulay
1975-78	John Champion
1978-80	Andrew Stuart

French:
1901-04	Gaudence-Charles Faraut
1904-08	Charles Bord
1908-09	Charles Noufflard
1909-11	Jules Martin
1911-13	Jules-Vincent Repiquet
1913-16	Jacques-Louis Miramenda (1st)
1916-17	Edmond Lippmann
1918-19	Lucien Nielly
1919-20	Alfred Solari
1920-21	Jacques-Louis Miramenda (2nd)
1921-23	Henri d'Arboussier (1st)
1923-25	Auguste de la Vaissière
1925-29	Henri d'Arboussier (2nd)

1929-30   Gabriel Thaly
1930-31   Maurice-Georges Tronet
1931-33   Antoine-Louis Carlotti
1933-35   Henri-Camille Sautot   (1st)
1935-37   Fernand Casimir
1937-40   Henri-Camille Sautot   (2nd)
1940-47   Robert Kuler
1947-49   André Menard
1949-58   Pierre Anthonioz
1958-60   Benjamin-Marcel Favreau
1960-65   Maurice Delauney
1965-69   Jacques Mouradian
1969-74   Robert Langlois
1974-78   Robert Gauger
1978-80   Jean-Jacques Robert

Presidents:

July 1980-Feb 1984   George Sokomanu   (b G.Kalkoa) (1st)
Feb-March 1984   Frederick Timakata   (acting)
March 1984-Jan 1989   George Sokomanu   (2nd)
Jan 1989-Jan 1994   Frederick Timakata
Jan-March 1994   Alfred Masengnalo   (acting)
March 1994-March 1999   Jean-Marie Léyé
March 1999-   John Bani

Chief Ministers:

Dec 1977-Dec 1978   George Kalsakau   (N)
Dec 1978-Nov 1979   Gerard Leymang   (TU)
Nov 1979-July 1980   Walter Lini   (VP)

Prime Ministers:

July 1980-Sept 1991   Walter Lini   (VP)
(18-19 Dec 1988   Barak Sopé - appointment declared illegal)
Sept-Dec 1991   Donald Kalpokas   (1st) (VP)
Dec 1991-Dec 1995   Maxime Carlot Korman   (1st) (UMP)
Dec 1995-Feb 1996   Serge Vohor   (1st) (UMP)
Feb-Sept 1996   Maxime Carlot Korman   (2nd) (UMP)
Sept 1996-March 1998   Serge Vohor   (2nd) (UMP)
March 1998-Nov 1999   Donald Kalpokas   (2nd) (VP)
Nov 1999-   Barak Sopé   (MPP)

MPP = Melanesian Progressive Party
N = Natatok
TU = Tan Union

UMP = Union of Moderate Parties
VP = Vanuaaka Pati

Secessionist state

VEMERANA (Espiritu Santo)

Capital: Luganville (Santo Town)

Prime Minister:

May-July 1980	Jimmy Stevens

VATICAN CITY STATE

Official name: Vatican City State, Statto della Citta del Vaticano
State founded: 11 February 1929

The Popes have exercised temporal authority over the See of Rome since the 1st century. In the 8th century their area was extended by the creation of the Papal States. In 1309 the papacy was moved to Avignon where it remained until 1377. During the Great Schism of 1378-1417 the Popes in Rome were challenged by anti-popes in Avignon and later in Spain. In 1860 the Papal States were incorporated into the newly united kingdom of Italy; the city of Rome was not incorporated until 1870 and the pope withdrew to the Vatican. The Concordat agreed between Pope Pius XI and Italy in 1929 established the Vatican City as a sovereign state.

PAPAL STATES

Capital: Rome (Avignon 1309-77)

Sovereigns (Popes):

756-April 757	Stephen II (elected Pope in 752)
May 757-June 767	Paul I
Aug 768-Jan 772	Stephen III
Feb 772-Dec 795	Adrian I
Dec 795-June 816	Leo III
June 816-Jan 817	Stephen IV
Jan 817-Feb 824	Pascal I
May 824-Aug 827	Eugenius II
Aug-Sept 827	Valentine
Oct 827-Jan 844	Gregory IV
Jan 844-Jan 847	Sergius II
Jan 847-July 855	Leo IV
July 855-April 858	Benedict III
April 858-Nov 867	Nicholas I
Dec 867-Dec 872	Adrian II
Dec 872-Dec 882	John VIII (assassinated)
Dec 882-May 884	Marcellus I
May 884-Sept 885	Adrian III
Oct 885-Sept 891	Stephen V
Sept 891-April 896	Formosus
April 896	Boniface VI
May 896-Aug 897	Stephen VI (assassinated)
Aug-Nov 897	Romanus

Dec 897	Theodore
Jan 898-Jan 900	John IX
Jan 900-July 903	Benedict IV
July-Sept 903	Leo X (deposed,murdered)
Jan 904-April 911	Sergius III
April 911-June 913	Anastasius III
July 913-Feb 914	Lando
March 914-May 928	John X (deposed,murdered)
May-Dec 928	Leo VI
Dec 928-Feb 931	Stephen VII
March 931-Dec 935	John XI
Jan 936-July 939	Leo VII
July 939-Oct 942	Stephen VIII
Oct 942-May 946	Marinus II
May 946-Dec 955	Agapetus II
Dec 955-Dec 963	John XII (Ottaviano) (deposed)
Dec 963-May 964	Leo VIII (1st)
May 964-March 965	Benedict V (deposed)
March-Oct 965	Leo VIII (2nd)
Oct 965-Sept 972	John XIII
Jan 973-June 974	Benedict VI (deposed,murdered)
Oct 974-July 983	Benedict VII
Dec 983-Aug 984	John XIV (Pietro Canepanova)
Aug 984-March 996	John XV
May 996-Feb 999	Gregory V (Bruno)
April 999-May 1003	Silvester II (Gerbert)
June-Dec 1003	John XVII (Sicco)
Dec 1003-July 1009	John XVIII (Phasinus)
July 1009-May 1012	Sergius IV (Pietro Buccaporca)
May 1012-April 1024	Benedict VIII (Teofilatto)
April 1024-Dec 1032	John XIX (Romanus) *brother*
Dec 1032-Dec 1044	Benedict IX (Teofilatto) (1st)
Jan-Feb 1045	Silvester III (Giovanni di Sabina)
Feb-May 1045	Benedict IX (2nd) (abdicated)
April 1045-Dec 1046	Gregory VI (Giovanni Graziano)
Dec 1046-Oct 1047	Clement II (Suidger)
Nov 1047-July 1048	Benedict IX (3rd)
July-Aug 1048	Damasus II (Poppo)
Dec 1048-April 1054	Leo IX (Bruno,Count of Dagsbourg)
April 1055-July 1057	Victor II (Count Gebhard of Dollenstein)
Aug 1057-March 1058	Stephen IX (Frédéric de Lorraine)
Dec 1058-July 1061	Nicholas II (Gerard)
Sept 1061-April 1073	Alexander II (Anselmo of Baggio)
April 1073-May 1085	Gregory VII (Hildebrand)
May 1086-Sept 1087	Victor III (Desiderius)

March 1088-July 1099	Urban II (Odo)
Aug 1099-Jan 1118	Pascal II (Ranieri)
Jan 1118-Jan 1119	Gelastius II (Giovanni Gaetani)
Feb 1119-Dec 1124	Calixtus II (Gui of Burgundy)
Dec 1124-Feb 1130	Honorius II (Lamberto Scannabecchi)
Feb 1130-Sept 1143	Innocent II (Gregorio Papareschi)
Sept 1143-March 1144	Caelestinus II (Guido de Castello)
March 1144-Feb 1145	Lucius II (Gerardo Caccianemici)
Feb 1145-July 1153	Eugenius III (Bernardo Paganelli)
July 1153-Dec 1154	Anastasius IV (Corrado)
Dec 1154-Sept 1159	Adrian IV (Nicholas Breakspeare)
Sept 1159-Aug 1181	Alexander III (Rolando Bandinelli)
Sept 1181-Sept 1185	Lucius III (Ubaldo Allucingoli)
Nov 1185-Oct 1187	Urban III (Uberto Crivelli)
Oct-Dec 1187	Gregory VIII (Alberto di Morra)
Dec 1187-March 1191	Clement III (Paolo Scolari)
March 1191-Jan 1198	Caelistinus III (Giacinto Buboni)
Jan 1198-July 1216	Innocent III (Lothario dei Conti di Segni)
July 1216-March 1227	Honorius III (Cencio Savelli)
March 1227-Aug 1241	Gregory IX (Ugolino dei Conti di Segni)
Oct-Nov 1241	Caelistinus IV (Goffredo Castiglione)
June 1243-Dec 1254	Innocent IV (Sinibaldo Fieschi)
Dec 1254-May 1261	Alexander IV (Rainaldo dei Conti di Segni) (*nephew of Gregory IX*)
Aug 1261-Oct 1264	Urban IV (Jacques Pantaléon)
Feb 1265-Nov 1268	Clement IV (Gui Fauçoi le Gros)
Sept 1271-Jan 1276	Gregory X (Theobaldo Visconti)
Jan-June 1276	Innocent V (Pierre de Tarentaise)
July-Aug 1276	Adrian V (Ottobono dei Fieschi)
Sept 1276-May 1277	John XXI (Pedro Juliani)
Nov 1277-Aug 1280	Nicholas III (Giovanni Orsini)
Feb 1281-March 1285	Martin IV (Simon de Brion)
April 1285-April 1287	Honorius IV (Giacomo Savelli)
Feb 1288-April 1292	Nicholas IV (Girolamo Moschi)
July-Dec 1294	Caelistinus V (Pietro del Morrone) (abdicated)
Dec 1294-Oct 1303	Boniface VIII (Benedetto Gaetani)
Oct 1303-July 1304	Benedict XI (Nicola Boccasini)
June 1305-April 1316	Clement V (Bertrand de Got)
Aug 1316-Dec 1334	John XXII (Jacques Duèse)
Dec 1334-April 1342	Benedict XII (Jacques Fournier)
May 1342-Dec 1352	Clement VI (Pierre Roger)
Dec 1352-Sept 1362	Innocent VI (Étienne Aubert)
Sept 1362-Dec 1370	Urban V (Guillaume Grimoard)
Dec 1370-March 1378	Gregory XI (Pierre-Roger de Beaufort)
April 1378-Oct 1389	Urban VI (Bartolommeo Prignano)
Nov 1389-Oct 1404	Boniface IX (Pietro Tomacelli)

Oct 1404-Nov 1406	Innocent VII (Cosimo dei Migliorati)
Nov 1406-July 1415	Gregory XII (Angelo Carrari) (abdicated)
Nov 1417-Feb 1431	Martin V (Oddone Colonna)
March 1431-Feb 1447	Eugenius IV (Gabriele Condulmer)
March 1447-March 1455	Nicholas V (Tommaso Parentucelli)
April 1455-Aug 1458	Calixtus III (Alfonso de Borja)
Aug 1458-Aug 1464	Pius II (Enea de'Piccolomini)
Aug 1464-July 1471	Paul II (Pietro Barbo)
Aug 1471-Aug 1484	Sixtus IV (Francesco della Rovere)
Aug 1484-July 1492	Innocent VIII (Giovanni Cibo)
Aug 1492-Aug 1503	Alexander VI (Rodrigo de Borja) *(nephew of Calixtus III)*
Sept-Oct 1503	Pius III (Francesco Todeschini-Piccolomini)
Oct 1503-Feb 1513	Julius II (Giuliani della Rovere) *(nephew of Sixtus IV)*
March 1513-Dec 1521	Leo X (Giovanni de'Medici)
Jan 1522-Sept 1523	Adrian VI (Adriaan Florenz)
Nov 1523-Sept 1534	Clement VII (Giulio de'Medici) *(cousin of Leo X)*
Dec 1534-Nov 1549	Paul III (Alessandro Farnese)
Feb 1550-March 1555	Julius III (Giovanni del Monte)
April-May 1555	Marcellus II (Marcello Cervini)
May 1555-Aug 1559	Paul IV (Giovanni Caraffa)
Dec 1559-Dec 1565	Pius IV (Giovanni de'Medici)
Jan 1566-May 1572	Pius V (Michele Ghislieri)
May 1572-April 1585	Gregory XIII (Ugo Boncompagni)
April 1585-Aug 1590	Sixtus V (Felice Peretti)
15-27 Sept 1590	Urban VII (Giambattista Castagna)
Dec 1590-Oct 1591	Gregory XIV (Niccolo Sfondratti)
Oct-Dec 1591	Innocent IX (Giovanni Facchinetti)
Jan 1592-March 1605	Clement VIII (Ippolito Aldobrandini)
1-27 April 1605	Leo XI (Alessandro de'Medici)
May 1605-Jan 1621	Paul V (Camillo Borghese)
Feb 1621-July 1623	Gregory XV (Alessandro Ludovisi)
Aug 1623-July 1644	Urban VIII (Maffeo Barberini)
Sept 1644-Jan 1655	Innocent X (Giambattista Pamfli)
April 1655-May 1667	Alexander VII (Fabio Chigi)
June 1667-Dec 1669	Clement IX (Giulio Rospigliosi)
April 1670-July 1676	Clement X (Emilio Altieri)
Sept 1676-Aug 1689	Innocent XI (Benedetto Odescalchi)
Oct 1689-Feb 1691	Alexander VIII (Pietro Ottoboni)
July 1691-Sept 1700	Innocent XII (Antonio Pignatelli)
Nov 1700-March 1721	Clement XI (Gianfrancesco Albani)
May 1721-March 1724	Innocent XIII (Michelangelo Conti)
May 1724-Feb 1730	Benedict XIII (Pietro Orsini)
July 1730-Feb 1740	Clement XII (Lorenzo Corsini)
Aug 1740-May 1758	Benedict XIV (Prospero Lambertini)
July 1758-Feb 1769	Clement XIII (Carlo Rezzonico)

May 1769-Sept 1774	Clement XIV (Giovanni Gangenelli)
Feb 1775-Feb 1798	Pius VI (Giovanni Braschi) (deposed - Pope until Aug 1799)
(Feb 1798-1809	Roman republic)
1809-June 1815	French occupation)
June 1815-Aug 1823	Pius VII (Barnaba Chiaramonti) (elected Pope March 1800)
Sept 1823-Feb 1829	Leo XII (Annibale della Genga)
March 1829-Nov 1830	Pius VIII (Francesco Castiglioni)
Feb 1831-June 1846	Gregory XVI (Mauro Cappellari)
June 1846-Feb 1849	Pius IX (Giovanni Mastai-Ferretti) (1st)
(Feb 1849-July 1850	Roman republic)
July 1850-Sept 1870	Pius IX (2nd) (Pope until Feb 1878)
(Sept 1870	Rome incorporated into Italy)

Heads of Government (Secretaries of State):

1815-Aug 1823	Ercole Consalvi
Oct 1823-June 1828	Giulio della Somaglia
June 1828-Feb 1829	Tommaso Bernetti (1st)
March 1829-Nov 1830	Giuseppe Albani
Feb 1831-Jan 1836	Tommaso Bernetti (2nd)
Jan 1836-June 1846	Luigi Lambruschini
Aug 1846-July 1847	Pasquale Gizzi
July 1847-Jan 1848	Carlo Vizzardelli
Jan-March 1848	Giuseppe Bofondi

Prime Ministers:

March-April 1848	Giacomo Antonelli
May-Aug 1848	Luigi Ciacchi
Aug-Sept 1848	Edoardo Fabbri
Sept-Nov 1848	Pellegrino Rossi († assassinated)
Nov-Dec 1848	Emanuele Muzzarelli
Nov-Dec 1848	Giovanni Soglia (rival government)
Dec 1848-Feb 1849	Giuseppe Galletti

Ruling Triumvirates:

Feb-March 1849	Carlo Armellini/Aurelio Saliceti/Mattia Montecchi
March-July 1849	Carlo Armellini/Aurelio Saffi/Giuseppe Mazzini
3 July 1849	Lirio Mariani/Alessandro Callandrelli/Aurelio Saliceti
July 1849-April 1850	Luigi Altieri/Annibale della Genga/Luigi Vannicella-Casoni

Head of Government:

April 1850-Sept 1870	Giacomo Antonelli (Secretary of State 1848-76)

From 1870 to 1929 the Popes were restricted to the Vatican in Rome; they did not rule over any sovereign territory.

Popes (1870-1929):

Sept 1870-Feb 1878	Pius IX (Giovanni Mastai-Ferretti) (elected 1846)
Feb 1878-July 1903	Leo XIII (Giocchino Pecci)
Aug 1903-Aug 1914	Pius X (Giuseppe Sarto)
Sept 1914-Jan 1922	Benedict XV (Giacomo della Chiesa)
Feb 1922-Feb 1929	Pius XI (Achille Ratti) (Pope until 1939)

VATICAN CITY STATE

Sovereigns (Popes):

Feb 1929-Feb 1939	Pius XI (Achille Ratti)
March 1939-Oct 1958	Pius XII (Eugenio Pacelli)
Oct 1958-June 1963	John XXIII (Angelo Roncalli)
June 1963-Aug 1978	Paul VI (Giovanni Montini)
Aug-Sept 1978	John Paul I (Albino Luciani)
Oct 1978-	John Paul II (Karol Woytyła)

Secretaries of State:

Feb 1929-Feb 1930	Pietro Gaspari
Feb 1930-Feb 1939	Eugenio Pacelli (later Pope Pius XII)
Feb 1929-Aug 1944	Luigi Maglione (†)
(Aug 1944-Nov 1952	post vacant)
Nov 1952-Oct 1958	Domenico Tardini/Giovanni Montini (later Pope Paul VI)
Oct 1958-July 1961	Domenico Tardini
Aug 1961-April 1969	Amleto Cicognani
April 1969-March 1979	Jean Villot (†)
April 1979-Dec 1990	Agostino Casaroli (acting April-July 1979)
Dec 1990-	Angelo Sodano

Presidents of the Papal Commission:

(Feb 1929-April 1984	post held by Secretary of State)
April 1984-Oct 1990	Sebastiano Baggio
Oct 1990-June 1999	Rosalio Castillo Lara
June 1999-	Edmund Szoka

VENEZUELA

Official name: Bolivarian Republic of Venezuela
Previous name: United States of Venezuela 1919-58, Republic of Venezuela 1958-99
Independence date: 11 May 1830
Capital: Caracas

The coast of Venezuela was visited by Columbus in 1498. Spanish settlements were established there early in the 16th century. Three attempts were made to throw off Spanish rule in the early 19th century before Venezuela became part of an independent Greater Colombia. In 1830 Venezuela seceded to become an independent republic.

Presidents:

April-July 1812	Francisco de Miranda
(July 1812-Aug 1813	Spanish rule)
Aug 1813-Jan 1814	Simón Bolívar (1st) (later President of Bolivia, Colombia & Peru)
(Jan 1814-Feb 1819	Spanish rule)
Feb 1819-Dec 1820	Simón Bolívar (2nd)
(Dec 1820-Jan 1830	part of Greater Colombia)
Jan 1830-Feb 1835	Juan Aguerrevere Páez (acting Jan 1830-March 1831) (1st)
March 1835-April 1836	José Vargas
April 1836-Jan 1837	Andrés Narvarte
Jan-May 1837	Juan Aguerrevere Páez (acting)
May 1837-Jan 1838	Carlos Soublette (1st)
Jan 1838-Jan 1843	Juan Aguerrevere Páez (2nd)
Jan 1843-1846	Carlos Soublette (2nd)
1846-Feb 1847	Juan Aguerrevere Páez (3rd)
Feb 1847-Feb 1851	José Tadeo Monagas (1st)
Feb 1851-Feb 1855	José Gregorio Monagas (*brother*)
Feb 1855-March 1858	José Tadeo Monagas (2nd) (deposed)
March 1858-June 1859	Juliano Castro
June 1859	Manuel Tovar (acting)
June-Aug 1859	Juliano Castro (acting)
Aug-Sept 1859	Pedro Gual (acting)
Sept 1859-March 1861	Manuel Tovar
Sept 1861-May 1863	Juan Aguerrevere Páez (4th)
June 1863-June 1868	Juan Falcon (acting June-Dec 1863)
June-Dec 1868	José Tadeo Monagas (acting)
Dec 1868-June 1870	José Ruperto Monagas (*son*) (acting Dec 1868-March 1869)
June 1870-Feb 1877	Antonio Guzmán Blanco (1st)
Feb 1877-Nov 1878	Francisco Linares Alcantara (†)

Nov 1878-Feb 1879	Jacinto Gutiérrez (acting)
Feb 1879-Feb 1884	Antonio Guzmán Blanco (2nd)
Feb 1884-Feb 1886	Joaquín Crespo (1st)
Feb 1886-Aug 1887	Antonio Guzmán Blanco (3rd)
Aug 1887-June 1888	Hermogenes López
June 1888-Feb 1890	José Rojas Paul
Feb 1890-June 1892	Raimundo Andueza Palacio (deposed)
June-Oct 1892	Guillermo Villegas Pulido
Oct 1892-March 1898	Joaquín Crespo (2nd) (†)
March 1898-Oct 1899	Ignacio Andrade (deposed)
Oct 1899-Dec 1908	Cipriano Castro (deposed)
Dec 1908-May 1915	Juan Gómez (1st) (acting Dec 1908-Feb 1910)
May 1915-May 1922	Victorino Márquez Bustillos
May 1922-May 1929	Juan Gómez (2nd)
May 1929-June 1931	Juan Bautista Pérez
June-July 1931	Pedro Itriago Chacin
July 1931-Dec 1935	Juan Gómez (3rd) (†)
Dec 1935-April 1936	Eleazar López Contreras (acting)
19-25 April 1936	Arminio Borjas (acting)
April 1936-May 1941	Eleazar López Contreras
May 1941-Oct 1945	Isaías Medina Angarita (deposed)
Oct 1945-Feb 1948	Rómulo Betancourt (1st)
Feb-Nov 1948	Rómulo Gallegos Freire (deposed)
Nov 1948-Nov 1950	Carlos Delgado Chalbaud († assassinated)
Nov 1950-Dec 1952	Germán Suárez Flamerich
Dec 1952-Jan 1958	Marcos Pérez Jiménez (deposed)
Jan-Nov 1958	Wolfgang Larrazabal Ugueto
Nov 1958-Feb 1959	Edgard Sanabria
Feb 1959-March 1964	Rómulo Betancourt (2nd) (DA)
March 1964-March 1969	Raúl Leoni (DA)
March 1969-March 1974	Rafael Caldera Rodríguez (1st) (CSP)
March 1974-March 1979	Carlos Andrés Pérez Rodríguez (1st) (DA)
March 1979-Feb 1984	Luis Herrera Campins (CSP)
Feb 1984-Feb 1989	Jaime Lusinchi (DA)
Feb 1989-Sept 1993	Carlos Andrés Pérez Rodríguez (2nd) (DA) (suspended May-Sept 1993; impeached)
May-June 1993	Octavio Lepage (acting)
June 1993-Feb 1994	Ramón Velasquez (acting June-Sept 1993)
Feb 1994-Feb 1999	Rafael Caldera Rodríguez (2nd) (NC)
Feb 1999-	Hugo Chávez Frías (FRM)

DA = Democratic Action
CSP = Christian Social Party (COPEI)
FRM = Fifth Republic Movement
NC = National Convergence

States

Prior to 1990 State Governors were appointed by the President - only subsequent elected Governors are listed.

AMAZONAS

Capital: Puerto Ayacucho

Governors:

Jan 1993-Jan 1996	Edgar Sayago Murillo
Jan 1996-	J. Bernabe Gutiérrez (DA)

ANZOÁTEGUI

Capital: Barcelona

Governors:

Jan 1990-Jan 1996	Ovidio González
Jan 1996-Jan 1999	Dennis Balza
Jan 1999-	Alexis Rosas (FE)

FE = Fatherland for Everyone

APURE

Capital: San Fernando

Governors:

Jan 1993-Jan 1996	Marcelo Oquendo Rojo
Jan 1996-Jan 1999	José Molina
Jan 1999-	José Montilla (DA)

ARAGUA

Capital: Maracay

Governors:

Jan 1990-Jan 1996	Carlos Tablante
Jan 1996-	Didalco Bolívar (MTS)

MTS = Movement Towards Socialism

BARINAS

Capital: Barinas

Governors:

Jan 1993-Jan 1996	Gerhard Carta y Ramirez
Jan 1996-Jan 1999	Rafael Rosales
Jan 1999-	Hugo de los Reyes Chávez (FRM) (*father of President Chávez*)

BOLÍVAR

Capital: Ciudad Bolívar

Governors:

Jan 1990-Jan 1996	Andrés Velazquez
Jan 1996-	Jorge Carvajal (DA)

CARABOBO

Capital: Valencia

Governor:

Jan 1990-Jan 1996	Henrique Salas Römer
Jan 1996-	Henrique Salas Feo (*son*) (PV)

PV = Project Venezuela

COJEDES

Capital: San Carlos

Governor:

Jan 1993-Jan 1999	José Felipe Machado
Jan 1999-	Antonio Galindez (DA)

DELTA AMACURO

Capital: Tucupita

Governor:

Jan 1993-	Emery Mata Millan (DA)

FALCÓN

Capital: Coro

Governors:

Jan 1990-Jan 1996	Aldo Cermeño
Jan 1996-	José Curiel (CSP)

GUÁRICO

Capital: San Juan

Governors:

Jan 1993-Jan 1996	José Malavé Risso
Jan 1996-Jan 1999	Rafael Silveira
Jan 1999-	Eduardo Manuit

LARA

Capital: Barquisimeto

Governors:

Jan 1990-Jan 1996	José Mariano Navarro
Jan 1996-	Orlando Fernández

MÉRIDA

Capital: Mérida

Governors:

Jan 1990-Jan 1996	Jesús Rondon Nucete
Jan 1996-	William Dávila (DA) (2nd)

MIRANDA

Capital: Los Teques

Governors:

Jan 1990-Jan 1996	Arnaldo Arocha Vargas
Jan 1996-	Enrique Mendoza (SCP)

MONAGAS

Capital: Maturin

Governors:

Jan 1990-Jan 1996	Guillermo Call
Jan 1996-	Luis Martínez (DA)

NUEVA ESPARTA

Capital: La Asunción

Governors:

Jan 1990-Jan 1996	Morell Rodríguez
Jan 1996-Jan 1999	Rafael Tovar (CSP) (†)
March 1999-Feb 2000	Irene Sáez
Feb 2000-	Juan Abraham

PORTUGUESA

Capital: Guanare

Governors:

Jan 1990-Jan 1996	Elías D'Onghia Colaprico
Jan 1996-	Iván Colmenares (MTS)

SUCRE

Capital: Cumaná

Governors:

Jan 1991-Jan 1993	Eduardo Morales Gil (1st)
Jan-Feb 1993	Ramón Martínez (1st)
Feb-June 1993	Eduardo Morales Gil (2nd)
June 1993-Jan 1999	Ramón Martínez (2nd)
Jan 1999-	Eduardo Morales Gil (DA) (3rd)

TÁCHIRA

Capital: San Cristóbal

Governors:

Jan 1990-Jan 1996	J.Francisco Ronn Sandoval

Jan 1996-Jan 1999   Ricardo Méndez   (2nd)
Jan 1999-   Sergio Calderón   (SCP)

TRUJILLO

Capital: Trujillo

Governors:

Jan 1993-Jan 1996   José Méndez Quijada
Jan 1996-   Luis González   (DA)

VARGAS

Capital: La Guaira

Governor:

Jan 1999-   Mario Laya Camacho

YARACUY

Capital: San Felipe

Governors:

Jan 1993-Jan 1996   Nelson Suárez Montiel
Jan 1996-   Eduardo Lapy

ZULIA

Capital: Maracaibo

Governors:

Jan-Dec 1993   Osvaldo Alvarez Paz   (SCP)
Dec 1993-Jan 1996   Lolita Aniyar de Castro
Jan 1996-March 2000   Francisco Arias Cárdenas
March 2000-   Germán Valero Chaćon

VIETNAM

Official name: Socialist Republic of Vietnam, Cộng Hõa Xâ Hôi Chu Nghĩa Viêt-Nam
Previous names: Empire of Annam 1802-1945, Democratic Republic of Vietnam 1945-76
State formed: June 1802
Independence date: 2 September 1945
Reunification: 2 July 1976
Capital: Hanoi

In 1802 the Nam-Viet kingdom was reunited under the emperors of Annam. France established a colony in Cochin-China in 1862 and by 1883 the whole country had become a French protectorate. Japan occupied Vietnam during World War II and after the Japanese defeat in 1945 a communist republic was proclaimed. In 1949 France established a monarchy in Saigon which gradually lost ground to the communist forces. In 1954 the country was divided between the communist republic in the north and the monarchy in the south, the latter becoming a republic in 1955. A guerilla war began in the south and the United States sent in troops. In 1975 the USA withdrew assistance and a communist government took over the south. In 1976 the two parts of the country were reunited largely under the former northern government.

Emperors:

June 1802-Jan 1820	Gia Long	(*b* Nguyen Phuc Anh)
Jan 1820-Jan 1841	Minh Mang	(*b* Nguyen Phuoc Chi Dam) (*son*)
Jan 1841-Nov 1847	Thieu Tri	(*b* Nguyen Mien Tong) (*son*)
Nov 1847-July 1883	Tu Duc	(*b* Nguyen Phuoc Hoang Nham) (*son*)
20-23 July 1883	Nguyen Duc Duc	(*b* Nguyen Ung Chan) (*nephew*)
July-Nov 1883	Nguyen Hiep Hoa	(*b* Nguyen Phe Hong Dat)
Nov 1883-Aug 1884	Kien Phuc	(*b* Nguyen Ung Dang)
Aug 1884-July 1885	Han Nghi	(*b* Nguyen Ung Lich)
July 1885-Jan 1889	Dong Khanh	(*b* Nguyen Canh Tong) (*brother*)
Jan 1889-May 1907	Thanh Thai	(*b* Nguyen Buu Lan)
May 1907-May 1916	Duy Tan	(*b* Vinh San) (*son*) (deposed)
May 1916-Nov 1925	Khai Dinh	(*b* Nguyen Buu Dao) (*son*)
Nov 1925-Aug 1945	Bao Dai	(*b* Nguyen Vinh Thuy) (see South Vietnam)

Presidents:
Chairman of the Council of State 1981-92
(Information prior to 1976 refers to North Vietnam)

Sept 1945-Sept 1969	Ho Chi Minh	(*b* Nguyen That Thanh) (†)
Sept 1969-March 1980	Ton Duc Thang	(†)

March 1980-July 1981	Nguyen Huu Tho (acting) (see South Vietnam)
July 1981-June 1987	Truong Chinh (*b* Dang Xuan Khu)
June 1987-Sept 1992	Vo Chi Chong
Sept 1992-Sept 1997	Le Duc Anh
Sept 1997-	Tran Duc Luong

Prime Ministers:

Chairman of the Council of Ministers 1981-92
(Information Sept 1945-July 1976 refers to North Vietnam)

April-Aug 1945	Tran Trong Kim
Sept 1945-Sept 1955	Ho Chi Minh
Sept 1955-June 1987	Pham Van Dong
June 1987-March 1988	Pham Hung (†)
March-June 1988	Vo Van Kiet (acting)
June 1988-Aug 1991	Do Muoi
Aug 1991-Sept 1997	Vo Van Kiet
Sept 1997-	Phan Van Khai

Communist Party* Leaders:

*Worker's Party of Vietnam
Chairman 1945-69
First Secretary 1969-76
General Secretary since 1976

Sept 1945-Sept 1969	Ho Chi Minh (†)
Sept 1969-July 1986	Le Duan (†)
July-Dec 1986	Truong Chinh
Dec 1986-June 1991	Nguyen Van Linh (*b* Nguyen Van Cac)
June 1991-Dec 1997	Do Muoi
Dec 1997-	Le Kha Phieu

Former independent state

SOUTH VIETNAM

Official names: State of Vietnam 1949-54, Empire of Vietnam 1954-55, Republic of Vietnam 1955-75, Republic of South Vietnam 1975-76
Independence date: 8 March 1949
Capital: Saigon (renamed Ho Chi Minh City in 1976)

Head of State:

Emperor 1954-55

March 1949-Oct 1955	Bao Dai (see Annam) (deposed)

Presidents:

Chief of State 1963-64 & 1964-65
Chairman of the Provisional Leadership Committee Sept-Oct 1964
Chairman of the Consultative Council 1975-76

Oct 1955-Nov 1963	Ngo Dinh Diem (deposed, assassinated)
Nov 1963-Jan 1964	Duong Van Minh (1st) (deposed)
Jan-Feb 1964	Nguyen Khanh (1st)
Feb-Aug 1964	Duong Van Minh (2nd) (deposed)
16-25 Aug 1964	Nguyen Khanh (2nd)
Sept-Oct 1964	Duong Van Minh (3rd)
Oct 1964-June 1965	Phan Khac Suu (deposed)
June 1965-April 1975	Nguyen Van Thieu
21-28 April 1975	Tran Van Huong
28-30 April 1975	Duong Van Minh (4th) (deposed)
April 1975-July 1976	Nguyen Huu Tho

Prime Ministers:

May-June 1949	Nguyen Van Xuan (see Cochin-China)
June 1949-Jan 1950	Bao Dai
Jan-May 1950	Nguyen Phan Long
May 1950-June 1952	Tran Van Huu
June 1952-Dec 1953	Nguyen Van Tam
Dec 1953-June 1954	Buu Loc
June 1954-Nov 1963	Ngo Dinh Diem (deposed, assassinated)
Nov 1963-Feb 1964	Nguyen Ngoc Tho
Feb-Aug 1964	Nguyen Khanh (1st)
Aug-Sept 1964	Nguyen Xuan Oanh (acting) (1st)
Sept-Oct 1964	Nguyen Khanh (2nd)
Oct 1964-Jan 1965	Truong Van Huong (1st)
Jan-Feb 1965	Nguyen Xuan Oanh (acting) (2nd)
Feb-June 1965	Phan Huy Quat (deposed)
June 1965-Oct 1967	Nguyen Cao Ky
Nov 1967-May 1968	Nguyen Van Loc
May 1968-Aug 1969	Tran Van Huong (2nd)
Sept 1969-April 1975	Tran Thiem Khiem
4-22 April 1975	Nguyen Ba Can
28-30 April 1975	Vo Van Mau (deposed)
April 1975-July 1976	Huynh Tan Phat

RIVAL GOVERNMENT 1969-75

No established headquarters
Communist government operating against the Saigon government. It took over Saigon in April 1975.

President:
Chairman of the Consultative Council

June 1969-April 1975   Nguyen Huu Tho

Prime Minister:

June 1969-April 1975   Huynh Tan Phat

COCHIN-CHINA

Capital: Saigon

Prime Ministers:

June-Nov 1946   Nguyen Van Thinth   († suicide)
Dec 1946-Sept 1947   Van Hoach
Sept 1947-May 1948   Nguyen Van Xuan   (see South Vietnam)

Cochin-China became part of the State of Vietnam in 1949

YEMEN

Official name: Republic of Yemen, Al-Jamhuriyah al-Yemen
Previous names: Mutawakelite Kingdom of Yemen 1918-62, Yemen Arab Republic 1962-90
Independence date: November 1918
Unification date: 22 May 1990
Capital: Sana

Yemen came under Turkish rule in 1536, but regained independence less than a century later. The northern area was re-occupied by Turkey in 1872, but declared itself an independent kingdom in 1918. In 1962 the monarchy was overthrown, but the royalists conducted a civil war until 1970. In the south, Aden was occupied by Britain in 1839, and by 1888 protectorates were established over most of the surrounding areas. In 1959 a federation was formed, but armed resistance forced Britain to withdraw in 1967 when a Marxist republic was proclaimed. In 1990 the North and South Yemen united, but differences between the two former states resulted in armed conflict in 1994 and the brief secession of the south which was ended by the northern army.

Information up to 1990 is for North Yemen

Kings:

Nov 1918-Feb 1948	Yahya (assassinated)
Feb-March 1948	Abdullah (usurper)
March 1948-Sept 1962	Ahmad (*son of Yahya*)
18-27 Sept 1962	Mohammed el-Badr (*son*) (deposed)

Presidents:

President of the Revolutionary Council 1962-67
Chairman of the Presidential Council 1967-78

Sept 1962-Nov 1967	Abdullah al-Sallal (deposed)
Nov 1967-June 1974	Abdel Rahman al-Iriani (deposed)
June 1974-Oct 1977	Ibrahim al-Hamadi († assassinated)
Oct 1977-June 1978	Ahmed al-Ghashmi († assassinated)
June-July 1978	Abdel al-Arashi (acting)
July 1978-	Ali Abdullah Saleh

Prime Ministers:

17-18 Feb 1948	Prince Ibrahim (*son of King Yahya*)
Feb-March 1948	Ali ibn Abdullah al-Wazir (deposed, executed)
April 1948-Aug 1955	Prince Hassan (*brother of Ibrahim*)
Aug 1955-Sept 1962	King Ahmad (*brother*)

18-27 Sept 1962	King Mohammed al-Badr (*son*)
Sept 1962-May 1964	Abdullah al-Sallal (1st)
May 1964-Jan 1965	Hamoud al-Jaifi
Jan-April 1965	Hassan al-Amri (1st)
April-June 1965	Ahmed Nooman (1st)
6-18 July 1965	Abdullah al-Sallal (2nd)
July 1965-Sept 1966	Hassan al-Amri (2nd)
Sept 1966-Nov 1967	Abdullah al-Sallal (3rd)
Nov-Dec 1967	Muhsin el-Aini (1st)
Dec 1967-July 1969	Hassan al-Amri (3rd)
(July-Sept 1969	post vacant)
Sept 1969-Feb 1970	Abdullah al-Khorshumi
Feb 1970-Feb 1971	Muhsin el-Aini (2nd)
Feb-May 1971	Abdel Sabra
May-July 1971	Ahmed Nooman (2nd)
Aug-Sept 1971	Hassan al-Amri (4th)
Sept 1971-Dec 1972	Muhsin el-Aini (3rd)
Dec 1972-Feb 1974	Abdullah al-Hagri (assassinated 1977)
Feb-June 1974	Hassan Makki
June 1974-Jan 1975	Muhsin el-Aini (4th)
16-23 Jan 1975	Abdel Deifallah (acting)
Jan 1975-Oct 1980	Abdel-Aziz Abdel-Ghani (1st)
Oct 1980-Nov 1983	Abdel Karim al-Iriani (1st)
Nov 1983-May 1990	Abdel-Aziz Abdel-Ghani (2nd)
May 1990-May 1994	Hayder al-Attas (see South Yemen)
May-Oct 1994	Mohammed al-Attar (acting)
Oct 1994-May 1997	Abdel-Aziz Abdel-Ghani (3rd)
May 1997-April 1998	Farag Said Ben Ghanem
April 1998-	Abdel Karim al-Iriani (2nd)

GOVERNMENT-IN-EXILE 1962-70

Royalist government based in Saudi Arabia during the civil war

Kings:

5-17 Oct 1962	Hassan (*brother of King Ahmad*)
Oct 1962-May 1970	Mohammed el-Badr

Prime Ministers:

5-17 Oct 1962	Ahmed al-Sayari
Oct 1962-Feb 1969	Prince Hassan
Feb 1969-May 1970	King Mohammed el-Badr

Former separate state

SOUTH YEMEN

Official names: Federation of South Arabia 1963-67, Southern Yemen People's Republic 1967-70, People's Democratic Republic of Yemen 1970-90, Democratic Republic of Yemen May-July 1994
Independence date: 30 November 1967, Seceded from united Yemen 21 May-7 July 1994
Capital: Madinet al-Shaab (*f*Al-Ittihad) (until 1968), Aden (after 1968)

High Commissioners:

1963-65	Gerald Trevaskis
1965-May 1967	Richard Turnbull (see Tanganyika)
May-Nov 1967	Humphrey Trevelyan

Presidents:
Chairman of the Presidential Council 1969-78
Chairman of the Presidium of the People's Supreme Assembly 1978-90

Nov 1967-June 1969	Qahtan as-Shaabi (deposed)
June 1969-June 1978	Salem Rubayyi Ali (deposed, executed)
June-Dec 1978	Ali Nasser Mohammed (1st)
Dec 1978-April 1980	Abdul Fattah Ismail
April 1980-Jan 1986	Ali Nasser Mohammed (2nd) (deposed)
Jan 1986-May 1990	Hayder al-Attas (acting Jan-Feb 1986)
(May 1990-May 1994	united with North Yemen)
May-July 1994	Ali Salim al-Bidh

Prime Ministers:

5-27 July 1967	Husain Bayoomi (acting)
(July-Nov 1967	post abolished)
Nov 1967-April 1969	Qahtan as-Shaabi
April-June 1969	Faisal as-Shaabi (*cousin*)
June 1969-Aug 1971	Mohammed Haithem
Aug 1971-Feb 1985	Ali Nasser Mohammed
Feb 1985-Feb 1986	Hayder al-Attas (1st)
Feb 1986-May 1990	Yasin Noaman
(May 1990-May 1994	united with North Yemen)
May-July 1994	Hayder al-Attas (2nd)

Party Leaders:
Secretary-General of the Socialist Party of Yemen

Oct 1978-April 1980	Abdul Fattah Ismail
April 1980-Jan 1986	Ali Nasser Mohammed
Feb 1986-May 1990	Ali Salem al-Bidh

Former states and protectorates of South Yemen

* = members of the federation

ADEN*

Capital: Aden

Governors:

1937-40	Bernard Reilly
1940-44	John Hathorn Hall
1944-51	Reginald Champion
1951-56	Tom Hickinbotham
1956-60	William Luce
1960-63	Charles Johnson
(1963-67	Functions transferred to High Commissioner)

Chief Ministers:

Jan-June 1963	Hassan Bayoomi (*brother of Husain Bayoomi*)
June 1963-Feb 1965	Zain Baharoon
Feb-Sept 1965	Abdul Mackawee
(Sept 1965	post abolished)

ALAWI*

Rulers:

1899-1920	Shaikh Ali bin Nasir
1920- ?	Shaikh Abdal-Nabi
? -1940	Shaikh Muhsin
1940-67	Shaikh Salih bin Sayil

AQRABI*

Rulers:

1940-57	Shaikh Mohammed bin Fadhl
1957-67	Shaikh Mohammed bin Mohammed

AUDHALI

Sultans:

? -1928	Qasim bin Ahmad

1928-67 Salih bin Hussain
(Regent 1928- ? Mohammed Jibil)

BEIHAN*

Emirs:

1900-35 Sharif Ahmad al-Muhsin
1935-67 Sharif Salih bin Hussain
(Regent 1935- ? Sharif Hussain)

BIRALI

Sultan:

? -1967 Alawi bin Muhsin

DATHINA*

Ruler:

? -1967 Abdul Qadir bin Shayi

DHALA*

Emirs:

1911-53 Shaikh Nasr bin Sharif al-Amiri
1953-67 Shaikh Sah'afal bin Ali al-Amiri

DHUBI

Ruler:

? -1967 Abdulrahman bin Saleh   (Regent:Salih Salim)

FADHLI*

Capital: Zingibar

Sultans:

1887-1907 Ahmad I
1907-24 Hussain bin Ahmad

1924-27   Abdul Qadar
1927-36   Abdullah
1936-41   Salih
1941-62   Abdullah bin Othman
1962-July 1964   Ahmad II   (deposed)
July 1964-Aug 1967   Nasir bin Abdullah

HADRAMI

Rulers:

 ? -1960   Mohammed Muhsin Ghalib
1960-67   Abdul Qavi

HAUSHABI*

Sultans:

1904-22   Ali bin Mani
1922- ?   Muhsin
 ? - ?   Sarur bin Mohammed
 ? -1955   Mohammed
1955-67   Faisal bin Sarur

KATHIRI

Capital: Sai'un

Sultans:

 ? -1880   Ghalib bin Muhsin
1880-1929   Mansur bin Ghalib
1929-38   Ali bin Mansur
1938-50   Jaafar bin Mansur
1950-67   Hussain bin Ali

LAHEJ*

Sultans:

1728-42   Fadhl I
1742-53   Abdul Karim I
1753-77   Abdul Hadi
1777-92   Fadhl II

1792-1827	Ahmad I
1827-Nov 1847	Mohsin
Nov 1847-Jan 1849	Ahmad II
Jan 1849-63	Ali I
1863-74	Fadhl III
1874-98	Fadhl IV
1898-1914	Ahmad III
1914-15	Ali II
1915-47	Abdul Karim II
1947-52	Fadhl V
1952-Dec 1958	Ali III al-Karim
Jan 1959-Nov 1967	Fadhl VI

LOWER AULAQI*

Sultans:

1912-24	Abubakhr bin Nasir
1924-30	Munazzar bin Ali
1930-47	Aidrus bin Abdullah
1947-67	Nasir bin Aidrus

LOWER YAFA'I*

Sultans:

? -1916	Abdullah bin Muhsin
1916-25	Muhsin bin Ali
1925-58	Aidrus bin Muhsin
1958-67	Mahmud bin Aidrus

MAFLAHI*

Ruler:

? -1967	Qasim Abdulrahman

MAHRI

Capital: Hadibo

Sultans:

? -1951	Ahmed bin Abdullah
1951-67	Isa bin Ali

MAUSATTA

Rulers:

| ? -1960 | Ahmed bin Babakr |
| 1960-67 | Salih Hussain |

QU'AITI

Capital: Mukalla

Sultans:

1866-1909	Awadh bin Omar
1909-22	Ghalib (I) bin Awadh
1922-36	Omar bin Awadh
1936-56	Salih bin Ghalib
1956-66	Awadh bin Salih
1966-67	Ghalib (II) bin Awadh

QUTEIBI

Ruler:

| ? -1967 | Shaikh Seif Hassan Ali |

SHAIB

Rulers:

| ? -1960 | Ahmed Mana as-Saqladi |
| 1960-67 | Yehia bin Mohammed |

UPPER AULAQI SHAIKHDOM*

Rulers:

| 1902-59 | Muhsin bin Farid al-Aulaqi |
| 1959-67 | Abdallah bin Muhsin |

UPPER AULAQI SULTANATE*

Sultans:

| 1887-1935 | Salih bin Abdullah |
| 1935-67 | Awadh bin Salih al-Aulaqi |

UPPER YAFA'I

Sultans:

? -1895	Mohammed bin Ali
1895-1903	Kahtan bin Omar
1903-27	Salih bin Omar
1927-67	Mohammed bin Salih

WAHIDI*

Sultans:

1905-19	Muhsin bin Salih
1919-48	Ali bin Muhsin
1948-67	Nasir bin Abdullah
1967	Ali bin Mohammed

YUGOSLAVIA

Official name: Federal Republic of Yugoslavia, Savezha Republika Jugoslavija

Previous names: Kingdom of Serbs, Croats and Slovenes 1918-29, Kingdom of Yugoslavia 1929-45, Federal People's Republic of Yugoslavia 1945-63, Socialist Federal Republic of Yugoslavia 1963-92

State founded: 1 December 1918

Capital: Belgrade (Beograd)

The 'Kingdom of Serbs, Croats and Slovenes' was created in 1918 under the Serbian dynasty. It united Montenegro and Serbia, which had gained independence from Turkish rule in 1799 and 1878 respectively; Bosnia and Herzegovina, parts of the Ottoman Empire annexed by Austria in 1908; and Croatia and Slovenia, parts of the Austrian Empire. In 1929 the name 'Yugoslavia' was adopted. During World War II the country was occupied by Germany which set up puppet states in Croatia and Serbia, while a government-in-exile operated from London. In 1945 a communist republic was set up, which from 1948 followed a line independent of Moscow. The dramatic political changes of eastern Europe resulted in multi-party elections in all the Yugoslav republics in 1990, and the coming to power of several non-communist governments. In 1991 Slovenia and Croatia declared independence. Civil war broke out in the latter between Serb-dominated federal forces and Croats. Declarations of independence by Bosnia-Herzegovina and Macedonia followed, leaving only Serbia and Montenegro.

Kings:

Dec 1918-Aug 1921	Peter I (see Serbia)
Aug 1921-Oct 1934	Alexander (*son*) (assassinated)
Oct 1934-April 1941	Peter II (1st) (Regent: Prince Paul)
(April 1941-Feb/May 1945	German occupation)
March-Dec 1945	Peter II (2nd) (Regency Council)

Presidents:

President of the Presidium of the National Assembly Dec 1945-Jan 1953
President of the Collective Presidency July 1971-June 1992

Dec 1945-Jan 1953	Ivan Ribar
Jan 1953-May 1980	Josip Broz-Tito (†)
4-15 May 1980	Lazar Koliševski (see Macedonia)
May 1980-May 1981	Cvijetin Mijatović (see Bosnia-Herzegovina)
May 1981-May 1982	Sergej Krajgher (see Slovenia)
May 1982-May 1983	Petar Stambolić (see Serbia)
May 1983-May 1984	Mika Spiljak (see Croatia)
May 1984-May 1985	Veselin Djuranović (see Montenegro)
May 1985-May 1986	Radovan Vlajković (see Vojvodina)

May 1986-May 1987	Sinan Hasani
May 1987-May 1988	Lazar Mojsov
May 1988-May 1989	Raif Dizdarević (see Bosnia-Herzegovina)
May 1989-May 1990	Janez Drnovsek
May 1990-May 1991	Borisav Jovi
(May-June 1991	post vacant)
June-Dec 1991	Stjepan (Stipe) Mesić (see Croatia)
Dec 1991-June 1992	Branko Kostić (de facto acting) (see Montenegro)
June 1992-June 1993	Dobrica Cosić
1-25 June 1993	Miloš Radulović (acting)
June 1993-June 1997	Zoran Lilić
June-July 1997	Srdja Božović (acting)
July 1997-	Slobodan Milosović (SSP) (see Serbia)

Prime Ministers:

President of the Federal Executive Council since 1963

Dec 1918-Aug 1919	Stojan Protić (see Serbia) (1st) (RP)
Aug 1919-Feb 1920	Ljubomir Davidović (1st) (DP)
Feb-May 1920	Stojan Protić (2nd) (RP)
May 1920-Jan 1921	Milenko Vesnić
Jan 1921-July 1924	Nikola Pasić (see Serbia) (1st) (RP)
July-Oct 1924	Ljubomir Davidović (2nd) (DP)
Nov 1924-April 1926	Nikola Pasić (2nd) (RP) (†)
April 1926-April 1927	Nikola Uzunović (1st) (RP)
April 1927-July 1928	Velja Vukicević (RP)
July 1928-Jan 1929	Anton Korošec
Jan 1929-April 1932	Petar Zivković
April-June 1932	Vojislav Marinkovic
July 1932-Jan 1934	Milan Serškić
Jan-Dec 1934	Nikola Uzunović (2nd)
Dec 1934-June 1935	Bogoljub Jevtić
June 1935-Feb 1939	Milan Stojadinović (YRU)
Feb 1939-March 1941	Dragisa Cvetković
March-April 1941	Dušan Simović
(April 1941-Feb/May 1945	German occupation)
Feb-March 1945	Ivan Subasić
March 1945-Jan 1953	Josip Broz-Tito
(Jan 1953-June 1963	post abolished)
June 1963-May 1967	Petar Stambolić (see Serbia)
May 1967-May 1969	Mika Spiljak (see Croatia)
May 1969-July 1971	Mitja Ribičić
July 1971-Jan 1977	Djemal Bijedić († air accident)
Feb 1977-May 1982	Veselin Djuranović (see Montenegro)
May 1982-May 1986	Milka Planinc (see Croatia)

May 1986-March 1989	Branko Mikulić (see Bosnia-Herzegovina)
March 1989-Dec 1991	Ante Marković (see Croatia)
Dec 1991-July 1992	Aleksandar Mitrović (de facto acting)
July 1992-Feb 1993	Milan Panić
Feb 1993-May 1998	Radoje Kontić (see Montenegro)
May 1998-	Momir Bulatović (see Montenegro)

DP = Democratic Party
RP = Radical Party
SSP = Serbian Socialist party
YRU = Yugoslav Radical Union

Communist Party* Leaders:

*League of Communists
Secretary-General 1945-66
President June 1966-Oct 1980
President of the Central Committee Presidium 1980-90

Dec 1945-May 1980	Josip Broz-Tito (†)
May-Oct 1980	Stevan Doronjski (see Vojvodina)
Oct 1980-Oct 1981	Lazar Mojsov
Oct 1981-June 1982	Dušan Dragosavac
June 1982-June 1983	Mitja Ribičić
June 1983-June 1984	Dragoslav Marković (see Serbia)
June 1984-June 1985	Ali Sukrija (see Kosovo)
June 1985-June 1986	Vidoje Zarković (see Montenegro)
June 1986-June 1987	Milanko Renovica (see Bosnia-Herzegovina)
June 1987-June 1988	Bosko Krunić (see Vojvodina)
June 1988-May 1989	Stipe Šuvar
May 1989-May 1990	Milan Pančevski (see Macedonia)
(1990	Party gave up leading role)

GOVERNMENT-IN-EXILE 1941-45

Headquarters: London (1941-43, 1944-45), Cairo (1943-44)
Operated during German occupation

King:

April 1941-March 1945	Peter II

Prime Ministers:

April 1941-Jan 1942	Dušan Simović
Jan 1942-June 1943	Slobodan Jovanović
June-Aug 1943	Miloš Trifunović
Aug 1943-June 1944	Bodizar Purić
June 1944-Feb 1945	Ivan Subasić

RIVAL GOVERNMENT

Formed by partisans in German-occupied Yugoslavia

Prime Minister:

Dec 1943-March 1945   Josip Broz-Tito

Republics

Bosnia-Herzegovina, Croatia, Macedonia and Slovenia seceded from Yugoslavia in 1991/92 and are listed separately.

MONTENEGRO

Official name: Republic of Montenegro, Republika Crna Gora
Previous names: Principality of Montenegro 1696-1910, Kingdom of Montenegro 1910-18, Socialist Republic of Montenegro 1945-91
Capital: Podgorica (Titograd 1945-92)

Princes:

July 1696-Jan 1735	Danilo I
Jan 1735-March 1782	Sava II (*cousin*)
March 1782-Oct 1830	Petar I (*cousin*)
Nov 1830-Oct 1851	Petar II (*nephew*)
Oct 1851-Aug 1860	Danilo II (*nephew*) (assassinated)
Aug 1860-Aug 1910	Nikola

King:

Aug 1910-Nov 1918   Nikola

Presidents:

President of the People's Assembly 1945-74
President of the State Presidency 1974-92

1945-47	Nikola Miljanić
1947-53	Nikola Kolaćević
1953-63	Blažo Jovanović
1963-65	Filip Bajković
1965-67	Andrija Mugoša
1967-69	Veljko Milatović (1st)
1969-74	Vidoje Žarković
May 1974-May 1982	Veljko Milatović (2nd)
May 1982-May 1983	Veselin Djuranović

May 1983-May 1984	Marko Orlandić
May 1984-May 1985	Miodrag Vlahović
May 1985-May 1986	Branislav Soskić
May 1986-May 1988	Radivoje Brajović
May 1988-Jan 1989	Bozina Ivanović
March 1989-Dec 1990	Branko Kostić
Dec 1990-Jan 1998	Momir Bulatović (LC, DPS)
Jan 1998-	Milo Djukanović

Prime Ministers:

President of the Executive Council since 1945

March 1879-Dec 1905	Božo Petrović-Njegos
Dec 1905-Nov 1906	Lazar Mijusković (1st)
Nov 1906-Jan 1907	Marko Radulović
Jan-April 1907	Andrija Radović (1st)
April 1907-June 1912	Laza Tomanović
June 1912-April 1913	Mitar Martinović
April 1913-Dec 1915	Janko Vukotić
Dec 1915-April 1916	Lazar Mijusković (2nd)
April 1916-Jan 1917	Andrija Radović (2nd)
Jan-May 1917	Milo Matanović
May 1917-Feb 1919	Evgenije Popović
(1919-45	post abolished)
April 1945-53	Blažo Jovanović
1953-62	Filip Bajković
1962-June 1963	Andrija Mugoša
June 1963-Dec 1966	Veselin Djuranović
Dec 1966-May 1967	Mijusko Sibalić
May 1967-Sept 1969	Vidoje Žarković
Sept 1969-May 1974	Žarko Bulajić
May 1974-April 1978	Marko Orlandić
April 1978-May 1982	Momćilo Cemović
May 1982-May 1986	Radivoje Brajović
May 1986-March 1989	Vuko Vukadinović
March 1989-Jan 1991	Radoje Kontić
Jan 1991-Feb 1998	Milo Djukanović
Feb 1998-	Filip Vujanović

DPS = Democratic Party of Socialists (fLC)
LC = League of Communists

Communist Party Leaders:

League of Communists (LC)

1945-63	Blažo Jovanović
1963-68	Djoko Pajković

1968-May 1977	Veselin Djuranović
May 1977-June 1982	Vojo Srzentić
June 1982-May 1984	Dobroslav Culafić
May-Oct 1984	Vidoje Žarković
Nov 1984-May 1986	Marko Orlandić
May 1986-Jan 1989	Miljan Radović
April 1989-91	Momir Bulatović
(1991	multi-party system introduced)

SERBIA

Official name: Republic of Serbia, Republika Srbija
Previous names: Principality of Serbia 1804-82, Kingdom of Serbia 1882-1918, Socialist Republic of Serbia 1945-90
Capital: Belgrade (Beograd)

Princes:

Feb 1804-July 1817	Djordje Petrović (Karadjordje) (assassinated)
Nov 1817-June 1839	Milos Obrenović I (1st) (abdicated)
June-July 1839	Milan Obrenović II (*son*)
July 1839-March 1843	Mihail Obrenović III (*brother*) (1st)
March 1843-Dec 1858	Aleksander Karadjordjević (*son of Djordje Petrović*) (deposed)
Dec 1858-Sept 1860	Miloš Obrenović I (2nd)
Sept 1860-June 1868	Mihail Obrenović III (2nd) (assassinated)
June 1868-Feb 1882	Milan Obrenović IV (*grand-nephew of Miloš Obrenović I*)
	Regents: 1868-72 Jovan Ristić/Milovoje Petrović-Blaznavac

Kings:

Feb 1882-March 1889	Milan Obrenović IV (abdicated)
March 1889-June 1903	Aleksander (*son*)
June 1903-Dec 1918	Peter (*son*) (later King of Yugoslavia)

Presidents:

President of the People's Assembly 1945-74
President of the State Presidency 1974-90

1945-53	Sinisa Stanković
1953-57	Petar Stambolić
1957-63	Jovan Vesalinov
June 1963-May 1967	Dušan Petrović
May 1967-May 1969	Miloš Minić
May 1969-April 1978	Dragoslav Marković
April 1978-May 1982	Dobrivoje Vidić
May 1982-May 1984	Nikola Ljubićić

May 1984-May 1986   Dušan Ckrebić
May 1986-Dec 1987   Ivan Stambolić
Dec 1987-March 1989   Petar Gračanin
March-May 1989   Ljubisa Igić   (acting)
May 1989-July 1997   Slobodan Milošević   (SSP)
July 1997-Feb 1998   Dragan Tomić   (acting)
Feb 1998-   Milan Milutinović   (SSP)

Prime Ministers:

President of the Executive Council since 1945

April 1862-Nov 1867   Ilija Garašanin
Nov 1867-June 1868   Nikola Hristić   (1st)
June 1868-July 1869   Djordje Cenić
July 1869-Aug 1872   Radivoje Miloković
Aug 1872-March 1873   Milivoje Petrović-Blaznavac
March 1873-Nov 1874   Jovan Ristić   (1st)
Nov 1874-Jan 1875   Acim Cumić
Jan-Aug 1875   Danilo Stevanović
Aug-Sept 1875   Stevča Mihajlović   (1st)
Sept 1875-April 1876   Ljubomir Kaljević
April 1876-Oct 1878   Stevća Mihajlović   (2nd)
Oct 1878-Oct 1880   Jovan Ristić   (2nd)
Oct 1880-Sept 1883   Milan Pirocanac
Sept 1883-Feb 1884   Nikola Hristić   (2nd)
Feb 1884-June 1887   Milutin Garašanin
June-Dec 1887   Jovan Ristić   (3rd)
Dec 1887-April 1888   Sava Grujić   (1st)
April 1888-Jan 1889   Nikola Hristić   (3rd)
Jan-March 1889   Kosta Protić
March 1889-Feb 1891   Sava Grujić   (2nd)
Feb 1891-Aug 1892   Nikola Pasić   (1st)
Aug 1892-April 1893   Ivan Avakumović
April-Nov 1893   Lazar Dokić
Nov 1893-Jan 1894   Sava Grujić   (3rd)
Jan-March 1894   Djordje Simić   (1st)
March-Oct 1894   Svetomir Nikolajević
Oct 1894-June 1895   Nikola Hristić   (4th)
June 1895-Dec 1896   Stojan Novaković   (1st)
Dec 1896-Oct 1897   Djordje Simić   (2nd)
Oct 1897-July 1900   Vladislav Djordjević
July 1900-March 1901   Aleksa Jovanović
March 1901-Oct 1902   Mihailo Vujić
Oct-Nov 1902   Petar Velimirović   (1st)
Nov 1902-May 1903   Dimitrije Cincar-Marković

May-Sept 1903	Jovan Avakumović
Sept 1903-Nov 1904	Sava Grujić (4th)
Nov 1904-May 1905	Nikola Pasić (2nd)
May 1905-March 1906	Ljubomir Stojanović
March-April 1906	Sava Grujić (5th)
April 1906-July 1908	Nikola Pasić (3rd)
July 1908-Feb 1909	Petar Velimirović (2nd)
Feb-Oct 1909	Stojan Novaković (2nd)
Oct 1909-June 1911	Nikola Pasić (4th)
June 1911-June 1912	Milovan Milanović
June-Aug 1912	Marko Trifković
Aug 1912-Dec 1918	Nikola Pasić (5th)
Dec 1918-Aug 1919	Stojan Protić
(1919-41	post abolished)
Aug 1941-April 1945	Milan Nedić
April 1945-48	Blagoye Nesković
1948-53	Petar Stambolić
1953-57	Jovan Vesalinov
1957-62	Miloš Minić
1962-65	Slobodan Penezić
1965-68	Dragi Stamenković
1968-69	Djurica Jojkić
1969-May 1974	Milanko Bojanović
May 1974-April 1978	Dušan Ckrebić
April 1978-May 1982	Ivan Stambolić
May 1982-May 1986	Branislav Ikonić
May 1986-Sept 1990	Desimir Jeftić
Sept 1990-Jan 1991	Stanko Radmilović
Jan-Dec 1991	Dragutin Zelenović
Dec 1991-Jan 1993	Radoman Božović (see Vojvodina)
Jan 1993-Feb 1994	Nikola Sainović
Feb 1994-	Mirko Marjanović

SSP = Serbian Socialist Party

Communist Party Leaders:

1945-48	Blagoye Nesković
1948-57	Petar Stambolić (1st)
1957-66	Jovan Veselinov
1966-68	Dobrivoje Radoslavljević
1968-71	Petar Stambolić (2nd)
1971-Oct 1973	Marko Nikezić
Oct 1973-June 1982	Tihomir Vlasković
June 1982-April 1984	Dušan Ckrebić
April 1984-May 1986	Ivan Stambolić

May 1986-May 1989   Slobodan Milošević
May 1989-July 1990   Bogdan Trifunović
(July 1990   Party merged with Socialist Alliance to form Serbian Socialist Party)

Autonomous Provinces of Serbia

KOSOVO

Previous name: Kosovo-Metohija 1945-71, 1990-99 (name still used by Serbia)
Capital: Priština

Autonomy abolished in 1990, but the ethnic Albanian population have organized a parallel government. After international attempts to reach a settlement failed, NATO forces attacked Serbia. A United Nations administration was set up in 1999.

Presidents:
President of the People's Assembly 1945-74
President of the State Presidency

July 1945-Feb 1953	Fadil Hoxha (1st)
Feb-Dec 1953	Ismet Shaqiri
Dec 1953-May 1956	Djoka Pajković
May 1956-April 1960	Pavle Jovićević
April 1960-June 1963	Dušan Mugosa
June 1963-June 1967	Stanoje Aksić
June 1967-May 1969	Fadil Hoxha (2nd)
May 1969-April 1974	Iliaz Kurtesi
April 1974-July 1981	Dzavid Nimani
Aug 1981-May 1983	Ali Sukrija
May 1983-May 1984	Sefcet Jasari
May 1984-May 1985	Nebi Gasi
May 1985-May 1986	Branko Skembarević
May 1986-May 1988	Bajran Seljani (1st)
May 1988-April 1989	Remzi Koljgeci
April-June 1989	Bajran Seljani (2nd)
June 1989-July 1990	Hisen Kajdomcaj
(July 1990	post abolished)

Prime Ministers:
President of the Executive Council 1945-90
Chairman of the Executive Council 1998-99

1945-63	Fadil Hoxha
1963-67	Ali Sukrija
1967-April 1974	Ilija Vakić
April 1974-May 1978	Bogoljub Nedeljković

May 1978-May 1980 Bahri Oruci
May 1980-May 1982 Riza Sapindzija
May 1982-May 1984 Imer Pulja
May 1984-May 1986 Nedeljko Borković
May 1986-May 1989 Nazmi Mustafa
May-Dec 1989 Nikola Skrelji
Dec 1989-July 1990 Jusuf Zejnulahu
(July 1990 post suspended)
1998-99 Zoran Andjelković

Communist Party Leaders:

1945-65 Dušan Mugosa
1965-71 Deva Veli   (1st)
June 1971-81 Mahmut Bakati
1981-82 Deva Veli   (2nd)
1982-April 1983 Sinan Hasani
April 1983-March 1984 Ilijaz Kurtesi
March 1984-May 1985 Svetislav Dolasević
May 1985-May 1986 Kolj Sirokov
May 1986-May 1988 Azem Vlasi
May-Nov 1988 Kacusa Jasari
Nov 1988-Jan 1989 Remzi Koljgeci   (acting)
Jan 1989-Oct 1990 Rahman Morina   (†)

U.N. Administrators:

June-July 1999 Sergio Vieira de Mello   (acting)
July 1999- Bernard Kouchner

PARALLEL/EXILED GOVERNMENT

Republic of Kosovo

President:

June 1992- Ibrahim Rugova

Prime Ministers:

Oct 1991- Bujar Bukoshi   (based in Germany)
May 1999- Hasim Thaci   (rival PM)

VOJVODINA

Capital: Novi Sad

Presidents:

President of the People's Assembly 1945-74
President of the State Presidency 1974-90
President of Assembly since 1993

1945-46	Jovan Veselinov
July 1947-Dec 1953	Luka Mrksić
Dec 1953-July 1963	Stevan Doronjski
July 1963-April 1967	Radovan Vlajković (1st)
April 1967-June 1973	Ilija Rajaćić
June 1973-May 1974	Sreta Kovaćević
May 1974-May 1983	Radovan Vlajković (2nd)
May 1983-May 1984	Djordje Radoslavljević (1st)
May 1984-May 1985	Nendor Major (1st)
May 1985-May 1986	Predrag Vasiljević
May 1986-May 1988	Djordje Radoslavljević (2nd)
May-Oct 1988	Nendor Major (2nd)
(Oct 1988-May 1989	post vacant)
May 1989-Sept 1990	Jugoslav Kostić
(Sept 1990	post abolished)
1993-97	Milutin Stojković
1997-	Zivorad Smiljanić

Prime Ministers:

President of the Executive Council

1945-47	Aleksandr Sević
1947-53	Luka Mrksić
March-Sept 1953	Stevan Doronjski
Dec 1953-July 1962	Geza Tikvicki
July 1962-July 1963	Jojkic Djuruca
July 1963-April 1967	Ilija Rajaćić
April 1967-Oct 1971	Stipan Marusić
Oct 1971-May 1974	Franjo Nadj
May 1974-May 1982	Nikola Kmezić
May 1982-May 1986	Zivan Marelj
May 1986-Oct 1989	Jon Srbovan
Oct 1989-Sept 1990	Sredoje Erdeljan
Sept 1990-Dec 1991	Radoman Božović
Dec 1991-July 1992	Jovan Radić
July 1992-Feb 1993	Koviljko Lovre
Feb 1993-	Bosko Perosević

Communist Party Leaders:

1951-69	Stevan Doronjski

1969-May 1972	Mirko Canadanović
May 1972-April 1983	Dušan Alimpić
April 1983-May 1984	Slavko Veselinov
May 1984-June 1987	Bosko Krunić
June 1987-Oct 1988	Milovan Sogorov
(Oct 1988-Jan 1989	post vacant)
Jan 1989-90	Nadeljko Sipovac

ZAMBIA

Official name: Republic of Zambia
Previous name: Northern Rhodesia until 1964
Independence date: 24 October 1964
Capital: Livingstone (until 1935), Lusaka (since 1935)

In 1889 Britain granted a charter to the British South Africa Company to administer territory north of the Limpopo River, and in 1897 a British resident was appointed to the two northern provinces of Rhodesia, as the territory had been named. In 1911 these two provinces (North-eastern and North-western Rhodesia) were united to form Northern Rhodesia, and in 1924 its administration was transferred to the British colonial office. From 1953 to 1963 Northern Rhodesia was part of the Federation of Rhodesia and Nyasaland. Self-government was granted early in 1964, with full independence following later in the year. After a period of one-party rule, a multi-party system was re-introduced in 1991.

Administrators:

1911-21	Lawrence Wallace
1921-23	Drummond Chaplin
1923-24	Richard Goode

Governors:

1924-27	Herbert Stanley
1927-32	James Maxwell
1932-34	Ronald Storrs
1934-38	Hubert Young
1938-41	John Maybin
1941-47	E.John Waddington
1948-54	Gilbert Rennie
1954-58	Arthur Benson
1958-64	Evelyn Hone

Presidents:

Oct 1964-Nov 1991	Kenneth Kaunda	(UNIP)
Nov 1991-	Frederick Chiluba	(MMD)

Prime Ministers:

Jan-Oct 1964	Kenneth Kaunda	(UNIP)
(Oct 1964-Aug 1973	post abolished)	
Aug 1973-May 1975	Mainza Chona	(1st)
May 1975-May 1977	Elijah Mudenda	

COUNTRIES AND REGIONS

May 1977-June 1978	Mainza Chona (2nd)
June 1978-Feb 1981	Daniel Lisulo
Feb 1981-April 1985	Nalumino Mundia
April 1985-March 1989	Kebby Musakotwane
March 1989-Nov 1991	Malimba Masheke
(Nov 1991	post abolished)

UNIP = United National Independence Party (sole legal party 1972-91)
MMD = Movement for Multi-party Democracy

Former protectorate

BAROTSELAND

Capital: Mongu

Kings:

1864-76	Sipopa (assassinated)
1876-78	Mwanawina II
1878-July 1884	Lubosi (1st) (deposed)
Sept 1884-Nov 1885	Tatila Akufuna (deposed, assassinated)
Nov 1885-Feb 1916	Lewanika (*f* Lubosi) (2nd)
1916-45	Yeta III (*b* Letia) (*son*) (abdicated)
1945-48	Imwiko (*brother*)
1948-Nov 1968	Mwanawina Lewanika (*brother*)
Nov 1968-Oct 1969	Godwin Mbikusita

Prime Ministers:

1864-72	Njekwa
1872-78	Mamili (executed)
1878-84	Silumbu
1884-85	Mataa (deposed, assassinated)
1885-98	Mwauluka (†)
1898-1919	Mokamba (†)
1919-28	Mataa
1928-Jan 1941	Mbwangweta Munalula (†)
1941-48	Shemakono Wina
1948-56	Muheli Walubita
1956-62	Akabeswa Imasiku
1962-Oct 1963	Silamelume Siyubo
(Oct 1963-March 1964	post vacant)
March 1964-Oct 1965	Hastings Noyoo (acting March-Dec 1964)
(Oct 1965	post abolished)

Barotseland is now a province of Zambia.

ZIMBABWE

Official name: Republic of Zimbabwe
Previous names: Southern Rhodesia until 1964, Rhodesia 1964-79 and 1979-80, Zimbabwe-Rhodesia June-Dec 1979
Independence dates: 11 November 1965 (not internationally recognised), 18 April 1980
Capital: Harare (*f* Salisbury)

In 1890 Southern Rhodesia came under the rule of the British South Africa Company until 1923 when it became a British colony. Self-government was granted in the same year, with political control in the hands of the European community. From 1953 to 1963 the country was part of the Federation of Rhodesia and Nyasaland. Britain refused to grant independence until a majority government was formed, and in 1965 the Rhodesian government declared independence. This was not recognized internationally, and United Nations economic sanctions were applied. In 1970 a republic was declared. A protracted guerilla war began and intensified, forcing the government to share power with some black politicians in 1979. However the war continued until agreement for temporary British rule and elections followed by legal independence was reached.

Administrators:

1894-96	Leander Jameson
1896-97	Earl Grey (Albert Grey)
1897-1914	William Milton
1914-23	Francis Chaplin

Governors:

Oct 1923-Nov 1928	John Chancellor (see Trinidad & Tobago)
Nov 1928-Jan 1935	Cecil Rodwell
Jan 1935-Dec 1942	Herbert Stanley (see Northern Rhodesia)
Dec 1942-Feb 1945	Evelyn Baring
Feb 1945-Jan 1947	William Tait
Jan 1947-Sept 1953	John Kennedy
Sept 1954-Dec 1959	Peverill William-Powlett
Dec 1959-Nov 1965	Humphrey Gibbs

Officer Administering Government:

Nov 1965-March 1970	Clifford Dupont

Presidents:

March 1970-Dec 1975	Clifford Dupont (acting March-April 1970)

Dec 1975-Jan 1976   Henry Everard   (acting) (1st)
Jan 1976-Aug 1978   John Wrathall   (†)
Aug-Nov 1978   Henry Everard   (acting) (2nd)
Nov 1978-March 1979   Jack Pithey   (acting)
March-May 1979   Henry Everard   (acting) (3rd)
June-Dec 1979   Josiah Gumede

Governor:

Dec 1979-April 1980   Lord Soames   (Christopher Soames)

Presidents:

April 1980-Dec 1987   Canaan Banana
Dec 1987-   Robert Mugabe   (ZANU-PF)

Prime Ministers:

Oct 1923-Aug 1927   Charles Coghlan   (RhP) (†)
Aug 1927-July 1933   Howard Moffat   (RhP)
July-Sept 1933   George Mitchell   (RhP)
Sept 1933-Sept 1953   Godfrey Huggins   (RP,UP)
Sept 1953-Feb 1958   R.Garfield Todd   (UFP)
Feb 1958-Dec 1962   Edgar Whitehead   (UFP)
Dec 1962-April 1964   Winston Field   (RF)
April 1964-May 1979   Ian Smith   (RF)
June-Dec 1979   Abel Muzorewa   (UANC)
(Dec 1979-April 1980   post vacant)
April 1980-Dec 1987   Robert Mugabe   (ZANU-PF)
(Dec 1987   post abolished)

RF = Rhodesia Front
RhP = Rhodesia Party
RP = Reform Party
UANC = United African National Council
UFP = United Federal Party (f UP)
UP = United Party
ZANU-PF = Zimbabwe African National Union-Patriotic Front

Defunct Federation

RHODESIA AND NYASALAND

Date formed: 1 August 1953
Date dissolved: 31 December 1963
Member states: Southern Rhodesia, Northern Rhodesia, Nyasaland
Capital: Salisbury

Governors-General:
Represented monarch who was concurrently British monarch

Sept 1953-Jan 1957	Lord Llewellin (John Llewellin) (†)
Jan-Feb 1957	Robert Tredgold (acting)
Feb-Oct 1957	William Murphy (acting)
Oct 1957-May 1963	Lord Dalhousie (Simon Ramsay)
May-Dec 1963	Humphrey Gibbs (acting)

Prime Ministers:

Sept 1953-Oct 1956	Lord Malvern (Godfrey Huggins) (UFP) (see Southern Rhodesia)
Oct 1956-Dec 1963	Roy Welensky (UFP)

INDEX

A Mya Lay, U, 609
Aandahl, Fred, 1020
Ab Egg, Alfred, 865
Aba, Edward, 683
Abächerli, Alois, 886
Abadie, Henry, 958
Abaijah, Josephine, 680
Abarca Alcaron, Raimundo, 580
Abashidze, Aslan, 362
Abayev, Solomon, 735
Abba Gana Terab, 642
Abba Kyari, 647
Abba Musa Rimi, 647
Abbas Djoussouf, 253
Abbas I (Egypt), 302
Abbas I (Iran), 466
Abbas II (Egypt), 302
Abbas II (Iran), 466
Abbas III (Iran), 466
Abbas Khalatbary, 7
Abbasi, S.M., 669
Abbe, Godwin, 640, 655
Abbett, Leon, 1014
Abbot, Anthony, 966
Abbot, Fernando, 174
Abbott, Charles, 101
Abbott, John, 198
Abd Abdullah Baihum, 528
Abd al-Halim al-Mutu'afi, 843
Abd al-Majid al-Qa'ud, 535
Abd al-Rahman al-Khatim, 840
Abd ar-Rahman Abu Madyani, 837
Abd-ar-Rahman I (Córdoba), 822
Abd-ar-Rahman II (Córdoba), 822
Abd-ar-Rahman III (Córdoba), 822
Abd as-Sayyar Ali Safar, 839
Abdal-Nabi, Shaikh, 1080
Abdalla Abu-Fatma Abdalla, 837
Abdallah al-Badro, 32
Abdallah bin Muhsin, 1084
Abdallah Mohammed Ahmed, 252
Abdallah Yakta, 54
Abdar-Raziq Sawsa, 535
Abdarrahman Yousifi, 603
Abddirizak Hussain, 797
Abdel al-Arashi, 1078
Abdel al-Badri, 535
Abdel al-Kasm, 913
Abdel al-Nayef, 472
Abdel-Azaz Abdel-Ghani, 1078
Abdel-Aziz bin Humaid al-Naimi, Shaikh, 946
Abdel-Aziz bin Rashid al-Naimi, Shaikh, 946
Abdel Aziz (Morocco), 602
Abdel Deifallah, 1078
Abdel Hafidh (Morocco), 602
Abdel Hegazy, 304
Abdel Karim al-Irani, 1078
Abdel Karim Kabariti, 506
Abdel Khleifawi, 913

Abdel Rahman al-Irani, 1077
Abdel Sabra, 1078
Abdelahi Mohammed, 253
Abdelazziz Bouteflika, 60
Abdelhamid Brahimi, 60
Abdellatif Filali, 603
Abdelmalek Benhabyles, 60
Abdelmuhsin al-Sudeary, 44
Abderrahman Khene, 32
Abderrahman (Morocco), 602
Abdessalam Bussairy, 536
Abdić, Fikret, 146
Abdirashid Shermarke, 797
Abdoh, Djalal, 464
Abdou Mohammed Hussain, 254
Abdou Mohammed Mindhi, 254
Abdoulaye Souley, 634
Abdrazyakov, Abdulkhak, 738
Abdu Bako, 648
Abdukarimov, Isatai, 507
Abdul Adisa, 654
Abdul Ajib bin Ahmed, 552
Abdul al-Bazzaz, 471
Abdul al-Obeidi, 534
Abdul Alisan, 36
Abdul Azaz bin Abdul Majid, 559
Abdul-Azaz bin Abdur-Rahman, 779
Abdul-Azaz bin Abdur-Rahman (Saudi Arabia), 778
Abdul Azaz bin Ahmad, 555
Abdul Aziz bin Abdul Majid, 553
Abdul-Aziz bin Mitab, 779
Abdul-Aziz bin Mohammed al-Qasimi, Shaikh, 947
Abdul Aziz (Brunei), 182
Abdul Aziz Shah, 556
Abdul Aziz (Turkey), 930
Abdul Azzem, 22
Abdul Bakkush, 535
Abdul-Bakr Tabit Damla, 229
Abdul el-Rifai, 506
Abdul el-Sarraj, 913
Abdul es-Saadun, 470, 471
Abdul Fattah Ismail, 1079
Abdul Ghafar bin Baba, 553
Abdul Ghani bin Ali, 553
Abdul Ghani Othman, 552
Abdul Hadi Awang, 560
Abdul Hadi I (Lahej), 1082
Abdul Hakim Khan, 667
Abdul Halim Muadzam Shah, 550, 552
Abdul Hamad Pasha, 912
Abdul Hamid bin Pawanteh, 557
Abdul Hamid Halim Shah, 552
Abdul Hamid I (Turkey), 930
Abdul Hamid II (Kalimantan), 463
Abdul Hamid II (Turkey), 930
Abdul Hamid Khan, 671
Abdul Hamid Khan Dasti, 669
Abdul Hassouna, 22
Abdul-Hossein Hajir, 468

Abdul-Hossein Mirza Farman Farma, 467
Abdul Jailul Akhbar (Brunei), 181
Abdul Jailul Jabbar (Brunei), 181
Abdul Jalil Saif an-Nasr, 536
Abdul Jalil Shah, 556
Abdul Jalloud, 535
Abdul Jamil bin Rais, 559
Abdul Kadir Sheikh, 669
Abdul Kahar, 181
Abdul Karami, 528
Abdul Karim I (Lahej), 1082
Abdul Karim II (Lahej), 1083
Abdul Kassem, 471
Abdul Kubar, 535
Abdul Mackawee, 1080
Abdul Mahid bin Yusof, 551
Abdul Majid Didi, 562
Abdul Majid Didi (Maldives), 561
Abdul-Majid Mirza Ayn od-Dowleh, 467
Abdul Majid (Turkey), 930
Abdul Malek bin Yusof, 553
Abdul Malik bin Yusof, 554
Abdul Malik (Indonesia), 463
Abdul Malik Mansur Shah, 555
Abdul Mejid, 930
Abdul Mirjan, 471
Abdul Momin Aminu, 642
Abdul Momin (Brunei), 181
Abdul Monem Khan, 123
Abdul Mshelia, 641
Abdul Mubin (Brunei), 181
Abdul Qadar, 1082
Abdul Qadir bin Shayi, 1081
Abdul-Qasim Ibrahim, 838
Abdul Qavi, 1082
Abdul Rahim bin Abubakar, 555
Abdul Rahim bin Tamby Chik, 554
Abdul Rahim Durrani, 666
Abdul Rahim Hatef, 54
Abdul Rahman, 551
Abdul-Rahman Ahmed Ali Tur, 798
Abdul Rahman Arif, 470, 472
Abdul Rahman Bazzaz, 32
Abdul Rahman bin Ya'akob, 558
Abdul Rahman Ghafurzai, 55
Abdul Rahman Khan, 671, 672
Abdul Rahman Muadzam Shah, 551
Abdul Rahman Osman, 570
Abdul Rahman Shah, 559
Abdul Rahman Swareddahab, 836
Abdul-Raouf Rawabdeh, 506
Abdul Rashid Khan, 667
Abdul Razak bin Hussein, 555
Abdul Sabur Fareed, 55
Abdul Salam al-Majali, 506
Abdul Salam Arif, 470
Abdul Samad Shah, 559
Abdul Sarwat Pasha, 303
Abdul Taib Mahmood, 558
Abdul Talib bin Abdul Karim, 553

Abdul Wahab bin Toh Muda Abdul Aziz, 556
Abdul Yehya Pasha, 303
Abdul Zahir, 54
Abdulahat Abdurixit, 233
Abdulkadri Kure, 652
Abdulkarim Mousswai-Ardebili, 467
Abdullah al-Hagri, 1078
Abdullah al-Khorshumi, 1078
Abdullah al-Sallal, 1077, 1078
Abdullah al-Yafi, 528
Abdullah Allajabo, 838
Abdullah Amiri, 838
Abdullah as-Selem as-Sabah, 519
Abdullah bin Ahmed al-Kalifa, 120
Abdullah bin Faisal, 779
Abdullah bin Jaafar, 551
Abdullah bin Jasim al-Thani, 707
Abdullah bin Khalifa, 919
Abdullah bin Khalifa al-Thani, 707
Abdullah bin Muhsin, 1083
Abdullah bin Othman (Fadhli), 1082
Abdullah bin Rashid al-Mualla, Shaikh, 947
Abdullah bin Saud, 779
Abdullah bin Thunaian, 779
Abdullah bin Tok Muda Ibrahim, 555
Abdullah Bishara, 20
Abdullah (Córdoba), 822
Abdullah Deng Nial, 843
Abdullah (Fadhli), 1082
Abdullah Hanga, 919
Abdullah I bin Hussein (Jordan), 505
Abdullah I bin Sabah as-Sabah, 519
Abdullah Ibrahim (Comoros), 254
Abdullah Ibrahim (Morocco), 602
Abdullah II bin Hussein (Jordan), 505
Abdullah II bin Sabah as-Sabah, 519
Abdullah Issa, 797
Abdullah Kamil, 292
Abdullah Khalil, 836
Abdullah Khan, 1054
Abdullah Mohamed Shah I (Perak), 555
Abdullah Mohamed Shah II, 556
Abdullah Muadzam Shah, 555
Abdullah Muktasim Billah Shah, 554
Abdullah Safi-al-Nur, 839
Abdullah Said Ahmad, 843
Abdullah Siahmed, 839
Abdullah Ubaydullah, 841
Abdullah (Yemen), 1077
Abdullahi Mohammed, 657
Abdullahi Mukhtar, 647, 648
Abdullahi Shelleng, 642
Abdullayev, Ilyas, 113
Abdullin, _, 738
Abdullojanov, Abdulmalik, 915
Abdulrab Rasul Sayyaf, 55
Abdulrahman bin Saleh, 1081
Abdulsalam Abubakar, 636
Abdulvasiyev, Muminsho, 916

Abdur al-Gailani, 470
Abdur Momin bin Ismail (Brunei), 182
Abdur Rahman, 53
Abdur Rahman Biswas, 121
Abdur Rashid Khan, 671
Abdurakhmanov, Abdudzhar, 1052
Abdurakhmanov, Yusup, 521
Abdürrahman Nureddin Paşa, 931
Abdus Sattar, 121
Abduwan Mohammed, 642
Abe, Nobuyaki, 503
Abegg, Alfred, 898
Abegg, Heinrich, 863
Abeid Karume, 919
Abeille, Jean-Pierre, 338
Abel, Jean-Baptiste, 59
Abel, Karl von, 368
Abel (Denmark), 286
Abel-Smith, Henry, 91
Abell, Anthony, 558
Aberdeen, Marquess of (John Gordon), 197
Aberhart, William, 200
Abernethy, George, 1023
Abeyawardena, Mahinda, 833
Abi, Anthony, 639
d'Abin, Ganier, 295
Abiodun Olukoya, S., 653
Abis, Lucio, 486
Abisala, Alexandras, 539
Ablyakimov, Enver, 724
Abolhassan Bani-Sadr, 467
Abolqassem Nasser ol-Molk, 466, 467
Abor Ayang, Matthew, 837
Aboud, César, 160
Aboud Jumbe, 919
Abraham, Alan, 206
Abraham, Hérard, 410
Abraham, Juan, 1071
Abraham, Kochakkan, 424
Abramenko, Valery, 731
Abramov, Kiyam, 738
Abramov, Ya.I., 733
Abrantes, Marquês de (Miguel du Pin e Almeida), 149
Abreu, Anísio de, 170
Abreu, Areolino de, 170
Abreu, Joaquim de, 171
Abreu, Júlio de, 216
Abrial, Jean-Charles, 59
Abrill, Carlos, 691
Absolum, Brian, 629
Abu Ali, 641
Abu Ali Majdhub Abu Ali, 840
Abu Bakar bin Baginda, 559
Abu Hassan Omar, 559
Abu Mohammed, 839
Abu Sarkar, 123
Abu Sayed Chowdhury, 121
Abu Zahar Isnin, 554
Abu Zaid Durda, 535
Abubakar, 551

Abubakar, D.S., 645
Abubakar Abu Hasheed, 646
Abubakar Atiku, 640
Abubakar Audu, 649, 650
Abubakar Barde, 639
Abubakar Maimalari, 647
Abubakar Musa, 649
Abubakar Riayatuddin Muadzam Shah, 554
Abubakar Rimi, 648
Abubakar Salihu, 639
Abubakar Tafawa Balewa, 636
Abubakar Umar, 647
Abubaker Abdul Rahim, 440
Abubakhr bin Nasir, 1083
Abubakr Awadallah, 836
Abula, Joseph, 640
Abullahi Adamu, 651
Abusadat Sayem, 121, 122
Acamapichtli (Aztec Empire), 574
Aceval, Emilio, 686
Acha, José de, 140
Acharya, Binayak, 443
Acheampong, Ignatius, 391
Achelkh bin Oumar, 221
Achike Udenwa, 646
Achilli, Leo, 774
Acholonu, E., 648
Achu, Simon Achidi, 195
Acióli, António, 155
Acioly, João, 151
Acker, Achille van, 131
Ackermann, Joseph, 870
Ackermann, Walter, 859, 860
Acosta, Santos, 249
Acosta Garcia, Julio, 271
Acosta Lagunes, Augustín, 590
D'Acquisto, Mario, 487
Acuña, Julio, 80
Acz, Lajor, 418
Ada, Joseph, 1045
Ada-George, Rufus, 655
Adair, John, 995
Adam Yusuf, 840, 841
Adamec, Ladislav, 281, 283
Adamkus, Valdas, 539
Adamovich, Iosif, 127
Adams, Alva, 980
Adams, Grantley, 124, 926
Adams, James, 1029
Adams, Jewett, 1011
Adams, John, 972
Adams, John Quincy, 972
Adams, John (Tom), 125
Adams, Peter, 959
Adams, Samuel (Arkansas), 977
Adams, Samuel (Massachusetts), 1001
Adams, Sherman, 1013
Adams, William, 980
Adamson, Harvey, 606
Adamu Aliero, 649
Adamu Atta, 650

Adberrahman Farès, 60
Addiego, Rafael, 1049
Addington, Henry, 951
Addis, William, 783
Ade Adefarati, 653
Adeang, Kennan, 615
Adebayo, Cornelius, 650
Adebayo, Robert, 638, 658
Adebunji Olurin, 654
Adekunle Lawal, 650
Adelaye, E.O., 655
Adelung, Bernhard, 371
Aden Abdullah Osman, 797
Adenhauer, Konrad, 366
Adenihun, S.A., 646
Adesogi Aderemi (Oni of Ife), 638
Adesu, Moses, 642
Adetoye Sode, 654
Adewumi Agbaje, 646
Adewusi, J.A., 640
Adeyemi Afolahan, 656
Adib es-Shishakli, 911, 913
Adib Pasha, Auguste, 527, 528
Adkins, Homer, 978
Adlercreutz, Axel, 851
Adleyba, Boris, 361
Adly Yeghen Pasha, 303
Adnan Menderes, 932
Adoboli, Koffi, 923
Adolf Fredrik (Sweden), 850
Adolf Friedrich III (Mecklenburg-Strelitz), 382
Adolf Friedrich IV (Mecklenburg-Strelitz), 382
Adolf Friedrich (Mecklenburg-Strelitz), 381
Adolf Friedrich V (Mecklenburg-Strelitz), 382
Adolf Friedrich VI (Mecklenburg-Strelitz), 382
Adolf I (Schaumburg-Lippe), 386
Adolf II (Schaumburg-Lippe), 386
Adolf (Nassau), 382
Adolphe (Luxembourg), 542
Adonaegui, Juan Sanfuentes, 222
Ador, Gustave, 854
Adoula, Cyrille, 259
Adre, Elías, 82
Adrian I (Pope), 1060
Adrian II (Pope), 1060
Adrian III (Pope), 1060
Adrian IV (Pope), 1062
Adrian V (Pope), 1062
Adrian VI (Pope), 1063
Aducci, Fúlvio, 176
Adulyadej, Bhumibol, 920
Adyebo, George, 938
Aebischer, Max, 870
Aeby, Stanislas, 869
Aedh (Scotland), 953
Aemmer, Friedrich, 864, 865

Aepli, Alexander, 896
Afakirye, B.L., 649
Afewerki, Issais, 310, 311
Affolter, Hans, 894
Afonso, Emiliano, 153
Afridi, K.K., 666
Afrifa, Akwast, 391
Aftab Ahmad Sherpao, 668
Aftab Shahban Mirani, 670
Afzal Khan, 53
Aga Mohammed Khan (Iran), 466
Agababov, _, 726
Agamaly, Samed, 113
Agapetus II (Pope), 1061
Agboneni, G., 639, 643
Aggarwal, S.P., 453, 454, 455
Agha Mohammed Ayhya Khan, 664
Agkatsev, V.M., 736
Agnew, James, 96
Agnew, Spiro, 1001
Agodino, Mario, 74
Agrawal, J.C., 453
Agrba, A.S., 360
Agripino, João, 166
Agt, Andreas van, 620
Aguado, Jorge, 71
Agudo, Adolfo, 827
Agüero, Rosendo, 412
Agüero Rocha, Fernando, 632
Aguerrevere Páez, Juan, 1066
Aguiar, Aristeu de, 157
Aguiar, Euripides de, 170
Aguiar, Francisco, 156
Aguiar, Francisco de, 157
Aguiar, Joaquim de, 704
Aguilar, Eugenio, 306
Aguilar, Francisco, 412
Aguilar, Jorge Ruiz, 81
Aguilar, Manuel, 270
Aguilar Barquero, Francisco, 271
Aguilar Castillo, Magdaleno, 589
Aguilar Pico, Rigoberto, 587
Aguilar y Maya, José, 580
Aguinaldo, Emilio, 694
Aguirre, António, 156
Aguirre, Arturo Cordón, 81
Aguirre, Carlos, 75, 77
Aguirre, José, 825
Aguirre, Marcelino Orega, 12
Aguirre, Ramón, 580
Aguirre, Vicente, 581
Aguirre Rivero, Angel, 581
Aguirre Samaniego, Manuel, 578
Aguirre y Salinas, Osmin, 307
Aguiyi-Ironsi, Johnson, 635
Agulla, Horacio, 83
Aguri, Anderson, 684
Ah, Alfred von, 887
Ahanda, Vicent, 195
Aharonyan, Avetis, 85
Ahern, Bertie, 474

Ahern, Michael, 92
Ahidjo, Ahmadou, 195
Ahmad bin Ali al-Thani, 707
Ahmad bin Mohamed Hashim, 556
Ahmad bin Said, 556
Ahmad Fuad II, 302
Ahmad I (Fadhli), 1081
Ahmad I (Lahej), 1083
Ahmad II (Fadhli), 1082
Ahmad II (Lahej), 1083
Ahmad II (Tunisia), 927
Ahmad III (Lahej), 1083
Ahmad Koroh, 557
Ahmad Matin-Daftari, 468
Ahmad Muadzam Shah, 559
Ahmad Raffae bin Omar, 557
Ahmad Razali bin Mohamed Ali, 559
Ahmad Shah Durrani, 53
Ahmad Shah (Kelantan), 552
Ahmad Shah (Pahang), 555
Ahmad Shah (Trengganu), 559
Ahmad Tajuddin Halim Shah, 552
Ahmad Tajuddin Mukarram Shah, 552
Ahmad (Yemen), 1077
Ahmadshah Ahmadzai, 55
Ahmadu Bello, 637
Ahmadu Muazu, 641
Ahman, S., 645
Ahmed, Gulsher, 432
Ahmed Abdallah Abderemane, 252, 253
Ahmed Abdou, 253
Ahmed Abdullahi, 650
Ahmed Abdullahi Yusuf, 798
Ahmed al-Bakr, 470, 471
Ahmed al-Ghashmi, 1077
Ahmed al-Sayari, 1078
Ahmed Ali Qunayf, 840
Ahmed Arifi Paşa, 931
Ahmed Baban, 471
Ahmed Bahnini, 603
Ahmed Balafrej, 602
Ahmed Ben bella, 60
Ahmed Ben Cheikh Attoumane, 253
Ahmed Benbitour, 60
Ahmed bin Abdullah, 1083
Ahmed bin Abdullah al-Mualla, Shaikh, 948
Ahmed bin Babakr, 1084
Ahmed bin Jabir as-Selem as-Sabah, 519
Ahmed bin Khalifa al-Khalifa, 120
Ahmed bin Rashid al-Mualla, Shaikh, 948
Ahmed bin Said (Oman), 663
Ahmed (Brunei), 181
Ahmed Cevad Paşa, 931
Ahmed Daku, 648, 655
Ahmed Daouk, 528
Ahmed Dini Ahmed, 292
Ahmed el-Mirghani, 836
Ahmed Hamdi Paşa, 930
Ahmed Hilmi, 476
Ahmed I (Tunisia), 927

Ahmed I (Turkey), 929
Ahmed II (Turkey), 930
Ahmed III (Turkey), 930
Ahmed Izzet Paşa, 931
Ahmed Khan Moshir od-Dowleh, 467
Ahmed Khatib, 305, 912
Ahmed Khudayer, 472
Ahmed Koulamallah, 221
Ahmed Kusumonegoro, 463
Ahmed Laraki, 603
Ahmed Lawzi, 506
Ahmed Maher Pasha, 304
Ahmed Mana as-Saqladi, 1084
Ahmed Markarfi, 648
Ahmed Mirza Shah (Iran), 466
Ahmed Mohamed Noor, 558
Ahmed Muadzam Shah, 554
Ahmed Nooman, 1078
Ahmed Osman, 603
Ahmed Ould Bousseif, 569
Ahmed Ould Sidi, 569
Ahmed Ouyahia, 60
Ahmed Qavam os-Soltaneh, 468
Ahmed Saif an-Nasr, 536
Ahmed Sani, 657
Ahmed Sékou Touré, 404
Ahmed Shah (Afghanistan), 55
Ahmed Shah (India), 421
Ahmed Shah (Malaysia), 550
Ahmed Shukairy, 477
Ahmed Tajuddin (Brunei), 181
Ahmed Tejan Kabbah, 786
Ahmed Tevfik Paşa, 931
Ahmed Toukan, 506
Ahmed Ubeidat, 506
Ahmed Usman, 653, 654
Ahmed Vefik Paşa, 930, 931
Ahmed Yar Khan, 665, 666
Ahmed Zaki, 562
Ahmed Ziwar, 303
Ahmed Zogu, 56, 57
Ahmeti, Vilson, 58
Aho, Esko, 321
Ahomadegbe, Justin, 137
Ahsam, S.M., 123
Ahsanuddin Chowdhury, 121
Ahtisaari, Martti, 319
Ahuad, Nestor Rufino, 77
Aidinbekov, S.M., 725
Aidrus bin Abdullah, 1083
Aidrus bin Muhsin, 1083
Aiken, George, 1036
Aiken, William, 1028
Aikens, James A., 202
Aikens, James C., 202
D'Aimmo, Florindo, 485
Aina Owoniyi, 656
Aird, John Black, 208
Aitakov, Nedirbai, 934, 1051
Aitowai, Semai, 684
Ajasin, Michael, 652

Ajaung, Joseph, 839
Ajobena, Frank, 639
Ajodhia, Jules, 846
Akaagerger, Joseph, 649
Akavitov, A.I., 742
Akayev, Askar, 521, 522
Akbar Ali Khan, 442, 450
Akbar Bugti, 666
Akbar (India), 421
Akel, Frederik, 312
Akerheilm, Johannes, 851
Akers-Jones, David, 245
Akgayev, Ata, 733
Akhazov, Timofey, 724
Akhigbe, Michael, 650, 652
Akhmatov, Tashtambek, 521
Akhmedov, Khan, 935
Akhokhov, Aslanbi, 727
Akhokhov, Kh., 727
Akhtar Ali Qazi, 670
Akhtar Hassain, 671
Akhunbabayev, Yuldash, 1051
Akhundov, Veli, 114
Akihito (Japan), 502
Akilov, Akil, 915
Akilu Habte Wold, 316
Akintola, Samuel, 638
Akintunde Aduwo, 658
Akirtava, N.N., 361
Akitonde, Daniel, 652
Akmadžić, Mile, 144
Aknazarov, Zekeriya, 719
Akonobi, Robert, 645
Akpan Isemin, 640
Aksić, Stanjoe, 1094
Aksyonov, Aleksandr, 127
Akuffo, Frederick, 391
Akufo-Addo, Edward, 391
Akulov, Ivan, 944
Akum George, 642
Al-Amin Dafa'alla, 838
Al-Amin Daffala, 839
al-Assad, Assad, 22
Al-Awad al-Hassan, 839, 840
Al-Hadi Bushra, 837
Al-Hakam I (Córdoba), 822
Al-Jaili Ahmed al-Sharif, 842
Al-Jayli as-Sharif, 840
Al-Jazouli Dafallah, 836
Al-Khatim al-Khalifa, 836
Al-Muayyad (Córdoba), 822
Al-Mundhir (Córdoba), 822
Al-Mustanir (Córdoba), 822
Al-Shaikh Bish Akor, 838
Al-Sharif Badr, 838
Al-Sherif Badr, 844
Al-Tijani Hassan al-Amin, 839
Ala Addin ar-Rubi, 912
Ala Hussain Ali, 519
Alaix, Isidro, 816
Alamgir II (India), 422

Alaniou, Eugène, 252, 344
Alanis, Joan Marti, 62
Alar, Koniel, 678
Alarcón Rivera, Fabián, 300
Alaungpaya (Myanmar), 606
Alawi bin Muhsin, 1081
Alayola Barrera, César, 590
Albani, Giuseppe, 1064
Albano, Elias Fernández, 222
Albano, Ildefonso, 155
Alberlings, Arhur, 526
Albert I (Belgium), 129, 131
Albert I (Monaco), 597
Albert II (Belgium), 130
Alberti, Jean-Baptiste, 340
Albertini, Remo, 488
Albertz, Heinrich, 369
Albiñana Olmos, José, 828
Albores Guillén, Roberto, 577
Albornoz, Alvaro de, 819
Albrecht, Ernst, 372
Albrecht, Luigi, 875
Albrecht (Brunswick), 378
Albrecht I (Hungary), 415
Albrecht (Saxony), 374
Albrecht (Schwarzenburg-Rudolstadt), 387
Albrekt (Bohemia), 282
Albrekt (Sweden), 849
Albuquerque, Caetano, 161
Albuquerque, Carlos de, 167
Albuquerque, Etelvino de, 169
Albuquerque, Fernando de, 177
Albuquerque, João de, 165
Albuquerque, Júlio de, 177
Albuquerque, Luiz, 151
Alcala Zamora, Niceto, 815, 818
Alcantara, Francisco Linares, 1066
Alcantara Herran, Pedro, 249
Alcorn, James, 1006
Alcorta, José, 69
Aldayev, A.B., 728
Aldeia, Ferdnando, 297
Alderdice, Frederick, 205, 206
Aldrich, Chester, 1010
Alebua, Ezekial, 794
Aleixo, Renato, 154
Alekander (Bulgaria), 183
Alekisander Karadjordjević (Serbia), 1091
Aleksander (Poland), 697
Aleksandr I, 358
Aleksandr I (Russia), 713
Aleksandr II (Russia), 713
Aleksandr III (Russia), 713
Aleksandrov, Ivan, 730
Aleksei (Russia), 713
Aleksevna, Sophia, 713
D'Alema, Massimo, 480
Alemán, Arnaldo, 632
Alemán, Miguel, 590
Alemán Valdás, Miguel, 574
Alemán Velasco, Miguel, 590

Alemao, Churchill, 429
Alemasov, Aleksandr, 738
A|len, Stephen, 768
Alencar, José, 171
Alencar, Marcello, 173
Alencar, Miguel de, 169
Alende, Oscar, 71
Aleskander (Serbia), 1091
Alessandro de Medici (Tuscany), 496
Alessandro (Parma and Piacenza), 494
Alessi, Giuseppe, 487
Aleucar, Miguel Arraes de, 170
Alevras, Ioannis, 393
Alexander, Archibald, 1046
Alexander, E., 969
Alexander, George, 1044
Alexander, James, 1044
Alexander, Lamar, 1032
Alexander, Lincoln, 208
Alexander, Moses, 990
Alexander, Nathaniel, 1018
Alexander, P. Cherian, 429, 438, 448
Alexander I (Scotland), 953
Alexander II (Pope), 1061
Alexander II (Scotland), 954
Alexander III (Pope), 1062
Alexander III (Scotland), 954
Alexander IX (Pope), 1062
Alexander (Lippe), 380
Alexander (Serbia), 1086
Alexander VI (Pope), 1063
Alexander VII (Pope), 1063
Alexander VIII (Pope), 1063
Alexandrenne, Louis, 46
Alexandros (Greece), 392
Alexis, Jacques, 411
Alfa, I., 647
Alfaro, Eloy, 299
Alfaro, José, 270
Alfaro, Ricardo, 674
Alfassa, Matthieu-Maurice, 255, 339, 563
Alfonsi, Prosper, 335
Alfonso Froíla I (Asturias), 820
Alfonso I (Aragon), 820
Alfonso I (Asturias), 820
Alfonso I (Modena), 491
Alfonso I (Naples and Sicily), 491
Alfonso I (Navarre), 823
Alfonso I (Portugal), 702
Alfonso I (Sicily), 493
Alfonso II (Asturias), 820
Alfonso II (Modena), 491
Alfonso II (Naples and Sicily), 491
Alfonso II (Portugal), 702
Alfonso II Ramón (Aragon), 820
Alfonso III (Aragon), 820
Alfonso III (Asturias), 820
Alfonso III (Modena), 491
Alfonso III (Portugal), 702
Alfonso IV (Aragon), 820
Alfonso IV (Asturias), 821

Alfonso IV (Modena), 491
Alfonso IV (Portugal), 702
Alfonso IX (León), 822
Alfonso V (Aragon), 820
Alfonso V (Asturias), 821
Alfonso V (Portugal), 702
Alfonso VI (Castile), 821
Alfonso VI (León), 822
Alfonso VI (Portugal), 703
Alfonso VII (Castile), 821
Alfonso VII (León), 822
Alfonso VIII (Castile), 821
Alfonso X (Castile), 821
Alfonso XI (Castile), 821
Alfonso XII (Spain), 815
Alfonso XIII (Spain), 815
Alford, Robert, 968
Alfred, James, 1033
Alfred (Saxe-Coburg-Gotha), 385
Alfred the Great (England), 949
Alger, Russell, 1003
Algirdas (Lithuania), 538
Ali, Ambrose, 644
Ali Adib, 536
Ali Akhbar Hashemi Rafsanjani, 467
Ali al-Ayoubi, 471
Ali al-Kamil Riayat Shah, 556
Ali Albania Saleh, 1077
Ali Amini, 468
Ali Aref Bourhan, 292
Ali Asghar Amin os-Soltan, 467
Ali bin Abdullah al-Mualla, Shaikh, 947, 948
Ali bin Abdullah al-Thani, 707
Ali bin Ahmad, 557
Ali bin Hamoud, 919
Ali bin Hussain (Hejaz), 778
Ali bin Kalifa al-Kalifa, 120
Ali bin Mani (Haushabi), 1082
Ali bin Mansur (Kathiri), 1082
Ali bin Mohammed, 1085
Ali bin Muhsin, 1085
Ali bin Nasir, Shaikh, 1080
Ali bin Said, 919
Ali Fartak, 842
Ali Hassan Mwinyi, 918, 919
Ali Haydar Midhat Paşa, 930
Ali I (Lahej), 1083
Ali I (Tunisia), 927
Ali ibn Abdullah al-Wazir, 1077
Ali II (Lahej), 1083
Ali II (Tunisia), 927
Ali III al-Karim (Lahej), 1083
Ali III Muddat (Tunisia), 927
Ali Kafi, 60
Ali Khamene'i, 467, 469
Ali Khan Amin od-Dowleh, 467
Ali Khan Ture, 229
Ali Lutfy, 304
Ali Mahdi Mohammed, 797
Ali Mansur, 468

Ali Mather Pasha, 304
Ali Mohammed, 840
Ali Mohammed Jaidah, 32
Ali Mroudjae, 253
Ali Nasser Mohammed, 1079
Ali (Pahang), 554
Ali Razamara, 468
Ali Rida Pasha ar-Rikabi, 912
Ali Riza Paşa, 931
Ali Saibou, 633
Ali Salem al-Bidh, 1079
Ali Salim al-Bidh, 1079
Ali Sastroamidjoyo, 462
Ali Soheily, 468
Ali Soilih, 252
Ali Sukrija, 1094
Alia, Ramiz, 57, 58
Aliasuk, Pavel, 126
Alibux, Errol, 846
Alier, Abel, 836
Aliesch, Peter, 876, 877
Aliev, _, 1053
Aliev, Akper, 116
Aliev, Geidar, 113, 114, 115
Aliev, Mir Ismail, 116
Aliev, Mukhu, 726
Aliev, P., 116
Aliev, Teimur, 115
Alieva, Sakina, 115, 116
Alikhanov, Enver, 114
Alikiagalelei, Patelise, 352
Alim Gan Akcurin, 1055
Alimadi, Otema, 938
Alimov, Arif, 1052
Alimpić, Dušan, 1097
Alingué, Jean Bawoyeu, 221
Aliou Mahamidou, 634
Aliyev, Gadsi-Kasum, 725
Aliyu, J., 647
Aliyu Karma, 654
Alla Kuli Khan, 1054
Allain, William, 1007
Allan, Colin, 783, 1057
Allan, John, 99
Allardyce, William (Bahamas), 118
Allardyce, William (Falkland Islands), 964
Allardyce, William (Newfoundland), 205
Allardyce, William (Tasmania), 95
Allen, Charles, 1045
Allen, Colin, 793
Allen, Frank, 1002
Allen, George, 1037
Allen, Henry, 994, 997
Allen, Milton, 762
Allen, Oscar, 997
Allen, Philip, 1026
Allen, William, 1022
Allende, Sebastian, 581
Allende Gossens, Salvador, 223
Allende Salazar, Manuel, 818
Allesbrook, Geoffrey, 962

Alley, Alphonse, 137
Alli Aranguren, Juan, 828
Alliegro y Milá, Anselmo, 278
Allin, Roger, 1020
Allison, Abraham, 984
Allon, Yigal, 475
Allston, Robert, 1029
Allys, Léopold, 340
d'Almahara, Marchese, 492
Almakayev, Petr, 733
Almazov, I.A., 722
Almeida, Alfeu de Andrade e, 156
Almeida, António de (Brazil), 160
Almeida, António de (Portugal), 703, 705
Almeida, Artur de, 428
Almeida, Baltasar, 604
Almeida, José de, 158, 160, 166
Almeida, Landulfo de, 154
Almeida, Luís de, 169
Almeida, Manuel de, 777
d'Almeida, João, 171
Almenara, Domingo, 690
Almendra, Jacob Gayoso e, 171
Almeyra, Guillermo Sánchez, 82
Almond, J. Lindsay, 1037
Almond, Lincoln, 1027
Aloisia Tautuu, 352
Alonso, Mariano (Equatorial Guinea), 308
Alonso, Mariano (Saharwi Republic), 761
Alonso, Sergio Fernández, 140
Alonso Roque, Mariano, 686
Alsina, Walter, 74
Alston, Joseph, 1028
Alston, Robert, 967
Altamirano, Luis, 222
Alterach, Miguel, 78
Altgeld, John, 991
Althann, Michael von, 492
Altherr, Gustav, 859, 860
Althouse, Adelbert, 1044
Altieri, Luigi, 1064
Altmeier, Peter, 373
Altorfer, Gottfried, 890, 891
Alturria, Agustín, 75
Altwegg, Paul, 896, 897
Aluku, S.B., 654
d'Alva, Leonel, 777
Alva Castro, Luis, 692
Alvarado Lavallade, Juan, 575
Alvaredo Aramburu, Alberto, 576
Alvares, Élcio, 157
Alvarez, Areces, Vicente, 824
Alvarez, Juan, 573
Alvarez, Mariano, 690
Alvarez Armelino, Gregorio, 1049
Alvarez del Castillo, Enrique, 582
Alvarez Lima, José, 590
Alvarez López, Manuel, 587
Alvarez Mandizábal, Juan, 815
Alvelino, Moises, 180
Alves, Aluízio, 174

Alves, Francisco, 148, 177
Alves, João, 180
Alves, Vasco, 65
Alves de Barros, António, 161
Alvim, José, 162
Alviso Mocenigo I, 498
Alviso Mocenigo II, 498
Alviso Mocenigo III, 498
Alviso Mocenigo IV, 498
Aly Sabry, 304
Alype, Marie-François, 291
Alzamora, José, 691
Amadeo (Spain), 815
Amador Guerrero, Manuel, 674
Amadou Boubacar Cisse, 634
Amadou Cheffou, 634
Amadou Karim Gaye, 31
Amagayev, _, 720
Aman Andom, 316
Amanbayev, Jumgalbek, 522
Amanullah Khan, 53
Amaral, Diogo do, 706
Amaral, Francisco do (East Timor), 298
Amaral, Francisco do (Portugal), 704
Amaral, João, 706
Amaral, Leopoldo do, 154
Amaral, Manuel, 776
Amarasiri, M.S., 833
Amarjargal, Rinchinnyamiyn, 600
Amati, Olinto, 770, 771
Amato, Giuliano, 480
Amatouni, A.S., 86
Ambane, Louis, 683
Ambartsumyan, Sargis, 85, 86
Ambrósio, Cordolino, 172
D'Ambrosio, Vito, 485
Ambrosy, Peter, 109
Amda Iyasu, 314
Amda Seyon I, 314
Amda Seyon II, 314
Amedeo IX (Piedmont-Sardinia), 495
Amedeo VIII (Piedmont-Sardinia), 495
Amedi Ikwechegh, 646
Amelunxen, Rudolf, 373
Ames, Adelbert, 1006
Ames, Benjamin, 998
Ames, Oliver, 1002
Amézaga, Juan, 1049
Amgarten, Beat, 887
Amici, Giuseppe, 773, 774
Amin, Esperidão, 177
Amin, M.A., 642
Amin Ahmad Khan, 432
Amin Ahmed Khan, 444
Amin al-Hafez, 912, 913
Amin Dada, Idi, 938
Amin Didi (Maldives), 561, 562
Amin el-Husseini, 476
Amin Gemayel, 527
Amin Hafez, 529
Aminu Kontagora, 642, 648

Aminuddin Ahmed, 122
Amir-Abbas Hoveida, 468
Amir Gulistan Janjua, 667
Amirkhanov, Kh.I., 725
Amirul Mengal, 666
Amit, Ismael, 76
Ammons, Elias, 980
Ammons, Tellor, 980
Ammosov, Maksim, 522
Ammosov, M.K., 736, 737
Ammosov, P.V., 736
Amod, Adam, 683
Amor, Anandyn, 599, 600
Amoral, Manuel, 216
Amoresano, Alberto, 83
Amoresano, Heraldo, 83
Amorim, Pedro de, 428
Amorin, Eládio de, 158
Amorin, Harry, 162
Amorin, Pedro de, 604
Amorin, Pedro do, 64
Amory, Vance, 763
Amsallem, Walter, 334
Amsler, Kurt, 891
Amstalden, Walter, 885, 886
Amurov, U., 915
Amus, A., 361
An-Nasir (Córdoba), 822
An Pingsheng, 232, 243
Anaja, J.U., 654
Ananyan, Armenek, 85
Anastasius III (Pope), 1061
Anastasius IV (Pope), 1062
Anaya, Aurelio, 587
Anaya, Carlos, 1048
Anaya, Pedro, 573
Anaya, Toney, 1016
Anchabadze, Givi, 360
Anchim, Khortek, 739
Anciaux, Jean, 342
Andaija, Andrew, 684
Andersen, Valdemar, 510
Anderson, C. Elmer, 1005
Anderson, Charles, 1021
Anderson, David, 89, 205
Anderson, Elmer L., 1005
Anderson, Forrest, 1009
Anderson, Hugh, 998
Anderson, J. Hugo, 1009
Anderson, J. Patton, 1039
Anderson, James, 213
Anderson, Jarl, 103
Anderson, John (Sri Lanka), 830
Anderson, John (United States), 995
Anderson, Kenneth, 965
Anderson, Sigurd, 1030
Anderson, Victor, 1010
Anderson, Wendell, 1005
Andjelković, Zoran, 1095
Andrada, António de, 163
Andrada, Marco, 45

Andrade, Alfredo de, 604
Andrade, Auro, 150
Andrade, Ignacio, 1067
Andrade, João de, 153
Andrade, José, 167
Andrade, Moacir de, 152
Andrae, Carl, 287
András I (Hungary), 414
András II (Hungary), 415
András III (Hungary), 415
Andrassy, Gyula, 416
d'Andrea, Héctor, 80
Andreeva, Zoya, 723
Andreoli, Barise, 774
Andreoli, Enrico, 772, 773
Andreoli, Paride, 774
Andreolli, Tarcisio, 488
Andreotti, Carlo, 489
Andreotti, Giulio, 480
Andres Rodríguez, Juan de, 824
Andrew, John, 1002
Andrews, Charles, 981
Andrews, John, 955
Andreyev, A.K., 736, 737
Andreyev, Petr, 733
Andriamahazo, Gilles, 547
Andriamihaja, 547
Andriananampoinimerina (Madagascar), 546
Andrianarivo, Tantely, 548
Andrić, Mato, 143, 144
Andrić-Luzanski, Ivo, 146
Andrione, Mario, 490
Andropov, Yury, 716, 717
Androutsopoulos, Adamantios, 397
Andrus, Cecil, 990
Andul al-Obeidi, 535
Anecoglyan, Gevorg, 85
Aneerood Jugnauth, 571
Aneke, J.J., 646
d'Anethan, Jules, 130
Aney, Madhavrao, 426
Ang Duong (Cambodia), 190
Angami, T.N., 442
Angammare, Raoul-Eugène, 347
Angarita, Isaías Medina, 1067
Angelescu, Constantine, 710
Angeli, Guiseppe, 770
Angeli, Pierluigi, 488
Angeli, Pierre-Louis, 346
Angelin, Angelo, 175
Angelini, Antoine-Marie, 340
Angelo, Euclides de, 250
D'Angelo, Giuseppe, 487
Angeloz, Eduardo, 74
Angers, Auguste-Réal, 211
Anglin, Francis, 197
Angoulvant, Gabriel-Louis (Congo, Brazzaville), 257

Angoulvant, Gabriel-Louis (Côte d'Ivoire), 272, 782
Angoulvant, Gabriel-Louis (India), 456
Angulo, Mauro, 589
Anhuitzotl (Aztec Empire), 574
Anibelli, António, 168
Aniebo, Augustine, 649
Anio, Pama, 681
Anis, Pedi, 681
Anisi, Alex, 678
Anjaiala, T., 424
Ankrah, Joseph, 391
Anna (Russia), 713
Annadurai, Conjeevaram, 448
Annaliev, Abdy, 934
Annan, Kofi, 42
Annand, William, 207
Anne (Great Britain), 951
Anne of Austria, 323
Annet, Armand-Léon, 136, 291
Annet, Armand-Léon (Djibouti), 291
Annet, Armand-Léon (Madagascar), 546
Annoni, Mario, 868, 869
Ansari, S.S., 442
Ansberg, Aleksandr, 313
Ansel, Martin, 1029
Ansell, Graham, 629
Anselme, Bernard, 132, 133
Anshuman Singh, 430, 445
Ansquer, Vincent, 334
Antall, József, 417
Anthamatten, Karl, 903
Anthonioz, Pierre, 568, 1058
Anthony, A.K., 436
Anthony, George, 994
Anthony, Henry, 1026
Anthony, Kenny, 765
Antich, Francesc, 825
Antognini, Isidoro, 899
Antoine, James (Jim), 214
Antoine (Monaco), 597
Anton (Saxony), 374
Antonelli, Giacomo, 1064
Antonescu, Ion, 710
Antonetti, Raphaël, 257, 272, 343, 563, 780
Antonia Martínez, María, 828
Antonin, Louis-Jean, 403
D'Antonio, Anna Nenna, 481
Antonio (Parma and Piacenza), 494
António (Portugal), 702
Antonione, Roberto, 483
Antonov, B.I., 727
Antonov, V.I., 729
Antrick, Otto, 378
Antrobus, Charles, 767
Antulay, Abdur Rehman, 438
Antunes, João, 703
Anund Jakob (Sweden), 849
Anvelt, Jaan, 313
Anyaoku, Chukwumeka (Emeka), 10
Anziani, Armand, 345

Anzilotti, Enrico, 797
Ao, P. Shilu, 441
Aoun, Michel, 529
Apang, Gagong, 425
Aparici, Ricardo de, 76
Apenisa Cakobau, 317
Aper Aku, 642
Aphaiwongse, Kovid, 920
Apio, Paul, 679
Apithy, Sourou-Migan, 137
Apodaca, Jerry, 1016
Apostol, Gheorghe, 711
Apostolski, Vanco, 544
Apryatkin, Semen, 723
Aqif Pasha Elbasini, 56
Aquino, Corazon (C. Cojuangco), 694
Arafat, Yasser, 476, 477
Aragão, António de, 154
Aragona, Giancarlo, 34
Aramburu, Pedro, 70
Araña Osorio, Carlos, 402
Arancibia, David Padilla, 141
Aranda, Jorge, 80
Aranda Osorio, Efraín, 577
Arandia, Ricardo, 84
Arango, Andrés Pastrana, 251
Arango, José, 674
Aranguren, Julio, 76
Aranha, Oswaldo, 174
Aranibar, José, 690
Araújo, António de, 159
Araújo, Arnaldo, 298
Araújo, Arturo, 307
Araújo, Bernardo, 158
Araújo, Joachim de, 158
Araújo, Joaquim de, 168
Araújo, José de (Acre, Brazil), 150
Araújo, José de (Paraíba, Brazil), 165
Araújo, José de (Rio Grande do Norte, Brazil), 174
Araújo, Manuel, 306
Araújo, Otávio de, 169
Araújo, Radir de, 174
Araújo, Teutônio de, 172
Araújo, Tibúrcio de, 151
Araújo, Urbano, 159
Araújo Góes, Manoel de, 151
Arawwawala, H.G., 832
Arbab Mohammed Jehangir Khan, 668
Arbab Sikandar Khan, 667
Arbenz Guzmán, Jacobo, 401
Arboleda, Julio, 249
Arboussier, Henri d', 347
d'Arboussier, Henri, 1057
Arbulú Galliani, Guillermo, 692
Arbuzov, Valery, 747
Arce, Aniceto, 140
Arce, Pedro, 306
Arce, Walter Guevara, 141
Archer, Geoffrey, 798, 835, 937
Archer, James, 101

Archibald, Adams, 202, 206
Archibong, Daniel, 643
Arciszewski, Tomasz, 700
Arcoverde, Dirceu, 171
Ardanza, José, 825
Arden-Clarke, Charles, 147, 390, 530, 558
Ardito Barleta, Nicolás, 675
Ardzinba, Vladislav, 360
Arenas, Antonio, 690
Arenas, Germán, 691
Arends, E., 621
Areosa, Danilo, 153
Arévalo, Juan, 401
Argetoianu, Constantine, 710
Argüello, Leonardo, 632
Argyle, Stanley, 99
Ariako, Andrew, 680
Arias, Carlos, 412
Arias, Dario, 76
Arias, Harmodio, 674
Arias, Juan, 412
Arias Espinosa, Ricardo, 675
Arias Madrid, Arnulfo, 674, 675
Arias Navarro, Carlos, 818
Arias Sánchez, Oscar, 271
Aribaud, Jean, 346
Ariburun, Tekin, 930
Ariembo, Bensen, 682
Arif Razzak, 471
Arista, Mariano, 573
Aristide, Jean-Bertrand, 411
Arisugawa, Taruhito, 502
Ariyoshi, George, 989
Arjit Singh, 5
Arjun Singh, 437, 444, 454
Arkhipov, N.V., 730
Armanini, Segundo, 77
Armansperg, Josef von, 392, 393
Armellini, Carlo, 1064
Armendariz, Alejandro, 71
Armendariz Ruiz, Gustavo, 577
Armero y Peñaranda, Francisco, 816
Armitage, Cecil, 355
Armitage, John, 355
Armitage, Robert, 279, 549
Armour, Jenner, 293
Armstrong, Ernest, 207
Armstrong, Samuel, 1001
Arn, Edward, 994
Arnall, Ellis, 987
Arnaud, Georges, 252
Arnaudo, Bernabé, 77
Arnim-Boitzeburg, Adolf, 383
Arnison, Peter, 91
Arnold, Anton, 902
Arnold, Franz, 901
Arnold, Karl, 373
Arnold, Lemuel, 1026
Arnold, Lynn, 95
Arnold, William, 956
Arny, W., 1015

Aroi, Kenas, 615
Aronshtam, _, 935
Arop Achur Akol, 842
Arosemena, Alcibíades, 675
Arosemena, Domingo Díaz, 674
Arosemena, Florencio, 674
Arosemena, Juan, 674
Arosemena, Justa, 674
Arosemena, Pablo, 674
Arosemena Gómez, Otto, 300
Arosemena Monroy, Carlos, 300
Arosemena Tola, Carlos, 300
Arrazola, Lorenzo, 816
Arrechea, Ricardo Barrios, 78
Arriaga, Manuel de, 703
Arriaga Rivera, Augustín, 583
Arrieta, Dario, 580
Arrigoni, Paolo, 484
Arrindell, Clement, 762
Arron, Henck, 846
Arrowsmith, Edwin, 293, 530, 964, 970
Arroyo del Rio, Carlos, 300
Arruda, João de, 162
Arsache, Apostol, 709
Arsala Rahmani, 55
Arsanov, Ahmed, 722
Arsenault, Aubin, 210
Arshad al-Umari, 471
Arsov, Ljupco, 544, 545
Artaza, Adolfo Navajas, 74
Arteaga, Rosalia, 300
Arteaga y Sontoyo, Armando, 584
Artelejo Campos, Adolfo, 603
Arteşanu, Gheorghe, 710
Arteta, Diego Noboa, 299
Arthur, Chester, 972
Arthur, Harold, 1036
Arthur, Oswald, 118, 964
Arthur, Owen, 125
Artigas, José, 1048
Arudjaba, François, 269
Arundell, Robert, 124
Arushanyan, Shmavon, 85
Arutinov, G., 86
Arutiuman, Grigor, 86
Arutiunyan, Gagik, 86
Arutiunyan, Khostrov, 86
Arutiunyan, Nagush, 85
Arutiunyan, Suren, 86
Arx, Ferdinand von, 894
Arx, Rudolf von, 893, 894
Arzhakov, Stepan, 737
Arzilli, Giovanni, 770, 771
Arzilli, Giuseppe, 771, 774
Arzú Irigoyen, Alvaro, 402
Arzumanyan, Grigory, 86
Asad al-Mulk, 466
Asadollah Alam, 468
Asbeck, Willem van, 845
Asbjörnsson, Jón, 419
Asbún, Juan Pereda, 141

Asche, Austin, 102
Ásgeirsson, Ásgeir, 419
Ashcroft, John, 1008
Ashe, John, 1018
Ashe, Samuel, 1018
Ashida, Hitoshi, 503
Ashimov, Baiken, 507, 508
Ashirbekov, Ubbiniyaz, 1053
Ashley, Francis, 793
Ashley, James, 1008
Ashraf Lutfi, 32
Ashraf Tabbani, 670
Asiake, Lusiano, 351
Askerov, M.G., 115
Askew, Reubin, 985
Askin, Robin, 90
Aslan Riaz Hussain, 668
Aslanov, Armais, 117
Aslonov, Kadreddin, 914
Asmar, Alfredo, 79
Aspin, Norman, 961
Aspinall, Owen, 1043
Asquith, Herbert, 952
Asribekov, Ye., 361
Assad Kotaite, 44
Assalé, Charles, 195
Asselin, Martial, 211
Asser, Joseph, 960
Assier de Popignan, Charles, 136, 353
Assoumani, Azzaly, 253
Assunção, Alexandre, 164, 165
Astaykin, Ivan, 734
Astley-Cubitt, Thomas, 960
Astraukas, Vytautas, 539
Asuquo, Bassey, 644, 645
Ata, Solomone, 924
Ata al-Ayoubi, 911, 912
Ata Mahdum, 1055
Atabayev, Kaigisyz, 934, 1056
Atahiru Bafarwa, 656
Atahuallpa, 693
Ataíde, Francisco, 157
Ataíde, José de, 156
Atal, H.L., 449
Atanasov, Georgi, 184
Atanda Yussuf, M., 645
Atassi, Loay, 912
Atatürk, Mustafa Kemal, 930, 931
Ataullah Mengal, 666
Ataur Rahman Khan, 121, 123
Aten, Erhart, 592
Atencio, Mario, 73
Atgeriyev, Turpal, 722
Athanasiadis-Novas, Georgios, 397
Athanasiu, Alexandru, 711
Athelstan (England), 949
Atif Obeid, 304
Atif Sidky, 304
Atiyafa, Robert, 678
Atiyeh, Victor, 1024
Atkinson, George, 1040

Atkinson, Harry, 626
Atkinson, William, 987
Atopare, Silas, 676
Atoto, Benstead, 682
Atta, Ernest, 643
Atta, M.E., 640
Attah, Victor, 640
Attlee, Clement, 952
Atun, Hakki, 280
Aubame, Jean-Hilaire, 354
Aubanel Vellajo, Gustavo, 575
Aubert, Pierre, 856, 906
Aubert, Pierre-Émile, 341
Auersperg, Karl von, 106
Augagneur, Jean-Victor, 257
Augagneur, Jean-Victor, 546
Augsburger, Ueli, 868
August II (Poland), 697
August III (Poland), 697
August (Oldenburg), 382
Augustin (Mexico), 572
Auld, Robert, 955
Aule, Navy, 680
Aung Pa, U, 609
Aung San, 607
Aura, Teuvo, 320
Auranzeb Alamgir I (India), 421
Aurelian, Petru, 709
Aurelio (Asturias), 820
Aurelio Soto, Marco, 412
Auriol, Vincent, 325
Aurousseau, Jean-Claude, 338
Aushev, Ruslan, 726
Ausseil, Jean, 598
Austin, Horace, 1004
Austin, Hudson, 400
(Australia), 88
Avakumović, Ivan, 1092
Avakumović, Jovan, 1093
Avalia, Pedro, 81
Avbelj, Viktor, 791
Avelin, Alfredo, 81
Avelino, Georgino, 173
Avellaneda, Nicolás, 69
Avellaneda, Roberto, 84
Avenol, Joseph, 24
Averescu, Alexandru, 709, 710
Averkiev, V.P., 729
Avery, William, 995
Avezmatov, Saparbay, 1053
Avezov, Kasym, 1053
Ávidos, Florentino, 157
Avila Bretón, Rafael, 589
Avila Camacho, Manuel, 574
Avila Camacho, Maximino, 585
Avila Camacho, Rafael, 585
Avila Heredia, Ricardo, 591
Avkhimovich, Nikolai, 127
Avril, Prosper, 410
Avturkhanov, Umar, 722, 723
Awad Khier Allah, 840

Awadh bin Omar, 1084
Awadh bin Salih, 1084
Awadh bin Salih al-Aulaqi, 1084
Awali Kazir, 650
Awang bin Hassan, 555
Awni Khalidi, 7
Axayácatl (Aztec Empire), 574
Axtell, Samuel, 1015
Axtell, S.B., 1034
Ayala, Eligio, 687
Ayala, Eusebio, 687
Ayala, Julio Turbay, 251
Ayandho, Bernard, 219
Ayang, Luc, 195
Ayatskov, Dmitry, 751
Ayauld, César, 78
Aycinena, Pedro, 401
Aycock, Charles, 1019
Ayer, Théodore, 870
Ayerra, Niceto, 73
Ayers, Henry, 94
Ayhya Khan, Agha Mohammed, 665
Aymerich, Joseph, 194
Ayora, Isidro, 300
Ayres, Roy, 1009
Ayson, Hugh, 627, 628
Aytmuratov, Yerezhep, 1053
Ayub Khan, 53
Ayub Khan, Mohammed, 665
Ayub Thabit, 527, 528
Ayushyev, Bolot, 754
Ayyangar, Ananthasayanam, 427
Ayyangar, B. Gopalaswami, 433
Ayyar, S.G.N., 452
Azad, Bhagwat, 428
Azam Khan (Afghanistan), 53
Azam Khan (Bangladesh), 123
Azaña y Díez, Manuel, 815, 818
Azcárraga, Gustavo, 584
Azcarraga y Palmero, Marcelo de, 817
Azcona del Hoyo, José, 413
d'Azeglio Marchese di, 495
Azeredo, Eduardo, 163
Azevedo, Ciro de, 179
Azevedo, Gregório, 153, 170
Azevedo, José de, 706
Azevedo, Milton de, 179
Azevedo, Temístocles de, 151
Azezedo, Albuíno, 157
Azikiwe, Nnamdi, 635, 636
Azim Daudpota, 670
Azimov, Yahya, 915
Azivov, M., 738
Aziz Sidky, 304
Aziza, Patrick, 649
Azizur Rahman, 121
Azlan Shah, 550, 556
Aznar García, Salomon, 576
Aznar López, José María, 826
Azócar, Patricio Aylwin, 223
Azzan bin Qais (Oman), 663

Azzara, Carmelo, 481
Azzedine Laraki, 31, 603

Ba Maw, 607
Ba Swe, U, 607
Ba U, 607
Baal, Jan van, 464
Baarenfels, Eduard Baar von, 109
Babakhanov, _, 522
Babayan, S.A., 117
Babayev, G., 115
Babayev, Khivali, 934
Babayev, Sukhan, 934, 935
Babbit, Bruce, 977
Babboni, Gustavo, 770, 771, 774
Babcock, Tim, 1009
Babel, Jean, 873
Babenko, Vladimir, 752
Babić, Milan, 276
Babiker al-Nur Osman, 835
Babikir Jabir Kabalo, 841
Babiuch, Edward, 699
Babkin, I.P., 730
Babrak Karmal, 54, 55
Babur (India), 421
Baca, Alberto Martínez, 78
Baca, Ezequiel de, 1016
Bacai Sanha, Malam, 406
Bacellar, Pedro, 153
Bach, Jacques, 350
Bachelder, Nahum, 1013
Bächler, Hans, 871
Bachman, Casar, 893
Bachmann, Aldo, 80
Bachmann, Arthur, 910
Bachmann, Ernst, 858
Bachmann, Rudolf, 895
Bačilek, Karel, 789, 790
Baciocchi, Antonello, 774
Baciocchi, Elisa, 496
Backer, Alfredo, 171
Bacmeister, Georg, 379
Bacon, James, 97
Bacon, Roger, 207
Bacon, Walter, 984
Badal, Prakash Singh, 445
Badaloni, Piero, 483
Badamdorji, Da Lama Shanzav, 600
Badar bin Seif (Oman), 663
Badarakho, Buyan, 739, 740
Badayev, Aleksei, 714
Badeni, Kasimir, 107
Badger, William, 1012
Badiev, Aleksandr, 720
Badjoko, Charles, 268
Badlani, K.G., 453
Badlishah, 552
Badmakhalgarev, Lag, 728
Badoglio, Pietro, 316, 479, 534
Badr al-Din Taha, 839

Badwai al-Kahir Idris, 843
Badwei al-Khair, 840
Baeda Mariam I, 314
Baeda Mariam II, 315
Baeda Mariam III, 315
Baena Soares, João, 28
Baeriswyl, Aloys, 870
Baéz, Buenaventura, 295
Báez, Cecilio, 686
Báez, Ramón, 296
Baezo Meléndez, Fernando, 578
Bagabandi, Natsagiyn, 599
Bagapsh, Sergei, 360
Bagautdinov, Anvar, 738
Bagaza, Jean-Baptiste, 188
Bagby, Arthur, 974
Bagchi, B.P., 453
Bagely, John, 1003
Baggio, Sebastiano, 1065
Bagirov, Kyamran, 115
Bagrat III, 357
Bagrat IV, 357
Bagrat V, 358
Bagrat VI, 358
Bagratyan, Grant, 86
Bagrianov, Ivan, 184
Bagrov, Nikolai, 943
Baguryan, Karen, 116
Bagyidaw (Myanmar), 606
Bahadur, Bupal Singh, 445
Bahadur, Martand Singh, 460
Bahadur, Sri Jaya Chamraya Wadiyar, 434, 448
Bahadur, Yadavendra Singh Mahendra, 459
Bahadur Sah (Nepal), 616
Bahadur Shah I (India), 421
Bahadur Shah II (India), 422
Bahi Ladgham, 928
Bahij al-Khatib, 912
Bahjat al-Talhouni, 506
Bahr Asgad, 314
Bahuguna, Hemavati, 450
Bai Enpei, 240
Bai Lichen, 233
Bai Qingcai, 241
Bai Rubing, 241
Baichurin, G.G., 738
Baidevletov, Rafael, 719
Baidwan, K.S., 453, 454
Bailey, Carl, 978
Bailey, Thomas, 1006
Bailey, William, 994
Bailhache, Philip, 959
Baille, Alastair, 959
Baillet-Latour, Henri de, 21
Bailly, Camille-Victor, 273, 346, 563, 780
Bairamov, Nurberdi, 934
Bairu, Tedla, 311
Baiteke, Atanraoi, 35
Bajković, Filip, 1089, 1090
Bajpai, Girijashankar, 458

Bajpai, Rajendra, 453
Bajpal, Rajendra, 457
Bakafa, 315
Bakarić, Vladimir, 274, 275
Bakary, Djibo, 634
Bakeer Marker, M., 833
Baker, Conrad, 992
Baker, Francis, 968
Baker, James, 997
Baker, John, 93
Baker, Nathaniel, 1012
Baker, Sam, 1008
Baker, Shirley, 924
Baker-Bates, M., 961
Bakirov, Mir, 114
Bakiyev, Rim, 719
Bako, Y., 640
Bakradze, Valerin, 359
Bakshi Ghulam Mohammed, 433
Bala Mohammed Mande, 651
Balaguer, Joaquín, 296
Balakau, Jeffrey, 679
Balakshin, Pavel, 744
Balametov, Yuz Ahmed, 115
Balarbe Musa, 647
Balbis, Zinovios, 394, 395
Balbo, Cesare, 495
Balbo, Italo, 534
Balboa Gojon, Praxedis, 589
Balda, Emilio della, 773
Balda, Giuseppe, delle, 773
Balda, Marino della, 771, 772
Baldasseroni, Giovanni, 497
Baldiserra, Antonio, 310
Baldomero Esparto, Joaquín, 815
Baldomir, Alfredo, 1049
Baldridge, H. Clarence, 990
Baldschus, August (Augustas Baldzius), 541
Balducci, Ezio, 771
Balducci, Guiseppe, 771
Balducci, Nullo, 770
Baldwin, Brian, 969
Baldwin, Henry, 1003
Baldwin, Raymond, 982
Baldwin, Roger, 981
Baldwin, Simeon, 982
Baldwin, Stanley, 952
Balfour, Arthur, 952
Balgynbayev, Nurlan, 508
Baliles, Gerald, 1037
Balista, Giuseppe, 488
Balkh Sher Mazari, 665
Balladur, Edouard, 329
Ballance, John, 626
Ballard, David, 989
Ballay, Noël, 403, 781
Ballbe, Oigimer Silva, 75
Ballivián, Adolfo, 140
Ballivián, José, 140
Ballmoos, Walter, 897

Ballot, Victor, 136, 338
Balmaceda, José, 222
Balmer, Paul, 872
Balogun, S.A., 652
Balsemão, Francisco, 706
Balsiger, Hans-Ernst, 879
Balsimelli, Carlo, 771, 772
Balsimelli, Francesco, 772
Balstad, Hakon, 662
Balta, José, 689
Baltayev, K.B., 1053
Baltić, Milutin, 274
Balyakov, Anatoly, 721
Balyjir-Beili, Sodnom (s. Bakhir), 739
Balza, Dennis, 1068
Balzar, Frederick, 1011
Bam, A.S., 456
Bamana, Younoussa, 343
Bamberger, Simon, 1034
Bamert, Kaspar, 892
Bamigboye, David, 650
Bamigboye, Theophilus, 641, 653
Bamina, Joseph, 189
Ban Fushang, 237
Banalzino, Sergio, 25
Banana, Canaan, 1101
Banda, Hastings Kamusu, 549
Bandara, R. Nimal, 833
Bandaranaike, Sirimavo, 831
Bandaranaike, Solomon, 831
Bandodkar, Dayanand, 429
Banerjee, A.N., 434
Banerjee, Asoka, 432
Banerjee, Shishir, 429
Banerji, Khrishna, 453
Banerji, Shishir, 453
Banffy, Deszö, 416
Bang, Peter, 287
Bangarappa, S., 435
Bangerter, Norman, 1034
Bani, John, 1058
Banks, Charles, 200
Banks, Nathaniel, 1002
Bannon, John, 95
Banuelos, J. Félix, 591
Bao Dai (Nguyen Vinh Thuy), 1073, 1074, 1075
Bao Dongcai, 239
Bao Erhan, 233
Bao Xuding, 244
Baptista, António, 705
Baptista, Lourival, 180
Baptista, Mariano, 140
Barabanov, Vladimir, 745
Barak, Ehud, 476
Barakhov, I.N., 736
Baranda García, Alfredo, 582
Barari, Hari, 431
Barata, Filipe, 297
Barata, Francisco, 776
Barata, Joaquim, 164, 165

Baratieri, Oreste, 310
Barau, Yves, 342
Barba González, Silvano, 581
Barbalho, Jader, 165
Barbara, Agatha, 566
Barbarigo, Augostino, 497
Barbarigo, Marco, 497
Barbeau, Charles, 348
Barber, Amos, 1042
Barberena Vega, Miguel, 575
Barberot, Roger, 347
Barbieri, Lazaro, 84
Barbosa, Artur, 246
Barbosa, Demócrito, 172
Barbosa, João (Macau, 246
Barbosa, João (Portugal), 705
Barbosa, Raul, 156
Barbosa, Raymundo (Amazonas, Brazil), 153
Barbosa, Raymundo (Bahia, Brazil), 154
Barbosa, Sebastião, 776
Barbosa, Theobaldo, 152
Barbour, James, 1037
Barbuy, Aldo, 82
Barcellos, Annibal, 152
Barceló, Carlos Romero, 1046
Barcelos, Wálter, 175
Barcena, Oscar, 72
Barclay, Arthur, 532
Barclay, Edwin, 532
Barclay-Harvey, Charles, 93
Bardaji y Azara, Eusebio, 815
Bardoloi, Gopinath, 426
Bardossy, László, 417
Bare, Edward, 683
Barerdi, Giancarlo, 773
Barge, Charles, 621
Barghash bin Said, 919
Bargues, Isaac-Robert, 547
Barillas, Manuel, 401
Barinaga, Manuel, 690
Baring, Evelyn, 509, 1100
Barkauskas, Antanas, 539
Barker, George, 960
Barker, Peter, 680
Barkhat Gourad Hamadou, 292
Barley, Jack, 510
Barman, Bhumidhar, 426
Barnala, Surjit Singh, 445, 448, 453
Barnard, Frank, 200
Barnard, Stephanus, 804
Barnes, Cassius, 1023
Barnes, Hugh, 606
Barnes, Leonard, 612
Barnes, Roy, 987
Barnet y Vinageras, 277
Barnett, Frederick, 793
Barnett, Ross, 1006
Baron, Charles, 456
Baron, George, 957
Baroni, Danilo, 72

Barra, Francisco de la, 573
Barraga, Miguel de, 572
Barrat, Roland, 337
Barre, Antoine, 336
Barre, Raymond, 329
Barreiro, Candido, 686
Barrelet, Jean-Louis, 881
Barrera y Luyando, Angel, 308
Barreto, Emygdio, 168
Barreto, João, 172
Barreto, Plínio, 177
Barrett, David, 201
Barrett, Frank, 1042
Barrette, Antonio, 212
Barrillot, Georges, 344
Barrio Terrazas, Francisco, 578
Barrios, Gerardo, 306
Barrios, Justo Rufino, 401
Barrios de Chamorro, Violeta, 632
Barroeta, Rafael, 270
Barron, Frank, 294
Barron, Harry, 95
Barron, Henry, 99
Barron, William, 1040
Barros, Ademar de, 178
Barros, Cassio de, 162
Barros, Eugênio, 160
Barros, Felipe de, 158
Barros, Francisco, 173
Barros, Helvídio de, 171
Barros, João de, 177
Barros, José, 173
Barros, Olegário de, 161
Barros, Pedro, 246
Barros, Pedro de, 604
Barros, Prudente, 148, 177
Barros, Togo de, 172
Barroso, Benjamin, 155
Barroso, José, 156
Barroso, Liberato, 173
Barrot, Odilon, 326
Barrow, Errol, 125
Barrow, Nita, 124
Barrowclough, Harold, 625
Barrows, Lewis, 999
Barry, John, 1003
Barschel, Uwe, 376
Barstow, John, 1036
Bartel, Kazimierz, 698
Barthes, René, 347, 782
Barthou, Louis, 327
Bartlett, Dewey, 1023
Bartlett, John, 1013
Bartlett, Josiah, 1011
Bartlett, Washington, 979
Bartlett Bautista, Manuel, 588
Bartlett Díaz, Manuel, 586
Bartley, Mordecai, 1021
Bartley, Thomas, 1021
Bartolini, Aldomiro, 774
Bartolini, Gianfranco, 489

Bartolomeo, Luigi Di, 485
Barton, Edmund, 88
Bartram, Walter, 375
Bärtsch, Konrad, 876
Bärtsch, Luzi, 876, 877
Bärtschi, René, 868
Barulli, Libero, 774
Barulli, Umberto, 774
Barwell, Henry, 94
Barwick, David, 963
Baryadayev, Konstantin, 721
Basadre, Enrique, 691
Basail, Miguel, 72
Basanov, Vladimir, 728
Basayev, Shamil, 722
Base, Clement, 795
Bashford, Coles, 1041
Bashir Azmah, 913
Bashir Magashi, 655
Bashir Rahmal, 842
Bashmakov, Lev, 750
Basiev, Oleg, 735
Basjir Gemayel, 527
Bass, Robert, 1013
Bassett, Richard, 983
Bassetti, Piero, 484
Bassoe, Johannes, 662
Bassolini, Antonio, 482
Bassos Lima, José de, 151
Bastedo, Frank, 212
Bastico, Ettore, 534
Bastos, João, 705
Bastyan, Edric, 93, 95
Basu, Jyoti, 452
Batagayev, Aleksei, 756
Bate, William, 1031
Bates, Frederick, 1007
Bates, John, 1002
Batista, Abdon, 176
Batista, Nilo, 173
Batista y Zaldívar, Fulgencio, 277, 278
Batliner, Gerard, 537
Batlle, Jorge, 1050
Batlle Berres, Luis, 1049
Batlle y Grau, José, 1049
Batlle y Grau, Lorenzo, 1049
Batmanov, Aleksei, 732
Batmounkh, Jambyn, 599
Batmouonkh, Jambyn, 600
Batryov, Shadahz, 935
Batsrow, William, 1041
Batt, Phil, 990
Battaglini, Antonio, 898
Battershill, William, 279, 918
Batthyany, Lajos, 416
Battle, John, 1037
Baturin, Viktor, 728
Batyev, Salikh, 738
Bauder, Robert, 868
Baudis, Dominique, 333
Baudouin, 130

Bauer, Gustav, 366
Bauer, Theodor, 387
Baum, Erwin, 376
Baumann, Johannes, 855, 859
Baumgartner, Gottlieb, 888
Baunsgaard, Hilmar, 288
Baup, J., 905
Baur, Charles, 334
Bautista Azmar-Cabanas, Juan, 818
Bautista Castillo, Gonzalo, 585
Bautista Ceballos, Juan, 573
Bautista Egusquiza, Juan, 686
Bautista Ezcurra, Juan, 686
Bautista Gil, Juan, 686
Bautista O'Farrill, Gonzalo, 585
Bautista Quiros, Juan, 271
Bautista Sacasa, Juan, 632
Bauzá, Eduardo, 70
Bavadra, Timoci, 318
Bavier, Simeon, 854
Bavin, Thomas, 90
Baxter, Elisha, 977
Baxter, George, 1042
Baxter, John, 204
Baxter, Percival, 999
Bay, Gustav, 862
Bayandin, Lev, 756
Bayar, Celâl, 930
Bâyar, Celal, 932
Bayardelle, Ange (Congo, Brazzaville), 255, 257
Bayardelle, Ange (Djibouti), 291
Bayezid I (Turkey), 929
Bayezid II (Turkey), 929
Bayh, Evan, 992
Bayinnaung (Myanmar), 606
Bayle, Pierre, 343
Baylon Chacón, Oscar, 576
Bayma, Henrique, 178
Baynes, Edward, 764
Bayo Lawal, 642
Bayon, Juan, 78
Bayulken, Umit, 7
Baz, Gustavo, 582
Bazarova, Roza, 934
Bazille, Wilhelm, 389
Bazin, Jean-François, 331
Bazin, Marc, 411
Bazzanella, Gianni, 488, 489
Beale, John, 968
Beant Singh, 445
Beards, William, 993
Beasley, David, 1030
Beatrix (Netherlands), 619
Beattie, Alexander, 766
Beattie, David, 626
Beattie, Peter, 92
Beauchamp, Laurent, 341, 343
Beaufort, Joan, 954
Beaufort, Leicester, 557
Beaujon, F.J.C., 621

Beaujon, Hendrik, 621
Beaujon, Jan, 624
Beaujon, Julius, 622
Beaujon, Oscar, 623
Beaujon, Otto, 622
Beaujon, Richard, 623, 624
Beaulieu, Wilhelm von, 383
Beaumont, J. Michael, 957
Beauvais, Armand, 997
Beaux, Henri, 252, 344, 350
Beaver, James, 1025
Beaver, Robert, 201
Beavogui, Lansana, 404
Bebb, William, 1021
Becerra de la Flor, Daniel, 692
Bech, Joseph, 543
Bechard, Paul, 782
Bechoff, Roland, 341
Bechvaya, Kiril, 361
Bechvaya, Kirill, 362
Bechvaya, M., 361
Beck, Heinrich, 374
Beck, Kurt, 373
Beck, Max, 107
Beckham, John, 996
Beda, Angelo, 837, 844
Bedell, Ralph, 35
Bedford, Frederick, 99
Bedford, Gunning, 983
Bedle, Joseph, 1014
Beebe, George, 994
Beeckman, R. Livingston, 1027
Beel, Louis, 620
Beernaert, Auguste, 130
Beetham, Edward, 147, 848, 925
Beevi, M.S. Fathima, 448
Begg, Varyl, 965
Begin, Menachem, 475
Begnis, Carlos, 82
Begole, Josiah, 1003
Béguin, Ernest, 880, 881
Béguin, Jacques, 881, 882
Béguin, Thierry, 882
Beichmann, Frederik, 662
Beirão, Francisco, 704
Beisebayev, Massimkhan, 508
Bekk, Johann, 377
Bekker, Simon, 805
Beknazarov, Soibnazar, 916
Bekov, Sergei, 722
Béla I (Hungary), 414
Béla II (Hungary), 414
Béla III (Hungary), 415
Béla IV (Hungary), 415
Belaid, Abdessalam, 60
Belaunde, Rafael, 691
Belaunde Terry, Fernando, 689
Belcredi, Richard, 106
Belgayev, Gambozh, 720
Beliayev, Nikolai, 508
Bell, Arthur, 956

Bell, Charles, 1012, 1036
Bell, Douglas, 215
Bell, Francis, 626
Bell, Frank, 1011
Bell, Gawain, 35, 637
Bell, Henry, 570, 937
Bell, Hugh, 293
Bell, John (New Hampshire, USA), 1012
Bell, John (Pennsylvania, USA), 1026
Bell, John (Prince Edward Island, Canada), 210
Bell, P. Hansborough, 1032
Bell, Samuel, 1012
Bell, Thomas, 35
Bell, William, 629
Bell-Irving, Henry, 201
Belleau, Narcisse, 198, 210
Bellmon, Henry, 1023
Bello, S.T., 649
Bellomo, Michele, 486
Belloni, Protogene, 771
Bellony, Emmanuel, 337
Belluzzi, Antonio, 770
Belluzzi, Ciro, 770
Belluzzi, Giovanni, 770
Belluzzi, M. Benedetto, 773
Belluzzi, Marino, 773
Belluzzi, Settimio, 771, 772
Belo, Newton, 160
Belo, Saturnino, 160
Belonogov, Anatoly, 744
Belotsky, M.I., 522
Belser, Eduard, 864
Beltrametti, Juan, 78
Beltrami, Vittorio, 485
Beltrán, Washington, 1049
Beltrán Espantoso, Pedro, 692
Beltrones Tapia, Manlio, 588
Belyakov, Aleksandr, 747
Belyayev, Ivan, 730
Belykh, Yury, 751
Belzú, Manuel, 140
Bembinov, Grigory, 728
Bembo, Giovanni, 498
Ben-Gurion, David (D. Grün), 475
Ben-Zvi, Izhak (I. Shimshelewitz), 475
Benavides, Oscar, 689
Bender, Arthur, 904
Bender, Ivan, 145
Benedettini, Ernesto, 774
Benedict III (Pope), 1060
Benedict IV (Pope), 1061
Benedict IX (Pope), 1061
Benedict V (Pope), 1061
Benedict VI (Pope), 1061
Benedict VII (Pope), 1061
Benedict VIII (Pope), 1061
Benedict XI (Pope), 1062
Benedict XII (Pope), 1062
Benedict XIII (Pope), 1063
Benedict XIV (Pope), 1063

Benedict XV (Pope), 1065
Benediktsson, Bjarni, 420
Beneš, Edvard, 282, 283, 284
Benítez de Lugo, Alfonso, 825
Benjamin, Edouard, 15
Benjamin, John, 786
Bennett, Alfred, 104
Bennett, Caleb, 983
Bennett, Charles, 205
Bennett, Gordon, 209
Bennett, Phillip, 96
Bennett, Richard, 199
Bennett, Robert, 995
Bennett, Thomas (Idaho, USA), 989
Bennett, Thomas (South Carolina, USA), 1028
Bennett, William A. (British Colombia), 201
Bennett, William (Belize), 134
Bennett, William R. (British Colombia), 201
Benningsen, Alexander, 379
Bennloch y Viva, Juan, 62
Benoit, Pedro, 296
Benoy John, 310
Bensch, Jean, 343
Benson, Elmer, 1005
Benson, Frank, 1024
Benson, Stephen, 532
Benson Arthur, 1098
Bent, Thomas, 98
Bentes, Dionisio, 164
Bentín, Antonio, 690
Bentsen, Niels, 289
Benvenuti, Ludovico, 12
Beraldo, João, 163
Beran, Rudolf, 283, 285
Bérard, Jean, 922
Beraudier, Charles, 335
Berber, Alberto, 580
Berdiev, Alla, 934
Beregfay, Károly, 416
Bérégovoy, Pierre, 329
Bereng bin Anyut, Louis, 558
Berenguer, y Fuste, Damaso, 818
Beresin, Anatoly, 735
Berestovoy, Viktor, 745
Berezin, Anatoly, 734
Berezovsky, Boris, 8
Berg, Carl von, 383
Berge, Abraham, 661
Bergmann-Pohl, Sabine, 367
Bergner, Christoph, 375
Berhane, Ghebray, 18
Beria, Lavrenti, 359, 364
Berinkey, Dénes, 416
Berisha, Sali, 57
Berlin, Eugène, 272
Berlusconi, Silvio, 480
Bernacchi, Michael, 510
Bernadet, Daniel, 331

Bernard, Denis, 960
Bernard, Henri, 252
Bernard, Joseph, 209
Bernard, Marie-Joseph, 353
Bernardes, Arthur, 148, 163
Bernardini, Domenico, 774
Bernardini, Eugenio, 772
Bernasconi, Agostino, 899
Bernasconi, Benito, 900
Bernetti, Tommaso, 1064
Bernhard II (Saxe-Meiningen), 386
Bernhard III (Saxe-Meiningen), 386
Bernier, Lucien, 339
Bernini, Carlo, 490
Bernstein, Klaus, 288
Berov, Lyuben, 185
Berquo, Pedro, 776
Berreta, Tomás, 1049
Berro, Bernardo, 1048
Berry, Graham, 98
Berry, James, 978
Berry, Nathaniel, 1012
Berry, Thomas, 1030
Bersani, Pier Luigi, 482
Bertaut, Maurice, 338
Berthoud, Jean, 880
Berti, Gian, 774, 775
Berti, Pietro, 774
Bertozzi, Mario, 75
Bertram, George, 959
Bertran, Francisco, 413
Bertrand, Jean-Jacques, 212
Bertrand, Jean-Marie, 350
Bertuleit, Wilhelm (Vilius Bertulitis), 541
Bervini, Rossano, 900
Berzanti, Alfredo, 483
Berzegov, Nukh, 717
Berzins, Andris, 526
Beshara al-Khuri, 527
Besouro, Gabino (Alagoas, Brazil), 151
Besouro, Gabino (Piauí, Brazil), 170
Besso, Santiago, 81
Besson, François, 871
Bessone, Ramón Díaz, 78
Betancourt, Carlos, 585
Betancourt, Rómulo, 1067
Betham, Gustav, 35
Bethlen, István, 417
Bethman-Hollweg, Theobald von, 366, 384
Bethune, W. Angus, 97
Betin, Oleg, 752
Betrian, Stanley, 623
Bettencourt, André, 332
Bettencourt, José de, 604
Bettschart, August, 892
Beuret, Jean-Pierre, 877
Beurnier, Maurice (Guadeloupe), 338
Beurnier, Maurice (Senegal), 780
Beust, Ferdinand, von, 106
Beust, Friedrich von, 374
Beveridge, John, 991

Beverley, James, 1045
Beyries, Jean-Louis, 568
Bezerra, Carlos, 162
Bezerra, José, 156
Beznosov, Pavel, 732
Bezuidenhout, David, 611, 612
Bezzola, Andrea, 876
Bezzola, Domenic, 875
Bgazhba, Mikhail, 360, 361
Bhadri, Bajrang, 432
Bhagat, Bali Ram, 432, 445
Bhaktavatsalam, M., 448
Bhan, Brish, 460
Bhan, Suraj (Bigar, India), 427
Bhan, Suraj (Uttar Pradesh, India), 450
Bhandare, R.D. (Andhra Pradesh, India), 424
Bhandare, R.D. (Bihar, India), 427
Bhandari, Nar Bahadur, 447
Bhandari, Romesh, 429, 449, 450, 453, 454
Bhandari, Sunder Singh, 427, 430
Bhanu Pratap Singh, 429, 434
Bhardawa, Kalka, 449
Bhargava, Gopichand, 444
Bhargava, Kant, 36
Bharqawa, R.B., 438
Bhatnagar, S.K., 447
Bhattal, Rajinder Kaul, 445
Bhend, Samuel, 869
Bhim Shumshere Jung, 617
Bhimsena Thapa (Nepal), 616
Bhishma Narain Singh (Assam & Sikkim, India), 425, 426, 446
Bhishma Narain Singh (Tamil Nadu), 448
Bhonphahuyasena, Bhanon, 920
Bhosale, Babasaher, 438
Bhunu (Ngwane, Swaziland), 847
Bhutti bin Suhail al-Maktum, Shaikh, 946
Bhutto, Benazir, 665
Bhutto, Mumtaz, 670
Bhutto, Zulfikar, 664, 665
Bia, Ajax, 677
Biagi, Germano de, 773, 774
Bianco, José, 175
Bianrifi Tarmidi, 253
Bias Fortes, Chrispim, 162, 163
Bias Fortes, José, 163
Biasotti, Sandro, 484
Biasutti, Adriano, 483
Bibb, Thomas, 974
Bibb, William, 974
Bicakćić, Edhem, 146
Bicakçiu, Ibrahim, 57
Bicheldey, Kaadyr-ool, 739
Bickett, Thomas, 1019
Bidault, Georges, 328
Bidegain, Oscar, 71
Bidou, Alain, 335
Biebrich Torres, Carlos, 588
Biedenkopf, Kurt, 375
Bielecki, Jan, 699

Biéler, Philippe, 907
Bielich, Vicente Merino, 223
Biella, Bernardino, 80
Bienert, Rudolf, 284
Bienerth, Richard, 107
Bierut, Bołeslaw, 698, 699
Biesheuvel, Barend, 620
Bigelow, Hobart, 981
Bigger, Samuel, 991
Biggs, Ansel, 993
Biggs, Benjamin, 983
Biggs, Frank, 1020
Bigi, Federico, 775
Bigirwenkya, Zerubaberi, 14
Bigler, John, 979
Bigler, William, 1025
Bignone, Reynaldo, 70
Biha, Leopold, 189
Bijedić, Djemal, 1087
Bijedic, Dzemal, 143
Biker, Joaquim, 216, 405
Bilbo, Theodore, 1006
Bildt, Carl, 852
Bildt, Didrik, 851
Bilić, Jure, 275
Billardon, André, 330
Billinghurst, Guillermo, 689
Billings, Franklin, 1036
Billini, Francisco, 295
Bilmezis, Juan, 77
Binaisa, Godfrey, 938
Bindsibadze, _, 362
Binger, Louis-Gustave, 272
Bingham, Francis, 958
Bingham, Hiram, 982
Bingham, Kinsley, 1003
Binhoure, Adrien, 291
Binney, Hugh, 95
Binns, Henry, 802
Binns, Patrick, 210
Bioley, Henri, 902
Bionaz, Cesare, 489
Biordi, Agostini, 772, 773
Biordi, Ubaldo, 773, 774
Biragov, Yury, 735
Birch, Ernest, 557
Bircher, Silvio, 859
Birchler, Usa, 908
Bird, Lester, 68
Bird, Vere, 67, 68
Bird, Wallace, 203
Birendra (Nepal), 616
Birgir Magnusson (Sweden), 849
Birgir (Sweden), 849
Birindwa, Faustin, 259
Birkavs, Valdis, 526
Birketvedt, Odd, 662
Birni-Kudu, A.S., 647
Biron, Ernst, 713
Biros, Casimir-Marc, 137, 347
Biryukov, Nikolai, 734

Biryukov, Vladimir, 746
Bisa Onabajo, 652
Bisatya, Oudhnarain, 458
Bishewar Koirala, 617
Bishop, Maurice, 400
Bishop, Richard, 1022
Bisi Akande, 653
Bisig, Robert, 908
Bislip, Pedro, 621
Bismark, Otto von, 366, 383, 384
Bissel, William, 990
Bissell, Clark, 981
Bissing, Moritz von, 129
Bistras, Leones, 539
Biswal, Hemananda, 443
Bittel, Deolindo, 72
Bittencourt, António, 153
Bittencourt, Augusto, 164
Bittencourt, Carlos de, 174
Bittencourt, João, 164
Bitto, István, 416
Bitwadded Makonnen, 316
Biya, Paul, 195
Bizimungi, Pasteur, 759
Bjegović, Djordje, 276
Bjelke-Petersen, Johannes, 92
Björkman, Carl, 321
Björnsson, Sveinn, 419
Blacas, d'Aulps, Pierre, 325
Blacher, Louis-Placide, 136, 403, 633
Black, Eugene, 43
Black, Frank, 1017
Black, George (Utah, USA), 1034
Black, George (Yukon, Canada), 214
Black, Robert (Robin), 245, 787
Black, Samuel, 1009
Blackburn, Luke, 996
Blackburne, Kenneth, 499
Blackwood, Ibra, 1029
Bladsel, Henry, 1011
Blaine, John, 1041
Blair, Andrew, 204
Blair, Anthony, 953
Blair, Austin, 1003
Blair, James (Australia), 91
Blair, James (USA), 1008
Blaize, Herbert, 399, 400
Blake, Edward, 208
Blake, Eugene Carson, 50
Blake, Henry, 245, 830
Blakeney, Allan, 213
Blanc, Jacques, 332
Blanc, Marcel, 906
Blanchard, Francis, 44
Blanchard, Hiram, 207
Blanchard, James, 1004
Blanchard, Newton, 997
Blanche, Bartolome, 223
Blanche (Blanca) (Navarre), 823
Blanchy, Pierre, 597, 598
Blanco, Antonio Guzmán, 1066, 1067

Blanco, José, 77
Blanco, Pedro, 140
Blanco, Salvador Jorge, 296
Blanco García, Jaime, 826
Blandin, Marie-Christine, 333
Blandy, Richard, 1057
Blangy, Michel, 342
Blanton, Ray, 1032
Blaser, Adolf, 868
Blaser, Ernst, 868
Blattler, Remigi, 884
Blättler, Remigi, 884
Blažević, Jakov, 274, 275
Bleackley, Peter, 970
Blease, Coleman, 1029
Blehr, Otto, 660, 661
Bleuler-Huni, Konrad, 908
Bley, João, 157
Blick, M., 968
Blignaut, Pieter, 803
Blinnikov, Sergei, 730
Bliss, Aaron, 1004
Blittersdorf, Friedrich, 377
Blix, Hans, 43
Blochausen, Félix de, 542
Blocher, Hermann, 864
Blodnieks, Adolfs, 526
Blomdal, Odd, 662
Blood, Henry, 1034
Blood, Hilary, 124, 355, 399, 570
Blood, Robert, 1013
Bloomfield, Joseph, 1014
Blos, Wilhelm, 388
Blount, William, 1031
Blount, Willie, 1031
Bloxham, William, 985
Bludov, Dmitry, 714
Blue, Robert, 993
Bluhme, Christain, 287
Blum, Léon, 328
Blumer, Cosmos, 874
Blumer, Eduard, 874
Blumeris, Arthur, 37
Blundell, Denis, 626
Blyth, Arthur, 94
Bo-Boliko Lokonga (André Bo-Boliko), 259
Boban, Mate, 145
Boboshevsky, Zvetko, 183
Bocaiúva, Quintino (Q. de Sousa), 171
Bocanegra, José de, 572
Boccia, Antonio, 481
Bochkaryov, Vasili, 750
Bock, Lorenz, 389
Böckli, Erich, 897, 898
Bode, George, 652
Bode, Hubert, 67
Boden, Wilhelm, 373
Bodenhausen, G., 47
Bodet, Jaime Torres, 46
Bodjollé, Emmanuel, 923

Bodman, Heinrich, 378
Bodmer, Adolf, 860
Bodo, Dogsomyn, 600, 601
Bodwell, Joseph, 999
Bodwin, James, 1001
Bodyul, Ivan, 595
Boe, Nils, 1030
Boeckh, Christian von, 377
Boegl, Hans, 108
Boer, K.H. de, 621
Boerma, Addeke, 43
Boeynants, Paul van den, 131
Boffa, Paul, 566
Bofondi, Giuseppe, 1064
Bogado, Floro, 75
Boganda, Barthélémy, 219
Bogdanov, E.S., 758
Bogdanov, Valery, 728
Bogdanski, Jezdimir, 544
Bogden, Curtis, 1019
Bogdo Gegen Khan, 599
Boggs, James, 984
Boggs, Lilburn, 1007
Bogoev, Ksente, 545
Bogolyubov, Nikolai, 522
Bogombov, Oleg, 747
Bogrond, Luis, 412
Bogsch, Arpad, 47
Bohi, Albert, 896
Bohmcker, Johann, 370
Boies, Horace, 993
Boileau, Guy, 350
Boillat, Pierre, 877
Boiossier, Jacques-Alphonse, 136
Boisadam, Philippe, 343
Boisdé, Raymond, 331
Boissier, Jacques, 340
Boisson, Pierre-François, 194, 257, 782
Boissonnas, Jean, 872
Bojanović, Milanko, 1093
Boji, Dieudonné, 265
Bokassa, Jean-Bédel (cousin), 219
Bokassa I (Jean-Bédel), 218, 219
Bokov, Khakhbikar, 722
Bokovikov, Aleksandr, 755
Bola Ige, 653
Bola Tinubu, 651
Bolack, Tom, 1016
Bolea Foradoda, Juan, 824
Bolesław I (Poland), 696
Bolesław II (Poland), 696
Bolesław III (Poland), 696
Bolesław IV (Poland), 696
Bolesław V (Poland), 696
Bolfing, Karl, 893
Bolger, James (Jim), 627
Bolin, Wesley, 977
Bolívar, Didalco, 1068
Bolívar, Simón, 140, 249, 688, 1066
Bolkiah, 181
Bolkiah, Sultan Hassanal, 182

Bolla, Fulvio, 899
Bollini, Domenico, 773
Bollini, Marino, 773, 774
Bollini, Paolo, 774
Bolotte, Pierre, 338
Bols, Louis, 960
Bolte, Henry, 99
Bolz, Eugen, 389
Bomboko, Justin, 259
Bömers, Otto, 386
Bommai, Somappa, 435
Bonaparte, Joseph, 814
Bonaparte, Louis Napoléon, 324
Bonaparte, Napoléon, 323, 324
Bonar Law, Andrew, 952
Bond, Christopher, 1008
Bond, Robert, 205
Bond, Shadrach, 990
Bondarenko, Mikhail, 941
Bondaz, Gianni, 490
Bondaz, Vittorino, 489
Bondevik, Kjell Magne, 661
Bone, Scott, 975
Bonekwe, _, 268
Bonelli, Giovanni, 770
Bonelli, Menetto, 770, 774
Bonelli Rubio, Juan, 308
Bonelly, Rafael, 296
Bonfiglio, Angelo, 487
Bonfils, Charles-Henri, 137, 403
Bongho-Nouarra, Stephane, 256
Bongo, Omar, 354
Bonham, Milledge, 1029
Bonham-Carter, Charles, 565
Bonhomme, Albert, 338
Bonhoure, Adrien, 272, 341, 345, 456
Bonhoure, Louis-Alphonse (French Guiana), 336
Bonhoure, Louis-Alphonse (Martinique), 339
Bonhoure, Louis-Alphonse (New Caledonia), 347
Boniface IX (Pope), 1062
Boniface VI (Pope), 1060
Boniface VIII (Pope), 1062
Bonifaz, Naftalio, 300
Bonilla, Adolfo, 589
Bonilla, Manuel, 413
Bonilla, Miguel, 413
Bonilla, Policarpo, 412
Bonilla Vázquez, Ignacio, 589
Bonnard, Claude, 906
Bonnecarrère, Auguste-François, 194, 922
Bonnefort, Pierre, 255
Bonnelle, François, 343
Bonner, John, 1009
Bonner, Yves, 343
Bonnet, Bernard, 335
Bonnet, Yves, 338
Bonnici, Ugo Mifsud, 566
Bono Martínez, José, 826

Bonomi, Ivanoe, 479
Bonvin, Louis (Benin), 136
Bonvin, Louis (Gabon), 353
Bonvin, Louis (Pondicherry), 353, 456
Bonvin, Roger, 856
Boon, Herbert, 67
Boon, Ratliff, 991
Booth, Newton, 979
Booysen, Harry, 611
Bór-Komoroski, Tadeisz, 700
Boradori, Marco, 901
Borba, Manoel, 169
Borbiconi, Marino, 770, 771
Borbidge, Robert, 92
Borbora, Golap, 426
Borchetas, Endrias, 540
Bord, André, 329
Bord, Charles, 1057
Borda, Juan, 1049
Bordaberry Arocena, Juan, 1049
Bordallo, Ricardo, 1044
Bordas Valdes, José, 296
Bordes, Pierre-Louis, 59
Bordier, Paul-Camille, 633
Bordier, Pierre-Camille, 218
Bordon, José, 78
Bordon, Mauro, 489
Bordon, Robert, 198
Borel, Alfred, 873
Borel, Antoine, 881
Borella, Achille, 898, 899
Boreman, Arthur, 1039
Boren, David, 1023
Borges, César, 155
Borges, Pedro, 155
Borghese, Marcantonio, 492
Borghesi, Angelo, 771, 772
Borghesi, Bartolomeo, 772
Borgia, Francesco, 486
Borgoño, Justiniano, 689, 690
Borgoño, Luis Barros, 222
Boris III (Bulgaria), 183
Boris (Russia), 713
Borisov, Semen, 737
Borja, Custodio de, 64
Borja Cevellos, Rodrigo, 300
Borjas, Arminio, 1067
Borje, Miguel, 586
Borković, Nedeljko, 1095
Börlin, Ernst, 863
Borner, Alain, 873
Börner, Holger, 372
Bornet, Bernard, 904
Bornhausen, Irineu, 176
Bornhausen, Jorge, 177
Borno, Louis, 410
Borodin, Petr, 595
Borooah, Deva, 427
Boross, Péter, 417
Borrego Estrada, Genaro, 591
Borrero, Manuel, 300

Borrero, Misael Pastrana, 251
Borrero y Cortazar, Antonio, 299
Borromeo, Carlo, 492
Borromeo, Giulio, 492
Borselli, Ricardo, 83
Borso (Modena), 491
Borsoyev, I., 720
Borten, Per, 661
Borunda Ortiz, Teofilo, 577
Bos du Thil, Karl du, 371
Bosanquet, Day, 93
Bösch, Josef, 892, 893
Bosch Gaviño, Juan, 296
Boselli, Enrico, 482
Boselli, Paolo, 479
Boshof, Jacobus, 803
Bosianu, Constantine, 709
Bošić, Boro, 144
Bösiger, Walter, 867
Boskaljon, C.F., 624
Bosque, Pio, 307
Bossa, José, 429
Bossano, José (joe), 965
Bosse, Pieter van, 619
Bosset, Norbert, 905
Bossi, Emilio, 899
Bossi, Johann, 875
Bossy, Aloys, 869
Boston, Henry, 785
Bostrom, Erik, 851
Boswell, Alexander, 956
Botashev, Magomet, 729
Botelho, Francisco, 171
Botha, Cornelius (Con), 803
Botha, J. Christoffel, 803
Botha, Louis, 800, 804
Botha, Pieter, 800
Bottcher, Otto (Otonas Betcheris), 541
Bottin, Aldo, 490
Botto de Barros, Advaldo Cardoso, 46
Bottolfsen, Clarence, 990
Boucaut, James, 94
Bouch, William, 1017
Bouchard, Lucien, 212
Boucherville, Charles, 211
Bouchet, Alfred-Léon, 345
Bouchraya Bayoune, 761
Boudinot, Auguste, 337
Bouge, Joseph-Louis, 345
Bouge, Louis-Joseph, 336, 338
Bouhid, Waldir, 165
Bouhin, Clement, 344
Bouilloux-Lafont, Maurice, 597
Bouisson, Ferdinand, 328
Boukango, _, 261
Boukary Adji, 634
Bouley, Roger du, 1057
Boulloche, Léon, 338
Bourassa, Robert, 212
Bourdillon, Bernard, 635, 937
Bourgarel, Adrien, 339

Bourgeois, Léon, 327
Bourges, Yves, 257
Bourges, Yvon (Burkina Faso), 186
Bourges, Yvon (France), 331
Bourges-Maunoury, Maurice, 328
Bourgine, Maurice-Léon, 136, 633, 922
Bourke, Martin, 970
Bourn, Augustus, 1027
Bournat, Gilbert de, 344
Bourne, Frederick, 122
Bourquin, Fritz, 881
Bourseiller, Herve, 337
Boutellier, Paul, 336
Bouterse, Desiré (Desi), 846
Boutwell, George, 1002
Bovet, Jules, 869, 870
Bowell, MacKenzie, 198
Bowen, John, 199
Bowen, Otis, 992
Bowen, Thomas, 989
Bowerman, Jay, 1024
Bowie, Oden, 1000
Bowie, Robert, 1000
Bowles, Chester, 982
Bowles, Richard, 202
Bowring, Charles, 549
Bowring, Walter, 293
Bowser, John, 98
Bowser, William, 201
Boyd, Alfred, 202
Boyd, Augusto, 674
Boyd, John, 203
Boyer, Eric, 342
Boyer, Jean-Pierre, 409
Boyle, Cavendish, 204, 570
Boyle, Emmet, 1011
Boyle, F.C., 102
Boynton, James, 987
Bozanga, Simon, 219
Bozhilov, Dobri, 184
Božović, Radoman, 1093, 1096
Božović, Srdja, 1087
Braamcamp, Anselmo, 704
Bracalente, Bruno, 489
Bracken, John, 202
Brackett, John, 1002
Bracks, Steve, 99
Braddon, Edward, 96
Braden, George, 214
Bradford, August, 1000
Bradford, Robert, 1002
Bradley, Lewis, 1011
Bradley, Michael, 970
Bradley, William, 996
Bradley, Willis, 1044
Bradshaw, Robert, 763
Brady, James, 989
Braga, António, 167
Braga, Joaquim, 703, 705
Braga, José, 159
Braga, Ney, 168

Braga, Wilson, 166
Bragança Neto, Raul, 777
Bragg, Thomas, 1019
Braghis, Dimitru, 595
Brahier, Gaston, 877
Braithwaite, Nicholas, 400
Brajović, Radivoje, 1090
Bramble, P. Austin, 966
Bramble, Wilfred, 966
Bramlette, Thomas, 995
Branch, Emmet, 992
Branch, John (Florida, USA), 984
Branch, John (North Carolina, USA), 1018
Branco, Eugenio, 776
Branco, Manuel, 149
Branco, Sergio Castelo, 177
Brand, David, 101
Brand, Johannes, 803
Brand van Zyl, Gideon, 799, 802
Brandão, António, 179
Brandão, Francisco, 163
Brandão, Júlio, 163
Brande, Luc van den, 132
Brandenberg, Paul, 893
Brandenstein, Carl von, 382
Brandenstein, Joachim von, 381
Brandli, Christoffel, 876
Brandon, Gerard, 1005
Brandon, William, 975
Brandt, André, 882
Brandt, Camille, 881
Brandt, David, 966
Brandt, Willy (Herbert Frahm), 366, 369
Branigan, Roger, 992
Brann, Louis, 999
Branstad, Terry, 993
Branting, Hjalmar, 851
Brantjes, Nicolaas, 621
Brar, Harcharan Singh, 431, 445
Brasil, Ptolomeu, 176
Brătianu, Ion, 709
Brătianu, Ionel, 709, 710
Brătianu, Vintilla, 710
Bratlie, Jens, 661
Bratteli, Trygve, 661
Brauer, Max, 371
Braun, Alexander, 374
Braun, Arthur von, 377
Braun, Friedrich, 896
Braun, Otto, 384
Bravo, Leopoldo, 81
Bravo, Nicolás, 572
Bravo Ahuja, Victor, 585
Bravo Murillo, Juan, 816
Brawand, Samuel, 867, 868
Bray, John, 94
Bray-Steinburg, Otto, 368
Brayman, Mason, 989
Brazauskas, Algirdas, 539, 540
Breathitt, Edward, 996
Breathitt, John, 995

Brechbühl, Fritz, 865
Breitenmoser, Franz, 861
Breithaupt, Louis, 208
Breitlung, Wilhelm von, 388
Brena Torres, Rodolfo, 585
Brenes Jarquin, Carlos, 632
Brennan, Joseph, 999
Brenner, August, 864, 865
Brenner, Ernst, 854
Bresis, Vilnis, 526
Bressoles, Louis, 340
Brett, Robert, 199
Brevie, Jules, 633, 782
Brévié, Jules, 272
Brewer, Albert, 975
Brewer, Earl, 1006
Brewster, Harlan, 201
Brewster, Owen, 999
Brezhnev, Leonid, 508, 595, 716, 717
Brial, Victor, 350
Briand, Albert, 344
Briand, Alfred-Léon, 344
Briand, Aristide, 327
Brice, James, 1000
Bricker, John, 1022
Bridges, George, 93
Bridges, H. Styles, 1013
Briggs, Edward, 1002
Brigham, Paul, 1035
Briner, Peter, 892
Briner, Robert, 909
Briscoe, Dolph, 1033
Brisson, Henri, 326, 327
Brito, Gratuliano, 166
Brito, Joaquim de, 776
Britto, António, 175
Brizan, George, 400
Brizio, Gian Paolo, 485
Brizola, Leonel, 172, 175
Brizuela, Guillermo, 71
Brizuela, Hermino Torres, 77
Brkić, Hasan, 144
Brkić, Zvonko, 275
Broadbent, Edward, 956
Brocklehurst, G.J., 628
Brodard, Remi, 871
Brodbeck, Adolf, 862
Brodeur, Louis-Philippe, 211
Brodie, Alexander, 976
Brody, Andreas, 285
Broger, Albert, 861
Broger, Raymund, 861
Broido, Grigory, 915
Bromet, Geoffrey, 957
Bromley, Robert, 762
Bromov, Boris, 748
Bron, Antoine, 872
Bronevich, Valentina, 755
Brons, Johannes, 845
Brooke, Charles, 558
Brooke, Charles Vyner, 558

Brooke, James, 558
Brooke, John, 277, 1045
Brooke, Robert, 1037
Brooke-Popham, Henry, 509
Brooker, Edward, 97
Brookes, John, 1001
Brooks, Bryant, 1042
Brooks, E.C., 969
Brooks, R. Dallas, 87, 97
Brooks, Ralph, 1010
Broom, Peter, 1014
Broome, James, 984
Broqueville, Charles de, 130, 131
Brosi, Georg, 876
Brosio, Manlio, 25
Brotzu, Giuseppe, 486
Brouckère, Charles de, 130
Brouckère, Henri de, 130
Brough, Charles, 978
Brough, John, 1021
Broughton, J. Melville, 1019
Brouwer, Abraham, 623
Brovikov, Vladimir, 127
Brovko, Feodor, 594
Broward, Napoleon, 985
Browm, John W., 1022
Brown, Aaron, 1031
Brown, Albert G., 1006
Brown, Albert O., 1013
Brown, Benjamin Gratz, 1007
Brown, D. Russell, 1027
Brown, Dean, 95
Brown, Edmund Jr (Jerry), 979
Brown, Edmund (Pat), 979
Brown, Ethan, 1021
Brown, Frank, 1001
Brown, Fred, 1013
Brown, George (Saskatchewan, Canada), 212
Brown, George (Upper & Lower Canada), 198
Brown, John C., 1031
Brown, John Y., 996
Brown, John Y. Jr, 996
Brown, Joseph E., 987
Brown, Joseph M., 987
Brown, Neil, 1031
Brown, Sinai, 678
Brown, Thomas, 984
Brown, W.G., 214
Browne, Joseph, 1007
Browning, Gordon, 1032
Brownlee, John, 200
Brownlow, William, 1031
Brownson, Nathan, 986
Broz-Tito, Josip, 1086, 1087, 1088, 1089
Bruce, Charles, 570
Bruce, Herbert, 208
Bruce, R. Randolph, 200
Bruce, Stanley, 88
Brücker, Josef, 902

Brucker, Wilbur, 1004
Bruckner, Edmund, 922
Bruderer, Jakob, 860
Bruderer, Otto, 860
Brugger, Ernst, 856, 910
Brugger, Friedrich, 874
Brugghen, Justinius van der, 619
Bruhin, Egon, 893
Brühlmann, Walther, 891
Brum, Baltasar, 1049
Brumbaugh, Martin, 1025
Brundage, Avery, 21
Brundtland, Gro Harlem, 47
Brunello, Duilio Rafael, 74
Brunet, Auguste (Mali), 563
Brunet, Auguste (New Caledonia), 347
Brunhart, Hans, 537
Brüning, Heinrich, 366
Brunner, Martin, 874
Brunon, Pierre, 338
Brunot, Richard, 194, 218, 220, 272
Brunschwig Graf, Martine, 873
Brunsdale, Norman, 1020
Bruschke, Werner, 375
Bruton, Charles, 848
Bruton, John, 474
Bruvelaitis, Juergis, 541
Bryan, Charles, 1010
Bryan, George, 1025
Bryan, Gerald, 962
Bryan, Henry, 1043
Bryan, Richard, 1011
Bryant, C. Farris, 985
Bryant, John, 629
Bryne, Brendan, 1015
Bu He, 232
Buachidze, Samuil, 758
Buaiz, Vitor, 157
Bubbicu, Filippo, 481
Bubyakin, N.V., 736
Bucaram Ortiz, Abdalá, 300
Bucci, Roberto, 774
Buchanan, James, 972
Buchanan, John (Canada), 207
Buchanan, John (USA), 1031
Buchanan, Thomas, 532
Büchel, Markus, 537
Buchez, Philippe, 324
Buchs, Victor, 869, 870
Buchtel, Henry, 980
Buck, C. Douglass, 984
Buck, Wilhelm, 374
Buckingham, William, 981
Buckley, Donal, 473
Buckner, Simon, 996
Buckson, David, 984
Budd, James, 979
Budrys, Jonas, 540
Büeler, Anton, 892
Bueno, António, 177
Bueno, Jerônymo, 158

Buffet, Charles, 103
Buffet, David, 104
Buffet, Louis, 326
Buffi, Giuseppe, 900, 901
Bufi, Ylli, 57
Bugallal Araújo, Gabino, 818
Bugdayev, Ilya, 728
Buggia, Jean-Jacques, 344
Bugli, Pietro, 774
Bugli, Primo, 772, 773
Bugotu, Francis, 35
Buhagiar, Francesco, 566
Buhl, Vilhelm, 288
Bühler, Robert, 879
Bühlmann, Werner, 879
Buhot-Launay, Émile (Central African Republic), 218
Buhot-Launay, Émile (French Guiana), 336
Buillard, Michel, 346
Buisignani, Pasquale, 770
Buiskool Johannes, 846
Buitrago, Pablo, 631
Bujang bin Othman, 558
Bujard, M., 905
Bukar Ibrahim, 656, 657
Bukleski, Tome, 544
Bukoshi, Bujar, 1095
Bulacios, Carlos, 76
Bulajić, Žarko, 1090
Bulashev, Zinatulla, 719
Bulat, _, 595
Bulatov, V.S., 944
Bulatović, Momir, 1088, 1090, 1091
Buldayev, Sergei, 720
Bülent Eçevit, 932
Bülent Ülüsü, 932
Bulganin, Nikolai, 715, 716
Bulkeley, Morgan, 981
Bulle, F.K., 758
Bulloch, Archibald, 985, 986
Bullock, Alexander, 1002
Bullock, George, 960
Bullock, Rufus, 987
Bulnes, Manuel, 222
Bülow, Bernhard von, 366, 384
Bulow, William, 1030
Bultin, Bato, 679
Bulundwe, Edouard, 264
Bulwer, Henry, 802
Bulyea, George, 199
Bumatsende, Gonchigiyn, 599
Bumçi, Luigi, 56
Bumpers, Dale, 978
Buncamper, Walter, 624
Bundu, Abbas, 15
Bunge, Juan Figueroa, 79
Bunge, Nikolai, 714
Bünger, Wilhelm, 375
Buniatzade, Dadash, 114
Bunn, William, 989
Bunyakat, Thawi, 920

Buol-Schauenstein, Karl, 106
Burbank, John, 1020
Burbury, Stanley, 95, 96
Burckhardt, Hans, 864
Burckhardt, Lukas, 865, 866
Burckhardt-Finsler, Albert, 864
Burckhardt-Schazmann, Christian, 864
Burdon, John, 134, 762
Buresch, Karl, 107, 109
Burgagni, Antonio, 771
Burgagni, Nelson, 771
Burgener, Joseph, 902
Burger, Kurt, 372
Burger, Schalk, 804
Burgers, Thomas, 804
Bürgi, Hermann, 898
Bürgi, Josef, 893
Bürgi, Urs, 910
Burgi, Walter, 895
Burgos García, Enrique, 586
Burhanuddin Rabbani, 54, 55
Buri, Dewet, 868
Burity, Tarcísio, 166
Burkart, Josef, 908
Burke, Andrew, 1020
Burke, Brian, 101
Burke, Denis, 102
Burke, John, 1020
Burke, Thomas, 1018
Bürki, Gottelf, 868
Burleigh, Edwin, 999
Burlet, Jules de, 130
Burman, Samir, 449
Burmov, Todor, 184
Burnett, David, 1032
Burnett, Peter, 978
Burney, Dwight, 1010
Burney, S.M.H., 431, 439
Burnham, Forbes, 408
Burnquist, Joseph, 1005
Burns, Alan (Belize), 134
Burns, Alan (Ghana), 390
Burns, Alan (Nigeria), 635
Burns, Haydon, 985
Burns, John, 989
Burnside, Ambrose, 1027
Burr, Dominique, 348
Burren, Fritz, 867
Burroughs, John, 1016
Burrowes, Hugh, 762, 966
Burrows, Thomas, 202
Burt, Francis (Australia), 100
Burt, Francis (USA), 1009
Burton, Hutchins, 1018
Burton, William, 983
Busbee, George, 987
Busch, Alberto Natusch, 141
Busch, Germán, 141
Buschor, Ernst, 910
Bush, George, 973
Bush, George W., 1033

Bush, John (Jeb), 985
Bushati, Maliq, 57
Bushfield, Harlan, 1030
Bushnell, Asa, 1022
Bushuev, P.I., 730
Busia, Kofi, 391
Busiel, Charles, 1013
Busignani, Aldo, 771
Busignani, Patricia, 774
Businger, Ferdinand, 882, 883
Businger, Josef, 885
Bussi, Antonio, 84
Bustamante, Alexander (W.A. Clarke), 499, 500
Bustamante, José, 583
Bustamante, Anastasio, 572
Bustamante, Manuel, 1048
Bustamante Belaunde, Alberto, 692
Bustamante y Bustamante, Alfonso, 692
Bustamante y Rivero, José, 689
Busti, Jorge, 75
Bustillos, Victorino Márquez, 1067
Butalia, H.S., 452
Butayev, Kasbek, 735
Butcher, James, 1000
Buteler, René, 78
Buthelezi, Mangosuthu, 809
Butler, Benjamin, 1002
Butler, David, 1009
Butler, Ezra, 1035
Butler, Harold, 44
Butler, Milo, 118
Butler, Montagu, 957
Butler, Pierce, 1028
Butler, Richard (ITU), 45
Butler, Richard (South Australia), 94, 95
Butler, Spencer, 606
Butov, Vladimir, 756
Butros-Ghali, Butros, 19, 42
Butros Pasha Ghali, 303
Buttel, Christian von, 383
Buttigieg, Anton, 565
Büttiker, Eugen, 893, 894
Buu Loc, 1075
Buyoya, Pierre, 188
Buys, Johannes, 804
Buzdugan, Gheorghe, 708
Buzek, Jerzy, 699
Byambasuren, Dashiyn, 600
Byatt, Horace, 917, 925
Byatt, Robin, 967
Bykin, Ya.B., 719
Bykov, Fedor, 722
Bylinski, Ivan, 127
Bynoe, Hilda, 399
Byrd, Charles, 1021
Byrd, Harry, 1037
Byrne, Frank, 1030
Byrne, Joseph, 509, 783, 785
Byrnes, James, 1029
Byrnes, Thomas, 92

Bystrzonowski, _, 700

Caabi el-Yachroutou Mohammed, 253
Caamaño, José Plácido, 299
Caamaño Deño, Francisco, 296
Caballero, Bernardino, 686
Caballero, Carlos, 73
Caballero, Tomás, 77
Caballero Aburto, Raúl, 580
Cabanellas Ferrer, Miguel, 819
Cabeçades, Joaquim, 705
Cabell, William, 1037
Cabral, Amancio, 216, 776
Cabral, Filomeno (Angola), 64, 65
Cabral, Filomeno (East Timor), 297
Cabral, José (Dominican Republic), 295
Cabral, José (Portugal), 429, 604
Cabral, Milton, 166
Cabral Lius, 406
Cabras, Antonello, 487
Cabrera Carrasquedo, Manuel, 585
Caccia, Fulvio, 900
Cáceres, Andrés, 689
Cáceres, Ramón, 296
Cadier, Edmond-Emilien, 353
Cadman, Radclyffe, 803
Cadruvi, Donat, 876
Caelestinus II (Pope), 1062
Caelestinus III (Pope), 1062
Caelestinus IV (Pope), 1062
Caelestinus V (Pope), 1062
Caetano, Marcello, 706
Café, João, 148
Cafiero, Antonio, 71, 78
Caflisch, Anton, 874
Cağatay, Mustapha, 280
Çağlayangil, Ihsan, 930
Cahannes, Augustin, 876
Cahen, Alfred, 49
Cahill, John, 90
Cahill, William, 1015
Caiado, Leonino, 158
Caicedo, Domingo, 249
Caillard, André, 348
Caillaux, Joseph, 327
Cain, John, 99
Cain, Jonathan, 99
Cairat, Francesc, 62
Cairns, Don, 962
Cairoli, Benedetto, 479
Cajander, Aimo, 319, 320
Cakobau, George, 318
Calabro, Victorio, 71
Calame, Albert, 880
Calame, Henri, 880, 881
Calasans, José de, 179
Calatrava, José, 815
Calawdewos, 314
Caldas, Cândido, 155
Caldecott, Andrew, 245, 830

Calderón, Climacho, 250
Calderón, Guido Vildoso, 141
Calderón, Guillermo Quintero, 250
Calderón, Serapio, 689
Calderon, Sergio, 1072
Calderón Guardia, Rafael, 271
Calderón Rodríguez, Enrique, 579
Calderón Sol, Armando, 307
Calderón Velarde, Alfonso, 587
Caldwell, Millard, 985
Calelia-Römer, Susanne, 622
Čalfa, Marián, 283
Calhoun, James, 1015
Călinescu, Armand, 710
Calixtus II (Pope), 1062
Calixtus III (Pope), 1063
Call, Guillermo, 1071
Call, Ramón Malla, 62
Call, Richard, 984
Callagahn, James, 953
Callandrelli, Alessandro, 1064
Callbeck, Catherine, 210
Callejas, Rafael, 413
Calleri di Sala, Edoardo, 485
Calles, Aureo, 588
Calles, Plutarco, 574
Calmon, Francisco, 154
Calonder, Felix, 854
Cals, Joseph, 620
Caluori, Joaquim, 876
Calvel, Auguste, 563
Calvet, Jean, 218
Calvo, Bartolomé, 249
Calvo, Bartolomeo, 674
Calvo, Mariano, 140
Calvo, Paul McDonald, 1044
Calvo-Sotelo y Bustelo, Leopoldo, 818
Calzada Urquiza, Antonio, 586
Camacho, Carlos, 1045
Camacho, Manuel, 604
Camacho, Mario Laya, 1072
Camacho Guzmán, Rafael, 586
Camacho Quiroz, César, 582
Camaco, Jaime, 706
Câmara, Jerônimo da, 173
Camara, José, 159
Câmara, José, 174
Câmara, Mârio, 173
Camargo, Afonso de, 167
Camargo, Alberto Lleras, 250
Camargo, Laudo de, 177
Camargo, Sergio, 271
Camata, Gérson, 157
Camdessus, Michel, 45
Camelli, Orleir, 151
Camenzind, Josef, 892
Camenzind, Richard, 893
Cameron, Donald (Nigeria), 635
Cameron, Donald (Nova Scotia, Canada), 207
Cameron, Donald (Tanzania), 917

Cameron, Douglas, 202
Cameron, Edward (British Virgin Islands), 962
Cameron, Edward (St Lucia & St Vincent), 764, 766
Cameron, Edward (The Gambia), 355
Cameron, Gordon, 215
Cameron, William, 1037
Camille-Paris, Jacques, 12
Caminos, Juan de, 77
Campanys, Lluis, 826, 827
Campaoré, Blaise, 186
Campbell, Alexander (Ontario), 208
Campbell, Alexander (Prince Edward Island), 210
Campbell, Barrington, 955
Campbell, Bennett, 210
Campbell, Carroll, 1030
Campbell, Clifford, 499
Campbell, David (Malta), 565
Campbell, David (Virginia, USA), 1037
Campbell, Douglas, 202
Campbell, Jack, 1016
Campbell, John, 1042
Campbell, Kim, 199
Campbell, Thane, 210
Campbell, Thomas (Arizona, USA), 976
Campbell, Thomas (Texas, USA), 1033
Campbell, W. Telfer, 510
Campbell, Walter, 91
Campbell, William, 1031
Campbell-Bannerman, Henry, 952
Campero, José, 578
Campero, Narciso, 140
Campestiguy, Juan, 1049
Camphausen, Ludolf, 383
Campins, Luis Herrera, 1067
Campion, William, 99
Campione, Giuseppe, 487
Campo, Carlos Ibánez del, 222, 223
Campo, Neudo, 176
Campo, Rafael, 306
Campora, Héctor, 70
Campos, Abelardo de, 76
Campos, Aristides, 157
Campos, Artur de, 216
Campos, Berbardo, 149
Campos, Bernardino de, 177
Campos, Carlos de, 177
Campos, Eleazar, 160
Campos, Frederico, 162
Campos, Guilherme, 179
Campos, Jaime, 162
Campos, João de, 168
Campos, Jorge Nocetti, 82
Campos, José Siqueira, 180
Campos, Julio de, 162
Campos, Martinho, 150
Campos, Milton, 163
Campos, Olympio, 179
Campos, Pedro, 177

Camsel, Charles, 213
Camus, Eloy, 81
Canadanović, Mirko, 1097
Canal, Boisrand, 410
Canalejas y Mendez, José, 817
Canales Clarion, Fernando, 584
Canalizo, Valentín, 573
Cañas, Antonio, 306
Candamo, Manuel, 689, 690
Candao, Zacaria, 695
Candeth, Kenneth, 429
Candía, Alfredo Ovando, 141
Candia, Isidro, 589
Candler, Allen, 987
Candole, Eric de, 796
Cañellas Fons, Gabriel, 825
Canepa, Adolfo, 965
Canet, Jayme, 168
Canevascini, Guglielmo, 899, 900
Canning, George, 951
Cannon, William, 983
Cano Ricardo Obregon, 73
Cánovas del Castillo, Antonio, 817
Cansanção, José, 151
Canseco, Enrique, 589
Cantacuzino, Gheorge, 709
Cantau, Julien-Edgard, 336
Cantave, Léon, 410
Canto Echeverría, Humberto, 590
Canty, Brian, 959
Canute (England), 949
Cao Diqui, 244
Capac Yupanqui, 693
Capagorry, André, 341
Capanema, Gustavo, 163
Capaul, Sebastian, 875
Capdeville, Robert, 332
Caperton, Gaston, 1040
Capet, Hughes (France), 322
Capgras, Émile, 341
Capiberibe, João, 152
Capitan, Cándido, 82
Capodicasa, Angelo, 487
Capper, Arthur, 994
Capper, John, 956
Capponi, Gino, 497
Caprivi, Leo von, 366, 384
Capstan, Yakin, 103
Car, Pero, 274
Caraccioli, Hector, 413
Carattoni, Federici, 773
Carattoni, Federico, 773
Carattoni, Piermatteo, 770
Carazo, Evaristo, 631
Carazo Odio, Rodrigo, 271
Carbajal, Francisco, 573
Carcagno, Jorge, 73
Çarçani, Adil, 57
Carde, Jules, 194, 255
Carde, Jules-Gaston, 59, 782
Cardelli, Luciano, 774

Cardelli, Virgilio, 773
Cárdenas, Adan, 631
Cárdenas, Alberto, 582
Cárdenas, Francisco, 584
Cárdenas, Francisco Arias, 1072
Cárdenas, Lazaro, 574
Cárdenas del Rio, Damasco, 583
Cárdenas González, Enrique, 589
Cárdenas Solorzano, Cuauhtémoc, 583
Cardinall, Allan, 964
Cardinaux, Louis, 869
Cardon, Philip, 43
Cardoso, António, 65
Cardoso, Clodimir, 160
Cardoso, Fernando Henrique, 149
Cardoso, Francisco, 166, 167
Cardoso, Hunald, 179
Cardoso, Joaquim, 175
Cardoso, Maurico, 179
Cardoso, Newton, 163
Carenco, Jean-François, 338, 344
Carey, D. Vic, 957
Carey, Hugh, 1018
Carey, Joseph, 1042
Carey, Peter, 956
Carey, Robert, 1042
Carey, T. Godfrey, 956
Carey, Victor, 956
Carey, William, 956
Cargo, David, 1016
Carías Andino, Tiburcio, 413
Carillo, Braulio, 270
Carillo Olea, Jorge, 583
Carillo Zavala, Abelardo, 576
Carinus, Johan, 802
Carl Alexander (Saxe-Weimar-Eisensach), 386
Carl August (Saxe-Weimar-Eisensach), 386
Carl Friedrich (Saxe-Weimar-Eisensach), 386
Carl IX (Sweden), 850
Carl (Saxe-Meiningen), 385
Carl VII Sverkersson (Sweden), 849
Carl VIII Knutsson (Sweden), 850
Carl X Gustav (Sweden), 850
Carl XI (Sweden), 850
Carl XII (Sweden), 850
Carl XIII (Sweden), 850
Carl XIV Johan (Sweden), 850
Carl XV (Sweden), 850
Carl XVI Gustaf (Sweden), 850
Carleson, Edvard, 851
Carletti, Tommaso, 796
Carlew, Frederick, 785
Carli, Désiré, 337
Carlin, John, 995
Carlin, Thomas, 990
Carlisle, John, 67
Carlo Alberto (Piedmont-Sardinia), 495
Carlo (Charles of Anjou, Sicily), 493
Carlo Emanuele I (Piedmont-Sardinia), 495

Carlo Emanuele II (Piedmont-Sardinia), 495
Carlo Emanuele III (Piedmont-Sardinia), 495
Carlo Emanuele IV (Piedmont-Sardinia), 495
Carlo Felice (Piedmont-Sardinia), 495
Carlo I (Naples and Sicily), 491
Carlo I (Parma and Piacenza), 494
Carlo I (Piedmont-Sardinia), 495
Carlo I (Sicily), 493
Carlo II (Naples and Sicily), 491
Carlo II (Parma and Piacenza), 494
Carlo II (Piedmont-Sardinia), 495
Carlo II (Sicily), 493
Carlo III (Naples and Sicily), 491
Carlo III (Parma and Piacenza), 494
Carlo III (Piedmont-Sardinia), 495
Carlo III (Sicily), 493
Carlo IV (Naples and Sicily), 492
Carlo IV (Sicily), 493
Carlo (Parma and Piacenza), 494
Carlo V (Naples and Sicily), 492
Carlo VI (Naples and Sicily), 492
Carlo VII (Naples and Sicily), 492
Carloman I (France), 322
Carloman II (France), 322
Carlos I (Spain), 814
Carlos II (Spain), 814
Carlos III (Spain), 814
Carlos IV (Spain), 814
Carlos (Portugal), 703
Carlotti, Antoine-Louis, 1058
Carlson, Arne, 1005
Carlson, Frank, 994
Carlson, George, 980
Carlsson, Ingvar, 852
Carlucci, Jorge, 72
Carmichael, Thomas, 97
Carmo, Aurelio do, 165
Carmona, António, 703, 705
Carnahan, Mel, 1008
Carneiro, João, 155
Carneiro, Rui, 166
Carnell, Katherine, 101
Carney, Thomas, 994
Carnieri, Claudio, 489
Carnighi, Ulderico, 83
Čarnogurský, Ján, 789
Caro, José, 572
Caro, Miguel, 250
Caroco, Jorge, 405
Carol II (Romania), 708
Carollo, Vincenzo, 487
Caron, René-Edouard, 210
Caroselli, Francesco, 796
Carossino, Angelo, 484
Carp, Petru, 709
Carpenter, B. Platt, 1008
Carpenter, Cyrus, 993
Carper, Thomas, 984

Carr, Elias, 1019
Carr, Ralph, 980
Carr, Robert, 91
Carraco Cardoso, Carlos, 580
Carranza, Bruno, 270
Carranza, Venustiano, 573
Carras, Hubert, 194
Carrasco Altamirano, Diodoro, 585
Carrera, Martin, 573
Carrera, Rafael, 401
Carrero Blanco, Luis, 818
Carrillo Marcor, Alejandro, 588
Carrington, Edwin, 6, 18
Carrión, Geronimo, 299
Carrizo, Luis, 82
Carroll, Beryl, 993
Carroll, Henry, 211
Carroll, John, 1000
Carroll, Julian, 996
Carroll, Thomas, 1000
Carroll, William, 1031
Carruthers, Garrey, 1016
Carruthers, Joseph, 90
Carstens, Karl, 366
Carta y Ramirez, Gerhard, 1069
Carter, Frederick, 205
Carter, George, 988
Carter, Gilbert, 118, 124
Carter, James (Jimmy), 973, 987
Cartier, George, 198
Carton, Doyle, 985
Carton de Wiart, Henri, 130
Cartraud, Raoul, 334
Caruana, Peter, 965
Carvajal, Angel, 590
Carvajal, Jorge, 1069
Carvajal, Meliton, 691
Carvalho, Álvaro de, 165
Carvalho, Antero de, 64
Carvalho, António de, 155
Carvalho, Aristides de, 179
Carvalho, Dionisio de, 165
Carvalho, Eronides de, 179
Carvalho, Evaristo, 777
Carvalho, Felipe de, 216
Carvalho, Fernando de, 155
Carvalho, Francisco de, 151
Carvalho, João de, 168
Carvalho, José (Angola), 65
Carvalho, José (Brazil), 160
Carvalho, José de (Brazil), 164
Carvalho, José Nobre de, 246
Carvalho, Júlio de, 163
Carvalho, Luiz, 165
Carvalho, Manoel, 151
Carvalho, Manuel de, 297
Carvalho, Osmar de, 172
Carvalho, Pedro de, 179
Carvalho, Sebastião de, 179
Carvalho e Silva, Joaquim de, 166
Carvallo, Héctor, 686

Carvel, Elbert, 984
Carvell, Jedediah, 209
Carville, Edward, 1011
Casado, Plínio, 172
Casai, Louis, 872
Casali, Alvaro, 772, 773
Casali, Bruno, 773
Casañas y Pages, Salvador, 62
Casardi, Alberico, 25
Cásares Quiroga, Santiago, 818
Casaroli, Agostino, 1065
Casas Alemán, Francisco, 590
Casati, Gabrio, 495
Casaulta, Giachen, 876
Cascardo, Hercolino, 173
Cascetta, Vittorio, 482
Case, Norman, 1027
Casey, Robert, 1026
Cash, Gerald, 118
Cashin, Michael, 205
Casimir, Fernand, 1058
Casimir-Périer, Jean, 324
Casimir-Périer, Jean (grandson), 327
Casis, Roberto, 82
Cass, Lewis, 1003
Cassam Moolam, 570
Cassam Uteem, 570
Cassebohm, Friedrich, 383
Casseres, Ronald, 623
Castaneda Castro, Salvador, 307
Castelan, Marcelino, 72
Castelar y Ripoll, Emilio, 815
Castellano, Gaspar, 824
Castellanos, Julio, 80
Castellanos, Victoriano, 412
Castellanos Dominguez, Absalon, 577
Castellanos Gerado, Milton, 575
Castelli, Nestor, 80
Castello, Egardo, 79
Castello Branco, Humberto, 149
Castellon, Francisco, 631
Castelo, Placido, 156
Caster, Lolita Aniyar de, 1072
Castilhos, Júlio de, 174
Castilla, Ramón, 688
Castillo, Arnoldo, 72
Castillo, Miguel, 307
Castillo, Oscar, 72
Castillo, Ramón, 70
Castillo Armas, Carlos, 402
Castillo Franco, Armando, 579
Castillo Lara, Rasalio, 1065
Castillo Ledón, Luis, 583
Castillo López, Jesús, 583
Castillo Tielmans, José, 577
Castle, Michael, 984
Castor, Elie, 337
Castorena, J. Jesús, 580
Castrén, Kaarlo, 319
Castrén, Urho, 320
Castro, Alvaro de, 604, 705

Castro, António, 164
Castro, Augusto de, 159
Castro, Cipriano, 1067
Castro, Emilio, 50
Castro, Fernando, 65
Castro, Joaquim de, 705
Castro, José, 270
Castro, José de, 705
Castro, Juliano, 1066
Castro, Laureano Gómez, 250
Castro, Manoel de, 156
Castro, Miguel, 173
Castro, Morris de, 1046
Castro, Raul, 977
Castro, Rodríguez, 81
Castro Jijón, Ramón, 300
Castro Rus, Fidel, 278
Castro Sánchez, Juventino, 586
Caswell, Richard, 1018
Caswell, Tod, 1019
Catalan Calvo, Rafael, 580
Catargiu, Barbu, 709
Catargiu, Lascar, 709
Catherine (Catarina) (Navarre), 823
Cato, Milton, 767
Catroux, Georges, 59
Cattori, Giuseppe, 899
Catts, Sidney, 985
Cauchon, Joseph, 202
Caulfield, Henry, 1008
Causey, Peter, 983
Cavaco Silva, Anibal, 706
Cavadini, Jean, 882
Cavaignac, Louis, 324, 326
Cavalcante, Luiz, 152
Cavalcanti, Ambrosio, 168
Cavalcanti, Carlos, 169
Cavalcânti, Clovis, 166
Cavalcânti, Joaquim, 170
Cavalcanti, José, 169
Cavalcânti, José de Melo, 169
Cavalcânti, José de Moura, 169
Cavalcanti, Newton, 161
Cavalcânti, Newton, 172
Cavalcânti, Odon, 166
Cavalcânti, Rivando, 166
Cavazos Lerma, Manuel, 589
Caveri, Severino, 489
Cavero, Armando, 77
Cavero, José, 691
Cavina, Sergio, 482
Cavour, Camillo, 479, 495, 496
Caxias, Marquês de (Luiz de Lima e Silva), 149
Cayetano, Benjamin, 989
Cayla, Léon, 782
Caylon, Léon, 546
Cea Bermudez, Francisco, 815
Ceaușescu, Nicolae, 708, 711
Cebuc, Ion, 595
Cecchetti, Alberto, 773, 774

Cecco, Giustino De, 481
Ceccoli, Edda, 774
Ceccoli, Egidio, 770
Ceccoli, Gino, 771, 772
Ceccoli, Mariano, 772
Cecil, Nigel, 957
Cecilia, A.J., 623
Cecotti, Sergio, 483
Cédile, Jean, 922
Cedras, Raoul, 411
Cejuela, Bonifacio, 78
Celeste, Richard, 1022
Celestin, Martial, 411
Celio, Bixio, 900
Celio, Enrico, 855, 899
Celio, Nello, 856, 899, 900
Celis, Francisco, 579
Celli, Lino, 773
Celluci, Paul, 1003
Celmán, Miguel Juárez, 69
Celmans, Hugo, 526
Celsi, Celestino, 84
Cemerski, Angel, 544, 545
Cemović, Momčilo, 1090
Cenac, Winston, 765
Cenić, Djordje, 1092
Ceniceros, Severino, 579
Censi, Marc, 333
Centeno Anchorena, José, 308
Centurion, Carlos Gómez, 81
Centurion, Luis Gómez, 74, 77
Centurioni, Francesco, 498
Centurioni, Nicolo, 498
Cepeda Dávila, Ignacio, 578
Cepeda Flores, Ramón, 578
Cepernič, Jorge, 83
Ceranić, Marko, 144
Cercus, Louis, 353
Cerda, Manuel de la, 631
Cerda, Pedro Aguirre, 223
Cerdan, Jorge, 590
Ceresole, Paul, 853
Cerezo Arévalo, Vinicio, 402
Cermño, Aldo, 1070
Cerna, Vicente, 401
Cernaux, Marcel, 342
Cerneaux, Marcel, 342
Černik, Oldřich, 283
Černius, Jonas, 539
Černý, Ján, 283
Cerqueira, Edgard de, 150
Cerqueira, Eduardo, 163
Cerrina-Feroni, Giovanni, 310, 796
Cervantes Corona, José, 591
Cervantes Delgado, Alejandro, 581
Cervantes Hernández, Anselmo, 589
Cervera Pacheco, Víctor, 591
Cesaire, Aimé, 341
César, António, 176
César, Carlos, 706

Cesar, José, 177
Cesare (Modena), 491
Céspedes y Quesada, Carlos, 277
Cetshweyo, 806
Cevera, Gabriel, 578
Cevey, Pierre, 907
Chaaudri Mohammed Ali (Pakistan), 664
Chaban-Delmas, Jacques, 329, 330
Chabdarov, Boris, 727
Chacaltana, Cesáreo, 690
Chacin, Pedro Itriago, 1067
Chaćon, Germán Valero, 1072
Chacon, Lazaro, 401
Chadli Benjedid, 60
Chadwick, Stephen, 1024
Chafee, John, 1027
Chagas, João, 705
Chagla, Mahomed, 458
Chai Songyue, 243
Chakdon Namgyal, 446
Chakdorjab, 601
Chakravarti, Birendra, 431
Chakravarti, Subramaniam, 432
Chakravorty, Nripen, 449
Chalbaud, Carlos Delgado, 1067
Chaliha, Bimala, 426
Chalk, Gordon, 92
Chalmers, Frederick, 615
Chalmers, Robert, 830
Chaloryoo, Sa'ngad, 921
Chalvet, Jean, 291, 568
Chamanand, Kriangsak, 921
Chamant, Jean, 330
Chamassi Sair Omar, 254
Chamay, Edouard, 873
Chamberlain, Abiram, 982
Chamberlain, Daniel, 1029
Chamberlain, George, 1024
Chamberlain, Joshua, 998
Chamberlain, Neville, 952
Chambers, George, 926
Chambers, John, 993
Chambon, Charles, 456
Chambon, Jean-Georges, 136
Chambon, Jean-Jacques, 255
Chamling, Pawan Kumar, 447
Chamorro, Diego, 632
Chamorro, Frutos, 631
Chamorro, Pedro, 631
Chamorro Vargas, Emiliano, 632
Chamoun, Camille, 527
Champ, William, 96
Champion, John, 1057
Champion, Reginald, 1080
Chan, Julius, 677
Chan, K., 103
Chan II (Cambodia), 190
Chan Kai Yau, 5
Chan Si, 192
Chancellor, John, 476, 570, 925, 1100
Chand, Krishan, 454

Chandernagor, André, 333
Chandler, Albert, 996
Chandler, E. Barron, 203
Chandler, Edward, 204
Chandra, J. Pravash, 455
Chandra, Naresh, 430
Chandra, Ramesh, 453
Chandra Sekkar Singh, 428
Chandra Shumshere Jung, 617
Chandravati, 456
Chandresvar Narain Singh, 448, 450
Chandy, Kizhekethil, 430, 436, 456
Chanel, Marc, 336
Chanewesvar Narain Singh, 444
Chaney, Frederick, 101
Chang Ching-hui, 230
Chang Do Yun, 517
Chang Hsiao-hsin, 230
Chang Myun (John Chang), 517
Chang Shao-tseng, 226
Chang Taik Sang, 517
Chang Tso-lin, 225
Changkhyim, 231
Chanis Pinzon, Daniel, 674
Chann Ak, 191
Channon, Newton, 1031
Chanot, Georges, 343
Chantelat, Pierre, 332
Chao Phraya Chakkri (Thailand), 920
Ch'ao Ping-chun, 226
Chao Shou-po, 248
Chapaprieta y Terragosa, Joaquín, 818
Chapital, Constantino, 585
Chapleau, Joseph-Adolphe, 211
Chaplin, Alan, 530
Chaplin, Drummond, 1098
Chaplin, Francis, 1100
Chapman, John, 766
Chapman, Reuben, 974
Chapman, Thomas, 96
Chapon-Baissac, Pierre, 291
Chappaz, Achille, 902
Chapple, John, 965
Chaptynov, Valery, 718
Charan Singh, 423, 450
Charbonnet, Victor, 871
Charbonniaud, Claude, 348
Charkviani, Kandid, 359
Charles, George, 765
Charles, Hochoi, 926
Charles, M. Eugenia, 294
Charles (Carlos) I (Navarre), 823
Charles (Carlos) II (Navarre), 823
Charles (Carlos) III (Navarre), 823
Charles Gasyonga II (Ankole), 938
Charles I (France), 322
Charles I (Great Britain), 950
Charles II (France), 322
Charles II (Great Britain), 950
Charles III (France), 322
Charles III (Monaco), 597

Charles IV (France), 323
Charles IX (France), 323
Charles V (France), 323
Charles VI (France), 323
Charles VII (France), 323
Charles VIII (France), 323
Charles X (France), 324
Charlman, Peter, 841
Charlotte (Luxembourg), 542, 543
Chartier, Elie, 345
Charykov, N.M., 724
Chase, Ira, 992
Chase, Salmon, 1021
Chasseling, Carlos, 74
Chassiron, C.L. de, 961
Chastonay, Oscar de, 903
Chastoney, Joseph de, 902
Chataigneau, Yves, 59
Châtel, Yves-Charles, 59
Chater, Arthur, 798
Chatterton, Fenimore, 1042
Chatton, Romain, 869, 870
Chattopadhyay, Debi, 445
Chaturvedi, T.N., 453
Chatzikyriakos, Alexandros, 396
Chauba, Samson, 360
Chaudet, Paul, 855, 906
Chaudhary, Amarsinh, 431
Chaudhary Altaf Hussain, 668
Chaudhry, Mahendra, 318
Chaudhuri, Nabakrushna, 443
Chaudhuri Khaliquzzan, 122
Chaudhury Randkir Singh, 447
Chaudie, Jean, 781
Chaudran, Tumkur Satish, 429
Chauhan, Ram Lal, 433
Chaussebourg, Fernand, 334
Chautala, Om Prakash, 432
Chautemps, Camille, 327, 328
Chauveau, Pierre, 211
Chauvet, Augustin, 330
Chauvet, Paul, 257
Chavan, Shankarrao, 438
Chavan, Yashwantrao, 438, 458
Chavanne, André, 873
Chavannes, Fortune de, 255
Chaves, Alfredo, 577
Chaves, Aloysio, 165
Chaves, António, 167
Chaves, Francesco, 65
Chaves, Joaquim, 173
Chaves de Mendoça, António, 163
Chaves González, Manuel, 824
Chávez, Coronado, 412
Chavéz, Federico, 687
Chavez Carrillo, Rodolfo, 578
Chavez Hernández, Ausencio, 583
Chavez Hernández, José, 583
Chazal, René, 568
Chazelas, Jean-Victor, 568
Chean Van, 191

Chechenov, Khusein, 727
Cheeseman, Joseph, 532
Cheikh el-Avia Ould Mohammed Khouna, 569
Chekhishky, Volodymir, 941
Chekoyev, Anatoly, 363
Chelebiev, Chelebi, 942
Chembulatov, Mikhail, 734
Chen Bangzhu, 238
Chen Cheng, 247, 248
Chen Chu-hsuan, 228
Chen Geng, 242
Chen Guangyi, 235
Chen Guodong, 244
Chen Huanyou, 239
Chen Kung-po, 229
Chen Lei, 237
Chen Mingren, 238
Chen Mingyi, 235
Chen Pixian, 238
Chen Puru, 240
Chen Shineng, 236
Chen Shui-bian, 247
Chen Weida, 244
Chen Xilian, 240
Chen Xitong, 244
Chen Yi (Shanghai), 244
Chen Yi (Taiwan), 248
Chen Yu, 235
Cheney, Person, 1012
Cheng Andong, 241
Cheng Heng, 190
Cheng Jian, 238
Cheng Kejie, 232
Ch'eng Ming-hsu, 225
Cheng Shiqing, 239
Ch'eng Tsu, 224
Cheng Weigao, 236, 237
Cheng Zihua, 241
Cherenkov, Vuiko, 184, 185
Cherian, P.V., 437
Cherkasov, Ishu, 726
Cherkesov, Georgy, 727
Cherkeziya, Otar, 358, 359
Chermont, Justo, 164
Chermoyev, Tapa, 757
Chermside, Herbert, 91
Chernenko, Konstantin, 716, 717
Chernogorov, Aleksandr, 744
Chernomyrdin, Viktor, 715
Chernousov, Boris, 715
Cherny, V.I., 742
Chernyshev, Aleksandr, 714
Chernyshev, Aleksei, 749
Cherry, Francis, 978
Cherry, R. Gregg, 1019
Chervyakov, Aleksei, 126, 127
Chessé, Henri, 186
Chevallez, George-André, 856
Chevance, Jean, 340
Chevènement, Jean-Pierre, 332

Chevigne, Pierre de, 547
Chhibbar, S.K., 440
Chhibber, Bakshi, 444
Chhiber, B.K.N., 453
Chhunga, Chal, 441
Chia Teh-yao, 227
Chiang Chao-tsung, 226
Chiang Ching-kuo, 247
Chiang Kai-shek, 225, 227, 247
Chiara, Jean-François di, 337
Chiararalloti, Giuseppe, 482
Chiari, Roberto, 675
Chiari, Rudolfo, 674
Chiaruzzi, Pietro, 773
Chibirov, Ludvig, 363
Chichester-Clark, James, 955
Ch'ien Neng-hsun, 226
Chifley, Joseph, 88
Chigir, Mikhail, 127
Chigogidze, Guram, 362
Chigoyev, Merab, 363
Chikovani, Mikhail, 360
Childerich III (France), 322
Childers, Erskine, 474
Chiles, Lawton, 985
Chiluba, Frederick, 1098
Chilvers, Merrilyn, 102
Chima, G.S., 455
Chimalpopoca (Aztec Empire), 574
Chimaroke Nnamani, 646
Chimba, Aleksandr (Saryg), 739
Chin A Sen, Henk, 845, 846
Chin Lee Chong, 518
Chin Yun-p'eng, 226
Ching Ti, 224
Chinwoke Mbadinuju, 641
Chiodo, Agostino, 495
Chirac, Jacques, 325, 329
Chirinos Calero, Patricio, 590
Chiryayev, Gavriil, 737
Chisholm, Brock, 47
Chisi, K.L., 442
Chiskov, Vikenty, 740
Chissano, Joaquim, 605
Chitanava, Nodar, 359
Chiti, Vannino, 489
Chittenden, Martin, 1035
Chittenden, Thomas, 1035
Chiu Chuang-huan, 248
Chkheidze, Zurab, 359
Chkhenkeli, Alaki, 358
Chkhubianishvili, Zakhari, 358, 359
Cho Man Sik, 515
Choi Kyu Hah, 517
Choi Too Sun, 517
Choi Yong Kun, 515
Choibalsan, Kharlogiyn, 599, 600
Chokier, Erasme Surlet de, 129, 130
Chokyi Gyaltsen, 231
Ch'oljong (Korea), 513
Chona, Mainza, 1098, 1099

Chong-hui (Korea), 512
Chong-sun (Korea), 512
Chongjo (Korea), 512
Chongjong (Korea), 512
Choonhavan, Chatichai, 921
Chopoe Namgyal, 446
Chopra, Inder, 447
Choskyi Gyaltsen Kundeling, 231
Chot-Plassot, Robert-Paul, 336
Choteau, Alphonse, 338, 341, 568, 633
Chou, Tsu-ch'i, 226
Chou Chih-jou, 248
Choudhury, Mahendra (Assam, India), 426
Choudhury, Mahendra (Punjab, India), 444
Chrétien, Jean, 199
Christain I (Denmark), 287
Christain II (Denmark), 287
Christain III (Denmark), 287
Christain IV (Denmark), 287
Christain IX (Denmark), 287
Christain V (Denmark), 287
Christain VI (Denmark), 287
Christain VII (Denmark), 287
Christain VIII (Denmark), 287
Christain X (Denmark), 287
Christen, Werner, 883
Christensen, Jens, 288
Christensen, Niels, 289
Christian, Charles Parkin, 967
Christian, Edgar, 967
Christian, Fred, 967
Christian, Frederick, 967
Christian, Gerard, 967
Christian, Ivan, 967
Christian, John, 967
Christian, Titi, 681
Christian, Warren, 967
Christian Gunther III (Schwarzenburg-Sonderhausen), 387
Christian II (Sweden), 850
Christian Ludwig I (Mecklenburg-Schwerin), 381
Christianson, Thomas, 1005
Christina (Sweden), 850
Christnacht, Alain, 348
Christoffer I (Denmark), 286
Christoffer II (Denmark), 286
Christoffer III (Denmark), 287
Christoffer (Sweden), 850
Christophe, Henri, 409
Chuang Leih-ti, 224
Chuard, Ernest, 905
Chuard, Ernst, 855
Chuard, Joseph, 869
Chuayffet, Chemor, Emilio, 582
Chub, Vladimir, 750
Chubar, Vlas, 941
Chubin, Yakov, 935
Chubinidze, Miron, 358
Chukwuemeka Ezeife, 640
Chulalongkorn (Thailand), 920

Chun Bo, 238
Chun Doo Hwan, 517
Chundokov, I.S., 717
Chung Ch'un, 227
Chung Il Kwun, 517
Chung Won Shik, 518
Chungjong (Korea), 512
Church, Louis, 1021
Churchill, Thomas, 978
Churchill, Winston, 952
Chwa II (Bunyoro), 939
Chyngyshev, Tursunbek, 522
Ciacchi, Luigi, 1064
Ciaffi, Adriano, 485
Ciampi, Carlo Azeglio, 478, 480
Ciavatta, Luciana, 774
Čič, Milán, 789
Cicogna, Pasquale, 498
Cicognani, Amleto, 1065
Cid, Francisco de Paulo, 216
Çiller, Tansu, 932
Cimoszewicz, Włodzimierz, 699
Cimpaye, Joseph, 188
Cincar-Marković, Dimitrije, 1092
Çindork, Hüsamettin, 930
Cioccari, Plinio, 900
Ciorba, Victor, 710
Cipriani, Luigi, 483
Cirillo, Ciro, 482
Cirisio, James, 837
Cisneros Molina, Joaquín, 589
Cisneros Sánchez, Manuel, 691
Cissey, Ernest de, 326
Citale, Carlo, 485
Civit, Joaquín Guevara, 77
Ckrebić, Dušan, 1092, 1093
Claes, Willy, 25
Claeys-Bouaert, Alfred, 189
Claflin, William, 1002
Claiborne, William (Louisiana, USA), 996
Claiborne, William (Mississippi, USA), 1005
Claireaux, Henri, 344
Clam-Martinitz, Richard, 107
Clarion Reyes, Benjamin, 584
Clark, Alonzo, 1042
Clark, Barzilla, 990
Clark, Charles, 1006
Clark, Chase, 990
Clark, Edward, 1033
Clark, Ernest, 95
Clark, Glen, 201
Clark, Helen, 627
Clark, Henry, 1019
Clark, James, 993, 995
Clark, John, 983, 986
Clark, Joseph, 199
Clark, Myron, 1017
Clark, William, 1007
Clark, William G., 203
Clark, William M., 208

Clarke, Charles, 565
Clarke, Ellis, 925
Clarke, Frederick, 764
Clarke, George, 993
Clarke, George (Australia), 97
Clarke, George (Canada), 204
Clarke, James, 978
Clarke, J.H., 202
Clarke, Lionel, 208
Clarke, Marshall, 530
Clarkson, Adrienne, 198
Clarkson, Frank, 962, 970
Clary-Aldnugen, Manfred von, 107
Clausen, Alden (Tom), 43
Clauson, Clinton, 999
Clavadetscher, Walter, 889
Clay, Clement, 974
Clayton, Joshua, 983
Clayton, Powell, 977
Cleaves, Henry, 999
Clech, Guy, 344
Cleland, Donald, 676
Clemenceau, Georges, 327
Clement, Frank, 1032
Clement, Percival, 1036
Clement, Wolfgang, 373
Clement II (Pope), 1061
Clement III (Pope), 1062
Clement IV (Pope), 1062
Clement IX (Pope), 1063
Clement V (Pope), 1062
Clement VI (Pope), 1062
Clement VII (Pope), 1063
Clement VIII (Pope), 1063
Clement X (Pope), 1063
Clement XI (Pope), 1063
Clement XII (Pope), 1063
Clement XIII (Pope), 1063
Clement XIV (Pope), 1064
Clementi, Cecil, 245
Clements, Earle, 996
Clements, Gilbert, 209
Clements, William, 1033
Clerc, Denis, 871
Clerides, Glafkos, 279
Cleveland, Chauncy, 981
Cleveland, Grover, 972, 1017
Clifford, Bede, 118, 570, 925
Clifford, George, 964
Clifford, Hugh (Ghana), 390
Clifford, Hugh (Malaysia), 557
Clifford, Hugh (Nigeria), 635
Clifford, Hugh (Sri Lanka), 830
Clifford, John, 1002
Clinton, De Witt, 1017
Clinton, George, 1016
Clinton, William (W. Blythe), 973, 978
Clodumar, Kinza, 615
Cloete, Cornelius, 613
Clottu, Alfred, 880, 881
Clottu, Gaston, 881

Clough, David, 1005
Clozel, Marie-François, 272, 563, 781
Cluchard, Jean, 344
Clyde, George (Grenada), 399
Clyde, George (Utah, USA), 1034
Coates, Joseph, 627
Çoba, Gjon, 56
Cobb, Howell, 987
Cobb, Rufus, 974
Cobb, William, 999
Cobo, Augusto Lavalle, 77
Coburn, Abner, 998
Cocatrix, Paul de, 903
Cochran, John, 983
Cochran, Robert, 1010
Cockburn, John, 94
Cockshut, Henry, 208
Codecido, Emilio Bello, 222
Coe, William, 1044
Coeffe, Jacques, 335
Coelho, Alfredo, 604
Coelho, António, 161
Coelho, João, 164
Coelho, Levindo, 163
Coelho, Manuel, 64, 405, 705
Coelho, Nilo, 155
Coelho, Nilo de Souza, 169
Coelho, Plínio, 153
Coëme, Guy, 132
Coetsee, Jacobus (Kobie), 800
Coffin, O. Vincent, 982
Coghlan, Charles, 1101
Cogo, Margherita, 488
Cohen, Andrew, 937
Coimbra, Estacio, 168, 169
Coke, Richard, 1033
Colagiovanni, Ulderico, 485
Colaković, Rodoljub, 144
Colarres, Alceu, 175
Colasanto, Giuseppe, 486
Colby, Anthony, 1012
Colby, Geoffrey, 549
Colcord, Roswell, 1011
Cold, Christian, 1046
Coldwell, Pedro, 586
Cole, George, 1039
Cole, W. Sterling, 43
Colebatch, Hal, 100
Coleman, Charles, 956
Coleman, James, 1006
Coleman, Peter Tali, 1043
Coleman, William, 532
Coleman, W.P., 104
Coles, Edward, 990
Coles, George, 209
Colidge, Carlos, 1035
Colijn, Hendrickus, 619
Colin, André, 331
Colin (Scotland), 953
Colina, Horacio de la, 81
Colindres, Vicente, 413

Collado Mena, Carlos, 828
Colle, Vicenzo Del, 481
Collet, Angelo, 171
Collet, Wilfred, 134, 407
Colley, George, 802
Collier, Henry, 974
Collier, Philip, 100
Collignon, Robert, 132
Collings, William F., 957
Collings, William T., 957
Collins, F.H., 215
Collins, John (Delaware, USA), 983
Collins, John (Newfoundland, Canada), 206
Collins, John (Rhode Island, USA), 1026
Collins, Leroy, 985
Collins, Martha Layne (M. Hall), 996
Collins, Michael, 473, 474
Collins, Thomas, 983
Collor de Mello, Fernando, 149
Collum, Shelby, 991
Colmenares, Iván, 1071
Colodrero, Nicolás Díaz, 74
Colombani, Antoine, 252
Colombani, Don-Jean, 633, 781
Colombani, Ignace, 218, 220
Colombi, Luigi, 898
Colombini, Enzo, 774
Colombo, Emilio, 480
Colombo, Juan Carlos, 75
Colon, Rafael Hernández, 1046
Colotka, Peter, 789
Colquitt, Alfred, 987
Colquitt, Oscar, 1033
Colton, George, 1045
Colton, John, 94
Colville, David, 458
Combes, Émile, 327
Combo, Ayouba, 253
Combs, Bert, 996
Comby, Bernard, 904
Comegys, Cornelius, 983
Comelli, Antonio, 483
Comer, Braxton, 975
Comet, Henri-Michel, 348
Comonfort, Ignacio, 573
Compain, Jacques, 291
Complesse, Robert, 854
Comptois, Paul, 211
Compton, John, 765
Compton, M. Robin, 962
Comstock, William, 1004
Conable, Barber, 43
Conant, Gordon, 208
Concha, José, 250
Condell, Claude, 966
Cone, Frederick, 985
Congacou, Tairou, 137
Congdou, Frederick, 214
Congreve, Walter, 565
Coniglo, Francesco, 487
Conley, Benjamin, 987

Conley, William, 1040
Conn, Neil, 102
Connally, John, 1033
Connelley, Henry, 1015
Connelly, Brian, 968
Connolly, Harold, 207
Connor, Martin, 1006
Connor, Seldon, 999
Conombo, Joseph, 187
Conrad, Peter, 857
Conradie, David, 610
Conradie, Johannes, 802
Consalvi, Ercole, 1064
Constantin, Daniel, 342
Constantine II (Scotland), 953
Constantine III (Scotland), 953
Constantine IV (Scotland), 953
Constantinescyu, Emil, 708
Constanza (Sicily), 492
Contarini, Alviso, 498
Contarini, Carlo, 498
Contarini, Domenico, 498
Conte, Floreal, 76
Conté, Lansana, 404
Conteh, Patrick, 786
Contendas, Barão de, 168
Conti, Pietro, 489
Contín, Carlos, 74
Contreras, Eleazar López, 1067
Converse, Julius, 1035
Convertino, Cosimo, 486
Conway, Elias, 977
Conway, James, 977
Cony, Samuel, 998
Cook, John, 982
Cook, Joseph, 88
Cooke, Howard, 499
Cooke, Lorrin, 982
Cooke, Nicholas, 1026
Cookman, Nathaniel, 962
Coolidge, Calvin, 973, 1002
Cools-Lartigue, Louis, 293
Cooney, Frank, 1009
Coontz, Robert, 1044
Cooper, Frank, 91, 92
Cooper, Job, 980
Cooper, Myers, 1022
Cooper, Prentice, 1032
Cooper, Robert, 1029
Cooper, Russell, 92
Cooper, William, 983
Cooreman, Gerhard, 132
Copertino, Giovanni, 486
Coppet, Jules-Marcel de, 136, 220, 291, 546, 547, 568, 782
Coquilhat, Camille-Aimé, 258
Coquoz, Jean, 903
Cor, Henri, 338, 780
Corallo, Salvatore, 487
Corbier, Claude, 347
Corboz, Richard, 870

Corcoran, Desmond, 95
Cordeaux, Harry, 118, 937, 968
Cordeiro, Hélsio, 157
Cordero, Luis, 299
Cordés, Ernesto, 82
Cordet, Jean-François, 337, 340
Cordoba, Gonzalo Hernández, 300
Córdoba, Manuel, 307
Córdoba Blanco, Dante, 692
Cordón Cea, Eusebio, 307
Cordova, Andrés, 300
Córdova, Henrique de, 177
Cordova, Jorge, 140
Cork, Philip, 764
Cornaz, Stefan, 866
Cornejo, Hernán, 80
Cornelis, Henri, 258
Cornell, Alonzo, 1017
Corner, Frank, 629
Corni, Guido, 796
Cornut-Gentille, Bernard, 257, 782
Cornwall, Clement, 200
Cornwall, Henry, 629
Cornwell, John, 1040
Corona del Rosal, Alfonso, 581
Coronado, Saturnino, 582
Corrado I (Sicily), 493
Corrado II (Sicily), 493
Corral Martínez, Blas, 579
Corrales Ayala, Rafael, 580
Correa, Esterão, 161
Correa, Francisco, 161
Correia, António, 216, 405
Correia, Carlos, 406
Correia, Innocêncio, 167
Correia, Joaquim, 160
Correia, José, 170
Correia, Luís, 246
Correira, José, 297
Corrias, Alfredo, 486
Corrias, Efisio, 486
Corrodi, Paul, 909
Cort van der Linden, Pieter, 619
Cortazar, Modesto, 816
Cortes Castro, Léon, 271
Corwin, Thomas, 1021
Cory, William, 213
Coryndon, Robert, 509, 530, 848, 937
Cosentino, Fernando, 73
Cosgrave, Liam, 474
Cosgrave, William, 473, 474
Cosgrove, Robert, 96, 97
Cosgrove, Samuel, 1039
Cosić, Dobrica, 1087
Cosimo I (Tuscany), 496
Cosimo II (Tuscany), 496
Cosimo III (Tuscany), 496
Cosio, Joaquín, 631
Cossiga, Francesco, 478, 480
Cossió Vidaurrin, Guillermo, 582
Cossy, R., 904, 905

Costa, Abel da, 216
Costa, Afonso, 705
Costa, Alberto da, 706
Costa, Alfredo da, 706
Costa, Cândido da, 174
Costa, Eduardo da, 64
Costa, Fernando, 178
Costa, Fernando da, 162
Costa, Francisco da, 428
Costa, Frederico da, 154
Costa, Irapuan, 158
Costa, João de, 159
Costa, Jorge, 73
Costa, Jorge Nova da, 152
Costa, José, 156
Costa, José de, 604
Costa, José Horta e, 246
Costa, Manuel da, 705
Costa, Mario de, 161
Costa, Pedro de, 161
Costa, Vasco Almeida e, 246
Costa Alegre, Norberto, 777
Costa e Silva, Arthur, 149
Costa Gomes, Francisco de, 703
Costa Gomez, Moises da, 622
Costello, John, 474
Costes, Jean-Paul, 343
Cota Montaño, Leonel, 576
Coté, Jean-Pierre, 211
Cotegipe, Barão de (João Wanderley), 150
Cottet, Joseph, 870, 871
Cotti, Flavio, 856, 900
Cottier, Marius, 871
Cotton, Alexander, 969
Coty, René, 325
Coubertin, Pierre de, 21
Couceira, Henrique, 64
Couchepin, Arthur, 902
Coudert, Pierre, 252
Coulibaly, Ouézzin, 186
Coulson, John, 16
Counsell, Marilyn Trenholm, 203
Cournarie, Pierre, 194, 347, 782
Cournoyea, Nellie, 214
Court, Charles, 101
Court, Joseph-Urbain, 341, 633
Court, Richard, 101
Courtois, Bernard, 337
Cousseran, Paul, 341, 346
Coussirou, Jean-Marie, 342
Cousturier, Paul, 343, 403
Coutinho, António Rosa, 65
Coutinho, Flávio, 166
Coutinho, Henrique, 156, 157
Coutinho, Vitor, 604
Coutinho, Vitor de, 705
Coutino, Pedro, 246
Coutino Coss, Amador, 577
Couto, Miguel, 172
Coutts, Walter, 766, 937
Couve de Murville, Maurice, 328

Covas, Mário, 178
Covert, Walter, 206
Coward, John, 956
Cowen, Zelman, 87
Cowper, Charles, 89, 90
Cowper, Steve, 976
Cox, Charles, 762
Cox, Henri, 345
Cox, Jacob, 1021
Cox, James, 1022
Cox, John, 1031
Cozzens, William, 1027
Cqmpbell, James, 1022
Craddock, Reginald, 606
Crafts, Samuel, 1035
Craig, George, 992
Craig, Locke, 1019
Crailshein, Krafft, 369
Cramer, Lawrence, 1046
Crane, Arthur, 1042
Crane, W. Murray, 1002
Crapo, Henry, 1003
Cravioto Cisneros, Oswaldo, 581
Crawford, Coe, 1030
Crawford, Frederick, 783, 937
Crawford, George, 986
Crawford, John, 208
Crawford, Samuel, 994
Craxi, Benedetto (Bettino), 480
Creagh, Charles, 557
Creasy, Gerald, 390, 565
Cremonese, Gianfranco, 490
Crescentini, Giorgio, 774
Crescenzi, Ugo, 481
Crespellani, Luigi, 486
Crespo, Joaquín, 1067
Crespo, Vitor, 605
Cresson, Édith, 329
Cresto, Enrique, 75
Cretulescu, Nicolae, 709
Crill, Peter, 959
Crispi, Francesco, 479
Cristea, Miron, 708, 710
Cristiani Burkard, Alfredo, 307
Critchley, T.K., 676
Crittenden, John, 995
Crittenden, Thomas, 1008
Crocicchia, Horace, 272, 403
Crocker, Walter, 93
Croes, P., 621
Croitoru, Dumitru, 596
Croix, Edouard, 340
Cromwell, Oliver, 950
Cromwell, Richard, 950
Crook, Kenneth, 963
Crosbie, John, 205
Crosby, J. Schluyer, 1008
Crosby, Robert, 1010
Crose, William, 1043
Cross, Burton, 999
Cross, Ronald, 95

Cross, Wilbur, 982
Croswell, Charles, 1003
Crothers, Austin, 1001
Crounse, Lorenzo, 1010
Crouse, Lloyd, 207
Crowe, E.N., 958
Crowther, William, 96
Crozby, William, 998
Cruce, Lee, 1023
Cruder, Giancarlo, 483
Cruikshank, John, 962
Crus, Raul, 297
Cruvinel, Belarmino, 158
Cruywagem Willem, 805
Cruz, Richardo, 587
Cruz Aguirre, Anastasio, 1048
Cruz Ramirez, Joaquín, 575
Cruz Uclés, Ramón, 413
Crvenkovski, Branko, 545
Crvenkovski, Krste, 545
Csia, Sándor, 416
Cuandra, Vicente, 631
Cuartas, Belisario Betancur, 251
Cuauhémoc (Aztec Empire), 575
Cubás Grau, Raúl, 687
Cudmore, Derek, 963
Cuéllar Abaroa, Cristano, 589
Cuello, Enrique Escobar, 80
Cuestas, Juan, 1049
Cuitáhuac (Aztec Empire), 575
Culafić, Dobroslav, 1091
Culberson, Charles, 1033
Cullen, William, 89
Cultiaux, Didier, 348
Cumber, John, 959, 963
Cumić, Acim, 1092
Cuming, Thomas, 1009
Cummin, Duncan, 310
Cumming, Alfred, 1034
Cumming-Bruce, Francis, 118
Cummings, Alexander, 980
Cummins, Albert, 993
Cummins, Hugh, 124
Cunha, Joaquim, 170
Cunha, José da, 169, 175
Cunha, Manuel de, 159
Cunha Linha, Ronaldo, 166
Cunningham, Alan, 476
Cunningham, Barry, 103
Cunningham, George, 667
Cuno, Wilhelm, 366
Cuomo, Mario, 1018
Curchad, Louis, 45
Cureau, Adolphe-Louis, 255, 353
Curiel, José, 1070
Curlewis, John, 799
Curley, James, 1002
Curmit-Tayishi, 739
Currie, Archibald, 845, 846
Currier, Moody, 1012
Curry, George (New Mexico, USA), 1016

Curry, George (Oregon, USA), 1024
Curti, Curzio, 898
Curtin, Andrew, 1025
Curtin, John, 88
Curtis, Edward, 989
Curtis, Kenneth, 999
Curtis, Oakley, 999
Curto, António, 64
Curton, Émile de, 345
Curzon, Marquess George, 422
Cusin, Gaston, 782
Cuthbert, Parminus, 682
Cutileiro, José, 49
Cutler, John, 1034
Cutler, Nathan, 998
Cutler, Roden, 89
Cvetković, Dragisa, 1087
Cvetković, Marijan, 274
Cxristian I (Sweden), 850
Cyilima II (Rwanda), 759
Cyrankiewicz, Józef, 698, 699

Dabain, B.D., 720
Dabčević-Kućar, Savka, 275
Dablanc, Christian, 292
Dabo Aliyu, 656
Dacko, David, 218, 219
Dacko, David (cousin), 219
Daclin-Sibour, Paul-Émile, 343
Dacosta, Claude-Antoine, 256
Dadjo, Kléber, 923
Dag, Bernardo, 73
Dagain, Charles, 220, 780
Daglish, Henry, 100
Dagnino, Gianni, 484
Dagonia, Georges, 339
Dagort, Henri, 344
Dahanayake, Wijeyananda, 831
Dahinden, Hansheiri, 902
Dahiru Mohammed, 641
Dähler, Edmund, 861
Dähler, Johann, 860, 861
Dai Suli, 237
Daibey-Ouattara, Aboubacar, 15
Daio, Daniel, 777
Daladier, Edouard, 328
Dale, Charles, 1013
Dale, David, 962, 966
Dalgat, Magomet, 725
Dalinger, Vladimir, 742
Dalkin, Robert, 104
Dalley, Brendan, 969
Dálnoki-Miklós, Béla, 417
Dalton, Charles, 209
Dalton, John, 1008
Daltro, Manoel, 178
Daltro, Manuel, 175
Daluege, Kurt, 284
Dalvit, Luigi, 488
Dalwigk, Karl, 371

Daly, Malachy Bowes, 206
Dam, Atli, 289
Dam, Peter Mohr, 289
Damad Ahmad Nami, 911, 912
Damad Ferid Paşa, 931
Damásio, Virgílio, 154
Damaskinos, Archbishop (Demetrios Papandreou), 393, 396
Damasus II (Pope), 1061
Damba, Dashiyn, 600
Dambadorji, Tserenvacharyn, 600
Dambinbadzar (Jalhansa Khutukhtu), 600
Dambui, Cherobim, 678
Damdinsuren, Jamtsangiyn, 599
Damianov, Georgi, 183
Damle, Kashinath, 429
Damodar Pande, 616
Dampilon, I.D., 720
Damseaux, André, 132
Dan Zhenlin, 238, 243
Dana, John, 998
Danas, António, 154
Dandl, Otto von, 369
Danev, Stoyan, 184
Daniel, Price, 1033
Daniel, Rowland, 147
Daniel, Simeon, 763
Daniel, William, 1044
Daniels, William, 989
Danieri Mwanga II (Buganda), 939
Danilo I (Montenegro), 1089
Danilo II (Montenegro), 1089
Danioth, Hans, 902
Danioth, Ludwig, 901
Daniyalov, Abdurakhman, 725, 726
Dankovtsev, A.G., 731
Dansouf, A., 536
Dantas, António, 173, 179
Dantas, Francisco, 150
Dantas, Lourenço, 178
Dantas, Manoel, 179
Dantas, Manuel, 150
Danzan, Khorloogiyn, 600
Daodiace, Giuseppe, 310
Dárányi, Kálmán, 417
Darbara Singh, 445
Darbinyan, Armen, 86
Darden, Colgate, 1037
Darden, Thomas Jr, 1043
Dare, Albert, 628, 629
Dariye, Joshua, 654
Darley, Frederick, 89
Darling, Clifford, 118
Darms, Gion, 875
Darsières, Camille, 341
Darsigov, Magomed-Bashir, 726
Dartiguenave, Philippe, 410
Dartout, Pierre, 337
Daruvar, Yves de, 252
Das, Banarasi, 451
Das, Biswanath, 443, 450

Das, B.S., 447
Das, Prafulla Kumar, 449
Das, Ram Sunder, 428
Dăscălescu, Constantine, 710
Dassanayaka, Ananda, 834
Daszyński, Ignacy, 698
Dato y Iradier, Eduardo, 817, 818
Datuk Ali bin Abdullah, 5
Daubigny, Jean, 342
Daud, Fortunato, 75
Daud Shah, 559
Daudi Chwa II (Buganda), 939
Daudi Kasagama (Toro), 939
Dauladi Zakari, 649
Daulataram, Jairamadas, 425
Daulataram, Jairamdas, 426
Daulenov, Salken, 508
Daun, Wierich von, 492
Daunt, Timothy, 957
Dave, Arvind, 425
Dave, Prasannabhai, 454
Davey, Martin, 1022
David, Heinrich, 864
David, Johnny, 593
David I (Scotland), 953
David II (Scotland), 954
Davidović, Ljubomir, 1087
Davidson, James (British Virgin Islands), 963
Davidson, James (Wisconsin, USA), 1041
Davidson, Walter (Australia), 89
Davidson, Walter (Newfoundland), 205
Davidson, Walter (Seychelles), 783
Davidson-Houston, Wilfred, 764, 965
Davie, Alexander, 201
Davie, Theodore, 201
Davie, William, 1018
Davier, Irenée, 344
Davies, David, 47
Davies, James, 997, 998
Davies, Louis, 197, 210
Davies, Myrick, 986
Dávila, Carlos, 28
Dávila, Fausto, 413
Dávila, Miguel, 413
Dávila, William, 1070
Dávila Arrondo, Fidel, 819
Davis, Cushman, 1004
Davis, Daniel, 999
Davis, David, 990
Davis, Deane, 1036
Davis, Edmund, 1033
Davis, George, 1045
Davis, Gray, 979
Davis, Harry, 1022
Davis, Jeff, 978
Davis, Jefferson, 926, 973
Davis, Jehu, 983
Davis, John (Jersey), 958
Davis, John (Massachusetts, USA), 1001, 1002

Davis, John (North Dakota, USA), 1020
Davis, John (Rhode Island, USA), 1027
Davis, John W., 1024
Davis, Jonathan, 994
Davis, Leslie, 628
Davis, Robert, 202
Davis, Steuart, 968
Davis, Thomas, 628
Davis, W., 1015
Davis, Westmoreland, 1037
Davis, William, 208
Davison, Ronald, 626
Davitadze, David, 362
Davitadze, Levan, 362
Davletyarov, Akhmetsafa, 738
Davlyatkadamov, Khushkadam, 916
Dawar Bakhsh, 421
Dawes, James, 1010
Dawit I, 314
Dawit II, 314
Dawit III, 315
Dawith III, 357
Dawith IV, 357
Dawith V, 357
Dawith VI, 357
Dawith VII, 357
Dawkins, Arthur, 966
Dawson, Andrew, 92
Dawson, John, 1034
Dawson, William, 1040
Day, P.A., 969
Daya Khan, 230
Dayendranath Burrenchobay, 570
Dayo Popoola, 652, 654
Daza, Hilarion, 140
De Alwis, Ananda, 832
De Chair, Dudley, 89
De Cosmos, Amor (William Smith), 201
Deakin, Alfred, 88
Dean, Howard, 1036
Dean, Roger, 101
Deane, William, 87
Deb, Dasarath, 449
Deb Shumshere Jung, 617
Debacq, Jean-Jacques, 343
Debbas, Charles, 527, 528
Debétaz, Edouard, 906
DeBlois, George, 209
Deblonde, Philippe, 350
Debré, Michel, 328
Debrot, Nicolaas, 622
Deby, Idriss, 221
Decharte, Maurice, 340
Decker, Pierre de, 130
Decoppet, Camille, 854
Décoppet, Camille, 905
Dedual, Julius, 875
d'Eeckhoutte, Iweins, 49
Deeke, Udo, 176
Deferr, Raymond, 904
Defferre, Gaston, 334

Degazon, Frederick, 293
Degutiene, Irena, 540
Dehaene, Jean-Luc, 131
Deheza, Miguel Ferrer, 73
Dehnkamp, Willy, 370
Dehousse, Jean-Marie, 132
Deichmann, Karl, 370
Deist, Heinrich, 377
Deitte, Adolphe, 218, 220, 255, 272
Dejeu, Gavril, 710
Del Sesto, Christopher, 1027
Delabarre, Michel, 333
Delacombe, Rohan, 97
Delacoste, Edmond, 902, 903
Delacroix, Léon, 130
Delamuraz, Jean-Pascal, 856
Delaneau, Jean, 331
Delaunay, Claudio, 495
Delauney, Jacques, 337
Delauney, Maurice, 1058
Delavignette, Robert-Louis, 194
Delba, Mikhail, 360
Delden, Reiner van, 624
Dele Olumilua, 653
Deleplanque, Jean, 338
Delgado, Alfredo, 587
Delgado Ortega, Enrique, 589
Delgado Ramirez, Celso, 584
Delgado Rannauro, Dante, 590
Deliau, Jean, 340
Deligeorgis, Epaminondas, 394, 395
Deliyiannis, Nikolas, 395
Deliyiannis, Theodoros, 395
Dellai, Lorenzo, 489
Delors, Jacques, 17
Delouvrier, Paul, 60
Delpech, Léonce-Joseph, 922
Deltiel, Pierre, 218
Delvaux, Albert, 267
Delvina, Suleyman, 57
Demange, Paul, 341, 598
Demas, William, 6
Dembélé, Mamadou, 564
Dementei, Nikolai, 126
Demerdzis, Konstantinos, 396
Demetros, 315
Demichelli Lizaso, Alberto, 1049
Demichyan, Karen, 86
Demirel, Süleyman, 930
Demo Thubten Jigme, 231
Demo Trinley Rabgyas, 231
Demo Trulku Jampel Delek, 231
Dempsey, John (Connecticutt, USA), 982
Dempsey, John (New Mexico, USA), 1016
Demydenko, Arkady, 943
Deneen, Charles, 991
Denegrí, Aurelio, 690
Deng Baoshan, 235
Deng Haijiong, 232
Deng Xiaoping, 227, 228
Denge, Michel, 261, 268

Denham, Digby, 92
Denham, Edward (Guyana), 407
Denham, Edward (Jamaica), 499
Denham, Edward (The Gambia), 355
Denis (Portugal), 702
Denise, Auguste, 273
Denktaş, Rauf, 280
Denney, William, 984
Dennison, William, 1021
Denoon, Lennox, 926
Denton, George, 355
Denver, James, 994
Deo, Rajendra Singh, 443
Depretis, Agostino, 479
Derbigny, Pierre, 997
Deren-Ayerlei, O., 943
Deriaud, Paul-Charles, 256
Dern, George, 1034
Derosi-Bjelajac, Ema, 274
Derqui, Santiago, 69
Deryagin, Aleksandr, 746
des Essarts, Frédéric-Jean, 345
Des Voeux, George, 317
Desai, Hitendra, 430
Desai, Khandubhai, 423
Desai, Morarji, 423, 458
Desanti, Jean-Hyacinthe, 563
Desbaillets, Alfred, 872
Descemet, Gabriel-Omer (Burkina Faso), 186
Descemet, Gabriel-Omer (Mauritania), 568
Deschamps, Hubert-Jules, 272, 291, 780
Deschanel, Paul, 324
Deschenaux, Eugène, 869
Desha, Joseph, 995
Deshmukh, Vilasrao, 438
Desimoni, Jorge, 82
Deslandes, Venancio, 65
Despland, Gabriel, 905, 906
Dessalines, Jean-Jacques, 409
Desyatnikov, Vasily, 747
Dettori, Paolo, 486
Deucher, Adolf, 854
Deukemejian, George, 979
Deuntzer, Johan, 288
Deustua, Alejandro, 690
Deva, Veli, 1095
Devan Nair, C.V., 787
Dever, Paul, 1002
Deverell, Colville, 570
Devesi, Baddeley, 793
Devi, Rabri, 428
Devi, V.S. Rama, 432, 434
Devine, Grant, 213
Devine, Joseph, 1020
Devpura, Heera, 446
Dewael, Patrick, 132
Dewar, Donald, 954
Dewatre, Jacques, 337, 342
Dewdney, Edgar (British Colombia), 200

Dewdney, Edgar (Northwest Territories, Canada), 213
Dewey, Nelson, 1040
Dewey, Thomas, 1018
Dhamal, Prem Kumar, 432, 433
Dhanis, François, 258
Dharmasaki, Sanya, 921
Dharsono, Hartono, 5
Dhavan, Shanti, 451
Dhebar, Uchharangarai, 460
Dhiyab bin Isa al-Nahayan, Shaikh, 945
Dhube, Hari, 440
Di Bello, Ruben, 75
Di Risio, Hugo, 82
Di Rupo, Elio, 132
Diakité, Yoro, 564
Diapari, 462
Dias, Álvaro, 168
Dias, Anthony, 449, 451
Dias, Fernando Mendoça e, 429
Dias, Manuel, 173
Diasamidze, David, 362
Díaz, Adolfo, 632
Díaz, Carlos, 402
Díaz, Manuel, 674
Díaz, Porfiro, 573
Díaz de Entresotos, Angel, 826
Díaz de la Vega, Romula, 573
Díaz del Rio, Víctor Suances, 308
Díaz Infante, Luis, 580
Díaz Ordaz, Gustavo, 574, 585
Dibbs, George, 90
Dibela, Kingsford, 676
Dichinson, Denver, 1011
Dickerson, Mahlon, 1014
Dickerson, Philemon, 1014
Dickinson, John (Delaware, USA), 982
Dickinson, John (Pennsylvania, USA), 1025
Dickinson, Luren, 1004
Dickson, James, 92
Dickson, John, 510
Dickson, Thomas, 848
Dickson, Y., 656
Didelot, Pierre, 336, 343, 456, 780
Didgov, Mukharbek, 726
Didgov, Tamerlan, 726
Didier, Alfred, 871
Diederichs, Georg, 372
Diederichs, Nicolaas, 800
Diefenbacher, Michel, 338, 341
Diefenbaker, John, 199
Diekmann, Bruno, 375
Diener, Verena, 910
Dieng, Diakha, 29
Diepgen, Eberhard, 370
Diepreye Alameyseigha, 641
Diergaardt, Johannes, 611, 614
Diergaardt, Reginald, 612
Diestel, Arnold, 371
Diete-Spiff, Alfred, 655

Diethelm, Josef, 893
Dietrich, Charles, 1010
Dietschi, Urs, 894, 895
Díez Conseco, Pedro, 688
Dighe, Madhukar, 440
Digo, Yves-Jean, 354, 922
Digvijay Singh, 437
Dijk, Marinus van, 621
Dijoud, Paul, 598
Dikambayev, Kazy, 522
Dikshit, Umarshankar, 434, 451
Dilawar Khan of Junagadh, 669
Dillier, Christian, 886
Dillingham, Paul, 1035
Dillingham, William, 1036
Dillon, Richard, 1016
Diman, Byron, 1026
Dimirtov, Georgi, 184
Dimitrov, Filip, 185
Dimitru, Sergei, 594
Dimond, Francis, 1026
Dimwkar, Ranganath, 427
Din Mohammed, 669
Dinardo, Raffaele, 481
Dine, Fiori, 57
Ding Ratang, U, 608
Ding Sheng, 235
Dingane, 806
Dingley, Nelson, 999
Dini, Lamberto, 480
Dinmukhametov, Galei, 738
Dinnyés, Lajos, 417
Dinsmoor, Samuel, 1012
Dinuzulu, 806
Dinwiddy, Bruce, 962
Diomedes, Alexandros, 397
Diomi, Gaston, 266
Diorditsa, Aleksandr, 595
Diori, Hamani, 633
Dios Orozco, Juan de, 631
Diouf, Abdou, 781, 782
Diouf, Jacques, 43
Dipico, E. Manne, 812
DiPrete, Edward, 1027
Dirat, Henri, 218
Direko, Winkie, 811
Diro, Ted, 677
DiSalle, Michael, 1022
Disraeli, Benjamin, 952
Dissanayake, Berty Premalal, 832
Dissanayake, Jayasena, 832
Dissanayake, W., 831
Distaso, Salvatore, 486
Dittli, Carlo, 902
Diumasumba, André, 263
Diur, Dominique, 264
Diwan, B.J., 424
Dix, John Adams, 1017
Dix, John Alden, 1017
Dixit, Sheila, 455
Dixon, Frank, 975

Dixon, Joseph, 1009
Dizdarević, Raif, 143, 1087
Djafarov, Safar, 113
Djarimov, Aslan, 717
Djerić, Branko, 145
Djimasta, Koibla, 221
Djordević, Vladislav, 1092
Djordje Petrović (Serbia), 1091
Djukanović, Milo, 1090
Djumhana, R., 464
Djuranović, Veselin, 1086, 1087, 1089, 1090, 1091
Djurhuus, Hakun, 289
Djurhuus, Kristian, 289
Djuruca, Jojkic, 1096
Dlamini, B. Sibusiso, 848
Dlamini, Maphevu, 847
Dlamini, Obed, 847
Dlamini, Sotsha, 847
Dmirty I (Russia), 712
Dmitri I, 357
Dmitri II, 357
Dmitri III, 358
Dmitrin, Aleksandr, 732
Dmitriyev, Gennady, 741
Dmitry II (Russia), 712
Dmitry III (Russia), 713
Do Muoi, 1074
Dobbie, William, 565
Dober, Klemens, 893
Dobi, István, 416, 417
Doble, Denis, 962
Dobler, Karl, 861
Doblhoff-Dier, Anton von, 106
Dobryatov, A., 750
Dobson, Henry, 96
Dockery, Alexander, 1008
Docking, George, 995
Docking, Robert, 995
Dodangoda, Amarasiri, 833
Dodd, Norris, 43
Dodds, John, 95
Dodge, Henry, 1040
Dodkhudoyev, Nazarsho, 914, 915
Doe, Samuel, 532
Doer, Gary, 203
Dohnanyi, Klaus von, 371
Dohpugh, Darwin, 440
Doiron, Joseph, 209
Doje Cedain, 234
Doje Cering, 234
Dokić, Lazar, 1092
Doksom, Damsranbelegiyn, 599
Dolanowski-Hryniewski, Jerzy, 700
Dolasević, Svetislav, 1095
Dolchanma, Bai-Kara, 739
Dole, Sanford, 988
Dolisie, Albert, 255
Dollfuss, Engelbert, 107
Dologuélé, Anicet, 219
Domato, José, 84

Domeniconi, Alberto, 81
Domett, Alfred, 626
Dominguez, Juan Jiménez, 83
Dominguez, Roberto, 76
Dominijanni, Bruno, 482
Dominique, Michel, 410
Domitien, Elizabeth, 219
Dompok, Bernard, 558
Dona, Nicolo, 498
Donaghey, George, 978
Donahey, Alvin, 1022
Donald, Alan, 963
Donald I (Scotland), 953
Donald II (Scotland), 953
Donald III Bane (Scotland), 953
Donald Stephens, 557
Donaldson, Stuart, 89
Donandt, Martin, 370
Donato, Francesco, 497
Donato, Leonardo, 498
Donato, Marcantonio, 497
Donduk, 739
Dong Biwu, 225
Dong Khanh (Nguyen Canh Tong), 1073
Dönges, T. Ebenhezer, 800
D'Onghia Colaprico, Elías, 1071
Donini, Gaetano, 898
Dönitz, Karl, 365
Donker Curtius, Dirk, 619
Donne, Gavin, 628
Donnell, Forrest, 1008
Donnelly, Phil, 1008
Donzé, Willy, 873
Dooge, James, 474
Dooley, James, 90
Doorly, Charles, 764
Dorey, Graham, 956
Dorgan, 225
Doria, João, 179
Dória, João, 167
Doria, José, 179
Dorig, Beat, 861
Dorion, Antoine, 198
Dorji, Debzumpon S.T., 139
Dorji, Jigme, 139
Dorji, Kazi Llhendup, 447
Dorji, Kazi Ugyen, 139
Dorji, Lendup, 139
Dorji, Yanglob Singye, 138
Dorman, Maurice, 565, 785
Dorman-Smith, Reginald, 607
Dorn, Edward, 1044
Dornelles, Ernesto, 175
Doronjski, Stevan, 1088, 1096
Dors, Christian, 347, 350
Dorsey, Hugh, 987
Dorticós Torrado, Osvaldo, 278
Dorvillé, Ernandes, 152
Dorzhiev, D.D., 720, 721
Dosanjh, Ujjal, 201
Dosière, René, 334

Dost Mohammed, 53
Doty, James (Utah, USA), 1034
Doty, James (Wisconsin, USA), 1040
Douglas, Adye, 96
Douglas, Archibald (Myanmar), 606
Douglas, Archibald (Scotland), 954
Douglas, Denzil, 763
Douglas, Francis, 565
Douglas, J. Robson, 206
Douglas, John, 92
Douglas, Roosevelt (Rosie), 294
Douglas, Thomas, 213
Douglas, William (Barbados), 124
Douglas, William (USA), 1002
Douglas-Home, Alexander, 952
Douglas-Smith, W., 958
Doumer, Paul, 325
Doumergue, Gaston, 324, 327, 328
Dousset, Maurice, 331
Doustin, Daniel-Marius, 220
Dovcsak, Antal, 417
Dovydaitis, Pranas, 539
Dowding, Peter, 101
Dowiyogo, Bernard, 615
Dowling, Otto, 1043
Downer, John, 94
Downey, John, 979
Doyle, Charles, 197
Doyle, Charles Hastings, 203, 206
Drago, Giuseppe, 487
Dragosavac, Dušan, 1088
Dragoumis, Stephanos, 395
Drake, Francis, 993
Drake, Heinrich, 380
Drake, Walton, 103
Draper, Eben, 1002
Drayton, Edward, 293, 399
Drayton, John, 1028
Drees, Willem, 620
Dreier, Karl, 387
Dreifuss, Ruth, 856
Dreschler, Otto-Heinrich, 381
Drew, Francis, 310
Drew, George (Canada), 208
Drew, George (USA), 985
Drew, Thomas, 977
Dreyer, Pierre, 870, 871
Dreyfus, Lee, 1041
Dring, Arthur, 666
Driscoll, Alfred, 1015
Driver, Arthur, 101
Drnovsek, Janez, 792, 1087
Drobotov, Anatoly, 943
Droz, Edouard, 880
Droz, Numa, 854
Druery, Daniel-Henri, 853
Druk, Mircea, 595
Drummond, J. Eric, 24
Drury, Ernest, 208
Dry, Richard, 96
Du Cane, John, 565

du Plessis, Abraham, 614
du Plessis, Wentzel, 610
Du Zheheng, 240
Duan Junyi, 237
Duarte, Jonas, 158
Duarte, José Napoleon, 307
Duarte, Manoel, 151
Duarte, Samuel, 166
Duarte, Teofilo, 216, 297
Duarte (Portugal), 702
Dubček, Alexander, 283, 790
Dubey, Bindeshwari, 428
Dubey, H.S., 425
Dubief, Henri, 59
Dubois, Pierre, 882
Dubois-Chabert, André, 336
Duboule, Charles, 872
Duboule, Gilbert, 873
Duboux, V., 905
Dubs, Jakob, 853
Dubuis, Alphonse, 905
Duca, Anselmo Zolio, 72
Duca, Ion, 710
Duchac, Josef, 376
Duchemin, Charles, 873
Duckwitz, Richard, 370
Duclerc, Charles, 326
Ducoing Gamba, Luis, 580
Ducotterd, Georges, 870
Ducret, Robert, 873
Ducrey, Henri, 902
Dudas, Ambrose, 667
Dudayev, Dzhokhar, 722, 723
Dudley, Edward, 1019
Dueñas, Francisco (El Salvador), 306
Dueñas, Francisco (Equatorial Guinea), 308
Dufaure, Jules, 326
Dufayard, André, 350
Duff, James, 1026
Duff, Lyman, 198
Duff (Scotland), 953
Duffy, Charles, 98
Dufour, J., 905
Dufus, Herbert, 499
Dugan, Winston, 87, 93, 97
Dugonjić, Rato, 143
Duhaga II (Bunyoro), 939
Duhalde, Alfredo, 223
Duhalde, Eduardo, 71
Dujany, Cesare, 490
Dukakis, Michael, 1003
Duke, Donald, 643
Dulio, Emilio, 796
Dumec, Roger, 350
Dumont, W. Yvon, 202
Dun, Robert, 35
Duncan, Joseph, 990
Duncan, Pat, 215
Duncan, Patrick, 799
Duncan I (Scotland), 953
Dundas, Ambrose, 957

Dundas, Charles, 118, 937
Dung, John, 644
Dunkel, Arthur, 47
Dunklin, Daniel, 1007
Dunlap, Robert, 998
Dunn, Winfield, 1032
Dunne, Edward, 991
Dunning, Charles, 212
Dunning, Paris, 992
Dunsmuir, James, 200
Dunsmuir, John, 201
Dunstan, Albert, 99
Dunstan, Donald, 93, 95
Duong Van Minh, 1075
DuPasquier, Léo, 881
Duplessis, Maurice, 211, 212
Dupong, Pierre, 543
Dupont, Christain-Raimond, 291
Dupont, Clifford, 1100
Dupont, Émile, 873
Dupont, Jacques, 598
Dupont, Jacques-Charles, 326
Dupont, Pierre, 984
Duprat, Pierre, 338, 341, 456
Dupre, Jacques, 997
Dupre Ceniceros, Enrique, 579
Dupuy, Charles, 327
Duque, José, 405
Duraković, Nijaz, 144
Durán Ballén, Sixto, 300
Durán Cartin, Carlos, 271
Durand, Oswald, 272, 780
Durand, Ricardo, 80
Durbin, Winfield, 992
Durdynets, Vasyl, 942
Durie, David, 965
Düring, Josef, 878
Durkee, Charles, 1034
Durnovo, Ivan, 714
Durnwalder, Luis, 488
Dürrenmatt, Hugo, 867
Durrer, Adalbert, 887
Durrer, Arnold, 886
Dusch, Alexander, 377
Dutoit, Jean, 873
Dutra, Eurico, 148
Dutra, Olívio, 175
Dutta, Sarat, 456
Dutton, Francis, 94
Dutton, Henry, 981
Duvakin, Sergei, 742
Duval, François, 340
Duvalier, François, 410
Duvalier, Jean-Claude, 410
Duvall, William, 984
Duvieusart, Jean, 131
Duvoisin, Pierre, 906, 907
Duy Tan (Vinh San), 1073
Duyshenev, Arstanbek, 521
Duysheyev, Arstanbek, 522
Dwinell, Lane, 1013

Dwiwedi, Surendra Nath, 425
Dwyer, Eric, 102
Dwyer, John, 100
Dwyer-Gray, Edmund, 96
Dyakonov, Ibad, 732
Dyakonov, Ion, 944
Dyal, R.S., 453, 456
Dyer, Elisha, 1026
Dyer, Elisha Jr, 1027
Dyer, George, 1044
Dysart, A. Allison, 204
Dzanagov, Vladimir, 735
Dzasokhov, Aleksandr, 735
Dzeliwe Shongwe, 847
Dzhailor, Afiyaddin, 116
Dzhalilov, Afiyaddin, 115
Dzhangildin, Ali, 507
Dzharfarov, Saftar, 115
Dzhashi, Irkali, 362
Dzhavakhishvili, Givi, 359
Dzhioyev, K., 363
Dzhosoyev, G.N., 363
Dzhumanazarov, Mateke, 1053
Dzotsenidze, Georgi, 358
Dzugayev, Dahibut, 736
Dzurinda, Mikulas, 790

Eagles, James, 978
Eanes, António, 703
Earl, Anthony, 1041
Earl, Robert, 962
Earle, George, 1025
Earle, John, 96
Early, Peter, 986
East, Julio, 691
Eastwood, Ralph, 965
Eaton, Benjamin, 980
Eaton, Horace, 1035
Eaton, John, 984
Ebeial, Tegi, 684
Eberhard, Bernhard, 380
Eberhart, Adolph, 1005
Eberle, Roland, 898
Ebermaier, Karl, 194
Ebert, Friedrich, 365, 366
Ebi, Fritz, 865
Ebiye, John, 640
Eboué, Adolphe, 338, 339
Éboué, Adolphe, 220, 338, 339
Eboué, Félix, 257
Ebri, Clement, 643
Eca, António de, 64
Echandi Jiménez, Mario, 271
Echaurrea, Federico Errázurez, 222
Echenique, José, 688
Echeverria, Antonio, 584
Echeverría Castellot, Eugenio, 576
Eddeh, Emile, 527, 528
Eddin, Burhan, 56
Edelman, Angel, 79

Eden, Anthony, 952
Eden, Nils, 851
Edgar, Henry, 103
Edgar, Jim, 991
Edgar I (England), 949
Edgar II (England), 950
Edgar (Scotland), 953
Edge, Walter, 1014, 1015
Edgerton, Sidney, 1008
Edis, Richard, 962
Edison, Charles, 1015
Edmondson, J. Howard, 1023
Edmund I (England), 949
Edmund II (England), 949
Edmund (Scotland), 953
Edmund (Sweden), 849
Edmunds, Newton, 1020
Edorhe Oyakhire, A., 654, 656
Edred (England), 949
Edstrom, J. Sigfrid, 21
Eduard (Anhalt), 376
Eduardo, Johnny, 65, 66
Edward I (England), 950
Edward II (England), 950
Edward III (England), 950
Edward IV (England), 950
Edward Mutesa II (Buganda), 937, 939
Edward (Scotland), 954
Edward the Confessor (England), 950
Edward the Elder (England), 949
Edward the Martyr (England), 949
Edward V (England), 950
Edward VI (England), 950
Edward VII (Great Britain), 951
Edward VIII (Great Britain), 951
Edwards, Edward, 1015
Edwards, Edwin, 998
Edwards, Henry, 981
Edwards, Hughie, 100
Edwards, James, 1030
Edwards, John, 1007
Edwards, Ninian, 990
Edwy (England), 949
Eekelen, Willem van, 49
Efendiev, Sultan, 113
Effiong, Phillip, 638
Eftaxias, Athanasios, 396
Egan, William, 976
Egbert, William, 199
Egbert (England), 949
Egerton, Walter, 407
Eggenberger, Mathias, 888, 889
Egger, Franz, 909, 910
Eggerath, Werner, 376
Eggerz, Sigurdur, 419
Eghagha, H., 652
Egli, Alphons, 856
Egli, Gotthard, 878, 879
Egli, Josef, 879, 880
Egloff, Johann, 896
Ego Aguirre, Julio, 691

Eguala Seyon, 315
Egwu, Sam, 644
Ehard, Hans, 369
Ehringhaus, John, 1019
Eichel, Hans, 372
Eichfeld, Johän, 312
Eigenmann, Guido, 889
Eigl, Adolf, 111
Einadi, Luigi, 478
Einbund, Karl (Kaanel Eenpalu), 312, 313
Eiroa, García, Emilio, 824
Eisenhower, Dwight, 973
Eisner, Kurt, 369
Ejoor, D.A., 637
Ek Yi Oun, 192
Ekanayake, Nandimithra, 831
Ekangaki, Nzo, 27
Ekaterina I (Russia), 713
Ekaterina II (Russia), 713
Eketebi, Laurent, 260, 261
Eklund, R. Sigvard, 43
Ekman, Carl, 851
Ekundayo Opaleye, 652
El-Awad el-Hassan, 843
el-Ganzouri, Kamal, 304
El-Rashid Bakr, 836
el-Sadat, Anwar, 303, 304, 305
El-Saeed el-Husseni, 844
El-Tayib Khayr, 843
Elbegdorj, Taskhiagiyn, 600
Elbert, Samuel (Colorado, USA), 980
Elbert, Samuel (Georgia, USA), 986
Elchibey, Abulfaz, 113
Eldarova, Roza, 725
Eldjárn, Kristán, 419
Eldring, Leif, 662
Elegbede, M., 643
Eleonore (Leonor) (Navarre), 823
Eliáš, Alois, 284
Elías, Carlos, 690
Eliava, Shalva, 359, 364
Elifas, Filemon, 613
Elim, D.S., 724
Elim, K.S., 720
Eliot, Edward, 293, 510
Eliot, H., 969
Elisa (Lucca), 490
Eliseveta (Russia), 713
Elistratov, Petr, 734
Elizabeth I (England), 950
Elizabeth II (England), 951
Elizagaray, Jorge, 79
Elizondo, Eduardo, 584
Ellauri, José, 1049
Ellefsen, Pauli, 289
Ellenberger, Jules, 147
Ellerbe, William, 1029
Ellington, Buford, 1032
Elliot, Andrew, 201
Elliot, Charles, 103
Ellis, John, 1019

Ellis, Maureen, 103
Ellsworth, William, 981
Elmhirst, Thomas, 956
Elmore, Alberto, 690
Elmslie, G.A., 98
Elrod, Samuel, 1030
Elthon, Leo, 993
Elvidge, Ford, 1044
Ely, Joseph, 1002
Eman, Hendrik (Henny), 621
Emanuele Filiberto (Piedmont-Sardinia), 495
Emanuels, Serverinus, 846
Emein, C.K., 651
Emerson, Frank, 1042
Emerson, Lee, 1036
Emery, George, 1034
Emiridze, G.K., 362
Emma (Netherlands), 619
Emmanuel, David, 986
Emmenegger, Emil, 879
Emmerson, Henry, 204
Emmerson, Louis, 991
Emparanza, Jorge Bermudez, 71, 73
Encalada, Manuel Blanco, 222
Encinas Johnson, Luis, 588
Endalkachaw Makonnen, 316
Endara Gallimay, Guillermo, 675
Ender, Otto, 107, 112
Enderley, Emmanuel, 195
Endreyas, 314
Engelberger, Eduard, 884
Engelbrektsson, Engelbrekt, 850
Engelhard, Alberto, 165
Engell, Hugo, 372, 381
Engholm, Bjorn, 376
England, John, 102
Engler, John, 1004
English, James, 981
Engulu, Léon, 261, 264, 265
Engwanda, Augustin, 261
Enhsayhan, Mendsayhany, 600
Enrico (Sicily), 492
Enrietti, Ezio, 485
Enrique (Castile), 821
Enrique II (Castile), 821
Enrique III (Castile), 821
Enrique IV (Castile), 821
Enriques Larrondo, Angel, 761
Enríquez, Alberto, 300
Enwerem, Evan, 646
Eocha (Scotland), 953
Episcopo, Eduardo, 76
Epp, Franz Ritter von, 369
Eps, Johan van, 623
Epureanu, Manolache, 709
Erasmus, Daniel, 804
Erbakan, Neçmettin, 932
Erbanov, Mikhail, 720, 721
Erbe, Norman, 993
Erckert, Karl, 488

Ercole I (Modena), 491
Ercole II (Modena), 491
Ercole III (Modena), 491
Erdeljan, Sredoje, 1096
Ereaut, Frank, 959
Erenroth, Iohan, 184
Erhard, Ludwig, 366
Eri, Vincent Serei, 676
Eriau, Jean-Gabriel, 347, 348
Erich, Rafael, 319
Erignac, Claude, 335
Erignac, René, 336
Erik I (Denmark), 286
Erik I (Norway), 659
Erik II (Denmark), 286
Erik II (Norway), 660
Erik III (Denmark), 286
Erik III (Norway), 660
Erik IV (Denmark), 286
Erik IX (Sweden), 849
Erik V Klipping (Denmark), 286
Erik VI Maendved (Denmark), 286
Erik VII (Denmark), 287
Erik VIII (Sweden), 849
Erik X Knutsson (Sweden), 849
Erik XI Eriksson (Sweden), 849
Erik XII (Sweden), 849
Erik XIII (Sweden), 850
Erik XIV (Sweden), 850
Eriksen, Erik, 288
Erikson, John, 1009
Eriksson, Sune, 321
Erizzo, Francesco, 498
Erkvania, Zurab, 360
Erlach, Rudolf von, 867
Erlander, Tage, 851
Erlandsson, Ragnar, 321
Ernazarov, Ye., 507
Erni, Anton, 878
Ernst, Frans von, 45
Ernst, Heinrich, 908, 909
Ernst August (Brunwick), 378
Ernst August (Hanover, 1692-1698), 379
Ernst August (Hanover, 1837-1851), 379
Ernst August I (Saxe-Weimar-Eisensach), 386
Ernst August II (Saxe-Weimar-Eisensach), 386
Ernst I (Saxe-Altenburg), 385
Ernst I (Saxe-Coburg-Gotha), 385
Ernst II (Saxe-Altenburg), 385
Ernst II (Saxe-Coburg-Gotha), 385
Ernst Ludwig (Hesse), 371
Erny, Ernst, 862, 863
Eroğlu, Derviş, 280
Errani, Vasco, 483
Erskine, George, 958
Erzer, Hans, 895
Esatrada, José, 631
Escalon, Pedro, 306
Eschenburg, Karl, 381

Escher, Joseph, 903
Escheverriá Alvarez, Luis, 574
Escobar, Bernardo, 401
Escobar, Jorge, 81
Escobar, Patricio, 686
Escobar Munñoz, Ernesto, 583
Escombe, Harry, 802
Escuredo, Rodríguez, Rafael, 824
Eshba, Yefrem, 360
Eshimbetova, Tursyn, 1053
Eshkol, Levi (L. Shkolnik), 475
Eskender, 314
Espaillat, Ulises, 295
Esparteiro, Joaquim, 246
Esparza Reyes, J. Refugio, 575
Espina Salguero, Gustavo, 402
Espinosa, Javier, 299
Espinosa Sánchez, Juventino, 584
Espinoza, Carlos Dávila, 223
Esponda, Juan, 577
Espriella, Ricardo de la, 675
Esquivel, Aniceto, 270
Esquivel, Ascensión, 271
Esquivel, Manuel, 135
Esquivel Medina, Humberto, 590
Esquivel Méndez, Eligio, 575
Estabillo, José, 84
Estèbe, Frédéric, 341
Estenssoro, Víctor Paz, 141
Esterházy, Mórić, 416
Estigarribia, José, 687
Estimé, Dumarsais, 410
Estrada, Emilio, 299
Estrada, José D., 632
Estrada, José J., 632
Estrada, Joseph, 694
Estrada, Palma, Tomás, 277
Estrada Cabrera, Manuel, 401
Estrella Urena, Rafael, 296
Estrup, Jacob, 287
Etchber, Salvador-Jean, 186
Etcheber, Salvador-Jean, 563
Etchegoyen, Julio, 73, 77
Etchegoyen, Martin, 1049
Etchepareborda, Roberto, 71
Etcheverría, Xavier, 572
Ethelbald (England), 949
Ethelbert (England), 949
Ethelred I (England), 949
Ethelred II the Unready (England), 949
Ethelwulf (England), 949
Etiebet, Donald, 643
Etienne, Henri, 45
Étienne, Jean-Claude, 331
Etier, Paul, 905
Etpison, Ngiratkel, 673
Etter, Philipp, 855, 907
Eugenius I (Pope), 1060
Eugenius III (Pope), 1062
Eugenius IV (Pope), 1063
Eugster, Arthur, 859

Eulenburg, Botho, 384
Eupu, Edric, 682
Eustace, Joseph, 766
Eustis, William, 1001
Evangheli, Pandeli, 57
Evans, Daniel, 1039
Evans, John (Australia), 96
Evans, John G., 1029
Evans, John (USA), 979
Evans, John V., 990
Evans, Luther, 46
Evans, Melvin, 1046
Evans, Waldo, 1043, 1046
Everard, Henry, 1101
Everett, Edward, 1002
Everingham, Paul, 102
Evertsz, Juancho, 622
Evison, John, 629
Evren, Kenan, 930
Ewald, Christian von, 371
Ewang, Sam, 652, 655
Ewans, M.K., 962
Ewen, William, 986
Ewing, William, 990
Exon, James, 1010
Eyadéma, Gnassingbé, 923
Eydoux, Pierre, 344
Eyschen, Paul, 542
Eyskens, Gaston, 131
Eyskens, Mark, 131
Eze, Herbert, 645
Ezeta, Carlos, 306

Fabbri, Edoardo, 1064
Fabela, Isidro, 582
Fabius, Laurent, 329, 332
Facklam, Peter, 866
Facta, Luigi, 479
Fadahunsi, Joseph, 638
Fadden, Arthur, 88
Faddeyev, Nikolai, 13
Fadhil al-Chalabi, 32
Fadhil bin Zikra, 536
Fadhl I (Lahej), 1082
Fadhl II (Lahej), 1082
Fadhl III (Lahej), 1083
Fadhl IV (Lahej), 1083
Fadhl V (Lahej), 1083
Fadhl VI (Lahej), 1083
Fadil Jamali, 471
Fadul, Francisco, 406
Fagerholm, Karl, 320
Fagnoul, Bruno, 133
Fagundes, Miguel, 173
Fahd bin Abdul-Azaz (Saudi Arabia), 778
Fahey, John, 91
Fahim bin Sultan al-Qasimi, Shaikh, 20
Fahri Özdilek, 932
Fahrländer, Karl, 857
Fahy, Frank, 473

Fairbanks, Erasrus, 1035
Fairbanks, Horace, 1035
Fairchild, Edward, 1041
Fairchild, Lucius, 1041
Fairfield, John, 998
Faisal as-Shaabi, 1079
Faisal bin Abdul-Azaz (Saudi Arabia), 778
Faisal bin Sarur (Haushabi), 1082
Faisal bin Turki (Oman), 663
Faisal bin Turki (Saudi Arabia), 779
Faisal I (Iraq), 470
Faisal II (Iraq), 470, 472
Faisal Mukhtar, 844
Faisal (Syria), 911
Fait, Raúl, 74
Fajuyi, Francis, 638
Fakhar Hekmat, 468
Fakhri Pasha, 303
Fakhruddin Ebrahim, 670
Fakruddin Ali Ahmed, 422
Fakudze, Andreas, 847
Falcam, Leo, 592, 593
Falcão, Sebastião, 152
Falcon, Juan, 1066
Falconio, Antonio, 481
Faleiro, Luizinho, 430
Falkenhausen, Alexander von, 129
Falkenhausen, Ludwig von, 129
Falkenstein, Johann, 374
Fälldin, Thorbjörn, 851
Fallières, Armand, 324, 326
Falvy, Maurice-Émile, 633
Fama, Albano, 903
Fanfani, Amintore, 478, 479, 480
Fang Zhichun, 239
Fannin, Paul, 977
Fanti, Guido, 482
Fantini, Antonio, 482
Farag Said Ben Ghanem, 1078
Faraut, Gaudence-Charles, 1057
Faria, Juvenal de, 173
Farias, Osman de, 152
Farias, Osvaldo de, 169
Farias, Oswaldo de, 175
Farias, Wilmar de, 162
Farina, Luigi, 479
Faris al-Khuri, 913
Farnell, James, 90
Farnham, Roswell, 1036
Farnsworth, Daniel, 1040
Faro, José, 65
Farooq Abdullah, 434
Farooq Khan Lodi, 666
Farooq Laghari, 664
Farouk (Egypt), 302
Farquharson, Donald, 210
Farrar, Frank, 1030
Farrell, Edelmiro, 70
Farrely, Alexander, 1046
Farrias, Luis, 584
Farrington, Wallace, 988

Farrukhsiyar (India), 421
Farwell, Leonard, 1040
Farziliyev, Bedzhan, 116
Fasanya, Moses, 639, 653
Faseyev, Kamil, 738
Fasildas, 315
Fasino, Mario, 487
Fassbind, Joseph, 892
Fasseri, José, 79
Fässler, Ulrich, 880
Fata'a-iki, 628
Fateh Jung Chautaria, 616, 617
Fateyev, Valery, 751
Fath Ali Khan (Iran), 466
Fathollah Khan Sardar Mansur Sepahdar Azam, 468
Fatkulov, _, 737
Fatmi Ben Slimane, 602
Fattigati, Ernesto, 83
Fattor, Mario, 84
Fattori, Domenico, 770, 771, 774
Fattori, Marino, 771
Fattori, Onofrio, 770, 771
Faubus, Orval, 978
Faucher, Léon, 326
Faulk, Andrew, 1020
Faulkner, Brian, 955
Faure, Edgar, 328, 332
Faure, François, 324
Faustin I (Haiti) (F. Soulouque), 409
Fauteux, Gaspard, 211
Favergiotti, Juan Carlos, 83
Fávila (Asturias), 820
Favon, Georges, 871
Favre, Charles, 907
Favre, Nehri-Louis, 868
Favre, Ricardo, 75
Favreau, Benjamin-Marcel, 1058
Fawcus, Robert, 147
Fawtier, William-Maurice, 336, 345
Fawzi al-Mulki, 506
Fawzi al-Sultan, 44
Fawzi Silo, 911, 913
Fayez al-Tarawneh, 506
Fayez el-Khoury, 912
Fayu Fegahabor, 644
Faz Riza, Paz, 578
Fazal Elahi Chaudri, 664
Fazan, E., 905
Fazil-ul-Haq Khalikyar, 55
Fazlollah Zahedi, 468
Fazy, Henri, 871, 872
Fazzerani, Rossano, 774
Fazzini, Héctor, 76
Featherstone, Eric, 848
Féaux, Valmy, 133
Febres Cordero, León, 300
Federico I Ruggiero (Sicily), 492
Federico III (Sicily), 493
Federico IV (Sicily), 493
Federigo (Naples and Sicily), 491

Federik, Eduardo, 81
Federov, Valentin, 751
Fedini, Jean, 338
Fedorov, Nikolai, 724
Fedoruk, Sylvia, 212
Feghabo, Walter, 644
Fehling, Emil, 381
Fehr, Hermann, 868
Fehrenbach, Konstantin, 366
Feijo, Diogo, 148
Feilitzsch, Friedrich von, 386
Feillet, Paul, 343, 347
Fejervary, Géza, 416
Felber, Hans, 878, 879
Felber, René, 856, 882
Felch, Alpheus, 1003
Feldges, Mathias, 866
Feldman, Markus, 855
Feldmann, Markus, 867
Felice (Lucca), 490
Felipe I (Portugal), 702
Felipe II (Portugal), 702
Felipe II (Spain), 814
Felipe III (Portugal), 702
Felipe III (Spain), 814
Felipe IV (Spain), 814
Felipe V (Spain), 814
Felix Serna, Faustino, 588
Felker, Samuel, 1013
Fellisch, Karl, 375
Fellmann, Klaus, 879, 880
Feltrin, Pietro, 490
Fenech-Adami, Edward, 566
Feng Jixin, 235
Feng Kuo-chang, 225
Fenner, Arthur, 1026
Fenner, James, 1026
Fenton, Reuben, 1017
Feo, Emilio de, 482
Feo, Vincenzo de, 310
Ferald, Bert, 999
Ferdinand (Austria, Emperor), 105
Ferdinand (Bulgaria), 183
Ferdinand I (Austria), 105
Ferdinand I (Bohemia), 282
Ferdinand II (Austria), 105
Ferdinand II (Bohemia), 282
Ferdinand III (Austria), 105
Ferdinand (Modena), 491
Ferdinand (Romania), 708
Ferdinando I (Sicily), 493
Ferdinando I (Two Sicilies), 493
Ferdinando II (Sicily), 493
Ferdinando II (Two Sicilies), 493
Ferdinando III (Naples and Sicily), 492
Ferdinando III (Sicily), 493
Ferdinando IV (Naples and Sicily), 492, 493
Ferguson, George, 208
Ferguson, Herbert, 399
Ferguson, Jack, 91

Ferguson, James, 1033
Ferguson, Thompson, 1023
Fergusson, Bernard, 625
Fergusson, Charles, 625
Ferhat Abbas, 60, 61
Feris, José Romero, 74
Feris, Raúl Romero, 74
Ferit Melen, 932
Fermin Zubiria, Alberto, 1049
Fernandes, Luis, 776
Fernandes, Raul, 171
Fernández, Benito, 73
Fernández, Jorge, 78
Fernández, Orlando, 1070
Fernández, Prospero, 271
Fernández Albarrán, Juan, 582
Fernández Albor, Gerardo, 827
Fernández Alverez, Rafael, 824
Fernández Crespo, Daniel, 1049
Fernández de Cordoba, Fernando, 816
Fernández de Villaverde, Raimondu, 817
Fernández-Galiano, Antonio, 826
Fernández López, Basileo, 829
Fernández Maldonaldo, Jorge, 692
Fernández Manero, Victor, 588
Fernández Martín, Fernando, 825
Fernández Martínez, Enrique, 580
Fernández Miranda, Torcuato, 818
Fernández Reyna, Leonel, 296
Fernández Viagas, Plácido, 824
Fernando, Elizondo, 72
Fernando I (Aragon), 820
Fernando I (Castile), 821
Fernando I (León), 822
Fernando II (Aragon), 820
Fernando II (León), 822
Fernando II (Spain), 814
Fernando III (Castile), 821
Fernando III (León), 822
Fernando III (Tuscany), 496, 497
Fernando IV (Castile), 821
Fernando IV (Tuscany), 497
Fernando (Portugal), 702
Fernando V (Castile), 821
Fernando V (Spain), 814
Fernando VI (Spain), 814
Fernando VII (Spain), 814
Ferrante I (Naples and Sicily), 491
Ferrante I (Tuscany), 496
Ferrante II (Naples and Sicily), 491
Ferrante II (Tuscany), 496
Ferrara, Aldo, 482
Ferrara, Maurizio, 483
Ferraro, Carlos, 76
Ferraz, Angelo, 149
Ferraz, António, 170
Ferraz, Arturo, 705
Ferraz, Luíz, 155
Ferraz, Valentin, 816
Ferré, Luis, 1046
Ferreira, Alvaro, 64

Ferreira, António (Angola), 65
Ferreira, António (Brazil), 168
Ferreira, Benigno, 686
Ferreira, Carlos, 405
Ferreira, Cipriano, 161
Ferreira, Fileto, 153
Ferreira, Gabriel, 170
Ferreira, João (Maranhão, Brazil), 160
Ferreira, João (Paranãa, Brazil), 167
Ferreira, João (Piauî, Brazil), 170
Ferreira, Jorge Washington, 75
Ferreira, José (Brazil), 158
Ferreira, José (Portugal), 704
Ferreira, José (Sao Tomé e Príncipe), 776
Ferreira, Leal, 154
Ferrer, Francisco, 412
Ferrero, Edmondo, 484
Ferrero, Francesc Escude, 62
Ferrero Rebagliati, Raúl, 692
Ferrier, Johan, 845, 846
Ferris, Woodbridge, 1004
Ferry, Elisha, 1039
Ferry, Jules, 326
Feudtenegg, Ernst Seidler von, 107
Feusi, Balz, 893
Feusi, Hermann, 874
Feusi, Josef, 893
Fevzi Paşa, 931
Feyide, Mesach, 32
Fiame Mata'afa F.M. II, 769
Ficquelmont, Karl, 106
Fida Mohammed Khan, 667
Fieandt, Rainer von, 320
Field, John (Cameroon), 195
Field, John (Kiribati), 510
Field, John (Saint Helena), 968
Field, Michael, 97
Field, Winston, 1101
Fielder, James, 1014
Fielding, William, 207
Fields, William, 996
Fierlinger, Zdenek, 283
Fifer, Joseph, 991
Figaroa, Francisco de, 621
Figelski, Vladislav, 1056
Figgures, Frank, 16
Figir, Vicent, 593
Figl, Leopold, 106, 107, 109
Fignole, Daniel, 410
Figueira, Manuel, 65
Figueiredo, Amadeu de, 216, 776
Figueiredo, João de, 216
Figueras Y Moracas, Estanislao, 815
Figueredo, Abel de, 165
Figueredo, António de, 161
Figueredo, Argemiro de, 166
Figueredo, Arnaldo de, 162
Figueredo, João, 149
Figuereo, Juan, 296
Figueres Ferrer, José, 271
Figueres Olson, José-Maria, 271

Figueroa, Ferdnando, 306
Figueroa, Genovevo, 583
Figueroa Alcocer, Rubén, 581
Figueroa Figueroa, Rubén, 580
Fikre-Selassie Wogderes, 316
Filangieri, Carlo, 494
Filbinger, Hans, 368
Filgueiras, Frederico, 159
Filho, Garibaldi Alvis, 174
Filho, Romero Jucá, 175
Filiberto I (Piedmont-Sardinia), 495
Filiberto II (Piedmont-Sardinia), 495
Filip (Sweden), 849
Filipenko, Aleksandr, 755
Filipov, Grisha, 184
Filipović, Nikola, 143
Filippi, Jean, 335
Filippi, Melchoirre, 771
Filippo I (Naples and Sicily), 492, 493
Filippo I (Piedmont-Sardinia), 495
Filippo II (Naples and Sicily), 492, 493
Filippo III (Naples and Sicily), 492, 493
Filippo IV (Naples and Sicily), 492, 493
Filippo (Parma and Piacenza), 494
Filippov, Vasily, 721
Fillmore, Millard, 972
Fillon, François, 334
Fillon, Victor-Marie, 291
Filmon, Gary, 203
Filonardi, Vincenzo, 796
Filov, Bogdan, 183, 184
Finant, Jean-Pierre, 268
Finca, Bongani, 807
Finch, Cliff, 1007
Finckh, Eugen von, 383
Findlay, William, 1025
Fine, John, 1026
Finger, Jakob, 371
Finn, Gilbert, 203
Finnbogadóttir, Vigdís, 419
Finney, Joan (J. McInroy), 995
Finniss, Boyle, 93
Fino, Bashkim, 58
Fiorini, Mauro, 774
Firmeza, Pedro, 156
Firoz Khan Noon, 122, 665, 669
Firuz (India), 421
Firyubin, Nikolai, 48
Fiscanni, Francesco, 497
Fischer, Abraham, 803
Fischer, Carlos, 1049
Fischer, E., 905
Fischer, Franz, 891
Fischer, Hanspeter, 898
Fischer, Peter, 45
Fiscoseco, José, 76
Fiset, Eugène, 211
Fish, Hamilton, 1017
Fishback, James, 978
Fisher, Andrew, 88
Fisher, Charles, 204

Fisher, Gerald, 798
Fisher, John, 1025
Fitto, Raffaele, 486
Fitto, Salvatore, 486
Fitzgerald, Frank, 1004
Fitzgerald, Garret, 474
Fitzpatrick, Benjamin, 974
Fitzpatrick, Charles, 197, 211
Fitzpatrick, Desmond, 958
Flach, Émile, 597
Flamerich, Germán Suárez, 1067
Flanagin, Harris, 977
Flanders, Alvan, 1039
Flanders, Benjamin, 997
Flandin, Pierre, 328
Flaxman, Hubert, 1057
Fleković, Petar, 275
Fleming, A. Brooks, 1040
Fleming, Francis (Sierra Leone), 785
Fleming, Francis (USA), 985
Fleming, Iolanda, 151
Fleming, J., 969
Fleming, Osbourne, 960
Fleming, William, 1037
Flemming, Hugh, 204
Flemming, James, 204
Fletcher, Allen, 1036
Fletcher, Arthur, 317, 925
Fletcher, Ryland, 1035
Fletcher, Thomas, 1007
Fleury, Luíz, 178
Fleytas, Victor, 72
Floissac, Vincent, 765
Floquet, Charles, 326
Flor Casanova, Noe de la, 588
Flores, Antonio, 299
Flores, Florencio, 675
Flores, Francisco, 307
Flores, Joseph, 1044
Flores, Juan, 299
Flores, Luis, 691
Flores, Manuel, 1049
Flores, Venancio, 1048
Flores Avendaño, Guillermo, 402
Flores Cunel, Rogelio, 584
Flores Facusse, Carlos, 413
Flores Muñoz, Gilberto, 584
Flores Sánchez, Oscar, 578
Flores Tapia, Oscar, 578
Florescu, Ion, 709
Florestan (Monaco), 597
Florias, Mario, 487
Florio, James, 1015
Flosse, Gaston, 346
Flottwell, Adalbert von, 388
Flower, Roswell, 1017
Floyd, John, 1037
Floyd, John Buchanan, 1037
Flynn, Edmund, 211
Flynn, William, 1027
Fock, Dirk (Indonesia), 461

Fock, Dirk (Suriname), 845
Fock, Jenö, 417
Fokin, Vitold, 941
Folaumahina, Mikaele, 350
Folgio Miramontes, Fernando, 577
Folk, Joseph, 1008
Follett, Rosemary, 101
Föllmi, Dominique, 873
Folsom, James, 975
Folsom, James Jr, 975
Foncha, John, 196
Fonin, M., 935
Fonjallaz, Eugène, 905
Fonnesbeck, Christian, 287
Fonseca, Clodoaldo de, 151
Fonseca, Deodoro da, 148
Fonseca, Hermes da, 148, 154
Fonseca, José de, 776
Fonseca, Manuel da, 604
Fonseca, Pedro de, 151
Fonseca, Roberto, 82
Fonseca Alvarez, Guillermo, 587
Fonseka, Gamini, 832
Font, Estanislau Sangrà, 63
Font, Pere, 62
Fontan y Lobe, Juan, 308
Fontanet, Guy, 873
Fontanini, Pietro, 483
Fontenelle, José, 155
Fontes, Jeremias, 172
Fontes de Melo, António, 704
Fontoura, Alvaro de, 297
Foot, Hugh, 279, 499
Foot, Samuel, 981
Foote, Henry, 1006
Foraker, Joseph, 1022
Forbes, George, 627
Forcade de la Roquette, Jean de, 326
Forcellini, Dominico, 772, 773
Forcellini, Giuseppe, 772, 773
Ford, Gerald (Leslie King), 973
Ford, Sam, 1009
Ford, Seabury, 1021
Ford, Thomas, 990
Ford, Wendell, 996
Forde, Francis, 88
Forde, Mary Leneen, 91
Fordyce, Kirk, 1007
Forester-Walker, Frederick, 964
Forget, Amedee, 212, 213
Forgia, Antonio La, 483
Forlani, Arnaldo, 480
Formigoni, Roberto, 484
Formosus (Pope), 1060
Fornani, Giovanni, 797
Fornerod, Charles, 853
Forni, Emilio, 899
Forrer, Ludwig, 854
Forrest, John, 100
Forster, Albert, 701
Forster, William, 89

Forsyth, John, 986
Forsythe, William, 35
Fort, John, 1014
Forte, George, 1014
Fortes Ramos, Jesús Cayetano, 829
Fortis, Alessandro, 479
Fortunato, Giustino, 494
Fortune, Gabriel-Émile, 255
Forzano, Lino Montiel, 84
Foscarini, Marco, 498
Foschi, Salvatore, 771, 772
Foss, Eugene, 1002
Foss, Joseph, 1030
Fosse, Roger, 332
Fossombroni, Vittorio, 497
Foster, Charles, 1022
Foster, Murphy, 997
Foster, Murphy (Mike), 998
Foster, Robert, 317, 318, 793
Foster, Walter, 204
Foteyev, Vladimir, 723
Fouché, Jacobus de, 804
Fouché, Jacobus (Jim), 800
Fouchet, Christian, 60
Foulkes, Raul Alfonsín, 70
Fourchier, Jacques, 334
Fourie, Adriaan, 802
Fourn, Gaston, 136, 922
Fourneau, Alfred-Louis, 353
Fourneau, Fernand, 339
Fourneau, Jacques-Georges, 255, 403
Fourneau, Lucien, 194, 255
Fournier, Alberic-Auguste, 186
Fournier, Hubert, 342
Fournier, Jean-René, 904
Fournier, Rafael Calderón, 271
Fournier, René-Victor, 255
Fousset, Louis, 339, 563
Fowle, Daniel, 1019
Fox, Channing, 1002
Fox, William, 626
Fox Quesada, Vicente, 580
Fox-Strangeways, Vivian, 510
Foz, A. Rodríguez, 75
Fraefel, Thomas, 908
Fraga Iribane, Manuel, 827
Fragelli, José, 162
Fraile, Carlos, 299
Fraire, Eduardo, 77
Francesco Giacinto (Piedmont-Sardinia), 495
Francesco I (Modena), 491
Francesco I (Tuscany), 496
Francesco I (Two Sicilies), 493
Francesco II (Modena), 491
Francesco II (Tuscany), 496
Francesco II (Two Sicilies), 493
Francesco III (Modena), 491
Francesco IV (Modena), 491
Francesco (Parma and Piacenza), 494
Francesco V (Modena), 491

Francher, Frederick, 1020
Franchet, Regis, 29
Francia, José Rodríguez de, 686
Francini, Ciro, 771
Francini, Francesco, 773
Francini, Loris, 774
Francini, Pietro, 770
Francini, Vincenzo, 771
Franciosi, Carlo, 774
Franciosi, Giovan, 773
Franciosi, Marino, 772
Francis, David, 1008
Francis, H., 629
Francis, James, 98
Francis, John, 1026
Francis, Nathaniel, 971
Franck, Edouard, 219
Franckuk, Anatoly, 943
Franco, Adolpho, 168
Franco, Albano, 180
Franco, Augusto, 180
Franco, Itamar, 149, 163
Franco, João, 704
Franco, Manuel, 687
Franco, Mario, 80
Franco, Rafael, 687
Franco, Wellington, 172
Franco Aguilar, Augustín, 591
Franco Bahamonde, Francisco, 815, 818, 819
Franco Rodríguez, David, 583
François, Joseph-Pascal, 345, 353, 456
François (Francisco) (Navarre), 823
François I (France), 323
François II (France), 323
François-Marsal, Frédéric, 327
Frank, Hans, 697
Frank, T. Hilbourne, 68
Frankenthurn, Paul Gratsch von, 107
Franklin, Benjamin, 976, 1025
Franklin, Jesse, 1018
Franque, Luis Ranque, 66
Frantz, Frank, 1023
Franz, 105
Franz Josef, 105
Fraser, Alistair, 206
Fraser, Duncan, 206
Fraser, F., 214
Fraser, John, 203, 204
Fraser, Malcolm, 88
Fraser, Peter, 627
Frashëri, Mehdi, 57
Frazier, James, 1031
Frazier, Lynn, 1020
Frear, Walter, 988
Frederick Hendrik (Netherlands), 618
Frederik (Bohemia), 282
Frederik I (Denmark), 287
Frederik II (Denmark), 287
Frederik III (Denmark), 287
Frederik IV (Denmark), 287

Frederik IX (Denmark), 287
Frederik V (Denmark), 287
Frederik VI (Denmark), 287
Frederik VII (Denmark), 287
Frederik VIII (Denmark), 287
Fredrik (Sweden), 850
Freeman, Orville, 1005
Freeston, Brian, 35
Freeston, Leslie, 317
Frei, Julius, 862
Frei Ruiz-Tagle, Edouardo, 223
Freire, Felissbello, 178
Freire, José, 156, 157
Freire, Oswaldo, 160
Freire, Ramón, 222
Freire, Rómulo Gallegos, 1067
Freitas, António de (Cape Verde), 216
Freitas, António (Guanabara, Brazil), 159
Freitas, António (Rio de Janeiro, Brazil), 172
Freitas, José, 705
Freitas, Pedro, 171
Freitas, Tertuliano de, 167
Freitas, Uladislau de, 166
Fremont, John, 976
French, Augustus, 990
French, Neville, 964
Frenette, J. Raymond, 204
Frère-Orban, Hubert, 130
Frey, August, 45
Frey, Emil, 854
Frey, Emile, 45
Frey, Josef, 878, 879
Frey-Herosee, Friedrich, 853
Freyburg, Alfred, 377
Freycinet, Charles de, 326
Freyenmuth, Robert, 896, 897
Frezouls, Antoine, 403
Frías, Hugh Chávez, 1067
Frias, Tomás, 140
Frick, Alexander, 537
Frick, Mario, 537
Frick, Simon, 888, 889
Frick, Wilhelm, 284
Fricker, Charles, 905
Frieden, Pierre, 543
Friedrich, István, 417
Friedrich August I (Saxony), 374
Friedrich August I (Warsaw), 701
Friedrich August II (Saxony), 374
Friedrich August III (Saxony), 374
Friedrich August (Oldenburg), 382
Friedrich (Baden), 377
Friedrich Franz I (Mecklenburg-Schwerin), 381
Friedrich Franz II (Mecklenburg-Schwerin), 381
Friedrich Franz III (Mecklenburg-Schwerin), 381

Friedrich Franz IV (Mecklenburg-Schwerin), 381
Friedrich (Germany), 365
Friedrich Gunther (Schwarzenburg-Rudolstadt), 387
Friedrich I (Anhalt), 376
Friedrich I (Baden), 377
Friedrich I (Prussia), 383
Friedrich II (Anhalt), 376
Friedrich II (Baden), 377
Friedrich II (Prussia), 383
Friedrich III (Austria), 105
Friedrich III (Prussia), 383
Friedrich Karl (Schwarzenburg-Rudolstadt), 387
Friedrich (Mecklenburg-Schwerin), 381
Friedrich (Saxe-Altenburg), 385
Friedrich (Waldeck), 388
Friedrich Wilhelm (Brunswick), 378
Friedrich Wilhelm (Hesse-Cassel), 380
Friedrich Wilhelm I (Prussia), 383
Friedrich Wilhelm II (Prussia), 383
Friedrich Wilhelm III (Prussia), 383
Friedrich Wilhelm IV (Prussia), 383
Friedrich Wilhelm (Mecklenburg-Strelitz), 382
Friedrich Wilhelm (Nassau), 382
Friedrich (Württemberg), 388
Friedrichs, Rudolf, 375
Fries, H. de, 845
Friesen, Alfred von, 374
Friesen, Richard, 374
Frigo, Franco, 490
Friis, Michael, 288
Frijs, Christian, 287
Fritsch, Ernst, 385
Fritsche, Johann, 861
Frogier, Pierre, 348
Froíla I (Asturias), 820
Froíla II (Asturias), 820
Frolich, August, 385
Frölich, August, 376
Fromm, Georg, 875
Frondizi, Arturo, 70
Froneman, Gabriel, 804
Frossard, Charles, 956
Frost, Leslie, 208
Frota, Júlio da, 174
Frouin, Jean-Paul, 335
Frouk Hamadalla, 836
Froute, Alain, 338
Fruchard, Louis, 334
Fructuoso Rivera, José, 1048
Frutos, Juan, 687
Fruytier, Leonard, 621
Fry, William, 957
Fryer, Frederick, 606
Fu Xishou, 234
Fuad Chehab, 527, 528
Fuad I (Egypt), 302
Fuad Maasum, 472

Fuad Mohieddin, 304
Fuad Rouhani, 32
Fuchs, Félix-Alexandre, 258
Fuchs, Hans, 893
Füeg-Hitz, Cornelia, 895, 896
Fuentes Rodríguez, José de la, 578
Fuerta, Federico, 79
Fuhrer, Rita, 910
Fujimori, Alberto, 690
Fukuda, Takeo, 504
Fuller, Alvin, 1002
Fuller, Frank, 1034
Fuller, George, 90
Fuller, John, 97
Fuller, Levi, 1036
Fullerton, William, 964
Fulton, Robert, 993
Fulton, William, 977
Fuluhea, Pelenato, 351
Fünfschilling, Hans, 864
Fuqua, Henry, 997
Furcolo, Foster, 1003
Furgler, Kurt, 856
Furnas, Robert, 1009
Furrer, Jonas, 853
Furrer, Josef, 901
Furrer, Viktor, 885
Furtado, Francisco, 149
Furtado, José, 171
Futkaradze, Ismail, 362
Futrell, Junius, 978
Fyodor I (Russia), 713
Fyodor II (Russia), 713
Fyodor III (Russia), 713
Fysh, Philip, 96

G. Zail Singh, 423, 445
Gabarayev, Vladislav, 363
Gabathuler, Johann, 888
Gabidullin, Zaki, 738
Gabites, R.O., 629
Gabre Krestos, 315
Gabrié, Marie-Louis, 339
Gabriel, Almir, 165
Gabriel, Sigmar, 372
Gabriel, Theodor, 883
Gabrielli, Francisco, 77
Gabrielli, Rodolfo, 78
Gabuka, Chris, 641
Gabuzzi, Stefano, 898
Gabyseb, Aleksandr, 736
Gadea, Héctor, 80
Gaden, Nicholas, 568
Gadgil, Narhar, 444
Gadient, Andreas, 875
Gadzhhiyev, Salekh, 115
Gafurov, Bodozhan, 915
Gafyatullin, Sulaiman, 738
Gagarin, Pavel, 714
Gage, Henry, 979

Gage, Jack, 1042
Gagern, Heinrich, 371
Gagner, Max, 867, 868
Gagnon, Onésime, 211
Gagulia, Gennadi, 360
Gaidar, Yegor, 715
Gailis, Maris, 526
Gailius, Viktoras, 540
Gaillard, Félix, 328
Gaines, John, 1023
Gair, Vincent, 92
Gairdner, Charles, 95, 100
Gairy, Eric, 400
Galan, Giancarlo, 490
Galassi, Clelio, 773
Galassi, Pio, 773
Galazov, Akhsarbek, 735, 736
Gale, Leo de, 399
Galeano, Manuel, 78
Galhardo, Eduardo, 428
Galiev, Mirza, 719
Galina, Jorge, 72
Galindez, Antonio, 1069
Galindo, Carlos Blanco, 141
Gallas, Johann, 492
Gallati, Rudolf, 874
Gallegos Alvarado, José de, 270
Gallen, Hugh, 1013
Gallet, Gustave, 345
Galleti, Giuseppe, 1064
Galli, Brenno, 899
Gallieni, Joseph-Simon, 546
Gallino, Oscar, 71
Gallmann, Heinrich, 907
Gallo Porras, Luis, 692
Gallotti, Luiz, 176
Gallwey, Henry (Saint Helena), 968
Gallwey, Henry (The Gambia), 355
Galo Thondup, 232
Galsworthy, Arthur, 967
Galtieri, Leopoldo, 70
Galusha, Jonas, 1035
Galvanauskas, Ernst, 539
Galvão, António, 169
Galves, Manuel, 690
Gálvez, Juan, 413
Galvez Betancourt, Carlos, 583
Galway, Henry, 93
Gama, Clovis da, 163
Gamarnik, Yan, 127
Gamarra, Augustín, 688
Gambetta, Léon, 326
Gamble, Geoffrey, 797
Gamble, Hamilton, 1007
Gamboa, Rafael, 577
Game, Philip, 89
Games Oroxco, Edmundo, 575
Gamiz Fernández, Salvador, 579
Gamma, Martin, 901
Gamma, Raymund, 902
Gamsakhirdia, Zviad, 358

Ganao, Charles, 256
Ganden Tripa Tsemoling, 231
Gandhi, Indira, 423
Gandhi, Rajiv, 423
Gandhi, Ruston, 432
Gandolfi, Antonio, 310
Ganev, Dimitar, 183
Ganev, Venelin, 183
Gangwal, Mishrilal, 459
Ganić, Ejup, 146
Ganilau, Peter, 318
Ganong, Gilbert, 203
Ganoza, Augustín, 691
Gans y Martínez, Oscar, 278
Ganzoni, Robert, 875
Ganzoni, Rudolf, 874, 875
Gao Dezhan, 239
Gao Yan, 239
Gaona, Juan, 686
Gapurov, Mukhamednazar, 934, 935
Garaicoetxea, Carlos, 825
Garašanin, Ilija, 1092
Garašanin, Milutin, 1092
Garate Legleu, Raúl, 589
Garawa, Douglas, 682
Garba Duba, 641, 655
Garba Mohammed, 655
Garba Nadama, 655
Garbai, Sándor, 415, 416
Garbani-Nerini, Evaristo, 898, 899
Garber, Silas, 1009
Garbit, Hubert-Auguste, 546
Garcá Barragan, Marcellina, 581
Garcelon, Alonzo, 999
Garcez, Arnaldo, 179
Garcez, João, 180
Garcez, Lucas, 178
Garcez, Martinho, 179
García, Américo, 81
Garcia, Carlos, 694
García, Fernando, 83
Gárcía, Fernando Aliaga, 84
García, Francisco, 591
García, Héctor, 83
Garcia, Hélio, 163
García, Lizardo, 299
Garcia, Luíz, 179
García Calderón, Francisco, 689
García Camacho, Carlos, 1044
García Corres, Bartolome, 590
García-Godoy Cáceres, Héctor, 296
García Gómez, Florencio, 816
García González, Alfonso, 575
García Granados, Miguel, 401
García I (Asturias), 820
García I Sánchez (Navarre), 823
García II (Navarre), 823
García III (Navarre), 823
García IV Ramirez (Navarre), 823
García Menocal, Mario, 277
García Mercado, Francisco, 584

García Montes, Jorge, 278
García Morena, Gabriel, 299
García Pérez, Alan, 689
García Toledo, Anastasio, 585
García Urrutia, Baltasar, 690
Gard, Marcel, 903
Gardiner, Anthony, 532
Gardiner, James, 213
Gardiner, William, 999
Gardner, Booth, 1039
Gardner, Frederick, 1008
Gardner, Henry, 1002
Gardner, O. Max, 1019
Gardon, Garde, 201
Garec, René, 330
Garfield, James, 972
Gariboldi, Italo, 534
Garland, Augustus, 977
Garnier, Jean-René, 344
Garoëb, Justus, 612
Garotinho, Anthony, 173
Garrahy, Joseph, 1027
Garrard, James, 995
Garraway, Edward, 147, 530
Garrido, José Rojas, 249
Garrioch, Henry, 570
Garro, Pedro, 83
Garrouste, Pierre, 344
Garsia, Rupert, 615
Garson, Stuart, 202
Garst, Warren, 993
Garula Mohammed, 651
Garvey, Dan, 977
Garvey, Ronald (Fiji), 317
Garvey, Ronald (Isle of Man & Belize), 134, 957
Garvey, Ronald (St Vincent and Grenadines), 766
Garvin, Lucius, 1027
Gary, Raymond, 1023
Garyayev, Naldzhi, 728
Garza, Arturo de la, 584
Garzo, Luis, 81
Gasanov, Gasan, 114
Gasanov, Natig, 115
Gascoine, Julian, 960
Gascón Mercado, Julian, 584
Gasiyev, Feliks, 363
Gasiyev, Znaur, 363
Gasmallah Rassas, 836
Gaspar, Alfredo, 705
Gaspari, Pietro, 1065
Gasparini, Jacopo, 310
Gasperi, Alcide de, 479
Gasperoni, Cesare, 774
Gasperoni, Pier-Paulo, 774
Gass, Michael, 793
Gasser, Hans, 886
Gaston, William, 1002
Gata, Falakiko, 350
Gates, Charles, 1036

Gates, Ralph, 992
Gatluak Deng, 844
Gatti, Gabriele, 775
Gattoni, Jorge, 81
Gaudin, Jean-Claude, 334
Gauger, Robert, 1058
Gaulle, Charles de, 325, 328
Gauna, Antenor, 75
Gaus Ali Shah, 670
Gaus Bizenjo, 666
Gaus Ralsani, 666
Gauzès, Jean-Paul, 332
Gavai, Padmakar, 454
Gavard, Jacques, 872
Gavenis, Juris, 943, 944
Gavillet, A., 906
Gayle, John, 974
Gayrbekov, Muslim, 722
Gazi Ahmed Mukhtar Paşa, 931
Gbenye, Christophe, 259
Gbezera-Bria, Michel, 219
Ge Hongsheng, 243
Gear, John, 993
Geary, Henry, 960
Geary, John (Kansas, USA), 994
Geary, John (Pennsylvanis, USA), 1025
Geay, Lucien-Eugène, 563, 568, 780
Geddes, John, 1028
Gediminas (Lithuania), 538
Gedvilas, Mečislovas, 539
Gedzhenov, Ch., 733
Geens, Gaston, 132
Geer, Dirk de, 619, 620
Geer, Ludwig de, 851
Geer, Ludwig Gerhard de, 851
Geer, Theodore, 1024
Geffrard, N. Fabre, 410
Gegeyo, Kingsley, 682
Gehlot, Ashok, 446
Gei, Konstantin, 127
Geiger, Willi, 889
Geiler, Karl, 372
Geingob, Hage, 611
Geisel, Ernesto, 149
Geismar, Léon, 922
Geiss, Anton, 378
Gekman, I., 742
Gelastius II (Pope), 1062
Gelling, Donald, 958
Gemperli, Albert, 888, 889
Gemperli, Paul, 889
Genda, Ambrose, 786
Gendun, Peljidiyn, 599, 600
Generali, Claudio, 900
Genga, Annibale della, 1064
Genoud, Claud, 870
Genoud, Guy, 904
Genoud, Paul, 870
Gent, Gerald, 550
Gentil, Émile, 255
Gentil, Johann, 623

Gentil, Manuel, 297
Gentilhomme, Paul-Louis de, 546
Genyatulin, Ravil, 745
Georg I (Hanover), 379
Georg I (Saxe-Meiningen), 385, 386
Georg I (Schaumberg-Lippe), 386
Georg II (Hanover), 379
Georg II (Saxe-Meiningen), 386
Georg II (Schaumberg-Lippe), 386
Georg II (Waldeck), 387
Georg III (Hanover), 379
Georg IV (Hanover), 379
Georg (Mecklenburg-Strelitz), 382
Georg (Saxe-Altenburg), 385
Georg (Saxony), 374
Georg (Schwarzenburg-Rudolstadt), 387
Georg V (Hanover), 379
Georg Viktor (Waldeck), 388
George, Hywel, 766
George, Hywell, 963
George, Robert, 93
George, Yosiwo, 592
George I (Great Britain), 951
George II (Great Britain), 951
George III (Great Britain), 951
George IV (Great Britain), 951
George Rukidi III (Toro), 939
George Tupou I (Tonga, Taufa'ahau), 924
George Tupou II (Tonga), 924
George V (Great Britain), 951
George VI (Great Britain), 951
Georghiev, Kimon, 184
Georgievski, Ljubcho, 545
Georgios I (Greece), 392
Georgios II (Greece), 392, 393, 398
Georgy, Guy-Noël, 256
Gerard, Bernard, 346
Gérard, Étienne, 325
Gerasimov, Valentin, 747
Geraue, Baptiste-Léon, 345
Gerbel, Serhy, 941
Gerbinis, Louis (Guadeloupe), 338
Gerbinis, Louis (Martinique), 339
Gerbinis, Louis (Pondicherry), 456
Gerbrandy, Pieter, 620
Gerdener, Theodor, 803
Gerhardsen, Einar, 661
Geringer, Jim, 1042
Gerlach, Manfred, 367
Germain, Gaëtan, 291
Germain, Paul, 330
Gerö, Ernö, 418
Gerry, Elbridge, 1001
Gertschen, Richard, 904
Gery, Frédéric de, 345
Gestido, Oscar, 1049
Getiya, S., 361
Gettuyev, Magomet, 727
Getty, Donald, 200
Geydarov, Nazar, 113
Géza I (Hungary), 414

Géza II (Hungary), 414
Ghafoor, Abdul, 427
Ghalib bin Muhsin (Kathiri), 1082
Ghalib (I) bin Awadh, 1084
Ghalib (II) bin Awadh, 1084
Ghazi (Iraq), 470
Gheorghiu-Dej, Gheorghe, 710, 711
Gheshov, Ivan, 184
Gheurghiu-Dej, Gheorghe, 708
Ghica, Dimitrie, 709
Ghica, Ion, 709
Ghigo, Enzo, 485
Ghilardotti, Fiorella, 484
Ghinami, Alessandro, 486
Ghiotti, Renzo, 774
Ghirelli, Francesco, 489
Ghironzi, Giancarlo, 773, 775
Ghisani, Rolando, 78
Ghisletta, Federico, 900
Ghiz, Joseph, 210
Gholam Azhari, 468
Gholson, Richard, 1039
Ghosh, Ajoy Kumar, 452
Ghosh, Prafulla, 452
Ghulam Faruk, 123
Ghulam Gilani Khan, 668
Ghulam Hidayatullah, 669, 670
Ghulam Ishaq Khan, 664
Ghulam Mohammed, 664
Ghulam Mohammed Shah, 434
Ghulam Mustafa Jatoi, 665, 670
Ghulam Mustafa Khar, 668
Ghulam Sadiq, 433, 434
Ghulum Mustafa Khar, 669
Gia Long (Nguyen Phuc Anh), 1073
Giacobbi, Félix, 403
Giacobbi, François, 335
Giacomini, Agostini, 772
Giacomini, Giordani, 772
Giacomini, Giordano, 772
Giacomini, Romolo, 772
Giacomino, Giordano, 775
Giacomo (Sicily), 493
Giagu, Nino, 486
Giampaoli, Rodolfo, 485
Gian Gastone (Tuscany), 496
Giancecchi, Pietro, 773
Giandomenico, Giovanni Di, 485
Gianecchi, Pietro, 773
Giannatasio, Luis, 1049
Gibben, J.E., 214
Gibbons, David, 961
Gibbs, Addison, 1024
Gibbs, Dennis, 966
Gibbs, Félix, 78
Gibbs, Humphrey, 1100, 1102
Gibbs, William, 1026
Giblin, William, 96
Gibril, Akim, 786
Gibson, A.H., 214
Gibson, Ernest, 1036

Gibson, Garretson, 532
Gibson, John (Canada), 208
Gibson, John (USA), 991
Gidada, Negaso, 316
Giddings, Marsh, 1015
Gierek, Edward, 699
Gies, Gerd, 375
Giesler, Paul, 369
Giffard, Henry, 956
Gigar, 315
Gigini, Amos, 795
Gigli, Rodolfo, 483
Gignoux, John, 872
Gigurtu, Ion, 710
Giheno, John, 677
Gikalo, Nikolai, 114, 127
Gil Preciado, Juan, 582
Gila, Samson, 681
Gilashvili, Pavel, 358, 360
Gilchrist, Albert, 985
Giles, Alexander, 530, 766
Giles, Leslie, 101
Giles, William, 1037
Gilgen, Alfred, 910
Gill, Lachman Singh, 444, 445
Gill, Moses, 1001
Gill, Partal Singh, 429
Gillespie, Danny, 102
Gillett, James, 979
Gillies, Duncan, 98
Gillies, William, 92
Gilligan, John, 1022
Gilman, John, 1011, 1012
Gilmer, George, 986
Gilmer, Thomas, 1037
Gilmer, William, 1044
Gilmore, James, 1037
Gilmore, Joseph, 1012
Gilpin, William, 979
Gilruth, John, 101
Gilson, Horace, 989
Giner Durán, Praxedes, 578
Gingell, Judy, 215
Gioacchino (Joaquim Murat, Naples and Sicily), 492
Gioberti, Vincenzo, 495
Giolitti, Giovanni, 479
Giorgi I, 357
Giorgi II, 357
Giorgi III, 357
Giorgi IV, 357
Giorgi IX, 358
Giorgi V, 357
Giorgi VI, 357
Giorgi VII, 358
Giorgi VIII, 358
Giorgi XIII, 358
Giovanna I (Naples and Sicily), 491
Giovanna II (Naples and Sicily), 491
Giovanna (Sicily), 493
Giovanni Cornari I, 498

Giovanni Cornari II, 498
Giovanni (Sicily), 493
Giovanoli, Fritz, 867, 868
Giovenzana, Giuseppe, 484
Gipoulon, Henri, 563
Giral y Pereira, José, 818, 819
Girão, Eduardo, 155
Girard, Marc, 202
Girardin, Brigette, 347
Giraud, Michel, 332
Giri, Varahagiri (Mysore & Kerala, India), 422, 434, 435
Giri, Varahagiri (Uttar Pradesh, India), 450
Giric (Scotland), 953
Girija Koirala, 617
Giró, Juan, 1048
Girvan (Nepal), 616
Giscard d'Estaing, Valéry, 325, 330
Gise, Friedrich, 368
Gisi-Willisegger, Ruth, 896
Gisler, Ambros, 902
Gisler, Konrad, 910
Gisler, Rudolf, 874
Gisler, Walter, 893
Gist, William, 1029
Giudice, Calogero Lo, 487
Giuliano I de Medici (Tuscany), 496
Giuliano II de Medici (Tuscany), 496
Giulio de Medici (Tuscany), 496
Giumarra, Vincenzo, 487
Giuseppe (Josef I of Austria, Naples and Sicily), 492, 493
Giuseppe (Joseph Bonaparte, Naples and Sicily), 492
Giustiniani, Marcantonio, 498
Gizenga, Antoine, 259
Gizikis, Phaedon, 393
Gizzi, Pasquale, 1064
Gladky, Dmitri, 595
Gladstone, William, 952
Glaesnapp, Ernst von, 388
Glaser, Heinrich, 862
Glass, Albert, 969
Glass, James, 969
Glass, Lewis, 969
Glass, William, 969
Glasscock, William, 1040
Glasson, Pierre, 870
Glasspole, Florizel, 499
Gleim, A.Ya., 741, 742
Gleim, Otto, 194
Gleisner, Wilhelm, 388
Gleissner, Heinrich, 111
Glenday, Vincent, 798
Glendening, Parris, 1001
Glenn, Robert, 1019
Glick, George, 994
Gligorov, Kiro, 544
Glogowski, Gerhard, 372
Glushenkov, Anatoly, 751
Glynn, Martin, 1017

Gnägi, Rudolf, 856, 868
Goad, Colin, 45
Gobat, Albert, 866
Gobbi, Maurizio, 774
Gobbo, James, 98
Goblet, René, 326
Godbout, J. Adelard, 211, 212
Goddard, Samuel, 977
Godden, Charles, 959
Godley, Alexander, 965
Godmanis, Ivar, 526
Godoy, Ruperto, 81
Godwin, Mills, 1037
Goebbels, Joseph, 366
Goebel, William, 996
Goedgedrag, Fritz, 623
Góes, Horácio de, 179
Goffin, Louis, 49
Gofman, Konrad, 741
Goga, Octavian, 710
Gogobaridze, Levan, 362
Gogoi, Keshab, 426
Gogovski, Gligorije, 545
Gogua, Vasili, 358
Goh Chok Tong, 788
Góis e Vasconcelos, Zacarias de, 149
Goldayev, Boris, 915
Goldenberg Schreiber, Efraín, 692
Golding, John, 970
Goldsborough, Charles, 1000
Goldsborough, Philips, 1001
Goldschmidt, Neil, 1024
Goldsworthy, Roger, 134
Golescu, Alexandru, 709
Golescu, Nicolae, 709
Golescu, Stefan, 709
Golfari, Cesare, 484
Golitsyn, Nikolai, 714
Gololoded, Nikolai, 127
Goloshchokin, Filipp, 508
Goltz, Colmar von der, 129
Golub, N.I., 595
Goma, Louis-Sylvain, 256
Gomang, Giridhari, 443
Gömbös, Guyla, 417
Gomensoro, Tomás, 1049
Gomes, Augusto, 179
Gomes, Ciro, 156
Gomes, Jary, 162
Gomes, Manuel, 703
Gomes, Nestor, 157
Gomes, Théofilo, 167
Gomes, Wenceslão Braz, 148, 163
Gomes, Wladislau, 161
Gomes Candau, Marcolino, 47
Gomes de Castro, José, 704
Gómez, Alberto Gordillo, 84
Gómez, Crescencio, 412
Gómez, Egardo, 81
Gomez, Emilio, 168
Gómez, José, 277

Gómez, Juan, 1067
Gómez, Marte, 589
Gómez Becera, Alvaro, 816
Gómez de la Serna, José, 308
Gómez de la Torre, Francisco, 300
Gómez de las Roces, Hipólito, 824
Gómez de Salazar y Nieto, Federico, 761
Gómez Farías, Valentin, 572, 573
Gómez Maganda, Alejandro, 580
Gómez Pedraza, Manuel, 572
Gómez Reyes, Roberto, 584
Gómez Sandoval, Fernando, 585
Gómez y Arias, Miguel, 277
Gomide, Francisco, 177
Gomolka, Alfred, 373
Gomulka, Władysław, 699
Gomwalk, Joseph, 657
Gonatas, Stylianos, 396
Gonçalves, Antonino, 161
Gonçalves, Caetano, 64
Gonçalves, Carlos, 174
Gonçalves, João (Brazil), 160
Gonçalves, João (Sao Tomé e Príncipe), 777
Gonçalves, Landry, 170
Gonçalves, Sigismundo, 168
Gonçalves, Vasco, 706
Gonçalves, Waldir, 171
Göncz, Árpád, 416
Gondim, Pedro, 166
Gondra, Manuel, 687
Gondry, Henri-Ernest, 258
González, Carlos, 76
González, Felipe, 575
González, Hugo, 589
González, Ignacio, 295
González, José, 82
González, Juan, 686
González, Juan Torres, 141
González, Luis, 1072
González, Manuel, 573
González, Ovidio, 1068
González, Roque, 73
González, Salvador, 270
González, Santiago, 306
González Alocer, Alejandro, 576
González Beytia, José, 590
González Blanco, Salomon, 577
González Bravo, Luis, 816
González Cosío, Manuel, 586
González Curi, José, 576
González de la Vega, Francisco, 579
González Fernández, Vicente, 585
González Flores, Alfredo, 271
González Garrido, José Patrocinio, 577
González Herrera, Saul, 578
González Laxe, Fernando, 827
González López, Luis, 402
González Lugo Jesús, 578
González Macchi, Luis, 687
González Marquez, Felipe, 818

González Navero, Emiliano, 686, 687
González Parra, Emilio, 584
González Pedreo, Enrique, 588
González Viquez, Cleto, 271
González y González, Antonio, 816
Gonzalvo, Maxime, 337
Good-Adams, Hamilton, 91
Goode, Richard, 1098
Goode, William, 557, 787
Goodell, David, 1012
Gooding, Frank, 989
Goodland, Walter, 1041
Goodrich, James, 992
Goodridge, Augustus, 205
Goodwin, Ichabod, 1012
Goodwin, John, 976
Goodwin, Thomas, 91
Goold-Adams, Hamilton, 147, 803
Goonetilleke, Oliver, 830
Goosen, Pieter, 807
Gopal Singh, 429, 441
Gopallawa, William, 830
Goppel, Alfons, 369
Gorbach, Alfons, 107
Gorbachev, Mark, 730
Gorbachev, Mikhail, 716, 717
Gorbenko, Leonid, 746
Gorbunov, Igor, 720
Gordo, Adolfo, 173
Gordon, Elmira, 134
Gordon, James, 1003
Gordon, John, 987
Gordon, Pamela, 961
Gordon, Walter, 1046
Gordon Ordas, Felix, 819
Gore, Christopher, 1001
Gore, Howard, 1040
Gore, Michael, 963
Gore, Robert, 1045
Goremykin, Ivan, 714
Gorges, Howard, 610
Görgey, Artur, 415
Gorghulho, Carlos, 776
Goria, Giovanni, 480
Göring, Hermann, 384
Gorinov, Trofim, 733
Gorjão, Manuel, 604
Gorlori, Horacio, 75
Gorm (Denmark), 286
Gorman, Willis, 1004
Gorodovikov, Basan, 728
Gorokhova, Yevdokiya, 736
Gorraez, Juan, 586
Gorsira, Michael, 623
Gorton, John, 88
Goryachev, Yury, 753
Goshwami, B.K., 429
Gosper, John, 976
Goss, Wayne, 92
Gosse, Clarence, 206
Gossett, Charles, 990

Goto, Fumio, 503
Gottwald, Klement, 282, 283
Gotzen, Adolf von, 917
Goubert, Edouard, 457
Gough, Hugh, 958
Gouin, Félix, 328
Gouin, Jean, 211
Gouin, Lomer, 211
Goujon, Daniel, 780
Goujon, Denis-Joseph, 336
Gouland, Sasao, 592
Goulart, João, 149
Gouldsbury, Valesius, 764
Goulyan, Abram, 86
Gounaris, Demetrios, 395, 396
Gourbeil, Jules (Guadeloupe), 338
Gourbeil, Jules-Maurice, 339
Gourbeil, Jules (Senegal), 780
Gouttes, Bernard de, 347
Gouzden, Helvio, 73, 76
Govind Narain Singh, 427, 434, 437
Govorin, Boris, 745
Gowda, Haradanahalli Deve, 423, 435
Gowers, William, 937
Gowon, Yakubu, 635
Gozi, Celio, 772
Gozi, Federico, 770, 771, 772
Gozi, Gernino, 770
Gozi, Gino, 771, 772
Gozi, Girolami, 771
Gozi, Giulano, 774
Gozi, Giuliani, 771, 772
Gozi, Manlio, 771, 772
Gqozo, Oupa, 807
Graber, Pierre, 856, 906
Grabski, Władysław, 698
Graça, Carlos da, 777
Gračanin, Petar, 1092
Gradnauer, Georg, 374
Graeff, Andries de, 461
Graf, Beat, 861
Graf, Ernst, 888
Graham, Horace, 1036
Graham, Robert, 985
Graham, Samuel, 766
Graham, Stephen, 1043
Graham, William (UK), 44
Graham, William (USA), 1019
Grajales, Francisco, 577
Grajales Reynosa, Victorio, 577
Granada, Jorge, 76
Granados Roldán, Otto, 575
Grand, Lucien, 334
Grandi, Tarcisio, 488
Grandy, John, 965
Granero, José, 83
Granet, Paul, 331
Gräni, Alfred, 884
Granjo, António, 705
Grant, Henry, 565
Grant, James, 980

Grant, MacCallum, 206
Grant, Ronald, 103
Grant, Ulysses, 972
Grantham, Alexander, 245, 317
Grantham, Guy, 565
Granzow, Walter, 381
Grasset, Bernard, 348
Grassett, Edward, 958
Grasso, Ella (E. Tambussi), 982
Grasso, Giovanni, 482
Gratiant, Georges, 340
Gratz, Leopold, 111
Grau San Martin, Ramón, 277
Grauss, Alois, 111
Graves, Bill, 995
Graves, D. Bibb, 975
Gray, Isaac, 992
Gray, John, 209
Gray, Robert, 97
Gray, William, 766, 968
Grayson, William, 1000
Grazia, Ignazio, 770
Graziani, Rodolfo, 316, 796
Graziono, Matteo, 487
Greatbach, Bruce, 783
Grechukha, Mikhail, 940
Green, Anne, 969
Green, Daniel, 205
Green, Dwight, 991
Green, Fred, 1004
Green, Guy, 95, 96
Green, Hamilton, 408
Green, Harold, 969
Green, Peter (Pieter Groen), 969
Green, Robert, 1014
Green, Theodore, 1027
Green, Warren, 1030
Green George, 399
Green Nehemiah, 994
Greene, William, 1026
Greeneys, Christopher, 995
Greenfield, Herbert, 200
Greenhalge, Frederic, 1002
Greenidge, Carl, 18
Greening, Leslie, 67, 762
Greenly, William, 1003
Greenway, Thomas, 202
Gregg, Hugh, 1013
Gregg, Judd, 1013
Gregh, François-Didier, 598
Gregory, John, 1037
Gregory, William, 1027
Gregory-Hood, Peter, 962
Gregory IV (Pope), 1060
Gregory IX (Pope), 1062
Gregory-Smith, Henry, 793
Gregory V (Pope), 1061
Gregory VI (Pope), 1061
Gregory VII (Pope), 1061
Gregory VIII (Pope), 1062
Gregory X (Pope), 1062

Gregory XI (Pope), 1062
Gregory XII (Pope), 1063
Gregory XIII (Pope), 1063
Gregory XIV (Pope), 1063
Gregory XV (Pope), 1063
Gregory XVI (Pope), 1064
Gregson, Thomas, 96
Gregurović, Franjo, 275
Greiner, John, 1015
Greiner, Nick, 91
Greiser, Arthur, 701
Gremaud, Edouard, 871
Grenfell, Georges, 269
Grenville, George, 951
Grevy, Jules, 324
Grewal, Sarla, 436
Grey, George, 626
Grey, Ralph, 118, 407
Grey-Wilson, William, 118, 964
Grib, Mecheslav, 126
Grieder, Albert, 862
Grieshaber, Robert, 890
Griffin, Marvin, 987
Griffith, Arthur, 473
Griffith, Samuel, 91, 92
Griffith, Thomas, 762, 783
Griffiths, Thomas, 615
Grigg, Edward, 509
Griggs, John, 1014
Grignon, Gérard, 345
Grigolli, Giorgio, 488
Grigoreva, Lyuliya, 736
Grimald, Aimé (Central African Republic), 218
Grimald, Aimé (French Polynesia), 346
Grimald, Aimé (New Caledonia), 347
Grimani, Antonio, 497
Grimani, Marino, 498
Grimani, Pietro, 498
Grimani, Vincenzo, 492
Grimble, Arthur, 510, 766, 783
Grimes, James, 993
Grimes, Michael, 102
Grimes, William, 1023
Grimm, Robert, 867
Grimson, Franklin, 787
Grímsson, Ólafur, 419
Grinius, Kazys, 538, 539
Gris, Gabriel, 39
Grishchenko, Pyotr, 741
Griskevicius, Piatras, 540
Griswold, Dwight, 1010
Griswold, Matthew, 981
Griswold, Morley, 1011
Griswold, Roger, 981
Gritti, Andrea, 497
Grivas, Ioannis, 397
Grlichkov, Aleksandar, 545
Grobbelaar, J.H., 804
Grobet, Christian, 873
Grobler, Esaias, 804

Grodet, Louis-Albert, 336
Groendal, Benedikt, 420
Groesbeck, Alexander, 1004
Gröger, Florian, 108
Grollemund, Michel, 340
Grolmann, Karl von, 371
Gromyko, Andrei, 716
Gronchi, Giovanni, 478
Grondahl, Jan, 662
Groom, Raymond, 97
Groome, James, 1000
Gros, Roger, 335
Grosjean, Carlos, 881, 882
Gross, Gerald, 45
Gross, Marcel, 903
Grossu, Semyon, 595
Grosz, Károlyi, 417, 418
Grotewohl, Otto, 367
Groth, Leif, 289
Grout, Josiah, 1036
Grover, Lafayette, 1024
Groza, Petru, 708, 710
Gruber, Karl, 111
Gruening, Ernest, 976
Grujić, Sava, 1092, 1093
Grünenfelder, Emil, 888
Grunitzky, Nicholas, 923
Grushetsky, Ivan, 940
Gschwind, Hugo, 862, 863
Gu Xuilian, 239
Guadelupe Victoria, Manuel, 572
Guaita, Osvaldo, 73
Gual, Pedro, 1066
Gualco, Giacomo, 484
Guarasci, Antonio, 481
Guardia, Ernesto de la, 675
Guardia, Ricardo de la, 674
Guardia, Santiago de la, 674
Guardia, Tomás, 270, 271
Guazzelli, Sinval, 175
Gubbrud, Archie, 1030
Gubelia-Mezmariashvili, S., 361
Gudgeon, Walter, 627
Gudino Díaz, Manuel, 578
Gudunov, Boris (Russia), 713
Guedes, António (Brazil), 166
Guedes, António (Sao Tomé e Príncipe), 776
Guédès, Auguste, 345
Guedes, Duarte, 164
Guedes, Paulo, 429
Guéi, Robert, 273
Guel Jiménez, Francisco, 575
Güell y Morales, Gonzalo, 278
Guena, Yves, 273
Guerard, Benjamin, 1028
Gueret, Emilio, 78
Guerios, Hélio, 165
Gueritz, Edward, 557
Guerkov, Artemi, 362
Guerra, Alessandro, 483

Guerra, Henrique, 405
Guerra, José Gutiérrez, 141
Guerra, Paulo, 169
Guerrazzi, Francesco, 497
Guerrero, Anacleto, 584
Guerrero, José, 631
Guerrero, Lorenzo (Larry), 1045
Guerrero, Manuel, 1044
Guerrero, Osvaldo Alvarez, 80
Guerrero, Vicente, 572
Guerrero Gutiérrez, Lorenzo, 632
Guerrero Martínez, Alberto, 300
Guerrero Mendoza, Niceforo, 580
Guerrero Mier, Angel, 579
Guerrier, Philippe, 409
Guerzoni, Luciano, 482
Guevara, Gabriel, 580
Guevara Rodríguez, Aníbal, 402
Guggiari, José, 687
Guggisberg, Frederick, 390, 407
Guggisberg, Paul, 867
Guglielmo I (Sicily), 492
Guglielmo II (Sicily), 492
Guglielmo III (Sicily), 492
Gugloev, Georgy, 735
Gugushvili, Vissarion, 359
Guiberti, Raul, 157
Guichard, Olivier, 334
Guido, José, 70
Guilarte, Eusebio, 140
Guild, Curtis, 1002
Guilhon, Fernando, 165
Guillaume I (Luxembourg), 542
Guillaume II (Luxembourg), 542
Guillaume III (Luxembourg), 542
Guillaume IV (Luxembourg), 542
Guille, John, 956
Guillen, Fernando, 76
Guillen, Nestor, 141
Guillermo, Cesáreo, 295
Guimarães, Algacir, 168
Guimarães, Bernardino, 703, 705
Guimarães, Francisco, 171
Guimarães, Hosannah, 158
Guimarães, João, 776
Guimarães, José (Paranã, Brazil), 166
Guimarães, José (Rio de Janeiro, Brazil), 171
Guimarães, Manoel, 167
Guimarães, Protógenes, 172
Guimarães, Vitorino, 705
Guinand, Edmond, 881
Guinand, Jean, 882
Guinchard, Alfred, 881
Guinn, Kenny, 1011
Guion, John, 1006
Guisan, Lucien, 906
Guise, John, 676
Guise, Robert de, 339, 403, 456, 922
Guitart y Vilardebo, Justino, 62
Guitiérrez, Santos, 250

Guizado, José, 675
Guizot, François, 326
Gukasyan, Arkady, 116
Gukasyn, Arkady, 117
Gul, Peter, 683
Gul Aurangzeb, 666
Gul Mohammed Khan Jogezai, 666
Gulbuddin Hekmatyar, 55
Gumbaridze, Givi, 358, 360
Gumbs, Emile, 960
Gumede, Josiah, 1101
Gun-Munro, Sydney, 766
Gunderson, Carl, 1030
Gungaadorj, Sharavyn, 600
Gunn, John, 94
Gunter, Julius, 980
Gunthard, Alois, 910
Gunther Karl I (Schwarzenburg-Sonderhausen), 387
Gunther Karl II (Schwarzenburg-Sonderhausen), 387
Gunther (Schwarzenburg-Rudolstadt), 387
Guo Feng, 240
Guo Shuyan, 238
Guo Yingqin, 242
Guo Zhengqian, 238
Gupta, Banarasi, 431, 432
Gupta, Chandra, 450
Gupta, I.P., 453
Gupta, Radhika, 449
Gupta, Ram Prakash, 451
Gurbanovs, Anatolys, 525
Gurber, Karl von, 374
Gurenko, Stanislav, 942
Gurgel, Walfredo, 174
Gurjal, Inder, 423
Gurjâo, Rafael, 173
Gurmukh Nihal Singh, 445, 455
Gurnam Singh, 444, 445
Gurney, Henry, 550
Gurr, Andrew, 964
Gurria Ordoñez, Manuel, 589
Gürsel, Cemal, 930, 932
Gurtler, Alfred, 110
Gurtler, Paul, 863
Gürün, Kamuren, 7
Gurung, B.B., 447
Gusarov, Nikolai, 128
Guseinov, Aslan, 116, 117
Guseinov, Mirza, 114, 915
Guseinov, Panakh, 114
Guseinov, Rakhim, 114
Guseinov, Surat, 114
Gusev, I.S., 733
Gusev, Vladimir, 718
Guslyannikov, Vasily, 734
Gusri, 230
Gustaf I (Sweden), 850
Gustaf II Adolf (Sweden), 850
Gustaf III (Sweden), 850
Gustaf IV Adolf (Sweden), 850

Gustaf V (Sweden), 850
Gustaf VI Adolf (Sweden), 850
Gustafsson, Henrik, 321
Gustov, Vadim, 747
Gut, Walter, 879
Gutch, John, 793
Guterres, António, 706
Gutiérrez, Carl, 1045
Gutiérrez, Eulalio, 573
Gutiérrez, J. Bernabe, 1068
Gutiérrez, Jacinto, 1067
Gutiérrez, Jaime, 307
Gutiérrez, José, 582
Gutiérrez, Leonidas Plaza, 299
Gutiérrez, Lucio, 300
Gutiérrez, Tomás Monje, 141
Gutiérrez Barrios, Fernando, 590
Gutiérrez Cazares, Jesús, 588
Gutiérrez de la Concha, José, 816
Gutiérrez Ezetas, Ramón, 306
Gutiérrez Rincon, Efráin, 577
Gutiérrez Ruiz, David, 586
Gutiérrez Treviño, Eulalio, 578
Gutknecht, Max, 377
Gutnisky, Luis, 75
Gutorm (Norway), 659
Gutt, Camille, 45
Guy, Camille, 339, 341, 403, 780
Guy, Geoffrey, 293, 968, 970
Guy, William, 1020
Guyon, Claude, 344
Guyon, Marie-Casimir, 353, 546
Guyon, Marie-Joseph, 347
Guzhvin, Anatoly, 744
Guzmán, Carlos, 582
Guzmán, Felipe, 141
Guzmán, Fernando, 631
Guzmán, Horacio, 76
Guzmán, Horacio G., 75, 76
Guzmán, Juan, 306
Guzmán Fernández, Antonio, 296
Guzzetti, Giuseppe, 484
Guzzoni, Alfredo (Albania), 56
Guzzoni, Alfredo (Eritrea), 310
Gwadabe, Lawrence, 651
Gwadiso, Dumisani, 810
Gwinnitt, Button, 986
Gyainvain Norbu, 234
Gylling, Edvard, 730
Gylys, Vytautas, 540
Gysin, Remo, 866
Gyulmamedov, I., 115
Gyurme, 230
Gyurme Namgyal, 446

Haab, Robert, 855
Haakon I (Norway), 659
Haakon II (Norway), 659
Haakon III (Norway), 659
Haakon IV (Norway), 660

Haakon (Sweden), 849
Haakon V (Norway), 660
Haakon VI (Norway), 660
Haakon VII (Norway), 660, 662
Häberlin, Heinrich, 855
Habib Bourguiba, 927, 928
Habib Chatti, 31
Habib Makhtoum, 841
Habib Pasha el-Saad, 527
Habib Rahimtoola, 668, 669
Habib Thiam, 781
Habibe, Bacharuddin, 461
Habibu Shuaibu, 651, 654
Habibullah Ghazi, 53
Habibullah Khan, 53
Habidullah, Wajahat, 455
Habré, Hissène, 221
Habyalimana, Juvenal, 759
Hácha, Emil, 282
Hache, Claude, 877
Hackzell, Antti, 320
Haddon-Smith, George, 118
Hadik, János, 416
Hadley, Herbert, 1008
Hadley, Ozra, 977
Hadzić, Goran, 276
Hadzivasilev, Mito, 544
Haedo, Eduardo, 1049
Haegi, Claude, 873
Hafez al-Assad, 912, 913
Haffter, Arthur, 898
Hafizullah Amin, 54, 55
Hafner, Karl, 909
Hafstein, Jóhann, 420
Hagaman, Frank, 994
Hagerman, Herbert, 1016
Hagerup, Georg, 660
Häggblom, Alarik, 321
Haglelgam, John, 592
Hagood, Johnson, 1029
Hahn, Michael, 997
Haider, Jörg, 109
Haight, Henry, 979
Haildi Abderamane Ibrahim, 253
Haile, William, 1012
Haile Selassie (Ras Taffari Makonnen), 316
Hailu Yimenu, 316
Haines, Daniel, 1014
Haines, John, 990
Haines, William (Australia), 98
Haines, William (USA), 999
Hainisch, Michael, 106
Haksar, Kailas, 433
Haldipur, R.N., 425, 447, 456
Hale, Samuel, 1012
Hale, William, 1042
Halifa Houmadi, 253
Halil Rifat Paşa, 931
Halilov, Kurban, 113
Halim, 462
Hall, Carl, 287

Hall, David (Delaware, USA), 983
Hall, David (Oklahoma, USA), 1023
Hall, Douglas, 798
Hall, Floris van, 619
Hall, Fred, 995
Hall, Hiland, 1035
Hall, John (Delaware, USA), 983
Hall, John Hathorn, 1080
Hall, John (New Zealand), 626
Hall, John (Oregon, USA), 1024
Hall, John (Uganda), 937
Hall, Joshua, 998
Hall, Luther, 997
Hall, Lyman, 986
Hall, Raymond, 95
Hall, Robert, 785
Hall, Willard, 1007
Hall, William, 1031
Hall-Jones, William, 626
Haller von Hallenburg, Józef, 700
Hallgrimsson, Geir, 420
Hallstein, Walter, 17
Halonen, Tarja, 319
Halsten (Sweden), 849
Halvorsen, Otto, 661
Hama Amadou, 634
Hamad bin Khalifa al-Thani, 707
Hamad bin Mohammed al-Sharqi, Shaikh, 946
Hamad bin Rashid al-Mualla, Shaikh, 948
Hamad bin Said, Shaikh, 947
Hamad bin Said (Oman), 663
Hamad Karoui, 928
Hamaguchi, Osachi, 503
Hamaid bin Abdullah al-Qasimi, Shaikh, 947
Hamani Diori, 634
Hamber, Eric, 200
Hamdan bin Zaid al-Nahayan, Shaikh, 945
Hamdan Shaikh Tahir, 555
Hamdi Pachachi, 471
Hamed Ali, 122, 647
Hamed bin Ali al-Kalifa, 120
Hamed bin Isa al-Kalifa, 120
Hamed bin Thwain, 919
Hamer, Rupert, 99
Hamid Abbar, 536
Hamid Algabid, 31, 634
Hamid Khoja, 913
Hamilton, Andrew, 1033
Hamilton, Edward, 956
Hamilton, James, 1028
Hamilton, John, 991
Hamilton, Liam, 474
Hamilton, Paul, 1028
Hamilton, Thomas, 1000
Hamlin, Hannibal, 998
Hamm, John, 207
Hammer, Bernhard, 854
Hammerskjöld, Dag, 42
Hammerskjold, Hjalmar, 851

Hammerstein, Wilhelm, 379
Hammill, John, 993
Hammond, Abram, 992
Hammond, James, 1028
Hammond, Jay, 976
Hammond, John, 958
Hammond, William, 1005
Hammuda (Tunisia), 927
Hamon, Francis, 959
Hamoud al-Jaifi, 1078
Hamoud bin Mohammed, 919
Hampton, Wade, 1029
Hamrin, Felix, 851
Hams, Charles, 205
Hamzah bin Abdullah, 559
Han-gun, 513
Han Kyu Sol, 513
Han Nghi (Nguyen Ung Lich), 1073
Han Ningfu, 238
Han Xianchu, 234
Hanazono (Japan), 501
Hanbidge, Robert, 212
Hancock, John, 1001
Hancock, Otho, 962
Handley, George, 986
Handley, Harold, 992
Handu, Lionel, 682
Hanfield, Eric, 103
Hang Thun Hak, 192
Hanger, Mostyn, 91
Hänggi, Franz, 893, 894
Hänggi, Peter, 895, 896
Hanin, Charles-Émile, 354
Hanington, Daniel, 204
Hank González, Carlos, 582
Hanley, J. Frank, 992
Hanlon, Edward, 92
Hanna, Louis, 1020
Hannah, Colin, 91
Hannah, Timothy, 4
Hannett, Arthur, 1016
Hannett, Leo, 682
Hans (Denmark), 287
hansen, Clifford, 1042
Hansen, Hans, 288
Hansen, Roberto, 76
Hansenne, Michel, 44
Hanson, Edward, 1043
Hanson, Richard, 93
Hansson, Per, 851
Hanstein, Carl von, 380
Häntzschel, Kurt, 382
Hanumanthaiya, Kengal, 434
Hanzo, Yamanashi, 513
Haq, Fazle, 667, 668
Haqqi al-Azm, 912
Har Mande Singh, 452
Har Swarup Singh, 457
Hara, Takashi, 503
Harahap, Burhanuddin, 462
Harald I Blaatland (Denmark), 286

Harald I (Norway), 659
Harald II (Norway), 659
Harald II Svendsen (Denmark), 286
Harald III (Denmark), 286
Harald III (Norway), 659
Harald IV (Norway), 659
Harald V (Norway), 660
Haramija, Dragutin, 275
Harang, Bernard, 331
Harcourt, F.S., 67
Hardee, Carey, 985
Hardeknut (Denmark), 286
Harden, Charles, 1008
Harder, Josef, 897
Hardicanute (England), 949
Hardie Boys, Michael, 626
Harding, Francis, 203
Harding, John, 279
Harding, Stephen, 1034
Harding, Warren, 973
Harding, William, 993
Hardman, Lamartine, 987
Hardwick, Thomas, 987
Hardy, Arthur, 208
Hardy, Francis, 334
Harford, James (Antigua and Barbuda), 67
Harford, James (Saint Helena), 968
Harford, James (St Kitts and Nevis), 762
Hargrove, R., 962
Harihar Prasad Singh, 427
Harington, Charles, 965
Harlem Brundtland, Gro, 661
Harley, Joseph, 1029
Harmel, Paul, 131
Harmois, Jules, 337
Harmon, Judson, 1022
Harnisch, Paul, 891
Harnum, E. John, 205
Harold I Harefoot, 949
Harold II (England), 950
Harper, Charles, 968
Harper, Josiah, 1012
Harrach, Aloys, 492
Harriman, Averell, 1018
Harriman, Walter, 1012
Harrington, Emerson, 1001
Harrington, Gordon, 207
Harris, Andrew, 1022
Harris, Elisha, 1026
Harris, Godfrey, 969
Harris, Ishan, 1031
Harris, Joe Frank, 987
Harris, Lagumot, 615
Harris, Michael, 209
Harris, Nathaniel, 987
Harris, René, 615
Harris, Robert, 959
Harris, Thomas, 962
Harris bin Mohamed Salleh, 558
Harrison, Albertis, 1037
Harrison, Benjamin, 972, 1037

Harrison, C.S., 959
Harrison, David, 202
Harrison, Faustino, 1049
Harrison, Henry, 981
Harrison, James (Australia), 93
Harrison, James (Jersey), 958
Harrison, William, 972, 991
Harroy, Jean-Paul, 189
Hart, Herbert, 768
Hart, John (Australia), 94
Hart, John (Canada), 201
Hart, Louis, 1039
Hart, Ossian, 985
Hart, Reginald, 956
Hartley, Roland, 1039
Hartling, Poul, 288
Hartmann, Eduard, 109
Hartmann, Emil, 387
Hartmann, Georg, 875
Hartmann, Siegfried, 894
Hartness, James, 1036
Hartranft, John, 1025
Hartridge, David, 47
Harun bin Idris, 559
Haruna Bonnie, 640
Harvey, James, 994
Harvey, Louis, 1041
Harvey, Matthew, 1012
Harvey, Ron, 102, 103
Harvey, Wilson, 1029
Harwood, Charles, 1046
Hasan, Naeenuddin, 36
Hasan, Syed Nurul, 451, 452
Hasan Saka, 932
Hasani, Sinan, 1087
Haseth, A.W. de, 624
Haseth, Carl de, 623
Haseth, Willem de, 623
Hashar bin Maktum al-Maktum, Shaikh, 946
Hashem el-Atta, 835
Hashim al-Atassi, 911, 912
Hashim Jailul Alam Akamuddin (Brunei), 181
Hashimoto, Ryutaro, 504
Hasina Wajed, 122
Haskard, Cosmo, 964
Haskell, Charles, 1023
Haskell, Robert, 999
Haslauer, Wilfried, 110
Haslett, Joseph, 983
Hasluck, Paul, 87
Hasner, Leopold, 106
Hasquin, Hervé, 133
Hassan, Joshua, 965
Hassan al-Amri, 1078
Hassan al-Hakim, 912, 913
Hassan al-Tuhamy, 31
Hassan Bayoomi, 1080
Hassan bin Mohamed Salleh, 553
Hassan bin Yunus, 551

Hassan (Brunei), 181
Hassan Gouled Aptidon, 292
Hassan I (Morocco), 602
Hassan II (Morocco), 602, 603
Hassan Katsina, 637
Hassan Khalid Abulhuda, 505
Hassan Khan Moshir od-Dowleh, 467, 468
Hassan Khan Mostowfi al-Mamalek, 467, 468
Hassan Khan Vossuq od-Dowleh, 467
Hassan Makki, 1078
Hassan Mansur, 468
Hassan Nur-ud-din Iskander II (Maldives), 561
Hassan Sa'ad Ahmed, 840
Hassan Suleiman, 842
Hassan (Yemen), 1078
Hassanal Bolkiah (Brunei), 182
Hassel, Kai-Uwe von, 375
Hassenpflug, Hans, 380
Hastie, William, 1046
Hastings, Daniel, 1025
Haszard, Francis, 210
Hata, Tsutomu, 504
Hatfield, Henry, 1040
Hatfield, Mark, 1024
Hatfield, Richard, 204
Hathaway, George, 204
Hathaway, Sibyl, 957
Hathaway, Stanley, 1042
Hathi, Jaisukh, 444
Hathi, Jaisukh Lal, 431
Hatoyama, Ichiro, 503
Hatton, Steve, 102
Hau Pei-tsun, 247
Haughey, Charles, 474
Haultain, Frederick, 213
Haumant, Jean-Camille, 345
Haüpl, Michael, 111
Hausen, Max, 374
Hauser, Edwin, 874
Hauser, Franz, 865, 866
Hauser, Fritz, 864, 865
Hauser, Johann, 111, 888
Hauser, Samuel, 1008
Hauser, Walter, 854
Hausherr, Paul, 858
Hautpoul, Alphonse, 326
Havel, Václav, 281, 283
Havelock, Arthur (Australia), 95
Havelock, Arthur (South Africa), 802
Havemann, Benjamin, 803
Haverstock, Lynda, 212
Havieta, Chris, 679
Haviland, Thomas, 209
Havilland, Peter De, 956
Hawke, Albert, 101
Hawke, Robert, 88
Hawkesworth, Edward, 134
Hawkins, Alvin, 1031
Hawkins, William, 1018

Hawley, James, 990
Hawley, Joseph, 981
Hay, David, 676
Hay, James, 785
Hay, Marion, 1039
Hayashi, Senjuro, 503
Hayat Sherpar, 667
Hayatou, Sadou, 195
Hayden, John (Mike), 995
Hayden, William, 87
Hayder al-Attas, 1078, 1079
Haydon, John, 1043
Hayes, John, 96
Hayes, Rutherford, 972, 1021, 1022
Hayl Sagad, 315
Hayne, Robert, 1028
Haynes, Thomas, 966
Hays, George, 978
Haythorne, Robert, 210
Hayward, Sarel, 800
Hazar Khan Khoso, 666
Hazarika, Jogendra, 426
Hazen, John, 204
Hazif Ibrahim, 444
Hazzaa el-Majali, 506
Hazzard, David, 983
He Guoqiang, 235
He Zhiqiang, 243
He Zhukang, 237, 239
Head, Natt, 1012
Heales, Richard, 98
Healy, Timothy, 473
Heap, John, 961
Heape, William, 399
Heard, Stephen, 986
Heard, William, 997
Hearnes, Warren, 1008
Hearst, William, 208
Heartz, Frank, 209
Heath, Edward, 952
Heatley, David, 629
Heaton, Herbert, 964
Héber Usher, Alberto, 1049
Hebert, Paul, 997
Hedemann, Carl, 1046
Héder, Leopold, 337, 339
Hedi Baccouche, 928
Hedi Nouira, 928
Hedtoft, Hans, 288
Heemskerk, Jan, 619
Heemskerk, Theodoor, 619
Heemstra, Arnoud, 845
Heemstra, Schelte van, 619
Heer, Heinrich, 874
Heer, Joachím, 854
Heer, Joaquim, 874
Heffron, Robert, 90
Hefti, Hans, 874
Hefti, Melchior, 874
Hegde, Ramakrishna, 435
Hegedus, András, 417

Hegnenburg-Dux, Friedrich, 369
Hei Bole, 233
Heiber, Johannes von, 388
Heider, Otto, 370
Heil, Julius, 1041
Heim, Raymond, 340
Heine, Wolfgang, 377
Heinemann, Gustav, 366
Heinlein, Max Hussarek von, 107
Heinrich II (Reuss-Greiz), 384
Heinrich IX (Reuss-Greiz), 384
Heinrich LXII (Reuss-Schleiz), 385
Heinrich XI (Reuss-Greiz), 384
Heinrich XII (Reuss-Schleiz), 384
Heinrich XIII (Reuss-Greiz), 384
Heinrich XIV (Reuss-Schleiz), 385
Heinrich XIX (Reuss-Greiz), 384
Heinrich XLII (Reuss-Schleiz), 385
Heinrich XX (Reuss-Greiz), 384
Heinrich XXII (Reuss-Greiz), 384
Heinrich XXIV (Reuss-Greiz), 384
Heinrich XXVII (Reuss-Schleiz), 385
Heinrich XXXVIII (Schwarzenburg-Sonderhausen), 387
Heintzleman, B. Frank, 976
Heinze, Rudolf, 374, 375
Heinzer, Josef, 893
Heisbourg, Georges, 49
Held, Gustav, 374
Held Heinrich, 369
Heldt, Max, 375
Helfrich, Oscar, 621
Helg, René, 873
Hellpach, Willi, 378
Hellwege, Heinrich, 372
Helm, Alexander, 835
Helm, John, 995
Helou, Charles, 527
Helou, Esperidão, 177
Helweg-Larsen, Lars, 1046
Hely-Hutchinson, Walter, 801, 802
Hemming Augustus, 499
Hempstead, Stephen, 993
Hendee, George, 1035
Henderson, Alexander, 214
Henderson, Charles, 975
Henderson, J. Pinckney, 1032
Henderson, James, 1032
Hendricks, Thomas, 992
Hendricks, William, 991
Hendricks Díaz, Joaquín, 586
Hendrickse, Helenand (Allen), 801
Hendrickson, Waino, 976
Hendrie, John, 208
Henegan, Barnabus, 1028
Heng Samrin (Cambodia), 191
Henggeler, Josef, 909
Henggeler, Otto, 907
Hennessy, James, 134
Heno, Gau, 677
Henri (Enrique) I (Navarre), 823

Henri I (France), 322
Henri I (Haiti), 409
Henri II (France), 323
Henri II (Navarre), 823
Henri III (France), 323
Henri III (Navarre), 823
Henri IV (France), 323
Henri (Luxembourg), 542
Henri V (France), 324
Henrique (Portugal), 702
Henriques, Arturo, 704
Henriquez, Oscar, 621
Henriquez y Carvajal, Francisco, 296
Henry, Albert, 628
Henry, Eugène, 258
Henry, Geoffrey, 628
Henry, George, 208
Henry, Guy, 1045
Henry, John, 1000
Henry, Patrick, 1037
Henry, Yves, 344
Henry I (England), 950
Henry II (England), 950
Henry III (England), 950
Henry IV (England), 950
Henry V (England), 950
Henry VI (England), 950
Henry VII (England), 950
Henry VIII (England), 950
Henryk (Poland), 697
Hensley, Joseph, 210
Hepburn, Mitchell, 208
Heraika Izz-Eddin, 841
Hérard, Charles, 409
Herbert, Charles, 104
Herbert, Robert, 91, 92
Herbert, Thomas, 1022
Hercelles, Oswaldo, 692
Herdman, J. Mark, 963
Herencia Zevallos, Mariano, 689
Herivel, Sydney, 957
Herly, Jean, 598
Hermann, Alois, 907
Hermann, Willy, 889
Hermannsson, Steingrímur, 420
Hermoso Rojas, Manuel, 825
Hernández de la Torre, José Maria, 824
Hernández Gómez, Tulio, 589
Hernández Martínez, Maximiliano, 307
Hernández Netro, Mateo, 587
Hernández Ochoa, Rafael, 590
Hernández Piedra, Rafael, 579
Hernández Ros, Andrés, 828
Heros, Alfonso de la, 692
Herreid, Charles, 1030
Herrera, Dionisio, 631
Herrera, Enrique Olaya, 250
Herrera, Federico, 690
Herrera, José, 573
Herrera, Vicenta, 270
Herrera y Franch, Alberto, 277

Herrera y Luna, Carlos, 401
Herrera y Obes, Julio, 1049
Herrick, Myron, 1022
Herring, Clyde, 993
Herring, Edmund, 97
Herriot, Edouard, 327
Herry, Jacques, 344, 350
Herschler, Edward, 1042
Herseth, Ralph, 1030
Hertenstein, Wilhelm, 854
Herter, Christian, 1002
Hertling, Georg, 369
Hertling, Georg von, 366, 384
Hertzog, Enrique, 141
Hertzog, James Barry, 800
Herzog, Chaim, 475
Herzog, Roman, 366
Herzog zu Mecklenburg, Adolf, 922
Hesling, Frérédic, 186
Hess, Fritz, 46
Hessling, Hendrik, 624
Hesteren, Antonius van, 623
Heureaux, Ulises, 295, 296
Heuss, Theordor, 365
Heusser, Jakob, 909, 910
Heutsz, Johannes van, 461
Hevia, Carlos, 277
Hewitt, John, 627
Heydrich, Reinhard, 284
Heyward, Duncan, 1029
Hezba Ared, 314
Hezkeyas, 315
Hickel, Walter, 976
Hickenlooper, Bourke, 993
Hickey, John, 1042
Hickinbotham, Tom, 1080
Hickman, Albert, 205
Hicks, Henry, 207
Hicks, Thomas, 1000
Hidalgo, Ernesto, 580
Hiester, Joseph, 1025
Higa, Shuhei, 504
Higashiyama (Japan), 501
Higgins, Edward, 1034
Higgins, Frank, 1017
Higgins, James, 1027
Hikmat Suleiman, 471
Hilbe, Alfred, 537
Hildebrand, Josef, 907
Hildreth, Horace, 999
Hildyard, Reginald, 960
Hilfiker, Walter, 862
Hill, Clause, 957
Hill, David, 1017
Hill, Hugh, 970
Hill, Isaac, 1012
Hill, John, 999
Hill, Lionel, 94
Hill, Philip, 207
Hillery, Patrick, 474
Hilly, Francis Billy, 794

Hime, Albert, 802
Himmatsinhji, M.S., 432
Hincks, Francis, 198
Hindenberg, Paul von, 365
Hinds, Samuel, 408
Hinkle, James, 1016
Hintze-Ribeiro, Ernesto, 704
Hipolito, Abel, 705
Hiro, Joseph, 795
Hirohito (Japan), 502
Hironuma, Kiichiro, 503
Hirota, Koki, 503
Hirsch, Paul, 384
Hirschy, Pierre, 882
Hirtsiefer, Heinrich, 384
Hisamuddin Alam Shah, 559
Hisamuddin Amal Shah, 550
Hisham I (Córdoba), 822
Hitler, Adolf, 365, 366
Hnatyshyn, Ramon, 198
Ho-A-Chuck, Claude, 337
Ho Chi Minh (Nguyen That Thanh), 1073, 1074
Ho Hau-wah, Edmund, 246
Ho Ying-ch'in, 227
Hoadley, George, 1022
Hoard, William, 1041
Hoareau, Mario, 342
Hobbs, Allen, 1043
Hobby, William, 1033
Hoby, Gottfried, 889
Hoch, Edward, 994
Hochleitner, Albert, 110
Höchli, Alexander, 887
Hochoy, Solomon, 925
Hockenhull, Andrew, 1016
Höcker, Wilhelm, 372
Hodges, George, 994
Hodges, Jim, 1030
Hodgson, Frederick, 124, 407
Hodgson, Robert, 209
Hodgson, Stuart, 213
Hodson, Arnold, 390, 785, 964
Hodža, Milan, 283
Hodzhibayev, Abdurrahim, 915
Hoegh, Leo, 993
Hoey, Clyde, 1019
Hofer, Erwin, 891
Hofer, Hans, 887
Hoff, Philip, 1036
Hoffherr, René (Cameroon), 194
Hoffherr, René (New Caledonia), 347
Hoffman, Arthur, 854
Hoffman, Johannes, 369
Hoffman, John, 1017
Hoffman, Josias, 803
Hoffmann, Harold, 1015
Hoffmann, Johannes, 373
Hoffmann, Karl, 377
Hofman, Emil, 896
Hofmann, Hans, 910

Hofmann, Karl von, 371
Hofmann, Meinrad, 885
Hofmeyer, Gys, 610
Hofmeyr, Jan, 805
Hofstetter, Alfred, 860
Hoft, Willem Visser 't, 50
Hogan, Edmund, 99
Hogg, James, 1033
Hoghes, Luther, 1019
Högner, Wilhelm, 369
Höhener, Hans, 860
Hohenlohe-Ingelfuigen, Adolf, 383
Hohenlohe-Schillingfurst, Chlodwig, 366, 368, 384
Hohenlohe-Schillingfurst, Conrad von, 107
Hohenwart, Karl von, 106
Hohenzollern-Sigmaringen, Karl, 383
Hohl, Hans, 860
Holanda, Francisco de, 165
Holbrook, Frederick, 1035
Holcomb, Marcus, 982
Holcomb, Silas, 1010
Holden, William, 1019
Holder, Frederick, 94
Hole, Lois, 200
Holenstein, Thomas, 855
Holgate, Harry, 97
Holkeri, Harri, 321
Holl, John, 209
Hollamby, David, 968
Holland, Sidney, 627
Holland, Spessard, 985
Holley, Alexander, 981
Holliday, Frederick, 1037
Hollings, Ernest, 1030
Hollis, Alfred, 925
Hollister, Nancy, 1022
Holloway, William, 1023
Hollway, Thomas, 99
Holman,w, 90
Holmes, David, 1005
Holmes, Gabriel, 1018
Holmes, Robert, 1024
Holmes, Simon, 207
Holomisa, Bantu, 810
Holquín, Carlos, 250
Holquín, Jorge, 250
Holshouser, James, 1019
Holstein, Johan, 288
Holstein, Ludvig, 287
Holt, Harold, 88
Holt, Homer, 1040
Holt, Thomas, 1019
Holt, W. Elmer, 1009
Holten, R.M., 102
Holton, Linwood, 1037
Holubovich, Vsevolod, 941
Holyoake, Keith, 626, 627
Holzgetham, Ludwig, 106
Homberger, Ernst, 910
Honah Jang, 639

Hone, Evelyn, 1098
Hone, Herbert, 557
Honecker, Erich, 367
Honegger, Eric, 910
Honegger, Fritz, 856
Honey, DeSymons, 783, 848
Hong Hu, 239
Hong Ji, 514
Hong Song Nam, 516
Hong Yon Sik, 513
Honjong (Korea), 512
Honoré II (Monaco), 597
Honoré III (Monaco), 597
Honoré IV (Monaco), 597
Honoré V (Monaco), 597
Honorius II (Pope), 1062
Honorius III (Pope), 1062
Honorius IV (Pope), 1062
Honourat, Jean-Jacques, 411
Hood, Alexander, 960
Hoogenhout, Petrus, 610
Hoole, Alan, 968
Hoop, Joseph, 537
Hooper, Ben, 1032
Hoover, Herbert, 973
Hophan, Willy, 886, 887
Hoppin, William, 1026
Höppner, Reinhard, 375
Hormaechea Cazón, Juan, 826
Hormat bin Rafei, 559
Horn, Guyla, 417
Horn, Waldemar, 922
Horner, Henry, 991
Horner, John, 1003
Hornsrud, Christopher, 661
Hørring, Hugo, 288
Horta, Henrique, 216
Horta e Costa, José, 428
Horthy de Nagybánya, Miklós, 415
Horton, Henry, 1032
Hoskyns-Abrahall, Theodore, 637
Hossein Ala, 468
Hossein Mousavi, 469
Hosseinali Khan Nezam os-Saltaneh Mafi, 467
Hostein, Charles, 345
Hou Jie, 237
Hou Zongbin, 241
Houari Boumédienne, 60
Hough, Daniel, 611, 805
Hough, Henry, 1046
Houngbédjie, Adrien, 137
Houphouët-Boigny, Félix, 273
House, A. Maxwell, 205
Houser, Harold, 1043
Houston, George, 974
Houston, John, 986
Houston, Sam, 1031, 1032, 1033
Houtte, Jean van, 131
Houx, Frank, 1042
Hovey, Alvin, 992

Hovsepyan, Haik, 86
Howard, Benjamin, 1007
Howard, Daniel, 532
Howard, Edmund, 473
Howard, George, 1000
Howard, Henry (British Virgin Islands), 962
Howard, Henry (St Kitts and Nevis), 762
Howard, Henry (USA), 1027
Howard, John (USA), 1000
Howard, Joseph, 566
Howard, William, 1021
Howe, Joseph, 206, 207
Howe, Robert, 835
Howell, Richard, 1014
Howlan, George, 209
Howland, William, 207
Howley, Richard, 986
Hoxha, Enver, 57, 58
Hoxha, Fadil, 1094
Hoyles, Hugh, 205
Höynck, Wilhelm, 34
Hoyt, Henry, 1025
Hoyt, John (Arizona, USA), 976
Hoyt, John (Wyoming, USA), 1042
Hoyte, Desmond, 408
Hrach, Leonid, 943
Hrawi, Elias, 527
Hristić, Nikola, 1092
Hrivnak, Pavel, 789
Hrushevsky, Myhaylo, 940
Hrytsenko, Anatoly, 943
Hseih Tung-ming, 248
Hsi Tung, 224
Hsiao Tsung, 224
Hsien Tsung, 224
Hsinbyushin (Myanmar), 606
Hsiung Hsi-ling, 226
Hsu Chih ch'ang, 225
Hsu Shih-chang, 226, 228
Hsu Shih-ying, 227, 228
Hsuan Tsung (1425-35), 224
Hsuan Tsung (1820-50), 225
Hsuan T'ung, 225
Hu Fuguo, 242
Hu Ping, 234
Hu Qili, 244
Hu Wei-teh, 227
Hu Yaobang, 228
Hua Guofeng, 227, 238
Huaman de los Heros, Benjamin, 691
Huang Chieh, 248
Huang Hsin, 226
Huang Jingbo, 240
Huang Ju, 244
Huang Oudong, 240
Huang Yan, 234
Huang Zhizhen, 238
Huascar Inca (Tupac Cusi Huallpa), 693
Huayna Capac (Tito Cusi Huallpa), 693
Hubbard, Henry, 1012

Hubbard, John, 998
Hubbard, Lucius, 1004
Hubbard, Richard, 1033
Hubener, Erhard, 375
Huber, Alois, 901
Huber, Claus, 877
Huber, Hans, 859
Huber, Henri, 868
Huber, Hermann, 857
Huber, Karl, 901
Huber, Paul, 880
Huber, Rudolf, 901
Huber, Vernon, 1043
Huber, Werner, 901
Huchon, Jean-Paul, 332
Huckabee, Mike, 978
Huda, M.N., 123
Huddleston, Hubert, 835
Huender, Willem, 845
Huerta, Adolfo de la, 573
Huerta, Roberto, 73
Huerta, Victoriano, 573
Huerta Sánchez, Luciano, 589
Hug, Gottlieb, 890
Huggins, Godfrey, 1101
Huggins, John, 499
Hughes, Charles, 1017
Hughes, Harold, 993
Hughes, Harry, 1001
Hughes, Hubert, 960
Hughes, Louis, 976
Hughes, Richard, 1015
Hughes, Simon, 978
Hughes, William, 88
Huh Chung, 517
Hui Liangyu, 234
Hui Ti, 224
Hui Yuyu, 238, 239
Huith, M.J., 624
Huitzilhuitl (Aztec Empire), 574
Hukam Singh, 432
Hülgerth, Ludwig, 109
Hull, Jane Dee (J.D. Bowerstock), 977
Hull, William, 1003
Hulse, Heriberto, 176
Humada, Julio, 79
Humaid bin Abdel-Aziz al-Naimi, Shaikh, 946
Humaid bin Rashid al-Naimi, Shaikh, 946
Humayan (India), 421
Humayan Mari, 666
Humbert, Jean, 881
Humbert, Jean-François, 332
Hummel, Hermann, 378
Humo, Avdo, 144
Humphrey, Lyman, 994
Humphreys, Benjamin, 1006
Humphreys, John, 557
Hun Sen, 192
Hunag Fu, 226
Hundseid, Jens, 661

Hungerford, Ralph, 1043
Hunley, Helen, 200
Hunn, John, 984
Hunt, A. Cameron, 980
Hunt, Frank, 989
Hunt, George, 976, 977
Hunt, Guy, 975
Hunt, James, 1019
Hunt, Lester, 1042
Hunt, Rex, 964
Hunt, Washington, 1017
Hunt, William, 1045
Hunter, Archibald, 964
Hunter, John, 134
Huntington, Samuel (Connecticutt, USA), 981
Huntington, Samuel (Ohio, USA), 1021
Hunton, Jonathan, 998
Hunziker, Bruno, 858
Huo Shihlian, 233
Huo Shilian, 241
Huonder, Emmanuel, 876
Huonder, Johann, 875
Huq, A.K. Fazlul, 122, 123
Hurley, Charles, 1002
Hurley, Robert, 982
Hürlimann, Alois, 908
Hürlimann, Hans, 856, 908
Hurtado, Ezequiel, 250
Hurtado Larrea, Osvaldo, 300
Hurtado Miller, Juan Carlos, 692
Hurulle, E., 831, 832
Husain Bayoomi, 1079
Husak, Gustáv, 283
Husák, Gustáv, 789, 790
Husbands, Clifford, 124
Hüseyin Hilmi Paşa, 931
Hüseyin Rauf, 931
Husi, Fritz, 893
Husni al-Berazi, 912
Husni el-Zaim, 911, 912
Hussain, Zakir, 422, 427
Hussain al-Oweini, 528
Hussain bin Ahmad (Fadhli), 1081
Hussain bin Ali (Hejaz), 778
Hussain bin Ali (Kathiri), 1082
Hussain (Egypt), 302
Hussain Ershad, 121, 122
Hussain Maziq, 535, 536
Hussain Rushdi Pasha, 303
Hussain Zaki, 36
Hussaini Abdullahi, 644, 648
Hussein bin Onn, 551
Hussein bin Talal, 472, 505
Hussein I (Tunisia), 927
Hussein II (Tunisia), 927
Hussein Khalidi, 506
Hussein Mohammed Aideed, 797
Hussein Sirry Pasha, 304
Hussein Suhrawardy, 122, 664
Husseni, A.G., 640

Husson, Louis, 257
Huszár, Károlyi, 417
Hutchings, Hugh, 966, 970
Hutson, Eyre, 134, 317
Huxley, Julian, 46
Huxley, Roger, 968
Huxman, Walter, 994
Huy Kanthoul, 191
Huynh Tan Phat, 1075, 1076
Huysmans, Camille, 131
Hwaga Niyaz Heggi, 229
Hwang In Sung, 518
Hyde, Arthur, 1008
Hyde, Douglas, 473
Hyndman, F. Walter, 209
Hyojong (Korea), 512
Hyon Soong Jong, 518
Hyonjong (Korea), 512
Hyppolyte, Louis, 410
Hyzler, Albert, 566

Ia Vega, Agustín de, 83
Iazkuliev, Bally, 934, 935
Ibarra, Juan, 690
Ibarra, Matías Laborda, 81
Ibarra Autran, José de, 308
Ibarretxe, Juan José, 825
Ibiam, Francis, 636
Ibim Princewell, 643
Ibori, James, 644
Ibragimov, Gadzhi, 116
Ibragimov, Mirzoalim, 1051
Ibragimov, Rakhim, 719
Ibrahim, 551
Ibrahim, A., 651
Ibrahim Abboud, 835, 836
Ibrahim Abd ar-Rahman, 842
Ibrahim al-Hamadi, 1077
Ibrahim al-Hilaly Pasha, 304
Ibrahim Ali Didi, 562
Ibrahim Ali Didi (Maldives), 561
Ibrahim Alkali, 650
Ibrahim as-Sanussi, 839
Ibrahim Barry Mainassara, 633
Ibrahim bin Mohammed (Brunei), 182
Ibrahim Didi, 561
Ibrahim Edhem Paşa, 930
Ibrahim (Egypt), 302
Ibrahim Fikri bin Mohamed, 560
Ibrahim Hadi Pasha, 304
Ibrahim Hakimi, 468
Ibrahim Hakki Paşa, 931
Ibrahim Hamid, 839
Ibrahim Hashim, 505, 506
Ibrahim Ismail, 551
Ibrahim Maiyaki, 634
Ibrahim Mohammed Didi, 562
Ibrahim Mohammed Didi (Maldives), 561
Ibrahim Nasir, 561, 562
Ibrahim Nur-ud-din, 561

Ibrahim Shah, 551, 559
Ibrahim Shah (Kelantan), 553
Ibrahim Taiwo, 650
Ibrahim Turaki, 647
Ibrahim (Turkey), 929
Ibrahim Ubaydullah, 838
Ibrahimov, Ali, 114
Ibrahimov, Mehmet, 943
Ibrahimov, Mirza, 113
Ibrahimov, Veli, 943
Ibraimov, Jumabek, 522
Ibraimov, Sultan, 521, 522
Ibru, Felix, 643
Idam-Syuryun, 739
Idenburg, Alexander, 845
Idenbyrg, Alexander van, 461
Idiatullin, Revo, 739
Idris Garba, 642, 648
Idris (Libya), 534, 535
Idris Murshid ul-Azam Shah, 556
Idris Shah, 559
Idris Wakil, 919
Idrisa al-Mutawakil Allahi Shah, 556
Idriss Jazairy, 44
Iferle, S.O., 650
Igbinedion, Lucky, 645
Igić, Ljubisa, 1092
Iglesia, Julio Arroyo, 81
Iglesias, Miguel, 689
Iglesias Ricou, Marcolino, 824
Iglesias y Castro, Rafael, 271
Ignacio, José, 157
Ignatev, Pavel, 714
Ignatov, Nikolai, 714
Ignatov, Semen, 719, 720, 721
Ignatyev, Semen, 738
Igumnov, Gennady, 750
Ihova, Conway, 682
Ike Nwosa, 639
Ike Nwosu, 654
Ikeda, Hayato, 503
Ikonić, Branislav, 1093
Ikpeme, I.D., 652
Ikramov, Akmal, 1052
Iléo, Joseph, 259
Ilg, Ulrich, 112
Iliescu, Ion, 708
Ilin, Ilya, 595
Ilin, K.S., 720
Illia, Arturo, 70
Illingworth, Frederick, 100
Illueca, Jorge, 675
Ilyashenko, Kirill, 594
Ilyumzhinov, Kirsan, 728
Im Hof, Adolf, 864, 865
Imabud, Carlos, 84
Imamov, _, 915
Imashev, Sattar, 507
Imasiku, Akabeswa, 1099
Imaz, Francisco, 71
Imbert Barreras, Antonio, 296

Imbulana, P.C., 831, 834
Imfeld, Oskar, 886
Imranullah Khan, 666
Imre (Hungary), 415
Imrédy, Béla, 417
Imru, Mikhail, 316
Imwiko (Barotseland), 1099
In-sun (Korea), 512
In Tam, 192
Inayatullah Gandapore, 667
Inayatullah Khan, 53
Inca Roca, 693
Indalecio Madero, Francisco, 573
Indergand, Josef, 901
Indinok, Ivan, 749
Indjova, Reneta, 185
Indulf (Scotland), 953
Inestrona, Francisco, 412
Infanger, Eduard, 886
Inge I (Norway), 659
Inge I (Sweden), 849
Inge II (Norway), 659
Inge II (Sweden), 849
Ingersoll, Charles, 981
Ingman, Lauri, 319, 320
Ingraham, Hubert, 119
Ingstad, Helge, 662
Inienger, John, 644
Injo (Korea), 512
Injong (Korea), 512
Innes, Charles, 606
Innes, Frederick, 96
Innes, James Rose, 799
Innes, William, 214
Innih, George, 644, 650
Inniss, Probyn, 762
Innocent II (Pope), 1062
Innocent III (Pope), 1062
Innocent IV (Pope), 1062
Innocent IX (Pope), 1063
Innocent V (Pope), 1062
Innocent VI (Pope), 1062
Innocent VII (Pope), 1063
Innocent VIII (Pope), 1063
Innocent X (Pope), 1063
Innocent XI (Pope), 1063
Innocent XII (Pope), 1063
Innocent XIII (Pope), 1063
Inönü, Erdal, 932
Insfrán, Gildo, 75
Inukai, Takashi, 503
Inzhiyevsky, Aleksei, 729
Ionatana, Ionatana, 936
Ionescu, Take, 710
Ionnisyan, Ashot, 86
Iorga, Nicolae, 710
Iorio, A. Michele, 485
Ioseliani, Jaba, 358
Ipatas, Peter, 679
Ippolito de Medici (Tuscany), 496
Iqbal Khan Jadoon, 667

Irakli II, 358
Iredell, James, 1018
Ireland, John, 1033
Ireta Viveros, Félix, 583
Iriart, Flavio, 76
Iribarren, Guillermo, 77
Irigoyen, Hipólito, 70
Irigoyen, Manuel, 690
Irina (Russia), 713
Irklis, P.A., 730
Irniq, Peter, 214
Ironside, Edmund, 965
Irrazabal, Juan, 78
Irvine, William, 97, 98
Irving, Clifford, 958
Irwin, Jared, 986
Irwin, John, 976, 989
Irwin, Robert, 206
Irwin, William, 979
Isa, L.J., 647
Isa, Ramez, 622
Isa bin Ali, 1083
Isa bin Sulman al-Kalifa, 120
Isaac, Pierre, 350
Isaacs, Isaac, 87
Isabela I (Castile), 821
Isabella, Queen (England), 950
Isabella I (Spain), 814
Isabella II (Spain), 814
Isabella Maria (Portugal), 703
Isah Mohammed, 639
Isaiah Bol Riyani, 842
Isakayev, Bayab, 521
Isaksson, Martin, 321
Isanov, Nasirdin, 522
Isarescu, Mugur, 711
Isayev, Geidar, 116
Isayev, Uraz, 508
Isenschmid, Josef, 879
Ishak bin Lofti Omar, 553
Ishaya Bakul, 642
Ishayev, Viktor, 743
Ishibashi, Tanzan, 503
Isiaka Adeleka, 653
Iskander Mirza, 664
Iskander Shah, 556
Iskanderov, Akbarsho, 914, 916
Iskanderov, Mamed, 113, 114
Islam Shah (India), 421
Islamov, Ahmed, 1056
Islesias, Roberto, 78
Isliukov, Semen, 724
Ismael Omar Gelleh, 292
Ismail Amri Sued, 29
Ismail Chundrigar, 665, 667, 668
Ismail (Egypt), 302
Ismail el-Azhari, 835, 836
Ismail I (Iran), 466
Ismail II (Iran), 466
Ismail Muabidin Shah, 556
Ismail Nasiruddin Shah, 560

Ismail Petra (Kelantan), 553
Ismail Shah, 551
Ismail Shah (Kelantan), 552
Ismail Sidky Pasha, 303, 304
Ismailov, R., 115
Ismay, Hastings, 25
Ismayil Aymat, 233
Ismet Inönü, 930, 932
Ismet Shaqiri, 1094
Isogai, Rensuka, 245
Isombuma, Paul, 269
Isong, Clement, 643
Issat en-Noss, 913
Issuri Riancho, Dulce María, 591
Isturiz y Montero, Francisco, 816
Isturiz y Montero, Manuel, 815
István I (St. Stephen, Hungary), 414
István II (Hungary), 414
István III (Hungary), 414, 415
István IV (Hungary), 414
István V (Hungary), 415
Iten, Andreas, 908
Iten, Bonaventura, 908
Iten, Leo, 908
Ito, Hirobumi, 502
Ito, Masayoshi, 504
Iturbide, Augustin de, 572
Iturre, César, 83
Itzcóatl (Aztec Empire), 574
Ivan I (Russia), 712
Ivan II (Russia), 712
Ivan III (Russia), 712
Ivan IV (Russia), 712, 713
Ivan V (Russia), 713
Ivan VI (Russia), 713
Ivanov, _, 722
Ivanov, Boris, 745
Ivanov, G.A., 740, 741
Ivanov, Igor, 729
Ivanov, Nikolai, 730
Ivanov, Solomon, 721
Ivanov, Yuri, 730
Ivanova, Tatyana, 725
Ivanović, Bozina, 1090
Ivarato, Aita, 678
Ivashko, Vladimir, 941, 942
Iwakura, Tomomi, 502
Iyam, B.A., 645, 650
Iyasu I, 315
Iyasu II, 315
Iyasu III, 315
Iyasu IV, 315
Iyasu V, 316
Izard, Mark, 1009
Izetbegović, Alija, 143
Izzard, George, 977

Jaafar al-Askari, 470
Jaafar bin Hassan, 556
Jaafar bin Mansur (Kathiri), 1082

Jaafar bin Mohamed, 551
Jaafar el-Nemery, 835, 836
Jaafar Pishevari, 469
Jaakson, Jüri, 312
Jaberg, Ernst, 868
Jabir al-Ahmed as-Sabah, 519, 520
Jabir bin Abdullah as-Sabah, 519
Jabir bin Mubarak as-Sabah, 519
Jablónski, Henryk, 698
Jack, David, 767
Jackman, Henry (Hal), 208
Jackson, Andrew, 972, 984
Jackson, Charles, 1026
Jackson, Claiborne, 1007
Jackson, Ed, 992
Jackson, Eliha, 1000
Jackson, Frank, 993
Jackson, Frederick, 937
Jackson, Hancock, 1007
Jackson, Henry, 317, 925
Jackson, Jacob, 1040
Jackson, James, 986
Jackson, Wilfred, 407, 570, 918
Jackson, William, 965
Jacob, Jack, 429, 444
Jacob, John, 1040
Jacob, M.M., 440
Jacobs, Wilfred, 67
Jacobsson, Per, 45
Jacomini di San Lavino, Francesco, 56
Jacot, Maurice, 882
Jacquemont, Francis, 347
Jacques I (Haiti), 409
Jacques (Monaco), 597
Jada Zakariya, Henri, 837
Jadallah at-Talhi, 535
Jadeya, Digvijayasinhji Ranjit Singh, 460
Jadwiga (Poland), 697
Jafar Muadzam Shah, 556
Jaffar Sharif-Emani, 468
Jagan, Cheddi, 408
Jagan, Janet (J. Rosenberg), 408
Jagdeo, Bharrat, 408
Jaggi, Jean-Claude, 882
Jagland, Thorbørn, 661
Jagmohan, 429, 433, 454
Jagvaral, Nyamyn, 599
Jahan Dad Khan, 670
Jahandar Shah (India), 421
Jahangir (India), 421
Jahn, Rudi, 370
Jaichandra Singh, 439
Jaime I (Aragon), 820
Jaime II (Aragon), 820
Jain, Ajit, 435
Jain, Takhatmal, 459
Jaivanon, François-Adrien, 456
Jakeš, Miloš, 283
Jakeway, Francis, 317
Jakobson, August, 312
Jakopic, Albert, 792

Jalilov, Afetin, 116
Jaloustre, Georges, 597
Jam Ghulam Qadir, 666
Jam Sadiq Ali, 670
Jamal Bashaga, 536
Jamali, Taj Mohammed, 666
Jameel al-Hujilan, 20
James, Arthur, 1025
James, Edison, 294
James, Forrest, 975
James, Stanislaus, 765
James, Walter, 100
James, William, 1009
James I (Great Britain), 950
James I (Scotland), 954
James II (Great Britain), 951
James II (Scotland), 954
James III (Scotland), 954
James IV (Scotland), 954
James V (Scotland), 954
James VI (Scotland), 954
Jameson, Leander, 1100
Jamil al-Midfai, 471
Jamil al-Ulshi, 912
Jamil al-Ushi, 911
Jamil Mardam Bey, 912
Jamir, S. Chubatoshi, 442
Jammeh, Yahya, 355
Jampal Gyatso, 231
Jampel Tsultrim Tsemoling, 231
Jamshed bin Abdullah, 919
Jamshid Amouzegar, 468
Ján (Bohemia), 282
Jan I Olbracht (Poland), 697
Jan II Kazimierz (Poland), 697
Jan III (Poland), 697
Janab Asaf Ali, 442
Janak, Ignac, 790
Janak Singh, 433
Janakiraman, R.V., 457
Jane (England), 950
Jang, David, 642
Jang, Nawab Mehdi Mawaz, 430
Jang, Raja Bahadur Shamshir, 435
Jangsa Tsang, 232
Janklow, William, 1030, 1031
Janner, Adolfo, 899, 900
Janot, Raymond, 330
Janotti, José, 172
Jansen, Ernest, 799
Jansen, Gerhard, 383
Janson, Paul, 131
Janssen, Camille, 258
Jansson, Roger, 321
Jaquet, Edouard, 906
Jara, Albino, 687
Jardim, Alberto, 7076
Jardin, Roger, 877
Jardine, Douglas, 557, 785
Jarma, S, 642
Jaroszewicz, Piotr, 699

Jarov, Ali, 116
Jaruzelski, Wojciech, 698, 699
Jarvie, Thomas, 1019
Jarvis, Thomas, 962
Jas, Frans, 622
Jasari, Kacusa, 1095
Jasari, Sefcet, 1094
Jasim bin Mohammed al-Thani, 707
Jasokie, John, 442
Jaspar, Henri, 130
Jasper, Heinrich, 378, 379
Jasray, Punsagiyn, 600
Jatti, Basappa, 422, 434, 442, 456
Jau, Michel, 346
Jaunutis (Lithuania), 538
Jaup, Heinrich, 371
Jauregui, Rafael Zenon, 76
Javad Khan Sa'ad od-Dowleh, 467
Jawara, Dauda, 355, 356
Jay, John, 1016
Jayaram, Jayalalitha, 448
Jayaratne, Lesley, 833
Jayathilaka Podinilame, H., 833
Jayawardene, Junius, 830, 831
Jayawardine, Asoka, 832
Jayaweera, Siripala, 832
Jayawickrema, Montague, 832
Jayawickrema Perera, Gamini, 833
Jayne, William, 1020
Jean I (France), 323
Jean II (France), 323
Jean-Joseph, Alphonse, 340
Jean (Juan) I (Navarre), 823
Jean (Juan) II (Navarre), 823
Jean (Juan) III (Navarre), 823
Jean (Luxembourg), 542
Jeandrin, Nicolas, 456
Jeanne III (Navarre), 823
Jeanne (Juana) I (Navarre), 823
Jeanne (Juana) II (Navarre), 823
Jeanneret, François, 881, 882
Jeckell, George, 214
Jedrzejewicz, Janusz, 698
Jefferson, Thomas, 972, 1037
Jeffrey, Michael, 100
Jeffries, Richard, 1029
Jeftić, Desimir, 1093
Jeger, Franz, 895
Jelavić, Ante, 143
Jelks, William, 975
Jembibewon, David, 653
Jen Tsung (1424-25), 224
Jen Tsung (1796-1820), 225
Jenkins, Charles, 987
Jenkins, John, 94
Jenkins, Roy, 17
Jenkins, William, 1023
Jenks, Wilfred, 44
Jenni, Paul, 863
Jennings, Jonathan, 991
Jennings, Patrick, 90

Jennings, William, 985
Jennison, Silas, 1035
Jenny, Caspar, 874
Jenny, Kurt, 866
Jensen, Carlos, 83
Jensen, Carlos Fernández, 76
Jensen, Leslie, 1030
Jereissati, Tasso, 156
Jerome, David, 1003
Jester, Beauford, 1033
Jesús Liman, José de, 582
Jeter, Thomas, 1029
Jette, Louis-Amable, 211
Jevtić, Bogoljub, 1087
Jewell, Marshall, 981
Jewkes, Gordon, 964
Jha, Adity, 454
Jha, Binodanand, 427
Jha Lakshmi Kanth, 433
Ji Yunshi, 239
Jia Qinglin, 234, 244
Jia Qiyun, 243
Jia Zhijie (Gansu), 235
Jia Zhijie (Hubei), 238
Jiang Chunyun, 241
Jiang Jianglin, 240
Jiang Minjuan, 242
Jiang Weiqing, 239
Jiang Yizhen, 234
Jiang Zemin, 226, 228, 244
Jiang Zhuping, 238
Jiao Ruoyu, 244
Jibril Yakubu, 657
Jiménez, Enrique, 674
Jiménez, Gustavo, 689
Jiménez, Jésus, 270
Jiménez, José, 690
Jiménez, Juan, 296
Jiménez, Manuel, 295
Jiménez, Marcos Pérez, 1067
Jiménez Cantú, Jorge, 582
Jiménez Coronado, Joaquín, 761
Jiménez-Coronado, Joaquín Agulla, 603
Jiménez de Ashua, Luis, 819
Jiménez de Cisneros, Francisco, 814
Jiménez Delgado, Ramón, 587
Jiménez Morales, Guillermo, 585
Jiménez Oreamuno, Richardo, 271
Jiménez Ruiz, Eliseo, 585
Jin Asgad, 314
Jin Jipeng, 240
Jinjolia, Sokrat, 360
Jirgalang, 225
Jiří (Bohemia), 282
Jiro, Minami, 513
Joachim Ernst (Anhalt), 376
João I (Portugal), 702
João II (Portugal), 702
João III (Portugal), 702
João IV (Portugal), 703
João V (Portugal), 703

João VI (Portugal), 703
Joas, 315
Joas II, 315
Jobim, Válter, 175
Jobin, Francis, 202
Joel, Georg, 383
Joensen, Edmund, 289
Jofili, Irineu, 173
Joga, Vicente, 75
Jogaila (Lithuania), 538
Johan I Sverkersson (Sweden), 849
Johan II (Sweden), 850
Johan III (Sweden), 850
Johann Albrecht (Brunwick), 378
Johann (Saxony), 374
Jóhannesson, Ólafur, 420
Johanns, Mike, 1010
Jóhannsson, Kjartan, 16
Johansen, Lars Emil, 290
Johansson, Hugo, 321
John, Anapparambal, 435
John, Anapparambil, 447
John, Patrick, 294
John, Rupert, 766
John Balliol (Scotland), 954
John (England), 950
John IX (Pope), 1061
John Paul I (Pope), 1065
John Paul II (Pope), 1065
John VIII (Pope), 1060
John X (Pope), 1061
John XI (Pope), 1061
John XII (Pope), 1061
John XIII (Pope), 1061
John XIV (Pope), 1061
John XIX (Pope), 1061
John XV (Pope), 1061
John XVII (Pope), 1061
John XVIII (Pope), 1061
John XXI (Pope), 1062
John XXII (Pope), 1062, 1065
Johns, Charles, 985
Johnson, Andrew, 972, 1031
Johnson, Byron, 201
Johnson, Charles, 1080
Johnson, Daniel, 212
Johnson, Daniel (son), 212
Johnson, David, 1029
Johnson, Donald, 30
Johnson, Edwin, 980
Johnson, Francis, 202
Johnson, Frederick, 212
Johnson, Gary, 1016
Johnson, George, 202
Johnson, Henry, 997
Johnson, Herschel, 987
Johnson, Hilary, 532
Johnson, Hiram, 979
Johnson, Isaac, 997
Johnson, James, 987
Johnson, John, 1005

Johnson, Joseph, 1036
Johnson, J.W. Fordham, 200
Johnson, Keen, 996
Johnson, Leslie, 676
Johnson, Lyndon, 973
Johnson, Mobolaji, 650
Johnson, Paul, 1006
Johnson, Paul Jr, 1007
Johnson, Philip, 969
Johnson, Pierre-Marc, 212
Johnson, Thomas, 999
Johnson, Walter, 980
Johnston, Eric, 102
Johnston, Henry, 1023
Johnston, James, 207
Johnston, John, 979
Johnston, Joseph, 975
Johnston, Olin, 1029
Johnston, Peter, 959
Johnston, Rita (R. Leichert), 201
Johnston, Samuel, 1018
Johnston, William, 1025
Jojkić, Djurica, 1093
Joliat, Louis, 866
Joller, Remigi, 883
Jolly, Julius, 377
Jolo Boba, Charles, 842
Joly de Lotbinière, Henri, 200
Jonas, Franz, 106, 111
Jonassaint, Émile, 411
Jónasson, Hermann, 419, 420
Jonathan, Leabua, 530
Jonckheer, Ephraim, 622
Jones, Alfred, 206
Jones, Anson, 1032
Jones, Ben, 400
Jones, Brereton, 996
Jones, Daniel, 978
Jones, Glyn, 549
Jones, Gwilym, 966
Jones, J. Walter, 210
Jones, James, 1031
Jones, John, 1011
Jones, Lawrence, 957
Jones, Mervyn, 970
Jones, Robert, 977
Jones, Sam, 997
Jones, Thomas, 975
Jones, William, 1026
Jong, Petrus de, 620
Jong Beek en Donk, Jan de, 621
Jonge, Bonifacuis de, 461
Jonguitud Barrios, Carlos, 587
Jonnart, Célestin, 59
Jónsson, Emil, 420
Jordan, Chester, 1013
Jordan, Frederick, 89
Jordan, Len, 990
Jordan, Rudolf, 377
Jordan-Martin, A., 904
Jore, Léonce, 345, 347

Jore, Léoncre, 780
Jorédié, Léopold, 349
Jorge, Marcelino, 179
Jørgensen, Anker, 288
José (Portugal), 703
Josef I, 105
Josef II, 105
Joseph (Saxe-Altenburg), 385
Josephe, Noël, 333
Joshi, Harideo, 426, 446
Joshi, Kailash, 437
Joshi, Kumudben, 424
Joshi, Liladhar, 459
Joshi, Manohar, 438
Joshua, Ebenezer, 767
Joshua, Haggai, 681
Jospin, Lionel, 329
Joss, Fritz, 867
Joubert, François, 802
Joubert, Petrus, 804
Joulia, Joseph, 347
Jourdain, Maxime, 781
Jovanović, Aleksa, 1092
Jovanović, Blažo, 1089, 1090
Jovanović, Slobodan, 1088
Jovellanos, Salvador, 686
Jovellar, Joaquín, 817
Jovi, Borisav, 1087
Jovićević, Pavle, 1094
Joxe, Pierre, 330
Joy, George (Saint Helena), 968
Joy, George (Vanuatu), 1057
Jozeau-Marigne, Léon, 330
Ju De, 225
Jua, Augustine, 196
Juan Carlos (Spain), 815
Juan I (Aragon), 820
Juan I (Castile), 821
Juan II (Aragon), 820
Juan II (Castile), 821
Juanita (Castile), 821
Juanita (Spain), 814
Juárez, Benito, 573
Juárez, Carlos, 83, 84
Juárez Cisneros, René, 581
Juchen Thupten Namgyal, 232
Judd, Lawrence (American Samoa), 1043
Judd, Lawrence (Hawaii, USA), 988
Juddha Shumshere Jung, 617
Judge, Thomas, 1009
Julia, Marcel, 340
Juliana (Netherlands), 619
Julien, Gustave, 345
Julius II (Pope), 1063
Julius III (Pope), 1063
Jullien, Philippe-Émile, 341, 343, 345
Jumagulov, Apas, 522
Jumaliyev, Kabanychbek, 522
Jumaniyazov, Bahram, 1053
Juncker, Jean-Claude, 543
Jung, Ali Yavar (Nawab Jung Bahadur),
437
Jung, Philipp, 372
Jung Bahadur, 617
Jungers, Eugène, 189, 258
Junke, August, 378
Junod, Raymond, 906
Juppé, Alain, 329
Jurasevskid, Peteris, 526
Juri, Amado, 84
Jusić, Zlatko, 146
Justo, Agustín, 70
Justo, António, 297
Juvanon, François-Adrien, 343
Juvanon, Frédéric-Adrien, 336
Juxon-Smith, Andrew, 786

Kaahumanu, 988
Kaan, Wilhelm Edler von, 110
Kabaloyev, Bilar, 736
Kabanov, A., 943
Kabila, Laurent, 258
Kabin, Johannes, 313
Kabiru Gaya, 648
Kablan-Duncan, Daniel, 273
Kablova, Tamara, 363
Kaboré, Roch, 187
Kabua, Amata, 567
Kabua, Imata, 567
Kabui, Joseph, 682
Käch, Adolf, 879
Kachaznuni, Ruben, 85
Kachmazov, Anatoly, 363
Kaczorowski, Ryszard, 700
Kádár, János, 417, 418
Kadgiehn, O. (O. Kadgienas), 541
Kadri Paşa, 931
Kadyrov, Gayrat, 1052
Kafandaris, Georgios, 396
Kafarova, Elmire, 113
Kagama, Paul, 759
Kaganovich, Lazar, 942
Kageni, Dennis, 682
Kägi, Jakob, 909
Kägi, Walter, 889
Kahaya II (Ankole), 938
Kahn-Ackermann, Georg, 12
Kahn Mohammed Ibrahim, 671
Kahr, Gustav von, 369
Kahtan bin Omar, 1085
Kaidama, Elliot, 680
Kaidyshev, Yury, 737
Kaifu, Toshiki, 504
Kaine, Trevor, 101
Kairon, Partap Singh, 444
Kaisen, Wilhelm, 370
Kaiser, Adolf, 887
Kaiser, Werner, 894
Kajdomcaj, Hisen, 1094
Kak, Ram Chandra, 433
Kakfwi, Stephen, 214

Kakharov, Abdulakhhad, 915
Kakodkar, Shashikala, 429
Kalakaua (Hawaii) (David), 988
Kalangula, Peter, 614
Kalau, James, 641
Kalchenko, Nikifor, 941
Kalema (Buganda), 939
Kaliel, B., 641
Kalifa bin Sulaiman al-Kalifa, 120
Kalifa bin Sulman al-Kalifa, 120
Kalin, Ivan, 594, 595
Kälin, Karl, 892
Kalinin, Mikhail, 714, 716
Kaljević, Ljubomir, 1092
Kalkas, V., 541
Kállai, Guyla, 417
Kállai, Miklós, 417
Kallio, Kjösti, 319, 320
Kallsberg, Anfinn, 289
Kálmán (Hungary), 414
Kalnberzin, Janis, 525, 526
Kalogeropoulos, Nikolas, 395, 396
Kaloi, Richard, 349
Kalonji, Albert, 260
Kalpokas, Donald, 1058
Kalsakau, George, 1058
Kalsang Yeshi, 232
Kaltenbach, Jean, 331
Kalu-Igboama, J.A., 640
Kalume, Jorge, 150
Kalyan Singh, 451
Kamakeza, Mark, 794
Kamal Azfar, 670
Kamal Hassan Ali, 304
Kamaleddin Hussein, 304
Kamalidenov, Zakash, 507
Kamalov, Kalibek, 1053
Kamalov, Sabir, 1052, 1053
Kamalov, Timur, 1053
Kamaluddin (Brunei), 181
Kamamalu, Victoria, 988
Kamamga, Gregoire, 263
Kamara-Taylor, Christian, 786
Kamaruddin bin Mat Isa, 556
Kambanda, Jean, 760
Kambarov, Tursun, 1053
Kamberov, Isa, 113
Kambola, Henri Ndala, 265
Kamehameha, Lot, 988
Kamehameha (Hawaii) (Lot Kamehameha), 988
Kamehameha I (Hawaii) (Paiea), 988
Kamehameha II (Hawaii) (Liholiho), 988
Kamehameha III (Hawaii) (Kauikeaouli), 988
Kamehameha IV (Hawaii) (Alexander Liholiho), 988
Kamenev, Lev, 713
Kamensky, Mikhail, 522
Kamil Idris, 47
Kamio, John, 656

Kamitatu, Cleophas, 266
Kampani, M.L., 425, 453
Kampmann, Viggo, 288
Kamruddin bin Idria, 560
Kamwanga, Sebastiaan, 613
Kanakarratne, Neville, 833
Kanaris, Konstantinos, 392, 394, 395
Kanatchikov, Semen, 738
Kane, Falilou, 29
Kane, Richard, 793
Kanellopoulos, Panayotis, 396, 397
Kang, Sukhdev Singh, 435
Kang Jianmen, 233
Kang Sheng, 241
Kang Song San, 515
Kang Teh, 230
Kang Young Hoon, 518
Kanga, Ignace, 266
Kania, Stanisław, 699
Kankulov, Masha, 726
Kannamwar, Marotrao, 438
Kanshal, Jagan, 427
Kant, Krishna, 424, 448
Kanthi, Shivalingappa, 434
Kanu, G., 646
Kanungo, Sityanand, 427, 430
Kanwar Bahadur Singh, 432
Kany, Sultanmurad, 1055
Kanyenkiko, Anatole, 189
Kao Lin-wei, 228
Kao Tsung, 225
Kapal, Philip, 684
Kapeistov, Anatoly, 742
Kapeliele Tufele dit Setu, 352
Kapetanović, Izudin, 146
Kapi, Don, 679
Kapodistrias, Augustinos, 392
Kapodistrias, Ioannis, 392
Kapour, Vijay, 454
Käppeli, Gottlieb, 857
Kappeyne van de Coppello, Johannes, 619
Kapur, Hari Krishnan, 454
Karabegović, Osman, 144
Karadžić, Radovan, 145
Karaglu, Koch, 1055
Karall, Lorenz, 108
Karam, Antoine, 337
Karamanlis, Konstantinos, 393, 397
Karamanov, Uzabakay, 508
Karamayev, Mikhail, 718
Karapetyan, Saak, 86
Karasek, Franz, 12
Karava, Sepoe, 679
Karavayev, A.V., 740
Karavelov, Petko, 183, 184
Karayev, Djuma, 934, 935
Kardanov, Z.K., 729
Karel (Bohemia), 282
Karemera (Rwanda), 759
Karibzhanov, Fazyl, 507
Karimov, Abdullah, 1051

Karimov, Islam, 1051, 1052
Karimov, Jamshed, 915
Karimov, M.S., 719
Karinyan, Artashes, 85
Karjalainen, Ahti, 320
Karkhutdinov, Igor, 751
Karl August (Nassau), 382
Karl (Austria, Emperor), 105
Karl (Baden), 377
Karl Eduard (Saxe-Coburg-Gotha), 385
Karl Friedrich (Baden), 377
Karl I (Austria), 105
Karl I (Brunswick), 378
Karl I (Norway), 660
Karl II (Austria), 105
Karl II (Brunswick), 378
Karl II (Norway), 660
Karl III (Brunswick), 378
Karl III (Norway), 660
Karl (Mecklenburg-Strelitz), 382
Karl (Nassau), 382
Karl (Norway), 660
Karl (Schwarzenburg-Sonderhausen), 387
Karl (Württemberg), 388
Károly, Guyla, 417
Károlyi, Mihály, 415
Károlyi I (Hungary), 415
Károlyi II (Hungary), 415
Karotamm, Nikolai, 313
Karpov, Ivan, 728
Karpov, Vladimir, 745
Karryev, Chary, 935
Karsunsky, Boris, 742
Kartawisjaja, Djuanda, 462
Kartelishvili, Lavrenti, 944
Kartvelishvili, Dmitri, 359
Kartvelishvili, Lavrenti, 358, 359
Karunakaran, Kannoth, 436
Karunanidhi, Muthuvel, 448
Kas, Jim, 680
Kasabuvu, Joseph, 258
Kasagić, Rajko, 145
Kasdi Merbah, 60
Kasenda, Mpinga, 259
Kaseng, Isidore, 684
Kashamura, Anicet, 265
Kashim Ibrahim, 637
Kashiwabara II (Japan), 501
Käslin, Hans-Peter, 884
Kassem Rimawi, 506
Kasteel, Petrus, 621
Kasumov, Mir, 113
Kasyan, Sargis, 85, 86
Kasyanov, Mikhail, 715
Katanandov, Serrgei, 730
Katay Sasorith, 523
Katayama, Tetsu, 503
Katayev, Yevgeny, 732
Katea, Mikaele, 351
Katjiuongua, Moses, 611
Katju, Kailas, 437

Katju, Kailash, 442
Katju, Kailish, 451
Kato, Takaaki, 503
Kato, Tomosabura, 503
Katschthaler, Hans, 110
Katsura, Taro, 502, 503
Katzir, Ephraim (E. Katchalsky), 475
Kauffmann, Léon, 542
Kaufman, Max, 863
Kaufmann, Hans, 894
Kaul, Sheila, 432
Kaunda, Kenneth, 1098
Kaushal, Swaraj, 441
Kavalerov, Timofei, 732
Kavanaugh, Edward, 998
Kavčič, Stane, 791
Kavtaradze, Sergei, 359
Kavunzu, Belunda, 267
Kavuvu, Demas, 681
Kawa, Tsewing, 138
Kay-Mouat, Jon, 957
Kayibanda, Gregoire, 759
Kayode Olukimo, 652
Kaysone Phomvihan, 523, 524
Kazadi, Ferdinand, 260
Kazakov, Arishtarkh, 1055
Kazakpayav, Abdisamat, 507
Kazanets, Ivan, 941
Kazhageldin, Akezhan, 508
Kazi Zafar Ahmed, 122
Kazimierz I (Poland), 696
Kazimierz II (Poland), 696
Kazimierz III (Poland), 697
Kazimierz IV (Poland), 697
Kazimierz (Lithuania), 538
Kazushige, Ugaki, 513
Ke Qingshi, 244
Kean, Thomas, 1015
Keating, Frank, 1023
Keating, Paul, 88
Kebich, Vyacheslav, 127
Kebreau, Antoine, 410
Kećmanović, Vojslav-Djedo, 143
Keel, Valentin, 888
Keenleyside, Hugh, 213
Keightley, Charles, 965
Keishang, Rishang, 439
Keita, Ibrahim, 564
Keita, Modibo, 564, 782
Kekauiouhi, M.A., 988
Kekkonen, Urho, 319, 320
Kekuanaoa, Mataio, 988
Keletaona, Keletaona, 351
Keletaona, Nasalio, 351
Keletaona, Sagato, 351
Keletaono, Alafosio, 351
Keller, Emil, 857, 858
Keller, Eugen, 866
Keller, Gustav, 909
Keller, Hermann, 892
Keller, Jakob, 890

Keller, Werner, 884, 885
Kellogg, Edward, 1043
Kellogg, William, 997
Kelly, Harry, 1004
Kelly, John, 970
Kelzang Gyatso, 230
Kemal Vlora, Ismail, 57
Kemchik-ool, 739
Kempenaer, Jacob de, 619
Kemper, James, 1037
Kempný, Josef, 281
Kempthorne, Dirk, 990
Kendall, C.B., 968
Kendall, H. Ernest, 206
Kendall, Nathan, 993
Kendrew, Douglas, 100
Kendrick, John, 1042
Kengava, Clement, 794
Kengo Wa Dondo (Léon Kengo), 259
Kenilorea, Peter, 794
Kennedy, John, 973
Kennedy, John (Zimbabwe), 1100
Kennedy, Thomas, 208
Kennedy-Cooke, Brian, 310
Kennel, Karl, 879
Kennerley, Alfred, 96
Kenneth I MacAlpin (Scotland), 953
Kenneth II (Scotland), 953
Kenneth III (Scotland), 953
Kennett, Jeffrey, 99
Kennon, Robert, 997
Kent, Edward, 998
Kent, John, 205
Kent, Joseph, 1000
Kenyatta, Jomo (Kamau wa Ngenge), 509
Kephas, I., 643, 644
Kerekou, Mathieu, 137
Kerensky, Aleksandr, 715
Kerferd, George, 98
Kerimbayev, Daniyal, 507
Kerimov, Musa, 722
Kern, Heinrich, 908
Kerner, Otto, 991
Kernmaier, Ferdinand, 109
Kerr, Alan, 104
Kerr, John, 87
Kerr, Robert, 1023
Kerrey, Robert, 1010
Kery, Theodor, 108
Kessler, Alfred, 888
Kessler, Bruno, 488
Kessler, Herbert, 112
Kessler, Philip, 343
Kestutis (Lithuania), 538
Ketskhoveli, Z, 359
Kevorkov, Boris, 117
Kewal Singh, 456
Keyes, Henry, 1013
Keyser, F. Ray, 1036
Kgosiemang, Constance, 614
Khabarov, Vladimir, 756

Khabibullayev, Pulat, 1051
Khabibullin, Ravmer, 720
Khachmandanov, _, 737
Khadzhiyev, Salambek, 722
Khai Dinh (Nguyen Buu Dao), 1073
Khair al-Ahdab, 528
Khakholov, Aleksandr, 720, 721
Khakhva, Tengiz, 362
Khaleda Zia, 122
Khalid al-Azm, 912, 913
Khalid bin Abdul-Azaz (Saudi Arabia), 778
Khalid bin Ahmed al-Qasimi, Shaikh, 947
Khalid bin Mohammed al-Qasimi, Shaikh, 947
Khalid bin Saud, 779
Khalid bin Sultan al-Qasimi, Shaikh, 947
Khalid Chehab, 528
Khalid (Tanzania), 919
Khalifa bin Barghash, 919
Khalifa bin Hamad al-Thani, 707
Khalifa bin Harub, 919
Khalifa bin Shakbut al-Nahayan, Shaikh, 945
Khalifa bin Zaid al-Nahayan, Shaikh, 946
Khalikov, M., 719
Khama, Seretse, 147
Khamchiyev, Belan, 726
Khamtai Siphandon, 523, 524
Khan, A.R., 666
Khan, Barkatullah, 446
Khan, H.K., 453
Khan, Khurshid Alam, 434, 435
Khan, M. Nur, 671
Khan Abdul Qayum Khan, 667
Khan Bahadur Allah Baksh, 670
Khan Choi, Fath Ali, 114
Khan Hamidullah Khan, 671
Khan Iftikar Hussein, 669
Khan Iftikhar Hussein, 669
Khan Rahimuddin, 670
Khan Saheb, 671
Khanbabayev, Shamsaddin, 116
Khandjyan, Aghasi, 86
Khanna, Tejendra, 454
Khare, N.B., 437
Kharitonov, Yevgeny, 743
Khatayevich, Mendel, 738
Khatissyan, Aleksander, 85
Khattak, Aslam, 667
Khawaja Mohammed Azhar Khan, 667
Khawaja Nazimuddin (East Pakistan), 123, 664
Khawaja Shahabuddin, 667
Khayayev, Izatullo, 915
Khayeyev, Izatullo, 916
Khendrup Gyatso, 231
Khenrab Wangchuk Dedrug, 231
Kher, B.G., 458
Khetagurov, Sergei, 735
Khetagurova, Tamara, 735
Khider, Akli, 343

Khieu Samphan, 191, 193
Khim Tit, 191
Khishby, Vladimir, 361
Khodhayev, Mumin, 915
Khodzha, Temur, 1055
Khodzhamuradov, Annamurad, 935
Khodzhan, Sultan, 508
Khodzhayev, Fayzulla, 1051, 1054
Khodzhayev, Mumin, 915
Khodzhayev, Nizam, 1055, 1056
Khokhlov, Ivan, 715
Kholov, Makhmadullo, 914
Khomutnikov, V.A., 1053
Khomutnikov, Vasily, 727
Khondakar Mushtaq Ahmed, 121
Khosla, Ayudhia, 442
Khrishna, S.M., 435
Khrishtof, G., 361
Khrissate, Kamel, 344
Khrushchev, Nikita, 716, 717, 941, 942
Khubayev, Vladimir, 729
Khubulov, Valery, 363
Khuda Bux Marri, 666
Khudaiberdyov, Narmakhonmadi, 1052
Khudaibergenov, Aitbay, 934
Khudayberdin, Shagit, 719
Khudyayev, Vyacheslav, 732
Khuen-Héderváry, Károly, 416
Khurana, Madan Lal, 455
Khurana, Sundar, 448, 454, 456
Khurshid Alam Khan, 429
Khurshid Ali Khan, 667
Khurshid Hasan Khurshid, 671
Khut, Malich, 717
Khwaja Ahmed Tariq Rahman, 668
Khwaja Shamsuddin, 433
Kibbelaar, Anno, 623
Kibbey, Joseph, 976
Kidrić, Boris, 791, 792
Kidston, William, 92
Kidwai, Akhaq, 427, 452
Kieber, Walter, 537
Kielmansegg, Erich, 107
Kielmansegg-Gulzow, Eduard, 379
Kielstra, Johannes, 845
Kien Phuc (Nguyen Ung Dang), 1073
Kiesinger, Kurt-Georg, 366, 368
Kigeri III (Rwanda), 759
Kigeri IV (Rwanda), 759
Kigeri V (Rwanda), 759
Kiggell, Launcelot, 956
Kihuyu, Étienne, 263
Kikalango, Jean-Marie, 262
Kilage, Ignatius, 676
Kilby, Thomas, 975
Kilganov, L.K., 727
Killinger, Manfred von, 375
Kiloe, Jackson, 794
Kim, Kurt, 858
Kim Chong Pil, 517, 518
Kim Chong Yul, 518

Kim Dae Jung, 517
Kim Du Bon, 515
Kim Gu, 514
Kim Hong Jip, 513
Kim Hyun Chul, 517
Kim Il, 515
Kim Il Sung (Kim Sung Choo), 515, 516
Kim Jong Il, 516
Kim Pyong Sik, 515
Kim Sang Hyup, 518
Kim Sun-won Whang ho, 512, 513
Kim Yong Ju, 515
Kim Yong Nam, 515
Kim Young Sam, 517
Kimave, Riddler, 679
Kimba, Everiste, 259
Kimball, Charles, 1027
Kin Hassan bin Nik Abdul Rahman, 560
Kinau, 988
King, Alvin, 997
King, Angus, 999
King, Austin, 1007
King, Bruce, 1016
King, Charles (Australia), 103
King, Charles (Liberia), 532
King, Cyril, 1046
King, Edward, 1003
King, George, 204
King, John (New Hampshire, USA), 1013
King, John (New York, USA), 1017
King, Kurleigh, 6
King, Leslie, 615
King, Merton, 1057
King, Samuel (Hawaii, USA), 989
King, Samuel (Rhode Island), 1026
King, William, 998
King-Harman, Charles, 764, 785
Kingston, Charles, 94
Kinigi, Sylvie, 189
Kinkead, John, 1011
Kinley, J. James, 207
Kinnear, Ian, 960
Kintu, Michael, 939
Kiosseivanov, Georgi, 184
Kioussopoulos, Demetrios, 397
Kipo, Paul, 677
Kirchensteins, August, 525, 526
Kirchner, Nestor, 83
Kirchschläger, Rudolf, 106
Kirichenko, Aleksei, 942
Kirimir, Jafar Seydahmet, 943
Kiriyenko, Sergei, 715
Kirk, Claude, 985
Kirk, Norman, 627
Kirker, Thomas, 1021
Kirkpatrick, George, 208
Kirkwood, Samuel, 993
Kirman, Richard, 1011
Kirner, Joan, 99
Kirov, Sergei, 114
Kirtinidhi Bista, 617

Kirzhanov, Nikolai, 730
Kisanga, Hilaire, 266
Kiselyev, N.M., 718
Kiselyov, Tikhon, 127, 128
Kishan, Ram, 444
Kishi, Nobusuke (N. Sato), 503
Kisialev, Kuzma, 127
Kislitsyn, Vyacheslav, 733
Kislyuk, Mikhail, 746
Kisseka, Samson, 938
Kistler, Heinrich, 893
Kiszczak, Czesław, 699
Kitbelle, Sumner, 1046
Kitchener, Frederick, 960
Kitchin, William, 1019
Kithahimbwa (Bunyoro), 939
Kitovani, Tengizviad, 358
Kittermaster, Harold, 134, 549, 798
Kitticachorn, Thanom, 920, 921
Kitzhaber, John, 1024
Kivimaki, Toivo, 320
Kiwanuka, Benedicto, 938
Kiwewa Mutabi II (Buganda), 939
Kiyoura, Keigo, 503
Klaasesz, Jan, 845
Klagges, Dietrich, 379
Klasnic, Waltraud, 110
Klaus, Gottfried, 895
Klaus, Johann, 107
Klaus, Josef, 106, 110
Klaus, Václav, 281
Klausson, Valther, 313
Kläy, Alfred, 867
Klein, Ralph, 200
Kleiner, Marianne, 860
Kleinubing, Vilson, 177
Kleppe, Per, 16
Klerk, Frederik de, 800
Klerk, Jan de, 800
Kleschev, Aleksei, 127
Klestil, Thomas, 106
Klibi, Chedli, 22
Klićković, Gojko, 145
Klima, Viktor, 108
Klimenko, F.T., 742
Kliment, Archbishop Vasil, 184
Klimmt, Reinhard, 374
Klimovski, Savo, 544
Klinte, Bent, 289
Kljusev, Nikola, 545
Klose, Hans-Ulrich, 371
Kluber, Friedrich, 377
Klutsé, Kwassi, 923
Klychev, Annamuchamed, 934
Kmezić, Nikola, 1096
Kneip, Richard, 1030
Knight, Goodwin, 979
Knight, Henry, 607
Knight, Nehemiah, 1026
Knilling, Eugen von, 369
Knischnik, Armando, 73

Knolek, Iván, 789
Knollys, Francis, 960
Knorinsh, Wilgelm, 127
Knorr, R. Willi, 377
Knott, J. Proctor, 996
Knous, William, 980
Knowles, Tony, 976
Knowles, Warren, 1041
Knud I (Denmark), 286
Knud II (Denmark), 286
Knud II (Sweden), 849
Knud III (Denmark), 286
Knud IV (Denmark), 286
Knudsen, Gunnar, 661
Knüsel, Alois, 893
Knusel, Josef, 907
Knüsel, Melchior, 853
Knüsel, Peter, 879
Knut I Eriksson (Sweden), 849
Knutsson, Carl, 850
Knutsson, Torgils, 849
Kobakhiya, Valerian, 360, 361
Kobelt, Karl, 855, 888
Kobozev, Petr, 1055
Koch, Adolf, 896, 897
Koch, Hermann, 380
Koch, Roland, 372
Kocharyan, Robert, 85, 86, 116
Kochetov, Andrei, 730
Kochinyan, Anton, 86
Kochlamuzaashvili, Iosef, 362
Kochubei, Viktor, 714
Koditsa, Ivan, 594
Kodituwakku, Karunasena, 832
Kodjo, Edem, 27, 923
Koellreuter, Andreas, 864
Koffigoh, J. Kokou, 923
Kogălniceanu, Mihai, 709
Koh Kun, 518
Koh Tsu Koon, 555
Kohl, Helmut, 366, 373
Köhler, August, 922
Köhler, Heinrich, 378
Köhler, Horst, 45
Kohler, Pierre, 877
Kohler, Simon, 868
Kohler, Urs, 908
Köhler, Walter, 378
Kohler, Walter Jr, 1041
Kohler, Walter Sr, 1041
Kohli, Dalip, 439, 454
Kohli, S.N., 440
Koimanrea, Francis, 678
Koiso, Kuniaki, 503
Koivisto, Mauno, 319, 320, 321
Kojong (Korea), 513
Kok, Wim, 620
Kokaku (Japan), 501
Kokov, _, 736
Kokov, Valery, 727
Kokovtsev, Vladimir, 714

Kolaćević, Nikola, 1089
Kolak, Rudi, 144
Kolapa Oshola, 654
Kolarev, Vasil, 184
Kolarov, Vasil, 183
Kolbin, Gennadi, 508
Kolchina, Olga, 735
Kolelas, Bernard, 256
Kolettis, Ioannis, 393, 394
Kolingba, André, 219
Kolisev, F.I., 1055
Koliševski, Lazar, 544, 545, 1086
Koljgeci, Remzi, 1094, 1095
Koller, Arnold, 856
Koller, Edwin, 889
Kollias, Konstantinos, 397
Kolokotronis, Gennaios, 394
Kolowrat, Franz, 106
Kolpakov, V.I., 731
Kolstad, Peder, 661
Kolta, Kostaq, 57
Kolumbegov, Torez, 363
Kolybanov, _, 738
Komakidze, R., 362
Komarov, Yevgeny, 748
Komarovsky, Yury, 756
Komatsu (Japan), 501
Komyo II (Japan), 501
Kombil, Banabas, 680
Komboni, Andrew, 683
Komo, D.M., 655
Kompongsong, Sunthorn, 921
Konan-Bédié, Henri, 273
Konaré, Alpha, 564
Konaté, Tissoulé, 18
Konda, Marboz, 838
Kondakov, Aleksandr, 730
Kônder, Adolpho, 176
Kondratenko, Nikolai, 743
Kondratev, Aleksandr, 750
Kondratyev, Grigory, 733
Kondylis, Georgios, 393, 396
Koné, Jean-Marie, 564
Kong Fei, 232
Kongor, George, 843
König, Walter, 910
Könitzer, Karl, 867
Konow, Henrik, 1046
Konow, Wollert, 661
Konoye, Fumimaro, 503
Konstantin I, 358
Konstantinos I (Greece), 392
Konstantinos II (Greece), 393
Konstantinov, Tikhon, 594, 595
Konstantopoulos, Konstantinos, 395
Konthi Suphamongkhon, 38
Kontić, Radoje, 1088, 1090
Konuk, Nejat, 280
Koolman, Lindo, 621
Kopf, Heinrich, 372
Kopp, Otto, 863

Kopsov, Anatoly, 719
Koraea, Thomas, 679
Körber, Ernst von, 107
Korčák, Josef, 281
Korfanty, Wojciech, 698
Korizis, Alexandros, 396
Korkmasov, D.E., 725
Korman, Maxime Carlot, 1058
Körner, Theodor, 106, 111
Korniets, Leonid, 940, 941
Koroka, Kagel, 684
Korolyov, Oleg, 748
Koroma, Johnny-Paul, 786
Koroma, Sorie, 786
Koromba, Yaungtine, 684
Korošec, Anton, 1087
Korostelev, Grigori, 522
Korotchenko, Demyan, 940, 941
Korotchenya, Ivan, 8
Korowi, Wiwa, 676
Korshunov, Lev, 743
Korutürk, Fahri, 930
Korvald, Lars, 661
Kosavac, Dragutin, 144
Koschnick, Hans, 370
Koshman, Nikolai, 722
Koshoyev, Temirbek, 521
Koslov, Frol, 715
Kosokawa, Morihito, 504
Kosrat Rasul, 472
Kossior, Stanislav, 942
Kossuth, Lajos, 415, 416
Kostanyan, Haik, 86
Kostić, Branko, 1087, 1090
Kostić, Jugoslav, 1096
Kostov, Ivan, 185
Kostrikov, S., 114
Kosygin, Aleksei, 715, 716
Kotalawala, John, 831
Kotsuba, Natalya, 730
Kou Abhay Og Long, 524
Kouandété, Maurice, 137
Kouchner, Bernard, 1095
Koumakoye, Delwa, 221
Koumoriko, Victor, 267
Koumoundouros, Alexandros, 394, 395
Koundouriotis, Georgios, 392, 394
Koundouriotis, Paulos, 392, 393
Kountché, Seyni, 633
Kouyalé, Lansama, 15
Kovač, Michal, 789
Kovaćević, Sreta, 1096
Koval, Nikolai, 595
Kovalev, Afanasi, 127
Kovalev, Aleksandr, 753
Kovalev, Mikhail, 127
Kovalev, V., 754
Kovlyagin, Anatoly, 750
Koya, C. Mohammed, 436
Koyambounou, Gabriel, 219
Kozayev, V.D., 363

Kozić, Dusan, 145
Kozikov, A.Ya., 734
Kozlov, Vasili, 126
Kozlowski, Leon, 698
Kozonguizi, Fanuel, 611
Kpera, John, 642, 645
Kpomakpor, David, 533
Kraag, Johan, 845
Krag, Jens-Otto, 288
Krähenbuhl, Hans, 868
Krainer, Josef, 110
Krainer, Josef Jr, 110
Kraivichien, Thanin, 921
Krajaćić, Ivan, 274
Krajgher, Boris, 791
Krajgher, Sergej, 1086
Krajgher, Sergij, 791
Kramář, Karel, 283
Krappe, Ernst, 380
Kraprayoon, Suchinda, 921
Krapušek, Tone, 791
Kraschel, Nelson, 993
Krasnoshchekov, Aleksandr, 758
Krasnoyarov, Yevgeny, 751
Krasts, Guntars, 526
Krause, Julio, 77
Kravchuk, Leonid, 941
Kreis, Alfred, 896
Kreisky, Bruno, 106, 107
Krejči, Jaroslav, 284
Krenz, Egon, 367
Kress, Viktor, 752
Kriakos, Demetrios, 394
Krieg, Pierre-Charles, 332
Kriel, J Hermanus (Hernus), 813
Kriezis, Antonios, 394
Krinitsky, Aleksandr, 127
Kripalani, M.K., 456
Kripalani, Sucheta, 450
Krishna Bhattarai, 617
Krishna Kumar Singh, 460
Krishna Kumar Singhji Bhavsinghji, 447
Krishna Pal Singh, 430
Krishna Rao, K.V., 439
Krishnatry, S.M., 452
Krishtopans, Vilis, 526
Kristensen, Knud, 288
Kristensen, Thorkil, 30
Kristian Frederick (Norway), 660
Kristnatry, S.N., 425
Kristofer (Norway), 660
Krivchenko, Albert, 744
Krogmann, Carl, 371
Krokidas, Sotirios, 396
Kroning, Rodolfo Prower de, 78
Kroon, Ciro, 622
Kruger, Hans, 382
Kruger, S.J. Paulus, 804
Krugers, Xavier, 623
Krunić, Bosko, 1088, 1097
Krutulović, Vicko, 274

Krylov, Aleksei, 731
Krym, Salomon, 943
Ku Wei-chun, 226, 227
Kuaj Miar Makwai, 839
Kuang Tsung, 224
Kubarev, Eduard, 724
Kubel, Alfred, 372, 379
Kubey, Mehmet, 943
Kubilis, Andrius, 540
Kubilius, J., 540
Kubiš, Ján, 34
Kubitschek, Juscelino, 149, 163
Kučan, Milan, 791, 792
Kucharzewski, Jan, 698
Kuchenthal, Werner, 379
Kucherov, Vasily, 737
Kuchma, Leonid, 941
Kudabayev, A., 1053
Kudyshev, Yury, 741
Kühn, Heinz, 373
Kuhut, Bernhard, 383
Kukk, Johan, 312
Kuks, A.N. (Fuchs), 741, 742
Kuks, G.M. (Fuchs), 742
Kulatov, Turabay, 521
Kulatov, Turabay, 522
Kulayev, Mstislav, 719
Kuler, Robert, 1058
Kuliev, Timur, 114
Kulihaapai, Vitolio, 351
Kulkarni, Bidesh, 456
Kulkov, Mikhail, 522
Kulov, Kubadi, 735
Kulumba, Joseph, 267
Kulumbetov, Uzakbay, 507
Kumar, Nitish, 428
Kumar, Shanta, 433
Kumaratunga, Chandrika, 831, 834
Kumekhhanov, _, 727
Kump, H. Guy, 1040
Kun, Reuben, 615
Kunayev, Dinmuhammed, 508
Kundeling, Woeser G., 232
Kündig, Hermann, 860
Kung Hsian-hsi, 227
Kung Hsin-chan, 226
Kunin, Madeleine (M. May), 1036
Kuniteru, Koiso, 513
Kunitsyn, Serhy, 943
Kunmunch, Michel, 350
Kuntschen, Joseph, 902, 903
Kunvar Singh, 617
Kunz, Gottfried, 866
Kunz, Hans-Jörg, 892
Künzi, Hans, 910
Kuoni, Tobias, 876
Kupa, François, 268, 269
Kuprianov, G.N., 730
Kuptsov, Valentin, 715
Kurakov, Lev, 724
Kurbanov, Dzhumbay, 1053

Kurbanov, Mamdali, 915
Kurbanov, Rakhankul, 1052
Kurdukar, Sidharkar, 444
Kurkauskas, V., 540
Kurnia Jasa Othman bin Talib, 553
Kuroda, Kiyotaka, 502
Kurondo, Siwi, 683
Kurtesi, Iliaz, 1094
Kurtesi, Ilijaz, 1095
Kurts, Vilgelm (Wilhelm Kurz), 742
Kürzi, Marcel, 893
Kurzmeyer, Werner, 879
Kushayev, Khafiz, 719
Kushhkov, Kishkuka, 727
Kutiyev, Fuad, 114
Kutlugh Murad Khan, 1054
Kuusinen, Otto, 730
Kuuskoski, Reino, 320
Kuyper, Abraham, 619
Kuznetsov, Boris, 750
Kuznetsov, Ivan, 734
Kuznetsov, Vasily, 716
Kuznetsov, Vladimir, 743
Kuznetsov, Yevgenny, 744
Kviesis, Alberts, 525
Kvirning, Emmanuil, 942
KwaMhlanga, 808
Kwanghae-gun (Korea), 512
Kwangmu (Korea), 513
Kwartsz, Lindoro, 621
Kwasniewski, Aleksander, 698
Kyburz, Rudolf, 893, 894
Kydrashev, Ch.K., 718
Kyemambe IV (Bunyoro), 939
Kyle, Wallace, 100
Kyndiah, P.R., 441
Kyongjong (Korea), 512
Kyprianou, Spyros, 279
Kyrsedi Oyun Kenden, 740
Kyselyov, Vasyl, 943

La Croix, Jean-Pierre, 335
La Follette, Philip, 1041
La Follette, Robert, 1041
la Fontaine, J.-T.-I. de, 542
la Vaissière, Auguste de, 1057
Laar, Mart, 313
Laatasi, Kamuta, 936
Labarrère, André, 330
Labastida Ochoa, Francisco, 587
Labotsibeni (Swaziland), 847
Labra García, Wenceslao, 582
Lacabanne, Raúl, 74
Lacalle Herrera, Luis, 1050
Lacascade, Étienne, 345
Lacayo Sacasa, Benjamin, 632
Lacerda, Carlos de, 159
Lacerda, Jorge, 176
Lachat, Ernest, 343
Lachat, François, 877

Lachenal, Adrien, 854, 872
Lachenal, Paul, 872
Lacoste, Robert, 60
Lacroix, Jean-Pierre, 337
Lacunza, José de, 574
Ladd, Herbert, 1027
Laely, Andreas, 875
Lafalla, Arturo, 78
Lafana, Damson, 678
Lafanama, Peter, 678
Laffitte, Jacques, 325
Lafleur, Jacques, 349
Lafontaine, Oskar, 374
Lafontant, Roger, 410
Lafoon, Ruby, 996
Lafranchi, Arturo, 900
Lagarde, Antoine, 291
Lagden, Godfrey, 530
Lages, Afrânio, 152
Lageula, Muni, 351
Lago, Joseph, 836
Lagomarsino, Angel, 76
Lagorio, Lelio, 489
Lagos, Ricardo, 223
Lagourgue, Pierre, 342
Lagrosillière, Joseph, 340
Laguarda y Fenollera, Juan, 62
Lahivi, Hario, 490
Lahoud, Emile, 527
Lahoz, Eleodoro Sánchez, 82
Lai Ruoyu, 241
Laigret, Charles, 255
Laigret, Christian, 340, 347, 568
Laina, Ned, 679
Laird, David, 213
Lajos I (Hungary), 415
Lajos I (Poland), 697
Lajos II (Hungary), 415
Lak, Robert, 684
Lakalaka, Keleto, 350
Lakas Bahas, Demetrio, 675
Lakatami, Sani, 629
Lakatos, Géza, 417
Lake, Everett, 982
Lake, Richard, 212
Lakina, Soane, 350
Lakoba, Nestor, 360
Lakoué, Enoch, 219
Lal, Bansi, 431, 432
Lal, Bhajan, 431, 432
Lal, Bipen Behari, 446
Lal, Brij Mohan, 427
Lal, Cheddy, 456
Lal, Devi, 431, 432
Lal, Ram, 433
Laldenga, 441
Lall, J.S., 447
Lallan Prasad Singh, 426, 439
Lalumière, Catherine, 12
Lam Adesina, 654
Lamar, Mirabeau, 1032

Lamb, Richard, 980
Lambert, John, 1014
Lambert, Yves, 44
Lambertin, Pierre, 340
Lambertz, Karl-Heinz, 133
Lamblin, Auguste, 218
Lambotte, Gerard, 350
Lambros, Spyridon, 395
Lambruschini, Luigi, 1064
Lamenha, António de, 152
Lami, Pierre, 273, 781
Lamizana, Sangoulé, 186, 187
Lammasch, Heinrich, 107
Lamodière, Fernand, 350
Lamont, Donald, 964
Lamontagne, Gilles, 211
Lampe, Willem, 624
Lampert, Marius, 903
Lamy, Julien-Georges, 336
Lamy, Robert, 341
Lanari, Luis, 79
Lanatta, Francisco, 691
Lanci, Giuseppe, 771
Lancís Sánchez, Felix, 278
Landeros Gallegos, Rodolfo, 575
Landi, Bruno, 483
Lando, Pietro, 497
Lando (Pope), 1061
Landolt, Franz, 874
Landolt, Jules, 874
Landon, Alfred, 994
Landouzy, Bernard, 342
Landsbergis, Vytautas, 539
Landsverk, Tollef, 662
Lane, George, 1023, 1024
Lane, Henry, 992
Lane, William, 1001, 1015
Laney, Ben, 978
Lang, Hedi, 910
Lang, John, 90
Lang, Louis, 858, 859
Lange, David, 627
Langelier, François, 211
Langenauer, Jakob, 860
Langer, William, 1020
Langley, Desmond, 960
Langlie, Arthur, 1039
Langlois, Robert, 1058
Langone, Losolyn, 599
Langro, Paul, 683
Langton, John, 1011
Lanham, Samuel, 1033
Laniel, Joseph, 328
Lansana, David, 786
Lansdowne, Marquess of (Henry Petty-Fitzmaurice), 197
Lanusse, Alejandro, 70
Lanza, Giovanni, 479
Lanzerac, Victor (French Polynesia), 345
Lanzerac, Victor (Pondicherry), 456
Lanzuela Marina, Santiago, 824

Lapade Ajiborisha, 653
Lapalud, Maurice-Pierre, 272, 341, 353
Lapang, D.D., 440
López Mateos, Adolpho, 574
Lapie, Pierre-Olivier, 220
Lapli, John, 794, 795
Lapointe, Hughues, 211
Laprida, Guillermo Sosa, 75
Laprida, Mario, 74
Laptev, Adolf, 746
Lapy, Eduardo, 1072
Lara, Juan, 270
Lara Ramos, César, 577
Larco Cox, Guillermo, 692
Lardelli, Albert, 875
Lardelli, Renzo, 876
Lardi, Bernardo, 876
Laredo Bru, Federico, 277
Lareida, Kurt, 859
Lares, Teodosro, 574
Largarcha, Froilan, 249
Largiadèr, Otto, 876
Largo Caballero, Francisco, 818
Larifla, Dominique, 339
Larminet, René de, 257
Larosière de Chapfeu, Jacques de, 45
Larrabee, William, 993
Larrabure y Unanue, Eugenio, 690
Larrain, Emiliano Figueroa, 222
Larrazabal Ugueto, Wolfgang, 1067
Larrazolo, Octaviano, 1016
Larrea Alba, Luis, 300
Larrechea, Juan de, 73
Larsen, Vibeke, 289
Larson, Cecil, 629
Larson, Morgan, 1015
Lascurain, Pedro, 573
Laslo (Naples and Sicily), 491
Lassen, Hans, 289
Lastiri, Raúl, 70
Lastowski, Vatslav, 127
Lastra Ortiz, Manuel, 588
Lasu, Joseph, 843
László I (Hungary), 414
László II (Hungary), 414
László III (Hungary), 415
László IV (Hungary), 415
László V (Hungary), 415
Lataste, Thierry, 348
Lateef Jakande, 650
Latham, Milton, 979
Lathbury, Gerald, 965
Latif, Idris, 429, 437
Latin, Ivo, 274
Latinwo, B., 650
Latorre, Lorenzo, 1049
Latorre Alcubierre, Pedro, 308, 761
Latrille, André (Chad), 220
Latrille, André (Côte d'Ivoire), 272
Latsis, Villis, 526
Laugerud García, Kjell, 402

Laur-Munchhofen, Eduard von, 386
Laura Frattura, Ferdinando Di, 485
Laurel, José, 694
Laurel, Salvador, 694
Lauret, Jules, 291, 336
Lauri, Hans, 868
Laurie, A. Dawn, 103
Laurier, Wilfred, 198
Lausche, Frank, 1022
Lauti, Toaripi, 936
Lava, Oscar, 80
Laval, Pierre, 327, 328
Lavalle Urbina, Eduardo, 576
Lavan, John, 100
Lavarack, John, 91
Lavaud, Frank, 410
Lavelua, Vito, 351
Lavil, Fernand, 220
Lawal, Adekunle, 646
Lawal, M.A., 652
Lawal Haruna, 643
Lawal Kaita, 647
Lawley, Arthur, 99
Lawrance, Arthur, 798
Lawrence, Carmen, 101
Lawrence, David, 1026
Lawrence, G.C., 919
Lawrence, John, 615
Lawrence, Robert, 685
Lawson, _, 956
Lawson, Harry, 98
Lawson, Ray, 208
Laxalt, Paul, 1011
Laycock, Robert, 565
Layng, Thomas, 936
Layva Mancilla, Gabriel, 580
Lázár, György, 417
Lazarenko, Pavlo, 942
Lazarovski, Jakov, 545
Lazebny, N.S., 718
Le Baron, Thomas, 958
Le Beau, Georges, 59
Le Bourdon, Raymond, 597
Le Brun, Albert, 325
Le Cheminant, Peter, 956
Le Cornec, Jacques, 338
Le Direach, Jean, 337
Le Duan, 1074
Le Duc Anh, 1074
Le Hénaff, Jacques, 350
Le Hunte, George Ruthven, 93
Le Kha Phieu, 1074
Le Layac, Paul, 255
Le Layec, Pierre, 220
Le Marchant, Robert, 956
Le Masurier, Robert, 959
Le Soavec, Bernard, 345
Le Vander, Harold, 1005
Le Vern, Alain, 332
Lea, Preston, 984
Lea, Walter, 210

Leader, George, 1026
Leahy, William, 1045
Leake, George, 100
Leake, Walter, 1005
Leal, Aurelino, 172
Leal, Francisco, 705
Leal, João, 170
Leal, Walfredo, 165
Leandro, José, 246
Leane, Edwin, 103
Leane, E.T., 101
Leanza, Vincenzo, 487
Leão, Humberto, 170
Leary, Richard, 1044
Leatham, Ralph, 960
Leather, Edwin, 960
Leavey, Thomas, 46
Leavitt, Michael, 1034
Lebailly, Paul, 344
Lebeau, Joseph, 130
Lebed, Aleksandr, 743
Lebed, Aleksei, 731
LeBlanc, Edward, 294
LeBlanc, Pierre-Evariste, 211
Leblanc, Roméo, 198
Lebouder, Jean-Pierre, 219
LeBreton, David, 959
Leburton, Edmond, 131
Lecanaut, Jean, 332
Leche, Richard, 997
Lecher, Robert, 995
Lechner, Hans, 110
Leclerc de Hautecloque, Philippe, 194
Leconte, André, 337
Leconte, Cincinnatus, 410
Leconte, Ricardo, 74
Lecsot, Elie, 410
Ledeganck, Herman, 258
Lee, Andrew, 1030
Lee, Anthony, 959
Lee, Blair, 1001
Lee, Dixty Ray, 1039
Lee, Fitzhugh, 1037
Lee, H. Rex, 1043
Lee, Henry, 1037
Lee, J. Bracken, 1034
Lee, James, 210
Lee, William, 96
Lee Bum Suk, 517
Lee Han Key, 518
Lee Hoi Chang, 518
Lee Hong Koo, 518
Lee Huan, 247
Lee Hyun Jae, 518
Lee Kuan Yew, 788
Lee Sang Yong, 514
Lee Si Yong, 514
Lee Soo Sung, 518
Lee Teng-hui, 247, 248
Lee Tong Hui, 514
Lee Tong Yong, 514

Lee Young Duck, 518
Leedy, John, 994
Leekpai, Chuan, 921
Leeuwen, Pieter van, 623, 624
Lefèbre, Gérard, 344
Lefèbre, Louis-Charles, 780
Lefèvre, Théodore, 131
Lefroy, Henry, 100
Legendre, Jean, 334
Legendre, Robert, 136
Léger, Jules, 198
Legitime, François, 410
Legqog, 234
Legrand, Léon, 350
Legros, Auguste, 342
Leguhavi, Jason, 795
Leguía y Martínez, Germán, 691
Leguía y Salcedo, Augusto, 689, 690
Leguina Herrán, Joaquín, 828
Lehen, Joseph, 685
Lehman, Herbert, 1017
Lehto, Reino, 320
LeHunte, George, 925
Lei, Hermann, 898
Leimbachner, Georges, 893
Leite, Avelino, 776
Leite, Benedito, 159
Leite, Duarte, 705
Leite, Eraldo, 169
Leite, João, 179
Leite, José, 179, 180
Leite, Sebastião, 161
Leito, Bernardito (Ben), 622
Leiva, Pariano, 412
Lejeune, Henri, 336
Lejeune, Leo, 863
Lekhanya, Justin, 530
Lekishvili, Nikoloz, 359
Lekota, Patrick, 811
Lekwot, Zamani, 655
Lelikov, A.Ye., 737
Lely, Cornelis, 845
Lemaire, Jean, 255, 339, 456
Lemari, Kunio, 567
Lemass, Seán, 474
Lemisch, Arthur, 108, 109
Lemke, Helmut, 375
Lemonoza, Vera, 734
Lemos, Eduardo de, 776
Lemus, José, 307
Lénart, Jozef, 283
Lénart, Jozef, 790
Lencastre, Julio, 65
Lendi, Charles, 45
Leng Ngeth, 191
Lengruber, Otávio, 157
Lenherr, Hans Peter, 892
Lenin, Vladimir, 715, 716
Lennep, Emile van, 30
Lennon, William, 91
Lenormand, Maurice, 348

Lentsch, Josef, 108
Leo III (Pope), 1060
Leo IV (Pope), 1060
Leo IX (Pope), 1061
Leo VI (Pope), 1061
Leo VII (Pope), 1061
Leo VIII (Pope), 1061
Leo X (Pope), 1061, 1063
Leo XI (Pope), 1063
Leo XII (Pope), 1064
Leo XIII (Pope), 1065
Léon Bejarana, Armando, 583
Léon Brindis, Samuel, 577
Léon Carpio, Ramiro de, 402
Léon Herrera, Santos, 271
Leonard, Roger, 59
Leone, Carlo, 482
Leone, Giovanni, 480
Leone, Mario, 489
Leong Yew Koh, 553
Leoni, Raúl, 1067
Leonicio Elías, Ricardo, 689
Leontieff, Alexandre, 346
Leontyev, Anatoly, 724
Leopold (Baden), 377
Leopold I (Austria), 105
Leopold I (Belgium), 129
Leopold I (Lippe), 380
Leopold II (Austria), 105
Leopold II (Belgium), 129
Leopold II (Lippe), 380
Leopold III (Anhalt), 376
Leopold III (Belgium), 129, 130
Leopold III (Lippe), 380
Leopold IV (Anhalt), 376
Leopold IV (Lippe), 380
Leopoldo I (Tuscany), 496
Leopoldo II (Tuscany), 497
Leopoldovna, Anna, 713
Lepa, A.K., 738
LePage, Bradford, 209
Lepage, Octavio, 1067
Leperveenche, Léon de, 342
Lepori, Alberto, 900
Lepori, Giuseppe, 899
Lepping, George, 793
Lepreux, Charles, 339
Leques, Jean, 348, 349
Lerchenfeld, Hugo von, 369
Lerdo de Tejada, Sebastian, 573
Lerma Blasco, Joan, 828
Lerner, Jaime, 168
Lerroux y García, Alejandro, 818
Lersundi Ormaechea, Francisco de, 816
Lesage, Jean, 212
Lescure, Frédéric, 330
Leser, Ludwig, 108
Lesik, Iosif, 126
Leslie, Harry, 992
Leslie, Prescott, 1009
Leslie, Preston, 995

Lessa, Marário, 151
Lessa, Ronaldo, 152
Lester, Seán, 24
Lesterlin, Bernard, 350
Leszek I (Poland), 696
Leszek II (Poland), 696
Leta, Norbert, 267
Letcher, John, 1037
Letellier, René, 336
Lethem, Gordon, 407, 783
Letimah, B.L., 655
Letsie III (Lesotho), 530
Leu, Ernst, 892
Leu, Franz, 878, 879
Leu, Georg, 891
Leuba, Jean-François, 906
Leuba, Pierre-Auguste, 881
Leupena, Tupua, 936
Leupin, Hans, 863
Leurquin, Bernard, 344
Leushkin, Sergei, 755
Leutenegger, Albert, 896, 897
Leutheusser, Richard, 376
Leuthold, Bruno, 884
Leutwein, Theodor, 610
Levallois, Michel, 342
Levashov, Vasily, 714
Levecque, Fernand, 339
Lévecque, Fernand, 780
Lévécque, Fernand (French Guiana), 336
Lévécque, Fernand (Pondicherry), 456
Lévéque, Michel, 598
Lévesque, René, 212
Levi, Noel, 39
Levingston, Roberto, 70
Levy, Georges, 336
Lewanika (Barotseland), 1099
Lewelling, Lorenzo, 994
Lewis, Allen, 764, 765
Lewis, David, 974
Lewis, Ernest, 964, 970
Lewis, James, 1041
Lewis, Meriweather, 1007
Lewis, Morgan, 1017
Lewis, Neil, 96
Lewis, Vaughan, 765
Leydin, Reginald, 104, 615
Léyé, Jean-Marie, 1058
Leygues, Georges, 327
Leymang, Gerard, 1058
Leyra Mortera, Xicotencatl, 576
Leyva, Velazquez, Gabriel, 587
Lezama, Arturo, 1049
Lho Bak Rin, 514
Lho Shin Yong, 518
Li Changchun (Henan), 237
Li Changchun (Liaoning), 240
Li Changyan, 241
Li Chi-sen, 229
Li Ching-hsi, 226
Li Choe Ung, 513

Li Chuting, 241
Li Dazhang, 242
Li Dengying, 235
Li Deshing, 234
Li Erzhong (Hainan), 236
Li Erzhong (Hebei), 237
Li Fanwu, 237
Li Fengping, 243
Li Gun Mo, 515
Li Jiating, 243
Li Jingquan, 242
Li Jong Ok, 515
Li Ken-yuan, 228
Li Keqiang, 237
Li Kum Myong, 513
Li Li, 236
Li Peng, 227
Li Qingwei, 241
Li Qiyan, 244
Li Ruihan, 244
Li Shenglung, 244
Li Tsung-jen, 225
Li Tzu-ch'eng, 225
Li Won Yong, 513, 514
Li Xiannian, 226
Li Xuefeng, 236
Li Yuan, 238
Li Yuan-hung, 225
Li Yuwen, 239
Li Zaihan, 236
Li Zhaozhuo, 232
Liamine Zeroual, 60
Liang Buting, 241
Liang Hung-chi, 229
Liang Lingguang, 235
Liang Shih-yi, 226
Liao Zhigao, 234
Liapchev, Andrei, 184
Liaquat Ali Khan, 664
Liaquat Ali Khan Jatoi, 670
Liberia Peters, Maria, 622
Liceaga Ruibal, Víctor, 576
Licht, Frank, 1027
Liddell, Clive, 965
Lie, Trygve, 42
Lieb, Ernst, 890, 891
Liebe, Otto, 288
Liebert, Eduard von, 917
Lien Chan, 247, 248
Liesch, Walter, 875
Liesching, Theodor, 388
Ligon, Thomas, 1000
Liinamaa, Keijo, 320
Likoinidov, _, 728
Likulia Bolongo, 259
Lilić, Zoran, 1087
Liliuokalani (Hawaii) (Lydia), 988
Lilley, Charles, 92
Lilley, George, 982
Lilo, Ruben, 795
Lim Chong Eu, 555

Lim Yew Hock, 788
Lima, Alexandre, 168
Lima, António de, 163
Lima, Felipe, 156
Lima, Floriano, 172
Lima, Francisco de, 159
Lima, Hermes, 150
Lima, Joaquim, 154
Lima, José, 167, 168
Lima, José de, 166
Lima, Noraldino, 163
Lima, Orestes, 174
Lima, Pedro, 148
Lima, Sebastião, 178
Lima, Valdomiro de, 178
Lima, Venceslau de, 704
Lima, Vicente, 167
Lima Alvaro, 170
Limann, Hilla, 391
Limboo, Sanchman, 447
Limburg-Stirum, Johannes van, 461
Limodin, Daniel, 343
Limon Gutiérrez, José, 584
Limpright, Peter, 1046
Lin Hujia, 244
Lin Qiming, 241
Lin Sen, 225
Lin Tie, 236
Lin Yang-kuang, 248
Linares, José, 140
Lincoln, Abraham, 972
Lincoln, Enoch, 998
Lincoln, Gatewood, 1043
Lincoln, Levi, 1001
Lind, John, 1005
Lindelof, Friedrich, 371
Linden, Joseph, 388
Lindenberg, Carlos, 157
Lindequist, Friedrich von, 610
Lindley López, Nicolás, 689, 692
Lindman, Salomon, 851
Lindo, Henry, 293
Lindo, Juan, 306
Lindo y Zelaya, Juan, 412
Lindoso, José, 154
Lindsay, Robert, 974
Lindsey, Washington, 1016
Linford, R.J., 103
Ling, Syargey, 127
Linhares, José, 148
Lini, Walter, 1058
Link, Arthur, 1020
Linkomies, Edwin, 320
Linkun, _, 725
Lins, Alcides, 163
Lins, Manoel, 177
Liosi, Jones, 680
Liotard, Victor-Théophile, 136, 347, 403
Lipinski, Richard, 374
Lippens, Maurice, 258
Lippitt, Charles, 1027

Lippitt, Henry, 1027
Lippman, Edmond, 1057
Lipponen, Paavo, 321
Lisboa, Aquiles, 160
Lise, Claude, 341
Lise, Pierre, 347
Lisette, Gabriel, 221
Lisiahi, Manuele, 350
Lisle Brock, Daniel De, 956
Lisnichenko, _, 729
Lissouba, Pascal, 256
List, Robert, 1011
Lister, Ernest, 1039
Listisyn, Anatoly, 754
Lisulo, Daniel, 1099
Little, John, 978
Little, Philip, 205
Littlefield, Alfred, 1027
Liu Bingyan, 237
Liu Geping (Ningxia-Hui), 233
Liu Geping (Shanxi), 242
Liu Guangdao, 237
Liu Jianfeng, 236
Liu Jianxun, 237, 238
Liu Jie, 237
Liu Maosheng, 237
Liu Mingchin, 243
Liu Minghui, 243
Liu Qi, 244
Liu Ruishan, 241
Liu Shaoqi, 225
Liu Tianfu, 235
Liu Xianquan, 240
Liu Xingyuan (Guangdong), 235
Liu Xingyuan (Sichuan), 242
Liu Xuefend, 236
Liu Yung-fu, 247
Liu Zheng, 238
Liu Zhenghua, 242
Liu Zihou (Hainan), 236
Liu Zihou (Hebei), 236
Liu Zihou (Hubei), 238
Liuzzi, Gennaro, 486
Livas Villarreal, Eduardo, 584
Liver, Peter, 875
Livingston, William, 1013
Livytsky, Andry, 941
Lizano Zabal, Augustín, 270
Lizarume, José, 73
Ljubicic, Nikola, 1091
Ljundberg, Ernst, 43
Lleras, Alberto, 28
Llerena, Francisco, 77
Lleshi, Hazhi, 57
Llewelyn, Robert, 764, 766
Llopis Ferrandiz, Rodolfo, 819
Lloque Yupanqui, 693
Llorente, Saturnino, 71
Lloyd, Edward, 1000
Lloyd, Francis, 848
Lloyd, G. Peter, 963

Lloyd, Henry, 1000
Lloyd, James, 399
Lloyd, William, 205
Lloyd, Woodrow, 213
Lloyd George, David, 952
Lluesma García, Estanislao, 308
Lo Sun Yin, Peter, 558
Loaiza, Rodolfo, 587
Loayza, José, 690
Lobão, Edison, 160
Lobato, Nicolau, 298
Lobb, Reginald, 766
Lobo, Arnaldo, 165
Lobo, Fernando Martín, 84
Lobo, José, 179
Lobo Cordero, Alfonso, 632
Locher, Albert (Bern, Switzerland), 867
Locher, Albert (Zurich, Switzerland), 908
Locher, Armin, 861
Locke, Gary, 1039
Lodewijk I (Netherlands), 618
Lodewijk II (Netherlands), 618
Lodge, John Davis, 982
Lodge, Ronald, 425
Lodkin, Yury, 745
Lodovico, Carlo, 490
Lodovico (Piedmont-Sardinia), 495
Lodovico (Sicily), 493
Loene, Giovanni, 478
Loepfe, Arthur, 861
Loet La Nabhalai (Thailand), 920
Logan, Robert, 768
Logan, William, 783
Loggia, Giuseppe La, 487
Logologofolau, Clovis, 350
Logothetopoulos, Konstantinos, 396
Lohner, Emil, 867
Lokendra Chand, 617
Loki, Christopher, 837
Lokoloko, Tore, 676
Löliger, Ernst, 863
Lomanto, António, 155
Lomardi, Alberto, 81
Lombardini, Manuel, 573
Lominadze, Vissarion, 364
Lon Nol, 190, 192
Lonardi, Eduardo, 70
Lonferini, Alberto, 773
Lonferini, Giovanni, 771, 772
Lonferini, Marino, 771
Lonfernini, Giuseppe, 773
Lonfernini, Luigi, 770, 771, 773
Lonfernini, Sante, 772
Lonfernini, Settimio, 774
Lonfernini, Teodoro, 772
Long, Athelstan, 963
Long, Earl, 997
Long, Huey, 997
Long, John, 1002
Long, Oliver, 47
Long, Oren, 989

Long Boret, 192
Long Shujin, 233
Lóngay, Menyhért, 416
Longequeue, Louis, 333
Longerstaey, Edouard, 49
Longino, Andrew, 1006
Longjam Thambou Singh, 439
Longley, James, 999
Longrigg, Anthony, 961
Longrigg, Stephen, 310
Longuet, Gérard, 333
Lony, Jacques, 337
Looker, Othniel, 1021
Loomis, Orland, 1041
Lopes, Cristiano, 157
Lopes, Francisco, 428, 703
Lopes, Henri, 256
Lopes, João, 428
Lopes, José, 156
Lopes, Paulo, 156
Lopes, Tarquínio, 159
López, Antonio, 83
López, Carlos, 82, 686
López, Carlos González, 76
López, Eurario, 582
López, Francisco, 686
López, Hermogenes, 1067
López, Javier, 577
López, Joaquín, 816
López, José (Argentina), 81
López, José (Colombia), 249
López, Varnancio, 401
López Arellano, Osvaldo, 413
López Arias, Fernando, 590
López Avelar, Norberto, 583
López Cardena, Fernando, 590
López Dávila, Manuel, 587
López de Nava, Rodolfo, 583
López de Romaña, Alejandro, 690
López de Romana, Eduardo, 689
López de Santa Anna, Antonio, 572, 573
López del Castillo, Raúl, 278
López Dominquez, José, 817
López Gutiérrez, Rafael, 413
López Hernández, Manuel, 576
López Nogales, Armando, 588
López Padilla, Benecio, 578
López Sánchez, Raúl, 578
López y Planes, Vicente, 69
Lopsakovi, Chulydym, 739
Lopsan-Osur, 739, 740
Lopukhin, Pyotr, 714
Lord, Bernad, 204
Lord, William, 1024
Loredano, Francesco, 498
Loredano, Leonardo, 497
Loredano, Pietro, 498
Lorenz, Heinrich, 386
Lorenzetti, Maria Rita, 489
Lorenzo I de Medici (Tuscany), 496
Lorenzo II de Medici (Tuscany), 496

Loret de Mola Medíz, Carlos, 591
Loretan, Raymond, 903
Loretan, Wolfgang, 903, 904
Loreto, Sergio, 169
Loro, James, 836
Lortkipanidze, Vazha, 359
Lortkipanidze, Zakaria, 361
Losada, Mario, 78
Losala, Simon, 268
Losco, Andrea, 482
Losol, Darzavyn, 600
Losonczi, Pál, 416
Lotbinière, Henri Joly de, 211
Lotfali Khan Vazir Akkham, 467
Lothair I (France), 322
Lothair II (France), 322
Loubet, Émile, 324, 326
Louden, James, 619
Loueckhote, Simon, 348
Lougheed, Peter, 200
Louis I (France), 322
Louis I (Monaco), 597
Louis II (France), 322
Louis II (Monaco), 597
Louis II (Navarre), 823
Louis III (France), 322
Louis IV (France), 322
Louis IX (France), 323
Louis (Luis) I (Navarre), 823
Louis-Philippe, 324
Louis V (France), 322
Louis VI (France), 323
Louis VII (France), 323
Louis VIII (France), 323
Louis X (France), 323
Louis XI (France), 323
Louis XII (France), 323
Louis XIII (France), 323
Louis XIV (France), 323
Louis XIX (France), 324
Louis XV (France), 323
Louis XVI (France), 323
Louis XVII (France), 323
Louis XVIII (France), 324
Louise-Hippolyte (Monaco), 597
Louisy, Allan, 765
Louisy, Perlette, 765
Lounsbury, George, 982
Lounsbury, Phineas, 981
Loureiro, José, 704
Loutsch, Hubert, 542
Louveau, Edmond-Jean, 563
L'Ouverture, François Toussaint, 409
Louw, Eugene, 802
Lovaglio, Dante, 80
Love, John, 980
Lovelace, Alec, 67, 293
Loveless, Herschel, 993
Loveridge, John, 956
Lovland, Jorgen, 661
Lovre, Koviljko, 1096

Lovrenović, Josip, 144
Low, Frederick, 979
Lowden, Frank, 991
Lowe, Douglas, 97
Lowe, Enoch, 1000
Lowe, Ralph, 993
Lowe, Richard, 1043, 1044
Lowndes, Rawlins, 1028
Lownes, Lloyd, 1001
Lowry, Mike, 1039
Lowry, Robert, 1006
Loyere, Paul de la, 338
Loyola Vera, Ignacio, 586
Lozada, Gonzalo Sánchez de, 142
Lozang Tashi, 231
Lozano Díaz, Julio, 413
Lozano Ramirez, Raúl, 581
Lozoya Solis, Jesús, 577
Lu Cheng-hsiang, 226
Lu Dadong, 242
Lu Rongjing, 234
Lu Ruihua, 235
Lu Ruilin, 236
Luakabwanga, François, 262, 267, 268
Luanghy, Pascal, 266
Lubaya, André, 262
Lubbers, Rudolphus (Ruud), 620
Lubbock, Francis, 1033
Lubennikov, Leonid, 730
Lubeth, Marcellin, 339
Lübke, Friedrich, 375
Lübke, Heinrich, 365
Lubohova, Ekrem, 57
Lubosi (Barotseland), 1099
Lubota, François-Xavier, 66
Lubys, Bronislovas, 539
Luca, Ramón Barros, 222
Lucas, Frank, 1042
Lucas, Robert (Iowa, USA), 993
Lucas, Robert (Ohio, USA), 1021
Lucas García, Romeo, 402
Lucas Jiménez, Juan, 826
Lucchesi, Riccardo di, 310
Luce, Cyrus, 1003
Luce, Richard, 965
Luce, William, 1080
Lucena, Alberto, 71
Lucena, Barão de (Henrique de Lucena), 168
Lucena, Solon de, 165
Lucero, Pedro, 78
Lucey, Patrick, 1041
Luchessi, Julio, 77
Luchette, Rodolfo, 82
Luchinsky, Pyotr (Petru Lucinschi), 595
Luciano de Castro, José, 704
Lucinschi, Petru, 594
Lucius II (Pope), 1062
Lucius III (Pope), 1062
Luckevich, Anton, 127
Luckham, Albert, 629

Luckoo, Edward, 407
Lucotte, Marcel, 330
Luddington, Donald, 793
Ludemann, Hermann, 375
Ludington, Harrison, 1041
Ludlow, George, 1014
Ludvik (Bohemia), 282
Ludvonga II (Swaziland), 847
Ludwig, Carl, 865
Ludwig, Siegfried, 109
Ludwig Friedrich II (Schwarzenburg-Rudolstadt), 387
Ludwig Gunther IV (Schwarzenburg-Rudolstadt), 387
Ludwig I (Baden), 377
Ludwig I (Bavaria), 368
Ludwig I (Hesse), 371
Ludwig II (Baden), 377
Ludwig II (Bavaria), 368
Ludwig II (Hesse), 371
Ludwig III (Bavaria), 368
Ludwig III (Hesse), 371
Ludwig IV (Hesse), 371
Luft, G.A., 741
Lufti al-Haffar, 912
Lugard, Frederick (Hong Kong), 245
Lugard, Frederick (Nigeria), 635
Lugo, José, 580
Lugo Guerrero, José, 581
Lugo Verduzco, Adolfo, 581
Lui, Frank, 629
Lui, Salesio, 630
Luigi (Tuscany), 496
Luipert, Daniel, 613
Luis, Juan, 1046
Luis I (Portugal), 703
Luis II (Portugal), 703
Luis (Spain), 814
Luizet, Charles-Jean, 257
Lukacs, László, 416
Lukanov, Andrei, 184
Lukashenko, Aleksandr, 126
Lukashin, Sargis, 86
Luke, Harry, 317
Lukhangwa, 231
Lukić, Vladimir, 145
Lukman, Rilwanu, 32
Lukodi, Agnes, 837
Lukyanets, I.K., 507
Lulach (Scotland), 953
Lule, Yusufu, 938
Lumpkin, Wilson, 986
Lumumba, Patrice, 259
Luna Kan, Francisco, 591
Luna y Peralta, Federico, 691
Lunalino (Hawaii) (William Charles), 988
Lunda Bululu, 259
Lundeberg, Christian, 851
Lundsteen, Poul, 289
Lungtok Gyatso, 231
Luns, Joseph, 25

Luo Guibo, 242
Lupéron, Gregorio, 295
Luque Loyola, Eduardo, 586
Lusinchi, Jaime, 1067
Lusser, Florian, 901
Lusser, Josef, 901
Lutali, Aififi, 1043
Lutaud, Charles, 59
Lutcken, Eduard von, 379
Luther, Hans, 366
Lüthi, Ruth, 871
Luthva, 441
Lutz, Jakob (Appenzell-Ausser Rhoden, Switzerland), 859
Lutz, Jakob (Zurich, Switzerland), 908, 909
Lutz, Johann, 369
Lutzow, Leo von, 388
Luvsan, Sonomyn, 599
Luyt, Richard, 407
Luz, Carlos da, 149
Luz, Hercílio da, 176
Luz, Kadish, 475
Luzhkov, Yury, 754
Luzuriaga, Pablo, 78
Luzzatti, Luigi, 479
Lvov, Georgy, 714
Lyashko, Aleksandr, 940, 941
Lyashko, Yury, 744
Lykke, Ivar, 661
Lynch, Charles, 1006
Lynch, John, 474
Lynch-Staunton, Frank, 199
Lynden van Sandenburg, Constantinius van, 619
Lyne, William, 90
Lyng, John, 661
Lyngdoh, Brington, 440
Lyon, Caleb, 989
Lyon, Sterling, 203
Lyons, Joseph, 88, 96
Lyra, Augusto de, 173
Lyubchenko, Panas, 941
Lyubimov, Isidor, 1056
Lyubimov, Vyacheslav, 750
Lyuh Woon Hung, 514
Lyzhin, N.M., 729
Lyzohub, Fedir, 941

Ma Hushan, 229
Ma Li, 236
Ma Mingfang, 240
Ma Qizhi, 233
Ma Wenrui, 241
Ma Xin, 233
Ma Xingyan, 234
Ma Zhongchen, 237
Maada Bio, Julius, 786
Maarshall, William, 1004
Maaruf Dawalibi, 913
Maati Bousbid, 603

Mabandla, Justice, 807
Mabandla, Zwelibanzi, 810
Mabey, Charles, 1034
Mabhena, Jonas, 808
Mabi Mulumba, 259
Mabry, Thomas, 1016
Mabus, Ray, 1007
Mabuza, Enos, 808
Macalister, Arthur, 91, 92
Macapagal, Diosdado, 694
MacArthur, Arthur, 1041
Macartney, William, 95, 99
Macbeth (Scotland), 953
Macchioro, Gino, 796
MacCorkle, William, 1040
MacCulloch, Edgar, 956
MacDonald, Andrew, 209
Macdonald, Angus, 207
Macdonald, Augustine, 209
Macdonald, Charles, 986
MacDonald, Donald, 208
Macdonald, Gordon, 205
MacDonald, H.B., 104
MacDonald, Hugh, 202
MacDonald, John Alexander, 198
MacDonald, John Sandfield, 198, 208
MacDonald, Malcolm, 509
MacDonald, Ramsay, 952
MacDonald, W. Ross, 208
MacDonald, William, 209
Macdonnell, Ronald, 44
MacDougal, Patrick, 197
Macedo, Joaquim Falcão, 150
Maček, Ivan, 791
MacEwen, J.W. Grant, 199
MacFarlan, Ian, 99
MacGregor, James, 147
Macgregor, William (Australia), 91
Macgregor, William (Newfoundland), 204
Machado, Alderico, 160
Machado, Alvaro, 246
Machado, Álvaro, 165
Machado, Brasil, 167
Machado, Dionízio, 179
Machado, Floriano, 153
Machado, João, 165
Machado, Joaquim (Goa), 428
Machado, Joaquim (Macau), 246
Machado, Joaquim (Mozambique), 604
Machado, José, 153
Machado, José Felipe, 1069
Machado, Londres, 162
Machado, Pedro, 776
Machado, Raul, 159
Machado y Morales, Gerardo, 277
Machar, Moses, 842
Machel, Samora, 605
Macheret, Augustin, 871
Machessou, Alexandre, 347
Mächler, Albert, 887, 888
Machold, Reinhard, 110

Machungo, Mario, 605
Maciá, Francesco, 826
Macías Nguema, Francisco, 309
Macías Valenzuela, Anselmo, 588
Macías Valenzuela, Pablo, 587
Maciel, Arthur, 161
Maciel, Leandro, 179
Maciel, Marco, 169
Maciel, Olegário, 163
Mackay, Aeneas, 619
Mackay, Alexander, 962
Mackay, J. George, 209
Mackay, John, 208
MacKay, Kenneth (Buddy), 985
MacKeen, David, 206
MacKeen, Henry, 206
MacKenzie, Alexander, 198
Mackenzie, George, 214
Mackenzie, Robert, 92
MacKenzie, Thomas, 626
MacKenzie, William (Botswana), 147
Mackenzie-Kennedy, Henry, 549, 570
MacKenzie King, W., 198, 199
Mackiewicz, Stanisław, 700
Mackilligin, David, 963
MacKinnon, Donald, 209
Mackintosh, Charles, 213
Mackwelung, Moses, 593
MacLaren, David, 203
MacLaren, Murray, 203
MacLean, Angus, 210
MacLean, G.I., 214
MacLean, John, 201
MacLehose, C. Murray, 245
MacLellan, Russell, 207
MacLennan, David, 962
MacMahon, M. Patrice, 324, 326
MacMichael, Harold, 476, 917
MacMillan, Alexander, 207
MacMillan, Gordon, 965
MacMillan, Harold, 952
MacMillan, William, 210
Macmillan Wallace, 399
MacNaughton, Terence, 762
MacPhail, Lloyd, 209
Macpherson, Campbell, 205
MacPherson, John (Australia), 98
MacPherson, John (Nigeria), 635
Madaki, John, 648
Madaki, Joshua, 641, 654
Madal, Dhanik Lal, 445
Madden, John, 97
Maddock, Walter, 1020
Maddocks, Kenneth, 317
Maddox, ester, 987
Mäder, Emil, 888
Madero González, Braulio, 578
Madero González, Raúl, 578
Madison, George, 995
Madison, James, 972
Madoux, André, 333

Madrazo, Carlos, 588
Madrazo Pintado, Roberto, 589
Madrelle, Philippe, 330
Madrid Hurtado, Miguel de la, 574
Madrid López, Demetrio, 826
Madrid Romandia, Roberto de la, 575
Madrid Virgen, Carlos de la, 579
Madriz, José, 632
Madsen-Mygdal, Thomas, 288
Madueke, Allison, 645, 646
Maein Chol, Michael, 841
Maestracchi, Pierre-Louis, 345
Maestracci, Pierre-Louis, 780
Maestre, Bonaventura, 62
Maestro, Carlos, 73
Maffey, John, 835
Maga, Hubert, 137
Magalhâes, Abel, 172
Magalhães, Agamenon, 169
Magalhães, António, 155
Magalhães, António de, 405
Magalhães, João, 246
Magalhães, José de, 604
Magalhães, Juracy, 154, 155
Magalhães, Manuel (Cape Verde), 216
Magalhães, Manuel (Macau), 246
Magalhães, Rafael, 159
Magalhães, Roberto, 170
Magalhães, Romildo, 151
Magaña, Alvaro, 307
Magande, Ng'andu, 18
Magariños, Carlos, 46
Maggini, Carlo, 899
Maglajlija, Seid, 144
Maglione, Luigi, 1065
Magliotto, Armando, 484
Magloire, Paul, 410
Magnago, Silvius, 488
Magnani, Rinaldo, 484
Magnus (Denmark), 286
Magnus I Ladulas (Sweden), 849
Magnus I (Norway), 659
Magnus II Eriksson (Sweden), 849
Magnus II (Norway), 659
Magnus III (Norway), 659
Magnus IV (Norway), 659
Magnus V (Norway), 659
Magnus VI (Norway), 660
Magnus VII (Norway), 660
Magnusson, Jón, 419
Magoffin, Beriah, 995
Magomedov, Dzhmalutdin, 725
Magomedov, Magomedali, 725
Magoon, Charles, 277
Magsaysay, Ramon, 694
Maguina, Alejandrino, 691
Maguire, Conor, 473
Maha Mongkut (Thailand), 920
Mahabir Singh, 452
Mahaffy, Arthur, 293
Mahajan, Mehr, 433

Mahamane Ousmane, 633
Mahamidou Issoufou, 634
Mahaña, Gildardo, 583
Mahanta, Prafulla, 426
Maharaj Singh, 458
Mahatab, Harekrushna, 443
Mahathir bin Mohamed, 551
Mahaud Witt, Jamil, 300
Mahavir, Bhai, 437
Mahcado, Manoel, 176
Mahendra (Nepal), 616, 617
Maheswari, Himmat Singh, 438
Maheu, Pierre, 46
Mahfoud Beida, 761
Mahindasoma, G.D., 832
Mahlangu, G. Majozi, 808
Mahler, Halfdan, 47
Mahmed Ould Louly, 568
Mahmood Ali, 437
Mahmood Haroon, 670
Mahmoud Riad, 22
Mahmud, 53
Mahmud al-Ayoubi, 913
Mahmud al-Maghreby, 535
Mahmud al-Zubi, 913
Mahmud bin Aidrus, 1083
Mahmud bin Mat, 555
Mahmud bin Suleiman, 560
Mahmud Buhadma, 536
Mahmud el-Bishti, 536
Mahmud Fawzi, 304
Mahmud I (Turkey), 930
Mahmud II (Turkey), 930
Mahmud Iskander, 551
Mahmud Jam, 468
Mahmud Muntasir, 535, 536
Mahmud Pasha Sami, 303
Mahmud Şevket Paşa, 931
Mahmud Shah II, 554
Mahmud (Trengganu), 560
Mahmut Bakati, 1095
Mahodil, Ananda, 920
Mahumd Iskander, 550
Mai, David, 683
Maia, Agripino, 174
Maia, Álvaro, 153
Maia, Jerônimo, 174
Maia, José, 174
Maia, José de, 246
Maia, Tarcísio, 174
Maia, Ubaldo, 157
Maiah, Joel, 680
Maiani, Ariosti, 774
Maiani, Giuseppe, 772, 773
Maidou, Henri, 219
Maier, Reinhold, 368, 389
Maigari, Bello, 195
Maillard, Guy, 338
Maillard, Pierre, 344
Maillet, Camille, 336, 780
Maillet, Raymond, 334

Maina, Charles, 14
Maiorescu, Titu, 709
Mair, Alexander, 90
Mairebam Koireng Singh, 439
Maissen, Aluis, 876, 877
Maitra, Sankar, 452
Maitre, Jean-Philippe, 873
Maituku, Petelo, 351
Maiziere, Lothar de, 367
Majano, Adolfo, 307
Majid al-Ali al-Mualla, Shaikh, 947
Majid bin Said, 919
Majko, Pandeli, 58
Majluta Azar, Jacobo, 296
Major, Elliott, 1008
Major, John, 953
Major, Nendor, 1096
Majumber, Sudhir, 449
Majzoub al-Khalifa, 839
Majzoub Babiker, 841
Makape Papilo, Sosefo, 350
Makarios III (Archbishop), 279
Makarov, G.M., 361
Makea Takau, 627
Makharadze, Filipp, 358, 359
Makhdoom Quraishi, 668
Makhkamov, Kakhar, 914, 915
Makhmudov, _, 1055
Makhmudov, Arzi, 1053
Makhmudov, Nazir, 1053
Makka, Fidelis, 642
Makmop, Norbert, 684
Makoni, Simbarashe, 37
Makoto, Saito, 513
Maksagak, Helen, 213, 214
Maksinov, Semen, 740
Maksyuta, Nikolai, 753
Maktum bin Bhutti al-Maktum, Shaikh, 946
Maktum bin Hashar al-Maktum, Shaikh, 946
Maktum bin Rashid al-Maktum, Shaikh, 945, 946
Makuza, Bernard, 760
Malafeyev, V., 753
Malago, Simon, 265
Malaisa, Francis, 679
Malan, Daniel, 800
Malan, Henri, 136
Malan, J. Nicolaas, 802
Malan, Magnus, 800, 802
Malau, Lafaele, 351
Malavé Risso, José, 1070
Malaviya, Chaturnarain, 458
Malbakhov, Timbora, 727
Malcampo y Monge, José, 816
Malcher, José, 164
Malcolm, D.K., 100
Malcolm I (Scotland), 953
Malcolm II (Scotland), 953
Malcolm III (Scotland), 953

Malcolm IV (Scotland), 953
Maldonado, José, 819
Maldonaldo Pérez, Caritino, 580
Maldonaldo Sánchez, Braulio, 575
Malebane-Metsing, Rocky, 806
Malecela, John, 918
Malembe, Charles, 266
Malendoma, Timothée, 219
Malenkov, Georgy, 716, 717
Malespin, Francisco, 306
Malet de Carteret, Charles, 959
Maleville, Gabriel, 83
Malewa, Najamuddin Daeng, 462
Maleyev, Valery, 756
Malfatti, Franco, 17
Malfeyt, Justin, 189
Malhotra, O.P., 444
Malietoa Laupepa, 768
Malietoa Mata'afa, 768
Malietoa Moli, 768
Malietoa Talavou, 768
Malietoa Tanumafili I, 768
Malietoa Tanumafili II, 769
Malik, Abdul (Bangladesh), 123
Malik, Bidhubhusan, 450
Malik Amir Mohammed Khan, 671
Malik Khiazar Hyat Khan, 669
Malik Meraj Khalid, 665, 669
Malines, Guy, 338
Maling, Irwin, 766
Malinov, Aleksander, 184
Malipiero, Pasquale, 497
Mallarino, Manuel, 249
Mallet, George, 765
Malloum, Félix, 220, 221
Malmud Nokrashy Pasha, 304
Malofeyev, Anatoly, 128
Malos, Ferdinand da, 246
Malossini, Mario, 488
Malou, Jules, 130
Malpartida, Elías, 691
Malsagov, Akhmed, 726
Malta, Euclides, 151
Malta, Joaquim, 151
Maluf, Paulo, 178
Malval, Robert, 411
Malvy, Martin, 333
Malvy, Pierre, 336
Malypetr, Ján, 283
Mamadou Dia, 781
Mamadou Lamine Loum, 781
Mamadu, A., 639
Mamaloni, Solomon, 794
Mamayev, _, 733
Mambaya, Paul, 269
Mambetov, Bolot, 522
Mamdouh Salem, 304
Mamedbekov, Kerim, 725
Mamedo, Jurandir, 169
Mamedov, Gusein (Dacestan, Russia), 725
Mamedov, Gusein (Nakhichevan), 115

Mamedov, Yagub, 113
Mamili, 1099
Mamkhegov, Mikhail, 727
Mamo, Anthony, 565
Mamohato (Lesotho), 530
Mamoun Kuzbari, 913
Mamsuriv, Taymuraz, 735
Mamudayev, Mahirbek, 722
Mamuladze, David, 362
Man Mohan Adhikari, 617
Mana, M., 654
Manbariev, Abdulla, 943
Mancham, James, 783, 784
Mancheno, Carlos, 300
Mancino, Nicola, 478, 482
Manco Capac, 693
Manco Inca Yupanqui, 693
Mandaba, Jean-Luc, 219
Mandal, Bindeshwari, 427
Mandal, Dhanik Lal, 431
Mandarini, Francesco, 489
Mandel, Marvin, 1001
Mandela, Nelson, 800
Mandić, Nikola, 275
Mandloi, Bhagwantrao, 437
Mandzhiev, Erdmi, 728
Manehatha, Philip, 795
Mănescu, Manea, 710
Manetiva, Peter, 794
Manfred (Sicily), 493
Manfredotti, Carlos, 84
Mangabeira, Octávio, 155
Mangefel, John, 593
Mangope, Lucas, 806, 807
Mani Uhita, Soane, 350
Manigat, Leslie, 410
Manin, Carles-Émile, 220
Manin, Daniele, 498
Manin, Lodovico, 498
Maniu, Iuliu, 710
Maniusis, Juuzas, 539
Manjappa, Kadilal, 434
Mankin, Ivan, 730
Mankulumana, 806
Manley, Michael, 500
Manley, Norman, 499
Manly, Charles, 1019
Mann, Edgar, 958
Mann, Frederick, 97
Mann, Leo, 863
Mann, S.A., 1034
Mann, William, 1037
Mannerheim, Karl, 319
Manning, Ernest, 200
Manning, John, 1029
Manning, Patrick, 926
Manning, Richard, 1028
Manning, Richard III, 1029
Manning, William (Jamaica), 499
Manning, William (Malawi & Sri Lanka), 549, 830

Mano, Manuel, 65
Manolić, Josip, 275
Manono, Dominique, 262
Manopakorn, 920
Mansfield, Alan, 91
Mansfield, Philip, 961
Mansholt, Sicco, 17
Mansoor Ali, 121
Mansor bin Othman, 554
Mansur, João, 168
Mansur, T., 463
Mansur bin Ghalib (Kathiri), 1082
Mansur Shah II (Trengganu), 559
Mansur Shah (Kelantan), 552
Mansurov, Burkhan, 737
Mansurov, S., 757
Mantere, Oskari, 320
Manteuffel, Otto, 383
Manu, Gheorghe, 709
Manuchehr Ikbal, 468
Manuel I (Portugal), 702
Manuel II (Portugal), 703
Manuella, Tulaga, 936
Manuit, Eduardo, 1070
Manukutu, J.H., 464
Manukyan, Vazguen, 86
Manusama, Johannes, 464
Manz, Paul, 863
Manzaneque Feltrer, Angel, 308
Manzanilla Shaffer, Víctor, 591
Manzikala, Jean Foster, 264, 265, 268
Manzoni-Borghesi, Angelo, 770, 771
Manzoor Wattoo, 669
Manzur Masud, 671
Mao Zedong, 225, 227, 229
Mao Ziyong, 238
Mar, José de la, 688
Mara, Kamisese, 318
Mara, Nambuga, 684
Maraite, Joseph, 133
Marak, Selsang, 440
Maranhão, Alberto, 173
Maranhão, Constantino, 169
Maranhão, José, 166
Maranhão, Pedro, 173
Marani, Primo, 772, 773
Marback, Guilherme, 154
Marble, Sebastian, 999
Marcellin, Raymond, 331
Marcello, Niccolo, 497
Marcellus I (Pope), 1060
Marcellus II (Pope), 1063
Marcey, William, 1017
Marchal, Charles, 136, 336
Marchal, Léon, 12
Marchand, Charles, 343
Marchand, Félix-Gabriel, 211
Marchand, Jean-Henri (Congo, Brazzzavile), 255
Marchand, Jean-Henri (Gabon), 353
Marchand, Maurice, 344

Marchand, Théodore-Paul, 194
Marchant, William, 793
Marchenko, Petr, 744
Marchesson, Marcel, 353
Marchessou, Marcel, 136
Marchuk, Yevheny, 942
Marcilese, Hugo, 82
Marcilio, Flávio, 156
Marco, Guido de, 566
Marco Bergós, José, 824
Marcos, Ferdinand, 694
Marcourt, Michael, 201
Marcoz, Oreste, 489
Marcucci, Francesco, 770
Marcucci, G. Vito, 773
Marcucci, Giacomo, 770
Marcucci, Gian Marco, 774
Marcucci, Giovannito, 773
Marcucci, Marco, 489, 771
Marcucci, Vincenzo, 770, 771
Marek, Bruno, 111
Marelj, Zivan, 1096
Marentes Miranda, Tomás, 590
Maresca, Niccolo, 494
Maret, Arthur, 906
Marett, Robert, 959
Marfini, Claudio, 489
Margadant, Christian, 875, 876
Margai, Albert, 786
Margai, Milton, 786
Margaret (Scotland), 954
Margherita, Clemente della, 495
Marghilman, Alexandru, 710
Margrete (Norway), 660
Margrethe I (Denmark), 287
Margrethe II (Denmark), 287
Margrethe (Sweden), 850
María Aznar López, José, 818
María Cristina I (Spain), 814
María Cristina II (Spain), 815
Maria (Hungary), 415
Maria I (Portugal), 703
Maria II (Portugal), 703
Maria Luisa (Lucca), 490
Maria Luisa (Parma and Piacenza), 494
Maria (Sicily), 493
Maria Teresa (Parma and Piacenza), 494
Maria Theresa, 105
María y Campos, Maurico de, 46
Mariani, Lirio, 1064
Mariano Navarro, José, 1070
Mariátegui, Sanfro, 692
Maricar, M.O. Hasan Farook, 457
Marich Man Singh Shrestha, 617
Marie, André, 328
Marie, Aurelius, 293
Marie Adelaide (Luxembourg), 542
Marie de Medicis, 323
Marie-Jeanne, Alfred, 341
Marie Louise (Tuscany), 496
Mariere, J.S., 637

Marijnen, Victor, 620
Marin, Ecolastico, 306
Marin, José, 178
Marín, Julio Andrade, 299
Marin, Rubén, 77
Marinć, Andrej, 791, 792
Marinho, José, 405
Marinho, Miha, 791
Marini, Anselmo, 71
Marini, Miguel, 74
Marinko, Miha, 792
Marinkovic, Vojislav, 1087
Marinus II (Pope), 1061
Marion, Daniel, 213
Marios, Francisco, 78
Marisov, Valery, 741
Mariz, António, 166
Mariz, Dinarte, 174
Mariz, José, 166
Marjanović, Mirko, 1093
Marjolin, Robert, 30
Mark, David, 651
Markaryants, Vladimir, 86
Markendaya Singh, 454
Markert, Richard, 370
Markezinis, Spyros, 397
Markham, Henry, 979
Markin, Sergei, 737
Markov, Arklady, 741
Marković, Ante, 274, 275, 1088
Marković, Dragoslav, 1088, 1091
Marković, Pero, 145
Markovski, Krste, 545
Marks, Albert, 1031
Marla Kachalla, 643
Marland, Ernest, 1023
Marland, William, 1040
Marlette, Ferrucio, 771
Marlow, Wolmar, 662
Marmaduke, John, 1008
Marmaduke, Meredith, 1007
Marmora, Alfonso la, 479, 496
Marques, Altino, 177
Marques, Eduardo (East Timor), 297
Marques, Eduardo (Macau), 246
Marques, Jaime, 65, 246
Marques, Joaquim, 161
Marques, José (Brazil), 159
Marques, José de (Colombia), 249
Marqués, Sergio, 824
Marques, Silvino, 65, 216
Marquie, Jean-Pierre, 344
Marquordt, Gerhard, 379
Marraco, Santiago, 824
Marroquín, José, 250
Marsal bin Maun, 182
Marschler, Willy, 376
Marsden, William, 961
Marsh, Reginald, 104
Marshall, David, 788
Marshall, Hugo, 637

Marshall, John, 627
Marshall, Thomas, 992
Martelli, Ferruccio, 771, 772
Martelli, Filippo, 772
Martelli, Horace, 958
Martelli, Renato, 772
Martelli, Rosolino, 773, 774
Martellotta, Giuseppe, 486
Martens, Gunnar, 290
Martens, Paulo, 178
Martens, Wilfried, 131
Martiarena, José, 76
Martić, Milan, 276
Martignac, Jean-Baptiste, 325
Martignoni, Angiolo, 899
Martignoni, Werner, 868
Martikyan, Sergei, 85
Martin, Alexander, 1018
Martín, Angel, 73
Martin, Charles, 1024
Martin, Clarence, 1039
Martin, Daniel, 1000
Martin, David, 89
Martin, Edward, 1026
Martin, Frank, 803
Martin, Frédéric, 872
Martin, Harold, 348
Martin, Jacques, 907
Martin, James (Australia), 90
Martin, James (USA), 1019
Martin, John, 986
Martin, John A., 994
Martin, John W., 985
Martin, Joseph, 201
Martin, Joshua, 974
Martin, Jules, 1057
Martin, Noah, 1012
Martin, Robert, 1023
Martin, William, 212
Martín Huerta, Ramón, 580
Martin I (Aragon), 820
Martin IV (Pope), 1062
Martin V (Pope), 1063
Martina, Dominico, 622
Martina, Ornelio, 623
Martineau, Alfred-Albert, 456
Martineau, Alfred-Albert (Djibouti), 291
Martineau, Alfred-Albert (Gabon), 353
Martineau, John, 978
Martinelli, Pietro, 900
Martínez, Carlos Ponce, 80
Martínez, Enrique (Chiapas, Mexico), 577
Martínez, Enrique (Coahuila, Mexico), 578
Martínez, Juan, 401
Martínez, Luis, 1071
Martínez, Patricio, 578
Martínez, Ramón, 1071
Martinez, Robert, 985
Martínez, Rogelio Nores, 73
Martínez, Tomás, 631
Martínez Adame, Arturo, 580

Martínez Alvarez, Jesús, 585
Martínez Barrio, Diego, 815, 818, 819
Martínez Bartolo, Bartolomé, 632
Martínez-Campos, Arsenio, 817
Martínez Corbala, Gonzalo, 587
Martínez de la Rosa, Francisco, 815
Martínez de la Vega, Francisco, 587
Martínez Domingues, Alfonso, 584
Martínez Laclaya, Roberto, 632
Martínez Manatou, Emilio, 589
Martínez Mera, Juan, 300
Martínez Ross, Jesús, 586
Martínez Sieso, José, 826
Martínez Trueba, Andrés, 1049
Martínez Villicaña, Luis, 583
Martini, Antonio Giagu de, 486
Martini, Ferdinando, 310
Martinitz, Georg von, 492
Martino, Enrico, 797
Martino, Francesco Di, 487
Martino, Nobile de, 796
Martino, Nobile di, 310
Martino I (Sicily), 493
Martino II (Sicily), 493
Martinoli, Sebastiano, 899
Martinović, Mitar, 1090
Martins, Alfredo, 405
Martins, Alfredo (Brazil), 159
Martins, Alfredo (East Timor), 297
Martins, Eneas, 164
Martins, José, 216
Martins, Mariano (Goa), 428
Martins, Mariano (Sao Tomé e Príncipe), 776
Martins, Wilson, 162
Martos, Boris, 941
Marty, Dick, 900
Marty, Franz, 893
Marusić, Stipan, 1096
Marvel, Joshua, 984
Marvin, William, 984
Marwah, Ved Prakash, 439
Marwick, Allan, 848
Marwick, Brian, 848
Marx, Wilhelm, 366, 384
Mary I (England), 950
Mary II (Great Britain), 951
Mary of Guise, 954
Mary (Scotland), 954
Marziani, Spartaco, 488
Marzorali, Alfred, 189
Masakata, Terauchi, 513
Masaliyev, Absamat, 521, 522
Masaryk, Tomás, 282
Masefield, J. Thorold, 960
Masengnalo, Alfredo, 1058
Maseribane, Sekhonyana, 530
Mashar, Riek, 837
Masheke, Malimba, 1099
Masherov, Pyotr, 128
Masi, Tito, 773

Masikita, Pierre, 267
Masimov, Ali, 114
Masipula, 806
Masire, Q. Ketumile, 147
Maskhadov, Aslan, 722
Maslennikov, G.M., 737
Masol, Vitaly, 941, 942
Mason, Stevens, 1003
Mason-MacFarlane, Noel, 965
Masoni, Marina, 900
Massa, Essio, 75
Massaccesi, Horacio, 80
Massamba-Débat, Alphonse, 256
Massendes, Jean, 344
Massengho, Ildephonse, 265
Masset, Ferdinand, 871
Massey, Vincent, 198
Massey, William, 626
Massi, Emidio, 485
Massingham, John, 968
Masson, Georges-Pierre, 353
Masson, Louis, 211
Masson, Paul, 186
Mata, João da, 153
Mata Millan, Emery, 1069
Mataa, 1099
Mataeialona, Sione, 924
Mataio Tuitoga, 628
Matanović, Milo, 1090
Matanzima, George, 810
Matanzima, Kaiser, 810
Matari II (Rwanda), 759
Matari III (Rwanda), 759
Matas Palou, Jaume, 825
Matchanov, Nazar, 1051
Matej I (Bohemia), 282
Matej II (Bohemia), 282
Mateša, Zlatko, 275
Mateus, António, 65
Mathabur Singh Thapa, 616
Mathers, Frederick, 206
Matheson, Alexander, 210
Matheson, Scott, 1034
Mathewes, John, 1028
Mathews, P.C., 438
Mathieson, John, 210
Mathieu, Pierre, 339
Mathur, Mohan, 453
Mathur, N.P., 440
Mathur, Shiv, 446
Mathy, Karl, 377
Matilda (England), 950
Matinović, Rodolfo, 83
Matjila, Andrew, 611
Matlala, Makgoma, 809
Matochkin, Yury, 746
Matos, Afonso de, 159
Matos, José de, 64
Matrika Koirala, 617
Matsepa-Casaburri, Ivy, 811
Matsukata, Masayoshi, 502

Matsuoka, Seiho, 504
Matsuura, Koichiro, 46
Matt, Adolf von, 884
Matt, Hans von, 883
Mattarella, Piersanti, 487
Matteson, Joel, 990
Matthew, John, 104
Matthews, Albert, 208
Matthews, Claude, 992
Matthews, George, 986
Matthews, Henry, 1040
Matthews, Joseph, 1006
Matthews, Norman, 966
Matthey, Francis, 882
Matthias, 105
Mattli, Peter, 902
Mattocks, John, 1035
Mattos, Carlos, 158
Mattos, Leonidas de, 161
Matucci, Emilio, 481
Matveev, A.M., 724
Matveyev, Nikolai, 758
Matyas I (Hungary), 415
Mätzler, Karl, 889
Mauberna, Jean, 403
Maude, Henry, 510
Maudit, Henri de, 220
Mauduit, Henri de, 568
Maulana Mufti Mahmood, 667
Maull, Joseph, 983
Maumon Gayoom, 561
Maumud (Tunisia), 927
Maung Maung, 607, 608
Maung Maung Kha, U, 607
Maura y Montaner, Antonio, 817, 818
Mauran, Henri, 597
Mauregato (Asturias), 820
Maurer, Andreas, 109
Maurer, Ion, 708, 710
Maurer, Rudolf, 909
Maurer-Mayor, Jacqueline, 907
Maurice, Émile, 340
Maurice, René, 344
Maurits (Netherlands), 618
Mauro, Max, 157
Mauroy, Pierre, 329, 333
Mautamakia, Sosefo, 351
Mavlyanov, Abdurrazak, 1052
Mavrocordatos, Alexandros, 392, 393, 394
Mavromichalis, Kyriakoulis, 395
Mavromichalis, Petros, 392
Mavromichalis, Stylianos, 397
Maw, Herbert, 1034
Mawlong, E.K., 440
Maximilian (Bohemia), 282
Maximilian I (Austria), 105
Maximilian I (Bavaria), 368
Maximilian II (Austria), 105
Maximilian II (Bavaria), 368
Maximilian (Mexico), 573
Maximos, Demetrios, 396

Maxwell, Christopher, 628
Maxwell, James, 1098
Maxwell, William, 1044
May, A.J., 846
May, Francis, 245, 317
Mayagoitia Dominguez, Héctor, 579
Mayamba, Emmanuel, 267
Mayanja-Nkangi, Joshua, 939
Mayavero, Alfons, 613
Mayawati, 451
Maybank, Burnet, 1029
Maybin, John, 1098
Mayer, Johann, 109
Mayer, René, 328
Mayner, Robert, 1015
Mayo, Rarl of (Richard Bourke), 422
Mayoral Heredia, Manuel, 585
Mayr, Michael, 107
Mayta Capac, 693
Maza, Angel, 77
Mazarin, Jules, 325
Mazarrasa, Felipe, 589
Mazepa, Isaak, 941
Mazin, _, 736
Mazo González, Alfredo del, 582
Mazo Velez, Alfredo del, 582
Mazowiecki, Tadeusz, 699
Mazurov, Kirill, 127, 128
Mazza, Luigi, 774
Mazza, Oscar, 72
Mazzilli, Ranieri, 149
Mazzini, Giuseppe, 1064
Mba, Casimir Oyé, 354
Mba, Léon, 354
Mbakwe, Samuel, 646
Mbandzeni (Swaziland), 847
M'Bareka el-Bekai, 602
Mbaukua, Gottlob, 613
Mbeki, Thabo, 800
Mbengele, François, 263
Mbida, André-Marie, 195
Mbikusita, Godwin (Barotseland), 1099
Mbombo, Robert, 263
Mbomua, William Eteki, 27
Mbonyumutwa, Dominique, 759
Mbopha, 806
M'Bow, Amadou, 46
Mbuende, Kaire, 37
McAleese, Mary, 474
McAlister, Hill, 1032
McArthur, Duncan, 1021
McBride, Henry, 1039
McBride, Richard, 201
McCain, Margaret, 203
McCall, Samuel, 1002
McCall, Thomas, 1024
McCallum, Henry (Canada), 204
McCallum, Henry (Natal), 802
McCallum, Henry (Sri Lanka), 830
McCandlish, Benjamin, 1044
McCarthy, C.D., 310

McCarthy, Charles, 988
McCarthy, Daniel, 985
McCartney, James, 970
McCaughey, Davis, 97
McCelland, Robert, 1003
McClelland, George, 1014
McClenan, Abner, 203
McCleod, Neil, 210
McCloy, John, 43
McClure, Herbert, 510
McClurg, Joseph, 1007
McComie, Valerie, 28
McConaughty, James, 982
McConnell, William, 989
McCook, Edward, 980
McCord, Jim, 1032
McCord, Myron, 976
McCormack, William, 92
McCormick, Richard, 976
McCoy, Edmund, 967
McCoy, James, 967
McCrae, John, 1006
McCrae, Thomas, 978
McCray, Warren, 992
McCreary, James, 996
McCreight, John, 201
McCuish, John, 995
McCulloch, James, 98
McCullough, John, 1036
McCurdy, John, 206
McDairmid, John, 202
McDaniel, Henry, 987
McDonald, G., 968
McDonald, H., 968
McDonald, James, 99
McDonald, Jesse, 980
McDonald, Piers, 215
McDonald, William, 1016
McDougal, John, 978
McDowell, James, 1037
McDuffie, George, 1028
McEnery, Samuel, 997
McEntee, Peter, 134
McEwan, John, 88
McEwen, Jock, 629
McFarland, Ernest, 977
McGarvie, Richard, 98
McGibbon, Pauline, 208
McGill, Andrew, 1004
McGillivry, Donald, 550
McGirr, James, 90
McGonigal, Pearl, 202
McGovern, Francis, 1041
McGowen, James, 90
McGrath, Andrew, 1029
McGrath, J. Howard, 1027
McGrath, James, 205
McGraw, John, 1039
McGregor, James (Manitoba), 202
McGregor, James (Nova Scotia), 206
McIlwraith, Thomas, 92

McInnes, Thomas, 200
McIntosh, Cameron, 212
McIntyre, Albert, 980
McIntyre, Alistair, 6
McIntyre, Peter, 209
McKay, Douglas, 1024
McKeag, William, 202
McKean, Thomas (Delaware, USA), 982
McKean, Thomas (Pennsylvania, USA), 1025
McKeithen, John, 998
McKeldin, Theodore, 1001
McKell, William, 87, 90
McKelvie, Samuel, 1010
McKenna, Frank, 204
McKenzie, W., 102
McKernan, John, 999
McKinley, William, 972, 1022
McKinly, John, 982
McKinney, Philip, 1037
McKinnon, Donald, 10
McKinnon, Ken, 215
McKinnon, Murdoch, 209
McLane, John, 1013
McLane, Robert, 1000
McLarty, Duncan, 101
McLaurin, Anselm, 1006
McLean, Allan, 98
McLean, Angus, 1019
McLean, George, 982
McLean, Hugh, 203
McLelan, Archibald, 206
McLeod, Thomas, 1029
McMahon, William, 88
McMahon-Box, Joseph, 629
McMaster, William, 1030
McMath, Sidney, 978
McMillan, Daniel, 202
McMillan, Robert, 99
McMillin, Benton, 1031
McMillin, George, 1044
McMinn, Joseph, 1031
McMullen, Adam, 1010
McMullen, Richard, 984
McMullin, Fayette, 1039
McNab, Alan, 198
McNab, Archibald, 212
McNair, Alexander, 1007
McNair, John, 203, 204
McNair, Robert, 1030
McNamara, Robert, 43
McNamee, Luke, 1044
McNeil, James, 473
McNichols, Stephen, 980
McNutt, Alexander, 1006
McNutt, Paul, 992
McPhee, John, 96
McPherson, W.H., 99
McSweeney, Miles, 1029
McVay, Hugh, 974
McWherter, Ned, 1032

McWilliams, Roland, 202
McWillie, William, 1006
Mdivani, P.G. (Budu), 359
Mdlalose, Frank, 812
Mead, Albert, 1039
Mead, John, 1036
Meade, Reuben, 966
Meadows, Clarence, 1040
Means, John, 1029
Mebiame, Léon, 354
Mecham, Evan, 977
Mechelli, Girolamo, 483
Mechem, Edwin, 1016
Mechem, Merritt, 1016
Mečiar, Vladimir, 789, 790
Medary, Samuel (Kansas, USA), 994
Medary, Samuel (Minnesota, USA), 1004
Mededo, Bernardo de, 216
Medeiros, António de, 174
Medeiros, José, 171, 173
Medeiros-Mallet, Frederico de, 161
Medici, Cosimo de (Tuscany, 1434-64), 496
Medici, Cosimo de (Tuscany, 1537-69), 496
Médici, Emilio, 149
Medill, William, 1021
Medina, José, 412
Medina Ascencio, Francisco, 582
Medina Plasencia, Carlos, 580
Meduri, Luigi, 482
Medvedev, Ye., 940
Meester, Theodoor de, 619
Megezhevsky, M.V., 736
Meguib, Esmat, 22
Mehdi, Bishnuram (Assam, India), 426
Mehdi, Bishnuram (Tamil Nadu, India), 447
Mehdi Barzagan, 469
Mehdiqoli Hedayat, 468
Mehmed Esad Saffek Paşa, 931
Mehmed Ferid Paşa, 931
Mehmed Kamil Paşa, 931
Mehmed Rüsdü Paşa, 931
Mehmed Sadik Paşa, 931
Mehmed Said Paşa, 931
Mehmed Talat Paşa, 931
Mehotra, Prakash, 426
Mehra, O.P., 445
Mehta, Balwantrai, 430
Mehta, Chhabildas, 431
Mehta, Jivraj, 430
Mehta, Sureshchandra, 431
Mehtab Ahmad Khan Abbasi, 668
Meienberg, Klemenz, 908
Meier, Hans, 874
Meier, Julius, 1024
Meier, Rudolf, 909, 910
Meier, Theo, 863
Meierhans, Paul, 909, 910
Meierovics, Zigfrids, 526

Meighen, Arthur, 198
Meigs, Return, 1021
Meiners, Johan, 623, 624
Meir, Golda, 475
Meira, Lúcio, 172
Meira, Otávio, 164
Meira, Raimundo, 297
Meiring, Jacobus, 802
Mejdani, Rexhep, 57
Mejía, Carlos, 79
Mejía, Marcelino, 412
Mejía Victores, Oscar, 402
Meker, Maurice, 291
Mekhiyev, Imran, 115
Meksi, Alexander, 58
Melancia, Carlos, 246
Meléndez, Carlos, 306, 307
Meléndez, Jorge, 307
Meles Zynawi, 316
Melgar Castro, Juan, 413
Melgarejo, Mariano, 140
Meline, Jules, 327
Melis, Mario, 487
Melis, Mario, 486
Melkumyan, G.A., 117
Melle, Werner von, 370
Mellette, Arthur, 1021, 1030
Mello, Américo, 177
Mello, Arnon, 152
Mello, Fernando Collor de, 152
Mello, Herculano de, 168
Mello, José, 168
Mello, Nélson de, 153
Melnikov, Leonid, 942
Melnikov, Vladimir, 732
Melo, António da Gama e, 165
Melo, Edelzio de, 179
Melo, Flaviano Baptista de, 151
Melo, Geraldo de (Alagoas, Brazil), 152
Melo, Geraldo de (Rio Grande do Norte, Brazil), 174
Melo, José, 249
Melo, Julio de, 169
Melo, Leônidas, 170
Melo, Matias de, 170
Melo, Oswalso, 166
Melo, Ubaldo de, 174
Melo, Wolney de, 180
Melo e Alvina, Diogo de, 405
Melo Egidio, Nuno de, 246
Meloni, Vittorio, 772
Melro, Hermilio, 151
Melville, George, 764
Memo, Marcantonio, 498
Mena, Fernando, 65
Mena Cordova, Eduardo, 576
Mena Palomo, Victor, 591
Menabrea, Luigi, 479
Menard, André (Pondicherry), 456
Menard, André (Vanuatu), 1058
Mendes, Álvaro, 170

Mendes, Amazonino, 154
Mendes, Francisco, 406
Mendès-France, Pierre, 328
Mendeshev, Seitgali, 507
Méndez, Aparisio, 1049
Méndez, Fernando Pérez, 81
Méndez, Gerónimo, 223
Méndez, Juan, 573
Méndez, Miguel Abadía, 250
Méndez, Ricardo, 1072
Méndez Montenegro, Julio, 402
Méndez Quijada, José, 1072
Mendieta, Carlos, 277
Mendivil y Elio, Manuel de, 308
Mendoça, Roberto de, 160
Mendonça, Roberto de, 156
Mendoza, Carlos (Argentina), 78
Mendoza, Carlos (Ecuador), 300
Mendoza, Carlos (Panama), 674
Mendoza, Enrique, 1070
Mendoza Aramburu, Angel, 576
Mendoza Berruto, Eliseo, 578
Mendoza Gutiérrez, Juan, 691
Mendoza Pardo, José, 583
Mendume, Mikhail, 739, 740
Meneghetti, Ildo, 175
Menelik II, 316
Menem, Carlos, 70, 77
Menemencioğlu, Turgut, 7
Menéndez, Andrés, 307
Menéndez, Francisco, 306
Menéndez, Luciano, 74
Menéndez, Manuel, 688
Menéndez, Mario, 964
Meneses, Paulo de, 180
Menezes, José, 179
Menezes, Josino, 179
Mengiardi, Reto, 876
Mengistu Haile Mariam, 316
Mengoni, Flavio, 488
Menicucci, Secondo, 772
Menon, C. Achutha, 436
Menon, E.P., 432
Menon, Govinda, 436
Menon, Vapal, 442
Mensdorff-Pouilly, Alexander, 106
Menzies, Robert, 88
Mercadier, Albert, 922
Mercado Jarrín, Edgardo, 692
Mercado Romero, Guillermo, 576
Mercatelli, Luigi, 796
Mercer, John, 1000
Mercier, Honoré, 211
Merewether, Edward, 785
Mergenthaler, Christian, 389
Meri, Lenart, 313
Merino, Ferdnando de, 295
Merino Fernández, Aaron, 585
Meriwether, David, 1015
Merkulov, Gennady, 750
Merkushkin, Nikolai, 734

Merkys, Antanas, 539, 540
Merlaud-Ponty, Amédée, 781
Merlaud-Ponty, Amédée-Guillaume, 563
Merlika-Kruja, Mustafa, 57
Merlin, Martial-Henri, 257, 337, 546, 782
Merlo, Antonio, 84
Merriam, William, 1005
Merrill, Samuel, 993
Merrill, Steve, 1013
Merriman, Frank, 979
Merriman, John X., 801
Merscheriakov, G.I., 758
Mertenat, François, 877
Merwart, Émile, 136, 335, 338
Merwat, Émile, 338
Merwe, Cornelius van der, 800
Merwin, John, 1046
Merz, Karl, 907
Merz, Leo, 867
Merzagora, Cesare, 478
Meshkov, Yury, 943
Mesić, Stjepan (Stipe), 275, 1087
Mesihović, Munir, 143
Meskill, Thomas, 982
Mesquita, Geraldo de, 150
Messervy, W.S., 1015
Messmer, Anton, 887
Messmer, Pierre, 195, 257, 273, 329, 333, 568, 782
Messner, Anthony, 104
Messner, Zbigniew, 699
Mestre, Ramón, 74
Mestrinho, Gilberto, 153, 154
Mesut Yilmaz, 932
Meta, Ilir, 58
Metaxas, Andreas, 394
Metaxas, Ioannis, 396
Metcalf, Ralph, 1012
Metcalf, Thomas, 995
Metternich, Clemens von, 106
Metzsch-Reichenbach, Georg von, 374
Meusho (Japan), 501
Mey (Cambodia), 190
Meyer, Albert, 855, 907
Meyer, Alfred, 380
Meyer, Eugene, 43
Meyer, Isidor, 901
Meyer, Kurt (Bern, Switzerland), 868
Meyer, Kurt (Luzern, Switzerland), 880
Meyer, Lucas, 805
Meyer, Oskar, 109
Meyer, Philipp, 907
Meyers, Franz, 373
Meylan, René, 882
Meylandt, Barthélémy Theux de, 130
Meza, Luis García, 141
Mgalobishvili, G., 359
Mgeladze, Akaki, 359, 361
Mhinga, Edward, 808
Mhlaba, Raymond, 811
Mian Aminuddin, 668, 669

Mian Mohammed Afzal Hayat, 669
Mian Mohammed Azhar, 668
Mian Mumtaz Daultana, 669
Miaoulis, Athanasios, 394
Mibambwe III (Rwanda), 759
Mibambwe IV (Rwanda), 759
Michael, Alan, 954
Michael, Heinrich von, 382
Michaelis, Georg, 366, 384
Michał (Poland), 697
Michaux-Chevry, Lucette, 339
Michel, Christian, 875
Michel, Smarck, 411
Micheloni, Federico, 772, 773
Micheloni, Giuseppe, 773
Micheloti, Simone, 771
Michelotti, Maria Dominica, 774
Michelotti, Marino, 771, 772
Michelotti, Romano, 773
Michelsen, Christian, 660
Michelson, Alfonso López, 251
Michener, Roland, 198
Michetti, Gaetano, 481
Michetti, Mario, 771
Michov, Nikolai, 183
Mickelson, George S., 1030
Mickelson, George T., 1030
Mickey, John, 1010
Micombero, Michel, 188, 189
Middleton, Henry, 1028
Middleton, John (Canada), 205
Middleton, John (Falkland Islands), 964
Midtboe, Finn, 662
Mieczysław I (Poland), 696
Mieczysław II (Poland), 696
Mieczysław III (Poland), 696
Miescher, Otto, 866
Miescher, Rudolf, 864
Miettunen, Martti, 320
Mifflin, Thomas, 1025
Mifsud, Ugo, 566
Mifsud-Bonnici, Carmelo, 566
Miftah Omar, 534
Miguel Eduardo, 83
Miguel Gil, José de, 827
Miguet, Robert, 338
Mihai (Romania), 708
Mihajlović, Stevča, 1092
Mihajlović, Svetoza, 144
Mijares Palencio, José, 585
Mijatović, Cvijetin, 144, 1086
Mijnals, Charles, 846
Mijusković, Lazar, 1090
Mikalapokoulos, Andreas, 396
Mikelić, Borislav, 276
Mikhail (Russia), 713
Mikhailov, Batyr, 728
Mikhailov, Viktor, 748
Mikhailov, Yevgeny, 750
Miki, Takeo, 504
Mikołajczyk, Stanisław, 700

Mikoyan, Anastas, 114, 716
Mikulić, Branko, 143, 144, 1088
Miláły, Károlyi, 416
Milanović, Milovan, 1093
Milatović, Veljko, 1089
Milazzo, Silvio, 487
Miles, Herbert, 964
Miles, John, 1016
Miljanić, Nikola, 1089
Milkas, Wilhelm, 106
Millán Lizárraga, Juan, 587
Milledge, John, 986
Miller, Benjamin, 975
Miller, Charles, 984
Miller, Dan, 201
Miller, Frank, 208
Miller, James, 977
Miller, John (Missouri, USA), 1007
Miller, John (North Dakota, USA), 1020
Miller, Keith, 976
Miller, Leslie, 1042
Miller, Nathan, 1017
Miller, Robert, 1011
Miller, Stephen (Minnesota, USA), 1004
Miller, Stephen (South Carolina, USA), 1028
Miller, Thomas, 212
Miller, Walter, 1031
Miller, William (Arkansas, USA), 977
Miller, William (North Carolina, USA), 1018
Miller, Zell, 987
Millerand, Alexandre, 324, 327
Milligan, Keith, 210
Milliken, Carl, 999
Milliken, William, 1004
Millon, Charles, 335
Mills, Charles, 956
Mills, William, 1016
Milne, MacGillivray, 1043
Miloković, Radivoje, 1092
Milongo, André, 256
Milos Obrenović I (Serbia), 1091
Milos Obrenović II (Serbia), 1091
Milos Obrenović III (Serbia), 1091
Milos Obrenović IV (Serbia), 1091
Milosević, Slobodan, 1087, 1092, 1094
Milović, Ante, 275
Milton, John, 984
Milton, William, 1100
Milutinović, Milan, 1092
Minas, 314
Mincev, Nikola, 545
Minčev, Nikola, 544
Minchetti, Raffaele, 770
Mindaugas (Lithuania), 538
Minder, Johann, 866
Mindon Min (Myanmar), 606
Minero Roque, José, 591
Ming, Arnold, 886
Ming, Peter, 885

Minger, Rudolf, 855
Minghetti, Marco, 479
Minh Mang (Nguyen Phuoc Chi Dam), 1073
Minić, Miloš, 1091, 1093
Minnikhanov, Rustam, 738
Minor, William, 981
Mintoff, Dominic, 566
Mir Afzal Khan, 668
Mir Hussein, 1054
Mir Nasrulla, 1054
Mir Omir, 1054
Miramenda, Jacques-Louis, 1057
Miramón, Miguel, 573
Miramontes, Candelario, 584
Miranda, Anibal Sanches e, 246
Miranda, António de, 152, 246
Miranda, Francisco de, 1066
Miranda, Julius de, 845
Miranda Andrade, Otoniel, 581
Miranda dos Santos, José (Zeca), 162
Mirando, Julio, 84
Mirgazyamov, Marat, 719
Miriung, Theodore, 682
Mirkasymov, Irakhmat, 1052
Mirkin, S.Z., 735
Miro, Ricardo, 72
Miro Cardono, José, 278
Mironas, Vladislovas, 539
Mironescu, Gheorghe, 710
Mironov, Nikolai, 741
Mirsaidov, Shakurulla, 1052
Mirtskulava, Aleksandr, 359, 360
Miruho, Jean, 265
Mirza-Akhmedov, Mansur, 1052
Mirza Baig, 7
Mirza Muhiddin, 1054
Mirzabekov, Abdurazak, 725
Mirzan Zainal Abidin, 560
Mirzoyan, Levon (Azerbaijan), 114
Mirzoyan, Levon (Kazakhstan), 508
Mirzoyev, Akbar, 915
Mishari bin Saud, 779
Mishra, Dwarka, 437
Mishra, Jagannath, 427, 428
Mishra, Loknath, 426, 441
Mishra, Shripati, 451
Misick, Washington, 971
Misier, Fred, 845
Misimoa, Afioga Afoafouvale, 35
Mita, Ciriaco de, 480
Mitchell, Alexander, 970
Mitchell, Charles, 317, 802
Mitchell, David, 986
Mitchell, Douglas, 803
Mitchell, George, 1101
Mitchell, Henry, 985
Mitchell, James (Australia), 100
Mitchell, James (Canada), 204

Mitchell, James (St Vincent and Grenadines), 767
Mitchell, John, 99
Mitchell, Keith, 400
Mitchell, Nathaniel, 983
Mitchell, Peter, 204
Mitchell, Philip (Fiji), 317
Mitchell, Philip (Kenya), 509
Mitchell, Philip (Uganda), 937
Mitchell, Robert, 1015
Mitchell, Roma, 93
Mitchell, Samuel, 101
Mithi, Mukut, 425
Mitkov, Vladimir, 544
Mitra, Biren, 443
Mitre, Bartolomé, 69
Mitrović, Aleksandar, 1088
Mitrovica, Rexhep, 57
Mitskevich-Kapsukas, Vikenti, 127, 539
Mitsotakis, Konstantinos, 397
Mittelholzer, Leo, 861
Mitterand, François, 325
Mittnacht, Hermann, 388
Miville, Carl, 865
Mixson, Wayne, 985
Miyazawa, Kiichi, 504
Mizanur Rahman Chowdhury, 121
Mizuno II (Japan), 501
Mizzi, Enrico, 566
Mkapa, Benjamin, 918
Mkrtchyan, Artur, 116
Mladenov, Petŭr, 185
Mnyamana, 806
Moaitz, Enny, 681
Moanda, Faustin-Vital, 266, 268
Moaouya Ould Sidi Ahmed Taya, 568, 569
Moawad, René, 527
Mobutu Sese Seko (Joseph Mobutu), 258, 259
Mocenigo, Giovanni, 497
Mocenigo, Pietro, 497
Mocenigo, Tommase, 497
Moco, Marcolino, 11
Moctezuma I Ilhuicamina (Aztec Empire), 574
Moctezuma II Xocoyotzin (Aztec Empire), 574
Mocumbi, Pascoal, 605
Modrow, Hans, 367
Mody, Hormasji, 450
Moeckli, Georges, 867, 868
Moeder, Max, 679
Moeen Qureshi, 665
Moeur, Benjamin, 977
Moffat, Howard, 1101
Mofford, Rose, 977
Mogae, Festus, 147
Mogodayev, Konstantin, 721
Mohamed Abdulaziz, 761
Mohamed Abid bin Mohamed Adam, 553
Mohamed Adnan Robert, 557

Mohamed Ali Rustam, 554
Mohamed Asri bin Muda, 553
Mohamed bin Jusoh, 555
Mohamed bin Mahbob, 551
Mohamed bin Mohamed Taib, 559
Mohamed bin Nasir, 553
Mohamed bin Yaacob, 553
Mohamed Daud bin Abdul Samad, 560
Mohamed Fuad (Donald Stephens), 557, 558
Mohamed Ghazali bin Jawi, 556
Mohamed Hamdan bin Abdallah, 557
Mohamed Hamzah bin Zainal Abidin, 553
Mohamed ibni al-Marhum Sultan Ahmed, 555
Mohamed Isa bin Abdul Samad, 554
Mohamed Ismail bin Abdul Latiff, 559
Mohamed Khalil bin Yaacob, 555
Mohamed Lamine ould Ahmed, 761
Mohamed Najib bin Abdul Razak, 555
Mohamed Parikesit, 463
Mohamed Razali bin Mohamed Ali Wasi, 556
Mohamed Said bin Keruak, 558
Mohamed Said bin Mohamed, 554
Mohamed Salahuddin, 558
Mohamed Sallah Said Keruak, 558
Mohamed Shah, 559
Mohamed Shah I (Kelantan), 552
Mohamed Shah II (Kelantan), 552
Mohamed Shah II (Trengganu), 560
Mohamed Shah III (Kelantan), 552
Mohamed Shah IV (Kelantan), 552
Mohamed Shamsuddin bin Mohamed Yaakub, 556
Mohamed Shariff bin Osman, 552
Mohamed Zin Abdul Ghani, 554
Mohammed Abbasi, 668
Mohammed Abd-el-Krim al-Khattabi, 603
Mohammed Abdelghani, 60
Mohammed Abdou Madi, 253
Mohammed Abdullah, 433, 434
Mohammed Adil Shah, 421
Mohammed Akbar Hydari, 425
Mohammed Akhtar Mengal, 666
Mohammed al-Adib, 911
Mohammed al-Amu, 839
Mohammed al-Attar, 1078
Mohammed al-Fadul, 842
Mohammed al-Halabi, 913
Mohammed al-Mangoush, 535
Mohammed al-Zubaydi, 472
Mohammed Alam (Brunei), 181
Mohammed Alauddin (Brunei), 181
Mohammed Ali Aden Qalineh, 797
Mohammed Ali (Brunei), 181
Mohammed Ali (Egypt), 302
Mohammed Ali Foroughi, 468
Mohammed Ali (Iran), 466
Mohammed Ali Jawid (Afghanistan), 55
Mohammed Ali Khan Ala os-Saltaneh, 467

Mohammed Ali (Pakistan), 664
Mohammed Ali Raja, 467
Mohammed Ali Raja'i, 469
Mohammed Ali Samatar, 797
Mohammed Alimuddin, 439
Mohammed Amanou, 3
Mohammed Amin Mohammed, 472
Mohammed Arif Bargash, 667
Mohammed Arif Nakai, 669
Mohammed Arnin Khan, 1054
Mohammed Attiqur Rahman, 668
Mohammed Ayub Khan, 664
Mohammed Ayub Khuhro, 670
Mohammed Babanigda, 636
Mohammed Bahonar, 469
Mohammed Bawa, 645, 646
Mohammed Beheshti, 467
Mohammed Benhima, 603
Mohammed bin Ali, 1085
Mohammed bin Fadhl, Shaikh, 1080
Mohammed bin Hamad al-Sharqi, Shaikh, 946
Mohammed bin Kalifa al-Kalifa, 120
Mohammed bin Mohammed, Shaikh, 1080
Mohammed bin Othman es-Said, 535
Mohammed bin Rashid, 779
Mohammed bin Sabah as-Sabah, 519
Mohammed bin Salih, 1085
Mohammed bin Shakbut al-Nahayan, Shaikh, 945
Mohammed bin Thani al-Thani, 707
Mohammed Boudiaf, 60
Mohammed (Brunei), 181
Mohammed Buhari, 636, 658
Mohammed Chamkani, 54
Mohammed Chenik, 928
Mohammed Daoud (Afghanistan), 54
Mohammed Daoud (Jordan), 506
Mohammed Egal, 797, 798
Mohammed el-Badr (Yemen), 1077, 1078
Mohammed el-Baradei, 43
Mohammed el-Sadri, 471
Mohammed Farid Didi, 562
Mohammed Farid Didi (Maldives), 561
Mohammed Farrah Aideed, 797
Mohammed Fuzal, 429
Mohammed Ghannouchi, 928
Mohammed Gharib Bilal, 919
Mohammed Ghazi, 469
Mohammed Goni, 642
Mohammed Habibur Rahman, 122
Mohammed Haithem, 1079
Mohammed Hamadi, 919
Mohammed Haneef Ramay, 668, 669
Mohammed Hatta, 461, 462
Mohammed (Haushabi), 1082
Mohammed Hawadle Madar, 797
Mohammed Hayat Khan, 671
Mohammed Hidayatullah, 422
Mohammed I (Córdoba), 822
Mohammed I (Tunisia), 927

Mohammed I (Turkey), 929
Mohammed Ibrahim (India), 421
Mohammed II (Morocco), 602
Mohammed II (Tunisia), 927
Mohammed II (Turkey), 929
Mohammed III al-Sadiq (Tunisia), 927
Mohammed III (Turkey), 929
Mohammed Imad-ud-din IV (Maldives), 561
Mohammed Imad-ud-din V (Maldives), 561
Mohammed Imad-ud-din VI (Maldives), 561
Mohammed Indan bin Kari, 557
Mohammed (Iran), 466
Mohammed IV al-Hadji (Tunisia), 927
Mohammed IV (Morocco), 602
Mohammed IV (Turkey), 930
Mohammed Jamalul Alam II (Brunei), 181
Mohammed Jega, 639
Mohammed Jinnah, 664
Mohammed Jukhdar, 32
Mohammed Kaak, 928
Mohammed Kanzul Alam (Brunei), 181
Mohammed Karim Lamrani, 603
Mohammed Khan Ala os-Saltaneh, 467
Mohammed Khan Barozai, 666
Mohammed Khan Junejo, 665
Mohammed Khatami, 467
Mohammed Khouna Ould Haydalla, 568, 569
Mohammed Lawal, 650
Mohammed Lemine Ould Guig, 569
Mohammed Lere, 647
Mohammed Mahdavi-Kani, 469
Mohammed Maina, 642
Mohammed Maiwandal, 54
Mohammed Malmud Pasha, 303, 304
Mohammed Marwa, 651
Mohammed Mili, 45
Mohammed Mossadegh, 468
Mohammed Muhsin Ghalib, 1082
Mohammed Muin-ud-din I (Maldives), 561
Mohammed Muin-ud-din II (Maldives), 561
Mohammed Murwa, 642
Mohammed Musa, 671
Mohammed Musa Khan, 666
Mohammed Mustafa Miro, 913
Mohammed Mzali, 928
Mohammed Nadir Shah, 54
Mohammed Naguib, 303, 304
Mohammed Nahgoub, 836
Mohammed Natsir, 462
Mohammed Omar, 54
Mohammed Osman, 840
Mohammed Qureshi, 427, 437, 450
Mohammed Rabbani, 55
Mohammed Rafiq Tarar, 664
Mohammed Ragab, 534, 535
Mohammed Rahmin Khan, 1054

Mohammed Reza Pahlavi (Iran), 466
Mohammed Saadulla, 426
Mohammed Sabir Shah, 668
Mohammed Sa'ed, 468
Mohammed Saeed, 839
Mohammed Safdar, 668
Mohammed Said bin Keruak, 557
Mohammed Said (Egypt), 302
Mohammed Said Pasha, 303
Mohammed Said (Sudan), 840
Mohammed Sakizly, 535, 536
Mohammed Salah Mzali, 928
Mohammed Salimoglu, 1055
Mohammed Shafeq, 54
Mohammed Shafiq, 667
Mohammed Shah (India), 421
Mohammed Shah (Iran), 466
Mohammed Shahabuddin, 122
Mohammed Shams-ud-din II (Maldives), 561
Mohammed Shams-ud-din III (Maldives), 561
Mohammed Sharq, 54
Mohammed Sidahmed, 840
Mohammed Siyad Barreh, 797
Mohammed Sobhi, 46
Mohammed Tajuddin (Brunei), 181
Mohammed Taki Abdoulkarim, 253
Mohammed Tewfik, 303
Mohammed Tewfik (Egypt), 302
Mohammed Umaru, 648, 650
Mohammed Usman Arif, 450
Mohammed V al-Nasir (Tunisia), 927
Mohammed V (Morocco), 602
Mohammed V (Turkey), 930
Mohammed Vali Khan Sepahdar Azam, 467
Mohammed VI al-Habib (Tunisia), 927
Mohammed (VI) bin Afra (Morocco), 602
Mohammed VI (Morocco), 602
Mohammed VI Vahideddin (Turkey), 930
Mohammed VII al-Munsif (Tunisia), 927
Mohammed VIII al-Amin (Tunisia), 927
Mohammed Yusuf, 54
Mohammed Yusuf bin Abdul Rahim (Brunei), 182
Mohammed Yusuf Shah, 671
Mohammed Zahir Shah, 54
Mohammedullah, 121
Mohan Shumshere Jung, 617
Mohieddine Fekini, 535
Mohsen Berazi, 912
Mohsin (Lahej), 1083
Moi, Daniel Arap, 509
Moily, M. Veerappa, 435
Moine, Mario, 75
Moine, Virgile, 867, 868
Moinuddin Haider, 670
Moisset, Jean-Pierre, 344
Mojsov, Lazar, 1087, 1088
Mokai, Albert, 684

Mokamba, 1099
Mokanu, Aleksandr, 594
Mokdad Sifi, 60
Mokgoro, Job, 807
Mokhehle, Ntsu, 531
Moktar Ould Daddah, 568, 569
Molas López, Felipe, 687
Moles, Pere, 62
Moley, Benezeth, 266
Molin, Francesco, 498
Molina, José, 1068
Molina, Justo Páez, 73
Molina, Raúl Aguirre, 80
Molina Barraza, Arturo, 307
Molina Pallochia, Omar, 692
Molina Urena, José, 296
Molinari, Pedro, 83
Mollayev, S.K., 722
Moller, Joseph, 623
Mollet, Guy, 328
Molné, Marc Forné, 63
Molofe, Popo, 813
Moloney, Cornelius, 134, 925
Molotov, Vyacheslav, 716
Molteno, John, 801
Moltke, Adam, 287
Mom, Manrique, 72
Mombello, Carlo di, 497
Momis, John, 682
Momoh, Joseph, 786
Momozono I (Japan), 501
Momozono II (Japan), 501
Momper, Walter, 370
Mon, Alejandro, 816
Monagas, José Gregorio, 1066
Monagas, José Ruperto, 1066
Monagas, José Tadeo, 1066
Moncada, Francesco, 64
Moncada, José, 632
Mondonça, Roberto de, 164
Mondou, Gaston, 272
Mondragon Guerra, Octavio, 586
Mones, José, 412
Money, B.W., 969
Monfeix, Jean, 336
Mong Geng Shir, 837
Mongagi, Newman, 682
Monge Alvarez, Luis, 271
Mongenast, Mathias, 542
Mongiya, Daniel, 267
Moni, S., 455
Monis, Ernest, 327
Monjardim, Argeu, 157
Monory, René, 334
Monrad, Ditlev, 287
Monreal Avila, Ricardo, 591
Monroe, James, 972, 1037
Monroe, Walter, 205
Montagne, Michel-Lucien, 345
Montagné, Michel-Lucien, 922
Montagne Markolz, Ernesto, 691

Montagne Sánchez, Ernesto, 692
Montague, Andrew, 1037
Montali, Sebastiano, 483
Montalva, Abelardo, 300
Montalva, Edouardo Frei, 223
Montanari, Attilio, 773
Montanelli, Giuseppe, 497
Montchamp, Marie-Henri, 347
Montealegra, José, 270
Montecchi, Mattia, 1064
Monteglas, Maximilian, 368
Monteiro, Bernardino, 157
Monteiro, César, 153
Monteiro, Edgar, 152
Monteiro, Ismar, 152
Monteiro, Jerônimo, 157
Monteiro, Leão, 216
Monteiro, Ricardo, 405, 776
Monteiro, Silvestre, 152
Monteiro, Vitoriano, 174
Montemayor Seguy, Rogelio, 578
Montenegro, Augusto, 164
Montenegro, Martinho, 216, 246
Montenegro, Severino, 166
Montero, Federico Toranzo, 80
Montero, José, 687
Montero, Juan Estaban, 222, 223
Montero, Lizardo, 689
Montero Ríos, Eugene, 817
Montes, Ismael, 141
Montgomery Moore, A.G., 197
Montiel, Alberto, 75
Montiel, Arturo, 582
Montiel, Hugo, 78
Montiel, Sergio, 75
Montilla, José, 1068
Montini, Giovanni, 1065
Montironi, Luigi, 772
Montironi, Stelio, 772, 773
Montoro, André, 178
Montoya, Alberto, 75
Montpezat, Jean, 346
Montt, Jorge, 222
Montt, Manuel, 222
Montt, Pedro, 222
Monzon, Elfego, 402
Moodie, Francis, 668
Moodie, Thomas, 1020
Moody, Dan, 1033
Moody, Zanas, 1024
Mook, Hubertus van, 461
Moonlight, Thomas, 1042
Moor, Frederick, 802
Moore, A. Harry, 1015
Moore, Andrew, 974
Moore, Arch, 1040
Moore, Arthur, 92
Moore, Charles, 990
Moore, Daniel, 1019
Moore, Gabriel, 974
Moore, Henry, 509, 785, 830

Moore, John, 978
Moore, Lee, 763
Moore, Marshall, 1039
Moore, Michael, 47, 627
Moore, Miles, 1039
Moore, Newton, 100
Moore, Samuel, 974
Moore, Thomas, 997
Moore, William, 1025
Moorehead, Charles, 995
Moorehead, James, 995
Moorehouse, Albert, 1008
Moores, Frank, 206
Moos, Ludwig von, 855, 856, 886
Moos, Paul von, 885
Mopeli, T. Kenneth, 810
Mora, António, 65
Mora, Manuel, 588
Mora Fernández, Juan, 270
Mora Otero, José, 28
Moracchini, Dauphin, 337
Moraczewski, Jędrzej, 698
Moraes, Domingos de, 177
Moraes, José, 157
Morais, Jaime, 64, 428
Morais, Luís de, 178
Moraitinis, Aristeidis, 394
Morales, Agustín, 140
Morales, Gerardo, 76
Morales, Melquiades, 586
Morales, Raimundo, 690
Morales Barud, Jorge, 583
Morales Bermudez, Francisco, 692
Morales Blumenkron, Guillermo, 585
Morales Gil, Eduardo, 1071
Morales Lauguasco, Carlos, 296
Morales Sánchez, Gregorio, 584
Moralez Bermudez, Francisco, 689
Moralez Bermudez, Remigo, 689
Moraliswane, Josiah, 612
Moran, Marie-Nicolas, 345
Moraques, Miguel, 71
Morauta, Mekere, 677
Moravčík, Jozef, 790
Morazan, Francisco, 270
Moreaux, Philippe, 133
Morehead, Boyd, 92
Morehead, John, 1010, 1019
Moreira, António Mascarenhas, 216
Moreira, Artur, 159
Moreira, Delphim, 148
Moreira, Guilherme, 153
Moreira, José, 161
Moreira, Traiaú, 160
Morel, Félicien, 871
Morellon, Jean, 330
Morena, Alfredo Baquerizo, 299, 300
Moreno, Julio, 300
Moreno, Manuel, 580
Moreno, Rafael Blanco, 82
Moreno Vale, Rafael, 585

Moret y Prendergast, Segismundo, 817
Moretti, Sergio, 77
Morgan, Arthur, 92
Morgan, Edwin, 1017
Morgan, Ephraim, 1040
Morgan, Rhodi, 954
Morgan, William, 94
Morgan Arthur, 91
Morgan David, 848
Morgans, Alfred, 100
Morganti, Antonio, 773
Morganti, Domenico, 772
Mori, Giancarlo, 484
Mori, Yoshiro, 504
Moriaud, Alexandre, 872
Mörikofer-Zwez, Stéphanie, 859
Morill, Anson, 998
Morin, Augustin, 198
Morin, Don, 214
Morin, Jean, 60
Morin, Michel, 340
Morina, Rahman, 1095
Morínigo, Higinio, 687
Morínigo, Marcos, 686
Morkel, Gerald, 813
Morkos, Elias, 623
Morley, Clarence, 980
Morna, Alvaro, 65
Moro, Aldo, 480
Moro, Cristoforo, 497
Morones Prieto, Ignacio, 584
Morosini, Francesco, 498
Morozov, Ivan, 732
Morri, Egisto, 771
Morri, Francesco, 771, 772
Morri, Germano, 489
Morri, Marino, 771, 772
Morri, Moro, 770, 771
Morri, Romeo, 774
Morri, Ruggero, 771
Morrill, David, 1012
Morrill, Edmund, 994
Morrill, Lot, 998
Morris, Alexander (Manitoba), 202
Morris, Alexander (Northwest Territories, Canada), 213
Morris, Edward, 205
Morris, Guy, 629
Morris, John, 95
Morris, Luzon, 981
Morrison, Cameron, 1019
Morrison, Frank, 1010
Morrison, John, 989
Morrow, Edwin, 996
Morrow, Jeremiah, 1021
Morse, David, 44
Mortezaqoli Bayat, 468
Mortier, Edouard, 325
Mortimer, Roger, 950
Morton, Julius, 1009
Morton, Levi, 1017

Morton, Marcus, 1001, 1002
Morton, Oliver, 992
Moruzi, Alexandru, 709
Móscicki, Ignacy, 697
Moscoso de Gruber, Mireya, 675
Moseley, William, 984
Moser, Fritz, 868
Moser, Karl, 867
Moser-Ott, Christoph, 890
Moser-Tobler, Albert, 890
Moses, Franklin, 1029
Moses, John, 1020
Moses, Resio, 593
Moshoeshoe II (Lesotho), 530
Mosimann, Jakob, 862, 863
Mosisili, Pakalitha, 531
Moskvichev, Ivan, 733
Mosquera, José, 80
Mosquera, Tomás de, 249
Mosquera y Arboleda, Joaquín, 249
Mosquero Narváez, Aurelio, 300
Moss, David, 967
Mossdorf, Albert, 910
Mossion, Jacques, 334
Mota, António, 155
Mota, Augusto, 428
Mota, Lourival da, 160
Mota, Wessels, 809
Mota Pinto, Carlos, 706
Mothe, Henri-Félix de la, 343
Motshekga, Mathole, 812
Mott, Hugo, 71
Motta, Apulchro, 179
Motta, Giuseppe, 854, 855
Motta, Luiz, 156
Mottet, Louis, 272
Motzfeldt, Jonathan, 290
Moudud Ahmed, 122
Mouloud Hamrouche, 60
Moultrie, William, 1028
Moungar, Fidèle, 221
Mount, James, 992
Moura, Aluízio, 173
Moura, Camile de, 161
Moura, Hastínfilo de, 177
Moura, Raul de, 163
Mouradian, Jacques, 1058
Mouradien, Jacques, 252
Mourages, Albert-Jean, 563, 568
Mourgues, Albert-Jean, 186
Mourgues, Gaston, 186
Moussa, Pierre, 256
Mousseau, Joseph-Alfred, 211
Mousson, Heinrich, 909
Moustache, José, 339
Moustapha Niasse, 781
Moutia, Sydney, 29
Mouton, Alexander, 997
Mouttel, Louis, 339
Mouttet, Henri, 867
Movisyan, Vladimir, 86

Mowat, Oliver, 208
Mowbray, Martin, 103
Mowinckel, Johan, 661
Moya, Rafael, 270
Moyano, Carlos, 80
Moyer, John, 1043
Moysés, Lupion, 168
Mpande, 806
Mphephu, Patrick, 811
Mpotokwane, Lebang, 37
Mratkhazin, Kh.I, 738
Mrazović, Karlo-Gaspar, 274
Mrksić, Luka, 1096
Msuya, Cleopa, 918
Mswati II (Swaziland), 847
Mswati III (Swaziland), 847
Mtei, Edwin, 14
Mtshali, Lionel, 812
Mtshweni, Klaas, 808
Mu Tsung (1566-72), 224
Mu Tsung (1861-75), 225
Muammar Gaddafi, 534, 535
Muaza, U., 647
Mubarak, Hosni, 303, 304
Mubarak al-Shamikh, 535
Mubarak bin Sabah as-Sabah, 519
Muchniewski, Zygmunt, 700
Mudar Badran, 506
Mudashiru, Gbolahan, 650
Mudenda, Elijah, 1098
Mudge, Dirk, 611
Muff, Erwin, 879
Mugabe, Robert, 1101
Mugglin, Carl, 879
Mugoša, Andrija, 1089, 1090
Mugoša, Dusan, 1094, 1095
Muhamadu Ibrahim, 651
Muheim, Anton, 879
Muheim, Gustav, 901
Muhinda Mamili, Richard, 612
Muhirwa, André, 188
Muhona, Paul, 263, 268
Muhsin, Shaikh, 1080
Muhsin bin Ali, 1083
Muhsin bin Farid al-Aulaqi, 1084
Muhsin bin Salih, 1085
Muhsin el-Aini, 1078
Muhsin (Haushabi), 1082
Muhyiddin (Brunei), 181
Muhyiddin Yassin, 552
Muin Gan bin Amin, 1054
Muirhead, James, 102
Mujibur Rahman, 121
Mujica, Carlos, 84
Mujica Gallo, Miguel, 692
Mukabya Mutesa I (Buganda), 939
Mukamba, Jonas, 261, 263, 268
Mukarji, Nirmal, 444
Mukashev, Salamat, 507
Mukenge, Barthélémy, 262
Mukha, Vitaly, 749

Mukhamedov, Kopleon, 1052
Mukhametshin, Farid, 738
Mukherjee, Arun, 441
Mukherjee, Ayoj, 452
Mukherjee, Harendra, 451
Mukherjee, Shanti Priya, 440, 449
Mukherjee, Sharada, 424, 430
Mukhitdinov, Nuritdin, 1052
Mukhtar Hussain, 797
Mukhtarov, _, 738
Muktar Muhammed, 647
Mukubenov, Maxim, 728
Mulamba, Leonard, 259
Mularino, Pier Marino, 774
Mularoni, Augusto, 771
Mularoni, Ermenegildo, 771
Mularoni, Fausto, 774
Mularoni, Filippo, 771, 772
Mularoni, Francesco, 771
Mularoni, Giuseppe, 771
Mularoni, Luigi, 772
Mularoni, Pier, 773
Mularoni, Piero, 774
Mulatier, Léon, 45
Mulatoni, Vincenzo, 770
Muldoon, Robert, 627
Mulele, Pierre, 267
Mulhall, Carlos, 80
Mulikihaamea, Leone, 351
Müller, Alois, 907
Müller, Bernhard, 868
Müller, Charles, 16
Müller, Eduard, 854
Müller, Fenelon, 161
Müller, Gebhard, 368, 389
Müller, Herman, 622
Müller, Hermann, 366
Müller, Jakob, 897
Müller, Josef, 901
Müller, Joseph, 874
Müller, Julio, 161
Müller, Lauro, 176
Müller, Max, 373
Müller, Paul, 888, 889
Müller, Peter, 374
Mullooly, Brian, 474
Mulroney, Brian, 199
Mulumba Lukoji, 259
Muluzi, Bakili, 549
Muminov, Abdulvali, 1051
Mumtaz Rathore, 672
Muna, Salmon, 196
Munalulu, Mbwangweta, 1099
Munasinghe, Susil, 834
Munazzar bin Ali, 1083
Munbayev, Zhalau, 507
Münch, Werner, 375
Münchhausen, Alexander, 379
Mundia, Nalumino, 1099
Mune, Dick, 684
Mungul-Diaka, Bernardin, 259

Muñiz, Pedro, 691
Munjong (Korea), 512
Münnich, Ferenc, 417
Munnik, Lourens, 802
Munongo, Godefroid, 264, 265
Muñoz, Francisco, 79
Muñoz, Marco, 590
Muñoz Marín, Luis, 1046
Muñoz Rivera, Luis, 1045
Munro, Alan, 962
Munro, Charles, 965
Munro, James, 98
Munroe, Hugh, 212
Munshi, Kanaiyalal, 450
Munu, Momodo, 15
Munzinger, Martin, 853
Munzinger, Oskar, 893
Murad, José, 160
Murad I (Turkey), 929
Murad II (Turkey), 929
Murad III (Turkey), 929
Murad IV (Turkey), 929
Murad V (Turkey), 930
Muradyan, Badal, 86
Murakhovsky, Vsevolod, 729
Muraliyev, Amangeldy, 522
Murat Casab, José, 585
Muratore, Renzo, 484
Muratov, _, 737
Muratov, Zinnyat, 738
Muratović, Hasan, 144
Muraviev, Kosta, 184
Muravsky, Valery, 595
Murayama, Tomiichi, 504
Murdanov, G.I., 363
Murer, German, 884
Muri, Alois, 46
Müri, Hans, 857
Murillo Karam, Jesús, 581
Murillo Vidal, Rafael, 590
Mürner-Gilli, Brigitte, 880
Murphee, Dennis, 1006
Murphy, Dermot, 968
Murphy, Francis, 1013
Murphy, Frank, 1004
Murphy, Franklin, 1014
Murphy, Isaac, 977
Murphy, John, 974
Murphy, Michael, 103
Murphy, Nathan, 976
Murphy, William (Bahamas), 118
Murphy, William (Zimbabwe), 1102
Murr, Wilhelm, 389
Murrah, Pendleton, 1033
Murray, Brian, 97
Murray, Charles, 764, 766
Murray, Eli, 1034
Murray, George (Australia), 93
Murray, George (Canada), 207
Murray, Jack, 676
Murray, James, 204

Murray, John, 98
Murray, Johnston, 1023
Murray, William, 1023
Murtala Mohammed, 635
Murtala Myako, 651
Murtinho, Manoel, 161
Musa, Said, 135
Musa, Solomon, 786
Musa al-Mak Kor, 841
Musa Ghiyatuddin Riayat Shah, 559
Musa Inuwa, 651
Musa Khan, 53
Musa Mohammed, 656
Musa Shehu, 654, 655
Musa Usman, 657
Musabekov, Gazanfar, 113, 114, 364
Musafir, Gurmukh Singh, 444
Musagaliev, M., 508
Musakotwane, Kebby, 1099
Museveni, Yoweri, 938
Musgrove, Ronnie, 1007
Mushanov, Nikola, 184
Mushin Sadr, 468
Mushtaq Gurmani, 668, 671
Musin, Rashid, 739
Muskie, Edmund, 999
Musoke, Kintu, 938
Musonge, Peter Mafany, 195
Mussad el-Nuweirri, 844
Mussard, Jules, 872
Mussolini, Benito, 479, 481
Mustafa al-Umari, 471
Mustafa Ben Halin, 535
Mustafa Hamed Moh Aberchán, 829
Mustafa I (Turkey), 929
Mustafa II (Turkey), 930
Mustafa III (Turkey), 930
Mustafa IV (Turkey), 930
Mustafa Khalil, 304
Mustafa Nahas Pasha, 303, 304
Mustafa Pasha Fehmi, 303
Mustafa (Tunisia), 927
Mustafayev, Feirus, 114
Mustafayev, Imam, 114
Mustafayev, Nurradin, 116
Mustaffa bin Jaafar, 551
Mustapha bin Harun, 557, 558
Mustapha Ismail, 639, 650
Mustapha Ould Salek, 568, 569
Musulamu, Lomano, 351
Musy, Jean, 869
Musy, Jean-Marie, 855
Mutaga II (Burundi), 188
Mutalibov, Ayaz, 113, 114, 115
Mutalov, Abdulkhashim, 1052
Mutambuka (Ankole), 938
Mutapćić, Abdulah, 144
Muthura, Francis, 14
Mutkurov, Sava, 183
Mutschmann, Martin, 375
Mutsuhito (Japan), 502

Muttasim Abdul-Rahim, 840
Mutter, André, 60
Müürisepp, Aleksei, 313
Muwandu, _, 265
Muwanga, Paulo, 938
Muyev, Boris, 728
Muzaffar-Ad-din (Iran), 466
Muzaffar Hussain Shah, 670
Muzaffar Qizilbashi, 671
Muzaffer-ed-Din, 1054
Muzahim al-Pachachi, 471
Muzanty, Carlos, 405
Muzanty, João, 405
Muzhir al-Raslan, 505
Muzorewa, Abel, 1101
Múzquiz, Melchor, 572
Muzzarelli, Emanuele, 1064
Mwamba-Ilunga, Prosper, 264
Mwambutsa III (Burundi), 188
Mwambutsa IV (Burundi), 188
Mwanawina II (Barotseland), 1099
Mwanawina Lewanika (Barotseland), 1099
Mwauluka, 1099
Mwezi II (Burundi), 188
Myasnikov, Aleksandr, 86, 127
Myasnikyan, Aleksandr, 86
Myburgh, Philippus, 802
Myers, Michael, 625
Myongjong (Korea), 512
Mzhavanadze, Vasili, 359

Nabiullin, Valei, 719
Nabiyev, Rakhman, 914, 915
Nabiyev, Yusif, 115, 117
Nabo, Francisco, 246
Nadar Kumaraswami Kamaraj, 448
Nadareishvili, Tamaz, 361
Nader Shah (Iran), 466
Nadig, Adolf, 875
Nadim Pachachi, 32
Nadj, Franjo, 1096
Nadjmuddin, Anak Agung, 462
Nadr bin Sharif al-Amiri, Shaikh, 1081
Nadzhafov, G., 116
Naeff, Wilhelm, 853
Naegelen, Marcel-Edmond, 59
Nägeli, Heinrich, 908, 909
Nagendra Rijal, 617
Nagoum Yamassoun, 221
Nagy, Ferenc, 417
Nagy, Imre, 417
Nahatab, Harekrushna, 458
Naidu, Chandrababu, 424
Naidu, Padmaja, 451
Naidu, Sarojini, 450
Naik, Ravi, 430
Naik, Sudakarrao, 432
Naik, Sudhakarrao, 438
Naik, Vasantrao, 438
Naim Talû, 932

Naine, Albert, 872
Nair, C.K. Balakrishna, 455
Nair, P. Vasudevan, 436
Nair, P.M., 455
Naire, C.H., 455
Naisali, Henry Faati, 39
Naiseline, Nidoïsh, 349
Najafqoli Khan Samsam os-Saltaneh, 467
Naji as-Suweidi, 471
Naji Shaukat, 471
Naji Talib, 472
Najib el-Rubai, 470
Najibullah, 54, 55
Naka-No-Mikado (Japan), 501
Nakajima, Hiroshi, 47
Nakamura, Kuniwo, 673
Nakashidze, Jemal, 362
Nakasone, Yasuhiro, 504
Nakayama, Tosiwo, 592
Nakkache, Alfred, 527, 528
Nalau, Jerry, 681
Naldo García, José, 826
Nallar, Jorge, 83
Nam Duck Woo, 518
Namaliu, Rabbie, 677
Nambudiripad, Sankaran, 436
Namgyal, Jigme, 138
Namgyal, Kyitselpa Dorji, 138
Namnansuren, Shiridambyn (Sain Noyan Khan), 599
Namphy, Henri, 410
Namsinov, Ilya, 727
Nan Ping, 243
Nance, Albinus, 1010
Nanclares, Jorge, 84
Nanda, Gulzarilal, 423
Nang Klao (Thailand), 920
Nanjappa, Venkatasubrami, 449
Nanke, Hugon, 700
Nanni, Mario, 772
Nano, Fatos, 57, 58
Naod, 314
Naon, Carlos Miranda, 73
Napier, J. Mellis, 93
Napoléon II (France), 324
Napoléon III (France), 324
Nara II (Japan), 501
Narantsatsralt, Janlaviyn, 600
Narayan, Shriman, 430
Narayanan, Kocheril, 423
Nardone, Benito, 1049
Narimanov, Nariman, 113
Narinamov, Nariman, 114
Narolin, Mikhail, 748
Nartakhova, Mariya, 736
Nartov, Dmitri, 718
Naruhiko, Higashikini, 503
Narutowicz, Gabriel, 697
Naryshkina, Natalia, 713
Nasau, Kuresa, 630
Nascimento, Lopo do, 65

Nash, Abner, 1018
Nash, George, 1022
Nash, Surendra, 432
Nash, Walter, 627
Nasir-Ad-din (Iran), 466
Nasir bin Abdullah, 1085
Nasir bin Abdullah (Fadhli), 1082
Nasir bin Aidrus, 1083
Nasiu, Ajalan, 795
Nasko, M.G., 655
Nasratollah Maksum, 914
Nasriddinova, Yadgar, 1051
Nasrollah Moshir od-Dowleh, 467
Nasrullah Khan, 53
Nasrullah Khan Babar, 667
Nasrullah Khan Khuttak, 667
Nassaruddin (Brunei), 181
Nasser, Gamal, 303, 304
Nassi Assar, 7
Nasuhi al-Bukhari, 912
Natalevich, Nikifor, 126
Natalicio González, Juan, 687
Natel, Laudo, 178
Natera, Panfilo, 591
Nath, Surendra, 444
Nathan, Matthew, 245, 390, 802
Nathan, Matthew (New Zealand), 91
Nathan, Sellapan, 787
Nattes, Ernest de (Côte d'Ivoire), 273
Nattes, Ernest de (Guadeloupe), 338
Nau, Rina, 677
Naudé, Jozua (Tom), 800
Nava Castillo, Antonio, 585
Navaka, J., 540
Navarra, Ramón Iglesias, 62
Navarro, Antenor, 166
Navarro, Armando, 71
Navarte, Andrés, 1066
Naveiro, Jorge, 81
Navinchandra Ramgoolam, 571
Navon, Yitzhak, 475
Navozov, _, 733
Nawab Zulfikar Ali Magsi, 666
Nawasasat, Dhamrong, 920
Nawaz Sharif, 665, 669
Nawinna, S.B., 833
Nayanar, Ezhambala, 436
Nazarbayev, Nursultan, 508
Nazarov, Aleksandr, 755
Nazarshoyev, M., 916
Nazdratenko, Yevgeny, 743
Nazim Akkari, 528
Nazim Kudsi, 912, 913
Nazimuddin, Khawaja (Bengal, India), 122
Nazmi Mustafa, 1095
Nazor, Vladimir, 274
Ndabuko, 806
Ndadaye, Melchoir, 188
Ndala, Bruno, 267
Ndamase, Tutor, 810
Ndaweni, J., 812

Ndebo, Bernard, 264
N'Dele, José, 65
Ndhlela, 806
Ndimira, Pascal-Firmin, 189
Ndjoba, Cornelius, 613, 614
Nduvungunye (Swaziland), 847
Nduwayo, Antoine, 189
Ne Win, U (Shu Maung), 607, 608
Neal, Eric, 93
Neame, Philip, 956
Néaoutyine, Paul, 349
Nebenius, Karl, 377
Nebi Gasi, 1094
Nedelin, Gennady, 756
Nedeljković, Bogoljub, 1094
Nedić, Milan, 1093
Nedunchezhian, V., 448
Neely, M. Mansfield, 1040
Neergaard, Niels, 288
Neff, Pat, 1033
Negi, Ramesh, 454
Negrín, Juan, 818
Nehru, Braj, 425, 426, 430, 433, 449
Nehru, Jawaharlal, 423
Nehta, Jivraj, 457
Neil, John, 989
Neill, James, 293
Neilson, William, 97
Neiva, Artur, 154
Neiva, Tude, 154
Neiva, Venâncio, 165
Nektora Ashik, 837
Nelson, Benjamin, 1010
Nelson, Gaylord, 1041
Nelson, Hugh (Australia), 91, 92
Nelson, Hugh (Canada), 200
Nelson, Knute, 1005
Nelson, Thomas, 1037
Neme Castillo, Salvador, 588
Nemeth, Károly, 416
Németh, Miklós, 417
Nemtsov, Boris, 748
Nena, Jacob, 592
Nepshekuyev, S.T., 717
Nerette, Joseph, 411
Nerfin, Paul, 906
Néry, António, 153
Néry, Júlio, 153
Néry, Paulo, 154
Néry, Silvério, 153
Nerysoo, Richard, 214
Nesković, Blagoye, 1093
Nestos, Ragnvald, 1020
Netanyahu, Binyamin, 476
Neto, Agostinho, 65
Neto, Dorgival, 166
Neto, Feitas, 171
Neto, Francisco, 179
Neto, Hugo, 171
Neto, João, 175
Neto, José (Mato Grosso, Brazil), 162

Neto, José (São Paulo, Brazil), 178
Neto, Manuel, 164
Neto, Mariano, 159
Neto, Martinho, 159
Neukomm, Ernst, 891, 892
Neumann, Johann, 381
Neurath, Konstantin, 284
Nevermann, Paul, 371
Neves, Graciano, 157
Neves, Jones, 157
Neves, José, 169
Neves, José das, 152
Neves, Leopoldo, 153
Neves, Tancredo, 149, 150, 163
Nevill, Geoffrey, 628
Neville, Keith, 1010
Neville, Robert, 118
Neville, Tim, 680
New, Laurence, 957
Newaya Krestos, 314
Newaya Mariam, 314
Newbold, Joshua, 993
Newdegate, Francis, 95, 99
Newell, William, 1014, 1039
Newlands, Harry, 124
Newlands, Henry, 212
Newman, William, 615
Newton, Francis, 147
Newton, Peter, 961
Ney, Hubert, 374
Neychev, Mintso, 183
Neyelov, Yury, 756
Neyhorst, Henry, 846
Ngala, Ronald, 509
Ngalula, Joseph, 260, 263
Ngapo Ngawang Jigme, 233, 234
Ngardou, Djidingar Domo (Michel Djidingar), 221
Ngawang Jigme Chogyal, 138
Ngawang Jigme Dakpa II, 138
Ngawang Jigme Norbu, 138
Ngendandumwe, Pierre, 188, 189
Ngeze, François, 188
Ngo Ding Diem, 1075
Ngodrup, Chokyul Yeshe, 138
Ngomane, 806
Ngouabi, Marien, 256
Ngoupande, Jean-Paul, 219
Ngubane, Baldwin (Ben), 812
Ngubane, Nyanga, 812
Nguema, Marc Nan, 32
Nguyen Ba Can, 1075
Nguyen Cao Ky, 1075
Nguyen Duc Duc (Nguyen Ung Chan), 1073
Nguyen Hiep Hoa (Nguyen Phe Hong Dat), 1073
Nguyen Huu Tho, 1074, 1075, 1076
Nguyen Khanh, 1075
Nguyen Ngoc Tho, 1075
Nguyen Phan Long, 1075

Nguyen Van Linh (Nguyen Van Cac), 1074
Nguyen Van Loc, 1075
Nguyen Van Tam, 1075
Nguyen Van Thieu, 1075
Nguyen Van Thinh, 1076
Nguyen Van Xuan, 1075, 1076
Nguyen Xuan Oanh, 1075
Nguza Karl-I-Bond (Jean Nguza), 259
Ngwane III (Swaziland), 847
Ni Xiance, 239
Nibbs, Arthur, 68
Nicchiara, Benedetto Majorana della, 487
Nice, Harry, 1001
Nichol, Walter, 200
Nicholas, Wilson, 1037
Nicholas I (Pope), 1060
Nicholas II (Pope), 1061
Nicholas III (Pope), 1062
Nicholas IV (Pope), 1062
Nicholas V (Pope), 1063
Nicholls, Francis, 997
Nicholls, Graham, 102, 103
Nicholls, Herbert, 95
Nichols, Douglas, 93
Nichols, George, 803
Nicholson, Gresham, 958
Nicholson, John, 201
Nicholson, William, 98
Nicita, Santi, 487
Nicklin, Francis, 92
Nicol, Willem, 805
Nicol, Yves-Maurice, 340
Nicola, Enrico de, 478
Nicolaas, E., 621
Nicolas, Henri-Pierre, 194
Nicole, Léon, 872
Nicolini, Marino, 770
Nicoll, John, 787
Nicolosi, Rino, 487
Nie Bichin, 244
Nie Rongzhen, 243
Niederberger, Paul, 884
Niederhauser, Rudolf, 864, 865
Niederl, Friedrich, 110
Niedra, Andrievs, 526
Niekerk, Gerrit van, 805
Niekerk, Sybrand van, 805
Niekerk, Willem van, 611
Nielly, Lucien, 1057
Niels (Denmark), 286
Nielsen, Carlos, 79
Nielsen, Finn, 289
Nielsen, Ove, 44
Nigg, Josef, 887
Nigh, George, 1023
Nigmadzhanov, Gilman, 719
Nihat Erim, 932
Nijalingappa, Siddavanahalli, 434
Nik Abdul Aziz bin Nik Mamat, 553
Nik Ahmed Kamil bin Nik Mahmud, 553
Nik Mahmud bin Ismail, 553

Nik Yusof bin Nik Abdul Majid, 553
Nikezić, Marko, 1093
Nikiferov, Petr, 758
Nikitin, A.N., 723
Nikola (Montenegro), 1089
Nikolai I (Russia), 713
Nikolai II (Russia), 713
Nikolajević, Svetomir, 1092
Nikolayev, Mikhail, 736, 737
Nikolayev, Stepan, 734
Nikonov, Viktor, 733
Nikulin, Vladimir, 728
Nikusiyar (India), 421
Nilangerkar, Shivajirao, 438
Nimani, Dzavid, 1094
Nimazhap, 739, 740
Nimba, Kabangui-Fortunat, 265
Nimitz, Chester, 1044
Nimley, David, 532
Ninan Cuyucho, 693
Ningkan, Stephen, 558
Ninko (Japan), 501
Nishani, Omer, 57
Nishanov, Rafik, 1051, 1052
Nishtar, Sardar, 668
Nistico, Giuseppe, 482
Nitti, Francesco, 479
Niveira, Fernando Piargine, 74
Nixon, Harry, 208
Nixon, Richard, 973
Niyazbekov, Sabir, 507
Niyazov, Amin, 1051, 1052
Niyazov, Saparmurad, 934, 935
Niyetullayev, Sagyndyk, 1053
Niyi Adebayo, 645
Nizamov, S.N., 738
Njekwa, 1099
N'Jie, Pierre, 356
Njotowijona, Umarjadi, 5
Nkanga, I.O., 640
Nkanu, Godwin, 650
Nkrumah, Kwame, 390, 391
Noad, Frederick, 762
Noble, Noah, 991
Noble, Patrick, 1028
Noboa Bejarano, Gustavo, 301
Nobs, Ernst, 855, 909
Nobuyuki, Abe, 513
Noe, James, 997
Noel, Edmond, 1006
Noel, Owen, 793
Noel, Philip, 1027
Nogueda Otero, Israel, 580
Nogueira, Arlindo, 170
Noirot-Cossin, Paul, 346
Noirot-Cosson, Paul, 340
Nokk, Franz, 377
Noli, Theophanes (Fan), 57
Nombe, Walter, 678
Noor, Rusli, 4, 5
Noor Adlan, 4

Noor Hassanali, 925
Norbeck, Peter, 1030
Norblad, Albin, 1024
Nord, Alexis, 410
Nordlien, Frederik, 1046
Nordli, Odvar, 661
Noriega, Zenón, 689, 691
Noriega Morena, Manuel, 675
Noriega Pizano, Arturo, 579
Norman, Colin, 104
Norman-Walker, Hugh, 147, 783
Norodom I, 190
Norodom Sihanouk, 190, 191, 192, 193
Norodom Suramarit, 190
Norquay, John, 202
Norrie, Charles, 93
Norris, Daniel, 213
Norris, Edwin, 1009
Norris, Tobias, 202
North, William, 38
Northcote, Geoffrey, 245, 407
Northcote, Henry, 627
Northcott, John, 89
Northen, William, 987
Northey, Edward, 509
Northmore, John, 99
Norton, Edward, 245
Nosov, Ivan, 944
Note, Kessai, 567
Nothomb, Jean-Baptiste, 130
Nott, Roger, 101, 104
Notte, John, 1027
Nouailhetas, Pierre, 291
Noufflard, Charles (Benin), 136
Noufflard, Charles (Vanuatu), 1057
Nouhak Phounsavanh, 523
Noumazalay, Ambroise, 256
Nouoel y Bobadilla, Adolfo, 296
Nourdine Bourhane, 253
Noutary, Jean, 922
Novaes, José de, 168
Novaković, Stojan, 1092, 1093
Novelo Torres, Ernesto, 590
Novosiltsev, Nikolai, 714
Novotný, Antonín, 282, 283
Novruzov, Neimat, 115
Nowack, Julian, 698
Nowigt, Paul, 381
Noyes, Edward, 1021
Noyoo, Hastings, 1099
Nozhikov, Yury, 745
Nsanzimana, Sylvestre, 760
Nsengiyaremye, Dismas, 760
Nsibambi, Apolo, 938
Nsibandze, Benjamin, 847
N'Singa Udjuu (Joseph N'Singa), 259
Ntare IV (Burundi), 188
Ntare V (Ankole), 938
Ntare V (Burundi) (Charles Ndideye), 188
Ntaryamira, Cyprien, 188
N'Tchama, Caetano, 406

Ntibantuganya, Sylvestre, 188
Ntikala, André, 263
Ntombi Thawala, 847
Ntoutoume-Emane, Jean-François, 354
Ntsanwise, Hudson, 808
Nu, U, 607
Nubarian, Nubar Pasha, 303
Nucci, Christian, 348
Nucete, Jesús Rondon, 1070
Nujoma, Dirk, 611
Nunes, Alacid, 165
Nunes, Lucídio, 171
Nunes, Manuel, 246
Nunes, Petrônio, 171
Nunes, Tibério, 171
Núñez, José, 631
Nuñez, Miguel, 581
Núñez, Osvaldo, 72
Nuñez, Rafael, 250
Nuñez de Cáceres, José, 295
Núñez de Prado, Miguel, 308
Núñez Portuondo, Emilio, 278
Núñez Rodríguez, Francisco, 308
Nunn, Louis, 996
Nuon Chea, 192
Nuorteva, A.F., 729
Nur Etemadi, 54
Nur Misuari, 695
Nur Taraki, 54, 55
Nureddin, Tarraf, 304
Nureddin al-Atassi, 912, 913
Nureddin Kuhala, 913
Nureddin Mahmud, 471
Nureddine Rifai, 529
Nuri es-Said, 471, 472
Nuriyev, Ziya, 720
Nurmakov, Nigmet, 508
Nurul Amin, 123, 665
Nussbaumer, Silvan, 908
Nutter, Donald, 1009
Nuvoli, Paolo, 485
Nuyens, Theodorus, 621
Nwachukwu, I., 646
Nwobodo, Jim, 645
Nxumalo, Samuel, 808
Nxumalo, Sishayi, 848
Nyabongo II (Bunyoro), 939
Nyame, Jolly, 656
Nyamoya, Albin, 188, 189
Nye, Archibald, 447
Nye, James, 1010
Nyerere, Julius, 918
Nyers, Reszö, 418
Nyffeler, Paul, 863
Nygaardsvold, Johan, 661, 662
Nzambimana, Edouard, 189
Nzondomyo, Alfred, 261

Oates, Thomas, 968
Oates, William, 975

Obademi, J.O., 642
Obafemi Awolowo, 638
Obaldia, José de, 674
Obaldia, José Domingo de, 674
Obame-Nguema, Paulin, 354
Obando, José, 249
O'Bannon, Frank, 992
Obasanjo, Olusegun, 636
Obasi, Godwin, 47
Obeid, Jorge, 82
Obeng, Paul, 391
Oberholzer, Alex, 889
Oberoi, Tirath, 453
Oberto, Giovanni, 485
Obi, Anthony, 653
Obi, Paul, 641
Obiang Nguema, Teodoro, 309
Obote, Milton, 938
Obrecht, Franz, 894
Obrecht, Max, 894, 895
Obregón, Alvaro, 574, 588
O'Brien, Charles, 124, 783
O'Brien, George, 317
O'Brien, J. Leonard, 203
O'Brien, Kolouei, 630
Obuchi, Keizo, 504
O'Callaghan, Donal, 1011
Ocana García, Samuel, 588
Occhilupo, Italo, 75
Ochab, Edward, 698, 699
Ochefu, Anthony, 657
Ochirbat, Gombojavyn, 600
Ochirbat, Punsalmaagiyn, 599
Ochoa, César, 83
Ochoa Zaragoza, Rigoberto, 584
Ochsner, Martin, 892
Ochulor, S.C., 643
O'Connor, Herbert, 1001
O'Connor, Raymond, 101
Oda, Isaiah, 677
O'Dalaigh, Cearbhall, 474
O'Daniel, W. Lee, 1033
Oddie, Tasker, 1011
Oddsson, David, 420
O'Dea, Fabian, 205
Odell, Benjamin, 1017
Odemegwu Ojukwu, C., 636, 638
Odendaal, Frans, 805
Odermatt, Gotthard, 886
Odermatt, Josef, 883, 884
Odermatt, Maria, 885
Odili, Peter, 655
Odintsev, Vladimir, 736
Odo (France), 322
Odoardo (Parma and Piacenza), 494
O'Donnell y Joria, Leopoldo, 816
Odorozzi, Tullio, 488
Odría, Manuel, 689
Oduber, Nelson, 621
Oduber Quiros, Daniel, 271
Oduoye, Simeon, 644, 651

Odzierzyński, Roman, 700
Oeake, Ope, 679
Oechslin, Stephan, 893
Oerter, Sepp, 378
O'Ferrall, Charles, 1037
Ogandzhanyan, M.G., 117
Oganesov, Nikolai, 725
Ogar, P.A.M., 650
Ogbeha, Jonathan, 640, 644
Ogbemudia, Samuel, 637, 644
Ogbonnaya Onu, 639
Ogden, Aaron, 1014
Ogi, Adolf, 856
Ogilvie, Albert, 96
Ogilvie, Richard, 991
Ogilvie, William, 214
Ogimachi (Japan), 501
Ogle, Benjamin, 1000
Oglesby, Richard, 990, 991
O'Grady, James (Australia), 95
O'Grady, James (Falkland Islands), 964
Oguey, Pierre, 906
Oguguo, A.E., 646
Ohandianyan, Hamazasp, 86
O'Higgins, Bernardo, 222
O'Higgins, Thomas, 474
Ohira, Masayoshi, 504
Ohrel, Alain, 346
Oiterong, Alfonso, 673
Ojanguren, Gerardo, 73
Okada, Keisuke, 503
Okalik, Paul, 214
Okello, Tito, 938
O'Kelly, Seán, 473
Okelo-Odongo, T., 18
Okilo, Melford, 655
Okonkwo, George, 638
Okoro Cole, Christopher, 785, 786
Okpara, Michael, 636
Okuma, Shigenobu, 502, 503
Okwesilieze Nwodo, 645
Okyar, Fethi, 931
Oladeinde, Joseph, 652
Oladipo Diya, 652
Olaechea, Manuel, 690
Oland, Victor, 206
Olano, Francisco, 79
Olarte Cullén, Lorenzo, 825
Olav I (Denmark), 286, 287
Olav I (Norway), 659
Olav II (Norway), 659
Olav III (Norway), 659
Olav IV (Norway), 660
Olav V (Norway), 660
Olayinka Sule, 647
Olcott, Benjamin, 1024
Olden, Charles, 1014
Olea Muñoz, Javier, 580
O'Leary, D.V., 104
O'Leary, Humphrey, 625
O'Leary, Terence, 967

Oleksy, Józef, 699
Oleson, Ole, 1020
Olewale, Tatie, 684
Olgiati, Oreste, 875
Olimi V (Bunyoro), 939
Oliphant, Mark, 93
Olivares Santana, Enrique, 575
Oliveir, José de, 168
Oliveira, Albano de, 246
Oliveira, António da Silva e, 176
Oliveira, Armando, 178
Oliveira, César de, 156
Oliveira, Dante de, 162
Oliveira, Eduardo de, 604
Oliveira, Francisco de, 173
Oliveira, Héctor, 75
Oliveira, Henrique de, 776
Oliveira, João de, 150
Oliveira, Joaquim da Mala e, 246
Oliveira, Jorge de, 175
Oliveira, José de, 604
Oliveira, Nísio de, 163
Oliveira, Rafael, 776
Oliver, James, 1046
Oliver, John, 201
Olivier, George Borg, 566
Olivier, Marcel, 546, 563
Olivier, Philippus, 802
Olivier, Sydney, 499
Oliviera, Domingos, 705
Olivo, Rosario, 482
Ollivier, Émile, 326
Olof (Sweden), 849
O'Loghlen, Bryan, 98
Olozaga, Salustiano de, 816
Olsen, Ann-Kristin, 662
Olsen, John, 95
Olson, Allen, 1020
Olson, Culbert, 979
Olson, Floyd, 1005
Olson, Horace (Bud), 200
Olszewski, Jan, 699
Olter, Bailey, 592
Oluka, M.A.S., 644
Olunloyo, Victor, 653
Olusegu Osoba, 652
Olusegun Osoba, 652
Olympio, Sylvanus, 923
Oman, Joseph, 1046
Omar al-Bashir, 836
Omar Ali Juma, 919
Omar Ali Saifaiddun II (Brunei), 181
Omar Ali Saifaiddun III (Brunei), 182
Omar Ali Saifuddin I (Brunei), 181
Omar Arteh Ghalib, 797
Omar bin Awadh, 1084
Omar el-Badri, 32
Omar Haroun Abdullah, 842
Omar Karami, 529
Omar Mansur al-Kikiya, 536
Omar Saif an-Nasr, 536

Omar Shah, 559
Omari, Dunstan, 14
Omari, Taris, 265
Omeruah, Samson, 645
Omeruo, T.U.N., 649
Omlin, Josef, 885
Omoboriowo, A., 652
Omu, Paul, 643
Ona, Francis, 681
Onario, Rota, 510
Ondar, Chimit-Dorzhu, 739, 740
Ondo Edu, Bonifacio, 309
O'Neal, Edward, 975
O'Neal, Emmett, 975
O'Neal, Ralph, 963
O'Neil, William, 45
O'Neill, Charles. William, 1022
O'Neill, Terence, 955
O'Neill, William, 982
Oneya, Dominic, 642, 648
Ong Tong Cheong, 787
Onganía, Juan, 70
Oni, G.O., 651
Onkelinx, Laurette, 133
Onn bin Jaafar, 551
Onoh, Christian, 645
Onoja, Lawrence, 648, 654
Onslow, Alexander, 99
Onu, Peter, 27
Onyearugbulem, Anthony, 645, 653
Oorzhak, Cherik-ool, 739, 740
Opangault, Jacques, 256
Opazo, Pedro, 222
Openg bin Sapi'ee, 558
Oplesnin, I.I., 732
Oquendo Rojo, Marcelo, 1068
Orakelashvili, Ivan (Mamia), 359, 364
Orantes, José, 401
Orazmukhamedov, Oraz, 934
Orban, Viktor, 417
Orbegoso, Luis, 688
Ordoño I (Asturias), 820
Ordoño II (Asturias), 820
Ordoño III (Asturias), 821
Ordoño IV (Asturias), 821
Ordorico Villamar, Rafael, 582
Ordway, Nehemiah, 1021
Orea, John, 677
Oreamuno, Francisco, 270
Oreamuno Flores, Alberto, 271
Örek, Osman, 280
Orellana, José, 401
Orellana, Manuel, 401
Orero, Baldassare, 310
Oresanya, S., 654
Oreshkov, A.G., 731
Oreste, Michel, 410
Orfila, Alejandro, 28
Organov, Nikolai, 714
Oribe, Manuel, 1048
Oriji, J.I., 646

Oriji Kalu, 639
Orkhan (Turkey), 929
Orlandić, Marko, 1090, 1091
Orlando, Vittorio, 479
Orlich Bolmarich, Francisco, 271
Orlov, Aleksei, 714
Orlov, Vladimir, 714
Orman, James, 980
Ormières, Louis, 353
Ormsbee, Ebenezer, 1036
Ornano, Camile d', 292
d'Ornano, Michel, 330
Ornelas Kuchle, Oscar, 578
Orozco Romero, Alberto, 582
Orr, Charles, 118
Orr, James, 1029
Orr, John Boyd, 43
Orr, Kay, 1010
Orr, Robert, 992
Orrico de los Llanos, Miguel, 588
Orselli, Georges, 272, 340, 345
Orsetti, Christian, 340
Orsi, René, 80
Orsino Saturnino, 586
Orsted, Andreas, 287
Ortega, Fausto, 585
Ortega, Melchor, 579
Ortega, Ramón, 84
Ortega Douglas, Luis, 575
Ortega Martínez, Lauro, 583
Ortega Saavedra, Daniel, 632
Ortigão, António, 216
Ortiz, René, 32
Ortiz, Roberto, 70
Ortiz Avila, José, 576
Ortiz Rubio, Pascual, 574
Ortiz Santos, Leopoldino, 587
Ortoli, François-Xavier, 17
Ortuño, René Barrientos, 141
Oruci, Bahri, 1095
Osadebay, Denis, 637
Osahito (Japan), 501
Osatkin-Vladimirsky, Aleksandr, 127
Osborn, Chase, 1004
Osborn, Thomas, 994
Osborne, Bertrand, 966
Osborne, John (Montserrat), 966
Osborne, John (USA), 1042
Osborne, Sidney, 977
Oscar I (Sweden), 850
Oscar II (Sweden), 850
O'Shanassy, John, 98
Osio, Arturo, 483
Osipov, Georgi, 732
Osipov, Georgy, 734
Oskar I (Norway), 660
Oskar II (Norway), 660
Osman al-Itadi Ibrahim, 839
Osman Ali Khan, 459
Osman bin Aroff, 552
Osman bin Mohamed, 559

Osmayev, Amin, 722
Osmeña, Sergio, 694, 695
Osóbka-Morawski, Edward, 699
Osório, Jacintho, 154
Osorio, Oscar, 307
Osorio, Pedro, 161
Osornio Camarena, Enrique, 575
Ospina, Pedro Nel, 250
Ospina Rodríguez, Mariano, 249
Osswald, Albert, 372
Ostapenko, Serhy, 941
Ostashek, John, 215
Ostrowski, Friedrich, 369
Ostrowski, Stanisław, 700
Osu Sukam, 558
Osundu, Christopher, 643
Oswald, Arthur, 878
Ota, Seisaku, 504
Otalora, José, 250
Otano Cod, Javier, 828
Otedolo, Michael, 651
Otero, Delfor, 84
Otero, Miguel, 1016
Othily, Georges, 337
Othman bin Mohamed Saat, 551
Othman I (Turkey), 929
Othman II (Turkey), 929
Othman III (Turkey), 930
Othman (Tunisia), 927
Othon (Greece), 392
Othonaos, Alexandros, 396
Otika, M.B., 652
Ott, Arnold, 878
Ottavio (Parma and Piacenza), 494
Otter, Frederik von, 851
Ottiker, Fritz, 909
Ottingen-Wallerstein, Ludwig, 368
Otto, Viktor von, 374
Otto (Bavaria), 368
Ouaidou, Nassour, 221
Ouattara, Alassane, 273
Ouedei, Goukouni, 221
Ouédraogo, Gerard, 187
Ouédraogo, Jean-Baptiste, 186
Ouédraogo, Kadré, 187
Ouédraogo, Youssouf, 187
Ouimet, Gédéon, 211
Oulevay, A., 906
Oum Cheang Sun, 191
Oumarou, Ide, 27
Oumarou Mamane, 634
Outerbridge, Leonard, 205
Ovchinnikova, Aleksandr, 736
Ovezov, Balysh, 733, 934, 935
Owen, John (Cayman Islands), 963
Owen, John (USA), 1018
Owen, Lemuel, 210
Owen, Walter, 201
Owens, Bill, 980
Owing, James, 1043
Owsley, William, 995

Oxenstiorna, Bengt Jonsson, 850
Oyakilome, Fidelis, 655
Oyandel, Abraham, 223
Oyansky, Platon (P. Sleptsov), 736
Oyegun, John, 644
Oyez-Ponnaz, Isaac, 904, 905
Oyinlola, O., 651
Øystein I (Norway), 659
Øystein II (Norway), 659
Oza, Ghanshyam, 430
Özal, Turgut, 930, 932
Ozanne, Edward Chepmell, 956
Ozdoev, Kureis, 722
Ozodunobi, V.A., 643
Ozolins, Karlis, 525
Ozov, Anatoly, 729

Paall, Edvard, 312
Paap, Johannes, 624
Paasikivi, Juho, 319, 320
Paasio, Rafael, 320
Paca, William, 1000
Pacagnini, Norberto, 78
Pace, Giovanni, 481
Pacelli, Eugenio, 1065
Pachacuti Inca Yupanqui (Casi Yupanqui), 693
Pacheco, Francisco, 151
Pacheco, Gregorio, 140
Pacheco, Romualdo, 979
Pacheco, Rondon, 163
Pacheco Arego, Jorge, 1049
Pacheco Iturribarria, José, 585
Pacheco y Gutiérrez, Joaquín, 816
Packer, William, 1025
Paddock, Algenon, 1009
Paddon, W. Anthony, 205
Padelford, Seth, 1027
Paderewski, Ignacy, 698
Padilha, Raimundo, 172
Padma Shumshere Jung, 617
Padmanabhan, A., 441
Paeniu, Bikenibeu, 936
Paes, Alvaro, 151
Paes de arros, António, 161
Paeva, Félix, 687
Páez, Federico, 300
Páez, Manuel, 587
Páez Urquidi, Alejandro, 579
Pagan Min (Myanmar), 606
Page, Carroll, 1036
Page, Earl, 88
Page, J. Percy, 199
Page, John (New Hampshire, USA), 1012
Page, John (Vermont, USA), 1035
Paghadia, Jagannath, 427
Paguaga Irias, Edmundo, 632
Pahadia, Jagannath, 446
Paia, Caesar, 838
Paiewonsky, Ralph, 1046

Paik Too Chin, 517
Paine, Charles, 1035
Painlevé, Paul, 327
Pairin Kitingan, Joseph, 558
Pais, Sidinio, 703, 705
Pajak, Antoni, 700
Pajković, Djoka, 1094
Pajković, Djoko, 1090
Pak Che Sun, 513
Pak Kyu Su, 513
Pak Sung Chul, 515
Pak Yong Hyo, 513
Paksas, Rolandas, 540
Pakvasa, Mangaldas, 436
Pal, Jagdambika, 451
Palacio, Francisco, 306
Palacio, Raimundo Andueza, 1067
Palacio López, Antonio Riva, 583
Palacios, Enrique, 829
Palacios, José Ruiz, 72
Palacios Alcocer, Mariano, 586
Palden Thondup Namgyal, 446
Paleckis, Justas, 539
Paljor Dorje Shatra, 231
Pallares, Roc, 62
Pallayev, Gaibnazar, 914
Palleschi, Roberto, 483
Palliwal, T., 446
Palma, Arturo Alessandri, 222, 223
Palma, Baudillo, 401
Palma Carlos, Adelino de, 706
Pálmason, Jón, 419
Palme, Olof, 851
Palmeira, Guiherme, 152
Palmer, Arthur, 92
Palmer, Edward, 209
Palmer, Geoffrey, 627
Palmer, Herbert, 355
Palmer, Herbert (Canada), 210
Palmer, Herbert (Cyprus), 279
Palmer, John, 991
Palmer, Reginald, 399
Palmer, William, 1035
Palomba, Federico, 487
Palomino Dena, Benito, 575
Pálsson, Thorsteinn, 420
Paluku, Denis, 261, 264, 266, 267
Pámanes Escobedo, Fernando, 591
Pamfilov, Konstantin, 715
Pan Cili, 233
P'an Fu, 227
Pančevski, Milan, 545, 1088
Pancheri, Enrico, 488
Panday, Basdeo, 926
Pande Bishambhar, 442
Pandey, Bhairab, 444
Pandey, Bhairub, 451
Pandey, Kedar, 427
Pandey, Vinod Chandra, 427
Pandit, Anand, 454
Pandit, Vijaya Lakshmi, 437

Pando, José, 141
Pandolfi Arbulú, Alberto, 692
Pandt, Th.M., 624
Panev, Zosima, 732
Pangalos, Theodoros, 393
Pangalos, Theoforos, 396
Pangandaman, Lininding, 695
Pangelinan, Del, 593
Pangelinan, Lourdes, 35
Panić, Milan, 1088
Panigrahi, Chintamani, 439
Panizzi, Gabriele, 483
Pant, Govind Ballabh, 450
Panyarachun, Anand, 921
Panzera, Francis, 147
Pao Birendra Singh, 431
Papadopoulos, Georgios, 393, 397
Papagos, Alexandros, 397
Papanastasiou, Alexandros, 396
Papandreou, Andreas, 397
Papandreou, Georgios, 396, 397, 398
Papen, Franz von, 366, 384
Papinaud, Pierre, 345
Papunidze, Vakhtang, 362
Papyan, Matsak, 85
Para, Arnaldo, 772
Paradelo, Mario Castulo, 82
Paranagúa, Joaquim, 170
Parant, Philippe, 344
Paraskevopoulos, Ioannes, 397
Pardee, George, 979
Pardo, José, 690
Pardo, Manuel, 689
Pardo y Barreja, José, 689
Pardos, Carlos, 83
Paredes, Beatriz, 590
Paredes, Mariano, 401
Paredes, Rubén, 675
Paredes y Arrillaga, Mariano, 573
Parent, Simon-Napoléon, 211
Parhon, Constantine, 708
Pariani, Alberto, 56
Parikh, Rasiklal, 460
París, Gabriel, 250
Parison, Georges-Hubert, 780
Parison, Jean-Paul, 568
Parisot, Georges-Hubert (Martinique & Gabon), 340, 353
Parisot, Georges-Hubert (New Caledonia), 347
Parisot, Jean-Paul, 403
Parizeau, Jacques, 212
Park, Guy, 1008
Park Choong Hoon, 517, 518
Park Chung Hee, 517
Park Eun Sik, 514
Park Tae Joon, 518
Parker, Carlos Gigena, 73
Parker, James, 964
Parker, Joel, 1014
Parker, John (American Samoa), 1043

Parker, John (Canada), 213
Parker, John (USA), 997
Parker, Reginald, 212
Parkes, Henry, 89, 90
Parkhurst, Frederick, 999
Parks, George, 975
Parmar, Yeshwant, 433
Parnell, Harvey, 978
Parnell, John, 103
Parolin, Orlando, 83
Parr, Cecil, 557
Parra, Aquillo, 250
Parra, Francisco (Mexico), 584
Parra, Francisco (OPEC), 32
Parreiras, Ari, 172
Parri, Ferruccio, 479
Parris, Albion, 998
Parsi, Jean, 340
Parsons, Andrew, 1003
Parsons, Lewis, 974
Partl, Alois, 111
Parushothaman, Vakkom, 453
Pascal, Pierre (Côte d'Ivoire), 272
Pascal, Pierre (Djibouti), 291
Pascal I (Pope), 1060
Pascal II (Pope), 1062
Pascal-Tourilot, Ertha, 410
Pasetto, Giorgio, 483
Pashi, Alphonse, 267
Pashkovski, Yu.G., 758
Pasić, Nikola, 1087, 1092, 1093
Paskar, Pyotr, 595
Pasolini, Gastone, 773
Pasquale, Francesco, 770, 771
Pasquale, Valerio, 771
Passarinho, Jarbas, 165
Pastore, John, 1027
Pataki, George, 1018
Patardze, Zurab, 359
Pataskar, Hari, 436
Patassé, Ange-Félix, 219
Patel, Babubhai, 431
Patel, Chimanbhai, 430
Patel, J.H., 435
Patel, Keshubhai, 431
Patenaude, Esioff, 211
Paterson, T.F., 102
Paterson, Thomas, 200
Paterson, William, 1014
Pathak, Gopal, 434
Patient, Serge, 337
Patil, Vasantrao, 438, 445
Patil, Veerebdral, 435
Patil, Veerendra, 435
Patita Vaimua, Soane, 351
Patnaik, Bijayanand, 443
Patnaik, Biju, 443
Patnaik, Janaki, 443
Patnaik, Naveen, 443
Patnaik, N.M., 449
Patolichev, Nikolai, 128

Patrick Olimi (Toro), 939
Patrón, Hernán Risso, 80
Päts, Konstantin, 312, 313
Patsatsia, Otar, 359
Patten, Christopher, 245
Patten, Paul, 996
Patterson, Dennis, 214
Patterson, Isaac, 1024
Patterson, James (Australia), 98
Patterson, James (Canada), 202
Patterson, John, 975
Patterson, Malcolm, 1031
Patterson, Paul, 1024
Patterson, Percival, 500
Patterson, William, 212, 213
Patteson, Okev, 1040
Pattison, John, 1022
Pattison, Robert, 1025
Pattison, Séamus, 474
Patton, John, 1037
Patton, Robert, 974
Pattullo, Thomas, 201
Patwa, Sunderlal, 437
Patwari, Prabhudas, 448
Paul, Hans, 110
Paul, John, 118, 134, 355, 957
Paul, José Rojas, 1067
Paul, Rudolf, 376
Paul-Boncour, Joseph, 327
Paul Friedrich (Mecklenburg-Schwerin), 381
Paul I (Pope), 1060
Paul II (Pope), 1063
Paul III (Pope), 1063
Paul IV (Pope), 1063
Paul V (Pope), 1063
Paul VI (Pope), 1065
Paula, Alejandro, 622
Paula, José de, 157
Paula Santander, Francisco de, 249
Paulen, Ben, 994
Paulisbo, Patrick, 680
Paulo Cid, Francisco, 776
Paulos (Greece), 393
Paulssen, Arnold, 376
Pauluks, Janis, 526
Pauncefort, Bernard, 968, 969
Pavate, Dadasaheb, 444
Pavel (Russia), 713
Pavelić, Ante, 274, 275
Pavetić, Vlatko, 274
Pavlov, Artem, 740
Pavlov, Georgy, 733
Pavlov, Valentin, 716
Pavlov, Yakov, 724
Paw Tun, 607
Pawar, Sharad, 438
Pawlak, Waldemar, 699
Pawley, Howard, 203
Payan, Eliseo, 250
Paye, Jean-Claude, 30

Payet, Christophe, 342
Payet, Roger, 342
Payne, Frederick, 999
Payne, James, 532
Paynter, Samuel, 983
Paz, Manuel da, 170
Paz, Osvaldo Alvarez, 1072
Paz Barahona, Miguel, 413
Paz García, Policarpo, 413
Paz Soldan, Carlos, 692
Pea Talavou, 768
Peabody, Endicott, 1003
Peabody, James, 980
Peacock, Alexander, 98
Peake, Archibald, 94
Pearkes, George, 201
Pearson, Arthur, 215
Pearson, Aylmer, 557
Pearson, Christopher, 215
Pearson, Lester, 199
Pearson, Paul, 1046
Pease, Elisha, 1033
Peay, Austin, 1032
Peçanha, Celso, 172
Peçanha, Nilo (Brazil), 148
Peçanha, Nilo (Rio de Janeiro, Brazil), 171
Pechoux, Laurent-Elisée, 347
Pechoux, Laurent-Élisée, 272
Péchoux, Laurent-Elisée, 922
Peçi, Sotir, 56
Peck, Ashael, 1035
Peck, George, 1041
Peckford, Brian, 206
Pedan, Nikolai, 717
Pedernera, Juan Esteban, 69
Pedersen, Torben, 289
Pedini, Vincenzo, 772
Pedini-Angellini, Maria, 773
Pedrazzini, Alex, 900, 901
Pedrini, Ferdinando, 80
Pedro I (Aragon), 820
Pedro I (Brazil), 148
Pedro I (Castile), 821
Pedro I (Navarre), 823
Pedro I (Pedro), 702
Pedro II (Aragon), 820
Pedro II (Brazil), 148
Pedro II (Portugal)), 703
Pedro III (Aragon), 820
Pedro III (Portugal)), 703
Pedro IV (Aragon), 820
Pedro IV (Portugal)), 703
Pedro V (Portugal)), 703
Pedrosa, Amaro, 169
Pedrosa, Jônathas, 153
Pedrosa, Silvio, 174
Pedrossian, Pedro, 162
Pedrozo, Miguel, 81
Peebles, Herbert (British Virgin Islands), 962
Peebles, Herbert (Montserrat), 966

Peebles, Herbert (St Vincent and Grenadines), 766
Peel, Robert, 952
Peel, Robert (Saint Helena), 968
Peel, William (Hong Kong), 245
Peel, William (Kiribati), 510
Peereboom, Julius van den, 130
Peery, George, 1037
Pehrsson-Bramstorp, Axel, 851
Pei Lisheng, 241
Peidl, Gyula, 417
Peien, Aloitch, 683
Peixoto, Dermerval, 169
Peixoto, Ernâni, 172
Peixoto, Floriano, 148
Peixoto, José, 151, 155
Pekar, Tsondu, 138
Peker, Recep, 932
Pekkala, Mauno, 320
Pelayo (Asturias), 820
Pelham, Henry, 951
Pelicier, Marie-Marc, 340, 347
Pelieu, Pierre-François, 272, 354
Pelivan, Jure, 144
Peliza, Robert, 965
Pella, Guiseppe, 479
Pellanda, Rubén, 74
Pellegrini, Angelo, 900
Pellegrini, Carlos, 69
Pellerin, Christian, 343
Pelletier, Charles, 211
Pelletier, Émile, 598
Pelloux, Luigi, 479
Pelse, Arvids, 526
Pen, Albert, 345
Pen Sovan, 192
Peña, Luis Sáenz, 69
Peña, Pedro, 687
Peña, Roque Sáenz, 69
Peña y Peña, Manuel de la, 573
Peñaranda, Enrique, 141
Penchoo Namgyal I, 446
Penchoo Namgyal II, 446
Penezić, Slobodan, 1093
Penfold, Peter, 963
Peng Chong, 239
Peng Dehuai, 233
Peng Zhen, 243
Pengel, Johan-Adolf, 846
Peni, Wilson, 681
Penikett, Tony, 215
Penn Nouth, 191, 192, 193
Penna, Affonso, 148
Pennewill, Simeon, 984
Pennington, John, 1020
Pennington, William, 1014
Pennington, William S., 1014
Pennoyer, Sylvester, 1024
Pennypacker, Samuel, 1025
Pensotti, Mario, 76
Penteado, Heitor, 177

Pentier, Robert, 339
Pepin III (France), 322
Peralta Azurdia, Enrique, 402
Peralta López, José, 588
Perassi, Oscar, 76
Perceval, Spencer, 951
Pércovich Roca, Luis, 692
Perdigão, José, 160
Perdomo, Elpidio, 583
Pereira, Americo, 166
Pereira, António, 776
Pereira, Aristides, 216
Pereira, Bráulio, 154
Pereira, Carlos, 405
Pereira, Domingos, 705
Pereira, Epitácio, 160
Pereira, Gabriel, 1048
Pereira, Lafaiete, 150
Pereira, Luiz, 155
Pereira, Manoel, 154
Pereira, Renato Costa, 44
Pereira, Waldo Bernal, 141
Pereira, Washington, 177
Peres, Haroldo, 168
Peres, Shimon (S. Persky), 475, 476
Perey, Claude, 906
Pérez, Aniceto, 73
Pérez, Joaquín, 1044
Pérez, José, 222
Pérez, Juan Bautista, 1067
Pérez, Manuel, 76
Pérez, Mariano Ospina, 250
Pérez, Santiago, 250
Pérez Arce, Enrique, 587
Pérez Balladares, Ernesto, 675
Pérez-Caballero, Joaquín Espert, 827
Pérez Camara, Carlos, 576
Pérez Crespo, Antonio, 828
Pérez de Castro, Evaristo, 815
Pérez de Cueller, Javier, 42
Pérez de Lema Tejero, José, 761
Pérez Gallardo, Reynaldo, 587
Pérez García, Alfonso, 585
Pérez Godoy, Ricardo, 689, 692
Pérez Martínez, Héctor, 576
Pérez Saénz, José, 827
Perham, Sidney, 998
Perie, Jean, 350
Périer, Casimir, 325
Perillo, Marconi, 158
Perisin, Ivo, 275
Perkins, George, 979
Perl, Nestor, 73
Permeti, Turkhan Pasha, 57
Pernambuco, Miguel, 164
Perneartti, Agustín, 71
Perneta, João, 167
Pernice, Hugo, 83
Pérodeau, Narcisse, 211
Perón, Juan, 70
Perón, María Estela de, 70

Perosević, Bosko, 1096
Perpich, Rudolph, 1005
Perréard, François, 872
Perréard, Jules, 872
Perreau-Pradier, Jean, 341
Perret, P., 905
Perrier, Ernest, 869, 870
Perrier, Louis, 880
Perriez, Franck, 338
Perron, Marshall, 102
Perrone, Ettore, 495
Perry, Benjamin, 1029
Perry, Edward, 985
Perry, Madison, 984
Perry, Roger, 969
Perry, Ruth, 533
Pershin, Nikolai, 730
Persico, Giovanni, 484
Persons, Gordon, 975
Persson, Göran, 852
Pertini, Alessandro, 478
Perugini, Pasquale, 482
Perumal, Annamalai, 832
Peruzzi, Ubaldino, 497
Pervez Mushahraf, 665
Pesaro, Giovanni, 498
Pessoa, António, 165
Pessôa, Epitácio, 148
Pessôa, Pantaleâo, 172
Pétain, H. Philippe, 325, 328
Petar I (Montenegro), 1089
Petar II (Montenegro), 1089
Peter, Carl, 865
Péter (Hungary), 414
Peter I (Oldenburg), 382
Peter I (Serbia), 1086, 1091
Peter II (Oldenburg), 382
Peter II (Serbia), 1086, 1088
Peterle, Lojze, 792
Peters, Arthur, 210
Peters, Frederick, 210
Peters, John, 981
Peters, Leonard, 621
Petersen, Carl, 371
Petersen, Hjalmar, 1005
Petersen, Marita, 289
Petersen, Rudolf, 371
Peterson, David, 209
Peterson, Russell, 984
Peterson, Val, 1010
Peterson, Walter, 1013
Petillon, Léon, 189, 258
Pétion, Alexandre, 409
Petit, Camille, 341
Petit, Edouard, 345
Petit, Raphaël, 340
Petitbon, Jean, 291, 346
Petitpierre, Max, 855
Petliura, Simon, 940
Petre, Léon, 633
Pêtre, Léon, 922

Petrić, Jaksa, 274
Petrochi, Julio, 72
Petronia, Ernesto, 622
Petronilla (Aragon), 820
Petrosyan, Georgy, 116
Petrosyan, Leonard, 117
Petrov, Aleksandr, 724
Petrov, Gennady, 733
Petrov, I.P., 732
Petrov, I.S., 730
Petrov, Ivan, 737
Petrov, Sergei, 724
Petrov, Vladimir, 718
Petrović, Dušan, 1091
Petrović-Blaznavac, Milivoje, 1092
Petrović-Blaznavac, Milovije, 1091
Petrović-Njegos, Božo, 1090
Petrovsky, Grigory, 940, 941
Petrulis, Vytautas, 539
Petrushkov, _, 734
Petrushkov, N.I., 1055
Petsun, E.G., 737
Pettavel, Louis-Auguste, 880
Pettus, John, 1006
Peuvergne, Jean, 136, 338, 403, 780
Pevznyak, P.M., 737
Peynado, Jacinto, 296
Peyrot, François, 873
Peyrouton, Bernard-Marcel, 59
Pezer, Jean, 336
Pezet, Juan, 688
Pezet, Michel, 334
Pfister, Max, 880
Pfister, Otto, 909
Pfisterer, Thomas, 859
Pflimlin, Pierre, 328
Pfordten, Ludwig, 368
Pfretzschner, Adolf, 369
Pfuel, Ernst von, 383
Pham Hung, 1074
Pham Van Dong, 1074
Phan Huy Quat, 1075
Phan Khac Suu, 1075
Phan Van Khai, 1074
Phan Wannamethee, 5
Phanomjong, Pridi, 920
Pharaon, Henri, 528
Phatudi, Cedric, 809
Phaya Khammao, 523
Phelan, Edward, 44
Phelps, John, 1008
Phelps, Phelps, 1043
Pherekyde, Mihai, 709
Philemon, Titus, 680
Philip, Pierre, 341
Philipp, Emmanuel, 1041
Philippe d'Orleans, 323
Philippe (Felipe) I (Navarre), 823
Philippe (Felipe) II (Navarre), 823
Philippe (Felipe) III (Navarre), 823
Philippe I (France), 323

Philippe II (France), 323
Philippe III (France), 323
Philippe IV (France), 323
Philippe V (France), 323
Philippe VI (France), 323
Philipson, Gilbert, 338
Phillips, Frederick, 762
Phillips, Harold, 970
Phillips, John, 977
Phillips, Leon, 1023
Phillips, Oladipo, 641
Phillips, William, 612
Philp, Robert, 92
Phinéra-Horth, Stéphan, 337
Pho Proeung, 192
Phola Sonam Tobgye, 230
Pholien, Joseph, 131
Phoofolo, Hae, 531
Phosa, Mathews, 812
Phoui Sananikone, 523, 524
Phoumi Vongvichit, 523
Phraya Taksin (Thailand), 920
Pi y Margall, Francisco, 815
Pianna, Osvaldo, 175
Piano, Rafael de, 73
Piastrellini, Guillermo, 77
Piatakov, Georgy, 941
Picado Michalski, Teodoro, 271
Picanon, Edouard, 336, 347
Picard, Paul, 342
Pichardo Pagaza, Ignacio, 582
Pickard, E.T., 104
Pickens, Andrew, 1028
Pickens, Francis, 1029
Pickens, Israel, 974
Pickering, William, 1039
Picornell, Jerónimo Albertí, 825
Picot, Albert, 872
Picot, François, 873
Picque, Charles, 132
Picquie, Albert, 546
Pidoux, Philippe, 907
Pieck, Wilhelm, 367
Piedra, Carlos, 278
Pienaar, J.Jacobus, 805
Pienaar, Louis, 611
Pier-Luiga (Parma and Piacenza), 494
Pierce, Benjamin, 1012
Pierce, Franklin, 972
Pierce, Gilbert, 1021
Pierce, Walter, 1024
Pieri, Claude, 347
Pierlot, Hubert, 131, 132
Piero I de Medici (Tuscany), 496
Piero II de Medici (Tuscany), 496
Pierola, Nicolás de, 689
Pierpont, Francis, 1037
Pierre-Alype, Marie-François, 338
Pierre-Louis, Joseph, 410
Pierret, Claude, 350
Pierrot, Jean-Louis, 409

Pierson, Nicolaas, 619
Piesch, Hans, 109
Pietro, Joaquín, 222
Pietro I (Sicily), 493
Pietro II (Sicily), 493
Piette, Maurice, 597
Pieve, Janis, 526
Pike, Theodore, 798
Piksayev, Aleksandr, 734
Piksin, Ivan, 734
Pilapitiya, Abeyratne, 833, 834
Pile, William, 1015
Pilet-Golaz, Marcel, 855
Pilgrim, Michael, 765
Piljak, Obrad, 143
Pillai, Pattom, 423, 435, 436, 444
Pillai, T.K. Narayana, 435
Pillar, Joseph, 870
Pillar, William, 958
Pillersdorf, Franz von, 106
Pilling, Henry, 968
Pillsbury, John, 1004
Piloko, Make, 352
Pilsudski, Józef, 697
Piłsudski, Józef, 698
Pimental, António, 704
Pimental, Francelino, 405
Pimental, Paulo, 168
Pimental, Pedro, 295
Pimental e Melo, Carlos, 776
Pimentel, António, 153
Pimentel, Francisco, 156
Pimputkar, M.C., 454
Piña Olaya, Mariano, 586
Pinard, Lionel, 399
Pinaud, Luís, 172
Pinay, Antoine, 328
Pinchback, Pinckney, 997
Pinchot, Gifford, 1025
Pinckney, Charles, 1028
Pinckney, Thomas, 1028
Pindall, Zenophon, 978
Pindling, Lynden, 119
Pineau, Christian, 328
Pineda, Laureano, 631
Pinelli, Pierdionigi, 495
Piñero, Jesús, 1045
Pingree, Hazen, 1004
Pingree, Samuel, 1036
Pinheiro, Edward, 165
Pinheiro, Israel, 163
Pinheiro, Severino, 169
Pinho, João, 154
Pinilla, Gustavo Rojas, 250
Pinilla Fábrega, José, 675
Pinkham, Lucius, 988
Pinkowski, Józef, 699
Pinney, Charles, 104
Pinochet Ugarte, Augusto, 223
Pintasligo, Maria, 706
Pinto, Aníbal, 222

Pinto, Carlos, 178
Pinto, Edmundo, 151
Pinto, Francisco, 222
Pinto, João, 165
Pinto, José, 163
Pinto, Liberato, 705
Pinto, Otomar, 176
Pinto da Costa, Manuel, 777
Pip, Ants, 312
Pipes, William, 207
Pipinelis, Panayotis, 397
Pir Allahi Baksh, 670
Pirchegger, Anton, 110
Pires, António, 162
Pires, Francisco, 777
Pires, José, 297
Pires, Manoel, 161
Pires, Mario, 298
Pires, Pedro, 217
Pirocanac, Milan, 1092
Piruzyan, Aram, 86
Pirzada Abdus Sattar, 670
Pisani, Alviso, 498
Pisani, Edgard, 348
Pistarini, Héctor Puente, 76
Pistulli, Antoine, 56
Pita, Juan, 74
Pitakaka, Moses, 793
Pitat, Joseph, 338
Pitcher, Nathaniel, 1017
Pithárt, Petr, 281
Pithey, Jack, 1101
Pitkin, Frederick, 980
Piton, Guillermo Pérez, 73
Pitra, František, 281
Pitt, William, 951
Pitteloud, Cyrille, 903
Pittet, Michel, 871
Pittius, Nicolaas Gey van, 805
Pittman, Vail, 1011
Pitu, Jacob, 795
Pius II (Pope), 1063
Pius III (Pope), 1063
Pius IV (Pope), 1063
Pius IX (Pope), 1064, 1065
Pius V (Pope), 1063
Pius VI (Pope), 1064
Pius VII (Pope), 1064
Pius VIII (Pope), 1064
Pius X (Pope), 1065
Pius XI (Pope), 1065
Pius XII (Pope), 1065
Piva, Ferruccio, 773
Pivovarov, Nikolai, 721
Pizano, Ernesto Samper, 251
Pizzey, Jack, 92
Plaisted, Frederick, 999
Plaisted, Harris, 999
Planinc, Milka, 275, 1087
Planta, Rudolf, 875
Plantegenest, Marc, 345

Plantz, William, 623
Plastiras, Nikolas, 396, 397
Plater, George, 1000
Platov, Vladimir, 752
Platteel, Pieter, 464
Plattner, Wilhelm, 875
Platts, Frederick, 627
Plavsić, Biljana, 145
Playford, E.C., 101
Playford, Thomas, 94
Playford, Thomas (grandson), 95
Plaza, José, 80
Plaza, Victorino de la, 69
Plaza Lasso, Galo, 28, 300
Pleasant, Ruffin, 997
Pleasants, James, 1037
Pleass, Clement, 636
Plehwe, Karl von, 49
Plenet, Henri, 337
Plessis, Johannes du, 804
Plessis, Josias du, 802
Pleven, René, 328, 331
Plimsoll, James, 96
Plow, Edward, 206
Plowman, George, 803
Plumer, Herbert, 476
Plumer, William, 1012
Poati-Souchlaty, Alphonse, 256
Poccard, Pedro Braillard, 74
Podeschi, Claudio, 774
Podewils-Durniz, Klemens, 369
Podgayev, G.Ye., 742
Podgornov, Nikolai, 753
Podgorny, Nikolai, 716, 942
Pogosyan, Genrikh, 117
Pogosyan, Zhirayr, 117
Poher, Alain, 325
Poincaré, Raymond, 324, 327
Poindexter, George, 1005
Pointer, Mike, 629
Pointexter, Joseph, 988
Poiret, Jean, 403
Pokawin, Stephen, 680
Pol Pot (Saloth Sar), 192, 193
Polamo Valencia, Florencio, 590
Polat, 739
Poleanov, Vladimir, 744
Poletti, Charles, 1018
Poletti, Rodolfo, 78
Polezhayev, Leonid, 749
Policarpe Vermont, 337
Polignac, Jules de, 325
Politis, Nikolas, 396
Poliuan, Yan, 757
Polk, Charles, 983
Polk, James, 972, 1031
Polk, Trusten, 1007
Pollard, John, 1037
Pollen, Daniel, 626
Pollock, Edwin, 1043
Pollock, James, 1025

Polonski, Vladimir, 114
Polozkov, Ivan, 715
Poluyanov, Nikolai, 755
Polyakov, Ivan, 126
Polyansky, Dmitry, 715
Pomare I (Tu Tinah), 352
Pomare II, 352
Pomare III, 352
Pomare IV (Aimata), 352
Pomare V (Teri'i Tari'Arthur), 352
Pomarez, Robert, 76
Pommies, Robert, 342, 350
Pompidou, Georges, 325, 328
Ponce, Generosa, 161
Ponce, Manuel, 689
Ponce de León, Ernesto Zedillo, 574
Ponce de León, Griselda Alvarez, 579
Ponce Enríquez, Camilo, 300
Ponce Vaides, Federico, 401
Ponchardier, Dominique, 292
Pond, Charles, 981
Ponder, James, 983
Ponikowski, Antoni, 698
Ponomarenko, Panteleimon, 127, 508
Ponomarev, Aleksandr, 758
Ponomarev, Mikhail, 728
Pons, Antonio, 300
Pont, René-Louis, 344
Ponte, Nicolo da, 498
Ponton, Louis, 340
Poonacha, Cheppudira (Coorg, India), 458
Poonacha, Cheppudira (Madhya Pradesh, India), 436
Poonacha Cheppudira, 442
Pope, James, 209, 210
Pope, John, 977
Popham, Henry, 293
Popit, France, 791, 792
Poplasen, Nikola, 145
Popok, Yakov, 742, 935
Popov, Blagoje, 545
Popov, Dimitar, 185
Popov, F.V., 718
Popov, Gavriil, 754
Popović, Evgenije, 1090
Porchet, F., 905
Porciúncula, José de, 159, 171
Porras, Belisario, 674
Porras, Meliton, 691
Porritt, Arthur, 626
Portela, Francisco, 171
Portela Valladares, Manuel, 818
Porteous, George, 212
Porter, Albert, 992
Porter, David, 1025
Porter, James, 1031
Portes Gil, Emilio, 574
Portillo, Anibal, 307
Portillo Cabrera, Alfonso, 402
Portillo y Pacheco, José López, 574
Pôrto, Dorval, 153

Portugal, Clotário, 167
Portusach, Francisco, 1044
Posada Herrera, José de, 817
Posada Moreno, Jesús, 826
Posey, Thomas, 991
Posibeyev, Grigory, 733
Posleman, Eduardo, 81
Posnett, Richard, 134
Posnette, Richard, 960
Posse, Arvid, 851
Posser da Costa, Guilherme, 777
Post, Regis, 1045
Potapov, Leonid, 720, 721
Pote Sarasin, 38
Pothier, Aram, 1027
Potocki, Alfred, 106
Potter, George, 1003
Potter, Philip, 50
Potts, Benjamin, 1008
Potts, Temphin, 1044
Poudroux, Jean-Luc, 342
Poulet, Georges, 344
Poulet, Georges-Virgile, 339, 353
Poulitsas, Panayotis, 396
Poullet, Prosper, 130
Poungui, Ange, 256
Pourchon, Maurice, 330
Pourier, Miguel, 622
Poveda Burbano, Alfredo, 300
Powell, Lazarus, 995
Powell, Wesley, 1013
Powers, Llewellyn, 999
Powers, Ridgely, 1006
Powles, Guy, 769
Pownall, Charles, 1044
Poyer, John, 1043
Poynter, William, 1010
Pozderac, Hamidija, 143, 144
Pozdeyev, Pavel, 744
Pozgalev, Vyacheslav, 753
Pozo, Agapito, 586
Pradeep Singh, 455
Pradervand, J.-P., 906
Pradhan, R.D., 425
Prado, Mariano, 689
Prado Proano, Eugenio, 577
Prado Ugarteche, Javier, 691
Prado y Ugarteche, Jorge, 691
Prado y Ugarteche, Manuel, 689
Praga, Herculano, 159
Prajadhipok (Thailand), 920
Prakasa, Sri, 425, 437, 447, 458
Prakasam, Tanguturi, 424, 448
Prakash, Chaudhary Brahim, 454
Pramoj, Kukrit, 921
Pramoj, Seni, 920, 921
Prasad, Baleshwar, 438, 439, 447, 454
Prasad, Mahabir, 431, 432
Prasad, Mata, 425
Prasad, Rajendra, 422
Prasad, Siddheshwar, 449

Prasad, Sukhdev, 445
Prasada, Shankar, 454
Pratadasinha Sah (Nepal), 616
Pratt, Thomas, 1000
Prawiraranegara, Sjarifuddin, 462
Pré, Roland (Burkina Faso), 186
Pré, Roland (Cameroon), 194
Pré, Roland (Djibouti), 291
Pré, Roland (Gabon & Guinea), 353, 403
Premachandra, G.M., 833
Premadasa, Ranasinghe, 830, 831
Premajayantha, Susil, 834
Premsyl Otakar I (Bohemia), 281
Premsyl Otakar II (Bohemia), 282
Prendergast, George, 99
Prescott, Benjamin, 1012
Preston, James, 1037
Preston, Lewis, 43
Preto, José, 705
Pretorius, Jacobus (Kosie), 614
Pretorius, Martinus, 803, 804
Preus, Jacob, 1005
Preux, Charles de, 902
Preval, René, 411
Priani, Pedro (Chubut, Argentina), 72
Priani, Pedro (Santa Cruz, Argentina), 82
Price, George, 135
Price, Henry, 1044
Price, James, 1037
Price, Rodman, 1014
Price, Sterling, 1007
Price, Thomas, 94
Prim y Prets, Juan, 816
Primakov, Yevgeny, 715
Primo de Rivera y Orbaneja, Miguel, 818
Primrose, Philip, 199
Prince, L. Bradford, 1015
Principe, Francesco, 482
Prinsloo, G.D.P., 614
Prio Socarras, Carlos, 277, 278
Prior, Edward, 200, 201
Prisching, Franz, 110
Pristina, Hassan, 57
Pritchett, Kintzing, 1023
Prithwi Natayana (Nepal), 616
Prithwi (Nepal), 616
Pritytsky, Sergei, 126
Priuli, Antonio, 498
Priuli, Girolamo, 498
Priuli, Lorenzo, 498
Prlić, Jadranko, 145
Probyn, Leslie, 124, 499, 785
Proctor, Fletcher, 1036
Proctor, Mortimor, 1036
Proctor, Redfield, 1035
Proctor, Redfield Jr, 1036
Prodi, Romani, 17
Prodi, Romano, 480
Proietti, Carlo, 483
Prokhorov, Aleksandr, 751
Prokkonen, Pavel, 730

Prokopev, Leonid, 724
Prokopovich, Viacheslav, 941
Prokopyev, Ilya, 724
Prokopyev, Yury, 737
Pröll, Erwin, 109
Propsting, William, 96
Protić, Kosta, 1092
Protić, Stojan, 1087, 1093
Proto, Félix, 339
Protopapadakis, Petros, 396
Protopopov, Dmitri, 915
Proust, Jean-Paul, 338
Prouteaux, Georges-David, 218
Prouty, George, 1036
Provenzano, Giuseppe, 487
Prowse, Thomas, 209
Prum, Pierre, 543
Prunskiene, Kazimiera, 539
Prusak, Mikhail, 749
Pryor, David, 978
Prystor, Aleksander, 698
Przemsyl (Poland), 696
Pu Chauzhu, 243
Pu Haiqing, 244
Pu Yamethin, U, 607
P'u-Yi, 230
Puapua, Tomasi, 936
Pućar-Sjari, Djuro, 143, 144
Puddu, Mario, 486
Puente Raygada, Oscar do le, 692
Puerreydon, Juan, 69
Puerta, Ramón, 79
Puertra, Luis la, 689
Pugin, Antoine, 872
Pugo, Boriss, 526
Pugsley, William, 203, 204
Pühringer, Josef, 111
Pujol Soley, Jordi, 827
Pulatkhodzhayev, Usman, 915
Pulatkodzhayev, Usman, 1054
Pulido, Guillermo Villegas, 1067
Pulja, Imer, 1095
Pumarejo, Alfonso López, 250
Punchinilame, G.V., 833
Pupillo, Giuseppe, 490
Pupp, Alois, 488
Puradiredja, Adil, 464
Puri, G.S., 441
Purić, Bodizar, 1088
Puricelli, Arturo, 83
Purtscher, Martin, 112
Pustovoitenko, Valery, 942
Putin, Vladimir, 714, 715
Putkamer, Jesko von, 388
Putte, Isaac Fransen van de, 619
Puttkamer, Jesko von, 194
Putuhena, 462
Puzanov, Aleksandr, 715
Pyke-Nott, James, 636
Pyle, Howard, 977
Pyotr I (Russia), 713

Pyotr II (Russia), 713
Pyotr III (Russia), 713
Pyrureyev, A.P., 728
Pyrureyev, Dorzhi, 727, 728
Python, Georges, 869
Python, José, 870
Pyun Yung Tai, 517

Qaboos bin Said (Oman), 663
Qadiruddin Ahmed, 670
Qahtan as-Shaabi, 1079
Qarban Ali Khan, 667
Qasim Abdulrahman, 1083
Qasim bin Ahmad, 1080
Qian Yunluo, 236
Qiao Xiaoguang, 232
Qin Yingji, 232
Quadros, Jânio, 149, 178
Quan Shuren, 240
Quandt, Bernhard, 372
Quarta, Nicola, 486
Quartenoud, Maxime, 870
Quartier-la-Tente, Edouard, 880
Quast, Jan, 621
Quay, Jan de, 620
Queiros, Barros, 705
Queiroz, Djenal de, 180
Quércia, Orestes, 178
Queriroz, José de, 155
Queuille, Henri, 328
Quevedo Moreno, Rodrigo, 577
Quezon, Manuel, 694, 695
Quie, Albert, 1005
Quinan, Onofre, 158
Quinby, Henry, 1013
Quinn, Robert, 1027
Quinn, William, 989
Quiñonez Molina, Alfonso, 306, 307
Quintana, Germán, 83
Quintana, Manuel, 69
Quintanilla, Carlos, 141
Quintans, José, 72
Quirasco, Antonio, 590
Quirno, Elpidio, 694
Quiroga, Pablo, 584
Quiros, Juan, 306
Quisling, Vidkin, 661
Quitman, John, 1006

Raab, Julius, 106, 107
Ra'ana Liaquat Ali Khan, 669
Rabaeus, Bengt, 16
Rabah Bitat, 60
Rabelo, Mandel, 177
Rabelo, Marcos, 155
Räber, Josef, 892
Raber, Joseph, 45
Rabie, Jakobus (Jac), 801
Rabin, Yitzhak, 475
Rabiu Kwankwaso, 648

Rabuka, Sitiveni, 318
Rabun, William, 986
Račan, Ivaca, 275
Rachaiah, Basavaiah, 429, 432, 435
Racicot, Marc, 1009
Raczkiewicz, Władysław, 700
Raczyński, Edward, 700
Rada y Gamio, José, 691
Radama I (Madagascar), 546
Radama II (Madagascar), 546
Radcliffe, Percy, 958
Radescu, Nicolae, 710
Radhakishun, Pretaapnarain, 846
Radhakrishnan, Sarvepalli, 422
Radić, Jovan, 1096
Radisić, Zivko, 143
Radmilović, Stanko, 1093
Radoslavljević, Djordje, 1096
Radoslavljević, Dobrivoje, 1093
Radoslavov, Vasil, 184
Radović, Andrija, 1090
Radović, Miljan, 1091
Radulović, Marko, 1090
Radulović, Miloš, 1087
Radus-Zenkovich, Viktor, 508
Rae, Robert, 209
Rafael Mora, Juan, 270
Raffarin, Jean-Pierre, 334
Rafi Ud-Daulat, 421
Rafik Hariri, 529
Raftery, P.A., 962
Raghbir Singh, 460
Ragimov, Kamran, 116
Ragimov, Mamed, 115
Ragone, Miguel, 80
Raharo, 547
Rahi, Michel, 46
Rahim Kuli Khan, 1054
Rahimbayev, Abdullah, 915, 1055, 1056
Rahimuddin Khan, 666
Rahm, Karl, 890
Rai, Daroga, 427
Raid es-Sulh, 528
Raifikesht, Vladimir, 743
Raina, Jagat Mohan, 438
Rainford, Roderick, 6
Rainier III (Monaco), 597
Rainiharo, 547
Rainijohary, 547
Rainilaiarivony, 547
Rainitsimbazafy, 547
Rais, Francesco, 486
Rais Yatim bin Yatim, 554
Raiser, Konrad, 50
Raj Kumaraswamy, Poosapati, 442
Raja, K., 425
Raja, K.A.A., 424, 440
Raja, P.S. Kumaraswami, 448
Raja Ahmad bin Raja Endut, 556
Raja Kerjan, 554
Raja Laboh, 554

Raja Lenggang, 554
Raja Nazrin, 556
Raja Radin, 554
Raja Sikander Zaman, 668
Raja Ulin, 554
Rajaćić, Ilija, 1096
Rajagopalachari, Chakravarti, 422, 448, 451
Rajapakse, Morris, 834
Rajbansi, Amichand, 801
Rajendra (Nepal), 616
Rajendram, M., 443
Rajeshwar, Thangavelu, 425, 447, 452
Raji, R.A., 641
Raji Rasabi, 651, 652
Rajkumar Dorendra Singh, 439
Rajniss, Ferenc, 416
Rajvade, M.V., 452
Rakhimov, Murtaza, 719
Rakhimov, Sadik, 114
Rakhman Gul, 669
Rakhmanov, Gusein, 114
Rakhmanov, Inamali, 914
Rakhmatov, Mirzo, 914
Rákosi, Mátyás, 417, 418
Rakotoarijaona, Desiré, 547
Rakotomalala, Joël, 547
Rakotomavo, Pascal, 548
Rakotoniaina, Justin, 547
Rakotovahiny, Emmanuel, 547
Rakovsky, Khristian, 941
Rakowski, Mieczysław, 699
Rallis, Demetrios, 395, 396
Rallis, Georgios, 397
Rallis, Ioannis, 396
Ralston, Samuel, 992
Ram Lal, Thakur, 424
Rama II (Thailand), 920
Rama IV (Thailand), 920
Rama IX (Thailand), 920
Rama V (Thailand), 920
Rama VI (Thailand), 920
Rama VII (Thailand), 920
Rama VIII (Thailand), 920
Ramabulana, Tshamano, 811
Ramachandran, D., 457
Ramachandran, Janika, 448
Ramachandran, Marudar, 448
Ramachandran, Parthasarathy, 435
Ramadhani Saki, 919
Ramadier, Jean-Paul, 195, 403, 633
Ramadier, Paul, 328
Ramaema, Elias, 531
Ramahatra, Victor, 547
Ramalho, José, 153
Ramallo García, Luis, 827
Ramanantsoa, Gabriel, 547
Ramanujan, Gopala, 429, 443
Ramaswamy, Subramanyan, 457
Ramatlhodi, Ngoako, 812
Ramchod, Bhadra, 801

Ramduth, Kassipershad, 801
Ramek, Rudolph, 107
Ramirez, Norberto, 631
Ramírez, Pedro, 70
Ramirez García, Leonel, 579
Ramirez Guerrero, Carlos, 581
Ramirez Guerrero, José, 579
Ramirez López, Heladio, 585
Ramiro I (Aragon), 819
Ramiro I (Asturias), 820
Ramiro II (Aragon), 820
Ramiro II (Asturias), 821
Ramiro III (Asturias), 821
Ramli, bin Ngali Talib, 556
Ramnuny, M., 455
Ramodike, Nelson, 809
Ramón Beteta, Mario, 582
Ramón Valdes, José, 579
Ramos, Aristiliano, 176
Ramos, Celso, 176
Ramos, Fidel, 694
Ramos, João, 170
Ramos, Nereu, 149, 176
Ramos, Paulo, 160
Ramos, Ramón, 588
Ramos, Vidal, 176
Ramos Izquierdo, Luis, 308
Ramos Santos, Matías, 591
Ramphal, Shridath (Sonny), 10
Rampton, Calvin, 1034
Ramsay, James, 91, 100
Ramsbotham, Peter, 960
Ramsbottom, Alfred, 804
Ramsdell, George, 1013
Ramset, Alexander, 1004
Ramseyer, Gérard, 873
Ramstedt, Johan, 851
Ramunay, M., 441
Ramushwana, Gabriel, 811
Ramzi Badri Shir, 837
Rana Bahadur Sah (Nepal), 616
Rana Jung Pande, 616
Ranadip Singh Bahadur, 617
Ranavalona I (Madagascar), 546
Ranavalona II (Madagascar), 546
Ranavalona III (Madagascar), 546
Ranbir, Rajkumar, 439
Rance, Hubert, 607, 925
Randall, Alexander, 1041
Randhavi, M.S., 453
Randolph, Beverley, 1037
Randolph, Edmund, 1037
Randolph, Peyton, 1037
Randolph, Theodore, 1014
Randolph, Thomas, 1037
Rane, Narayan, 438
Rane, Pratap Singh, 429, 430
Rangarajan, Chakravarty, 424, 443
Rangel, Rafael, 580
Rangel, Rubens, 157
Rangel Frias, Raúl, 584

Rangell, Johann, 320
Rankine, John, 637
Ranocchini, Gloriana, 774
Ransom, Ephaphroditus, 1003
Ranuccio I (Parma and Piacenza), 494
Ranuccio II (Parma and Piacenza), 494
Rao, B. Ramakrishna, 435, 450, 459
Rao, J. Vengal, 424
Rao, K. Prabhakara, 456
Rao, Kona Prabhakara, 447
Rao, Kona Prabkakara, 438
Rao, K.V. Krishna, 433
Rao, N. Bhaskara, 424
Rao, Nandmuri Rama, 424
Rao, P.V. Narasimha, 423, 424
Rao, R. Gundu, 435
Raoul, Alfred, 256
Rapava, Avksenti, 360
Rapenne, Jean, 336, 563, 633
Rarewala, Sardar, 460
Ras Abebe Aragai, 316
Ras Taffari Makonnen, 316
Rasahei, Papi, 680
Rasanjy, 547
Raschein, Paul, 875
Rasheed Raji, 656
Rasheed Shekoni, 650
Rashid al-Gailani, 471
Rashid al-Solh, 529
Rashid al-Tali, 505
Rashid bin Ahmed al-Mualla, Shaikh, 948
Rashid bin Humaid al-Naimi, Shaikh, 946
Rashid bin Majid al-Qasimi, Shaikh, 947
Rashid bin Maktum al-Maktum, Shaikh, 946
Rashid bin Said al-Maktum, Shaikh, 945, 946
Rashid Karami, 528, 529
Rashid Sfar, 928
Rashidi Kawawa, 918
Rashidov, Sharaf, 1051, 1052
Rasizade, Artur, 114
Rasmussen, Poul Nyrup, 288
Raso, Manuel Pio, 73
Rasoherina (Madagascar), 546
Rason, Cornthwaite, 100
Rason, Ernest, 1057
Rastrelli, Antonio, 482
Rasul Baksh Talpur, 669
Rasulov, Djabar, 915
Rataj, Maciej, 697
Ratieta, Naboua, 511
Rating Rimpoche, 231
Ratnayake, Tilak, 834
Ratner, Payne, 994
Rato, José, 776
Ratsimandrava, Richard, 547
Ratsirahonana, Norbert, 547, 548
Ratsiraka, Didier, 547
Rattani, Maurizio, 774
Rattazzi, Urbano, 479

Ratzenbock, Josef, 111
Rau, Bengal, 433
Rau, Eduard, 389
Rau, Johannes, 366, 373
Rauhofer, Josef, 108
Raupp, Vladir, 175
Rausch, Jean-Marie, 333
Rausching, Herman, 701
Rausnitz, Alfred, 108
Rava, Maurizio, 796
Ravaul, Jacques, 338
Ravele, Frank, 811
Ravize, Manuel, 589
Ravnelli, Carlos, 83
Ravony, Francisque, 547
Ravussin, Marc-Henri, 906
Rawlings, Jerry, 391
Rawson, Arturo, 70
Rawson, Harry, 89
Ray, James, 991
Ray, R.K., 449
Ray, Robert, 993
Ray, Siddharta, 444, 452
Raymond, Alex, 333
Razak bin Zain, 552
Razanamasy, Guy, 547
Razl, Stanislaus, 281
Razzakov, Ishak, 522
Read, George, 982
Read, Herbert, 570
Read, John, 103
Reagan, Roland, 973, 979
Real, Carlos, 579
Rebelo, Arnaldo, 428
Rebelo, Arnaldo de, 216
Rebelo, Arnoldo, 246
Rebelo, Horacio, 65
Rebeque, Benjamin de, 325
Rebmann, Gustav, 862
Rebolledo, Guillermo, 590
Rebollo, Pedro, 78
Recchi, Gaetano, 485
Rechberg und Rothenlöwen, Johann, 106
Rechenberg, Albrecht von, 917
Rector, Henry, 977
Reddiar, O.P. Ramaswami, 448
Reddiar, V. Venkatasurba, 457
Reddy, Bezwada Gopala, 450
Reddy, Bhavanam, 424
Reddy, Gopala, 424
Reddy, Jayaram, 801
Reddy, K. Brahmananda, 424
Reddy, K. Brahmanandu, 438
Reddy, K.C., 444
Reddy, Kotla Vijayabhaskara, 424
Reddy, K.V. Raghunath, 439, 447, 449, 452
Reddy, Kyasambally, 434, 436
Reddy, Marri Chenna (Andhra Pradesh), 424

Reddy, Marri Chenna (Pondicherry & Rajasthan & Tamil Nadhu), 445, 448, 457
Reddy, Marri Chenna (Punjab & Uttar Pradesh), 444, 450
Reddy, N. Janarhan, 424
Reddy, N. Sanjiva, 422, 424
Reddy, Obul, 424
Reddy, Satya Narain, 427, 443, 450, 452
Reddy, Vijaya, 424
Redern, Wilhelm von, 388
Redha Malek, 60
Redler, Ferdinand, 112
Redman, Harold, 965
Redstom, C.F., 969
Reece, Eric, 97
Reece, Gerald, 798
Reed, Amos, 1034
Reed, Clyde, 994
Reed, Harrison, 985
Reed, John, 999
Reed, Joseph, 1025
Reeder, Andrew, 994
Reedtz-Thott, Tage, 288
Reese, Heinrich, 864
Reeve, Harold, 615
Reeves, Paul, 626
Reffell, Derek, 965
Reffi, Adriano, 774
Reffi, Alberto, 772
Reffi, Alfredo, 770, 771
Reffi, Eugenio, 771, 773
Reffi, Eusebio, 772
Reffi, Giordano, 773, 775
Reffi, Orlando, 772
Reffi, Pietro, 772, 773
Regaldo Ezetas, Tomás, 306
Regan, George, 207
Regazzoli, Aquiles, 76
Regi, Joos, 875
Regla-Motta, Manuel de, 295
Rego, Benedito do, 170
Rego, Clovis, 165
Rego, Jaime do, 776
Rêgo, Pedro, 151
Rehrl, Franz, 110
Rehrl, Josef, 110
Rei, August, 312
Reiber, Ernst, 897
Reibey, Thomas, 96
Reibnitz, Kurt von, 382
Reichlin, Karl, 892
Reichmuth, Xaver, 893
Reid, David, 1019
Reid, George, 88, 90
Reid, Gordon, 100
Reid, Marion (M. Doyle), 209
Reid, Pyolemy, 408
Reid, Richard, 200
Reid, Robert, 984
Reid Cabral, Donald, 296

Reig, Oscar Ribas, 63
Reigen (Japan), 501
Reigersberg, Heinrich, 368
Reilly, Bernard, 1080
Reilly, Edward, 1045
Reina Andrade, José, 401
Reina Barros, José, 401
Reina Idiaquez, Carlos, 413
Reinart, Egon, 374
Reinhard, Carl, 496
Reinicke-Bloch, Hermann, 381
Reis, Américo dos, 159
Reis, António, 177
Reis, Arthur, 153
Reis, Francesco, 64
Reis, Henoch, 153
Reis, João dos, 179
Reisch, Georg, 16
Reisgys, Martynas, 541
Reither, Josef, 109
Reitz, Francis, 803
Relander, Lauri, 319
Relvas, José, 705
Remeliik, Haruo, 673
Remengesau, Thomas, 673
Remmele, Adam, 378
Remón Cantero, José, 675
Remy, Marie-Emmanuel, 252
Ren Rong, 233
Ren Zhongyi, 240
Renard, Georges, 257
Renaud, Edgar, 880, 881
Rencher, Abraham, 1015
René, F. Albert, 783, 784
Renfrow, William, 1023
Renggli, Jakob, 878
Renier, Paolo, 498
Renison, Patrick, 134, 407, 509
Renkin, Jules, 130
Renner, Karl, 106, 107
Rennie, Gilbert, 1098
Rennie, John, 570, 1057
Renovica, Milanko, 143, 144, 1088
Rensburg, Johannes van, 804
Rensburg, Willem Janse van, 804
Renshaw, John, 90
Renteria, Daniel, 583
Renzi, Giuseppe, 772
Renzi, Renzo, 774
Reol Tejada, Juan, 826
Repetto, William, 969
Repiquet, Jules-Vincent, 194, 341, 347, 1057
Reptenlov, Turar, 521
Requeijo, Roberto, 79
Requião, Roberto, 168
Resende, Eurico, 157
Reshetnikov, _, 740
Respini, Renzo, 900
Reste, Dieudonné, 136, 220, 257, 272
Restivo, Franco, 487

Restrepo, Carlos, 250
Restrepo, Carlos Lleras, 251
Resulzade, Mehmet, 113
Reumann, Jakob, 111
Reutemann, Carlos, 82
Reuter, Émile, 543
Reuter, Ernst, 369
Reutern, Mikhail, 714
Reutlinger, Hans, 897
Reutlinger, Rudolf, 860
Révay, Julius, 285
Revidatti, Gustavo, 74
Reviglio, Victor, 82
Revoil, Amedée, 59
Revoredo, Armando, 691
Rex, Robert, 629
Rey, Charles, 147
Rey, Georges-Pierre, 272, 780
Rey, Jean, 17
Rey, Victor, 336, 345
Rey-Bellet, Jean-Jacques, 904
Rey de Castro, Alberto, 691
Reyes, Juan Carlos, 73
Reyes, Narciso, 5
Reyes, Rafael (Chile), 222
Reyes, Rafael (Colombia), 250
Reyes Chávez, Hugh de Los, 1069
Reymond, Jean-Émile, 598
Reynaud, Paul, 328
Reynolds, Albert, 474
Reynolds, John (Illinois, USA), 990
Reynolds, John (Wisconsin, USA), 1041
Reynolds, J.W., 1016
Reynolds, Robert, 983
Reynolds, Thomas (Australia), 94
Reynolds, Thomas (USA), 1007
Reynoso, René, 579
Reynosos, Leobardo, 591
Reza Shah Pahlavi (Iran) (Mohammed Reza Khan), 466, 468
Rezende Machado, Iris, 158
Rhee, Syngman (Lee Syn Man), 514, 517
Rhijn, Albertus van, 610
Rhinera, Rodolfo, 75
Rhodes, Cecil, 801
Rhodes, Edgar, 207
Rhodes, James, 1022
Rhodio, Guido, 482
Rhyner, Kaspar, 874
Riak Gai Kok, 838
Riart, Luis, 687
Riaz Pasha, 303
Riba, Tomo, 425
Ribar, Ivan, 1086
Ribas, Emilio, 158
Ribas, Manoel, 167
Ribeiro, Benedito, 163
Ribeiro, Delfim, 163
Ribeiro, Eduardo, 153
Ribeiro, Eurico, 160
Ribeiro, João, 173

Ribeiro, Joaquim, 179
Ribeiro, José (Goa, India), 428
Ribeiro, José (Mozambique), 604
Ribeiro, Manoel, 151
Ribeiro, Vicente, 179
Ribeyre, Paul, 335
Ribicic, Ciril, 792
Ribičić, Mitja, 1087, 1088
Ribicoff, Abraham, 982
Ribó, Julià Reig, 62
Ribot, Alexandre, 327
Ricasoli, Bettino, 479, 497
Riccardi, Marino, 774
Ricciuti, Romeo, 481
Rice, Alexander, 1002
Rich, John, 1004
Richa, José, 168
Richard, Gustavo, 176
Richard, Henri-Marius, 339
Richard, Ralph, 964
Richard, Xavier, 346
Richard I (England), 950
Richard II (England), 950
Richard III (England), 950
Richards, Albert, 200
Richards, Ann, 1033
Richards, Arthur, 317, 355, 499, 557, 635
Richards, Charles, 204
Richards, De Forest, 1042
Richards, Edmund, 530, 549
Richards, Edward, 961
Richards, John, 1029
Richards, Robert (Australia), 94
Richards, Robert (Nauru), 615
Richards, William, 1042
Richardson, Dennis, 624
Richardson, Friend, 979
Richardson, George, 768
Richardson, James, 1028
Richardson, John, 1028
Richardson, John Jr, 1029
Richardson, M.G., 961
Richardson, Ralph, 624
Richardson, William, 1009
Richaud, Léon-Félix, 353
Riché, Jean-Baptiste, 409
Richey, Matthew, 206
Richner, Adolf, 858
Richter Prada, Pedro, 692
Rickards, John, 1009
Rickenbach, Victor, 859
Rida al-Rikabi, 505
Rideout, Thomas, 206
Ridge, Thomas, 1026
Ridgely, Charles, 1000
Ridgeway, Joseph, 830
Ridgeway, Mark, 615
Ridolfi, Cosimo, 497
Riecke, Hans, 380
Riedel, K., 376
Riedener, Josef, 888, 889

Riegg, Alfred, 887, 888
Riera, Fernando, 84
Riesco, Germán, 222
Riesen, Jean, 870
Riggs, Thomas, 975
Righetti, Argante, 900
Righi, Antonio, 770
Righi, Michele, 773
Righi, Pompeo, 771, 772
Rigotard, Jean, 343
Riley, Richard, 1030
Rimaz, Raphaël, 871
Rinaldo, Henri, 339
Rinaldo (Modena), 491
Rinaldo (Naples and Sicily), 491
Rinck, Julius, 371
Ringier, Arnold, 857
Ringstorff, Harald, 373
Rintelen, Anton, 110
Rio, Giovanni de, 486
Rion, Anita, 877
Rios, Juan, 223
Ríos Montt, Efraín, 402
Ripoll, Luis, 78
Rissik, Johann, 805
Risterucci, Jean, 347, 354
Ristić, Jovan, 1091, 1092
Ritch, William, 1015
Ritchie, Albert, 1001
Ritner, Joseph, 1025
Ritschard, Johann, 866
Ritschard, Rolf, 895, 896
Ritschard, Willi, 856, 895
Riu y Calañas, Raimundo, 62
Riva Agüero, Enrique de la, 690, 691
Riva Agüero, José de la, 688
Riva Palacio, Emilio, 583
Rivadavia, Bernardino, 69
Rivara, Horacio, 71
Rivarola, Cirilio, 686
Rivas, Patricio, 631
Rivas Guillen, Genevevo, 587
Rivera Aceves, Carlos, 582
Rivera Carballo, Julio, 307
Rivera Crespo, Felipe, 583
Rivera Paz, Mariano, 401
Riveri, Carlo, 796
Rivero Agüero, Andrés, 278
Rivers, Eurith, 987
Rivet, Louis, 345
Riyong, Yauwe, 683
Rizzo, Socrates, 584
Ro Jai Bong, 518
Roan, Archibald, 1031
Roane, John, 977
Robati, Pupuke, 628
Robb, Charles, 1037
Roberdeau, Henri, 272
Robert, Jean-Jacques, 1058
Robert, Jocelyn, 338, 345, 353
Robert I (France), 322

Robert I the Bruce (Scotland), 954
Robert II (France), 322
Robert II (Scotland), 954
Robert III (Scotland), 954
Roberto, Holden, 66
Roberto (Naples and Sicily), 491
Roberto (Parma and Piacenza), 494
Roberts, Barbara (B. Hughey), 1024
Roberts, C.A., 629
Roberts, Henry, 982
Roberts, John, 208
Roberts, Joseph, 532
Roberts, Oran, 1033
Roberts, Thomas, 1032
Robertson, James (Nigeria), 635
Robertson, James (USA), 1023
Robertson, John, 89, 90
Robertson, R. Gordon, 213
Robertson, Thomas, 996
Robertson, William, 124
Robertson, Wyndham, 1037
Robichaud, Hedard, 203
Robichaud, Louis, 204
Robie, Frederick, 999
Robinel, Tertillien, 340
Robins, Charles, 990
Robinson, Alfred, 805
Robinson, Arthur, 925, 926
Robinson, Charles, 994
Robinson, Clifford, 204
Robinson, George, 1002
Robinson, James, 995
Robinson, John (Canada), 208
Robinson, John (South Africa), 802
Robinson, John (USA), 1035
Robinson, Joseph, 978
Robinson, Lucius, 1017
Robinson, Mary, 474
Robinson, Moses, 1035
Robinson, Robert, 984
Robinson, William, 209
Robitaille, Théodore, 211
Robledo Rincon, Eduardo, 577
Robles, Francisco, 299
Robles, Marco, 675
Roblin, Dufferin, 202
Roblin, Rodomond, 202
Roblot, Émile, 597
Robson, John (British Indian Ocean Territory), 961, 962
Robson, John (Canada), 201
Robson, W. Geoffrey, 956
Roburt, Hammer de, 615
Roca, Julio, 69
Roca, Vicente Ramón, 299
Roçadas, Carlos, 216
Rocadas, José, 64, 246
Rocafuerte, Vicente, 299
Rocard, Michel, 329
Rocca-Serra, Jean-Paul de, 335
Rocha, Acrísto da, 156

Rocha, Caetano da, 167
Rocha, Domingos da, 162
Rocha, Francisco da, 150
Rocha, José da, 155
Rocha, Luiz da, 160
Rocha, Nabor Teles de, 150
Rocha Cordero, Antonio, 587
Rocha Lins, Tibúrcio da, 151
Rocha Neto, Bento da, 168
Rochaix, John, 872
Rochas da Costa, Celestina, 777
Rochat, Philippe, 44
Rochebouet, Gaëtan de, 326
Rochev, Ivan, 731
Rochfort, Alexander, 958
Rochussen, Jacob, 619
Rockefeller, John IV, 1040
Rockefeller, Nelson, 1018
Rockefeller, Winthrop, 978
Röder, Franz-Josef, 374
Rodger, John, 390
Rodier, François-Pierre, 336, 341, 455
Rodil y Gallaso, José, 816
Rodionov, Mikhail, 715
Rodney, Caesar, 982
Rodney, Caleb, 983
Rodney, Daniel, 983
Rodrigo, Nihal, 36
Rodríguez, Abelardo (Mexico), 574
Rodríguez, Abelardo (Sonora, Mexico), 588
Rodríguez, Andrés, 687
Rodriguez, Bettenco, 405
Rodríguez, Carlos Andrés Pérez, 1067
Rodriguez, Francisco, 171
Rodríguez, Francisco, 675
Rodríguez, Jorge, 70
Rodríguez, Jorge Alessandri, 223
Rodríguez, José, 271
Rodríguez, Luis (Argentina), 78
Rodríguez, Luis (Mexico), 580
Rodríguez, Morell, 1071
Rodríguez, Rafael Caldera, 1067
Rodríguez, Raúl Bercovitch, 74
Rodriguez, Rodrigo, 246
Rodríguez, Roque, 413
Rodriguez, Vasco, 405
Rodríguez Barrera, Rafael, 576
Rodríguez de la Borbolla, José, 824
Rodríguez Echeverría, Miguel, 271
Rodríguez Elías, José, 591
Rodríguez Familiar, Ramón, 586
Rodríguez Flores, Jesús, 575
Rodríguez Gaona, Jesús, 580
Rodríguez Ibarra, Juan, 827
Rodríguez Lara, Guillermo, 300
Rodríguez Martínez, José, 826
Rodríguez Mercado, Roberto, 580
Rodríguez Rodríguez, Román, 825
Rodríguez Solorzano, Angel, 579
Rodríguez Triana, Pedro, 578
Rodríguez-Vigil Rubo, Juan, 824

Rodwell, Cecil, 317, 407, 1100
Roell, Johan, 619
Roemer, Adolf, 888, 889
Roemer, Charles (Buddy), 998
Roger, Clifford, 1042
Rogers, Benjamin, 209
Rogers, Daniel, 983
Rogers, John, 1039
Rogers, Robert, 201
Rogger, Hans, 879
Roggo, Alphonse, 870
Rogier, Charles, 130
Rogue, Jacques, 568
Rogué, Jacques, 220
Roh Tae Woo, 517
Rohan, Josselin de, 331
Rohrer, Hans, 889
Roika, Lukas, 684
Rojas, Hugo Ballivián, 141
Rojas, Liberato, 687
Rojo Gómez, Javier, 581
Rojo Lugo, Jorge, 581
Rojumana, Clement, 795
Roketsky, Leonid, 752
Rokh (Iran), 466
Roldós Aguillera, Jaime, 300
Rolland, Pierre, 347
Rollandin, Augusto, 490
Rollet, Louis-Félix, 633
Röllin-Weber, Margrit, 893
Rollins, Frank, 1013
Rolón, Raimundo, 687
Rolph, James, 979
Rolvaag, Karl, 1005
Rolz-Bennett, José, 464
Roman, André, 997
Roman, Petre, 710
Roman y Reyes, Victor, 632
Romanov, John, 213
Romanov, Vitaly, 733
Romanus (Pope), 1060
Romer, Friedrich von, 388
Römer, René, 622
Romer, Roy, 980
Romero, Eulogio, 691
Romero, Juan Carlos, 80
Romero, Julio, 74
Romero, Roberto, 80
Romero de Velasco, Flavio, 582
Romero Esquival, Benjamin, 576
Romero Mena, Carlos, 307
Romero Pereira, Tomás, 687
Rommey, Cyril, 963
Romney, George, 1004
Romo Gutiérrez, Arturo, 591
Ronai, Sándor, 416
Roncali, Federico, 816
Roncière, Paul, 346
Rondeau, José (Argentina), 69
Rondeau, José (Uruguay), 1048
Rondon, José, 161

Ronn Sandoval, J. Francisco, 1071
Roon, Albrecht, 384
Roos-Niedermann, Rita, 889
Rooseboom, William, 461
Roosevelt, Franklin, 973, 1017
Roosevelt, Theodore, 973, 1017
Roosevelt, Theodore II, 1045
Root, Edmund, 1044
Rooth, Ivar, 45
Roper, Albert, 43
Rosa, Afonso, 156
Rosa, César, 297
Rosa, Miguel, 170
Rosa, Pompílio, 175
Rosa, Riccardo, 488
Rosado, Tomás, 604
Rosales, Rafael, 1069
Rosas, Alexis, 1068
Rosauer, Rodolfo, 79
Rose, Daniel, 998
Rose, David, 67, 407
Rose, Jack, 963
Rosellini, Albert, 1039
Rosenberg, Felix, 898
Rosenthal, Charles, 104
Rosetti, Teodor, 709
Rosier, William, 872
Rosón, Antonio, 827
Ross, C. Ben, 990
Ross, Charlesworth, 966
Ross, Edmund, 1015
Ross, Frank, 200
Ross, George, 208
Ross, James, 214
Ross, John, 197, 211
Ross, Lawrence, 1033
Ross, Nellie (N. Wynns), 1042
Ross, Rudolf, 371
Ross, William (Canada), 208
Ross, William (Delaware, USA), 983
Ross, William (Wyoming, USA), 1042
Rossel, Eduard, 751
Rossell de la Lama, Guillermo, 581
Rosselló, Pedro, 1046
Rossi, Angel, 78
Rossi, Dante, 773
Rossi, Giovanni, 899
Rossi, José, 335
Rossi, Marino, 771, 772
Rossi, Mario, 773
Rossi, Ottaviano, 774
Rossi, Peelgrino, 1064
Rossi, Raimondo, 899
Rossing, Peter, 383
Rossini, Massino, 774
Rossini, Simone, 773
Rossini, Vittorio, 773
Roten, Ernst von, 903, 904
Roth, August, 897
Roth, Jean-François, 877
Rothe, Karl, 371

Rotheli, Alfred, 895
Rother, Timothy, 45
Röthlin, Anton, 887
Röthlin, Arnold, 886
Rotimi, Christopher, 658
Rotolo, Nicola, 486
Rotwitt, Carl, 287
Roufos, Benizelos, 392, 394
Rougier, Ferdinand, 563
Rouher, Eugène, 326
Roullier, Jean, 44
Roume, Ernest-Nestor, 781
Roure, Jean-Claude, 340
Rousset, Alain, 330
Routray, Nilamani, 443
Routt, John, 980
Rouvier, Maurice, 326, 327
Roux, Jean-Louis, 211
Rouys, Ernest-Eugène, 255
Rovaletti, Hugo, 80
Rover, Carl, 383
Rovio, G.S., 730
Rovirosa Wade, Leandro, 588
Rowatt, Hugh, 213
Rowe, W. Earl, 208
Rowland, James, 89
Rowland, John, 982
Rowling, Wallace (Bill), 627
Roxburgh, Thomas, 762
Roy, Bidham, 452
Roy, Étienne, 410
Roy, Rajni, 457
Roy, Vesta, 1013
Royal, Joseph, 213
Royce, Stephen, 1035
Roych, Angelo, 487
Roye, Edward, 532
Roynette, Jacques, 348
Royo, Arístides, 675
Roz Nuri Shawez, 472
Rozas, Angel, 72
Rozas y Acuna, Manuel, 694
Rozenberger, David, 741
Rozendal, Silvio (Boy), 622
Rozins, F., 525
Rúa, Antonio de la, 76
Rüa, Fernando de la, 70
Ruas, Oscar, 297
Rubattel, L., 905, 906
Rubattel, Rodolphe, 855, 905
Ruben, Vitaly, 525, 526
Ruben, Yury, 526
Rubial, Ramón, 825
Rubiks, Alfreds, 526
Rubin, Abram, 757
Rubio Ortiz, Noradino, 586
Ruchet, Marc-Émile, 854
Ruchonnet, Louis, 854
Ruchupan, Meechai, 921
Ruck, Jeremiah, 1041
Ruckauf, Carlos, 71

Ruckstuhl, Hans, 859
Rud, Gerasim, 595
Rudhart, Ignaz von, 393
Rudini, Marchese di (Antonio Starabba), 479
Rudloff, Marcel, 329
Rudolf, Alfred, 867
Rudolf (Bohemia), 282
Rudolf (France), 322
Rudolf V (Austria), 105
Rudzutak, Yan, 1056
Rueda, Alberto, 73
Rueda Villagran, Quintin, 581
Rueff, Jacques, 597
Rüesch, Ernst, 889
Ruey, Claude, 907
Rufai Garba, 656
Rufari Garba, 640
Rufenacht, Antoine, 332
Ruffieux, André, 873
Ruffo Appel, Ernesto, 576
Ruffy, Eugène, 854
Ruger, Konrad von, 374
Ruger, Thomas, 987
Ruggiero, Renato, 47
Ruggiero II (Sicily), 492
Rugova, Ibrahim, 1095
Ruh, Jakob, 890
Ruhollah Khomeini, 469
Ruhstrat, Franz, 383
Ruhstrat, Friedrich Andreas, 383
Ruhstrat, Friedrich Julius, 383
Ruis-Gallardon Jiménez, Alberto, 828
Ruiz Cortines, Adolfo, 574, 590
Ruiz Ferro, Julio, 577
Ruiz González, Faustino, 308
Ruiz González, Pedro, 591
Ruiz Massieu, José, 581
Ruiz Zorilla, Manuel, 816, 817
Rukstuhl, Edwin, 888
Rukstuhl, Johann, 887
Rumor, Mariano, 480
Runde, Ortwin, 371
Rundle, Anthony, 97
Rundle, Henry, 565
Runkorem, Seth, 465
Runnels, Hardin, 1033
Runnels, Hiram, 1006
Runyon, William, 1015
Ruoss, Anton, 892
Ruppel, António, 168
Ruprecht, Hans Peter, 898
Rusadan, 357
Rusch, Carl, 861
Ruskulov, Turar, 1056
Russell, Alfred, 532
Russell, Charles, 1011
Russell, Daniel, 1019
Russell, Donald, 1030
Russell, Frederick, 205
Russell, Lee, 1006

Russell, Richard, 987
Russell, Thomas, 963
Russell, William, 1002
Russo, Gaspare, 482
Rustomji, Nari, 447
Rutgers, Abraham, 845
Ruth, Earl, 1043
Rutherford, Alexander, 200
Rutherford, John, 1037
Rutledge, Edward, 1028
Rutledge, John, 1028
Rutskoi, Aleksandr, 747
Rüttimann, Josef, 858
Ruttin, Martin, 258
Rutty, Jacques, 872
Ruud, Morten, 662
Rüütel, Arnold, 313
Ruys de Beerenbrouck, Charles, 619
Ruzzini, Carlo, 498
Rwigema, Pierre-Celestin, 760
Ryabchikov, Nikolai, 733
Ryabov, Aleksandr, 752
Ryan, George, 991
Ryan, Thomas, 92
Ryckmans, Pierre, 258
Rycroft, William, 557
Rye, Thomas, 1032
Rykov, Aleksei, 715, 716
Ryskulov, Turar, 1055
Ryti, Risto, 319, 320
Ryzhkov, Nikolai, 716
Rzayev, Kamal, 1053

Sá, Alfredo, 153
Sá Cardoso, Alfredo de, 705
Sá Carneiro, Francisco, 706
Sa Chen-ping, 226
Sá e Albuquerque, Lourenço de, 159
Saa, Adolfo Rodríguez, 82
Saad al-Abdullah as-Sabah, 519, 520
Saad Jumaa, 506
Saad Zaghlul Pasha, 303
Saadi, Ramón, 72
Saadi, Vicente, 72
Saadi Munlah, 528
Sa'adoun Hammadi, 472
Saadullah al-Jabiri, 912
Saavedra, Angel de, 816
Saavedra, Juan Bautista, 141
Saavedra Acevedo, Jerónimo, 825
Saavedra y Magdalena, Diego, 308
Sabah Abu Abdullah bin Jabir as-Sabah, 519
Sabah as-Selem as-Sabah, 519
Sabah bin Jabir as-Sabah, 519
Sabanov, Tobaz, 735
Sabbat, Kazimierz, 700
Sabines Gutiérrez, Juan, 577
Sabirov, Mukhammat, 738
Sabo Bakinzuwo, 648

Saborin, Maurice, 338
Sabri el-Assali, 913
Saburov, Evgeny, 943
Sacasa, Roberto, 631
Sachar, Bhim Sen, 423
Sachar, Bhimsen, 442, 444
Sachinda Lal Singh, 449
Sacko, Soumana, 564
Saddam Hussein, 470, 472
Saddiq Hussein Qureshi, 668
Sadi-Carnot, François, 324
Sadi Irmak, 932
Sadiq Ali, 437, 438, 448
Sadiq el-Mahdi, 836
Sadiq Hussein Qureshi, 669
Sadis, Ugo, 900
Sadler, Reinhold, 1011
Sadoul, Numa, 255, 291, 353
Sadoveanu, Mihai, 708
Sadovsky, Stefan, 789, 790
Sadunts, S.K., 915
Sadykov, I.Kh., 738
Saeb Salam, 528
Sáez, Irene, 1071
Saffi, Aurelio, 1064
Safford, Anson, 976
Saffores, Augusto, 83
Safi I (Iran), 466
Safi II Suleiman (Iran), 466
Saganov, Vladimir, 721
Sagar, J., 455
Sagasta, Praxedes, 817
Sagdiyev, Makhtay, 507
Saget, Louis, 252, 291, 292
Saget, Nissage, 410
Sagredo, Nicolo, 498
Saguier, Adolfo, 686
Sah'afal bin Ali al-Amiri, Shaikh, 1081
Sahan, Kidar, 455
Sahay, Bhagwan, 432, 433, 435, 454
Sahay, Krishna, 427
Sahay, Vishnu, 425, 426
Sahibzada Mohammed Khurshid, 667
Sahidan Kassim, 557
Sahla Dengel, 315
Sahm, Heinrich, 701
Sahoulba, Gontchome, 221
Said Abdullah Shah, 670
Said Abeid, 254
Said Ali Mohammed, 253
Said Asfendiar, 1055
Said bin Ahmed (Oman), 663
Said bin Bhutti al-Maktum, Shaikh, 946
Said bin Maktum al-Maktum, Shaikh, 946
Said bin Ngah, 553
Said bin Sulat, 919
Said bin Sultan (Oman), 663
Said bin Tahnun al-Nahayan, Shaikh, 945
Said bin Taimur (Oman), 663
Said el-Ghazzi, 913
Said el-Mufti, 505, 506

Said-Galiyev, Sakhibgarey, 738, 943
Said Ghawas, 667
Said Halim Paşa, 931
Said Mir Alim Khan, 1054
Said Mohammed Cheikh, 253
Said Mohammed Djohar, 253
Said Mohammed Jaffar, 252, 253
Said Mohammed Soefou, 254
Saida, S., 655
Sa'idu Madaki, 648
Saidullayev, Malik, 723
Saifuddin, 233
Saiful Rijal, 181
Saigal, O., 455
Saiin (Japan), 501
Saikia, Hiteswar, 426, 440
Sailain, S.L., 456
Sailo, Thenphunga, 441
Sainović, Nikola, 1093
St. John, Bernard, 125
Saint-Alary, Jean de, 922
St Aubyn, Geoffrey, 970
St Clair, Arthur, 1021
Saint Félix, Charles de, 336
Saint-Félix, Charles de, 218, 255
Saint-Jean, Alfredo, 70
Saint Jean, Ibérico, 71
St John, John, 994
St Johnston, Thomas, 762
Saint-Just, Luc Letellier de, 211
St Laurent, Louis, 199
Saint-Mart, Paul de, 546
Saint-Mart, Pierre de, 218, 546
Saint-Mleux, André, 598
Saionji, Kimmochi, 502, 503
Saito, Makoto, 503
Saiyad Fazl Ali, 442
Saiyid Fazl Ali, 425
Sajid Mohammed Rahim Khan, 1055
Sak Sutsakham, 191
Sakalauskas, Vytautas, 539
Sakaran bin Dandai, 557, 558
Sakarinthone (Laos), 523
Sakhai, A.S., 522
Sakhatmuradov, Halmurad, 935
Sakirov, Gennady, 728
Saklecha, Virendra, 437
Sakombi, Denis, 261
Saksena, K.P., 460
Sakuramachi I (Japan), 501
Sakuramachi (Japan), 501
Saladrigas y Zayas, Carlos, 278
Salah Ali al-Ghali, 842
Salah Bitar, 913
Saleheddin Baccouche, 927, 928
Salahuddin Abdul Azaz Shah, 550
Salahuddin Abdul Aziz Shah, 559
Salamanca, Daniel, 141
Salamon (Hungary), 414
Salan, Robert, 60
Salandra, Antonio, 479

Salas, Ismael, 587
Salas, José de, 573
Salas, Juan Manuel, 71
Salas Feo, Henrique, 1069
Salas Römer, Henrique, 1069
Salato, Esika, 35
Salazar, António, 703, 706
Salazar Martínez, Florencio, 587
Salazar y Baquíjano, Manuel, 688
Saldanha, Álvaro, 160
Saldanha, Ivar, 160
Saldanha, Sinval, 174
Saldern, Ernst von, 388
Saldern, Johannes von, 388
Saldias, Roque, 691
Saleem, Yunus, 427
Saleh, Jaime, 622
Saleh, Raymundo, 623
Saleh Michika, 639
Salem bin Mubarak as-Sabah, 519
Salem Rubayyi Ali, 1079
Sales, Manoel, 177
Salgar, Eustorjio, 250
Saliceli, Pierre-Jean, 922
Saliceti, Aurelio, 1064
Salih bin Abdullah, 1084
Salih bin Ghalib, 1084
Salih bin Hussein, 1081
Salih bin Omar, 1085
Salih bin Sayil, Shaikh, 1080
Salih (Fadhli), 1082
Salih Hussain, 1084
Salih Jabr, 471
Salih Paşa, 931
Salii, Lazarus, 673
Salikhov, Murad, 521, 522
Salilsbury, George, 1044
Salim Ahmed Salim, 27, 918
Salim Ben Ali, 253
Salim bin Sultan al-Qasimi, Shaikh, 947
Salim bin Thwaini (Oman), 663
Salimov, Akil, 1051
Salinas, Luis Siles, 141
Salinas de Gortari, Carlos, 574
Salinas Leal, Bonifacio, 584
Salini, Rocco, 481
Saliya Mathew, C.N., 833
Saller, Michel, 291
Salles, Colombo, 176
Salles, Ephigênio de, 153
Salles, Francisco de, 163
Salles, Manuel, 148
Salmeron y Alonso, Nicolás, 815
Salmin Amur Juma, 919
Salmon, Thomas, 1036
Salnave, Sylvain, 410
Salogor, Nikita, 595
Saloman, Edward, 1039
Salomon, Alberto, 691
Salomon, Louis, 410
Salote Tupou III (Tonga), 924

Saltonstall, Leverett, 1002
Saltykov, Nikolai, 714
Salvafeka, Ismail, 507
Salvago-Raggi, Guiseppe, 310
Salvatori, Pedro, 79
Salvatori, Reves, 774
Salvi, Héctor, 82
Salykov, Kakimbek, 1053
Sam, T. Simon, 410
Sam Sary, 191
Sama Duwa Sinwa Nawng, 608
Samadov, Abduljalil, 915
Samaila Chama, 649
Samaitis, Eduard (Simmat), 541
Samana, Utula, 681
Samanez Ocampo, David, 689
Sámano Torres, Alfonso, 583
Samaranch, Juan Antonio, 21
Samaraweera, G., 832
Samaraweera, Percy, 834
Samarco, Louis, 354
Samary, Paul, 336, 341, 343
Samban, Bruce, 678
Sambu Jamsarangiyn, 599
Sambwa Pida Nbagui, 259
Samedin, Ibrahim, 943
Samford, William, 975
Sami al-Jundi, 913
Sami Hinnawi, 912
Samigulov, G., 719
Samir el-Rifai, 505
Sampaio, António, 704
Sampaio, Jorge, 703
Samper Ibáñez, Ricardo, 818
Sampião, Cid Feijo, 169
Samprieto Casamarrona, Antonio, 829
Sampson, Flem, 996
Sampson, Nikos, 279
Sampson, Ronald, 964
Sampurnanand, 445, 450
Samsonov, Boris, 943
Samuel, Herbert, 476
Samuel (Hungary), 414
Samuels, Gordon, 89
Samuels, Voldemars, 525, 526
Samuelsen, Andreas, 289
Samuelson, Don, 990
Samurski, Nazhmuddin, 725
San Juan, Carlos, 80
San Kho Lian, U, 608
San Luca, Ferdinando Clemente di, 482
San Martin, José de, 688
San Martín y Ulloa, José, 306
San Román, Miguel, 688
San Souci, Emery, 1027
San Yu, U, 607
San Yun, 191
Sanabria, Edgard, 1067
Sanakoyev, Feliks, 363
Sanakoyev, V.G., 363
Sanatescu, Constantine, 710

Sánchez, Hugo Garay, 74
Sánchez Albornoz, Claudio, 819
Sánchez Anaya, Alfonso, 590
Sánchez Cano, Edmundo, 585
Sánchez Celis, Leopoldo, 587
Sánchez Cerro, Luis, 689
Sánchez Colin, Salvador, 582
Sánchez de Toca, Joaquín, 818
Sánchez Díaz, Raúl, 575
Sánchez Guerra, José, 818
Sánchez Guerra Saéz, Luis, 308
Sánchez Hernández, Fidel, 307
Sánchez Piedras, Emilio, 589
Sánchez Sánchez, Luis, 692
Sánchez Unzueta, Horacio, 587
Sánchez Vilella, Robert, 1046
Sánchez Vite, Manuel, 581
Sáncho I (Asturias), 821
Sáncho I Garces (Navarre), 823
Sancho I (Portugal), 702
Sáncho I Ramirez (Aragon), 820
Sáncho II (Castile), 821
Sáncho II Garces (Navarre), 823
Sancho II (Portugal), 702
Sáncho III (Castile), 821
Sáncho III Garces (Navarre), 823
Sáncho IV (Castile), 821
Sáncho IV (Navarre), 823
Sáncho V Ramirez (Navarre), 823
Sáncho VI (Navarre), 823
Sáncho VII (Navarre), 823
Sanclemente, Manuel, 250
Sander, Carl, 987
Sanders, Jared, 997
Sandford, George, 118
Sandiford, Erskine, 125
Sandlar Richard, 851
Sandoval, José, 631
Sandoz, André, 881
Sandwith, John, 766
Sanetomi, Sanjo, 502
Sanfa Asgad, 314
Sanford, Francis, 346
Sanford, Terry, 1019
Sangayev, Erenzhen, 727, 728
Sange Gyatso Lhabzang Khan, 230
Sanger, Elrich, 32
Sangheli, Andrei, 595
Sangma, Purno, 440
Sangma, Williamson, 440, 441
Sangster, Donald, 500
Sanguinetti, Julio, 1050
Sani, M.S., 641
Sani Abacha, 636
Sani Bello, 648
Sanjiviah, Damodaran, 424
Sankara, Thomas, 186, 187
Sankawulo, Wilton, 533
Sanlini, Ruggiero, 796
Sanmarco, Louis, 218
Sanni Daura Ahmed, 656

Sanni es-Solh, 528
Sanos, Máximo, 1049
Sanots Guardiola, José, 412
Sansores Pérez, Carlos, 576
Sant, Alfred, 566
Santa Cruz, Andrés, 140, 249, 688
Santa Cruz, Wilde, 78
Santa Maria, Domingo, 222
Santamaria, Francisco, 588
Santana, Jerônimo, 175
Santana, João de, 171
Santana, Miguel, 578
Santana, Pedro, 295
Santana, Pedro de, 160
Santarelli, Giulio, 483
Santer, Jacques, 17, 543
Santiago Salaverry, Felipe, 688
Santiago y Díaz, Fernando de, 818
Santiago y Díaz de Mendevil, Fernando, 761
Santillan, Eduardo Contreras, 79
Santillan, Manuel, 589
Santillo, Henrique, 158
Santin de Castilo, Miguel, 306
Santini, Rinaldo, 483
Santoro, Enrico, 485
Santos, António dos (Cape Verde), 216
Santos, António dos (Macau), 246
Santos, Artur, 157
Santos, Augusto dos, 604
Santos, Benedito dos, 156
Santos, Cipriano dos, 164
Santos, Edouardo, 250
Santos, Emilio dos, 296
Santos, Francelino dos, 163
Santos, Francisco, 172
Santos, Generosa dos, 167
Santos, Gonzalo, 587
Santos, Joachim Dos, 246
Santos, José dos, 705
Santos, José Eduardo dos, 65
Santos, Manuel dos, 604
Santos, Roberto, 155
Santos, Vitor, 246
Santos, Zelaya, José, 631
Santos Lombardo, José, 270
Sanusi Junid, 552
Sanz Alonso, Pedro, 827
Sanz Sesma, Miguel, 828
Sao Hkun Hkio, 609
Sao Shwe Thaike, 607
Saouma, Edouard, 43
Sapag, Felipe, 79
Sapelli, Alessandro, 796
Sapin, Michel, 331
Sapindzija, Riza, 1095
Sapozhnikov, Nikolai, 741
Saqr bin Khalid al-Qasimi, Shaikh, 947
Saqr bin Mohammed al-Qasimi, Shaikh, 947
Saqr bin Sultan al-Qasimi, Shaikh, 947

Saqr bin Zaid al-Nahayan, Shaikh, 945
Saracco, Giuseppe, 479
Saragat, Guiseppe, 478
Saraiva, José, 149, 150
Sarajoğlu, Şükrü, 932
Sarap Singh, 430, 435
Sarasin, Pote, 920
Sardar Abdul Qayyum Khan, 671, 672
Sardar Bahadur Khan, 667
Sardar Hukam Singh, 445
Sardar Jogendra Singh, 442, 445
Sardar Mohammed Ashrad, 672
Sardar Sikander Hayat, 671, 672
Sardar Ujjal Singh, 448
Sardinha, Francisco, 430
Sardo, Modesto, 487
Sardon bin Jubir, 555
Sarewi, Alexis, 682
Sargent, Francis, 1003
Sargent, Winthrop, 1005
Sarinić, Hrovje, 275
Sarkar, Manik, 449
Sarkis, Elias, 527
Sarkisov, Babken, 85
Sarkisyan, Agasi, 86
Sarkisyan, Aram, 86
Sarkisyan, Armen, 86
Sarkisyan, Fadei, 86
Sarkisyan, Vazguen, 86
Sarles, Elmore, 1020
Sarmento, Siseno, 153
Sarmiento, Domingo, 69
Sarney, José, 149, 160
Sarney, Roseana, 160
Saroop Khan, 668
Sarović, Mirko, 145
Sarrault, Albert, 328
Sarrien, Ferdinand, 327
Sarrulle, Oscar, 84
Sarsa Dengel, 314
Sartorius, Luis, 816
Sartzetakis, Christos, 393
Sarue Iyasu, 314
Sarup Singh, 438
Sarur bin Mohammed (Haushabi), 1082
Sarwate, Manohar, 45
Saryev, Akmamed, 934
Sassou-Nguesso, Denis, 256
Satarawala, K.T., 429
Satarwala, K.T., 444
Sato, Eisaku, 503
Satorlino Afika, 844
Satpathy, Nandini, 443
Saturnino da Costa, Manuel, 406
Saucedo, Salvador, 578
Sauckel, Fritz, 376
Saud bin Abdul-Azaz (Saudi Arabia), 778
Saud bin Abdul-Aziz, 779
Saud bin Faisal, 779
Sáude Maria, Victor, 406
Saukham Khoy, 191

Saul, Bruno, 313
Saul, David, 961
Saulsbury, Gove, 983
Saunders, Albert, 210
Saunders, Norman, 971
Sausgruber, Herbert, 112
Sausmarez, Havilland de, 956
Sautot, Henri-Camille, 218, 343, 345, 347, 1058
Sauvé, Jean-Paul, 212
Sauve, Jeanne, 198
Sava II (Montenegro), 1089
Savage, Alfred, 124, 407
Savage, Ezra, 1010
Savage, Frank, 963, 966
Savage, John, 207
Savage, Michael, 627
Savang Vathana (Laos), 523
Savary, Alain, 333
Savary, Alain-François, 344
Savchenko, Oleg, 746
Savchenko, Yevgeny, 745
Savea, Patita, 351
Savea, Petelo, 351
Savelyev, Viktor, 729
Savignac, Gabriel, 252
Savill, Louise, 962
Savimbi, Jonas, 66
Savino, Vito, 486
Savisaar, Edgar, 313
Savonarola, Girolamo, 496
Savoretti, Zaccaria, 772
Savoy, Émile, 869, 870
Savy, Robert, 333
Saw, U, 607
Saw Hla Tun, 609
Saw Maung, 607
Saw Wunna, 609
Sawar Khan, 668
Saward, M.H., 955
Sawyer, Amos, 533
Sawyer, Charles, 1012
Sawyer, Grant, 1011
Saxena, Girish, 433
Sayago Murillo, Edgar, 1068
Saydam, Refik, 932
Sayed Nazrul Islam, 121
Sayers, Joseph, 1033
Sayid Abdul Ahad, 1054
Sayid Ameer Hyder, 1054
Scadden, John, 100
Scales, Alfred, 1019
Scalfaro, Oscar, 478
Scanlen, Thomas, 801
Scavenius, Erik, 288
Scelba, Mario, 480
Schädler, Gustav, 537
Schaefer, William, 1001
Schaer-Born, Dori, 868
Schaerer, Eduardo, 687
Schafer, Edward, 1020

INDEX

Schaffer, Friedrich (Fritz), 369
Schaffl, Joseph, 110
Schaffner, Hans, 856
Schaller, Alfred, 865
Schaller, Gérald, 877
Schaller, Veronica, 866
Schärf, Adolf, 106
Schärf, Friedrich, 372
Scharping, Rudolf, 373
Schärrer, Otto, 890
Schärrer, Robert, 891
Scharzenberg, Felix, 106
Schausberger, Franz, 110
Scheel, Walter, 366
Scheffer, Friedrich, 380
Scheidemann, Philipp, 366
Schele, Eduard, 379
Schele, Friedrich von, 917
Schemel, Adolf, 110
Schenk, Karl, 853, 854
Scherbakov, P.V., 733
Scherer, Anton, 908
Scherer, Eduard, 887
Scherer, Jakob, 854
Scherf, Henning, 370
Schermerhorn, Willem, 620
Scherrer, Albert, 889
Scherrer, Heinrich, 887, 888
Scherrer, Theodor, 891
Scheurer, Karl, 855
Schibler, Oskar, 857
Schieck, Walter, 375
Schiele, Pierre, 329
Schild, Jörg, 866
Schimmelpenninck, Gerrit, 619
Schindler, Dietrich, 874
Schläpfer, Albert, 897
Schläppy, Rémy, 881, 882
Schlatter, Jakob, 890
Schlayer, Johannes von, 388
Schlebusch, Hubert, 379
Schlegel, Florian, 889
Schlegel, Josef, 111
Schleicher, Kurt von, 366, 384
Schley, William, 986
Schloifer, Johann, 383
Schlumpf, Leon, 856, 876
Schlüter, Poul, 288
Schmedeman, Albert, 1041
Schmid, Anton, 896, 897
Schmid, Arthur, 858, 859
Schmid, Carlo, 861
Schmid, Eugen, 896
Schmid, Franz, 901
Schmid, Hansruedi, 866
Schmid, Jacques, 894
Schmid, Johann, 874
Schmid, Josef (Luzern, Switzerland), 877, 878
Schmid, Josef (Zug, Switzerland), 907
Schmid, Peter (Basel-Landschaft, Switzerland), 864
Schmid, Peter (Bern, Switzerland), 868
Schmid, Rudolf, 908
Schmid, Theodor, 878
Schmidli, Ulrich, 898
Schmidt, Felipe, 176
Schmidt, Helmut, 366
Schmidt, Max, 857
Schmieding, Wilhelm, 388
Schmitt, Charles, 346
Schmitt, Henri, 873
Schmitt, Josef, 378
Schmitz, Richard, 111
Schmuki, August, 889
Schmutz, Daniel, 906, 907
Schnee, Heinrich, 917
Schneider, Arnold, 865, 866
Schneider, Elisabeth, 864
Schneider, Erwin, 868
Schneider, Friedrich, 864
Schneider, Fritz, 895, 896
Schneider, Hans, 889
Schneider, Roy, 1046
Schnieper, Xaver, 878
Schnyder, Karl, 866
Schnyder, Oskar, 903
Schnyder, Wilhelm, 904
Schober, Johann, 107
Schobinger, Josef, 877, 878
Schoch, Gustav, 891
Schoeman, Stephanus, 804
Schoeppel, Andrew, 994
Schoers, Johannes, 370
Schollaert, François, 130
Schönenberger, Peter, 889
Schöpfer, Robert, 894
Schotborgh, Herman, 621, 623
Schott, Max, 388
Schrameck, Abraham, 546
Schrattenbach, Wolfgang von, 492
Schreibar, Ottomar (Otomaras Streibens), 541
Schreiber, Germán, 691
Schreiber, Martin, 1041
Schreiber, Walter, 369
Schreiner, Anton, 108
Schreiner, William, 801
Schrenk, Karl, 368
Schreuer, Karl, 867
Schreyer, Edward, 198, 203
Schröder, Gerhard, 366, 372
Schröder, Luise, 369
Schröder, Paul, 381
Schroeder, Seaton, 1044
Schubiger, Johann, 887, 888
Schuler, Josef, 892
Schuler, Meinrad, 893
Schulthess, Edmund, 854, 855
Schultz, Arnaldo, 405, 406
Schultz, John, 202
Schultz-Ewerth, Erich, 768

Schulz, Peter, 371
Schumacher, Edmund von, 878
Schumacher, Feli von, 878
Schumacher, Joseph, 110
Schumacher, P., 906
Schumacher, Wolrad, 388
Schuman Robert, 328
Schümperli, Rudolf, 897
Schumy, Vinzenz, 108
Schüssel, Wolfgang, 108
Schussnigg, Kurt von, 107
Schuster, Rudolf, 789
Schutz, Jakob, 876
Schutz, Klaus, 369
Schwabe, Karl, 382
Schwalb López, Fernando, 692
Schwaller, Urs, 871
Schwander, Albert, 862
Schwander, Vital, 892, 893
Schwarz, Ernst, 858
Schwarz, Henning, 376
Schweigaard, Christian, 660
Schweinsberg, Schenk von, 380
Schweitzer, Pierre-Paul, 45
Schwimmer, Walter, 12
Schwinden, Edward, 1009
Scillingo, Adolfo, 83
Scofield, Edward, 1041
Scoon, Leo, 399
Scott, Abram, 1006
Scott, Alan, 963
Scott, Charles, 995
Scott, David, 967
Scott, Robert (Mauritius), 570
Scott, Robert (North Carolina, USA), 1019
Scott, Robert (South Carolina, USA), 1029
Scott, W. Kerr, 1019
Scott, Walter, 212
Scott, Winston, 124
Scranton, William, 1026
Screiber, Edmond, 565
Scrugham, James, 1011
Scuckman, Bruno von, 610
Scullin, James, 88
Scupham, William, 796
Seabra, José, 154
Seabrook, Whitemarsh, 1029
Seaga, Edward, 500
Seaman, Keith, 93
Searell, Warren, 629
Seay, Abraham, 1023
Seay, Thomas, 975
Sebastian, Cuthbert, 762
Sebastião, António, 777
Sebastião (Portugal), 702
Sebe, Lennox, 807
Sebree, Uriel, 1043
Seddon, Richard, 626
Sedki Solomon, 304
Sedney, Jules, 846
See, John, 90

See-chai Lam, David, 201
Seeley, Elias, 1014
Seematter, Arnold, 867
Seeto, Robert, 681
Seewoosagur Ramgoolam, 570, 571
Segizbayev, Sultan, 1051
Segni, Antonio, 478, 480
Segond, Guy-Olivier, 873
Segrt, Vlado, 143
Sehested, Hannibal, 288
Seidov, Gasan, 114
Seif Hassan Ali, Shaikh, 1084
Seif Sharif Hamad, 919
Seignoret, Clarence, 293
Seiler, Adolf, 862
Seiler, Hermann, 902
Sein Lwin, U, 607, 608
Sein Win, U, 607, 608
Seite, Berndt, 373
Seitniyazev, D., 1053
Seitov, P., 1053
Seitz, Karl, 106, 111
Seitz, Theodor, 194, 610
Sejo (Korea), 512
Sejong (Korea), 512
Seleki, Z.T., 809
Seligman, Arthur, 1016
Selim Hoss, 529
Selim I (Turkey), 929
Selim II (Turkey), 929
Selim III (Turkey), 930
Seljani, Bajran, 1094
Sellheim, Victor, 103
Selmer, Christian, 660
Seltzer Marseille, Elmar, 577
Selwyn-Clarke, Percy, 783
Selyukin, M., 734
Sema, Hokishe, 432, 442
Semenov, Bato, 720
Semenov, Vladimir, 729
Semernov, Aleksandr, 745
Semisi, Peniuto, 630
Semlin, Charles, 201
Semple, Eugene, 1039
Sen, Binay, 43
Sen, Nakul, 429
Sen, Shyamal Kumar, 452
Senanayake, Donald, 831
Senanayake, Dudley, 831
Senanayake, E.L., 831, 832
Senanayake, Maithripala, 832
Senarclens, Aymon de, 872
Sendall, Walter, 407
Sendwe, Jason, 264, 265
Senevitatne, Athanda, 833
Senevitatne, Nalin, 832
Senghor, Léopold, 781, 782
Sengi, Jonathan, 678
Sengupta, Sukhamoy, 449
Senkin, Ivan, 730
Şenseddin Günaltay, 932

Senter, De Witt, 1031
Seoane Corrales, Edgardo, 692
Sequeira, João de, 604
Sequeira, José, 405
Sequeira, Valfredo de, 169
Serada, Ivan, 126, 127
Seraphine, Oliver, 294
Serbini Ali, 4
Serdyuk, Zinovi, 595
Serdyukov, Valery, 748
Serfyukov, Valery, 747
Sergent, René, 30
Sergeyenkov, Vladimir, 747
Sergius II (Pope), 1060
Sergius III (Pope), 1061
Sergius IV (Pope), 1061
Seriche Bioko, Cristino, 309
Seriche Dougan, Angel, 309
Serna, Donaciano, 581
Serpa, Justiniano de, 155
Serra, Astoldo, 160
Serrano, Antonio, 72
Serrano, José, 140
Serrano, José Campo, 250
Serrano Elías, Jorge, 402
Serrano y Domínguez, Francisco, 815, 816
Serrato, José, 1049
Serrini, Giuseppe, 484
Serškić, Milan, 1087
Serva, Cesar, 161
Servais, Emmanuel, 542
Servan-Schreiber, Jean-Jacques, 333
Service, James, 98
Servidio, Alberto, 482
Seryakov, Vladimir, 740
Sethi, Prakash, 437
Sette, José, 157
Seval, Jacques, 342
Sevellec, Pierre, 343
Sever, Albert, 109
Severino, Rodolfo, 5
Sevic, Aleksandr, 1096
Sevier, John, 1031
Sevryugin, Nikolai, 752
Sewall, Sumner, 999
Seward, William, 1017
Sewell, Henry, 626
Sewell, William, 1044
Sexto, José, 160
Sexwale, Tokyo, 812
Seydewitz, Max, 375
Seyed Sheh bin Syed Abdullah, 555
Seyfullin, Saken, 508
Seyid Mohammed Khan, 1054
Seymour, Horatio, 1017
Seymour, Thomas, 981
Seyss-Inquart, Arthur, 107
Seyss-Inquart, Artur, 619
Seyyid Zia Ed-Din Tabataba'i, 468
Sha Wenhan, 243
Shaari bin Shafi, 556

Shaba Lafiaji, 650
Shabanov, Ivan, 753
Shabozov, Garibsho, 916
Shabunin, Ivan, 753
Shafer, George, 1020
Shafer, Raymond, 1026
Shaffer, J. Wilson, 1034
Shaffner, John, 206
Shafik al-Wazzan, 529
Shafranik, Yury, 752
Shafroth, John, 980
Shagadayev, Minovar, 914
Shagari, Shehu, 636
Shagimardanov, Fazil, 719
Shah, Kardardas, 448
Shah, Viren, 452
Shah Alam II (India), 422
Shah Berunai, 181
Shah Jahan I (India), 421
Shah Jahan II (India), 421
Shahabuddin Ahmed, 121
Shahbaz Sharif, 669
Shaheen, Jeanne, 1013
Shahib Hamid, 668
Shaimardanov, _, 737
Shaimiyev, Mintimer, 738, 739
Shaiza, W., 455
Shaiza, Yangmasho, 439
Shakbut bin Dhiyab al-Nahayan, Shaikh, 945
Shakbut bin Sultan al-Nahayan, Shaikh, 945
Shakhnazarov, N.S., 117
Shakhnazaryan, Levon, 117
Shakhramanyan, R.T., 116
Shakirov, Midkhat, 720
Shallenberger, Ashton, 1010
Shamir, Yitzhak (Y. Yezernitsky), 475
Shamkholov, Shakhruddin, 725
Shamshetov, Dauletbai, 1053
Shamshin, Vladislav, 737
Shamsuddin bin Nain, 554
Shamurzin, Sultankul, 521
Shankar, R., 436
Shankar, Ramsewak, 845
Shankar, Shiv, 435, 447
Shanks, Lyle, 629
Shanmughan, P., 457
Shannon, John, 982
Shannon, Wilson (Kansas, USA), 994
Shannon, Wilson (Ohio, USA), 1021
Shao Qihui, 237
Shao Shiping, 239
Shapdyrzhap, Irgit, 740
Shapiro, Lev, 742
Shapley, Lloyd, 1044
Shapour Bakhtiar, 468
Shapp, Milton, 1026
Sharaborin, Kh.P., 737
Sharafeyev, Said, 738
Sharangovich, Vasili, 127

Shardyr, 740
Sharett, Moshe (M. Shartok), 475
Sharif Ahmad al-Muhsin, 1081
Sharif Ahmad Umar Badr, 838
Sharif Ali (Brunei), 181
Sharif Salih bin Hussain, 1081
Sharifuddin Pirzada, 31
Sharipov, Isagali, 507
Sharkey, William, 1006
Sharma, Anand, 451
Sharma, A.P., 444
Sharma, Bhagwat, 431, 436, 442
Sharma, Hari, 429
Sharma, K.D., 445
Sharma, Shankar, 423, 438, 444
Sharma, Shanker, 424
Sharma, Udit, 441, 449
Sharma, Yagya Dutt, 443
Sharpe, Alfred, 549
Sharpe, John, 961
Sharpe, Merrell, 1030
Sharples, Richard, 960
Sharvananda, S., 834
Sharwood-Smith, Bryan, 637
Shashipapo, Limus, 613
Shastri, Bhola, 427
Shastri, Lal Bahadur, 423
Shastri, M., 430
Shave, Alan, 959
Shaw, John, 925
Shaw, Leslie, 993
Shaw, Vernon, 294
Shaw, Walter, 210
Shawa, Loi Mohammed, 221
Shayakhmetov, Zhumabay, 508
Shazar, Zalman (Z. Rubashov), 475
Shcherbitsky, Vladimir, 941, 942
Shchukin, Nikolai, 944
Shearer, Hugh, 500
Sheares, Benjamin, 787
Sheboldayev, Boris, 725
Sheffield, William, 976
Shehu, Mehmet, 57
Shehu Kangiwa, 655
Shein Htang, U, 608
Shekani, R.A., 647
Shekari, A., 648
Shekhar, Chandra, 423
Shekhawat, Bhairon, 446
Shelby, Isaac, 995
Sheldon, Charles, 1030
Sheldon, George, 1010
Sheldon, Lionel, 1015
Shelest, Pyotr, 942
Shen Ta-ching, 248
Shen Tsung, 224
Shen Zulum, 243
Sheng-tsu, 225
Sheppard, John, 1029
Shepstone, Denis, 803
Sher Ahmed, 671

Sher Ali Khan, 53
Sher Bahadur Deupa, 617
Sher Shah (India), 421
Sherif Abdul Sharaf, 506
Sherif Hussein bin Nasser, 506
Sherif Pasha, 303
Sherman, Buren, 993
Shershunov, Viktor, 747
Sherwell, Ambrose, 956
Shevardnadze, Eduard, 358, 359
Shevchenko, Valentina, 940
Shick Gutiérrez, René, 632
Shidehara, Kijuro, 503
Shiels, William, 98
Shih Hun, 513
Shih-tsu, 225
Shih Tsung, 224, 225
Shihabuddin Riayat Shah, 555
Shiimi, Ushona, 613
Shikhsaidov, Khizri, 725
Shilowa, Mbhazima, 812
Shiminas, Albertas, 539
Shimnashvili, _, 362
Shin Hyon Hwack, 518
Shin Ki Sun, 513
Shin Kyu Sik, 514
Shinkuba, Bagrat, 360
Shipanga, Andreas, 611
Shipley, Jenny, 627
Shippard, Sidney, 147
Shir Ghiyam, 54
Shirindzhanov, M., 916
Shirshin, Grigory, 740
Shivers, Allan, 1033
Shkele, Andris, 526
Shobaram, 459
Shoku (Japan), 501
Shol Yak, Gabriel, 837
Sholkhang, 231
Sholtz, David, 985
Shonekan, Ernest, 636
Short, Apenera, 628
Shorter, John, 974
Shortridge, Eli, 1020
Shotemor, Shirinsho, 914
Shotman, Aleksandr, 729
Shoup, George, 989
Shoup, Oliver, 980
Shricker, Henry, 992
Shrinagesh, Satyavant, 423, 425, 434
Shtygashev, Vladimir, 731
Shtyrov, Vyacheslav, 737
Shu Shenyou, 239
Shugur, _, 943
Shuja-ul-Mulk, 53
Shukla, Ravishankar, 437
Shukla, Sambhu, 460
Shukla, Shyam, 437
Shukri al-Kuwatli, 911
Shulze, John, 1025
Shum Sun Tek, 513

Shumshere Jung, 617
Shumyatsky, Boris, 758
Shunk, Francis, 1025
Shurchanov, Valentin, 724
Shushkevich, Stanislav, 126
Shuteyev, Vasily, 747
Shvab, Ivan (Johannes Schab), 741, 742
Shvernik, Nikolai, 714, 716
Shvetsov, Valery, 734
Siadious, Bernard, 347
Siadous, Bernard, 336
Siale Bileka, Silvestre, 309
Siazon, Domingo, 46
Sibalić, Mijusko, 1090
Sibbeston, Nick, 214
Sibghatullah Mujaddi, 54, 55
Sibley, Henry, 1004
Sibomana, Adrien, 189
Sicaud, Pierre, 344, 346
Sicotte, Louis, 198
Sicurani, Jean-Charles, 346
Sicuranti, Jean-Charles, 563
Sid Ahmed Ghozali, 60
Sidar Hasan Mahmud, 7
Sidar Hashim Knah, 54
Sidar Mahmud Knah, 54
Sidar Shir Amhed Suri-i-Milli, 54
Sidebottom, R.A., 989
Sidhu, Shivinder Singh, 44
Sidi Ahmed Ould Bneijara, 569
Sidi Mohammed Ould Boubaker, 569
Sidibe, Mande, 564
Sidimi, Lamine, 404
Sidler, Rudolf, 892, 893
Sidor, Karol, 789
Sidorov, S.P., 736
Siebert, Ludwig, 369
Siedel, Hans, 369
Siegelman, Don, 975
Siegenthaler, Peter, 868
Siegenthaler, Walter, 867, 868
Siegrist, Rudolf, 858
Siegrist, Ulrich, 859
Siembo, Sylvanus, 683
Siepel, Ignaz, 107
Sierra, Terencio, 412
Sierro, Serge, 904
Sievking, Kurt, 371
Siew, Vincent, 247
Sifton, Arthur, 200
Sigcau, Botha, 810
Sigcau, Stella, 810
Sigismund (Bohemia), 282
Sigismund (Hungary), 415
Sigismund (Sweden), 850
Sigler, Kim, 1004
Sigrah, Rensley, 593
Sigrist, Albert, 910
Sigrist, Jakob, 878
Sigua, Tengiz, 359
Sigurd I (Norway), 659

Sigurd II (Norway), 659
Sigwald, Adolfo, 71, 74
Siiman, Mart, 313
Sikhyong Namgyal, 446
Sikorski, Władysław, 698, 700
Silajdžić, Haris, 144, 146
Silapaarcha, Banharn, 921
Silayev, Boris, 522
Silayev, Ivan, 715, 716
Silbersahn, Claude, 337
Silerio Esparza, Maximiliano, 579
Siles, Hernando, 141
Silkevich, Suleyman, 943
Sillery, Anthony, 147
Silo (Asturias), 820
Silong Yakkyi Langdun, 231
Silumbu, 1099
Silva, Aderbal da, 176
Silva, Alberto, 171
Silva, Álvaro de, 172
Silva, Aníbal de, 150
Silva, António da, 705
Silva, Augusto da, 178
Silva, Benedito de, 152
Silva, Bertino da, 173
Silva, Coriolano de Carvalho e, 170
Silva, Edmundo Soares e, 172
Silva, Francisco da Fonseca e, 171
Silva, Francisco da (Paraná, Brazil), 167
Silva, Francisco da (São Paulo, Brazil), 178
Silva, Frederico da, 163
Silva, Henrique da, 246
Silva, Herculano de Carvalho e, 178
Silva, Hugo, 172
Silva, João da, 162, 163
Silva, João de Sabóia e, 155
Silva, Joaquim de Carvalho e, 167
Silva, José da (Brazil), 154, 168, 169
Silva, José da (East Timor), 297
Silva, José de Alcantara e, 156
Silva, José de Azevedo e, 604
Silva, José de Morais e, 170
Silva, José dos Santos e, 164
Silva, José Gomes da, 166
Silva, Lauro Sodré e, 164
Silva, Luíz da, 159
Silva, Manuel, 172
Silva, Manuel Castro e, 173
Silva, Manuel Vasalo e, 429
Silva, Mario da, 167
Silva, Moacyr da, 157
Silva, Raimundo da, 153
Silva, Samuel da, 175
Silva, Sebastião da, 160
Silva, Stênio da, 156
Silva Antóninio da, 170
Silva Cienfuegos-Jovellanos, Pedro de, 824
Silva García, Pablo, 579
Silva Jr, António da, 246
Silva Nieto, Fernando, 587
Silveira, Carlos da, 171

Silveira, Ivo, 176
Silveira, Joaquim da, 173
Silveira, Manoel da, 170, 176
Silveira, Rafael, 1070
Silveiro, Badger de, 172
Silveiro, Roberto, 172
Silvela y Le-Vielleuze, Francisco, 817
Silvester II (Pope), 1061
Silvester III (Pope), 1061
Silvestre, Achille, 291
Silzer, George, 1015
Sim Lee, Thomas, 1000
Sim Var, 192
Sima, Hans, 109
Sima, Horia, 711
Simen, Rinaldo, 898
Simeon II (Bulgaria), 183
Simeon (Russia), 712
Simi, Lepaio, 630
Simić, Djordje, 1092
Simitis, Kostas, 397
Simmonds, Kennedy, 763
Simms, John, 1016
Simon, Antoine, 410
Simon, Henri, 905
Simon, Jules, 326
Simon, Pedro, 175
Simon August (Lippe), 380
Simon Heinrich Adolf (Lippe), 380
Simonaitis, Erdmonas, 540
Simone, Carlo De, 796
Simonenko, Valentin, 941
Simonet, Jacques, 132
Simoni, Paul, 291
Simonin, Henri, 867
Simonis, Heide, 376
Simons, Mathias, 542
Simons, Walter, 365
Simonyi-Semadam, Sándor, 417
Simović, Dušan, 1087, 1088
Simpson, George, 89
Simpson, Milward, 1042
Simpson, Oramel, 997
Simpson, William, 1029
Sinan Hasani, 1095
Sinato, Gerard, 682
Sinchi Roca, 693
Sinclair, Peter, 89
Sindermann, Horst, 367
Sindhia, George Jivaji Rao, 459
Sindikubwabo, Théodore, 759
Singh, H., 453
Singh, L.R.S., 456
Singhhatek, Farimang, 355
Sinha, Dip Narain, 427
Sinha, Mahamaya, 427
Sinha, Rama Dulari, 435
Sinha, Sarat, 426
Sinha, Satya Narain, 436
Sinha, Satyendra, 428
Sinha, S.K., 425, 426

Sinha, Sri Krishna, 427
Sinibaldi, Alejandro, 401
Sinigoj, Dušan, 791
Sinimalé, Joseph, 342
Sinimbu, João de, 149
Sinner, George, 1020
Sinowatz, Alfred, 107
Sint Jago, Alfred, 623
Sione, Tomu Malaefono, 936
Sipoetz, Hans, 108
Sipopa (Barotseland), 1099
Sipovac, Nadeljko, 1097
Siqueira, Otavio de, 158
Siriex, Paul-Henri, 291, 403
Sirik Matak, 192
Sirokov, Kolj, 1095
Siroky, Vilem, 283
Sirotković, Jakov, 275
Sisavang Vong (Laos), 523
Sisavat Keoboumphan, 524
Sisile (Swaziland), 847
Sisowath, 190
Sisowath Monivong, 190
Sisto, José, 1044
Sital, Badresein, 846
Sitarammaya, B. Pattabhi, 436
Situp, Tsewing, 138
Siune, Matthew, 683
Sivasankar, Tumkur, 429
Sivertz, Bent, 213
Sixtus IV (Pope), 1063
Sixtus V (Pope), 1063
Siyubo, Silamelume, 1099
Sjahrir, Sutan, 461
Sjarifuddin, Amir, 461
Skaha, 806
Skate, Bill, 677
Skembarević, Branko, 1094
Skhthankar, Yeshwant, 442
Skinner, Carlton, 1044
Skinner, Richard, 1035
Skippings, Oswald, 971
Skirmunt, Roman, 127
Sklyarov, Ivan, 748
Skoropadsky, Pavilo, 940
Skosana, Simon, 808
Skouloudis, Stephanos, 395
Skrelji, Nikola, 1095
Skrzynski, Aleksander, 698
Skujenieks, Margers, 526
Skulkov, Igor, 741
Skulski, Peopold, 698
Skvortsov, Nikolai, 508
Slade, William, 1035
Sladen, Charles, 98
Slater, Alexander, 390, 499, 785
Slaton, John, 987
Slaughter, Gabriel, 995
Slavik, Felix, 111
Sławej-Składkowski, Felician, 699
Sławek, Walery, 698, 699

Sleeper, Albert, 1004
Sleeswijk, George, 624
Sleževičius, Mykolas, 539
Sleževičus, Adolfas, 540
Śliwiński, Stanisław, 698
Sloan, Richard, 976
Slobbe Bartholomaeus van, 621
Sloley, Herbert, 530
Slutsky, Anton, 943
Slyunkov, Nikolai, 128
Smail Hamdani, 60
Small, Len, 991
Smallman, David, 968
Smallwood, Robert, 206
Smallwood, William, 1000
Smarth, Rosny, 411
Smedley, Harold, 967
Smet de Nayer, Paul de, 130
Smetona, Antanas, 538, 540
Šmidke, Karel, 789
Smilevski, Vidoje, 544, 545
Smiljanić, Zivorad, 1096
Smirnov, Igor, 596
Smirnov, Yevgeny, 731
Smit, Jacobus, 805
Smith, Albert, 204
Smith, Alfred, 1017
Smith, Arnold, 10
Smith, Benjamin, 1018
Smith, C. de Witt, 989
Smith, Charles (Malaysia), 557
Smith, Charles (South Carolina, USA), 1029
Smith, Charles (Vermont, USA), 1036
Smith, David, 962
Smith, Edward, 1036
Smith, Elmo, 1024
Smith, Forrest, 1008
Smith, Francis, 96
Smith, George (Australia), 104
Smith, George (Canada), 207
Smith, George (Malawi), 549
Smith, George (Turks & Caicos Islands), 970
Smith, George (Virginia, USA), 1037
Smith, Green, 1008
Smith, Henry (Rhode Isand, USA), 1026
Smith, Henry (Texas, USA), 1032
Smith, Hoke, 987
Smith, Hulett, 1040
Smith, Ian, 1101
Smith, Isaac, 1035
Smith, James (Canada), 215
Smith, James Eman, 627
Smith, James (Liberia), 532
Smith, James M., 987
Smith, James Y., 1027
Smith, Jennifer, 961
Smith, Jeremiah, 1012
Smith, John, 510

Smith, John B., 1013
Smith, John Cotton, 981
Smith, John Gregory, 1035
Smith, John W., 1001
Smith, Kenry, 87
Smith, Miles, 101
Smith, Nels, 1042
Smith, Peter, 963
Smith, Preston, 1033
Smith, Reginald, 796
Smith, Robert, 1009
Smith, Roy, 1044
Smith, Samuel, 998
Smith, Stephen, 628
Smith, Stephenson, 628
Smith, W. Forgan, 92
Smith, William, 1037, 1038
Smith, William E., 1041
Smith, William H., 974
Smith, Wycliffe, 624
Smith-Dorrien, Herbert, 964
Smith-Rewse, Geoffrey, 1057
Smithers, Peter, 12
Smole, Janko, 791
Smuts, Jan, 800
Smylie, Robert, 990
Smythe, Charles, 802, 803
Smythe, Frederick, 1012
Smythe, William, 201
Snegur, Mircea, 594
Snell, Earl, 1024
Snelling, Richard, 1036
Snieckus, Antanas, 540
Snopek, Carlos, 76
Snow, Wilbur, 982
Snowball, Jabez, 203
Snyder, Simon, 1025
Snyman, Esaias, 803
Soares, Adrúbal, 157
Soares, Jair, 175
Soares, João, 64
Soares, José, 178
Soares, Marcelo, 162
Soares, Mario, 703, 706
Soares, Vital, 154
Sobarzo, Horacio, 588
Sobchak, Anatoly, 754
Sobhuza I (Swaziland), 847
Sobhuza II (Swaziland), 847
Sobisch, Jorge, 79
Sobolev, Anatoly, 747
Sobolev, Leonid, 184
Sobral, Teodoro, 170
Sobreira, Ivan, 166
Sobrinho, Alexandre, 169
Sobrinho, Gustavo, 170
Sobrinho, Lavoisier, 174
Sodano, Angelo, 1065
Soddu, Pietro, 486
Soden, Julius von, 194, 917
Soderini, Piero, 496

Sodnom, 740
Sodnom, Dumaagiyn, 600
Sodré, Constante, 156, 157
Sodré, Feliciano, 172
Sodre, Roberto, 178
Sofianski, Stefan, 185
Sofoulis, Thermistocles, 396, 397
Soglia, Giovanni, 1064
Soglo, Christophe, 137
Soglo, Nicéphore, 137
Sogorov, Milovan, 1097
Soguel, Frédéric, 880
Sohlman, Staffan, 30
Soidri Ahmed, 254
Soisson, Jean-Pierre, 330, 331
Sökman, Tayfur, 933
Sokoine, Edward, 918
Sokolov, Yefrem, 128
Sokomanu, George, 35
Sokomanu, George (G. Kalkoa), 1058
Sola, Pedro Remy, 80
Solana, Javier, 25, 49
Solanki, Madhavsinh, 431
Solar, Pedro, 690
Solari, Alfredo, 1057
Solari, Jean, 345
Soldini, Mario, 900
Soleano, George, 623
Solens, Josep Pintat, 63
Soler i Clodera, Cristófol, 825
Solf, Wilhelm, 768
Solf Muro, Alfredo, 691
Solís Palma, Manuel, 675
Soljić, Vladimir, 146
Solkin, A.F., 1055
Sollberger, Charles, 906
Soloman, Albert, 96
Solomentsev, Mikhail, 715
Solomiac, Léon, 456
Solomon, Vaiben, 94
Solomon I, 314
Solomon II, 315
Solomon III, 315
Solomon Lar, 654
Solórzano, Carlos, 632
Solórzano, Carlos (Ecuador), 300
Solórzano, Carlos (Nicaragua), 632
Solorzano, José, 582
Solovev, Vadim, 745
Soltan Ali Keshtmand, 54
Soltan Hosein (Iran), 466
Solyakov, Petr, 730
Somaglia, Giulio della, 1064
Somare, Arthur, 678
Somare, Michael, 676, 677, 678
Somaviá, Juan, 44
Sommer, Henri, 868
Sommerfeld, Hugo von, 388
Somov, A.V., 724
Somoza Debayle, Anastasio, 632
Somoza Debayle, Luis, 632

Somoza García, Anastasio, 632
Son Ngoc Thanh, 191, 192
Son Sann, 192, 193
Sonam Togyal, 232
Sonderegger, Karl, 860
Song Baorui, 242
Song Fatang, 237
Song Peizhang, 234
Song Pyung Jo, 514
Song Qingling, 225
Song Ruixiang, 240
Song Yo Chang, 517
Song Zhaosu, 235
Songaila, Ringaudas, 539, 540
Songgram, Pibul, 920
Songjong (Korea), 512
Sonjo I (Korea), 512
Sonjo II (Korea), 512
Sonnino, Sidney, 479
Soong Chu-yu, James, 248
Sopé, Barak, 1058
Sophoulis, Thermistocles, 396
Sorbie, Arthur, 1020
Sorhaindo, Crispin, 293
Sorin, Constant, 338
Sorokin, Karp, 1056
Sorokin, Maksum, 725
Sorsa, Kalevi, 320, 321
Sorton, Sydney, 624
Sorzano, Luis Tejeda, 141
Soskić, Branislav, 1090
Soslan, Dawith, 357
Sostoa y Sthamer, Gustavo de, 308
Sota, José Manuel de la, 74
Sotiropoulos, Sotirios, 395
Soto, Ignacio, 588
Soto Maynes, Oscar, 577
Soto y Alfaro, Bernardo, 271
Soublette, Carlos, 1066
Souçadaux, Jean, 547
Soucadeux, Jean, 194
Souda, Marcondes de, 157
Soult, Nicolas, 325, 326
Soum, Henri, 597
Soumialot, Gaston, 265
Soupault, Jean-Michel, 256
Souphanouvong, 523
Sourdille, Jacques, 331
Sousa, António de, 704
Sousa, António de Melo e, 173
Sousa, Aurelio, 691
Sousa, José Abreu e, 704
Soustelle, Jacques-Émile, 59
Southard, Samuel, 1014
Southorn, Wilfred, 355
Southwell, C.A.Paul, 763
Souto, Paulo, 155
Souto-Maior, Abel, 65
Souza, Ernâni Satyro e, 166
Souza, Francisco, 171
Souza, Francisco Pires de, 155

Souza, José de (Bahia, Brazil), 154
Souza, José de (Rio Grande do Sul, Brazil), 175
Souza, Paul-Émile de, 137
Souza, Pedro de, 168
Souza, Washington de, 148
D'Souza, Wilfred, 430
Souze, Faustino de Albuquerque e, 156
Sow, Abdoulaye Sékou, 564
Spaak, Paul-Henri, 25, 131
Spadaccini, Felice, 481
Spadolini, Giovanni, 478, 480
Spaeth, Lothar, 368
Spalding, Warner, 103
Spangenberg, Ricardo, 80
Spano, Salvatorangelo, 486
Sparks, Chauncey, 975
Sparks, John, 1011
Spasov, Luka, 724
Spaulding, Huntley, 1013
Spaulding, Roland, 1013
Speekenbrink, Antonius, 622
Speiser, Paul, 864
Spellman, John, 1039
Spénale, Georges-Léon, 922
Speziali, Carlo, 900
Spiljak, Mika, 1086, 1087
Špiljak, Mika, 275
Spillmann, Fritz, 907
Spinelli, Antonio, 494
Spinelli, Gennaro, 494
Spinnler, Carl, 862
Spinola, António de, 405
Spínola, António de, 703
Spiridonov, Yury, 732
Spitaels, Guy, 132
Spitteler, Werner, 863, 864
Spitz, Georges-Aimé, 340
Špoljarić, Djuro, 275
Spore, Steen, 290
Sprague, Charles, 1024
Sprague, William, 1026, 1027
Spraight, Richard Jr, 1018
Spraight, Richard Sr, 1018
Sprenger, Jakob, 372
Sprigg, Gordon, 801
Sprigg, Samuel, 1000
Spring, Heinrich, 386
Springer, Hugh, 124
Springzak, Joseph, 475
Sprockel, C.G., 622
Sproul, William, 1025
Spry, William, 1034
Spühler, Willy, 855, 856
Spychalski, Marian, 698
Squire, Watson, 1039
Squires, Richard, 205
Squnders, Alvin, 1009
Sramek, Ján, 283, 284
Sraponyan, S., 86

Srbovan, Jon, 1096
Sremec, Zlatan, 274
Srivastava, Chadrika, 45
Srivastava, Oudh Narain, 439, 441
Srzentić, Vojo, 1091
Staaf, Karl, 851
Staal, Gerard, 845
Stabel, Anton von, 377
Staccini, Cesare, 770, 771
Stack, Lee, 835
Stadler, Hansruedi, 902
Stadlin, Hermann, 907
Stafford, Robert, 1036
Stafford, William, 626
Stähelin, Philipp, 898
Stähelin, Willi, 897
Stähl, Hans, 867
Ståhlberg, Kaarlo, 319
Stainbeck, Ingram, 989
Stakun, Mikhail, 126
Stalder, Xaver, 857, 858
Stalin, Iosef, 716, 717
Stallard, Peter, 134, 957
Stambolić, Ivan, 1092, 1093
Stambolić, Petar, 1086, 1087, 1091, 1093
Stamboliski, Aleksander, 184
Stambolov, Stefan, 183, 184
Stamenković, Dragi, 1093
Stamm, Bernhard, 891, 892
Stämpfli, Jakob, 853
Stampfli, Oskar, 894, 895
Stampfli, Otto, 894, 895
Stämpfli, Walter, 855
Stanfield, Frank, 206
Stanfield, Robert, 207
Stanford, Leland, 979
Stanford, Rawghlie, 977
Stang, Emil, 660
Stang, Frederik, 660
Stanisław I (Poland), 697
Stanisław II August (Poland), 697
Stankevičius, Laurynas Mindaugas, 540
Stanković, Sinisa, 1091
Stanley, Arthur, 97
Stanley, George, 203
Stanley, Herbert, 830, 1098, 1100
Stanley, Robert, 793
Stanley, Thomas, 1037
Stanley, William, 994
Stanovnik, Janez, 791
Stapleton, Robert, 636
Stapleton, Robert de, 118
Starckenbrogh-Stachower, Alidius van, 461
Starhemberg, Ernst, 107
Stark, Lloyd, 1008
Starodabtsev, Vasily, 752
Starr Jameson, Leander, 801
Staryi, Grigory, 594
Stasi, Bernard, 331
Stasi, Giovanni Di, 485
Stassen, Harold, 1005

Stassinopoulos, Michael, 393
Staub, Carl, 908
Staub, Karl, 907
Stauffer, Alfred, 867
Stauning, Thorvald, 288
Staveley, Martin, 963
Stearns, Marcellus, 985
Stearns, Onslow, 1012
Steczkowski, Jan, 698
Steeg, Jules, 59
Steeg, Théodore, 327
Steele, George, 1022
Steele, John (Illinois, USA), 991
Steele, John (New Hampshire, USA), 1012
Steen, Johannes, 660
Stefan I (Poland), 697
Stefani, Albert, 900
Stefani, Mario de, 797
Stefansson, Stefan, 419
Stegerwald, Adam, 384
Steiger, Edmund von, 866
Steiger, Eduard von, 855
Steimer, Emil, 907, 908
Steinberger, A.B., 769
Steinbock, Johann, 109
Steinbrecher, Erich, 386
Steiner, Franz, 904
Steiner, Josef, 907
Steiner, Leopold, 109
Steinhauer, Ralph, 199
Steinhauser, A., 875
Steinhoff, Fritz, 373
Steinhoff, Karl, 370
Steinmann, Hans, 878
Steinmetz, Pierre, 342
Steinthórsson, Streingrímur, 419
Stelling, Johannes, 381
Steltzer, Theodor, 375
Stengel, Franz, 377
Stenkil (Sweden), 849
Steno, Michele, 497
Stepan, Karl, 110
Stepanenko, _, 737
Stepanov, Viktor, 730
Stepashin, Sergei, 715
Stephanopoulos, Kostas, 393
Stephanopoulos, Stephanos, 397
Stephen, Alexander, 987
Stephen, Ninian, 87
Stephen (England), 950
Stephen II (Pope), 1060
Stephen III (Pope), 1060
Stephen IV (Pope), 1060
Stephen IX (Pope), 1061
Stephen V (Pope), 1060
Stephen VI (Pope), 1060
Stephen VII (Pope), 1061
Stephen VIII (Pope), 1061
Stephens, Lon, 1008
Stephens, Stanley, 1009
Stephens, William, 979

Stephensen, Stephen, 662
Stephenson, Charles, 1011
Stephenson, Edward, 989
Stephenson, Hugh, 606
Stepovich, Michael, 976
Sterling, Ross, 1033
Stern, Ernest, 43
Sterndale, Robert, 968
Steuble, Adolf, 860, 861
Steunenberg, Frank, 989
Stevanović, Danilo, 1092
Stevens, Bertram, 90
Stevens, Clark, 1043
Stevens, Isaac, 1037
Stevens, Jimmy, 1059
Stevens, Samuel, 1000
Stevens, Siaka, 786
Stevenson, Adlai, 991
Stevenson, Coke, 1033
Stevenson, Hubert, 785
Stevenson, John, 995
Stevenson, Malcolm, 279, 783
Stevenson, William, 1040
Stewart, Charles, 200
Stewart, Douglas, 762
Stewart, Duncan, 558
Stewart, Edwin, 1025
Stewart, Henry, 783
Stewart, James, 210
Stewart, John (Scotland), 954
Stewart, John (USA), 1035
Stewart, Murdoch, 954
Stewart, Robert (Bermuda), 960
Stewart, Robert (Scotland), 954
Stewart, Robert (USA), 1007
Stewart, Sam, 1009
Steyn, Lucas, 799
Steyn, Marthinus, 610
Steyn, Martinus, 803
Sthamer, Gustav, 370
Stich, Otto, 856
Stichtenoth, Fritz, 382
Stickney, William, 1036
Stiernberg, Carl von, 380
Stiffker, Hans, 876
Stiffler, Johann, 874
Stikker, Dirk, 25
Stimson, Robert, 968
Știrbai, Barbu, 710
Stisted, Henry, 207
Stitt, T., 962
Stix, Karl, 108
Stobbe, Dietrich, 369
Stock, Christian, 372
Stockdale, Fletcher, 1033
Stockhausen, Carl von, 388
Stöcki, Clemens, 864
Stockley, Charles, 983
Stöckli, Clemens, 863
Stöcklin, Armin, 864
Stöckling, Hans, 889

Stockmann, Josef, 886
Stockmann, Karl, 885
Stockton, Thomas, 983
Stofile, Makhenkosi, 811
Stoiber, Edmund, 369
Stoica, Chivu, 708, 710
Stoilov, Constantin, 184
Stojadinović, Milan, 1087
Stojanović, Ljubomir, 1093
Stojanović, Nikola, 144
Stojćević, Stanko, 275
Stojković, Milutin, 1096
Stokes, Edward, 1014
Stokes, Montford, 1018
Stolojan, Teodor, 710
Stolpe, Manfred, 370
Stoltenberg, Gerhard, 375
Stolypin, Pyotr, 714
Stone, David, 1018
Stone, Edward, 99
Stone, John, 1000, 1006
Stone, Shane, 102
Stone, William (Iowa, USA), 993
Stone, William (Missouri, USA), 1008
Stone, William (Pennsylvania, USA), 1025
Stoneman, George, 979
Stooke, George, 785
Stoph, Willi, 367
Storace, Francesco, 483
Storey, John, 90
Storrs, Ronald, 279, 1098
Stössel, Johann, 908, 909
Stottenberg, Jens, 661
Stout, Robert, 626
Stoutt, H. Lavity, 963
Stoutt, Jacob, 983
Stoutt, Robert, 625
Stow, John (Barbados), 124
Stow, John (St Lucia), 764
Stoyanov, Petŭr, 183
Strakhov, Aleksei, 751
Strakhov, I.K., 731
Strandfeldt, Victor, 321
Strandmann, Otto, 312, 313
Strangeways, Henry, 94
Stráský, Jan, 283
Strasser, Valentine, 786
Stratos, Nikolas, 396
Stratton, Charles, 1014
Stratton, Richard, 967
Stratton, William, 991
Straub, Bruno, 416
Straub, Hans, 908
Straub, Robert, 1024
Strauss, Franz-Josef, 369
Strautmanis, Peteris, 525
Stravrev, Dragoljub, 544, 545
Straw, Ezekiel, 1012
Strechaj, Rudolf, 789
Streeruwitz, Ernst, 107
Street, Kenneth, 89

Street, Philip, 89
Streibel, Hans-Rudolf, 866
Streibl, Max, 369
Stremayr, Karl von, 106
Stresemann, Gustav, 366
Stresny, N.P., 594
Streuli, Adolf, 909
Streuli, Hans, 855, 909
Streuli, Rudolf, 909
Strickland, Gerald, 89, 95, 99
Strijdom, Johannes, 800
Stroessner, Alfredo, 687
Stroev, Aleksandr, 594
Strom, Harry, 200
Strong, Caleb, 1001
Strong, John, 970, 975
Štrougal, Lubomír, 283
Stroyev, Yegor, 749
Struycken, Anton, 622
Stuart, Alexander, 90
Stuart, Andrew, 1057
Stuart, Carolyn, 103
Stuart, Henry, 1037
Stubbs, Reginald, 245, 279, 499, 830
Stubbs, Walter, 994
Stubmann, Peter, 382
Stucka, Peteris, 525
Stucki, Fridolin, 874
Stucki, Jakob, 910
Stucky, Georg, 908
Studler, Albert, 857, 858
Stulginskis, Aleksandras, 538
Stumpf, Franz, 110
Sturdza, Dimitrie, 709
Sture, Sten the Elder, 850
Sture, Sten the Younger, 850
Sture, Svante, 850
Sturgkh, Otto, 107
Sturmer, Boris, 714
Sturrock, John, 530
Sturua, Georgi, 358, 361
Sturza, Ion, 595
Sturzenegger, Fritz, 890
Stüssi, Christoph, 874
Stutz, Christoph, 866
Su Gang, 236
Su Yirian, 241
Su Zhenhua, 244
Suárez, Hugo Banzer, 141, 142
Suárez, Marco, 250
Suárez del Rondo, Joaquín, 1048
Suárez González, Adolfo, 818
Suárez Molina, José, 581
Suárez Montiel, Nelson, 1072
Suárez Veintemilla, Mariano, 300
Suassuna, João, 165
Suat Ürgüplü, 932
Suazo Córdova, Roberto, 413
Subarna Shumshere, 617
Subasić, Ivan, 1087, 1088
Subbarayan, P., 437

Subhi Bey Barakat, 912
Subramaniam, C., 438
Subroto, 32
Sucher, Arnold, 109
Suchocka, Hanna, 699
Sucre, Antonio de, 140
Sudarenko, Valery, 746
Sudre, Camille, 342
Sudre, Marguerite, 342
Sudreau, Pierre, 331
Sueldo, Julio, 84
Suharto, 461, 462
Suhr, Otto, 369
Sui Tamole, Fololiano, 351
Sukarno, Ahmed, 461, 462
Sukawali, Tjokordo, 462
Sukchong (Korea), 512
Sukhadia, Mohahlal, 446
Sukhadia, Mohan, 423
Sukhadia, Mohan Lal, 434
Sukhadia, Mohanlal, 448
Sukhishvili, L., 359
Sukiman, Wirjosandjojo, 462
Sukrija, Ali, 1088
Sukselainen, Väinö, 320
Sulaiman bin Ahmed al-Kalifa, 120
Sulaiman (Brunei), 181
Suleiman, Dan, 654
Suleiman Badrul-Alam Shah, 560
Suleiman Franjieh, 527
Suleiman I (Turkey), 929
Suleiman II (Turkey), 930
Suleiman Mohammed Suleiman, 843
Suleiman (Morocco), 602
Suleiman Shah, 559
Süleyman Demiral, 932
Suliman Nabulsi, 506
Sulimov, Daniil, 715
Sullivan, James, 1001
Sullivan, John, 1011, 1012
Sullivan, Michael, 1042
Sullivan, Timothy, 473
Sullivan, William, 210
Sulman bin Hamed al-Kalifa, 120
Sultan bin Ahmed (Oman), 663
Sultan bin Mohammed al-Qasimi, Shaikh, 947
Sultan bin Salim al-Qasimi, Shaikh, 947
Sultan bin Saqr al-Qasimi, Shaikh, 947
Sultan bin Zaid al-Nahayan, Shaikh, 945
Sultan Mahmud Chaudhary, 672
Sultan Singh, 449
Sultanov, Faizullla, 719
Sultanov, Gamid, 115
Sultanov, Uktir, 1052
Sultanuddin Ahmed, 122
Sulzer, William, 1017
Sumauskas, Matejas, 539
Šumauskas, Matejas, 539
Sumaye, Frederick, 918
Sumbu, Paul-Marcel, 263

Sumin, Petr, 745
Summers, Gerald, 798
Sumner, Increase, 1001
Sumokil, Christiaan, 464
Sun Fo, 227
Sun Gouzhu, 238
Sun Pao-chi, 226
Sun Wensheng, 242
Sun Yat-sen, 225, 228
Sun Yun-suan, 247
Sun Zuobin, 240
Suna II (Buganda), 938
Sunay, Cevdet, 930
Sundlun, Bruce, 1027
Sundquist, Don, 1032
Sundstein, Jogvan, 289
Sung Ping, 235
Sung Tsu-wen, 227
Sungrab, 231
Sunia, Tauese, 1043
Sunila, Juho, 320
Sunjong (Korea), 513
Sunthorn Hongladarom, 38
Sununu, John, 1013
Suprunyuk, Evgeny, 943
Surat, Aleksandr, 744
Surdin, N.G., 734
Surendra (Nepal), 616
Surganov, Fyodor, 126
Surikov, Aleksandr, 743
Surlemont, Jules-Eucher, 336
Suruagy, Divaldo, 152
Survana Prabha (Nepal), 616
Surya Bahadur Thapa, 617
Surzhikov, Viktor, 747
Suslov, Vladimir, 752
Susneyos, 315
Suter, Walter, 908
Sutherland, Peter, 47
Sutton, George, 802
Sutton, John, 958
Šuvar, Stipe, 1088
Suyerkulov, Abdy, 522
Suyumbayev, Akhmatbek, 522
Suzuki, Kantaro, 503
Suzuki, Zenko, 504
Suzzi-Valli, Domenico, 770, 771
Suzzi-Valli, Leonido, 770, 771, 772
Suzzi-Valli, Pietro, 771
Svanidze, Nikoli, 361, 362
Švehla, Antonín, 283
Svelnys, V., 541
Svend I (Denmark), 286
Svend II Estridsen (Denmark), 286
Svend III (Denmark), 286
Sverdlov, Yakov, 713
Sverdrup, Johan, 660
Sverker I (Sweden), 849
Sverker II Carlsson (Sweden), 849
Sverre (Norway), 659

Svetin, Mikhail, 741
Svinhufud, Pehr, 319, 320
Svoboda, Ludvik, 283
Swain, David, 1018
Swainson, John, 1004
Swaminathan, D.M.S., 834
Swan, John, 961
Swann, Thomas, 1000
Swanson, Claude, 1037
Swaraj, Sushma, 455
Swarap Singh, 445
Swaroop, Shiva, 425
Swart, Charles, 799, 800
Swartz, Carl, 851
Swayne, Charles, 510
Swayne, Eric, 134
Sweet, William, 980
Sweet-Escott, Ernest, 134, 317, 783
Swettenham, James, 407, 499
Sweyn (England), 949
Sweyn Knutson (Norway), 659
Swierzyński, Józef, 698
Swift, Henry, 1004
Swift, William, 1044
Świtalski, Kazimierz, 698
Swoboda, Gustav, 47
Syabikov, _, 757
Sychev, Vyacheslav, 13
Sydow, Oscar von, 851
Syed Abdul Kadir bin Mohamed, 551
Syed Ahmad bin Syed Mahmud Shahabudin, 552
Syed Mir Qasim, 434
Syed Nahar bin Sheh Shahabudin, 552
Syed Nurul Hasan, 443
Syed Omar bin Syed Abdullah Shahabudin, 552
Syed Qaim Ali Shah, 670
Syed Zahiruddin bin Syed Hassain, 553
Sykes, James, 983
Sylvain, François, 410
Sylvester, Hans, 108
Symes, George, 835, 917
Symington, Fife, 977
Symonette, Roland, 119
Symphor, Paul, 340
Symphorien, Joseph, 337
Syrový, Ján, 282, 283
Syrtsov, Sergei, 715
Syse, Jan, 661
Sysoev, Petr, 740, 741
Syutkin, Albert, 732
Szakartis, Árpád, 416
Szálasi, Ferenc, 417
Szarpáry, Gyula, 416
Szczepanik, Edward, 700
Szell, Kálmán, 416
Szermere, Bertalan, 416
Szindler, Jan (Johann Schindler), 701
Szlávy, József, 416
Szoka, Edmund, 1065

Szótjay, Döme, 417
Szüros, Mátyás, 416

Taaffe, Eduard von, 106, 107
Tabacci, Bruno, 484
Tabai, Ieremia, 39, 510, 511
Taban, Timothy, 841
Taban Deng Gai, 841
Tabayev, Daniil, 718
Tabeyev, Fikryat, 739
Tablante, Carlos, 1068
Tabone, Censu (Vincent), 566
Tabunshchik, Gheorghe, 596
Tacfifenua, Atelemo, 352
Tache, Étienne, 198
Taddei, Primo, 772
Tadjidine Ben Said Massonde, 253
Tadzhiev, _, 915
T'aejo (Yi Songgye, Korea), 512
T'aejong (Korea), 512
Taft, Bob, 1022
Taft, Royal, 1027
Taft, William, 277, 973
Tagirov, Afzal, 719
Tagle, José de, 688
Taha al-Hashimi, 471
Tahar Ben Ammar, 928
Taher Bekir, 536
Taher Masri, 506
Taher Yahya, 471, 472
Tahiliani, Radhakrishnan, 447
Tahmasp I (Iran), 466
Tahmasp II (Iran), 466
Tahnun bin Shakbut al-Nahayan, Shaikh, 945
Tahnun bin Zaid al-Nahayan, Shaikh, 945
T'ai Tsu, 224
Taibekov, Yelubai, 508
Tailby, William, 628
Tailhades, Edgar, 332
Taillon, Louis-Olivier, 211
Taimur, Syeda, 426
Taimur bin Faisal (Oman), 663
Tait, William, 1100
Taj Addin el-Husni, 911, 912
Tajan-Sie, Banja, 785
Tajes, Máximo, 1049
Tajuddin Ahmed, 121
Takahashi, Korekiyo, 503
Takasi, Esipio, 351
Takatai, Petelo, 350
Takeshita, Nobaru, 504
Takhtarov, Adil-Girei, 725
Takieddine Solh, 529
Takizala, Henri-Desiré, 264, 265, 267, 268
Takla Giyorghis, 315
Takla Giyorghis II (Ras Gobaze), 315
Takla Haymanot I, 315
Takla Haymanot II, 315
Takla Mariam, 314

Takoyev, _, 757
Taktra Rimpoche Ngawang, 231
Talal bin Abdullah (Jordan), 505
Talamantes, Gustavo, 577
Talbot, Charles, 399
Talbot, Matthew, 986
Talbot, Ray, 980
Talbot, Reginald, 97
Talbot, Thomas, 1002
Taleski, Blagoje, 544
Taleyarkhan, Homi, 446
Talib, Sufi, 303
Talibov, Vasif, 115
Talis, Jacob, 683
Talleyrand-Peregord, Charles de, 325
Tallmadge, Nathaniel, 1040
Talmadge, Eugene, 987
Talmadge, Herman, 987
Talwar, Pajeev, 455
Tamayo, José, 299
Tambiev, Yusup, 721
Tambroni, Fernando, 480
Tameura, Tekire, 511
Tamirat Laynie, 316
Tamur Dawamat, 233
Tan Furen, 243
Tan Qilong, 240, 241, 243
T'an Yen-kai, 227
T'an Yen-k'ai, 228
Tanaka, Giichi, 503
Tanaka, Kakuei, 504
Tancrède, Auguste, 410
Tancrede (Sicily), 492
Tandja Mamadouo, 633
T'ang Ching-sung, 247
Tang Fei, 247
T'ang Shao-yi, 226
Tangaroa Tangaroa, 628
Tanjong (Korea), 512
Tanka Achariya, 617
Tanko Ayuba, 647
Tanner, Carl, 862
Tanner, John, 991
Tanner, Väinö, 320
Tantzen, Theodor, 383
Tao Zhu, 235
Tap, Pierre, 336
Taparelli, Juan, 78
Taparelli, Juan Carlos, 75
Tapase, Ganpatrao, 450
Tapase, Sri Ganpatrao, 431
Tapgun, Fidelas, 654
Taplashvili, A.I., 362
Tarand, Andres, 313
Tarasov, Mikhail, 714
Tarazevich, Georgi, 126
Tardieu, André, 327
Tardini, Domenico, 1065
Tarfa, P.C., 653
Tarhan, Ilias, 943
Tarik bin Taimur, 663

Tarjanne, Pekka, 45
Tarrandellas, Josep, 826, 827
Tarschys, Daniel, 12
Tartara, Julio, 83
Tartari, Luigi, 490
Taschereau, H. Elzear, 197
Taschereau, Louis-Alexandre, 211
Taschereau, Robert, 198
Tasfa Ilasu, 314
Tashenev, Zhumabek, 507, 508
Tashi Namgyal, 446
Tassamma Nadaw, 316
Tatarashvili, Shota, 360
Tătărescu, Gheorghe, 710
Tatari Ali, 641
Tate, Robert, 768
Tatham, David, 964
Tatiashvili, Dzhumar, 359
Tatila Akufuna (Barotseland), 1099
Tatliev, Suleyman, 725
Tatliyev, Suleiman, 113
Tattnall, Josiah, 986
Taua, Mark, 682
Taufa'ahau Tupou IV (Tonga, Tupouto'a Tungi), 924
Tauguinas, Rolando, 72
Tauhavili, Mikaele, 350
Taupongi, Francia, 795
Taureka, Opa, 677
Taureka, Reuben, 677
Tavares, Alvaro, 65
Tavares, Álvaro, 405
Tavares, Francisco, 174
Tavares, José, 152
Tavares, Pedro, 159
Távora, Manoel, 155
Távora, Virgílio, 156
Tawa Sli, 558
Tawes, J. Millard, 1001
Tayley, John, 1017
Taylor, A.D., 102
Taylor, Alfred, 1032
Taylor, Bill, 102, 103
Taylor, Charles, 533
Taylor, David, 964, 966
Taylor, Derek, 971
Taylor, Henry, 118
Taylor, John (UNESCO), 46
Taylor, John (USA), 1028
Taylor, Leon, 1014
Taylor, R.B., 629
Taylor, Robert, 1031
Taylor, William (Kentucky, USA), 996
Taylor, William (Wisconsin, USA), 1041
Taylor, Zachary, 972
Tazewell, Littleton, 1037
Tazhiev, Ibrahim, 508
Tchakste, Janis, 525
Tchoungi, Simon-Pierre, 195
Te Tsung, 225
Teakle, Joseph, 1008

Teannaki, Teatao, 510
Teao, Falima, 630
Teao, Gabriel, 795
Teaotai, Ata, 511
Teardo, Alberto, 484
Tebet, Ramez, 162
Techenor, Isaac, 1035
Teemant, Jaan, 312
Teferi Benti, 316
Teheiura, Jacques, 346
Teixeira, Constantino, 406
Teixeira, Gabriel, 246, 604
Teixeira, Mauro, 158
Teixeira, Pedro, 158
Tejada, Lidia Gueiler, 141
Tejedor Sanz, Ramón, 824
Tekwie, John, 683
Teleki, Pél, 417
Télémanque, Seide, 410
Teles, Leonor, 702
Teles, Sebastião, 704
Telfair, Edward, 986
Telfer-Smollett, Alexander, 956
Teli, Isidore, 685
Tell, Wilhelm, 385
Telleriarte, Ricardo, 77
Tellez Cruces, Augustín, 580
Telli, Diallo, 27
Tellier, Théophile, 136, 338, 633
Temi Ejoor, 639, 645
Temmer, Irvin, 624
Temple, William, 983
Templer, Gerald, 550
Templer, Philip, 293
Templeton, Charles, 982
Tenchio, Ettore, 876
Tener, John, 1025
Tenev, Florencio, 72
Tengku Abdulla, 555
Tengku Nadzaruddin, 554
Tenoch (Aztec Empire), 574
Tenorio, Froilan, 1045
Tenorio, Pedro T., 1045
Tenpai Gonpo Kindeling, 231
Tenpai Nyima, 231
Tensung Namgyal, 446
Tenzin Dalai Khan, 230
Tenzin Gyatso, 231
Tenzin Namgyal Tethong, 232
Tenzing Namgyal, 446
Teo, Penitala Fiatau, 936
Ter-Gabrielyan, Saak, 86
Ter-Petrosyan, Levon, 85
Terán, Horacio, 589
Terán Terán, Héctor, 576
Terauchi, Matsakate, 503
Terblanche, Jan, 802
Terboven, Josef, 660
Terenzi, Gian, 774
Terenzi, Giovanni, 772
Terepai Moate, 628

Tereshchenko, Sergei, 508
Terhune, Warren, 1043
Terra, Gabriel, 1049
Terrac, Edouard, 403, 568
Terrade, Jean, 340
Terragno, Rodolfo, 70
Terral, Thomas, 978
Terrason de Gourgèes, Jean-Henri, 563
Terrell, Joseph, 987
Terry, Charles, 984
Terry, Peter, 965
Tesfaye Dinka, 316
Tesfaye Gebre-Kidan, 316
Tessio, Aldo, 82
Teufel, Erwin, 368
Tevernier, Jean, 330
Tewary, Tribhuvan, 456
Tewfik Abulhuda, 505, 506
Tewfik Nessim Pasha, 303, 304
Tewfiq el-Suweidi, 471, 472
Tewodoros I, 314
Tewodoros II (Kassa Haylu), 315
Teziyev, Oleg, 363
Thaci, Hasim, 1095
Thakur, D.D., 425, 426
Thakur, Karpoori, 427, 428
Thaly, Gabriel, 336, 1058
Thamar, 357
Than Shwe, 607
Thanarat, Sarit, 921
Thanh Thai (Nguyen Buu Lan), 1073
Thanhawla, Lal, 441
Thant, U, 42
Tharp, William, 983
Tharrawaddy Min (Myanmar), 606
Thatcher, Margaret, 953
Thatcher, Ross, 213
Thayer, John (Nebraska, USA), 1010
Thayer, John (Wyoming, USA), 1042
Thayer, William, 1024
Theiler, Mathe, 892
Thélin, Adrien, 904, 905
Thelps, Willard, 215
Themtander, Oscar, 851
Théodore, Davilmar, 410
Theodore, Edward, 92
Theodore (Pope), 1061
Theophilos, 315
Theotokis, Georgios, 395
Theotokis, Ioannis, 397
Theraulaz, Alphonse, 869
Thériault, Camille, 204
Thérond, Fernand-Ernest, 336, 353
Theunis, Georges, 130
Theus, Arno, 876
Thibault, Lise, 211
Thibaw (Myanmar), 606
Thibodeaux, Henry, 996
Thielen, Frits, 623
Thielen, Jacob, 623
Thiercy, Georges, 292

Thiers, Adolphe, 324, 325, 326
Thieu Tri (Nguyen Mien Tong), 1073
Thilges, Edouard, 542
Thill, Robert, 350
Thinault (Teobaldo) I (Navarre), 823
Thinault (Teobaldo) II (Navarre), 823
Thinley, Jigme, 139
Thomas, Arthur, 1034
Thomas, Charles, 980, 983
Thomas, Christopher, 28
Thomas, Francis, 1000
Thomas, James, 1000
Thomas, John, 68
Thomas, M.M., 441
Thomas, Philip, 1000
Thomas, Thomas, 390, 549
Thomnas, Albert, 44
Thompson, Aubrey, 147, 530
Thompson, David, 989
Thompson, Eric, 637
Thompson, Harry, 764, 766
Thompson, Hugh, 1029
Thompson, James, 991
Thompson, John, 198, 207
Thompson, Lindsay, 99
Thompson, Martin, 680
Thompson, Meldrim, 1013
Thompson, Melvin, 987
Thompson, P. Forsythe, 969
Thompson, Tommy, 1041
Thompson, Willoughby, 959, 966
Thomson, Graeme, 407, 635, 830
Thomson, John, 963
Thomson, Vernon, 1041
Thone, Charles, 1010
Thorbecke, Jan, 619
Thorburn, James, 390
Thorburn, Robert, 205
Thordarson, Björn, 419
Thorhallsson, Tryggvi, 419
Thorlaksson, Jón, 419
Thorn, Gaston, 17, 543
Thorn, George, 92
Thorn, Victor, 542
Thornburgh, Richard, 1026
Thornley, Colin, 134
Thornton, Dan, 980
Thornton, Matthew, 1011
Thornton, William, 1015
Thoroddsen, Gunnar, 420
Thorpe, John, 764, 783
Thorpe, W.G., 629
Thors, Ólafur, 419, 420
Thotub Namgyal, 446
Thow, Ian, 968
Throckmorton, James, 1033
Throop, Enos, 1017
Throssell, George, 100
Thuau, Rémi, 344
Thubten Gyatso, 231
Thullner, Johann, 108

Thun und Hohenstein, Franz, 107
Thungon, Prem, 425
Thurmond, J. Strom, 1029
Thurn, Everard, 317
Thurston, John, 317
Thwaini bin Said (Oman), 663
Thye, Edward, 1005
Thyselius, Carl, 851
Tiago, Henrique N'Zita, 66
Tian Bao, 234
Tian Chengping, 240
Tian Fengshan, 237
Tiberi, Dino, 484
Tibiriça, Jorge, 177
Tieh Ying, 243
Tiemann, Norbert, 1010
Tienhoven, Cornelius van, 619
Tiffin, Edward, 1021
Tijmstra, G.J., 624
Tikhomirov, Vladislav, 746
Tikhonov, Nikolai, 716
Tikka Khan (Bangladesh), 123
Tikka Khan (Pakistan), 668
Tikvicki, Geza, 1096
Tilak, Raghukul, 445
Tilburg, Jan van, 845
Tilden, Samuel, 1017
Tildy, Zoltán, 416, 417
Tilekeratne, Stanley, 831
Tilkens, Auguste-Constant, 258
Tilley, Benjamin, 1043
Tilley, Leonard, 204
Tilley, Samuel, 203, 204
Tillman, Benjamin, 1029
Timakata, Frederick, 1058
Timele, Jacob, 678
Timmerman, George, 1029
Timur, 53
Tindemans, Leo, 131
Tindiwi, Danley, 679
Tingayev, I.Ya., 734
Tingley, Clyde, 1016
Tinoco, Tasso, 151
Tinoco Granados, Federico, 271
Tinoco Rubi, Victor, 583
Tinsulanond, Prem, 921
Tirant, René, 137, 291
Tirard, Pierre, 326
Tirtoprodjo, Susanto, 462
Tiscornia, Roberto, 74
Tiso, Jozef, 789
Tiso, Stefan, 789
Tisza, István, 416
Tisza, Kálmán, 416
Tito, Teburoro, 511
Titov, Fedor, 722
Titov, Konstantin, 751
Tiwari, Narain, 451
Tizard, Catherine (C. Maclean), 626
Tizoc (Aztec Empire), 574
Tjakraningrat, 463

Tjamuaha, Thimoteus, 613
Tjejamba, Erastus, 613
Tjibaou, Jean-Marie, 348, 349
Tjokroaminoto, Anwar, 464
Tkharkakhov, Mukharby, 717
Tkhiliashvili, Aleksandr, 362
Tlactozin (Aztec Empire), 575
Tlekhas, Mugdin, 717
Tlostanov, K., 726
Tobaining, Ereman, 678
Tobey, Charles, 1013
Tobin, Brian, 206
Tobin, Maurice, 1002
Tobler, Ernst, 909
Tobler, Johann, 859
Toby, Jean-François, 346, 633
Tod, David, 1021
Todd, J.R., 962
Todd, R. Garfield, 1101
Todd, William, 203
Todorov, Stanko, 184
Todorov, Todor, 184
Tofilau Eti Alesana, 769
Tohian, Paul, 681
Tojiev, Amin, 1053
Tojo, Hideki, 503
Toka, Salchak, 740
Tokobayev, Moldagazi, 521
Toksin, Vasily, 724
Tolbert, William, 532
Toledo, Anibal de, 161
Toledo, Pedro de, 177
Toledo Corro, Antonio, 587
Tolkonsky, Viktor, 749
Tolmie, Simon, 201
Toloube, Jeffrey, 680
Tolubayev, Asanali, 521
Toma, Jugo, 504
Tomanović, Laza, 1090
Tomás, Américo, 703
Tomás, Emilio, 75
Tomasi Kulimoetoke I, 351
Tomasi Kulimoetoke II, 352
Tomassoni, DomenicoBugli, Primo, 772
Tomassoni, Maurizio, 774
Tomaszewski, Tadeisz, 700
Tombalbaye, Ngarta, 220
Tombolbaye, François, 221
Tombura, Joseph, 836
Tomćić, Zlatho, 275
Tomelleri, Angelo, 490
Tomić, Dragan, 1092
Tomislav (Croatia), 274
Tomlinson, Gideon, 981
Tompkins, Daniel, 1017
Tomsić, Vida, 791
Ton Duc Thang, 1073
Tončić-Sorinj, Lujo, 12
Tonckens, Warmolt, 845
Tonelli, Salvatore, 774
Tonfik, Timothy, 841

Tongia, 628
Tonisson, Jaan, 312, 313
Tonkin, David, 95
Tonkin, John, 101
Tonnino, Luigi, 770
Toole, Joseph, 1009
Toome, Indrek, 313
Topa, Raúl, 84
Topa Amaru, 693
Topa Huallpa, 693
Topa Inca, 693
Topal, Stepan, 596
Topete, Everardo, 581
Topete y Carballa, Juan, 816, 817
Toptani, Abdi, 56
Toptani, Refik, 56
Toptani Pasha, Essad, 57
Torado, Rafael, 72
Torche, Fernand, 869
Torche, Paul, 870
Torcuato de Alvear, Marcello, 70
Toreno, Conde de (José Ruiz de Saravia), 815
Torey, L. Mike, 645, 653
Toribio, René, 339
Torlopov, Vladimir, 732
Tornaco, Victor de, 542
Törngren, Ralf, 320
Toro, David, 141
Toro, Manuel Murillo, 249, 250
Torp, Oscar, 661
Torré, Xavier-Antoine, 195
Torrens, Robert, 93
Torrenté, Henri de, 902
Torres, Alberto, 171
Torres, José, 160
Torres, Paulo, 172
Torres, Pere, 62
Torres Corzo, Teofilo, 587
Torres Landa, Juan, 580
Torres Manzo, Carlos, 583
Torres Mesias, Luis, 591
Torres Ortiz, Pedro, 578
Torres Sánchez, Enrique, 579
Torres y Torres Lara, Carlos, 692
Torrijos Herrera, Omar, 675
Tory, James, 206
Toshov, Andrei, 184
Tošovský, Josef, 281
Tosta, Vicente, 413
Toucey, Isaac, 981
Touré, Amadou Toumani, 564
Touré, Sidia, 404
Touré, Younoussi, 564
Tourinho, Mario, 167
Touzet, Antoine, 220
Tovar, Augustín, 690
Tovar, Manuel, 1066
Tovar, Rafael, 1071
Tovar de Revilla, Carlos, 308
Tovmassyan, Artur, 116

Tovmasyan, Suren, 86
ToVue, Ronald, 678
Towers, Gordon, 200
Towner, Horace, 1045
Towns, George, 987
Townsend, Clifford, 992
Townsend, John, 984
Toxqui Fernández, Alfredo, 585
Toyayev, Kasymzhomart, 508
Trad, Petro, 527, 528
Tragant, Carlos, 81
Traikov, Georgi, 183
Trajkovski, Boris, 544
Trammell, Park, 985
Tran Duc Luong, 1074
Tran Thiem Khiem, 1075
Tran Trong Kim, 1074
Tran Van Huong, 1075
Tran Van Huu, 1075
Traoré, Diallo, 404
Traoré, Moussa, 564
Trapaglia, Angel, 76
Trapp, Martin, 1023
Travanut, Renzo, 483
Treacher, William, 557
Treacy, Seán, 474
Treadwell, John, 981
Trebilco, E., 104
Tredgold, Robert, 1102
Treen, David, 998
Trees, S.G., 969
Treina, Jean, 873
Trejos Fernández, José, 271
Trelles Montes, Oscar, 692
Trench, David, 245, 793
Trench, Martin, 1046
Trepov, Fyodor, 714
Tresch, Peter, 901
Treutlen, John, 986
Trevaskis, Gerald, 1079
Trevelyan, Humphrey, 1079
Trevín Lomban, Antonio, 824
Treviño Martínez, Jorge, 584
Treviño Zapata, Norberto, 589
Trianthophilakos, Nikolas, 396
Tribbit, Sherman, 984
Tribhuvan Narayan Singh, 450, 451
Tribhuwan (Nepal), 616, 617
Triches, Euclides, 175
Trifimov, Aleksandr, 722
Trifković, Marko, 1093
Trifunovic, Bogdan, 1094
Trifunović, Miloš, 1088
Trikoupis, Kharilaos, 394, 395
Trikoupis, Spyridon, 393
Trimarco, Manuel, 79
Trimble, Allen, 1021
Trimble, David, 955
Trinidad Cabañas, José, 412
Trinkle, E. Lee, 1037
Trinley Gyatso, 231

Tripathi, Kamlapati, 450
Tripathy, Sadasiba, 443
Tritle, Frederick, 976
Trivedi, Chandulal, 423, 442, 444
Trivedi, Ram, 430
Troadec, Jean-René, 220
Trochu, Louis, 326
Troillet, Maurice, 902, 903
Trolle, Erik, 850
Trollip, Alfred, 803
Tromp, Felipe, 621
Tromp, F.J. (Jossy), 621
Tron, Niccolo, 497
Troncoso de la Concha, Manuel, 296
Tronet, Maurice-Georges, 1058
Tronin, Andrei, 741
Trooz, Jules de, 130
Trotha, Lothar von, 610
Trouillé, Pierre, 340
Troup, George, 986
Trousdale, William, 1031
Trouvoada, Miguel, 777
Trowbridge, Richard, 100
Troy, John, 975
Troya, Carlo, 494
Troya Fernando di, 494
Trucco, Manuel, 223
Trudeau, Pierre, 199
Trueba Urbina, Alberto, 576
Truitard, Léon-Hippolyte, 136, 341
Truitt, George, 983
Trujillo, César Gaviria, 28
Trujillo, Julian, 250
Trujillo García, Mario, 588
Trujillo Gurria, Francisco, 588
Trujillo Molina, Héctor, 296
Trujillo Molina, Rafael, 296
Truman, Harry, 973
Trumbull, John, 982
Trumbull, Jonathan Jr, 981
Trumbull, Jonathan Sr, 981
Trumbull, Joseph, 981
Trummer, Rolph, 110
Trunk, Gustav, 378
Truong Chinh, 1074
Truong Chinh (Dang Xuan Khu), 1074
Truong Van Huong, 1075
Trutch, Joseph, 200
Trygger, Ernst, 851
Tryjillo, César Gaviria, 251
Tsaava, Londer, 361
Tsagarayev, Mikhail, 735
Tsalderis, Konstantinos, 396
Tsalderis, Panayotis, 396
Tsankov, Aleksander, 184
Tsankov, Dragan, 184
Ts'ao K'un, 225
Tsatsos, Konstantinos, 393
Tsavelos, Kitsos, 394
Tschiggfrey, Hans, 111
Tschudi, Hans-Martin, 866

Tschudi, Hans-Peter, 856, 865
Tschumi, Hans, 867, 868
Tsedashiev, Gurodarma, 754
Tsedenbal, Yumjagiyn, 599, 600
Tsekov, Sergei, 943
Tsemoling Ngawang Tsultrim, 231
Tserenchimit, 599
Tserendorji, Balingiyn, 600
Tserkinov, Anatoly, 741
Tsewongroutsen, 231
Tshering, Netuk, 447
Tshisekedi, Étienne, 259
Tshomba-Fariah, Joseph, 266
Tshombe, Moïse, 259, 260
Tsilumba, Constantin, 262
Tsiranana, Philibert, 547
Tsirimokos, Elias, 397
Tskhakaya, Mikhail, 358, 359
Tskhovrebashvili, V., 358
Tskhovrebashvili, Valentin, 363
Tsolokoglu, Georgios, 396
Tsouderos, Emmanouil, 396, 398
Tsuchi-Mikado II (Japan), 501
Tsultrim Gyatso, 231
Tsulukidze, Ilya, 362
Tsvetkov, Valentin, 748
Tsyrempilon, Dorzhu, 720
Tu Duc (Nguyen Phuoc Hoang Nham), 1073
Tu Hsi-Kua, 227
Tuan Ch'i-jui, 225, 226, 227
Tuanka Abdul Rahman, 550
Tuanka Syed Putra, 550
Tuanku Abdul Rahman, 554
Tuanku Abdul Rahman Putra, 551
Tuanku Antah, 554
Tuanku Ismail Nasiruddin Shah, 550
Tuanku Jaafar Abdul Rahman, 550, 554
Tuanku Mohamed, 554
Tuanku Munawir, 554
Tuanku Syed Ahmad, 556
Tuanku Syed Alwi, 556
Tuanku Syed Husain, 556
Tuanku Syed Putra, 556
Tuanku Syed Safi, 556
Tuanku Syed Sirajuddin, 556
Tubelis, Juozas, 539
Tubino, João, 152
Tubira, John, 680
Tubman, William, 532
Tubylov, Afanasy, 740
Tubylov, Valentin, 740
Tuck, William, 1037
Tucker, Henry, 961
Tucker, Jim Guy, 978
Tucker, Tilghman, 1006
Tudela y Varela, Francisco, 691
Tudjman, Franjo, 274
Tufele, Mikaele, 351
Tugwell, Rexford, 1045
Tui, Basile, 350

Tui A'ana Tamasee, 768
Tuia, Pio, 630
Tuiasosopo, Palauni, 35
Tuikalepa, Nofeletu, 351
Tuile'epa Sailele Malielegaoi, 769
Tu'ipelehake, Siaosi, 924
Tu'ivakano, Tevita, 924
Tuka, Vojtech, 789
Tulenheimo, Antti, 320
Tuleyev, Aman, 746
Tulku Namgyal, 446
Tulo, Sam, 682
Tulsi Giri, 617
Tumanov, Vladislav, 750
Tumen Delgerjab, Durdet Khan, 601
Tumenas, Antanas, 539
Tun, Petrus, 593
Tun Abdul Razak bin Hussain, 551
Tun Aye, U, 609
Tun Tin, U, 607
Tunde Idiagbon, 642
Tung Chee-hwa, 245
Tunka Abdul Rahman Putra, 31
Tunku Abdul Malik, 552
Tunku Ismail bin Tunku Yahya, 552
Tunku Sulaiman, 556
Tunnell, Ebe, 984
Tunuslu Hayreddin Paşa, 931
Tuomioja, Sakari, 320
Tuoyo, S., 652
Tupouniua, Mahe, 39
Tupper, Charles, 198, 207
Tupper, William, 202
Tupua Tamasese Leolofi IV, 769
Tupua Tamasese Mea'ole, 769
Tupuola Taisi Efi, 769
Tura, Severino, 774
Turban, Friedrich, 377
Turbott, Ian, 67, 399
Turci, Lanfranco, 482
Turcke, Ludwig von, 386
Turello, Vinicio, 483
Turki bin Abdullah, 779
Turki bin Said (Oman), 663
Turkur, B., 639
Turnbull, Alfred, 768
Turnbull, Charles, 1047
Turnbull, Richard, 918, 1079
Turnbull, Roland, 557
Turner, Christopher, 966, 970
Turner, Daniel, 993
Turner, Farrant, 989
Turner, George, 98
Turner, James, 1018
Turner, John (British Columbia), 201
Turner, John (Canada), 199
Turner, L. Jay, 1039
Turner, Roy, 1023
Turner, Thomas, 1026
Turney, Peter, 1031
Turnquest, Orville, 118

Turrubiartes, Ildefonso, 587
Turtulli, Mihal, 56
Turyshev, _, 732
Tusar, Vlastimil, 283
Tuttle, Hiram, 1012
Tutu'aho, Siaosi Uiliame, 924
Tuugahala, Paino, 350
Tuxworth, Ian, 102
Tuyaa, Nyam-Osoriyn, 600
Twagiramungu, Faustin, 760
Tweedie, Lemuel, 203, 204
Twerenbold, Paul, 908
Twigt, Bernardus, 44
Twining, Edward, 557, 764, 918
Twistleton-Wykeham-Fiennes, Eustace, 783
Tyazhlov, Anatoly, 748
Tyler, J. Hoge, 1037
Tyler, John, 972, 1037
Tyler, John Sr, 1037
Tyncherov, A.Kh., 738
Tyndall, Joseph, 6
Tyssowski, Jan, 701
Tyuryakulov, Nazir, 1055, 1056
Tzannetakis, Tzanis, 397
Tz'u-An, 225
Tz'u-Hsi, 225

Uatioa, Reuben, 511
Ubah, J.I.P., 649
Ubico Castañeda, Jorge, 401
Ubilava, Yuza, 360
Ubiparip, Gojko, 144
Uchaykin, Vasily, 734
Uchida, Yasuya, 503
Uda bin Mohamed, 555, 559
Udenhout, Wim, 846
Udofia, A., 653
Udržal, František, 283
Udugov, Movladi, 722
Uduokaha Esuene, 643
Ugarteche, Manuel, 691
Ugazhakov, Vasily, 731
Ugolini, Pietro, 770
Uhalde, Navio, 79
Uhrich, John, 212
Ukaegbu, Emmanual, 641
Ukbabi Asiki, A., 657
Ukéïwé, Dick, 348
Ukiwe, O.E., 650, 651
Ukpo, Anthony, 655
Ulanfu, 232
Ulate Blanco, Otilio, 271
Ulázló I (Hungary), 415
Ulázló II (Hungary), 415
Ulbricht, Walter, 367
Uldzhabayev, Tursunbai, 915
Uldzhhabayev, Tursunbai, 915
Ulloa, Nestor, 76
Ulloa, Roberto, 80
Ulloa Elías, Manuel, 692

Ullsten, Ola, 851
Ulmanis, Guntis, 525
Ulmanis, Karlis, 525, 526
Ulrica Eleonora (Sweden), 850
Ulrich, Carl, 371
Ulrich, Josef, 893
Ulufa'alu, Bartholomew, 794
Uluots, Jüri, 312, 313
Uly, Johannes den (Joop), 620
Umakhanov, Magomed-Salam, 725, 726
Umalatov, Alipasha, 725
Umar al-Muntasir, 535
Umar Farouk Ahmed, 643, 647
Umar Musa Yar'adua, 649
Umaru Muhammed, 655, 658
Umberto I (Italy), 478
Umberto II (Italy), 478
Ume, Emmanuel, 677
Umurzakov, Nurbapa, 507
Umwech, Marcellino, 592
Unánue, Hipolito, 688
Undasynov, Murtas, 507, 508
Underwood, Cecil, 1040
Underwood, Charles, 1043
Ung Huot, 192
Ungiadze, Yuri, 362
Ungku Abdul Aziz bin Abdul Majid, 551
Uniacke, James, 207
Uno, Sosuke, 504
Unstead, William, 1019
Unsworth, Barrie, 91
Upadhayaya, Hari, 457
Upham, William, 1041
Upington, Thomas, 801
Uranga, Raúl, 74
Urayev, Petr, 733
Urazbayev, Nasir, 719
Urazbekov, Abdulladyv, 521
Urban II (Pope), 1062
Urban III (Pope), 1062
Urban IV (Pope), 1062
Urban V (Pope), 1062
Urban VI (Pope), 1062
Urban VII (Pope), 1063
Urban VIII (Pope), 1063
Urbánek, Karel, 283
Urbański, Alfred, 700
Urbina, José, 299
Urco, 693
Urcuyo Maliaño, Francisco, 632
Urdaneta, Rafael, 249
Uriarte, Higinio, 686
Uriburu, José, 73
Uriburu, José E., 69
Uriburu, José F., 70
Uricoechea, Juan, 249
Uriondo, Carlos, 83
Urquhart, Frederick, 101
Urquiza, Justo de, 69
Urraca (Castile), 821
Urraca (León), 822

Urralburu Taínta, Gabriel, 828
Urriola, Ciro, 674
Urriologoitia, Mamerto, 141
Urrutia Lleo, Manuel, 278
Urs, D. Devaraj, 435
Ursprung, Jorg, 858, 859
Uruçui, Barão de (João da Cruz Santos), 170
Usa, Siriako, 794
Useni, J.T., 644
Usman Faruk, 658
Usman Jibrin, 647
Usmankhodzayev, Inamzhon, 1051, 1052
Usmanov, Gumer, 738, 739
Ustiyanu, Ivan, 595
Ustymovich, Mykola, 941
Usubaliev, Turdakun, 522
Usupov, Magomed, 725, 726
Utama Syed Ahmed bin Syed Mahmud Shahabuddin, 553
Utermarck, John, 956
Utsumi, Yashio, 45
Utter, George, 1027
D'Uva, Giustino, 485
Uwilingiyimana, Agathe, 760
Uyanayev, Chomai, 726
Uzelac, Milan, 144
Uzunović, Nikola, 1087

Va'ai Kolone, 769
Vacaroiu, Nicolae, 710
Vacher, Joseph, 339
Václav I (Bohemia), 282
Václav II (Bohemia), 282
Václav III (Bohemia), 282
Václav IV (Bohemia), 282
Vader, Arthur, 313
Vadier, Joseph, 403
Vafiades, Markos, 398
Vagapov, Sabir, 719, 720
Vaghela, Shankarsingh, 431
Vagneti, Marino, 774
Vagnetti, Marino, 773
Vagnorius, Gediminas, 539, 540
Vagov, Aleksei, 522
Vagris, Janis, 525, 526
Vagts, Erich, 370
Vähi, Tiit, 313
Vahia, Culwick, 795
Vahlqvist, Magnus, 16
Vaida-Voevod, Alexandru, 710
Vaino, Karl, 313
Vaithilingam, V., 457
Vaitoianu, Arthur, 710
Vajiravudh (Thailand), 920
Vajpayee, Atal Bihari, 423
Vakhayev, Ramazan, 722
Vakhnin, Nikolai, 732
Vakić, Ilija, 1094
Vakrushev, Vasily, 715

Val, Ricardo del, 83
Val Cismon, Cesare de, 796
Valadão, Ary, 158
Valadares, António, 180
Valade, Jacques, 330
Válcarcel, Mariano, 690
Valcárcel Siso, Ramón, 828
Valdemar I (Denmark), 286
Valdemar II (Denmark), 286
Valdemar IV (Denmark), 286
Valdemar (Sweden), 849
Valdes, Ramón, 674
Valdes, Rodolfo, 588
Valdez, Manuel Fernández, 77
Valdez Montoya, Alfredo, 587
Valdéz Sánchez, Jesús, 578
Valencia, Guillermo, 250
Valencia, Ramón Gonzáles, 250
Valente, João, 405
Valenti, Sanzio, 772
Valenti, Vittorio, 772
Valentić, Nikica, 275
Valentin-Smith, Victor, 353
Valentine (Pope), 1060
Valéra, Éamon de, 473, 474
Valera Aparicio, Fernando, 819
Valerio, Vicente, 578
Valier, Bertuccio, 498
Valier, Silvestro, 498
Valk, Frans van der, 622
Valladão, Manuel, 179
Valladares, Tomás, 631
Valle, Alberto del, 575
Valle, Eric Arturo del, 675
Valle, Eurico, 164
Valle Riestra, Javier, 692
Valles, Andrés, 306
Valli, Francesco, 770, 773
Valluy, Claude, 136
Vals, Francis, 332
Valuyev, Pyotr, 714
Valverde, José, 295
Vam Thu Maung, 608
Vamuzo, S., 442
Van Buren, Martin, 972, 1017
Van-Dúnem, Fernando, 65
Van Dyke, Nicholas, 983
Van Hoach, 1076
Van Ness, Cornelius, 1035
Van Sant, Samuel, 1005
Van Zandt, Charles, 1027
Vanai, Sosepho, 351
Vance, Joseph, 1021
Vance, Zebulon, 1019
Vander-Horst, Arnoldus, 1028
Vanderbilt, William, 1027
Vanderhoof, John, 980
Vandiver, Ernest, 987
Vanier, Georges, 198
Vannicell-Casoni, Luigi, 1064
Vannucci, Gino, 773

Vanuawaru, Kone, 677
Vaquero, José, 74
Vardaman, James, 1006
Varela, Eleutério, 159
Varela, Enrique, 691
Varela, José, 174
Varela, Pedro, 1049
Varela, Rodolfo, 73
Vares, Johannes, 312, 313
Vargas, Antonio, 300
Vargas, Arnaldo Arocha, 1070
Vargas, Getúlio, 148, 174
Vargas, Jesus, 38
Vargas, Jorge, 694
Vargas, José, 1066
Vargas, Virgilio Barco, 251
Vargas Lugo, Bartolomé, 581
Vargas Prieto, Oscar, 692
Varma, Virendra, 432, 444
Varnbuler, Karl, 388
Varnier, Maurice, 59
Varona y Loredo, Manuel de, 278
Varonka, I., 127
Varshalomidze, Guram, 362
Vasconcellos, Albino de, 168
Vasconcelos, Augusto de, 705
Vasconcelos, Doroteo, 306
Vasconcelos, Eduardo, 585
Vasconcelos, Jarbas, 170
Vasconcelos, José de, 151, 157
Vasconcelos, Raimundo de, 170
Vasilchikov, Ilarion, 714
Vasile, Radu, 711
Vasiljević, Predrag, 1096
Vasily I (Russia), 712
Vasily II (Russia), 712
Vasily III (Russia), 712
Vasily IV (Russia), 713
Vasilyev, Arklady, 733
Vasquez, Domingo, 412
Vásquez, Horacio, 296
Vassiliou, Georgios, 279
Vasylenko, Mykola, 941
Vatchenko, Alexis, 940
Vaterlaus, Ernst, 909, 910
Vaudeville, Jean, 341
Vaughan, Charles, 94
Vaughan, Vernon, 1034
Vaugoin, Karl, 107
Vauzelle, Michel, 334
Vaxtang, II, 357
Vaxtang, III, 357
Vaxtang, IV, 358
Vaz, António Guedes, 216
Vaz, Camilo Rebocho, 65
Vaz, José, 159
Vaz de Almeida, Armindo, 777
Vaz de Almeida, Damião, 777
Vázques, Eladio, 82
Vázques Colmenares, Pedro, 585
Vázquez, Alberto, 81

Vazquez, José, 761
Vázquez Vela, Gonzalo, 590
Veazey, Thomas, 1000
Véber, René, 336, 339
Veera, Dharma, 431, 434, 444, 451
Veersamy Ringadoo, 570
Veg, Béla, 418
Vega Alvarado, Renato, 587
Vega Dominguez, Jorge de la, 577
Veiga, Carlos, 217
Veiga, Raul, 171
Veikune, Siosateki, 924
Veillon, Pierre-François, 907
Veimar, Arnold, 313
Veintemilla, Ignacio de, 299
Velarde, Manuel, 690
Velasco, Daniel, 580
Velasco, José de, 140
Velasco Alvaredo, Juan, 689
Velasco Curiel, Francisco, 579
Velasco Ibarra, Enrique, 580
Velasco Ibarra, José, 300
Velasco Suárez, Manuel, 577
Velasquez, Andrés, 1069
Velasquez, Ignacio, 829
Velasquez, Ramón, 1067
Velazquez Perdomo, Elpidio, 579
Velesinov, Jovan, 1093
Velimirović, Petar, 1092, 1093
Vellegal, Carlos, 73
Velli, Georg, 876
Vellodi, M.K., 459
Veloso, António, 777
Veloso, Djalma, 171
Velsh, A.A. (Welsch), 741, 742
Venables-Vernon, William, 959
Venetiaan, Ronald, 845
Veneziale, Marcello, 485
Venier, Francesco, 498
Venier, Sebastiano, 498
Veniot, Peter, 204
Venizelos, Eleutherios, 395, 396
Venizelos, Sophocles, 397, 398
Venkatachalam, Jyoti, 435
Venkataraman, Ramaswami, 423
Vennola, Juho, 319, 320
Ventatasubbiah, Pondakainti, 427, 434
Venter, Jacobus, 803
Ventura, Jesse, 1005
Venturni, Marino, 773, 774
Venturnini, Gian Carlo, 774
Veprev, A.F., 743
Veraldi, Donato, 482
Verani, Pablo, 80
Verda, Giorgio, 484
Verdeţ, Ilie, 710
Verendyakin, V.V., 734
Verger, Louis, 347
Vergès, Paul, 342
Vergnes, Charles, 255
Verhoefstadt, Guy, 131

Verin, Eidoxie, 337
Verlaçi, Shefqet, 57
Verma, Manik Lal, 445
Verma, M.C., 455
Verma, Sahib Singh, 455
Vermudo I (Asturias), 820
Vermudo II (Asturias), 821
Vermudo III (Asturias), 821
Vernet, Jaques, 873
Vernet, José, 82
Veronese, Vittorino, 46
Verran, John, 94
Verrastro, Vincenzo, 481
Vershinin, Pavel, 741
Verwoerd, Hendrik, 800
Vesalinov, Jovan, 1091, 1093
Veselinov, Jovan, 1096
Veselinov, Slavko, 1097
Vesnić, Milenko, 1087
Vessey, Robert, 1030
Vetoshkin, G., 732
Vetoshkin, Gennady, 731
Vetsch, Burkhard, 889
Veulle, John De, 958
Vezirov, Abdul, 115
Vian, Dominique, 337
Viana, Aurélio, 154
Viana, Cesario, 297
Viana, Eduardo, 65
Viana, Fernando, 163
Viana, Godofredo, 160
Viana, João, 154
Viana, Jorge, 151
Viana, Luiz, 154
Viana Filho, Luiz, 155
Vicente, Fernando, 76
Vicini, Domenico, 771
Vicini Burgos, Juan, 296
Victor II (Pope), 1061
Victor III (Pope), 1061
Victoria, Eladio, 296
Victoria (Great Britain), 951
Vidal, Francisco, 1048
Vidaurri, Santiago, 574
Vidayev, S.M., 734
Videau, Daniel, 346
Videla, Gabriel González, 223
Videla, Jorge, 70, 84
Videnov, Zhan, 185
Vidić, Dobrivoje, 1091
Vidmar, Josep, 791
Vidot, Roger, 342
Viegas, Luís, 405
Vieillescazes, Claude, 341
Vieira, Casemiro, 159
Vieira, João, 406
Vieira, Manoel, 159
Vieira, Paulo, 177
Vieira, Severino, 154
Vieira, Vasco, 246
Vieira de Melo, Sergio, 298

Vieli, Balthazar, 874
Vieli, Josef, 875
Viera, Feliciano, 1049
Viera, Félix, 71
Vierin, Dino, 490
Vierira de Mello, Sergio, 1095
Viglione, Aldo, 485
Viglione, Atilio, 73
Vignarajah, K., 834
Vignon, Robert, 336
Vijayavargiya, Gopikrishan, 459
Vike-Freiberga, Vaira, 525
Vikelas, Dimitros, 21
Viktorov, Valerian, 724
Vilanova, Amaro, 169
Vilanova, Josep, 62
Vilbrun-Guillaume, Joseph, 410
Vilela, Maguito, 158
Vileroy, Augusto de, 153
Viljoen, Daniel, 610
Viljoen, Gerrit, 611
Viljoen, Marais, 800
Villa, Celso Torrelio, 141
Villalba, Julio Díaz, 80
Villanueva, Eliseo Vidart, 78
Villanueva, Rafael, 691
Villanueva del Campo, Armando, 692
Villanueva Madrid, Mario, 586
Villard, R., 906
Villareal, Rafael, 589
Villareal Guerra, Americo, 589
Villaroal, Gualberto, 141
Villarubia, Bonaventura, 62
Villaseñor Peña, Eduardo, 583
Villazon, Eliodoro, 141
Villeda Morales, Ramón, 413
Villedeul, Marc de, 136
Villegas, Guillermo, 79
Villegas, Ofilio, 581
Villéger, Gaston, 338, 340
Villèle, Joseph, 325
Villere, Jacques, 996
Villiers, Jacob de, 799
Villiers, Michael, 958
Villiger, Hans, 901
Villiger, Kaspar, 856
Villot, Jean, 1065
Vilmain, Jean, 333
Vilsack, Tom, 993
Vincent, Alfred, 871
Vincent, Sténio, 410
Vinnichenko, Volodymir, 940, 941
Vinogradov, Nikolai, 753
Vinokurov, Ilya, 737
Vinokurov, I.N., 736
Viola, Enrique, 82
Viola, Roberto, 70
Violette, Maurice, 59
Viotelier, Pierre, 336
Vir Bahadur Singh, 451
Virabhadra Singh, 433

Viracocha I (Huatan Tupac), 693
Virata, Cesar, 694
Virieux, F., 904, 905
Virolainen, Johannes, 320
Virolainen, V., 730
Vischer, Ueli, 866
Vishvanathan, Venkata, 454
Vishwanath Pratap Singh, 423, 451
Vishwanatham, Kambanthodath, 430
Vishwanathan, Venkata, 432
Viswanathan, Venkata, 435
Vita, Silvestro, 770
Vital, Andreas, 874
Vittorio Amedeo I (Piedmont-Sardinia), 495
Vittorio Amedeo II (Piedmont-Sardinia), 495
Vittorio Amedeo III (Piedmont-Sardinia), 495
Vittorio Amedeo (Sicily), 493
Vittorio Emanuele I (Piedmont-Sardinia), 495
Vittorio Emanuele II (Piedmont-Sardinia), 495
Vittorio Emmanuele II (Italy), 478
Vittorio Emmanuele III (Italy), 478
Vivanco, José, 584
Vivas, Angel, 82
Viveros, Ernesto, 581
Vivian, John, 980
Vivian, M. Young, 35
Vivian, Young, 629
Viviani, René, 327
Vizol, 442
Vizzardelli, Carlo, 1064
Vladiminsky, Mikhail, 714
Vladislav II (Bohemia), 282
Vladislav III (Bohemia), 282
Vlahović, Miodrag, 1090
Vlajković, Radovan, 1086, 1096
Vlasi, Azem, 1095
Vlasković, Tihomir, 1093
Vlasov, Aleksandr, 715, 723
Vlasov, Ivan, 714
Vlasov, Valentin, 729, 744
Vlasov, Vasily, 737
Vlasov, Yury, 753
Vlok, Adriaan, 800
Vo Chi Chong, 1074
Vo Van Kiet, 1074
Vo Van Mau, 1075
Vodoz, A., 905
Vodoz, Olivier, 873
Voelcker, Francis, 768, 769
Vogae, Bernard, 685
Vogel, Bernhard, 373, 376
Vogel, Hans-Jochen, 369
Vogel, Julius, 626
Vogel, Sebastian, 877
Voges, Russel, 624
Vogt, Werner, 895

Vohor, Serge, 1058
Vohra, Motilal, 450
Voinovich, George, 1022
Voisin, Charles, 189
Voizard, Pierre, 597
Vokinger, Walter, 884
Voldermaras, Augustinius, 539
Volkavich, Daniil, 127
Volkov, Aleksandr, 740, 741
Volkov, Aleksei, 127
Volkov, Nikolai, 742
Volkov, Vladilen, 718
Volkov, Vladimir, 734
Vollenhoven, Joost van, 403, 781
Volmar, Friedrich, 867
Voloshin, Augustin, 285
Volpe, John, 1003
Volpinari, Antonio, 773
Von Stecher, Jorge, 71
Vonderweid, Marcel, 869, 870
Vonmoos, Johann, 875
Voorhees, Foster, 1014
Vora, Motilal, 437
Vorobev, Georgy, 741
Voronchikhin, I.T., 740
Voronin, Aleksei, 741
Voronov, Gennady, 715
Voronovich, Yefstafi, 594
Voronovski, Nikolai, 724
Voroshilov, Kliment, 716
Vorotnikov, Vitaly, 714, 715
Vorster, B. Johannes, 800
Voscherau, Henning, 371
Voskanyan, Grant, 85
Vosloo, Andries, 802
Voss, August, 526
Votintsev, V.D., 1055
Voulgaris, Demetrios, 392, 394
Voulgaris, Petros, 396
Vranitzky, Franz, 108
Vratsyan, Simon, 86
Vratusa, Anton, 791
Vrhovec, Josip, 275
Vries, Gerrit de, 619
Vrioni, Elias, 57
Vrioni, Omer, 56, 57
Vuillaume, Paul, 353
Vujanović, Filip, 1090
Vujić, Mihailo, 1092
Vukadinović, Vuko, 1090
Vukicević, Velja, 1087
Vukotić, Janko, 1090
Vunagi, Stanley, 795
Vyan, Ram, 456
Vyas, Jainarain, 445, 446
Vyelyas, Vaino, 313
Vytautas (Lithuania), 538
Vytenis (Lithuania), 538
Vyvere, Alois van der, 130

Waal, N. Frederik de, 802
Waardenburg, Simon van, 464
Wachter, Johann, 388
Wacław I (Poland), 696
Wacław II (Poland), 696
Waddell, Alexander, 558
Waddell, Thomas, 90
Waddington, E. John, 124, 1098
Waddington, William, 326
Wade, Abdoulaye, 781
Wade, Charles, 90
Waeber, Arnold, 870, 871
Wagemaker, Isaac, 621
Wagner, Carl-Ludwig, 373
Wagner, Johann, 108
Wagner, Leopold, 109
Wagner, Robert, 378
Wagoner, Murray von, 1004
Wahengbam Nipamacha Singh, 439
Wahid, Abdurrahman, 461
Wahis, Théophile, 258
Wahlen, Friedrich, 855
Wai, Simeon, 683
Waidner, José Martínez, 79
Waihee, John, 989
Wailing, Donald, 962
Wainwright, J., 968
Wainwright, Robert, 970
Wairisal, Albert, 464
Waite, Davis, 980
Waka, Lukas, 685
Wakatsuki, Reijiro, 503
Waldeck-Rousseau, P. René, 327
Waldheim, Kurt, 42, 106
Waldvogel, Karl, 891
Waldvogel, Kurt, 891, 892
Waldvogel, Traugott, 890
Wałęsa, Lech, 698
Walheim, Alfred, 108
Wali, Maumohan, 454
Waligo, Abraham, 938
Walkem, George, 201
Walker, Clifford, 987
Walker, Daniel, 991
Walker, David, 985
Walker, Gilbert, 1037
Walker, Joseph, 997
Walker, Ludwig, 901
Walker, Miles, 958
Walker, Robert, 994
Walker, William, 631
Wallace, Charles, 200
Wallace, David, 991
Wallace, George, 975
Wallace, J.G., 962
Wallace, Lawrence, 1098
Wallace, Lewis, 1015
Wallace, Lurleen, 975
Wallace, Reginald, 510
Wallace, William (Idaho, USA), 989
Wallace, William (Washington, USA), 1039

Wallaced, Walter, 963
Waller, Thomas, 981
Waller, William, 1007
Wallgren, Monrad, 1039
Walliman, Hermann, 886
Wallmann, Walter, 372
Wallner, Thomas, 896
Wallnofer, Eduard, 111
Walpen, Oscar, 903
Walpole, Robert, 951
Walser, Eduard, 875
Walser, Willi, 860
Walsh, Albert, 205
Walsh, David, 1002
Walsh, Frank, 95
Walsh, William, 199
Walt, Barend van der, 610
Walt, Tjaart van der, 807
Walter, Ansito, 592
Walter, Emil, 909
Walter, George, 67
Walter, Neil, 629
Walter, Robert, 293
Walters, David, 1023
Walther, Heinrich, 878
Walton, George, 986
Walton, John, 1023
Walubita, Muheli, 1099
Walwyn, Humphrey, 205
Wamaro, Dere, 685
Wan Abdul Azaz bin Ungku Abdullah, 555
Wan Idris bin Ibrahim, 551
Wan Li, 234
Wan Mohamed bin Wan Teh, 556
Wan Mokhtar bin Ahman, 560
Wan Mutahir, 554
Wan Xueyuan, 243
Wanchoo, Niranjan, 435, 436
Wang Chaowen, 236
Wang Cheng-t'ung, 226
Wang Ching-hui, 227
Wang Ching-wei, 228, 229
Wang Ch'ung-hui, 226
Wang Chung-wei, 227
Wang Daohan, 244
Wang Enmao, 239
Wang Feng, 233
Wang Guangyu, 234
Wang Huaixiang, 239
Wang Jiadao, 237
Wang Key-min, 229
Wang Qian, 242
Wang Senhao, 242
Wang Shih-chen, 226
Wang Shiying, 242
Wang Shoudai, 238
Wang Shousen, 241
Wang Ta-hsieh, 226
Wang Taihua, 234
Wang Xiaofeng, 236
Wang Xiayu, 241

Wang Yunkun, 239
Wang Yuzhao, 234
Wang Zhao, 240
Wang Zhaoguo, 234
Wang Zhongyu, 239
Wangchuk, Jigme, 138
Wangchuk, Jigme Dorji, 138, 139
Wangchuk, Jigme Sangye, 138, 139
Wangchuk, Ugyen, 138
Wangchuk Gyalpo Shatra, 231
Wangdu Dorjee, 232
Wanick, Américo, 160
Wanis al-Geddafi, 535, 536
Wanké, Douda Mallam, 633
Wanner, Christian, 896
Wanner, Hermann, 891
Wanner, Theo, 891
Wanner, Traugott, 891
Waqqas, Ismail, 508
Warburton, Alexander, 210
Ward, Alfred, 965
Ward, Deighton, 124
Ward, Joseph, 626, 627
Ward, Marcus, 1014
Warfield, Edwin, 1001
Warioba, Joseph, 918
Warmoth, Henry, 997
Warner, Daniel, 532
Warner, Fred, 1004
Warouw, S.J., 462
Warren, Earl, 979
Warren, Francis, 1042
Warren, Fuller, 985
Warren, Jay, 967
Warren, William, 205
Warton, Thomas, 1025
Wase, M., 648
Wasfi Tell, 506
Washburn, Cadwallader, 1041
Washburn, Carlos, 690
Washburn, Emory, 1002
Washburn, Israel, 998
Washburn, Paul, 1035
Washburn, William, 1002
Washington, George, 972
Wasim, Sajjad, 664
Wasmosy, Juan Carlos, 687
Wat, Louis van der, 804
Waterhouse, George (Australia), 94
Waterhouse, George (New Zealand), 626
Waterman, Robert, 979
Wath, Jahannes van der, 610
Wathelet, Melchoir, 132
Watkins, Brian, 969
Watkins, David, 1014
Watkins, Frederick, 965, 970
Watson, Arthur, 959, 966, 970
Watson, Herbert, 803
Watson, John, 88
Watson, Lepani, 680
Watson, William, 984

Watt, Hugh, 627
Watt, Lindsay, 629
Watt, William, 98
Wattenwyl, Friedrich von, 866
Watts, Thomas, 974
Wauchope, Arthur, 476
Way, Samuel, 93
Way Rojas, Victor Joy, 692
Wayne, Richard, 67
Waziri, A., 642, 644
Weare, Meshech, 1011
Weatherby, Lawrence, 996
Weaver, Arthur, 1010
Webb, C.H., 102
Weber, Alfred, 901
Weber, Edward, 46
Weber, Fritz, 874
Weber, Karl von, 892
Weber, Leo, 858
Weber, Otto, 888
Webster, Ronald, 959, 960
Weck, Bernard, 869, 870
Weck, Charles, 869
Weck, Louis, 869
Weddel, R.H., 101
Wedemeier, Klaus, 370
Wedenig, Ferdinand, 109
Wee Chong Jin, 787
Wee Kim Wee, 787
Weeks, Frank, 982
Weeks, John, 1036
Weerawani, Samaraweera, 834
Wegern, Martin von, 386
Wei Chunshu, 232
Wei Guoqing, 232, 235
Wei Heng, 242
Wei Jinghui, 234
Wei Tao-ming, 248
Weichmann, Herbert, 371
Weicker, Lowell, 982
Weigall, William, 93
Weil, Alain, 343
Weingartner, Wendelin, 111
Weir, Walter, 203
Weissgatterer, Alfons, 111
Weizmann, Chaim, 475
Weizmann, Ezer, 475
Weizsäcker, Karl, 388
Weizsäcker, Richard von, 366, 370
Wekerle, Sándor, 416
Welagedra, D.B., 832
Weld, Frederick, 626
Weld, William, 1003
Welensky, Roy, 1102
Welford, Walter, 1020
Weller, John, 979
Wellhauser, Pierre, 873
Wells, Clyde, 206
Wells, Heber, 1034
Wells, Henry, 1037
Wells, James, 997

Wells, Roger, 962
Wells, Samuel, 998
Welsch, Heinrich, 374
Welsh, Matthew, 992
Welti, Emil, 853, 854
Weltschi, Ernesto, 77
Wen Minsheng, 237
Wen Shizhen, 240
Wen Tsung, 225
Wenban-Smith, W. Nigel, 961
Wenckheim, Béla, 416
Wendorff, Hugo, 381
Wendt, Carl, 662
Wenk, Gustav, 865
Wenzl, Erwin, 111
Wereat, John, 986
Werleigh, Claudette, 411
Werner, Aloys, 873
Werner, Ferdinand, 372
Werner, Pierre, 543
Werra, Raphaël von, 902
Werth, Albert, 610
Wertli, Peter, 859
Werts, George, 1014
Wessels, Cornelis, 804
Wessenberg-Ampringen, Johann, 106
West, Caleb, 1034
West, John, 1030
West, Oswald, 1024
Weston, Hilary, 208
Weston, James, 1012
Weston, William, 96
Wet, Christian de, 803
Wet, Johannes de, 611, 614
Wet, Nicolaas de, 799
Wetmore, Andrew, 204
Wetmore, George, 1027
Wetshindjadi, Benoît, 263
Wettengel, Ivan, 1044
Wetter, Ernst, 855
Wettstein, Oskar, 909
Wey, Max, 878
Weyer, Sylvain, van de, 130
Wheatley, Willard, 963
Wheeler, P., 969
Whitaker, Frederick, 626
Whitaker, José, 177
Whitcomb, Edgar, 992
Whitcomb, James, 992
White, Albert, 1040
White, Benjamin, 1009
White, E. Wyndham, 47
White, Edward, 997
White, Frank (Arkansas, USA), 978
White, Frank (North Dakota, USA), 1020
White, Frederick, 213
White, George (Gibralter), 964
White, George (USA), 1022
White, Herbert, 606
White, Hugh, 1006
White, Hugo, 965

White, J.G., 102
White, John (British Antarctic Territory), 961
White, John (Nauru), 615
White, Mark, 1033
Whiteaker, John, 1024
Whitehead, Edgar, 1101
Whiteley, Peter, 958
Whiteway, William, 205
Whitfield, Henry, 1006
Whitfield, James, 1006
Whitlam, E. Gough, 88
Whitman, Charles, 1017
Whitman, Christine Todd, 1015
Whitney, James, 208
Whittaker, Geoffrey, 959
Whittleton, Jack, 4
Whyte, James, 96
Whyte, William, 1000
Wibaux, Félix, 348
Wickham, Denis, 796
Wickliffe, Charles, 995
Wickliffe, Robert, 997
Wickremasinghe, Ranil, 831
Widmer, Peter, 868
Wiebe, John (Jack), 212
Wiederkehr, Peter, 910
Wieloglowski, Gaspar, 700
Wiesli, Alois, 896
Wiin-Nielsen, Akel, 47
Wijdenbosch, Jules, 845, 846
Wijetunge, Dingiri, 830, 831, 832
Wilbur, Isaac, 1026
Wilcocks, Carl, 804
Wild, August, 896
Wild, Laurence, 1043
Wild, Richard, 626
Wilder, Douglas, 1037
Wiles, Donald, 966
Wilhelm (Brunswick), 378
Wilhelm Ernst (Saxe-Weimar-Eisensach), 386
Wilhelm (Hanover), 379
Wilhelm I (Germany), 365
Wilhelm I (Hesse-Cassel), 379, 380
Wilhelm I (Prussia), 383
Wilhelm I (Württemburg), 388
Wilhelm II (Germany), 365
Wilhelm II (Hesse-Cassel), 380
Wilhelm II (Prussia), 383
Wilhelm II (Württemburg), 388
Wilhelm (Nassau), 382
Wili, Felix, 879
Wilkes, Michael, 958
Wilkie, Alexander, 1057
Wilkins, Michael, 956
Wilkinson, James, 1007
Wilkinson, Richard, 785
Wilkinson, Wallace, 996
Willard, Ashbel, 992
Willcock, John, 100

INDEX

Willeimina (Netherlands), 619, 620
Willem I (Netherlands), 618
Willem II (Netherlands), 618
Willem III (Netherlands), 618
Willem IV (Netherlands), 618
Willem V (Netherlands), 618
Willey, Norman, 989
Willi, Georg, 875
Willi, Gion, 876
William I (England), 950
William I (Scotland), 954
William II (England), 950
William III (Great Britain), 951
William IV (Great Britain), 951
William-Powlett, Peverill, 1100
Williams, A. Leonard, 570
Williams, Abraham, 1007
Williams, Arnold, 990
Williams, Benjamin, 1018
Williams, Boswell, 765
Williams, Charles, 1035
Williams, Daniel, 399
Williams, David (Gibralter), 965
Williams, David (USA), 1028
Williams, Denys, 124
Williams, Eric, 926
Williams, F.R., 962
Williams, G. Mennen, 1004
Williams, Henry, 766
Williams, James, 992
Williams, Jared, 1012
Williams, John Bell, 1007
Williams, John (Jack), 977
Williams, Joseph (New Zealand), 628
Williams, Joseph (USA), 998
Williams, Martin, 967
Williams, Philip, 1046
Williams, Ralph (Botswana), 147
Williams, Ralph (Canada), 204
Williams, Ransome, 1029
Williams, Robert (Mississippi, USA), 1005
Williams, Robert (Oklahoma, USA), 1023
Williams, William, 206
Williamson, Isaac, 1014
Williamson, William, 998
Willich, Friedrich, 383
Williman, Claudio, 1049
Willis, Edward, 958
Willis, Eric, 90
Willis, Errick, 202
Willis, Frank, 1022
Willis, Simeon, 996
Willmar, Jean Jacques, 542
Willoch, Kaare, 661
Willocks, James, 960
Wills, William, 1036
Wilmot, Lemuel, 203
Wilmot, Robert, 203
Wilopo, 462
Wilsoe, Elmer, 623
Wilson, Alexander (Australia), 104

Wilson, Alexander (Jersey), 958
Wilson, Augustus, 996
Wilson, David, 134
Wilson, E. Willis, 1040
Wilson, Frank, 100
Wilson, George, 993
Wilson, Harold, 952
Wilson, James, 96
Wilson, John, 1028
Wilson, Leslie, 91
Wilson, Malcolm, 1018
Wilson, Peter, 979
Wilson, Samuel, 499, 925
Wilson, Selwyn, 629
Wilson, Stanley, 1036
Wilson, Woodrow, 973, 1014
Wiltord, Laurent-Marcel, 780
Wiltz, Louis, 997
Wimalasena, Noel, 833
Win Maung, U, 607
Wina, Shemakono, 1099
Winans, Edwin, 1003
Winant, John (ILO), 44
Winant, John (USA), 1013
Winder, Levin, 1000
Windham, Charles, 197
Windisch-Grätz, Alfred von, 106, 107
Windley, Edward, 355
Wingate, Francis, 835
Wingti, Paias, 677, 684
Winiker, Vinzenz, 878, 879
Winkel, Christiaan, 622
Winkler, Alois, 109
Winneke, Henry, 97
Winsauer, Ernst, 112
Winship, Blanton, 1045
Winslow, Warren, 1019
Winston, John, 974
Winter, Georg, 377
Winter, Gordon, 205
Winter, James, 205
Winter, William, 1007
Winterberg, Carl, 388
Winthrop, Beekman, 1045
Winyi IV (Bunyoro), 939
Wipfli, Josef, 901
Wippermann, Konrad, 386
Wiranatukusamah, Ario, 464
Wirth, Karl, 366
Wirz, Adalbert, 885
Wirz, Theodor, 885
Wise, Frank, 100, 101
Wise, Henry, 1037
Wismer, Josef, 878, 879
Wisner, Moses, 1003
Wissman, Hermann von, 917
Witasse, Pierre de, 597
Withycombe, James, 1024
Witos, Wincenty, 698
Witte, Sergei, 714
Wittek, Heinrich von, 107

Wittemann, Josef, 378
Witteveen, Hendrickus, 45
Władysław I Herman (Poland), 696
Władysław I (Poland), 696
Władysław II Jagiello (Poland), 697
Władysław II (Poland), 696
Władysław III (Poland), 697
Władysław IV (Poland), 697
Władysław (Lithuania), 538
Wodehouse, Joscelyn, 960
Wodzicki, Stanisław, 700
Woelfel, Adolf-Louis, 922
Wohleb, Leonhard, 378
Woivalin, Folke, 321
Wojciechowski, Stanisław, 697
Wolcott, Oliver, 981
Wolcott, Oliver Jr, 981
Wolcott, Roger, 1002
Woldemar (Lippe), 380
Woldemikael, Fitaurari, 311
Wolfe, George, 1025
Wolfensohn, James, 43
Wolff, Albert, 100
Wolfisberg, Anton, 887
Wolfley, Lewis, 976
Wollman, Harvey, 1030
Wong Pow Nee, 555
Wong Wen-hao, 227
Wonters, Gielliam, 621
Wood, George, 1032
Wood, James, 1037
Wood, John, 990
Wood, Josiah, 203
Wood, Leonard, 277
Wood, Reuben, 1021
Woodall, John, 960
Woodbridge, William, 1003
Woodbury, Levi, 1012
Woodbury, Urban, 1036
Woodford, Charles, 793
Woodring, Harry, 994
Woodruff, Rollin, 982
Woods, George (Oregon, USA), 1024
Woods, George (Utah, USA), 1034
Woods, George (World Bank), 43
Woodson, Silas, 1007
Woodward, Eric, 89
Woodward, William, 200
Wool-Lewis, Cyril, 970
Woolley, Charles, 279, 407
Wootten, Francis, 1034
Wordsworth, Robert, 104
Workman, Charles, 793
Wörner, Manfred, 25
Worobetz, Stephen, 212
Worth, Jonathan, 1019
Worth, W., 102
Worthington, Thomas, 1021
Wos y Gil, Alejandro, 296
Wran, Neville, 91
Wrathall, John, 1101

Wray, Martin, 147
Wright, Andrew, 279, 355
Wright, Arthur, 764, 766
Wright, Fielding, 1006
Wright, John, 769
Wright, Joseph, 992
Wright, Robert, 1000
Wright, Silas, 1017
Wroblewski, Władysław, 698
Wu De, 243, 244
Wu Guangzheng, 241
Wu Guanzhong, 239
Wu Kuo-chen, 248
Wu Liji, 232
Wu T'ing-fang, 226
Wu Tsung, 224
Wu Yixia, 235
Wu Zhipu, 237
Wullschleger, Eugen, 864
Wullschleger, Max, 865, 866
Wyer, Hans, 904
Wyk, Abraham van, 804
Wyl, Leo von, 886
Wymann, Otto, 883
Wyn-Harris, Percy, 355
Wyne, Ghulam Hyder, 669
Wyrsch, Jakob B., 882, 883
Wyrsch, Jakob S., 883
Wyrsch, Richard, 893
Wyser, Alfred, 895
Wyss, Edmund, 865, 866
Wyss, Gottfried, 895
Wyss, Heinrich, 892
Wyss, Johann, 907
Wyss, Michel von, 882

Xi Zhongxun, 235
Xian Henghan, 235
Xiao Yang, 242
Xie Feng, 236
Xie Fuzhu, 243
Xie Jinping, 235
Xie Xuegung, 244
Xie Zhenhua, 242
Xing Zhaotang, 233
Xiong Qingquan, 238
Xowie, Robert, 349
Xu Jiatun, 239
Xu Kuangdi, 244
Xu Shiyou, 239
Xu Zhongling, 234
Xue Ju, 243
Xuereb, Paul, 566

Yaber, Felipe, 78
Yadav, Lallu Prasad, 428
Yadav, Mulayam Singh, 451
Yadav, Ram Naresh, 451
Yadav Kant Silval, 36
Yadgarov, Damir, 1053

Yager, Arthur, 1045
Yagudin, M., 738
Yahuar Huacac, 693
Yahya Abdulkarim, 655
Yahya bin Mohamed Seh, 555
Yahya Petra, 550
Yahya Petra (Kelantan), 553
Yahya (Yemen), 1077
Yakabov, Mir, 114
Yakimov, Anatoly, 755
Yakob, 315
Yakolev, Ivan, 508
Yakovlev, Aleksandr, 722
Yakovlev, Vladimir, 754
Yakub Khan, 53
Yakubu Muazu, 655
Yallá, Kumba, 406
Yalu, Egbert, 683
Yamagata, Aritomo, 502
Yamamoto, Gonnohyoe, 503
Yameogo, Maurice, 186
Yan Haiwang, 235
Yanayev, Gennady, 716
Yandarbayev, Zelimkhan, 722
Yandarbeyev, Zelimkhan, 723
Yanepa, James, 678
Yanes Urias, César, 307
Yañez, Augustín, 582
Yañez Maya, J. Jesús, 579
Yang Jingren, 233
Yang Ki Suk, 514
Yang Shangkun, 226
Yang Xiufeng, 236
Yang Xizong, 242
Yang Yi-chen, 237
Yang Yong, 236
Yang Zhengwu, 238
Yanjmaa, Suhbaataryn, 599
Yapur, Tamer, 78
Yaput, Parson bin, 103
Ya'qub Shura, 840
Yara, Chobyo, 504
Yarrington Ruvalcaba, Tomás, 589
Yarvisalo, I.A., 730
Yasid (Morocco), 602
Yasin al-Hashimi, 470, 471
Yasin Noaman, 1079
Yaskina, Yefimya, 734
Yasnov, Mikhail, 714, 715
Yates, Joseph, 1017
Yates, Richard, 990, 991
Yates, W., 102
Yazrov, Yury, 8
Yberg, Alois ab, 892, 893
Ydígoras Fuentes, Miguel, 402
Ye Fei, 234
Ye Jianying, 226, 235, 243
Ye Liansong (Hainan), 236
Ye Liansong (Hebei), 237
Ye Xuanping, 235
Yefremov, Anatoly, 744

Yefremov, Stepan, 741
Yegorov, A., 730
Yegorov, Nikolai, 743
Yegros, Fulgencio, 686
Yehia bin Mohammed, 1084
Yehia Hammouda, 477
Yehya Ibrahim Pasha, 303
Yeiwene, Yeiwene, 349
Yejong (Korea), 512
Yelagin, Vladimir, 749
Yelena (Russia), 712
Yeliseyev, Yevgeny, 727
Yell, Archibald, 977
Yeltsin, Boris, 714, 715
Yem Sambaur, 191
Yemelyanov, N.S., 736
Yen Chia-kan, 247, 248
Yen Hsi-chan, 247
Yen Hsi-shan, 227, 228
Yen Hui-ch'ing, 226, 227
Yeoh Ghim Seng, 787
Yeremey, Grigory, 595
Yeri, J., 644
Yerlakov, A.S., 724
Yermoshin, Vladimir, 127
Yerovi Indaburu, Clemente, 300
Yesayan, Oleg, 117
Yeshak, 314
Yeshe Gyatso Rating, 231
Yeshimbetov, Davlet, 1053
Yeta III (Barotseland), 1099
Yevdokimov, Yury, 748
Yhombi-Opango, Joaquim, 256
Yildirim Akbulut, 932
Ying Tsung, 224
Yocupicio, Roman, 588
Yodoyman, Joseph, 221
Yohanna Madaki, 639, 642
Yohannes I, 315
Yohannes II, 315
Yohannes III, 315
Yohannes IV, 316
Yon Hyong Muk, 515
Yonai, Mitsumasa, 503
Yonas, 315
Yong Teck Lee, 558
Yong Yin Fatt, Roderick, 5
Yong Yong Son, 513
Yongchaiyudh, Chavalit, 921
Yongjo (Korea), 512
Yonsan-gun (Korea), 512
Yoo Chang Soon, 518
Yoshida, Shigeru, 503
Yoshihito (Japan), 502
Yoshimichi, Hasagawa, 513
Yostos, 315
Youde, Edward, 245
Youlou, Fulbert, 256
Young, Albert, 967
Young, Andrew, 967
Young, Brian, 967

Young, Brigham, 1034
Young, Clement, 979
Young, Colville, 134
Young, Dennis, 676
Young, H. Norris, 967
Young, Hubert, 549, 925, 1098
Young, Hugh, 213
Young, John (Australia), 97
Young, John (Hawaii, USA), 988
Young, John (New York, USA), 1017
Young, Mark, 124, 245, 917
Young, Pervis, 967
Young, Thomas, 1022
Young, W., 103
Young, William (Canada), 207
Young, William (Dominica & Falkland Islands), 293, 964
Young, William (Pitcairn Island), 967
Young, William (St Lucia), 764
Young, William (Turks & Caicos Islands), 970
Youngdahl, Luther, 1005
Younis al-Hussein, 840
Youssef Ben Khedda, 60, 61
Yozei II (Japan), 501
Ypi, Xhafar, 56, 57
Yu Han-min, 228
Yu Ke, 239
Yu Kui Hwai, 513
Yu Kuo-hwa, 247
Yu Mingtao, 241
Yu Taizhong, 232
Yu Yichuan, 242
Yuan Chin-kai, 230
Yuan Renyuan, 240
Yuan Shih-kai, 225
Yuan Shih-k'ai, 226
Yudin, Nikolai, 749
Yue Qifeng (Hainan), 236
Yue Qifeng (Liaoning), 240
Yugov, Anton, 184
Yuhi I (Rwanda), 759
Yuhi III (Rwanda), 759
Yuhi IV (Rwanda), 759
Yui Hung-chun, 247, 248
Yuldashev, Rajapbay, 1053
Yumagalov, Kh., 719
Yun Bo Sun, 517
Yun Longbo, 232
Yury (Russia), 712
Yushchenko, Viktor, 942
Yushchiev, N.A., 729
Yushunev, N.L., 723
Yusof bin Ishak, 787
Yusofbeli, Nasib, 114
Yussif Zeayan, 913
Yusuf Haroon, 670, 671
Yusuf Issidin Shah, 556
Yusuf (Morocco), 602
Yusuf Pahlawan Niyaz, 1055
Yusuf Sharifuddin Mufzal Shah, 556

Yusuf Wahba Pasha, 303
Yusupov, Ismail, 508
Yusupov, Marat, 1053
Yusupov, Usman, 1052
Yuvraj Karan Singh, 433

Za-Dengel, 315
Za Hre Lian, U, 608
Zaandam, Remy, 621
Zacca, Edward, 499
Zadionchenko, Semen, 719
Zafarullah Khan Jamali, 666
Zafferani, Luigi, 772
Zafferani, Rosa, 774
Zafferani, Rossano, 773
Zafy, Albert, 547
Zagafuranov, Fairakhamany, 719
Zahle, Carl, 288
Zaid bin Khalifa al-Nahayan, Shaikh, 945
Zaid bin Shaker, 506
Zaid bin Sultan al-Nahayan, Shaikh, 945
Zaid el-Rifai, 506
Zaimis, Alexandros, 393, 395, 396
Zaimis, Thracyvoulos, 394
Zain Baharoon, 1080
Zain-Ul-Rashid Muadzam I, 552
Zain-Ul-Rashid Muadzam II, 552
Zainal Abdin Muadzam Shah, 559
Zairov, Mukhitidin, 916
Zaitsev, Nikolai, 724
Zaitsev, Vladimir, 748
Zakaria Mohieddin, 304
Zakharov, Vladimir, 728
Zakhurdayev, Vasily, 734
Zaki-Valodiv, Ahmed, 719
Zakir Hussein, 122
Zaldívar y Lazo, Rafael, 306
Zaldúa, Francisco, 250
Zaleski, August, 700
Zalikin, Aleksandr, 719
Zalkauskas, K., 540
Zalm, William Vander, 201
Zamalloq, Gómez, 603
Zaman Mirza, 53
Zamboni, Angel, 81
Zamor, Oreste, 410
Zamora, Jaime Paz, 141
Zan Hta Sin, U, 608
Zanardelli, Giuseppe, 479
Zañartu, Federico Errázurez, 222
Zangabie, Gabriël, 267
Zangiyev, B.D., 735
Zangpo, Chogyal, 138
Zangpo, Kawa, 138
Zanichelli, Arturo, 73
Zanora Verduzio, Elías, 579
Zanotti, Marino, 774
Zapata, Fausto, 587
Zaplana, Eduardo, 828
Zápotocký, Antonín, 282, 283

Zara Yakob, 314
Zaragoza, Federico Mayor, 46
Zárate Albarran, Alfredo, 582
Zárate Aquino, Manuel, 585
Zarković, Vidoje, 1088, 1089, 1090, 1091
Zarobyan, Yakov, 86
Zatonsty, Vladimir, 940
Zatysev, Mikhail, 724
Zauditu, 316
Zaugg, Fritz, 857, 858
Zavala, Joaquín, 631
Zavalia, Benjamin, 83
Zavgayev, Doku, 722, 723
Zavoli, Aldo, 773
Zawadski, Aleksander, 698
Zawisza, Aleksander, 700
Zayas y Alfonso, Alfredo, 277
Zaydin y Marquez Sterling, Ramón, 278
Zečević, Zdravko, 276
Zech, Julius, 922
Zee, J. van der, 624
Zeeland, Paul van, 130
Zegarra, Enrique, 690
Zehnder, Émile, 870
Zeigner, Erich, 375
Zejnulahu, Jusuf, 1095
Zelaya y Ayes, Francisco, 412
Zelencuk, Stepan, 595
Zelenović, Dragutin, 1093
Zeller, Adrien, 329
Zeltner, Karl, 863
Zeman, Miloš, 281
Zemgals, Gustavs, 525
Zemljarić, Janez, 791
Zemp, Heinrich, 879
Zemp, Joseph, 854
Zen-Ruffinen, Ignace, 902
Zeng Shaoshen, 240
Zeng Siyu, 238
Zeng Xisheng, 234
Zeng Yongyu, 233
Zentani Mohammed al-Zentani, 535
Zentner, Georg, 368
Zepeda, José, 631
Zeppenfeldt, Gerard, 620
Zerbo, Saye, 186, 187
Zernatto, Christof, 109
Zeyer, Werner, 374
Zgraggen, Anton, 883
Zgraggen, Ernst, 884
Zhamsuyev, Bair, 754
Zhang Binghua, 238
Zhang Boxing, 241
Zhang Chunqiao, 244
Zhang Dingcheng, 234
Zhang Guogang, 240
Zhang Guohua, 242
Zhang Guosheng, 240
Zhang Haoruo, 242
Zhang Jingfu, 234
Zhang Lichang, 244

Zhang Shuguang (Hainai), 236
Zhang Shuguang (Hebei), 237
Zhang Tixue, 238
Zhang Wule, 235
Zhang Yunyi, 232
Zhang Zgongliang, 240
Zhang Zgongwei, 242
Zhao Boping, 241
Zhao Jianmin, 241
Zhao Leji, 240
Zhao Shoushan, 240, 241
Zhao Xinchu, 238
Zhao Xiu, 239
Zhao Zengyi, 239
Zhao Zhihao, 241
Zhao Ziyang, 227, 228, 235, 242
Zhapakov, Naruz, 1053
Zhdanov, Zinovi, 733
Zhelev, Zheliu, 183
Zheng Silin, 239
Zhezlov, N.I., 728
Zhilunovich, Dmitri, 127
Zhivkov, Todor, 184, 185
Zhivov, D., 738
Zhordania, Noe, 359
Zhou Enlai, 227
Zhou Jianren, 243
Zhou Lin, 236
Zhou Xing, 243
Zhou Zijian, 234
Zhu Rongji, 227, 244
Zhu Senlin, 235
Zia-Ud-Din Muadzam Shah, 552

Zia ul-Haq, Mohammed, 664, 665
Ziaur Rahman, 121, 122
Ziegler, Alberik, 902
Ziegler, Bernard, 873
Ziehm, Ernst, 701
Zijl, Ebenzei van, 611
Zijlstra, Jelle, 620
Zilhão, João, 405
Zilius, Jonas, 540
Zilk, Helmut, 111
Ziltener, Meinrad, 892
Zimmerer, Eugen von, 194
Zimmerman, Fred, 1041
Zimmermann, Carl, 371
Zinawi, Meles (Legesse Zinawi), 316
Zine el-Abidine Ben Ali, 927, 928
Zinn, Georg-August, 372
Zinsou, Émile, 137
Zitha, M. Cephas, 808
Zivković, Petar, 1087
Zlatev, Pencho, 184
Znamensky, Yury, 718
Zobaran, Rui, 176
Zog I, 56
Zographos, Konstantinos, 393
Zoitakis, Georgios, 393
Zolatas, Xenophon, 397
Zölch-Balmer, Elisabeth, 869
Zoli, Adone, 480
Zoli, Corrado, 310
Zollikofer, Ludwig, 887
Zoramthanga, 441
Zorilla Martínez, Pedro, 584

Zorzi, Franco, 900
Zotin, Vladislav, 733
Zschinsky, Ferdinand von, 374
Zschokke, Peter, 865
Zsedyi, Béla, 416
Zu-Rhein, Friedrich, 368
Zuazo, Hernán Siles, 141
Zubairu, Tanko, 646
Zubak, Kresimir, 145, 146
Zubakin, Semen, 718
Zubov, Valery, 743
Zucconi, Oscar, 72
Zufferey, Antoine, 904
Zukhbaya, Otar, 360
Zulick, C. Meyer, 976
Zuloaga, Félix, 573
Zuloaga, Juan, 691
Zumakulov, Boris, 727
Zumbuhl, Norbert, 884
Zumbuhl, Robert, 910
Zurfluh, Hans, 902
Zust, Albert, 878
Zutt, Richard, 864
Zuviria, Gustavo Martínez, 73
Zuylen van Nijevelt, Julius van, 619
Zvyagilsky, Yukhim, 942
Zweifel, Edwin, 865
Zweifel, Esajas, 874
Zygmunt I (Poland), 697
Zygmunt II August (Poland), 697
Zygmunt III August (Poland), 697
Zyndram-Kościałkowski, Marian, 699